Looking Forward

Looking

LIFE IN THE TWENTIETH CENTURY

Forward

AS PREDICTED IN THE PAGES OF
AMERICAN MAGAZINES
FROM 1895 TO 1905

CREATED AND COMPILED BY
Ray Brosseau

INTERPRETIVE TEXT BY
Ralph K. Andrist

AMERICAN HERITAGE PRESS · NEW YORK

for Margot, W.I.A.

This volume was prepared for American Heritage Press by the following staff: Kenneth W. Leish, editor; Annette Jarman, assistant editor; Helen C. Dunn, copy editor; Jonathan L. Weber, production; Susan Faxon, editorial assistant. The art director was Tom Bevans, who was assisted by Wayne Young, Constance Doyle, Lynn Capeheart, Judy Stern, Karen Bowen, and Daphne Cook.

COPYRIGHT © 1970 BY RAY BROSSEAU
ALL RIGHTS RESERVED.
PUBLISHED BY AMERICAN HERITAGE PUBLISHING CO., INC., A SUBSIDIARY OF McGRAW-HILL, INC.
LIBRARY OF CONGRESS CATALOGUE CARD NUMBER: 72-95723
SBN: 07-008131-x

Contents

Foreword
by Ralph K. Andrist

LOOKING FORWARD

When the twentieth century opened, there was a great deal of looking into the future by men of note and much forecasting of great things for America and the rest of the world. Humans endow certain years—the ends of decades, for instance—with a mystique; such years stand like eminences, providing heights from which men can view the way they have just come and possibly also get a glimpse of the road ahead. And the most commanding height of all is the year when one century gives way to another; from it one can look back upon an entire hundred years and strain one's eyes to see ahead into a future that stretches into distant mists.

There were arguments about when the twentieth century began. Logic proves that 1900 was the last year of the nineteenth century (a century begins with 1 and ends with 100), but for most citizens the heady sensation of writing 1900 for the first time was proof enough that a change had taken place, logic notwithstanding. As 1899 gave way to 1900, newspapers from coast to coast printed long editorials explaining why a prosperous nation could look forward to an almost utopian future. On the closing day of 1899 *The New York Times* listed the many inventions of the nineteenth century, but considered them only small steps upward into the bright promise of the 1900's: "We step upon the threshold of 1900 which leads to the new century facing a still brighter dawn of civilization." Most papers, however, commented more on the state of business than on the state of civilization—and that was understandable, for the United States at that time was deeply absorbed in the task of making itself more affluent. "If one could not have made money this past year, his case is hopeless," the Boston *Herald* wrote.

But there were also some who saw beyond mere money and envisioned a world becoming better in every way. Many of these sentiments, of course, came from "impractical" people such as clergymen. The Reverend Newell Dwight Hillis, who had very recently taken over as pastor of Plymouth Church in Brooklyn, watched the world outside his study window and told his congregation, "Laws are becoming more just, rulers humane; music is becoming sweeter and books wiser; homes are happier, and the individual heart becoming at once more just and more gentle." The Reverend Mr. Hillis had apparently overlooked many things in his euphoric view of an improving world: slums and sweatshops and the indignities suffered by a deprived minority. Mr. Hillis, like *The New York Times* and the Boston *Herald* and most other newspapers across the land, was a spokesman for the upper middle class.

Chauncey Depew, a big man in the New York Central Railroad and a new United States Senator in 1899, did a little spread-eagling as he told an audience what the arrival of the new century meant: "There is not a man here who does not feel 400 per cent bigger in 1900 than he did in 1896, bigger intellectually, bigger hopefully, bigger patriotically, bigger in the breast from the fact that he is a citizen of a country that has become a world power for peace, for civilization and for the expansion of its industries and the products of its labor."

Along with self-congratulation about the glorious present, there was much probing of the future. John Jacob Astor saw magnificent cities in which pedestrians would stroll high above the rumble and crash of traffic—and on transparent sidewalks at that, although he did not say what this eerie sensation might, do to those suffering from acrophobia. Edward Everett Hale, who had once written the moving story "The Man Without a Country," thought that by 1975 people might be shot from city to city across the country through tubes. Ray Stannard Baker, an informed magazine writer, believed that the automobile, which was just beginning to appear on streets, would put an end to the roar of city traffic. "In the first place," he wrote, "it will be almost as quiet as a country lane—all the crash of horses' hoofs and the rumble of steel tires will be gone, and since vehicles will be fewer and shorter than the present truck and span, streets will appear less crowded."

Time has shown how wrong Mr. Baker was. But it is not surprising that many prophets missed the mark widely—and often so completely that their predictions are ludicrous today. Never before had the development of technology been so rapid, and it was either a brave man or a foolish one who ventured a guess as to what his society would be like in another generation. The hazards of prediction were increased because some of the most significant developments of the time coincided with the change in centuries. When 1799 gave way to 1800, it was merely a change in dates; the nation and the world went on pretty much as before. But in 1900 America was changing even as the old leaf was torn off the calendar. In April of 1898 the first American automobile manufactured for sale had been purchased, and the nation would never be the same again. By 1900 some eight thousand automobiles were registered in the country, and in the summer of 1903 the auto car was advanced enough to enable two motorists to make the first coast-to-coast trip in their Packard in only fifty-two days, a feat that takes on a new dimension when it is remembered that over great stretches of the way roads were almost nonexistent. At the turn of the century, too, the Wright brothers were experimenting with gliders at Kitty Hawk, and one December day in 1903 they made the first flight in a powered aircraft, another event that would change the direction of history. The telephone was an infant in 1900, but with every passing month it reached more homes and places of business and became more indispensable. There were many inventions, most of them unimportant by themselves, but in the aggregate they brought about great changes in the nation.

Moreover, the differences were not only material ones effected by advances in technology. There were social and political changes as well. The United States had fought a war with Spain in 1898 and had thereby become a world power. Victory brought us the Philippines, Puerto Rico, and Guam, and while many Americans were intoxicated with the idea of holding dominion over strange peoples in faraway places, others were troubled by the idea of imperialism. In any event, possession of the Philippines quickly involved the United States in the affairs of the Far East, from which it still has not been able to extricate itself.

New and revolutionary technologies, a role for America in world affairs, attempts to introduce new meaning and morality into an essentially crass society, these and many other elements made the turn of the century a fast-moving and often confusing time. It was to view that time, not through the measured perspective of history but as the people living at the moment saw it, that this volume was assembled. On the following pages are gathered opinions, facts, musings, and sometimes dogmatic assertions of those who lived and wrote between 1895 and 1905. These published pieces, which during that long-ago time were part of the current reading matter of educated Americans, are a reasonably representative cross-section of what the popular magazines of the period were printing; they come from the files of such journals as *The Saturday Evening Post, Harper's Weekly, Collier's, Puck, Life* (the long-defunct humor magazine), *Judge, Woman's Home Companion, Scientific American, Popular Mechanics, Country Life in America, Ladies' Home Journal,* and others.

The title of this book, *Looking Forward,* does not signify that the reader will find merely a collection of prophecies and predictions made when this century was new, except to the extent that the future is always contained in the present. Rather, in the articles, editorials, cartoons, and advertisements (for an advertisement can reveal much about a bygone time) on the following pages, one will find the philosophies, ideas, and also the misconceptions that have led, with many changes and modifications, to our American society of the 1970's.

One thing becomes quickly apparent on reading this material from the past: the world was different back then. It was a world where the rich were very rich and the poor were hardly mentioned, where John Jacob Astor could say condescendingly, "A man with a million dollars is as well off as if he were rich." But times change, and men change with them, and that is what *Looking Forward* is all about.

1

The City of Tomorrow

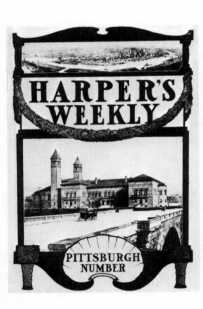

Ever since Ur of the Chaldees was the metropolis of the ancient world, big cities have been irresistible magnets for the young and the ambitious. Through the centuries young people have grieved their parents by leaving home to flock to the busy urban centers: sons and daughters of Mesopotamian shepherds, of Norwegian cod fishermen, of Minnesota wheat farmers.

For the people back home on the farm and in the village, the metropolis represented temptation and evil. There are still people in small-town America who look on New York or Los Angeles or Chicago as the Babylon of the New World.

Technology created the modern city. The New York or New Orleans of four or five decades before the Civil War was not basically different from the Rome of fifteen hundred years earlier. In both eras travelers depended on animals — usually horses — for motive power on land and they moved on water at the whim of the wind or by the strength of an oarsman's muscles. Buildings were low; the flames of candles or lamps lighted them in the evening, and fires in stoves or fireplaces dispelled the winter chill. Messages were still transmitted from person to person by hand.

The great change began with the invention of the steam engine, which provided an entirely new source of power not only for factories, but for ships and steamboats and a little later for railroads, which were tying communities together even before the Civil War. Then came the telegraph, to carry, almost instantaneously, important messages. By 1875 no large city was without gas for illumination, and well before the end of the century electric arc lights were brightening street corners. The telephone had ceased to be a curiosity by 1900, although it was hardly commonplace. Trolleys clanged through the streets and out into the suburbs that they and the railroads were creating.

More than anything else, the skyscraper changed the physical appearance of the metropolis. For many centuries it was not so much lack of architectural knowledge or the absence of suitable building materials that kept the profile of cities low. It was simply that tenants did not relish walking up many flights of stairs, and upper floors therefore rented for less money. Few buildings, consequently, rose above five stories. Then the elevator was invented; it was the elevator that created the skyscraper, and not the other way around. Architects began pushing buildings upward. In order to do so, they had to make the lower walls thicker to bear the increased weight, and there was a limit to the height buildings could go without making the lower walls impossibly thick. Architectural thinking then turned in the direction that gave the world the structure of the modern skyscraper: a steel skeleton with masonry and glass curtain walls.

An article titled "Wonders of the Skyscraper," which is reproduced in the following pages, tells something of the techniques involved in building a skyscraper, but unfortunately it stops short of describing early problems and their solutions. Other articles and editorials cover a range that shows how complex an organism a modern city is. The articles on the present and future of Washington, Chicago, and New York were, unhappily, written by politicians. The mayor of Chicago and the president of the Board of Commissioners of Washington both write as though they were cribbing from the latest official report. The information is there, but it does not sing. On the other hand, former mayor Gilroy of New York talks of his city with an intimacy and gusto that make him sound as though he were getting ready to run again.

The commuter was an established part of the urban scene even at the turn of the century. In the article "How People Come and Go in New York," the author estimates that even at that time more than three hundred and fifty thousand people came into the city to work every day. This phenomenon was common also to other large cities—Philadelphia, Chicago, Boston—where the railroad and the trolley were making it possible for people to work in the city and live in the suburbs. The railroads deliberately encouraged this movement toward the country: commuting meant more traffic for the railroads and more income. This is a fact that the railroads would rather forget now.

In 1901 British writer H. G. Wells wrote an essay in which he quite accurately foresaw the coming of the megalopolis, which is now hard upon us, although we are still unprepared for it: "We are on the eve of a great development of centrifugal possibilities. And since it has been shown that a city of pedestrians is inexorably limited by a radius of about four miles, and that a horse-using city may grow out to seven or eight, it follows that the available area of a city which can offer a cheap suburban journey of thirty miles an hour is a circle with a radius of thirty miles. . . . But thirty miles is only a very moderate estimate of speed, and the available area for the social equivalent of the favored season-ticket holders of today will have a radius of over one hundred miles, and be almost equal to the area of Ireland. The radius that will sweep the area available for such as now live in the outer suburbs will include a still vaster area. Indeed, it is not too much to say that the vast stretch of country from Washington to Albany will be all of it 'available' to the active citizen of New York and Philadelphia. . . ."

The megalopolis is with us today, although man does not always travel about in it as freely as Wells imagined he would. The railroads, which could be such an efficient mover of people, are shedding their passenger services as fast as they can obtain permission to do so. The automobile, in spite of its potential for covering distance in a hurry, often holds its frustrated driver immobilized in the midst of monumental traffic jams.

Many of the problems that we like to think are peculiar to the cities of today were already causing concern at the beginning of this century. The article called "Policing a Modern Metropolis" deals with a very old problem and one rooted more in human nature than in technology. The author, Chicago's superintendent of police, speaks mostly of political pressures on policemen and judges, but he does hint delicately that some police succumb to graft. We have not yet found a way to keep them all honest.

In 1900 there was also concern about the proliferation of advertising billboards, which were so ubiquitous that the mayor of Chicago spoke of them as defacing the city. Today zoning laws have largely done away with unrestricted billboards as a city problem, but the regulations have merely moved them out beyond the city limits; highways in some states are almost lined by two walls of billboard art. However, the cities still cope, and in ever-growing desperation, with another problem the mayor of Chicago mentioned: the paper scatterers. Even the alarmed voices recently warning that we are fouling our nests beyond redemption have not halted the tide of discarded paper blowing about the streets.

As for pollution of the atmosphere, *Life,* the old humorous weekly, got an early whiff of bad air in 1898, when it published the picture captioned "A Sunny Day in 1910." The magazine was right in predicting increasingly foul air, but it was wrong in particulars, for the smoke that darkens the air of the city streets in *Life*'s drawing rises from the smokestacks of steam locomotives on the elevated railroads. Steam locomotives had disappeared from the elevated railroads before 1910, but the rise of air pollution continued unchecked: from the chimneys of homes, from factory smokestacks, and especially from the exhaust pipes of motor vehicles. Today the situation has become perilous.

Another portent that although developing technology was making the modern city possible, it was not necessarily making it more livable or comfortable, appeared in the *Scientific American* after the opening of New York's first subway. The editors, disappointed that the subway was proving stuffy and uncomfortable with the coming of spring, learnedly discoursed on air currents and ventilation and concluded that "if the oppressive symptoms continue to increase as the midsummer heat comes on, some steps will certainly have to be taken to mitigate the nuisance." Many subways have been built since then, but little or nothing has been done to "mitigate the nuisance," for new subways are still unbearable in summer heat. It is almost an axiom of city life that what once seemed intolerable soon becomes the norm.

There are, in fact, few problems of the modern city that were not foreshadowed at the turn of the century. The only difference is that most of them have grown larger with the passing of time.

The New Cities

OUR cities sprang up so suddenly and spread so swiftly that the country has been pushed beyond the easy reach of the urban population before there was a chance to prevent it. At enormous expense and with results that cannot be wholly satisfactory American cities are now trying to repair the really deplorable omission. But what are the towns doing?

In a few years hundreds of towns will become cities. Now they have the country in their very streets; soon it will be gone—unless the parks are set apart and space for trees is left on either side of the new streets and extensions of streets.

No town is too small or too far away from the present lines of swift development to take the necessary precautions; and the way to begin is for some public-spirited citizen—man or woman—to stir the matter up.

The Wonderful Growth of Cities

A hundred years ago no city in America had 100,000 people.

To-day there are sixty-two cities in this country that have a greater population than New York or Philadelphia had one hundred years ago.

We have not space to enumerate all of them; but here, in the order of size, are the fifteen leading cities of the country. There are also the figures for 1890, giving their order in that year, thus showing that even in cities there are changes in position:

		1900		1890
New York, N. Y.	1	3,437,202	1	2,492,591
Chicago, Ill.	2	1,698,575	2	1,099,850
Philadelphia, Pa.	3	1,293,697	3	1,046,964
St. Louis, Mo.	4	575,238	4	451,770
Boston, Mass.	5	560,892	5	448,477
Baltimore, Md.	6	508,957	6	434,439
Cleveland, Ohio	7	381,768	9	261,353
Buffalo, N. Y.	8	352,387	10	255,664
San Francisco, Cal.	9	342,782	7	298,997
Cincinnati, Ohio	10	325,902	8	296,908
Pittsburg, Pa.	11	321,616	12	238,617
New Orleans, La.	12	287,104	11	242,039
Detroit, Mich.	13	285,704	14	205,876
Milwaukee, Wis.	14	285,315	15	204,468
Washington, D. C.	15	278,718	13	230,392

A Man of Straw

WHY do the problems of the so-called slums of our great cities tend to increase in gravity? These slums are made up almost wholly of the newly arrived. The only just measure of immigration is its proportion to the population. In the preceding great influx, that of half a century ago, the average yearly immigration was fifteen-tenths of one per cent. of the total population; in the present wave the average has been about six-tenths of one per cent. of the total population—or not much more than one-third as great as the immigration of the late forties and early fifties.

Are we making an undue fuss about our slums, being misled by surface signs, by squalor and by ignorance, both eradicable in one generation? Are the ever increasing rich of the cities, especially their sympathetic women eager for pastimes, pottering about too much with the poor, exaggerating the evils of poverty, which is only an evil to the unambitious and incompetent? Are we regarding as slums places that are, in fact, Nature's breeding-grounds for the best possible citizenship? Are we molly-coddling the poor into false self-pity and tempting them into pauperization?

It is a crime to tempt a man to lean when by making an effort he might stand alone.

The Rush to Failure in the City

SOME published fragments of the new census statistics are very depressing to the old-fashioned yet very sensible people who have been hoping that the movement of villagers and country people to the large cities had been checked.

What is the meaning of the continuous rush to the cities? The old explanation was that farmers' sons and daughters wearied of work that was never finished; they had heard of city demands for labor and of city wages, payable always in cash and at stated dates. They had also heard of city pleasures, some of which were said to cost nothing, while others were very cheap. But young people do not constitute the whole body of people who are crowding into the cities, for mechanics and artisans of all kinds are in the throng, for in the villages and country districts employment is irregular and pay uncertain. The more aspiring of them hope for the larger opportunities and recognition that the country dares not promise; they know, too, that such of their children as incline to study may become fairly, even highly, educated in the city without special cost to their parents. Of the "seamy" side of city life they know nothing, for their acquaintances who "went to town" have not returned to tell of it; few of them could return if they would. The few who go back to the old homesteads are the men who have succeeded, and in any village such a man in effect resembles a gold-laden miner from Cape Nome or the Klondike; his example threatens to depopulate the town.

Nevertheless, the rural districts are not going to be depopulated, except when their soil is very poor and their malaria over-rich. A countryward movement started in some cities a few years ago, and it has been increasing in volume; it may be almost invisible in some localities, for three million square miles is an area so great that any city's overflow might be lost in it. The men who are trying scientific farming are all from the cities and they have carried their city ideas with them. As a rule, city brain and city money are suggesting and backing the rural attempts to have good roads, pure water, perfect drainage, high farming, high-grade schools, free libraries and many other ameliorations of old-time conditions. Yet in one respect the city man in the country is a disappointment to all classes of the dissatisfied, for when they talk of going to the city he persistently says "Don't," and he supports his advice with a dismal array of facts and figures. —JOHN HABBERTON.

Our Crowding Habit

WHATEVER may be the trouble with our American birthrate, to talk about overcrowding is sheer nonsense. Take the matter of area alone. We have eighty million people and we talk of a density—a sparsity rather—of twenty-seven to the square mile of our three million square miles. But one-third of our eighty millions live in cities and towns that take up practically no room at all. One American in every twenty is a New Yorker; one in every ten is a resident of New York, Chicago, Philadelphia, St. Louis, Boston and Baltimore; if you add Cleveland, Buffalo, San Francisco, Cincinnati and Pittsburg, you have one-eighth of our whole population. In fact, cutting out the cities and towns, you have a "density" of less than fifteen to the square mile of land area, or six hundred and forty acres to every four families.

No, there is plenty of room; we are too far apart to be comfortable; we need nearer neighbors. The trouble is that a few of us, a few hundred out of fourscore million, have been allowed to get that crowding habit, and to "get it bad." But we will stop that presently.

Policing a Modern Metropolis—By Francis O'Neill

General Superintendent of Police, City of Chicago

THE official life of the chief police executive of a large city is mainly an unremitting effort to say "No"—and to say it with the least possible offense to those whose requests and demands are denied. If he is a forceful and honest man, who enters his office with a determination to give a good, sound police administration, he puts his shoulder against the powerful coil-spring of political influence the moment he enters upon his duties. Not only must he maintain his pressure without an instant of relaxation, but this must be steadily increased until the repression of adverse influences reaches that point which will win the approval of the people—or rather, of the reasonable portion of the public, which realizes that a great city cannot be transformed into a Sunday-school by the application of brute force as represented by the policeman's baton.

The instant the pressure is relaxed the spring flies back with a force proportioned to the pressure which has been exerted upon it. It will not do to push part of the time and then relax into easy-going methods. The successful Chief must keep pushing evenly and steadily, and during every moment of his official existence.

THE "FRONT OFFICE" WIRE-PULLERS

That automatically alert, stubborn and aggressive resistance to police pressure which forms the spring against which the executive of the Department must keep his shoulder sternly set comprises various forces, but mainly they are evident in efforts to get at the public crib, to secure special privileges, and to prevent the punishment of criminals and transgressors of the law. Other elements enter into the problem, but these are the principal ones which may profitably be taken into account and carefully analyzed.

First and foremost is political influence. No layman who is not brought in daily contact with the routine of business at police headquarters in a big city can form any idea of the demands made upon the time of a Chief of Police by the place hunters. When the force is not under strict civil service rule the volume of these supplications passes understanding. If the policemen's clubs were made of gold instead of locust wood, competition for them could scarcely be more strenuous. In this particular I speak from long and painful experience. For more than eight years I served as private secretary, or in other confidential positions, in the office of Superintendent of Police, and during most of that time a place on the force was considered one of the legitimate spoils of party victory. Now, however, civil service in the Police Department of Chicago is "not a theory, but a condition." Ever since the passage of the civil-service law there has been a constant tightening of lines, until the conditions which prevail at present may be well covered by the statement that I am working to-day with absolutely the same force with which my predecessor worked and which he handed down to me.

Even under these conditions, however, there are many political visitors to this office, who come here on behalf of friends whom they wish to place on the force, or who, being already there, desire promotion. These ward politicians are slow to learn that civil service, when it is the real thing, shuts the flood-gate on the old channel of entrance into police life and changes the whole direction of the stream by which the Department receives its influx of fresh materials. But those who now come here to exert their "drag" are but a corporal's guard when compared with the legions which stormed the Department in the older days.

In order to assist those unfamiliar with the actual conditions, let me attempt to show the persistency with which a Chief of Police is preyed upon when positions on the force are subject to political pull. During my service as private secretary to a former Superintendent of Police I had two experiences which stick in my memory as thoroughly typical of scores of others which might be recalled.

HOW THE ALDERMAN WAS SAVED

One day a very efficient alderman, who was not afraid to exert himself in the interests of his constituents, came to me with a troubled face and a wearied manner. Dropping dejectedly into a chair he made known his mission.

"I am being slowly but surely driven to insanity," he said. "There is a certain patrolman on the force who is determined that I shall secure his promotion to the position of sergeant. He never sleeps! It is impossible to shake him. No matter how early I rise in the morning or how late I return home at night, he or one of his emissaries is camped on my front door steps, and he has a faithful lookout posted at the rear of the house so that I cannot make my escape by way of the alley. The importunate widow of Scriptural celebrity was a shy, shrinking and purposeless creature compared with this patrolman! Time and again I have discussed his case with the Chief, and I understand that there is not the slightest chance in the world for his promotion under present conditions. If I had a dozen interviews with the Superintendent I couldn't grasp the hopelessness of this man's case any better than I do now; and I have explained every circumstance to him over and over again, but without making the slightest impression upon his hopes or determination. He will not listen to reason, and now I am ready to resort to other methods. Is there not some ordinance or rule of the Department which says that officers who annoy the Department Chief with delegations in their behalf shall be subject to discipline?"

"Yes," I replied; "there is such a rule, and your best plan is to bring your man in for an interview. Meantime, I will acquaint the Chief with the circumstances of the case and call his attention to the ruling which covers the case."

This scheme was carried out, and the next morning the alderman and the patrolman appeared—the latter smiling with satisfaction over the prospect that the "boss" had "weakened," and that a short interview with the Superintendent of the Department would "fix things all right" and secure his promotion to the pay and dignity of a sergeant. After the alderman had defined the object of their call the Chief put on his severest expression and, turning suddenly to the policeman, said:

"Do you know that you are violating one of the rules of the Department in coming here to take up my time in order to secure promotion by political influence? Well, you are; and the penalty for it is suspension or dismissal from the service, according to my discretion. I guess that suspension will answer while I take your case under advisement."

This turn of affairs was a terrible shock to the patrolman, and nearly threw him into a spasm of fear. His irrepressible ambition to wear the uniform of a sergeant suddenly left him and all his thought became instantly centred on saving himself from disgrace and retaining his position. Then the alderman made an earnest plea that the man be spared the penalty, on condition that the offense should never be repeated. After seeming carefully to weigh this argument of intercession, the Superintendent finally acceded to the alderman's request. When they came out of the Chief's private office the patrolman grasped the alderman's hand and wrung it with a grip which told of the gratitude which he could not put into words. That patrolman never asked for promotion after this experience; he was content to let new honors seek him instead of seeking them.

AN EASY WAY OF PAYING DEBTS

Another incident which even more effectively illustrates the great volume of demands made upon the time of the chief executive of the Police Department concerns an alderman who took care of his people in the manner most approved by the prevailing standard of ward politics. He hustled persistently on the errands of his constituents, no matter how hopeless the missions which engaged his energy. Early one morning he came into Chief Brennan's office with a big, muscular man in tow. They were pleasantly welcomed by the Chief, who informed them, in as few words as possible, that there was no vacancy on the force and no likelihood that one would occur in the near future. Half an hour later the same alderman returned with another man, bent on securing a similar appointment. Again the Chief patiently made the explanation. Four times this rôle was repeated by the alderman. When he brought in the fifth man, however, the patience of the Chief was exhausted and he exclaimed:

"Can't you understand, sir, that I am here to do police work and that I must have time in which to do it? This is the fifth call you have made here this morning for the purpose of getting a constituent appointed on the force. In every instance I have told you plainly that there are no vacancies and that no appointments as patrolmen are possible. And still here you come again with another man! This is carrying things altogether too far. I hope you will not annoy me further."

Placing his hand on the shoulder of the Chief the alderman interrupted him by saying:

"I know that as well as you do, but can't you see that I must square myself with my constituents and particularly with those who run the ward and who gave me my seat in the Council? I dislike to come here and take up your time, over and over again, on a mission which I know is hopeless, quite as much as you dislike to be interrupted, but there is no other way out of it. My men will not be satisfied unless I bring them here so that they may hear from your own lips the statement that they have no chance to secure appointment to places on the force—and I may as well tell you right now that I have just two more such calls to make to-day and that you will materially injure my interests if you do not give me a hearing, however brief."

And this alderman was only one of many, all working to keep the favor of their political henchmen by the same method—that of robbing the Chief of the time he should have to master the problems of actual police business, the maintenance of good order and the apprehension and punishment of criminals. The pay-roll of the Police Department of Chicago now numbers more than three thousand names. What if these places were subject to the exigencies of political pull? Under such an unfortunate condition the Superintendent of Police could not claim one hour a day for undivided attention to the non-political duties of his office. Generally, where appointments to the force are at the mercy of political influence, there is some person high in the confidence of the administration who makes an effort to adjust or distribute the political patronage. Even then, however, the Chief is perpetually handicapped by the political exigencies of the moment. He cannot make a move, even in the enforcement of discipline, without taking the time to learn if he is thereby about to tread upon the toes of some politician who is able, perchance, to reach up to the very head of the Department with disturbing results. Consequently he must consult the political thermometer every hour—almost every minute—of each day, and this paralyzes his usefulness as an active director of the police powers of the city.

HOW A JUDGE KEPT STRAIGHT

Thus far I have told only how the time, the energy and the hopes of the head of the Police Department are consumed by the place hunters. When there is no civil service they have full sway. When a civil service law is rigidly enforced, as it is in Chicago under the present administration, this pest is reduced to a minimum.

Years ago I stood beside the desk of a certain police magistrate who presided over one of the most crowded police courts in Chicago. At his right hand, when he opened court, was a stack of letters. Invariably the envelopes were left unopened until after the close of court. It impressed me as a little strange that a wide-awake officer of the law should not open his morning mail until noon or after. He saw that this practice interested me, and when we were alone he volunteered this explanation:

"Almost every letter which reaches me in the morning delivery contains a message calculated to influence my decision of some case to be heard in the course of the day. If I allow myself to read the letters before listening to the cases it is almost impossible not to be influenced by the statements, arguments and even threats which they contain. Some of them come from sources which are practically irresistible to the man who has run the political gantlet necessary in order to secure appointment to the position of police magistrate. The only way by which I can secure even partial immunity from such pressure is to leave the letters unopened until the cases are heard. Then, of course, I can write to my correspondents that the contents of their important communications were not known to me until after the cases in question were decided."

This effort to evade the wholesale pressure of political influence had a pathetic and inevitable ending. The men whose letters failed to produce the desired results in his decisions secured his official scalp and his name was not included among those forwarded to the Governor for reappointment. He was among the exceptions in his class. Most of his associates on the police bench read their letters before making their decisions.

Some magistrates have been known to resort to a shifty scheme by which to placate the powerful influences. They would announce orally a decision precisely the reverse of that actually entered in the docket. Of course, the clerk would make a minute of the oral decision—but upon the blotter and not on the pages of the docket! Under this plan the prosecuting witness would leave the court-room with the satisfaction of having scored a victory, while the defendant would remain to take a later and leisurely departure.

CONTESTS FOR THE POLICE-COURT BENCH

When a private citizen starts out to secure an appointment to a police justiceship he enters upon a long race, every step of which adds to the handicap of obligations with which he must inevitably be weighted. First, he must get one of the circuit judges to place his name in nomination for justice of the peace. This means, as a rule, that he must get the indorsement of the political organization of his ward or of other powerful influences in the community. To do this implies starting with the backing of the political leaders of his own precinct. When these are won to his standard the contest moves into the large field of the ward, and here he is likely to encounter a dozen competitors who are working the wires with tried skill and cunning. He must get men to hustle for him, to indorse him, to see their friends in his behalf, and to checkmate his competitors. By the time he has gained the backing of the ward powers he has received enough favors to sink a ship. After his judicial nomination his name is sent to the Governor of the State. This carries the battle to the State Capitol. Again he must gather his forces and get his friends to see the Governor in his behalf. If this assault of the hustlers is successful, the Chief Executive of the State sends his name to the State Senate for confirmation. Sometimes the work of months is blasted by the antagonism of one powerful political "knocker" who can make himself felt at the State Capitol. The appointment of the Governor secured, the guns of influence are next called into action to secure Senatorial confirmation. If this is won, the candidate is now a justice of the peace, but not, be it remembered, a police magistrate. From the list of justices of the peace the Mayor selects the police justices. Here comes a far more severe test of political influence than any yet encountered, for such a position is very profitable. Once more the candidate must get his backers "to the front" and inspire them with renewed diligence and activity. Then there is still the supreme test — that of securing assignment to the police court of paramount importance and profit. By the time this long and wearisome gantlet has been run the candidate who secures a place in one of the principal police courts has placed himself under obligations not only to almost every man of his own acquaintance, but to his friends' friends as well. And before he is fairly settled in his long-sought chair in the police court he is reminded, by hundreds of demands, that his shoulders are loaded with political debts.

These claims are presented to him for liquidation every day of his political life. He may be a man of strong integrity and fully determined to discharge his duties with strict judicial impartiality, but he cannot escape the haunting presence of his obligations; and his official life is bound to be a constant struggle between conscience and the demands of political creditors. Under a good administration the police magistrate who pays his political debts at the expense of judicial impartiality will be found out and dispensed with, but under a bad one he will thrive and fatten.

A SUPERINTENDENT'S HANDICAPS

The same observation will apply in general to the Superintendent of Police. If he secures his appointment through political influence and wire pulling he will be encumbered with obligations which will be pressed upon him with merciless importunity and under the most embarrassing circumstances. When such an appointment is made absolutely without the foreknowledge of the appointee, and without any application on his part for the place, he comes to his duties under the most favorable circumstances possible; and his failure to give a good, sound administration, under genuine civil service rule, must be either his own fault or that of the Mayor by whom he is appointed. It is safe to say, however, that the burden of responsibility will rest with

himself, for the Mayor who resists all political pressure and selects as his chief political executive a man not pushed by any clique or group of politicians, can have but one motive for such independence — that of giving a police administration free from all political entanglements and designed for legitimate and courageous police work.

There is a wide difference of opinion as to what constitutes a good police administration for a big city. A certain element will not be satisfied with anything short of the absolute ideal in morals. But the reasonable portion of the public realizes that this is an impossibility. Ideal morality cannot be universally enforced in any community, particularly in a large city, even by a police force made up of men having the moral courage of martyrs and the stern convictions of Puritans. What, then, is the best that can be expected in the line of approximating the ideal, with human nature as it is now constituted? How much can be demanded, in the limits of human reason, in suppressing vice and crime and preserving order in a modern metropolis? My own definition of a good police administration, as it has been worked out by twenty-eight years of service in the department, is this:

WHAT THE POLICE OUGHT TO ACCOMPLISH

First. The suppression of public gambling to a point where the police force does not know of its existence, and where honest and vigilant effort is constantly put forth to discover its outcropping and to punish its appearance.

Second. The suppression of vice to a point where it cannot directly affect those who do not, of their own unaided choice, seek its haunts.

Third. The placing of the saloon thoroughly under the control of the law.

Fourth. The reduction of crime and disorder to that minimum which results from a knowledge, on the part of the potential lawbreakers, that punishment shall be impartial and exempt from the influence of political pull or other form of official corruption.

These are the main points in my definition of a sound police administration; and if the conditions I have outlined are fairly approximated the people may well be satisfied and should give that administration their hearty confidence and support, resting assured that they will never know at what cost of vigilance, hard work and perpetual warfare such a result has been attained.

It must be apparent to any thoughtful and well-informed man of the world that the materials with which a chief of police has to work are not ideal. The policeman's pay and the nature of his duties are hardly attractive to a man of acute moral sensibilities or highly developed intellectuality, and this is not in any sense a reflection upon the mental or moral make-up of the men who constitute the police force.

They are human; their wage is comparatively small, and their work mainly of a rough sort and repulsive to the man of refined sensibilities. They are constantly brought in contact with the harsh, the corrupt, the vicious and the sordid sides of life, and it is not to be wondered at that many of them yield to the unwholesome influences of such a contact. This makes it necessary for the conscientious and energetic Chief of Police to exercise unflagging vigilance to see that his honest efforts are not thwarted by the men under him. He must keep as close a surveillance upon his men as they are supposed to keep upon the public.

LETTERS OF COMPLAINT FROM THE PUBLIC

In addition to this means of detecting corruption, connivance and inattention to duty, he has also the private communications which reach him from the public at large. I receive scores of these letters daily. They must, however, be considered with great care and acted upon with conservatism. All of them are thoroughly investigated, mainly by secret agents, and many are found to have been inspired by malice, spite, envy, rank unreasonableness and other equally unworthy motives. The sifting of complaints is one of the most delicate duties which a Superintendent of Police is called upon to discharge. Though he should be able to locate any "grafting" on the part of the men in his force, that is not always so easy and simple a matter as might be supposed. More than one Chief has gone well-nigh to the end of his administration without finding out the source of certain influences which constantly thwarted his good intentions, and he has exclaimed, when about to retire: "Oh for one month more in which to make good the record!"

But, to recur to the topic first discussed, the bane of police service is political influence. This is the drone-maker. The officer who has the "soft snap," who is shocked and almost insulted if required actually to perform police duty, is a perpetual annoyance and stumbling-block to the head of the Department.

Those who are inclined harshly but sincerely to criticise Chicago for a supposed unreasonable prevalence of crime, in the line of confidence workers and easy-money men, fail to take into account the unwelcome legacy left us by the World's Fair, which brought here many strange devices and many clever workers in this field. This sinister influence has been more far-reaching and difficult to uproot than can be realized by any person except the conscientious police officer. It was an educational campaign which introduced the "panel house," the "knock-out drops," and a score of other modern developments in the arts of the professional criminal, unknown here before the great Exposition. To uproot the harvest of that sowing has been a larger task than can easily be appreciated.

THE TRAFFIC SQUAD OF THE FUTURE.

How Bachelors Live in New York
By Robert Shackleton

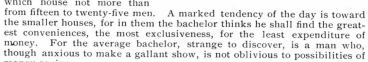

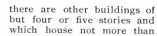

A millionaire bachelor's silver closet

A vista in a Fifth Avenue apartment

A bachelor's strait and narrow way

IN NEW YORK CITY, so it is estimated, there are some 10,000 men who live in bachelor apartments. There is, of course, no way of arriving at the number with accuracy, scattered throughout the city as the myriad apartments are, with many tucked away in unexpected or practically unknown quarters, but the opinion of those best qualified to judge points to the total named.

And in the term "bachelor apartments" I do not include every bachelor room. Wide is the difference in condition between the young man who creeps to a garret in an East Side tenement, or who lives in a hall bedroom in a West Side boarding-house, and the man who pays thousands of dollars a year for his expensively furnished suite. I am speaking only of those whose home is of more than one room and of those who live in the distinctively bachelor apartment buildings.

From four hundred to four thousand dollars a year—that may in a general way express the range of cost for the one item of rent of a bachelor apartment. It used to be said by many a young man in New York that he could not afford to be married. Now there is many a young man who thinks that he cannot afford to be a bachelor. For when to the rent of an expensive apartment is added the general cost of living that goes with an expensive house—the cost of eating, of clothes, of entertainment, of service, of tips, of theatres—such a total is reached that it need not be a matter of surprise that many a man turns to matrimony for reasons economical.

Between Forty-second and Twenty-third Streets to the north and south, and between Madison and Sixth Avenues to the east and west, may be said, in a general way, to lie the bachelor apartment houses.

Bachelors like to live in the centre of things: of life, of theatres, of amusement. For them the suburbs have no charms; for them the commuter sounds the praises of the country in vain. Within touch of the clubs and theatres and hotels and of the busy life of Broadway and Fifth Avenue the average bachelor must be.

Some bachelor apartments there are, indeed, which lie to the southward of the district mentioned, anchored there by association so firmly as to resist the northward-moving current of the city's population; and others there are which, answering that current, have been located far above Fifty-ninth Street, to either the eastward or the westward of Central Park; but the greatest amount of bachelor apartment house life is within the limits I have named.

There are large bachelor houses and there are small; there are buildings which tower far upward, with story piled upon story, and which contain from a hundred and twenty-five to a hundred and fifty suites, and

there are other buildings of but four or five stories and which house not more than from fifteen to twenty-five men. A marked tendency of the day is toward the smaller houses, for in them the bachelor thinks he shall find the greatest conveniences, the most exclusiveness, for the least expenditure of money. For the average bachelor, strange to discover, is a man who, though anxious to make a gallant show, is not oblivious to possibilities of money saving.

But in most bachelor houses there is no outward and visible sign of money saving. Granite-pillared entrances, lobbies ringed round with massive columns, hallways marble-walled and rich-tiled: it is through such as these that many a bachelor goes to his apartments. Dining-rooms there are with oval ceilings of multi-colored glass through which the sunlight shines subdued, and in some rooms there is a soft glow that comes from hidden electric lights. One may not dispute the truth of the assertion that it is not good for man to be alone, and yet there is many a New York bachelor who somehow seems to get on more than comfortably.

There is not in New York, as yet, the charm that goes with the chambers where bachelors dwell in some of the Old-World cities. We have no buildings, for example, which, like some in the heart of busiest London, are rich in historical and literary association and in memories that reach back for generations. Nor have we an Albany, closely reminiscent of such famous men as Macaulay and Byron and Lytton. In New York the tendency is all for newness, and seldom is a building allowed to stand long enough to acquire the gray atmosphere of age. Buildings are cut off in their youth.

But the bachelor homes of New York can show—and this, to the New York bachelor, is the important point—conveniences and luxuries far beyond those of Old-World bachelor houses. Elevators run throughout the night; steam heat warms the rooms in winter and ventilating appliances cool them in summer; electric light is in every room; in a few buildings there is even a cold-storage attachment for every tenant, operated by an apparatus in the basement, and giving to each bachelor the opportunity to have bottles or game, icy cold, ready to his hand. For modern comfort the New York bachelor is content to forego picturesque associations.

A notable characteristic of New York bachelor apartments is the fireplace. The bachelor seems to look on that as a necessary adjunct to his home, and therefore in the great majority of bachelor apartments it is in marked evidence. A cheerful glow it makes and serves to give to the bachelor a sense of homelike coziness.

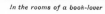

In the rooms of a book-lover

Entrance to one of the big houses

A bachelor's paintings by Corot and De Chavannes

Our Cities in the Twentieth Century

IT IS the destiny of New York to be the Empire City of the World. She will be the chief centre of commerce, of finance and of population. This destiny may be delayed through misgovernment and other causes, but it is inevitable. Another fifty years, with the rate of increase recorded in the past century, will give her the lead in population. Such reasonable shipping facilities as we have a right to expect for our extensive water-front, in view of our tremendous commercial development, will give her control of the world's commerce. The great prosperity of the country, and our amazing development as a manufacturing nation, will shift the financial centre from Threadneedle Street to Wall Street. New York will be the world's clearing house within the next few years unless the unexpected happens. Altogether, there have never been before any city in the world, at any time, such prospects as are before New York. The difficulty in forecasting these prospects lies in the inability of any human mind to grasp them.

The natural advantages of New York are greater than those enjoyed by any other city in history, ancient or modern. Athens, Rome, the great trading ports of the East which flourished in the olden time, had not one-hundredth part of the natural advantages that belong to us. London, Paris, Berlin, Vienna, and all the other great cities of Europe to-day are hampered by a thousand and one restrictions and difficulties unknown to us. In America there is not another city that is even approximately in the same

citizens will make their permanent homes, winter and summer, along these magnificent beaches.

When we can go to the easterly limit of our great city in fifteen minutes, embarking at Wall Street in luxurious cars that will carry us without change, the Long Island Boulevard will offer all the advantages of a residence on Fifth Avenue. The time when we shall be able to do this is almost in sight. It will come as soon as the tunnels already planned for the East River are completed. With electric propulsion the trip will be swift, clean and pleasant. It will involve no more trouble and hardship than is now involved in a trip from Wall Street to Central Park.

Nor will the rich alone take advantage of this new section. Those in moderate circumstances will find on the Long Island shore homes at moderate prices. The tendency in this direction has manifested itself already, even with the limited transportation facilities we now enjoy. Brooklyn has grown out more and more to the eastward, until now there is a continuous and unbroken stretch of well-built dwellings clear to the limits of Coney Island, where a few years ago there were potato patches and cornfields. Fort Hamilton, Gravesend, New Utrecht, Bensonhurst, Bath Beach, have grown up almost over night.

Thousands of beautiful houses, fronting on streets that are finely paved, thoroughly lighted and perfectly clean, have been built and are occupied. The inhabitants have all the conveniences that are to be found in the heart

class with New York, so far as Nature has provided. It seems almost as though Providence had here deliberately arranged all the conditions to make possible the creation of a city unequaled elsewhere in the world. Not only have we the greatest extent of water-front, and the finest harbor on earth, but we have in addition over twenty-five miles of ocean-front. From Coney Island Point to Far Rockaway there is a stretch of beach seventeen miles long within the city limits, capable of most picturesque improvement. On Staten Island, which is now the southern section of the city, there is an ocean frontage of over eight miles.

Sooner or later this entire stretch of land, washed by the tides, will be an unbroken parkway. Already the development of this plan has begun. From South Brooklyn to Fort Hamilton a magnificent parkway and boulevard has been laid out along the water-front, which, when completed, will be the finest ocean driveway on earth. This driveway will at no distant day extend the full length of that part of the city which margins the sea. Here will be located the magnificent dwellings and summer homes of the rich. Once the era of development has set in, the men of affairs who now make their homes during the hot season in Newport, Narragansett, and the other so-called fashionable watering-places will locate within the city's boundary, where they can remain in close touch with their business, and at the same time enjoy to the full all the advantages found farther away. As our transportation facilities improve, many of our foremost

of New York. Electricity is on tap everywhere. The sanitary appliances are perfect. There are hundreds of square miles of territory where land, ten years ago, could have been bought at $500 an acre, which to-day sell for $500 a lot. Such development as this forecasts accurately what is to come when there is unbroken and continuous transit from the heart of New York.

To the south the development will be as great as it has been to the east. Already it has set in, and in a few years more the beautiful hills on Staten Island will all be crowned with fine homes facing on perfect streets, "fanned by ocean breezes." At present, access to the south is to be had only by the Staten Island ferryboats, but by means of tunnels every part of Staten Island will be brought within fifteen or twenty minutes of the City Hall. And the trip will be made under the most perfect conditions, in well-lighted, smooth-running, comfortable cars.

When the development that may reasonably be expected along the ocean-front section of New York City has come there will be presented a picture unparalleled on earth. Already there is unfolded to the incoming passengers on ocean steamships a panorama that beggars anything to be seen elsewhere. When the Staten Island heights are crowned, and the Long Island plains are fully populated, the beauty of this panorama will be increased a hundredfold. Day and night the scene will be equally fascinating. Under the sunlight, the green slopes, the beautiful streets, the

New York—Its Present and Its Future *By Ex-Mayor Gilroy*

E. 69th St.   E. 68th St.

magnificent parks and the winding boulevards will offer such a picture as will inspire the most unimaginative. At night, under the glow of thousands of brilliant electric lamps, it will be like a bit from fairyland to the eyes of the travelers on incoming ships. No stage scene ever set will compare with it.

I have laid great stress on the development of New York to the southward and eastward because the field here is comparatively new. In the past, before consolidation, New York had only one way of growing—that was to the north. When Brooklyn, Staten Island and Queens County were taken into the Greater City the complexion of things changed entirely, and to-day we are restricted only in one direction—that is to the west.

There has at times been some speculation which contemplated the extension of the city into New Jersey. That, however, may be considered a dream. The Hudson River will probably always remain as the boundary between the two States. New Jersey will, of course, derive a substantial increase of population from New York. To-day there are undoubtedly a hundred thousand people whose business lives are spent in New York City, but whose homes lie across the North River. These people are really New Yorkers to all intents and purposes. Most of their waking hours are spent on Manhattan Island. The true census of the city should, perhaps, embrace them in its population; but as the census figures are based on the sleeping places, these people will always be considered apart.

third Street, people used to go to witness balloon ascensions. It was the country. To-day the Fifth Avenue Hotel is out of the hotel district, the centre of which is about Forty-second Street. When the City Hall was built it was considered that it marked the northernmost limits of the city. The main front and the sides of the building were finished in white marble, but the back was built of brownstone, on the theory that there would never be anybody behind it to look at it.

Forty years ago the principal theatres were located about City Hall Park. The Park Theatre was on Chambers Street, Burton's Theatre was on Broadway, between Worth and Anthony—Anthony being Pearl Street to-day. In 1850 Park Place was still a street of residences. Bond Street and Great Jones Street were the uptown residence streets.

The New York, New Haven and Hartford station was at Canal Street, near Broadway. The Harlem Railroad ran its cars to Tryon Row. Just north of the Tombs, where the Criminal Court House stands to-day, at White and Centre Streets, was a huge freight depot. The only passenger station of the New York Central Railroad in New York was at Thirtieth Street and Eleventh Avenue—a location now practically out of the world.

Had any one prophesied the changes that have since come he would have been deemed a visionary. Fifty years are, after all, not such a very long period, but fifty years have changed things so completely in New York that, looking backward, it is almost impossible to give a picture of the things

E. 71st St.   E. 70th St.

In the future, however, they are certain to be bound even more closely to us than they have been in the past. There will undoubtedly be a number of tunnels under the North River, and the Great Bridge, which has been so long under contemplation, is certain to come within a comparatively few years. Then it will be about as easy to reach points in New Jersey as it will be to reach points on Long Island, Staten Island and the territory across the Harlem. Necessarily there will be a tremendous growth of population throughout that section of New Jersey that is in touch with Manhattan Island. In an article on New York this growth cannot properly be considered.

After looking over the field to the south and east, we must turn to the north. Here will come a development that I believe will be the most remarkable in the history of any city. It will date almost from the moment that the first train is run through the Underground Railroad, now building.

No better prophecy of what may be expected can be made than through a retrospect of what has been. Fifty years ago it was common to picnic in the woods just north of what is now Forty-second Street. To-day Forty-second Street is the centre of the city. Every one who has his eyes open must know that, amazing as was the era of development in the latter half of the last century, it will be proportionately very much greater in the first half of the new.

Half a century ago all the hotels of any account were located in or about Cortlandt Street. Where the Fifth Avenue Hotel stands to-day, at Twenty-

as they were and as they are to-day. If, with the comparatively limited resources, scientific, mechanical, financial and industrial, that have been at our disposition since 1850, we have made such strides, what is going to happen in the next fifty years, when our scientific, mechanical, financial and industrial resources are unlimited?

New York collects in taxes each year almost as much as the city's total wealth of fifty years ago amounted to. Necessarily, her expenditure in all directions must be proportionately greater than it ever was. I believe there will come a time when the largest part of the entire Island of Manhattan will be given up to business. Our commerce will grow to such an enormous extent that the wholesale district will be well up to Central Park, and the retail centre will be north of One Hundred and Tenth Street. We have seen the retail stores go up, and still farther up, and the process is certain to continue.

Only ten years ago Fourteenth Street was the main shopping street. To-day it is Twenty-third. Forty-second Street is given up entirely to stores, where ten years ago it was practically all residences. One Hundred and Twenty-fifth Street, from end to end, is given up to business. One of the largest department stores in the country is located there.

As the Underground Railroad draws people uptown, this development is bound to continue. The only difference is that its progress will be much

(Concluded on Page 19)

E. 80th St.   E. 79th St.

more rapid. Retail business always follows the population, and, that being the case, I look for change early in the century that will transfer the upper part of Sixth and Seventh Avenues, St. Nicholas Avenue, and the entire section thereabouts into a business centre. The hotel centre, too, will crowd up into that neighborhood. True, the palatial hotels of to-day are at and below Fifty-ninth Street. New York has been increasing at the rate of thirty per cent. every ten years. This increase, maintained, will give us in fifty years a population very closely approximating ten millions. Such a population will, of necessity, upset entirely all our preconceived notions.

The Progress in Municipal Architecture

In nothing has New York shown greater progress than in her architecture. We have entered on a new era in the construction of our private and public buildings. Fifteen years ago there were few, if any, cities on earth whose architecture was quite so hideous as ours. Of public buildings we had none worth speaking about except our City Hall and the famous old "Tombs," which was a beautiful example of the Egyptian style. Our domestic architecture gave us nothing to be proud of. With a few exceptions, we lived in square boxes built of brick, or, where we were very pretentious, of brownstone. The brownstone invariably peeled under our climatic conditions, and we had great rows of ugly, monotonous structures that looked as though they had some virulent skin disease. The brick buildings it was possible to keep in better shape through the liberal application of paint, but, so far as art was concerned, they were little more pleasant to the eye than the adobe dwellings of the Mexicans. Interior decoration was practically unknown.

To-day all this has changed. On upper Fifth Avenue and the side streets hundreds of dwellings have been erected that are perfect examples of high art; beautiful buildings of marble and other ornamental building stones. The sculptor, the iron-worker and the glass-worker have joined hands to produce effects that are a feast for the eye.

With our public buildings we have made even greater strides. The great library that is building on Fifth Avenue, the two museums in Central Park, the new buildings that are going up in the Bronx Park, the Columbia College buildings, St. Luke's Hospital, the Cathedral, and the other groups planned for Morningside Heights, all show that New York is preparing for her destiny as a centre of art and beauty, as well as a centre of commerce. We shall have the most beautiful, as well as the most prosperous, city on earth.

A Splendid Driveway of Twenty Miles

Even New Yorkers have, as a general thing, little idea of the change that is coming over New York in respect to its external appearance. The improvement that has been wrought by the great system of beautifully paved streets, and the cutting through of parkways and driveways, is unknown to most of our people. I wonder how many there are who know that, with the finishing of the viaduct across Manhattan Valley at Riverside Drive we have practically completed a twenty-mile driveway. As soon as the new avenue that is to connect this viaduct with the French Boulevard to the north of One Hundred and Twenty-fifth Street has been finished there will be a continuous stretch of roadway from Seventy-second Street and Central Park to One Hundred and Tenth Street, to Riverside Drive, to the Viaduct, to the French Boulevard, to Dykeman Street, to the Speedway, to St. Nicholas Avenue, and back to the Park. This beautiful drive, nearly twenty miles long, is lined for almost its entire length with handsome dwellings, and the pavement is the most perfect in the world.

New York's park area to-day is sufficient for any growth that she may experience. It is greater than that of any other city in America. The only additions that will probably be made to it will be in the creation of numerous small parks in the congested districts. The work is already well advanced, and will no doubt be continued. These small parks reduce the death rate, and improve the living conditions of those who most need such improvements. Their establishment will lead ultimately to the remodeling of our tenement-house system. The tenement house, as we are now situated, we must always have. The people who work for a living cannot afford the time, as a general thing, that would be lost in going to and fro between their places of labor and dwellings in the suburbs. But with improved sanitation laws and the development of the artistic sense that is taking place, we shall make the tenement of the future a model institution. The workingman's home of the twentieth century will be as much in advance of that of the nineteenth century as the nineteenth century home was an improvement over that of the eighteenth century.

I expect to see a complete revolution in the water-front of the city. This revolution has begun, and will be completed through the municipal ownership of every foot of water-front. Already New York owns most of this property, and the rest will be acquired as rapidly as is consistent with safe management. I do not look for the ornate docks of Liverpool. Our own straight, long, open docks are much preferable.

I look to see practically the entire water-front faced with enormous storage-houses, ornately built, thereby adding vastly to the appearance of the river streets, without at all interfering with their utilitarian character. New York must live and thrive on her commerce, and nothing will ever be permitted to interfere with its development.

The system of pier roof-gardens already inaugurated will be very generally extended. The piers themselves will be regularly and handsomely built of wood and iron, and this will do away entirely with the ragged appearance now presented by the city on an approach by water.

Municipal Ownership of Utilities

How far municipal ownership of public utilities will extend it is hard to say. That the city will always own her own water supply, and that she will finally own all her dockage, is certain. The people are too wide awake to permit any private corporation of the future to control even a portion of either of these two utilities. The wisdom of the public ownership of lighting and heating facilities is yet to be determined.

As to the city's owning and operating the street railways, that, as a general proposition, seems to me to be out of the question. The system under which the city controls the Underground Railroad, now building, is nearly perfect. To attempt to acquire control of the surface systems would be ruinous. Confiscation, no matter under what method it should be effected, would be robbery, and the people are too honest to permit anything of the kind. Purchase on a fair basis would mean an outlay of many hundreds of millions, and the people are too wise to sanction it.

The greatest hardship under which New York suffers to-day in her government is the crude system of taxation. Some plan must be devised by which it will be possible to throw a fair share of the public burden on personal property.

At present the personal tax is administered in a manner that is almost childish. The burden of our great public expenditures falls almost entirely on real estate, so that the property owner finds it difficult to obtain any revenue from his holdings. The assessed valuation for real estate for 1900 was $3,168,-547,700. The total assessed valuation on personal property was only $485,574,493. No reasonable man doubts that the real value of personal property held in this city is many times that amount.

If this personal property could be made to bear a proper proportion of the public burden, our tax rate would fall at once to little more than one per cent. Our present tax rate, which is $2.40 on every hundred dollars, is outrageous. The rate has grown in less than ten years from $1.79 to its present figure, and, if the rate of expenditure continues, there is no telling where the increase will stop. Outlays are permitted on the most ruinous scale. Apparently all care for the well-being of the taxpayers has been thrown aside in the wild scramble to get out of them as much money as possible.

This condition of affairs is a tremendous handicap. Once it is removed, and our municipal government is run on a business basis, as it should be, New York will continue her march toward her destiny as the Empire City of the World at a rate that will fill the people of the earth with amazement.

SIGHTSEEING IN 1920.

The caption on this 1902 cartoon from *Life* reads as follows: "That depression down there is where New York City stood. But with all its skyscrapers and underground tunnels it suddenly sunk one day and they haven't been able to find it since."

How Money is Burned in New York

By Paul Latzke

A LADY, and a very pretty lady she was, good to look at from the crown of her head to the soles of her feet, entered the shop. A demure saleswoman, faultlessly gotten up in black, met the lady at the threshold. They greeted each other pleasantly and then conversed for a few minutes in low tones. What they said did not reach my ears. There was a clock on the opposite side of the street, and, being prohibited from paying too close attention to the pretty lady and the demure saleswoman, I watched the clock. It had ticked off seven and a half minutes when the conversation that had been beyond my ears increased in volume. The lady and the saleswoman were approaching the front of the shop where I was standing. What followed could not escape me.

"We are very much obliged to you, indeed, Mrs. Blank."

"I am sure the obligation is on my part," was the gracious response, "for a prettier gown I have rarely seen in my life. You don't know how pleased I am at securing it."

"Thank you, indeed, for your good opinion. Good-morning."

"Good-morning."

The pretty lady had reached the door, which was held open by a page in buttons, when she suddenly seemed to remember something.

"By the way," she said, "I forgot to ask the price of the gown. How much is it?"

"Seventeen hundred dollars," was the calm answer.

"Isn't that rather high?" suggested the lady, as the ordinary woman might have suggested that peaches at sixty cents a basket were high.

"No, I think not," replied the saleswoman, as demure as ever, and also apparently looking at the transaction as the most commonplace thing in the world. "You know it's an exclusive design and the very latest importation. Then the fur trimming——"

"Yes, I suppose that's true; I had forgotten it. All right; be sure and get it around early."

And the thing was over. A dress costing seventeen hundred dollars had been bought by this woman as freely as the average maid would have bought a kerchief. It hadn't even occurred to her to ask the price, except as an afterthought.

The Greenback Bonfires on Fifth Avenue

And that is the whole tone in New York to-day. It is the Era of Burning Money. There are bonfires on every corner of Fifth Avenue, from Twenty-third Street to Forty-second, and they are being fed with greenbacks at a rate that would have made the ancients, fabled for their luxury, stare and write themselves down novices. This dress transaction that I have attempted to describe is simply an incident, and a very small and unimportant one; an incident that is repeating itself in scores of shops every day, almost every hour of every day. In the jeweler's, the florist's, the furnisher's; everywhere it is the same. Ask any tradesman in the fashionable district which lies along Fifth Avenue between the streets I have mentioned, and, if he knows you well enough, he will tell you that his sales have increased fifty per cent. during the last eighteen months, and that his prices have gone up in proportion.

On a nasty, rainy morning I was standing in a jeweler's store on Fifth Avenue. The place was about eighteen feet wide and something like twenty-five feet deep. It would not have made more than a fair-sized bedroom in the home of a prosperous country merchant. Business was evidently dull.

"Trade isn't rushing?" I suggested to the proprietor.

"Oh, no; not this morning," he answered cheerfully; "the ladies are not fond of coming out in wet weather even in carriages."

"And expenses go on?"

"Yes; but who minds expenses when times are what they are to-day? We pay an annual rental of seven thousand dollars for this place. A few years ago it would have gone begging at three thousand. At this moment, if I should indicate to the landlord that I consider the rent too high, or that I am in any way displeased, or that I desire to relinquish my lease, he would rent it over my head inside of an hour at an increase of anywhere from fifteen to fifty per cent. It is practically impossible to find a street store location on Fifth Avenue to-day, and even the upper floors are held at figures that would make country people stare. A building with a twenty-five-foot front will bring, in a year's rent for a single upper story, more money than one would get for the outright sale of the ordinary store property in many cities. It is simply a question of what landlords have the conscience to ask. Would-be tenants are clamoring at their doorsteps."

Some Fifth Avenue Golcondas

This is literally true. There is a piece of unimproved property near Thirty-second Street on Fifth Avenue on which stands an old-fashioned dwelling-house, one of the few that remain in that section. It has a frontage of twenty-five feet and a depth of less than a hundred. It is owned by a wealthy tailor who bought it some years ago on speculation for $45,000. To-day he holds it at $200,000. He has declined an offer of $13,000 a year for ground rent, or more than $500 a front foot. He wants $15,000, and he will get it, and in addition will get a rental equal to ten per cent. per annum for all improvements. As the old building will have to be torn down and a new one erected for business purposes, at an expense of perhaps $40,000, this means that the property will bring, in rents, when improved, $19,000 a year under a ten-years' lease, or an assured income of $190,000 on an investment of less than $85,000.

That is the way fortunes are being made in New York real estate. And the boom is by no means confined to Fifth Avenue. It extends through all the side streets, and is even stronger on certain sections of Broadway than it is in the district I have mentioned. A conservative estimate shows that the property from Twenty-third Street to Forty-seventh Street, between Fifth Avenue and Seventh Avenue, has enhanced in value, within the last year, over sixty million dollars. This is not mere paper valuation. Rents are being collected in proportion. Purchasers stand ready with good gold to snap up every parcel that comes into the market, and the fortunate holders, who are not inclined to sell, are besieged by a horde of agents, the great majority of whom have standing offers of cash. It is an ordinary occurrence for a man owning a twenty-five-foot lot in this district to raise the price a thousand dollars overnight. Two thousand dollars a front foot is asked for property on the side streets, in fair locations, and eight thousand dollars a front foot is asked, and given, for parcels located in particularly choice spots, as, for example, on Broadway about Herald Square at Thirty-fourth Street, and Long Acre Square at Forty-fourth Street.

The Thirty-Fourth Street Boom

There have been some great stock booms during the past years in Wall Street, but even they were not more spectacular than this marvelous real-estate boom. Values have not alone doubled, but trebled and quadrupled in places. A hundred stories could be told of men who started out with a "shoe-string," as the saying goes, and who, through good fortune backed by some foresight, have become millionaires.

Thirty-fourth Street and Forty-second Street property was for years a drag. The boom hit Forty-second Street about a year and a half ago, when it was announced that one of the chief stations of the Underground Road was to be located on the flatiron at the junction of Broadway and Seventh Avenue at Forty-second Street. Instantly all the property around went up by leaps and bounds. A tradesman who had secured a ninety-nine years' lease on a small lot on one of the corners sublet at an increase over his rental of $35,000 a year. He was not required to spend a dollar for improvements or to invest more than a year's rental at the figure he paid. Now he and his heirs are assured of an income of $35,000 a year for ninety-nine years.

The Thirty-fourth Street boom began when it was announced that two large department stores had secured the entire Broadway fronts from Thirty-third to Thirty-fifth Streets, running back well into the block. Shortly afterward rumors began to spread that the Pennsylvania Railroad was going to put a huge terminal station somewhere in the same neighborhood. This sent values up like skyrockets. When the official announcement was made the other day that the Pennsylvania depot was to occupy all the space between Seventh and Tenth Avenues, from Thirty-second to Thirty-fourth Street, and that the Long Island Railroad was going to have an underground terminal at the same place, those who had sold, even at the enhanced values, groaned aloud at their misfortune.

A twenty-five-foot lot with an ordinary old-fashioned dwelling-house, on Thirty-fourth Street near the corner of Eighth Avenue—that is, two long blocks from Broadway—was purchased seventeen years ago for $15,000. In the interval there were long periods when it did not pay two per cent. on the investment. Three days before Christmas this piece of property was sold for $42,000, and the ink was hardly dry on the title deeds when the old holders received an offer of $48,000. They tore their hair with rage, and then set to work to get the property back, if possible, at something near the figure at which they had sold, in order to take on the other purchaser. Through a third party they approached the holder to whom they had transferred with an offer of $44,000, showing a clear profit of $2000 in two hours on a real-estate proposition that, ordinarily, would have been a dead proposition for a couple of years. The man laughed at them. "Why," he said, "as soon as I could get downtown with the title deeds I sold that piece of property for $50,000, and I've got the cash in bank for it now."

A Profit of $355,000 on a Tiny Plot

A Broadway corner in the vicinity of Herald Square is a tiny triangular plot, fifteen feet front on Broadway and eighteen feet deep on the cross street. This lot was bought in the seventies for $20,000. One of the department stores I have mentioned secured all the property on the block with the exception of this little corner. When the agents of the proprietors sought the owner of the little corner they found that he was in Europe. They wrote and asked him to cable a proposition. He replied that he would sell for $125,000. They laughed at him and offered him something less. He didn't even answer. Finally they offered him $125,000, and he told them that his price had risen and was now $150,000. They offered him $140,000 and he declined. Then they rose to $150,000, and he told them that his price was $175,000. Before they could close he had jumped it to $190,000, then to $210,000, to $225,000, and finally to $375,000. This for a bit of ground that has in it two hundred and sixteen square feet, or at the rate of nearly two thousand dollars for every square foot! The department-store people indignantly declined to buy. When they woke up they found that a little merchant with a speculative mind and considerable backing had snapped up the parcel at the owner's figure. All this occurred inside of three months. The proprietors of the department store now find themselves in this predicament: they have a huge plot of ground containing about four acres, for which they have paid enormous prices and on which they are proceeding with the construction of a building to cost several million dollars, while the vital corner, a mere speck of ground, is denied them, except at a price that makes even New York stare.

At first glance this would seem to be like a bit of extortion; but shrewd real-estate men have figured it out that, even at this figure, the owners can make this little plot pay over ten per cent. It is impossible, of course, to erect a skyscraper on such a small parcel, because an elevator would cut off so much floor space that there would be nothing left.

But the difficulty may be solved in a unique way. Provided the department store does not finally capitulate, and pay a big profit over $375,000, the owners of the corner, it is said, intend to put up a six-story building, which they will rent to a rival department store farther downtown as a branch where samples will be shown. Then the space above is to be let for advertising purposes, the scheme being to erect a huge steel tower with electric signs and other up-to-date devices.

It is figured that, when the Pennsylvania and Long Island terminals are completed, when the department stores are going at full blast, and when all the surrounding property facing Herald Square has been improved according to the present plans, over five hundred thousand people, on an average, will pass within sight of this corner every twenty-four hours throughout the year. This estimate includes the passengers on the elevated road and the passengers on the three great surface roads that intersect here.

On this advertising proposition, it is figured, a net revenue of $38,000 a year can be cleared for the ground value of the little plot, or ten per cent. on the investment, enormous as it is in proportion to the square feet of land.

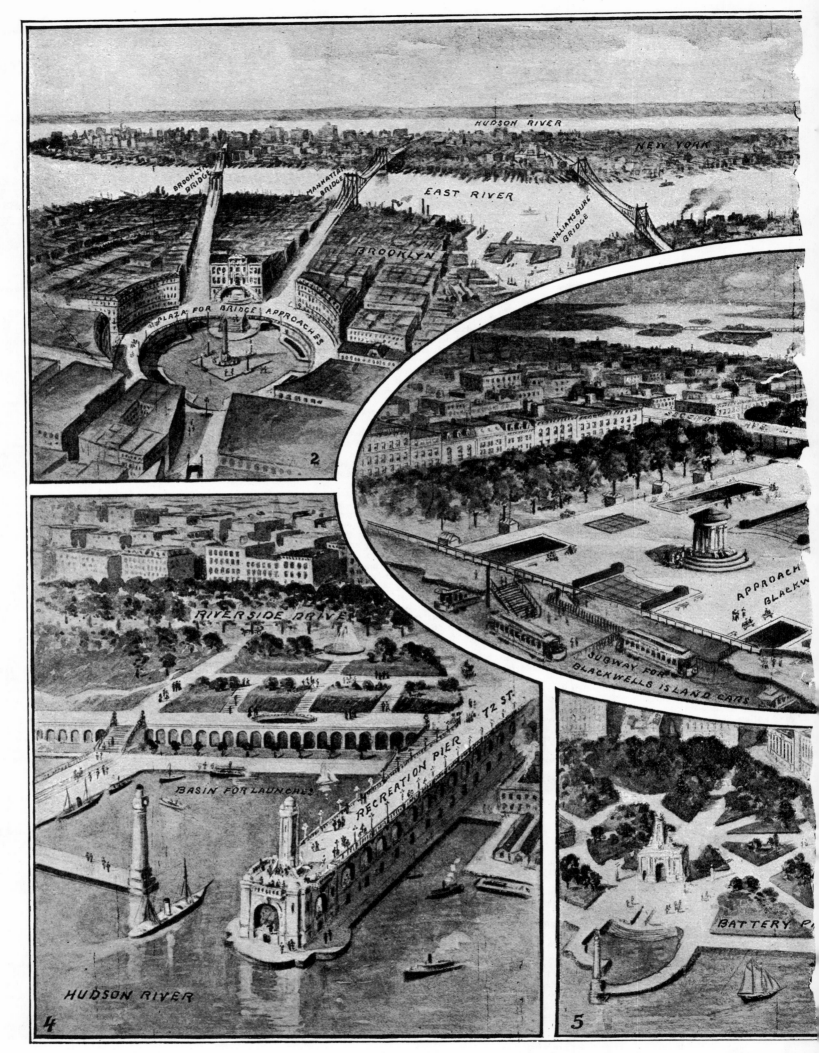

HUDSON RIVER

NEW YORK

EAST RIVER

BROOKLYN BRIDGE

MANHATTAN BRIDGE

WILLIAMSBURG BRIDGE

BROOKLYN

PLAZA FOR BRIDGE APPROACHES

2

SECOND AVE.

APPROACH BLACKW

SUBWAY FOR BLACKWELLS ISLAND CARS

RIVERSIDE DRIVE

BASIN FOR LAUNCHES

RECREATION PIER

72 ST.

HUDSON RIVER

4

BATTERY P.

5

PLANS FOR IMPROVING AND

In December, 1903, Mayor McClellan approved the appointment by the Board of Aldermen of a Commission to pre
Mayor and the Board of Aldermen a report embodying an elaborate scheme for the city's development, involv
numerous other matters essential to the project. An extra appropriation has been given to the Commission, and
the prosecution of the work, will probably be submitted to the Mayor at the end of the year. The drawings on this
for approaches to the East River and Manhattan bridges; (3) a panorama of upper Manhattan and the Bronx, look
Drive; (5) the proposed improvement of Battery Park, showing Union Ferry terminal and water-stairs for the reception

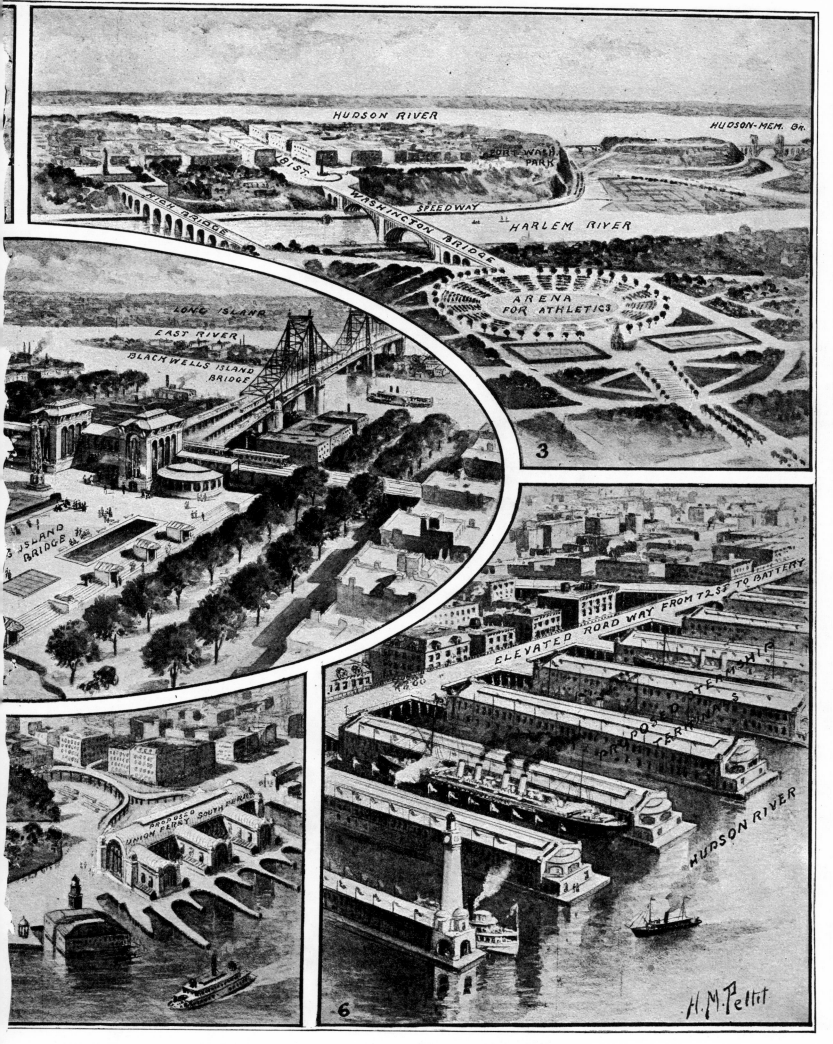

BEAUTIFYING NEW YORK

pare plans for the improvement and beautifying of New York City. Last January the Commission presented to the
ing the laying out of parks, streets, and highways, the location of city buildings, improvement of water fronts, and
several architects of prominence are at work perfecting plans. The final report, embodying definite measures for
page show (1) the proposed Subway loop terminal for the Blackwells Island Bridge; (2) a common plaza in Brooklyn
ing west. showing improvements and extensions; (4) the proposed improvement of Seventy-second Street and Riverside
of distinguished guests; and (6) the proposed new West Side elevated roadway from Seventy-second Street to the Battery

HOW PEOPLE COME AND GO IN NEW YORK.

BY RICHARD BARRY.

ILLUSTRATED BY T. DART WALKER AND L. A. SHAFER.

PROBABLY over three hundred and fifty thousand brain-workers, manual toilers, and wage-earners daily enter the artery centre of the Greater New York—the place where its pulse is to be felt, the commercial heart, which might now well include the busy district from Thirty-fourth Street south to the Battery. Between the hours of seven and ten o'clock in the morning this great inrush is going on, and the hordes of Uitlanders are settling down to begin the work-day.

But to digress at the outset to gain an idea of proportion: Supposing that a city of the size and importance of Cincinnati should be threatened with some direful disaster, making it expedient and necessary to move every man, woman, and child to a distance of from twelve to forty miles in a limited space of time, what hubbub and confusion would follow! How long would it take for this to be accomplished? It would be a hard thing to state; and yet more people than the city of Cincinnati holds pour regularly into New York and regularly pour out again every day!

Where do they come from, where do they go, and how do they do it? Where stand the towns and villages that are populous at night and as deserted in the daytime as if the country had called their young and the willing to the defence of her frontiers. Where are they? They are scattered in so many directions and at such varying distances that the exodus and the influx of the inhabitants are hardly noticeable. It is only when they gather at the congested points where they deliver their bodies into the care and keeping of the common carriers that the strength of the commuter army is recognized.

Although these men (some of whom travel a distance equal to the circumference of the earth at the equator every year, and spend a large proportion of their lives on train or trolley or boat) arise with the crowing of cocks and the early morning twitter of birds in their ears, and at night may awaken to listen to the melancholy hooting of an owl in the orchard, they are nevertheless men of the city. Town has stamped them in appearance, speech, and manner, and so accustomed do they become to the diurnal pilgrimage that they have grown to regard it in a philosophical spirit. With the adaptability of the American temperament, they have begun to utilize it in one way or another to their advantage. To a man unaccustomed to this life and forced to make these journeyings for a week, say, they would seem most probably a bore; but to the philosophical commuter the time is not altogether spent amiss. He makes business appointments on the train, or finds time for amusement in conversation and companionship; he devotes himself to contemporary literature, or familiarizes himself with the news of the day; and in some cases he carries his club with him, as it were, claims his favorite seat and corner, and gains the relief and excitement that the "whister" derives from the game of "Master Cavendish."

The comic papers have taken the commuter for one of their butts in stock; but over this he triumphs, and his absolute importance to the business life of the metropolis is evident. It was noticed at the time of the great blizzard, when suburban traffic was blocked completely and business came almost to a standstill.

But various are the classes and distinctions of these workaday pilgrims, and the routes and methods they take of reaching shop, store, or office have developed individual habits—habits of promptness and habits of perpetual haste. Many, alas! are at the mercy completely

WALL STREET WHEN THE BANKERS SHUT UP SHOP FOR THE DAY.

of the corporation that for a yearly price contracts to start them on time, deliver them safely, and return them to the bosom of their families. There are some who boast with proper pride that they have never missed a train; there are others who apparently never succeed in catching one without having to run for it. They chase from the breakfast table to the suburban railway station, and from the uptown surface cars they rush through the waiting-room, greet the ticket-taker with a friendly nod of recognition, and settle themselves in the smoking-car just as the train-despatcher rings his bell. The railway

hands know them by name and sight, the conductor is a conspicuous friend, and the brakeman is especially polite at the Christmas season.

The inhabitant who lives south of the Harlem River cannot be classed among the pilgrims. He is independent of time-tables. He has no intimacy with minor officials, and he disdains the carrying of bundles. But the citizen of the Greater New York who depends upon these things is often the shopper for the family. He disdains disguise, and boldly carries out a pocket full of quail, a basket of peaches, or a sugar-cured ham, and is willing to tell you where he *always* procures them. There is one class, however, limited in numbers, but none the less to be recognized, whose daily goings and comings are somewhat in the sense of the recreations of a prince of royal blood. His pilgrimage is witnessed by thousands, and the money he spends in one week going from his mahogany desk to his mahogany dinner table would keep the average pilgrim's coal-cellar filled for a decade. His yacht anchors near the river-bank up the Hudson or in one of the shallow inlets of the Sound, where the rich man's sloping lawn reaches down to his private pier-head. He enters his gig or launch, puts off to his graceful craft, dons a yachting-cap, leans back in a wicker chair, and is transported as smoothly and delightfully as the prince in a fairy tale, into the world of turmoil and the country of bonds and stocks and profits. Late in the afternoon he drives to the city water-front, gives his orders to the belettered sailors in true naval fashion, is greeted at the gangway by a steward with the latest popular beverage, and off he goes homeward, the cool breeze fanning him, while countless thousands of his kind swelter in the crowded cars, or cling helplessly to the greasy straps of the suburban trolley lines.

It would be rather interesting to draw the distinction between these, and to note the methods that are employed by some of the latter class to reach their journey's end. They are men whose fingers are ink-stained from handling the pen, and whose forefingers are calloused from following columns of figures in the ledger, who every night and every morning pull in small boats some two or three miles from their little cottages along the Great South Bay.

From Brooklyn, over bridge and ferry, comes a mighty army. See the net-work of surface and elevated roads that land them at their doors!

Others leave the trolley at the corner of some country lane and strike out through the dust or mud or snow to be welcomed at the hill-top like returning mariners by their expectant youngsters and their faithful spouses—sometimes at night to be guided by cheerful lights placed in the windows.

It would be hard to estimate the number of people who cross from Brooklyn by ferry and bridge to their daily work. But, beyond all doubt, this army, a fair proportion of which is women, amounts to something in the neighborhood of one hundred thousand. From the towns of Long Island come about thirteen thousand, while the ferry-boats from Staten Island and the south carry about seven thousand. New Jersey adds its great proportion to the total sum. The five great railroads and their branches terminating along the western shore of the North River carry commuters in the following proportions: the New York, Susquehanna, and Western, two thousand; the New Jersey Central, eight thousand; the Delaware, Lackawanna, and Western, twenty-five thousand; the Erie, thirty-eight thousand; the West Shore, two thousand; and the Pennsylvania road, thirty thousand.

But it is surprising to learn what a great proportion enters the city from the north through the Grand Central Station, coming in by the net-work of roads that terminate in that small and confined space. It is marvellous how such crowds can be handled. But what is yet more

THE HEIGHT OF LUXURY.

ALONG THE SHORES OF THE HARLEM RIVER.

keeps many large industries going. The steam - railroads give more care to the comfort of these customers than of the people who come and go. The elegant (a word that just fits) vestibule trains give them all the luxury of barber shops, reading - rooms, valets, maids, and stenographers as they roll toward the Mecca of their hopes. The luggage of the money-spender is taken direct from the railway station to the number- ed room at the chosen hotel; a special cab-service, at reasonable rates, takes the owner of the luggage and deposits him at the doorway. Nothing could be more simple or more comfortable. He finds nothing to complain of in all this, and, beyond all doubt, is satisfied with the common carriers and the terminal facilities; he is a preferred patron, and tips his way along regardless of expense. But let him go out to spend a day or so with a suburban friend; he will find that a different matter. Crowded and jostled and packed and steamed, he will regard a trip to Chicago in "the Limited" as a pastime; he will lose all sense of personal importance, and vote that of all criminally good-natured individuals the New York commuter is the worst offender. A Chicagoan once stated that "New York was only intended to be 'so big' anyhow," and lacked the power of limitless expansion. "You have to go either up or down or out of it," said he. Perhaps that is true enough, but it has grown to be a pretty long "up or down," and is still growing; as for the getting out, that implies a getting in, and is becoming another question to face. Another bridge or two across the East River would help out the difficulty —comparatively a simple matter of investment of capital. What has been done once so successfully can be done again. The bridges will come in good time, and there may be before long one linking us to the Jersey shore. Few people know that the tunnel underneath the North River was ever completed. The gigantic failure of the

remarkable is the facility and the mystery of their disappearance once they reach the street. From all the downtown ferries, during the opening and closing of the business day, march columns of hurrying figures. They overrun the sidewalks, and, unless it is too muddy, often take to the middle of the streets. Like a daily tide they set in and out at stated hours, gathering numbers from every doorway and corner. But at the entrance of the Grand Central Station one sees no such evidence of the march to a common dispersing-point—which downtown is Broadway. At Forty - second Street the crowds scatter in all directions—across town they go in the horse - cars, or up or down by elevated roads or the trolley. A few figures readily show the amount of this augmentation of New York's mercantile and business army. New York Central carries about forty thousand; the New Haven and Hartford, twenty - eight thousand; the Harlem, twenty thousand; the New York and Northern, ten thousand; the Suburban, that joins the Third Avenue Elevated, carries twenty thousand.

The sojourners or the visitors for pleasure cut but small figures when compared with these daily travellers, but a glance at the number of great hotels shows that New York is growing to be the great pleasure city of the continent. Every facility is pushed to its utmost to accommodate the transient public. During one week of the early winter every hotel in town was full of visitors and sight-seers, and some thoughtless people who counted on finding plenty of room at the fashionable and expensive hotels were forced to take lodgings or go to boarding-houses—*pensions* they would call them on the other side. The money spent in the city by the dwellers in other places, spent in the mere gratification of pleasure,

AN AUCTION SALE OF LOTS IN SUBURBAN GREATER NEW YORK

THE LONELY POLICEMAN ON ONE OF GREATER NEW YORK'S COUNTRY ROADS.

THE BUSINESS MAN'S HOLIDAY—CITY ISLAND AS A YACHTING RENDEZVOUS

LATE FOR BUSINESS—THE NEXT TROLLEY WILL PASS IN HALF AN HOUR.

UP-TO-DATE ROAD-BUILDING—ON THE NEW PELHAM ROADWAY.

scheme, the great sums of money lost in the undertaking, would make a story worth the reading. The tunnel is filled with water, and the project is as good as abandoned. The bridge is the more feasible proposition now. But the Borough of the Bronx will soon be densely populated, and here will be the quandary for the "rapid-transit" people.

The great problem that confronts the city is how to handle the multitudes that in the future will inhabit the upper reaches of the great avenues that at present stretch through the sparsely settled city blocks above the Harlem River. These lands, principally owned by syndicates and land companies, are being bought by people who wish to own their own homes, and yet whose active interests centre about the markets and business of the great city to the south.

Every now and then excursions are run to these "parks," or "hursts," and there, on the spot, the lots are sold by auction. Building and Loan Associations are eager and willing to put up houses on tempting terms. Values are increasing, the country is becoming thickly settled, and the number of those who come and go is swelling to vaster proportions every month. No one can look ahead fifty years hence and state exactly what will be the methods of handling or managing the multitudes. The lack of an adequate system of rapid transit is now felt sorely; the need for some decisive plan of action grows each day. But the situation will have to be faced sooner or later. Even with the introduction of better means of transportation and the passing of the car-horse it is imperative to adopt some design of adequate proportions to the magnitude of the proposition. In fact, the daily pilgrim, although perhaps the most long-suffering and the most patient of men, is growing to be a force in the community, and now that the majority of him has a voice in municipal affairs, he had best be considered before, rising in his might, he presents a *sine quâ non* at some election-time that will be discomfiting to present property-holders in the heart of the Borough of Manhattan.

Whether it is possible to adopt the underground system, a crude and unsatisfactory first edition of which is in vogue in London, is a question; but the continued inability of the Rapid Transit Commission to formulate plans for the proposed tunnel that meet the unrestricted approval of the courts and the city government leads the casual observer to the conclusion that the urgency of the demand is not sufficiently recognized by those in authority.

The construction of any system that will meet the situation will be the result of long labor and the overcoming of what appears at the first glance to be an insurmountable difficulty. But the vexatious delays and obstacles placed in the way of the commission might cause it to be supposed that New York was waiting for the invention of a successful air-ship. This may come all in good time, perhaps, but from present indications people would rather travel on terra firma or below it. At least they demand some tangible and structural connection with Mother Earth. A man bound for Wall Street has no anxiety to put in at the Azores because of a strong westerly gale.

As the various boroughs of our new and ponderous city lose their *rus in urbe* aspect, the problem becomes more and more formidable. For the lack of building-space (judged by ground-space) will never prevent the city from its commercial expansion. There is the atmosphere above in which to project business enterprises; and if we should take and form a city, composing it alone of the buildings shorn of their six lower stories, we would have yet a city of the first magnitude, for more people, by six or eight times, travel perpendicularly in the elevators or lifts of the city than ride on the cars of the combined railroads.

And now the only person who is undisturbed by all this—so far as his bodily comfort is concerned—is the man with the steam-yacht who owns his private pier.

STATEN ISLAND FERRY
THE NEWSPAPER HABIT

NORTHWARD FROM THE
GRAND CENTRAL STATION
THE WHIST HABIT

L.A.S.

AT THE BROOKLYN END OF THE BRIDGE.
Slightly confusing to a Stranger.

23

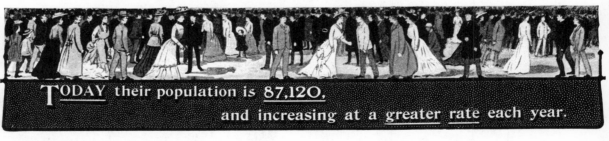

VENTILATION OF THE SUBWAY.

During the construction of the New York Rapid Transit Subway, the SCIENTIFIC AMERICAN frequently drew attention to the fact that one of the most serious and difficult problems connected with the undertaking, was that of ventilation. At that time we contended that for the circulation and renewal of air within the tunnel something more would be required than the piston-like action of the trains, which the engineers believed would prove sufficient for the purpose. After the opening of the Subway we were agreeably surprised to find that, although a moving train filled only about one-fourth of the cross-sectional area of the four-track tunnel, it proved sufficient to produce strong currents, which caused a liberal inflow and outflow of air at the station entrances. Moreover, the renewal of the Subway atmosphere thus brought about was greatly assisted by the action of the easterly and westerly winds at the Subway entrances and exits, the strong downward current at the entrances facing the wind and the equally strong upward currents at the opposite entrances facing away from the wind, clearly proving that a very thorough circulation of air was taking place, at least at the stations. Nevertheless, now that the warm weather has come, it cannot be denied that the condition of the atmosphere in the Subway is very disappointing. That the oppressiveness is not altogether due to lack of circulation and renewal of the air, is proved by the fact that the air currents at the entrances and on the platforms are as strong in the warm as they were in the cold weather. Just what the unpleasant symptoms are due to is a question difficult to determine, but they are probably caused by the increased temperature acting upon the naturally humid atmosphere in the tunnel, and upon the odors due to exhalation from the enormous crowds that use the tunnel, especially at the rush hours.

Much of the discomfort is due to the fact that a refreshing drop in temperature on the street is not felt until some hours afterward in the Subway, and a person entering from the cooler outside atmosphere is apt to suppose that the heated air is an evidence of vitiated atmosphere. The problem of properly ventilating the system will be one of the most difficult yet undertaken by the engineer. Some relief may be obtained by installing a system of fans, but it would have to be put in upon a very costly scale before it would add materially to the renewal of air that is now taking place at the station entrances. It is of course unreasonable to expect that travelers in the Subway will enjoy as pure an atmosphere as that of the elevated system; but if the oppressive symptoms continue to increase as the midsummer heat comes on, some steps will certainly have to be taken to mitigate the nuisance.

THE BLIZZARD IN BOSTON—ELECTRICITY'S FATAL WORK AMONG THE HORSES.
ANOTHER ILLUSTRATION OF THE GREAT DANGER FROM OVERHEAD WIRES IN A CITY.—DRAWN BY MAX F. KLEPPER.

Why Not a Permanent World's Fair?

IT IS estimated that the World's Fair at St. Louis has cost $50,000,000. Six months hence there will be nothing to show for that outlay except a modest art gallery and a devastated park. It is hardly surprising that many people are asking whether it would not be possible to lay out the money to better advantage.

The great white marble Public Library of New York is to cost less than $3,000,000. Sixteen such buildings could be put up for $50,000,000. Suppose a city desirous of spending that amount of money on a World's Fair should pay $5,000,000 for a site and for landscape effects to beautify it, and then should group in the most imposing way a dozen marble palaces, each equal to the New York Public Library, at a cost of $35,000,000 more, leaving $10,000,000 for installing and maintaining exhibits: would not that city have a possession that would attract the admiration of the world?

Such an exhibition would be small compared with the wildernesses of staff at Chicago and St. Louis, but would it not be large enough? Who ever sees everything at a World's Fair? The marble exposition would be permanent, and it could be made more perfect from year to year. Everything could be excluded but the very cream of the world's achievement. All the vulgar advertising features, the miles of canned goods, the flaunting Pikes and Midways, the slot machines, popcorn and frankfurters could be eliminated. There would be a vision of pure beauty and the sublimation of instruction.

No city on earth would have a spectacle to match such a university of human progress.

The next time it is proposed to spend $50,000,000 on a summer's riot of glass and plaster, to fade away like a dream, would it not be worth while to consider the possibility of putting the money into a form that would be a permanent enrichment of the community and of the world?

The Reform of the Trolley Car

RALPH WALDO EMERSON, who lived in Boston before the literary centre was moved to Philadelphia, and in whose honor a monument should be erected by the sombre persons who compile books of quotation, once wrote: "There is a remedy for every wrong, and a satisfaction for every soul." This is a broad statement, and at first glance it seems beyond reason; but though the compensations in life may not always be equal, yet, in some form or other, they are bound to come. For the past dozen years since the trolley car came into existence it has been riding over people's limbs and feelings. The increase of nervous exhaustion and nervous prostration might possibly be attributed to the trolley era in American life. There is a heartlessness about the average trolley car which hurts. There is a lack of consideration that is distinctly unpleasant. With it our manners have grown worse. It has kept men in their seats hiding in shame behind open newspapers when every instinct of gallantry told them they ought to get up and cling to the strap while the lady sat down. Even worse has been its absolute unresponsiveness to responsibility. It has never willingly done restitution for any injury to life or limb.

For this very reason we hail with a special joy the action of the court whose strong arm took this monster of iniquity by the throat and compelled it to pay damages. The case was one of modest yet of far-reaching significance. A lady was—strange to say—occupying a seat in the car. Opposite her stood, or rather wobbled, a fat man. The car was going its merry way, and when it reached a curve it jumped forth with that glee which is so familiar. The consequence was that the fat man landed suddenly and somewhat heavily in the lap of the innocent passenger, greatly to the perturbation of her spirit and to other annoyances and injuries which were brought forth fully in the court proceedings. The jury promptly gave her a verdict of $2300. Of course, we should all feel better if it had been $23,000, but the precedent has been established, and the trolley companies must either give fat men seats or see that they are securely propped up.

By this good work of justice it may be that the trolley car will gradually be tamed and made to behave itself. A reform that is very necessary is that of the market basket. There must come a time when the unoffending passenger may get satisfaction for the kind of locomotion that places in his lap the week's marketing of a large and hungry family. Akin to this, of course, would be something that would take into account the industrious person who tries to carry home three satchels or a wheelbarrow-load of bundles in the busy hours of the day. These things are often more troublesome than fat people. It is especially so in Philadelphia, which is the headquarters of the street-car trust of the country. The passengers are so firmly wedged together—solidified, as it were, in one unhappy mass—that no one of them can fall down without upsetting the whole crowd, but in other cities it is said that there is sometimes room in trolley cars.

—LYNN ROBY MEEKINS.

Saved to be Wasted

IN NEW YORK they are calculating how much the new subterranean system of swift transit is prolonging the lives of the millions who use it. The figures are amazing; the figures for the totals of all the time savings through all our modern machines would be overwhelming. And still we are not all comfortable and happy. The modern man of forty has distanced Methuselah with his 969 years. The modern youth starts life with all the past as his equipment. Yet the most of us waste with lavish hand the enormous treasure-chests of saved time which science bestows.

A great many brains are puzzling over the problem of how to utilize the vast energies in the currents of air and the rise and fall of tides and waves. But how much vaster is this problem of turning to use the infinite energies of the science-equipped man!

No one ever got any pleasure out of wasting money. As soon as the pleasure begins the waste stops. And the same thing is true of time.

The Ideal City—By Tom L. Johnson

Mayor of Cleveland

DRAWN BY ANNA RICE

Mr. Tom L. Johnson
PHOTO. BY THE DECKER STUDIO CLEVELAND, O.

IN THE ideal municipality the people will be very close to the government. Under our present system the people and their servants who conduct the affairs of the city are too wide apart. A mayor and council are elected, and thereafter no one among the citizens seems especially to concern himself with the business affairs of the city unless some great and special occasion arises. Of the ordinary affairs and, generally speaking, of the extraordinary affairs, that come up from day to day the citizens know little or nothing. Their interest is listless. They skim the newspaper accounts concerning municipal transactions, but know nothing of the details of government.

Under an ideal system, or under the system as nearly ideal as we can hope for in the immediate future, all this will be changed. The citizens, whether they pay taxes directly or indirectly, will take as much interest in the affairs of their government as do stockholders in the affairs of their corporations. Vital questions will not be left to the decision of the executive and council alone. They will come directly before the people for a vote. No franchise for a public utility will be sold or given away or voted away by delegated powers. All such matters will be decided at the ballot-box. The spectacle that we often see now, of invaluable rights bartered by politicians, will disappear forever; for when a question is left for the people to decide it is pretty safe to say that the right will prevail.

Of course, under such a system, the mayor and city council will be shorn of considerable power, but no more so than is wise or just. I am fully in favor of giving to the chief officer of a municipality very extensive powers, but they should be purely executive. No private corporation dreams of vesting its president and directors with unlimited power to buy, sell, give away or exchange any part of the property placed under their control. Matters such as these are passed on by the stockholders, and so it should be in municipal affairs. The mayor, like the president of a corporation, should be simply the administrator who executes the wishes and directions of the people as expressed at the polls. He should be held to a strict accountability and every voter should feel a personal responsibility for the action of the executive. The city, so far as its industrial affairs are concerned, should be considered to be simply a big business machine, in which every man who has a vote will also have the right to demand an accounting from the officers intrusted with the administration of affairs.

In explaining what should be the relation of the citizens to the government, I have spoken of the condition under which no franchise would be given away or sold without a direct submission of the question to the people at the polls. In making this statement, of course, I am taking the conditions as they are to-day and not as I should wish them to be. Under an ideal system there would be no franchises to vote away. The city, and not a private corporation, would own and operate the public utilities, such as street-car lines, gas works and lighting plants.

Such a condition is undoubtedly coming, but how soon no one can tell. It may come much more suddenly than even the most sanguine of us expect. Such an incident as was witnessed recently in Philadelphia, where a gang of politicians deliberately gave away, with the connivance and active aid of the mayor, street-railway franchises worth millions of dollars, may occur even in a city whose citizens are more alert. In that event it would not be too much to expect that the whole system would be upset at a moment's notice, and that the people would come into their own. Municipal ownership is such a rational and common-sense proposition that the wonder is it has not long ago been adopted. The process of evolution from private to public ownership is not nearly so difficult and involved a matter as most people seem to imagine. Nor does it mean that a municipality must of necessity load itself down with a great burden of debt.

I do not advocate the confiscation of street-car lines or other semi-public properties for the benefit of the municipality. But neither do I advocate the purchase of such properties by the people at the artificial values at which they are now held under private ownership. I would squeeze the water out first. This can be done by a very simple process—by imposing the proper burden of taxation and compelling the lowering of fares to a reasonable basis, three cents. Such a course would bring the value of the property down to a sound and proper basis, and on such a basis a city could buy without injustice to the private corporation or to its own citizens.

Free Street-Car Transportation for the Public

Here in Cleveland we are striving to bring about a state of public mind that will, we hope, enable us to see municipal ownership in practical operation at a comparatively early date. All the street-car franchises in this city expire by 1913; most of them expire much earlier. The companies admit the expiration of some of their franchises in 1904. The city claims an even earlier expiration than 1904 and proceedings to declare these franchises expired will be brought at the proper time. With the aid of these expirations we mean to get our rights without waiting for the special laws that would otherwise be necessary to secure lower fares.

The ideal system of municipal ownership of street railways would give free transportation to everybody. At first blush this may seem an extreme step, but that is because we have not been used to looking at the matter in the right light. In every great office building a system that is in many respects the counterpart of the one I suggest is maintained in the elevator service. All comers are carried in the elevators free of charge. No one dreams of collecting a toll or of insisting that, in the absence of such a toll, the person wishing to be sent to the upper floors use the stairs. The maintenance of the elevator service falls upon the tenants of the building, for it is included when the rent schedules are fixed. The tenants in turn pass it along to their customers and clients. Every one who pays a lawyer's bill has the elevator service charged somewhere though he may not find it set out in detail. The burden scattered among all the tenants and their clients is so minute, and the results in comfort are so decided, that no one dreams of abridging the service even though by so doing the rents might be somewhat lowered.

Our free streets and roads form another instinctive precedent for free street-car service. There was a time when every road leading into and out of our cities had a toll-gate. Experience showed the restrictive influence of such institutions, and to-day it is only the backward and unprogressive community that maintains toll roads. How recent has been the change in this direction is made manifest by the fact that it is only a few years since the big bridge from New York to Brooklyn was made free to foot passengers.

It may be asserted that a system of free street-car transportation would involve a hardship on the tax-paying residents, in that strangers coming to the city would be given privileges for which they did not pay. In times of great public gatherings, such as conventions, the strangers might even crowd off some of the regular taxpayers. This objection loses its force when it is remembered that every stranger must spend money for food and lodging, and that a great gathering invariably means a considerable increase in business for merchants, hotel-keepers and citizens generally. The money left in the city by the strangers would more than pay for the free street-car rides. In the big office buildings where the free elevator service exists the tenants do not demand that the privilege of riding be restricted to themselves. They realize that persons who come into the building bring them business and aid them in making money. It is to their interest to make the transportation of these people up and down as easy and comfortable as possible. Out of consideration for its best business interests no progressive concern will take offices in a building where there is no elevator service.

Street-Car Lines Operated by the City

In case, however, in spite of its manifest advantages, the system of free transportation should be deemed too radical for immediate acceptance, the next best plan would be the operation of the roads by the city, and the imposition of a fare as low as is consistent with the expense of management and maintenance. The lower the fare the better for all concerned. Such a system would have many advantages over the system of private ownership for profit besides that of securing lower fares. It would eliminate the most prolific source of political corruption in our municipal government. Take away the private control of public utilities and there would be an end to much tax dodging and to much bribery of public servants. This bribery comes in various forms. Often it is in the shape of the direct payment of money to secure certain privileges and immunities. Often it is in the shape of political preferment made possible through the control of the machine by the corporations, which always remain in close and responsive touch with machine workers. The gain in the direction of a higher moral tone would in itself be sufficient compensation for adopting municipal ownership even if all the other advantages fell away.

Pending municipal ownership in one form or another, every city should henceforth be most careful, in awarding franchises for public utilities, to restrict the term of years the franchise has to live and to provide very definitely for the acquisition of the rights by the city. All street-car franchise rights should be based on three-cent fares, and it should be explicitly stipulated that the streets turned over must remain "free territory." By this I mean that no city government having the rights and interests of the citizens at heart will grant to any street-car company, henceforth, the privilege of operating over any street to the exclusion of any other line. The ideal way for the city, under the system of private ownership, to grant franchises, would be simply for the operation of the road, the city itself building and maintaining the tracks and holding them in ownership. If, however, this cannot be done, then the corporation seeking a franchise should be required to give the use of its tracks to all comers on the payment of a proper compensation for such use.

An Improved Scheme of Taxation

The most important feature in the administration of the ideal city government will be its system of taxation. If we could reach it, the most satisfactory system would be the single tax, advocated by Henry George. Land values should be made to bear the entire burden of the cost of government. All improvements made by citizens should be exempt in order to encourage their extension. In the absence of the single tax the first thing to be considered in adopting a taxation system is the equalization of land values for purposes of assessment. The conditions existing in Cleveland to-day are undoubtedly typical of those in every city in America, and may very properly be taken as a guide. Here we find the most gross inequalities in valuation. Some land properties are assessed at ten per cent. and others at one hundred and ten per cent. of their real value. This is due, in different cases, either to the ignorance, incompetence or corruption of the tax-levying bodies. It is due, too, in some cases, to the unscientific and inaccurate system for ascertaining values that is in vogue. Instead of accurate facts and mathematical methods, we leave matters to the individual judgment of assessors.

As a first step toward righting things here, Cleveland is ascertaining values under what is known as the "Somers Unit System of Taxation." Under the direction of Mr. Somers himself, a tax bureau has been established and a force is now at work ascertaining the true value of our real estate, regardless of the opinion and judgment of the assessors. It is unnecessary to explain at length here the Somers system. Suffice it to say that, under its workings, values in all parts of the city are fixed with something approximating mathematical accuracy. The system works almost automatically, and makes it difficult for under or over valuation to exist. It is our belief that its adoption will raise very materially the total valuation of land and of franchise values. The increase will be mainly at the expense of the large holders of valuable sites and franchises. The burden of inequality has fallen almost invariably upon the small property-holder, on the workingman who owns his own home, and on the small merchant. A number of the large owners have been assessed only on from ten to twenty per cent. of the true value of their land.

The result of our work in this direction, we think, will be either the lowering of the general assessment ratio, which at present is sixty per cent. of the selling value, or the lowering of the general tax rate. In either event there will be a decided relief to the great body of our taxpayers, and, we hope, a nearer approach to the idea of putting the burden as much as possible on land and franchises instead of on improvements which stand for progress and prosperity, for lower rents, and for better accommodations. Unfortunately we shall not be able to reap the benefits of the new system of land taxation for a year to come, as, under the laws of Ohio, the work of the Board, performed under the old system, cannot be upset for that period. When we do, however, put our new system in operation we hope to furnish an object-lesson for every municipality in the country.

Selling Value the Right Basis of Assessment

Further relief for the mass of the people along the line of just taxation will come almost everywhere through a more scientific assessment of municipal privilege. Heretofore, in nearly every city, street-car companies, electric-light and gas companies, telephone companies and the like have been taxed only on a small part of the tangible value of their physical assets. The city government which does its duty to the people will go beyond this. It will tax the corporation on the real value, the selling value, of its property, just as it taxes the ordinary citizen. It is absurd to say that a street-car company, for example, shall be taxed simply upon the valuation of its tracks, ties, rolling stock, power-houses, etc., or an electric-light company only on its wires, conduits and plant.

The real basis of assessment should be the selling value of the property as a going concern, and this can very readily be ascertained from the selling value of its stocks and bonds. Operating under this idea we, here in Cleveland, have raised the assessment of the five companies controlling our public utilities (two street-car companies, two gas companies and one electric-light company) $18,000,000. This is about twelve per cent. of the total valuation of all the real estate in the city, and the new assessment which has been placed on

these corporations has to that extent relieved the small taxpayer. It has lowered the general tax rate from three per cent. to 2.67 per cent.

This, it seems to me, is a very long step in the direction of shifting the burden to the shoulders that should justly bear it. The corporations affected have threatened all sorts of legal proceedings to enjoin us from enforcing our levy. But so far nothing has come of these threats, and as we have the law on our side we have no great apprehension. We are proceeding on the cardinal principle that underlies or should underlie all taxation: namely, that man owes to society in proportion to what he takes from society.

The proper taxation of steam railroads is a more serious and difficult proposition than the taxation of municipal privileges. In Ohio the railroads are not paying more than thirty per cent. of their just taxation. In other States the conditions are about the same. The assessment of railroad property is, under the present system, under the control of bodies that are subject to corrupt influences in one form or another. That they often respond to this influence is made manifest by the low assessments that have been levied. Sometimes these influences take the form of a direct cash payment.

In other cases the influence comes through the issuing of passes and sometimes through political pressure. In any event, the result is the same.

Getting at the Real Value of Stock

This condition in Ohio is so grave that it has been made a State issue. We have tried by every means in our power to get the taxation due us, but under the present laws we have so far failed. As with the street railways, so the steam roads have always returned their property on the basis of a small part of their tangible physical assets, with extreme allowances for depreciation. The amounts so returned have been accepted, and assessments have been made on this basis, each county assessing in proportion to the mileage within its boundaries. We propose to get at the true value of the railroad property by taking the selling value of its stocks and bonds as with the other public corporations.

The present political compaign in Ohio is of special importance because of this taxation issue against the railroads, and if we carry the State we will secure a condition that, I believe, will be emulated by every other State in the Union, establishing a source of taxation that will go far to helping along ideal municipal government by solving the question of income, which must always determine the extent and effectiveness of city government. Properly solved it will bring about many improvements and new ideas. It will enable the municipalities to improve the schools, to lay out additional parks, and to secure suitable public buildings without mortgaging the future and without going too deeply into the pockets of the working citizens. In all these matters all the cities of the United States are below what should be the standard. Every city should have parks scattered plentifully throughout its limits and especially in its congested districts. Nothing so directly affects the welfare of the people as a comprehensive park system. Such a system should include free baths.

We should go just as far in this park matter as our income will permit. The parks should not only be beautiful but useful. There should be no "Keep Off the Grass" signs. There should be nothing to interfere with the pleasures and comforts of the people within the limits of reason. Of course, there will be vandals here and there who will perhaps destroy some shrub or pick some flowers. They should be dealt with individually. The park system should establish all manner

of institutions that can contribute to the welfare of its citizens. There should be playgrounds, refreshment places, and public gymnasiums.

In the matter of public buildings every city should strive to have something that is not alone useful but ornamental. Every public building should be a public monument. It should be a lesson to the people in art and architecture. As a sheer business proposition it pays a city to make itself attractive, and nothing will help it along so much as imposing public buildings.

Getting the Best School Buildings

Special attention should be devoted to the character of the school buildings, both inside and out. Without undue extravagance, the school buildings should be of the best and the appointments as perfect as they can be made. As a primal proposition there should be ample school accommodations for every child of school age. The spectacle that we see in many of our cities, where thousands of children are denied the benefits of an education for the lack of school room, is one of the most disgraceful exhibitions of the inefficiency of our present system of city government.

The ideal police system is yet to be found. One thing is certain: the system so generally in vogue of making sporadic raids on disorderly places fails entirely of effectiveness. No permanent good was ever accomplished by a police raid on a disorderly resort. The keepers pay their fines and resume business. They make good their losses by perpetrating additional outrages on the public. My father was at one time the Superintendent of Police in Louisville, Kentucky. The most difficult question he had to deal with was the regulation of low saloons, dance halls and other resorts. He found, after repeated experiment, that the most effective measure with places against which complaint was made was to station a policeman in uniform at the door. The policeman was instructed to inquire the name and address of every one who went in and out. Of course, in most instances the man declined to give either, but the presence of the policeman and the query were sufficient to keep that particular person away from there, and the result was that the business of the place was ruined.

Since the present administration has come into power in Cleveland this method has been tried with excellent results. We have driven six disorderly establishments out of business, and have closed up twelve dives that were the resorts of notorious thieves. The disorderly and criminal element, having lost its choicest meeting-places, has found Cleveland very unattractive. Some of the resorts that we closed made a considerable show of resistance. One man who kept a particularly vicious dive withstood the presence of a policeman at his door for six months. He brought all sorts of political and personal influence to bear to secure the withdrawal of the policeman, and when he found this unavailing he declared he would run anyhow. At the end of six months, however, he threw up the sponge.

Having large discretionary powers, policemen should be exceptionally intelligent and should be endowed with more than the average amount of common-sense. In their selection all questions of politics should be carefully eliminated. They should be appointed under a strict civil-service system, and undergo a careful mental as well as physical examination.

In every city department as conducted to-day there are openings for improvement. I have picked out only a few of what I consider the most important toward the realization of ideal municipal government.

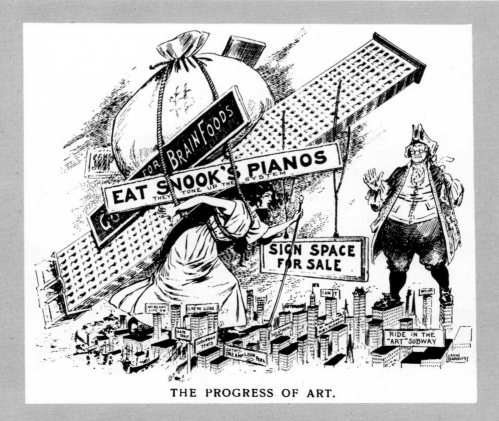

THE PROGRESS OF ART.

Our Cities in the Twentieth Century

The Chicago River, in which the canal begins   *Looking from the Lake Front Park*   *The end of the Sanitary Canal in Joliet*

NOT as having already attained, but pressing forward—this, and not a boastfulness of present achievements, epitomizes the true Chicago spirit. Put into briefest space, the genius of this city is expressed in one word, PUSH. Every phase of its development bespeaks this irrepressible capacity for doing things. It is more keenly concerned with the affairs of to-day than of yesterday and of to-morrow than of to-day.

As a young city its main interests are inevitably of commercial and industrial character. Its foremost concern is expressed in the question: What are the movements on foot which promise most in the promotion of Chicago's commercial prominence?

This may be unhesitatingly answered. The conversion of the Chicago Sanitary Canal into a waterway navigable by light ocean vessels. This carries with it the kindred problem of deepening the Chicago River to a depth sufficient to accommodate vessels of the heaviest draft that will ply the lakes for the next half century; of depressing the tunnels under the river to meet this progressive move, and of supplanting the present centre-pier bridges with bascule structures which will permit the use of the centre of the channel by the huge crafts engaged in modern lake commerce. Here is the biggest project on foot to-day, so far as the business future of this city is concerned. The ramifications of this plan are almost endless and vitally touch almost every industry of the City of the Lakes. Its execution implies a complete remodeling of the present river and harbor frontage and of all that is covered by the term shipping facilities. Most important of all, it carries an inevitable, compulsory reduction of freight-carrying rates to a minimum, and it is this factor which finally determines the commercial supremacy of any great centre of population which has a fair share of other industrial advantages.

$30,000,000 Spent on a Waterway

What basis, it will be asked, has Chicago for the expectation that it will come into possession of so vital and stupendous a public improvement as a free and direct channel from its grain elevators, its lumber, coal and commercial docks, to the sea and thence to the ports of the world? A very definite and tangible one! At a cost of more than thirty million dollars Chicago has just completed a waterway which lacks only a connecting link to fill this requirement. To make a ship canal leading into the Mississippi and navigable for vessels of light ocean draft needs only the additional expenditure of half the sum already invested to complete a deep-water connection with the Illinois River and to deepen the channel of the latter. The city of Chicago offers to the National Government the present great waterway with this condition: Spend fifty cents for each dollar Chicago has invested and receive a deep ship canal from the centre of the United States to the ocean, which will multiply the commerce of the great West, afford

an invaluable means of military protection and operation in time of war, and develop the industrial resources of a vast region of country rich in all that will contribute to the nation's wealth. That the Federal Government could have well afforded to bear the entire expense of constructing such a waterway will scarcely be questioned by any person who looks well into the future and sees things in their larger perspective. Much less can it be doubted that the Government will hasten to accept this canal when two-thirds of its cost has been paid by the city of Chicago.

In its present condition the great sanitary canal, connecting Chicago and the Illinois River, is equivalent to a forty-mile harbor, twenty-five feet deep. The deepening of the Illinois, which connects it with the Mississippi, will be the signal which will line the banks of the great inland ocean harbor with manufacturing and commercial plants of every description. If this connecting link be made navigable for only the lightest type of ocean-going vessels—say those of fourteen feet draft—the benefits to commerce will be immediate and effective before a single vessel can carry its cargo by this new route to the ocean, for the carrying rates by land would drop to meet this potential competitor.

It is impossible that the Federal Government can overlook the value of this ocean connection as a means of war protection. The wisdom of the principle that times of peace are the most propitious in which to prepare for war has never been controverted. According to our present treaty with England, the United States is permitted to maintain only one war vessel on the Great Lakes, but England has the absolute control of the Welland Canal, the only gateway to the ocean. There is more danger that the United States will become involved in hostilities with Great Britain than with any other power. In event of such a calamity the proposed deep waterway between the Gulf of Mexico and the Great Lakes would give a ready means of sending light-draft war vessels to protect our cities of the great inland seas and to blockade the Welland Canal. The motive of self-protection is alone sufficient to induce the Federal Government to carry forward the work already two-thirds done by Chicago.

Commercial Benefits of Vast Promise

But the commercial consideration is the one which is of paramount interest to the general public, and this benefit would be felt not only by Chicago and all the territory and cities along the route to the Gulf, but by all the States of the great Middle West. Surveys and estimates show that an additional expenditure of fifteen million dollars will give a waterway navigable for vessels of fourteen feet draft, and will permit ocean vessels of the smaller type to load with grain at Duluth or Chicago and deliver their cargoes at Liverpool. How the interest of every merchant and shipper on the Great Lakes will respond to this waterway may be illustrated by the effect which the old Illinois and Michigan Canal

The new 39th Street conduit, Chicago   *In the heart of the retail district*   *The largest elevator in the world*

Chicago: Its Present and its Future.

By Mayor Carter H. Harrison

Controlling Works at Lockport on the Sanitary Canal

A fleet loading in the Chicago River

PHOTO BY J. W. TAYLOR, CHICAGO

COPYRIGHT, 1900. PHOTO BY LAWRENCE, CHICAGO

The Chicago Board of Trade, showing the pits where corn and wheat are dealt in

PHOTO BY J. W. TAYLOR, CHICAGO

On Madison and State Streets

PHOTO BY J. W. TAYLOR, CHICAGO

The pens in the Union Stock Yards

PHOTO BY J. W. TAYLOR, CHICAGO

A busy State Street corner

and the Erie Canal have on carrying rates. Both these canals have long outlived their period of large, active traffic, but if they were not in existence the land freight rates would be very greatly increased. It is through their influence in holding down the cost of land transportation that these effete waterways render their great service and amply repay the cost of their maintenance. And so it would be with the proposed ship canal.

Of allied interest and importance to Chicago commerce is the deepening of the Chicago River. In this the future must be discounted. Although the largest vessel now plying the lakes draws but twenty-one feet, the tendency is toward greatly increased tonnage as affording economy in transportation. Unless the Chicago River is speedily made accessible to the largest vessels in the carrying trade Chicago must be prepared to see her shipping slip away from her. Delay in this respect has already been costly. It is feasible to deepen the channel of the river to a depth of twenty-five feet, and this move would add millions of dollars to her commerce. To-day larger vessels are engaged in the lake trade than were to be found on the ocean twenty years ago, and every year witnesses the launching of still larger craft. Not to make ample provision for this tendency would be the most suicidal blow that could be dealt to the commerce of this city. When the business public of Chicago becomes thoroughly aroused to the significance of this problem its representatives in Congress will reflect this awakening, and Federal action will follow.

To make this improvement possible, the old centre-pier bridges which now span the river must be removed and replaced with new ones of the bascule type, giving to vessels the full use of the stream. The strong current created by the opening of the sanitary canal makes these piers an especial menace to smaller craft, while the tunnels shut out steamers of the larger kind. This expensive change is a necessity of the immediate future, and plans for its execution are being worked out by the municipal authorities and the trustees of the Sanitary District. As these two bodies derive their support from the same source their interests are mutual. Although the tunnels which now obstruct the passage of heavy draft vessels are used by the street railways of the city, the question of depressing the tunnels must be wholly divorced from the problem of the future relationship between these corporations and the municipality. To permit the former to use the problem of depressing the tunnels as a club with which to obtain franchise advantages is not to be considered. Independent action in this particular is the only course which the city can afford to follow.

The Difficult Problem of a Big Subway

A subway to relieve the congestion of surface traffic is another problem of the immediate future vitally related to the city's commercial advancement. The precise scope and nature of this public improvement are not so clear as those of the shipping problem. No city approaching the size of Chicago has so compact a retail and wholesale district. It is a caldron boiling with business, its rim described by the union loop of the four elevated railroads. The mention of this boundary suggests one of the most difficult conditions with which the city has to deal in settling the subway question. A few years ago, before access to the heart of the city from every outlying section was made quick and easy by this rapid transit system, thousands of smaller tradesmen and shopkeepers drove a prosperous traffic along the main arteries of surface travel. Now hundreds of them have been forced into bankruptcy, and the more fortunate of their proprietors and clerks are filling clerical positions in the big department stores in the centre of the city—the very institutions which forced them to the wall by the powerful leverage of concentration of capital and convergence of quick transit facilities. I am unalterably opposed to any movement which will further aid and increase this concentration of retail traffic, believing it must result in the benefit of the few at the expense of the many. The ideal community is one in which the small tradesman is prosperous and independent. Whatever threatens this widespread proprietorship and independence is undesirable. Only a very few years ago the great thoroughfares threading the three grand divisions of Chicago from the suburbs to centre—Cottage Grove Avenue, North Clark Street, West Madison Street, Milwaukee Avenue, and other arteries of this character—were alive with busy and prosperous stores and shops in which everything that can now be obtained in the downtown department stores could be bought. Some of these were large establishments which would have done credit to a city of a hundred thousand inhabitants. To-day, it is doubtful if a single dry-goods store worthy the name can be found outside the downtown district.

Any subway scheme which would add to the present concentration of retail business in the overcrowded downtown district has a fatal defect which merits the disapproval of all who have the interest of the whole people at heart. The subway scheme sprang from the idea that something must be done to relieve the congestion of Chicago's concentrated business district. A tentative plan for an elaborate subway system, which shall put under ground all the surface lines of street railways in the business centre, has been prepared. This contemplates the elimination of grade crossings by the construction of a series of non-intersecting underground loops which shall make a transfer from the lines of one grand division of the city to those of another an easy matter. How to reconcile this movement with that which looks to the upbuilding of new business centres instead of further concentration in the present one is as yet an unsolved problem.

One thing, however, is certain. The great retail houses and the property owners in the centre of the city could well afford to bear a large part of the expense of constructing a downtown subway.

The Paving of Streets with Asphalt

The rapidly increasing amount of asphalt paving in the streets of Chicago's business district indicates that the section bounded by the Union Elevated loop will be almost entirely paved with this material within the next five years. At their private expense many of the largest merchants have already replaced the old paving with asphalt, estimating that thus securing diminution of loss in the destruction of goods by dust will more than repay their expenditure. As asphalt is not a hardy and permanent pavement, its great increase in the business centre of the city must be met with the passage of a wide-tire ordinance. The street railways should be compelled to put in grooved rails.

The ideal paving has not yet been discovered. The wood block is dead, except as replaced so frequently as to make its cost almost prohibitive; macadam paving is too filthy; brick will not stand sufficient wear and is too noisy; asphalt is too delicate for heavy traffic. A perfectly dressed granite

block is undoubtedly the best paving now known, but it is very expensive.

When a property owner has paid his special assessment for the paving of his street frontage this should settle his score for all time. The maintenance of the improvement should be provided for by the city—but not by funds raised from general taxation. All moneys for the maintenance and cleaning of streets should come from funds paid to the municipality by corporations or individuals enjoying special privileges. Every special privilege extended to a corporation or to a person for the use of streets, conduits or sidewalk space should bring in to the city a fair compensation, and the money gained from this source should be put in a fund sacredly dedicated to expenditure on the streets of the municipality. When this is done in Chicago no city in the world will surpass her in well-kept streets and cleanliness. In the lesser matters of compensation for special privileges, Chicago has already made considerable headway. One State Street merchant pays nearly $10,000 a year in rentals for space under sidewalks, for bridges across alleys, and for other items of this character. The city has 1,400,000 square feet of sidewalk space in its central business district which will, in time, be made to bring in such rentals. At twenty-five cents a square foot this rental would amount to $350,000.

Proposed City Revenue from Conduit System

An imperative and immediate necessity of utmost importance to Chicago is the construction of a system of underground subway conduits for sewers, telegraph and telephone wires, and pipes and mains for gas and water. This would yield the city a splendid revenue. But its chief benefit would be the elimination of the necessity for constantly digging up the streets to stop leaks, repair damages and extend systems. At present this work costs private corporations hundreds of thousands of dollars every year, impedes traffic and mutilates and destroys streets. Concessionaires would no doubt gladly contribute to the expense of such a subway, to save heavy maintenance and repair costs. The lines and pipes of concessionaires already holding franchises could be placed in the new subway without rental charge until the expiration of their franchises, when the value of the conduit space required for their use would be considered in the granting of an extension of franchise. An equipment for furnishing a high-pressure water service to the public, for the operation of elevators and other hydraulic machinery could be easily installed in these conduits and made to yield a good revenue.

In one particular, at least, Chicago is to-day ripe for municipal ownership. The first step to be taken in this direction is to secure from the Legislature authority to operate a public lighting system equipped for both gas and electricity. The immediate effect of such a measure would be the material reduction of the gas rates charged by the private corporations now in operation. Of course, the proposition to permit the municipality to own and operate a gas and electric lighting plant for public patronage immediately raises the cry that this is another step in the spoils system, an expansion of the army of office holders, and that the service furnished under such system would be imperfect and incompetently administered. To this I would answer that a step of this kind must be accompanied by a rigorous and absolute civil service administration—a real civil service, not a fad! As a matter of fact, Chicago is now in position to go into the electric lighting business by a change so slight that it would be scarcely perceptible, and would simply amount to an expansion of the municipality's present electrical system and the addition of a small force of meter readers, clerks and collectors. The only difference apparent to the private citizen would be that he would pay much less for his electric lights and would go to the City Hall instead of the office of the private corpora-

tions to settle his bills. Chicago already has the largest exclusively municipal electric lighting plant in the world. When I was first elected Mayor the annual cost of maintaining an arc light was found to be $95; now it is $58. In certain sections of the city the municipality is obliged to secure a limited number of arc lights from a private corporation, and is compelled to pay a minimum rate of $103 a year for each lamp, or $45 more than the expense of a lamp in its own system. Before the latter was put into operation, however, the price charged by the private corporation was $137.50. This indicates the value of municipal competition.

Water Power and its Big Possibilities

A factor not to be overlooked in this problem is the fact that, in its sanitary canal, Chicago has a magnificent source of power capable of easy and economical adaptation to the operation of a vast lighting system. At a point twenty-nine miles from the city the great canal has a fall of twenty-nine feet and a volume of 230,000 cubic feet of water a minute. Careful estimates by a number of competent engineers go to show that this fall of water will yield 12,000-horse power at the water wheels and will generate power enough to operate some ten thousand arc lights within the corporate limits of the city. The cost of the requisite plant and system entire would not exceed $2,500,000, and would effect an annual saving in the operating expenses of the city of fully $400,000. As the power is only required for the street lights at night, the same machinery can be used to produce and transmit the necessary power for operating all the pumping stations in the city during the day. The problem of adapting to the present machinery the electrical power to be used requires only standard machinery, purchasable in the open market.

Years ago Chicago parted with her gas privilege but retained ownership and control of the water system. The result is that her citizens have now a water service which is one of the most efficient and low-priced in this country. At the same time the municipality receives from the water consumers within its borders a net annual income of almost $2,000,000. This system was originally acquired at a cost of $200,000 and to-day represents an expenditure of a little more than $30,000,000. It has been operated for forty-eight years in a manner as sound, businesslike, economical and free from scandals as has been the management of any private corporation. The opponents of municipal ownership will find in the history of the water system of Chicago a most forceful refutation of their stock arguments. As to the quality of the service afforded, it may be incidentally mentioned that Chicago is to-day spending, for her magnificent system of intercepting sewers and lateral conduits alone, more than $3,300,000. These are marvels of engineering skill and of sanitary efficiency, guaranteeing the purity and healthfulness of Chicago's drinking water.

Not long ago a reputable business man entered my office and made a serious proposal that the city transfer its water system to the corporation which he claimed to represent, the consideration to be $50,000,000. This I treasure as one of the most absurd and picturesque experiences of my official service. Chicago's water service is now provided for on a scale ample for half a century ahead. She owns it and will never part with it! What would be the present value of a municipal gas plant had Chicago preserved this splendid property for herself forty-five years ago?

Municipal Ownership of Railways

The air is full of agitation of the question of municipal ownership of street railways in Chicago. Whatever may be said on this subject, one thing must be made clear: nothing should be done which will afford the slightest basis for the charge that Chicago has any political party or body of citizens inclined to countenance anything which might be termed the confiscation of private property. Such an impression would be absolutely baseless and slanderous. My own convictions are that this city is ripe for the first steps leading toward municipal ownership of its street railroad lines. In other words, in the granting of new franchises the city should prepare for ultimate ownership of the tracks and right of way of such lines.

For the protection of the private citizens who invested in these corporations in good faith, before the present agitation of municipal ownership arose, the franchises of these corporations should undoubtedly be extended for a limited period of years, but on terms of advantage to the municipality, instead of hardship. Such an extension should contain a clause permitting the city to come into possession of the systems on terms of mutual fairness at the expiration of the extended franchises. To secure proper maintenance of the systems the city should agree to recoup such expenditures as it should approve during a certain period immediately previous to the time of its actual acquirement of the property. In this connection I must insist upon a firm belief in the referendum. When men in positions of authority know that any large measure of this kind must be referred to the people for their approval they are relieved of many temptations to connivance and corruption. Stringent measures must be provided to protect every step in the direction of municipal ownership from politics, favoritism and "pull" of any kind or class.

The actual operation of a street railway system by a municipality would be a civic calamity unless safeguarded by a civil-service administration of the most ironclad character.

Notwithstanding the fact that Chicago is generally conceded to have the most elaborate and magnificent system of public parks and boulevards possessed by any city of the United States, one of its most urgent needs to-day is that of small parks and breathing spots in its most overcrowded sections. Fully 800,000 people in Chicago live more than a mile from any of the large parks. The distribution of the present park and boulevard system may be described as exceedingly uneven, 1814 acres of the system being inside eleven wards, while the other twenty-four wards contain only 224 acres. The former section has 358 people to one acre of park land, while the latter has 4605 persons to each acre of park or boulevard ground. These figures are sufficient to indicate that those districts of the city containing the densest population, the working people who have the least of this world's goods, are so far from the large parks as to be shut out from their benefits.

Small Parks for the Good of the Masses

There is no project now on foot in Chicago in which I have a keener personal interest than that of establishing a system of small parks—twelve or fourteen in number—in the centres of the most congested river and tenement wards. These should be provided with shade trees, benches, and devices for games and athletic exercises. Each of these breathing spots should also be provided with a few cages of inexpensive animals, to divert and entertain old and young. Most important of all, there should not be a single restriction placed upon the free use of every inch of these parks, and "keep off the grass" signs should be absolutely unknown. A careful estimate indicates that tracts of this character, of about five acres in extent, can be bought at prices ranging from $100,000 to $150,000 each. They will not, however, be obtainable at these prices unless secured in the immediate future. This is therefore a movement which must be brought to a successful end during the first year or two of the new century, if at all.

Chicago provides extensive and absolutely free baths to the public. These public bath houses are known as the Carter H. Harrison, the Martin B. Madden, the No. 3, and the Robert A. Waller baths. Three of these are already in active operation, and the other will be open before the publication of this article. In the year 1899, 303,640 free baths were furnished at the Harrison and Madden baths alone. A novel plan for extending the free-bath movement is that of equipping each municipal pumping station with bathing facilities comprising from four to ten compartments. As the water and heat necessary for these baths would otherwise be wasted, the additional expense to the city is the very slight one of towels and soap. Three pumping stations have already been so equipped and the number will soon be doubled.

Chicago has no achievement to which she is inclined to point with greater pride than the elevation of her steam railroad tracks. It already contains more than twice the mileage of elevated tracks to be found in all the other cities in the United States combined, and has cost the private corporations owning the railroads $17,000,000. The expense to the city for this improvement has been practically nothing. In the early days of this work, pleading, cajoling and threats were required to bring railroad managers to a frame of mind in which they would consent to the elevation of their tracks. Such has been their experience of the economy and increased efficiency of the new service that representatives of the municipality and of the railroad corporations now meet with the firm resolve on both sides that the tracks must be elevated; the only subject of controversy being the best way to meet existing conditions and to avoid unnecessary loss to established business.

Drawn by Sydney Adamson

UNDERGROUND MOVING SIDEWALKS IN NEW YORK

An interesting phase of New York's transportation problem is the proposal to construct underground moving sidewalks or platforms. The first one planned, of which the details are shown in the above drawing, is to go from Williamsburg to Bowling Green, and is to connect on the way with the surface and elevated cars. The fare will be one cent, and the speed will be from five to nine miles an hour.

THE KITCHEN.

THE BED ROOM.

THE PRIVATE HALL.

THE DRAWING ROOM.

BLUFF

SAL

ALL IS NOT GOLD THAT GLITTERS.

THE APARTMENT HOUSE TRAP AND ITS ALLURING BAIT.

Greater Atlantic City

The Story of How the Popular Watering Resort is Making Poor Men Rich and Rich Men Richer.

FIFTY years ago Absecon Island was a stretch of surf-washed sand on the Jersey Coast. To-day the same island is celebrating its Golden Anniversary as the greatest watering resort on the globe, the Mecca of millions of tourists seeking health and pleasure. Its wind-blown dunes have become the site of beautiful Atlantic City, with its permanent population of 35,000, and an estimated summer population of 250,000.

Busy streets, handsome cottages, palatial hotels cover the Island from shore to shore, from the Inlet to Longport, making it necessary for Atlantic City to seek a new direction in which to expand.

WONDERFUL GROWTH

Little did Jeremiah Leeds think, when paying forty cents an acre for Absecon Beach, little did his family think when selling it for $17.50 an acre, that to-day a moderate valuation of the real estate within Atlantic City's limits would total $70,000,000. Yet such is the fact.

This wondrous growth is due apparently, not to booming or speculation, but to entirely natural causes which exercise a peculiar fascination over visitors. So long as her beach is the finest, her surf the coolest, her skies the brightest, her breezes the balmiest, her boardwalk the gayest, access to her glories the easiest, so long must Atlantic City hold her sway, and so long will sweltering inland millions crowd her healthful shores. With this combination of excellences, the growth and prosperity of Atlantic City are practically as certain as the rising and setting of the sun.

Within ten years land in the heart of Atlantic City has risen 800 per cent., and Atlantic City is yet in its infancy. Unlike some shore resorts, as Newport, which was made by millionaires, Atlantic City has made comfortable fortunes for almost everybody who has invested in her real estate. The next ten years, in the judgment of those who know best, is bound to see as great a rise in the city's suburban property.

CITY MUST EXPAND

A glance at the map bears out this opinion. There rests Atlantic City on Absecon Island as on a throne—beauteous Queen City of the Coast, but with no room for expansion. Land is just as scarce about her as water is plenty. The salt marshes, five miles in width, stretch toward the mainland, affording no outlet for growth. To build on these is to build on mud washed by tide-water.

But Atlantic City must expand; homes must be built somewhere. There is but one direction —on the highland at Pleasantville Terrace, adjoining the town of Pleasantville. In this direction is absolutely all the natural high ground unoccupied within seven miles of the city. Accordingly attention is now being turned to this section.

This large tract of highland, formerly known as the Doughty Estate, belonged to General Doughty, of Revolutionary fame, whose log cabin still stands, a relic of that stirring period. This estate has remained in the Doughty family until this spring, when they sold it, thus allowing it to be placed on the market for the first time in over a hundred years.

ON THE HIGHLAND

Situated sixty feet above the ocean, Pleasantville Terrace affords the only natural outlet for the growth of Atlantic City, and promises an opportunity to investors not unlike that which made the wealth of the early owners of property on the Island.

Here the tonic air of the pines mingles with the healing ocean breezes, making it a natural resort of persons seeking restoration to health. Here also a beautiful natural lake, one mile in length, provides boating, fishing, swimming. The woods of pine and oak afford hunting in season, and artesian wells furnish the purest water.

EASY OF ACCESS

Access is easy, the handsome new station being just twelve minutes' ride on the Reading Railroad from the famous Boardwalk. All trains, except through express, make regular stops. A trolley line runs from Pleasantville, tickets being sold at the rate of six for twenty-five cents. The Delaware and Atlantic City Trolley line is surveyed direct through the property, and the Washington Avenue trolley will pass nearby.

The Atlantic City Estate Company, who are the purchasers of this property, have divided it into lots, 25 by 100 feet, which they are offering to investors and home-builders at prices that will seem insignificant five years hence. Since this is nearly all the unoccupied land there is within seven miles, such an opportunity to secure a home-site suburban to the world's greatest shore resort is not likely to occur again.

The price of these lots is $25; but for a short time only $10 will be deducted from the price of every other lot. Corner lots command $5 extra, a few choice lots being valued at $35.

It should be remembered that this is within easy reach of the wonderful Boardwalk, twelve minutes' ride by rail, and a five cent fare by trolley.

These lots may be had on the following remarkably easy terms: $1 down, each lot; $1 weekly for 1 or 2 lots; $2 weekly for 3 to 5 lots. No charge for deed; no mortgages; no interest; no taxes until 1906.

It can be readily seen that a fortune is not required to own a valuable piece of real estate. One may become an investor or a home-builder on a very small capital. Here a family may live inexpensively, amid quiet shade and cooling breezes, within a few minutes' ride of the world's greatest Ocean Sanatorium.

SAFETY OF INVESTMENT

So sure is the Company of the goodness of the investment that it gives a black and white guarantee that the lots will increase in value at least *25 per cent.* within one year, based on the price at which our corps of salesmen will

then be selling similar lots, or money will be refunded with six per cent. interest. Titles are guaranteed by Integrity Title and Trust Company of Philadelphia. Should the owner of property in Pleasantville Terrace die before his lots are fully paid for, his heirs will receive a clear deed, thus insuring him against risk or loss. Should he desire to build before September 1st, half the purchase price will be returned, and every assistance given him in his enterprise.

In this way men of moderate means may invest on the easiest terms and under the safest guarantee, with practically no risk. It is certainly a most unusual proposition. Land is the safest form of investment. It cannot burn, be stolen, or affected by financial panic. Pleasantville Terrace is the only land convenient to Atlantic City which can be bought as low, or on such terms.

Franklin P. Stoy, Mayor of Atlantic City, was among the first to recognize the advantages of Pleasantville Terrace, and among the first to purchase. He has consented to reply to all inquiries as to the standing of the Company and the goodness of the investment. Prominent officials of the Reading Railroad, clergymen and hundreds of business men, have also purchased largely. Property is sold under wise permanent restrictions, and to white people only.

Every facility is offered for investigation. Excursions are run every Sunday from Atlantic City, leaving the Reading Station at 2.30 P. M. Agents furnish tickets at the station, or they may be had at the Company's Offices, 410 Bartlett Building, Atlantic City.

A NEW SECTION

To those who cannot visit the property in person, a booklet and plans, from which to make selection, will be sent upon request. Section B opens June 25.

By enclosing $1 with name and address as many lots may be secured as desired, up to five, which is all that can be sold to one person. Satisfaction is guaranteed or the dollar will be returned. Or, send name and address for booklet and further information to The Atlantic City Estate Co., Victor J. Humbrecht, President. Philadelphia Offices, 1039-1050 Drexel Building, Fifth and Chestnut. Atlantic City Office, 410 Bartlett Building; Pittsburg Office, 308 Frick Building; Camden, N. J., Office, 304 Market St.; New York Office, Room 925, 1133 Broadway; Newark, N. J., Office, 412 Prudential Building; Washington, D. C., 209 Jenifer Building.

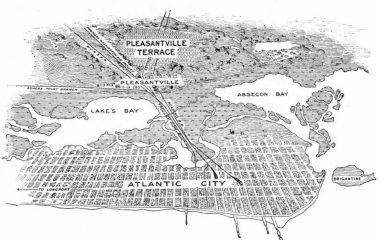

PLEASANTVILLE TERRACE, ATLANTIC CITY'S NEW SUBURB

The Saturday Evening Post Advertiser.

The Defacement of the Modern City

By Carter H. Harrison
Mayor of Chicago

Mayor Carter H. Harrison at his summer home

TO PROTECT his city from defacement is one of the most difficult problems with which the public-spirited citizen or the municipal officer is confronted. While other questions outrank this in importance, it is quite as easy to undervalue as to exaggerate the significance of this task. Cities, like women, cannot afford to be indifferent to the impression which they make on passing acquaintances.

For a city to become popular implies that it also becomes populous, and this also carries the natural inference of prosperity. Nothing that is intended to increase the popularity of a city, to enhance the general good impression it makes upon the visiting stranger and the outside world in general, can be called insignificant.

The whole problem resolves itself into a warfare between short-sighted commercial greed and far-sighted regard for the general good, including the most generous and substantial share of individual gain. Resistance to these encroachments of selfishness and commercialism is to be made by a strict application of the police powers of a municipality and by educating the people to a better appreciation of the need and value of firmly resisting all that threatens to detract from beauty of view.

The men who are mainly instrumental in defacing a city or a neighborhood by permitting, for hire, the erection of unsightly bill-boards are also to be divided into two classes: the non-resident owners of vacant property, and those resident owners to whom a rental fee of one hundred dollars from a bill-board company is larger and more tangible than twice that amount gained through the appreciation in value of their property by reason of its share in the general advancement of the neighborhood in appearance and conditions.

There is far more excuse for the former class of offenders than for the latter. The non-resident landholder, who does not see the advantage of an immediate improvement of his holdings, next looks about for some means of making his vacant property pay a portion, at least, of its own taxes, while waiting for the time when it may be advantageously improved or sold. His agent reports that the largest revenue is to be had by renting the frontage to a bill-board company.

Boulevards Spoiled by Bill-Boards

Perhaps it is a specially choice lot facing a boulevard. If so, it commands a still higher price for purposes of defacement. Owners of the adjoining property may protest until they are exhausted. They are told that the non-resident owner of the ground has ordered its rental for bill-board purposes and that there is no recourse from such a decision; that taxes must be paid, and the non-resident owner is not worrying about the æsthetic appearance of a city in which he does not live.

But what effect does this have on the property in the long run? Does it pay when the final results are summed up? No! And one of the best means of promoting the good looks of a city and of preventing its defacement is the establishment of a systematic propaganda for convincing non-resident owners of unimproved lots that they cannot afford to rent their frontage for bill-board purposes.

In some cases a peculiarly favorable location may render the bill-board privilege so valuable that the income from this source would actually pay both interest and taxes on a lot. One hundred dollars, however, is a liberal annual bill-board rental for a fifty-foot lot in the central portion of a large city. In most cases, probably, half that amount would be a liberal estimate of the income from the frontage privilege of a lot of standard or ordinary size.

Therefore the amount involved in this problem is never a large one to the individual property owner. Only a slight advance in the value of the holding would be required to cover the income from this defacement; for it may be taken for granted that the bill-board at its best, wherever placed and however constructed, is a defacement of the landscape.

Attractiveness Helps Real-Estate Values

Does any person doubt that the abolition of the bill-boards in Chicago, for instance, would add greatly to the general attractiveness of the city? And this is only another way of saying that the visiting stranger would be far more favorably impressed with the appearance of Chicago were these unsightly barriers to free vision removed. It is upon a consensus of just these "impressions" concerning a certain locality that the price of land within its limits is advanced. Anything which contributes to make these impressions more favorable is important. And it is surprising to notice how many dollars a little improvement in the appearance of a certain locality will add to the value of every lot in the neighborhood.

But the plain, unæsthetic property owner is inclined to underestimate the possible appreciation in value of his land from causes of this kind, and to overestimate the size of the check which has been placed temptingly within his reach by the bill-board company. It is to be feared that a long, persistent and well-directed campaign of education will be necessary to effect a general and marked change in the attitude of the men who constitute this large and unimaginative class of property owners.

This brings us to the point of the remedies by which the tide of city defacement may be stayed and driven back within reasonable bounds. Unfortunately, most American cities are in a situation about similar to that of Chicago, so far as the legal status of this problem is concerned. The only basis of action in law open to those who would take active steps to curtail such wholesale injury to the city's good appearance is found in that clause of the charter which gives the municipality authority to enact, in relation to property or persons, any regulations necessary to the public health or safety.

No ground for municipal legislation or interference can be found in the fact that a certain use of property violates the æsthetic sense of a neighborhood or of a city. Only when property is so used as to threaten the health or safety of the public can the municipality correct this violation of the canons of civic patriotism.

Legislative Remedies for the Evil

The first step for any city to take in a war against defacements is to determine the extent of the powers granted by its charter. Then its legislative body should pass enactments which provide for the exercise of all the power conferred by the charter and upheld by a sound interpretation of the common law. Right here, however, is a danger into which more than one city has fallen. In their zeal to frame an effective ordinance the friends of this kind of reform are very likely to exceed the limits of the charter and of good law and to enact an ordinance which will not stand in the courts. This difficulty has been encountered in Chicago and no doubt in scores of other cities. We cannot by ordinance compel a city to make itself beautiful any more than we can legislate the private citizen into a state of morality.

What can be done to fight the defacement nuisance, however, is this. Regulations and restrictions can be made so exacting, under the police powers of the city, that the number and the size of its bill-boards will be greatly diminished, that the citizen will hesitate before renting his frontage for that purpose, and will be inclined to refuse the tempting offer of the advertising companies rather than attempt to comply with the rigid police exactions.

Chicago has already accomplished something in this direction, although there is still room for improvement. The "triple-decker" sign-board has been practically abolished. This was an actual menace to the safety of the public, as a high wind was liable to dash any of these towering structures upon pedestrians passing along the street. Some "double-deckers" still remain with us, where they are of specially strong construction and are not so dangerous. But these, too, will have to go sooner or later—and the sooner the better. Of course the bill-board on a boulevard in the fine residence portion of a city is far more objectionable than in the business district, and this distinction should always be borne in mind in attempting to solve this problem.

One regulation which has been found effective is that requiring all bill-boards to be mounted a certain distance above the ground. The vacant lot, shut from the street by a huge bill-board which comes tight down to the ground, at once becomes a receptacle for all manner of filth and makes the place an offense to the community. This nuisance has been abated by compelling the elevation of the boards—a restriction which has a tendency to reduce the size of the bill-boards and to render them more expensive and difficult of construction. Thus, while the city cannot prevent a man from putting up a huge bill-board on the ground that the structure will shut off from a neighbor a desirable view, it can discourage the bill-board mania in general by keeping the police regulations, in that particular, up to the limit of good law and by enforcing them to the letter, curtailing their size, demanding that they be of heavy construction, and that their anchorage be of so elaborate and substantial a character that they are not likely to be uprooted by a strong wind.

What Private Citizens May Accomplish

I am convinced, however, that the private citizen can do more than the municipality in protecting a city from defacements in every way. Let us suppose a certain vacant lot, on a handsome boulevard, is owned by a man living in another part of the city. The property adjacent to the lot is owned by two men who have their homes there. A bill-board is to be erected on the frontage of the vacant lot. This will seriously obstruct the view of the neighbors across the street, will be an annoyance and an offense to those living alongside of it, and tends to make the whole immediate locality less attractive. Let all those neighbors form themselves into a delegation, go to the owner of the vacant lot and, in a reasonable and friendly way, place before him their objections to the bill-board, putting particular stress upon the fact that his intended move is certain to exert a depressing influence on the price of property in the block. If they cannot convince the owner of the unimproved property that he cannot afford to offend his whole neighborhood, and that he should not take such action as certainly will not help the price of his own holdings, they are below the average of delegation members in powers of persuasion. The man who will stand out, in a comparatively small matter, against the united protest of his "property neighbors" has more than the ordinary amount of fortitude and stubbornness. This spontaneous, private, unorganized manner of curtailing the encroachment of the bill-board and the big sign is unquestionably the most effective means of warfare.

Clubs and "improvement associations," however, may wield a powerful influence in this direction. They are the best channels for pushing a general campaign of education by which to elevate the sentiment of the whole city or community. In scores of smaller cities organizations of this kind have accomplished marvels and have changed the whole face of their landscapes. A notable example of such a work is to be seen at Geneva, Illinois, where the persistent labors of the local improvement association have preserved and protected the beauty of the valley of the Fox River for a course of many miles. The non-resident owner of vacant property should be carefully looked after by the club or association engaged in this line of work. He should be communicated with and made to feel that he owns property in a live city, that his "property neighbors" there recognize that he has a mutual interest, with them, in the advancement of the city's general welfare, and that he should help instead of hinder this dignified and businesslike effort to make the city in every way handsomer and more attractive. When appealed to in this manner he will think twice before instructing his agent to again give to an advertising company the right to put a bill-board on his property in a community where such a wholesome and vigorous agitation is in progress.

The Crusade Against Paper Scatterers

There seems to be a somewhat general impression that European cities have solved this problem, but such is not the case. Though their bill-boards are unquestionably covered with matter of a superior artistic standard, the boards are almost as numerous as in the larger cities of America.

The big signs painted on the exposed walls of large buildings are almost as flagrant defacements as are the bill-boards, and they are much more difficult to remedy than the latter. Practically speaking, they cannot be touched through the police powers of a city, and the arousal of public sentiment is about the only method by which they may be effectively discouraged.

Another very common and offensive disfigurement of cities arises from the wholesale scattering of papers of all kinds. This may be remedied by compelling the people properly to separate their garbage, instead of throwing into the box, along with food scraps and other household refuse, paper that will be lifted and blown about the streets by the first high wind that whistles down the alleys. In the residence districts of Chicago this reform has been so well enforced through the police department that it is certainly well established. Persons caught wantonly scattering papers were taken into custody and brought to the police station, despite the fact that they were steady-going citizens of high character and standing. A few examples of this kind exercised a most salutary influence.

Protruding stairways, and all signs which obstruct the sidewalks, are directly under the control of the city, and are permitted through the influence which their owners have with the aldermen or members of the council. When public sentiment demands it, defacements of this kind will speedily vanish. These things come through the aldermen and may be abolished through the same agency.

OUR CITIES IN THE TWENTIETH CENTURY
Washington—its Present and its Future

Front view of the White House

PHOTO. BY CLINEDINST, WASHINGTON, D. C.

The Washington Monument

FROM THE COLLECTION OF WILLIAM H. RAU, PHILA.

The National Capitol

PHOTO. BY CLINEDINST, WASHINGTON, D. C.

THE District of Columbia is the national capital. The city of Washington is the immediate seat of the Government of the United States. The Federal District, which was provided for in the Constitution, and in the act of Congress of 1790, was originally, as selected by President Washington out of the territory on the Potomac offered by Maryland and Virginia, ten miles square. But since the retrocession, in 1846, of the territory on the Virginia side of the Potomac, the land area of the District amounts to about seventy square miles. The District of Columbia, placed by the Constitution in the exclusive control of Congress, is governed, under the act of Congress of 1878 (which the Supreme Court of the United States has termed "the Constitution of the District of Columbia"), by a Board of three Commissioners, one of whom is always an officer of high rank of the Corps of Engineers of the Army, the other two being civilians, appointed by the President and confirmed by the Senate. The Commissioners serve for a term of three years, under the direction of the President, to whom they make an annual report; but the District has been held, nevertheless, by the United States Supreme Court, to be a municipal corporation. Under the act of 1878 the people of the District of Columbia lost the elective franchise, and the United States Government, which owns more than one-half of the land of the District, and had paid no taxes and made no regular contribution to the expenses of the District for seventy-eight years, promised to pay one-half of the expenses for the future. Before that time there had been no permanent government for the District of Columbia, and very little recognition of it in Congressional legislation, except during the period from 1871 to 1874, when Congress maintained a full-fledged territorial form of government, with a legislature, a delegate in Congress and a Governor. The Commissioners of the District of Columbia are the successors of the Governor of the District of Columbia and not of the Mayor of Washington, who was the chief ruler of the District of Columbia before 1871. It seems necessary to repeat these facts about the government of the District of Columbia because so many educated people do not seem to know them. It is a constant cause of surprise to Americans, as well as foreigners, that there is no voting for any political officer in the District of Columbia, and comparatively few people seem to understand that the city of Washington has no government except that of the District of Columbia.

The Growth and Beauties of Washington

Under the present form of government, the District of Columbia, so long retarded in its development by the neglect of the general Government, has greatly improved, and has nearly doubled in population and in wealth. The city of Washington now includes Georgetown, the old Scotch town that antedates the District of Columbia, and which is the seat of the famous old institution of the Jesuits, Georgetown College. It also includes several smaller places, and has spread out over the hills to the north of the old-time city limits until it is almost coterminous with the District of Columbia. At the present rate of growth practically the entire District of Columbia, outside of the park reservations, will in fifty years be built up with the city of Washington. The rapid transit provided by what is considered the best street railway system in the United States, all underground electric, there being no overhead trolleys within the city limits, has made the suburbs available, and, in some respects, the most desirable residence quarters, especially in hot summers when the elevation of one or two hundred feet above the old city, which is almost at tide level, makes a delightful difference.

Besides the suburbs within the District line, there are a dozen prosperous towns and villages a few miles out, along the lines of the railroads entering Washington, which are practically part of the District; while Alexandria, and even the city of Baltimore, which is only forty-five minutes away on the railroad, are used as places of residence by many people in Government employ or in private business.

The official reports of the United States census taken in June last give the population of the District as 278,718, but there is every reason to believe that this is at least 10,000 less than the real number, for fully that many people would be away for the summer on the first of June. The census of all large cities ought to be taken on the first of January.

While the District of Columbia is primarily a place for government and residence uses, it has considerable manufacturing and commercial interests, although it sells very little to the outside world.

An Industry that no Panic can Affect

The great industry, so to speak, is that of the United States Government, which gives employment to about 20,000 persons, to whom is paid about $23,000,000 a year, which gives the unique economic condition of practical commercial stability. No matter what panics or industrial depressions may occur in the country, the business of the Government goes on and the steady stream of Government expenditure continues, increased in volume from time to time when any new public building is erected or any other unusual outlay is made. It is estimated that, besides salaries, the Federal Government expended in the District of Columbia during the century just closed about $200,000,000, the greater portion for Government buildings, Government parks and other things owned absolutely by the Government, although since 1878 it has paid on an average about $3,000,000 a year as its share of the general expenses of the government of the District of Columbia. It is interesting to know that the total valuation of all property in the District of Columbia is about $410,000,000, of which about forty-seven and one-half per cent. is taxable, the rest belonging to the United States, and being, therefore, exempt. These figures represent a considerable amount of capital invested in commercial and manufacturing enterprises demanded by the local needs. The 2295 manufacturing establishments reported in the census of ten years ago produced a product valued at $39,296,259, on an aggregate capital of $28,876,258, and it is believed that there has been a large increase since that time.

The White House Conservatories

PHOTO. BY CLINEDINST, WASHINGTON, D. C.

Corcoran Art Gallery

PHOTO. BY CLINEDINST, WASHINGTON, D. C.

Pennsylvania Avenue, looking east from the Treasury Department

PHOTO. BY CLINEDINST, WASHINGTON, D. C.

PHOTO. BY CLINEDINST, WASHINGTON, D. C.
The Pension Bureau

HENRY B. F. MACFARLAND.

PHOTO. BY CLINEDINST, WASHINGTON, D. C.
The Treasury Department

But Washington is not the place to make fortunes and people do not come to Washington for that purpose. It is rather a resort; first, for the winter months, and then for most of the year, of people who have made fortunes, small or great, in the distinctively commercial or manufacturing cities elsewhere. Since, under the Civil Service Act of 1883, as administered with more or less fidelity by every President, the tenure of the civil servant in the executive departments has been made stable, it is probable that more people come to Washington merely to reside than come to seek or to take offices, except when the Census Bureau is organized, once in ten years, when, for a short time, a large temporary force of clerks is employed. The heads of the departments and the higher officials change with the political complexion of the Administration, but the great majority of the subordinates remain from one Administration to another, and, with their families, amount to something less than a third of the entire population of the District of Columbia. The other two thirds are made up of the people of leisure, those engaged in commercial and manufacturing enterprises, and its servants and laborers.

A Government Without Rings or Bribery

The government of the District of Columbia is the best in the United States, since there are no political bosses or rings, and neither bribery nor corruption. The cosmopolitan character of its social life is due to the presence of the Government, the Diplomatic Corps, prominent officers of the Army and Navy, and visitors from all over the United States and the world. Intellectual opportunities are afforded by the Library of Congress, by the great scientific collections of the Government, by the colleges, and by the scientific societies, which are maintained by scientists in Government employ, who are more numerous than in any other city in the United States, if not in the world. The opportunity of hearing the debates in Congress, the frequent interesting spectacles and gatherings of distinguished men, the mild climate and the peculiar attractiveness of the beautiful city and its surroundings, bring to Washington every year an increasing number of most desirable citizens. They find that it has admirable churches and a fine public school system, besides excellent private institutions of learning, first-class newspapers, good clubs and all the other necessaries of a modern city. They find that it has efficient municipal service—street, fire, police and scavenger; good lighting arrangements, and a fairly good water supply and sewage system. Its parks and its hundred thousand trees, the noble Government buildings and the fine private residences, all free from the soot and dirt which make some cities so unattractive, are always praised. Yet Washington, beautiful though it is, can be improved, and those who love it best are the most anxious to see improvements made.

Some of them, long desired, are already under way. Mr. Andrew Carnegie's gift of $350,000 and the appropriation by Congress of part of a small park in the centre of the city make possible the free public library which Washington has never had. It is now under

construction and will be ready for use in March, 1902, when, for the first time, the residents of Washington will have a first-class circulating library; for except for the use of Congressmen and a limited number of officials, no books are allowed to leave the Library of Congress.

Millions to Abolish Grade Crossings

The abolition of grade crossings on the steam railroads within the District of Columbia, for which the citizens and the Commissioners have been laboring so long, will probably be provided for at this session by act of Congress, and soon be begun under plans whose carrying out will cost about $11,000,000, including the expenditure on two new railway stations. The Baltimore and Ohio Railroad has had a station near the Capitol for over half a century, and has occupied, in a great Y, a good deal of the northeast portion of the city and the District. The Pennsylvania Railroad, or, rather, the Baltimore and Potomac, which it operates, has had, since 1876, a station on the Mall just south of Pennsylvania Avenue, and its tracks have occupied streets in southeast Washington, while the Southern railroads, connecting with it over the Long Bridge, have occupied streets in southwest Washington. The "servitude" thus imposed upon the streets of Washington has been more than a legal term. It has cost human lives every year; it has hindered the advancement of large sections of the city; it has caused vast annoyance and inconvenience. Of late years the railroad companies have shown a desire to change all this by doing away with the grade crossings, and after much discussion and negotiation between their representatives and those of Congress and of the District of Columbia, plans have been agreed upon which have been embodied in legislation. Under these bills, all the tracks are to be either depressed or elevated so as to abolish grade crossings within the District of Columbia, and two handsome terminal stations are to be erected. These features of the legislation are, of course, very popular in the District of Columbia. But the provision made for partial compensation to the railroads is not so generally approved. Under this provision, the Baltimore and Ohio Railroad is to receive a million and a half in money; half to be paid by the United States and half by the District of Columbia; and the Pennsylvania Railroad is to receive rights in the park known as the Mall, and in certain streets, which are estimated to be worth two million dollars. The railroads, of course, contend that they are making the changes in response to public demand and not primarily for their own advantage, and that this is only just compensation.

Pressing Need for a New Water Supply

Perhaps the most pressing needs of the District of Columbia are a better water supply and a better system for the disposal of sewage. Plans for the extension of the water supply service, and for a filtration plant in connection with it, have been matured by the United States Army Engineers charged with the task, and work under the plans for the former has been begun. A scientific

The Smithsonian Institution
PHOTO. BY CLINEDINST, WASHINGTON, D. C.

The Congressional Library
FROM THE COLLECTION OF WILLIAM H. RAU, PHILA.

The Agricultural Department
PHOTO. BY CLINEDINST, WASHINGTON, D. C.

system for the sanitary disposition of the sewage of the city has also been planned by the United States Army Engineers, and is partially completed. But it is regarded by everybody in Washington as very desirable that all these plans should be executed more expeditiously than the appropriations made by Congress have hitherto permitted, and in the name of the health and comfort of the city the Commissioners of the District have asked Congress to provide means for larger annual expenditures on this account, so that the work may be completed at the earliest possible day. The Commissioners coupled with these two projects the great need of the government of the District for a building for its offices. The District government has never had a building of its own, but since the organization of the Territorial government, in 1871, has gone from one rented building to another, and is now paying a large annual rental for inadequate quarters, which are not fireproof, and in which are necessarily stored archives and records (including all the records of the underground constructions) that could not be replaced except at a great cost, if at all. The need for a District government building has been admitted for years by Congress after Congress, but lack of money, or, perhaps, lack of interest, has prevented Congress from providing for it. Now, however, there is, apparently, a desire on the part of Congress to meet this need, and it is hoped that the purchase of a suitable site and the erection of a worthy building will soon be authorized.

The very successful celebration on the twelfth of December, 1900, of the centennial of the establishment of the seat of government in the District of Columbia, in which the President, his Cabinet, the Supreme Court, Congress, the Diplomatic Corps, the Governors of the States and Territories, and the Commissioners of the District of Columbia, with others, participated, strongly drew the attention not only of the National Government but of the entire country to the District of Columbia, and gave it an interest which it has never had before. This was apparent in the new vigor infused into all projects for the beautification of the city of Washington and its surroundings. The intense pride of the nation in its capital, and its generous purpose to make it all that it ought to be, were brought out clearly by this celebration, which gave a great stimulus to all ideas for the improvement of the District of Columbia, especially on the æsthetic side. The speeches delivered during the celebration, at the Executive Mansion and at the Capitol, dwelt on this, and immediately afterward propositions were broached in both houses of Congress for the creation of a commission of experts to form plans for the enhancement of the beauty of the District on a more comprehensive scale than ever before. The construction of the proposed magnificent memorial bridge to connect the city of Washington, west of the Executive Mansion, with Arlington, across the Potomac; the improvement of the parks, and especially of the Mall, extending from the Capitol to the White House, and of what is called Potomac Park, a great tract of land reclaimed from the former "flats" or marshes; and suggestions for the sites of future Government buildings with regard to their relation to other architecture, are among the subjects which, it was proposed, such a commission of experts should consider, together with the question as to whether the Executive Mansion should be enlarged, and if so, how, or whether some other provision should be made elsewhere for the better accommodation of the President of the United States, whose private quarters in the Executive Mansion are entirely too small, and who also needs larger apartments for the exercise of official hospitality.

The experts might also take into consideration the grouping and distribution of a number of Government buildings which have long been urgently required. Indeed, every one of the great executive departments has had to rent buildings, and ought to be provided with new ones. The rentals paid by the Government in the District of Columbia are more than the interest on a sum sufficient to construct all the new buildings that are needed by the Government.

It is evident that the improvements which might be called local to the District of Columbia, including, besides those which have been enumerated, the completion of the harbor work on the Potomac River and the proper treatment of the Eastern Branch, or Anacostia River, on which the United States Navy Yard is situated, cannot be made promptly and properly with the annual revenues of the District of Columbia and the corresponding appropriations out of the National Treasury. The Commissioners of the District of Columbia have recommended to Congress that one of two plans be adopted for providing the necessary money: first, that it be advanced from the United States Treasury, the District's half to be repaid in annual installments without interest; or, second, that two per cent. bonds be issued for the District's half, with principal and interest guaranteed by the United States. Unless one of these plans be adopted the improvements will go forward in a very unsatisfactory manner, and be more costly in the end.

The District of Columbia is, to use Senator Vest's phrase, "the eternal capital of the eternal Republic." It is hard to realize now that the removal of the national capital to Senator Vest's own State of Missouri was talked about as late as thirty years ago. The removal of the national capital, however, has never been seriously considered since the Civil War. As the nation expanded across the continent in the early part of the century the proposition to remove the capital to a more central point, in order to provide for better communication, seemed entirely natural, especially as the District of Columbia was not then attractive. But the steamboat, the locomotive and the telegraph destroyed the argument for removal based on distance in time and space. Then, when the North and South had contended in the Civil War over the national capital, it became impossible to remove it. Washington had become not only the seat of the Government, but of the sovereignty of the nation. Indeed, it symbolized the preserved Union.

The future of the national capital is as bright as the future of the nation. It is certain to grow in size and beauty, and to have continued prosperity. At the end of its second century it may have a million inhabitants, and it will certainly have such wealth and attractiveness as can hardly be imagined now. It may become necessary to enlarge the present District of Columbia, not only by securing again what Virginia gave and then took back, but perhaps by enlarging the original boundaries, with the coöperation of Maryland and Virginia. It will be the most splendid capital in the world.

The Æsthetics of "Sky-Scratchers"

ONLY a few years ago persons of culture everywhere were accustomed to throw up the hands of holy horror at the prodigious buildings which the pressure of American life, coupled with the newly-developed possibilities of steel construction, are raising in all the big cities of the land. One firm of architects, which had made its reputation by copying, or at best adapting, the masterpieces of European architects, went so far in passionate protest as to build a two-story edifice on one of the most valuable lots in New York City.

A few independent spirits, however, have always maintained that any art-form which has its origin so deep in the vital necessities of the life of a nation, and which so strikingly expresses them, cannot be essentially bad. One of them went so far as to suggest that the monstrous Flatiron Building was architecturally far more interesting and significant, at least to Americans, than the copy of the beautiful tower of Seville across the tree-tops of Madison Square.

Meantime the illustrators were discovering in the sky-scraper a new and striking picturesqueness. Jules Guérin, standing on Brooklyn Bridge, saw that the light of sunrise, as it played among the big buildings of lower Manhattan, had much of the richness of color, the vastness of aërial space, of an Alpine landscape. Joseph Pennell saw, and transferred to his etcher's plate, the clifflike majesty of the sky-scraper as seen from the level of the city street. A Frenchman wrote and published a treatise on what it pleased him to call The Sky-Scratchers of New York. Finally Sir Caspar Purdon Clarke, the new English director of the Metropolitan Art Museum, refused to condemn the architecture of his adopted city, though in refusing to do so he felt that he had to proclaim himself an anarchist in art. What Americans need, he said, is to have greater confidence in their own artistic judgment, their own resources, their own artists and their own arts.

It is not probable that the sky-scraper will take its place among the beautiful buildings of the world — alongside of the Parthenon and the Palace of the Doges — at least in its present state of development. It is more likely that its extravagances will require to be curtailed by law — in spite of Sir Caspar's anarchism. Meantime its development has given Americans a lesson. What we most need in order to become great intellectually and spiritually is the firm conviction that we are already very nearly so.

WHY THE ENGLISH NEED SKY-SCRAPERS—SKETCH MADE IN NEW YORK BY TOM BROWNE, THE ENGLISH CARTOONIST

Cockney. "Thank the Lord there is one thing we've not got in England."
New-Yorker. "Say, what's that?"
Cockney. "Sky-scrapers."
New-Yorker. "Well, you want 'em; your skies are so bad they need scraping."

THE WONDERS OF THE SKY-SCRAPER

By Corydon T. Purdy
An Eminent New York Engineer Whose Specialty is the Construction of High Buildings

STEEL FRAMEWORK OF THE DOME OF CHICAGO'S NEW POST-OFFICE

THE FAMOUS BROADWAY CANYON
Looking Down Broadway from City Hall Square, New York

DERRICK AT THE TOP OF A TWENTY-STORY BUILDING LIFTING THE STEEL GIRDERS

The building of the mammoth hives where modern business men work has become almost an exact science.

These most marvelous buildings are distinctly an American idea and the wonder of the rest of the world.

The sky-scraper is a work of engineering rather than of architecture. The parts are made from the architect's drawings, of which thousands are needed, then brought on the ground and put together.

It is a most intricate structure of steel, often extending many stories underground as well as upward. The walls are fastened onto the framework instead of being built up from the ground.

Every bit of weight, every bit of wind-pressure, are calculated to the fraction of a pound before a rivet is placed in the structure. For instance, in the Flatiron Building provision is made for the swaying in a heavy storm.

An intensely interesting and popular, yet thoroughly accurate, description of the methods pursued in putting up these monster towers by the engineer who has constructed more sky-scrapers than any other man in the world.

I WELL remember how New York looked the first time I visited the city some thirty years ago. I hastened forward on the ferry-boat, and gazed eagerly at the scene. The low-lying roofs formed a sky-line almost as level and uniform as the water in the bay, and unbroken except by Trinity Church spire and a few other projecting points. The individuality of the buildings was lost, as are the trees of a forest on a distant shore. Now all this is changed. Massive structures many stories high loom up above the old roof-line in all parts of the city, while they are bundled so solidly together at the lower end of the island that an entirely new sky-line has been formed high above the old one. On a clear day I can pick out and identify some of these great buildings with the naked eye from my home in the Jersey hills, fifteen miles away.

The incoming traveler looks at the scene with surprise and wonder as he sails down the bay. One of the greatest artists living said of the first few buildings that they were ugly. Recently, however, he looked upon them again from an ocean-steamer, and after looking at them long, he said, "How wonderful! It is grand now!" This is the spectacular side of modern buildings. It is their bigness, more than anything else, which impresses every one who sees them for the first time. It is so in all cities in which such buildings have been erected, but is more evident in New York, because that city can be viewed so splendidly from the water front.

These great buildings are the product of a new era in architecture. They have all been constructed during the past fifteen years, and mostly during the past ten years. They are distinctly American. There are probably no important features in their construction that have not been employed separately at earlier dates and in other countries; but it remained for Americans in this present generation to put together its various features, to formulate them as a distinct method, and to show its superiority over older methods by its wide adaptation in many cities.

To the inexperienced eye these new buildings look like the older ones, and even men familiar with their construction cannot always distinguish between them when they are only eight or nine stories high. It is not primarily in appearance, then, that they differ, and this is true in spite of the fact that bigness is the most noticeable characteristic of the modern building. Dwelling-houses, farm-barns, and small buildings generally, are built with timber frames, and the strength of such buildings depends chiefly upon the good character of the frame. Other and more important buildings are built with masonry walls, and the stability of such buildings depends upon the good character of the walls. The former arrangement is called "frame construction," while the latter is ordinarily called "masonry construction." It would be less confusing, however, to call the latter "massive construction." In one class the inherent strength is in a frame, in the other class it is in the solid wall.

The two ideas are fundamentally different. If the distinction is well understood, the way in which the "sky-scraper" is built will be better appreciated. It looks as though it were of masonry construction, but it is actually a frame building. Steel is used in place of wood in the construction of the frame, and brick, stone and mortar take the place of clapboards. In massive construction the walls carry the floors and roof, and make the building strong in every way, but in the steel-frame building the walls do not do this; indeed, they do not carry their own weight except for the height of one story. In a typical building the wall is supported on the steel frame at every floor. In appearance it seems to be continuous, like other walls, but really it is nearly, if not quite, cut in two horizontally at the height of every floor. This is a feature of the construction which always seems strange to people who are not familiar with it. When the first buildings of this type were erected in Chicago, throngs of spectators continually watched the progress of the work, and no feature of it interested them more than the construction of the masonry walls, started on one of the upper floors, as is often done, apparently in midair. These walls of course add something to the strength of the building, but the truth remains that the chief dependence for strength is in the steel frame, and the walls are mainly to inclose the building, to protect and perpetuate the steel construction, and to afford opportunity for exterior embellishment.

In the actual construction of great buildings the types of construction are often mixed. One wall or a part of the walls may be self-supporting, or even made to carry floors and roof, while the other walls are made with a steel frame; but many buildings of ordinary height, and all of the very high ones, are of typical construction, with all walls carried on steel.

The frame is composed of steel columns extending from the foundations of the building to the roof, arranged to carry conveniently all the loads of the building, and connected with each other at each floor-level with a system of steel beams and girders. These beams and girders in each floor system are connected with each other and with the columns at every point of contact, and they are so arranged that all points of the floor are supported by the nearest columns as directly and simply as possible. All members of the steel frame are completely fabricated before they

are brought to the building, and all the connections are made with rivets driven hot as the work of erection proceeds. As many rivets are used in each connection as are required, and always enough in well-constructed work to make the connection as strong as the members themselves. Such a frame can be erected completely and alone, without any of the exterior walls, and without any other construction whatever in the interior. This is not ordinarily done, because it is generally more economical to keep all parts of the work going at the same time.

Each individual member of the frame has some special work to do—some bit of floor to carry, or some wall, some opening to span, or some parts to tie together—and each piece is dimensioned and fitted for its special purpose. Then the frame as a whole should not only be strong enough to carry the weight of the building, and hold the different parts of the building together in proper form, but it should also be strong enough to resist injurious effects of all kinds from wind and storm.

The steel frame, therefore, stands in the modern building as the principal element of its construction. It is at the center of everything—everything else depends upon it, everything else is built around it—and it not only stands up strong in its own strength to carry the weight of all the material that enters into the construction of the building, but it stands there rigidly, as capable of resisting an explosion from within as it is to resist the pressure of a strong wind on the outside.

In generations past the details of the construction of a building, the character and size of the materials used, and the exact way in which they were put together, were largely fixed by precedent, and copied from one building to another. In steel-constructed buildings all this is changed. Constructive problems have become susceptible of calculation and definite determination. The strength of steel and iron can be measured, and the effect of the weights which they carry can be figured. It follows, therefore, that every part of a steel frame can be made just strong enough to carry its load. To make it smaller would be criminal, to make it larger would be wasteful; therefore it is necessary to make it just right.

But the problems of strength are not the only ones. The arrangement of the different parts of the frame, and particularly the position and number of the columns, must be determined. In

THE FRAMEWORK OF THE FIRST TWO STORIES OF THE FAMOUS FLAT-IRON BUILDING AT BROADWAY AND FIFTH AVENUE, NEW YORK

all particulars this arrangement must be suited to the proper use of the building. In structures of a public character columns generally must be few and far apart, while they often can be spaced quite closely together in office-buildings and hotels. The openings in the floors must also be accurately determined, so that no part of the frame will interfere with the plan of the building. Each piece of steel must be figured to fit into its own place, and a drawing must be made of it, so that the workmen in the shop can frame it and put every bolt and rivet-hole in it in exactly the right place. For this purpose over three thousand separate drawings are sometimes required for the steel framework in a single large building, and the location of each cut and each rivet-hole is figured on all these drawings to within one sixteenth of an inch.

The use of steel frames has added greatly to the labor of planning buildings. Not only is the work for the steel construction itself great, but there has been a remarkable development in every department of building-construction. This development has gone on hand in hand with the extension of the steel frame, each step bringing with it new problems and added labor. A generation ago an architect himself could do all the work required, if necessary, but now he must surround himself with specialists in different departments. He must, more than ever, be a student of affairs. If he is to design a store, he must master the necessities of that business; and in these days of great department-stores, that means much. Every building to be successful must be especially fitted to its use.

The artistic treatment of his problem often makes the greatest demand upon him, and it should never be slighted. Then there is the heating, the ventilation, the electric-lighting, the sanitation, the elevators and the power-plant all calling for technical knowledge. The more ordinary work in the finish of the building must also have special care; for the larger the building, the more important it is sure to be. The interior wood-finishing, plastering, marble-work, tile-work and ornamental-metal work must all be planned and specified and shown by drawings.

The foundations of these modern buildings, although made in various ways, are always scientifically planned. Until recently architects depended largely upon their experience and judgment; now well-established laws of mechanics control the designs, and the correctness of their application is the chief concern. The weight of every part of a building is figured, and whatever kind of foundation is used, it is calculated and proportioned to the weights it has to carry. Of course, as the size and cost of great buildings have increased, the importance of having good foundations has also increased. A fault in the superstructure might be remedied, but a mistake in the foundation is ordinarily irreparable. For this reason the methods that are most certain to be enduring and unchanging are preferred to others less certain in these respects, though the additional cost is often very great. The first high building erected in Chicago was carried on foundations made of steel and concrete spread out over a rather soft bed of clay. At first it seemed as though this material, within a small limit, was incompressible, but time has shown that this is not true. Many of these earlier buildings have settled materially, but very few of them have been really injured by this settlement. It is always better that a large building should stay exactly where it is put, and now all the best buildings in that city are built on piers of concrete extending down eighty feet or

more below the street to the rock level. Open wells are dug in this clay, through which material water scarcely penetrates. The sides of these wells are supported by wooden staves and iron rings as the work progresses, and when the bottom is reached, the holes are filled with the concrete up to the bottom of the steel columns.

In New York the ground varies greatly. In some places the rock-formation comes so closely to the surface that the steel columns can be started immediately upon the rock; in other places, and particularly at the lower end of the island, the rock bottom is covered with silt and quicksand forty to seventy feet below the street. This material is so fine that it flows freely with water, even for considerable distances. The construction of foundations in such places is therefore a work of great difficulty and of considerable danger to all surrounding property that is not founded on rock. Compressed air is generally used to make the excavation through such material and to hold the water in check. A chamber is constructed of iron or wood the size of the pier, and closed on all sides except the bottom. The compressed air in the chamber prevents the water from coming in, and as the men excavate the material from the bottom of the chamber, which is comparatively dry, the chamber itself gradually sinks until it rests on the solid rock. In the meantime the pier above the chamber has been built, and when the chamber and the entranceway to the chamber have been filled with concrete, the work is completed.

Floors are mostly made of hollow blocks of burned clay material. These are laid in flat arches between the steel beams, plastered on the bottom for the ceiling of the rooms below, and covered on the top with concrete, in which is bedded the wood or tile flooring. Concrete with iron bars or metal in other forms is frequently used in place of the flat arches, and a mixture of plaster of Paris and wood-shavings, reinforced with iron, also makes a satisfactory construction. A floor should be proof from warping by fire, a satisfactory protection to the iron beams which carry it, not too heavy, not too costly, simple in form and easy to put in place. If the building is very high in proportion to its size, and especially if the spans between the beams are long, thickness and body of material is also desirable.

Partition walls are likewise made in different ways and of different materials. They do not need to be strong to carry loads, for they have none to carry, but they should have considerable lateral strength, so that in case of accident or fire they cannot be broken down. A partition wall should prevent a fire from spreading from one room to another. In most cases a partition should also be sound-proof.

The interior finish of very high buildings ought to be made of materials that will not burn, in case a fire should occur, and a few of the best modern buildings are being made in that way; but any finish can be used, except as the law may intervene and dictate.

In most office-buildings the entrances and the elevators, as well as the halls and offices, can be arranged in different ways, and fortunate is the owner whose architect solves this problem happily. It may be done so that the building will always attract tenants, and it may very easily be done so that it will repel them. It may make the most of its areas, or it may waste space, and so materially lessen its income. The extreme importance of securing the best possible design in this respect is of course without question, and yet many of the older buildings and some of the modern ones are lacking either in attractive qualities or in renting capacity, or in both.

The modern high building is really a monument to the commercial activity of the present generation. Some of them, costing millions of dollars, are as beautiful as marble and bronze and mahogany can make them. Within their walls commerce is planned and directed. Within a single building is the life of a city. In the biggest of the office-buildings the business man finds everything that will add to his comfort, convenience and even luxury. His chief object is to save time, and he is usually able to do this in these buildings. He buys his morning paper at a news-stand in the corridor; he has his boots polished by a man who goes the rounds; an excellent restaurant in the basement or at the top of the building provides all that he wants in the way of good eating; telephone and telegraph are at his elbow; if he wishes to send a box of flowers or bonbons to his wife or his sweetheart, there are a florist and a confectioner at hand to meet his wants. Two thousand or three thousand people work under one roof, and they stand for a population of six thousand or eight thousand. Badly lighted, ill-kept and poorly furnished rooms in old buildings are not wanted, while the bright and attractive rooms in the new buildings are always in demand. The steel-frame method of construction and the modern high building in American cities have come to stay.

THE PROPOSED FORTY-FIVE-STORY MUNICIPAL BUILDING,
NEW YORK CITY
When Completed This Will Be by Far the Tallest and Most Impressive
Building in the World

THE FLATIRON BUILDING
The Grand Campanile Facing Madison
Square, New York City, Considered
the Most Wonderful Example of
Sky-Scraper Buildings

THE OLD AND THE NEW
St. Paul's Church, Where Washington Used to Worship, at the Right;
at the Left the Thirty-Two-Story Park Row Building, the
Highest in New York; in the Middle an
Ordinary Eight-Story Building

"A Sunny Day in 1910" was the title of this prescient cartoon from an 1898 *Life*.

2 The Breadwinner

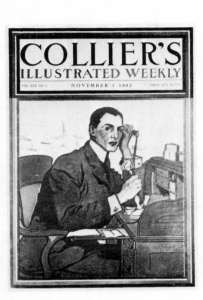

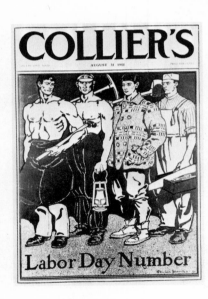

If the following group of items about the head of the family is representative, the American middle class at the turn of the century was obsessed with the subject of how to acquire money. It would be almost unthinkable today for magazines of general circulation to publish article after article on such topics as "Brokerage as a Business for Young Men" and "The Gospel of Saving," but these subjects were obviously considered important in the first half-dozen years of this century.

Exaltation of money and denigration of culture and higher education appear to sum up the spirit of the times. "The Gospel of Saving," by Russell Sage, which is reprinted here, tells a great deal about the period, not only because of what Sage says, but because Sage was asked to write it. In 1900, when the article appeared in *The Saturday Evening Post,* Russell Sage was in the fullness of his years, a ripe eighty-four. He would live another six years, to an even ninety, before learning that even he could not take it with him. He had been a congressman from New York, but his fame came from his adeptness as a handler of money. He was associated with Jay Gould, who made millions by watering stock and bankrupting the Erie Railroad, though Sage seems not to have become involved in those deals. He did well enough by himself, though; by sharp railroad promotions and later through what are euphemistically referred to as "shrewd money manipulations," he had put together a fortune estimated at about seventy million dollars by the time he passed on to glory.

This, then, is Russell Sage, who opens his article on saving by stating, "Thrift is so essential to happiness in this world that the failure to practice it is, to me, incomprehensible." Thrift is a splendid virtue, but one smells in Sage the vice of miserliness. Here is a man who could not understand spending two dollars for a book to read when those two dollars could be put out at 8 per cent. Or again: "A man should at no time spend more than is necessary for decent living. Extreme luxury and lavishness are signs, not of cultivation, but of barbarism." Probably more than one aspiring businessman copied that dictum down and pasted it inside his hat for instant reference. "Out of every dollar earned save twenty-five cents. Save seventy-five cents if you can, but never less than twenty-five." Sound advice, but only up to a point. It is meant for those who find pleasure in accumulating money, not for those who would rather enjoy what money buys.

Sage also has general advice for the aspiring millionaire. He urges the young man with wide horizons to lead a good, clean life

("Don't do anything that you would be ashamed to discuss with your mother"), to be a pillar of the community (join a church), and to "be prepared to work eighteen or twenty hours a day, if necessary." And finally he shows the suspicion of higher education that was so common to this period, the odd idea that the human brain is diverted from its main business of making money when it is crowded with too much extraneous information and that a boy is better off getting an early start on a career of getting rich. "With many of us," Sage writes, "in fact most of us, I believe it would be better if we were turned into the active work of the world at fifteen or sixteen."

Although it was a holdover from the nineteenth century, Sage's philosophy of money seemed to fit the new century very well. Not everyone had his singleness of purpose or his genius for making dollars multiply, but a great many persons were trying, and the journals of the time were doing their best to help ambitious young men up the ladder of success. The reader could get some tips on how millionaire J. P. Morgan operated. He could learn what opportunities awaited him in Hawaii or China; or if he had more modest aspirations, he could discover what to expect out of life as a farmer or as a conductor or motorman on a street railway system. He was told that the future was bright in the new telephone business. For the young man toying with the idea of making it big as a stockbroker, there is an article from the pen of a former president of the Chicago Stock Exchange telling what is required, but warning that those who cannot stand the heat had better turn to something less demanding: "In no other business is the candle of human vitality burned as rapidly as it is in the broker's office. The man who cannot stand sustained work under high pressure has no place in this calling and had better keep out of it."

There is nowhere any mention of what teaching or art may offer as a career. Among this welter of make-a-success-of-yourself material, one is arrested by an editorial entitled "Culture and Success"; this is the first time the word "culture" has obtruded itself. One finds that the editors, using a contemporary dictionary of biography, have discovered that almost all Americans of note claim some higher education. The writer, obviously a college man himself, comments, looking down his nose a little, "That leaves only . . . 3 per cent with no more than the common-school education which some gentlemen of note think all that is good for a business man."

(So much for you, Mr. Sage.) But unhappily one reads on: "Colleges are not primarily designed to teach a man to make money, but they teach him to measure his mental powers and make the most of them. When he turns his disciplined faculties in the direction of money-making he is more likely to succeed than if his mind were untrained." So an education, like everything else, has a dollar sign pasted on its face.

The subject of this chapter is the breadwinner, and although the foregoing makes it appear that he had no function other than to go forth into the marketplace, he was also a man who returned to his home at night. And when they wrote about his nonbusiness activities, the same journals that were so deadly serious about tycoons and careers and investments lightened their tone. "Why Whiskers?" an editorial asks, and goes on to discuss the completely insignificant matter of the mustache. Not beards: the age of beards had passed; the new time of whiskers and hair was more than sixty years in the future. This, of course, is the kind of editorial produced when the editor is faced with a blank sheet of paper and must think of something to fill it. The results are seldom earthshaking, but they often reveal what was in the air at the moment. For instance, there is an editorial on limited marriages, which would be binding only for the period of raising a family (although it seems doubtful that either principal would have strength for new adventures after that). The item is not an important one, but that such a matter was even mentioned tells us that even in Victorian America it was possible to question some of the ancient verities.

And, of course, there was the matter of what the breadwinner should wear when he went down to earn his living. The styles look uncomfortable and apparently were, for an editorial asks, "Have Men a Right to be Cool?" and then discusses the plight of the man who swelters in the summer in coat and vest and the trauma he suffers when he dares to shuck the two garments. Possibly the one sentence that sums up the summer discomfort of the time is this: "In spite of the theory that it is not man who is the slave of fashion, the only people who look cool in hot weather are women, who have learned the comfort and the beauty of the crisply clean shirtwaist." If women, clad in neck-to-ankle dresses and undergirded by the formidable corsets of the time, were considered comfortable, then God alone knows what the men of the time must have undergone.

Where the Money Goes

A YOUNG couple, after living along for nearly a year at the rate of $30 a week on an income of $25, reached the place where a sober, serious, heart-to-heart talk was imperative—a situation of the greatest delicacy, with the breakers upon the reefs of matrimonial disaster roaring in their ears. But they remained cool-headed and learned, among other things, that during the preceding week they had spent $3.15 on just nothing at all, $7.40 by paying too high prices for necessities when a little thought and care would have prevented it, $2.25 for things they could have very well done without, $2 for which they could not account at all; total, $14.80. They had spent in all during that week $34.50.

Subtract what was "fooled away" from what was spent, and you have $19.70—that is, they spent for value received $5.30 less than their income. The hint in this incident is as valuable to the single as to the married.

In Double Harness

IN A LATE collection of the unconscious humor of school-children is this: "The marriage customs of the ancient Greeks were that a man had only one wife, and it was called monotony." In a recent case in an American State in which the divorce laws are notoriously lax the plaintiff actually charged that the husband was so uniformly considerate that their wedded life had become humdrum beyond endurance; so she asked for separation on the ground of incompatibility of temper.

Matrimony and monotony make a favorite alliteration, and they are joined together in the cheap wit and problem plays of the times until the idea has grown stale; and yet it is an ever-present and increasingly prolific source of unhappiness. Wed and yawn, say the skeptics, and many of those who marry find themselves nursing their ennui, while

Languid Love,
Leaning his cheek upon his hands,
Droops both his wings.

It is not the fault of the institution. From the days of Cicero we have been told that "a man would have no pleasure in discovering all the beauties of the universe, even in Heaven itself, unless he had a partner to whom he might communicate his joys." The trouble is that too many men quit discovering after marriage, and either have no joys to communicate, or substitute for the pleasanter things ordinary, every-day grouches. Ruskin had the higher ideal when he said marriage was "only the seal which marks the vowed transition of temporary into untiring service, and of fitful into eternal love."

With untiring service marriage never grows dull. In fact, it acts as the finest sort of stimulus. "To tell the truth," confessed Tyrone Power, "family and poverty have done more to support me than I have done to support them. They have compelled me to make exertions that I hardly thought myself capable of; and often, when on the eve of despairing, they have forced me, like a coward in a corner, to fight like a hero, not for myself, but for my wife and little ones." That confession would fit many a man's life—and it explains, too, why we have so little patience with the husband who complains of his domestic burdens; instead of finding excuses he ought to be working harder to obtain the material results that would make the excuses unnecessary.

Real service finds plenty of things to do not only for self but for others, and in the doing of them come the precious satisfactions which drive out monotony. Doctor Johnson laid down the law: "Marriage is the best state for man in general; and every man is a worse man in proportion as he is unfit for the marriage state."

As has often been observed, it takes a little time to decide, after a man and a woman are made one by a clergyman, which is the one; but there is really no use in worrying about that. Simply get on fair terms with Fate, and do your best!

The Wifely Touch

LIGHT-MINDED paragraphers the country over have been making game of a Missouri judge who, although granting a husband's suit for divorce, disallowed the plea that the injured man regarded as of especial weight—namely, that his wife had been accustomed to extract from his trousers' pockets while he was asleep such treasure as diligent search revealed there. In the eyes of the law, as it seems, it is neither a crime nor a misdemeanor for a wife thus to share her husband's lot. A Chicago paper, meanwhile, rebukes both the learned, wise and upright judge and the flippant scribes. "The moment that husbands and wives," it says, "begin to play sly tricks upon each other, the beauty of the marriage relation is gone." To question, as a New York paper does, why the Chicago editor felt so keenly on the subject, is both irrelevant and base. The whole future of wifehood is at stake in the question.

Through all the ages marriage, while legally a contract in partnership, has been a relation in which money talked, and the man put the records on the financial gramophone. Like the Irishman of anecdote, the husband has said: "What's yours is mine, and what's mine's me own." The very physical being of women is evidence of this fact, for it is a matter of scientific record that, as is the case with rabbits, deer and other graceful but terror-driven animals, the retina of her eyes takes in a larger field of vision than that of dominant and cruel man. And her nature, even more than her physique, is all compact of shifts, evasions and dissimulations. If Solomon had been half as wise as he is said to have been, he would have found that fifth and greatest thing that passeth understanding, the way of a maid with a man. The so-called prose laureate of pessimism, Edgar Saltus, deposed that, in all his lifelong hunt for the true and the beautiful, he had never seen but one happy marriage. In that the wife was a deaf mute and the husband blind. Even then, Mr. Saltus added, the husband did not always know what she was thinking.

The idea that masculine comradeship and honor are possible in the relations of men and women is very recent. Those who profess it most prominently are suffragists, socialists and other queer creatures. In literature the most prominent and perhaps the first exponent of it is Trilby—and even Du Maurier did not venture to show us what that frank and manly girl would have become in matrimony. Yet the time is coming, however distant, when no good husband will close his eyes in sleep without first putting his wad in plain sight on the bureau, and no wife worthy of the name will take a red cent from it without ringing up the exact amount on the conjugal cash-register.

When the Honeymoon Wanes

THIS is peculiarly the season for the launching of matrimonial enterprises. All over the land each morning the bride and the groom, just back from the honeymoon, are parting for the day with smiling neighbors peeping from behind curtains. Usually the bride's last word is: "Come home early." And usually her evening greeting is: "Now, dear, forget all about the business, and let us be happy."

A natural start; but a mighty bad one. "Dear" ought not to come home early; "dear" ought not to forget all about the business. The honeymoon vacation is over; life has begun—not a bird-life of twittering and singing in the branches all day long with no necessity for thought of the morrow, but human life with its many and ever pressing serious matters. And "dear" should stay at the office until his business there is finished, and his wife should realize that it is her business as well as his, and should urge him to let her know all about it. They've got to talk about something while they hold hands; why not about that which must be the main source of the development of their characters and careers?

PROTECT YOUR FAMILY

A sense of security pervades the home which shelters a **SMITH & WESSON** Revolver.

SMITH & WESSON,

15 Stockbridge Street, Springfield, Mass.

Catalogue for a stamp.

Have Bachelors Any Rights?

VIRGINIA will soon vote upon the adoption or the rejection of a new constitution, and whatever may be the decision the instrument that will be passed upon will go down into history for a very interesting and somewhat curious reason. The convention that framed it was regarded as unusual in standing and ability, but it had one weakness that was soon pointed out—an undue proportion of its membership consisted of single men. There was no explanation for this, not even the claim that many good lawyers in Virginia were too poor to marry. But the bachelors, being without excuse and modest in the bargain, even if they were lawyers, banded together for the common defense. They formed a bachelors' club and tried to maintain their position before a scornful public.

The married men proved their superiority by practical demonstrations. They showed that on the floor they were much more self-possessed and far cooler than the bachelors. To this the bachelors made reply that the married men were used to joint debates at home, and that being interrupted did not feeze them. This is a fair illustration of the arguments of the single men—shallow, specious and scandalous. The married men further proved that they could talk longer and better than the single men, and they pointed to the records to show that they had accomplished by far the larger part of what had been done. The bachelors—still frivolous—responded that the benedicts were making up for time lost when the speakers of their own houses shut them off and did the talking themselves. Then it was established that the married men of the nation had done most of its fighting and had held most of its offices. The bachelors—worse than ever—asseverated that the married men went to war to escape hostilities and ran for office because they had to run somewhere, and that an office was about the safest place.

But soon the women of the country knew of the single-blessedness club and the members began to get letters. These epistles varied from stinging truths to flat proposals. Then the Virginia girls, than whom there are none lovelier in the world, took a hand. The club lost members. The assessments for wedding presents became onerous, and finally Captain Miller, the president, threw up his hands and surrendered, saying that there should be a provision in the State constitution they were framing providing that no man should be eligible to any office in Virginia who was not married or who had never been married, and he added: "I have come to the conclusion that bachelors have no rights and are incompetent as legislators, and that the sooner they are relegated to private life the better."

If such a provision were in, there could be no doubt that the whole of the new constitution would go through the polls with flying colors—but really, it is not necessary. A nation which has for its motto, In Union there is Strength, has already placed its stamp of disapproval upon bachelorhood.

❧

When Clubs are Trumps

ROMANTIC writers and those of the Richard Harding Davis type must still be trembling from the solar plexus blow recently delivered by a prominent New York clubman who declared that a bachelor could live at any one of several leading Fifth Avenue clubs with less expense than at a hotel of the better class. Since the time when the memories of Monsieur and Madame Grundy run not to the contrary so-called clubmen have been wearing halos—at least in the feminine fancy—such as only wealth and immaculate exclusiveness are supposed to command.

But "at least six members of the Metropolitan Club are spending no more than $1000 a year, which includes, in each case, an apartment and bath and breakfast, dinner and the very best of service," says this recognized authority. When it is remembered that the club in question is a favored rendezvous of multi-millionaires, and is considered as one of the smartest and most exclusive social organizations in the country, this statement savors of iconoclasm to a marked degree.

Had it been known some years ago that the clubable Van Bibber was perhaps worrying along on twenty dollars a week, a great many romantic young women might not have rejected so scornfully the advances of otherwise eligible bachelors who unfortunately must have forgotten that clubs were trumps.

Penalties for Bachelors

FADS, fashions and newspaper humors have the cycle habit. They come around every few years, wearing new trimmings, but essentially the same as before. The tax on bachelors is one of them. Some of the colonies taxed bachelors. The practical lawmakers of those practical days looked upon the man who did not marry as one shirking a manifest responsibility, and a revenue burden was placed on his unwilling shoulders. The scheme is attractive. Bachelors are increasing, and the governments—city, state and national—all need money. The bachelor is supposed to have money. He centres his efforts and his finances largely upon himself, and on the face of things he offers an opportunity.

But, of course, there will be no direct tax on bachelors. It might be unconstitutional, or class legislation, or something to bother the Supreme Court. Therefore, suggestions. Let the bachelor be compelled to play a more important part in the problems that afflict society. Miss Clark, secretary of the State Charities Aid Association of New York, comes forward with a new idea. She explained it at a public meeting. Unmarried persons of both sexes should adopt children, she said. Bachelors are too selfish; they become soured; they need more joy, more employment, more light and laughter; a child in the house or in the flat will supply this. No longer will the bachelor brood on the gray future if he has a youngster with well-developed lung power to fill his time and apartments with multitudinous demands.

The other sex is included in the scheme, for in these days, when old maids are out of fashion, there are no old maids—only bachelor girls. And the bachelor girl has her isolation. Often she gets weary of making things out of Sunday supplements. The work palls. She can, of course, take a cracker-box, a flour-barrel and four yards of material, and manufacture a Turkish corner at a cost of eighty-seven cents, not including arnica and court-plaster. But what does it amount to if no Romeo sits on the nails she forgets to hammer down? A child would pleasantly interrupt the monotony of that corner, would investigate its geography—and the bachelor girl would not be lonesome.

But, as usual, there is an obstacle. Adopting children requires courage. Bachelors and bachelor girls are not brave. If they were they would get married.

❧

CASEY: "FAITH, WE HEV ONE CONSOLATION, FLANAGAN. I'M INFARMED THAT MARRIED MEN LIVE LONGER THAN BACHELORS."
FLANAGAN: "IT'S A FALLA-ACY, ME BHOY. THE TIME ONLY SEEMS LONGER TO THIM THOT'S MARRIED."

The Beauty of Fatherhood

"WHY is it," asks a subscriber of his local newspaper, "that, with all the pother about the beatitude of motherhood, no one has a good word to say for fatherhood?" Why, indeed? When woman is caught neglecting the halo which religion and art have placed on her head, our good President takes it reverently off, polishes it up, and gently but firmly puts it back again. Fatherhood never had any halo, and nobody has missed it. Who ever heard of a man's shirking his duty to the race, and who ever praised him for performing it?

But are his sacrifices less momentous? In war he fights for his home unquestioningly, and dies for it without a murmur. In peace he is the provider, and what goes out in baby clothes cannot go out in golf, motoring or clubs. For the most part, it may be objected, what he loves is business; he has no care for such luxuries. Be it so. Even then he has his natural desires—to leave a salary and go in on his own hook; to branch out here, or to venture there on a flyer. He can't, for that would endanger the stability of the family finances, and even risk the future of his offspring.

Without a thought of his hard lot, he keeps to the highway of mediocrity, and is perhaps despised for doing so by the very wife and children to whom he has sacrificed his dearest ambition. His family shine intellectually, morally and socially. He holds down his chair before a rolltop desk, and pays for the metaphorical gold leaf. There is only one day in the month on which he can reckon on being popular, and that is pay-day.

Even his sins pass unnoted, unless they rise to the magnitude of a public scandal. If he had more glory to gain as a father, perhaps he would be less given to the tortuous ways of corners in wheat or frenzied finance. It is a subject of vital interest to the Republic, and we earnestly recommend that when the President has shot up enough bears he will give it his patriotic and strenuous attention.

A Self-Imposed Tyranny

WHAT has become of the "comic spirit" upon which Mr. George Meredith used to pride himself? In advocating marriages for a limited period only—the period of bringing up a family—he is voicing an idea as old as Plato. If the truth were known it would probably be found to be quite as old again as Plato. And in these matters age does not lend dignity or authority.

The trouble with all such propositions is that they ignore the essential principle of human institutions. If social laws were mere arbitrary enactments, emanating from Mars or from the moon, successful rebellion against them would, perhaps, be possible. But they are the deliberate and hard-won expression of the deepest necessities of man. In point of fact, monogamous marriages, as the latest authorities assure us, are not merely a human arrangement—they are found in the animal world, and were in all probability evolved æons before the anthropoidal ape.

It is, of course, inevitable that law should work wrong to many individuals, that the social ideal should bear upon many men and women with crushing tyranny. It is also true that certain well-recognized motives urge men and women to live alone, to change partners, even to indulge in a grand right and left. But such motives are exceptional and aberrant. It is possible that in the past they have been unduly condemned; but it is not possible that in their behalf the great institutions of life should ever be radically changed. As long as the human race remains what it is it will love, honor and live in mutual obedience to all high impulses until death.

Holmes somewhere remarks that if social anarchy were to reduce all property to ashes some promoter would arise and make a fortune out of potash. It is but varying the epigram to say that if marriage was abolished the severed couples would move Heaven and earth to put their necks again under the conjugal yoke. In Mr. Meredith's earlier years nothing would have been more delightful to his comic spirit than to write the novel of an advanced, an Ibscene couple who attempt the social revolt in behalf of free love, only to find that their human hearts are human.

Matrimonial Possibilities

The rising young dentist

Son of the Congressman

Son of the pork-packer

The Governor's son

Son of the village Banker

The rising young lawyer

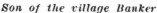

The Man Beautiful

NOT the least interesting or important development of science is what may be called æsthetic surgery—the artistic science of improving upon Nature's handiwork in the shaping of the face and its environs. And the curious fact has come out that in the crowds that respond to the "beauty surgeon's" perhaps too optimistic proclamations there are more men than women!

The women have every excuse for agitation about their personal appearance. They are on the matrimonial market, and the thing that most pleases the most customers in that market is beauty. But what excuse have the men? They, too, are on the matrimonial market, but the quality that most pleases the most of the customers that will look them over seriously is not beauty, but manliness. Manliness, of course, includes the ability to play a man's part in the mad rush at the bread counter. Why, then, are the men so eager to look pretty? Can it be just plain vanity?

A Sure Way to "Get Rich Quick"

THERE is no disputing the fact that in America, at least, the men are coming to have a terror of baldness fully equal to the similar terror in the women. It is not difficult to understand this phenomenon in the women, even in the married ones with the husband problem comfortably settled. But how explain it in the men?

The women never did love them for their umbrageous locks, or, indeed, for any other quality of beauty which men recognize in each other; and though there are instances of men having failed or succeeded in life according as they were beardless or endowed with patriarchal face-draperies, where is there an instance of a man having lost numbers in the line of promotion in any business or profession through loss of hair on the head?

Can it be that this growing hatred of baldness is the result of a growing fondness for the pleasures of youth and a growing distrust of the substantiality of the pleasures of old age, whereof sad-faced old men have discoursed so lengthily? Let us hope not. But—what a fortune awaits the discoverer of a sure-enough hair-retainer!

Why Whiskers?

LE GAULOIS' earnest and exhaustive inquiry into mustached men's reasons for wearing mustaches is attracting world-wide attention. More than half the men thus far interrogated say frankly that they do it "to please the ladies"; only a few hide behind the ancient pretext that it saves the trouble of shaving—as if an energy that can scrape the large expanse of jaws and jowls would faint before the light task of two dashes at the upper lip! In fact, the further the inquiry is pursued, among all nations, the truth will stand out, which we all, smooth and bearded, know *a priori*: that the mustached men think they look prettier, and think the ladies think so, too; also, that the smooth-faced men may not be unduly exalted, be it said of them that they clean their faces because they think them thus at their best for the delectation both of their owners and of the ladies.

As it is a vital part of our duty to give as little offense to each other's eyes as possible, who will chide man for putting so much time and thought on such questions as Whiskers or No Whiskers? And if Whiskers, how much and why?

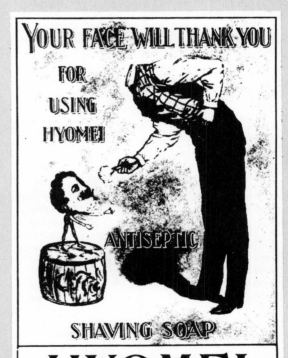

LATEST STYLES IN MEN'S FINE MADE TO ORDER CLOTHING.

Style 9   Style 7   Style C   Style 15   Style 4

Style B

Style 16   Style 17   Style 8   Style 5   Style 6

STYLE 9—Clerical, Standing Collar on Coat and Vest. Give Size of Collar.
STYLE 7—Full Dress.
STYLE C—Single Breasted Vest, no Collar.
STYLE 15—Tuxedo, no Buttons on Coat.
STYLE 4—Three-Button Cutaway Frock.
STYLE B—Single Breasted Four-Button Vest.
STYLE 16—Chesterfield Frock.
STYLE 17—Soft Roll Frock.
STYLE 8—Single Breasted Prince Albert **Frock.**
STYLE 5—Four-Button Frock.
STYLE 6—Double Breasted Prince Albert.

Have Men a Right to be Cool?

CIVILIZATION has not yet taught man to take his coat off when the weather grows hot. She has done much within the last decade to make the dog-days bearable. Man may now wear a soft shirt and pack his waistcoat away in camphor to await the approach of autumn. He may have his trousers made of duck, or the lightest of flannel. He may even reduce the thickness of his coat to a minimum. But coat of some sort he must have.

The millions of men who sit in their shirt-sleeves to do their work or to take their rest do so in defiance of what are supposed to be the unchangeable rules of polite and decent behavior. In the country, which is cooler than the city, and where, if anywhere, a man might wear a coat in August, he is allowed to go without one. He may cycle, play tennis, go yachting, or rowing, or golfing comfortably. In town he is doomed to increase his sufferings by sitting encased in woolen cloth. It is useless to argue that even in town in the seclusion of the home the rigor of the code is relaxed. Of course it is. But no man dares walk to his office, dine in a restaurant or sit in a theatre without the inevitable coat.

In spite of the theory that it is not man who is the slave of fashion, the only people who look cool in hot weather are women, who have learned the comfort and the beauty of the crisply clean shirt-waist. Would not men in fresh, cool-looking shirts be equally improved in appearance? It is true that a man who has removed a coat and thereby displayed a waistcoat is an unattractive sight. The waistcoat by the nature of its construction is essentially an underneath garment. And if one goes a step farther and, discarding the waistcoat, shows the unlovely mechanism of a pair of "galluses," the result is no better. The ordinary "boiled shirt" of white, with a stiff front indicating by its very shape that the rest of the garment is meant to be concealed, is only an argument for keeping the coat on. But the man in a soft shirt of pleasant color, with a neat belt around his waist, would be the fit companion of the shirt-waist girl, and would make the city on a hot day look less sodden with heat.

The world has been so occupied during the past ten or fifteen years with the emancipation of woman that it has quite forgotten the emancipation of man. Poor man now lags behind his sister in many matters, notably this of dress reform. His summer costume is ridiculous and stupid. How is something rational to be made the fashion? It is disputed whether tailors or the Prince of Wales decide what shall be the modish thing. No help can come from tailors—they make coats. And the weather in England is rarely so hot that the Prince wants to sit in his shirt-sleeves. The sufferer must make the effort himself. But, ridden by tradition as he is, he should have woman's help. If she will smile brightly on downtrodden and despised man when he comes to her dressed comfortably, man may perhaps gather courage to break his shackles—and take his coat off.

—H. G. RHODES.

DOUBT.

"Der fagt is I haf n't quvite made up my mind."

"No?"

"No. Sometimes I t'ink if a man has a bald head, vot is der use of him calling attention to it by vearing a vig?"

NOT AN ADMIRER.

"Gee! I wish I had de money to git a coat like dat!"

"You do?"

"Yes, but dat 's de last t'ing I 'd do wit' it."

The Case for the Fur Overcoat

THAT man, and not woman, is the greater slave to conventional rules of costume is a doctrine which has already found expression in these columns. And the amazing spectacle of "the shirt-waist man" has, during the last two summers, shown that when once goaded on to it by the newspapers and the intolerable heat, even poor man can yield to the dictates of common-sense. Woman no longer has a monopoly of comfort in the summer. But in the winter she still maintains her superiority, for to her sex alone is it allowed to wear furs.

Women apply some logic to dress. In summer they put on muslins and in winter snug furry jackets, tippets, and so forth. The average man would not dare to wear a fur overcoat, and he can probably give no better reason than that he would look like an actor. Leaving aside for the moment the criticism of a class which having not too much luxury at home takes a childish delight in seeming to have as much as possible in the streets, is there anything more than a false, inexplicable shame at the bottom of this feeling? There is in St. Louis a tall, weedy boy, with a narrow chest and a hereditary tendency to consumption, whose mother, gracefully evading the officials of the custom-house, brought him from England a fur-lined coat. The boy admitted that it would be a most unusually snug and pleasant garment, and that it would very probably prevent some of the racking colds which winter usually brought. But the other boys would laugh at him, he said, and neither commands nor entreaties would induce him to wear the coat. It was put away, and the moths ably attended to it. It is unnecessary to point the moral of this tale, and relate the youth's untimely death.

In fact, he went farther west, to a ranch, and no living doctor could now find any trace of illness about him. But it was a silly convention that prevented his wearing the coat a devoted mother had smuggled in for him.

The conditions of American life peculiarly demand an outer garment of great proportionate thickness to be put on when leaving the house. We keep our interiors hot enough, and there is very little need for thick clothing when indoors. Therefore those who resist the outer cold by fleece-lined underwear or a chamois-skin vest, make the mistake of wearing the greater part of their clothing at a time when they least need it.

The drivers of trolley cars, and truckmen in remote districts, are allowed to make themselves comfortable. Actors are tolerated as they stroll up Broadway appropriately clad to meet a blizzard. A few men who have come in contact with the effective civilizations of a continent which has not half the excuse which America has for the fur-lined coat, flaunt themselves in warmth. But the ordinary American finds in them something subtly vicious and "un-American." Your tailor would ask you a ridiculous price for a furred coat. But he would ask much less if comfort rather than luxury were the object to be attained. Sable is not the only wear. The skin of the rabbit keeps out the blast. Perhaps even that of the domestic cat—who knows? Women somehow manage to buy furs. Besides, they are not dear abroad, and no one any longer believes American tariffs immutable.

Pratt Fasteners
save time and trouble

Copyright, Pratt Fastener Company.

EVERY Travelling man, Professional man, Business man, Club man, and busy man will acknowledge without argument that "hard" knots and tangles in shoe-strings are among the most exasperating nuisances of daily existence.

THE PRATT FASTENERS hold shoe-laces securely without tying any knot at all. When shoes are made with Pratt Fasteners the extra length of shoe-string required to tie a bow-knot is not used (is saved), and short laces are used instead. When the Pratt Fasteners are put on old shoes, then the laces are cut off about two inches from the fasteners, and thus no long ends of the shoe-string are left to dangle.

THE PRATT FASTENERS are "a good idea"; they appeal to the common-sense of every one who understands what they are for and how they "work," and it is only a question of "finding out" about them for every one to wear them. One hundred million are being worn now by intelligent people in Sweden, Spain, and Switzerland, Austria, South Africa, Australia, Great Britain, France, and America. The United States Government has adopted them; in England they have been adopted for policemen's shoes; they are a feature of almost every bicycle shoe now made in America, and the general demand for this new method of fastening instead of tying shoe-strings is increasing steadily and surely—all because they **save time** and **are reliable.**

THE PRATT FASTENERS are being used by almost all of the larger manufacturers of boots and shoes in America, and you are sure to find them at the best shoe-stores everywhere. If you wear "Hanan," or "Emerson," or "Douglas" shoes, French, Shriner & Urner's, Hathaway, Soule & Harrington's, or Stacy, Adams's, De Muth's, Foreman's, or Holden's, Harris's, Hefflefinger's, or Kast's shoes—wherever you live, from New York to San Francisco, from Minneapolis to St. Louis, you can have the Pratt Fasteners on them. Or if you want Pratt Fasteners on the shoes you are now wearing, go to the nearest Emerson shoe-store in any of the twenty-seven large cities where there are Emerson stores and they will put them on for you **without expense to you**; or to the Hanan stores, or De Muth stores, or Foreman stores, in the different cities; they use them and have them. In Boston, Thayer, McNeil & Hodgkins; in Philadelphia, Sylvan Dalsimer & Co.; in Washington, Rich; in St. Louis, Harris; in Chicago, Marshall Field and Co., are headquarters for Pratt Fasteners and carry shoes that have been made with Pratt Fasteners for **Men and Women, Youths and Misses, Boys and Girls, and Children,** always in stock, or will gladly put a set of Pratt Fasteners on the shoes you are now wearing for you.

Here is a picture of the Pratt Fasteners as they look on shoes in place of the upper set of lacing-hooks or eyelets. You will never wear long shoe-strings and tie knots again if you will once wear Pratt Fasteners to hold the short strings instead of tying them. They can be put on in a minute! Ask, please, for **Shoes with Pratt Fasteners** when you buy another pair.

If you cannot get them where you live, write to us and we will see that you have them.

PRATT FASTENER COMPANY, 72 Lincoln St., Lincoln Bld., Boston, Mass., U.S.A.

Shoes can be laced with one hand.

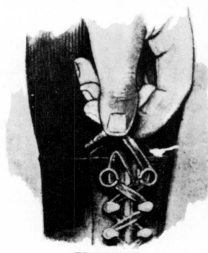

TRADE-MARK PATENTED.

FEB. 28, 1888.   MAY 5, 1896.

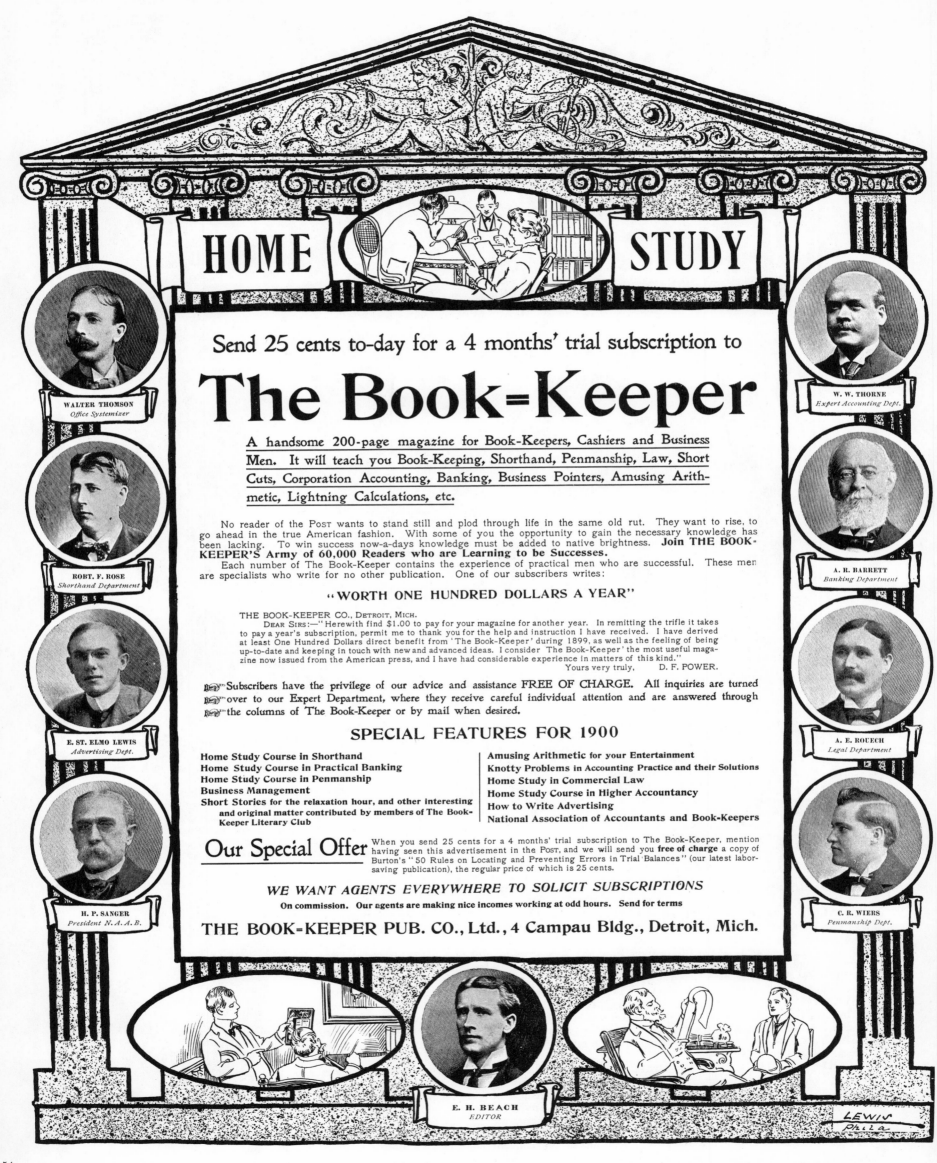

How Business Success Will be Won in the Twentieth Century

By CHARLES R. FLINT, President of the United States Rubber Company

THE specialist will be the dominating force in the business world of the twentieth century. The road to success lies along that line. Let the young man who starts out in life to-day or to-morrow concentrate on one thing and he has the golden key.

The day of the all-around man is over. New conditions have come into business life; and they have come to stay. These new conditions are unfavorable to the man who can do half a dozen things. He must master one business.

Under the readjustment there is no place for the all-around man. Nobody wants him, nobody cares for his peculiar kind of ability. Industries have been rearranged. They are now separated into departments instead of plants. At the head of each of these departments is wanted a man who knows all about this particular division, who has concentrated his entire mind and ability on its requirements and possibilities, who is in fact a highly trained, highly developed specialist. Men like these are scarce to-day. Hundreds of institutions are looking for them. Salaries ranging from $5000 to $15,000 are waiting for them. My own concern is looking for half a dozen specialists to-day, rubber men, lumber men, etc. We would cheerfully pay them $5000 a year, and even more cheerfully $15,000, for a $15,000 man is a great deal more valuable to his concern than the $5000 man. But he has got to be a $15,000 man. Naturally he is not plentiful.

Business in a concrete form has existed as long as the world's record runs; and until recently its course of development has been practically the same as in the beginning. Now, however, we are suddenly face to face with a new scheme. There has been a complete revolution. It is doubtful if the mass of the people appreciate this, yet it is as palpable to the man who has his eyes open as is the knowledge that to-day electricity is the motive power of the world. In a few years we shall wonder that we continued in our own time the crude business system of our forefathers.

Let no young man delude himself with the belief that we shall ever again go back to the old methods. As soon might we expect to see the electric cars put away in the sheds to give place to the old stages. And unless the boys who are starting out to-day in business life appreciate this and train themselves accordingly, they will be woefully handicapped.

The new method is the scientific, the civilized one. It is built on the knowledge of the interdependence of men. It explodes the fallacy of " independence." There can be no independence in the world except among savages: the wild man is the only human being who is really independent. The moment you get away from the savage state you leave independence behind. All government, all society are interdependent. The new business idea, call it the " trust " if you will, recognizes this principle and develops it to its highest form. That this recognition did not come long ago simply argues a backward mental state. The old order of " independence " in business ranks with the times when every baron was " independent," when he levied on the crops of his feudal retainers and was the master of their lives and families. As constitutional, scientific government has come to supplement the feudal system, so the " consolidation era " in business has come to supplant the old system.

How the New Business Idea Actually Works

Consolidation in business has bred the demand for the specialist, and as consolidation grows, as it will, the demand for specialists will grow. That it is subversive of independence and manhood is absurd. The man who directs a department for a big corporation to-day is more independent than he could possibly be under the old conditions when he went into business for himself. He is not worried with financial troubles and a thousand and one details that consumed his time without adequate return. He devotes all the time he has to that which he can do best. Naturally the result is higher production, and a consequent betterment for the world dependent on production. Nor does the new system make for concentration of wealth as is so generally stated. The reverse is the fact. Out of my own experience this is proven. When I was in business under the old scheme there were two profit sharers in the firm, my partner and myself. Everybody else connected with our business was a salaried employee. They had no share in the earnings. Everything they produced they produced for us. Later another partner was added, but there we remained. And what is the condition now? I have 300 partners, men who share in the profits of the concern, and who are interested in preventing losses. Last year $150,000 in profits was divided among the heads of departments with us. Our clerks own $60,000 worth of stock in our establishment. Carnegie, the greatest business man in the world, has thirty-two partners, young men who, having demonstrated their fitness for special lines of work, were given interests. And we are in the infancy of the new order of things.

Such a distribution of interest is possible only under a corporate system. No man in his senses would dare risk business association with 300 men under the old partnership plan, where any one of the 300 might involve the firm. Therefore the business remained a close corporation; the good things were distributed among relatives when they were distributed at all. Now everybody comes in on his merits. There are stock allotments, so that the able, frugal, painstaking man may almost any time acquire an interest. That this works to the interest of the man controlling the corporation is made evident from the better service we get. Almost any evening you may see clerks at work in our office. They put in this overtime because of the interest they take in the affairs of the house under the new conditions. It is never required of them that they work out of hours. It is entirely voluntary.

All these things work for the general success of business by the modern methods, and they emphasize the necessity of preparing to work under these methods. Naturally where there are great consolidations the work must be systemized. Production falls into departments, and at the heads of these departments must be specialists. The science of consolidation is not to bring competing interests together in order that prices may be raised. That is a foolish system and can only beget more competition. A combination to be persistently successful must be so managed that the same goods, or better goods, may be produced at lower prices. This can only be brought about by scientific supervision. And there is the source from which springs the demand for expert specialists. It is for the young men to take advantage of this demand.

Of course, the young man who starts out with an inherited fortune is not constrained to follow this plan. He can diversify his interests. It is the part of wisdom for him to do so. He protects himself if he is not dependent on one industry alone. But even a rich man's son might very well train himself as a high-class specialist. It will give him knowledge and power that in after life may prove exceedingly useful.

The Necessity for Being a Specialist

Mr. J. J. Hill, president of the Great Northern Railway, is a magnificent example of the possibilities that lie before a specialist. Mr. Hill is a specialist, has always been a specialist. He has devoted his entire time, attention and ability to railroading. He is to-day the greatest railroad operator in the world. There is nothing about the business that he doesn't know thoroughly. He has studied the business from A to Z and is master of all its details. Thanks to this thorough knowledge Mr. Hill has made himself one of the richest men in America.

Capital is always eager to associate itself with such men. But capital is mighty shy in having to do with men who are not master specialists. In my own case I always insist that my associates shall be specialists. I am always open to a good business enterprise; but I make sure that the men who are to handle the enterprise know all about it. And I also insist that they go into nothing else. It is distinctly stipulated in all our business contracts that the men in charge of our lumber interests have no other interests, that our rubber men confine themselves to rubber, and so all along the line. It is to this rule and its enforcement that I attribute much of such success as we have met with in our business enterprises. It has brought and holds for us a class of thoroughly trained specialists whose minds dwell continually on the one thing in which they are engaged. Thus we get better results than do concerns whose managers have to diversify themselves.

Everybody who amounts to anything is ambitious. He wants to get to the top, to become rich, to control things, to be a power. This laudable ambition, under the new way of the business world, will prove exceedingly dangerous if it leads the young man into general industries. In the formation period it was possible for men to go into different things and carry them through successfully. I myself, for example, without any particular qualifications as a specialist, have been enabled to aid in organizing a number of divers industries. But the situation with me was peculiar and unusual. I had been for years a member of a large commission firm which was the largest buyer in the United States of general manufactures for export. We handled everything from needles to locomotives. When the era of consolidation came I was in a position to deal intelligently as the representative of the different interests. I knew all the principals from years of business association, and, in a superficial way, I was familiar with the requirements and shortcomings of the various industries.

Now the formation period is practically over. We have settled down to doing business under the new plan. We have done very well so far; we are going right along the same line. Nothing can stop the development and expansion of the new trade scheme. The business of the world is going to be divided up more and more into departments.

Success is to be won in getting at the head of one of these departments. It is the twentieth century method.

Fortunes and Freaks in Advertising

By Paul Latzke

SOME STORIES OF FAMOUS SUCCESSES MADE BY MEN WHO HAVE USED PRINTERS' INK

BY SOME STRANGE WHIM OF RECKLESSNESS HE LEFT THE PAPER BEHIND

WHEN the January wind comes at a certain angle across Boston Common wise men keep indoors and animals seek the sheltered way. The air cuts through to the body like a knife. The heaviest overcoat is scant protection. Furs turn to feathery icicles. There is then comfort nowhere except indoors before a blazing fire. Those who must be abroad take the nearest way, and the street-car companies for once reap a harvest of "short riders."

Out of such conditions it requires rare favor of the gods to build success, but the story of a family from Lynn shows that it is possible. It happened that a rich man, having a directors' meeting to attend on such a January forenoon, jumped aboard the car on which the elder brother of this family—a young elder brother—was journeying to his home in Lynn. The rich man carried in his hand a copy of a Boston newspaper, and at the end of his short ride, by some strange whim of recklessness he left the paper behind. The elder brother, having a long, cold ride before him, and having no pennies to waste on newspapers, picked up the abandoned paper with eager satisfaction. And from this incident grew the making of millions out of an $84 check, and the beginning of an advertising romance that probably has no parallel.

This young man from Lynn was taking the $84 check home, and he had it very closely buttoned in his inside pocket. It represented the first substantial sum he and his family had had in their possession for several years. At the other end of the car line his mother and brothers and sisters were waiting hungrily for his appearance with the small fortune. They had been living on very thin provender for months, and looked to this check for a taste of good, strong food. The family originally had been among the most substantial people in Lynn. The father was a wealthy builder, and in 1874 had over one hundred houses, finished and under construction. Then a financial squeeze came, and he lost every dollar he had in the world. Fortunately, there remained the home, which was in the mother's name, and somehow the family managed for four years to keep from starving. Then in 1878 the elder brother had an idea. His mother, in the years of their prosperity, had brewed a certain medicinal compound, the recipe for which had been given her by an old German woman. Of this compound she had given away thousands of bottles, refusing pay even from strangers who asked the medicine of her. Her son's idea had to do with this medicine.

"Why not make up the compound and sell it?" he suggested.

The mother was doubtful.

"Who would buy it?"

"The people to whom you used to give it and lots of others when they hear of it. You've got nearly a thousand letters upstairs from the people who wrote to thank you for the medicine. We'll take some of these letters and have them printed; then we'll distribute them as advertisements."

With considerable misgiving, $2.65 was taken out of the slender family stock to pay for a thousand small, four-page circulars. The three brothers distributed these circulars from house to house. Next day they went over the same route, carrying in canvas bags a supply of the medicine which their mother had meanwhile brewed over the kitchen stove. Wherever a circular had been left they rang the doorbell and offered their wares. It was slow work, but it brought in enough money to keep the family from want. Here and there a drug store took several bottles, and circulars were left on the drug-store counters. Finally the demand reached a wholesale drug house in Boston and they ordered a gross. It was the payment for this first big sale, the $84 check, that the elder brother was carrying home when he happened to pick up the rich man's newspaper. He was too cold to take deep interest in the new "stories" spread out before him, but he finally lighted on a line that held his eye. It was printed on the editorial page in black type, and read:

Circulation, 54,000 Copies Daily.

The line fascinated him. It brought a wicked temptation to his mind.

"It takes us," he said to himself, "about three days to put out a thousand circulars, and they cost us $2.65 undelivered. At that rate 54,000 would take over half a year to put out, and the printing would come to $143. Now if we only had the money we could put them all out in one day through this newspaper, and the cost would probably be no greater."

Just then the car passed the newspaper office.

The young man ran to the door and jumped out.

"I'll just see what it *would* cost," he explained to himself. Inside, he handed the man a copy of his circular.

"What would you charge to put that in to-morrow morning's paper?"

"All of it?"

"Yes."

Mechanically the man counted the lines.

"$63.40."

"On the front page?"

"We don't put 'ads' there."

"Then it would do me no good."

"Very well, I'll put it there so you can try the effect."

The young man drew his breath hard. He knew what the sum asked meant at home; but the fever was on him. So steadying his voice as best he could he said:

"All right, you may print it if you will take in payment a check for $84 and give me the change."

The advertising man was willing and five minutes afterward his customer was on his way to Lynn again, but his precious hoard had melted to $20.60. At the house he was met by the whole family.

"Did you get the check?"

"Yes," he answered sententiously.

"Where—where is it? Let's see it?"

The questions came from all sides. They were hungry, clamorous for a sight of the precious paper. They wanted to handle it, feel of it, look at the figures.

Panic suddenly seized the boy. His intoxication passed away, and he realized what he had done. For a few minutes longer he fenced. Then, in desperation, he blurted out the story, and a wail of anguish and accusation went up. It was the most terrible tragedy that had come to this family since the dark days of 1874. The storm of words wore itself out after a while. The mother and daughters settled to deep, bitter crying. His brothers sulked in angry, hopeless silence. The little business that had at last promised a livelihood was ruined. The money left out of the $84 was not enough to face the most pressing demands of the butcher and the grocer. To buy more bottles, to put up a fresh supply of the medicine, to pay the printer for more circulars, was out of the question. For forty-eight hours the family remained in black despair. Then something happened. A messenger boy came with a telegram. It was from another wholesale drug house and read:

"Ship at once five gross compound by express."

It took the messenger boy a long time to get over the impression that the family had all gone suddenly crazy. They hugged each other and laughed and cried, and carried on generally as properly brought up lunatics do on the stage.

With reflection came quiet. There were no bottles and no labels and no compound. But somehow the bottles and labels were forced from reluctant dealers and printers, and a big fire was made in the kitchen stove under the medicine kettle. All day and all night and all of the next day the family brewed and bottled, and then the "five gross" were ready for the express company.

During the nine years following, through H. P. Hubbard, of New Haven, then one of the great advertising agents of America, the family spent over one and a half million dollars for advertising. They began on $1000 worth of credit extended them by Mr. Hubbard on the strength of their sales in and around Boston. When the mother died she left a business valued at several million dollars.

What the Woman Left with the Change

ANOTHER fine advertising story, almost as fascinating as that of the family from Lynn, had its inception on a hot summer's afternoon in the thriving Ohio town of Tiffin. Its final chapters cannot be written, but the action of the story has already carried to New York, and finds expression there in the finest building to be seen in the wholesale dry-goods district of that city. This building, only recently completed, is located on Mercer Street near Eighth. The street door leads into an outer office as spacious as an assembly hall, and here is generally to be seen the man out of whose idea the house grew—A. J. Stewart.

Mr. Stewart was a dry-goods clerk in Tiffin. On the summer day when his real life story started he had gone to work as usual, put his stock in order as usual, and waited on his customers as usual, without dreaming that he was at the turning point in his career. In the course of the afternoon there entered a woman who asked for two yards of black velveteen. After he had cut it off and wrapped it up for her and she had left the counter Stewart turned to one of his fellow-clerks, John U. May.

"John," he said, "did you see what that woman bought?"

"No."

"Two yards of velveteen for skirt-binding."

"Well, that's nothing remarkable," replied John.

"No," admitted Stewart. "It isn't. But it has given me an idea. Women are coming in here constantly for the same thing. After they get the velveteen they cut it into strips, sew it together and finally turn out a very inferior material with which to bind skirts. Now, why wouldn't it be a good thing to save them all that trouble?"

"And how would you do that?" inquired May.

"Why, get a machine that will cut the velveteen and sew the strips together. Then put it up in rolls and sell it ready for use."

May instantly saw the value of the idea. When business closed that evening and for many evenings after they talked the matter over, and finally concluded they would go into the business, then unknown, of manufacturing velveteen skirt-binding. They interested one of their friends named Potter, and organized the firm of Stewart, Potter & May. Stewart and May resigned their positions and moved to Cleveland, where they secured the services of a mechanic to work out Stewart's idea for a machine. With their machine finished they started into business and found a limited market for their wares. The dry-goods merchants were quite alive to the merits of ready-made skirt-binding, but the processes of introducing it to the customer was necessarily very slow. About this time there appeared in Cleveland a salesman for a Boston jobbing house, named L. F. Howe. Stewart and May made it their business to interest him in the new invention and succeeded so well that Howe bought Potter's interest, the firm being reorganized as Stewart, Howe & May, as it stands to-day. These three young men worked along until 1892, when, feeling the need of advanced methods, the firm was incorporated and moved to New York. Mr. May retired and George S. Curtis, of New York, an expert in financial matters, took his place.

"WHERE—WHERE IS IT? LET'S SEE IT?"

Mr. Curtis, even more than his associates, appreciated the field open to the new company if only the women of America could be educated to the use of ready-made velveteen skirt-binding. This seemed a difficult proposition, for at this time —only ten years ago—probably less than one per cent. of the dresses worn were bound with this material. Mr. Curtis had had no more experience in educational work of this kind than had his associates, but thinking the matter over he made up his mind that there was one certain way to achieve the end he was after.

"What we want to do," he said to the other members of the concern, "is to advertise. If we continue in the way we are it will take us forever to get the business on the basis it ought to be. We must continue to depend on the good will of the retailer to push our goods. As he's got other things to do, and skirt-binding is a small item with him, our progress

IN THE COURSE OF THE AFTERNOON THERE ENTERED A WOMAN WHO ASKED FOR TWO YARDS OF BLACK VELVETEEN

will be slow. If we go directly to the women of the country, telling them of the great saving of time and money and labor that may be effected by buying skirt-binding ready made, we shall create a natural demand and our goods will sell themselves."

At first this proposition was received coldly, especially when Mr. Curtis announced that they ought to appropriate at least $5000 as a starter. Five thousand dollars was a very large sum of money to the firm at that time and to invest this in an unknown field was considered foolhardy.

But Mr. Curtis is a man who rarely lets go, and before he finished he had his $5000 appropriation. This was in the spring of 1894. Within five months the business had jumped twenty per cent. Even Mr. Curtis was amazed. As for the other members of the company they were fairly carried off their feet, and when Mr. Curtis asked for additional funds for advertising they told him he could have any amount he thought necessary. At his suggestion $100,000 was voted in a lump sum. In less than a year the business had doubled, and orders were coming in faster than they could be filled.

From one floor the business spread to two, then to three, then to four, and then to five. Finally the company bought the present site on Mercer Street, and erected there the building that stands a monument to the genius of advertising. The yearly output of the company is to-day sufficient to encircle the earth several times. Its wares are found in every hamlet in the land, and it is doubtful if there is a woman, even in the backwoods, who does not know their trademark.

The Necessity for "Sticking to It"

IT IS a characteristic of most conspicuous advertising campaigns that their success is generally to be traced, as in the case of Mr. Stewart's ready-made skirt-binding, to an underlying idea, but the failure to understand the necessity for perseverance has caused the ruin of some of the most promising properties that have ever been advertised into great success. An instructive example is that of a Philadelphia concern whose founder made millions out of the exploitation of an excellent laundry soap. For ten years his advertisements were the talk of the country.

At the outset of his career he called on the publisher of one of the great daily New York newspapers one day and asked the rate for a whole page. The price given him was satisfactory and then he said:

"Suppose I split my advertisement up and make two half-

pages of it in different parts of the paper, would the price still be the same?"

The publisher told him it would.

"Well, then, suppose I split it up into quarter pages?"

"As long as you use the space of a page in one issue the price will be the same."

Before the soap-maker had finished he had an agreement from the unsuspecting publisher under the terms of which he was permitted to use the space of a page split up into inch advertisements to be scattered throughout the paper. Next morning the New York public was startled by the injunction: "Don't be a Clam," which appeared in big letters in 140 places throughout the paper. This was followed up in a few days with: "Don't be a Clam; a Clam Never Moves." Then: "A Clam is Not Progressive; a Clam Never Uses So-and-So's Soap; Don't be a Clam."

This man spent enormous sums in advertising along this line. Nothing like it had ever been seen in the country. It was freely prophesied that no concern could stand the strain of such an expenditure; but a business was built up that was among the largest of its kind in America. Unfortunately this policy was not continued. The company concluded that printers' ink was no longer necessary to them—that the soap had been so enormously advertised that it would carry itself for the future. The sales began to drop off so slowly that they did not realize their mistake for a long while. Then they made a valiant effort to regain the lost ground. But the mischief had been done, and done irreparably. Even the most extravagant use of the art of publicity failed to bring back the lost sales.

Robert Bonner's Idea of a Small "Ad"

IT MAY be argued that what would apply to such an article as soap would not apply to a more important and serious institution. But that this is not true may be readily shown by any number of instances. One of the most instructive is that furnished by the career of Robert Bonner, in his day prob-

"HOW MUCH SPACE DO YOU WANT, MR. BONNER?"

ably the most famous publisher in America. Mr. Bonner built up a paper that was known and read everywhere. It made him a millionaire many times over. His success was founded primarily on his bold advertising, and never before

nor since has there been such a lavish outlay of money by any publisher. On one occasion he called on James Gordon Bennett, the elder, saying that he wanted to contract for a big advertisement the following day in the New York Herald.

"How much space do you want, Mr. Bonner?"

"As much as you'll sell."

"Oh, I guess not," replied Mr. Bennett with a smile. "We've got lots of space, you know, for our advertisers."

"That's good," replied the other cheerfully. "Here's copy for one page, and here's copy for another, and here's copy for a third, and here's——"

"Hold on, there, hold on," cried the astonished publisher of the Herald. "Bless my heart, man, we can't give you the whole paper."

"Why," declared Bonner with an injured air, "you told me I could have all I wanted."

"Well, in Heaven's name, how much do you want?"

"Why, I figured on about six pages."

"I'm sorry, but there is a limit, you know, beyond which we can't go and get our paper out; and three pages about marks this limit."

"I'm sorry to hear that. Still if you can't, you can't, and I'll have to be satisfied with a little advertising. But I must say I'm very much disappointed."

A few days after this "little advertising" appeared Mr. Bonner received a call from Henry Ward Beecher, who was then writing for him the novel Norwood, which was appearing in serial form.

"I've come," said Mr. Beecher, "to remonstrate with you against the dreadful way in which you are throwing away your money."

"I? How?"

"Why, through your foolish extravagance in advertising. A dozen men of prominence, friends of yours and friends of mine, have come to me within the last few days, asking me to see you and stop you in your course. Your recklessness is the talk of the town. Everybody is prophesying that you'll be a bankrupt unless you stop."

"Good, good," chuckled Bonner. "That's the very thing. Don't you see that my advertising is a distinct success if it has the effect of making the whole town talk about me? The result will be that the whole town will buy my paper."

And it did. Mr. Beecher went away only half convinced. But it wasn't long before he admitted the wisdom of Mr.

"YOUR RECKLESSNESS IS THE TALK OF THE TOWN"

Bonner's course, convinced by circulation figures that were stupendous for those days. Mr. Bonner retired some years before his death to devote himself to the enjoyment of the large fortune he had accumulated. His successors believed themselves in possession of a property that need no longer be advertised. They felt that, as it was known almost as well as New York itself, it would be "folly to waste money." Something like six or seven years ago the circulation of this great property had dwindled to such an extent that it was no longer deemed wise to continue it as a weekly publication. There were several bursts of tardy advertising, but they failed utterly to revivify this property that had made its founder one of the richest men in America.

The publishers learned by costly experience what is to-day impressed on all advertisers by experts—that you must "keep everlastingly at it" to win and hold success with printers' ink, and that it is a practical impossibility to revivify any property that has been once advertised into great success and then allowed to die down for want of persistent effort.

Chances *for* Young Men
1. *In the* Hawaiian Islands
By Frank G. Carpenter

HONOLULU HARBOR

THE Hawaiian Islands are of their own kind. They are not like the Philippines, Puerto Rico, or any other colonial or territorial part of the United States. Their social, financial and material conditions are peculiar to themselves, and they can be appreciated only by one upon the ground.

They are among the richest islands of the globe and have already more rich men to the number of their Anglo-Saxon population than any part of the United States; but they are not a Klondike where gold can be picked up in the streams and the gullies. They have the most fertile of soils, but the supply of land is limited, and that still belonging to the Government is subject to many restrictions. They have a business which last year showed exports amounting to more than $15,000,000—almost double the value of the imports—but the business is of its own kind, so that the investor should study its character before he attempts to venture to compete with the capitalists who now have it well in hand. With all this, there are opportunities here well worth consideration, opportunities in which a limited number of our young men may realize the El Dorado of their hopes.

A BIRD'S-EYE GLANCE AT THE WHOLE HAWAIIAN GROUP

First, let us take a look at the country. It is not a large one. All told, the islands have not as much land as the State of Massachusetts, although the larger and only inhabited ones are scattered over the ocean for a distance as wide as that between Boston and Washington. The whole group, east and west, is wider than from New York to the Mississippi River, but the most of the western islands are barren rocks, some of which are mere dots on the surface of the Pacific. Some have not been prospected and others are said to contain valuable guano and phosphate deposits. Upon one, for instance, millions of sea birds roost every night, laying so many eggs that the Japanese laborers who are kept there gather them in wheel-barrows and carts, just as our farmers load potatoes and apples.

The Hawaiian Islands that we know, however, consist of the eight larger islands at the eastern end of the group. These are situated just about as far from San Francisco as Chicago is east of that city, and farther away from any Australian or Asiatic port than the distance from New York to London. The inhabited islands are not close to one another, some of them being a hundred miles and more away from Honolulu, with tempestuous seas between and only weekly passenger service of small steamers.

The inhabited islands range in size from Hawaii, which is almost as large as the State of Connecticut, to Kahoolawe, which is only about half as large as the District of Columbia. Oahu, the island on which Honolulu is situated, contains 600 square miles, while Kauai, the Garden Island of the group, has only 500 square miles, being 22 miles wide and 25 miles long.

The general character of all the islands is the same: they are wildly rugged, each being made up of one or more mountains, seamed with valleys and gorges, some of which are more than a thousand feet deep. Between the mountains lie rolling plains, and in many places at their feet there is a narrow plain sloping out to the sea. The plains, valleys and lower parts of the mountain sides contain the only lands suited to cultivation. They are covered with decomposed lava, often to the depth of twenty or thirty feet, furnishing a soil which produces rich crops of sugar, coffee, and all sorts of vegetables and tropical fruits. Some parts of the islands, on the other hand, are rocky and barren; still other portions are extremely ragged, being composed of extinct craters, while some are so high that upon them nothing can grow. In coming from San Francisco to Honolulu you are struck with the barren look of the islands. That part of Oahu which you first see is as bare as the Death Valley of California. It is composed of ragged craters long since burnt out, the sides of which are seamed and gullied by the lava flows of days gone by.

THE METROPOLITAN ADVANTAGES OF HONOLULU

As you go farther on you see other hills covered with a fuzz of emerald green and, rounding Diamond Head, come to low mountains covered with green. Palm trees with quivering branches wave you a welcome, and the houses of Honolulu look out at you through a forest of palms and other tropical trees as you come to anchor. Farther down the coast with your glass you can see the pale green of rich sugar plantations, and as you land and walk through the wide streets you find yourself in a very botanical garden of tropical plants and trees and beautiful flowers.

You may have expected to find a new country and may look for the ragged features of a frontier town in the city of Honolulu. If so, you will be disappointed. Honolulu has only 30,000 people, but in wealth and business it compares favorably with any town of five times the population in the United States. Its residences in many cases have large grounds about them, with lawns as velvety as those of England, beautiful trees and well-cared-for walks and drives. The town, in fact, has many rich men, and it is one of long-established businesses and families. It was in existence before San Francisco had a place upon the map.

The Honolulu of to-day has all the aspects of a modern American city. The signs over the best stores are in English and their proprietors have English names. The stores are of all kinds, with large stocks of goods and fine plate-glass show windows. Telephone wires run through all the streets, and you learn that more than a thousand telephones are in use. The streets and houses are lighted at night by electricity, and there is a system of waterworks and other modern improvements. The city has excellent public schools. Attendance is so vigorously compelled in city limits and throughout the islands that it is said it would almost require a search warrant to find a native Hawaiian or a white who cannot read and write. There are colleges of various kinds, numerous churches, a theatre which will seat more than a thousand people, a Young Men's Christian Association which has a well-equipped gymnasium and school, twenty miles of macadamized streets, an excellent public bicycle track, a half dozen or more large banks, three of which are savings banks, a stock exchange, a safe deposit company, and, in fact, every kind of modern business institution.

PASSAGE MONEY AND LIVING RATES FOR THE ISLANDS

At present everything that goes from and comes to the islands must pass through Honolulu, and it will always be one of the chief cities, if not the chief city, of the region. The only place that can ever hope to compete with it is the town of Hilo on the Island of Hawaii, but this has now a population of only 5000 and will need some millions of dollars expended on its harbor before it can be a landing place for the larger steamers. Honolulu will always be the seat of government and probably always the business and financial centre of the islands. It has, however, but a small harbor, which is taxed to its utmost with the shipping which calls here on its way to and from Australia, China and Japan, and the United States.

CUTTING THE SUGAR CANE

The young man who comes to the Sandwich Islands will first land at Honolulu. His passage from San Francisco to that point will cost him seventy-five dollars first cabin, or twenty-five dollars steerage, but the latter quarters on the ships are chiefly taken up with Chinese passengers and the accommodations are not at all comfortable. He will probably stop at Honolulu until he can look about him and get some idea of the chances. He will find that he is in a high-priced town and that his board will cost him as much, or more, than it did at home. If he goes to a hotel he will pay from two to five dollars the day, or if he rents a room he will be charged from six to twenty dollars the month, and his meals will cost him from four to six dollars the week. If he has a family and attempts to keep house his rent will be high, and he will find provisions more expensive than in the United States. His butter will cost him from forty to fifty cents the pound; eggs from thirty to fifty cents the dozen; flour two dollars and a half the hundred; beef about fifteen cents the pound, and other things in proportion. Even fruits and vegetables will be about one-third higher than at home, and the general extravagance of the people about him will be such that he will be tempted to spend more freely than at home. The average living expenses are, it is estimated, about one-third higher in Honolulu than they are in the United States.

If the young man is without capital he will have to rely on the labor market for his chances of a start; if he has a little money he may perhaps be able to engage in coöperative sugar planting; or if he has five thousand dollars or more there are opportunities for him to buy or lease Government lands and engage in raising coffee. The chief industry of the islands is sugar, but this, as I shall show further on, is one requiring large capital and expensive machinery. The best of the Americans here do not advise men to come to the islands unless they have at least five or ten thousand dollars, but others tell me there are opportunities for young men who are willing to work in almost every line.

WHAT YOU CAN EARN WITH YOUR HANDS, AND HOW

Let us first look at the labor market. It seems to me to be fairly well supplied. The sugar plantations are operated with Chinese and Japanese labor, there being 21,000 Asiatics on the sugar estates alone. In other branches of common labor there are from 20,000 to 30,000 more Chinese and Japanese and about 15,000 Portuguese, making a total of more than 60,000 of these classes of laborers in a population which is, all told, not more than 110,000. Taking out the natives, who in round numbers are about 40,000, there are 10,000 left, of whom perhaps 4000 are Americans. In Honolulu itself there are, I am told, not more than 4000 whites.

The young man from the States will come hoping to get a job in Honolulu or on one of the plantations as overseer or bookkeeper or engineer; he can hardly hope to take the places of the Chinese or Japanese. The demand for overseers is of course limited, and the man should not expect to get a position much more readily than he would at home. He will find, however, that wages are higher, both in Honolulu and in the country, than in the United States. The following are the sums paid for the different classes of work named: overseers and foremen on the plantations receive from $100 to $250 the month; sugar boilers and engineers from $100 to $175 the month; locomotive engineers from $40 to $75 the month, and plantation carpenters and blacksmiths from $50 to $100 the month. All of the higher-priced men on the plantations, including the above, have their houses and firewood furnished. White teamsters get from $30 to $40 the month, and the Chinese and Japanese common laborers about $15 the month.

In Honolulu mechanics are now in demand. There is considerable building going on and masons and carpenters are needed. The wages of carpenters and painters are from three to five dollars for the day's work of nine hours. Bricklayers receive five dollars and machinists from three to five dollars the day. There are at present about 2000 mechanics on the islands, of whom about 500 are Chinese and Japanese. There are about 300 American mechanics and perhaps 250 Portuguese. The drivers of the carts and wagons are principally natives, and the handling of freight at the wharves is done by the same class. I am told that they are preferred to the whites by the shippers. Outside of skilled mechanics, I should not advise any of our young men who have nothing but their muscle as capital to come to Honolulu.

HOW MUCH YOU CAN EARN WITH YOUR HEAD

As to clerks and bookkeepers the situation is much similar. There are frequent opportunities to get positions, but not more so than in the United States. There are already here about 1400 clerks and salesmen who get wages of from $50 to $125 the month and upward. Some are employed in the stores, on the plantations, and others in the smaller towns, but the most are here in Honolulu. Every large establishment must have a variety of clerks large enough to cover all the languages in general use in the islands—that is, Chinese, Japanese, Portuguese, Hawaiian and English. If a clerk can speak German and English, or both English and Portuguese, he is considered the more valuable on that account. There are some large German firms in Honolulu who will not employ a clerk who cannot speak and write German.

In the line of commercial traveling there is little done in the Hawaiian Islands, and the commercial man from the United States, who expects to visit the islands to work up trade, upon landing at Honolulu will be asked to pay $500 for the privilege of selling goods or taking orders on the Island of Oahu. He will have to pay $250 for the same privilege on the larger of the other islands, and, if he should make this his residence and engage in business, he will find that the city charges from fifty dollars the year upward for a license. In all small businesses he will have the competition of the Chinese and Japanese who now have the petty

Editor's Note—This is the first of a series of articles on Chances for Young Men in the far East. Each article is complete in itself.

retail trade of the islands, running the restaurants, the fruit stands and small grocery stores. They are good traders and are satisfied with small profits.

The professions are also fairly well supplied, there being about ninety doctors and one hundred and one lawyers. Under the Republic there were four circuit courts, a supreme court and about thirty district courts, but these may be changed under the new government inaugurated by the United States. Among the doctors are four American women and twenty-seven Japanese and Chinese practitioners. The Board of Health employs thirty physicians in the hospitals and dispensaries throughout the country, but these positions are filled. Doctors and dentists must take out a license, which is granted only upon the applicant showing a diploma from some reputable college or upon passing an examination. The children of rich or well-to-do Honolulu residents are graduating from the American colleges and universities every year and coming back here to practice in their chosen professions. They, of course, have the advantage over the newcomers in their local acquaintance and business connections.

THE OPENINGS IN THE GREAT SUGAR BUSINESS

The best chances and, in fact, almost the only chances for fortune-making in the Hawaiian Islands are from agriculture. The islands have neither mines nor manufactures, but they have a soil which will raise more sugar to the acre than any other land upon earth. On some plantations as many as ten tons of sugar to the acre are annually raised, a product from five to eight times as great as the average product of the sugar plantations of Louisiana.

The most of the money now made in the islands is from sugar. There are sixty large plantations, comprising altogether about 80,000 acres and yielding a product which annually sells for more than $15,000,000. These plantations are managed after the most modern methods. They are chiefly owned by corporations, the capital stocks of which range from half a million to four millions of dollars. The stock in the various companies is regularly bought and sold in the Honolulu stock exchange and nearly all of the companies pay big dividends. There is, all told, about $30,000,000 invested in the industry, of which about $22,500,000 belongs to Americans. The chief officers and overseers of the plantations are Americans, but the laborers are chiefly Chinese and Japanese who have been brought here under contract for this work. At present one-fourth of the whole population and fully one-half of the Asiatic population are employed on the sugar estates.

The chief opportunities for young men in connection with sugar raising are in what is here called coöperative farming—that is, in buying or leasing a small tract of land from one of the large companies and raising cane to be sold at the great factories. This is comparatively a new plan and quite a number of men are doing it at a profit. There is little opportunity to buy wild land which will raise sugar, and there are practically no sugar lands left in the hands of the Government. The profits from such land are so large that the best of it was bought or taken up on long leases from the Government years ago.

A BRIGHT FUTURE FOR MARKET GARDENERS

Outside of sugar there are many opportunities for the young man to succeed here in the different kinds of intensive farming which can be profitably undertaken on the islands. There is so little land, that the opportunities for doing things on the bonanza scale have long since gone by. In the raising of fruits and vegetables, in producing grain and meat for home consumption and in coffee plantations there would seem to be many openings. The soil here will produce almost any kind of tropical fruit. It will produce the choicest of pineapples and bananas and every kind of vegetable, including potatoes. Nevertheless, fruits are exceedingly high in the Honolulu markets and most of the potatoes used come from California. The same can be said of the wheat, notwithstanding the fact that during the first days of the gold excitement in California the bulk of the wheat and potatoes used there was raised in the Hawaiian Islands.

This is a land of oranges, but the fruit sells in Honolulu at twenty-five cents the dozen; strawberries can be easily grown, but they bring twenty-five cents the pound; grapes thrive, but if you buy them at the fruit stands you pay fifteen cents the pound for them, and it is so with similar fruits. As to bananas and pineapples, it is claimed the islands could produce enough of them to supply all the markets east of the Mississippi River. The taking off the tariff and the reduction of freight rates, which will probably follow the annexation to the United States, will make this country the tropical fruit garden of our Western States.

So far there has been so much money in sugar raising that everything else has had to give way to it, the planters lazily preferring to buy their supplies from the outside, just as the cotton planters of the Southern States did when they received such high prices for that crop. Now that the sugar lands are all taken up, other possible crops are receiving consideration.

PHOTO BY THE DAVEY PHOTO CO., H. I.

PACKING PINEAPPLES AT PEARL CITY, OAHU

THE BEST CHANCE FOR THE SMALL CAPITALIST

The chief of the new industries is the raising of coffee, and this is perhaps the best opening for the young man of small means. The coffee lands lie high up above the sugar plantations, which are chiefly found close to the sea. The coffee tree will bear as high up as half a mile above sea level, or as low as five hundred feet above that point. Coffee raising is comparatively a new industry, bringing a new class of land into use; hundreds of small capitalists have gone into it within the past few years.

The Hawaiian coffee is far superior to that raised in Brazil. It ranks with the best Mocha and Java in the markets of the Pacific slope, selling at retail there for thirty-five and forty cents the pound. It brings from fifteen to eighteen cents the pound at wholesale in the markets of San Francisco, where Rio sells for six or seven cents. At these rates the planters of Hawaii can figure on a clear profit of about ten cents the pound, and as a good plantation in bearing will annually produce about 1500 pounds to the acre, the profits are very large. One plantation on the Island of Hawaii produced last year 3400 pounds to the acre, or a net profit of $340 the acre, so that it will be seen that even a small coffee plantation might bring in a considerable income.

To raise coffee, however, requires some capital, and no young man should come to the islands for that purpose unless he has a capital of from three to five thousand dollars. The latter amount is considered by some low and by others ample for a start. For this sum he could take up a hundred acres of Government land on the Island of Hawaii, about the only island on which there is any land left. He would secure it on what is known as the purchase-lease system, agreeing to pay for it at its appraised value, say at from seven to ten dollars the acre, at any time within twenty-one years, provided he pay the Government eight per cent. interest on the value of the appraisement until the purchase money be paid. He would also agree to make certain improvements, and to live on the land, the understanding being that he could complete the purchase at any time after two years.

PHOTO BY THE DAVEY PHOTO CO., H. I.

UNHULLED COFFEE BERRIES

THE PROCESS OF BUILDING UP A PLANTATION

The coffee raiser first clears the land of forest and jungle. This will cost him perhaps thirty dollars the acre; but he can clear a little at a time, putting in, say, ten acres more every year, until at last he has the whole clear and in coffee. He buys his coffee trees of a nursery for two or three cents apiece and sets them out. They are cultivated from year to year, and at the third year begin to produce. They should be in full bearing the fifth year, at which time they will have cost him from $150 to $200 the acre. From that time on for twenty years or more they should annually pay him $100 the acre—a generous profit on his investment.

The process of building up such a plantation can be graduated by the amount of capital in the hands of the farmer, the larger plantations requiring, of course, more money and labor. A hundred-acre plantation with fifty acres only in coffee should produce an income of $6000 a year after the fifth year. This is, estimating the yield to be one pound to the tree, at a profit of ten cents the pound. Not counting the labor of the planter, the net cost of making and stocking such a plantation would be $12,000. The man with $5000 would start with less cultivated land, do his own work at least as far as management is concerned, and perhaps add to his income by raising bananas and vegetables.

The young man in this case will probably realize considerable off of the rise in the value of his land. There is but little good Government land left. The amount, all told, is less than two million acres. Of this, much is sterile, a great part inaccessible, and other parts are covered with lava. There are perhaps 500,000 acres that are of some value, and half of this amount is excellent land. The best coffee lands are on the Island of Hawaii, and about 60,000 acres of this character will be opened to settlement by the Kohala and Hilo Railway, which is now being surveyed.

THE CONDITIONS ON WHICH LAND CAN BE HELD

The Government is anxious that this land should be taken up by small planters, and, according to law, land can only be sold or leased in lots not to exceed one hundred acres, and only to persons who will agree to keep one-fourth of the land in cultivation for a period of years, and who will agree to live upon it. To such persons the land is sold at a low appraisement, often at one-fourth and less than the value of private lands in the same vicinity and of the same character. If all the good Government land as above estimated, 250,000 acres, were so divided, it would only accommodate 2500 families, so it will be seen that the supply is limited and the value of such lands must eventually increase.

At present the islands are divided up into great baronial estates owned or leased by rich men or corporations. Oahu has no public land available to settlers; Kauai, the Garden Island, is practically controlled by six corporations, and the Bishop Estate owns 600,000 acres outright. The Parkers control 700,000 acres on the Island of Hawaii, including 250,000 acres under irrigation, and the small island of Niihau has 25,000 sheep all owned by one family. The chances of the young investor are almost exclusively limited to the Government lands, and these are comparatively so few that they will, in a short time, be exhausted.

How They Treat Cub Reporters in Ohio

HARRY D. JONES, a well-known New York editor, tells a story illustrating the trials of one cub reporter:

"It was in Cleveland, Ohio, some years ago, when I was engaged in daily newspaper work in that city. A young man had just joined the reportorial staff of a rival paper. He came from an out-of-the-way town, and had never before lived in a large city. He was elated over this position, and assumed so much dignity and even haughtiness that the other reporters determined to teach him a lesson. He had been sent to the lake front to get an exclusive story concerning the ship-building industry, and he announced that fact to several other reporters, one of whom looked at him in mock amazement and remarked solemnly:

"'By Jove, old man, that's work they give to the oldest reporters on the staff! You see, these millionaire ship-builders won't talk to the ordinary reporter. If you have influence you can get a great beat from Keelson's yard. Everybody has been trying to get in there for two weeks.'

"The new reporter said that he had all the influence he needed and went post-haste to the yard. Here he was received by the second conspirator, who had taken on the guise of a member of the firm, and filled up with a technical story in which keels and main trucks, rudder posts and cutwaters, rolling chocks and deadeyes, were hopelessly and absurdly mingled. He closed the interview by presenting the reporter with a photograph of what he called the newest idea in naval architecture, but which was, in fact, a snap-shot picture of a factory taken at an unusual angle, with the factory chimney seeming to spring from the deck of a small boat lying in front of the building.

"The next day this remarkable picture appeared in print. Early in the afternoon the reporter was called up on the telephone by the third conspirator, who said angrily:

"'I am the agent of the ship-building company whose boat you libeled to-day, and you have described it so incorrectly that I shall sue you for damages unless you print a retraction and make the proper corrections. The chimney as you have printed it looks as if it were on my boat. It does not belong to my boat at all, but is part of a factory near by.'

"And this statement appeared in the paper the next morning just as it had been sent over the telephone. That same afternoon the new reporter started on one of the longest vacations on record in Ohio journalism. It is not ended yet."

The Gospel of Saving

By Russell Sage

THRIFT is so essential to happiness in this world that the failure to practice it is, to me, incomprehensible. It is such an easy, simple thing, and it means so much. It is the foundation of success in business, of contentment in the home, of standing in society. It stimulates industry. I never yet heard of a thrifty man who was lazy. It begets independence and self-confidence. It makes a man of the individual who practices it.

I think the greatest fault that characterizes our education of the young to-day is the failure to teach thrift in the schools. From the very outset a child ought to understand the value of saving. In some schools, I understand, penny savings funds are now established. Out of these funds, if they are administered with practical common-sense, will grow more sound teaching than out of anything else in the curriculum. I mean teaching that will make for success; and that, after all, is what the mother hopes for for her child and a nation for its citizens.

Failure in the world is impossible if a young man will start out right. If society will take hold of the matter in the proper spirit, every young man will start out right. Of course, even under the most favorable conditions there will be exceptions to this rule. But there are exceptions to every rule. Of them we can take no account. But the great body of young men would go right if they were taught the road at the outset. You may not be able to make good morals by legislation, but you can make a successful man by proper teaching and example.

As matters stand now, all that the average child ever hears in school of the value of saving is contained in some dry textbook or essay. There is nothing living, vital or forcible in such material as this. It is of very much greater importance that a child or young man should know how to proceed on the road to success in the world than it is that he should know the road to Cape Town or London, or that he should know the involved principles of the higher sciences.

Resolve that You Will Not be Hard Up

This is a tremendously practical world, and that man is going to get the most out of it who is not hampered by a constant want of money. It is absurd to suppose that great riches always bring happiness, or even that the accumulation of great riches is essential to success. The man of moderate means is, on the whole, perhaps happier than the extremely rich man, and he who makes for himself a safe place in any field can be set down as being quite as successful as the man who accumulates millions. But the man who is perpetually hard up cannot under any circumstances be happy, no matter what the foolish in the world may say, and no man can win a safe place in the world if he is hampered with debts. Helpless poverty is the most crushing affliction that can come to a family, and is the affliction most easily avoided. The man who starts out right will never be poor in the extreme sense, no matter how limited his income, or how circumscribed his opportunities.

Let him lay down the rule for himself that he will invariably spend less than he makes; then he is safe. No man can be happy in this life for any length of time if he does not live up to this principle, no matter how dazzlingly he starts out, or what his prospects are. If he deviates from this rule he will sooner or later come to grief. He must save to succeed. He must succeed in something to be happy. That man surely faces acute misery who at thirty is not better off than he was at twenty. It is a simple process, and for its non-observance there can be no possible excuse. Let the boy or man live so economically that he always has something to lay by, and he is certain to have, in the end, a competence to protect him against all ordinary worries. Of course, there may come unavoidable accidents; but even these will be more easily combated if, as a young man, the habit of economizing has been cultivated. I wonder constantly, when I meet examples of misery caused by unthriftiness, how such things can be with a human being whose brain is normal.

Much of the fault lies in the strenuous and unnatural life that we find in cities. Country people rarely suffer such extreme poverty as we find in the great centres of population. The farmer's boy is instinctively saving and careful. He sees all about him examples of husbandry. The bees, the ants and the squirrels all provide carefully for a rainy day. Man alone violates this natural instinct, and he violates it more generally in the luxurious life of the city than in the plainer and simpler life of the country.

Avoid the Barbarism of Luxury

A man should at no time spend more than is necessary for decent living. Extreme luxury and lavishness are signs, not of cultivation, but of barbarism. Their existence sets a very vicious example. It is because they see on all hands such an extreme waste of money that the youth who grow up in cities go into the world with perverted ideas. They want to dress beyond their means, eat beyond their means and live in houses that are beyond their means.

"Out of every dollar earned save twenty-five cents"

COPYRIGHT BY VANDER WEYDE

RUSSELL SAGE

No matter how fast a man may make money, he owes it to society as well as to himself to be economical. He should always make all the money he can in an honest, legitimate way, and save all he can. He should try to live not for himself alone, but for others. He should manage to give away something to charity. If his income is so limited that he can afford only ten cents a week for charity, let him give that ten cents. Besides doing good to others, he will stimulate himself and help his own character.

Nothing is more harmful and nothing is sillier than the endeavor to emulate others in the spending of money or in extravagant living. The young man working at a desk wants the most stylish cut of clothing and the most expensive pleasures, simply because his neighbor indulges in these extravagant fancies. He is not strong-willed enough to resist, and of course that leads to inevitable ruin.

I am no prophet, but I venture to assert that any young man who will live up to the following set of rules will get more genuine happiness out of life than his neighbor who violates them. I will also prophesy that he will inevitably win success. Not, necessarily, such success as will lift him above the seventy-five million people in this country, but moderate, comfortable success.

Follow These Rules of Life for Success

Out of every dollar earned save twenty-five cents. Save seventy-five cents if you can, but never less than twenty-five.

Get up at a regular hour every morning, and work until the things that are before you are finished. Don't drop what you have in hand because it is five o'clock.

Be honest; always have the courage to tell the truth.

Don't depend on others. Even if you have a rich father, strike out for yourself.

Cultivate independence at the very outset.

Learn the value of money. Realize that it stands, when honestly made, as the monument to your value as a citizen.

Be jealous of your civic rights. Take a wholesome interest in public affairs, but do not let politics, or anything else, interfere with the rigid administration of your private duties. The State is made up of individuals.

Be clean and decent. Don't do anything that you would be ashamed to discuss with your mother.

Don't gamble.

Be circumspect in your amusements.

In connection with amusements, I have never been able to understand why the young men of to-day deem the theatre an absolute essential in seeking diversion. After all is said and done, the theatre, even at its best, is neither so elevating, nor so instructive, nor so satisfactory as a great many other avenues of pleasure. An evening with a good book is, or ought to be, more satisfying to the young man of brains than an evening in a hall where a lot of make-believe characters are strutting up and down the stage, like children at a masquerade. When the human race reaches its highest mental development there will probably be no theatres. The people will then require neither stage settings nor actors to interpret the writings of their poets, scholars and storytellers. But that time is probably still far away. Meanwhile, it behooves the young man to get all the satisfaction that he can out of books rather than out of theatres. It is less costly, and from any standpoint more desirable.

Every young man who wishes to succeed should study carefully the human race. There is even more instruction in the people who are about us than in the books that lie on shelves. All we want is the faculty to read the people as we read the books. And this faculty may, with patience and perseverance, be cultivated with reasonable certainty.

Few things so well equip a man for competition with his fellows as a thorough knowledge of human nature. It will teach him that men are not bad, but weak. He need but avoid their weaknesses to avoid their failures. Not that a negative character is desirable. But as matters stand, even such a character is almost sufficient to insure a reasonable degree of success. But to make this success certain a positive character is necessary. The young man must not only avoid the vice and weakness of his neighbors, but he must practice the virtues that they do not possess or do not give evidence of possessing.

Join a Church and Help to Support It

At the very outset a young man ought to join a church. He ought to bear the burden of the church support to the full extent of his ability. What this ability is he must judge for himself. As in charity, he should give a dime if he can give no more; and this dime, if it represents the full measure of what he can spare, is just as important as the dollar or the thousand dollars of the rich man. Communion with the church helps tremendously in building up a solid character. There will be met clean, wholesome men and women. Acquaintances will be formed that are helpful in every way. It is natural that the people of a church should take more interest in the success of one of their young communicants than they do in the success of an outsider. That is human nature, and human nature prevails in a church just as much as it does outside. The only difference is, that the church human nature is cleaner. But unless a young man joins a church through conviction it is far better for him to remain away. If the utilitarian advantages are uppermost in his mind, if he has no true religion, church communion, instead of helping, will harm him. He may find success more easily, but not happiness. The man who joins a church simply because he can make something out of the connection is a hypocrite of the meanest stripe, and a hypocrite is not only a very unhappy man, but he must also be the most contemptible being in the sight of the Lord. I can conceive of no more miserable existence than that which is led by a pretender. And the more carefully a boy realizes the hollowness of shams, religious and otherwise, the more placidly he will sleep of nights. The man who joins a church because it offers an easy short-cut to a competence will probably find some pretty unpleasant experiences in his way. There are sincere young men who may be deterred from joining a church from this very reason. They have not a sufficient religious conviction, or perhaps no religion at all. In such cases (always providing that he is honest and sincere) it will nevertheless benefit a young man to attend a church. With most of us religion has come as a matter of education. It is never too late to begin this education, and, as a purely ethical problem, it is a fine thing for a thinking young man to spend part of his Sunday in a place where he can hear good, instructive discourse on religious topics.

Always Keep in Training for Hard Work

A certain portion of every young man's time ought to be given up to outdoor exercise. Most of the men who win riches and distinction in the great cities come from the country. They are farmers' boys as a general thing. The free outdoor life they have led equips them with a physique that defies hard work and long hours. Boys raised in the cities have no such advantages. Consequently they cannot stand the physical strain that is thrown on every man who comes to the front. Of late years this fact is becoming better understood. The boys are going to gymnasiums in the evenings, where they can get a taste of active life. But even a gymnasium, to my mind, does not produce the same result that exercise in the open brings. No sickly lad can in these days hope for a place in the front ranks. The struggle is too fierce, too trying.

The boy who will win must be prepared to work eighteen or twenty hours a day, if necessary. He can do this only if he has taken such good care of his body that he is a good specimen of manhood. All the outdoor games that are coming to the front of late are excellent things, especially for city boys. I don't believe the advantage in the next generation will be with the farmer's boy so much as it has been in the past generation. Thanks to the better understanding of physical culture, the city boy now has excellent opportunities for getting all the healthy sort of exercise that he needs. And he has, in addition, the advantage of being in close touch with his fellow-beings. He has also numberless opportunities for cultivating and improving his mind. This ought to give, and no doubt will give, the city boy a big start in the new century. In a measure, of course, this start is offset by the fact that the farmer's boy of to-day has advantages for securing education that were denied to his father. Every little settlement now aspires to its college or high school, and the courses are so arranged that a farmer's boy may still do a good day's work and yet find time for acquiring an education. When all other means fail, we have the correspondence schools, which, when honestly conducted, as most of them presumably are, are a boon to the ambitious boy who lives hundreds of miles away from the nearest institutions where he could hope for higher education.

Chances for Young Men - IV - In China

IRON WORKS AT HANKOW

By Frank G. Carpenter

WHAT are the chances for young Americans in China? I have asked this question at the chief treaty ports and have discussed it with both foreigners and Chinese in different parts of the Empire. I find that there are already opportunities for the right men in a limited number of places and that these opportunities are steadily increasing. If China is to be opened up as the great Powers have decided, the field for money-making will be one of the best in the world, and the demand for intelligent young foreigners trained along Western lines will be very great.

In order to understand the possibilities it is necessary to look at the curious position which China now holds among the countries and nations of the world. It is a country undeveloped and unprospected so far as the possibilities of modern times are concerned. It is a slice out of the human muscle-working, ignorant, superstitious, industrial past, dropped down without change into the practical, scientific, steam and steel age of the industrial present. It is a country larger in area than the United States, including its outlying islands, and one which has five people to our one. Its people are as human as we are, and, as their country develops and wages rise, their wants will increase and the trade between them and the rest of the world will be enormous.

They will want all sorts of modern improvements. They are not savages, and they can appreciate a good thing if it is forced upon them. They have now about four thousand walled cities and countless villages. They have, at vast expense, constructed a system of canals which is unsurpassed in the world; they have redeemed thousands of acres by dikes and stone walls, and when they realize the benefits to be had from railroads and factories they will be quick to build them. To do so they will need foreigners, and our young men will have their chance with those of Europe in the work.

At present China has not one mile of railroad track to each million of its inhabitants. It has, all told, just about 350 miles, although several thousand miles have been projected. The building of the new roads goes on very slowly. There are now only four places where work is being done, and, so far as I can learn, these are fully equipped with foreign employees. Two of the constructing parties are Chinese. They are working on the trunk line which is being built from Hankow to Peking through the central and northern parts of the Empire. The third plant is a line from Kiachow Bay, the new German concession, to coal mines in the province just back of it, and the fourth is the Russian road which is being constructed from Port Arthur north through Manchuria to connect with the trans-Siberian road. These roads are respectively managed by the Germans and the Russians, the foreigners connected with them coming from the home countries.

The railroads now in operation in China are worked by Chinese, with a few foreign engineers and foreign advisers. They consist of the northern railway system embracing the roads from Tien-Tsin to the Yellow Sea, to the Kaiping coal mines and the great wall at Shanhaikwan, the line from Tien-Tsin to Peking, the little extension toward Hankow, and the little line of about fourteen miles which connects Shanghai with Woosung on the Yang-tse-Kiang.

What Railways Can Do for China

These railroads do not begin to tap the population of China. They are but a drop in the sea in comparison with what the country should have. They are chiefly military lines, and do not reach the most populous sections nor touch those where manufacturing and trade are the greatest. The transportation of goods in China is done almost altogether upon boats, carts or wheelbarrows. There are cities of from one hundred thousand to a million, lying within fifty miles or less of one another, which are connected only by canals and wheelbarrow tracks.

Some of these towns lie in the vicinity of coal fields by which electricity could be cheaply produced and made to carry both passengers and freight, and there will in the future be many openings for electrical engineers here. There are no electric railroads in the cities of China, the most of them being so closely built that it will be impossible to put roads through them. Still Peking, the capital, with more than a million of inhabitants, has wide streets and at this writing no railroad within its walls. Indeed, until within two or three years the only way to reach Peking was by boat or cart. Its port and chief trading centre, Tien-Tsin—a city of more than a million—was only eighty miles away over a plain as flat as a floor, but all the traffic between the two cities was by wheelbarrows and carts, and by boats on the Pei-ho and the Grand Canal.

Since the railroad has been built I understand its traffic has so increased that it is now paying enormously. I am told that the new roads which are being constructed begin to earn a profit almost as soon as the rails are laid. This shows that the Chinese will patronize their railways, and the moment that one of the great trade lines has been completed the traffic upon it will be so great that it will probably lead to the rapid opening of other roads. Factories will come with the railroads and the mines along the roads will be developed.

In all these undertakings men with modern educational ideas and business training will be needed. There will be opportunities for civil and mining engineers and for men of special training along all lines of modern manufacturing adapted to Chinese wants. Foreigners will be required to superintend the establishment of the plants and they will be needed to run them for some time thereafter, although the Chinese will displace them as soon as possible with their own men.

When China Shall Be Open to Our Trade

The greater part of such opportunities are, however, in the future. So far the foreigners are confined to twenty-eight treaty ports where they may live and do business. At present the total number of foreigners in China is not more than fifteen thousand, or about one foreigner to twenty-seven thousand Chinese. A large number are missionaries, so that it will be seen that the supply can by no means meet the demand when all China is thrown open to trade.

The foreigners already employed here are making money, and many have amassed fortunes. Some of them are agents of the importing and exporting firms which connect China with the markets of the world. The foreign trade of China amounts to about a quarter of a billion dollars a year, and these men handle it. The chief firms have big houses and their employees are well paid. Some of the firms have their own steamship lines, others are interested in docks and real estate, others in tea-packing houses, modern cotton factories and silk filatures. In all such establishments there are opportunities for young men of the right sort who can come with proper credentials as to their character and efficiency. Such credentials are, however, an absolute necessity.

In the Employ of Government

In the opening up of China there will be places for a number of our young men in the employ of the Chinese Government as teachers, civil engineers, mining experts and clerks. Already a number of Americans are holding good positions of this nature. The chief Chinese colleges are presided over by Americans. The Imperial Foreign University at Peking has as its President Dr. William A. M. Martin, one of the oldest and best known of our missionaries. He organized this school and has been at its head for years. The school is largely intended to fit the young nobility of China for the diplomatic service. Doctor Martin has the confidence of the Chinese Government. His salary is probably equal to about $10,000 gold a year. He has some Americans among his professors, one of whom is Dr. R. Coltman, of Pennsylvania, formerly a medical missionary, but now professor of anatomy in the Imperial College.

At Tien-Tsin there is a Chinese Imperial University presided over by an American, Professor C. D. Tenney. Mr. Tenney was once a tutor in Li Hung Chang's family, and he has been connected with our Consulate at Tien-Tsin. He is a young man of ability and culture.

At Shanghai the Chinese have lately established the Nan-Yang College. They have erected a number of excellent buildings and will soon have accommodations for six hundred students. The President of this college is Mr. John C. Ferguson, who was formerly in charge of the missionary college at Nanking. Mr. Ferguson came to China as one of the missionaries of the Methodist Episcopal Church, but he is doing more good in his present position than he possibly could in any other. He is the foreign adviser of some of the leading Chinese officials, and as such is a man of great influence. He probably receives a large salary.

Among the other Americans who have made money and reputation out of their knowledge of Chinese in connection with the Government is Mr. W. N. Pethick, who was, for years, closely associated with Li Hung Chang, and Mr. E. T. Williams, formerly interpreter of the Consulate at Shanghai and now employed at the great Kiagnan arsenal.

All of these men have gotten their positions owing to their knowledge of the Chinese language. The schools with which they are connected are intended to fit young Chinese to take places under the Government where intercourse with foreigners is necessary, as the Chinese do not like to have such places filled by foreigners. It will be long, however, before there will be sufficient English-speaking Chinese to fill this demand, and as the country is opened up there will be employment at high prices for young Americans who have learned Chinese.

The Open Sesame to Position

The knowledge of Chinese is, in fact, already the open sesame to a good position in China, and it will be more and more so as time goes on. At present there are no places here for foreign teachers who come without such knowledge. The foreign schools are already well supplied, and when new men are needed by the missionary colleges they are sent out from the home churches,

A group of Mandarin civil officers, Canton

while the Government schools import their teachers direct from America.

The man who understands Chinese and can speak it has many openings before him, and if a young man can afford to come out here and devote a couple of years to study he can get a position. He will be in demand at the American Consulates as interpreter, will have a chance at a place in the different offices of the Chinese Government or in the Imperial Maritime Customs, and also in the many foreign enterprises managed and financed by Chinese capitalists.

The need of such men as interpreters is so great that our American Minister and the Consul-General have petitioned the State Department to send out ten young men to learn Chinese, with the view of using them as interpreters in our Consulates and in the Legation at Peking. Such men will probably receive salary and expenses from the time of their leaving America, but employers should make time contracts with them, as otherwise they can easily leave the Consulates for the higher salaries sure to be offered by the Chinese Government or by Chinese business men who need such clerks to carry on their foreign correspondence and act as interpreters. There have been numerous cases of this kind in the past. Only a few months ago a young American who spoke and wrote Chinese was in the employ of one of our Consulates as interpreter at $1700 a year. He was offered $3300 by the Chinese and he is now working for them.

The opportunities for such men in the collection of the foreign customs of China are many and excellent. The Imperial Maritime Customs Service, which has to do with all imports, is entirely in the hands of foreigners, and it is supposed to be recruited, other things being equal, from the various countries in proportion to their trade with the Chinese. At present America has nothing like her share of the places, and a judicious pushing on the part of our Minister would give many young Americans such positions if they were only fitted for them.

This customs service is one of the best paid of its kind in the world. It is under the direction of an Englishman, Sir Robert Hart, who is said to receive something like $75,000 a year besides a large allowance for entertaining. There are between three and four thousand men in its employ who are paid good salaries. The indoor staff, or the men who have to do the clerical and supervisory work, get from $1000 to $10,000 gold and at the same time their quarters. There are, I am told, many men in the customs who receive annual salaries which equal in value five thousand gold dollars. In addition to their salaries these customs officials get two years' vacation, with half pay at the end of every five years, and at the end of every seven years, including the vacations, a present of one full year's pay. Their positions are practically for life and they are treated as though they were under the civil service.

No Chance for the Mechanic

In other departments of the Chinese Government there are at present but few foreign employees. The railroads have some, such as Mr. C. W. Kinder and others, who have had to do with building the lines of North China; and there is Captain M. W. Rich, the foreign scientific adviser to Sheng, the director of railroads at Shanghai. Captain Rich is one of our well-known civil engineers and railroad men. He is from Minnesota and was, I believe, the builder of the "Soo" road. He came here, I am told, on a five years' contract at a salary of $10,000 gold a year.

As to the minor positions connected with the Chinese railroads, such as mechanics, locomotive engineers, conductors and so on, these are now all filled by Chinese, and they will probably continue so. Such men can be had here at wages upon which an American would starve. In the north of China locomotive engineers receive about seventeen dollars a month, firemen about eight dollars, and first-class telegraph operators twelve dollars and a half.

There is really no chance here for the ordinary mechanic nor for any one who has nothing but muscle and the common amount of brains and education to recommend him. All of the manual labor of the empire is done by Chinese. The large modern silk and cotton factories of China now employ tens of thousands of hands, but they are Chinese men and women, boys and girls. I visited one factory at Shanghai which had 3000 workmen. Of these only one was a foreigner, and he was the expert who built the mill. The only foreigners employed in the other factories are as managers, engineers

Editor's Note—This is the fourth and last of a series of papers from the special correspondent of The Saturday Evening Post on Chances for Young Men in the far East. The first paper appeared in the issue of March 10.

and foremen, chosen for their special knowledge of some branch of the business.

The same is true of mechanics, ordinary skilled labor and petty clerkships. In the silk filatures I saw little girls working thirteen hours for less than three cents a day, and in a big cotton mill I was told that the average wages paid adults did not exceed fourteen cents. This was in Shanghai where wages are at their top notch, where carpenters, blacksmiths and cabinet-makers get thirteen cents a day; bootmakers and bricklayers ten cents, and barbers three cents.

Credentials a First Requisite

During the past year I have traveled much in the interior of China and have visited many of the inland cities. In such localities unskilled laborers are paid about three cents a day, and farm hands are lucky when they receive more than two dollars of our money a month.

Every Chinese store has a number of clerks or salesmen. These are paid on the average about four dollars a month and board. In the foreign stores of Shanghai and elsewhere, and in the minor clerical positions of the big exporting and importing establishments, half-castes and Portuguese are largely used. These men receive from twenty to forty dollars a month. They are recruited from the annual overflow of the various ports where the schools are semi-commercial colleges and give such a business training as fits their graduates for clerkships.

Notwithstanding this, there are many opportunities here for good young men with push, energy and modern education, especially if they have business ideas and business

New business block in Hongkong

China is a land of canals and fine bridges

Transportation is now by wheelbarrows

training. *They must not come, however, without letters and credentials showing who they are and what their experience has been.* They should, if possible, bring personal letters of introduction to some of the foreigners vouching for their character, ability and previous employment. The young man who can bring these and in addition enough money to enable him to stay here for a month or so and look around for a position, and who, for lack of amusement, will not drift into dissipation, has a fair chance of making a place for himself. He must come with the intention of devoting his life to the work, and not with the idea that a year or so will suffice to make him enormously rich.

As to the professions, I am told there is no chance for foreign doctors in China and that the Chinese will not employ them. This is to some extent a mistake. There are hundreds of thousands of Chinese annually treated at the missionary hospitals. I know of one missionary doctor who turns in fees to the missions to the amount of $5000 a year, and I have been told that our present Minister to Korea, Dr. H. N. Allen, did an even greater business among the Koreans while he was practicing as a medical missionary before he entered the diplomatic service. These fees all come from the rich, the poor being treated for nothing. The foreign medicine is steadily growing in favor in the far East, and I can see no reason why there should not be a profitable practice for American physicians when the country is thoroughly opened up. As to dentists, there are Americans at Shanghai and elsewhere who are doing well. They charge about ten dollars for pulling teeth, and for other work in proportion.

There are in Shanghai several American lawyers and a small number of American exporters, importers and agents. In the past the Americans have made a great deal in trading in the far East. For three-quarters of a century the chief firm in China was the great American establishment of Russell and Company. It had its great houses at every port. Its ships carried the American flag along the coast and on the rivers, and it made fortune after fortune for its owners. As the men connected with it grew rich they drew out their capital and retired. After a long while the business began to droop for lack of funds, and a few years ago it had so dwindled that the firm passed out of existence.

A Better Opening than Ever Before

There has never been a better time for a young man to go out to trade out here than just now, and the young American who can bring some money and good business connections with him can find here ample field for his energy and abilities. There are such men now in China who came out only a few years ago and are now making from eight to ten thousand dollars gold a year, and who will make much more as time goes on. They are men with a keen eye to business, who have studied the situation and who are taking advantage of their opportunities. They are men of character and commercial honesty, whose word is as good as their bond. Such attributes are a necessity here. Business is largely done on faith, and large contracts are often carried out with only verbal agreements behind them. The man who goes back on a bargain cannot last in his dealings with the Chinese. They have their guilds, or commercial and bankers' unions, and the breaking of one contract will often discredit a foreigner in all future operations.

There should be an increased sale of many kinds of American goods in China, and the young man who can persuade some of our large manufacturing or exporting houses to send him out here to introduce their goods has a chance to make a good place for himself. He can add other imports to his list from time to time and can gradually build up a business. I know of one such man who was laughed at when he asked the Shanghai merchants to handle his goods. He opened a place himself and sold $100,000 worth in six months.

At present the Germans are studying the field for new things more than are either the Americans, the French or the English. Their young men are the most enterprising, the most industrious and the most successful. They are learning the language and are gradually working their way into all parts of the empire. They study the wants of the Chinese and try to import such things as will please them. The young American who will do the same is sure to succeed.

As to the chances here for the young American speculator, the fellow with a genius for knowing a good thing when he sees it and with the nerve to take hold of it, I believe they are now good and that they will be very great in the future. This man will have his eye upon mines, lands, stocks and all kinds of investments for which he may have, or can interest those who have, the capital.

The opportunities for real estate investments at the treaty ports have made many men rich within a few years. In Shanghai property has doubled in value again and again within a very short time, and at all of the cities opened to foreigners the land of the concessions has steadily risen. It will probably continue to rise as the foreign trade of China and the opportunities for foreigners increase.

BROKERAGE AS A BUSINESS FOR YOUNG MEN

By Alfred L. Baker

Former President of the Stock Exchange, Chicago

IN NO other business is the candle of human vitality burned as rapidly as it is in the broker's office. The man who cannot stand sustained work under high pressure has no place in this calling and had better keep out of it.

For this reason the young man who contemplates becoming a stock-broker should subject himself to candid self-examination before making it his choice for a life career. It is not enough that he should feel himself fully equal to a steady grind of hard work, or even to an uncommon degree of close mental application. He may be above the average in both physical and mental ruggedness and still be unfitted for this particular, exacting and strenuous line of commercial effort.

Before he casts the die in favor of this calling let him ask himself: "Am I endowed with a disposition which will enable me to endure excitement with comparative complacency and at the same time to work at 'concert pitch'?" Both of these requirements are essential to success in brokerage. Not possessing these characteristics, a broker is liable to give out at a most important and critical time.

Still other qualifications must not be overlooked. First of these is the broker's instinct. Unless a young man feels a natural and compelling inclination to get into the swift stream of the Exchange he should stifle his ambitions to shine as a broker. This instinct differs from the taste for the slower barter and sale of industrial products as the instinct of the thoroughbred race horse differs from the plodding disposition of the draught horse. Time, it is said, is the essence of all contracts, but especially does this apply to the transactions on the Stock Exchange floor, where time means instant action.

The Value of Making Friends

SO MUCH for the qualifications demanded in the actual discharge of the brokerage business; but business must be got before it is transacted, and it therefore follows that the young man who is equipped for this calling must possess the faculty for getting trade as well as the ability to handle it. A friendly approach to the world at large—to the chance acquaintance as well as to the intimate associate—is a prime requisite in the bearing of the young broker, for it is mainly by this means that he will enlarge the list of his customers. Many a broker has lost thousands of dollars in commissions which would have been his had he not repulsed the stranger who chanced to be introduced to him on the street, in the club, at the summer resort, or wherever men of the world are wont to meet in casual intercourse.

At the outset of his career the young man who elects to follow this business and follow it successfully must make up his mind that he will be a broker only and not a trader—that is, not a speculator himself.

Ninety-nine out of every hundred who have attempted to be traders and speculators on their own account have ended in disaster. Having once determined that he will be a broker he should steel himself to look without covetousness upon the profits of his customers and not allow these to tempt him upon a path of personal speculation. A broker who plays the market is a house divided against itself which must fall.

Naturally, the first thing for the novice in the broker's office to master is a knowledge of the terms and phrases peculiar to the business. Most beginners gain this information in the routine of their daily tasks, but their progress might be materially facilitated by a little home study. The only textbook required is one of the pamphlets used by the leading brokerage offices for distribution among the customers and prospective customers, and distributed as advertising matter.

Commercial printing-houses largely patronized by brokers furnish these pamphlets in large quantities. In addition to a comprehensive definition of brokerage terms and phrases these booklets generally contain the principles governing transactions on the New York Stock Exchange, and also a description of the processes by which such transactions are effected, together with a collection of miscellaneous information of a technical character which the beginner must thoroughly understand before he can grasp the meaning and ramifications of a trade. The pamphlet of this character which happens to be at hand is issued by the Financial Publishing Company, Chicago.

A Valuable Course of Study

WHEN the beginner in the broker's office has learned the terms of the business and gained a general idea of its processes he may at once begin a course of study which is ample enough to satisfy the energies of the most ambitious and tireless student. Although there is a broad and definite foundation to be laid in this line of research, and one which will prove a substantial and abiding asset, the oldest as well as the youngest broker must faithfully pursue this line of inquiry or he will be a poor counselor for his customers and must speedily become a "back number."

This important field of study is found in the official literature of the great railroad organizations of the country, for the stocks, bonds and securities of these corporations are the principal commodities in which the broker traffics. Mainly this literature is in the form of the annual reports of the various railway companies and they are obtained by application to the railway offices. Brokers are generally supplied with these bulky volumes and are glad to give studious employees access to them.

The value of a careful perusal of these documents is easily indicated. Foreknowledge of values or of their general trend is the one thing to be desired by the broker. Of course, he is ne er able actually to know that a certain railway security will advance or decline to a given limit, but it is his business—and the very essence of his business—so to inform himself on the conditions governing the values of that security that he may form a practical opinion of the merits of the property.

In the annual reports of the railroads the student will find the materials from which to build a foundation knowledge of the great properties, and this foundation will at all times serve him as a basis for calculations on the one essential point regarding any security: *its dividend-paying power*.

After learning the main traffic dependence of each road—whether lumber, wheat, corn, live-stock, fruit, coal, oil, manufactured products or a combination of several of these elements—let him dig into the finances of the company, the condition of the property, the personnel of the management and controlling shareholders.

What has the road cost? What is the condition of the property; of the physical plant, consisting of roadbed, rails, rolling-stock, shops, stations and buildings? How much does the company owe and what are the terms of interest and payment governing its various debts? Are costly improvements or extensions in progress? If so, how are the funds for these to be provided—from the surplus, from current earnings or from special issues of bonds? Is the percentage of operating expenses on the increase or decrease? Are any new and promising industrial developments, such as may be expected to swell the dividends of the company, coming to the front in the territory of the road? Are any large expansion movements planned or imminent which, although of a sound character, will temporarily decrease the dividend percentage? Or is there a falling away in any source of traffic which will tend to produce a shrinkage of the earnings of the road?

But the value of this groundwork of research will depend upon the quickness and intelligence with which the young broker applies this knowledge in relation to current events, to labor and crop conditions in the various sections of the country, to discoveries of mineral, oil and other valuable deposits, to the activity in special lines of manufacture and commerce. Unless he can put together the information gained from the morning paper, from the financial journal, from the ticker tape and from correspondence and conversation, and combine it with the knowledge gained from the railroad report, he will be working in the dark, guessing upon "general conditions," and following impulses.

No amount of intuition can take the place of definite knowledge of securities and of the elements which have made and will make their values.

This must be supplanted by a large amount of information of a less definite and authentic kind which must come to him in conversation and general talk. Although the "gossip of the street" is often misleading, it cannot be ignored, and the young broker must accept or reject it according to his own best judgment. In many, and perhaps most, instances he may be able to judge of its worth by reference to his knowledge of the road and its management. So far as possible he should learn something of the character of the men who dictate the policy of each great property. Another important thing for him to learn is who are the smaller as well as the larger holders of securities—particularly of those likely to be eagerly sought after? There is no rule by which this information is to be obtained aside from the very general one of keeping one's ears always open.

Nothing will take the place of a regular and careful reading of one or more of the ablest financial journals of the day. The ambitious young broker will do well to read closely The Commercial and Financial Chronicle, of New York, and The Economist, of Chicago. For a view of the foreign market the London Statist is to be commended. These journals are very sound and reliable, and will greatly assist in the education of the young broker—an education which, to a peculiar degree, is never finished until he quits.

While digging after the hard facts in the railroad reports and the current financial papers, the student will find it both pleasant and helpful to read some of the more entertaining literature of the Exchange. His ambitions will be sharpened and his knowledge of personalities greatly enlarged by the perusal of Mr. Henry Clews' delightful and chatty volume of reminiscences, called Twenty-Eight Years in Wall Street, and published by the Irving Publishing Company, New York.

A List of Useful Reading

ANOTHER interesting and unique work is Benners' Prophecies. This deals with the rise and fall of prices and the various theories regarding the principles underlying price movements. Much that is curious and entertaining is here mixed with considerable information of a useful character.

Of solid books there are many which may well find their way into the library of the young man who is determined systematically to study for brokerage as he would for a profession. Poors' Manual of Railroads (H. V. & W. H. Poor, New York), and Moody's Manual of Industrial and Miscellaneous Securities (O. C. Lewis Co., 6 Wall Street, New York), are essential. In connection with the latter volume it should be said that information regarding the industrial securities is exceedingly difficult to obtain, as these institutions do not issue anything in the line of official literature which corresponds with the elaborate annual reports put out by the railroad companies.

Another excellent handbook of this class is the Manual of Statistics, edited by Henry E. Wallace, and published by Chas. H. Nicoll, New York. This covers all kinds of securities. American Investments Classified is a useful volume by Curtis G. Harraman, 35 Nassau Street, New York. Its information is taken from official sources and relates to investors as well as investments of all classes.

American Street Railway Investments, issued as a supplement to the Street Railway Journal, 120 Liberty Street, New York, is a valuable annual which covers, in a very comprehensive and systematic way, the entire street railway situation of this country, giving the population of every city or town in the country having a surface system, the conditions governing franchises, the amount and nature of stock and bond issues, the time of annual meetings, and the value of plants and equipment.

If the young broker has followed the course of study indicated as essential to his groundwork and still longs for more, he may well spare the time to read Maurice L. Muhleman's Monetary Systems of the World, published by Chas. H. Nicoll, New York. However, he should remember that much of the reading here suggested is of a perpetual character, that the crop of official reports and annuals is perennial, and that the broker who is thoroughly alive must keep up with this fresh harvest of information.

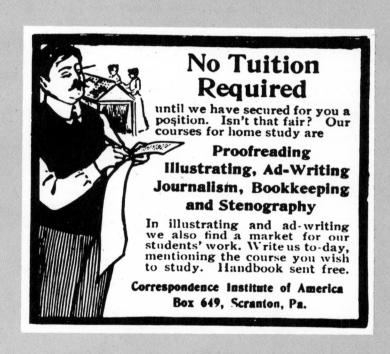

To Young Men Beginning Business

The Magic Telephone

By WILLIAM HENRY McDONOUGH
Editor American Telephone Journal

THE village of Wauseon, Ohio, had reached the conclusion that it wanted a telephone service. A number of business men in the place formulated a petition, addressed to the Central Union Telephone Company, which controls the Bell rights for that part of Ohio. In due time there came a communication from the main office at Chicago, refusing the application. Wauseon, with less than three thousand people, the telephone company said, was entirely too small to warrant the installation of a plant. This was in the spring of 1895.

What followed sounds like a romance. A campaign of competition was inaugurated that has revolutionized the telephone situation in the United States.

The leader in the movement for telephone service in Wauseon was Edward L. Barber, a young man of thirty-three, head of a private banking institution inherited from his father. He was a graduate of Cornell, had lived for a few years in Cleveland, but for ten years he had been back in Wauseon, his birthplace. One of Mr. Barber's closest friends was James S. Brailey, Jr., who was born in Wauseon twenty-three years before. He had attended the Northwestern College, and from there had gone to the University of Cincinnati and the Ohio State University, graduating as a lawyer in 1894. He had just about settled down to practice his profession in his native place when the Bell people made the foolish mistake of denying Wauseon. But for this mistake Mr. Brailey would, in all human probability, be a country lawyer to-day, looking after a comfortable but limited practice, and Mr. Barber would be a country banker as his father had been before him. Instead, these young men are the controlling factors in forty-six telephone companies and a few years more will see them millionaires several times over. They have inaugurated telephone systems, larger than the Bell, in Louisville and Lexington, Kansas City, Toledo, Utica, and some forty other places of lesser importance. Their systems are valued at many millions, and they are only at the beginning of their careers. And all this grew out of the Bell people's refusal to accommodate Wauseon. The act aroused Mr. Barber's ire. He hunted up his friend Brailey and laid the case before him.

The Beginnings of the Independents

"Now," said he, "can't we compel these people to give us service?"

"No," said young Brailey, "we can't. But I'll tell you what we can do. We can get together with the other business men here and install our own system."

"But how about the patents on the telephone?"

"They expired last year. The Bell people assert they are still protected in their monopoly by the Berliner patent, but I am sure that will not hold water. There are already plenty of people in the field who are making telephones, and who will be only too glad to supply us with instruments. If they can afford to take the chance, we certainly can."

The two young men associated themselves then and there for the purpose of building a telephone system for the village. They didn't know anything about the business, but that didn't deter them in the least. They set to work to learn. Some other young men in the town were interested in the proposition, and one fine morning there was a central in Wauseon. There were only sixty subscribers; to-day there are four hundred and more, or one for every seven men, women and children in the place. At this time neither Barber nor Brailey had any idea of going into telephone construction. But it happened that the neighboring towns of Napoleon, Ohio, and Adrian, Michigan, seeing how smoothly the telephone scheme worked in Wauseon, determined to have a similar service. Messrs. Barber and Brailey were requested to do the construction work. This was the real inception of the firm. The profit in Napoleon and Adrian was small, but it opened the eyes of the two young men to the possibilities that lay in this line of work. They organized the Central Construction Company, a partnership concern in which they hold equal shares, and went regularly into the installation of independent telephone systems. They worked all through Northern and Central Ohio, and then branched out into Indiana, New York, and afterward into Kentucky, until to-day their interests extend into many of the principal States.

THE NEWS IS RECEIVED BY SOME MEMBER OF THE HOUSEHOLD

In this connection it is interesting to note that practically all the people who are engaged in independent telephone construction to-day were novices, men without training who drifted into the industry through circumstances. The independent field is so new and the development has been so enormous, that it has been wholly impossible to pick up in sufficient numbers men who have been regularly trained for the business. There is no other work in the United States that offers such prospects for bright, energetic, pushing young men who are looking about for business openings. I doubt whether any one not actively engaged realizes what has been going on in the telephone industry during the past seven years and what may be expected in the next seven. We have only so recently emerged from the absolute domination of the Bell companies that the general public is not yet awake to the fact that there is such a thing as a first-class telephone service outside of Bell control. This is true particularly in the East, where independent telephony is just beginning to develop. It will probably be news, therefore, to the public, that on the first of May there were in use in this country, in round numbers, three million four hundred thousand telephones. Of these only one million four hundred thousand were controlled by the American Bell Telephone Company, as against two million and over controlled by the independent companies. This is not mere guesswork. The figures have been carefully compiled. They are not absolutely accurate, simply because it is impossible to keep up with development in the independent field. Figures that are official to-day are dead to-morrow. Independent companies are springing up over night, and almost without exception they are successful from the very start. It is of record that there were more failures of national banks last year than of independent telephone companies for the last three years. Yet a dozen telephone companies are organized where one national bank is organized. And we have always been accustomed to look on a national bank as the soundest institution in the country. It is difficult, even with figures, to give an adequate idea of the telephone situation. In 1894, there were less than three hundred thousand telephones in use throughout the country. Three million new telephones, in round numbers, have been put in service in the last seven years, or ten times as many as had been installed during the preceding eighteen years. If this ratio of increase is to continue we shall have over fifteen million telephones in use in 1920. There are plenty of people qualified to pass an opinion who put it down that we shall have a great many more.

The Tremendous Gains of New Companies

In discussing telephony, even the best informed people will often make the mistake of underestimating the strength of the new movement. They will tell you that the Independents are all right in the country and in small towns, but that they will never be factors in the large cities where the Bell people have from the start been firmly intrenched. The facts do not bear this out. To-day independent companies are operating in St. Louis, Baltimore, Cleveland, Pittsburg, Newark, Louisville, Minneapolis, Indianapolis, St. Paul, Rochester, Toledo, and so on down the list. In Philadelphia an independent company has about completed its plant, and is already giving a partial service. Buffalo, Detroit and Kansas City are building. Thus of the first twenty-six American cities, fifteen have independent services and in the others prospects are promising. It is a question of time, and a very short time, I believe, when the situation will be cleared up in New York and Boston and the Bell people will meet with competition in these two cities. Chicago gave a franchise some time ago to a company which is at present constructing conduits for its cables. San Francisco has granted a franchise, and an independent company is now in the field seeking a grant for Cincinnati. New Orleans had an independent company until recently, when the Bell people bought it out at a fancy figure. Applications for telephone rights are pending in Milwaukee and Washington. Of the seventy-four lesser cities having a population of between thirty-eight thousand and one hundred and thirty thousand, fifty-two have independent exchanges, and franchises are now being actively sought in a majority of the remaining twenty-two.

THEN THE EXCHANGE MANAGER PROCEEDS TO READ

In the past it has been the policy of the Bell Company to buy up its rivals when they showed signs of becoming formidable. But experience has shown the unwisdom of this course, for no sooner has one company been put out of business by purchase than another has sprung up. In New Orleans, for example, where a big price was paid for the control of the independent company that had been built up there, a company of important capitalists is now organizing a new independent concern. Detroit was bought out, but a new plant is now under way. The Bell people have, therefore, practically abandoned the practice of purchasing and are meeting competition by cutting rates and improving service, a state of affairs that is bringing great joy to their subscribers.

Telephones Popular With Progressive Farmers

Since 1895 more than two hundred thousand instruments have been put into farmhouses. The farmers of the Middle West have been particularly progressive. Farmers' exchanges have sprung up everywhere in Ohio, Indiana, Michigan and the neighboring States. The manner in which these exchanges go up is well illustrated by what are now known as the Stafford lines, in Geauga County, Ohio. In the spring of 1896 a number of farmers living about five miles east of Chagrin Falls, which is on the western border of Geauga County, concluded that it would be a pretty good thing to get into closer touch with each other by installing a telephone line running from house to house. They cut and set their own poles and here and there the fences were used to run wires. There were not over half a dozen in the original combination. The results were so satisfactory that the news spread in the neighborhood, and by fall several others concluded to build a line, using, with some extensions, the poles already erected. Up to this time it was simply possible under this scheme to talk from one house to the other. But as the number grew it was finally decided that it would be a good scheme if they could exchange conversations. One of the farmers, George W. Stafford, volunteered the use of his house as a "central" and here a switchboard was installed. Pretty soon the families in the neighborhood were fairly clamoring for connection, and as the exchange business grew Mr. Stafford realized that it would take some one's entire time to look after it. He therefore made a proposition to his neighbors to handle the exchange on a business basis. To-day this exchange, which is five or six miles away from the nearest railroad and which stands about a half mile from its nearest neighbor, controls forty-five miles of pole lines and has a hundred and fifty subscribers paying twelve dollars a year. It has a modern switchboard and its list of instruments is growing every day. It has long-distance connection with Cleveland, Painsville, Ashtabula, Warren, Youngstown and other centres of population, besides giving free service throughout the entire county of Geauga.

A telephone promoter is welcomed in rural communities with more eagerness than Santa Claus. An excellent example, though by no means an exceptional one, of what may be done, is furnished by the experience of a newspaper editor at Sturgeon, Missouri. He had a country weekly, and in order to get in closer touch with his people for stock and crop reports he concluded to build a little telephone line out through a certain section, where he could tap a number of houses. His neighbors laughed at him as a scatterbrain who didn't know what to do with his money, but he kept on building. To-day he is making more money out of his telephone line than he is out of his paper, and he is extending the system in all directions.

At Tipton, Indiana, a place of thirty-eight hundred population, forty miles from Indianapolis, there is an exchange manager who is going through the same process, only reversed. From a telephone man he is rapidly going into the field of an editor. He has a number of farm lines running out along the roads that lead to Tipton. With few exceptions, the houses along these roads are connected. The Indianapolis evening papers get into Tipton shortly after supper. The telephone man takes these papers, clips the headlines bearing on the main features, prepares a short synopsis, carefully written out, and pastes up what is known among newspaper men as a "dummy." When this is finished at a certain hour every evening he connects with all his lines, and gives a prescribed number of rings that brings every subscriber to his telephone. Then the exchange manager proceeds to read to the farmers his summary of the latest news. This is followed by stock reports, weather probabilities and other special information that is certain to interest subscribers all along the line. At the other end the news is received by some member of the household, who repeats it aloud to the other members of the family gathered about the telephone. In this way the farmers know the chief happenings of the world almost as soon as they appear on the bulletin-boards of the newspapers in the great metropolitan centres. This system, original with Tipton, has spread all through the Middle West and is now general in every farming community.

It is this sort of growth in entirely new fields that has brought all sorts and conditions of people into telephony. Doctors, lawyers, ministers, politicians, butchers, bakers, blacksmiths are all to be actively found promoting, building, operating. Sometimes mere children, boys of seventeen and eighteen, will be found in little stations in out-of-the-way localities. In El Paso, Texas, there is a company of which a woman, Mrs. Brett, is president. Her husband was a telephone contractor, and had built up a prosperous business when he died. She bravely took up the work and has succeeded splendidly. She operates several companies herself and in addition does general construction work. She has built up an excellent business reputation throughout the West and has all the contracts she can handle.

In Newton, New Jersey, Dr. H. A. Miller had built up a considerable practice. Ill health forced him to retire. He became interested in telephony and in order to employ his leisure time built a little line in and about Newton. To-day he has two hundred subscribers, an exchange that is equipped with all the modern appliances, and is making over eight per cent. on the money he invested.

Instances such as these could be multiplied by the score. People who have taken up telephony as a pastime or as a side issue have invariably ended by becoming fascinated by it and giving it their entire time. Many of these have started practically without capital, most of them without experience.

Some Good Books for Telephone Students

When the telephone field was thrown open to all comers in 1894 there was no one in the field except employees or ex-employees of the Bell Company who had any knowledge of the subject. The Bell people from the start had impressed a policy of silence. No officer, engineer or manager of any company was allowed to write on the subject of telephony or to give to the public any information. For such literature as there was this country had to depend upon Europe. Now and then if a Bell man ventured into print, either through technical journals or otherwise, he was promptly taken to task and advised that a further transgression would result in trouble. When the break came, however, at the expiration of the patents, a number of writers appeared in the field, and to-day we have excellent textbooks, including American Telephone Practice, by Kempster B. Miller; The Telephone Hand-Book, by Herbert Laws Webb; Practical Features of Telephone Work, by A. E. Dobbs, and The A B C of the Telephone, by J. E. Homans. There are also one weekly and two monthly telephone journals in the field, and all the important electrical papers devote special departments to the work. It was generally the policy of the old company to buy up all the telephone patents and shelve them. This naturally retarded improvements, and the United States up to 1894 was far behind some of the other countries in its appliances, though it was the home of the telephone. In Sweden, for example, where the Bell Company had never been able to obtain a monopoly and where the field was open to all comers, the mechanism of telephony was far ahead of the United States, and to this day the use of the telephone is much more general there than it is here, though we are rapidly catching up. When the

Independents came into the field all this was changed, and to-day we are producing a higher grade of instrument than is to be found anywhere else in the world.

Under the leases granted by the Bell Company for territorial rights all instruments have had to be rented from the parent company, and all switchboards and central office apparatus must be purchased from the Western Electric Company, a manufacturing concern controlled by the parent company. As soon as the field was thrown open a host of independent manufacturers started up and their growth has been phenomenal. Their factories employ thousands upon thousands of men and represent the investment of many millions of capital. All this since 1895.

A volume could be written about the rise of this manufacturing branch of the independent telephone industry. A few examples that have come under my own observation will give an indication of what has taken place.

A few years ago two emigrants landed in Chicago. They were unable to speak English, but having had a little experience in their native land they got positions with the Chicago Telephone Company as repairmen at a dollar and a half a day. They were hard workers and ambitious. They set themselves to learn English and put in their spare hours studying the mechanism of the telephone. In 1895 they had a few hundred dollars saved between them. They resigned their positions and opened a little workroom where they began to make telephone instruments. Their working force, besides themselves, consisted of two men and three boys. They were threatened with infringement suits and all manner of pressure was brought to bear to force them out of business. But they hung on. A few weeks ago one of these men took me over the factory he and his partner had built up out of that little workroom. There I saw a plant that occupied half a city block and employed twelve hundred people. They were turning out a complete telephone every minute. Recently these two manufacturers reorganized their company and now they are about to add fifty per cent. to their facilities, and still they doubt their ability to keep up to their orders, though with their new force they will ultimately be able to turn out close to a thousand telephones a day.

Another well-known manufacturer who has an enormous plant was a boy operator for the Bell Company. When the independent field was opened he branched out in a small way for himself. To-day he is president of a big corporation that makes telephones by the hundred thousand.

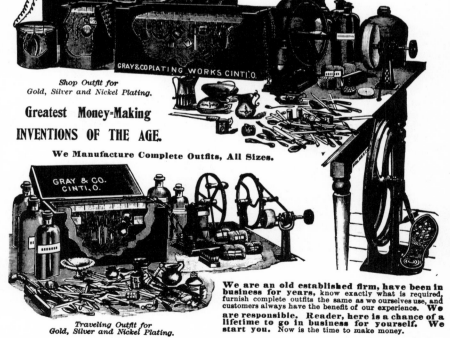

The Reign of the Mechanic

AMERICANS have a cheerful habit when things go wrong of assuming that all will come out right in the end. And their history gives them much reason for this assumption. Not many ills in American life run on very long without a remedy. For instance, moralists have complained that our young men have been getting false ideas of life. They have pointed to the crowded classes in the professional schools, and have asked what the country would do when everybody forsook manual labor and tried to make a living by his wits. They have foreseen the time when the land would be overrun by half-starved lawyers and doctors, and left destitute of mechanics.

But the industrial revolution now under way has changed all this. The great prizes of modern life are no longer for the men who practice the traditional professions, but for those who begin by working with their hands and end by controlling gigantic industries. The road to million-dollar salaries and royal power in these days is not through the law school or the theological seminary, but through the machine shop and the freight caboose.

The recent descriptions in THE SATURDAY EVENING POST of the methods by which millionaires are made at the Carnegie Works and of the progress of bright young men elsewhere from brakemen to railroad presidents must have a potent effect on the aspirations of the rising generation, and the new organization of industry will tend more and more to make such cases the rule instead of the exception. Under the old system, a bright workman in a shop employing half a dozen men might become the foreman of that shop, but he had little chance of making himself known outside. Now, such a man is in the direct line of promotion to the control of a whole national industry employing half a million men. Each step in his advancement is a preparation for another step. As every soldier in Napoleon's army carried a marshal's baton in his knapsack, so every workman in a modern factory carries potentially the presidency of a trust.

If this system continues to prevail it must have great social results. It will not only send the brightest young men of the country to mechanical occupations, instead of to the so-called professions, but it will prevent the segregation of the community into classes. The natural leaders of the workmen will be continually drafted off to become the managers of the industries as a whole. Whether this will be injurious or not to the men who stay in the ranks remains to be seen. At all events, it will prevent the creation of castes, either of employers or of employed. The blood of the community will be kept in constant circulation, and that ought to mean national health. —SAMUEL E. MOFFETT.

Culture and Success

MORE light on the question whether higher education is a hindrance to success in life is furnished by the latest edition of a biographical dictionary that includes practically everybody in America who is known outside of his own block. In this hospitable Hall of Fame are found the names of 11,551 persons, of whom 9760 furnished details about their education. Of these 4521 are graduates of American colleges and universities, 289 are graduates of West Point and Annapolis, 965 attended college without graduating, 366 were educated abroad, and 2059 are graduates of medical, scientific, theological and law schools. Thus 8200 out of 9760 persons, or 84 per cent. of the whole, have had some sort of higher education. In addition, 282 were privately educated, their training in many cases reaching collegiate grade, and 1249 were trained in academies, seminaries, normal schools and high schools. That leaves only 315 out of 9760, or 3 per cent., with no more than the common-school education which some gentlemen of note think all that is good for a business man.

The people with college, or even high-school, training constitute a very small percentage of the population of this country. Yet it appears that they furnish 97 per cent. of the men and women successful enough to have attracted any sort of public attention. Among the vast little-educated majority who furnish the other 3 per cent. there are doubtless nearly or quite as many persons of ability, proportionately, as among the small minority of higher training. If education were merely ineffective, not to say harmful, this great majority should swamp the minority in the lists of successful men. That its contribution to the total is scarcely perceptible looks like pretty conclusive evidence that higher education gives a man some advantages that he would not have without it.

Colleges are not primarily designed to teach a man to make money, but they teach him to measure his mental powers and make the most of them. When he turns his disciplined faculties in the direction of money-making he is more likely to succeed than if his mind were untrained. College men have learned to test all things and hold fast that which is good. They are not likely to be deceived by transparent swindles. They do not furnish many customers for gold bricks or green goods. They do not waste time in hunting perpetual motion. They do not patronize 520 per cent. "get-rich-quick" syndicates. In short, they have learned how to see things as they are, to avoid mirages, and to take advantage of genuine opportunities.

And of course there are other kinds of success infinitely higher than money-making. In attaining these an academic training is of incalculable advantage. Poets may be born, not made, but making has a great deal to do with other forms of intellectual distinction. Mr. Roosevelt might possibly have reached the Presidency if he had never gone to Harvard, but he would have had to get along without a good many of his other varied titles to fame.

The Value of Knowing How

IT WAS this magazine that first called general attention to the remarkable demand for the graduates of the technical schools. It did this in two ways: first, in statements of the fact, and then more intimately and interestingly in articles from the heads of the leading technical schools of the country. Recent inquiry has shown that the call for the services of these young men has increased rather than diminished. The writer of this recently spent a day with the head professor of one of the important scientific and technical schools, and it was a revelation. The young men were, with few exceptions, of the sturdy type, full of good spirits, cheerful in their labors, and not at all backward in having as much fun with the professor as he could get from them. The high stimulus of fine, intelligent work was never better shown. The thoroughness of it, too, was astonishing, for the students had to know how to do carpenter work as well as how to build bridges and great structures, and how to manage immense mills.

"Already," said the professor, "places are offered to every graduate student we have for the year, and some of them will have their choice of several important positions. Here is a letter which I received from one of our last year's men—an unusually capable man." The professor laughed a little as he added: "He is already getting a much larger salary than I am receiving at this university. It almost tempts me to become a graduate student myself."

The other side of this remarkable condition has just been told by Mr. E. J. Buffington, President of the Illinois Steel Company, one of the largest concerns of its kind in the world. "We want educated young men—graduates of technical schools," he said. He referred to the case of President Schwab—what a wonderful case that is!—and remarked that he worked almost into his position under the old school, and that the gift of business genius, which is always rare, did the rest in elevating him to his present unprecedented success. "There will be Carnegies and Schwabs in the future," said Mr. Buffington, "men who, through a powerful personality and great ability, will rise in spite of circumstances;" but the average young man of good, even of unusual, gifts must know technical science if he expects to win the larger prizes.

So quickly does modern civilization move, so imperative are its demands and so exacting its specifications, that the young man must know not only the textbook facts but how to use them practically.

The industrial situation is a lesson for all callings, and never was the Jack of all trades and the master of none so doomed to a bare existence as he is to-day.

To Young Men Beginning Business

The Young Farmer—By F. A. WARNER

MANAGER OF THE SIBLEY ESTATE FARMS

THERE is no event in life of so much importance as the choosing of the business of life. That time comes, or should come, to every young man, and to many it is a source of much anxiety. It is a step well worthy of his very best thought and his most careful decision.

It is for the purpose of assisting young men in making the choice of a business that this article is written.

Self-reliance, ability and energy are three requirements for success in any vocation. Without these any success achieved is more a matter of chance than a reward for correctly directed effort. An earnest desire to succeed, with a keen appreciation of the difficulties and obstacles to be surmounted, yet with a firm determination to attain the desired end by one's own effort, honestly applied, is half the success, attained already.

As a rule, wealth unearned by his own brain and hand is more likely to be a curse than a blessing to the average young man. Rich men's sons who can get money for the asking, with no thought of giving any value in effort for it, are not our best citizens nor is society benefited by their example. Sons making the right use of inherited wealth are the exception and not the rule.

There is an immense attraction in the sudden acquisition of wealth. The idea of getting rich at thirty-five or forty and using the rest of one's life in spending the money is firmly rooted in the mind of the average young American. He first sets a mark of perhaps $200,000 as the size of the fortune he wants, but if able and fortunate enough to secure that amount he immediately sets about doubling it, and then, if he follows in the usual course, he not only fails in the new effort but loses all he had first won, and is rarely able, afterward, to gain more than a mere livelihood.

In these days there is too much plunging and not enough conservatism, too much venture and not enough caution, too much trickery and not enough honesty, too much self and not enough thought for one's neighbor.

In the consideration of agriculture, which I think is an ideal business, I want the reader to follow me for a few minutes while I describe the ideal young farmer engaged in the real business of farming—a description made from the standpoint of studied and careful observation and of practical work for a period of over fifty busy years.

Starting out with the assumption that the young man was raised on the farm with only moderate country-school advantages, with possibly a winter or two in some city academy, I should advise him to attend, if possible, and even at some sacrifice, the College of Agriculture and the Experiment Station of his State. He should take up especially the study of soils and their adaptability to produce certain varieties of product, and the study of the proper preparation, cultivation and preservation of field crops, the care and feeding of stock—both for beef and dairy—and also swine husbandry. Even winter terms at such a college will add an interest to farm work and will greatly aid in explaining the various problems which arise to puzzle the farmer. The principles taught in these State Agricultural Colleges are broad in the scope of their work and are exceedingly helpful.

A Course of Reading for the Farmer

If, however, the privilege of attending such a college is denied, I should advise a young man to spend as much of his time as possible in the deliberate, thoughtful reading of some selections from the following list of publications, nearly all of which can be obtained from the Orange Judd Publishing Company, New York or Chicago. For a general survey of agriculture: First Principles of Agriculture, by Vorhees; Principles of Agriculture, by Professor L. H. Bailey, of Cornell University; New American Farm Book Revised and Enlarged, by Lewis F. Allen. These all treat of general farm matters in detail.

Fertility of the Land, by Professor I. P. Roberts, discusses soils and their composition, and remedies for the renewal of lost fertility. How Crops Grow, and How Crops Feed, by Johnson, are excellent for study and reference. Soil and Crops of the Farm, by Professor George E. Morrow, is a carefully compiled work relating to the most approved methods of making available the plant food and to methods of cultivation, and it pertains more especially to the great grain-growing and stock-raising Western States.

Land Draining, by Miles, gives most complete directions regarding open and tile drainage, and it is well illustrated.

The Book of Corn, compiled under the direction of Herbert Myrick and now in the printer's hands, promises to be, from what I know personally of the contributors, an invaluable book for the corn grower. The enthusiast on corn would be greatly interested also in Indian Corn Culture, by Professor C. S. Plumb; Corn Plants, Their Uses and Ways of Life, by F. L. Sargent, and Manual of Corn Judging, by A. D. Shamel.

All the crops grown by the farmer are more or less subject to insect pests or diseases, and Insects and Insecticides, by Weed, and its companion, Fungi and Fungicides, by the same author, treat of these matters very comprehensively.

Weeds and How to Eradicate Them, by Thomas Shaw, ought to be in every farmer's hands and should receive his earnest attention. Breeds of Livestock, by J. H. Sanders, editor of the Breeder's Gazette, gives an exhaustive treatment of the distinguishing characteristics of the various breeds of farm animals.

As for specialties, there are Swine Husbandry, by F. D. Coburn; American Dairying, by H. B. Gurler; Shepherd's Manual, by Henry Stuart; Youatt and Spooner on the Horse, and Wright's Practical Poultry-Keeper—all of them interesting and instructive.

Feeds and Feeding, by W. A. Henry, is a standard work and modern in every respect. Diseases of Horses and Cattle, by Donald McIntosh, should be owned by every stockman and carefully studied so that he may be ready to make prompt use of the suggestions and remedies when needed. Silos, Ensilage and Silage, by Manly Miles, tells how to build and fill silos and feed silage.

It would certainly be only in keeping with advanced ideas in farming to buy the young wife The Woman's Manual for the Household. This book is a veritable directory for the thousand and one things indispensable to know in a well-regulated household. The Practical Fruit Grower, by S. T. Maynard; Gardening for Young and Old, by Joseph Harris, and The Beautiful Flower Garden, by Mathews, would all add to the comfort and pleasure of the farm home if read and heeded. I have also read with interest and profit Clover Farming, by Henry Wallace, and Horse Useful, and Forage and Fodders, by F. D. Coburn.

Rules that the Young Farmer Should Follow

The reader will understand that these books mentioned are only a few of the general agricultural works. I have sought to cover in a general way the leading industries on the farm. There are a great number of books discussing specialties, and any of them can be obtained through the agricultural publishing houses.

I should recommend the reading, first, of such of these books as treat of matters connected with the young man's immediate work on the farm, and those which relate most directly to his particular surroundings. If he is to start as a strictly grain-raising farmer he should read those works which most fully relate to that subject. If he is to be a stock farmer then let him read the works treating directly of that subject.

The ideal young farmer is the one who will heed the helpful suggestions to be found in the reading of most of the books mentioned. In them will be found the results of years of research and experiment, and if he will make use of the knowledge he gains in their reading it will set him in the forefront, ready equipped to do battle in his chosen business and to gain a signal victory. Accompanying this reading there must be keen observation and the desire to verify the statements of the authors by actual trials under his own eye.

The young farmer should determine to be the very best farmer, and then he should use every honest endeavor to attain that mark. Such a determination is inconsistent with speculation and with going into extremes in anything. Own about the same amount of stock; plant about the same acreage of corn and oats, the same amount in pasture, in meadow, in fruit, in garden; arrange for the rotation of crops and conserve the fertility of the soil by sowing clover, by carefully preserving and spreading all manure, by keeping as much stock as will consume all the "roughage" grown and will make return to the land through manure.

I should have him start with economy in mind. Buy those things *necessary to do the work*. *Do not run in debt*. *Pay as you go*. Notes are easy to *sign* but hard to *pay*. And there is no independence so enjoyable as that which comes from "Owe no man anything but the love you owe a fellow-being." I should want him to keep right on with the special branch he chooses—not changing from one kind to another like a farmer I knew, who, seeing his neighbor have a fine crop of oats one year, planted nearly all his farm to oats the following year. Oats were poor and corn was better. Then he tired of oats and planted nearly all corn; and corn was not so profitable as hogs, and so he turned to hogs for profit, and when he was well stocked the hogs nearly all died of cholera. The neighbor who had followed the plan of having about the same amount of each product each year had done very well, for the reason that, having a variety of products, some one or more of them were of the profitable kind.

Our ideal young farmer must be a man of courage. Any disappointment, or any failure to accomplish the end he desires, should be the means of giving him a knowledge of things to avoid and of things to cultivate with greater care.

Business Methods Applied to Farming

He should, moreover, be a man of method. Every hour of every day should count for something. The movements of the body in doing work are entirely under the direction and control of the brain. The knowledge stored in the brain, therefore, should be of such a nature as shall seek to economize the strength of the body, bringing into the best use those parts of the body needed to do the work with the least waste. Many farmers are looked upon as great workers because they seem to be always in a hurry. They rush here and there, or pick up this article and drop that, and their useless movements are greatly in excess of the useful.

I call to mind a good-natured, strong, German farmer who was one of these hard workers. He was always up early in the morning. He would hurry into the field to plow—only to find that he had left the whiffletrees at the house, having used them on the wagon the evening previous. He could pitch more bundles of oats upon a wagon in the field than could most men, but would do it in such a manner that the wagon rarely reached the stack or thresher without a reloading. He was the same with all work on the farm. He had been twelve years a renter and was likely to be a renter for twelve years more.

By the proper care and use of the body health can usually be conserved and life really prolonged. The eating, sleeping, resting and working should be so controlled as to preserve the proper healthy equilibrium. I cannot pass this point without the remark that the use of liquor and tobacco has a direct tendency to weaken brain, nerve and muscle, and to cause an early collapse. I should like to see my ideal farmer have a sufficient amount of pride to appear at any time and place well clothed and in his right mind.

I should like him to know just what he is doing, financially, from year to year, and for keeping his accounts he should obtain a book with what is called "journal ruling." About two hundred pages will last a long time. He should open up the following accounts: *eighty-acre piece of corn, eighty-acre piece of oats, thirty-acre piece of wheat, sixty-acre pasture, sixty-acre piece of meadow, ten-acre piece of orchard and garden.* Charge against each piece the seed furnished and all work done and the acreage proportion of repairs, taxes, insurance, etc.; and when a crop is harvested credit to the proper account the product obtained. Also open an account with horses, cattle, hogs, farm machinery and expense account. Charge the stock with their feed, the farm machinery with the tools bought and their repairs, and the expense account with the items of expenditure not enumerated in the other headings. Credit horses with the work done and with money received from any sold. Credit cattle and hogs with increase, or with money from sales made. Credit farm machinery with the use per acre. It will take only a few minutes at evening to make the proper entries, and thus at any time the farmer can take an inventory value and find how he stands. Things which, as the book shows, do not have a balance on the credit side can be abandoned, and those which show a good credit can be increased.

The above is only what any man in any mercantile business always does, and as farming is just as much a business, there should be account books to show what is made or lost.

What it Costs to Begin Farming

If our ideal young farmer shall be so fortunate as to own the necessary teams, tools, seed and livestock for a 160-acre farm, and should further be so fortunate as to own the land, too, that land to be situated in the central part of the State of Illinois—if he shall be industrious and frugal, with a helpmeet of like mind, shall be the thorough farmer that we should wish him to be, then I should place him a little above the average farmer in production, and, allowing all things else to figure upon the average prices obtained for the past thirty years, I should expect his book of accounts to show the following entries as nearly as may be. If he started with new things his inventory account at the start would be as follows:

1 riding plow	$ 37.50
1 three-section harrow	15.00
1 disk, 7½ feet cut	24.00
1 corn planter and check wire	33.00
1 oats-seeder, 11 feet	16.00
1 riding cultivator	22.00
1 walking cultivator	15.00
1 farm wagon	55.00
1 mowing machine	40.00
1 hay rake	20.00
1 harvester, self-binder	120.00
1 hay rack	7.00
3 sets work harness at $26	78.00
3 horses (geldings) at $110	330.00
3 brood mares (2 in foal) at $130	390.00
4 cows at $40	160.00
4 steers and heifers, 2 years past, at $35	140.00
4 yearling heifers and steers at $20	80.00
4 calves, heifers and steers, at $8	32.00
2 brood sows, 250 lbs. each, at 4½c. lb.	22.50
4 doz. poultry (44 pullets, 4 cockerels) at $3 doz.	12.00
Furniture and household supplies	200.00
Seed corn, 12 bu. at $1	12.00
Seed oats, 125 bu. at 32c	40.00
Feed for six horses, March 1 to September 30, 168 bu. corn at 35½c	59.64
168 bu. oats at 29½c	49.56
Hay for four months, 1½ tons each, 6 tons at $5	30.00
Feed for 2 brood sows, 4 months, 10 bu. corn at 35½c	3.55
Total	$2043.75

Hence our young farmer must have about $2000 in money to make the above purchases in order to start farming and be what we call *fully equipped* to do good work and produce the best results. He might start with considerably less equipment but it would be at the expense of much more labor, and in the exchanging of work with neighbors there would be possible neglect of his own fields and a consequent less production and a slower accumulation of profits. I believe that our young farmer could safely start farming if he had $1000 in money to purchase the horses and tools needed to the close of corn cultivation; the other expenses could be provided for out of the earliest returns from the farm of the most salable products.

The First Year's Dividend

We shall now still further show what entries, debit and credit, should be made in his book of accounts. The 160-acre farm would produce per acre as follows:

70 acres in corn, 50 bu. an acre, 3500 bu. at 35½c	$1242.50
50 acres in oats, 45 bu. an acre, 2250 bu. at 29½c	663.75
16 acres in hay, 1½ tons an acre, at $5 per ton	120.00
20 acres in pasture, to graze cattle; increased value, 8 head unsold	120.00
4 acres in garden, orchard and roads, etc.; produce worth	25.00
Sold 4 head cattle, coming 3 years old, at $50	200.00
Sold 10 head hogs, 250 lbs. each, at 4½c. lb	112.50
Sold 2 brood sows, 400 lbs. each, at 4½c. lb.	36.00
Sold 6 doz. chickens at $3 doz	18.00
" 100 lbs. butter at 15c. lb.	15.00
" 250 doz. eggs at 12c. doz.	30.00
	$2582.75

In addition to the above he has on hand of increase stock:

6 calves at $10	$60.00	
2 brood sows at $9	18.00	
2 colts at $20	40.00	
6 doz. chickens at $3 doz	18.00	—136.00
Total		$2718.75

What His Expenses Will Be

His expense account will be about as follows:

1 hired man, 9 months at $20	$180.00
Extra help — harvesting, threshing, husking, etc.	50.00
Help in the house, sundry busy times	30.00
Feed for horses, hogs, cattle, etc., 400 bu. corn at 35½c	142.00
Feed for horses, 150 bu. oats at 29½c	44.25
Feed for horses and cattle, 9 tons hay at $5	45.00
Threshing bill, 2250 bu. oats at 1¼c	28.12
Shelling 3100 bu. corn at ¾c	23.25
Board hired man, 9 months at $10	90.00
" " girl, 3 months at $10	30.00
" " extra help, visitors, etc	25.00
Groceries, dry goods, clothing, shoes, etc	250.00
Miscellaneous, unprovided above	20.00
Wear and repairs on all tools, 10 per cent	38.00
Total	$995.62

This would leave net for him $1723.13, being the product of his labor and investment. This would be six per cent. on $80 per acre and nearly $1000 to save or to invest in more stock and improvements.

If our young farmer should start on a rented farm his expenses would be about the same; and if he should pay cash rent of $5 an acre he would have $923.13 profit. If he will cut up some of his corn before frost, and if he will carefully stack his oats and straw and properly house and paint his farm tools, his expenses can be considerably lessened and the rough feed used to save grain and hay, with a possible surplus of fruits, potatoes, melons, etc., to sell.

Careful rotation with clover sown in the oats, the persistent spreading of the manure made, and the timely doing of the seasonable farm work will increase his income as the years come and go.

The Most Profitable Farm Acreage

I should not advise any young man in the Western country to try to get rich upon an 80-acre farm. It may do to start with for a year or two, but it is too large for one man to work with success and too small in product to justify buying the tools and employing the help to do good farming.

Only in fruit farming or market gardening, or in the two combined, would that size farm pay.

On half-section farms he would do proportionately better than on 160 acres, but must have the necessary experience to be gained by two or three years on 160 acres, and when he has a large farm of from 1000 to 1280 acres he must have the capacity and ability to manage the work of his men to the best advantage and should be a thorough stockman, breeder, feeder and seller, and an earnest student of the rotation of crops, as it is now quite well understood; and on any size farm he must know intimately the How, Where and When of all things pertaining to his chosen business.

I should not have our young farmer neglect the social functions prevailing in his neighborhood, only I should advise that they be of such as character as shall in no instance have a tendency to belittle the dignity of his position. I realize there must now and then be some relaxation and diversion from the day-by-day duties on the farm. I think the Grange meetings, the township farmers' clubs, the farmers' institutes and the various farm and livestock associations, serve both to divert and educate, if I may so express it. The exchange of ideas and opinions and the object-lessons furnished are often of great benefit.

I should have our young farmer be a leader in these affairs by reason of his superior knowledge of the matters to be discussed, secured by his Agricultural College training or from the reading of some of the books referred to in this article.

The Young Farmer's Home Life

The home surroundings on the farm are of much more importance than is usually given to that feature. The arrangement of the buildings, for both convenience and health, is very important. Lack of shade trees and fruit trees gives an undesirable barrenness to the view. We repeat with reverence the line, "The moss-covered bucket that hung in the well." That sentiment did very well for our long-ago forefathers, but give us now the bucket that is so busy that no moss can cling to it.

The surroundings and interior of the farm home are indicative of the progressiveness of the owner. Let our ideal young farmer start out with the view of making the farm home a fitting place for his chosen life partner, who, at least in the courting days, expected to reign over a home dominion to be pointed at with pride and pleasure.

I should have this young farmer be a power in his neighborhood though showing an example of industry, honesty, ability and good judgment. I should have him bear in mind that quality, as well as quantity, is to be considered in every transaction, both in buying and selling. I should wish that he might always consider that "A good name is rather to be chosen than great riches."

The world wants live, progressive men whose works will live after them as an example to succeeding generations.

Agriculture is taking its place in the world's progress, and is a science and a business worthy of the united efforts of the unselfish wisdom of the best men. May our ideal young farmer be one of these men. He can be if he will.

THE CORRECT ARTICLE.

FARMER GREENE.—Oh, yes; there are several "gentlemen-farmers" around here.

THE FAIR STRANGER.—And what is a "gentleman-farmer"?

FARMER GREENE.—Oh, a feller that knows enough ter run a farm as it should be run, and rich enough ter stand th' loss!

THE AGE OF PROSPERITY.

UNCLE JOSH.—The boys won't stay on the farms no more.

UNCLE SILAS.—No; an' you can hardly expect 'em to. Nowadays, even the mortgages don't stay on the farms

3 Science and Invention

The crystal ball of prophecy is often clouded, and it is apt to be at its murkiest when man tries to predict what lies in store for him in the fields of science and technology. Prognostication in these areas is a chancy business at best: an invention, a discovery, an improved technique, new materials, can throw the most careful forecast into a cocked hat.

On the following pages is a good example of the scientific forecast gone awry; "How the World Will End," by Hudson Maxim, an American inventor of some note, details for the fearful readers of the *Woman's Home Companion* the various possible death throes of our earth. His article was based on the best knowledge of the time—and indeed, of many subsequent decades, for similar articles continued to appear in magazines and Sunday supplements until quite recently. The earth, Maxim says, may be struck by a giant meteor. A huge comet may swish its tail across our world and sweep away its atmosphere. The sun may explode and burn our planet to a cinder. And if none of these events happens, he continues, it is inevitable that on some incredibly distant day the sun will grow dim and our earth become icy cold and dead. Though these possibilities were unpleasant, they were all either highly unlikely or unimaginably remote in time.

Then, just about a generation ago, man's own technology suddenly wiped out his comfortable remoteness from annihilation. Doomsday no longer lay in the billion-to-one chance that a giant meteor would strike the earth; the end of mankind had become something that might be only half an hour away, and utter destruction had been placed within the power of men with fallible judgments and red telephones.

And just as humanity was coming to feel a nervous security in the very horror of mutual destruction—in the conviction that a balance of terror would protect the world—a new danger arose as the result of our onrushing technology and the so-called progress that follows hard in its wake. Man was fouling his air, his water, his earth, at a rate that would soon make the question of whether he learned to control his nuclear weapons academic.

The point is that neither Maxim nor anyone else at the time he wrote could have anticipated the discoveries that would lead to atomic weapons. And in his day pollution was no more than a local

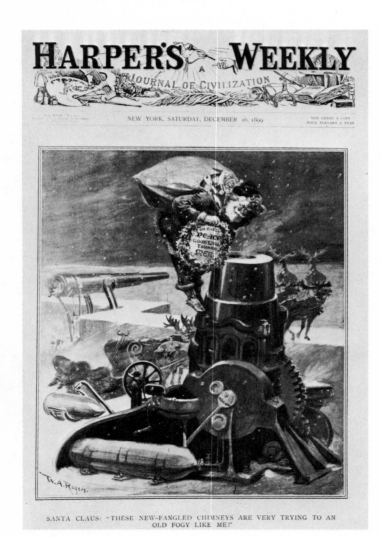

SANTA CLAUS: "THESE NEW-FANGLED CHIMNEYS ARE VERY TRYING TO AN OLD FOGY LIKE ME!"

nuisance, a breeder of flies and a creator of stenches.

A year after he wrote his article about the end of the world, Maxim gave the lady readers of the *Woman's Home Companion* another look into the future, although a far less cosmic one. In his "Inventions That Ought To Be Invented" he fires off a number of ideas. Some of them miss, but a surprising number anticipate later developments.

Scientists are still working on a source of light that Maxim advocated: one that can provide illumination without any loss in heat. Some progress has been made, but at present only the firefly knows the complete answer. And scientists today can produce energy from sunlight—not the most efficient and inexpensive way of producing energy but good enough to power artificial satellites.

Maxim's suggestion that nitrogen be removed from the air and fixed in a chemical usable as an agricultural fertilizer became fact more than half a century ago. In his article he proposes radio (he calls it wireless telephone), although Marconi had barely begun his experiments of sending dots and dashes through space. Maxim also advocates more vigorous work on color photography (and surprises us by mentioning that even at that early date a start, albeit "feeble," had been made on the problem).

There is more, however, on the following pages than the foresight of Mr. Maxim. Perhaps more informative are some of the period pieces; they are tidemarks of the time, permitting us to measure how far our knowledge has advanced in the years since. "Is There Snow on the Moon?" may seem a ridiculous question, but in the first years of the century serious men using the data then available asked it. The same is true of a discussion of men and canals on Mars; we have no right to smile indulgently, because it is only within the last few years that we have definitely disproved the existence of man-made structures on Mars.

The brief piece "How To Use the Telephone" is, on the surface, merely a charming bit of lavender and old lace, but it also points up how short a distance a great deal of progress may sometimes take us. There is no doubt that the telephone was originally a great convenience, handy for ordering groceries, a comfort when the doctor was needed, almost indispensable in case of fire.

Then into this simple but admirable system was injected a surfeit of progress. The friendly operator ("central," whom you often knew by first name) was replaced by clicking circuit-makers in some unknown place, and it became possible, with a few twists of the finger, to call anyone in town, or in the state—and finally in the nation. But when you could call anyone, anyone could call you. And does. The telephone rings: a magazine salesman is calling. It rings, and on the other end are moppets whose mother has left them alone for the afternoon and told them to dial the phone if they get bored. It rings for any number of wrong reasons.

At the same time many of the early warm comforts provided by the telephone have faded. Once it brought kindly Doc, the family physician, in case of an emergency. Today the only way to get Doc—who probably does not make house calls anyway—is to send someone after him, for now an answering service takes his calls, and it may be three or four hours before he ever calls back, no matter how urgent one's plea.

The telephone has been attacked here only because it is the available target; had there been instead a piece on how to drive a horseless carriage the same argument—that man is often enslaved by his technology—could have been pointed up even more sharply. The automobile has the capability of getting us about at seventy miles an hour with ease, but much of the time it sits immobilized in monstrous traffic jams; it was once touted as a way to get town dwellers out into the country and fresh air—and the sequel to that needs no comment.

The articles reproduced here were chosen arbitrarily; the field was vast, and despite attempts to make the selections representative, they are undoubtedly quite different from what other editors would have chosen. But the theme of the articles would very likely be the same no matter who did the selecting: a new age of science and technology will solve many of the problems and cure the ills of mankind. That was the expectation in the first years of the 1900's. Today that bright promise is a long, long way from being fulfilled.

INVENTIONS THAT OUGHT TO BE INVENTED

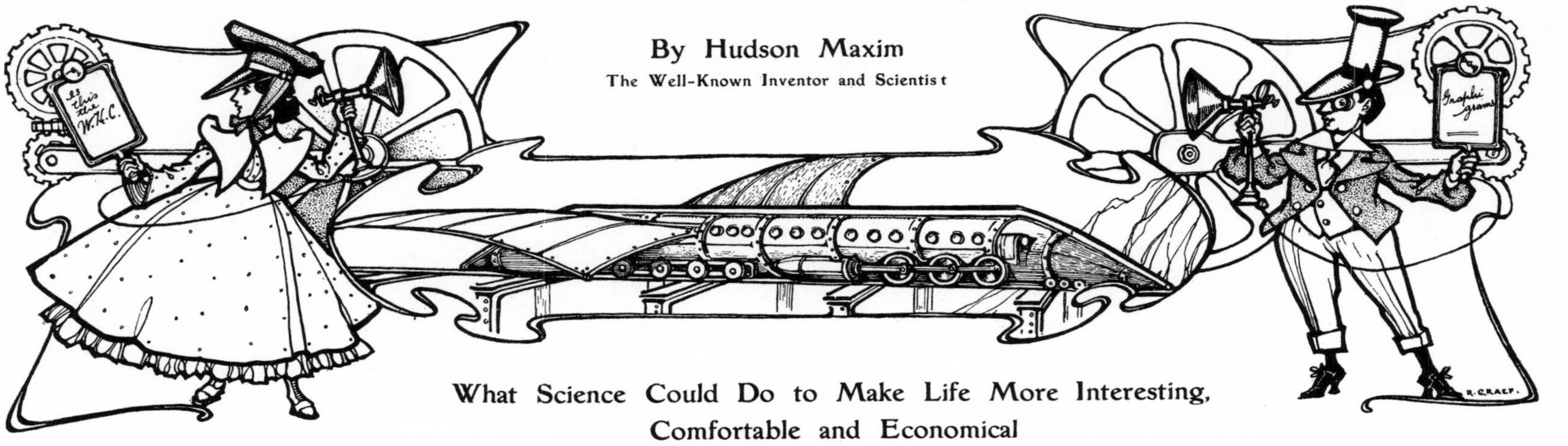

By Hudson Maxim

The Well-Known Inventor and Scientist

What Science Could Do to Make Life More Interesting, Comfortable and Economical

ONE of the most startling characteristics of the new age of civilization is the accelerating velocity of exploration, discovery and invention. The nineteenth century witnessed greater progress in the sciences and in the practical arts of life than all other epochs of history put together; but even those who know most about the achievements of that marvelous period are already amazed at the promise of incalculably greater accomplishments during the twentieth century.

One of the distinctive features of the new era is the prompt application to material uses of each and every result of scientific research. In the Middle Ages inventors were few, and slow in action, but in these days every fresh discovery is seized upon with eager utilitarian aims. Ardent expectations are cherished respecting many definite, practical and useful expedients not yet contrived, but looked upon as sure of realization. Some of these I may specify. They are but samples of coming wonders, but they are among the things likely to be soonest invented.

I will commence with what may be reckoned our domestic primaries, or the matters which affect us immediately in the familiar circle of home life. I refer to inventions which have to do with light, heat and food. Obviously there is scope for an immense revolution. Hundreds of electricians are at this moment striving to construct lamps in which nothing is consumed save the electrical energy applied to them—lamps that have the radiance of the sun and the coldness of the moon. The reason why determined study is thus being prosecuted with respect to illuminants is the need for lamps of longer life and purer light than the arc and incandescent lamps now in vogue. The economy of these is not high enough. They are not really very superior to the best forms of gas, which for cheapness still holds its own.

With regard to the great fuel problem, it is well known that Mr. Edison is concentrating much of his attention on the higher economics of the use of coal. Coal is King to-day. The immediate task of scientists is to draw from this commodity something like its real value in work, so as to obviate the enormous waste involved in present methods. Mr. Edison declares that a bucketful of coal should drive an express-train from New York to Philadelphia, and a few tons be sufficient for the largest ocean steamship, whose bunkers must now hold thousands. The *Oceanic* consumes a ton of coal every three minutes, or about five hundred tons a day, during her voyage between New York and Liverpool. But a single pound of coal burned under perfect conditions would do as much work as the strongest hod-carrier climbing stairs or ladder with brick and mortar during a weary day of ten hours' working-time. At present we waste six sevenths of the value of coal. Our inventors will know no rest until they have found the furnace, the engine or the appliance, or whatever it may turn out to be, which will substitute absolute economy for this immense extravagance.

Both for domestic and for manufacturing purposes engineers and men of science are diligently studying the art of harnessing the direct rays of the sun. They anticipate the time when the world's supplies of coal, petroleum and other combustibles will be practically exhausted. Vast regions of the earth's surface are sunburnt to aridity, and everywhere the sun's heat is constantly deluging that surface with stores of latent potential energy which might be made available for the purposes of civilized humanity. Water-power and wind-power both derive their energy from the sun's rays, and many clever inventions yet unheard of will have for their special object the application of each of these sources of activity. But the defect in each case is the lack of certainty. Wind and tide are variable and intermittent. Therefore, scientists look with great expectations to the perfection of the solar engine, which was produced by Ericcson in an elementary form. Some day there will be discovered a method of gathering and storing the energy of the direct rays of the sun for use in producing a heat-motor. But the practical sun-engine is still among the "uninvented inventions."

Science will be more and more concerned with problems of food-supply. Here the chemist comes into evidence. Scientists predict wonderful results as the ultimate rewards of the research now going on quietly in many a laboratory. The way will be found of growing strawberries as large as fine apples, and raspberries and blackberries will be produced of such dimensions that one will suffice for the fruit course of each person. Cranberries, gooseberries and currants will be as large as oranges. One cantaloup will supply a large family. Melons, cherries, grapes, plums, apples, pears and peaches will be seedless. All varieties of summer fruits will be of such a hardy nature that they will be capable of storage all through the winter, as potatoes now are. Cheap native rubber will be grown, and will be harvested by machinery all over this country. Roses will be as big as cabbages, violets will attain the size of fine orchids, and a heart's-ease will be of the sunflower magnitude. There will be practised the constant transfer of the perfume of any scented flower to another that is naturally inodorous. Plants will be rendered microbe-proof. How will all these wonders in culture be achieved? By the discovery of new methods of applying electric agency in glass gardens, so that at one and the same time currents will be passed through the soil to make plants grow faster and larger, and also to exterminate weeds and to destroy bacteria; while plants will be bathed all night in electric-light, to stimulate their progress. All this will be done, but the way to bring it to pass has yet to be invented.

This further brings up the question of the supply of nitrogen, that infinitely abundant elementary gas on which agriculture is absolutely dependent. Some way must be devised of restoring to their old fertility the vast worn-out fields of the world. The agricultural chemist declares that fixed nitrogen is indispensable for this vital redemption. Now, nitrogen, though everywhere so plentifully diffused, is exceedingly difficult to fix. It forms in bulk and weight three fourths of the atmosphere, yet it challenges man to bring it into subjection. To catch the elusive and flirtatious floating nitrogen is one of the most cherished objects of present-day explorers among Nature's secrets. Experiments conducted under the direction of William H. Bauldin, Jr., formerly of Baltimore, seemed to promise a solution of this problem, when a disastrous explosion ended the life of the chief engineer of the works. Thus the question is still in abeyance, but undoubtedly, before the great niter-beds of Chili and Peru are exhausted, some means will have been devised of making nitric acid cheaply from the air.

One of the dreams of medical men is likely to be realized in the near future. Few drugs will be swallowed or taken into the stomach unless needed for the direct treatment of that organ itself. The methods of administration of healing medicaments will be revolutionized in the days of our great-grandchildren. With the aid of diagnosis by X-rays, and by the medium of electric currents, drugs will be applied to various organs through the skin and flesh, and the treatment will be painless. It will be easy with the instruments that are certain to be invented—of which the microscope, the photographic camera and the X-ray apparatus are but the pioneers—for the pathologist, physician and surgeon to see the interior of the body and to explore its recesses as it is now to survey the exterior. Furthermore, food will be made for travelers in the pemmican style known to our North American Indians. All kinds of nutriment will be condensed into tabloids containing in very tiny compass the essentials to sustain life in full vigor for long periods.

The inventors of the future will revolutionize the culinary department. The kitchen and scullery will no longer be repellent or suggestive of domestic slavery. Drudgery will be a thing of the past for the cook. Electricity will be the cheap handmaid of the dining-room, for the electric current will be utilized with small expense, while when the new and miracle-working metal called radium is better known, and possessed in sufficient quantities, agencies for supplying both heat and light will be available which are as yet unthought of.

Though the means are as yet undevised, there will be no intermission of research until everybody can see and hear everybody without the slightest regard to intervals of space, no matter how great. The coming age will demand wireless telephone and telegraph circuits which will span the circuit of the globe, so that it will be as easy to telephone from New York to Pekin as from New York to Brooklyn. Our descendants will not be satisfied if the scientists of the next generation do not enable them with greatest facility and economy to witness by perfected kinematographs the weddings of any of their friends at the antipodes, the battles being fought on the other side of the world, and the races of horses, yachts and boats in every land. Balloons will rise high above contending armies, and with automatic cameras will "snap-shot" the whole scene, bringing down forthwith to the respective generals perfect pictures of their enemies' forces.

There is much to be done in the way of improving transportation. In this sphere invention has but initiated its attempts. Many observers imagine that aërial navigation is to be the realm of immediate scientific advancement, but though the aëronaut is one of the foremost of present-day scientific sensationalists, the engineer knows that he really holds the field. The possibilities of navigating the air, although its navigation is sure to come, offer to practical minds a far less inviting field of achievement in the lines of transportation than the necessary improvements on terra firma. On land and sea vehicles for travel will be in use which will render all those known at this hour only eligible for a museum of antique and obsolete curiosities. The automobile has come, but that is only pointing out the way of possibility. So far as velocity is concerned, the automobile has accomplished wonders, but it attains speed only on deadly conditions. What inventors have to contrive is a train that will cover two miles a minute, and cross the American continent at that rate without danger of disaster. They have to produce a ship which will cross from Liverpool to New York in three days. They must ponder the problems involved until they can solve the difficulty of avoiding collisions by the invention of automatic stoppage of trains and ships the moment there is any danger ahead.

One of the most essential items for the inventor of the near future to supply is a cheap and practical storage-battery. This is a desideratum which so far has baffled the electrical student. An inventor who can supply the want here indicated will find his fortune assured. He will be the magician of his time, for he will inaugurate a new era for the electric railway and accelerate the day of electric propulsion of long-distance trains for mail and passengers.

Inventions are now being waited for which will bring science and art into closer relationship. Color-photography affords a most eligible field for the scientist's ingenuity. A very feeble beginning has been made in this direction, which affords a mere hint of stupendous possibilities. Perhaps the thing most eagerly looked for is the actual portrait of an absent friend transmitted by telegraph. Allied to color-photography is the difficulty of producing multicolor printing. The best printing-presses yet invented can print in three colors at one impression; but the presses of the future will transfer to paper imprints embodying perhaps a dozen different tints.

This allusion to art colors brings to mind that the manufacturers of dress-fabrics have not yet been enabled to produce delicate hues in their stuffs which defy the influence of sun or rain. Inventors will yet produce expedients for preventing every delicate art shade from fading, so that all dress-colors will be "fast." Moreover, the mercerizing process will be so perfected that cheap cotton and wool fabrics cannot be distinguished from silk.

In all departments of common every-day life there are outcries for new products of the inventor's genius. Take, for instance, the solicitude of manufacturers of popular and genuine beverages for a non-refillable bottle. One of the most notorious of the swindles of the commercial world is the great "wine fake." For many a year the proprietors of the vineyards of Germany, France, Italy, Spain, Portugal and Hungary have complained with no little bitterness of the adulteration of their choicest wines by unscrupulous middlemen. They therefore ask for a bottle which can be used only once—that is to say, when it is filled in their own cellars at the vineyards. Distillers, manufacturers of medicine and makers of choice perfumery all suffer immense loss through the lack of some receptacle which when once its contents have been poured out can never be refilled with an inferior article and sold as the original.

Most interesting of all, because of their bearing on philanthropy, are the discoveries connected with the operation of certain attributes of radium, the remarkable element which has created so memorable a sensation in scientific circles. This astonishing substance gives out both heat and light to an almost incredible degree of intensity. It holds out hopes of giving to the blind at least some possibility of visual perception. If a tube containing radium is held to the closed eye or against the temples, a very powerful impression of light is produced. This is supposed to be due to the action of the radium on the phosphorescence in the pupil of the eye, and possibly also to its action on the nerve-centers. It is reported from Berlin that Doctor Lunden by means of the action of radium rays has actually restored the sight of two blind Russian boys, enabling them to see more or less clearly.

Prize-fighting will be such an elevated sport that no state will need to pass laws forbidding it.

Eloping young ladies will go up the ladder, instead of down.

The Advertising Sign Fiends will become more audacious than ever.

We may even hope to have *real* "Rapid Messenger Boys."

USE BIGGS SOAP

DISTRICT MESSENGER SERVICE

A great saving for racing men — Every horse-owner his own jockey.

The Air-Ship will revolutionize the exploration business — No more hardships; everything safe and comfortable.

J. Ottmann, Lith. PUCK BUILDING, N. Y.

WHEN THE AIR-SHIP IS PERFECTED.

THE FIRST VOYAGE BY AIRSHIP OVER MANHATTAN

A. Roy Knabenshue, in his dirigible balloon, Toledo No. 2, rising from his starting point at Sixty-second Street and Central Park West. Mr. Knabenshue made two flights from this point—the first, on August 20, to Forty-second Street, and the second, on the 23d, to Eighteenth Street, returning in each case to Central Park. The airship is sixty-two feet long and sixteen feet in diameter. It weighs 200 pounds complete and is supported by 7,000 cubic feet of hydrogen gas. The gas bag is of Japanese silk and weighs 65 pounds. The vessel is drawn along by a two-bladed propeller in the bow, driven by a 10-horsepower gasoline engine weighing 92 pounds

A FLYING MACHINE THAT ACTUALLY FLIES

The Brothers Wright succeed where Langley failed, in driving an airship that is not a balloon

TO SAIL three miles through the air at a speed of eight miles an hour against a breeze blowing twenty-one miles an hour is the most notable achievement in flying-machine experiments. Three years ago, two brothers named Wright, of Dayton, Ohio, went down among the sandhills of the North Carolina coast. They were expert mechanics, and brought their own tools and machinery. They had studied the experiments of flying-machine inventors here and abroad. They were going to put their study and ingenuity to practical use. They tried the "multiple wing" machine with its large number of sails. Then they turned to the gliding machine invented by Octave Chanute, and modified it to their purpose. Their first machine carried one of them three hundred and sixty feet, and after another year a new apparatus sailed an eighth of a mile. Last year they made changes, and added a gasoline engine and propellers, with the final successful test late in December as a result.

The machine, in which the operator lies at full length, is in some ways like a box kite with a rudder instead of a tail. The framework is covered with cloth at top and bottom. It is buoyant enough of itself to float its own weight and that of one man. During their three years of experiments, the brothers had added considerably to their knowledge of air-currents and of the resistance of canvas. Keeping these things in view, they designed and built their propelling apparatus. One propeller, revolving horizontally, is placed underneath the centre of the machine's body. The other is like the screw of a steamship, whirling vertically at the rear. The gasoline engine, with 4-inch pistons and 16-brake horsepower, operates at will either or both of the propellers. The one beneath helps to hold up the machine; the one at the rear drives it in the direction toward which the operator points it.

The machine is launched from a hill by merely "pushing off." It can be pointed in any direction and can be landed at will. It is strong enough to stand the strain of repeated trips, and its wings have been tested with six times the load they carried last month. The horizontal position of the man in the machine saves about one-half horsepower, by diminishing the wind resistance. The Wrights have used larger cloth surfaces than their predecessors. Their successful machine has three hundred square feet of cloth. Its wings measure more than forty feet from tip to tip, and it weighs, entirely equipped, about seven hundred pounds. The achievement marks an impressive step in advance toward the every-day navigation of the air.

The test in question was made at Kitty Hawk, in North Carolina, in the neighborhood of which place the machine was launched from the top of a sand dune. The aeroplane first took a downward course, but, as the propeller under the engine increased its revolutions, began to rise slowly and steadily into the air. When the machine was sixty feet above the ground, the rear propeller began to do its work, sending the "flyer" forward against the wind. Wilbur Wright was able to steer his craft as he pleased, with the aid of the horizontal steering-gear—as shown in our illustration—and after going three miles brought the machine gently to the ground without difficulty or mishap.

Professor Langley and Maxim experimented along the lines of a real flying machine, as distinct from the dirigible balloons of Santos-Dumont and Lebaudy. But the eminent scientist and the brilliant inventor, with fortunes at their disposal, have not been rewarded with the success of these amateurish mechanicians. A machine, not a kite, that propels itself against a strong wind, is under steerage control, and lands without converting itself into a scrap heap, is something new under the sun.

Carrying the machine uphill to the starting point

Taking a trial flight of a few yards

The aeroplane in position for "pushing off"

The machine in midair, traveling against the wind

The Aeroplane leaving the Ground at the Beginning of its Flight

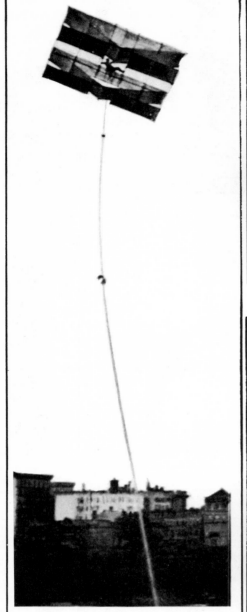

The Ludlow Aeroplane, with Hamilton, an Aeronaut, aboard, at an Elevation of Three Hundred Feet

The Aeroplane making one of its Careening Swoops just after its Rise

The Rescue of Hamilton from the Aeroplane after it had settled in the Middle of the North River

THE TRIAL FLIGHT OF THE LUDLOW MAN-CARRYING AEROPLANE IN NEW YORK

After many hazardous and unsatisfactory trials ashore, the Ludlow man-carrying aeroplane, "Air-ship No. 4," was recently successfully flown over the North River, New York, in tow of a tug. Charles Hamilton, an aeronaut, went up in the kite to an altitude of several hundred feet. So long as the tug maintained its speed and course the "air-ship" flew, but the tug was forced to come about, and the kite and its passenger were subsequently dipped into the river, but without serious mishap. The inventor hopes to adapt the kite to observation purposes in war-time, the device to be towed by a swift torpedo-boat

Photographs by Peter A. Juley

Skeptics and Believers

Rear-Admiral George W. Melville, Chief Engineer of the United States Navy, has declared: "If God had intended that man should fly He would have given him wings." He refers to all the airship business as a "fake," and says that it has been so since it was started, two hundred years ago.

Professor Langley's work is quite familiar to Americans and to scientists all over the world. He has made a life study of the problem, and several years ago he wrote in one of the official publications of the United States Government: "I wish to put on record my belief that the time has come for these questions to engage the serious attention not only of engineers but of all interested in the possibly near solution of a problem, one of the most important in its consequences of any which has ever presented itself in mechanics, for this solution cannot longer be considered beyond our capacity to reach."

Since those words were written there have been numerous flying machines which were announced as successful, but which subsequently failed to carry out their claims. Some of them — machines such as the Maxim machine, which is an arrangement of planes — made short flights, and others descended from high elevations without always killing their inventors, although there were a few tragedies.

When All the Air is Cornered

IT IS reported that Professor Moore, the Chief of the Weather Bureau, has invented a cold-air stove which, when charged with certain unnamed substances, will give off from the bottom a constant current of air at about 36 degrees, and keep the room in which it is placed at a temperature of between 60 and 70, no matter how hot the day. The invention comes with particular appropriateness from the Weather Bureau; disappointed so often in not seeing its predictions fulfilled, it has wisely decided not only to promise but to deliver the goods. With all the old ways of warming the air, with the new stove for cooling it and with the National Irrigation Bill become a law, we seem to have the weather at our mercy. There is still excessive rainfall to be contended with, but this is not a common occurrence; besides, there are umbrellas.

The announcement of the cold-air stove is a reminder that never before was the air we breathe so freely tampered with. Is there, soon, going to be any air to breathe? Apparently the cold-air stove does not consume air; it simply cools it; and if we wish we can warm it up again with an old-fashioned stove in the next room. But the manufacture of liquid air uses gaseous air in quantities, and now it is announced that at Niagara Falls it is proposed, with the abundant electric supply, to make nitrates from air for fertilizers and other purposes. It is even predicted that the time is approaching when the wheat fields of the world will be fertilized by nitrates produced directly from the atmosphere.

But to fertilize the wheat fields of the world is going to take up a prodigious quantity of air. Where is the air coming from? Is Nature turning out air all the time, or was the world at the start provided with its air stock, and do we breathe the same air made use of by Adam, with a slight loss of Eden flavor and a touch of soft-coal smoke? If the last is true some genius must soon invent an air-making process, and air plants will have to be set up here and there. The time may even come when we shall get our air from the corner grocery, put up in convenient parcels. But, if the wheat crop is trebled by the air-drawn fertilizers, bread will be cheap and we can afford to buy air. Think, however, of the possibilities of an air trust, or a strike at the air-works!

The Man and the Machine

THIS is an age of automatic devices. There is an ever-increasing tendency toward the elimination of the human factor from all possible problems. Little more than a century ago a boy stood by the cylinder of the engine and opened the escape-valve after every stroke of the piston. Then some one discovered that the opening and closing of the valve could be made automatic. This not only did away with the need for a boy but served the purpose much better, for the boy might forget or delay or move too soon or not soon enough, while the machine never made a mistake.

Right here is the value of the automatic arrangement. It is to be trusted. The banker is never quite certain that his cashier will not betray him, but the automatic time-lock is to be trusted to a finish. The tradesman may make a mistake in giving change, but the automatic register does not. Railroads once left the manipulation of switches and signals to their telegraph operators. Now and then one would go to sleep or delay or forget, and when he did something undesirable happened. Hence the railroads adopted the automatic arrangements now in use. The automatic switch is never open at the wrong time, and the automatic signal never says "Safe" when it should say "Danger."

Mathematically speaking, the reliability of any system of enterprise varies inversely as the human element involved, or directly as the mechanical element. Here lies the difficulty of conducting a government or an army or a large business. It is all human. The parts will persist in acting differently and less accurately than do those of a machine.

It is probable that more senseless things are said over defects in government arising from the imperfections of human service than over almost any other one thing. From blaming this official or that we come gradually to blame the whole lot. And since this element of human uncertainty is in any given number of persons a constant quantity — something that may be counted on as surely as the death calculation of an insurance company — our railing at officials in general is railing at humanity, and that is very unphilosophical. Then, too, we suggest all sorts of senseless expedients in the way of laws for the improvement of the departments of government and of the branches of politics. Some men's minds are built on geometric principles. They would have everything done by law. They would have laws not only for keeping the public in the way of righteousness but for making the officials enforce those that exist. The failure of all such propositions is due to the fact that those lines of activity must be carried out, not by machines which act automatically, but by men who never act just alike and seldom quite normally.

ABOUT the biggest thing of the new century's opening was the problem of signaling to the people of Mars. One imaginative scientist thought he received a message from the people in that far-away planet, and thousands and thousands of columns were printed showing how it might be possible to let the Martians know that there was another ball rolling around the sun and that it was having its joys and sorrows, its progress and its wars. But the whole sensation was short-lived.

In the matter of communication, it is important not so much to reach another planet, but to stimulate the district messenger boy and to improve the telephone service so that one need not spend all day helloing in order to get a five-minutes' conversation.

History by Snap-Shot

SNAP-SHOT history! The very idea seems odd; yet many of those who are idly snap-shotting at what goes on about them are providing the strongest and most vital historical material for those who, many generations hence, are to write of the conditions and happenings of the opening years of the twentieth century.

How Americans under the administration of President Roosevelt ate, how they walked, how they met each other on the street, how they dressed—all such matters will be before the future historian in little four-by-fives that shall be irrefragable proofs. How pleased we should be if we of this twentieth century could have similar pictures showing social conditions of the time of the ancient stately Romans, of the seafaring Tyrians, of the early Britons.

How our Presidential conventions are held, how our Presidents walk, ride and jump fences, how our Senators engage in fisticuffing bouts, how our elections are carried on, how fires are fought, how railroad accidents occur, how ambassadors are received, how princely visitors are welcomed, how battles are fought—all these things will be pictured for the men of the future. And we must not overlook the fact that the happenings of to-day will, to the people of the future, be as full of interest as are to us the details of the life, the public events, and the battles, of the past—of which we have no snap-shots.

True, we already have, of some great men and women, and of great events, paintings by eminent hands, but we cannot be sure that the painters did not flatter their subjects, that they did not make homely people handsome, that they did not make foolish people look wise, that they did not, in picturing battles, follow imagination rather than fact, that they were not looking for a substantial reward when they flatteringly placed King Ironsword or General Pothelmet in the very centre of his army, cheering on his troops, while at the same time he is the target for every one of the enemy. Had the snap-shot been anciently in use such matters would have been authentically pictured once for all.

And how the snap-shot will prevent the growth of mysteries! How shap-shots would have made impossible some of the greatest mysteries of the past! We should have

had a snap-shot showing "the author of Hamlet in his study writing his new play, Richard the Third," and we should know whether it was really Shakespeare or Bacon; we should have had another snap-shot, perhaps taken through a keyhole, showing "the actual author of the Junius Letters, and how he works"; we should have had another showing the "Man with the Iron Mask fitting on a new one in his cell"; we should even learn, pictorially, who it really was that "struck Billy Patterson."

And, outside of mysteries, how delightful it would be to have, for example, a snap-shot of the Signers gathered about the table in Independence Hall; another, this one a flashlight, of course, which should incontrovertibly show whether or not Washington did really stand up so recklessly in his boat as he went over the Delaware; another showing precisely how Cæsar looked as he crossed the Rubicon; another picturing Romulus and Remus at their lupine luncheon. But the acts of the Cæsars and the Romuli, of the Shakespeares and the Washingtons, of the twentieth century, will be set forth in pictured truthfulness—that is, if the chemicals last.

How to Use a Telephone

By Angus S. Hibbard

General Manager
Chicago Telephone Company

THE man who knows how to use a telephone properly is comparatively a rare personage, and the observance of a few simple rules and suggestions in relation to telephone usage would accomplish, for any busy man, a great economy in money, time and vital energy.

The telephone has done more to lay bare a latent strain of belligerency in all mankind than any other feature of modern experience, and this element offers the greatest obstacle known to the universal success of telephone operation. But this attitude is not the only abnormal development attending the act of telephoning. A man refuses to recognize plain physical conditions that would be apparent to a child in the primary grades. What man of affairs would willingly give a second audience to a caller who turned his back to his host and directed his voice in a direction away from him? Yet the majority of business men keep their faces a foot or more from the telephone and turned away from the instrument. To expect satisfactory results under such conditions is preposterous. The lips should not be an inch away from the rim of the receiver and the voice should beat squarely upon the drum to which the little "sound hopper" leads. Give a telephone instrument a "square chance" and it will do its work, unless radically deranged or defective.

This, however, is not the main difficulty. It is only the symptom of the disease. Lack of mental focus is the real trouble, both in talking and hearing—or, in telephone parlance, in transmitting and receiving. If your thought is not concentrated on the transmission of your message you will not make yourself heard or hear what is said to you. This is where a failure to realize that you are holding actual conversation is apparent. No person understands this phase of telephonic trouble better than the operator of long-distance lines, where conversations are important and comparatively expensive, and time is limited. He knows that, in case the two on the line do not readily hear each other, he must make each realize he is not talking into a hole in the end of an iron arm, but speaking into the ear of a man.

Shocking a Man into Attention

Sometimes it takes a sound shock to effect this focus of mental faculties. Once, when hard pushed, I resorted to a desperate expedient, which demonstrated this point with indisputable force. That was several years ago, when prominent men were not so accustomed as at present to use the telephone. They generally delegated the task to their assistants—a practice now much in vogue in England, where it is well-nigh impossible personally to engage the head of an establishment in telephonic conversation.

But in case of calls on the long-distance wires the conversations were generally of a confidential nature. Therefore the "parties," although not thoroughly accustomed to using the telephone, must be made instantly to understand each other, despite the added disadvantages of the "long range." At that time I was in charge of certain long-distance lines in the East, and was called upon to engineer a conversation of the utmost importance between a Baltimore capitalist and a Boston financier. Time was an essential in

the transaction, which involved thousands of dollars.

The Boston man seated himself at the instrument, in my office, and waited for me to get the Baltimore capitalist properly started. At the first sound of the latter's voice I knew he was "not there," mentally speaking. Then I resorted to the usual expedients to impress on him the realization that he was talking with a person instead of at an inanimate object.

"Don't hear a word! This thing is——" he was saying.

"I'm not a thing, Mr. Smith," I interrupted; "I'm a man, about thirty years old, prematurely bald, with dark hair and gray eyes. I can hear you because I know you're a real, live man doing business with your voice, right now. I can hear you because I'm thinking right to the point—and you're that point! Now listen to Mr. Jones."

But still I heard an irascible repetition of: "Can't hear! Can't hear! Better give the thing up and telegraph. No use trying this old thing! It's no account. I tell you I can't hear a word!"

Meantime my Boston man was growing restless and excited. Every moment was of great value in the affair. Turning to him I said:

"If I were to tell Mr. Smith that he lies he'd learn how to hear every word you say in one second. Shall I do it?"

"Yes," was the quick response; "and I'll square it completely, later."

Very clearly I spoke into the receiver the words:

"Mr. Smith, you lie!"

"What's that, sir?" came the instantaneous answer. "You call me a liar? Why, I'll, I'll——"

"You will understand," I interrupted, "that I mean nothing of the kind—only that you *do* hear distinctly every word I say and you are proving it. Now listen, quick, to Mr. Jones!"

He had no difficulty in hearing the Boston financier and the day was saved—simply because he was shocked into realizing that he was not talking at a thing, but conversing *with a man*.

Women are keenest to grasp the personality of the invisible conversationalist. A telephone is not a dead thing to them. They bow and smile into it and even stop before the mirror to touch up their hair when about to answer a call on a telephone in their own rooms.

Only a few days ago a man in Chicago decided to give his wife a novel surprise on her birthday anniversary. He arranged that, at a certain moment, her mother, whom she had not seen for years, should be at the long-distance telephone office in Philadelphia and should call up the daughter in Chicago. There was a telephone in the Chicago house and the husband answered the prearranged call. Turning from the instrument he said to his wife:

"Helen—here's your mother on the wire in Philadelphia."

The wife seated herself at the instrument and heard the familiar voice of her mother. It uttered one word: "Daughter!"

Suddenly the young matron in Chicago gripped the instrument and poured out her heart in the response: "Oh, mother! mother!"

Then, as she heard the sob that came over the wire from the aged mother, she answered in kind, still keeping the receiver at her ear. Speaking literally, those two women cried to each other until the tolls amounted to fifteen dollars. Later they both said that it was the sweetest experience they had known since their long separation began! Nothing could more effectively demonstrate the sympathetic possibilities of the telephone or better illustrate the vital point of realizing the personality behind the voice.

Telephones in the Country

A QUIET revolution is taking place in Western country life, which promises to accomplish results within a year more important and far-reaching than any since the advent of the transcontinental railroads. Already the pioneer life of the isolated farmer has disappeared and the tide of industrial and educational advance has swept over the Northwest. The national telephone system, which until recently extended its arms only to the large cities, has within a few months entered the houses of thousands of Western farmers and bound together city and country, producer and consumer, in bonds of actual contact and constant communication.

To the economist the results of this extension through the rich farm lands of the Northwest are of most profound interest, and must be the basis of an entire revision of the theories of the relations between producer and consumer. The immobility of the country is destroyed at a blow, and the farmer is raised from a passive agency to an aggressive economic force.

To the sociologist the results are no less important, as the telephone does away with the seclusion of rural life, binds together scattered communities, creates social interests, and destroys the barrier between city and country. Henceforth the country is but a vast suburb, in touch with the metropolis of its neighborhood, unified by the voice of one leader.

It is only within the past year that the farmer has opened his eyes to the possibilities of the telephone, but since he has recognized them there has been such a demand upon the telephone companies that it has been impossible to fill the orders, and local geniuses have built lines out of fence wire and china knobs. No farmer is considered up to date without his telephone. In the early morning the rattle of the bell arouses him to the day's work, and he hastens to care for his cattle. After breakfast he calls the post office several miles away, and inquires for his mail. There he is sure to hear the news of the town and to have a talk with some of the gossips of the place.

On the great ranches of the Southwest a use of the telephone more startling and really novel has been made. There, in the past few years, the vast free range of the early days has been checkered by the dreaded wire fence. Across the old trails of ante-railroad days, around the green-edged springs where wild herds used to water, and about the choicest pastures of the range, the wire fence—the enemy of cowboy and hunter, of wild beast and roving cattle—has drawn its magic circle. The ranchman of to-day has made this dreaded wire do him a noble service. He has made of it a line of communication across the barren hills from cattle round-up or sheep-dip to the ranch-house. He is a strange mingling of the old West and the new West, this rancher with the telephone.

All the forces of rural society are organized and controlled by the little wire which bobs over the hills and down the shady lanes. Through the telephone it seems inevitable that the farmer will assume a new economic position. Keeping in touch with the market, he is able to dispose of produce directly to the city dealer or to the consumer without the assistance of any middleman. Fluctuations in the market will be felt immediately by the producer, and he will be able to prevent any advantage being taken of him. He may talk to his town buyer and to his city broker the same hour and sell his produce at the top of the market.

This was recently shown in the broom-corn district of Illinois in a most graphic way. This district, which lies in the southern part of the State, was visited by buyers who offered sixty dollars per ton for broom-corn. This was the ruling price at the end of the previous season, and was generally accepted. The buyers had almost covered the district, buying the entire output, when an official of the telephone company, quick to see the possibilities of the corner, caused the farmers who had telephones to be notified that the price had risen and that they had better consult the market. These more enterprising farmers consulted the magnates of Troy, Ohio, the centre of the broom-corn market, and, as a result, sold their crop for four times the price paid to their neighbors, two hundred and forty dollars a ton. This lesson of progress has sunk deep into the broom-corn district, and, needless to say, every farmer in the county has been convinced of the practical value of the telephone.

—Wilbur Wheeler Bassett.

Talk Preserved by Celluloid

The final perfecting, after much travail by inventors, of the celluloid record cylinder for phonographs, has opened up entirely new fields of usefulness for the talking machine. It will soon be widely utilized for advertising purposes, thanks to this new invention—an idea much thought of hitherto, but which could not be carried out owing to the perishable character of the waxen tubes. One man, for example, wished to construct a talking crow, which would utter exclamatory remarks regarding his wares, but it was found that the record cylinder inclosed in the bird's stomach became indistinct at the end of a week or ten days. A well-known company, a few years ago, put some talking dolls on the market, and they spoke very intelligibly, but their conversational powers lasted so short a time that their manufacture was discontinued.

The celluloid cylinder is made in a very simple way. An electrotype is made of the wax record and from this a perfect impression is taken in the celluloid. The resulting cylinder of celluloid is practically unbreakable—a great advantage.

The customer who opens the door of a shop will thereby pull a string that actuates a phonograph, which will yell out a few suggestions as to accessible bargains. A man who operates a cigar-cutter on a tobacconist's counter will quickly discover that he has let loose a mechanical voice, which cries: "Hello! Try the Li Hung Chang five-cent cigar!" It is believed that this sort of advertising will be excellent for trade, inasmuch as, while a person may not read a sign, he cannot help hearing the howl of the phonograph.

One of the novelties in phonographs is an automatic instrument which enables a person, after dropping a nickel into a slot, to make a choice among half a dozen or more cylinders by pushing the button controlling the one he wants. In this manner one machine is made to do the duty now performed by a number. Another newly patented contrivance has a panorama attachment which shows a series of photographs as the customer gazes through an eye-hole. The story belonging to each picture is told by the talking machine in a sort of running commentary, the arrangement being such that the verbal description is given coincidently with the exhibition of each photograph.

The reproducer now in use is a tiny ball of sapphire, which is not entirely satisfactory, for the reason that, owing to its shape, it does not go down to the bottom of the record-track when the latter happens to make a sharp cut. The inventor thinks that he has found a great improvement for this in a small cylinder of sapphire, which is drawn along the track and enters the deepest parts of it, thus making a much more perfect reproduction of the sounds. In fact, the improvement is so great that a little cylinder gives as good a reproduction as has been obtainable hitherto with a big cylinder. Every one may not be aware that the records are made with a little rod of sapphire that cuts a path one two-thousandth of an inch deep.

The Age of Wireless Miracles

IF THE enthusiasts on the subject of the wireless transmission of electricity were to be believed we should feel ourselves on the verge of a revolution in all the conditions of life. Telegraphing, telephoning, lighting lamps, steering torpedoes and exploding mines at a distance without wires have already been accomplished, and the inventors tell us that these things can be done hundreds and even thousands of miles away. They say that the earth is a vast reservoir of electricity, and that when we know how to tap it we can carry little instruments in our pockets and make our power felt as if by magic wands in any direction and at any distance. The miracles of Bulwer Lytton's Vril seem within our grasp.

But it is not necessary to believe all that these enthusiasts tell us to see that we are on the eve of great changes. The things that have already been accomplished are enough to prove that, even if improvements stop short. For instance, consider the meaning of that incident at sea the other day when the Lucania and the Campania talked to each other in mid-ocean, a hundred and seventy miles apart, and a passenger on the westbound ship sent a message to a friend in Philadelphia which was transmitted from the eastbound vessel by wireless telegraphy to Ireland and thence by cable to America, enabling the Philadelphian to be at the dock in New York when his friend's ship came in.

That means that we already have a weapon that can conquer all the dangers of fogs, darkness and mistaken observations at sea. It means that in war it will be impossible henceforth for a fleet to drop out of sight as Cervera's squadron did in 1898, but that a hostile squadron can be traced with the help of relays of scouts from one side of the Atlantic Ocean to the other. It means that every group of islands in the world can be made a unit, as the Hawaiian group is already, without the expense of laying cables. It means that telegraph and telephone monopolies will be enormously impaired.

Draw a circle two hundred miles in diameter in any of the more densely populated parts of the country and see what a tremendous field there is for a device that has already proved its ability to cover such an area. The revolution may not be so great as the inventors predict, but that there will be a revolution is clearly manifest. And it is already upon us.

—SAMUEL E. MOFFETT.

Bad Form in Courtship

WHEN the typewriter first came out divers courageous young men tried it in communicating with the ladies of their choice, but, so far as the records go, always with disastrous results. Even the married man who ventures to address his wife on the machine takes his chances, and is usually brought to see his error. There is a suggestion of "Your esteemed favor of the 24th inst. received and contents noted" about the typewritten letter which will not down. As for the telephone, it seems scarcely credible that any man should ever have tried a proposal over it; but cases are not wanting, such is the hardihood of youth. These instances, however, statisticians note, all occurred when the telephone was new, and it need not be recorded that in every case the misguided man (let us not call him lover) soon found himself helloing alone, and met the information from "central" that "the party has rung off." Though, after all, the telephone still has its important functions in courtship; as a means of ascertaining the views of the lady's father it must ever remain a deserving favorite.

Of course, in the case of wireless telegraphy, if the lover had a private plant which he was capable of working personally, and the lass was similarly equipped, perhaps any objection to the device for courtship purposes might disappear; but this at present is out of the question. The time may come when every man will be his own wireless telegrapher, and perhaps wear an extensible pole down the back of his neck which he can project at pleasure, and flash messages to the man across the street. Conversation, with the wasteful wear and tear on the vocal organs, may be done away with, and we may yet sit about a room, each clicking off his wireless remarks from his own pole.

But this is of the future. At present the young man in love would do well to avoid wireless courtship.

The X-Ray a Wonderful Aid to Science.

How the Photographs Are Taken—New Method of Illuminating the Body.

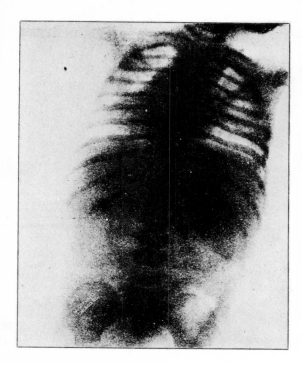

X-RAY PHOTOGRAPH OF 6-INCH HAT PIN IN STOMACH.

The ordinary light that we are accustomed to, makes glass, water and air transparent. But there is another light which does not make glass transparent, but which renders diaphanous every other substance except lead. This is the X-ray. It has been a wonderful revelation to surgical science in that it makes the human body pervious to light, enabling the surgeon to see and locate any foreign substance. We give herewith the picture of a little girl showing a hat pin she had swallowed. She resides in Indiana and her life was saved by means of the X-ray.

It is easier to take the picture of a thin person than a fleshy one with an X-ray machine. To take the picture the negative plate is placed under the patient instead of in the camera. The plate, which in size corresponds to the portion of the body to be photographed, is laid flat on a board and the board rests on a common surgical chair. The person whose interior is to be photographed is laid flat on the negative plate, the board being placed between the the plate and the chair cushion to keep the former from breaking. An X-ray tube is then placed over the part of the body to be photographed. From this is extended the leading-in wires, which connect the tube with the static machine, the source of electrical energy. Thus the X-ray light is produced in the X-ray tube and to this light the patient is exposed from one-half to three minutes according to the density of the part of the body to be photographed. After the exposure the negative plate is developed by the ordinary photographic process.

Looking into the interior of a person with the eye, aided by a spy-glass, was made possible by the invention of W. C. Fuchs, manager of the Chicago X-ray laboratory. This is accomplished with the aid of salts, which when taken internally has a peculiar effect on the X-ray, causing it to brightly illuminate the stomach. The salts are by scientists called tongstate of calcium, barium platinum cyanide and uranium. The patient is made to drink a full glass of these salts dissolved in water. An X-ray machine is so placed as to cast its rays on the stomach. This causes the liquid to light up the interior of the stomach. An instrument called a cystoscope, which is a sort of telescope, fitted with a small mirror so that a person can see out at right angles to the end, is then pushed down the patient's throat into his stomach and the physician makes his examination. Formerly the cystoscope was used with a small electric light attached to its end, but the light grew so hot that the patient suffered great torture.

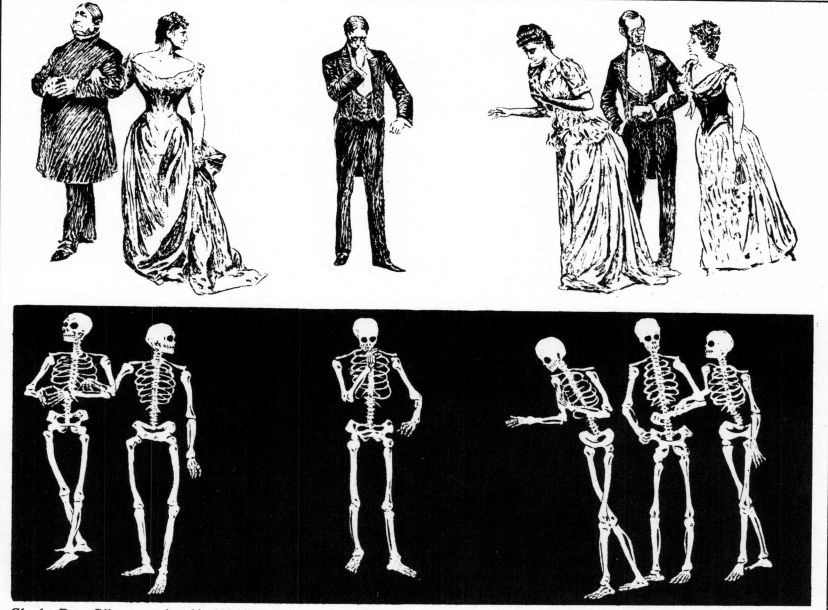

Charles Dana Gibson wondered in 1896 if a new kind of see-through photography (above) might result from Roentgen's discovery of x-rays.

EVOLUTION OF THE TALKING MACHINE

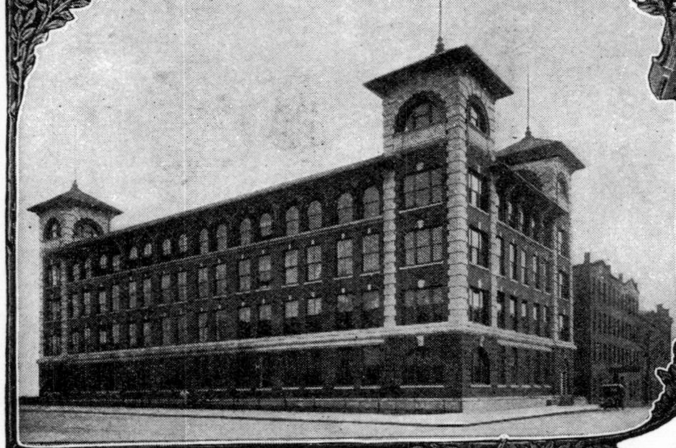

This building, containing the Executive Offices and Motor Factory, is the newest addition to the plant of the Victor Talking Machine Company.

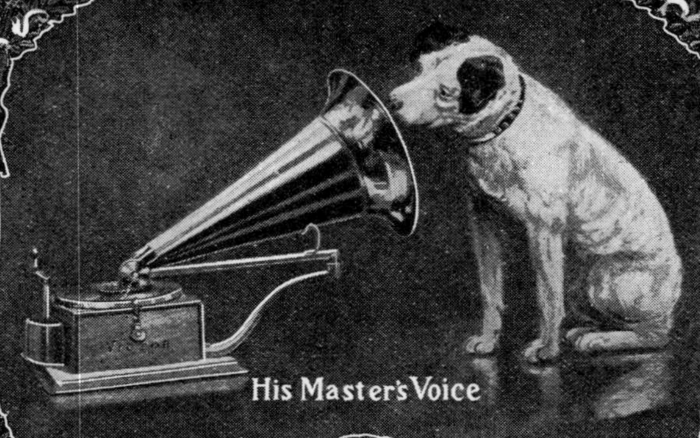

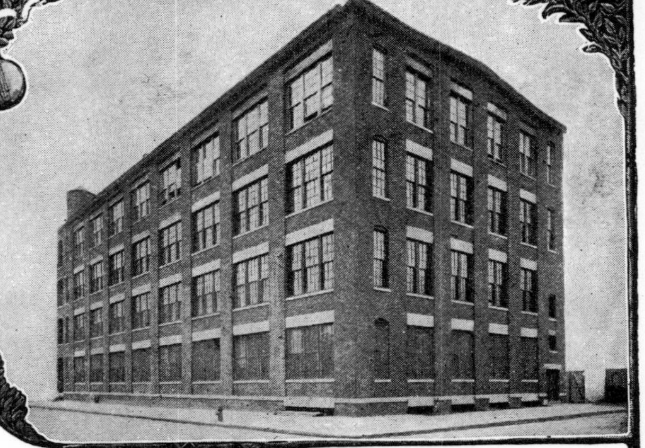

Warehouse and Shipping Department for the finished product of the Victor Talking Machine Company.

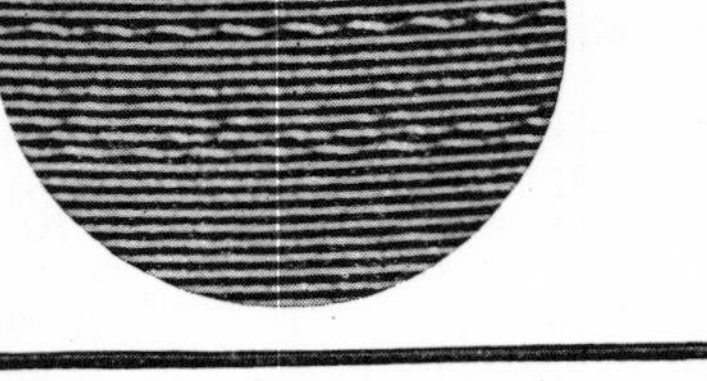

Photographic Enlargement of Victor Disk Sound Waves.

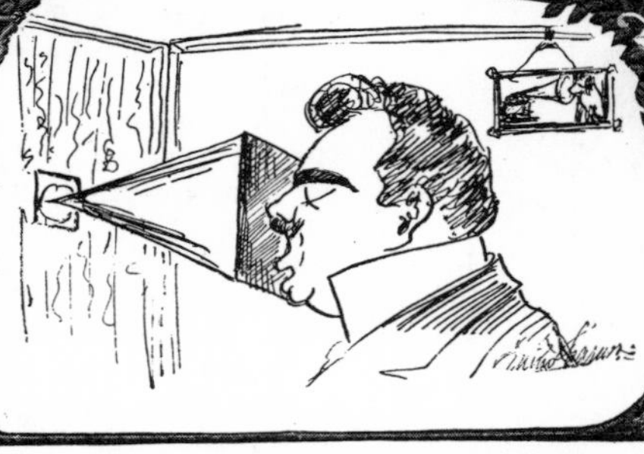

Car:cature of Caruso drawn by himself singing to a Victor Talking Machine.

SOUND is least understood of all the things which have baffled the brains of science. It is known that sound consists of vibrations or waves of air of greater density than the surrounding atmosphere, radiating from a common center of agitation like the concentric wavelets caused by dropping a pebble into a pool. But the laws which govern the vibrations and the exceptions under which they are modified have remained one of the inscrutable mysteries of nature. If an architect be asked to build an auditorium in which speech or music can be heard to advantage he does not know how to go about it. The auditorium when completed may have good acoustic properties or very bad; it is all a matter of luck. At Woodside and at Willow Grove Park in the suburbs of Philadelphia there are two band shells identical in size and design, planned by one architect and built of like material by the same carpenter. In one the acoustics are superb; in the other atrocious.

But inventive genius has at last stumbled upon a clue which promises to lead to the solution of the mystery of sound.

The clue is the talking machine.

It is as true as it is paradoxical that while the evolution of the talking machine is leading to a comprehension of the laws of acoustics that evolution has been possible only through a working knowledge of these same laws. Emil Berliner, the telephone inventor, cleared the way for achievement about twelve years ago when he produced a queer contrivance which he called the "gramophone," that possessed the remarkable power of receiving sounds and repeating them again at the will of the operator. A lively imagination could even fancy that it recognized in the gramophone record the particular voice which had made the sounds.

Eldridge R. Johnson, of Philadelphia, saw that Berliner's gramophone contained the vital principle through which alone the perfect talking machine could be produced. He also saw, or thought he saw, great commercial possibilities in the idea. So he purchased Berliner's patents, and with Leon F. Douglas, his brilliant Vice President, set to work to develop the talking machine. Possibly if he had realized the magnitude of the difficulties he was to encounter he might have left the undertaking to some one else.

Berliner had started in the right direction by evolving the theory that the right way to make a talking-machine record was on a flat disk instead of on a cylinder, because the stylus which writes the sound waves can only move up and down, or in and out of a cylinder. The deeper the stylus goes into the cylinder the greater the resistence it meets, so that there is always a tendency to cut short notes of a certain kind with the inevitable result that they are imperfectly rendered. On the other hand, a stylus which has only to swing from side to side has perfectly free play, for it meets exactly the same degree of resistence at every part of its movement. The laterally-moving stylus is thus able to record all shades of all tones with equal facility.

Perhaps this may be clearer if it be borne in mind that when sound is recorded by a talking machine the vibrations are caught in a bell-mouthed horn and poured through its little end, like water through a funnel, into a round box, the size of a five-cent box of blacking, filled with air. The outer lid of the box is a diaphragm of mica but 4-1000 of an inch thick, or about the thickness of a sheet of writing-paper. Attached to the center of this diaphragm by a dainty dab of cement is a delicately adjusted needle or stylus. When a sound wave is poured through the receiving horn against the cushion of air the diaphragm and the stylus attached to it are caused to vibrate in exact accord with the wave. The vibrations of the stylus are traced upon a plastic disk which revolves at a fixed speed in contact with its point, making an irregular spiral line. When the disk is filled with this spiral record it is called a "master record." It is hardened by a secret process, after which endless copies may be taken from it by another secret process. When one of these copies is placed in a talking machine and the stylus is caused to retrace the spirals, it vibrates exactly the same number of times per second as it did in making the lines. These vibrations are communicated through the diaphragm to the air cushion, thus repeating the sounds which were poured into the horn. Why? Well, some day after they have learned a great deal more about acoustics than any one now knows, perhaps the talking-machine experts may find out.

Meanwhile the above greatly enlarged photograph of a small section of a talking-machine record, which shows all that the inexperienced eye can hope to see of the mysterious tracings, may be found interesting. Those simple lines happen to be a photograph of a song by Melba. If the record were placed in a talking machine it would become the song itself in the living voice of the prima-donna.

Once the fundamental principle was pretty well understood the next step was to produce a motor to run the talking machine, so carefully regulated that it could be as absolutely depended upon as a chronometer, for any variation in speed causes a discord. Next it was necessary to learn at a cost of infinite experiment the exact size, shape, material and method of construction of the arm which connects the horn with the sound-box. Here, as elsewhere, trifles seemed to have an effect out of all proportion to their apparent importance. It was finally found that the best results could be obtained with an arm stamped out of a single piece of brass and swaged into shape without joint or seam. Other details in the seemingly simple mechanism which the inexperienced eye would never notice were worked out at the same high cost of time and toil, until at last the evolution of the talking machine had reached a stage where the product was considered worthy to make its public début as the Victor Talking Machine, under the auspices of the Victor Talking Machine Company, of Camden, New Jersey, of which Mr. Johnson is President, and Leon F. Douglas Vice President. While the Victor Company was developing the talking machine it was frequently obliged to fight legal battles to defend its rights in its many patents. These rights have been fully confirmed to the Victor Company, however, and their position today is well-nigh impregnable.

Inexhaustible patience and hypercritical pains were found to be as necessary in the making of Victor records as they were in the production of the talking machine itself. Every record is made in the presence of two, and often three, of the ablest musical critics in this broad land. If a reed squawks, or a trumpet blares, or a cornet piston sticks, or a singer accents a vowel in a high register, everything is stopped instantly, fresh disks are put in and a new beginning is made. Think of stopping Sousa's famous band right in the middle of a brilliant passage and compelling it to play the entire selection over again! No audience ever assembled would dare do such a thing, yet Sousa's band has been obliged to play one composition over four times before the talking machine would accept it as satisfactory. Even when the selection is rendered to the satisfaction of the jury of musical critics the performer is not excused until the record has been copied and played over several times, for the talking-machine record is more sensitive than any human ear and it may call attention to a fault which may necessitate the making of a new record. The other day a record of "The Angelus," played by the famous Victor Orchestra of twenty-three members, every man an artist, was rejected, because the talking machine revealed the fact that the second clarinet had run short of breath and skipped two notes. The fault was so trifling that even the musical jury had not noticed it at the time. Certainly the ordinary listener never would have detected it. It was necessary to have "Dear Old Georgia," the latest popular song craze, sung no fewer than fifteen times before the musical jury would accept a record as satisfactory. Nothing is ever accepted as "good enough"; every record must be the best that can be produced.

Such hypercritical care may seem to the outsider altogether unnecessary, yet it is the secret of a success which seems incredible. It looks like a deliberate sacrifice of one's reputation for veracity to assert that the specialists employed around the shops and laboratory not infrequently mistake the talking machine for the human voice, yet the assertion is true.

Melba, Sembrich, Homer, Calvé, De Lussan, Caruso, Scotti, Plançon, Campanari, Gadski, Ballistini, De Lucia, Crossley, Nuibo, Blauvelt and other famous stars have sung, and Kubelik and Maud Powell, the violinists, have played to make Victor records. It seems reasonable to assume that none of these great artists would have been willing to have their names connected with a talking-machine record unless it was a worthy reproduction of their actual voices, even when tempted by an offer of $35,000 for thirty songs, which was the price at which Caruso was secured. Melba didn't think the talking machine could amount to very much. But when she had been induced to listen to records by Sembrich and Caruso she went so far as to say that it might be a nice thing to send some of her best songs to her father in Australia. When she heard the records played she was so delighted she readily gave her consent to their sale—(for a consideration which made it necessary to set a price of $5 each on them). Kubelik played a violin obligato for Melba while she sang Gounod's "Ave Maria." When the Melba records reached Australia they were played to a delighted audience of four thousand persons, which included the best society of Melbourne.

Tamagno, the greatest of all tenors, is dead; but his voice still lives. An operator was sent to Tamagno's estate at San Remo to get some records. It required fourteen days to secure ten songs, for the great tenor would sing only what and when he chose.

Nordica paid the Victor Talking Machine the most beautifully poetic tribute it has ever received when she said:

"No, I cannot sing for the talking machine. If I were to have my voice recorded by it I should feel as if I were giving up a part of my soul."

When Pope Pius X decided to revive the use of the Gregorian chant the entire mass, by order of the Gregorian congress, was recorded by the Victor Talking Machine, and the records were sent to all the Catholic churches and institutions of the world that they might have in absolutely correct form the true liturgical music.

A prominent member of the American Dancing Masters' Association was engaged to give the correct tempo while a more notable assemblage of musicians than were ever before gathered for such a purpose played several long programmes of dance music. The records are quite loud enough for dancing and are already extensively used for that purpose, for they afford a far higher grade of music than was ever before available for dancing.

Patti, Calvé, Eames, Jean de Reszke, Melba, Sembrich and many other great artists, the Kings of England, Greece and Spain, the Emperors of Germany and Russia, and the Presidents of France and of Mexico, are all talking-machine enthusiasts.

It might reasonably be supposed that such an extraordinary popular and artistic hit as is shown in the story of the talking machine would be accompanied by a somewhat spectacular commercial success. But it does rather stagger one to learn that, starting practically at zero four years ago, the sales of Victor goods throughout the world have already reached the amazing total of $12,000,000 a year.

So great is the demand, in fact, that the one thousand employes housed in three buildings, with a total floor area of six acres, in Camden, New Jersey, to say nothing of a large laboratory and a cabinet shop in Philadelphia, an auxiliary plant in Newark and outside firms in New York and Hartford which manufacture special parts, find difficulty in supplying it. Yet only four years ago the Victor Talking Machine plant consisted of one corner of a little old machine shop doing a miscellaneous business in Camden, and it wasn't overcrowded at that. The entire plant was run by a twenty-horse-power engine; today one thousand horse-power is not sufficient.

Already the Victor Talking Machine is a scientific instrument through which great singers may have the whole world for an audience, and through which the present may speak in living accents to posterity. If the rate of evolution of the talking machine for the past four years be continued through the next decade what secrets may not be wrested from nature?

VICTOR TALKING MACHINE

Loud enough for dancing

The New Victor Dance Records

At last the perfect Record for Dancing ! It took us a long time and lots of money. Not so easy as it sounds to get the exact time and bring out the instruments and notes that produce perfect dance-rhythm, and yet have a

loud clear beautiful tone

Prof. Asher of the American Society of Professors of Dancing says :

"I have listened to the Victor Records for Dance Music and find the time to be perfect in every respect, and the records well adapted for dancing."

No more need of asking a friend to play the piano while the others enjoy their dancing. Better music and perfect time.

Between the dances, you can hear the greatest grand opera and light opera singers, and music of every kind.

Send for book of **Victor Dance Records.**

Victor Talking Machine

"His Master's Voice"

Victor Talking Machine Co Philadelphia
The original makers of the Gram-O-phone

IDEAS WORTH MILLIONS By Emile Berliner

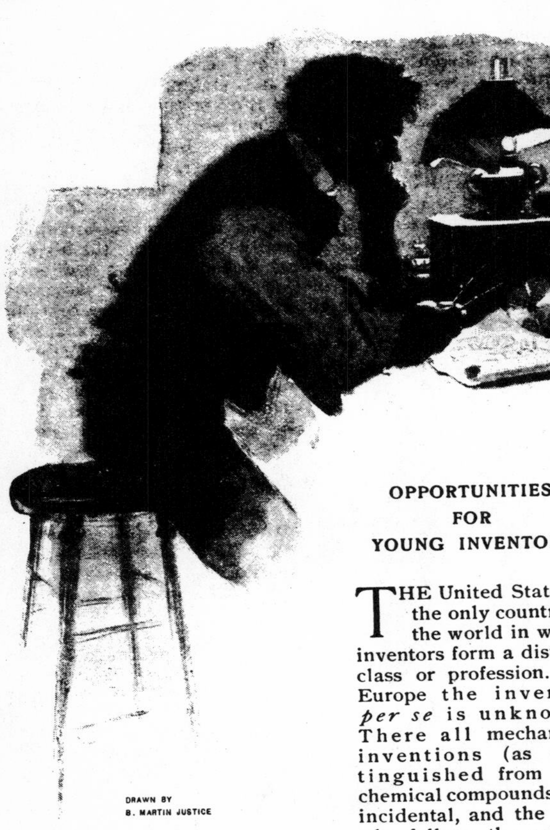

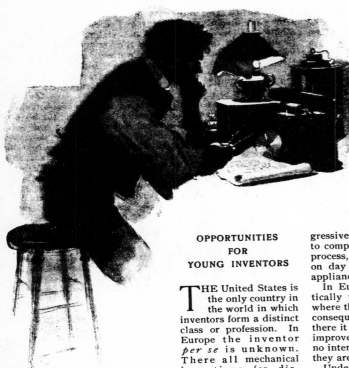

DRAWN BY B. MARTIN JUSTICE

OPPORTUNITIES FOR YOUNG INVENTORS

THE United States is the only country in the world in which inventors form a distinct class or profession. In Europe the inventor *per se* is unknown. There all mechanical inventions (as distinguished from new chemical compounds) are incidental, and the man who follows the calling of inventor as a distinct profession has no existence. With us, inventors have grown into a large class. Laboratories, as their workshops are known, have sprung up almost everywhere, and to-day there is no great manufacturing concern that has not in its employ one or more men of whom nothing is expected except the bringing out of improvements in machinery and methods.

The dominating position which the United States has taken in manufacturing is due primarily to the fact that we recognize the inventor to a greater extent than does any other country. Many reasons have been advanced by learned theorists, practical business men and experienced manufacturers to account for the tremendous prosperity which has come to this country. The credit has been ascribed to all sorts of causes, ranging from our superior political institutions to our superior soil and resources. As a matter of fact, this prosperity could not have come without the genius of the American inventor.

Marvels of Automatic Machinery

That we dominate the world in the iron and steel industry is due principally to the fact that our method of manufacturing and handling the raw material is entirely mechanical. From the time that the ore is taken out of the earth until the finished product is delivered, scarcely a human hand has been called into play except in the manipulation of levers and wheels. The American inventor has devised machinery for everything.

That America dominates in electricity and electrical appliances is due to the fact that our inventors have produced the most ingenious devices for applying a power that is still an unknown quantity.

That our crops are the greatest in the world is due to the fact that we were first in the field with a system of agricultural machinery that challenges the admiration of the world, and which, by cheapening all farm labor, enables us to control the cereal markets.

That we are the greatest nation of newspaper readers on the globe is to be attributed to the perfection of our printing presses and the ingenuity of our paper-working machinery. A spruce log is felled in the virgin forest; it is fed by machinery into the pulp-mill hoppers and comes out, at the other end of the mill, a roll of white paper several miles long. The human hand has not come in contact with the product from the time that the tree was cut down. The paper roll is swung by machinery on the web perfecting press, and comes out at the other end a magnificently printed newspaper, cut, pasted, folded. Thanks to typesetting and other machinery the cost of all this is so small that we can have this newspaper delivered at our breakfast table for one cent a copy.

And so it is in every pursuit in America. Yet with all the perfection we have reached and with all the progress that has been made we are barely on the threshold of what may be.

Encouragement Given by Our Patent Laws

But if the inventor has done all this for America, it is because America has done much for the inventor. It has been the wise policy of our Government to give him such protection as is elsewhere unknown. This is true particularly of the inventor of small improvements. The man who devises an improvement on a machine or a process already covered by patent is as fully protected and as much encouraged under our system as the original patentee. It is rarely that an invention, no matter how important, is perfect and unimprovable at the outset. Perfection comes only through practical application, and through the ideas of the men who are employed in handling the original invention. The workman at the bench who uses a tool is taught by experience that a spring here, or a ratchet there, or a lever elsewhere will materially increase the productiveness of the implement he is using, and improve the quality of the output. He works out his idea, makes a model, and then goes to the Patent Office with his application. Here he finds every encouragement. He finds that his improvement is just as fully protected and just as thoroughly his own property as is the original invention the property of the man who devised it. The Government issues a patent which gives him absolute control of the improvement. Then the workman goes to his employer and points out what he has done, and as the American manufacturer is a most progressive person he rarely fails to buy the improvement and to compensate the workman in a liberal manner. It is this process, this accumulation of small improvements, carried on day in and day out, that has brought our mechanical appliances to such great perfection.

In Europe, small improvements on a machine are practically unpatentable. The only country besides our own where there is any examination of patents, carrying with it a consequent protection to the inventor, is Germany. Yet even there it is next to impossible to obtain protection for a minor improvement. The result is natural. The workmen take no interest in their machines beyond manipulating them as they are told.

Under our system we have evolved a distinct, inventive mind. Men are born to-day in America with a genius for invention just as men are born here and elsewhere with a genius for art or letters. The laws of heredity have begun to operate in the field of invention as clearly as they have operated since the beginning of the world in other well-defined fields. As our national life continues this process will bring out an ever-increasing crop of men who create things.

The Qualities an Inventor Must Possess

There is no pursuit that is more fascinating or more promising than that of the inventor. He is privileged to dip into every calling. If he has the right sort of mind, it is not at all essential that he understand everything connected with the art in which he desires to operate; such nowadays is well-nigh impossible. He need only take that particular corner wherein the problem that he is after lies, and work it thoroughly. But thorough the work must be. He must have more than the patience of Job, more than the perseverance of the beaver, more than the industry of the bee. He must work hard, and be content to work for months at a time without making any apparent progress. He must be content to travel over the same field again and again and again, indefatigably. That is the secret of the inventor's success—never-ending application. The idea that an inventor is necessarily a genius is entirely fallacious. Genius for invention is merely the capacity for concentration and for work. Given these qualities, and a power of close observation, and you have the make-up of a successful inventor. He need be no learned scientist, and yet he may be able to work up most valuable inventions in many sciences. He need be no perfectly trained electrician, and yet he may be able to work up a valuable electrical appliance. But always he must be prepared to take advantage of new phenomena, and to know all about the field in which they lie. Many of our most important inventions are the result not so much of deep knowledge as of the power of observation and the ability to appreciate the possibilities of phenomena that the less observing would pass by without seeing.

Doctor Bell's Invention of the Telephone

The telephone is a fine illustration of this fact. When Mr. Bell finally discovered the principle that made possible the invention of the telephone, he was experimenting with the idea of perfecting a system of harmonic telegraphy. His father-in-law, Mr. Gardiner G. Hubbard, had made up his mind to fight the Western Union Telegraph monopoly. To do this he felt the need of a system by which one wire could be made to do the work of half a dozen or a dozen wires of the Western Union, so that a competing system could be built without spending the millions it would require to duplicate the old company's plant, line for line and pole for pole.

Mr. Hubbard encouraged Mr. Bell to experiment with a system of harmonic springs, keyed like piano tuning-forks. A telegraph wire was strung from one room to another, where the instruments were set up, and for months Mr. Bell and his assistant, Mr. Watson, carried on their work, reaching out slowly toward the attainment of great results. One day it happened that one of the harmonic springs over an electro-magnet at Mr. Watson's end of the line refused to respond. Somehow, it seemed caught and gave out no sound in the key in which it was tuned. Thinking to release it, he snapped it with his finger. He was just preparing to repeat the act when Mr. Bell rushed into the room and said:

"What did you do then, Watson?"

"Why, I snapped that spring with my finger. It won't work."

"That's most remarkable. I wish you would do it again."

Mr. Bell retired and Mr. Watson snapped the spring again. Mr. Bell returned to the room very much interested. He said that he had noticed that there was a physical response to Mr. Watson's act on the corresponding harmonic spring in the other room. It had jerked just as Mr. Watson's spring had been jerked. The trained mind of the inventor at once saw in this the key to a previous general conception of a speaking telephone.

"This act," he said, "was doubtless due to the electrical transmission of an undulatory current over that wire. If that is true, electrical waves produced by the voice can be sent over the wire and can be made to reproduce that voice at the other end."

Out of that incident, trivial to the unobserving mind, grew the telephone of to-day.

Observation the Soul of Invention

The invention of the constant contact telephone transmitter which made long-distance telephony possible and rendered short-distance talk clear and intelligible was the result of something of the same kind. I had for years been studying the science of electricity and the physics of sound when Mr. Bell's patent was issued in 1876, and it occurred to me at once that the knowledge I had absorbed in my studies might be very profitably applied to improving the telephone.

At that time I was engaged in commercial pursuits in Washington and my experiments and studies were more in the nature of a recreation than anything else. I paid frequent visits to the central office of the Fire Department, the electrical superintendent of which, Mr. Richardson, was a particular friend of mine. He had a dummy telegraph instrument on which he had taught me telegraphy, and on this particular evening I was working the instrument as usual, when he said:

"You don't press hard enough, Berliner."

"Does that make any difference?"

"Certainly; it makes all the difference in the world in the strength and clearness of the message at the other end. That is why women do not make good and effective operators as a rule. They are not strong enough—their touch is too light. They do not give thorough contact."

That was a revelation to me. Under Mr. Bell's invention the voice had to vibrate a diaphragm against a magnet and the volume of electricity thus produced was not sufficient to transmit sound waves sufficiently strong. That night, before I went to sleep, I had set up the movable diaphragm used in the telephone to-day, which keeps in constant contact, but with varying pressure, with the transmitting end of the telephone wire, simply pressing back and forth as the sound waves produced by the voice diminish or strengthen.

How a Queer Discovery was Made

Another case illustrating this point occurred not so many years afterward. Upon the completion of my invention of the constant contact sound transmitter, the Bell telephone people engaged my services as expert to aid in perfecting the telephone, which was still in a crude state. Mr. Blake had just invented his form of transmitter and the instrument was placed in my hands for final development. It secured a very much clearer transmission than had been possible before, but one of its troubles was that the carbon button used would rapidly wear holes at the contact. The material was so soft that it kept us busy replacing or refacing the carbon buttons. These buttons were made from the ordinary long soft carbons used in arc lights, which had only just appeared in the market. They were made by sawing the long carbons into thin circular buttons. We conducted all sorts of experiments with a view to securing a hardening of this carbon, but for a long time we failed in effecting any improvement. It was well known that the hardest carbon in the world was that which is deposited in gas retorts. This carbon deposit had always proved a serious source of trouble since the manufacture of coal gas was invented, because it has to be cleaned out from time to time, and this is a difficult job.

It occurred to me to have a little iron cage built, into which I put a lot of our soft carbon buttons. This cage I asked the gas people in Boston to put into their retort on the next occasion when they were ready for a charge. I left it there during six charges; then, when I took it out, I found my carbons all shriveled and shrunken. The intense heat had half burned them up. They were all rough, and for a little while I thought there was another failure. In a contemplative mood I began to rub one of the roughened buttons on a piece of emery paper to see what polishing might do for it. Soon I had rubbed away entirely the spongy rough surface and got down to the original button. Examining this closely, I found to my great surprise that the carbon itself was practically unchanged except that it had become tremendously hardened. A closer inspection showed that not alone had the carbon in the gas deposited itself on the surface of the buttons, but that it had also penetrated the pores of my carbon, filling them up absolutely and making the buttons as hard as any one could desire. That was in the year 1879.

By exposing to fewer gas charges we thereafter produced a carbon button that was at once hard and smooth, and to this day this process is employed. Nothing has ever been found that hardens carbon buttons for telephone use better or more economically.

A few years ago while I was experimenting with the gramophone we found that in tracing our records the sound lines were blurred by the particles of dust in the air that settled on the fatty film. To obviate this we kept the disk constantly flooded with a spray of alcohol as the tracing proceeded. This gave us much better results, and we flattered ourselves that we had achieved all that was possible in the way of perfection, until accident revealed to us still another improvement. I had just lifted one of the disks, after the tracing was finished, and was about to put it on a shelf to dry, when some water was splashed on it. Instantly it became spotted where the water had touched it.

"That's too bad," I said to my assistant. "There is a good record spoiled."

He agreed with me, and was about to put it to one side when I said:

"Wait a moment; let us see how it will etch."

After immersing into the etching tray we found that it etched more rapidly and smoother where the water drops had washed the alcohol away, and we then traced another record and washed the alcohol off under a hydrant. When I put it in the reproducing machine we found that it gave a clearer tone than any of the other disks.

The alcohol, while it kept the settling dust washed off, had dissolved some of the fatty film, and in drying had redeposited it on the record lines. The portion of the fat dissolved was very minute, but it was sufficient to interfere somewhat with the etching process. Water alone had no value in carrying off the dust particles that were our first greatest objection, because it did not adhere to the fat of the surface to be washed, but the water mixed very readily with the alcohol afterward and carried it off instantly, so that there was no drying process, and consequently no interfering with the etching. Ever since we have used this process, first the alcohol bath, and then the water bath.

These experiences, and hundreds like them, show that there is nothing so trifling that the inventor can afford to let it pass unobserved, and that the man who does not see things and is not a close observer will never make a success as an inventor, no matter how great his scientific knowledge.

The Age Most Fruitful in Inventions

The true inventor will manifest himself pretty early in life, though it is of record, according to the late James J. Storrow, that the most prolific age of invention is about the age of twenty-five and twenty-six years. That is to say, the most original inventions in the world, and the greatest number, have come from men who were up to or about twenty-six years of age. Long before this, however, the inventive faculty will have come to the surface in those who possess it. The boy who wants to know the "why" of things, who takes things to pieces, who is not content merely to absorb the joy that comes from a mechanical toy, but wants to see the wheels go round; the boy who seeks to find out how it is that powdered alum clears water, and is not content to drink the water without question, has in him the groundwork of the inventor.

However, the faculties required of the inventor are so peculiar that it will perhaps be a difficult matter to devise a course of training to help him along, except by teaching him to observe and how to observe. The ordinary college training gives little or no help except by its laboratory work — in fact too much accepted theory is very often a hindrance to the inventor. It is the first duty of an inventor to question all things, and very often to violate and upset such fixed rules as are principally based on theoretical deductions.

In college a young man is filled with knowledge built entirely on past experience. Certain rules — scientific, physical and mechanical — are laid down for his guidance, and he is told to consider them as regulating everything and as being absolutely indispensable. Out of this sort of training comes a mind that, though on the whole it is eminently fitted for routine work, is seldom adapted to grasp new propositions. Most college graduates are in the position of the city boy whose father promised that some day he would take him into the country and show him a forest. The appointed day came and the boy and his father jogged along over mile after mile of road. Finally, the youngster said:

"Father, where is this forest you are going to show me?"

"Why," replied the old man, busy with his own thoughts, "here it is all around you. We are in the forest."

"I don't see it. I don't see anything but trees."

And so it is often with the college graduate — he cannot see the forest for the trees.

This is no reflection on college training which forms the basis of our scientific progress, but the proposition is merely put forward to show that the position of inventors is generally one distinct from that of the theoretical scientist.

The Value of Theoretical Knowledge

Some few noted inventions have been brought into the world because of the fact that the inventor possessed great theoretical knowledge. A most important one, recently, of this sort is that of Doctor Pupin, who has just perfected a system by which trans-Atlantic telephony may become feasible. Doctor Pupin's invention is purely scientific, based on exact mathematical deductions. He worked for five years, but he knew that sooner or later he must find what he was looking for.

There are a few other similar inventions, but the inventor must generally depend not upon what he knows, but on what his trained faculty of observation enables him to find out by ceaseless experimenting.

One inventor may have something that, as it stands, appears to show only a comparatively small field of usefulness, but which, worked out under given conditions, will become a gold mine. The telephone again illustrates this. None of the men who worked at this idea originally had any conception of its possibilities. For some time after the apparatus was perfected by Mr. Bell, and even after Mr. Edison, Mr. Blake and myself had made our improvements, nobody appreciated the vast possibilities of the telephone. It was declared useful only as a means of communication between two points on a private line; between a man's office and his factory, his place of business and his home.

It was only when there was applied to it the central office idea that the telephone became important and really valuable. None of the men originally concerned with the invention thought of it immediately in connection with a central office. This idea grew out of the working of what was known as the Law Telegraph Company of New York, and the credit of applying the idea undoubtedly belongs to the late Gardiner G. Hubbard and to Mr. Theodore N. Vail. Mr. Vail was General Manager of the Bell Company. Mr. Hubbard from the first was the main factor in the initial development of the scheme.

The Law Telegraph Company was an institution organized for the benefit of the lawyers of New York. There was a central office, out of which ran private lines to the offices of the lawyers who subscribed. When one lawyer wanted to communicate with another, his operator called up the central office and the latter's line was connected by the usual plug system with the line of the man he desired to telegraph to. In other words, they did exactly what is now done in the telephone central office, only using the telegraph keys and skilled operators instead of telephone transmitters and receivers. To-day there are more patents on central office appliances than on the telephone instruments proper.

Sound Advice for Young Inventors

It is very advisable that a young inventor should know something of the Patent Office practice, and if possible have a good general idea of the principles of Patent Law. Next, he should be well up in the state of the particular art, the particular corner, in which he is working. Lacking this, grievous results and disappointments will be his lot.

Then, having an idea, the young man should allow nothing to stand in the way of his working it out; of course, practicing due economy in his laboratory expenditures. As soon as his conception has assumed shape he should take into his confidence some friend upon whom he can rely. This will give him valuable protection in case his invention comes to be important and is attacked or infringed. No particular good is achieved in hurrying to the Patent Office until everything is ready. The main thing is to have the invention as perfect as possible, and to have it viewed by one or more friends who can be depended upon. When the time comes the inventor should file his application for a patent through a reputable attorney. If it is sufficiently important and he has capital to justify it, he should secure his European patents and then publish his invention broadcast to the world. Publication then is the best policy, as it gives him prestige and invites honest criticism — an important consideration.

There are few inventions that justify European patents at the outset, and few inventors at the beginning can afford this luxury. The ordinary young man who has a device which he considers useful can very well rest content with the protection given him by the United States Patent Office.

His next step, after his patent is secured, should lead him to put its value to a practical test. This can be done most effectually by placing it before men with capital. The young inventor should guard against deceiving himself as to the commercial value of his patent. It is often impossible for a man who has worked over a device to take an impartial view of the possibilities that lie in it. It is almost a fatal error for a man to try to exploit his own inventions. There are few inventors who are good managers. They have generally little business talent. Therefore an inventor should join hands almost immediately with some good business man, and he should not hesitate to give a very substantial share of his invention to the man who pushes it.

There is as much in the proper development and the commercial exploitation of an invention as there is in its production, and the man or men who undertake the business end of the enterprise are entitled to as much credit as the inventor, and often more. Many inventors come to grief through the failure to recognize this fact at the outset. But it behooves the inventor to be very careful in his dealings with business men, for capital is cold-blooded and wants all it can get. But, though cold-blooded, capital is always eager for good things, and the young man who has a promising invention need have no fear that he cannot find men with money who will back him.

Often inventions look very ingenious on paper which fail when you come to work them out practically. The thing to do, therefore, is to get in touch with people who have special use for the invention. Preference should be given to great corporations — they are the safest to deal with. They are constantly looking for improvements; they are willing to pay better and more fairly than the average private individual.

The Defects in Patent-Law Proceedings

So far as the Patent Office is concerned, the inventor may put in his plans there with perfect assurance that he will be honestly dealt with. There have been numerous charges of collusion in the Patent Office, but there is not a single case where collusion has been proved. The record of the Office is clean, notwithstanding that there have been hundreds of thousands of patent litigations.

Of course the system is not perfect: no system is. The most serious defect, however, is not in the Patent Office, but in the method or procedure in our courts in patent cases. In case of infringement, a meritorious inventor, after having fought his way through the Patent Office, has again to fight expensive law suits before he can get a preliminary injunction. I think that after the severe examination in the Patent Office, a patent claim should be *prima facie* evidence against the man who comes into the market after the patentee. The burden of proof should be on the man who hasn't the patent. And the patentee should be entitled to a preliminary injunction on reasonable proof.

At present the infringer is encouraged because it takes years before a patentee can get his patent adjudicated, and in the meantime the infringer reaps his profits and simply skips the field should the patent be proven against him.

If inventors are useful adjuncts to American civilization, then the laws should rather be stretched in their favor; and because once in a while an invention is in great demand, and, under fine business management, has become a public necessity, that should be no ground for a public clamor for turning the law in favor of infringers as much as possible.

Once the public appreciates that nothing has more strongly helped this land of high wages to compete with Europe than has the encouragement given by our patent laws to inventors, they will see that their sympathy should rather be on the side of the inventor. But there are unfortunately many who would thoughtlessly kill the goose which lays the golden egg, and who consider an inventor a monopolist who should be downed on principle. Otherwise, our patent system is about as perfect as can be desired, and it is a decided blessing to the people of the United States.

Great Care Needed in Applications

There is, however, one thing that all inventors should carefully observe — that is, the drawing up of their applications for a patent. Ordinarily, this is left to some clerk in the office of the patent attorney, and often the inventor has bitter cause to rue it if he is not careful to supervise and study heedfully the wording of his application before it is sent to the Patent Office. It is not that the patent attorneys as a class are unreliable, but that they have so much to do that they frequently leave important work to assistants who are incompetent to deal with it. A recent decision of a United States Court against a telephone transmitter patent is an illustration of the danger of leaving the wording of the application entirely to patent attorneys' clerks. The inventor had filed a caveat covering his invention. He wrote the description himself and took it to the Patent Office. Instruments made from the drawing and description of this caveat did talk at the time with very imperfect receivers and they talk perfectly to-day, and the description and the claims of this caveat are concise and without a flaw. The only mistake the inventor made was that when, several months later, it came to the drawing up of the patent application, he trusted more to a patent attorney's clerk who didn't know anything about telephones (few people then did) than to his own ability to write things down, and the application when first filed was defective and needed subsequent amendments.

The Patent Office knew the circumstances and repeatedly examined them and decided invariably that he was entitled to a broad patent, but the recent decision against this patent makes no allowance for the circumstances cited, and holds the inventor down to the application as it read when first filed and as drawn by a clerk wholly ignorant of the subject. Since the application had been suspended by the Patent Office and had been fought for fourteen years on account of other claimants, it is hardly probable that other inventors would have permitted the patent to be granted if the invention had been antedated by them. This emphasizes the fact that every inventor should very carefully superintend the drawing up of his application for a patent.

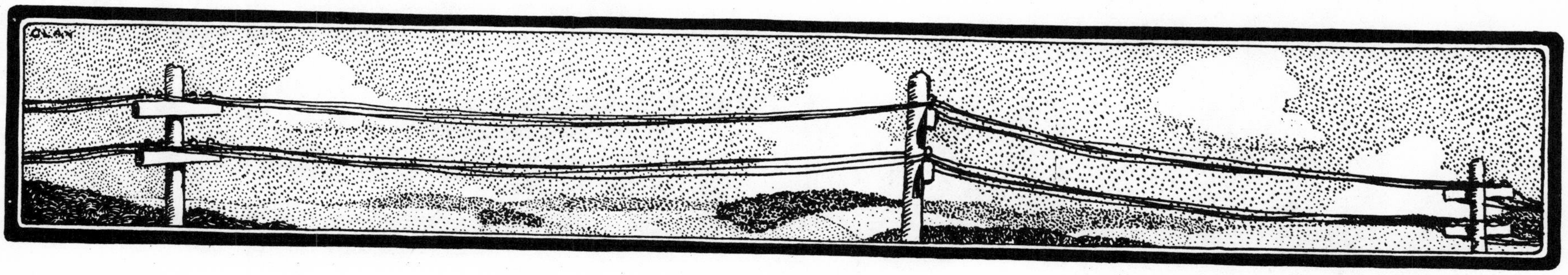

Electric Cooking

EDISON FLUOROSCOPE

Listening to the Roar of Niagara

Electricity in the Laundry

Photographing by Electric Light

General View from gallery

Watching the Electric Trolley Canal

THE ELECTRICAL EXPOSITION.

If you attend the National Electrical Exposition, which is now being held in New York city, and begin your tour of the exposition in the generating-room downstairs, about in the centre you will be attracted by an engine set up on three steel pivots, very much as you would mount your camera on its tripod. It has no anchorage; there is, indeed, nothing to hold it on these delicate pinions save its own weight. Its huge fly-wheel spins at the rate of hundreds of revolutions per minute. This machine is an electric generator, and develops a power sufficient to draw a small railway train, and it runs without a shock or a jar, and with hardly a sound. Upstairs the force that this machine is generating is being applied to a thousand uses. It is filling a great hall with a flood of marvellous light; it is making it possible for you to talk with a friend a hundred or a thousand miles away; it is cooking a meal; it is driving an automatic piano; it is furnishing heat for the iron which a maid is pushing over her ironing-board; it is taking pictures while you wait; it is sending alarms and warnings, ringing gongs and printing messages; it is even making it possible for you and me to look into a clumsy black stereoscope and, with the aid of the Röntgen rays, to see the bones of our arms, or to look through a heavy plank of oak. Outside it is running street cars, inside is the model showing how it will run canal-boats. The mind seems hardly able to discover the field of mechanical activity where this Protean force is not felt, is not doing useful work.

Upstairs Dr. Park Benjamin and Mr. Commerford Martin have been at work to sketch in a striking and novel way exactly the same story that the engine downstairs has been telling. Dr. Benjamin has perhaps the most valuable and interesting electrical library in the world; and if there were absolutely nothing else in the exposition, and you were interested in such matters at all, it would be worth your while to go and look over this curious collection. Instead of being laid out as such things usually are, in haphazard fashion, Dr. Benjamin has taken each volume in its chronological order, and opened it at its most striking page. In between each volume he has slipped a little card of explanation and succinct comment, so that as you move along slowly, looking over these rare old treasures, you may read the full story of the history of electricity, as it were, from earliest times to the present day.

Then when you have done with the literary side you may go a little further, and something of the same story, in even a more vivid and pictorial way, will be told you in the collection which Mr. F. B. Morse, son of the "Father of Telegraphy," has with like liberality placed at the disposal of the exposition, and in the remarkable collection of models which has been sent over from the Patent Office at Washington. Here you may see the earliest beginnings of the mechanical side of the electrical art, and step by step you may follow the path of its progress. Here you may see the first tentative models of Morse, you may see the first inventions of Edison, and Elihu Thompson, and Brush, and Houston, and Bell, and Gray, and Essick, and Westinghouse, and Tesla, and all the others who have contributed towards establishing the primacy of American inventive genius, and towards developing electrical devices to their present stage.

You will see here miniature designs of the first instrument that ever carried a telegraphic message, the first that ever conveyed the sound of the human voice, the first that ever developed a high potential current; you may view the first lamp that ever gave forth the brilliant glow of the electric arc, the first that ever shone with the milder radiance of the incandescent light, the first motor that ever set spinning a wheel, the first that ever heated a kettle of water, the first that ever propelled a car, and finally the first that ever enabled a human eye to see through an opaque and solid mass. And here, too, you will find instruments of the most bewildering variety and the most amazing delicacy for taking measurements and weights. You will see instruments so sensitive and of such precision that they will weigh a tiny bit of your hair and determine its thickness; that will detect and register the electric currents of your body; that will split the difference in the weights of the gas you burn and the air you breathe, that will tremble with the polar currents that flow about the earth. They do more than this; they give promise of the day when it will be possible for a machine to trace upon a sheet of paper the course and intensity of the thoughts that team in your brain.

All these things you may see, and when you have thoroughly grounded yourself in what you may call the first principles and the history of the art, you may turn to the industrial display—that is to say, to the exhibit of the various devices and instruments and wares which are now upon the market for the promotion of your ease, your comfort, and your pleasure. There are huge electrical engines, fetching effects and novelties without end, ranging from a 150-horse-power motor to an electrical jardinière. But it is not within the scope of this article to go over these in detail: you may readily see them all for yourself, or read of them in the electrical papers.

There are many things of other than purely commercial interest; for instance, the light which Professor Moore makes, and which is generated by means of an induction current passed through partially exhausted glass tubes. The vibrations set up by the current induce in the tube a peculiar glow or phosphorescence, much similar to, though far more brilliant than that which comes from a stick of phosphorus on a dark night. It is a beautiful light to look at, and peculiarly grateful to tired or over-sensitive eyes.

But I take it that above all others the most significant event of the exposition has been the sufficiently noteworthy feat of bringing power from the Niagara Falls. It is true that the actual amount of power brought is small, and anything but economical. Nevertheless, the mere fact that a current of electricity generated by the new giant turbines at the Falls has been carried so far as New York city, carried 465 miles over an ordinary Western Union wire, opens up wide vistas for the future. The longest distance through which a high potential current has hitherto been carried and made to do actual work is, I believe, 109 miles. An advance to four times this distance, and by ordinary means at that, indicates beyond peradventure that the day is not far distant when a large part of the mechanical work of New York, and other cities as well, will be undertaken by currents drawn from the great cataract and from the countless waterfalls scattered everywhere over the country. It means that our mills and factories, our railroads and surface ways, and not less the lighter work of the household and the kitchen, will be performed by this latest and efficient slave. Where, again, sufficient water-power is not available, successful long-distance transmission means the generation of electricity at the mouth of the coal-mine, and with far greater economy than at the present time. Thus the Pennsylvania Railroad is already taking steps to burn the countless culm banks which years of operation of the coal-mines have heaped up about the tunnel mouths. This culm is a sort of coal-dust, or refuse, which is not available for transportation, but which may be burned successfully in a new type of furnace, which provides for a wellnigh perfect combustion. These culm banks are scattered at intervals all over the country, from Pennsylvania and Alabama to Wyoming, and even to the far distant shores of Puget Sound, and they offer fuel to generate electricity and run our railways for years to come. It is hardly necessary to add that this is a fuel whose cheapness rivals that of water-power, and, with the latter, insures such an economical production of electricity as to offer the practical prospect that within a few years coal will have almost ceased to be transported from the point where it is mined. We shall have electricity everywhere.

Is there Snow on the Moon?

By GARRETT P. SERVISS

SPECULATION is once more rife about the moon. Professor William C. Pickering of the Harvard Observatory is the immediate cause of it.

One of the great sights of the moon, with which every possessor of a telescope is fond of astonishing his non-astronomical friends, is the mountainous district known as the Lunar Apennines. In eccentric grandeur this region on the moon is beyond comparison with any of the great landscape spectacles of the earth. It covers a triangular area of some four hundred miles on a side, situated near the centre of the moon's northern hemisphere, and as the sunshine crawls over it during the long lunar day, with gradually altering inclination of the rays of light, there is brought into view by successive steps a series of Alpine scenes that excite the imagination, and defy at once the pencil of the artist, the skill of the photographer, and the pictorial power of language.

A singular view of the Lunar Apennines, showing them in only one of their rapidly changing aspects, is not enough to convey an idea of their extraordinary constructure. The observer should, if possible, watch them during many successive nights, noting the pointed black shadows of the mighty peaks, shortening as the sun rises higher upon them, and finally vanishing, to reappear on the opposite side when the illumination changes from the morning to the afternoon slope (on the moon morning and afternoon are each about a week in duration), and noting also the appearance, disappearance, and reappearance of craters, ridges, pinnacles, ravines, and gorges as the contrasting lights and shadows play over them. Far away though they are, on the surface of a foreign globe, the tremendous precipices where the Lunar Apennines suddenly descend to the prairie-like level of the *Mare Imbrium* (Sea of Showers) produce almost a dizziness of the head for the imaginative observer who, knowing their height and steepness, long gazes upon them.

This wonderful lunar region has recently acquired fresh interest through the asseveration of Professor Pickering's belief that its mountain peaks and slopes are periodically covered with snow. Nobody has studied the moon longer, or more patiently, than has Professor Pickering, and his opinion naturally excites much interest among astronomers, and among all who are accustomed to watch and admire the queen of night, even though they take little interest in the scientific problems she presents. The series of photographs of lunar scenery made by Professor Pickering, and published in the latest volume of the "Harvard Observatory Annals," are unique in the opportunity which they afford for discussion of the actual conditions prevailing on the earth's satellite.

During the progress of the lunar day very remarkable changes occur in the brightness of the landscape. Professor Pickering's interpretation of these changes is that they are due to the deposition and melting away of snow, which not only gathers on the high mountain backs, but during the chill of night forms over the elevated plains also, and, after sparkling for a time in the slowly rising sun, at length disappears. It is to be supposed that the snow mantle, if one really exists, has no great thickness, as the quantity of watery vapor on the moon must be very slight.

The photographs of the Lunar Apennines in the "morning," in the "forenoon," at "noon," in the "afternoon," and in the "evening" certainly show that, if Professor Pickering's theory is not correct, some peculiarity of the moon's rocks, or soil, exists capable of creating the appearance of a white blanket alternately displayed and withdrawn. The spectacle is especially imposing along the crest of the range, where peaks from 16,000 to 21,000 feet in height tower almost perpendicularly over the *Mare Imbrium*. In the forenoon light the long gentle slopes on the side opposite the *Mare Imbrium* show white, while the great vertical cliffs overhanging the *Mare* are invisible in shadow. But in the afternoon the sun strikes these cliffs full upon their faces and they gleam like glaciers.

The snow theory, however, has not met with universal assent. The English astronomer, Mr. E. Walter Maunder, dissents from it, and holds to the view that the observed changes are simply due to contact between the broken superficies of the steep mountain slopes and the more uniform surface presented by the comparatively level portions, where meteoric dust and tarnished mineral débris cover the ground.

Intimately connected with the question whether there is snow on the moon is the still more interesting question whether there is life there. To this latter Professor Pickering, running counter to the generally accepted opinion, replies that there probably is life. But the indications of lunar animation which he has found do not encourage romantic expectation. They do not relate to animal, and much less to intelligent, forms of life. They concern only a kind of vegetation springing up on low ground at the touch of the sun and perishing with the day that brings it forth.

H. G. Wells's "The First Men in the Moon," which appeared in *Cosmopolitan* in 1900, was illustrated with this picture of a scientist and a businessman approaching the moon in a space ship.

THE DEMIGODS OF MARS

By GARRETT P. SERVISS

THERE is no use in denying the fact that the measure of human interest in a foreign planet depends upon the probability or possibility that the planet in question is an inhabited world. Astronomers absorbed in technical work may decry speculation of this kind as much as they like, but the intelligent public will continue to ask: "Are there people up there, or are there not?" And if the time should ever come when it can be stated, definitely and conclusively, that there is no possibility of life on other planets, there will not remain one reader in a thousand who will pay the slightest attention to anything else that may be said about them.

Fortunately there is little likelihood that the planet Mars will in this manner cease to be an object of general interest. On the contrary, every new study of his remarkable disk furnishes fresh material for speculation concerning the life and doings of his alleged inhabitants; and the latest observations of Percival Lowell, who has made himself the special student of Mars before all others, afford us a glimpse of the possibilities of that strange planet as fascinating as a dip into the "Arabian Nights," or the stories of Theseus and Hercules.

That such inhabitants actually exist is, of course, simply an inference from suggestive appearances. But these appearances are so extraordinary that no thoughtful observer can very well help trying to interpret their meaning, and it must be confessed that the interpretation which pronounces them to be correlatives of intelligent life is at least as good as any.

The Martians are Wonderful Creatures

It has generally been assumed, for a variety of reasons, that the Martians greatly excel us in their mastery over physical nature as well as in their bodily stature and intellectual experience, but the new picture of their achievements which Mr. Lowell presents in outline in a bulletin from his Arizona observatory shows them as virtual demigods, whose labors throw those of Hercules entirely into the shade.

Their task, it seems, has been and is to preserve the life of a planet. There is no room for petty politics on Mars. There can not even be any international complications. War is unimaginable on the surface of the planet to which we have given the name of the god of war, because all the races and nations that may dwell upon it must be blended into a common brotherhood by the one universal purpose of maintaining their world in a state of habitability. From that purpose there can be no flinching. Every power of mind and body must be bent to serve it. If a message could reach us from Mars it would surely be a cry of despair. From the cradle to the grave the inhabitant of Mars lives always under the shadow of an impending catastrophe which threatens the extinction of all life upon his globe. While we can look serenely forward to the ending of our world some millions of years in the future, on Mars they see planetary death knocking at their doors and must keep him out as long as they can. And the manner in which they are holding him back must awaken our liveliest admiration.

The Canals Accounted For

All these things seem fairly inferable from Mr. Lowell's studies. The clew to the whole situation is the scarcity of water. The notion prevalent a few years ago that there are oceans on Mars has been abandoned. Apparently there are not even lakes, unless of slight extent and of artificial origin. There are no natural streams or rivers. All the available moisture by which vegetation can be stimulated is locked up during half the Martian year, which is 687 days in length, in the polar snows. When those snows begin to melt—a phenomenon easily observed with the telescope—the "canals" make their appearance. The first canals are seen at the edges of the disappearing snow-cap, high up in polar latitudes. Then, as the melting continues, the canals increase in number, darken, broaden, and extend downward over the disk, until finally they reach, and even pass, the equator. The observed sequence of the phenomena exactly fits the hypothesis that the canals, hundreds in number, are brought into existence, or into visibility, as a result of the melting of the polar snow.

But now we come to a most important point. The canals are not to be regarded as water, but rather as a product of water. They are, says Mr. Lowell, probably lines of vegetation, quickened into growth by the water from the melted snow-caps. A little thinking about this brings out a very singular conclusion. *The annual awakening of vegetable life on Mars takes a course precisely opposite to that followed on the earth.* With us, on a world abundantly supplied with water, the march of life in the springtime is from the equator toward the poles; on Mars, where there is practically no water except that which winter has locked up at the poles, the direction of this vivifying procession is reversed, and vegetation springing up first near the polar circles advances down across the middle latitudes to the equator, and even beyond the equator with the other hemisphere.

But how is all this brought about—what causes the water to flow from the poles toward the equator? Here is where the cunning and all-powerful hands of the demigods of Mars appear. Gravitation will not account for the transfer of the water—at least not for any great distance. As far as we can see, some intelligence above the ordinary forces of nature must interfere in the phenomenon. *In a word, the lines of vegetation called canals must be of artificial origin.* The real canals, the irrigating ditches, which are the active agents in distributing the water and forcing it away from the poles, must be concealed in the larger visible lines which are thousands of miles in length and average perhaps a hundred miles in width. Along those lines, and within their borders, life is maintained. All around them the face of the planet is a desert!

There is one circumstance which distinctly favors the supposititious engineers of Mars—the planet is extraordinarily flat. There is little of any indication of the existence of mountains or even of hills upon it. Still, however, the problem of conveying enormous quantities of water from the polar circles to the equator is one that would seem too great for any beings less than demigods to solve. They must create a gigantic head of water. They must have pumping apparatus of unimaginable power and magnitude. They must raise the water again and again, and send it forward from one artificial level to another until the whole thirsty planet is satisfied.

"Impossible!" do you say? Well, perhaps so, and perhaps not so. In fighting for their lives men do wonders; and if it is the life of a whole world that is at stake who shall set a limit to the achievements of intellect?

A Hot, Little Planet

The astronomer in charge of the Harvard Observatory, at Arequipa, Peru, announces that in April last he succeeded in obtaining four photographs of the recently discovered planet Eros. This tiny orb—a veritable toy world, it might be called—is only about nine miles in diameter. One reason for the interest attaching to it is that it is the nearest to the earth, and nearest likewise to the sun, of all the minor planets. In 1894 it was only 15,000,000 miles away from us, a mere trifle of distance from an astronomical point of view, and next November it will approach within 28,000,000 miles.

There are about four hundred minor planets so far discovered, though doubtless many more, as yet unfound, exist. The first ones were located early in the present century, one of them being Vesta, which is, perhaps, the biggest of the whole lot, being about 240 miles in diameter. In area these baby sisters of the Earth may be said to equal various States of the Union, ranging from Rhode Island to some of the larger ones.

Eros, being nearest to the sun, must be warmer than any of the other minor planets—a fact that has a bearing on the possibility that it may be inhabited. The question whether these toy worlds are occupied by any forms of life is extremely interesting, though likely to remain unanswered. So slight is the gravity power of a planet nine miles in diameter that an ordinary man on Eros would be able to hurl away a half-ton stone with such velocity that it would never come back out of the realms of space. The photographs taken at Arequipa were made by Dr. Delisle Stewart.

HOW THE WORLD WILL END

THE ERUPTION OF MOUNT PELEE, MARTINIQUE—DRAWN FROM THE DESCRIPTION OF AN EYE WITNESS

BY HUDSON MAXIM

The Well-Known Inventor and Scientist

THE awful disaster which has recently befallen the inhabitants of the Caribbean Archipelago is, without doubt, one of the most serious in human history. It has a counterpart only in the destruction of Herculaneum and Pompeii, and a superior only in the great calamity in the Indian Archipelago in 1883, when the extinct volcano Krakatoa was blown into the sky by pent-up subterranean forces, while fifteen other volcanoes simultaneously belched forth to keep her company. It is estimated that in that eruption from fifty thousand to eighty thousand persons lost their lives.

Had all the energies of the human race been devoted to the manufacture of gun-powder and dynamite during historic time, the total product of this labor placed deep in the earth, and exploded, would have been infinitely insignificant compared with that terrific explosion of Krakatoa.

Mother Earth is herself the greatest manufacturer of high explosives. When a volcano breaks out afresh, the accompanying earthquake shocks and convulsions open great seams beneath the sea for renewed inception of water, which is quickly converted into steam or dissociated gases, which rush to vent themselves at the volcano, carrying along with them great quantities of lava and broken rock, to be belched forth sometimes to enormous heights. The force with which scoria and fragments of rock are propelled up the shaft of a volcanic crater is comparable with that which would be exerted by a continuous explosion of dynamite. When an oil-well is torpedoed, we have, while it lasts, a volcano in miniature.

The appearance and the effect to the inhabitants of St. Pierre when Mount Pelee exploded was essentially the same as though the world had come to an end—as though the crust of the earth had been broken up and all the pent-up fires of the interior let loose. The question, therefore, naturally arises, May not the human race be ultimately destroyed, with all other life, by similar causes, but of such magnitude as to embrace the whole earth? Even if the earth be not destroyed, even though other life in many forms might not disappear, still might not the human race be swept out of existence? No; there is no possibility of a general volcanic eruption over the whole earth.

By examining into the causes of volcanoes we learn that they are simply vents in the earth's crust for the escape of gases generated within the interior by the constant warfare between the water of the seas and the fire underneath, which are separated by an imperfect barrier of earth rent with fissures and broken by seams and faults. The water, working its way through these cracks and faults into the subterranean fires, is converted into steam, and the steam is heated until it is dissociated into its original elements of oxygen and hydrogen.

It is possible that a pressure may sometimes be generated in this way equal to that exerted by the most powerful dynamite at the instant of detonation. These pent-up gases naturally force their way to the nearest outlets along lines of least resistance, and the melted silica and lava become charged with the heated gases, as soda-water charged with carbonic-acid gas, so that the molten earth is forced along toward some volcanic outlet or to some thinner spot in the earth's crust capable of being lifted or displaced by the pressure of the gas. This causes earthquakes. An extinct volcano, which has served as a former vent, may be plugged up by the solidified

CROSS-SECTION OF A VOLCANO

lava in its crater, and still be the line of least resistance for the escape of the fiery dynamite underneath; consequently the whole top of the mountain may be blown into the air, as was Krakatoa, and a column of escaping gas and earth will belch forth miles in height, or the cone may be rent from summit to foundation, letting loose rivers of lava.

We frequently hear the suggestion that the earth may some time explode from the pent-up forces within, and we often read theories about explosions of heavenly bodies, but the earth can never explode from its own pent-up forces. Under our very feet at this moment, between the earth's solid crust and the molten interior, there is a pressure exerted more than double that which is capable of being exerted by the most powerful dynamite in the world.

It is a generally accepted and probably true theory that the whole interior of the earth is a molten mass of rock and metals heavier than the crust above, and upon which the crust floats in a relatively thin layer. The thickness of the earth's crust within the great continents is probably from fifty to one hundred miles. If we estimate the pressure exerted by the weight of one mile of earth and rock at ten thousand pounds, which is well within the truth, then fifty miles of earth would exert a pressure of about five hundred thousand pounds, and one hundred miles would exert a pressure of one million pounds, to the square inch. Now, as the pressure capable of being exerted by the most powerful dynamite, exploded in a space equal to its own volume, is about three hundred thousand to three hundred and fifty thousand pounds, it is evident that if the whole interior of the earth were filled with dynamite, and exploded, it would be capable of exerting a pressure only about one third great enough to raise the continents or to disrupt the crust of the earth.

Of course, it goes without saying that vents would be found on the lines of weakness; still could the great gulf underneath a volcano be filled with dynamite extending far down into the bowels of the earth, the effects of its explosion would not be more disastrous or far-reaching than are produced by the pent-up gases spontaneously generated there. Were it possible to bring up from those depths a cubic yard of the highly compressed incandescent gases and gas-charged silica, and then give it sudden release upon the surface of the earth, the effect would be quite equal to that produced by the detonation of an equal volume of dynamite.

We know, therefore, that the earth can never be destroyed from within.

The earth can never commit suicide. As the great terrestrial globe continues

A SHOWER OF METEORS MIGHT DESTROY ALL LIFE ON THE EARTH—WHAT MIGHT HAPPEN TO CITY HALL PARK, NEW YORK CITY

to shrink from loss of heat, high mountain-chains are formed along lines of weakness, and valleys are likewise deepened in the ocean-bed, exactly in the same manner that ridges of ice on a deeply frozen lake are formed, with corresponding depressions, due to the expansion of the water in freezing. The warping of the earth's crust will continue to produce volcanoes with occasional disasters until the ocean shall disappear by absorption in the earth, and our planet continue to revolve—a

THE WORLD MAY BE DESTROYED BY A COLLISION WITH SOME HEAVENLY BODY

dead world, like the moon. By that time, too, our sun may have so much cooled down as to be darkened by the formation of a crust upon its surface, and the whole solar system become a tomb of the dead, rolling on through infinite night. But that time is yet a long way off, and neither ourselves nor our children need to worry.

Although it is exceedingly improbable that the earth may be destroyed by collision with a comet or some huge meteor, still the fact that such a contingency is possible is sufficient ground for discussion on the subject, and for imagining what the result might be.

The earth is moving around the sun at a velocity of eighteen miles a second, while the sun, with all its attendant planets, is being hurried on toward the great fiery constellation of Hercules at a far greater velocity. The very fact that small meteors exist proves the possibility of the existence in space of meteors of inconceivable magnitude—even great black dead worlds may lie in our path, like breakers in the path of

a ship. Fifty miles a second is not an unusual velocity for heavenly bodies, and some are known to move at a speed even in excess of one hundred miles a second—five hundred times the speed of a rifle-ball. Small meteorites, which reach the earth at a velocity of from twenty to thirty miles a second, are instantly consumed by the friction generated with the atmosphere. Large meteors, however, occasionally reach the earth, escaping destruction from their size, but are found to have their surfaces fused from heat generated by the passage through the atmosphere. Although it is not probable, still it is possible, that the earth may some time encounter such a shower of small meteors, perhaps in the form of a comet, that the heat of combustion from friction with our atmosphere, and the poisonous gases thereby generated, might destroy all terrestrial life.

Expression was given to this theory in a series of articles published some time ago by Camille Flammarion, the eminent astronomer-author.

Again, it is known that not many years ago a huge bolide, something like eight miles in diameter, fairly grazed our earth. What would happen should a bolide, or meteor, a hundred miles, or even a thousand miles, in diameter strike the earth fairly and squarely?

Were we to suspend an egg by a small cord, and fire at it with a rifle, so that the bullet would strike it in the center, the effect would be somewhat similar on a small scale to what might be expected to happen to the earth if struck by a huge bolide a thousand miles in diameter, moving at a velocity of fifty miles a second.

We may ignore probabilities still further, and yet be within the possible, and conceive of a huge comet, or dead world, bigger than Jupiter, and that this great body might cross our path and rush toward our sun, and on its way catch up Mars like a speck of dust, and drop him in the earth's path; or the earth might be drawn along so near to the sun that we would be consumed by its furnace heat; or we might be drawn far out into space, and abandoned in the dark and frigid realm of Neptune.

In the wise economy of Nature it is so ordered that all vegetable life purifies the air for animal life, and vice versa. Animals consume oxygen and exhale carbonic acid, while vegetation absorbs carbonic acid, robbing it of its carbon and setting the oxygen free. The original atmosphere of the earth before animal life existed consisted essentially of nitrogen and carbonic acid. Our supply of atmospheric oxygen has been furnished by the great forests of vegetation, such as the coal-ferns, which covered the

THE TAIL OF A COMET MIGHT SWEEP AWAY THE EARTH'S ATMOSPHERE

earth in the Carboniferous Age, when the coal-beds were formed. The same conditions, only on a smaller scale, continue to prevail; but it is not likely that the oxygen given out by present vegetation is, or will be, sufficient to keep pace with its enormously increasing consumption by man. Lord Kelvin has estimated that if the present consumption of coal in human industries continues with anything like its present ratio of increase, the great coal-measures will be exhausted, and the oxygen of our atmosphere practically consumed by its combustion, within the next four or five centuries. This is the most likely, perhaps, of all possible calamities to generally affect the human race, and it more directly concerns us at the present time, from our realization that we are extravagantly wasting the breath of life of those who are soon to follow.

Let us hope, however, that long before our fuel shall be consumed and our oxygen exhausted man will have discovered some way of providing fresh supplies of oxygen from new sources.

"A DEAD WORLD, LIKE THE MOON"

4 The Other Americans

THE SATURDAY EVENING POST

An Illustrated Weekly Magazine
Founded A.º D.º 1728 by Benj. Franklin

AUGUST 8, 1903   FIVE CENTS THE COPY

Americans of To-Day and To-Morrow—By Albert J. Beveridge

THE CURTIS PUBLISHING COMPANY, PHILADELPHIA

HARPER'S WEEKLY

NEW YORK, APRIL 26, 1902

"THE RIGHT OF WAY"

HARPER'S WEEKLY

NEW YORK, JANUARY 4, 1902

A MEMORY OF EMANCIPATION DAY

Early in the 1900's the only really bothersome problem of race or nationality was that of the Negro. The Indian had been finally and brutally humbled a dozen years earlier, and those who survived were tucked away on remote reservations where they would not disturb the national conscience. The Chinese were proving to be a problem, but only in California. There was still a great deal of shoving and jostling and some snarling here and there as immigrants continued to pour into the country, but that was fairly normal—though there might have been a bit more of it than usual because strange and outlandish people were coming from southern and eastern Europe for the first time. For a while the nation had had difficulty in absorbing the tremendous wave of Irish immigration, but even in Boston, where they were most numerous, the Irish were so thoroughly Americanized in the opening years of the twentieth century that they controlled the city government and sat in the mayor's chair.

But not only did the black man remain outside the mainstream of American society; he appeared not to have the slightest prospect of ever entering into it. The South had created a completely effective Jim Crow system, and in 1896 the Supreme Court, in its celebrated *Plessy v. Ferguson* decision, gave its blessing to segregated facilities provided the accommodations for the races were equal. The case itself involved only a Louisiana law requiring segregated railroad facilities for colored people and whites, but by implication it extended to every other public facility. Though the decision required that segregated facilities be equal, it was a sham, for every enforcement agency and court of appeal in the South was in the hands of whites. Thus Jim Crow insured that the Negro would always be forced to live apart, with few opportunities for advancement. The black man in the North was in a better position legally; but he had little social standing, he stood a poor chance in the competition for jobs, and he was alternately viewed as a minstrel-show comic type and as a creature one step removed from a jungle savage.

There was no way up for the Negro. The most noted colored man of the time was Booker T. Washington, head of Tuskegee Institute, who was widely respected for his philosophy that the way for the Negro to advance was by learning to be a good farmer or mechanic. Yet when President Theodore Roosevelt invited Washington to the White House as a dinner guest there was a national uproar, most of it in the South but a good amount from bigots in other sections. Negroes were qualified to work in the White House kitchen, cooking and serving the President's food, but if one sat down at the same table with him he somehow defiled food and atmosphere.

Several articles that follow indicate that while many people were sensitive to the depressed economic and educational situation of the Negro, there appears to have been little awareness of his degraded and anomalous social position. There is no word to suggest that a dualistic society was not ordained from on high. One looks in vain for the word "integration" or a synonym. Negro poet Paul Lawrence Dunbar writes about Negro society in Washington and tells the same story: blacks were as separate from whites as if they were on different continents. Yet while they were separate socially, the two races often worked together during the day.

Rebecca Harding Davis (the mother of swashbuckling correspondent Richard Harding Davis) was astute enough to see that what the Negro needed most was a chance to work, that this was more important to him even than education. Mrs. Davis carried a cudgel for the Negro; one of her novels was faulted by the critics as being too openly pro-Negro, and yet it is interesting that even she was a little surprised to find that ability went with blackness: "I know one man, coal black, illiterate, who 'stole the trade' of a carpenter . . ." and again, "I know a jet-black boy of twenty-two . . . who has for years managed a small hotel. . . ." Would it have been less remarkable if either man had been only dark brown?

Joel Chandler Harris, creator of the Uncle Remus stories, gives a Southerner's view, but it is a very measured and dispassionate one; he cannot get excited even when he goes through the ritual blaming of the North and Reconstruction for all that is wrong in the South, including the Negro problem. The real bigot's viewpoint comes from Thomas Dixon, Jr., in his piece "Booker T. Washington and the Negro." Dixon at that time (1905) was best known as the author of *Leopard's Spots,* a novel about Reconstruction and the Ku Klux Klan. In 1905 he published *The Clansman* and in 1907 *The Traitor,* both sequels to his first book. And in 1915 he wrote the story for the motion picture *Birth of a Nation,* which was based on *The Clansman.* His novels were viciously anti-Negro, portraying the black man as sometimes childlike and helpless, sometimes lazy and shiftless, sometimes savage and bestial. This is the man *The Saturday Evening Post* invited to write about the Negro.

Dixon opens with the classic disclaimer: he is a good friend of the Negro race; although his books have antagonized colored people, he has only told the facts for the Negro's own good; from childhood some of his best servants have been Negroes. Having established his credentials, he goes on to prove that neither Booker T. Washington and his Tuskegee Institute nor any other kind of education can do the black man any real good. ". . . no amount of education of any kind, industrial, classical or religious, can make a Negro a white man or bridge the chasm of the centuries which

separate him from the white man in the evolution of human civilization."

Very few, even in 1905, were likely to have agreed with Dixon that one of the aims of education was to lighten the skin of Negroes. However, this is not the place to dissect Dixon's article; he should be read in the same spirit that one examines those drawings labeled "How many mistakes can you find in the picture?" And if one needs help in finding the mistakes in the picture, he can certainly get it from Albert Bushnell Hart's article "The African Riddle," which *The Saturday Evening Post* subtitles "Another Side of Mr. Dixon's Negro Question." Professor Hart, a historian at Harvard during almost half of a very long life, demolishes Dixon's emotional arguments. He does not hesitate to take up the subject of miscegenation, in an era when such matters were considered somewhat indelicate for discussion in mixed company, and makes it plain that the large number of persons of mixed Negro-white blood were the result of what amounted to the forced prostitution of slaves by their white masters. Hart points up very sharply the irrationality of the anti-Negro position: on one hand is the argument that the colored man is too simple and childlike to take care of himself without guidance from whites; at the same time there is the fear (which Dixon expresses very clearly) that widespread education for Negroes will result in their taking jobs away from the superior white man.

There is one piece of racist literature in this section that is not directed against the Negro but is as intemperate as most of the Southern arguments against giving rights and privileges to the black man. James D. Phelan's "The Case Against the Chinaman" lists every accusation that has ever been made against the Chinese —they do not adapt to American customs, they are opium addicts, they breed disease, they keep women in slavery, and on and on. Phelan was mayor of San Francisco at the time, and it is quite easy to see through his game. There was no great emotional content to his feeling against the Chinese—it was economic. The Chinese had been brought in when cheap labor was needed to build a transcontinental railroad and to do other hard labor, but by 1901, when Phelan wrote, they were competing with whites for jobs. Hence the tremendous resentment expressed by Mr. Phelan in his plea not to let any more Chinese into California.

Among all the words, one should not overlook the cartoons and the use of race stereotypes in advertisements. There, in a few pen strokes, a cartoonist can express his whole attitude and that of the times. And the attitude about race did not make the early 1900's the best of times for someone of a different color.

Booker T. Washington and the Negro

By *Thomas Dixon, Jr.*
Author of The Leopard's Spots

Some Dangerous Aspects of the Work of Tuskegee

FOR Mr. Booker T. Washington as a man and leader of his race I have always had the warmest admiration. His life is a romance which appeals to the heart of universal humanity. The story of a little ragged, barefooted piccaninny who lifted his eyes from a cabin in the hills of Virginia, saw a vision and followed it, until at last he presides over the richest and most powerful institution of learning in the South, and sits down with crowned heads and Presidents, has no parallel even in the Tales of the Arabian Nights.

The spirit of the man, too, has always impressed me with its breadth, generosity and wisdom. The aim of his work is noble and inspiring. As I understand it from his own words, it is "to make Negroes producers, lovers of labor, honest, independent, good." His plan for doing this is to lead the Negro to the goal through the development of solid character, intelligent industry and material acquisition.

Only a fool or a knave can find fault with such an ideal. It rests squarely on the eternal verities. And yet it will not solve the Negro problem nor bring us within sight of its solution. Upon the other hand, it will only intensify that problem's dangerous features, complicate and make more difficult its ultimate settlement.

It is this tragic fact to which I am trying to call the attention of the nation.

I have for the Negro race only pity and sympathy, though every large convention of Negroes since the appearance of my first historical novel on the race problem has gone out of its way to denounce me and declare my books caricatures and libels on their people. Their mistake is a natural one. My books are hard reading for a Negro, and yet the Negroes, in denouncing them, are unwittingly denouncing one of their best friends.

I have been intimately associated with Negroes since the morning of my birth during the Civil War. My household servants are all Negroes. I took them to Boston with me, moved them to New York, and they now have entire charge of my Virginia home. The first row I ever had on the Negro problem was when I moved to Boston from the South to take charge of a fashionable church at the Hub. I attempted to import my baby's Negro nurse into a Boston hotel. The proprietor informed me that no "coon" could occupy a room in his house in any capacity, either as guest or servant. I gave him a piece of my mind and left within an hour.

As a friend of the Negro race I claim that he should have the opportunity for the highest, noblest and freest development of his full, rounded manhood. He has never had this opportunity in America, either North or South, and he never can have it. The forces against him are overwhelming.

My books are simply merciless records of conditions as they exist, conditions that can have but one ending if they are not honestly and fearlessly faced. The Civil War abolished chattel slavery. It did not settle the Negro problem. It settled the Union question and created the Negro problem. Frederic Harrison, the English philosopher, declared that the one great shadow which clouds the future of the American Republic is the approaching tragedy of the irreconcilable conflict between the Negro and White Man in the development of our society. Mr. James Bryce recently made a similar statement.

The Argument of the Ostrich Man

IF ALLOWED to remain here the Negro race in the United States will number 60,000,000 at the end of this century by their present rate of increase. Think of what this means for a moment and you face the gravest problem which ever puzzled the brain of statesman or philosopher. No such problem ever before confronted the white man in his recorded history. It cannot be whistled down by opportunists, politicians, weak-minded optimists or female men. It must be squarely met and fought to a finish.

Several classes of people at present obstruct any serious consideration of this question—the pot-house politician, the ostrich man, the pooh-pooh man, and the benevolent old maid. The politician is still busy over the black man's vote in doubtful States. The pooh-pooh man needs no definition—he was born a fool. The benevolent old maid contributes every time the hat is passed and is pretty sure to do as much harm as good in the long run to any cause. The ostrich man is the funniest of all this group of obstructionists, for he is a man of brains and capacity.

I have a friend of this kind in New York. He got after me the other day somewhat in this fashion:

"What do you want to keep agitating this infernal question for? There's no danger in it unless you stir it. Let it alone. I grant you that the Negro race is a poor, worthless parasite, whose criminal and animal instincts threaten society. But the Negro is here to stay. We must train him. It is the only thing we can do. So what's the use to waste your breath?"

"But what about the future when you have educated the Negro?" I asked timidly.

"Let the future take care of itself!" the ostrich man snorted. "We live in the present. What's the use to worry about Hell? If I can scramble through this world successfully I'll take my chances with the Hell problem!"

My friend forgets that this was precisely the line of argument of our fathers over the question of Negro slavery. When the constructive statesmen of Virginia (called pessimists and infidels in their day) foresaw the coming baptism of fire and blood ('61 to '65) over the Negro slave, they attempted to destroy the slave trade and abolish slavery. My friend can find his very words in the answers of their opponents. "Let the future take care of itself! The slaves are here and here to stay. Greater evils await their freedom. We need their labor. Let the question alone. There is no danger in it unless you stir it."

The truth which is gradually forcing itself upon thoughtful students of our national life is that no scheme of education or religion can solve the race problem, and that Mr. Booker T. Washington's plan, however high and noble, can only intensify its difficulties.

This conviction is based on a few big fundamental facts, which no pooh-poohing, ostrich-dodging, weak-minded philanthropy or political rant can obscure.

The first one is that no amount of education of any kind, industrial, classical or religious, can make a Negro a white man or bridge the chasm of the centuries which separate him from the white man in the evolution of human civilization.

Expressed even in the most brutal terms of Anglo-Saxon superiority there is here an irreducible fact. It is possibly true, as the Negro, Professor Kelly Miller, claims, that the Anglo-Saxon is "the most arrogant and rapacious, the most exclusive and intolerant race in history." Even so, what answer can be given to his cold-blooded proposition: "Can you change the color of the Negro's skin, the kink of his hair, the bulge of his lip or the beat of his heart with a spelling-book or a machine?"

What Abraham Lincoln Said

NO MAN has expressed this idea more clearly than Abraham Lincoln when he said: "*There is a physical difference between the white and black races which, I believe, will forever forbid them living together on terms of social and political equality.*"

Whence this physical difference? Its secret lies in the gulf of thousands of years of inherited progress which separates the child of the Aryan from the child of the African. Buckle in his History of Civilization says: "The actions of bad men produce only temporary evil, the actions of good men only temporary good. The discoveries of genius alone remain: it is to them we owe all that we now have; they are for all ages and for all times; never young and never old, they bear the seeds of their own lives; they are essentially cumulative."

Judged by this supreme test, what contribution to human progress have the millions of Africans who inhabit this planet made during the past four thousand years? Absolutely nothing. And yet, Mr. Booker T. Washington in a recent burst of eloquence over his educational work boldly declares:

"The Negro race has developed more rapidly in the thirty years of its freedom than the Latin race has in one thousand years of freedom."

Think for a moment of the pitiful puerility of this statement falling from the lips of the greatest and wisest leader the Negro race has yet produced!

Italy is the mother of genius, the inspiration of the ages, the creator of architecture, agriculture, manufactures, commerce, law, science, philosophy, finance, church organization, sculpture, music, painting and literature, and yet the American Negro in thirty years has outstripped her thousands of years of priceless achievement!

Education is the development of that which *is*. The Negro has held the Continent of Africa since the dawn of history, crunching acres of diamonds beneath his feet. Yet he never picked one up from the dust until a white man showed to him its light. His land swarmed with powerful and docile animals, yet he never built a harness, cart or sled. A hunter by necessity, he never made an ax, spear or arrowhead worth

preserving beyond the moment of its use. In a land of stone and timber, he never carved a block, sawed a foot of lumber or built a house save of broken sticks and mud, and for four thousand years he gazed upon the sea yet never dreamed a sail.

Who is the greatest Negro that ever lived according to Mr. Booker T. Washington? Through all his books he speaks this man's name with bated breath and uncovered head—"Frederick Douglass of sainted memory!" And what did Saint Frederick do? Spent a life in bombastic vituperation of the men whose genius created the American Republic, wore himself out finally drawing his salary as a Federal office-holder, and at last achieved the climax of Negro sainthood by marrying a white woman!

What Education Cannot Do

SAYS the author of Napoleon, Honorable Thomas E. Watson: "Education is a good thing, but it never did and never will alter the essential character of any man or race of men."

I repeat, education is the development of that which *is*. Behold the man whom the rags of slavery once concealed—nine millions strong! This creature, with a racial record of four thousand years of incapacity, half-child, half-animal, the sport of impulse, whim and conceit, pleased with a rattle, tickled with a straw, a being who, left to his will, roams at night and sleeps in the day, whose native tongue has framed no word of love, whose passions once aroused are as the tiger's—equality is the law of our life!—when he is educated and ceases to fill his useful sphere as servant and peasant, what are you going to do with him?

The second big fact which confronts the thoughtful, patriotic American is that the greatest calamity which could possibly befall this Republic would be the corruption of our national character by the assimilation of the Negro race. I have never seen a white man of any brains who disputes this fact. I have never seen a Negro of any capacity who did not deny it.

One thought I would burn into the soul of every young American (and who thinks of a Negro when he says "American?")—this: Our Republic is great not by reason of the amount of dirt we possess, or the size of our census roll, but because of the genius of the race of pioneer white freemen who settled this continent, dared the might of kings, and blazed the way through our wilderness for the trembling feet of liberty.

A distinguished Negro college professor recently expressed himself as to the future American in one of our great periodicals as follows:

"All race prejudice will be eradicated. Physically, the new race will be much the stronger. It will be endowed with a higher intelligence and clearer conception of God than the whites of the West have ever had. It will be much less material than the American white of to-day. It will be especially concerned with the things of the mind, and moral excellence will become the dominant factor in the life of the new nation. The new race is to gain more from the Black element than from the White."

We have here an accurate statement of the passionate faith of ninety-nine Negroes out of every hundred. Professor Du Bois, author of The Souls of Black Folk, undoubtedly believes this. His book is a remarkable contribution to the literature of our race problem. In it for the first time we see the naked soul of a Negro beating itself to death against the bars in which Aryan society has caged him! No white man with a soul can read this book without a tear. Mr. Charles W. Chesnutt, the Negro novelist, believes in amalgamation, for he told me so. Professor Kelly Miller, the distinguished Negro teacher of Washington, believes it. In a recent article he declares:

"It is, of course, impossible to conceive of two races occupying the same area, speaking the same language, worshiping according to the same ritual, and endowed with the same political and civil privileges without ultimately fusing. Social equality is not an individual matter, as many contend, but is rigorously under the control of public sentiment."

I commend the solid logic of these sentences from a thoughtful Negro to the illustrious Society of Pooh-Poohs.

What is the attitude of Mr. Booker T. Washington on this vital issue? You will search his books and listen to his lectures in vain for any direct answer. Why? Because, if he dared to say what he really in his soul of souls believes, it would end his great career, both North and South. In no other way has he shown his talent as an organizer and leader of his people with such consummate skill as in the dexterity with which he has for twenty years dodged this issue, holding steadily the good-will of the Southern white man and the Northern philanthropist. He is the greatest diplomat his race has ever produced.

Yet he who reads between the lines of his written and spoken words will find the same purpose and the same faith which his more blunt and fearless brethren have honestly and boldly proclaimed. He shows this in his worship of Frederick Douglass. In his book, The Future of the American Negro, we find this careful sentence:

"To state in detail just what place the black man will occupy in the South as a citizen when he has developed in the direction named is beyond the wisdom of any one."

Yet on page 69 he says:

"The surest way for the Negro to reach the highest positions is to prepare himself to fill well at the present the basic occupations"—independent industries, of course—for, mark you, "*Tuskegee Institute is not a servant-training school!*"

Again on pages 83 and 85 we are told: "There is an unmistakable influence that comes over a white man when he sees a black man living in a two-story brick house that has been paid for. I need not stop to explain. Just in so far as we can place rich Negroes in the South who can loan money to white men, this race question will disappear."

Why?

The conclusion is obvious: The Negro who holds a mortgage on a white man's house will ultimately demand and receive social recognition from him.

On page 66 of his Future of the American Negro he says: "The Jew, who was once in about the same position as the Negro is to-day, has now recognition because he has entwined himself about America in a business and industrial way."

Again his conclusion is obvious. The absurdity of the comparison, however, is the important point in this sentence, not only for the pathetic ignorance of history it displays but for the revelation of the writer's secret hopes and dreams.

The Jew has not been assimilated into our civil and social life because of his money—but for a very different reason. The Jew belongs to our race, the same great division of humanity. The Semitic group of the white race is, all in all, the greatest evolved in history. Their children have ever led the vanguard of human progress and achievements. A great historian and philosopher once said: "Show me a man of transcendent genius at any period of the world's history and I'll show you a man with Hebrew blood in his veins." Our prejudice against the Jew is not because of his inferiority, but because of his genius. We are afraid of him, we Gentiles who meet him in the arena of life, get licked and then make faces at him. The truth is the Jew had achieved a noble civilization—had his poets, prophets, priests and kings—when our Germanic ancestors were still in the woods cracking cocoanuts and hickory-nuts with monkeys. We have assimilated the Jew because his daughter is beautiful and his son strong in mind and body!

The Danger of a Nation Within a Nation

THE trouble with Mr. Booker T. Washington's work is that he is silently preparing us for the future heaven of Amalgamation—*or he is doing something equally dangerous*, namely, he is attempting to build a nation inside a nation of two hostile races. In this event he is storing dynamite beneath the pathway of our children—the end at last can only be in bloodshed.

Mr. Washington is not training Negroes to take their place in any industrial system of the South in which the white man can direct or control him. He is not training his students to be servants and come at the beck and call of any man. He is training them *all* to be masters of men, to be independent, to own and operate their own industries, plant their own fields, buy and sell their own goods, and in every shape and form destroy the last vestige of dependence on the white man for anything.

I do not say this is not laudable—I do not say that it is not noble. I only ask what will be its end for the Negro when the work is perfect? Every pupil who passes through Mr. Washington's hands ceases forever to work under a white man. Not only so, but he goes forth trained as an evangelist to preach the doctrine of separation and independence.

The Negro remains on this Continent for one reason only. The Southern white man has needed his labor, and therefore has fought every suggestion of his removal. But when he refuses longer to work for the white man, then what?

Mr. Booker T. Washington says on page 65 of his book: "The Negro must live for all time beside the Southern white man."

On what sort of terms are they to live together? As banker and borrower? Hardly, if the Negro is the banker. Even now, with the white man still hugging the hoary delusion that he can't get along without the Negro, he is being forced to look to the Old World for labor. The simple truth is, the South will lag behind the world industrially in just so far as she depends on Negro labor. The idea that a white man cannot work in the fields of the South is exploded. Only one-third of the cotton crop is to-day raised by Negro labor. Even now the relations of the races, with the Negro an integral part of the white man's industrial scheme, become more and more difficult.

A Gulf that Grows Wide

PROFESSOR KELLY MILLER says: "It is a matter of common observation that the races are growing further and further apart."

Mr. Washington says on this point: "For the sake of the Negro and the Southern white man there are many things in the relations of the two races that must soon be changed" (page 65). The point I raise is that education necessarily drives the races further and further apart, and Mr. Washington's brand of education makes the gulf between them if anything a little deeper. If there is one thing a Southern white man cannot endure it is an educated Negro. What's to be the end of it if the two races are to live forever side by side in the South?

Mr. Washington says: "Give the black man so much skill and brains that he can cut oats like the white man—then he can compete with him."

And then the real tragedy will begin. Does any sane man believe that when the Negro ceases to work under the direction of the Southern white man, this "arrogant," "rapacious" and "intolerant" race will allow the Negro to master his industrial system, take the bread from his mouth, crowd him to the wall and place a mortgage on his house? Competition is war—the most fierce and brutal of all its forms. Could fatuity reach a sublimer height than the idea that the white man will stand idly by and see this performance? What will he do when put to the test? He will do exactly what his white neighbor in the North does when the Negro threatens his bread—kill him!

Abraham Lincoln foresaw this tragedy when he wrote his Emancipation Proclamation, and he asked Congress for an appropriation of a billion dollars to colonize the whole Negro race. He never believed it possible to assimilate the Negro into our national life. This nation will yet come back to Lincoln's plan, still so eloquently advocated by the Negro Bishop, Henry M. Turner.

It is curious how the baldheaded assertion of a lie can be repeated and repeated until millions of sane people will accept the bare assertion as an established fact. At the close of the War, Mr. Lincoln, brooding over the insoluble problem of the Negro's future which his proclamation had created, asked General Benjamin F. Butler to devise and report to him immediately a plan to colonize the Negroes. General Butler, naturally hostile to the idea, made at once his famous, false and facetious report, "that ships could not be found to carry the Negro babies to Africa as fast as they are born!" The President was assassinated a few days later. This lie is now forty odd years old, and Mr. Booker T. Washington actually repeats it as a verbal inspiration though entirely unconscious of its historic origin.

We have spent about $800,000,000 on Negro education since the War. One-half of this sum would have been sufficient to have made Liberia a rich and powerful Negro state. Liberia is capable of supporting every Negro in America. Why not face this question squarely? We are temporizing and playing with it. All our educational schemes are compromises and temporary makeshifts. Mr. Booker T. Washington's work is one of noble aims. A branch of it should be immediately established in Monrovia, the capital of Liberia. A gift of ten millions would do this, and establish a colony of half a million Negroes within two years. They could lay the foundations of a free black republic which within twenty-five years would solve our race problem on the only rational basis within human power. Colonization is not a failure. It has never been tried.

We owe this to the Negro. At present we are deceiving him and allowing him to deceive himself. He hopes and dreams of amalgamation, forgetting that self-preservation is the first law of Nature. Our present attitude of hypocrisy is inhuman toward a weaker race brought to our shores by the sins of our fathers. We owe him a square deal, and we will never give it to him on this Continent.

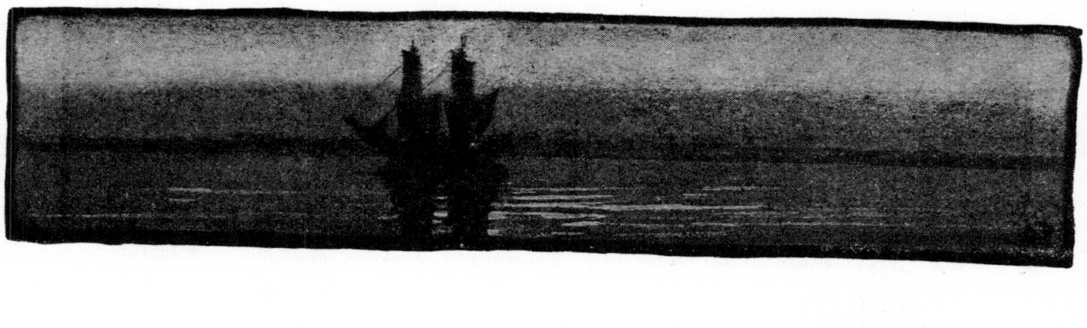

THE AFRICAN RIDDLE

Another Side of Mr. Dixon's Negro Question

By ALBERT BUSHNELL HART

Professor of History in Harvard University

"OUT of the eater came forth meat, and out of the strong came forth sweetness"—so ran Samson's famous riddle, which turns upon the familiar fact that in the midst of the evil and the foul there is often an unexpected industry and plenty. To nothing is the homely contrast of the swarm of bees and honey in the midst of a decaying carcass more applicable than to the results of African slavery in America, so strong, so fierce, so overcoming in its life, yet furnishing such materials for a new and busy social organization, now that it is gone.

All is not honey and sweetness in the South by any means, and from week to week new books and new articles from Southern whites, from negroes and from Northern observers show that the riddle is not yet solved; at the same time they bring out striking and often humorous contrasts between the points of view, not only of different writers, but of the same writers. It may be worth while to recall that these difficulties of understanding and explaining what we call the negro question, or the race question, or the Southern question, are

DRAWN BY EMLEN McCONNELL—

almost as old as American history; and that anybody who attempts to solve that problem by an offhand generalization will find himself in conflict with some of the deepest-laid principles of American character and government, and will very likely discover that he is fighting his own fundamental conceptions.

The first of the queer things about the negro question is that it should exist at all in America. From the dawn of time that race has had its seat in Africa; it has never been a conquering people; the Egyptians and the Moors are not negroes, and if they had been, their relations would have brought about a negro question in Southern Europe, and not across a tempestuous ocean. We might expect to find a race of negro slaves, or former slaves, in Spain, or France, or Italy; but what the devil did the negro want in our galley?

A Shameful Legacy

TRULY he wanted nothing. To this day there are practically no voluntary immigrants of the African race in the United States; Africa had to run with blood and resound with shrieks for centuries in order to push a few hundred thousand poor wretches to the coast so that our ancestors could get at them, and thereby hand down to us anxiety, sectional strife and race hostility. It is whimsical that to the Indian problem, which was acute for two centuries and a half, should have been added a negro problem. And all that woe in Africa and confusion in America could have been avoided if our ancestors had had the sense to understand that there were plenty of whites to colonize the new world! The South and Southwest might have been peopled, exactly as the North and Northwest have been, by swarms of European immigration, without a single slave or a single negro. How much happier America would be if we could solve the negro problem by turning the clock backward three centuries!

A special reason why our ancestors ought to have saved us our present troubles is that they not only introduced a savage race, but made them slaves, and thereby deliberately violated their own principles, religious, political and social. Since chattel slavery, except as a punishment for crime, died out in England before colonization, our ancestors had to reinvent it; and although after the Revolution they attempted to throw back the responsibility upon the British Government, it was a poor subterfuge. That Government, to be sure, systematically

annulled most of the colonial laws for regulation of the slave trade; but the colonies passed those laws either to get a revenue out of the trade or to prevent a dangerous increase in the number of slaves; they did not object to a profit in the slave trade, but that somebody else should get that profit. From the beginning to the end it was in the power of the colonies to drive slavery out by humane legislation and discriminating taxes; yet all sections, New England, Middle and Southern, received slaves, held slaves, and defended slavery.

In doing so, all sections sinned against their own religious principles; they saw as clearly as we do that slavery was in its nature a denial of the brotherhood of man and the common fatherhood of God. At first they claimed the right only to enslave pagans, but when masters refused to allow their slaves to be baptized, the kind-hearted colonial governments stepped in and enacted that it was also lawful to hold a Christian in bondage. The religious argument against slavery, although frequently put forward, produced very little effect until the abolitionists took it up seventy years ago; and then it was met by the most delightfully selfish and naïve perversions of Scripture: "Cursed be Canaan; a servant of servants shall he be unto his brethren." "Thou shalt not covet thy neighbor's house, . . . nor his manservant, nor his maidservant." "Servants, obey in all things your masters according to the flesh!" That settled the intention of the Almighty that the Anglo-Saxon should hold the African in bondage. Yet side by side with this Biblical privilege of enslaving the negro went a queer sense of moral responsibility to him, and a self-congratulation that the barbarous African had been drawn out of the bottomless pit of his native heathendom, and brought within the Christianizing influence of the overseer and the hoe gang. Here was confusion worse confounded: if the negro was to be Christianized, he ought to have the Bible and the right of private judgment on religion; but to more than nine-tenths of the slaves the Bible was always, and necessarily, a sealed book.

Quite as abrupt and bizarre was the contrast between slavery and the magnificent appeals to human freedom which our ancestors made, especially during the Revolution. What did it mean when the Declaration of Independence declared that all men "are created equal," and the Virginia Declaration of Rights held that "all men are by nature free and independent"? They meant, of course, all men who participated in the political community; but that left out not only the slaves but about three-fourths of

the adult white men, who, under the property qualifications of the time, were not voters; and it included a few negroes who, even in some of the Southern States, had the necessary qualifications for the suffrage. The truth is that the Declaration of Independence and slavery were mutually incompatible; and later the slave power recognized that truth by scoffing at the Declaration, and even came to the point where one advocate of slavery declared that "Slavery is the foundation of every well-designed and durable republican edifice."

With or without any declaration to that effect, there was a practical equality among the American farmers and frontiersmen; they moved when they liked, set up new communities, and chose their own careers; the great American principle of equality of opportunity was open to all free men. No, not to all free men, for there was a numerous and increasing class of free negroes who were in themselves a whimsical but humane contradiction to the excuses for slavery. If the negroes were degraded, incapable of taking care of themselves, dangerous, why should not they all be slaves? On the other hand, if only the brutal and incapable could rightfully be made slaves, why should not that principle cover the lowest stratum of the whites, many of whom, in the opinion of the slaveholders, were inferior to good slaves? In the heat of the abolition controversy some Southern writers accepted the latter horn of the dilemma, and urged that Northern mechanics, and even their own poor white neighbors, ought to be enslaved.

The Paradox of Slavery

THAT difficulty still exists whenever the negro question is discussed. If the race is to be kept down because it is ignorant and debased, why does not the same principle apply to white people of the same degree of intellectual and moral advancement? If men are to be treated on their merits, what are you going to do with black men? The only short-cut out of this difficulty has occasionally been put forward by extreme Southern writers, namely, that the negro is not a man at all, not one of those for whom Christ died, not subject to the lofty principles of government of the people, by the people and for the people, no part of the political community; an individual, as Chief Justice Taney expressed it, "not entitled to any rights that the white man is bound to respect." This theory, though distinctly put forth by very few persons, does undoubtedly lie at the root of much of the so-called discussion of the Southern question, which assumes that the negro exists only for the use and benefit of the white race; but it is contrary to the practice of centuries in allowing free negroes; and it is absolutely contradicted by the notorious and patent fact that two million or more of the so-called negroes have white blood, and some hundreds of thousands are more white than black.

Whenever a Northern writer mentions this question of the mixture of races he is accused by the Southern press of indelicacy, although no question is so frequently discussed and with such plainness of phrase by Southerners of all classes. This mixture of races began at the very outset of negro slavery in America. It was noticed by every traveler and observer throughout slavery times. It involved the most hideous of all the results of slavery: a master's son or daughter working in the fields under the driver's whip, or sold under the hammer to pay the father's debts. In not one case in ten thousand was the mulatto the child of a white mother; they sprang from the passions of the men of the dominant race. These are ugly truths, and we hope that they represent a bygone régime. Certainly the reprobation of Southern public opinion is much stronger on this matter than it used to be; and most of the young mulatto children are the children of mulatto parents, and not of white fathers.

No part of the whole negro question is so beset with grotesque contradictions as this. On one side we are assured that there is a divinely implanted racial aversion, which must forever keep the races from uniting; on the other hand, whole volumes, like Professor Smith's Color Line, are devoted to showing the awful and imminent danger of amalgamation. Some of the most intelligent and public-spirited Southern people feel sure that the real race question is whether, in the long run, the lowest stratum of white men will not marry daughters of the well-to-do negro families in their neighborhood.

Through the two millions or more of mulattos in the United States chiefly comes the question of personal relations with the whites which in the minds of the Southerners always means a disturbance of crystallized society; for the mulattos undoubtedly include most of the best-endowed, best-provided and best-mannered members of the race. There is the usual contradiction of opinion with regard to these mixed bloods: the same writer will tell you that the mulattos are feebler, more vicious and more unhealthy than the pure negroes, and in the same breath that all the negro leaders are mulattos. If Booker Washington founds a great school, or Du Bois writes a great book, they are told that their white blood is responsible for such achievements; if they offer to ride in the same car with a white man, they are bidden to betake themselves to the Jim Crow car.

By all American principles, the discrimination against respectable colored people, and especially against persons who are almost indistinguishable from whites, is unjust and absurd. The college catalogues of the land are starred with the names of Irishmen, Scotchmen, Germans, Italians, Armenians, Poles, Finns, Russians, and a dozen other nationalities, and the bearers are admitted without question to the society of their fellows. Indian full-bloods and half-breeds can ride on any train or attend any public performance. Chinese and Japanese gentlemen are treated as gentlemen throughout the world, except by the customs authorities of the United States. In European countries even the negroes are received on the same terms as other people of equal intelligence. It is this one race which, in one part of this one country, is selected out for absolute exclusion from every form of social intercourse which includes the breaking of bread together.

Yet even if the prejudice be unreasonable and illogical, it does exist, and exhibits itself almost as clearly in the North as in the South. It is somewhat akin to the feeling of social inequality between employers and domestic servants of every kind, but it has deeper roots; and it is of little use to criticise it, because there is not the slightest prospect of its eradication in several generations.

Inside of this contradiction of race prejudice with the religious and political tenets of America, there is another contradiction, which would be amusing if it were not fateful. Southern society, so proud, so exclusive, so efficient in protecting itself from the undesired, is in terror lest it should be found admitting the fearful curse of social equality; and there are plenty of Southern writers who insist that the negro shall be deprived of the use of public conveniences, of education, of a livelihood, lest he, the weak, the despised, force social equality upon the white race. What is social equality if not a mutual feeling in a community that each member is welcome to the social intercourse of the other? How is the negro to attain social equality so long as the white man refuses to invite him, or to be invited with him? It sounds like a joke.

It ceases to be comical, however, when the South insists that the North must join in protecting the South from hobnobbing with the negro, as evidenced to all the world by the cyclone of wrath raised by the invitation by President Roosevelt to Booker Washington to lunch with him at the family table, culminating in the open declaration of a Senator from South Carolina: "Now that Roosevelt has eaten with that nigger Washington, we shall have to kill a thousand niggers to get them back to their places." What sort of logic is this? The whole basis of the Southern treatment of the negro is that he is by nature hopelessly inferior, that he never can rise, that everybody with the slightest strain of negro blood is thereby naturally degraded; and then, on the other hand, that a courtesy by the President of the United States to the most eminent member of the negro race, conspicuous for the example of a noble character, and using all his influence against any political action or combination unfavorable to the whites—that such courtesy lifts the negro up to the hated equality. If the negro, or any member of the race, is the equal of the white man, no venomous attack upon the Chief Magistrate of the Nation can deprive him of that status; if he is not the equal, where is the danger?

There is really the crucial point in the whole controversy. Has the negro the intellectual and moral power to raise himself out of his present inferiority into a position of equality of achievement with the white man? The South is a unit that the negro is inferior, but there is no unity of opinion as to the possibilities of the future. A publication which has had a considerable sale among the poor whites of late declares that the negro is a beast, and that the white man would be justified in killing him off like a colony of monkeys. Thomas Nelson Page says that the negro "has indeed in the main behaved well" and that "he may individually attain a fair, and, in uncommon instances, a considerable degree of mental development." There is no doubt that the best friends of the negro are much disappointed by the paucity of result from his education since the Civil War, and numerous threats are heard to cut off the negro schools from support by general taxation. The South is not the first community to learn that ability to read and write does not necessarily mean uprightness, but nobody who knows the condition of the Southern rural schools, and especially of the negro schools, can suppose that the results so far prove very much either way. So long as the South finds itself able to spend only six millions a year on the education of about three million negro children, it is idle to argue from the intellectual results of negro education.

As to the capacity and conditions of the negro, the world is really very much in the dark, and the Southern people contribute astonishingly little of that first-hand and expert knowledge which they think they possess. Except some significant pamphlets by A. H. Stone, of Greenville, Mississippi, no Southern planter has described his own experience with his black laborers; few Southerners travel outside of the main highways, or know anything of the conditions, either of negroes or of poor whites, outside their own county; and, as Edgar S. Murphy points out, the white people know a great deal more about the bad negroes in their neighborhood than of what is passing in the minds of the quiet and industrious blacks. Northern people now, just as in slavery times, are rated for presuming to take interest in or express an opinion upon the negro question; but, unless they take an interest and investigate the subject on the ground, nobody is likely to have data for a sound judgment.

However, one thing is evident about the white opinion of the negroes—namely, that the South repeats, apparently with very little notion that a gun can both shoot and kick, the common argument of slavery times, the double-barreled statement that the negroes as a race are now much inferior to the whites, are steadily declining, are incapable of combined effort, and are probably doomed to die out; while at the same time it is a malicious and dangerous race, determined to establish domination over the whites, and to mix the blood of the two peoples, from which awful consequences it is restrained only by continuous threats and violence!

One would think that the easiest way of freeing the community from these fearful dangers would be to remove the negro race altogether, and ever since 1816 there has been a propaganda in favor of colonization, which springs up occasionally in such a suggestion as that made by Mr. Dixon in The Saturday Evening Post, that "Liberia is capable of supporting every negro in America; . . . a gift of ten millions . . . would establish a community of half a million negroes in two years." Without dwelling on this magical power of twenty dollars a head, it is sufficient to quote Mr. Page, who says: "They never will be deported . . . the negroes have rights; many of them are estimable citizens; and even the great body of them, when well regulated, are valuable laborers." This last opinion seems to be shared by the farmers and the legislatures of the Southern States, who instantly interpose whenever any effort is made to take any considerable number of negroes even from one State into another.

One would think that the most obvious and elemental remedy is that the negro should improve, and should show that it is not his purpose to attack or destroy white civilization. That is precisely the doctrine of Booker Washington, and the purpose of Tuskegee and Hampton and all the other institutions for the higher training of the negro in the South. Many white people have doubted whether the remedy could be applied on a sufficient scale, and whether the race could respond, but the thing itself seems absolutely desirable. Now comes Mr. Thomas Dixon, Jr., in The Saturday Evening Post, to assail this method. "Mr. Washington," says he, "is training the negroes to be masters of men, to be independent. . . . If there is one thing a Southern white man cannot endure it is an educated negro." In so far as Mr. Dixon is authoritative—and he appears to be accepted as spokesman by a considerable number of Southern people—he is simply going back to the real basis for slavery, namely, that the colored race exists to contribute to the comfort and ease of the white man. Mr. Dixon's argument is just as good against the poor whites as against the negro; it is just as good against the Russian Jew or the Hungarian laborer.

Here we come straight back to the fun of the negro question, to the delicious discrepancy of the two sides of the argument: the poor negro, inferior, weak, helpless, "half child, half animal, the sport of impulse, . . . pleased with a rattle, tickled with a straw," is about to compete with the white man, "take the bread from his mouth . . . and place a mortgage on his house"; the negro who cannot support himself is, by industrial competition, to drive the white man to desperation!

Under this doctrine, for the negro there remains only the alternative suggested by a preacher of his own race: "My bretherin, here is two roads befo' you; which will you choose? One of 'em leads to perdition, and de udder to everlastin' damnation." If the negro shows capacity to support himself, to manage his own affairs, to think and plan, to calculate, to be a full man, to become a consumer, to benefit his country by improving his own condition, then the white man, says Mr. Dixon, apparently with approval, will simply "kill him."

There is a negro question, the gravity which has hardly been touched in this article. There is doubtless misunderstanding in the North, there is often rancor in the South; but the question is not going to be solved now, or in the future, by killing off one of the parties to the conflict, nor by arguments and remedies which fail to agree with each other, with the American system of free government, or the world's experience of human nature.

HARVARD'S FOOTBALL ELEVEN OF 1909, UNDER PRESIDENT ROOSEVELT, OF HARVARD

James Montgomery Flagg drew the cartoon above for *Life* in 1904 after a Negro had won a place on Harvard's football team. Teddy Roosevelt, mentioned in the caption, had incurred the wrath of segregationists by inviting Booker T. Washington to dine at the White House.

THE NEGRO OF TO-DAY

His Prospects and His Discouragements

By Joel Chandler Harris

IT WAS not so long ago that he has forgotten it that a friend of mine from the North called on me—sought me out, so to say, on my snap-bean farm—and, without the least apology, renewed a discussion that had been broken off several years before by a railway time-table which informed me that I had just time to catch an outgoing train from New York. As the train was headed for the South it was hardly necessary for me to apologize for interrupting the discussion in a somewhat summary way; and so it hung in the air by loose ends for several years until my friend, with pardonable impatience, determined to have the matter out with me on ground of my own choosing.

Meanwhile, much to the surprise of both of us, our positions had been reversed. In New York he was of the opinion that if the South gave the negro half a chance he would show what metal he was made of, while I, at the time and place aforesaid, could see no hope in the future of the negro. But he had traveled to some extent in the South before reaching the snap-bean farm, and his views had undergone a complete change. On every other subject he was sane and sunny, but when it came to the negro he was a hopeless pessimist.

My friend had whirled through parts of the South in a Pullman car, had viewed the situation from the flying window, and had come to the conclusion that the negro had no future. Indeed, there was not much future for anybody in this region, though he was willing to admit that Atlanta had a smart appearance. His pessimism reached out over the negro and embraced the poor whites, the tackies, the crackers, and all others of that class.

Now, in discussing the negro question with my friend at the North I had been compelled in self-defense to put forward views that were foreign to my mind and belief. I had supposed that they would be accepted as half-humorous hinges for the discussion to swing back and forth upon; but I found that they had not only been taken seriously, but had been adopted bodily; and I was extremely sorry, for my friend is a genuine philanthropist, full of love for all things human.

I soon discovered why his views had changed, and the reason was such a small one that I could but laugh behind my hand. He had been made the astonished victim of the insolence of a negro porter of a sleeping-car. What the porter said or did I was never able to discover, but it was something that had the effect of shocking the sensibilities of my friend. It was in vain that I tried to convince him that the porter belonged to one of the classes of irresponsibles that are to be found in every race on the face of the globe; the porter was a negro and fitted in well with the other fleeting glimpses of various individuals of the colored race; and that was the end of it so far as my Northern friend was concerned—the end of it, that is to say, for a time, for since then I have seen his name in a list of those who had made liberal contributions to aid the practical education of the negro in the South.

I have mentioned my friendly discussion with this Northerner for the purpose of emphasizing the fact that it is the little things that count in the formation of opinions. A stranger in the South sees the helpless array of loafers, both white and colored, at the railway stations, and he comes to the conclusion that the whole population is thriftless and shiftless; he visits a city, and he observes the negro barbers and the hotel-waiters performing their antic follies on the guitar or zither, or he witnesses the insolence of a negro porter, and he concludes that all the negroes are of the same irresponsible order.

But it is not so, nor even measurably so. The guitar and zither players and the crap-shooters are all parts of the furniture of the house of sorrows, and I suppose have a definite place in the scheme of Providence; but it is this class of irresponsibles that is made to stand for the race in the comic papers, where the " coon " plays a leading part.

One thing is certain: when we come to form our conclusions and make up our judgment on the testimony of little things we make a confession of prejudice and intolerance, and we find it impossible to take a broad and catholic view of the whole question, whatever it may be. We cannot fairly judge a race, or a country, or a religious institution, or a social organization, or society itself — nay, not even the republic in which we take pride — unless we measure it by the standards set up by the men who are its best representatives. Unless we judge every human institution by its best products, instead of its worst, we shall find ourselves far from the truth; and this being so, who are we that we shall judge the products of the Almighty by their worst, instead of their best, results?

During the course of our talk at the snap-bean farm many things that deserve consideration in an article of this kind were touched on. There were some things that my friend could look straight in the face, and he mentioned — though without any display of regret — that there was a kind of mysterious periodicity with respect to the South's attitude toward the negro. Sometimes he would read in the newspapers of the day that the negroes were getting along as well as could be expected — in fact far better than any one could have hoped under the circumstances; and then, within the course of a few short months, he would find in the same newspapers long articles going to show that, in spite of the fact that Northern philanthropists had poured out their money like water for the educational advancement of the negro, he was going backward instead of forward; that his book-learning, such as he could imbibe, was unfitting him for the practical duties that his station would call on him to perform; that every student at a school meant a hand taken permanently from the cotton-patch and the cornfield — and so forth and so on.

My friend is a very busy man at home, and I judged that he read the Southern newspapers, such as came his way, with more attention than he gave to those published next door; otherwise, he would have discovered, almost without any effort on his part, that the hopeful and friendly tone of the Southern newspapers at various times was usually coincident with an absence of agitation at the North on the negro question, and vice versa — if I may be permitted to employ the choice dialect of Uncle Cæsar.

There can be no doubt that since the day of emancipation the negro has experienced the seamy side of justice; but who has been all along responsible for this state of things? There can be but one answer to this question: whatever form or system of injustice he has been made the victim of has been almost entirely due to the unwise and unnecessary crusade inaugurated in his behalf by the politicians of the North, who

DRAWN BY EMLEN McCONNELL

—THEIR ANTIC FOLLIES ON THE GUITAR

neither knew nor cared anything for the situation at the South. Indeed, there was a time when negro outrages at the South were deemed so essential to the welfare of these politicians that when real ones failed to occur their newspaper organs made a business of inventing them.

In addition to this, there was an assiduous effort made to convince the negro that the Southern people were his worst enemies, bent on subjecting him to some form of permanent servitude. These things had their inevitable effect, and in many instances the negro has been made to suffer for the folly of his political friends. These politicians, by way of showing what queer pranks ignorance — to call it by no severer name — can cut in the presence of great questions, endeavored to hand over to the negro, but a few months from slavery, the reins of political power. They did this, they said, that he might be able to protect himself.

In pursuance of this policy they placed in his hands the governments of several States and kept him there for a time by means of American bayonets; but it was only for a time, for when the bayonets were withdrawn the negro governments fell to pieces like houses of cards. This experiment was the beginning of all the troubles and difficulties that the negro has been made the victim of. He, the poor tool, has been practically held responsible for all the ills and all the evils that have followed the effort to make him a citizen and a political power before his time.

The truth is, the responsibility of the negro was no more than that of a little child who had wandered, quite by accident, into the halls of legislation, and remained, pleased at the novelty of the situation, and yet wondering what it was all about. Like a novice learning to play chess, he moved whatever pieces he was told to move, and when no one was observing him closely he moved others for his own amusement. Behind him was the imported carpet-bagger and the native scalawag, and these, receiving their orders from Washington, played havoc with things in general, and with the negro in particular; and when it was thought that the temper of the Southern people had been tried to the utmost, and when there were no more State treasuries to loot, carpet-bagger and scalawag retired to their original obscurity,

leaving the unfortunate negro to bear the brunt of the whole business.

If the politicians, who were the moving cause, had been filled with undying hate for the negro their attitude and acts would betray some show of consistency; but all of them were old enough to know something of human nature, and they knew that the outcome of their folly would manifest itself in some form of reprisal in the South; and when the reprisals came they were used as campaign material to keep the politicians in power. I am not referring to this matter in terms that my knowledge thereof would justify; if I were to do so I should be accused of carrying the discussion back to a weary time, when all was hate and confusion.

It was unfortunate, as a matter of course, that the South should have permitted itself to be goaded, or that it should have turned something more than a cold shoulder to the negro, or that it should have allowed him to suffer for the sins of the white leaders; but the South has never claimed to be superior to human nature. In fact the people here have always had a little more than a fair share of human nature; and it would be too much to expect them, in the heat of the moment — and there have been many heated moments since the war — to rise superior to the instincts of human nature and practice the philosophy that has been commended to us by the wise men of all ages. In fact neither the South nor the North practices it, for it is one of the weaknesses of human nature that the average man, no matter what his race or his ambition, would rather perform a hasty act than deprive himself of the momentary pleasure of performing it.

It is, of course, possible to take a large view of the matter, and to say that whatever has happened to the negro, and to the white man by his side, has been for the best, and will count as helpful elements in the future; but it is always so easy to dispose of doubtful human actions by saddling them bodily on Providence that I cannot but regret the foolish, futile and revengeful policy of the Northern politicians and the unreasoning irritability of the Southern people.

I believe that, at bottom, a majority of the American people are at one with respect to the negro and his future, and the reason I have for making the statement is a sound one, namely: that a large majority of the people of this country are blessed with common-sense in a larger measure than those of any other country on the globe. This innate common-sense has brushed away so many difficulties, and solved so many problems, and carried the country safely through so many crises, and has come to the front in so many emergencies, that it may confidently be depended on in the future.

In saying this I do not lose sight of the fact that this element has been conspicuously absent in the political treatment of the negro since the war. But I am convinced that this has been due to the ignorance of the average voter. Of late the North seems inclined to take a reasonable view of the difficulties by which the negro is surrounded — difficulties that concern the white people of the South even more intimately than they do the rest of the country. These difficulties have been and are still very serious, and on many occasions they have been rendered acute by the blind policy of certain politicians, or by a newspaper controversy based on dense ignorance on one side and unreasoning irritability on the other.

If any one can show me that discussion or agitation of the negro question or controversy over the political or social

DRAWN BY EMLEN McCONNELL

Emlen McConnell

status of the negro has tended in the slightest degree to improve his condition, or add to his welfare, or promote his best interests, I shall be the first to stir it up and hark it on and applaud its continuance; but I think that the contrary can be shown. I know that it has done harm. In the first place, as I have already said, it has always tended to irritate the South; and though I am willing to deplore such irritation as unnecessary, nevertheless I am bound to recognize the limitations of human nature, whether at the North or at the South. In the second place, this agitation, whether in the halls of Congress or in the newspapers, has had a tendency to give a majority of the negroes totally false ideas as to their status in the communities in which they live—so much so that a majority of them have felt themselves to be divorced from the interests of the whites and therefore from their responsibilities as citizens, and they have felt it to be their duty to antagonize every policy that the whites have put forward.

But the negro is not directly responsible for this attitude; it is a part of the first lessons that he learned from the carpetbaggers. At the very beginning of emancipation he was placed in a false position. When the Freedman's Bureau was in operation, and for a long time after it passed away, he considered himself the ward of the nation, and, if the truth were told, some such idea dimly haunts his dreams to this day. He was not only the ward of the nation, but he was to have special privileges, and in every contingency that arose he was to be taken care of.

Under the circumstances he was more than justified in drawing such a conclusion. He could point to hundreds of demonstrations and declarations in political campaigns, to exhortations in pulpits, to wild and whirling denunciations on the floor of Congress and elsewhere, and to thousands of editorial articles from the pens of men absurdly ignorant of the damage they were doing. The negro knew no better than to believe that he had been singled out for special favors at the hands of the Government, and it was, and is, a pity that he should have been held responsible for this belief.

The reader will say that I am repeating myself, but sometimes a little wholesome iteration is necessary where a fact is concerned, and the fact that I am emphasizing is responsible for all the misunderstanding that has arisen between the whites of the South and the negroes. In spite of it all, however, the condition of the negro has been steadily growing better. His relations with his white friends are no longer strained; he is beginning dimly to perceive that the welfare and progress of the individual is of more importance both to him and his neighbors than politics and promises that are made to be broken. He is beginning to realize that the best interests of all the members of the community in which he lives are also his best interests, and he is ordering his affairs accordingly. He is beginning to perceive that a negro's surest road to the respect and confidence of the white man is along the old route of individual industry and thrift and general usefulness to the community that is useful to him; and he is discovering for himself that the material things that make for prosperity and progress are as close to the trained hand and brain of the negro as they are to the hand of the white man.

Nevertheless, there are many Southern people who steadily refuse to believe that the negro has any wholesome future before him, and some of them even write communications to the papers in order to demonstrate the shiftless characteristics of the race; and there are men of the highest character and intelligence who claim that the two races can never live under the same government and in the same communities without inviting a race war on the one hand or amalgamation on the other, and that one or the other of these contingencies can only be averted by deportation to some country or territory where the negro can have everything his own way. Moreover, there are to be found individual instances where the assertion is made that the negro is going backward instead of forward; but individual instances of this kind are worth no more than the individuals themselves. In such cases you cannot argue from the particular to the general without doing wholesale injustice, for the facts are all the other way.

Then there is the subject of negro education, and this is a fruitful source of pessimism. We are told that the average negro is so incapable of taking an education that he cannot even attempt it without unfitting himself for those duties in which he has been most useful; and some go so far as to say that it destroys his usefulness altogether. We hear, also, that he is getting too much of what is called the higher education, and that the result is ruinous.

Again, there is complaint made that, although Booker Washington's Tuskegee Institute has been in successful operation for several years, and has made such progress as to arrest the attention of thoughtful men everywhere, he is not yet engaged in supplying our people with a superior article of house-servant. In short, it is possible to gather up numerous complaints of all kinds from various uneasy and contentious sources; and if you dispose of one another will soon fly in your face.

I know of a young negro who is a good Latin scholar—and he helps his father make boots and shoes. This may be pretty bad, but if any one can show me that he makes a worse

The first step towards lightening

"The White Man's Burden"

is through teaching the virtues of cleanliness.

Pears' Soap

is a potent factor in brightening the dark corners of the earth as civilization advances, while amongst the cultured of all nations it holds the highest place—it is the ideal toilet soap.

All sorts of people use it, all sorts of stores sell it.

shoe with his Latin than he would without it I shall turn a readier ear to complaints that at present strike me as far-fetched. Moreover, although Booker Washington has entered into no contract, so far as I know, to supply the country with house and farm servants, his school would make small impression on the demand for those desirable adjuncts even if he sent out forty thousand graduates a year.

But I desire to call attention to a fact which, at first sight, seems to be of no importance, but which, on a closer view, becomes highly important. When it is said of the negro that he is not capable of assimilating the learning taught in the schools, or that he is unable to utilize the benefits to be derived from education, there must be some standard by which he is measured or with which he is compared. Necessarily, that standard is the present capabilities of the white race; but how unjust to the negro to compare his infantile efforts to the

accomplishments of the white race! He is only about three centuries from a state of barbaric slavery in Africa compared with which his term of servitude in the United States was Christian freedom.

But if such a comparison is to be made, why not go back to the first forty years of the freedom of those who, in Great Britain, were held as serfs by England's invaders. There can be no doubt, though history has a gap here, that these English serfs were brothers to the ox, just as it has been said that the negroes are brothers to the mule. If we are to make any comparisons at all, why not measure what the negro is doing with what our ancestors were doing at the same stage of development?

The negro is of a different race, it is true, and his mind may fail to respond to the different processes of civilization and enlightenment; but this remains to be seen. It has not failed to respond thus far. He seems to be getting along remarkably well considering all the circumstances by which he has been surrounded. He is acquiring property quite rapidly, and in our modern civilization this faculty is regarded, whether rightly or not, as the highest possible test of progress.

The negro is also acquiring an education, slowly, as a matter of course, but surely; and by so much as the minds of the present generation are prepared and equipped, by just so much will the minds of the generation to come be prepared to assimilate knowledge. Public opinion in the South—the opinion that controls and leads—has no such views with respect to the negro, for the Southern States have spent millions and are still spending millions to educate the negro.

So far as education is concerned, I am fully persuaded that both blacks and whites are getting too much of the wrong kind and not half enough of the right kind. There seems to be an educational craze on all sides that must be left to wear itself out. Such has been the nature of the popular clamor that the real purpose of education has been lost sight of, and we are turning out heathen by the million, who enter on the business of life with the dimmest ideas of religion or morals.

Education for its own sake—the education that more than compensates for the time and effort necessary to acquire it—has been put bodily out of the schools.

And we are in such a furious hurry about the education that has become the national fetish, for the reason that it is quickly over with, that we are impatient with what the negro has accomplished. We are placed in the position of expecting a race but a few years from the inevitable ignorance imposed on it by the conditions of slavery to make the most remarkable progress that the world has ever heard of; and when we discover that, in the nature of things, this is impossible, we shake our heads sadly, and are ready to lose heart and hope.

If Booker Washington is pointed out as an example of what may be done by a negro who, in his youth, was in touch with slavery, the reply is that he is a phenomenon, and that, in the nature of things, we cannot expect the race to produce many such; or we are told that the white blood in his veins is a sufficient explanation of his remarkable career. But is it not true that a man like Booker Washington is an exception in any race? He is an orator of great power, a writer of unusual ability, and an extraordinary administrator of large and complicated interests. And as to his negro blood, why not state the fact in a different way? Why does it not operate to hamper and hinder him?

I do not ask any one to share my hopefulness with respect to the negro, nor is it necessary that the views I am putting forth should be accepted. There have been many developments of one sort and another well calculated to fatigue and disappoint and disgust those who are all the time hoping for the best. There have been among the negroes manifestations of brutality unparalleled, so far as I know, since the dawn of civilization, and the reprisals that have been made are but the natural result of the horror that must fill the bosoms of the best men who are brought sharply face to face with such cruelty and bestiality. Both the crime and the nature of the reprisals are nauseating and horrible, but where there is one the other must be expected, even in the North.

Has the Free Negro Failed?

What Forty Years of Independence Have Brought Him

By Rebecca Harding Davis

FOR seven years we have visited, every winter, a lonely little inn for sportsmen on the western coast of Florida. You reach it after days of travel through the poorest districts of the South. In Alabama, Georgia and Florida you pass through interminable forests of pine trees, most of which are girdled, dying or dead. Now and then you come to a wretched little "cl'arin'," with a few coal-black negroes lounging in the doors of the huts, with nothing apparently to do in life but to wave a friendly greeting to the train. The ground is yellow with millions of the little sand-hills thrown up by the wood-rats or gophers. What if these hidden myriads of hungry rats should some night attack the hungry negroes, you think, shuddering, as the train rushes on, leaving them in the great, solitary woods alone together.

The west coast of Florida, you find when you reach it, has in certain quarters a motionless, melancholy, tropical beauty of its own which seems to put it outside of our brisk, up-to-date United States. It does not change from year to year. There are the broad, shining bays debouching into the Gulf. They scarcely move. The alligators hide in the mud of their banks—the fish literally leap out of the creeping water. The little islands with their plumes of feathery palms are always the same, so are the great live oaks, draped with funereal moss, that line the banks. Beyond them stretch the "hummocks," or swamps and forests, filled with small game and deer. In the wilder parts the bear and panther still hide. Through the thin herbage that covers the coral rock which passes itself off as Mother Earth in this part of the world creep the moccasin and copperhead. Even in winter the jasmine trails her yellow blossoms over the trees, and magnolias light their white lamps in the thick woods.

The beauty of the place, you think, is too weird and unchanging, too melodramatic to be quite real. You feel that you have lost yourself in some enchanted, disreputable suburb of the world. Somewhere, you are sure, it abuts upon hell.

But I did not set out to paint a fanciful picture for you of Nature in Florida, but to give you a fact or two about the human nature there—facts which are not at all fanciful but most ugly realities.

Before the Civil War this quarter of the coast was a great sugar plantation. The owner was a leader in Congress and in the Confederate army. He has long been dead. His slaves, when freed, scattered—nobody knew or cared where. Some of them remained on the plantation and squatted in the swamps or woods, building themselves huts in which their grandchildren now live. There are tens of thousands of negroes in the Gulf States who are the descendants of field hands, and it is of them and their condition that I wish to speak here a few plain words.

White Americans in the North are just now a little tired of the everlasting, insoluble negro problem, and are tempted to drop it, to let the black folk settle it for themselves—work out their own salvation or damnation as they choose.

The majority of negro leaders hold that there are two things essential, first of all, for the uplifting of their race: education and the right of suffrage.

But surely, when a man has sunk to the level of the brute, his first chance of manhood lies in the quickened desire in him not to be a brute, to work, to make a home for himself, his wife and children, and to live in it honestly and decently. Booker Washington, by the simple, rational method of providing self-respecting work for them, is lifting thousands of his race out of brutality to manhood.

Understand me. I do not question the fact that education is a mighty lever in the hands of a human being, or that suffrage is an inestimable blessing to the man who casts his vote intelligently and does not sell it for twenty-five cents or a drink of gin.

But how first to make these men human and intelligent? What is to be done with these idle millions of negroes in the Gulf States?

Look at the plain facts. Take these villages in Florida and the cotton States, made up, as I said, of the descendants of field hands. In many of them is neither school nor church—nor ever has been, either. These blacks live from hand to mouth. They seine or hunt, beg or steal. Northern capitalists come down here enthusiastic about cheap negro labor, and put them into mills, phosphate works and the like. They are good for two days' work in the week; the other five they live on their wages, gorge and sleep. Why not? What do they know that is better? Then the Northern capitalist brings down white labor and declares "nothing can be done for the negro."

In one of the poorest hamlets in Florida a Sunday-school was started lately by some good Christian folk for the children of the fishermen.

"And the colored children?" I asked.

"Oh!" cried the superintendent, shuddering, "if a black child should come in that door every white would walk out of it! Oh, no! We keep the niggers out!"

This missionary was a Pennsylvanian, by the way.

They have virtually been kept "out" since the days of slavery. What is the result? What are they? They are blacker than their yellow kinsfolk in the North; they are not so shrewd or imitative. But they are kindlier, more affectionate and courteous, and, I cannot but think, show stronger brain power when their brains have a chance to work. Sometimes they make the chance. I know one man, coal black, illiterate, who "stole the trade" of a carpenter, worked at odd jobs in an Alabama town, and ended by being a builder, prosperous and respected. I know a jet-black boy of twenty-two who cannot read or write, but who has for years managed a small hotel, bought the provisions, controlled the work and looked after the guests.

One negro who acted as guide for the Northern sportsmen decided to "do better for himself," went into the interior and started a melon-patch on an acre of ground which cost him a few dollars. But he planted only the rarest and best kinds of cantaloups and with his own hands packed them for the market.

His Northern friends furnished him with the names of the dealers in New York who sold choice fruit. He carries on the same business to-day, and still oversees every detail of it, from the planting of the seed to the packing of the melon; but his fruit is sought for by the best dealers, and his capital is rated at over $100,000.

Another negro has built himself a snugly-furnished little cabin on an island below Tampa. There his wife and babies live, clean, comfortable and happy, while Otho makes a good income by trading in alligator and otter skins.

Last winter a man was lynched in a neighboring hamlet to us, and this year another in one still nearer—both for good cause.

But what will you have? No man has cared for their souls. When men and women are left for generations to herd together like brutes they will act like brutes. Who is to blame?

A great deal of philosophic nonsense is talked about "inferior races," "racial antagonism," "inherent difference in human types." The fact is, as all history shows to us, that a race or a family acquires its character through the treatment it receives from the world. The original Bourbon, for instance, was not more selfish, or cruel, or voluptuous than other men. But when his family were set apart and worshiped for centuries, while five millions of people slaved and starved that they might indulge the passions of beasts in their gilded cages, they became beasts.

What has black Toby to do, left here idle to live like an animal in his hut in the swamps with the wood-rats, but indulge the passions of an animal?

No observer with ordinary common-sense can come into actual contact with these people and not feel that what they need now, to-day, is the desire to work and the chance to work.

Education is not the most urgent necessity of life for them now, nor even the right to vote. These, it may be, are blessings for to-morrow. Simply to know how to read and write does not change a brute into a man. And as for the right of suffrage ——

For more than a century it has been justly denied to more than thirty millions of white educated Americans, who have well served their country and their God without it. The majority of them have wisely decided that they do not want it.

We women, at least, need not wring our hands in despair at the legislation which keeps Toby away from the polls a year or two longer.

The one thing that he wants to-day, as I said, is work.

An institution like Tuskegee or Hampton in the lower South would accomplish good results. Still more effective would be the promulgation of Mr. Washington's scheme of the working of small tracts by individual owners.

True, the negro in Mississippi who is able to grow one bale of cotton usually mortgages it, before it is planted, to the village storekeeper for his year's food and clothes. That is cruel enough. But, after all, he is fed and clothed. He is not drunk. It is not he who is lynched.

Mechanics are needed in all parts of the South, and the negro is not there barred out from work by the trades unions. Many of the finest buildings going up now in Southern cities are in the hands of negro workmen. They have ten chances of work in Charleston or Jacksonville to one in Philadelphia.

The black problem in the Gulf States will not be solved by any one sweeping act of legislation or political strategy. It is the individual negro that must be taught to work, to be honest, to be Christian. They are an imitative race. Virtue is quite as contagious among them as the smallpox.

This childish folk need to be taught the first lessons of life, which we teach to children: not to read or to vote but to stand on their feet, to use their hands, to help themselves.

Here is a great work which, it seems to me, is waiting for the young negro men and women who have had college training: surely a more wholesome, higher task in life than the pouring out of morbid essays or poems in which they bewail the injustice of Fate in giving them colored skins.

The Colored Brother at Work

By Samuel E. Moffett

THE time is past when the only careers in life open to a negro were to pick cotton, make up berths in a Pullman car, or wait on a table. The study of the negro population of the United States recently published by the Census Bureau discloses some facts that show very clearly that the colored race is steadily developing a complete social and industrial system of its own. There is hardly any branch of industry in which negroes are unrepresented, and that statement includes the women as well as the men.

A large city could be formed without a single white man in it, and yet lack for no trade or profession. There are 21,268 negro teachers and college professors in the United States, and 15,530 clergymen. The negroes could finance a railroad through their eighty-two bankers and brokers, lay it out with their 120 civil engineers and surveyors, condemn the right-of-way with their 728 lawyers, make the rails with their 12,327 iron and steel workers, build the road with their 545,980 laborers, construct its telegraph system with their 185 electricians and their 529 linemen, and operate it with their 55,327 railway employees.

Colored people complain that they have to sit in the gallery in white theatres, but their 2043 actors and showmen might give them theatres of their own in which they could occupy the boxes in solitary grandeur. They have fifty-two architects, designers and draftsmen, 236 artists and teachers of art, 1734 physicians and surgeons, 212 dentists, 210 journalists, 3921 musicians and teachers of music, and ninety-nine literary and scientific persons. The colored baby can be introduced to the world by negro physicians and nurses, instructed in every accomplishment by negro teachers, supplied with every requisite of life by negro merchants, housed by negro builders, and buried by a negro undertaker.

There are negro bookkeepers and accountants, clerks and copyists, commercial travelers, merchants, salesmen, stenographers and telegraph operators. Negroes are in every manual trade—carpenters, masons, painters, paperhangers, plasterers, plumbers, steam-fitters, chemical workers, marble-cutters, glass-workers, fishermen, bakers, butchers, confectioners, millers, shoemakers, tanners, watchmakers, gold and silver smiths, bookbinders, engravers, printers, tailors, engineers, photographers, glovemakers—everything that statisticians think it worth while to count. And the curious thing is that in whatever line a negro man is at work there also is a negro woman. The only occupations which the colored women have allowed their men-folk to monopolize are those of the architect, the banker and broker, the telegraph and telephone lineman, the boilermaker, the trunkmaker and the patternmaker. You can hire a negro civil engineeress or an electricienne. There are 164 colored clergywomen, 262 black actresses, and ten Afro-American female lawyers. One negro woman works as a plumber, another as a plumber, and forty-five of them are blacksmiths, iron and steel workers and machinists. Three are wholesale and 860 retail merchants. Others are journalists, literary persons, artists, musicians, government officials, and practitioners of an infinite variety of skilled and unskilled trades.

In many respects the colored populations bear a marked resemblance to a European peasantry. Take, for instance, the extensive employment of women in agriculture. Nearly 600,000 negro women and girls—almost as many as the numbers in all other occupations combined—are engaged in farming. Over half a million of them are employed as farm laborers, outnumbering the white women three to one.

Negroes operate about one-eighth of all the farms in the United States, which is rather more than their proportion of the population. But, of course, their share of the acreage and value of the land is much smaller—only 4.6 per cent. of the former and 2.7 per cent. of the latter. In South Carolina, Mississippi and Louisiana more than half of all the farms are worked by negroes.

Moreover, half of all the cotton plantations in the United States are under black control, although, of course, they average less in size than those run by white men. The black farms of all kinds produce greater values to the acre than the white. There is a great stretch of land, extending from the Atlantic to the Gulf Coast of Texas, in which more than half of all the farms are operated by negroes. In three counties more than nineteen-twentieths of the farms are in colored hands; in thirteen counties more than nine-tenths; in fifty-four counties more than three-fourths, and in 205 counties in eleven States more than half.

Negro barbers, porters, servants and waiters loom large in the popular imagination, but they really form an insignificant part of the colored race. The barbers are little over half of one per cent. of the income-earning negro men. Servants and waiters are four and one-half per cent. Over fifty-eight per cent. of those men are engaged in agriculture.

It is noteworthy that the proportion of self-supporting negroes is much larger than that of self-supporting whites. Of all over ten years old, 84.1 per cent. of the colored males and 40.7 per cent. of the colored females are engaged in gainful occupations, against 79.5 per cent. of the white males and 16 per cent. of the white females similarly occupied. These are figures to which the negro can "point with pride" when he is accused of preferring the midnight chicken and the surreptitious watermelon to the joys of labor.

LOOKING FORWARD.

MIRANDY.—Yo' am de laziest human bein' I ebeh sot eyes on!

PETE.—Ah, quit yo' flattehin', honey;—I 'se li'ble teh git de big head an' nebeh be any use.

Negro Society in Washington

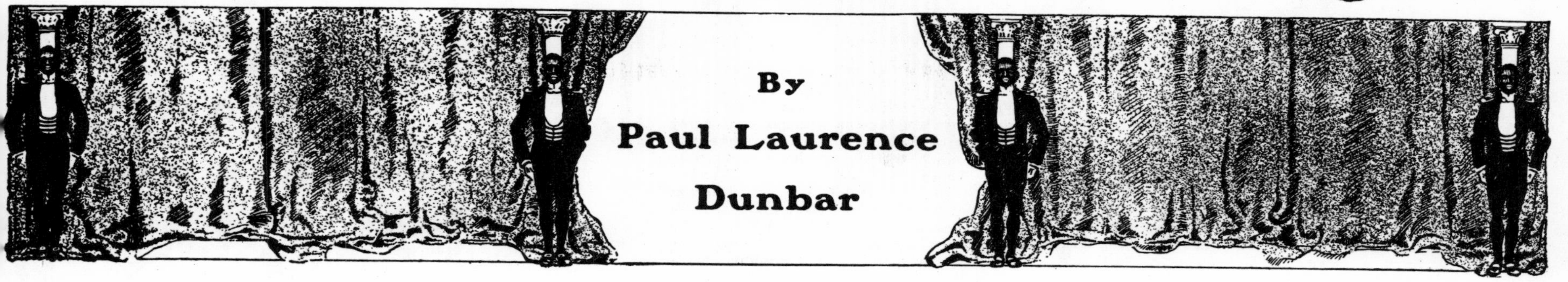

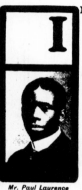

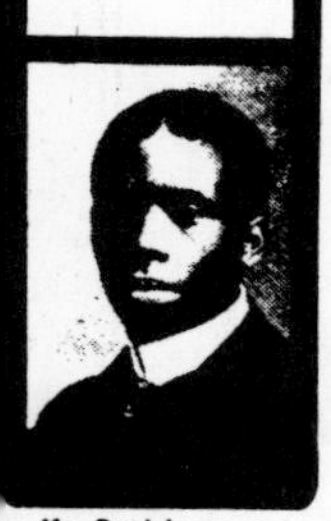
Mr. Paul Laurence Dunbar
PHOTO. BY BAKER'S ART GALLERY, COLUMBUS, O.

IN SPITE of all the profound problems which the serious people of the world are propounding to us for solution, we must eventually come around to the idea that a good portion of humanity's time is taken up with enjoying itself. The wiser part of the world has calmly accepted the adage that "All work and no play makes Jack a dull boy," and has decided not to be dull. It seems to be the commonly accepted belief, though, that the colored people of the country have not fallen into this view of matters since emancipation, but have gone around being busy and looking serious. It may be heresy to say it, but it is not the truth.

The people who had the capacity for great and genuine enjoyment before emancipation have not suddenly grown into grave and reverend philosophers. There are some of us who believe that there are times in the life of a race when a dance is better than a convention, and a hearty laugh more effective than a Philippic. Indeed, as a race, we have never been a people to let the pleasures of the moment pass. Any one who believes that all of our time is taken up with dealing with knotty problems, or forever bearing around heavy missions, is doomed to disappointment. Even to many of those who think and feel most deeply the needs of their people is given the gift of joy without folly and gayety without frivolity.

Nowhere is this more clearly exemplified than in the social doings of the Negro in Washington, the city where this aspect of the colored man's life has reached its highest development. Here exists a society which is sufficient unto itself—a society which is satisfied with its own condition, and which is not asking for social intercourse with whites. Here are homes finely, beautifully and tastefully furnished. Here come together the flower of colored citizenship from all parts of the country. The breeziness of the West here meets the refinement of the East, the warmth and grace of the South, the culture and fine reserve of the North. Quite like all other people, the men who have made money come to the capital to spend it in those social diversions which are not open to them in the smaller and more provincial towns. With her sister city, Baltimore, just next door, the Negro in Washington forms and carries on a social life which no longer can be laughed at or caricatured under the name "Colored Sassiety." The term is still funny, but now it has lost its pertinence.

A Society Sufficient to Itself

The opportunities for enjoyment are very numerous. Here we are at the very gate of the South, in fact we have begun to feel that we are about in the centre of everything, and that nobody can go to any place or come from any place without passing among us. When the soldiers came home from the Philippines last summer, naturally they came here, and great were the times that Washington saw during their stay. At a dinner given in honor of the officers two Harvard graduates met, and, after embracing each other, stood by the table and gave to their astonished hearers the Harvard yell at the top of their voices. One was a captain of volunteers, and the other, well, he is a very dignified personage, and now holds a high office.

And just here it might not be amiss to say that in the social life in Washington nearly every prominent college in the country is represented by its graduates. Harvard, Yale, Princeton, Cornell, Amherst, Pennsylvania, with women from Smith, Wellesley, Cornell, Oberlin, and a number of others of less prominence.

The very fact of our being so in the way of traffic has brought about some very amusing complications. For instance, and this is a family secret, do any of you uninitiated know that there were three inaugural balls? The whites could only afford one, but we, happy-go-lucky, pleasure-loving people, had to have two, and on the same night. There were people coming here from everywhere, and their friends in the city naturally wanted to show them certain courtesies, which was right and proper. But there are cliques, and more cliques, as everywhere else, and these cliques differed strenuously. Finally, they separated into factions: one secured the armory, and, the other securing another large hall, each gave its party. And just because each tried to outdo the other, both were tremendous successes, though the visitors, who, like the dying man, had friends in both places, had to even up matters by going first to one and then the other, so that during the whole of that snowy March night there was a good-natured shifting of guests from one ballroom to the other. Sometimes the young man who happened to be on the reception committee at one place and the floor committee at the other got somewhat puzzled as to the boutonnière which was his insignia of office, and too often hapless ones found themselves standing in the midst of one association with the flower of the other like a badge upon his lapel.

Each faction had tried the other's mettle, and the whole incident closed amicably.

The War of the Social Cliques

One of the beauties and one of the defects of Washington life among us is this very business of forming into cliques. It is beautiful in that one may draw about him just the circle of friends that he wants, who appeal to him, and from whom he can get what he wants; but on the other hand, when some large and more general affair is to be given which comprises Washington not as a home city, but rather as the capital of the nation, it is difficult to get these little coteries to disintegrate. The only man who is perfectly safe is the one who cries, "The world is my clique!" and plunges boldly into them all.

Of course, there are some sets which could never come together here. And we are, in this, perhaps imitators; or is it the natural evolution of human impulse that there should be placed over against each other a smart set?—yes, a smart set, don't smile—and a severe high and mighty, intellectual set, one which takes itself with eminent seriousness and looks down on all the people who are not studying something, or graduating, or reading papers, or delivering lectures as frivolous. But somehow, in spite of this attitude toward them, the smart young and even the smart old people go on having dances, teas and card parties, and talking small talk, quite oblivious of the fact that they are under the ban.

Washington has been card crazy this year, and for the first time on record the games did not end with the first coming of summer, but continued night after night as long as there was anybody in town to play them. For be it known that we also put up our shutters and go to the mountains or seashore, where we lie on the sands or in the open air and get tanned, if our complexions are amenable to the process, and some of them are.

There are to my knowledge six very delightful card clubs, and I know one couple who for twenty-five years have had their friends in for cards on every Thursday night in the autumn and winter. If the charitable impulse overtakes us there is a run on the department stores of the city for bright new decks of cards and bisque ornaments, the latter to be used as prizes in the contests to which the outside world is invited to come and look on.

Even after the shutters are put up, when our Negro lawyers lay aside their documents, and our doctors put their summer practice on some later sojourner in town, the fever for the game follows the people to their summer resorts, and the old Chesapeake sees many a game of whist or euchre under the trees in the daytime or out on lantern-lighted porches at night.

But let no one think that this diversion has been able to shake from its popularity the dances. And how we dance and dance, summer and winter, upon all occasions, whenever and wherever we can. Even when, as this year, we have not been compelled by the inauguration of a President to give something "socially official," there is enough of this form of amusement to keep going the most earnest devotee. There are two leading dancing clubs formed of men, and one which occasionally gives a dance, but mostly holds itself to itself, formed of women. The two first vie with each other winter after winter in the brilliancy of their affairs, one giving its own especial welcome dance with four assemblies; the other confining itself to one or two balls each year.

Not the Comic Balls We Know

Do not think that these are the affairs which the comic papers and cartoonists have made you familiar with; the waiters' and coachmen's balls of which you know. They are good enough in their way, just as are your butchers' picnics and your Red Men's dances, but *these* are not of the same ilk. It is no "You pays your money and you takes your choice" business. The invitations are not sent to those outside of one particular circle. One from beyond the city limits would be no more able to secure admission or recognition without a perfect knowledge of his social standing in his own community than would Mrs. Bradley-Martin's butler to come to an Astor ball. These two extremes are not so far apart, but the lines are as strictly drawn. The people who come there to dance together are people of similar education, training and habits of thought. But, says some one, the colored people have not yet either the time or the money for these diversions, and yet without a minute's thought there come to my mind four men, who are always foremost in these matters, whose fortunes easily aggregate a million dollars. All of them are educated men with college-bred children. Have these men not earned the right to their enjoyments, and the leisure for them? There are others too numerous to mention who are making five or six thousand a year out of their professions or investments. Surely these may have a little time to dance?

There is a long distance between the waiter at a summer hotel and the man who goes down to a summer resort to rest after a hard year as superintendent of an institution which pays him several thousand a year. In this connection it afforded me a great deal of amusement some time ago to read from the pen of a good friend of mine his solemn comments upon the Negro's lack of dramatic ability. Why? Because he had seen the waiters and other servants at his summer hotel produce a play. Is it out of place for me to smile at the idea of any Harriet of any race doing The Second Mrs. Tanqueray?

View us at any time, but make sure that you view the right sort, and I believe you will not find any particular racial stamp upon our pleasure-making. Last year one of the musical societies gave an opera here, not perhaps with distinction, but brightly, pleasantly, and as well as any amateur organization could expect to give it. Each year they also give an oratorio which is well done. And, believe me, it is an erroneous idea that all our musical organizations are bound up either in a scientific or any other sort of study of rag-time. Of course, rag-time is pleasant, and often there are moments when there are gathered together perhaps ten or twelve of us, and one who can hammer a catchy tune, rag-time or not, on the piano is a blessed aid to his companions who want to two-step. But there, this is dancing again, and we do not dance always.

Indeed, sometimes we grow strongly to feel our importance and to feel the weight of our own knowledge of art and art matters. We are going to be very much in this way this winter, and we shall possibly have some studio teas as well as some very delightful at-homes which will recall the reign, a few years ago, of a bright woman who had a wealth of social tact and grace, and at whose Fridays one met every one worth meeting resident here and from the outside. The brightest talkers met there and the best singers. You had tea and biscuit, talk and music. Mostly your tea got cold and you forgot to munch your biscuit because better things were calling you. This woman is dead now. Her memory is not sad, but very sweet, and it will take several women to fill her place.

A Season of Literature, Music and Art

There are going to be some pleasant times, though different in scope, in the studio of a clever little woman artist here. She is essentially a miniature painter, but has done some other charming and beautiful things; but above all that, and what the young people are possibly going to enjoy especially, she is a society woman with all that means, and will let them come, drink tea in her studio, flirt behind her canvases, and talk art as they know it, more or less. Her apartments are beautiful and inspiring. The gatherings here, though, will be decidedly for the few. These will be supplemented, however, later in the year by one of the musical clubs which is intending to entertain S. Coleridge Taylor, who is coming over from London to conduct his cantata, "Hiawatha." Mr. Taylor is a favorite here, and his works have been studied for some time by this musical club. It is expected that he will be shown a great many social courtesies.

An article on Negro social life in Washington, perhaps, ought almost to be too light to speak of the numerous literary organizations here, the reading clubs which hold forth; but, really, the getting together of congenial people, which is, after all, the fundamental idea of social life, has been so apparent in these that they must at least have this passing notice.

In the light of all this, it is hardly to be wondered at that some of us wince a wee bit when we are all thrown into the lump as the peasant or serving class. In aims and hopes for our race, it is true, we are all at one, but it must be understood, when we come to consider the social life, that the girls who cook in your kitchens and the men who serve in your dining-rooms do not dance in our parlors.

To illustrate how many there are of the best class of colored people who can be brought thus together a story is told of a newcomer who was invited to a big reception. A Washingtonian, one who was initiated into the mysteries of the life here, stood beside him and in an aside called off the names of the guests as they entered. "This is Doctor So-and-So," as some one entered the room, "Surgeon-in-chief of Blank Hospital." The stranger looked on in silence.

(continued.)

Negro Society in Washington

Concluded

"The man coming in now is Judge Somebody Else, of the District." This time the stranger raised his eyebrows. "Those two men entering are consuls to Such-and-Such a place." The newcomer sniffed a little bit. "And ah!" his friend started forward, "that is the United States Minister to Any-Place-You-Please." The man who was being initiated into the titles of his fellow-guests said nothing until another visitor entered the doorway; then he turned to his friend, and, in a tone of disbelief and disgust remarked, "Well, now, who under the heavens is that? The Prime Minister of England or the King himself?"

Last summer was the gayest that Washington has seen in many a year. It is true that there are hotels and boarding-houses at many summer resorts and that some of our people gather there to enjoy themselves, but for the first time there was a general flocking to one place taken up entirely and almost owned by ourselves. The place, a stretch of beach nearly two miles long with good bathing facilities, and with a forest behind it, has been made and built up entirely by Negro capital. Two men, at least, have made fortunes out of the sale and improvement of their property, and they, along with many others, are the owners of their own summer homes and cottages at Arundel-on-the-Bay and Highland Beach, Maryland. Here the very best of three cities gathered this last summer. Annapolis and Baltimore sent their quota and our own capital city did the rest. It was such a gathering of this race as few outside of our own great family circle have ever seen.

There is, perhaps, an exaltation about any body of men and women who gather to enjoy the fruits of their own labor upon the very ground which their labors have secured to them. There was, at any rate, a special exaltation about these people, and whatever was done went off with éclat. There was a dance at least once a week at one or another of the cottages, and the beauty of it was that any one who was spending the summer there needed to look for no invitation. He was sure of one by the very fact of his being there at all, a member of so close a corporation. The athletes did their turns for the delectation of their admirers, and there were some long-distance swimming contests that would have done credit to the boys in the best of our colleges. There were others who took their bathing more complacently, and still others who followed the injunction of the old rhyme, "Hang your clothes on a hickory limb, but don't go near the water." Cards, music and sailing parties helped to pass the time, which went all too swiftly, and the Izaak Waltons of the place were always up at five o'clock in the morning and away to some point where they strove for bluefish and rocks, and came home with spots. The talk was bright and the intercourse easy and pleasant. There was no straining, no pomposity, no posing for the gallery. When September came we began to hear the piping of the quail in the woods away from the beach, and our trigger-fingers tingled with anticipation. But the time was not yet ripe. And so the seal is to be set this winter upon our Maryland home by a house party, where the men will go to eat, smoke and shoot, and the women to read, dance and—well—women gossip everywhere.

This is but a passing glimpse of that intimate life among our own people which we dignify by the name of society.

Professional Trouble-Breeders

MANY Southern politicians are showing a disposition to try to revive the race question in its full fury of twenty years ago. That is a traitorous work, and will fail as it deserves to fail. The last election showed pretty clearly—see the Maryland and Missouri returns—that the race question as a means of keeping worthless and wicked political parasites in office has about run its course in the South, just as robbery in the name of protection has about run its course in the North.

The race question, bad though it may be, is certainly in a better state than it was fifty years ago. For then the South was morally, and it was in the way to be industrially, prostrate under the curse of slavery—and slavery is the most acute and dangerous phase of a race question.

Time and human sympathy will solve the race question; the politicians cannot help. And it is a happy augury that the Southern people are realizing the fact.

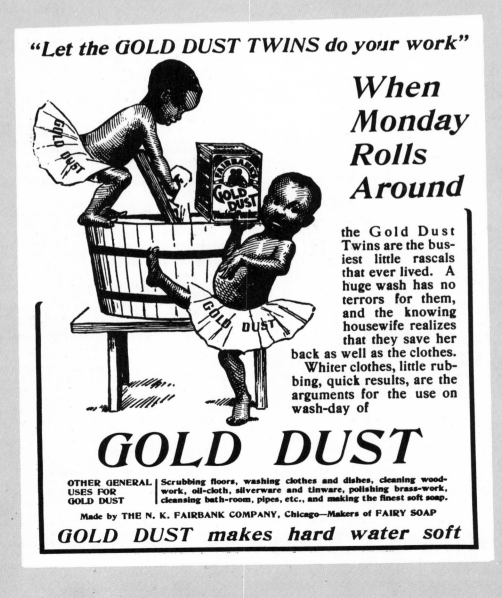
Too Much Cheese

DURING one of his campaigns "Private" John Allen stopped at a cross-roads store. While he was exchanging news with the proprietor an old darky from one of the plantations came in. When his purchase of "middlin' an' meal" had been wrapped up he started out. At the door he paused. "Got enny cheese, boss?" he asked.

"Why, yes," said the clerk, pointing to a freshly opened can of axle-grease on the counter; "box just opened."

The darky looked at it hungrily. "How much?" he asked.

"Give it to him for ten cents, and throw in the crackers," said Mr. Allen.

"All right," said the clerk, filling a bag with crackers. "Here you are."

The darky laid a greasy dime on the counter, picked up the box and the bag, and going out, seated himself in the shade of a cotton-bale. When he had finished the crackers he ran his finger around the box and gave it a good long lick. In a few moments he put on his hat and started for his mule. As he passed the store Mr. Allen hailed him.

"Well, Jerry, what did you think of that lunch?"

The old darky scratched his head, then he said, "I tell you de truf, Mars John, dem crackers wuz all right, but dat wuz de ransomest cheese I uver et!"

WILLIAMS' SHAVING SOAP

Christmas Morning on "de Ole Plantation"

"Christmas comes but once a year" with its joy and gladness for "little shavers."

Williams' Shaving Soap, with its big, thick, glorious lather, brings joy and gladness, comfort and satisfaction to all "shavers" every day in the year.

Williams' Soaps sold everywhere, but sent by mail if your dealer does not supply you.

The Negro in New York

A STUDY OF THE SOCIAL AND INDUSTRIAL CONDITION OF THE COLORED PEOPLE IN THE METROPOLIS

BY JNO. GILMER SPEED

THE prospect for the negro in New York city is not very encouraging. His race is not numerically very strong in the metropolis, and the number is not rapidly increasing either by births or by migrations from the South. The riot of August, when a mob attacked negroes in the streets without much, if any, restraint from the police, was even more of a surprise than it would have been at almost any time during the preceding quarter of a century. There have been no times when the negroes in New York were increasing with rapidity. At this time the opportunities of negroes are less in New York than they have ever been, and there does not seem any likelihood that present conditions will be immediately changed. This riot, however, has directed the attention of the people to the negro population, and if the truth be disclosed it may be that their present hard lot may in time be ameliorated.

The negro is not a new-comer in New York. He has been here for two centuries and a half. In the beginning and until 1785 he was a slave, but even during the time of bondage his condition was not much worse than now. The slavery that existed in New York was of a very mild sort, and the amiable Dutchmen who were the first slave-owners were very good and considerate masters. The English were not so gentle, and in the first half of the eighteenth century there were two severe disturbances, each marked with a loss of life. In 1709 there was so much traffic in slaves that a slave-market was opened in Wall Street, and black men and women were dealt in as though they were cattle or swine. The negroes were quite numerous in proportion to the white population, and there was always apprehension that there might be a slave uprising. In 1712 a house was burned, the slaves attacked the whites, and after killing several, were suppressed by the Royal troops of the garrison. For twenty-nine years there was comparative quiet, though one-fifth of the population was black. In 1741 there were ten thousand inhabitants of New York. Of these two thousand were negro slaves. There was an epidemic of incendiary fires. The investigations were not more scientifically judicial than the witchcraft trials in Salem. The most improbable and contradictory stories were believed, and many negroes were condemned in consequence. Some were hanged and some were burned at the stake. It was an anxious time in the little island city, and the officers of justice seem to have lost their heads pretty completely. This anx-

iety made slavery itself unpopular, and in 1785 the new State was quite willing to abolish the institution. At that time there were about 22,000 negro slaves in the State, a considerable proportion of these being held in and around the city. This abolition of slavery in New York did not cause the death of the slave trade, however, for this was participated in by New York merchants until the whole wretched business was wiped out by the civil war and the emancipation proclamation. Free negroes continued to live in New York from the time of the abolition of slavery until now, but they have always kept very much to themselves, living in colonies and engaged in a few special occupations in which they were reasonably prosperous. In 1850, when New York had a population of 515,547, there were 13,815 negroes in the city. This was not a formidable proportion, only about two and a half per cent., but the negroes then in the city were in many regards much better off than their successors are fifty years later. At that time the chief caterers of the city were negroes, as they continued to be in Philadelphia till a very few years ago. There were many barber shops manned by colored men. The white-washing trade belonged almost exclusively to negroes. Negroes also were the private coachmen of the town, and not a few drove public hacks. The bootblack business was theirs, and very many, if not most, of the hotel dining-rooms and restaurants had negro waiters. This was half a century ago, when the opportunity for negro employment in New York was at high-water mark. From that mark it has been receding ever since. At first slowly, but in the past dozen years very rapidly.

In the decade between 1850 and 1860 the negro population in New York actually decreased. This was due to the immense influx of foreign population and the consequent competition in all the unskilled branches of labor, and also to the prejudice against the race incident to the fierce political passions which culminated in the civil war. In 1860 the population of New York was 805,651, while of negroes there were 12,472, or one and a half per cent. The occupations of these colored people were just about what they had been ten years before. And, indeed, there was no appreciable change in this until after 1880. During the decade ending in 1870 there was a slight increase in the colored population, but a decrease in the percentage. The whole population was 942,-292, and the negroes numbered 13,072, or one and one-third per cent. By 1880 the

number had increased to 19,663, which was a little in excess of one and a half per cent. of the total population of 1,206,-299. This was the period when the decline in the industrial opportunities of the negroes in New York became very apparent. Nevertheless, they increased during the next decade both in numbers and in percentage of the whole. In 1890 the city's population was 1,515,301, and that of the negroes 25,674, or one and seven-tenths per cent. of the total. By this time there were few callings open to the men of the race, and the women who worked were chiefly employed in domestic service. But the increase up to the present year was steady, and the population now is estimated at 35,000. The census of this year puts the population of the Borough of Manhattan (all of these figures have had to do with this borough and not with the Greater New York) at 1,950,000, so the percentage is now slightly higher than it was ten years ago, having increased about one-tenth of one per cent.

It will be seen from the figures given above that the negroes in New York do not constitute a very considerable proportion of the population. The Irish, the Germans, the Italians, the Russians, and even the Scandinavians outnumber them, in the order given, while they are about as numerous as the French. Why there should be any race feeling against such an insignificant element of the population seems superficially strange. It is quite true that the Irish seem to have a natural antipathy to the negroes, but the other north-of-Europe races seem to have no natural feeling of repugnance and the Italians are quite devoid of it. The strangest thing about this strange problem is that so many native Americans should feel hostile—not actively hostile, but in sympathy with the lawless negro-baiters. I heard many native Americans, even New-Englanders, say after the riot that they would have been glad if many of the negroes had been killed. For this feeling, which there is no doubt of, there must be some other cause than mere race prejudice. It may be that this cause will be made clearer as I proceed.

Why, let us inquire, have the negroes in New York lost so many of the old-time opportunities for employment? Take the waiters in hotels and restaurants. This twenty-five and even twenty years ago was a great source of employment for negro men. Every middle-aged man can recall when very many of the best metropolitan hotels had negro servants. Some may continue to employ them. But very few. The trade of waiting, so far as negroes is concerned, has practically died out in New York. But why? The general introduction of French cooks had something to do with it, and the quicker intelligence of the white men who went into this trade had something more, while fashion completed the revolution which has supplanted the negroes in this employment. Your French cook rarely knows English; your negro never knows French. So these two could not communicate, and the negro waiter and the French cook had to part company. The young Germans and Frenchmen who make up the great body of dining-room servants in New York are much better educated than any save very exceptional negroes, and they undoubtedly seem more in earnest in the work that they do. That the negroes should suffer by this competition was as inevitable as any of the laws of nature. Fashion began to frown on the negro in hotel and domestic service many years ago. This attitude was partly one of prejudice and partly due to a love of comfort. The pigment in the skin of the black has an odor which is not agreeable to delicate olfactory nerves. At any rate, the negro waiters were displaced by whites in one place and another until the trade was practically no longer open to them.

Fifty, thirty, even twenty, years ago there were a great many negro coachmen in New York, and in the social scale the coachmen ranked next perhaps to the caterers. When we began to use English styles of equipage, to bang and dock our horses' tails, then we also cultivated a preference for English and Irish coachmen and stable hands. There was no race prejudice in this; it was to a very great extent a matter of style. But in this occupation also white men are more efficient. They are not only better drivers, but they are better horsemen. The negro is often most careless of the horses in his charge, and when he is in a temper he is very frequently cruel. There are negro coachmen still in New York, but compared with the number employed in the sixties and seventies they are very few.

Now, the negro caterers used to be men of much consideration and substance. Several of the men who flourished a generation ago left comfortable estates to their progeny. There may be negro caterers still in New York, but I do not recall to have been to an entertainment in twenty years where one was employed. In the old days there were colored men who ranked as Sherry and Delmonico do now. There are none such now, because the men of the race do not seem to be able to keep step in the march of progress.

As New York grew richer the people demanded greater luxury and more elegance. The negroes did not have enterprise enough to see this, and they have dropped out of the race. Then again the taste has changed as to cooking. The homely things which pleased our fathers and grandfathers do not completely satisfy us, and we require a French cook in a white cap instead of an old black mammy in a bandanna turban. In this field, as in others, the competition has been too strong for the colored men, and so the old caterers who used to serve the people who dwelt in the fashionable precincts of Bleecker Street and Washington Square have either been gathered to their fathers or shut up shop; and they have left no successors.

There were also a great many negro barbers in New York twenty-five years ago. There may be some still, but they are mostly engaged in barbering the men of their own race. Prejudice probably had much to do with killing this trade, but the indisposition on the part of some white people to get close to negroes had also something to do with it. At any rate, the trade is dead.

Then the whitewashing business used to seem to belong to negroes as though it was theirs by right. But there are few negroes now employed in this trade in New York. The house-painters and decorators and paper-hangers have taken it up, and the peripatetic darky whitewasher might walk his legs off in the metropolitan streets before finding a job. The boot-blacking business also once was his. But the Italians now have it. They conquered it. They put up thrones on the street corners, paying in work for the privilege, and then by doing better jobs they drove the negroes out of business.

There are no colored artisans in New York. The trades unions would prevent any such from receiving employment. As common laborers they are received on almost equal terms with others, but this is not an attractive occupation for the ambitious negroes who have come to New York to make fortunes. Even the women are not as much in demand for household servants as formerly. This decadence is due no doubt to the change in fashion, and possibly somewhat to a greater efficiency on the part of white servants. But the women are not sought as they once were. Even the people who came here from the Southern States, where negro servants are universal, prefer the Irish, German, and Scandinavian women as cooks, chambermaids, and waitresses.

In this rapid survey we have seen that the industrial opportunities for colored people have been lessening all the time, and now the sphere of their activities has become so narrow that it is a wonder that even thirty-five thousand of them can earn honest livings.

And they do not. The proportion of criminals among the negroes in New York is alarmingly large, and their influence is very dangerous. The birth-rate among the negroes in New York is small and the death-rate is large, being thirty in a thousand, as against nineteen in a thousand for the white population. If it were not for accessions from the South the negro population in New York would by no means hold its own. It is in these accessions that there is great danger. The best of the race in the country know or soon learn that the opportunities in New York are limited in comparison with those in Southern cities, so they stay away. They are not influenced in the same way that white people are towards New York.

A white man of ability, when he feels his strength to be above that of his fellows in his own neighborhood, is much inclined towards New York, where success means so much more than it does in smaller places. New York's white population, therefore, is always being re-enforced by the strongest and hardiest and most adventuresome of the men of the country. So also the particularly alert among the vicious and criminal know that their opportunities for wrong-doing are wider in the metropolis, and they hurry to it. The good negro in the South knows there is scanter chance for him in New York than at home, so he stays at home. The vicious and criminal negroes in the South know that their field of vice is broader in New York, so the more sturdy of these rogues come hither. The good stay away and the evil pour in. This is very bad, but it is made a hundredfold worse by reason of the necessity which compels all classes of negroes to huddle together in New York.

Property is not rented to negroes in New York until white people will no longer have it. Then rents are put up from thirty to fifty per cent., and negroes are permitted to take a street or sometimes a neighborhood. There are really not many negro sections, and all that exist are fearfully crowded. Nor are there good neighborhoods and bad neighborhoods. Into each all classes are compelled to go, and the virtuous and the vicious elbow each other in the closest kind of quarters. This is a great source of moral contagion, and vice spreads with great rapidity among the women of such quarters. During the day the decent men are at work. Then the vicious and the idle have full sway. If it were possible to make a census of the negroes and go into this phase of their social condition. I have no doubt that it would be found that more men of the race are idle and without visible means of support in proportion to the total number than in any other neighborhood in the world except those frankly given over to the criminal classes.

The testimony of clergymen and other religious workers among the negroes is to the effect that the harm done by this crowding is so serious that it is always threatening to undo the good work of the churches. This is very disheartening to the more intelligent among the negroes, and they see no remedy so long as this dreadful overcrowding continues. One clergyman said to me that when he saw the dreadful discomforts of the places that negroes in New York had to call home he could not in his heart blame them for drinking, if that mitigated the hardships of their unwholesome dwellings.

The landlords undoubtedly treat the negroes with very little kindness. They charge enormous rentals for very inferior houses and tenements, which yield more when the negroes have taken possession than they did in time of seemingly greater prosperity. Of course negroes in a neighborhood put a blight upon it, but the owners get a very large reward by reason of the higher rentals. Moreover, they make no repairs, and the property usually goes to rack and ruin. The negroes are not responsible for this, even though they are the cause. I knew a negro adventurer who took advantage of this prejudice against his people and made profit out of it. He would select a promising land-and-improvement scheme and through a white man would buy a lot. After a dozen houses had gone up he would appear on the scene with a gang of Italians and begin digging a cellar. The neighbors, always interested in new improvements, would ask who was to build. "I am," the negro would reply. "I am building a home for myself and family." In a little while there would be consternation in that neighborhood, and the promoter of the scheme would be visited. His scheme would be ruined if the negro persisted. The negro would express great determination to go ahead. Then in self-defence the promoter would buy him out at a handsome profit to the negro. He did this half a dozen times in as many years, making in the aggregate a handsome profit. As a rule, however, the negroes in New York are not beholden to the property-owners for anything except discomfort and extortion. If they stay in New York they are compelled to live in places where health, decency, and privacy are all but impossible. Housed as they are it is wonderful that they should be as good as they are; it is wonderful that they are not all entirely worthless.

Nearly all of the negroes in New York are literate—that is, nearly all can read and write. Few, however, have even a common-school education, and those who are liberally educated are but an insignificant remnant. Dr. DuBois of the University of Pennsylvania has made an exhaustive study of the negro in Philadelphia and also in other places further south. He says: "The great deficiency of the negro is his small knowledge of the art of organized social life—that last expression of human culture. His development in group life was abruptly broken off by the slave-ship, directed into abnormal channels, and dwarfed by the Black Codes, and suddenly wrenched anew by the Emancipation Proclamation. He finds himself, therefore, peculiarly weak in that nice adaptation of individual life to the life of the group which is the essence of civilization. This is shown in the grosser forms of sexual immorality, disease, and crime, and also in the difficulty of race organization for common ends in economic or in intellectual lines."

The Man—Not the Money

ARE nations as blind as individuals to the real meaning of their own lives?

A keen-eyed Englishman said the other day that the only picturesque features in American life were our colored races. But how many of us would agree with him? We should look on a brisk day in the Stock Exchange or a Chicago skyscraper as far finer and more suggestive sights than a Navajo studying electrical engineering, or an old negro Maumer peering with her bleared eyes into the coming years to find what they were bringing to her black sons.

Probably no stranger sight was offered in this country last year than a meeting held in Philadelphia in behalf of a training school for colored working-people.

An ex-President of the United States presided, and the chief speaker was a negro, born a homeless, nameless chattel, but who ranks now among the foremost genuine orators of the country.

The significance of the incident was not in the school, nor in the white man, nor in the black. It was in the Chance which this country offers to the individual, the possibility in it for a black slave to push his way up and up.

The Chance for the strange live force in a man to do something, to take its share in the work of the big, seething world —that is the real significance of this country among nations, after all.

One of the most important events in American history occurred about twenty years ago in a dusty little court-room in a Nebraska town.

A peaceable Indian tribe that had tilled the same ground for three hundred years were robbed of it by swindling agents at Washington, and were driven to the marshes of the Bad Lands, leaving their grain uncut and the fires burning on their hearths. They died like poisoned sheep. At the end of a year, gathering up the bones of their dead, they came back. The journey of the Israelites through the desert or the famous flight of De Quincey's Tartar tribe was not more tragic than the march of these red men, seeking again the homes of which they had been robbed. They were arrested in a town of Nebraska and the head men were brought into court. The agent for the Government demanded that they should be sent back to the Bad Lands on the plea that not being legally recognized as human beings in this country they could not own their homes nor farms, nor appeal to the law for restitution.

One of the chiefs gathered the meaning of these words. He rose, drew himself to his full height, and looking slowly around on the whites that filled the court-room, tapped himself gravely on the breast and said:

"Am I not, too—a man?"

The Judge, a just, sane man, decided that an Indian was a person, not a chattel, and entitled to the full protection of the law.

That decision still stands. It opened the Chance for the red man.

Do we see what that means?

We are apt nowadays to think that the work before each of us and the country is to get money and things. Money and things don't last. Let Professor Heilprecht tell you of the great Babylonish empire which he is digging out of the sand.

It is the Man who lasts, and the work of this Republic is the making of the man, not money.

Red Names for Red Men

SOME of the Indian chiefs and headmen whose boys and girls have been sent to Carlisle and other schools to be educated have just made a strong protest against any change in the names of their children. They say that it is the Indian custom to give to a child at birth a name with some family or spiritual significance, but that those forced on them on entering the schools have to an Indian no meaning whatever.

The protest is popularly regarded as absurd and fantastic; the average American usually takes the red man's ideas as a huge joke. But isn't there a basis of sound common-sense in this one idea?

The name which is given a boy when he comes into the world, by the time that he has carried it for a dozen or fifteen years, has become as much a part of him as his head or his hand; it is his property; it is he. What right have we to take it from him?

We don't stop the thousands of Podavitches and Maritskas who are crowding into Castle Garden every day to dub them Jim and Nancy. Why should not the red-skinned American boy keep his name as well as the foreign Hun or Pole?

Or, for that matter, why is one name preferable to another? Is there any more civilization or righteousness dormant in "Bill" and "Bob" than in the sonorous titles of the Omaha and Navajo?

A great Indian chief, the last of the Mohicans, was known as Uncas. The whites dubbed him Job Smith, and he sleeps now under a stone with that name upon it in the old Moravian graveyard at Bethlehem. What was gained by that christening?

The whole difficulty grows out of a curious belief cherished by every English-speaking man. It is that to be a civilized human being or a Christian you must not only believe but dress, speak and eat your dinner as he does.

The White Brothers going out to convert a heathen meet him as near to his own standing ground in life as they can. They adopt his language, his clothes, his customs. These, they hold, are only outside, unimportant matters. They seek to influence his soul and his principles of action.

We may not believe in their church nor its doctrines, but there is no doubt that they are the most successful missionaries in the world.

Bishop Coleridge Pattison, one of the foremost of modern Christian apostles, adopted these methods. He did not even urge civilized clothes upon his convert, provided his soul kept near to God.

"The South Sea Islander," he once said, "may sometimes be a cannibal, but he is always a gentleman; though, when he puts on English clothes," he slyly added, "he looks like a gent!"

Our ordinary method with the savage is to make him learn English whether he learns Christ or not.

Red, Yellow and Brown Americans

SENATOR CHAUNCEY M. DEPEW the other day rushed from the conference of the New York bosses exclaiming: "The optimist wins! The optimist always wins!" He had had a close call and he came near losing his Senatorship, but in politics a miss is as good as a unanimous vote so far as the election certificate is concerned.

However, we are mainly concerned with the gospel this young man of seventy-one summers preaches and practices, especially its usefulness in desperate cases. For more than a century the American Indian was our shame and our despair. We cheated him, debased him, killed him. We found him the noble red man and we made him an ignoble exhibit of thriftlessness and uncleanliness. We spent over $400,000,000 on him and let a large part of it go into the pockets of grafting politicians and other white thieves. We reduced the Indian population of our present territory from 600,000 to 270,000.

Rather a woeful opportunity for optimism, isn't it? And yet if we take into account what has been done within the past few years — conveniently forgetting what went before — we have many pleasant facts. Two years ago a new policy went into effect: able-bodied Indians were given work instead of pensions. Result, 12,000 Indians dropped from the ration-rolls and earning livings for themselves and their families. The old Indian agency system was honeycombed with evil. This year there are only twenty-three agencies compared with forty-three two years ago, and these are under educators instead of politicians. Schools are being greatly improved, and they show over 25,000 pupils — an increase of a thousand in a year. Much was done to deprive the red man of cheap whisky; as an alternative he took to patent medicines, which proved more devastating than the whisky; now the patent-medicine evil will be removed. Even the bad Indian is being sobered. So, after all, isn't the showing calculated to inspire optimism even in the Indian problem?

Now note the importance of it all. We are greatly troubled over the dozen millions of brown and yellow beings whom we are trying benevolently to assimilate in our new islands. Pessimism has run riot over that proposition. But need we be hopeless? What we have seen from our treatment of the Indian ought to be illuminating. What we are doing ought to be the starting-point of what we shall do to the alien races. We have lived and learned. Why should not our knowledge lift us above the fog and make us cheerful and confident?

We are accused of sending canned freedom to the Filipinos. That, at least, is better than the other brand they had, and we might improve our opportunity by including in the new cargoes some choice lots of preserved optimism.

Changing the Indians' Government

This brings us to the future of the Indian Territory. Three-fourths of the people are white, and the rest — of mixed and Indian blood — are opposed to Statehood.

At the present time a commission appointed by the Government is at work settling up the affairs of the Indians. For years the Government's representatives have been at work trying to persuade the Indians to give up their tribal governments, and now there is a prospect that it may be successful. When it is done the Indians will have enough money to keep them in comfort as long as they live, for the lands are valuable and will bring high prices.

There are five of these tribes which have stood out against the Government — the Cherokees, the Choctaws, the Chickasaws, the Creeks and the Seminoles.

An idea of what will be coming to these former savages can be had from this statement made by one of the officers of the Government: "In the Cherokee Nation every Indian citizen will get 120 acres of land of average value; in the Creek Nation every citizen will get between 160 and 200 acres of average-valued land; in the Seminole and Choctaw Nations they will get 500 acres per head. All of this land is either of fine agricultural, mining or grazing quality. It can be rented for enough to keep every Indian without work. The invested funds of the Indians, to be paid them when the land is all allotted, will be sufficient to give them a start, if they have no cash."

It may be, of course, that the amalgamation will never take place, and that instead of having one State we shall have two.

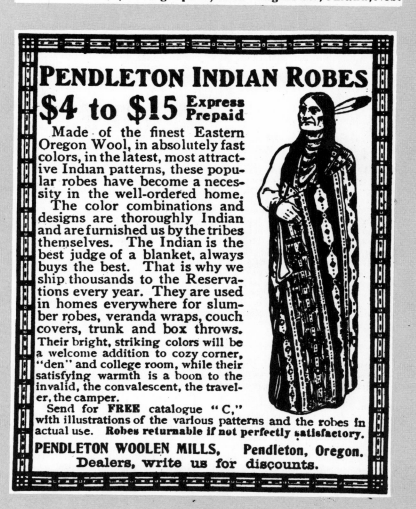

Mayor Phelan at his desk in the City Hall

The Case Against the Chinaman

By James D. Phelan, Mayor of San Francisco

THE expiration, on May 5 next, of the Geary Exclusion Law has again brought before the country the consideration of the Chinese question. That law and the treaty with China embodying its provisions, dated May 8, 1894, exclude Chinese laborers and admit merchants, students and travelers.

The reason why Congress limited the duration of the Exclusion Law was, no doubt, to observe the condition of the people affected and to be guided thereby in its future action. Taking advantage of this, the Chinese Minister at Washington, Mr. Wu Ting-fang, and the Chinese Consul-General at San Francisco, Mr. Ho Yow, have inaugurated an extra-diplomatic movement whose object is to influence public opinion and the deliberations of Congress against the reënactment of the expiring law.

Seeing, therefore, the necessity of taking immediate action, the municipal authorities of San Francisco called a convention for November 21 last, which met in San Francisco to express the sentiments of the State. Three thousand delegates from county boards, municipal bodies, labor unions and commercial and civic associations assembled, and after two days' discussion, without a dissenting voice, memorialized the President and the Congress of the United States asking them to reënact the Geary Exclusion Law and to continue the present treaty with China.

The Menace of Coolie Invasions

It may be recalled that in 1868 the Burlingame treaty was negotiated, and under its protection 75,000 Chinese coolies had, before the year 1880, found their way to California under contracts for work. The State was ablaze with indignation when it realized that the white population had been thus driven out of employment, and that men, women and children were marching the streets of the cities, hungry for bread. Kearnyism, which stood simply for vigorous opposition to Chinese coolieism, swept the State, carried the new constitution and elected the Mayor of San Francisco.

In 1882 Congress passed the first Exclusion Law, which was reënacted in 1892, and is now again before Congress. The effects of exclusion have been satisfactory and beneficent. According to the census of 1900 the 75,000 Chinese population of California in 1880 has been reduced to 45,500. Industrial conditions have greatly improved and a desirable Caucasian population has flowed naturally into the State.

The people, of course, want a continuation of a policy that has brought them prosperity and population. They object to the Chinese on the ground that they are a non-assimilative race, and claim that the experiences of the last thirty-five years have demonstrated it. For twenty years, or ever since the passage of the first Exclusion Act, the Chinese have not been disturbed. They have taken employment freely in every branch of industry, and yet they are the same sullen, non-assimilative people that they were at that time and have maintained their racial peculiarities intact. In fact, Ho Yow admits in a recent article that they work more cheaply than the white man; they live more cheaply; they send their money to China; most of them have no intention of remaining in the United States. They do not adopt American manners, but live in colonies and not after the American fashion. He might have said that they are governed by their own laws; that they have tribunals of their own; that in most cases they are not free agents, but exist and find employment under the patronage, if not the ownership, of the Six Chinese Companies; that they are slaves to the opium habit; that the vast majority of them are single men who sleep on shelves in crowded cellars or rooms, subsisting principally on rice; that as members of Tongs they wage war upon one another after the manner of the Corsican vendetta; that Highbinders, professional blackmailers and assassins are paid for protection and to execute revenge; that the Chinese breed disease, and that the unsanitary condition of their quarters is a constant menace to the public health.

The Impossibility of Americanizing the Mongol

The San Francisco Board of Health says, in a recent report, that there is no remedy for the evils of Chinatown apart from its utter demolition. Its vices, its gambling, its female slavery and its opium joints make a police problem most difficult of solution. Fines amounting to upward of $3000 a month are collected from Chinese; the jails and prisons are full of them, and still the conditions remain which give contributing force to the conclusions of the Board of Health.

The Chinese do not bring their wives in their immigration because they intend, when a competency is earned, to return to their native land. Until this year no statute had been passed by the California Legislature forbidding the intermarriage of whites and Chinese, and yet very few such marriages have ever taken place. The issue of them develop the virtues of neither race, but exhibit the vices of both.

The Chinese cannot, therefore, be moulded, as are other nationalities, into the American stock, the composite of many assimilative peoples. The Chinese have been and are a permanently foreign element, and, like every foreign substance in the body or the body politic, yield no nourishment, derange the system, produce disease, and unless encysted, as in the case of the San Francisco Chinatown, will ultimately imperil the life.

We are therefore presented with a simple question, whether we shall admit the Chinese coolies in unlimited numbers, first to overwhelm California, the most exposed and accessible State, and then to inundate the rest of the country. The Chinese work incessantly. They possess a certain imitative ability which enables them to enter all skilled employment. They take no holidays, their hours for labor are unlimited, and they are willing to work for the lowest wages. The consequences of their immigration are therefore inevitable — they will drive the American laborer and artisan out of employment, displace the sons and daughters of the pioneer, and, by their presence, arrest the settlement of the country by a desirable population.

There is nothing new or local in the policy of Exclusion. The Federal immigration laws to-day exclude the contract and the pauper labor of Europe, and the coolies coming from the best of the Chinese lands, the Canton Province, whence most immigration so far has come, are both contract and pauper labor.

The Perils of Cheap Coolie Labor

"Cheap labor" is the only defense made for the Chinaman. It is urged that cheap labor is a good thing for a country and that it contributes largely to the production of wealth. But America is not solely concerned in the production of wealth. It has other interests and duties. Its per capita productive energy to-day is, however, greater than any other country — due to the invention and improvement of machinery, which has been made for the most part by its own intelligent workingmen. Progressively will the productive capacity of the people increase. At the rate of twelve per cent. per decade of growth, this country, one hundred years hence, will have a population of two hundred and thirty millions. Production and population will advance together, and the home market, to which Chinese labor does not contribute, will be preserved.

Do we therefore need to stimulate our production by letting down the bars to the immigration of non-consuming and non-assimilative coolies? Is it not, after all, a question of holding this continent for development by Caucasians, who have so far succeeded so well? Regarded solely as a laboring class, as you would look upon the slaves of the South prior to the war, the Chinese are, no doubt, entitled to consideration; but can we, in consonance with our institutions, segregate a labor class and regard it simply by its capacity for work? If so, the Chinese meet nearly every requirement. They work for low wages, and they are not concerned about their political, religious or social condition.

But America has dignified labor, has invested its people with political rights and civic duties. In fact, the Government is controlled by majorities, and the majority of the people of this country, were Chinese immigration unlimited, would be directly and most harmfully affected. The effect would be disastrous. It would be putting an army of single men, inured to ceaseless and unremitting toil, content with the longest hours and the lowest wages and the most meagre food, without wives, appetites or aspirations, in competition with the American citizen, who has been bred by our civilization to family life and civic duties. The result would be either he would come down to the Chinese standard or be destroyed; or, again, after long suffering, during which our form of Government, dependent upon an intelligent and prosperous suffrage, would be shaken to its foundations, he would rise up and, perhaps outside the forms of law, resist the invasion.

I am, however, absolutely convinced that as soon as the question is understood, if it be not fully understood now, the majority of our countrymen, who would thus be directly affected, will give, as they have given in the past, their support to the peaceful and wise remedy now proposed, namely, the reënactment of the Chinese Exclusion Law.

Why Yellow Citizens are Undesirable

This country has been warned by the experience of the South and knows the bitterness of racial animosity. Suffrage is a privilege conferred by the several States upon citizens where it is believed that its exercise will be for the benefit of the State. The Chinese, having no appreciation of the blessings of liberty and not being attached to our institutions, socially and physically non-assimilative, mere contract laborers, subject to the orders of their masters, could not be safely intrusted with the right to vote. And yet, Ho Yow intimates blandly that they not only should be admitted freely, but should be admitted to all the privileges of citizenship. There are four hundred millions of human beings in China. They are attached to their land by a superstitious bond, and, when they are dead, their bones must repose in its sacred soil. It is the Celestial Kingdom. They make incursions into other lands; spoil-seekers, but never permanent residents.

In Hawaii to-day there are 25,000 Chinese. They receive good wages according to their standard. At home they are paid no more than two dollars a month for farm work, and there they are paid thirty dollars, but they cannot be induced to remain after they have accumulated $1000, which they consider a fair competency.

So, far from seeking an asylum, offering allegiance and understanding our institutions, necessary prerequisites to citizenship, they are not even bona-fide settlers; they are automatons wound up for work. They make no contribution to the country's enduring interests. In the contemplation of the Constitution they are mere machines. This is a republic of men. They come along after the country has been discovered, wrested from despotism, made free, opened up, settled by the pioneer and occupied by his posterity, to participate in the prosperity which liberty, invention and industry have developed and civilization has crowned.

The only thing they can offer in exchange is their labor; but the labor is already provided by those of our own household. Chinamen can make no contribution to citizenship, and, if their services are accepted, those who are capable of doing the work, supporting our schools, churches and institutions, recruiting our free population and fighting our battles, are crowded out. We abandon our fields and our factories to a servile class.

The Mongolian Immigrant a Social Parasite

The question before the country to-day is not so much the increase of more wealth as the equitable distribution of the great wealth we produce. The reorganization of labor and capital must be on lines of greater sympathy and better understanding, and the introduction of the Chinese, a race so alien to our own, would permanently prevent the improvement of the relations between the employer and the employee. Industrial monopoly, taking a short-sighted view, might be able, in the presence of a vast Chinese population, to coerce labor and reduce the standard of wages, hours and living. In fact, the tendency of unenlightened selfishness would be to give preference in employment to the Chinese themselves. Land monopoly, which destroyed Rome, when slaves tilled the soil and drove the farmer to the capital, would find an easy means of repeating history under conditions which the presence of the Chinese would create.

The brotherhood of man is a doctrine which deters many a well-meaning American from taking advanced grounds against the exclusion of undesirable peoples; but the East has shut out the pauper and contract labor of Europe, and the West demands only the same treatment of the aliens who are pressing for admission at her gates. The brotherhood of man can be best served by the Chinese realizing that they have a great industrial destiny in their own country, and that there, under the stimulus of American ideas, energy and invention, they can improve their own conditions. Then, merchants, travelers and students may come here as before and carry back the benefits of our improvements and experiments; and, when they have more merchants and more travelers and more educated men, our gates shall be opened to them as guests, but not as parasites. The Chinese coolies, by every test, are parasitical. They live off the body on which they alight, because their wages, instead of being reinvested, are taken out of the country. They are neither a necessary nor desirable part of our American system. The policy of protection, which guards us against the trade, logically should also guard us against the man.

The Old Solution of the Problem the Best

There have been timid protests against exclusion on the ground that our commerce with China and the friendly relation produced by our island possessions, and our participation in Oriental affairs, should be encouraged. Granted. But since 1880 exclusion has had no deterrent effect upon our Chinese commerce. Indeed, it has increased fifty per cent. during that period. We stand second to Great Britain alone in the volume of our export and our import trade, according to the Consular Reports of August, 1901. Our diplomatic relations with China have never been more cordial. By treaty, she acquiesced in our domestic policy of exclusion.

So, as a race, labor, trade and political question, there seems to be no good reason for departing from the solution which we have already found, or from the policy which we have based upon it.

Europe, in the last two thousand years, has been frequently exposed to invasion by Asiatic hordes, which, had it not been resisted by force of arms, the civilization which we enjoy to-day and of which we are a part would have gone down in barbarism.

A peaceable and insidious invasion from China would constantly reduce the standards which have been established by American civilization, and what force could not accomplish in past centuries might ultimately be accomplished on this free continent under the fostering influences of mistaken and foolishly generous laws.

The duty before this country is the betterment of man. It is by the improvement of political conditions and not by their debasement through the infiltration of inferior races that we shall succeed. Let us accept the settled law of the country with respect to Chinese Exclusion and turn our minds to higher and more important things. Let our influence radiate over the world, and for that purpose, if brotherhood be one of our objects, let us keep the patriotic fires burning and not suffer them to be dimmed.

The "Yellow Peril" Again

ALL our truly great journalists, statesmen and volunteer thinkers agree upon the existence of the "yellow peril"; but they radically disagree as to what the yellow peril is. Some hold that the triumphant Japanese will set the teeming millions of the Orient at work manufacturing cheap goods with which they will flood the Occident. Others hold that the yellow peril is military—the Japanese arming the teeming millions aforesaid and flinging them upon the Occident in such wars as those that submerged ancient Rome. Happily, both perils cannot coexist. If the teeming Orient millions are at home manufacturing cheap goods they cannot be away from home making war. Further to allay fear, if the Orient sends forth floods of cheap goods the millions of buyers of those goods will, at least, survive the inundation—else, how could goods be sold? Finally, if Japan means civilization—and who now doubts that she does?—then she does not mean war; for civilization means peace, except in the minds of boy-men, who remain forever at the blood-and-thunder-novel stage of life.

"Yellow peril" is not a bad subject for debating societies; but as a serious proposition it ranks with a pumpkin-shell with eyes, nose and mouth cut in it and a candle inside.

SAN FRANCISCO.

EVERY week sees several of the wretched unsanitary hovels in Chinatown torn down by the health officer and his assistants; and if this zeal in good works does not abate, a few months will witness the end of a long-standing nuisance. The Chinese are the most gregarious of people. Give four Celestials a room as large as a public hall and you will find them all bunked together in one corner. It is a great pity that the Chinese of San Francisco could not be moved to a separate quarter in the suburbs, for the district which they now occupy is one of the choicest in the city, sheltered by high hills from the keen ocean winds, and with a superb outlook on the noble bay of San Francisco.

The "Little Brown Men"

WE ARE often reading and hearing nowadays the phrase "the little brown men." It comes almost in a tone of top-lofty, patronizing approval—the tone the man who feels that women are the mental inferiors of men uses in addressing a good-looking woman who has what would in a man be intelligence.

It comes from men of no great stature full as glibly and condescendingly as from the men who are as much as seventy-two whole inches above the dirt. It comes from men of all complexions—the jaundice colored, the blue-gray and the gray-green and the mottled brown and blue.

Why "little"? And why "brown"? Why not just plain "men"? Above all, why the patronizing tone toward a people who had become proficient in the arts of civilization and had attained a courtesy and kindliness in their inter-relations which we are still struggling toward when our ancestors were shinning unclad up the primeval trees to escape from their stronger fellow wild beasts of a little lower order?

The patronizing tone is always rash. Used toward the Japanese it is ridiculous.

LINES TO A CHINK.

LI MUCH.— Hully Glee! Jim, gotee flive-pound flish on line, sure!

JIM HOP.— Hie! You likee him more lan flive-dollah washee on line!

Japan. "The Russians must be brutes."
U. S. A. "Those Japs are just savages, after all."
Russia. "Those Americans are horribly cruel."
—Chicago Tribune.

The Flood of Immigration

NOT a day passes without some striking reminder that we have no real history of our country — no interesting narrative that gives in clear, compact and concise form just the *essentials*.

For instance, one of the great factors in the upbuilding of America has been immigration. And so vast is our empire and so little have we done toward conquering it from the wilderness and so many are the new appliances for the work of conquest that to-day we have greater need of immigration than ever before. Yet we hear talk of shutting the gates against the immigrant on the ground that nowadays our immigration has enormously increased and is of a most undesirable kind.

If we knew history better our statesmen and our editors would not display such ignorance. If immigration were as great to-day as it was half a century ago we should be getting nearly three times as many foreigners each year as we are. And from no place in civilization to-day could there come such floods of illiterate, turbulent, starved peoples as were flooding us in the forties and fifties. Nor had we then any facilities for transforming them into Americans such as we now have.

It is a fact not without significance that some of the most conspicuous advocates of restraining immigration are also conspicuous examples of that type of supercilious, ignorant man of education which is such a deplorable feature of our public life of to-day.

CITIZENS FOR TROUBLE-MAKING ONLY.

Our Factory of Americans

TWENTY-ONE years ago we touched high-water mark in immigration, with three-quarters of a million arrivals. It looks as if that tremendous record would be beaten this year. In one day in April more than ten thousand immigrants landed at New York — the greatest day's work in the history of that port. One steamer brought 1341 Scandinavians, another nearly 1400 Italians, another almost 1600 Greeks, Italians, Arabs, Turks and Persians, a fourth over 2500 Poles and other Slavs, a fifth 270 Scotchmen, a sixth 525 Greeks, Turks and Arabs, and a seventh nearly 2600 Germans. In the first eleven days of April 41,200 immigrants of all nationalities invaded Ellis Island.

No wonder some of our kind friends across the Atlantic, looking at this appalling mixture, believe that we never can turn its varied ingredients into Americans. No such gigantic amalgamation of diverse races has ever been attempted since Caracalla made Roman citizens of all the inhabitants of his empire, and we may say that never in the history of the world has such an undertaking been successfully consummated.

But that does not prove that we shall fail. Indeed, there is every reason to believe that we shall succeed. We have been peculiarly fortunate in our preparation for the mighty work that is reversing the catastrophe of Babel. We have been a composite people from the beginning. The Thirteen Colonies were settled by Englishmen, Scotchmen, Scotch-Irish, Irish, Dutchmen, Swedes, Germans, Frenchmen and Negroes. Before the Revolution substantially all these, except the Negroes, had been welded into one homogeneous people, with a common language and common political ideals. For fifty years after that this people increased and solidified with little admixture from immigration, so that when new currents began to flow from Europe it was prepared to absorb them. It was a quarter of a century later still before the first great flood broke upon us. That deluge was Irish. In the fifties the problem of immigration was regarded as an Irish problem. The Know-Nothing protest was an anti-Irish movement. Irishmen captured our city governments, and our foreign policies were swayed by the prejudices of the "Irish vote."

But gradually the Irish freshet subsided, to be succeeded by a German stream. A quarter of a million German immigrants entered the country in a single year. German newspapers, theatres and churches sprang up and flourished. Had this continued there might have been some reason to fear that the Kaiser's dream of a huge, alien German colony in the United States would be realized. But it stopped in good time. Meanwhile the earlier Irish immigrants and their children had become thorough Americans, and were helping the original Americans to assimilate the Germans. The work was successfully accomplished, and now the Irish and Germans both are parts of that wonderful solvent that is Americanizing the newer arrivals.

We are receiving a good many Italians, Poles, Hungarians and Russian Jews at present, but it will be many years before their numbers compare with those of the Irish and Germans who have been already successfully assimilated. And by that time no doubt the stream will slacken, as the former streams have done. Meanwhile the races that have produced Marconi and Tesla will still further enrich a stock which the mixture of blood has made already the richest in the world.

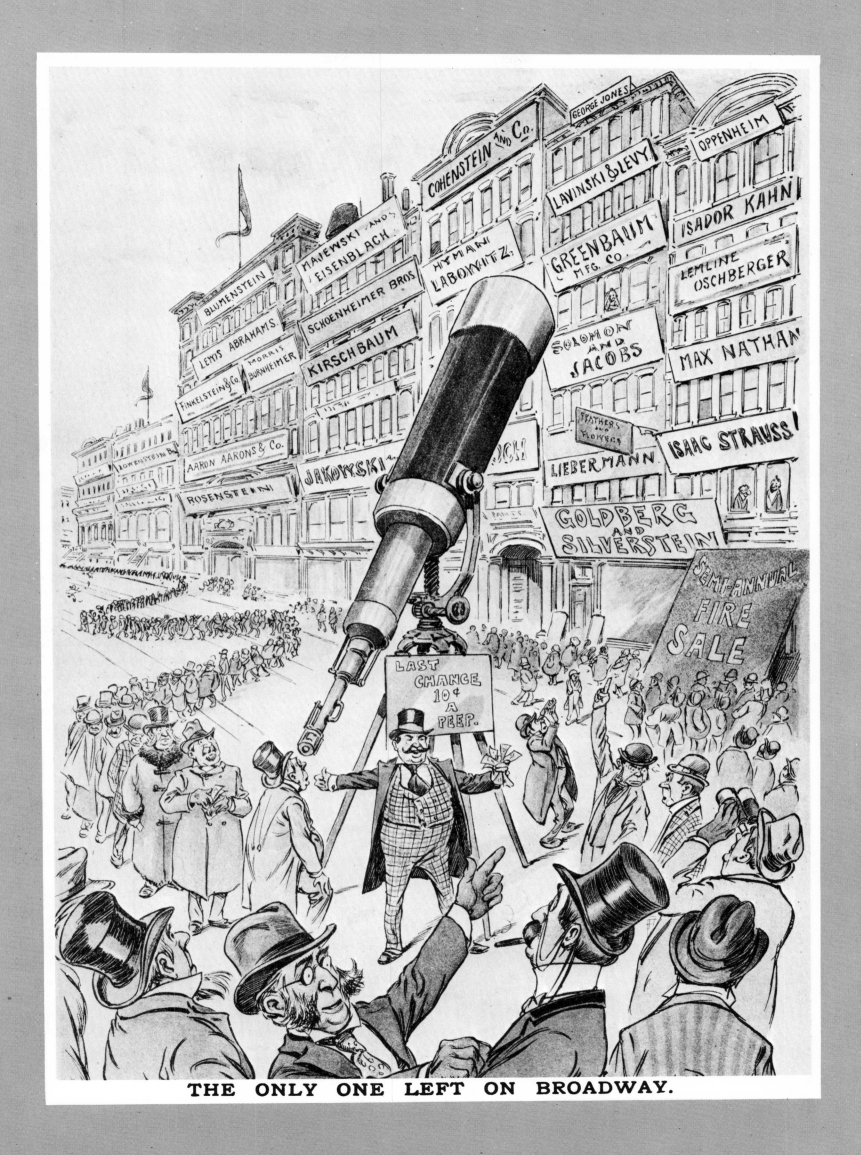

THE ONLY ONE LEFT ON BROADWAY.

5 The New Woman

WOMAN'S HOME COMPANION

FEBRUARY 1904

THE CROWELL PUBLISHING CO.

Collier's

Third Anniversary Number.   PRICE TEN CENTS.

THE SATURDAY EVENING POST
An Illustrated Weekly Magazine
Founded A·D· 1728 by Benj. Franklin

APRIL 11, 1903   FIVE CENTS THE COPY

EASTER

The Curtis Publishing Company Philadelphia

The special world of women is a strange and wonderful one, which no man can ever hope to understand entirely. It includes discussions of fashion, of coiffures, of recipes, of the cleverness of children (one's own), of draperies, of romance. Judged by the evidence available, it is a world that has remained pretty much the same in essentials, whatever its change in outward appearances, from the close of the Civil War to the turn of the century, and indeed until today. The illustrations in the journals changed, of course: the bustle disappeared, the hobble skirt came and went, the miniskirt had its day, but the women's pages reported one as extravagantly as they had the others.

The weakness of the women's pages in magazines and newspapers was that they told only part of the story of what went on in the special world of women. If a woman made superlative brandied peaches she was featured on the women's page; if she became a physician or a famous actress she was described in the general news or theater section. Thus over the years the women's page has become institutionalized; barring an occasional attempt to include news of women in general, it has changed very little.

This section of *Looking Forward* includes typical examples of women's page fare during the first half-dozen years of the 1900's: "What Women Will Wear in the Twentieth Century," "The Very Latest Autumn Fashions" (they were, though it scarcely seems to matter now, fashions for the autumn of 1903), a panel of pictures called "These Are the New Hats" (also from the autumn of 1903, although to a mere male they seem little different from those of the autumns of 1902 or 1904).

Then there are those items about which a man hesitates to comment out of sheer ignorance of the elements involved: the corset ads, for instance, which seem to proclaim a high degree of structural engineering during the period. And there were such now-forgotten devices as bustles and "fairy bust forms," which must have made any man who read such ads wonder what he was really getting in his own hourglass-shaped, swaying vision of loveliness—did artifice hide a long, lean, and hungry-looking girl?

What really was the status of women as this century opened? There is always talk about a "new woman"; every time she shortens her skirt or asks for the vote or begins to smoke she is hailed as a new woman. By and large, she has remained the same age-old model; changes in outer trappings and behavior have not brought any basic changes. However, it is true that as she has won certain fundamental rights her confidence in herself, which is something quite different, has changed.

From early history woman had been definitely a second-class citizen, with a long way to go before she could stand beside men instead of behind them. In the early days of this nation, a woman who married gave all her property to her husband and even lost her separate legal identity. Those property rights had been slowly won back, state by state, by the beginning of the twentieth century. After the Civil War women started working in earnest for the right to vote, but before 1900 only four states had granted the franchise to women. All four states were in the West—Wyoming, Utah, Colorado, and Idaho—which was hardly coincidental, because men on the frontier had seen their wives perform under the hardships of opening a new land and had no doubt that they could handle any problem, including the intelligent use of the vote. Washington and California, two other Western states, approved female suffrage in 1910 and 1911.

It was easier for a woman to get a higher education than to vote. Mount Holyoke Seminary opened its doors in 1838, though it was not until the birth of Vassar in 1865 that a college-level education became available to women. After that a good number of women's colleges opened in the East, and at the same time colleges and universities in the Midwest and West became coeducational.

A woman was granted a degree from a medical school as early as 1849, and the first woman to practice law was admitted to the bar in Iowa in 1869. With pioneers opening the way so early, it would seem that by 1900 the road would have been prepared for the movement of women into many fields that had traditionally been closed to them. However, it was still not easy in 1900 or 1905 for a young woman to become a physician or a lawyer, and the sad fact is that even today there are still lingering prejudices against women in professions. In law school moot courts, where students practice their skills by trying hypothetical cases, it was long the custom in many colleges—and may still be in some of the reactionary ones—to assign young women a preponderance of sordid cases, such as those involving rape, sodomy, and the like, in the hope that embarrassment would discourage them from pursuing a legal career. If they are rare today, such tactics were much more common in 1900. If nothing else, the would-be professional woman then had to face the superciliousness of the dominant male.

Yet in spite of the discouragements that she faced, the American woman as doctor or lawyer was accepted, albeit reluctantly in many quarters, by the beginning of this century. Included here is a cartoon showing a clergyman deploring the "steady decline of womanhood from its old ideals," while at the same time the woman of that time is depicted in some of the roles she has entered. She is shown not only as a student receiving her law degree and as a doctor with her little black bag, but also as a teacher, an artist, a stenographer, a sportswoman, a battlefield nurse, a crusader against cruelty to animals, and a newspaper reporter. Indeed, the world was opening to her.

More than for a career, perhaps, most women still hoped for beauty and romance, and Charles Dana Gibson seemed to epitomize these hopes with his "Gibson girl," who came into being during the Gay Nineties and reached her full elegance during the first few years of the 1900's. The Gibson girl did not aspire to a medical degree; she did not spend her time over law books; she did not hope to be a teacher. She was unbearably handsome with her piled-up hair and her shirtwaist dresses and she was always more interested in handsome men than in righting the wrongs of the world. But she was also an outdoor girl who played golf and tennis. The ideal was no longer the vaporish, fainting Victorian lovely; now the nation was admiring a type with a good stride and a joy in fresh air. A woman, in other words, who could do and act.

The Economics of the New Woman

WHAT is taken for progress is very often only the invention of a new name for something as old as the hills. Sappho is the prototype of what we used to call "the female poets of America," and now call magazine writers. Molière won his spurs by satirizing the "new woman," ambitious for intellectual distinction. A very real and vital difference, however, is that which Professor Simon N. Patten notes between the self-supporting girl of to-day and her no less self-supporting grandmother.

Whereas the girl of to-day goes out into the world to gain her bread, the elder dame paid her way by household industry. She made butter, raised chickens, cooked, wove clothing and carpets. Instead of disrupting the home she became one of the main supports of it. Folks married young because it was as cheap to live together as separately. They had large families because large families were the natural incident of home life, and where chores were the chief item in education, children were economically practicable.

The modern girl, no less eager than her grandmother to earn her own way, is too proud, perhaps, to become an employee in a commercial dairy, or to sew in a dressmaker's. Even if she were not, to do so would deprive her of her position at the head of her own establishment, and make the proper rearing of children impossible. Similarly, she is schooled and colleged not so much because she is brighter and more ambitious, but because the shifting of social conditions has left her no nearer and more homelike employment for her time. The new woman is so little of a woman not because she is different, but because economic conditions are different.

In effect, however, the educated, experienced modern girl is vastly different from her homekeeping grandmother of homely wit; and—in spite of all sentimentalization of the brave days of old—the difference is vastly in her favor. It is possible that she is even worth a young man's doing double work to get her and to keep her.

But there is one more thing to think of. In the upward trend of progress it is easier to gain a new point of vantage than to keep it. If the modern girl, once married, is to maintain her status in the world, to say nothing of advancing it, it can only be by passing on to another generation the advantages she receives in this. What, to her grandmother, came unconsciously and all in the course of nature she has to do in the exercise of the greater intelligence and the conscious ideals of her ampler life—perhaps at the cost of a far greater sacrifice of momentary comfort and ambition. According to the best of definitions, those things only are natural, and have a lasting place in the scheme of the world, which tend to reproduce themselves.

ADDICKS AND THE WHIPPING POST have contributed to Delaware's notoriety. It is frequently assumed that Delaware is the only commonwealth in the Union subject to either of these afflictions. The decree of an Oregon court, however, reveals the fact that in the Valley of the Willamette the mediæval penalty for wife-beating still prevails. Brutality reaches its maximum when a sordid husband strikes down and beats his wife because she refuses to satisfy his alcoholic thirst with the money earned at the tub, that her seven children may not starve. In urging in extenuation the excuse that he was "drunk at the time" the defendant exhibits

WHIPPING POSTS
IN OREGON
powers of reasoning and appeal that are somewhat short of final. So long as our own statutes hold to capital punishment for the crime of first degree, clinging to the Mosaic law of "a life for a life," it is clearly inconsistent to argue that the whipping post is not the penalty which "fits the crime." The argument against the whipping post is, of course, not based on sympathy for the husband. His sufferings would give joy to any honest heart which had not reached a degree of saintliness fitting the possessor for a better world. It is simply one of the pleasures that, without injury to our taste, we can not permit ourselves to indulge.

THE FLUSH OF EXCITEMENT that follows any broken superstition leads to some shallow theorizing. The removal of restraints has led woman to imitate man, with his different structure and function—to copy his education and work too closely along his lines. The most excessive exhibitions of this kind have probably had their day. The prosperous American girl now takes more exercise and more air, and lives more in the country, than she ever did before; a sound body, firm nerves, and a sane mind will be the consequence; and such physical vigor will express itself in an enjoyment

ATHLETICS AND
MOTHERHOOD

of natural functions. We like to do what we can do easily and well. The class which has been accused of avoiding children is coming to live more as the English aristocrats do, and one of the results will be to make the women of that class have as many children as the corresponding British women have. The decrease in fertility among the prosperous, in the last half century, has been mainly in the cities.

What the Century has Done for Women

NO LESSON that the nineteenth century taught us is more directly impressive than its exhibition of the unused resources which it brought into use. Its inventions and discoveries multiplied man's power over Nature by taking hold of common things and familiar facts, and putting them to use. Chemical and dynamical agencies at the close of the century were rendering service to the race in every direction, although at its opening they were useless through our ignorance or contempt for them.

A parallel fact was the great increase of woman's activity during the past century. At its beginning, the stage was almost the only career open to a woman of distinguished abilities. Even literature was practically closed through the common contempt for "bluestockings." Monk Lewis, who himself had perpetrated some of the worst novels in the language, wrote to his mother, on hearing that she had a novel in hand: "I cannot express to you in language sufficiently strong how disagreeable and painful my sensations would be if you were to publish any work of any kind, and thus hold yourself out as an object of newspaper animadversion and contempt. I always consider a female author as a sort of half-man." And "the little cock-sparrow," as Mrs. Oliphant calls him, spoke the feelings of his generation.

Already, indeed, England had a few woman authors of note, such as Fanny Burney and Mrs. Radcliffe; and several others were about to appear, notably Mrs. Shelley, Jane Austen and Jane Taylor. These, however, were but the first drops of the shower which, by the middle of the century, had reached such a volume as showed that the woman of letters was an established fact. Let any lover of good literature look over the list of English writers of the Victorian period, and consider what a loss it would have been to human enjoyment, what a detraction from the "gayety of nations," and what a diminution of the moral and civilizing forces of good literature, if woman had been "kept in her place" during those years, as were the women of the century preceding. Think of Charlotte Brontë living the demure and inarticulate existence of a country parson's daughter, Elizabeth Barrett timidly stealing under a feigned name into the Poets' Corner of an old magazine, and George Eliot using her splendid powers of imagination for the delight of a London coterie!

Literature is not the only gate that the nineteenth century threw open to women. Science, law, medicine, philanthropy, and social reform of every kind have welcomed her with more or less heartiness. She has been admitted to many forms of business activity, which have been created by our new conditions, or were closed to her and monopolized by men before. In a word, woman is allowed to make what she will of her own life, and to work out any kind of power that is in her, as she never was before; and she has laid us all under obligations by the splendid use she has made of her new opportunities.

It is objected that she has grown less feminine and attractive through the change. But this is not the fact. The woman of a century ago did cultivate some social accomplishments, which have been allowed to slip out of use. They worked samplers when they were young, and they could faint at discretion in their riper years. But to judge by the records of that age, in both memoir and fiction, there was an amount of coarseness in women's speech and behavior which has disappeared. Smoking, swearing, and roundly abusing those who offended them, although not universal accomplishments, were yet far more common among women than they are to-day. They read books and sat out plays which to-day they would be ashamed of. In fact, being taught that they were an inferior kind of men, they naturally thought that imitation of men was the road to perfection. They now know better.

Matrimony Versus A Career

By Lavinia Hart

DOES THE BACHELOR GIRL GET HER EQUIVALENT FOR HER RENUNCIATION? THE QUESTION AND THE ANSWER

THE "career" evil is getting its roots well fixed in the feminine population. It has advanced the marrying age and decreased the marriage rate. It likewise threatens the population. It has sent lovely woman, in short skirt and tailor coat, out into the world with "her way to make." It has put spectacles on her nose, worldly wisdom in her eyes, determination in her stride. It has relegated numberless victims to existence in family hotels—numberless others to life in the clubs. Also it has introduced a sexless species known as the bachelor girl. We almost hesitate to say that we live in a real home, the kind that mother used to make, and that our women folk are not struggling for night keys and everlasting fame.

Whence comes this new condition? We remember days when women's nerves, and husbands, and homes, and natural tendencies were not sacrificed for ambition and big headlines. But those were days before the "higher education." The "co-ed" was yet unborn.

It is not the present intention to depreciate the value of the college education for woman. Indeed it is to be deplored that the institutions of higher learning were not opened to them centuries ago; for this country would then have been spared the hysteria attendant upon adjustment to the new conditions. Women should have all the learning they can digest. But when the higher education tends to unfit rather than to fit them for their work in life, it savors strongly of mental and moral indigestion.

The highest purpose of the college is culture. The quickest means to culture is education. But education is not culture. Culture is the moral and ethical application of education. It does not consist in the memorizing of facts and figures, but somewhat in how much of them we forget. It is not the text of the fable but its moral that avails.

The Real Aim of Education

The Greek and Latin and mathematics of the college curriculum are not inflicted for the sake of conversational gymnastics, nor yet as a guarantee for counting-house employment. The study of these subjects does not aim toward a greater or less familiarity with Greek and Latin and mathematics, but toward the foundation and formation of character. This is the aim of the university and of all higher education. When women have come fully to realize this; when they can view education as a means rather than an end; when they can appropriate its forces to their own use, rather than be appropriated by them; when they can view the college course as a whole and dedicate it to its proper place as a good and wholesome influence upon character, then they will know just what to do with their Greek and Latin and mathematics, and a perplexing crisis in the history of the feminine intellect will have passed.

But that day is distant; and until it dawns women are going to fuss about the uses to which they shall put their newly acquired learning. We know more about women than their male biographers who attribute to them extravagance. Their trend is toward economy, and they have a natural horror of waste. The four years of college life must therefore be properly invested and the acquisitions thereof capitalized and made to bear fruit. There are the arts, professions, sciences. Man, in either the mood generous or the mood compulsory, has opened wide to his sisters the door to the enchanted grounds. If he has not yet extended the full privileges, at least there are "Ladies' Days." There is also matrimony; and all days are "Ladies' Days." But gracious! One's great-great-grandmothers went in for that in Puritan times, before there were any female colleges, or co-eds, or even public schools; and "higher education" and "culture" and "ethics" and all those desirable-sounding things were yet unheard of. If woman isn't to make a name for herself and have a career and do things, what is the use of all this educational advancement? Of course there are women who will take to matrimony. They are gifted for that sort of thing—keeping house and rearing children and puttering over pie recipes—the clinging-vine type of the old school. But it is different with the co-ed. The light of the higher education has fallen upon her and disclosed the path that leads to fame. She hears a voice calling from the heights and she must go. Whatever the sacrifice, Fate has beckoned, and it is her life.

Besides, *sotto voce*, it is easy, and the gains are great. The secret of fame is to tickle the public—not at the moment when it would weep. She is not unfamiliar with the ways and means of genius. In her college course she has hobnobbed with great minds. She has a generous smattering of the things they did and knows a thing or two about the elements of luck and public caprice. A painting, a poem, a statue, a brief, a delicate operation or a scientific discovery, and, presto! the fortunate favorite of Fate rubs the sleep from his eyes one fine morning to discover the world at his feet and laurels on his lucky brow! That this fortunate of Fate is usually old when the laurels arrive is a detail; that the loved ones to whom they would have mattered have deserted or starved is another; that worry and work and unsatisfied longing have wrecked his nervous system, and failure and humiliation and deprivation have whitened his blood and laid a withering finger on his spiritual nature—details all. Fame came as the result of his labor, and that lives. There is no record of his toil, his failures, his hopes, his despairs, his curses, his prayers. He just "wakes one fine morning" to find that the world has understood. "Lucky dog," says the public verdict. "And such is fame," says the co-ed.

But fame is not public caprice, nor is it a popular hit. The shout of the multitude dies on its lips if the popular hit be not based on something solid and worthy. No man or woman ever gained lasting fame by chance. The success that flashes suddenly upon the world is no mushroom growth. It is the result of courage and patience and unceasing toil. Fame does not come by wishing for it; it comes by the sweat of one's brow. We attain its heights more often by scaling the solid piles of successive failures than by floating upward on the tidal wave of a success. All result is the effect of effort; all happiness is the effect of content with what we have; all character is the effect of successful struggle with untoward conditions. No life can be worth while if it have not its shadows as well as its high lights; no character can be worth while if it have not the enduring power born of suffering; no virtue can be worth while if it have not proved its power of resistance; no goal can be worth while that does not demand, by test, proof of the aspirant's character and enduring power and good intent.

The aspirant for fame has no rosy road to follow. The roses are all at the top and the path is briar-strewn. The woman who chooses a career to escape the drudgery of married life will learn that the duties of home are but playthings compared with the toil and strife that are her portion. She will glance back at the "humdrum" life which she has scorned, as cattle look back toward the brook or a field of clover. She will think of the great-great-grandmother, who hadn't any ambition nor any "career," who loved her husband and kept his house, and reared his children and got their blessing, and she will wonder where, in the name of the higher education, she got her wisdom from.

The Shipwreck at the Isle of Content

All the women who yearn for a "career," however, are not impelled by motives of greed or vanity. Some really are searching for the best; they are aiming to realize the highest life of which their capabilities give promise. Can such a realization be found in marriage? They put away their caps and gowns and go out into society. They look around—and shudder. Can this be the best of which women are capable? Competition, rivalry, envy, unrest, a life of sham and glitter and weak pretension, a struggle for prestige that has no power, a striving for place that has no security—a price unheard of for Dead Sea fruit. And out of this turmoil of unreal living, homes called such by courtesy only, friction, emptiness, discontent. Certainly not an inspiring outlook for a girl with high ideals, and earnest endeavor, and fresh, young hope. No wonder the thought of celibacy and a career and honest attainment is garbled into a high ideal and lofty purpose, compared with this empty estate of the modern marriage. But the girl who judges does not go deep enough. Not the effect but the cause solves the problem. She sees women bought and sold in the matrimonial market for gold, for title, for position, and in humbler circles for the mere comfort of "a living"; and for these they give up their lives, their liberty, their selves; for these they stunt the growth of their immortal souls and sacrifice their certain chance of knowing happiness. And she sees men and women marry for love and start with all sails set for the Isle of Content; and presently they have run aground or sprung a leak or foundered on a rock, and folks look on and shake their heads and declare the marital bark is unseaworthy. But it isn't the marital bark that's ailing; it's the men and women who sail her. Marriage is not a success or a failure as a national but as an individual institution. Its fulfillment must depend upon the character and intention of every man and woman who enter into it. The happiness it yields will depend upon the direction of their efforts; whether they seek it from without or whether it comes from within. The measure of their content will depend upon their capacity for envy. The strength and quality and continuity of their love will depend upon their discernment in sifting the things that are real from the things that are not; in grasping the distinction between pleasure and happiness, and in living in those good and wholesome conditions that leave no bitter after-taste, no withering reaction.

The Kite Without a String

There is an ideal state in marriage, and, in spite of appearances that belie, it is often found. But these realized ideals have little in common with the ideals of the girl wavering between matrimony and a career. To her the ideal has to do with things lofty, and perfect, and unattainable. It is a matter of heroics. She has reached an age and a crisis where she must go out into a practical world, with a knowledge that is not at all practical; and with a judgment born of book-learning deal with the vital, palpitating problems of life. She has ideals, but they are like a kite flying high in air with no string attaching it to earth. Such ideals are useless. They are empty, unadaptable day-dreams. The ideals that count rise out of practical knowledge and every-day conditions. They are not things we vaguely long for, but things we intend to get. They are not standards made of clouds and floating comfortably out of reach. They are made of honest intention, and purpose, and grit; and they rise out of healthy consideration of conditions as they exist. Sound, healthy ideals result from a normal, healthy viewpoint; and the woman with such a viewpoint knows that whatever talent she may have, whatever qualification for a successful career, her greatest achievement and most magnificent fulfillment must be found in marriage and the home. For this Nature has endowed her. Not only are these her gifts, her talents, her privileges, but her responsibilities also. All other talents are inferior and secondary; all other careers are makeshifts and substitutes. It is a splendid achievement for a woman to be a successful lawyer, or doctor, or minister, or scientist, or artist, if she be qualified and if she have the time. But men can do these things, and they do them more or less well. What man cannot do, however, is to be the mother of a family and the inspiration of a home. If the woman who might have been a successful artist or doctor or lawyer turns to the duties of wife and mother instead, there will be numerous others to take her place and collect the fee. But no one else in the world can bear her children, or make the home she might have builded, or instil her character and purpose into the minds of a new generation of little men and women.

(Continued)

It is true that the demands of marriage upon women are exacting. It is true that because of these demands women have been unable to compete with men in the arts and professions and sciences. But even in this hardship there is virtue. The arts and professions and sciences have been sufficiently overcrowded with mediocre talent and inferior ability without their help. If we are to have women entering into these fields, let us have women who excel; women who will reflect honor and glory upon their sex; women of will, and wisdom, and judgment, and genius; extraordinary women, if you please, of high ideals and practical demonstration, normal, well-poised, and broad and clear as to view. That these women will marry need be in no sense disparaging.

Marriage Never Killed a Genius

Marriage never killed a genius. It could not. Genius will out. Not homely living, nor practical conditions, nor the exigencies of a bad marriage, nor yet the more formidable comfort and content of a good one, can put down genius or stifle its expression. For genius is not a matter of time spent in practice. It is not evidenced by a trick of the hand that carves or paints, nor is it the output of the polished intellect. That which we call genius is the voice of the soul, speaking through these mediums its message of beauty and love and truth. It is not by the manual labor of drilling at these various arts that the notes are found which strike the chord for lasting fame, but by the development of the individual soul. When that soul has grown to such magnificence and fullness that its message is ripe and ready to benefit, it overflows; and no power on earth can confine the greater soul to the limits it has outgrown.

When genius confronts us we marvel at the beauties of finesse, of technique, of color and form. When genius speaks we are dumb. We are awed by something greater than art, which is Nature — the soul of Nature — flashing forth its message as a spark that passes criticism, passes admiration, and seeks and finds the soul of man, as swift and straight as steel goes to the loadstone.

Thus does genius work. It does not demand for the fulfillment of its purpose the setting apart of a life or the abnormal twisting of one's natural instincts and inclinations. To make every hour as famous as we can; to do the best there is in us; to carry out, in less illumined hours, the promptings of those enlightened moments when the divine within us wakes; to be what we would seem; to have within us the genius with which we would impress the world; to live simply and sincerely and naturally, these are the ways and means to lasting fame. That which we are, nor more nor less, is embodied in that which we do. Our accomplishment suffers by our limitations and thrives with our development. For the great work, the complete life is necessary; the complete mental and physical and spiritual life; and these are not attained in the single state, which is one of incompletion. Marriage is popularly called a discipline, but it is more than that. Through its new and certain responsibilities men and women acquire character; through its suffering they gain enduring power; through its joys they learn gratitude, and touch the beauties of humility. A happy marriage is a compact of unselfishness; and out of unselfishness springs all the good of living. There is no emotion that falls to the lot of man so good and so far-reaching in result as unselfish love. There is no surer, quicker means of finding happiness than the wish and effort to make another happy. There is no better equipment for stirring the heart and mind and soul of mankind than by developing the heart and mind and soul of one's self by these means of marriage which God has put at our disposal. No man or woman is of himself a perfect whole; but it rests with himself to obtain the perfection of the unit, by uniting with some heart and mind and soul and self which shall supply, or complement, or round out that which he lacks or wherein he is weak.

A Girl Doctor of Philosophy

Miss Helen Bradford Thompson, one of the youngest and keenest doctors of philosophy in Chicago, finds herself in a somewhat amusing predicament. It was but very recently that she received from the University of Chicago her final doctor's degree. However, she is already being buried alive, as it were, by the influx of epistles from various portions of the United States and Canada. These are inquiries relating to her new discoveries in the line of experimental psychology.

She credits the general confusion to the misapprehension concerning her work on the part of some scores of newspapers throughout the country who insist she is striving to prove, by a series of experiments, that the feminine mind is the equal, if not the superior, of the mind masculine. This view of her work has caused her no end of embarrassment. When she has vigorously denied to a reporter that this was the object of her labor, she has been met later with a part column reiterating the erroneous surmise, and with no greater modification than, possibly, the following: "Miss Thompson will not admit that this is the whole aim of her experiments."

In her experiments to discover the normal characteristics of the mental power of the average being, she examined fully fifty students as to the acuteness of their physical senses, spending about twenty hours with each subject. In measuring the pulse curves she watched the lines carefully, and when a sudden break occurred she made a practice of asking what the student was thinking about. But her subjects, being human, often occasioned her a good deal of trouble during this part of the ordeal. One young man whose pulse showed decidedly erratic movement sometimes found his thoughts sidetracked from the subjects upon which he was supposed mainly to dwell. When asked to give an outline of his thoughts he generally looked helplessly at the serious but charming face of the future doctor of philosophy, blushed and would not tell. Despite these amusing freaks of human nature Miss Thompson believes she will be able to "strike an average" and determine the mental norm, and that this will be of immense value and assistance to school faculties.

Lotta's Shower of Gold

Miss Lotta Crabtree
PHOTO. BY GILBERT & BACON
PHILADELPHIA

LOTTA, the actress, after a retirement of many years, has come anew into public attention, this time as manager of a theatre in Boston which she has owned for some years but which heretofore she had leased.

In private life Lotta is Miss Charlotte Crabtree, a most charming and dignified lady of petite figure and middle age. She has lived in retirement for nearly twenty years. She left the stage at the height of her popularity for reasons that have never been definitely stated. She had always been singularly successful, so successful that when she quitted active life it was said that she was worth nearly a million dollars.

Lotta was born in San Francisco amid very humble surroundings, and long before she was out of short clothes had made her appearance as a banjo player in the San Francisco music halls. She could play so well, and sing so well, and tell stories so well, that she became an innocent favorite with the rough element before which she appeared, and it is of record that the utmost decorum always prevailed when she was on the stage.

Her singular influence over rough men was exemplified by an incident that occurred when she was about seventeen. In charge of her mother, she was making a tour of the Nevada mining camps. She landed at Hamilton, one of the roughest camps in the Territory. An expectant crowd of particularly rough miners was at the tavern to meet her when the stage drove up. The great theatrical event had been announced somewhat in advance, and the miners had looked forward with boundless joy to the appearance of the gay soubrette who was coming to entertain them.

When there alighted from the stage a spare, elderly lady, who was Mrs. Crabtree, and a little girl in short frocks, who was Miss Crabtree, the disappointment was loudly and vociferously expressed. However, any show was better than none, and that evening the miners fairly packed the place where the show was to take place. Two billiard tables had been pushed together to make a stage, a curtain being dropped between for purposes of retirement. At the hour set for the opening there stepped from behind this curtain, on to the front billiard table, a demure little creature with skirts reaching to the knees, and carrying a banjo slung negligently over her shoulders.

The audience was very cold. In less than half an hour, however, Lotta had every mother's son of them in a state of high-wrought enthusiasm.

She sung to them, danced for them, and told them funny stories with tireless energy, and they encored her again and again. Finally one man in the audience, carried entirely away by enthusiasm, came down to the front with a whoop, and, throwing something on the stage, cried out:

"There; you can have my pile!"

The example was contagious. In less than a minute every man in the place was scrambling eagerly forward to divest himself of riches in order to lay them at Lotta's feet.

The result of that night's work was the most profitable in the history of Miss Lotta's career on the stage, either in Nevada or anywhere else.

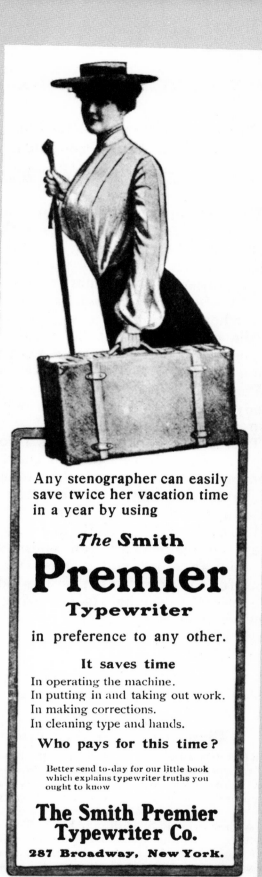

WHY FLIRTING STENOGRAPHERS FAIL.

They Are Rewarded With Candy, But Never With Promotion.

By Mrs. Juliet Shumaker, Principal of the Lancaster School, St. Paul, Minn.

The stenographer who, in the mildest and most harmless way flirts with her employer, her fellow clerks, or callers at the office, who is called to the telephone on an average of five times a day by some one to whom she talks in a honeyed voice, and whose giggle is a well known sound in the office, need not be surprised if she is pushed to one side and a man preferred when a responsible duty is to be performed.

Feminine graces will be rewarded with candy and compliments, never with promotion or confidence.

The stenographer who goes into an office expecting to win recognition and compensation on an equality with men must remember first and distinctly that she is not a woman, but a stenographer.

It is all well to talk about a woman's presence inculcating gentleness and courtesy in an office, but a busy man has no time for an extra word; he has no time for the effort to make that word a pleasant one when he does not feel pleasant.

The Voice of the Peacock

THE American woman, according to an observer who lately returned from an extensive tour in Europe, is one of the best in the world to look at: "but I never knew how bad they were to listen to till I came back. I really think it must be worse than when I left, and if there are any statistics on the subject I should be willing to bet on it."

All observing Americans who have lived among Europeans have noted this national trait; so that, bad as the voices of our women are, there is hope that they are not getting worse so fast. In point of fact, they are probably growing better. In all the great cities—San Francisco, Chicago, New York and Boston—women of cultivation have acquired, or are born to, the sort of voice King Lear praised in Cordelia:

> ever soft,
> Gentle and low—an excellent thing in woman—

and in smaller centres the case is probably the same.

In the mass, however, American voices still leave much to be desired. The matter is a serious one, for, even more than a seemly countenance and beautiful clothes, a voice "soft, gentle and low" is an index of a rich nature thoroughly cultivated. The modiste and the milliner make fine birds, and a little policy may succeed in controlling the features; but the voice is the organ of the heart. Petulance, hatred, envy color it—or discolor it—in a moment. That most potent factor in bad manners, overwrought nerves, raise the voice to the highest pitch of shrill and exasperating discord.

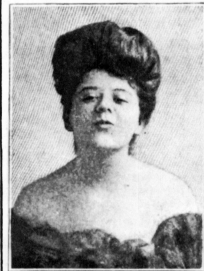

Words of Wisdom from the Wealthiest Woman in America
The Benefits of a Business Training for Women
By Hetty Green*

AMERICAN women would be much happier to-day if before the close of their girlhood their parents had provided them with a course of instruction in business. Every girl who enters upon her womanhood with her mind fully equipped with a business education will be saved from a great deal of pain, and will find much more happiness in every-day life than the girl who becomes a woman with only the conventional sort of schooling—the schooling that teaches her how to read, write, sing, cook and sew.

The notion that women should not "bother their little heads about business matters" was all right enough in the old days, when things were very different from what they are now. That notion began in an age when success in life meant the possession of great strength and great physical endurance, and it has continued to the present day, when success means possessing a lot of mental activity. It was, indeed, the only thing a woman could do, in those days, to confine her efforts to making herself as pretty a wax doll as possible for her husband, so that after the physical strain of the day it would relieve his eyes to look at her in the evenings, and thus go forth next day eager for fresh work. But the primitive idea of success having died out long ago, there is no reason why the primitive idea of what a woman should be to her husband should continue to exist in the sense it once did.

WHEN I say that all women should have a business training, I mean women of all classes—poor, middling rich and well-to-do. The assertion does not apply merely to those whose circumstances seem to indicate that they may one day be compelled to make their own way in the world. Every class of girl will make a better and happier woman if she has a business education, whether her womanhood sees her a maid, wife, mother or widow. I have heard it stated that for a woman to get a business training is to crush all the poetry out of her life. This is sheer nonsense. A woman with a knowledge of business appreciates music, painting and the other finer things of life just as much as the woman who is ignorant of all business matters; and the former has the decided advantage, in that she is able to turn her knowledge of business into securing more opportunities of seeing and appreciating these fine things. She can get more tickets to concerts and art-galleries, she will have more money to become the possessor of more beautiful things than a woman without business training, and a woman with a sure income before her feels a great deal more like studying poetry than a woman who is compelled to worry about her future bread and butter. I have been a business woman for fifty years, and I am just as fond of pictures and music as any one of my age. A business training is but one more accomplishment added to the list which the young woman of to-day is expected to acquire, and it is absurd to say that its possession will interfere with the proper enjoyment of any of the other accomplishments.

FOR a girl to get a business education it is not necessary for her to go to a "business college," although in many cases that would be a good thing for her to do. There are a thousand ways in which girls can get a business training, and each girl should select that particular way which is most accessible to her, and most to her taste. By the necessity for a girl's getting a business training I do not mean that she should necessarily go out to work. The business training she should have is one that will enable her to best look after the management of her own private affairs, the training that will make her counsel valuable to her father, her brother, her husband and her sons; the training that will enable her to look after her own business interests—her bread-and-butter matters—if she is suddenly thrown upon her own resources, and the business training that will make her a good housekeeper, for every housekeeper is a business woman, the degree of

MRS. HETTY GREEN
The Richest Business Woman in the World

her excellence as a housekeeper being the degree of the business training she was provided with before she entered upon her domestic duties. The successful and economical management of the house calls for the same kind of ability and judgment that is necessary to the successful management of a commercial enterprise.

THE first step to be taken, however, is probably the most important of all, and it is the same no matter in what station of life the girl may be. This first step is to learn the value of money; to learn how much it costs to earn it; to learn how necessary it is to have it in order to get along. Unfortunately, nearly all young children to-day are led to think that a nickel is nothing but a sort of token by which the corner candy-seller is to know that the child's parents wish him to give the child a handful of candy. And as a matter of fact many girls grow up to womanhood in the same childish ignorance of the true meaning of money, or how it is obtained, so that if by any chance they should be thrown upon their own resources, with no one to keep them supplied with the necessaries of life, they would be entirely helpless. Every child should be taught from the beginning that a piece of money is something that is hard to obtain, and that it ought to be taken care of accordingly. If indulgent parents desire to give their children sweets, they should make the habit of giving the children the sweets direct, and not the money to buy the sweets. It is very pretty, no doubt, to have a child do things simply to oblige her elders, and to conduct herself nicely because her "mamma doesn't like bad girls;" but tactful parents will do well to early accustom their children to also earn a little money for doing little things they are not ordinarily expected to do—the labor of earning the amount being an impressive and ever-enduring object-lesson to the child of the value of money.

A CHILD never appreciates a thing that she gets for the mere asking as much as she appreciates the same thing if she is compelled to work for it. We all know how much more satisfaction there is in the possession of a thing when we can truthfully say that we have earned it. I remember the first money I ever earned—it was my commission for selling a piece of my father's property —and although it was a comparatively small amount, I felt it to be a matter of the greatest magnitude and importance, simply because I had worked for it.

As the girl grows older she should be given a certain allowance every week from which to buy her own clothing. At first her mother should go with her to the shops to supervise the purchasing, but later the girl had better be allowed to purchase the articles herself, her mother simply accompanying her to approve of them. Then the girl should be taught to keep a little book, in which to enter the amounts she receives, and the amount she pays for what she purchases, and be taught to put some part of the money away, with which to buy presents for brothers and others at holiday-time. The keeping of the book will mean she will look it over often, and in doing so she will see where such and such was a good expenditure, and such and such a bad one. There is nothing better than this sort of training to teach a girl to economize. She acquires the habit of keeping track of every cent, and thus gets the most value for every dollar she spends.

IF A girl's parents are poor, and she wishes to go to work early to help them, it is wrong for her parents to take all her earnings every week, as it is customary to do, the parents buying the girl's clothing for her. It would be much better for the girl—and for her parents themselves, if they only knew it—if she were allowed to keep so much of her salary every week for clothes—it need not be more than the parents would spend for her—and let her buy her clothing herself. The girl knows how hard her money is to earn, and her spending it is a profitable experience. Of course, at first she will make injudicious purchases—buy the wrong sort of things, and pay too much for them in the eyes of her experienced mother—but if the mother will quietly point out to the girl how she could have done better with her money, it will be found that eventually the girl will not only be equally as economical—as good a business woman—as her mother, but much more so, she having been allowed an earlier beginning. Another great mistake that poor people as a rule make is that because the girls of the family are workers—in shops and the like—they are excused from all home duties and domestic responsibilities. Mothers whose daughters are employed during the day should manage it so that the daughters assist in the purchasing of household needs—food, additional furniture and the like—for in this way they get to know the market value of things which they will probably be called upon some day to purchase for their own homes.

BECAUSE a girl's father happens to be well off financially is no reason why she should not have a business training. Besides being allowed a certain amount for her clothing, she should be allowed to have a share or more in some corporation in which her father owns stock, and she should be allowed to manage this stock herself, not through a lawyer. A business man would do well to give his daughter a small interest in his business—let it be ever so small—so that she will set her mind to working as to how it can be improved. Parents who have real estate would be wise to give their daughter the title to a house, and let her manage it herself—collect the rental, bargain for repairs, etc.—always with her parents' consent, of course.

Now, where does all the benefit come in? Well, in the first place, the father's own business interests will improve by having the girl take an interest in them—provided, of course, she be a sensible young woman; and in the second place, the girl will make a better wife when she marries, knowing how to counsel her husband at critical times; in the third place, she will make a better mother, in that she can begin her sons' business training almost from their infancy; and in the fourth place, she is prepared in case she should happen to be thrown upon her own resources. Then, many wives are happier if they have a little income of their own which they can spend in any manner they please without feeling they are depriving their husbands. Such women will certainly be happier if they have learned how to get an income, and how to handle it themselves.

*This article is the result of an interview with Mrs. Green by C. Montgomery M'Govern, for the Woman's Home Companion.

The steady
DECLINE
of
WOMANHOOD
from its
OLD IDEALS

CONCERNING THE

PUCK. — Do you really think, my clerical friend

AMERICAN GIRL.

that the old ideals were better than these?

Will Women Vote?

SHALL women go into politics? may be an interesting question, but it is for debating clubs, not for the arena of practical life. *Will* women go into politics? is the practical question.

Fifty years ago the debating clubs discussed, "Shall women go into business?" It was decided that they should not, the women themselves being most eager advocates of the negative. Yet here the women are, swarming into business, and thinking out new lines of work. And they are protesting the while that they much prefer the "sphere of the home." May this not be the result in politics, too? How long will it be before the business woman demands the franchise? And, when she is numerous and determined, how is mere man to stand out against her?

The world moves. We may not like it; usually we don't. But move it will, and the only certain thing about its movements is that what was yesterday, and what is to-day, will not be to-morrow.

When Women Go to War

NOW comes Hans Eschelbach, writing in the North and South Review of Breslau that women ought to be forced into military service just as the men are. He points out that the women are more and more engaged, on equal terms with the men, in the far more arduous labors of the routine of peaceful toil, that the hand-to-hand encounter is no longer important in modern scientific warfare, and that it is the absence of the wives and sisters and mothers from the military camps that makes them so utterly demoralizing morally.

Herr Eschelbach is, to say the least of it, premature. But his suggestion is highly interesting and most suggestive. If, for instance, the women did go forth to war, instead of sending the men, would they continue to be the great propagandists of the war spirit that they now are? It is undoubtedly sad to sit at home, waiting for news from the battlefield; but is it quite so sad as being on the battlefield and getting all shot up and torn up, and having a band of vultures sitting near by waiting for you to lose the power of menacing motion?

Alien Eyes and American Women

HENRY JAMES and other observers abroad find our women so much more developed, so much more interesting, than our men. It is not unnatural that men should find women more interesting than they find men, though these particular men seem to think so. But, aside from the sex charm, there are two reasons why these foreign observers—studying women of a certain small class—should come to believe them far removed above the men.

The first reason is, the women of that particular idle, luxurious class make less sorry figures in luxurious idleness than do their husbands, fathers, brothers and sons. The second reason is that the women of that class are devotees of the false, un-American, actually ignorant "culture" which dominates foreign upper-class life. They feel delightfully at home with foreigners, so ignorant are they of the great realities of life and of the splendid and pulsing action of modern people.

UNION AGAINST UNION.

THE UNION MAN. — WHO EVER PUT THEM UP TO THAT PIECE OF IMPUDENCE?

DIAMONDS ON CREDIT

Diamonds on Credit under the LOFTIS SYSTEM means that any person of honest intentions, without regard to their cash resources, may open a CONFIDENTIAL CHARGE ACCOUNT for a Diamond, Watch or other valuable article of Jewelry, and pay the same in a series of easy monthly payments.

How to Do It: Write today for our beautifully illustrated Catalogue, and from it select any article which you would like to wear or own—or perhaps use as a gift to a loved one. We will send your selection on approval to your home, place of business or express office as you prefer. Examine it at your leisure and as carefully as you wish, then, if it is all that you anticipated and the best value you ever saw for the money asked — pay one-fifth of the price and keep it. The balance you may send to us in eight equal monthly payments.

On the Other Hand, if you decide not to buy, simply return the article to us at our expense. Whether you buy or not we pay all express and other charges—you pay nothing, neither do you assume any risk or obligation whatever. We submit our goods on their merits, with absolute confidence that their quality, low price and our easy terms of payment will command your favor.' We ask but one opportunity for adding your name to the largest list of pleased patrons with which a Diamond house was ever honored.

We Are One of the Largest Houses in the Diamond business and one of the oldest—Est. 1858. We refer to any bank in America — ask your local bank how we stand in the business world. They will refer to their Commercial Agency books and tell you that we stand very high, and that our representations may be accepted without question.

Our Guarantee Certificate given with every Diamond is the broadest and strongest ever issued by a responsible concern. Our exchange system is the most liberal ever devised, for it permits you to return any Diamond bought of us and get the full amount paid in exchange for other goods or a larger Diamond. Further, we give the broad guarantee of satisfaction to every customer.

Your Christmas Plans will not be complete until you have looked through our Catalogue, and considered what you can do in gift-making in conjunction with the LOFTIS SYSTEM. The $5. or $10. which you might pay for something cheap and trashy will make the first payment on, and put you in immediate possession of, a splendid Diamond or Watch. You can thus make a gift commensurate with and appropriate to the circumstances, without any considerable initial expenditure. There can be no more favorable time than the present for a Diamond purchase. Dealers agree in this view.

TO THE CASH BUYER of Diamonds, we have a proposition to make which is thoroughly characteristic of our house. It is nothing less than a written agreement to return all that they pay on a Diamond—less ten per cent., at any time within one year. Thus, one might wear a fifty-dollar Diamond for a whole year, then return it to us and get $45., making the cost of wearing the Diamond less than ten cents per week.

Write Today for Catalogue

LOFTIS BROS. & CO., Diamonds—Watches—Jewelry
Dept. L 51, 92 to 98 State St., Chicago, Ill.

THE EVOLUTION OF THE BATHING COSTUME.

TEN YEARS AGO
The good old-fashioned bathing suit, plenty of it and chock full of fun and comfort.

THE PRESENT DAY
Corsets, silk stockings, and all that. Attractive? Well, that's what we go there for!

TEN YEARS FROM NOW
The above design for a bathing costume has been handed us by a lady who summers at Narragansett Pier, and who is said to be ten years in advance of her time.

What Women Will Wear in the Twentieth Century

By Octave Uzanne

WHEN the question is of feminine fashions, one may, without any fear of ridicule, skirt all the paradoxes, weave all the fantasies, and festoon in zigzag all the suppositions possible; expose without order researches into and combinations of costume the most fabulous and the most imaginary—nothing that a writer devoted to the art of the toilet might invent or suggest could be taxed with being incontestable foolishness. There is no possible paradox on the question; everything conspires to render possible the most unlikely things. Fashion permits one to irrationalize at will, for at the most often she is herself irrational. She would no longer be Fashion if she did not know how to escape the laws of ponderation and stability. Her symbol is the weather vane, which whirls on the slightest whimsy of the wind, and which may not be fixed without losing its usefulness; it is also the butterfly, which bursts its chrysalis to spoil the earth of perfume and of color.

THE STAMP OF STYLE

Woman seems to have invented Fashion to hold in constant curiosity and eager mystery her loving physiologists, her painters, and her historiographers. Across the evolutions of the centuries she appears continually differing from herself, and her metamorphoses of toilet, in the far-off of the ages as well as in the nearer present, are so complex and so extravagant that they defy the most learned scholars utterly to lay bare their successive expressions.

It was not unworthy of the character of Adam Smith, the celebrated Scotch economist, to write in his Theory of the Sentiments two curious and subtle chapters on Fashion; the one relating to its influence on the conceptions of beauty and of deformity, the other, entirely physical, showing the impression that custom and costume may exercise on the moral sentiments. Fashion, who is the Goddess of Appearances, could only be further exalted by contact with our modern civilization, where ostentation has become more than ever a necessity of the wealthy. Without Fashion the fair elegants of the smart set would not be endlessly hurried away, indefatigable equestrians in an extraordinary steeplechase through the workrooms of the famous drapers, costumers and modistes of the great cities of the world. The toilet has assuredly become for the woman of to-day the first of the arts; it is in some sort the outward sign of the taste of her who wears it; it gives the stamp of her personality. The fashionable of to-day strives to exteriorize, through the costume which shapes to her form, her more intimate distinctions. Furthermore, in following blindly the decrees of the Goddess of Fashion, the woman of to-day plays also a part of charity, exercises surely a charitable action; for never has the remark of Chamfort appeared more judicious, that change of Fashion appears as the disguised tax which the industry of the poor imposes upon the vanity of the rich.

THE TRIUMPH OF THE ETERNAL FEMININE

What inspires a capital idea of the charm, of the beauty and the seductiveness of woman, from the hour when she began to clothe herself in primitive garments worked up from the first fruits of Nature, is the manner in which she has succeeded in triumphing, always and without interruption, as by some powerful enchantment, over the often pro-

digious plainness and the too-frequent deformations which the habit of Fashion seems to have imposed upon her at various intervals of history.

In the days of the sixteenth century, when farthingales, when skirts starched and plaited, came to imprison her in ells of heavy stuffs, when ruffs tilted high her head over enormous wide-crimped collars, when puffed sleeves in the German style pinned balloons to her arms, and inflexible corsets of iron flattened out those long and waspish waists whose rigorous and haughty expression Velasquez rendered so marvelously—in that armor more difficult to wear than the battle harness of a warrior—woman found means of being at her ease.

How many other tortures, undergone by her in the course of those times with the unconsciousness even of being their victim, she supported! For Fashion, like Religion, works her miracles.

The desire to be beautiful and in the taste of the day has transformed into veritable fakirs of the Occident, insensible at once to the contortions and to the rigors required, almost all women worthy of the name since first coquetry appeared upon the earth.

Run over in your mind the costumes of our grandmothers: the binding frocks of the Grand Siécle; the hoopskirts of the eighteenth century; those costumes of *nymphes légères*—of the time of the French Directorate especially—which made so many consumptives; then the crinolines of forty years ago—those horrible circles of steel, which so ridiculously cooped our grandmothers; what sufferings must such styles have implied had not an overmastering desire to please come to dominate the constraint of wearing them. When one thinks of the unbelievable combinations that feminine hair-dressing alone has caused to be invented and tolerated, one stands aghast. After the topknots and powdered wigs, the headdresses terraced to a yard above the cranial box, the woolsacks, cropped *à la Titus*, worn toward the epoch of Napoleon the First, how many other tonsorial crimes against the laws of Nature may not one imagine! Tressed fillets, chignons trussed up *à la chinoise*, corkscrew-curled pigtails, puffs built up above the occiput like confectioners' cakes!—surely, if Dante should return to earth he might conceive the idea of adding a new circle to his inferno: that of the devotees of Fashion. Their tortures would be to continue in the infernal regions precisely what they did in our earthly society; to give themselves over without respite to masseuses, hair-dressers, corset-makers, lingères, costumers, shoemakers and glovers, with long hours of trying on, mornings given over to cosmetics, nights to greased masks, to drugs, to soporifics—and that but shortly after the excitements of the evening. On the pediment of this last circle might be read this *résumé* of the life of the coquette:

> *S'habiller — babiller —*
> *se déshabiller*
> (To dress — to babble —
> to undress).

But why philosophize further? Whatever the human passion to which each one of us surrenders, it could not undergo cold-blooded analysis without revealing itself tainted with folly. We all of us, more or less deeply, channel our life in the impermeable shell of a dominating function, which gives us the illusion of a happiness seen in the outcome, like the glow one makes out at the far end of a railway tunnel. We all progress toward happiness by a thousand paths, all equally misleading — including that of fortune, which, as well as any other, creates so many bondages, such torture, envy and moral indigence.

WOMAN'S FIELD OF STRATEGY

The toilet is, after love — or parallel with love — the principal goal of the great majority of the daughters of Eve. Many know no literature but that of Fashion. Fashion becomes the manœuvring field of their strategy, the theme of their scientific ambition. They love this Fashion, this daughter of Proteus, who changes each season the decorative treatment of the figure.

Can we blame them for it?

And are not we men recompensed for such fervor for perfection in the setting forth of beauty when we contemplate at each spring-time the metamorphoses of feminine charms, and the new-blown grace of so many pretty women who give the streets of our great cities the appearance of fairy gardens, of which they might be the human flowers?

Although it seems difficult to affirm anything with positiveness upon a subject so delicate, so airy — one might add so illusive — as that which we are treating, it may be permitted us to think that the day of wide eccentricity in dress has definitely passed, and that we enter with this twentieth century into a period of calm, or relative, wisdom, and, so to speak, into the adult age of Fashion. Henceforward, Fashion will evolve about one and the same æsthetic sentiment without return to the extravagance of our mothers. Our cosmopolitanism — this age of leveling commercialism, of uniform apparel, of travel, of utilitarianism — will always bring us back to a necessary simplicity — even in excessive luxury — and will prevent the makers and promoters of new styles from disregarding too brutally a dress appropriate to contemporary life and the habit we have formed of reading the anatomy of the figure in the drapery which closely follows it, or which at the least allows it to be imagined.

THE INFLUENCE OF THE TAILOR-MADE GOWN

The modern woman, who more and more emancipates herself from the barbarous prejudices which long time held her in check, is less, even than recently, a dressmaker's model — or, if one prefers, a pretty manikin, whose laziness formerly lent itself easily to furbelows which precluded physical exercise. Both traveler and student, a lover of sport, of cycling and of motor-driving, in mind more independent than ever, in bearing more boyish, it would be hard to see in her to-day the sickly and capricious child she was so long in the Latin countries. It is for this that Fashion, do what she may, cannot from to-day henceforward clothe her like a Spanish Madonna or like an eccentric doll. Farewell pokes and crinolines, immoderate guimpes, pagoda sleeves, and coiffures that scale the heavens! We shall see you no more in days to come, for, aside from the fact that woman will be less frivolous, her time will seem too precious to surrender to the tyranny of the toilet so many hours which might be filled with work or pleasure more interesting and no doubt more healthful.

A definite step was taken the day when the tailor-made gown became part of our life. That day the doll, the fashion automaton, felt, in the appropriateness and the simplicity of her semi-masculine attire, something like an indication of her force, of her rights, of the less subordinate part which might fall to her in the future. She began to draw nearer man with that feeling of kinship, which was, at the outset, but a comrade's playfulness, but which has since so singularly strengthened, especially among the Anglo-Saxon races, where the feminine type has grown to such remarkable perfection in the last fifty years.

Some few sociological writers have expounded the idea that we should consider our fair contemporaries as the vanishing point of a race. Such is not our opinion, and, far from deeming the women of to-day as the last examples of a state of civilization on the verge of disappearing, we believe that they present to us an advanced type of a fortunate evolution, or rather the embryo already formed of that future Eve who shall conspire in our social re-birth.

What manner of woman will she be? A serious problem, the solution of which could be expressed only at great length, and the nature of which many inquisitive minds have attempted to set forth. But to those who more logically should say to us: "What will be the fashions of this coming woman, she who is growing up to-day and will begin to enter into the flower of her beauty toward 1915?" we should attempt to reply, half seriously, half whimsically: "What will be these fashions? Just this: simple and complex." Our beguilers will abdicate only transitorily the empire of the beautiful and ornate, and their kingdom of pretty trifles, of chiffons, of silk and supple crêpon can never be forfeit. They will reign there, as in the past, but provisionally — chrysalides through the long day, in comfortable gowns and easy to wear; at night they will reveal themselves as butterflies, in holiday resplendence, in sumptuous robes, diversely draped, masterpieces of taste, which will be still the admiration of artists and still the despair of husbands; for signed work being without other price than that fixed by the signatory, the art of adorning our companions will be in consequence at least as onerous for the purse of the head of the house as now — if not more so.

Toilets will multiply by so much the more as they will be needed for every use. A fair fashionable of the twentieth century will need extremely complex wardrobes, divided into as many departments as the ordinary occupations of life shall make necessary. We shall see a compartment for hunting dress, riding jackets and habits, hussars' pelisses for the hunting field, Scotch kilts, leggins, toques and riding hats; a compartment for easy and ample waists for traveling wear, plaited skirts, loose-fitting polonaises and comfortable cloaks; a compartment for town gowns and calling frocks; one for wheeling and motor-driving; those for tennis, for cycling, for the shore — and what not else! Numerous ladies' maids will be assigned the keep and count of all these costumes, and it would be no sinecure to have to watch over such considerable provisions of strict necessities for all the contingencies foreseen by and to be foreseen of My Lady. The life of a fashionable, under these conditions, would be nearly comparable to that of William the Second of Germany, whose cloakroom, packed with civil and military uniforms of all countries, is famous the world over. Several times a day the pretty woman who wishes to make good her social standing will hurry to one or another of her wardrobes for a morning walking coat, a riding habit or driving coat, the roomy leather tunic for automobile or autocycle, light skirt and shirt-waist for the bicycle, gauze and scarf for tennis, seashore costume of lawn, or some undress caprice for afternoon tea or garden party. Life, become more feverish through the rivalry of riches, the ease of travel, the rage for appearing everywhere, the necessity of being at one and the same time sportswoman and homekeeper, of carrying always the standard of the latest style, whether in the country or in town, the obligation to read everything, to know everything — or to have the air of knowing everything — will render existence furiously agitated and hard to bear for all those who do not enjoy physical and moral health of the first order.

THE COSTUMES WE MAY EXPECT TO SEE

Ten or fifteen years from now and we shall see the arrival of this intensive life, which has yet barely shown in outline but whose movement will be infinitely more complicated than even that of our day. Feminine dress will become more nearly that of man, but the small-clothes which will be worn underneath for outdoor jaunts will be never noticeable and always masked beneath a skirt of light fabric, sometimes transparent, which, plaited on the hips, will do away with any feeling of ridicule or shame, any shock to modesty. The ankles, cased in pretty embroidered stockings, will often be seen, or will read themselves, as the artists say, into the lace, gauze or guipure which, from the knees down, will form a wide flounce, as it were, around the bottom of the skirt. The habit of seeing women gaitered for the wheel, the hunt or the ride will no longer allow us to regard such an appearance as immodest. It would be, on the contrary, one more coquetry to the good to make capital of the neatness of one's footwear, the arch of the instep, the slenderness of the ankle. But good taste, delicacy and æsthetic sensitiveness alike forbid any of those get-ups in which certain female cyclists have presented to us the unpleasant appearance of deformed Coleoptera, such as we meet with pinned to the cards of natural history collections.

A BETTER OUTLOOK FOR GOOD HEALTH

The skirt will become short, cut at the ankle, or rising to attach itself by drawstrings to the beginning of the calf, thus giving every facility for walking, with every desirable guarantee of seemliness. Not only will trailing skirts be no longer the style, but they will be forbidden for reasons of public health. As the result of long discussions among the European hygienists, showing what an unsanitary part in town life women, with their dragging skirts, constantly sweeping and stirring the dust of the streets, have played, decrees will later be formulated recommending and imposing a dress which cannot gather filth.

Moreover, the methods of hygiene and antisepsis will soon govern the coming fashions. We shall understand before fifteen years have gone how many victims the corset actually in use makes. In place of corsets our women will wear supple physiological girdles, comformable to the movement of the torso and of the lungs. And the veil, so favorable to the complexion of pretty women of uncertain age, so sought after by young girls fond of this trellis — this screen to modesty, as it were — will be likewise marked as contrary to healthful respiration and to the order of general prophylaxis, or the prevention of disease. We shall expose the misdeeds of the veil, the network of which retains no end of hurtful bacteria which are sucked in by the breath to the mucous membrane of the throat. We shall allow veils for one day's use only, easy to wash the day after, like handkerchiefs — which also should be antiseptically treated.

THE RETURN TO OLD LOVES

As to fashions rightly so called (and thereby we understand those which have to do with the designing of corsages, of hats and headdresses), they will be in some sort a simplification of those which we know or have known. There will be something like a resumption of the models of 1830 to 1840, which set off so charmingly the feminine contours and graces. We shall borrow from all times and all nations becoming costumes, whose styles we shall modify and which we shall endeavor to make as practicable and as easy to wear as possible. We have imagined some types which our illustrators here on these pages have interpreted to the best of their powers. Perhaps our oversea fashionables will appreciate their practical side without our going into the details of their make.

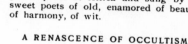

For evening dress the Neo-Greek style will prevail; tunics of crêpon, skillfully draped, requiring no corset, leaving perfect freedom of carriage, giving to every movement the beautiful and seductive unction, the suppleness, of a body free and richly clothed. Jewels, girdles of chased gold, necklaces of pearls streaming down in long pendants, casques of gold to bind up the hair, long kid gloves decorated with floral painting, signed by the masters, Roman togas for the matron, and tunics of linen or of silk plaited across the breast for the young girls — such will be, we believe, the principal expressions of receiving costumes and even of ball gowns. No more tight-laced busts and swelling necks; no more whalebone compression and misshapen chests — instead, free bodies, supple, clothed like the statuettes of Tanagra in floating folds; Indian crêpons, transparent gauzes cut low across the shoulders, but without exposing the neck, yet leaving the arms bare; costumes calling to mind, in short, the famous heroines of antiquity, those beloved by the philosophers of Attica and sung by the sweet poets of old, enamored of beauty, of harmony, of wit.

A RENASCENCE OF OCCULTISM

Such do we hope and foresee for 1915.

We shall no longer choose the colors of our garments on the freak or frivolity of the moment. Astral influences and the occult sciences, which are to win anew their vogue and which will again be the rage in society (still another fashion to foresee), will lead women rather to search — with due allowance to the indications given — for the tint corresponding to the star whose influence they desire to attract. They will learn that black predisposes them to the melancholy of Saturn; that blue holds them tributary to lunar fantasies; that gray binds them to Mercury and to his happy hests of financial prosperity; that reds lay them under the Olympian rule of Jupiter; that old gold puts them at outs with the sun, distributor of success; that, finally, green surrenders them wholly to Venus and the dizzy sleight of hand of Cupid.

This renascence of occultism will, by the evocatory symbolism of individual tones and the inevitable pleasantries derived therefrom, to a great degree stimulate liveliness of social intercourse.

Shall I prophesy further? To what end? "We little know what we are," said Lord Byron, "and still less what we may become." Heaven which hides from us the Scroll of Fate conceals equally that of the future fashions. It is permitted, however, to trace the course of the evolution of costume and to determine the almost immediate consequences of changing customs. We hope that our provisions, which we have made as conformable to Nature as possible, will be realized, and that we all of us shall be blithely alive, fifteen years from now, to verify and to applaud them. Perhaps we are too optimistic or even too little revolutionary. What odds! Woman should permit the wise to establish her fashions; she would at least win this advantage by it—that she could follow them without putting herself out of breath.

THE VERY LATEST

By Miss Grace

Newest Designs in Tailor-Made Costumes

Illustrations by Frank L. Fithian

ASHIONS this fall are interesting for two reasons—for what they are, and for what they foretell. There is a decided change which shows itself most conspicuously in the street-costume. It is the triumph of the figure. The American woman knows she has a good figure, and this season she is determined to show it. She is tired of wearing baggy blouses and loose coats which entirely conceal every pretty curve of her form.

And so it is that the old-fashioned tight-fitting basque is coming in in a new, attractive guise, and that the three-quarter coat, which is the height of fashion, is to be made as if molded to the figure. There are exceptions, of course, for this is a day of individual taste in dress, but the newest fashion is the one which modestly reveals, rather than conceals, the figure.

For street wear the mannish tailor-made costume is the ultra-smart thing. It is made generally with an instep-length gored skirt and a three-quarter tight-fitting coat, which may be of the corset variety or cut with an unseamed skirt-piece.

In buying or making this style of costume the wise woman will have two skirts for her coat, and in this way make one costume serve duty for two gowns. For shopping, traveling and morning wear in general she will have an instep-length skirt—a lined skirt bound with mohair braid or velveteen around the bottom, and finished with a little stiffening to give it the correct new flare. For calling, church and more or less formal occasions she will wear the same three-quarter-length coat with a long skirt that touches the ground all around, and has a little train at the back. When she wears this skirt she wears also a dressy silk blouse, while with the instep-length skirt a shirt-waist of one of the new heavy white cottons, either a Bedford cord, an Oxford or a silk-and-wool Jacquard, is the correct thing. All the skirts fit as smoothly over the hips as they ever did. The majority of the plain instep-length skirts which are made with five or seven gores have a habit-back or an inverted plait at the back. The long skirts are fuller than they have been, and are finished at the back in a variety of ways. With these skirts the habit-back is but seldom used. The fullness is confined in plaits and shirrings, while the plainer of these long

No. 166—CLAYTON BASQUE
No. 167—CLARENDON SKIRT

No. 168—GARRET SKIRT-COAT
No. 169—LANLEY SKIRT

No. 170—PALMER BASQUE
No. 171—LENOX SKIRT

No. 172—NEWPORT THREE-QUARTER COAT
No. 173—WHITNEY SKIRT

No. 174—COLLIER BASQUE
No. 175—CLEVELAND SKIRT

quarter coat, which is the height of fashion, is to be made as if molded to the figure. There are exceptions, of course,

AUTUMN FASHIONS

Margaret Gould

Gowns for Calling, Church and Home Wear

Illustrations by Anna May Cooper

skirts have the inverted plait. If the long skirt is fashioned of tweed or cheviot, it is made with a silk lining; if of broadcloth, panne cloth or the new fashionable veiling, it is made over a silk drop-skirt.

No. 176—BRADLEY COAT
No. 177—GILBERT SKIRT

No. 181—DORIS WAIST
No. 182—DUER SKIRT

In materials there is an astonishingly wide range of fabrics from which to choose, each one as popular as the other. Fleecy zibelines are the vogue, both plain and fancy. Those which have one color for both the foundation and the nap are worn, as well as the splashed, striped and plaided zibelines in charmingly artistic color-combinations. Mannish black-and-white tweed will be worn, as well as tweeds showing three or more rich colors. Cheviots are as popular as ever. There is a new herring-bone cheviot having a zibeline surface and scattered with hair-lines and splashes

No. 179—SERITA WAIST
No. 180—BARRINGTON SKIRT

No. 178—KENILWORTH CLOAK

usual, all the tints of castor—cream, fawn and champagne.

The woman who is ready to start her fall wardrobe will do well to remember two things. One is, that her street-costumes to be right in line with the newest fashions should be more or less severe in style and tight-fitting, while her gowns for evening and home wear are soft, fluffy and often bouffant in effect, with an air of quaintness about them.

No. 166—Clayton Basque
No. 167—Clarendon Skirt

This is the new tailor-made gown—the most advanced style of the season. It was designed, as it plainly shows, purposely for the woman with a good figure.

which is much the vogue. The illuminated zibelines are high-class novelties. Velvets and velveteens will be worn all through the autumn and winter. Dark blue serge is more fashionable than ever, and for certain costumes nothing is in better taste than panne cloth, broadcloth, and the new French goods known as drapes, which have a smooth surface with a slight pattern. For separate coats, wraps and trimmings astrakhan cloth and angora cloth are both in demand. The astrakhan cloth is an excellent imitation of the fur, and angora cloth resembles the silky baby lamb and has a long, wavy nap.

In colors all the violet shades are fashionable, from the pale pinkish violet of the wax begonia to the deep brownish shade of purple known as prune. There are many varying tints of gray in favor—the gun-metal shade, silver-gray, also the colors known as nickel and platinum. Dark blue and Havana brown are good colors to choose for a street-gown. The new reds which promise to be very fashionable, particularly in combination, are ruby, tokay and claret. The new russet-brown, which resembles burnt orange, is in favor, and as

No. 183—BERYL WAIST
No. 184—VAUGHN SKIRT

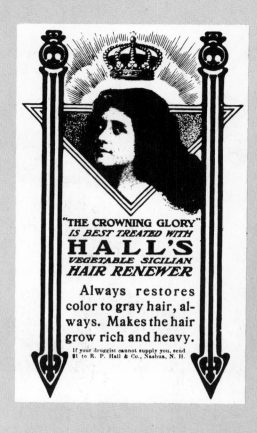

THESE ARE THE NEW HATS

By Grace Margaret Gould

Fancy envelope-shaped turban of black panne velvet. Rolling underbrim of black velvet and white chenille cords. Two white ostrich-feathers are the trimming.

New sailor, with broad, high crown, of scarlet velvet and twisted taffeta in three shades of red. The coque pompon is red with red velvet motifs.

Toque of dark blue plush and mixed silk and chenille braid in dark blue and white. Blue-gray wing passes through the brim.

New flat, pointed turban, of wild-rose pink angora, trimmed with medallions of cream lace and twisted mink tails.

Hat of cream-color felt. Fancy quill in brown, cream and peacock-green caught through the crown. Brown velvet bow.

Picture-hat of shirred slate-colored velvet, with high crown. Cluster of pale blue and gray ostrich-tips at the side.

Hat of navy-blue silk plush. Brim and folds outlined with white chenille cord. Bronze coque-feathers at the left side.

White beaver plateau with rolling brim trimmed with black ostrich-feathers. Brim caught up at back with white ribbon.

WHEN CRINOLINE COMES IN STYLE.

SHOWN TO REMIND THE FASHION MAKERS OF THEIR FEARFUL RESPONSIBILITY.

L. M. GLACKENS

The Woman of Thirty

By Temple Bailey

TO MOST women the thirtieth birthday is a day of reckoning. Before it there has been nothing to force upon her the knowledge that her girlhood is slipping away; and if occasionally the dark visages of increasing responsibility and lost youthfulness have frowned upon her, she has waved them back with a laugh of derision, and has continued to trip along the pathway of life with steps that have grown less light as the "twenties" have receded and the "thirties" advanced.

No matter how sensible she may be, however, the fatal "thirty" strikes a note of fear in the heart of the average woman. Lost girlish beauty, lost opportunities and lost enthusiasms confront her, and with a sigh she submits to what seems to her inevitable insignificance.

It is not easy for any woman to be laid on the shelf. It is not easy for the older sister to give way to the younger. It is not easy, in fact, for any one, man or woman, to become a spectator when he or she has occupied the center of the stage. It is the purpose of this article, therefore, to help as far as possible the woman who has noted the first gray hair, or looking relentlessly into her hand-glass, has discovered the tiny wrinkles in her own smooth complexion, and who mistakenly believes that the rest of life is a dreary thing to be endured rather than enjoyed.

AN ENTHUSIASTIC Christian Scientist who had been complimented upon the youthfulness of her appearance—she was nearly fifty and did not look thirty—said, lightly, "Oh, I hold always the thought of youth." And whatever else they may not have in common with her, all women would do well to adopt her controlling idea. Many a woman is so grieved by the knowledge that she is growing old that she worries herself into the appearance of old age, when otherwise she might have retained her youthful looks in spite of advancing years.

Insignificance is *not* inevitable if a woman will understand that certain adjectives to which she has always "lived up" must be changed. For prettiness she must substitute grace. She must be charming rather than coquettish or piquant, interesting rather than lively, and amiable instead of willful. Is the substitution unpleasant? Is not an amiable, interesting, graceful, charming woman as much to be envied as a pretty, willful, lively, coquettish girl?

"But," says some woman, "I cannot be all of that." Perhaps not all of it. But were you all of the other? Every woman *can* have at least one, and most women two, three or all of the adjectives applied to her.

IS THERE any woman who cannot be amiable? Do not understand me to mean the forced sweetness that degenerates into flattery. Such an attitude is unworthy. The first definition of "amiable" given in the dictionary is "worthy of love." To be worthy of love we must get ourselves into right relationship with the world. Love begets love, and the woman who would be amiable in the highest sense must learn to love her fellow-man. She should seek out the older people, and find what delightful companionship she has hitherto missed. If she will sympathize with the younger boys and girls she can be most helpful in their affairs of heart and ambition. The love affair of Jack of twenty-one and Betty of eighteen may seem to her foolish in the light of her larger, deeper experience, but if she will remember her own life-story, and bring some of the great tenderness which seeks for an outlet to the unraveling of their tangled skeins of perplexity, some day she will hear Betty say that she is "just sweet," and will find herself liking the girlish praise better than the applause of the multitude.

AMIABILITY is, primarily, a matter of heart, but to be interesting is a matter of brain. Ruskin says that "The ordinary habits of life produce great plainness of mind in middle-aged women." And women should at this turning-point avoid getting into the rut that shall lead to such depressing conditions. Perhaps the remark would not be as true to-day as it was a few years ago, for women are entering new fields and are more in touch with the world than they then were. It must be remembered, however, that a vast accumulation of unassimilated knowledge does not make a woman *interesting*. Therefore, she should study only that which she can absorb. To interest she must be interested. She must not make the mistake, if she is fond of music, of joining a club devoted to historical research. She should not agonize over the subtleties of Browning if she likes amateur photography better. By following the lines of study

which most appeal to her she will develop enthusiasm, and there is nothing more contagious, nothing more entertaining. Moreover, she should study people as well as books. Would that this last might be shouted from the house-tops to aspiring speakers, preachers and writers.

WHEN we come to the third adjective the average woman draws a long breath. Amiability and interesting qualities are states of mind and heart, she affirms, and can be controlled if one has the will-power, but gracefulness— She must not be too sure that this state of *body* is not also a matter of will. If she will give up the late suppers, the candy and other small luxuries; if she will remember that there can be dissipation in reading and studying as well as in eating and drinking, whereby nerves are set on edge and shoulders made round, and if she will stand patiently in front of a mirror and learn correct poise and how to walk, she may acquire some new ideas as to the control of mind over matter. One can sometimes cultivate an easy, natural, unconstrained carriage as readily as she can acquire those qualities of mind, manner and disposition which go to make up the sum of gracefulness.

SOME people are charming without effort. They possess the indefinable quality of magnetism, and draw people to them whether they will or not. But there are others who are charming because they have willed it so, and the woman who is amiable, interesting and graceful can let the fourth adjective take care of itself. But if she wishes to fulfill her full mission of attractiveness she must be a happy woman. It is contented, happy women that the old world needs. Stevenson says:

> If I have faltered more or less
> In my great task of happiness;
> If I have moved among my race
> And shown no glorious morning face;
> If beams from happy human eyes
> Have moved me not; if morning skies,
> Books and my food, and summer rain,
> Knocked on my sullen heart in vain—
> Lord, thy most pointed pleasure take,
> And stab my spirit broad awake.

"Task of happiness." Does the average woman think of it in that way?—that it is just as much her duty to be happy as it is to be busy and useful? In most American women there lurks just enough of Puritan blood to make them feel that whatever they don't want to do is the thing they ought to do, and so we have many self-immolated martyrs. Where her necessary work is disagreeable, and she can't reach the heights of liking it, the busy woman should promise herself a treat at the end of the day, a good book or a visit with a congenial friend, and then "look forward." If she can't find material things to be happy about let her build air-castles. Some day she may be able to "put foundations under them."

At every public gathering you can pick out brilliant women and useful women, discontented women and embittered women, energetic women and self-sacrificing women, restless women and clever women, but how many women with "glorious" faces? And yet they all have "morning skies, books and food, and summer rain" to be thankful for.

THERE are women who insist on regarding the full bloom of their womanhood blemished because it does not come up to the promised perfections of the bud of girlhood. Then it is that the sting of remembrance of unrealized ideals rankles in the soul of the woman passing her thirtieth milestone. She takes the dolorous view that these ideals are shattered which have not been realized during the formative period of her young womanhood, when it is not the ideals that have come to grief, but only the fleeting hopes she founded upon those ideals. Let the hopes go; new and better ones can be formed every day one lives. But cling to the ideals in all the purity of aim and highness of purpose put into them by girlhood, untainted with the pessimism of life. Yet to hold to these ideals through the stress and disappointments of every-day life calls for an attitude of cheerful hopefulness which is in itself one of the most potent agencies in gaining beauty of soul and face.

"The ugliest women are those unwilling to be old," says Ruskin again. Therefore, while she is yet young this average woman must decide that she will not degenerate into any of the types which have long been the glory of the cartoonist; that tea and toast and tabby-cats are no more inevitable than are strong-mindedness, blue spectacles and universal suffrage tendencies; and that, not rebelling, serene and true, henceforth she will not "creep along the coast, but steer out in mid-sea by guidance of the stars."

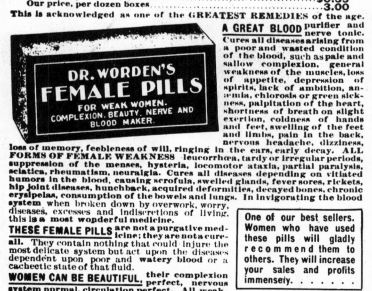

The Biology of Flirtation

THE American woman abroad is corrupting the manners of her English cousins—and also her morals. This, at least, is the serious conviction of no less an observer than Lucas Malet, who has raised an interesting protest in the Fortnightly Review. The evil of the American girl's communication lies in the fact that, being a creature of "light without heat"—the result of "a climate which makes for the production of nervous energy rather than of sex"—she is able to flirt with greater *éclat* than the Englishwoman, or even the woman of the Continent, and to go to greater lengths in the game with impunity.

This is very hard on the "duller," but "more inflammable," English girl, who is not only outclassed in competition with her electrical American cousin, but is destined to be consumed untimely in the furnace of her own heart. Many sad things happen to poor Joan Bull, the very best of which is that, as Congreve's Millicent phrased it, she "dwindles into matrimony," restless and rebellious against the normal and beautiful graces of the home. The remedy for her *malaise* Lucas Malet finds in the country responsible for the disease, and ups and quotes President Roosevelt at both offenders.

Let us grant that (as Benedick discovered three centuries before our President) the world must be peopled. Does it follow that, because the English girl is dull and inflammable, her American cousin shall have no cakes and ale? Measured by old-fashioned standards, perhaps, she is a bit cold-blooded, like the brook trout of our American waters; but she is game, and, if she enjoys the contest, why should she not dart and glide, and even flaunt her jeweled beauty in the sunlight, on the way to the matrimonial landing-net? The sport is expensive, perhaps, and when she is landed she is, at times—the culinary metaphor is Wordsworth's—a creature somewhat too bright and good for human nature's daily food. But our girls are what they are, and the consequences will be what they will be; why, therefore, should they not be flirted with?

The fact is that the American girl—and this is what European observers never see—represents a new and very significant phenomenon in the human comedy. L. F. Ward, in his recently published Pure Sociology, shows that the human race has developed three forms of sex-selection: first, that in which the female chooses; second, that in which the male chooses, and, finally, that in which choice is mutual. The Continental girl, because of the convention of the marriage of convenience, and the English girl, because of her dullness and inflammability, still fall somewhat short of the third and highest form. As for the American girl, may not her reputed coldness, and her propensity to be superfine and exacting, be due in part to the fact that she is endeavoring to make reason consort with instinct? The enterprise is perilous, and there is plenty of occasion for the warnings of wise men, from Benedick to Roosevelt. But if, in the end, wisdom and passion can be made housemates, it will be worth all the tragic-comic vagaries of the emancipated feminine intelligence.

Romance and the Main Chance

THE recent adventure of a young Philadelphia woman with a tramp proves that romance is not yet dead, but redoubles our worst fears that it is dying. While she was driving her brake in the country her horses got away with her, and she shrieked for help as lustily as any distressed damsel of yore. The tramp rushed from the woods, caught the horses, and stopped them, further damaging his already tattered raiment in the process. The lady, according to her own report, offered him money; "but he just quoted Byron and other poets about my hair and eyes, and said that a kiss from my ruby lips would amply repay him. Well, I hesitated, but I finally kissed him quick, jumped into the brake, and drove away." Then she added, with doubtful modesty: "I think he deserved it."

Deserved it? Of course he did! Our only quarrel is that he deserved more—not kisses, but far solider reward. When Cyrano flung to the actors the purse that contained his last livre, he consoled his regrets with the exclamation: "But what a gesture!" That Cyrano, however, was a hero of feigned romance. Your true troubadour was made of sterner stuff. In his songs he died nightly for love; but after he had sung them he accepted all the food, drink and shelter that came his way. When Horace sang and made Rome howl, Sir Mæcenas (as Eugene Field reminds us) paid the freight; and the magazine poet of to-day sticks hard and fast to his rate per line. There can be little doubt that, as this Weary Willie surveyed his tattered unmentionables, and saw the brake disappearing down the road, he was more than ever tired.

The greatest joy of the poet is to

Do good by stealth, and blush to find it fame.

And his greatest torment is to strike an attitude, and then himself have to pay the piper. When Weary Willie rescues another damoiselle, he will first get next to the long green, and then quote the poets.

HEAD AND SHOULDERS.

"Now, there's a girl you never see wearing a low-cut gown."
"Is that a sign of an old head on young shoulders?"
"Oh, no. On the contrary."

QUITE A DIFFERENCE.

ETHEL. — He has promised to give me every dollar he earns!

PAPA. — Better make him promise to give you every dollar he *gets*. He has a political job, you know!

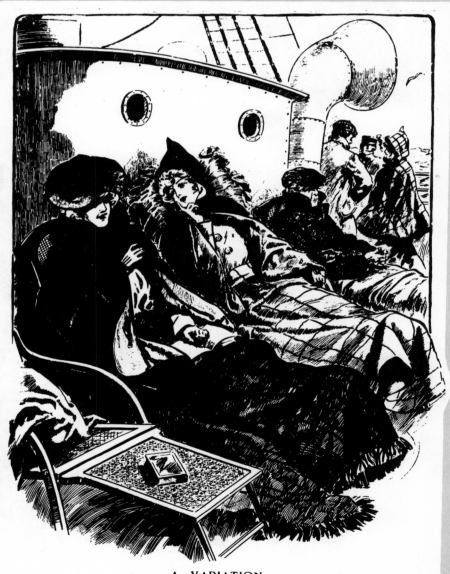

A VARIATION.

"She will marry the Count, but she wishes to omit the word 'obey' in the marriage service."

"Yes? Perhaps she'll promise to love, honor and support him."

FORE!

THE AMERICAN GIRL TO ALL THE WORLD

THE GIBSON GIRL

COPYRIGHT, 1895, BY LIFE PUBLISHING CO.

THE COMING. GAME.

YALE VERSUS VASSAR.

PICTURESQUE AMERICA.
ANYWHERE ALONG THE COAST.

HER FACE AND—*HER* FORTUNE

DRAWN BY CHARLES DANA GIBSON

6 Getting There

The year 1900 marks rather precisely the beginning of the automobile era in American history. The Europeans were ahead of us; Americans did not start to tinker with cars until the 1890's. The first vehicle driven by an internal-combustion engine produced in this country appears to have been built by the two Duryea brothers in 1893. The next year Elwood Haynes produced one, in 1896 it was Henry Ford and Charles Brady King, and soon after, Alexander Winton and R. E. Olds each created his version of a horseless carriage. By 1900 the infant industry was well under way; that year an even dozen firms produced 4,192 vehicles. Ten years later there were sixty-nine manufacturers busily at work, and that year they made some 187,000 machines.

The love affair between the American and his automobile began immediately. There were automobile clubs, motoring magazines, speed trials, reliability trials, hill climbs, and in 1908 an unbelievable race from New York to Paris by way of Alaska and Siberia. Everywhere the reek of exhaust fumes began to assault the nose, the beginning of the pall that today threatens to do us in.

The auto was not greeted everywhere with glad shouts. Woodrow Wilson, president of Princeton University, in 1905 called the vehicle a "picture of the arrogance of wealth" and predicted that it would spread socialistic feelings by emphasizing the difference between rich and poor. Tens of thousands of draymen, farmers, and other drivers of horses cursed the new contraptions roundly when their animals were frightened by backfiring gasoline engines.

Some of the material that follows shows that Wilson was not alone in his mistrust of the new machine. One editorial writer bluntly calls the motorists road hogs and complains that "the automobile wants the middle of the road and as much more as it can get." Another writes that automobile owners think they deserve "not merely the right of way, but all the way there is." Cartoons gibe at speeders; a doctor learnedly discourses on "speed mania." But as we well know, nothing stopped the motorization of America.

In those early years the nation had not yet discovered what its relationship to the automobile was going to be. As the following articles indicate, the country was not sure whether it had a plaything, something for fun and frolic, or a machine for serious business. Thus the automobile was discussed from every angle: What were its potentialities in warfare? Was it suitable for women? Could it be used for fire engines or ambulances? Some of this deep earnestness seems a little humorous today, but people were trying to reach an accommodation with a machine that was beginning to affect their lives. One man who saw something of its meaning for the future was Arthur Brisbane, famous pundit of the Hearst newspapers, who looked ahead and saw an entire nation on wheels: "In less than fifty years from now the working man, the mechanic and the laborers will go to their work from their cottages in the country in automobiles." Brisbane, for all his faith in the future, would surely have been amazed at how much less than fifty years it was before the average American workingman had his own car.

Already in 1900 a writer in *Collier's Weekly* was calling for a "national highway" for automobiles, to run across the continent, with branches down the Atlantic and Pacific coasts. "Such a highway, at certain seasons of the year would bear upon its surface innumerable vehicles, forming an almost continuous line from ocean to ocean. . . ." The early automobile owners were rich in faith in their future: at a time when there were only a few thousand autos in the entire United States they confidently predicted an "almost continuous line from ocean to ocean."

In 1901 British writer H. G. Wells, in a series of articles for the *North American Review* predicting the shape of the future, also had a few words to say about the highway of the future, which he thought would be built by private operators of buses and truck lines: "These special roads will be very different from macadamized roads; they will be used only by soft-tired conveyances; the battering horseshoes, the perpetual filth of horse traffic, and the clumsy wheels of laden carts will never wear them. . . . Their traffic in opposite directions will probably be strictly separated. The promoters will doubtless take a hint from suburban railway traffic, and where their ways branch the streams of traffic will not cross at a level but by bridges. . . ."

What Wells describes is something much like a modern limited-access highway with separated traffic lanes and noninterfering traffic at junctions, to be made possible by at least rudimentary versions of the crossovers and cloverleaves of today's highways.

The railroads receive only cursory attention in the magazines of the time, probably because they were familiar parts of the landscape and were not considered newsworthy. There is an article on the pains that were taken by one railroad to insure that its passenger coaches and sleeping cars were clean and germfree. Today, alas, very little seems to be done to keep most of the nation's few remaining passenger trains even reasonably presentable, while in the New York area travel on some commuter coaches is a distinct hazard to health.

A brief valedictory entitled "The Passing of the Locomotive" gives one a start until it is discovered that the writer is mourning the passing of the steam locomotive in the face of competition by the electric trolley. But the writer wept too soon. There was a tremendous upsurge in the growth of electric railway mileage in the United States during the first decade of this century, until in 1912 there were about 41,000 miles of electric railway track. But from that point it was downhill; the automobile was taking passengers away from the trolleys, and by 1920 many of the systems were losing money. As for the steam locomotive, it still had a good deal of life left in it, and not until after World War II did the sound of its mellow whistle fade from the landscape, victim of the unromantic but efficient diesel locomotive.

Like the steam locomotive, gracious passenger travel has faded into oblivion. The few railroad advertisements on the following pages are nostalgic reminders of a day when a trip on one of the trunk line railroads was something to boast about. Today, however, Phoebe Snow would find it no easy matter to get from New York to Buffalo on the Lackawanna; at this writing there is but a single scheduled train, departing at an hour not designed to attract travelers. The New York Central spoke with unconscious prophesy when it proclaimed: "You may fly some day, but the *Quickest Way Now* is the 20th Century Limited." Well, you can fly today, and the 20th Century Limited has been gone these several years now, done in partly by the airplane but partly by a management that would rather get out of the passenger business.

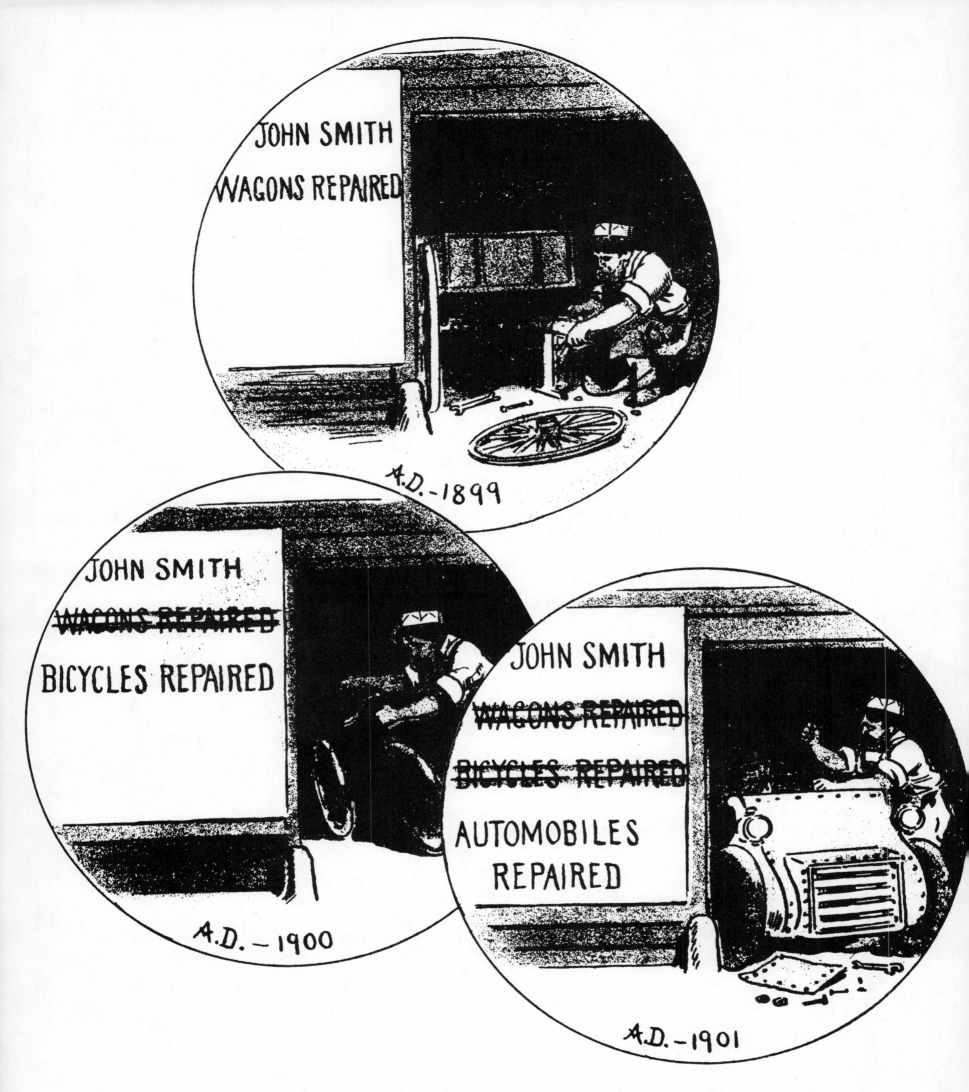

AMERICAN PROGRESSION OF THREE YEARS. *(NEXT!)*

Our Buffalo Heavy Concord Truck Harness, $27.98 and $32.25

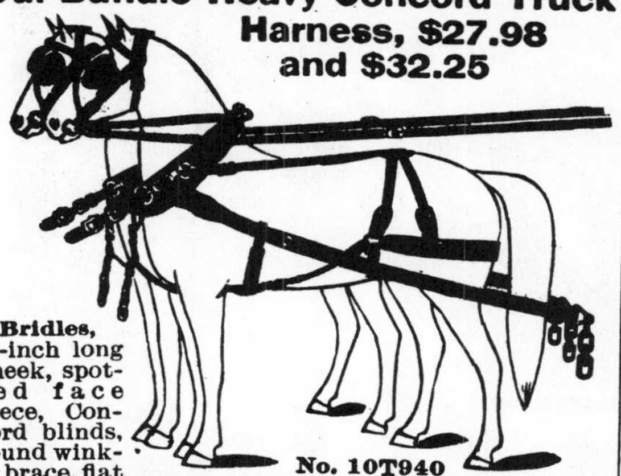

Bridles, ⅝-inch long cheek, spotted face piece, Concord blinds, round winker brace, flat rein; **lines,** fine selected Dundee oak leather, 1-inch wide and 18 feet long, with snaps; **hames,** oiled Concord bolt hames with brass balls; **traces,** heavy selected stock, double and stitched, 1½-inch, with heel chains, 1¼-inch bellyband, billet and heavy folded bellyband, traces made as shown in illustration; **breeching,** heavy folded body, with 1¼-inch layer, 1-inch side strap running to hame, 1-inch double hip strap, 1-inch side strap to snap in pole strap ring under horse; **breast straps,** 1½-inch with roller snaps; **pole straps,** made Chicago style. This harness is full size for 1,000 to 1,250-pound horses.

No. 10T940

No. 10T940 Our special price, **without collars,** per set....................................**$27.98**

No. 10T941 Same style of harness as No. 10T940, only made extra heavy, 2-inch traces, extra heavy breeching with 1¼-inch double hip straps, 1¼-inch double back straps and 1¼-inch side straps. Balance of the harness same as No. 10T940. **This is a very heavy truck harness.** Brass trimmed bridles and hames. Our special price, without collars....**$32.25**

Add for Extras to Price of Harness.

Add extra for 1¾-inch traces..................**$1.50**
Add extra for 1⅛-inch by 20-foot lines..........**.65**
Add extra for No. 10T2485 breeching in place of breeching on harness..........**1.60**
Add extra for harness large enough for 1,400 to 1,600-pound horse..........**2.00**
Our No. 10T3480 curled hair face collars, each add..........**2.95**

For price on collars, see collar page.

Weight, boxed, about 88 pounds.

Buffalo Center Plush Robe, $3.79.

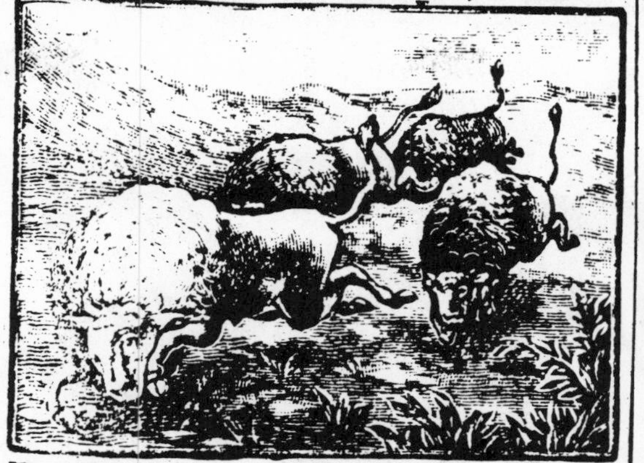

No. 10T10501 Our Special Buffalo Center Plush Robe. This robe is made of fine quality of plush with four buffalo pattern center, light shaded green border. Buffalos are light and dark brown. This robe has had a very large sale, it is not an extra loud pattern, but very handsome. Size of robe, 48x60 inches. Weight, about 5 pounds. Price..........**$3.79**

Our Dover Meda lion Double Plush Robe.

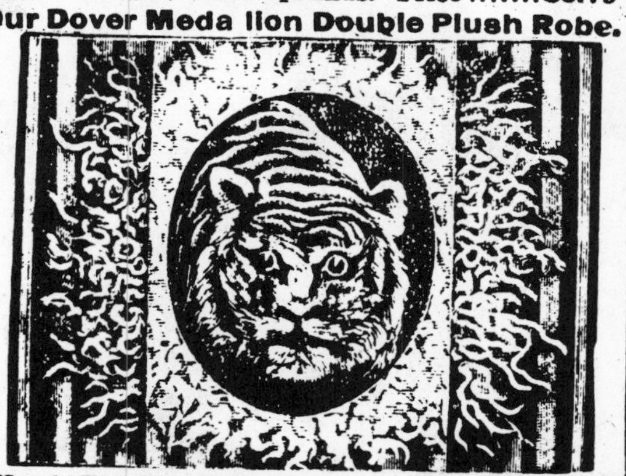

No. 10T10515 This robe is made with plain black plush on one side and fancy medallion pattern on the other side. Light green body with dark green stripes running across the robe, light and dark red circle of fancy figures and fine medallion tiger head center. Size, 48x60 inches. Weight, about 5½ pounds. Price..........$3.30

Milwaukee Fly Net, Lemon and Wine Body. $1.55

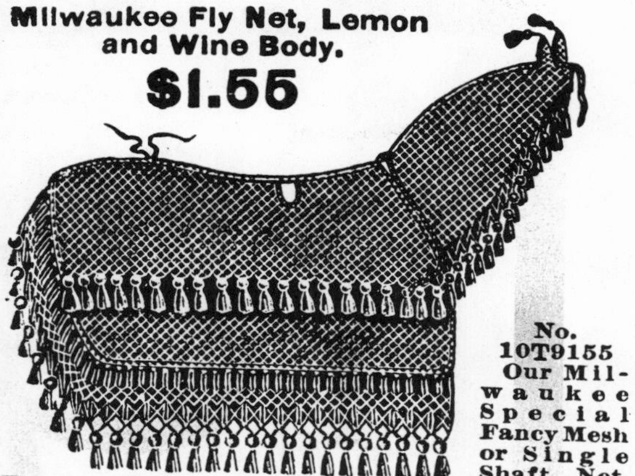

No. 10T9155 Our Milwaukee Special Fancy Mesh or Single Shaft Net. Heavy cord, fancy round border, ¾-inch diamond mesh, two rows tassels; body, neck and ear tips. Body fits around breast. Large size and deep woven center bar; detachable neck, made in two color color patterns. Pattern 4, lemon body, black border, lemon tassels. Pattern 7, wine body, green border, lemon tassels. Weight, about 32 ounces.

Price, each, for one horse..........**$1.55**

No. 10T9215 Our Fine Light Howard Round Leather Buggy Net. Made with fine round bars, improved Huston knot, string round and 6½, 7½ and 8 feet long. This is the best light net made. **The price is for one horse.** Body and breast net. Well made, selected Dundee net leather, all round, black, long string.

40-string, weight, 1¼ pounds.	Price, each....	**$1.35**
50-string, weight, 1¾ pounds.	Price, each....	**1.50**
60-string, weight, 2 pounds.	Price, each....	**1.67**
75-string, weight, 2¼ pounds.	Price, each....	**1.90**
90-string, weight, 2¾ pounds.	Price, each....	**2.25**
100-string, weight, 3 pounds.	Price, each....	**2.50**

Mesh Ear Tips.

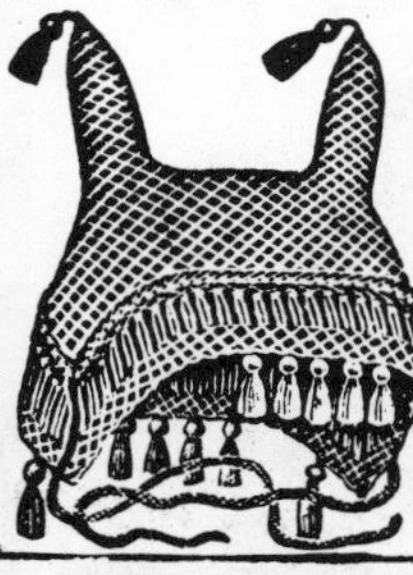

No. 10T9201 Our Fine White Shell Cotton Ear Tips. Made of fine white cotton cord with tassels. Weight, about 3 ozs. Price, each..........**50c**

No. 10T9202 Sears, Roebuck & Co.'s Special White Ear Tips. Made of double hard twisted cord; large shell pattern. A very handsome white ear tip. Weight, about 3 ounces.' Price, each..........**75c**

$46.75 THREE-QUARTER TOP BUGGY.

We have had so many requests for a three-quarter size buggy built in our factory that we have arranged to build this handsome three-quarter job in both our Brighton, Ohio, and Kalamazoo, Mich., factories, and find we can sell same to you for $46.75.

$46.75

DON'T FAIL TO STATE WIDTH OF TRACK

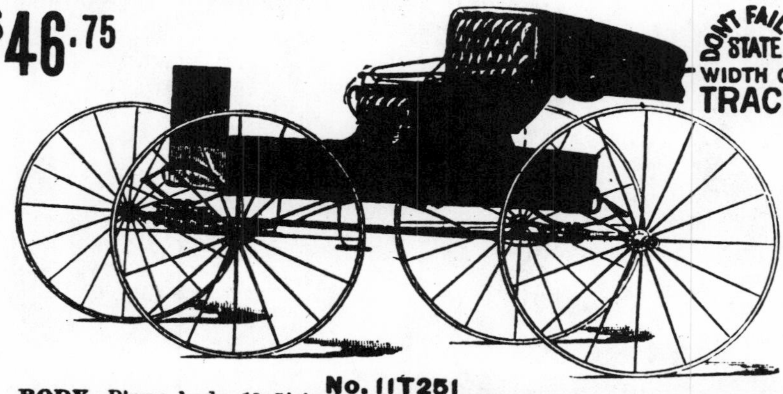

No. 11T251

BODY—Piano body 19x54 inches bottom measurement, panels convexed worked out of ⅝-inch selected lumber. Concave seat risers with concave seat panels; seat 24x16 inches with solid panel spring back.

GEAR—⅞ long distance felt pad axles with dust proof bell collar. All wood parts made of select second growth hickory, axle caps cemented to axles and sanded to smooth surface, making a non-perceptible joint.

SPRINGS—Celebrated Armstrong single leaf spring with Bailey body loop, and has in addition the longitudinal spring running from front to rear axle giving additional strength and keeping the body from pitching frontward or backward.

WHEELS—Sarven's patent wheels, 38 inches front and 42 inches rear, or 40 inches front and 44 inches rear, ⅞ inch tread, select second growth hickory, screwed rims and oval edge steel tires, full bolted. Axle boxes leaded and put in hub by hydraulic pressure. We put quick shifting shaft couplers on this gear.

TOP—Three-bow leather quarter, with quarter cut extra deep, leather back stays and leather valance stitched front and rear. Good quality head lining with lined back curtains. Rubber dust hood reinforced by leather for covering top when down. Higgins' patent curtain fasteners.

UPHOLSTERING—We use good quality dark green wool dyed body cloth in this job, and pad and line seat panels. Can upholster with leather if ordered for $1.50 extra.

PAINTING—Body given our Acme Royal finish painted jet black, highly polished; gear dark green with glazed carmine striping in wheels. Can paint gear all carmine if ordered. Comes regular with ¾ length carpet and body panels lined, whipsocket on dash, shafts, storm apron and boot. Either 4 foot 8 inches narrow or 5 foot 2 inches wide track, as ordered.

No. 11T251 Price, as described, with shafts..........**$46.75**

EXTRAS.

Leather upholstering in place of cloth..........	**1.50**
Leather roof and back curtain..........	**3.00**
Pole in place of shafts..........	**1.50**
Both pole and shafts..........	**3.00**
⅞-inch Goodyear rubber tires..........	**12.45**

Weight, about 425 pounds.

OUR HEAVY CONCORD TOP BUGGY FOR $51.10.

DON'T FAIL TO STATE WIDTH OF TRACK

$51.10

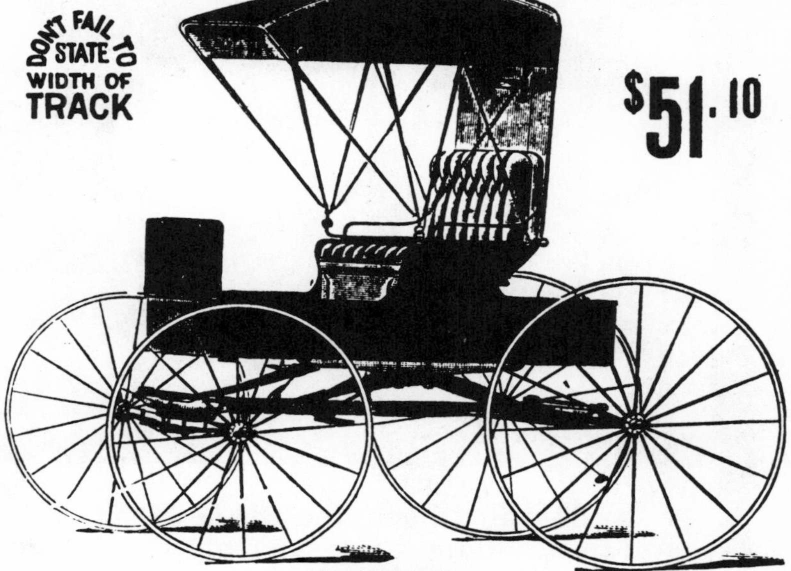

No. 11T263

GENERAL DESCRIPTION.

BODY—Large and roomy, 27 inches wide by 58 inches long; panels, 8½ inches high. The frame is made of air seasoned ash.

SPRINGS—Full Concord side springs, four plates, 1¼ inches wide, hung on steel equalizers supporting body on a wood truss, securely bolted with wrought iron clips and bolts. Can furnish arched axles.

GEAR—1-inch long distance axle. Full three perch Concord gear.

PAINTING—Body plain black, ebony finish; gear, dark Brewster green or red, neatly striped, as ordered.

WHEELS—Sarven's patent hub with sand bands, sixteen spokes, tire bolted to rim between each spoke. 1-inch or 1⅛-inch oval edge steel tires. Height, 38 inches front, 42 inches rear, or 40 inches front, 44 inches rear, as ordered. Easy shifting shaft coupler.

TRIMMINGS—Seat cushion, seat ends and back upholstered with all wool dark green body cloth, or genuine leather, as desired (leather $1.50 extra).

TRACK—Narrow, 4 feet 8 inches, or wide, 5 feet 2 inches.

TOP—Three or four bows, leather quarters, leather back stays.

No. 11T263 Price, complete, with shafts, at Kalamazoo, Mich., or Brighton, Ohio, factory..........**$51.10**

EXTRAS.

Complete brake attachment..........	**4.00**
Full leather top, except side curtains (which are rubber)..........	**4.00**
Pole in place of shafts..........	**1.75**
Both pole and shafts..........	**3.50**
Genuine leather upholstering..........	**1.50**

Weight, crated ready for shipment, about 550 to 600 pounds.

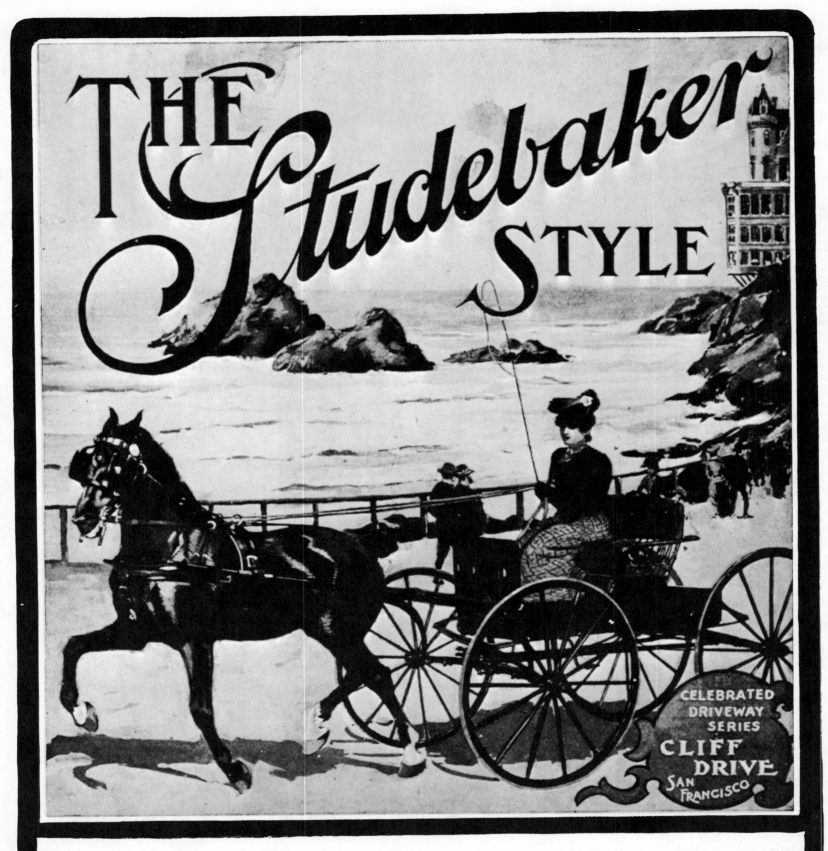

CELEBRATED
DRIVEWAY
SERIES
CLIFF
DRIVE
San Francisco

In buying "a genuine Studebaker" you experience the same satisfaction that you would feel in becoming the owner of any masterpiece of human skill.

Throughout the land, from the Atlantic to the Pacific, Studebaker style sets the fashion for the vehicle world, and on these bright summer days every fashionable driveway becomes an outdoor showroom.

Those who wish to examine our vehicles more closely are cordially invited to call at any of the following repositories. Just fifty years of experience and improvement represented in each vehicle shown. We also make harness and accessories.

STUDEBAKER BROS. MFG. CO.

NEW YORK CITY, Broadway and Prince St.
CHICAGO, Ill., 378-388 Wabash Avenue.
KANSAS CITY, Mo., 810-814 Walnut St.
SAN FRANCISCO, Cal., Cor. Market and Tenth Sts.

DENVER, Col., Cor. 15th and Blake Sts.
SALT LAKE CITY, Utah, 157-159 State St.
PORTLAND, Ore., 328-334 Morrison St.
DALLAS, Tex., 194-196 Commerce St.

Local Agencies Everywhere.   FACTORY AND EXECUTIVE OFFICE: South Bend, Ind.

BICYCLE-RIDING.

THE bicycle is the fastest vehicle propelled by animal power. As for the distance that may be gone over in a given time, the bicycler and his machine have far outstripped both trotters and runners. Bicycling, moreover, has great charms for those who have neither the capacity nor desire to attain great bursts of speed. The exercise is as pleasant as horseback-riding, and very much cheaper. But no matter how general the use of the bicycle may become, walking is not likely to lose its devotees. Daily walks must be taken within a limited horizon, however, while the regular bicycle-rider's area is extended amazingly. It has been asserted with some authority that the same effort that is required to walk one mile will propel a bicycle six miles. Bicycle-riders, at least, will not dispute this assumption. Now let us see what are the consequences of this increased capacity. A man who lives in a suburban district, in his walks around his home, if he be an average walker, will go two and a half miles out and the same distance back, making his walk five miles. In his various excursions he is likely to explore the district about his home for two and a half miles in every accessible direction, and if roads be plenty he may become acquainted with the general features of the landscape within an area of about twenty square miles. The same man on a bicycle will extend his radius to six times two and a half miles, and will therefore make fifteen miles out and fifteen miles back. He will thus have so broadened the domain of his observation that he may explore the country embraced within 707 square miles. Vigorous walkers who go five miles out and back enjoy a territory of seventy-eight miles; but this vigorous and ambitious man, if the six to one assumption hold good, would on the bicycle extend his excursions to thirty miles out and thirty back, so that he in time would have for his own all there is of beauty and instruction in 2827.4 square miles.

The cheapness of bicycling as compared with horseback-riding is worthy of consideration. A bicycle costs from $100 to $150; a horse costs from $200 to very much larger sums. The keep of a horse is at least $30 a month, including the charges of the farrier and veterinary; the cost of a bicycle for repairs ought not to be $3 a month; indeed, many of the makers guarantee them for a certain time, and make repairs without charge. So first cost and maintenance are both in favor of the machine.

With good roads in this country the rule, instead of, as now, the exception—and we shall surely have good roads before the next century is very old—the bicycle will enable its riders to learn their land more intimately and extensively than they dream of knowing it now.

FIVE representatives of American and French newspapers have been racing around the world with the probability of making the trip in something like sixty days. The chief joy in such a journey for those who take it is said to be that most of the time the traveler is out of reach of the colored supplements of the Sunday papers.

The Bicycle as a Street-Cleaner

ALMOST everything that it is possible to say about "what the bicycle has done" would seem to have been said, but there is a point of view which has not been sufficiently emphasized. And as it is one which appeals even more to those who do not ride than to those who do, to those who revile bicycles in general and in particular, a few words on the subject may not be amiss. They may help soften the revilings of these people, and to those who believe in the wheel they may give it a new attribute. This point of view is one which regards the bicycle as a street-cleaner—not a gatherer of mud, or a maker of good roads, but a moral street-cleaner. If any one will send his mind back some six or eight years and recall the city streets on summer evenings, and go down town some evening now and notice the difference, he will get the point.

Formerly the main thoroughfares and all the street corners were occupied by a mob of boys and girls, from twelve to twenty years old, who behaved in a most unseemly fashion—fooling objectionably, "guying," nudging and hugging, promenading with arms about each other, and doing and saying all the rest of the things so indicative of lower and debasing thought. Many of the short streets, where there was music of some sort or other, were positively blocked by these unpleasant young persons.

Now all is quite different. There will always be, of course, a certain amount of this sort of thing, but the improvement is very noticeable, and it is distinctly due to the bicycle. This is made evident to any observer who goes into the parks or the outlying asphalted streets where one now sees these same young persons on wheels. "But," some one may say, "are they not acting in the same fashion there?" No, distinctly not, to any noticeable extent. For the exhilaration of fresh air and exercise, and the necessary attention to the wheel itself, remove the desire and the opportunity for unpleasant familiarity, and youth disports itself in a decent manner. Let any one observe, and think of this for a little, and another honor must be added to the bicycle.

THE "FAMILY-CYCLE"—A NEW INVENTION TO KEEP COACHMEN OUT OF THE FAMILY CIRCLE.

146

The Road Hogs

ALREADY more than fifty thousand motor machines rush along the city streets and over the country roads of the United States. Every month fifteen hundred are added to the total, and with the present rate of increase in new factories the total addition will be a hundred automobiles a day before we are very much older. Indeed, we may look forward now to more than a hundred thousand machines in this country within the next two years.

It brings a mighty change. The immediate thought is the gain it gives to man in getting about quickly. It makes the automobilist independent of train and trolley. It provides new delight in swift motion. It is a new era in travel and recreation. But the larger significance is the effect upon the public highways.

Our roads are the records of civilization. Primarily, every inch of them belongs to the people. They are thoroughfares for all. No favorites own special privileges. A very considerable part of man's work in legislation has been in saving them from special classes. Vehicles came and laws had to be passed restraining their encroachments. Railroads multiplied the dangers and stricter laws became necessary. Trolley lines were even more rapacious and there was more than one pitched battle to keep them from monopolizing the common rights. Now the automobile is the most selfish of them all. It demands almost unlimited prerogatives, and the fifty-odd thousand drivers of automobiles are united in the plan to secure from legislatures the most favorable statutes regarding velocity and privileges. Committees on highways in every part of the country are busy with hearings and petitions.

It all represents the greater crowding of the roads under the stress and strain of progress. In this the people will have to stand up for themselves or they will lose much that they can never regain. Of course, they should not be illiberal or foolishly prejudiced. But the roads belong to them, and any radical encroachment on their rights means a loss that will be serious and permanent. It was possible to restrain the bicycle in some cases to special paths, but the automobile wants the middle of the road and as much more as it can get.

We find the contest assuming large proportions on both sides of the sea. Until 1878 the roads in England were under the control of the turnpike trusts, but in that year an act of Parliament abolished these monopolies and the old tollhouses gradually disappeared. The public enjoyed a new sense of personal liberty in getting back their highways. The bill recently passed by Parliament relating to the velocity of automobiles is attracting more acute attention than even Mr. Chamberlain's new proposal regarding free trade and protection. Canada, which has spent as much as five thousand dollars a mile for good roads, is discussing measures to keep them free and safe for the people. In the United States every village, every city, every county and every State has the question before it.

So the road rises to a new importance and to a larger appreciation than ever before, and the great contention is that the few shall not possess it at the cost of the many.

The Automobile—For and Against

IN THIS war between the automobile and the rest of the world we have a perfect example of what follows whenever a new idea is projected into human society. The automobile is a grand, good thing—good in itself, better in that it is the forerunner of one of the very best things that have boosted man high above his relations in the animal kingdom. Its advocates and users think that this gives them not merely the right of way, but all the way there is.

That is, they display the invariable intolerance of the pioneer of progress—the intolerance that makes the first propagators of a new scientific idea delay its adoption by their superciliousness, hasty temper and dogmatism; the intolerance that makes the pioneers in industrial organization use the admirable device of the corporation to ride roughshod over everybody. This intolerance of the exploiter begets an even more stubborn intolerance in those whom he exploits. Drivers and pedestrians take up arms against the automobile and wish to banish it from the earth; the victims of captains of industry order into the statute-books all sorts of silly laws that only aggravate the ills they aim to cure.

Certainly, a new idea has the best of reasons for echoing the Frenchman's cry, "Heaven save me from my friends!"

Future of the Automobile.

In less than fifty years from now the working man, the mechanic and the laborer will go to their work from their cottages in the country in automobiles.

You smile at this?

Don't smile too confidently.

Do you remember when the present model of bicycles first came into fashion?

Who used and paid for the first bicycles, at one hundred dollars or more each?

The rich men and women.

Who made fun of the first bicycle riders, laughing at their sensible costumes, throwing tacks on bicycle paths, doing everything to delay the manufacture of the cheap bicycle by discouraging those who paid for the first experiments?

You did, you who now laugh, or throw tin cans at the fast automobile did the same for the bicycle, not so many years ago.

And who uses the bicycle now? Get up early in the morning, especially in the country, and you will see the bicycle carrying the mechanic to his work. The cheap bicycle is almost exclusively used by working men. It is used exclusively by people of moderate means.

The rich have long since tired of it. The bicycle at Newport used to fill the foolish "society" columns. It now carries the butcher boy to and from work. It enables the workman to save his carfare, to get cheaper rent and fresh country air for his children by living far from his task. It gives these advantages, in addition to fresh air and daily exercise to thousands of clerks with small salaries.

Suppose that public jeering, sprinkling of tacks, etc., had prevented the development of the bicycle. The rich would simply have been deprived of one toy. They would never have missed it. The great loss would have fallen upon the poor, to whom the bicycle now offers many economical advantages, and their sole chance of reaching the country and of knowing nature's beauties.

Wanted: A Popular Craze

THE hour seems ripe for the bringing forward of a new outdoor pastime. What are we going to do the coming summer? The old recreations seem a little to pall. Where is the individual who will provide us with a popular craze?

It may be suggested that there are enough old crazes, but this argues a lack of familiarity with the subject. The essence of a craze is newness. The bicycle, golf, the automobile, may be pointed to. In the matter of bicycling, it is a melancholy fact that as a popular craze it is a thing of the past. Many people ride bicycles, but they do it because desirous of arriving at a certain point, or to reduce their weight, or to add to their weight, or simply for pleasure. The good old times when everybody rode a bicycle because everybody else did are past. Here, in fact, is the true test of a popular craze — it is when you do a thing because everybody else is doing it, and not from base reasons of pleasure or business.

Some maintain that golf is only just beginning, but this may be doubted. It will continue to be played rather largely, but only by those who really enjoy it.

Of course, automobiling is not worn out, but it is a question if it can ever become a popular craze. There is in connection with it a serious and very delicate matter to be taken into consideration. It may as well be said first as last that some of us cannot afford to buy an automobile. It is not necessary to name names in the case of anything so humiliating, but the fact may as well be faced. The most we can do is to stay at home and write letters to the newspapers denouncing the speed of automobiles. This shows that our hearts are in the right place, but does little to add to the popularity of the pastime.

What, then, is to take the place of these waning or impossible sports? There is nothing in sight. It looked a few months ago as if historical novel writing might do so. It was rumored that the sporting-goods shops were about to put in pads of manuscript paper, demijohns of red ink, gross boxes of double-hardened stub pens and local color in the form of historical dictionaries; but nothing came of it. This is to be regretted, as the writing of the modern historical novel should certainly form an agreeable and health-giving exercise.

Spring is almost upon us, and summer treads close behind. Where is the popular craze?

The Gypsy Life—Old and New

Some Twentieth-Century Automobiles

WITH the achievements of the nineteenth century yet fresh in mind, only the extreme of perversity would be apt to declare that anything is impossible in the prospective achievements of the twentieth. It is not alone that the logically impracticable has been proved the actually feasible in instance after instance within our recollection, but that the process of elaborating and perfecting an invention is, in these days, so rapid that public interest is given no time to flag, from the moment when the theory is first promulgated until the thing itself is an established fact. An illustration of this rapidity of development is furnished by the wireless telegraphic system of Signor Marconi, the progress of whose experiments has been so steady and so speedy that, from first to last, he has been almost continually in the public eye. At no stage of his proceedings have the scoffers been able to get fairly into print with their ridicule and hostility before his announcement of another proof of his theory's practicability, an additional experiment, or a further success.

In quite another field of modern science, however—that of auto-locomotion—it must have appeared to casual observers that, in this country at least, the inventors have recently come to a practical standstill, with their task but imperfectly done, at best. There is, it may frankly be said, not a motor carriage in existence to-day which is not far from being a complete solution of the problem, nor has there been, during, say, the last two years, that advance in development which the possibilities of the time, as illustrated, in other directions, by the performances of Monsieur Santos - Dumont or Signor Marconi, would lead us to expect. But these are surface indications only. The activity of invention is there, below the surface, and great changes are near.

What is difficult for an American to understand is that, for once, in a competition demanding a combination of scientific research, mechanical skill, and practical ingenuity, the Yankee inventor has been outstripped at, if not absolutely from, the start, by alien rivals. It is not often that the crow of the French cock can drown the scream of the American eagle, but, so far as auto-locomotion is concerned, we have been fairly and squarely beaten, and may as well admit it gracefully, and turn our attention to what the French are doing, with an idea of profiting thereby, rather than to be flying off at tangents without rhyme or reason, oftentimes merely to repeat, at the cost of time, capital, and labor, experiments which such men as De Dion, Panhard, Girardot, Fournier, or Charron have proved impracticable.

The subject of the French automobile in its commoner forms has been too exhaustively treated in the American reviews to make it advisable to go into the question here. What is of more interest at the moment is a brief comment upon the directions in which the fantastic, though far from unpractical, imagination of French inventors is turning, now that the perfection of the automobile, as a racing or road carriage, is, to all intents and purposes, merely a question of time.

While Paris—and, for that matter, practically all France—is on terms of but casual acquaintance with ice and snow, the present close relation of French and Russians has naturally turned the minds of Parisian inventors toward the question of auto-sleds and auto-sleighs. In a rudimentary form, the auto-sled has been for some time an actuality. It was a feature last winter on the Neva at St. Petersburg, but, it must be confessed, as poor an affair, when compared with the sleigh which has been built by a French inventor for one of the Russian grand-dukes, as would have been Fulton's first steamboat contrasted with a steam-yacht of to-day. The grand-duke's auto-sleigh is an actuality as well, though not till now made public. It is a thing of beauty, too, designed and executed in the style of Louis XV., and the inventor himself, whose name is known throughout the length and breadth of France for his former triumphs in automobilism, is authority for the statement that in one of the northern provinces of France, where snow was to be found, the grand-duke's new toy has already swept smoothly and swiftly along the winter roads, sending the snow flying from its paddles in a fine silver dust, while the superstitious peasants crossed themselves and fingered their beads at the passing of this new demon. There will be other auto-sleighs, now that the thing has been proved possible, but they will never be abundant, for not only is their cost of proportions which will restrict them to the possession of millionairedom, but there is barely a locality, with the exception of portions of Canada, where the winters are sufficiently severe, and, at the same time, society sufficiently ambitious, to insure a market which would repay their manufacture.

But the auto-sleigh is by no means designed to be simply the toy of a grand-duke. If the House of Savoy is not destined to be crowned with the glory of the discovery of the north pole, it will not be the fault of one of its younger princes. That royalty is only partially typical of conservatism is evinced by the fact that in the hands of the same French inventor the prince in question has placed a sum too large for even an enthusiast to waste on a chimera, to be expended in experiments and in the construction of an auto-sleigh to be used in a dash for the pole.

But while Italy is preparing to skim over the ice - pack in a miraculously swift and powerful machine, France herself proposes to make the interior of Africa as accessible as her own inland towns, by means of huge touring - carriages, built of aluminum, shaped like a submarine boat, water-tight, and able to navigate rivers as readily as to run on land. The calculations by which our French inventor arrives at the potential practicability of such a machine, for use, say, in the Sahara, are as ingenious as they are intricate, being based primarily on the weight of a camel

Touring-Carriage for Use in Africa

and his burden combined, per pound to the square centimetre of surface represented by the two feet which, in walking, rest simultaneously on the ground. It is, of course, common knowledge that hard or high-pressure tires assure greater speed as well as greater ease over firm roads, while soft or deflated tires are equally effective in travelling through sand. A calculation proves that the four great tires of the desert automobile, when deflated, give several times the area of the camel's feet, making possible a proportionate increase in the weight to be carried.

This desert machine, as it will appear when completed for the use of French explorers and engineers, will be a huge affair of tremendous power, capable of three separate and distinct methods of auto-loco-motion. In addition to the ordinary action of the motor upon the driving-wheels, there is a means of throwing the power onto another clutch, operating directly upon a propellor at the stern. The machine, as we have said, is water-tight, and the front wheels differ from the ordinary in that the spokes are replaced by disks of aluminum. As a result, they not only serve to steer the automobile when on land, but provide an effective rudder while afloat. There is, in addition, a powerful sail, for use in a favoring wind; the wind is counted upon in the case of the arctic automobile as well, it being fitted with a lee outrigger.

Finally, this desert-touring machine has a capstan in front, on which the motor can at any moment be made operative, enabling it, with a chain-and anchor, to lift the car up unusually steep inclines, or drag it, when in use as a boat, against the swiftest rapids. More than anything else, it sounds like a chapter from the prophecies of Mr. H. B. Wells, this prospect of aluminum caravans flying across the deserts, plunging over lakes and rivers, and bringing stores of gold, frankincense and myrrh, ivory, spices, and scented woods, to the borders of civilization in less time than a camel requires for a single day's journey. Indeed, the camels and the borders of civilization alike will soon be things of the past, if all this be possible. And we are told not only that it *is* possible, but that it is imminent, and these are no days in which to doubt assertions of the kind.

So long ago as the French Automobile Show of 1900 there was exhibited, in the Grand Palais des Champs Elysées, an enormous touring-car, with a dinner table completely set for eight persons. At the time it seemed a fantastic affair, and, in all probability, "for exhibition purposes only." Yet now it is known that the King of the Belgians already has such an auto-car, only on a scale even more elaborate—a car with a state-room, saloon, kitchen, and office. It is likely to be the only one of its kind, for an appreciable time at least. As the builder said, his Majesty is not desirous, in the first year of possession, to meet others on the road, no doubt filled with Americans. Therefore, up to this time, the plans, even the appearance, of the King's car have been kept secret.

Such are a few of the potentialities of the automobile. The French inventor and manufacturer with whom we have been speaking is confessedly the final authority among his compatriots, but, nevertheless, a man who believes that the motor vehicles of to-day are little more than baby-carriages, and that the immediate future will see some developments in auto-locomotion beside which even auto-sleighs and desert-cars will be as negatively interesting as the ordinary automobiles now seen in our streets and parks. "For the time being," he adds, "we in France shall set the example, and the rest of the world will follow. But in the end you in America will outstrip us all."

Proposed Auto-Sleigh for the Polar Regions

Auto-Sleigh built for a Russian Grand-Duke

A novel device, the object of which is to remove the discomfort of steering an automobile in cold weather, owing to the hands becoming numbed by contact with the metal of the wheel, has been patented by an English inventor. The steering wheel is warmed by the water after its passage through the water jackets of the engine. This is done by means of a flexible tube connected to a hollow spoke, from which the water flows round the wheel, thence returning to the water tank. It is claimed that in half a minute the wheel is rendered thoroughly warm. This invention promises to be largely adopted in public service automobiles, where great inconvenience arises in wintry weather from this cause.

The Dog: "Thank heavens, I'm out of it this time!" —From "Punch."

THE AUTOMOBILE IN WARFARE

By BRIGADIER-GENERAL A. W. GREELY, Chief Signal Officer, U.S.A.

IT WAS a dictum of the great military organizer, von Moltke, that the matter of the science of war levies tribute on all other sciences. More and more it became evident that in this century successful warfare must very largely depend on the assimilation of scientific inventions and their timely and practical adaptation to military uses. Yet most armies are slow to measure the scope and import of great industrial advances, especially if the invention pertains not to arms and ammunition. The automobile is an excellent example of the sort. Despite its importance and the dictum that "an army moves on its belly," the subject of mechanical traction has but slowly commended itself to military authorities. Indeed Colonel Layris, of the German Army, in his late work on this subject, says that mechanical traction has been viewed by most military authorities with indifference, and indeed almost with contempt. In this connection he mentions the officers of the German Artillery, almost at their wits' ends to mount heavy guns in a most difficult position, who declined the proffered aid of traction engines from a civilian at the cost of some twenty days of exhausting labors on their men, and with a corresponding delay in military operations.

In America, the necessity of mechanical traction is not urgent from a military standpoint, but in Europe it is one of the problems of the day. The obvious necessity of Great Britain, in drawing on the United States for its draught animals for the Boer War, is only one of many indications of the waning European supply. For several years Italy has been barely able to gather sufficient animals for mobilization, despite the lowering to four years of the age limit of animals subject to requisition. In France, the gradual decrease in the number of draught animals is nearing the point of embarrassment for war contingencies. Most military authorities believe that this new form of transportation will play a very important part in future warfare. The change of animal for mechanical traction on tramways in and near the great cities, and the extraordinary extension of such railways into rural districts have materially affected the supply.

Automobiles are Not New in War

Disregarding motor bicycles the application of automobilism, or mechanical traction, to military uses has been along three lines: freight, passenger, and express. The moving of heavy freight by traction engines is not new for foreign armies. In 1854, 1870, and from 1873 to 1883, experiments were made and engines used, in peace and in war, by the armies of Great Britain, Germany, Italy, France, and Russia.

Originally devised for road-making, plowing, harvesting, etc., steam motors were first applied to military uses by Great Britain in the Crimean War, in 1854. An engine equipped with endless rails moved artillery and heavy ammunition from Balaklava over roads impassable for other vehicles.

In 1870, in addition to its magnificent management of railways and utilization of permanent telegraphs, Germany tried automobilism (plowing engines), which was most serviceable when animals failed during the invasion. Von der Goltz tells us that two traction engines moved six loaded military wagons thirty miles in two and a half days. Their greatest service was the transportation of a railway locomotive around a broken tunnel. Similarly, Russia found such engines most valuable in the Plevna campaign and siege. But the invention was not sufficiently developed to merit permanent adoption, and imperfect machinery, breakdowns, etc., marked the first period of military use.

Eight Thousand Traction Engines Used in England

The grand manœuvres in France and Germany especially developed the need of supplementary transportation to that of rail, and the marked advances in mechanical devices applicable to automobilism brought it forward a few years since.

With improved devices the traction engine became so serviceable that in 1894 there were eight thousand in use in Great Britain. It was therefore natural that traction engines should be employed in South Africa during the Boer War. Not only did they prove of great value for transportation, but they were useful for constructing temporary defences, as their attached deep trenching plows threw up at once intrenchments thirty inches high and twenty-four inches wide. Coincident with advances in mechanical methods there have developed new types. The express or private automobile most engages public attention, but for military purposes it is far inferior to the freight machine which, in the shape of van or omnibus, will carry from eight to ten persons, or loads of several tons' weight, at a moderately rapid speed.

Germany and France have in late years given special attention to automobilism in their annual military manœuvres. Probably the experiences of the German imperial manœuvres of 1901 offer a fair indication of the applicability of this new method of military transportation. The machines were of three different types: express, freight, and traction. There were twelve express automobiles from five different manufacturers, all German, using as fuel either benzine or petroleum. The machines could travel from twenty-five to forty miles per hour, and the greatest distance made in a single day was about two hundred miles. One large covered automobile, besides having accommodations for map-reading, carried six persons. One steam carriage of the Serpollet type, using petroleum as fuel, was highly praised, while another was of such simple mechanism that it was easily handled by a novice. The benzine type carried enough fuel to travel a distance of over three hundred miles, so that it would have traveled a day and a half without renewing its supply.

The attitude taken by Germany regarding mechanical traction is timely and wise. It recognizes the utility and even the necessity of automobiles for war purposes. It, however, considers it inadvisable to adopt a standard type at present, and advances two excellent reasons for this policy. Important improvements are reasonably certain from industrial sources, and again the enormous expense is prohibitive of an immediate and complete traction equipment of the German Army in time of peace. In case of war, requisitions of suitable private machines would be made and the necessary residue obtained by emergency purchases.

It should be remembered that military transportation is done by the wholesale in Germany. In the 1901 manœuvres there were moved over one railroad in two days, without materially interfering with the regular passenger traffic, 56,000 men, 5,200 horses, 228 wagons, and 590 tons of baggage.

Successful Use of Automobiles at Army Manœuvres

During the late manœuvres, despite the unfavorable weather and the bad state of the roads, the freight automobiles provisioned large bodies of detached troops. The experimental traction engines, weighing six tons, each dragged three loaded wagons. Although the main roads were muddy, the machines managed very well and even made short distances across open fields. In bivouac grounds, much cut up, it is said, they were obliged to detach the loaded wagons and,

The Kaiser (on the back seat, to the left) returning from the German army manœuvres near Berlin

United States Signal Corps Automobile with General MacArthur and Staff

Motor-car used by Italian officers at the manœuvres near Rome

acting as stationary engines, handle them by cable and drum.

Automobilism gave such promise in the manœuvres of 1901 that the German Minister of War determined to investigate the subject scientifically. It was wisely recognized that all the derivable benefits of automobilism in war can only be guaranteed by experiments in time of peace, for the purpose of ascertaining the best types for various phases of military transportation. It was decided to intrust this investigation to a special detail, which should thoroughly investigate all matters connected with military automobiles.

Some German and French Experiments

In December, 1901, a detail from the Second Railway Regiment commenced experimental work with both express and freight automobiles. As far as can be learned, light three or four wheel machines, with two or three horsepower, are viewed with disfavor in Germany, although France expects much from this type. German authorities appear to favor machines of from six to fifteen horsepower. The heavier motors readily drag three heavily laden wagons over difficult hills without much trouble and with very rare breakdowns. The French Army has experimented more or less intermittently in automobilism since 1892, and systematically since 1900. Encouraged by successful experiments on country roads, oil-motor machines were used in the manœuvres of 1896.

At Peugot, in the autumn of 1900, the automobile was used most satisfactorily, both in connection with the field telegraph train and with the ambulance work of the medical corps.

During recent French manœuvres automobiles have been extensively used, especially for courier, searchlight, and freight service. Staff officers collecting reports have traveled one hundred miles in a day. In another instance an auto-train transported ten tons of forage fifty miles in a single day, saving two days' time over similar work by thirty-six horses. In time of war the military authorities look to requisitioning automobiles, and an officer of rank says:

"The State has the greatest interest in the rational development of mechanical traction on ordinary roads, and should devise means to persuade manufacturers to build, and citizens to possess, vehicles not only suitable for commercial needs, but also able to render good military service."

An outgrowth of this idea is the Automobile Volunteer Corps, organized in 1902 in Great Britain. It has received the sanction of the British War Office, which has agreed to allow the members seven dollars and a half per day when on service. In time of war they will be expected to place themselves and their cars, fully equipped, for home duty as couriers, patrols, etc. Rudyard Kipling and a number of other notables are included in the corps.

Russia renewed its experiments at its last army manœuvres with the Belgian express motor of six horsepower using benzine as a fuel and having an average speed of thirteen miles per hour. The roads were very bad and the ground unfavorable, the chauffeur being often obliged to take to uncultivated fields. Notwithstanding these conditions, which caused twenty-eight breakdowns, the machine covered about six hundred and forty miles in ten days.

The fortunate condition of the United States as regards draught animals renders automobilism a matter that can be safely deferred as a standard equipment until commercial needs have developed automobiles simpler in form, more reliable in action, and more economical in use than they are at present. Nevertheless, there should be timely provision along the lines followed by the German Army.

What Has Been Accomplished in this Country

Excepting a self-propelled battery of light artillery constructed at one of the Western military academies under the direction of an army officer, and which, manned by students, made an unsuccessful effort to reach Washington, the only experimental work thus far has been done by the Chief Signal Officer of the Army, who has confined his investigations or experiments to special vehicles suited for use as telegraph wagons for the speedy restoration of interrupted communication. There has been an endeavor to obtain what the Italian authorities have lately advanced as the ideal military machine; that is, an electrical automobile developing by dynamo its own motor power. No satisfactory electrical type could be obtained, and the obvious impossibility of regularly recharging automobile batteries in the field caused the temporary abandonment of this type. Experiments with steam automobiles using gasoline as fuel were tried with moderate success.

Military needs require material modifications in fuel and in form, which will make it possible to move small detachments and emergency supplies with considerable rapidity for special service. It is unquestioned that automobiles will play important parts in future wars, but it will be many years before they constitute the major transportation of an army. Motors can not replace mounted couriers or the military telegraph. For special uses, however, they are indispensable to every modern army, although the evolution of the types must be necessarily slow and tedious, especially in the United States.

Drawing a trainload of supplies into the yard of the fort, at Vincennes, France

A BRITISH EXPERIMENTAL WAR-CAR
This machine is fully armored and comes to a point at each end. It is armed with rapid-fire guns and can carry a dozen men

Traction engine hauling 6-inch siege guns during the recent French manœuvres

The Automobile in the Public Service
By Waldon Fawcett

FOR no product of the closing years of the century is the future replete with greater possibilities than the automobile.

Considering the position occupied by the self-propelled vehicle as a recent topic of discussion during the past eighteen months, there has been a surprising oversight of its possible value to municipalities and the State. That this is being so speedily and effectually remedied just now is due to a sudden avalanche of practical demonstration. Seemingly almost simultaneously the more progressive officials of the National Government and a number of the larger cities have enlisted the services of the automobile, and the result, from the standpoint of accomplishments, has been as gratifying as surprising. Indeed, the achievements thus far placed to its credit entitle the horseless carriage to a place beside the locomotive, the telephone and the telegraph as a revolutionary factor in the evolution of the methods of administration of public business.

The automobile as an engine of war is likely to be first made an established fact by the war in South Africa. The type which the British authorities have selected as best suited for use as a gun platform ought to turn a Maxim machine gun of the ordinary type into a very effective weapon indeed. The automobile in question is capable of carrying the gun and a thousand rounds of ammunition at a speed of almost twenty miles an hour for more than a hundred miles without the necessity of a replenishment of the fuel supply.

In the United States the initiative in the employment of the automobile as a war agent was taken by Brigadier-General A. W. Greeley, Chief of the Signal Corps of the United States Army, who recently secured three electric wagons, the maximum speed of which is ten miles an hour. Two of the vehicles are designed to carry the instruments and paraphernalia of the corps, while the third is to provide transportation for officers of the corps detailed for experiments with military balloons or wireless telegraphy, as an adjunct to which the automobiles are to serve. The wagons are fitted with electric lights, and later a searchlight will be provided.

Appreciation of the benefits of the automobile is likely to come first to the great mass of the people in America as an adjunct to improved postal service. Already most favorable records have been made. In the city of Buffalo, recently, 150 pounds of mail were collected from thirty boxes, including eight package boxes, in exactly thirty-three minutes, the distance covered being slightly more than eight miles.

There are at present employed in the rural free delivery service almost four hundred carriers, and the aggregate length of their combined routes is something under nine thousand miles. It is apparent that the territory served could be doubled in area were the carriers provided with automobiles.

To farmers this would mean pecuniary benefit, for with late information from the markets promptly available there would arise countless instances when farm products could be disposed of to better advantage, and, also, there is to be considered the rise of value in farm lands which follows the improvement of highways as a natural sequence.

In the field of municipal administration the advent of the automobile has naturally been made first in the twin departments of police and fire. Ultimately there will hardly be any limit to its usefulness in both. The usefulness of the steam roller, which has come to be regarded as a virtual necessity, probably helped to pave the way for the automobile steam fire engine, which first made its appearance in Boston. Arrangements have been made by other cities to follow this with automobile hose wagons, and hook and ladder trucks.

It is a question, however, whether the motor vehicles which are now being constructed at a Western manufactory for the fire chiefs of several cities will not in the end prove most valuable of all. The automobiles destined for this work are, in all the essentials of strength and weight, racing machines, and they are built to maintain a speed of twenty-eight miles an hour over rough roads. Each is to be provided with two acetylene gas lamps and a powerful signal horn. The premise that these vehicles will prove of unusual value is based on the fact that it is frequently necessary for fire chiefs to cover distances at a speed to which a horse would prove unequal. The qualities which make the automobile advantageous for fire department work apply with equal force to police patrol work.

*

Unquestionably the kindliest mission of the automobile will be found in the ambulance service. It will insure prompt medical attendance while affording greater comfort for sufferers while en route to hospitals. In point of fact many physicians already use it.

That the automobile is to play a part in the important problem of the cleansing of our cities is proven by the action of a Western city in placing an order for several automobile garbage carts. In street-sweeping machines, too, there is room for further saving.

Nothing can be more certain than the total displacement of the omnibus by the autocar, and the close watch which electric railway officials everywhere are keeping on this newcomer in the transportation world demonstrates that they

In 1901 *Judge* predicted that motorists of the future would wear costumes like these to protect themselves from dust churned up by their vehicles on unpaved roads.

This *Puck* cartoon envisioned the automobile as a killer; it also predicted that airships would fly to Alaska in a few hours, that steamships would reach Europe in four days, that electric trolleys would travel between Chicago and New York in twenty hours, and that trains would cross the continent in three days.

do not regard competition from that source as an impossibility. In various cities, notably Chicago and Cleveland, there have been projected systems of automobile service wherein the vehicles in service will each carry as many passengers as an ordinary street car and run with the same regularity. As yet, however, none of these projects has materialized.

In New York City shoppers have already had an opportunity to observe how the automobile expedites mercantile delivery, and it is therefore not difficult to give credence to the claims made for it as a successor to the bicycle in the delivery of telegrams and special letters. Even in the development of our new possessions the motor vehicle holds a future, for already a

line to run regularly across Puerto Rico is projected. Finally, the vehicles are to be put to many unique uses, not the least of which will be their employment as a motive power on the Erie Canal, should the automobile now building at Hartford for this purpose prove a success. It is believed that it will prove powerful enough to haul a string of six canal boats.

The future of the automobile in public and private service depends much upon its cheapening, but with two hundred manufacturers of the vehicles in this country and two thousand in Europe it is altogether likely that the decrease in price will be far more rapid than in the case of the bicycle.

Women and the Automobile

By Waldon Fawcett

RUNABOUT CARRIAGE

A PARK TRAP

READY FOR A SPIN

WOMEN have taken possession of the automobile quite as quickly and absolutely as they did the bicycle. Very manifestly and naturally they feel that this new type of vehicle is something distinctively within their province, and evidently there is to be no uncertainty in their dominion in the field. Although this early appreciation of the value of the horseless carriage as an adjunct of feminine life was wholly to be expected, it must nevertheless be regarded as particularly fortunate, since this new mode of locomotion undoubtedly holds greater possibilities for its feminine devotees than has any invention which has appeared in years.

In the French capital women utilize the automobile in a variety of services embracing pretty nearly everything, from a morning shopping tour to a jaunt into the country, such as was formerly only possible with a coach and four. Of late one of the chief uses of the automobile has been in connection with fashionable weddings, and at many prominent nuptial ceremonies the bride and bridegroom as well as all the guests have arrived in autocars. In some cases the vehicles have been decorated with a degree of elaborateness which would fill with despair the practical jokers to whom, in America, the task is usually relegated, but the ornamentation is with flowers instead of old shoes, and a highly artistic effect is presented.

THE general popularity of the automobile with American women may be said to have dated from the summer of 1899, when the use of the motor vehicles became a recognized diversion at Newport and other summer resorts. A number of ladies rapidly attained to proficiency in the management of the vehicles, and the entire country opened its eyes in wonder at the accounts of the automobile parade which was held late in the season at the Rhode Island resort above mentioned.

From that time forward the automobile gained in popularity with women just in proportion to the degree of attention bestowed upon it. With the advent of the feminine automobilist in considerable numbers the manufacturers began to devote more attention to designing vehicles which could be managed by the comparative novice, and wherever the mechanism could be simplified without the efficiency being impaired it was done. The ladies also acted as missionaries in a good cause by their objections to the unsightliness of some of the earlier vehicles, and the improvement which has been made in this respect is most noticeable.

In compliance with a demand from prospective lady customers several of the principal manufacturers of automobiles have opened academies, where instruction is given regarding the operation of the motor-carriages. The action taken in a number of the larger cities in opening the public parks to the horseless vehicles has also proven a fostering influence in the development of the feminine enthusiast.

There are at present in the city of Chicago twelve ladies who are entitled to classification as full-fledged automobile operators, since they regularly make trips about the city in automobiles, unattended or accompanied only by lady friends. In New York City there are twice as many. The city of Philadelphia has two or three feminine automobilists, and upward of a score of other ladies are to be found in the smaller communities throughout the country.

From a feminine standpoint the first thought with reference to the automobile is of the new pastimes to which it constitutes the gateway, but in reality these represent but a small portion of the advantages which it will introduce in woman's sphere, once its full possibilities have been developed.

One benefit which it will confer, which will doubtless be appreciated to a greater or less extent by pretty nearly every woman in the land, is in the improvement of the postal service. Especially will this be true in the rural districts, where the automobile will do much to hasten the day of universal free delivery. What this avenue of closer touch and speedier communication with the great world outside and all its varied interests will mean to

A ROAD-WAGON OWNED BY A CHICAGO ENTHUSIAST

farmers' wives and daughters can only be appreciated by women who have experienced the disadvantages of life in some of the more isolated farming districts.

SEVERAL women physicians in various sections of the country are already using automobiles regularly in making their professional calls, and the new mode of travel has so many advantages that it is certain of a very general adoption. Two classes of women to whom the automobile will mean much—strange though it may appear at first thought—are the professional nurses in the hospitals and kindergarten teachers in the large cities. The automobile ambulance, with its greater speed and reduced jarring and jolting of patients, will indirectly prove helpful in many ways to the white-aproned workers in wards of suffering. To the kindergarten instructors the horseless vehicles will prove a great convenience in returning the little pupils to their respective homes.

The feminine shoppers of many of the larger cities have already been brought to an appreciation of some of the good qualities of the automobile by a more prompt delivery of parcels. It is believed that by its use it will eventually be possible to insure delivery on the day of purchase, even if the latter have been made late in the afternoon, thus realizing one of the fondest dreams of the patron of the bargain-counters.

THE displacement of the horse, if it is to come, will certainly mean cleaner streets and probably far less noisy ones, two boons which will be deeply appreciated by all citizens. In New York City, where over a hundred electric cabs are regularly in service in the streets, the preference of women for the new mode of locomotion has been markedly discernible. Moreover, no announcement made in the metropolis in many a day gave its fair residents greater pleasure than that of the intention to displace by automobiles the dilapidated Fifth Avenue stages which have so long been the butt of the funmakers, but the eccentric characteristics of which have been no humorous matter to the hundreds of women obliged to ride on them daily.

The growth of the automobile in popularity among people of moderate means will naturally be dependent for its rapidity largely upon the lowering of the prices of the machines. That this cheapening process is likely, however, to be far more rapid than many persons suppose, and, indeed, far more speedy than in the case of the bicycle, would seem probable from the fact that there are now in America more than two hundred firms manufacturing upward of three hundred different types of vehicles. A further incentive to reductions in price is found in the fact that automobiles may be propelled by no less than half a dozen distinct motive powers, prominent among which are electricity, steam, compressed air, gasoline and petroleum. Indeed, some firms are already offering automobiles at prices less than a third those asked a year ago.

ONE of the problems which early confronted the women operators of automobiles was that of the necessity of sometimes recharging their machines when out on a trip. Like all the other obstacles in the way of enjoyment of the new sport, this is now, however, in a fair way to be remedied, for in New York and other cities charging-stations are being fitted up at regular intervals, where attendants will take charge of storing the power for another spin. Charging-stations in the country will come later, when the automobile tally-ho parties extend their radius beyond the city limits.

One of the surest indications of the permanency of the automobile as an adjunct of feminine enjoyment is found in the universality of its adoption. In England, France and Germany many of the aristocracy and nobility have been most devoted in their allegiance to the new vehicles for months past, and country tours of several hundred miles have not been uncommon. Even Queen Victoria, who is known to be far from partial to innovations of any kind, evidently realizes the dawn of the new era, for recently she ordered that all her driving-horses be trained to become accustomed to the sight of the automobiles.

LARGE VICTORIA, ONE OF THE METROPOLITAN TYPE

STANHOPE, OWNED BY TWO NEW YORK GIRLS

A SMALL VICTORIA OFTEN SEEN IN CENTRAL PARK

SPEED MANIA

By WILLIAM LEE HOWARD, M.D.

SPEED mania, the resistless desire to dash along public highways, that is an increasing habit of the automobilists, is the objective symptom of the high nervous tension which characterizes the present day civilization. It is the psychologic result of the high pressure which controls the active participants in the world's material movements. It is a sociologic toxin, and the antidote, mental and bodily relaxation, is as yet but little understood or desired by the victims.

This uncontrolled impulse for ever moving restlessly, and often objectlessly, enters into all the acts of the neurotic; is seen at the lunch-counter, on the railroads, and in the divorce courts. However, it is not necessary to study this subject beyond the speed mania of the automobilists. The facts we have to seriously consider are not those dealing with accidents or risks to lives, nor with the effects on the adult of middle life, but the harmful effects on the very young who are being literally whirled through the world at an age when their nervous systems need quiet and normal development.

Motoring a Safety-Valve

There always exist a certain number of people whose excess of nervous energy will display itself in apparently dangerous and useless acts. Such acts may be injurious to the individual or to the community. When carried to excess this uncontrollable energy is a symptom of mental alienation—*tête-exaltée*—which frequently makes the individual a criminal from the legal standpoint. What the unthinking often call courage is in reality a psychic blindness to reason. Aristotle long ago pointed out that true courage was the mean between foolhardiness and cowardice. Foolhardiness is often a mixed kind of insanity, or a condition of mental unrest. I believe that in many cases the automobile is the best method we have of controlling and satisfying this high psychic pressure or mental unrest. Individuals who would at times give way to uncontrollable impulses of an injurious nature find relief in the reckless flying of the racing machine. The neurotic, who, after a tense day on the Exchange, wants "to do something," gets rid of this awful feeling by dangerous dashes into the country. It is a wholesome vent for the reckless courage that otherwise would go to disorder and riotous excess.

Those affected with speed mania demonstrate most of the symptoms shown in other functional disturbances of the nervous system, even those produced by alcohol. They first become exalted, then hilarious and reckless, and when the race is finished they react. A marked effect is seen when women take part in these contests over long distances. It is hard for the opposite sex to brook rivalry, hence they often drive the men to reckless and fatal speed. I have seen some act as though they would "fling the dust aside and naked on the air of Heaven ride!" I have often, when watching the result of this speed mania on neurotic women, thought the cause might be a broken neurological fragment, or parts of old chains of activity in driving on of their men in the pursuit and combat of enemies, for it must be remembered that the customs, institutions and beliefs of our ancestors are related to ours somewhat as instinct is related to reason. In those who to-day show an atavistic vein reason is not predominant. This fact alone should show us that it is a colossal assumption that what we call civilization is the end of man, or the best thing in the world.

The present civilization is a novelty, full of artificialities, and hence superficial; the children of to-day who are whirled around in automobiles are going to be the nervous wrecks of to-morrow. The child needs normal animal exercises, and should be kept free from a state of tension and suspense. The constant use of auto-machines by very young persons produces undergrowth of accessory muscles of movements and powers, and nervous diatheses that make steady and continual mental toil seem monotonous, dull and boresome. The increasing use of automobiles by schoolboys is to be deplored; the effect will be seen later when the student is obliged to concentrate his mind on abstruse subjects. Study-hours will be tiresome, the allotted mental tasks irksome, and complete muscular relaxation impossible.

When the mental worker finds it difficult to work easily, when he realizes his inability to concentrate his faculties, he is approaching a nervous breakdown. The child who has been taken daily over roads at an exciting pace soon shows the effect of the strain on his nervous system. He may not be directly conscious of this, but to the careful observer he will be seen to do the simple things of life with excessive energy and a constant expenditure of nerve force. This child is a spendthrift in bodily capital, and the result will be nervous bankruptcy.

A short time ago I had an opportunity to watch this condition in three children. They were traveling through the country with the father and mother and a chauffeur whose every thought was of speed and whose conversation was largely of narrow escapes. This mental condition was contagious, for the little tot of five years was as full of expectation of thrilling runs and risks as his elder brother of eleven. They wore khaki suits, automobile caps, and their delicate eyes were goggled in dark green. The whole effect was sad but ludicrous—the paradox is allowable. When they sat down, which was seldom, their little hands clutched the sides of the chairs and their feet pressed hard on the floor. Throughout their undeveloped bodies, muscle-groups were in tension, demonstrating the unnatural expenditure of nervous force which will later in life exact strict and lawful accounting.

It is this unnatural waste of nervous force that should be carefully guarded and prevented, for, when the stress and storm comes, all the natural and reserved nervous energy the individual can give is called for, and where there is little to give failure of health is certain. This is the warning I wish to give to unthinking parents. Let your child sport in Nature's playground; let him get muscular development like any other little animal; let him go to bed physically tired and perhaps bruised, but with such an increase of nervous force that muscular relaxation is unconscious and sleep natural.

WE STOPPED THE BICYCLE SCORCHER;—NOW LET US HAVE THE MOBILE POLICE.

A NATIONAL HIGHWAY FOR AUTOMOBILES

By S. E. TILLMAN, U. S. MILITARY ACADEMY

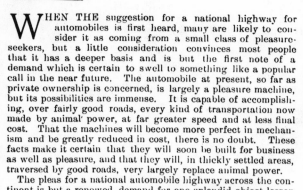

WHEN THE suggestion for a national highway for automobiles is first heard, many are likely to consider it as coming from a small class of pleasure-seekers, but a little consideration convinces most people that it has a deeper basis and is but the first note of a demand which is certain to swell to something like a popular call in the near future. The automobile at present, so far as private ownership is concerned, is largely a pleasure machine, but its possibilities are immense. It is capable of accomplishing, over fairly good roads, every kind of transportation now made by animal power, at far greater speed and at less final cost. That the machines will become more perfect in mechanism and be greatly reduced in cost, there is no doubt. These facts make it certain that they will soon be built for business as well as pleasure, and that they will, in thickly settled areas, traversed by good roads, very largely replace animal power.

The pleas for a national automobile highway across the continent is but a renewed demand for one splendid object lesson in good road-making. The owners of pleasure mobiles may not all fully grasp the importance of this plea and of this lesson, but many do, and the manufacturers of mobiles see the broad field opening up to the new vehicle and are anxious and materially interested in having its range as widely and rapidly extended as possible. While private interests are here involved, they are directed to the public good. In addition to the above indicated interested parties, there are many others equally anxious for a *good highway*—let it go by *any name*. In this class we may include all the riders of bicycles. The advent of the bicycle gave a great impetus to good road-making. The bicycle riders are numerous and have much influence, which, joined with that of other progressive citizens, have in several States been able to get annually larger appropriations for road-building. Massachusetts last year appropriated a half-million dollars and New Jersey nearly one-third as much. These States have taken similar action for several years past. The roads thus built are valuable object-lessons for all classes in the sections through which they run; thus the farmers, who have the greatest material interest in good roads, have been induced to lend assistance in their proper construction. This class in many places now see their two-horse teams drawing from four to five tons, where they used to stall with less than two tons.

There is a limit to the ramifications of the railway, but there is none to the extension of good highways, until every hamlet and every farm is touched. The advent of the automobile is the precursor of universal good roads and marks the beginning of a revolution in the carrying business of the country, as well as many other material and social changes. The construction of a national automobile highway is a worthy labor with which to begin the twentieth century.

The route tentatively suggested for such a highway at a recent dinner of the Automobile Club is the following: Starting from Boston, to pass through Albany, Rochester, Niagara, Cleveland, Chicago, Omaha, Denver, Salt Lake to San Francisco. From Boston along the coast a branch would extend to Portland, another to New York, Philadelphia, Washington and eventually to St. Augustine, Fla. On the west coast a branch would extend to Portland, Ore., and to Los Angeles.

The conception is a grand one, and its realization will be a great national achievement. Such a highway at certain seasons of the year would bear upon its surface innumerable vehicles, forming an almost continuous line from ocean to ocean, with far mightier streams extending along the coasts. The main and important branch lines of the highway would eventually become the avenues of the adjacent villages which would spring up along the lines, forming continuous suburbs of the important cities.

The expense of the undertaking will be very large, but it is thought that national, State, county and individual support will bring it within reasonable and practicable limits.

CYCLE RACING OUTLOOK
BY F. ED. SPOONER

CYCLE RACING is not limited to the Eastern country this season. With the settlement of the racing controversy, which cast its blight upon the sport in 1898, every one interested in cycling cast to one side the spirit of war and all joined hands to upbuild the game upon a sounder basis than ever. The National Cycling Association won the fight, but the L.A.W., after keeping the new organization in suspense a year longer than was necessary, retired and welcomed the victors with a cordial handshake. The harmony which exists in the cycling field is responsible in a large degree for the enthusiasm manifested everywhere to-day. From the furthermost western points to New England, and from the southernmost points where racing flourishes to Montreal, promoters are planning for a grand season of successes.

Everything in a cycle racing way will be conducted upon new lines this year. Tracks will give weekly meets instead of promoting only a few events. The success attained at a number of tracks last year which promoted these weekly meets acted as an object lesson for all of the others. By steady promoting the patrons became familiar with the riders, and there was created an army of cycle-race followers quite as rabid, quite as cranky, as the baseball enthusiasts who are never known to miss a baseball game throughout a season, providing the sport is maintained upon a successful basis. Vailsburg track at Newark, the Coliseum at Baltimore and the Salt Lake City Coliseum cleared from $8,000 to $15,000 on the season through promoting a regular run of meets. These successes brought about the announced policy of Minneapolis, St. Paul, Milwaukee, Chicago, Indianapolis, Louisville, Cincinnati, Cleveland, Terre Haute, Fort Wayne, Des Moines, Burlington, Buffalo, Syracuse, Baltimore, Washington, Atlantic City, Philadelphia, Manhattan Beach, New York, New Haven, Providence, Fall River, Brockton, New Bedford, Charles River, Waltham, Mass., and many more, to give these regular weekly events.

Over fifteen of these cities will have new tracks. For the past two years not over five new tracks have been constructed throughout the United States. Success with the many new tracks which will be completed this month will result in the formation of new companies in a score of other cities to build before the summer is fairly on.

With such an increase of racing the problem has been presented again and again regarding the entry lists. It has been held that there would not be enough riders of prominence to go round. Not so, however; for old-time champions have returned in great numbers and the score or more stars who had practically booked their passage to Europe have given up the trip. Amateurs in great number have taken out professional registration. Some of these have done so voluntarily, while others have been requested to do so by the new body which aims to clear up the field and start anew in many ways.

One of the Contestants on Top of Mount Washington after the Race

Mr. F. E. Stanley climbing the Steps to the Hotel on the Summit of the Mountain

Mr. Winton crossing the Tape at the Finish

Mr. Otto Nestman skirting the Mountain a Half-Mile from the Summit

THE AUTOMOBILE HILL-CLIMBING CONTEST ON MOUNT WASHINGTON

The photographs are snap-shots of scenes during the recent automobile hill-climbing contest on Mount Washington, in which such prominent automobilists as Harry Harkness, James L. Breese, and F. E. Stanley took part. The contest was won by Mr. Harkness, his 60-horse-power Mercedes machine making the eight-mile climb in 24 min. 37 3-5 sec. Record runs were made by Mr. F. E. Stanley, in his 6-horse-power Stanley steamer; by Mr. E. E. Morrison, in his 24-horse-power Peerless; and by Mr. James L. Breese in his 40-horse-power Mercedes

Photographs by Penfield

A Scorching Issue

THIS is the day of consolidation, and if the persons who enjoy a proprietary interest in the several hundred burning issues of the hour could be induced to get together and merge them all in the automobile issue an important economic advantage would result. Missouri, having gained a good place on the rush-line with her Folk, seems to be shrewdly manœuvring to maintain her position with the gasoline-wagon. At any rate, she has had a State convention about it.

The automobile question, in fact, logically includes most of the others. There are autoists who think that any statutory regulation is an outrage upon the sacred rights of ownership, and who assert it with all the impassioned stupidity of a railroad president who maintains that Congress has no right to interfere at all with the stockholders' management of the road. In fact, the Stone Age notion that a man can "own" anything whatever—in the sense that ownership carries an absolute right to do what he pleases with it regardless of the effect upon others—nowhere appears more clearly than in the automobile question.

On the other hand, we have large numbers of red-hot agriculturists who find ample, even superabundant, justification of homicide in the fact that the fright which horses take at the cars sensibly diminishes their pleasure in life, and who will be as little satisfied as a dyed-in-the-wool trust-buster with any remedy that stops short of complete extirpation.

The matter of speed and other regulations for different communities presents as many opportunities of hopeless confusion as the tariff itself. Besides, while the principles would be as old as the hills, the terms in which they were expressed would be rather new, and this would be a great advantage. For many good people on both sides have gotten into an incurable habit of snorting and rearing up over the old terms without in the least understanding what they mean.

An Embarrassment of Time-Savers

THE running-time of the fastest train between New York and Chicago, patronized largely by stock-brokers, has been reduced from twenty to eighteen hours, making it possible for the broker to follow the nerve-racking fluctuations in Steel Preferred up to half-past one instead of having to tear himself away from the ticker a whole hour earlier.

Anybody with a turn for statistics can figure out that we are now saving more time than there ever was before, but nobody seems to know where the saved time goes to. The telephone stands on the business man's desk. By aid of this marvelous instrument a man scores of miles away can call him up at any moment and ask any fool question that comes into his head. The swift — professionally swift —stenographer sits at his elbow, so that by merely speaking he can take two hundred and fifty words to say something which, if he had to use a goosequill, he would say in twenty, or not say at all and never feel the loss. The automobile or swift electric car takes him to and from his office. If he walked he would lose two hours a day and a good deal of fat and some of his appetite for highballs. The crack liner, with all the luxury and bustle of a first-class hotel, carries him across the Atlantic in five days, making it entirely practicable to get nervous prostration in mid-ocean. One can hardly imagine how men did business at all before they had these time-saving devices. But they did do it, and had rather more time to spare than the time-savers have.

Progress of Science

Alcohol for Automobiles

WITHIN recent years the production of alcohol in Germany has been stimulated by beneficial legislation, whereby for industrial purposes it is free of revenue duty, and the result has been that in addition to an extensive use in chemical and manufacturing processes it is being increasingly employed for small internal combustion motors. Alcohol has been found particularly useful for automobiles, and as the combustion under full load is practically complete, there are no offensive odors as in the case of gasoline and naphtha. Since gasoline has a higher heat of combustion than alcohol in the ratio of 2 to 1, to perform the same work a greater weight of the latter is required, but this is diminished by the fact that with alcohol a greater amount of heat is obtained in the form of work. Consequently, it takes four parts of alcohol by weight to accomplish the same amount of work as three parts of petroleum, and the question resolves itself into one of cost, in Germany this being in favor of alcohol. Furthermore, the question has to be considered in European countries such as Germany, that petroleum is a foreign product, while alcohol is produced from the extensive fields of potatoes which are universally cultivated throughout the empire. For an alcohol motor there are certain differences from the internal combustion motor using petroleum. As there is water present with the alcohol more heat is required to evaporate it so as to render it ready for explosion, but this is readily supplied by either the exhaust gases or from the cylinder walls. Also a greater degree of compression for the air and alcohol vapor is required than is necessary with gasoline. It would appear that the alcohol motor has been sufficiently developed to compete with other internal combustion motors for automobiles where the fuel can be provided at a suitable price and this is now a matter of industrial and legislative conditions.

THE AUTOMOBILE OF THE FUTURE.

Automobiling

What might be called "A Run along the Boards"

A MOTOR vehicle seems an incongruous element in connection with polo, yet an amusing game was played a short time ago on the field of the Dedham Polo Club of Boston. The players had the regulation mallets, but were seated in light steam runabouts instead of on ponies. No difficulty was found in keeping up a fast game, the ball could be hit with great precision, and the flexibility of control by throttle permitted very skilful manœuvres. Near side strokes are obviously out of the question on a machine of the regulation type, but with specially constructed bodies, if the wheels were protected by metal guards, it would be quite possible to "ride off" the opposing player and play the ball from any side. Other necessary changes would be the substitution of a wheel for the steering lever, and a narrow single seat of the racing type for the wide touring body. The game of "mobile" polo should not prove as expensive as the regular game. Instead of a string of from four to six ponies, which "eat their heads off" all winter, or else must be sold in the fall at a considerable loss, the well-equipped player would need two steam motors, which would not cost more than the price of four good ponies, and should last several seasons with proper care. Two cars seem necessary in a fast game, because of large steam consumption; while one machine was in play the other would have its supplies replenished, oil-cups filled, and other adjustments made. The steam vehicle seems obviously the most suited to the game of "mobile" polo.

The spectacular features of the motor have attracted so much attention that little consideration has been given to what is, after all, of the most importance—the use of the road-car from the view-point of the average owner.

The first idea of every purchaser seems to be the possibility of possessing a vehicle which will, with no trouble or care on his part, transport him safely, comfortably, and swiftly wherever he may wish to go. Among those who have approached the subject of the management of the motor-carriage with a full appreciation of the limitations and possibilities of the machine, no one is better qualified than Professor Frederic R. Hutton, Professor of Mechanical Engineering in the Columbia School of Mines, who has for some time operated a steam motor-car of the locomobile type. His remarks, which follow, concerning the use of the car should be appreciated by owners of similar machines:

"The light runabout construction, on account of its diminished weight, gives the greatest manœuvring facility in starting and stopping in crowded streets. With three-to-one gear—that is, three turns of the engine to one turn of the driving axle—the link motion can be put in the notch half-way between full and mid gear, for levels and slight inclines. This makes an invisible and quiet exhaust for summer and dry weather. In winter and on damp days some exhaust shows, but the engine uses less water than when run by the throttle and with the

"Unhorsed!"

link full forward. With gear three to one the vehicle will take two people and the extra load of tourist hand-luggage up any hill that is usually laid out on highways. I have been caught in *very* deep moist sand on a steep hill. The carriage will take any grade of any length on macadam up to twenty per cent. and never whimper. As the road deteriorates, the grade or its length grows less. I have lost adhesion in a mud-hole of greasy slime and on drenched grass, so that the wheels have spun. For this, however, skilful handling and slow speed are requisite, or the boiler pressure will run down, and the machine will stall at some slight increase.

Professor Hutton's remarks on his experiences in meeting horses on the road are timely and interesting. He says: "I have not stampeded a horse yet, in over 2000 miles of country touring. But this is because I always examine the horse coming towards me, and if he seems nervous and shy, I stop at the side of the road and speak to him. If he has any sort of a driver he will get by without danger of bolting. For women and children I usually get out and help by leading the horse. As a result I have known only the most courteous and kindly treatment from horsemen wherever I have gone. I use my bell very little; it alarms more than it warns; I usually dodge behind pedestrians. A very potent argument for steam machines versus the explosive type is the silence of the steam machine and the ease of starting from rest."

"A Throw-in!"

AUTOMOBILE POLO

To Protect the Health of Railway Travellers

By William W. Sanford, M.D.

THE danger of infection in railway-cars is a subject which is commanding the keenest attention of railroad companies, as well as that of physicians and the general public. The possible results of the association of such great numbers of persons in confined areas where precautions are not taken to guard against the spread of disease are thoroughly well known. It is the aim of the writer of this article to direct attention to methods now employed by competently managed railway companies to offset, as far as possible, these dangers.

The methods employed seem practical and efficient, and the care with which they are pursued offers the travelling public clean and hygienic surroundings.

At Melrose, New York, about six miles from the Grand Central Station, there is a railway yard where sleeping-cars, day coaches, and chair-cars are treated to a thorough cleansing and sterilization. Not a nook nor a cranny of any car is overlooked in the process. Should a train conductor's report show that a car of his train has conveyed a person suffering with a contagious disease or

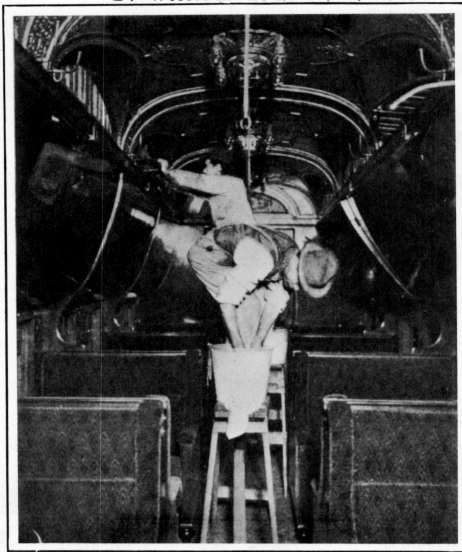

Cleansing the Interior of a Car by Washing

other illness, or that a death has occurred therein from any cause, that car is not again occupied until it has been cleaned from end to end. When its destination is reached, it is promptly conveyed

to special quarters, sealed, and treated for a period of four hours with formaldehyde gas. This is always done when emigrants have occupied the car.

When an ordinary train, consisting of day coaches, arrives at New York, it is taken as soon as possible to the cleaning-yard. The aisle carpets and all furnishings are removed, and the flooring thoroughly flushed and scrubbed with soap and water. Once every three months each coach is washed with soap and water from top to bottom. During the winter the interior is washed weekly. The removal of dust is effected by means of compressed air, this task being a weekly process. At the end of every car's journey, the lavatory with which it is equipped undergoes a thorough scrubbing with soap and boiling water, and is then treated with a solution of muriatic acid.

Exceeding care is exercised in cleaning glasses used for drinking water, also the tank containing it. Four times a year the car flooring and the seat legs are painted; and every twelve months the aisle carpets are removed, washed, and recolored. The same process is applied to leather seats and backs.

Within a short time after the arrival of a train of Pullman cars at the Grand Central Station it is run out to the Melrose yards, where the work of cleaning is admirably systematized. Provided

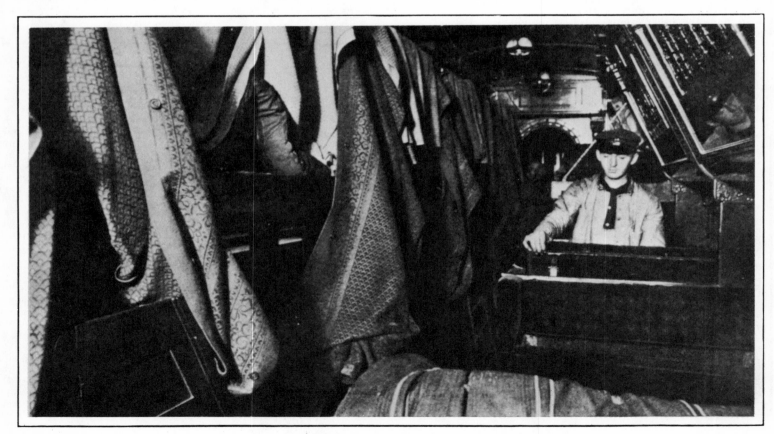

Preparing a Sleeping-car for Disinfection with Formaldehyde Gas

Blowing the Dust from every Nook and Cranny in a Car with a Jet of Compressed Air

a Pullman conductor has reported no death, either from contagious disease or other cause, and no contagious case has been transported, every car of the train is at once entered by a squad of cleaners, whose duty it is to remove all portable fittings of the car, such as the aisle carpet, bottoms and backs of seats, the curtains, berth springs, mattresses, all linen, and blankets, hairbrushes, combs, and other minor articles.

The blankets are thrown over an especially constructed rack in the sunlight, where they are treated with compressed air, forcing from them, at very high pressure, all particles of dust, and restoring the blanket to its original freshness. If, during the removal of the blankets from the car, a soiled one is observed, it is not used again until washed. The operator of the compressed-air jet passes evenly over every inch of the blankets, blowing out the dust from each side. Afterward the blankets are hung for several hours in the open air.

Blankets are washed as a routine duty every six months, and if a death has occurred in a berth a special fumigation and washing of the blankets used therein is ordered. The linen, consisting of sheets and pillow-slips, is collected and sent to a laundry, where it is actually boiled. The carpets, mattresses, and curtains also are blown out with compressed air.

Dismantling a Car in order that the Fittings may be thoroughly Cleaned

Big Things of the Century's End

Just about ten years ago a young woman went around the world in eighty days, and everybody who read newspapers was talking of her performance. Before the present year is over it will be possible to make the trip in forty days, and before the earth is very much older man will probably get around it within the limits of a month. The one tremendous maker of miracles has been transportation, and it is filling this very year with wonderful performances. On the ocean the whole tendency is toward bigness. The North German Line had scarcely finished the Kaiser Wilhelm der Grosse, 13,800 tons and 27,000 horse power, before the White Star Line had the Oceanic, with 17,040 tons and 27,000 horse power, and now two other lines are building ships that will exceed both of these leviathans. Every shipyard in the world is busy. Newport News, which a generation ago was a cornfield, is now a centre of ceaseless activity, with 6000 men building fourteen vessels, some of which have a tonnage of nearly 12,000. There are nearly 4000 men at work on vessels in the Union Iron Works at San Francisco, and in the yards of the Cramps, at Philadelphia, 6000 men are busy. More than 100,000 skilled workmen are engaged at the different yards on the two coasts. In addition to all this, the Government has over 200,000 tons of warships either on the stocks or under contract.

To quicken our commerce, vast schemes are under way, the greatest of them being a canal across the Isthmus, which will save more than 10,000 miles in the trip from New York to San Francisco, and which will cost, according to one of the estimates, at least $125,000,000.

For land transportation the projects exceed everything in the history of the world. The longest tunnel on earth is now being built through the Alps to open a new route between north and south Europe. It will be twelve and two-fifths miles long, will be completed in five and one-half years, and will cost $14,000,000. In this country a great tunnel is to be built under New York at a cost of $35,000,000, for the local traffic of that crowded city.

The Great Railroad Through Africa

Every one understands that one of the certain results of the South African war will be a railroad and telegraph line down the backbone of Africa. A few days ago there arrived at Cape Town a man who had made the entire journey of 5500 miles from Cairo, and he reported that the route was practicable for a continuous line of road. From Cairo south there are now 1100 miles in operation. Then there is a break of 3000 miles. Thence to Cape Town 1400 miles are built, and would be in regular operation were it not for the temporary embarrassments caused by the war. The vast wealth which Africa will yield will easily pay for this great line, and it will not be too much to predict that within five years, or at the outside ten, there will be through trains from the metropolis of the Nile to the Cape of Good Hope.

The Wonderful Progress of Modern Russia

Few of us have the slightest idea of the astonishing growth of enterprise and industry which is going on throughout Russia. With characteristic promptness the Americans have recognized the opportunities, and are not only selling tens of millions of dollars' worth of material in that country, but are now planning to invest at least $15,000,000 of American capital in Russian manufactures.

You probably do not know that to-day at Moscow you may take a train that combines the elegance and the convenience of the best modern travel, so that in your trip through Siberia you could not only bathe in a porcelain tub, get all the reading matter you wanted from a complete library, dine sumptuously and sleep comfortably, but that you would have at your command a complete gymnasium where you might take exercise as the train sped along. To many of us the road has simply been a line across the map, but the news comes that it is almost completed and that it will not be very long before trains can run all the way to Vladivostock. Already there are under construction numerous branch lines. Russia has also plans and partial concessions that will take a line thousands of miles through Persia to the Persian Gulf.

Millions for New Railroads in Asia

In Asia there are already 30,000 miles of railroad, and it is a safe prophecy to say that within five years there will be over 50,000. European syndicates have now concessions for nearly 4000 miles in China; Japan is rapidly increasing its 3200 miles, and in the French possessions over 2000 miles are projected. Russia will add thousands more, including a very important line on the left shore of the River Volga, which will connect with the general system, and will be of the utmost importance to the commerce of Russia, Central Asia and Persia. Down in Asia Minor there is an interesting rivalry between several of the nations, but Germany is ahead. The German syndicate will build 2000 miles that will unite the Persian Gulf with Europe, thus giving Germany entrance into the chief markets of the East. Already the Germans control Constantinople and Smyrna. In India, Great Britain has something like 20,000 miles of railway, and thus the great work of opening and modernizing Asia with its hundreds of millions of people goes on.

Transportation Development in this Country

The development of transportation in this country is mostly along railroad lines. The Great Lakes, which almost equal ocean travel in the cheapness of a long haul, will always have an increasing commerce. The tendency there is the same as upon the ocean — big ships that can carry big cargoes. Senator McMillan, who got a large part of his wealth from lake transportation, predicts still greater things in the size and importance of its trade.

Navigation on the Missouri River, which, next to the Mississippi and the Amazon, is the greatest waterway in the world, has been practically abandoned. If any one had predicted this twenty years ago he would have been laughed at, but the railroads, by increasing the size of their trains, and reducing the cost of their operation, have come closer and closer to water rates, and thus what was a wonderful river commerce has been diverted to the land.

The New Cable to the Far East

A few weeks ago the United States Ship Nero, Lieutenant-Commander H. M. Hodges, reached San Francisco after several months of interesting work in the Pacific Ocean. It is perfectly well understood that we must have cable communication with our possessions in the East. Several years ago a practicable route for this cable was established between San Francisco and Honolulu. Rear-Admiral R. B. Bradford, Chief of the Bureau of Equipment, after a very careful study of the conditions, laid out a route from Honolulu by way of Guam to the Philippines, and also to Japan. His selection met with opposition from some of the cable authorities; but Commander Hodges, after a careful survey of the whole route, found that Rear-Admiral Bradford was right. The work was a peculiarly difficult one, and was brilliantly performed by Lieutenant-Commander Hodges, so that the whole result was most gratifying.

In the 240 days the ship was at sea she steamed over 30,000 miles. Here is an experience on one of the Midway Islands where there was no human life: " The number of sea birds on this island is infinite. Our visit was made during the nesting season, and on fully half the island the sand was literally covered with sea birds. It was quite impossible to cross it without stepping on the nesting birds and their eggs, unless precaution was taken to drive them away by means of a shrub branch. The noise of the retreating birds as they hovered overhead, screeching and darting threateningly, was deafening."

The bill in Congress to contract with the cable company which is to construct this line, provides that the cable shall be of American make, that the cable ships shall fly the American flag, and that the line to Honolulu shall be completed January 1, 1902, and the line to Manila and Japan by July 1, 1903. This will add largely to the cables of the world, of which there are now more than 170,000 miles.

To Connect the Three Americas

On December 4, 1890, a remarkable gathering took place in the State Department at Washington. It was composed of three of the leading railroad men of the United States, and representatives from Central and South American countries, including Brazil, Venezuela, Peru, Mexico and Colombia. Secretary Blaine called the gentlemen to order, and the Intercontinental Railway Commission began its official existence. Mr. A. J. Cassatt, now President of the Pennsylvania Railroad, was elected President. In a few months this commission had organized surveying parties to find out the feasibility of what was then called the Three Americas Railway. Three corps of engineers were sent to South America, and twice the Congress of the United States voted $65,000 for this country's portion of the cost of the work. Contributions of smaller sums were made by the other countries, and altogether something like $200,000 was spent. Nothing very definite came of the labors except a corroboration of the idea that the line is entirely practicable. The engineering difficulties are not so great as those which have been solved in railway construction in the United States, especially in Colorado. From New York to Buenos Ayres is 9000 miles, and to-day more than one-half of this distance is covered by railroads. Mexico has been pushing southward. The Argentine Republic has been pushing northward. Chili has a good railway system, and the time will undoubtedly come when there will be railway service all the way from Alaska to the southern part of South America. As in South Africa, the enormous natural wealth of South America will easily pay for the several thousand miles of line which will one day be built. The extreme cost of the whole work has been placed at $300,000,000.

A. J. CASSATT
PHOTO BY DAVIS & SANFORD, NEW YORK

JAMES McMILLAN
PHOTO BY C. M. HAYES & CO., DETROIT

REAR-ADMIRAL R. B. BRADFORD
PHOTO BY GILBERT PHOTO CO., PHILA.

NEXT TO FLYING

You may fly some day, but
the Quickest Way Now is

The 20th Century Limited

Fig. I.

Diagram of the Albertson Magnetic Train, showing the Force required to move an empty Car

Professor A. C. Albertson

Fig. 2.

Diagram showing that the same Car with an increased Weight is propelled by a smaller Force

Across the Continent in Ten Hours

FROM New York to San Francisco in ten hours, on a train of cars without wheels, drawn at the rate of 300 miles an hour by a one-horse-power locomotive, and operated at one-sixth the cost of an ordinary railway — this is the achievement promised for a new system of railroading invented by Professor A. C. Albertson, an electrical engineer, late of Copenhagen University, Denmark. The American and European governments have granted letters patent on the invention; a working model of the system is now on exhibition in this city; and the facilities of the Delaware, Lackawanna, and Western Railroad have been placed at the disposal of Professor Albertson for the working out of his scheme.

If the invention proves to be practicable, it upsets a law hitherto regarded as immutable, namely, that the heavier the load, the more power is needed to move it; instead, Professor Albertson seems to have demonstrated the truth of the seeming paradox that the heavier the load, the *less* power is needed to move it. The scheme is, in brief, as follows:

The train is equipped with a set of powerful electric magnets, which slide along under the rails and lift the cars from the track. If, for instance, a car weighs ten tons, the engineer of the train would merely turn on a magnetic force of eleven tons, which would thus overcome the weight of the train and allow it to be propelled with a friction of only one ton. In other words, the entire weight of the train is held up by the magnetic force, and experiments have actually shown that the more the train weighs, the less force is needed to propel it. The great speed claimed by the inventor for the magnetic train is made possible largely by the fact that friction is almost wholly done away with.

With the under surfaces of the rails kept fairly clean by properly attaching sweeping devices travelling ahead of the magnets, and lubricated at the same time, the moving of a car, whether loaded or empty, will be accomplished by only a fraction of a horse-power; since nearly the entire weight of the car in both cases is suspended in the air. Instead of the cars pressing downward upon the rails, they would, on the contrary, pull upward. When it is necessary to turn off the magnetic force, the cars will drop down upon the tracks and rest on eight small wheels. The current necessary to supply 1000 electric lights of ordinary power would hold suspended a weight of 120 tons, or six rail-road cars weighing twenty tons each. Such a train, according to Professor Albertson, could be moved at immense speed by a motor of less than ten horse-power, as the friction would be inconsiderable.

On such a railroad system as this, smoke and vibration would be eliminated; there would be no possible chance of grade-crossing accidents, no derailing, no hot boxes. It would not be necessary to purchase land for the construction of the road, as the structure could be supported by single iron pillars.

Heavy and expensive locomotive engines of from two to three thousand horse-power in capacity would no longer be needed, as their place would be taken by small motors acting upon large driving-wheels. This, in turn, would necessitate but comparatively light-weight rails. Sleeping-cars would be superfluous, as the distance between the oceans could be covered in one day. No mechanical or pneumatic brakes would be needed, for the train is itself a brake: for, in order to stop, the engineer would simply turn on more magnetic power, thus making the pressure upward greater.

As shown in the diagrams at the top of the page, the heavier the weight of the train the less power is needed to propel it. For instance:

The suspended weights (8) represent motive power, drawing a small car (3) along the two iron bars (2-2) resting on the framework, which are supposed to be a short section of rails. The car is equipped with two electromagnets (4-4), which are excited by an electric current taken from any source; in this case from a lamp-socket. When the car is empty, it requires seven pounds to move it along the bars. When loaded with twenty-one pounds, only three pounds are required to move it. It might be moved by two pounds if the load on the car were increased, and by still less if loaded to its full capacity.

At first glance it might seem that whatever is gained by the reduction of locomotive power must be applied to the establishment of magnets strong enough to lift a given weight. But this is not so. Five hundred amperes, for example, will lift at least 60 tons, the moving of which, ordinarily, requires a steam-locomotive, but which, suspended, can be drawn by a few horse-power. The current for the purpose could be picked up from a wire along the track or from storage batteries placed in the cars.

Model of the Albertson Magnetic Train from a Drawing made by the Inventor

7 Home and Hearth

THE LADIES' HOME JOURNAL
JANUARY, 1901 — TEN CENTS

THE CURTIS PUBLISHING COMPANY, PHILADELPHIA

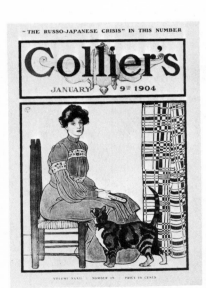

"THE RUSSO-JAPANESE CRISIS" IN THIS NUMBER

Collier's
JANUARY 9th 1904

VOLUME XXXII — NUMBER 15 — PRICE 10 CENTS

JANUARY 1901 — TEN CENTS
WOMAN'S HOME COMPANION

THE CROWELL & KIRKPATRICK CO. PUBLISHERS.

DECEMBER, 1902
Vol. III. No. 2

COUNTRY LIFE
IN AMERICA

Christmas Annual

The American home in 1900: the term evokes a picture of pleasant white houses with deep porches and broad lawns along the elm-shaded streets of hundreds of towns and villages. The picture was still essentially the prevailing one, but it was changing fast: the proportion of Americans living in cities was rapidly increasing, and the kind of places they were calling home was changing too.

Like many other things, home decorating styles were in a state of flux at the beginning of the century. As some of the advertisements on the following pages prove, the horribly tufted and tasseled creations that appear to have been survivals of the "Moorish craze" of a few years earlier were still in demand, although the height of the fashion was passing. The movement known as Art Nouveau reached its peak during the two decades just before and after the turn of the century; it was an international style marked by an abundance of sweeping curves usually based on floral motifs. It was in Art Nouveau that Louis Comfort Tiffany worked, designing the fantastic creations in colored glass—screens and vases and lampshades—that are having a minor revival in poor imitations today.

A completely different type of furnishing also became very popular just at the beginning of the century: Mission furniture, which was just as heavy and square and no-nonsense as Art Nouveau was curving and frivolous. And to further confuse the picture, there were a great many admirers of objects that were lumped together as "colonial," a term that could mean colonial, post-Revolutionary, or even copies of medieval furniture. It was difficult to predict just what one would find behind the front door of a home in the early 1900's.

Not only the interior decoration but the kind of home was undergoing changes. The urbanization of the United States was in full swing; every train that came into Chicago, St. Louis, New York, or any other large city unloaded its freight of eager young men and women certain that the answer to their dreams lay somewhere along the strange streets of the big city. And as the cities grew, new ways of living developed. The apartment house of many stories, made possible by the elevator, central heating, improved plumbing, and other services, had become common; as early as 1881 apartment buildings were reported to be going up in great numbers, not only in New York but in other cities—one of them being built that year was fourteen stories tall. The apartment house inevitably had its effect on ways of living; for one thing, it consigned to oblivion the largely ceremonial front parlor, which had been a fixture of American homes for many generations.

While apartment houses were creating a new way of life in the city, urban growth was having quite another effect on those who preferred to live in the suburbs and commute to work. Suburban living, then as now, was conducive to a more informal kind of existence, and simple one-storied houses in large numbers went up along hundreds of streets in the communities ringing the cities. It was at this time that the bungalow enjoyed great popularity; the term was used for a wide-eaved, one-storied house, usually with a porch supported by heavy square columns. The bungalow was the progenitor of the ranch house so popular in today's suburbs.

Whatever or wherever the home, its heart was the kitchen. In any progressive household, kitchen planning had become important by the beginning of the new century. Light, ventilation, convenience, proper storage facilities for perishable foods, good drainage, and other considerations were all taken into account in planning a kitchen.

Refrigerators at the time depended on ice for cooling (not until 1926 did the first self-contained household refrigerator, a gas type, become practical), and the iceman bearing a large block of ice to replenish the refrigerator called at every home two or three times each week. The icebox supported a major winter industry in Northern rural regions: cutting and storing lake ice for use during the summer.

The huge, fancily ornamented cast-iron range was the center of every kitchen, although gas was quite generally used for cooking by the beginning of the century. Some manufacturers put out combination models, with gas burners at one end. In general, the gas was used for top-of-the-stove cooking that had to be done in a hurry or in warm weather; no cook worth her salt would think of trying to do any serious baking in anything but the oven of a range with a good, dependable fire of wood or coal. Even as late as the 1930's, when electric stoves began to be widely used, a frequent remark of housewives was "They're all right for some things, but for baking, give me the old-fashioned kitchen range."

Central heating had become widespread by the beginning of the century, and as a result homes were more comfortable, but no one appeared to like much about central heating except its comfort. In 1902 *The House Beautiful* wrote that the open fire, although an inadequate method of heating, was the one beautiful way and that "as an ornament it is so superior to all others that if forced to choose, everything else had better be sacrificed to it." For the interior decorators, central heating, especially by steam or hot water, was a headache, because they never succeeded in devising a way to beautify the radiators or even to hide them from view.

Lighting in the modern home of the day was largely by gas, although electricity was coming on strong and there were many more homes with electric lightbulbs in 1905 than there had been in 1900. The same was true of the telephone, whose lines were each year entering hundreds of thousands of homes where the lady of the house had never before experienced the ineffable pleasures of whiling away half a morning exchanging confidences with a friend through Mr. Bell's invention. Between 1900 and 1905 the number of telephones in the United States more than trebled; in the latter year there were more than four million of the instruments in use. It was a time when laborsaving devices for the home were being developed at a rapid rate; there were improved washing machines and sewing machines, and there was even a flatiron with its own self-contained gas burner to keep it hot—electric irons were a long way in the future. Nor were the arts forgotten in this outburst of creativity: for the first time in history it became possible to have music in the home without a musician, for by 1900 the new phonograph, invented almost twenty years earlier, had been developed enough to reproduce sound passably well. That year more than one hundred fifty thousand of the machines and more than three million records were sold.

Of course, the bright new aspects of hearth and home at the turn of the century were not enjoyed by all Americans. If four million telephones were in use in 1905, tens of millions of homes were still without this connection to the outside world. Middle-class homes in the city may have depended mainly on illuminating gas for lighting, but farmers everywhere still hunched close to the yellow gleam of kerosene lamps to read the latest farm journal. There were a great many homes in the cities, too, that depended on lamps for lighting—not only the blocks of foul and vicious tenements, but also many modest small homes. And there was the matter of plumbing. Every modern urban home had its bathroom with porcelain fixtures, but the bathroom was unknown in rural regions, where the water for the Saturday night bath was heated on the kitchen range and the galvanized iron washtub served also for the bath. The outdoor toilet was a necessary adjunct to every farm home where lack of running water made indoor facilities impossible. However, the privy was also common in village and city, because the standard of living was much lower and the tolerance of unsanitary conditions far greater at the turn of the century than today.

The Dwelling-House of the Twentieth Century ❧ By Otis T. Mason

DRAWN BY B. MARTIN JUSTICE

The abolishment of stairs has been made practicable by the introduction of a pair of small elevators, which, being perfectly automatic, require no attendant

A HOUSE is a suit of clothes for a number of persons, shielding them from observation and protecting them against extremes of temperature. It affords to the biped mammal a refuge, and in its improvement and sanitation is to be found the most important cause of the wonderful lengthening of human life within the last few generations. Mortality figures seem to prove that we live at least a decade longer than did our ancestors one hundred years ago, and it is safe to predict that our descendants, one hundred years hence, will surpass ourselves in this respect—thanks in no small degree to beneficial changes in the construction and management of the dwellings they occupy.

The average white citizen of Philadelphia or Boston lives to be fifty years old; the average Indian does not survive sixteen. Think of this fact when you hear people say that the "artificial conditions of civilization have multiplied diseases," and you will realize that such a statement is pure nonsense. On the contrary, the dwelling-house—most important of all things that go to make up a civilization—is, in its highest development, a disease-proof fortress and a conserver of life. No feature of nineteenth-century progress has been more striking than the improvement accomplished in domestic architecture and in the internal arrangements of houses; yet even now the human domicile is far from having completed the process of evolution which began ages ago with the savage shelter of boughs, and it is probable that we should be greatly surprised if, by setting the clock ahead, we were able to step to-day into a typical residence—the dwelling, that is to say, of a man of moderate means—of the year 1950.

To begin with, let us survey this twentieth-century house from the outside, in front. It is a modest yet dignified structure bearing no likeness to other residences in the same block. Indeed—if one may judge from a multitude of examples afforded by neighboring streets—the mid-century is an epoch of individualism in domestic architecture. Dwellings are no longer put up in solid blocks, all exactly alike outside and inside—a style most popular in the latter part of the nineteenth century—and the party-wall is rarely used. Each house stands alone, mainly because, in the year 1950, people have come to realize that the lumping together of buildings renders them less attractive to the eye and deprives them in large degree of their power to express the individuality of their owners.

Stairs Replaced by Automatic Elevators

Suppose that we enter the dwelling with a view to ascertaining what novelties, structural and in respect to equipment, it has to exhibit. The abolishment of stairs has been made practicable by the introduction of a pair of small elevators, which, being perfectly automatic, require no attendant. They are run by electricity, noiselessly, and any one who wishes to ascend or descend has only to call one of the cars by touching a push-button. Thus summoned, it glides swiftly to the floor where it is wanted; the passenger gets aboard, and a touch applied to a numbered button inside causes it to pause at the story desired. Then the occupant steps out, and the vehicle is at the disposal of the next person who may need its services. Such elevators, indeed, were in use in a few rich men's houses so long ago as the end of the nineteenth century, and their general introduction at a later period in place of staircases is attributable chiefly to the cheapening of electricity.

Fifty years ago it was not realized that all the electricity required for the largest city could easily be obtained from the water-power of the river flowing by. To-day (A. D. 1950) it all seems so obvious that we marvel how the problem could have escaped solution by our intelligent ancestors. They failed to see the way out, however, whereas we, having produced electrical power in this manner at a small fraction of its former cost, distribute it underground everywhere, so that it furnishes all the light, heat and power needed for a great population. Every dwelling-house of moderate pretentions nowadays is filled with a network of copper wires, concealed by mouldings and decorations, which carry a current for illuminating the establishment, warming it, and running the domestic machinery.

The luxury of a perfectly warmed house, kept always at exactly the proper temperature, was unknown to the people of fifty years ago. In 1900 a dwelling, in winter, was either too hot or too cold most of the time, and to maintain the air of a single room at the correct degree of Fahrenheit for more than a few minutes together was almost out of the question. How uncomfortable it must have been, and how strange it seems from our viewpoint of the present day, when we have only to set the automatic governor of the heating apparatus at seventy-two degrees, let us say, and the temperature of the whole establishment is maintained at that point for months together. If the weather grows colder more electricity will flow in, and this in a proportion so nicely regulated that the thermometer within does not rise or fall by so much as a quarter of a degree. Supposing it to be desired, one room may be kept at a different temperature from another—the bed-chambers cooler than the drawing-rooms, for example.

Houses Cooled by Liquid Air

In 1900 no means were known for cooling the air of houses save by fans, and in hot weather the healthy languished, while the sick and feeble died. How differently things are managed in this mid-century epoch, when a residence without cooling apparatus for use in summer would be considered as incomplete as if it lacked heating arrangements for winter, the one being as much a matter of course as the other. In the twentieth-century mansion we find liquid air employed for this purpose, and here again the mechanism is perfectly automatic, the outflow of the substance being so controlled by a governor that the temperature is kept always at the same point. The receptacles containing the liquid air are hidden in the ceilings of the rooms, the fluid descending as it is liberated.

The dwelling of the twentieth century is lighted, of course, by electricity, but the light-bulbs are not exposed to view, as was formerly the case, and thus a great improvement has been made. Obviously, it is much better to conceal the sources of illumination, avoiding dazzle, and to diffuse the light by the help of reflecting surfaces, so that a warm and cheerful glow is distributed, rather than to have one part of a room extremely bright and the rest in relative darkness. More important, however, is the contrivance by which the light, under control of an automatic governor, turns itself on in exactly the degree that may be needed to keep the apartment at the requisite point of illumination. The fading of the daylight turns on the electricity, and vice versa. Indeed, one may fix the lighting of a house for a year ahead.

Damp House Cellars a Thing of the Past

Five elements go to make up a dwelling, no matter how gorgeous and elaborate the establishment may be, or how humble. They are, first, the cooking-place; second, the eating-place; third, the sleeping-place; fourth, the place for chatting and amusement; fifth, the storage-place. A Vanderbilt palace or an Eskimo hut is equally divisible into these parts, and we find them all, of course, in the house of the twentieth century. As for storage, one finds no cellar beneath the mansion of 1950, this subterranean room having been done away with for sanitary and other reasons. Electricity having rendered a stock of fuel unnecessary, and no furnace or other heating apparatus being required underground, the *raison d'être* of the cellar has vanished. The fashion of keeping food supplies in the family pit went out long ago, and now the housewife buys her groceries in insect-proof packages, putting them away on shelves, while her provisions go into a cold-storage compartment chilled by liquid air.

The twentieth-century house, instead of being sunk in the ground, is uplifted above it, and in this way a number of advantages are gained. To begin with, it is insulated by this means to a considerable extent, both electrically and as to temperature, so that there is less difficulty in regulating the heating, cooling and lighting of the mansion. Secondly, ventilation is assisted by a clear sweep of air beneath the dwelling; and, thirdly, the arrangement helps to make the establishment rat-proof and bug-proof. No properly constructed residence in 1950 is infested by roaches and mice, as all houses were to a greater or less extent fifty years ago—that is, in 1900.

How people managed to endure such vermin is beyond imagining, but the fact seems to be that they regarded the nuisance as unavoidable. While nominally keeping cats to destroy mice, they did in reality, had they but known it, keep the mice for the benefit of the cats.

Nothing in this wonderful dwelling, for the sake of visiting which we have jumped to the year 1950, is more remarkable than the cooking-place. It is different from the nineteenth-century kitchen in nearly every respect, the most striking point about it being its absolute cleanliness. In 1900 the kitchen was necessarily the dirty part of a house, owing chiefly to coal that blackened everything, ashes that made things untidy, and smoke that coated walls and ceiling. To-day, in the culinary department of the twentieth-century mansion, there is no smoke, no coal, no ashes, no smell, and no fire to inflame the face and the temper of the cook. No time is lost in kindling fires, and there is no waste of fuel in starting them and in keeping them up when they are not wanted. When a meal is to be prepared the current is turned on by a twist of a button, and immediately the electric range is ready for service. Incidentally, it may be mentioned that the sadirons employed for ironing in the laundry are made hot simply by attaching them to a wire, and, being kept at a constant temperature by the electric current, they never scorch the clothes. Then, too, they are always clean and bright. In a corner a little motor attends to the business of beating eggs.

One does not find in 1950 that ingenious automata have taken the place of domestic servants, as some imaginative persons long ago suggested might happen, and it seems unlikely that a machine will ever wait on the table satisfactorily. It is not apparent that many changes have been accomplished during the first half of the twentieth century in the eating department of the house; but, thanks to the new and perfect cleanliness of the kitchen, the latter has been brought into closer relations with the mid-century dining-room, and thus has come about an odd sort of reversion to primitive habits. Of this perhaps the first suggestion was given by the introduction of the chafing-dish into the dining-room—an instrument resembling in its mode of use the pot from which the appetite of the savage is gratified direct. However, it is not implied that the utensil in question is less satisfactory on this account, and nowadays we have the electric chafing-dish, which is attachable to a wire at a moment's notice by a plug-switch. Electricity has been substituted for the alcohol lamp in making tea, and dishes on the table are kept hot by a current conveyed through the cloth from copper plates beneath.

Not a battery is to be found in the twentieth-century dwelling here described. The electricity used in the establishment comes in a single current through a heavy wire from a distributing station, and on the premises is split up as required for heating, for lighting, for cooking, for running the elevators, and so on. The dumbwaiter runs by electricity, as well as the housewife's sewing machine, and the same fluid both runs and regulates all the clocks in the house. It works the automatic piano, and might be made to agitate the baby's cradle, only that people in 1950 have learned to know that infants are apt to be rendered stupid, or even idiotic, by rocking them. If the daughter of the house wants to crimp her hair, she fastens her curling-iron with a little plug to a convenient wire, and enjoys a certainty that the instrument will not scorch her curls.

Twentieth-Century Furniture

It is a marvelous convenience, the running of all the business of a dwelling by an invisible fluid furnished from without and convertible into power, light or heat as desired. The Genie summoned by Aladdin was less strong and far less clever; besides, he did only odd jobs, and took no contract by the year. Electricity has the obvious advantage of coolness when used for lights in summer, but of much more importance is the safety of its employment with reference to fires. In 1950 houses are rarely burned—not only on this account, but also because the furniture is of fireproof wood, and the floors, doors and wainscoting are fireproof likewise. Here, indeed, is one of the most notable improvements accomplished in the architecture of the twentieth century. In the nineteenth century people did not build their residences of unbaked mud, because they knew that, if so constructed, they would tumble down; but they did not hesitate to compose them of lively combustibles, ignoring the fact that they were likely to burn up.

The household furniture of 1950 is slighter than that of fifty years ago, though much more metal is utilized in its construction. In fact, during the last hundred years the idea has steadily gained ground that a dwelling should first afford space for its inmates, and that the furnishing should be considered as of subordinate importance. How queer the ancient four-post bedsteads, massive wardrobes and chests of drawers look nowadays! It must have been very uncomfortable to live with them. To-day we make our chairs, tables, beds and bureaus as light in weight as possible, consistently with strength, so that they may be easily moved, and they are not allowed to take up more room than is necessary. Of domestic appliances and conveniences there are many, of course, which were unknown in 1900. To attempt a catalogue of them is scarce worth while, but mention suggests itself of the photographs in natural colors which, since the discovery of the simple secret of that long-sought art, have lent at small expense such beauty to the walls of houses.

People must rise to a certain degree in the scale of civilization before they are able to grasp the idea of property in land—a conception not entertained by the primitive savage. Later comes the notion of property in water, illustrated by the holding of irrigation rights. With both of these forms of property our ancestors were familiar as far back as 1900, but it had never occurred to them that there could be such a thing as a property right in air, though there was a germ of its recognition in their laws for the abatement of nuisances. They said that ownership in a square foot of land extended downward to the centre of the earth; nowadays we say that it extends upward into space for an indefinite distance. In the twentieth century we regard smoke or waste air turned out above our premises as an infringement and a cause of action for trespass.

In the study of a house one must consider the street in front, which is to the dwelling what the river is to the city—a carrier of the traffic upon which it depends. The anthropologist tells us that the primitive street is a trail made by the tramp of human feet and widened to a path. Houses are set up along it, and it becomes a village thoroughfare. The rest is easy; but one must realize that the street of 1950 is very different from the street of the nineteenth century. There is now no dust, mainly because there are no horses in the towns. Other modes of transportation vastly superior and safer have replaced vehicles drawn by horses, and with the departure of those banished animals many evils have disappeared. For example, there are no longer many house-flies, which breed almost exclusively in

street filth, and certain infectious diseases long suspected of propagation by those insects are much less common than formerly.

Bricks and Wall-Papers Out of Date

No wall-papers are used in the typical dwelling of the twentieth century here described. In fact, they have ceased to be employed in the houses of the well-to-do, largely because they assist the accumulation of dirt and disease-germs. Sensible people in 1950 prefer walls that may be scrubbed and kept clean, and it is not considered that the handsomest papers are comparable in a decorative sense to modern art-frescoing and other methods of treatment now practiced. The substitution of artificial for natural wood in floors has been a very notable improvement, the counterfeit having all the smoothness and elasticity of real wood. It has the advantage of being fireproof, and, having no cracks, does not afford hiding-places for dust and insects. There is no respect in which the twentieth-century mansion has improved upon the nineteenth-century house more markedly than in cleanliness. It has come to be realized that cleanliness is not only a source of satisfaction in itself, but the best

possible defense against the physical ills which threaten the human body.

In 1950 nearly all dwellings, save those of the very poor, are built of artificial stone, which is preferred to the natural because it is better for the purpose, as well as cheaper. Brick, which is a species of artificial stone, has gone out of employment almost entirely. The experts who first made a scientific study of this subject found that there were certain specific properties which a building-stone, whether imitation or natural, ought to possess. For one thing, it ought to be porous, so as to afford a dead-air space to serve as a non-conductor. They declared that an ideal material of this kind was furnished by the tertiary lava from beneath which the famous Calaveras skull is said to have been dug out, and it is a fact that the best artificial stone utilized for building in 1950 closely resembles the volcanic tufa referred to. Being silicious, it is extremely durable—an essential point, of course.

The invention of artificial stone is one of enormous importance, inasmuch as over a large part of this country there is no rock suitable for building. This is true, for example, of all the eastern edge of the United States, from Northern New Jersey to Florida, and it applies likewise to the Gulf States and to the Mississippi Valley as far north as Cairo, Illinois. In the Cotton Belt of the South there is not even stuff for tombstones. Happily, however, Nature has provided plenty of material that is convertible into stone—a supply so vast, indeed, that we may build all of our cities out of it for centuries to come without diminishing it perceptibly. We dissolve flint to get silica, and combine the latter with soda in a liquid which we pour over sand, cementing the particles together. Such mixtures of silica are the great cements employed in Nature. In fact, it may be said that the processes used in the manufacture of artificial stones are the same as those followed by Nature herself. So far back as 1900 imitation sandstone was produced in immense quantities, while artificial marble was even then made by subjecting ordinary chalk first to a bath of mineral oxide to give it color, and then to the action of a silicate solution, the result being a substance indistinguishable from real marble and capable of an exquisite polish. The advantages which this ability to duplicate on the spot the processes of Nature confers are so much a matter of our daily life that we rarely stop to reckon them, or value their importance.

A judicious person, writing in 1900, must hesitate to attempt any serious prediction as to modifications in the building and equipment of dwellings which will be accomplished by the middle of the next century. There are ventured here only a few guesses as to what changes may come to pass. It will remain for a future generation to discover how far these surmises are accurate, though, of course, a good many people who have already arrived at adult age will survive long enough to live in and enjoy the luxuries and the improvements of the houses of A. D. 1950.

A HANDSOME RESIDENCE AT MODERATE COST

By Herbert C. Chivers

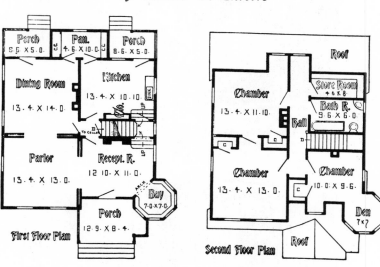

First Floor Plan

Second Floor Plan

IN SUBURBAN domestic architecture the aim of the designer is usually to secure cottage-like effects, even in a full two-story house. Where this can be done without the roof cutting into the second-story rooms it promotes economical construction, as the main roofs can often be carried over the porches at much less cost than separate roofs could be constructed. This style of roof, if well ventilated, makes a house cool in summer and warm in winter. Moreover, it is capable of graceful lines, and may lend beauty and picturesqueness to the general appearance of the building.

In the accompanying design this low-roof effect is obtained by carrying the main roof-lines down over the front and rear porches, gaining full-story heights where the roof passes over the front and rear chamber walls. The cottage-like roof is relieved by the full two-story portion above the parlor and the tower at the corner.

THE general appearance of the completed structure is clearly shown in the above illustration, while the interior arrangement, names, sizes of the rooms, etc., are indicated by the floor plans.

It will be seen that on the first floor there is a large reception-room, from which the other apartments may readily be reached, and from which also rise the main stairs. At the left one enters the parlor, and beyond it the dining-room, the two being separated by sliding doors. A noticeable feature is the wide fireplace which faces the front door as you enter the house.

The kitchen is at the right of the dining-room, communication between the two being established by means of a commodious pantry fitted with china-closet, shelving, etc. The kitchen and dining-room both have porches. The porch off the dining-room could be used as a conservatory in winter by means of portable sash.

AN INTERESTING feature is the combination front and rear stairs, which is reached directly from the hall and also from the kitchen, the first landing serving for both. As will be seen by the illustration, there is a neat panel of art-glass at this landing.

Another noticeable feature is the octagon tower at the corner, which serves as a cozy-nook on the first floor and gives a good outlook from the chamber on the floor above.

On the second floor are three chambers, a commodious bath-room and a good-sized store-room, which could be utilized as servants' quarters if desired. The space in the attic could be reached by stairs from the front chamber, and would afford splendid storage-room.

The cellar walls are of strictly hard-burnt brick, nine inches in thickness and seven feet in height, securely bonded and laid in cement. The walls above grade are of dark-red brick, laid in cement colored to match. The basement is separated into four divisions by means of wood partitions.

THE tower has a substantial foundation to the grade-line, above which it is of frame, with the portion shown as stonework covered with sheathing and stamped galvanized iron, in imitation of rock-face ashlar stonework.

The interior finish consists of yellow pine left the natural color and varnished. All doors are horizontally five-paneled.

The heating is by means of hot air, with registers in all rooms, and the plumbing consists of enameled sink in the kitchen, and closet, tub and basin in bath-room.

The exterior walls are covered with sheathing and building-paper, with narrow weather-boards on the first story colored a rich light olive-green, while the walls above, including gables and dormer, are covered with shingles of even dimensions and colored a light terra-cotta. All trimmings, as will be seen by the illustration, are pure white.

THIS building has just been built at a cost of $1,700, all complete as above described, for a man residing in an Illinois town. Since it was built, however, there has been a slight advance in building materials, and of course its cost at the present time would be correspondingly higher. It will be seen by a careful study of the floor plans that the space has been utilized to the best advantage throughout the house, with an eye to convenience, comfort and economy.

There are a number of feasible modifications which could be had in this plan without increasing its cost materially, such as a balcony around the rear dormer window, accessible from the rear chamber and hall, which would be quite a convenience for airing bed-clothing, etc. The front porch could be carried around the front tower in octagon shape. There could be a wide front vestibule by reducing the front porch and reception-room slightly; a bay-window could be had in the dining-room, and a front bay-window would look well at the parlor, as it could be roofed without additional expense, by the projecting cornice which shows at this point.

The Twentieth-Century Dwelling

THE typical dwelling of the twentieth century has not been built yet, but we are near enough to it to be able to forecast, at least in a general way, what it will be like. It will be made of concrete, or some similar material that will be comparatively unaffected by the weather and that will provide thorough protection against changes in the external temperature. On the outside the building will, of course, be tinted and decorated to suit the taste and means of the owner. Inside it will be given a hard, durable, smooth finish that will not hold dust and that will be impervious to moisture. Not only walls and ceilings but floors will be finished in this way, and at a moment's notice the furnishings can be taken out and a room or the whole house washed down with a stream from a hose and wiped dry with the utmost ease.

The lighting of the twentieth-century dwelling will be by diffusion from tubes of electrified vapor that will give an even and soft illumination all over the house — an illumination that, in many respects, will be better than daylight. But it is in respect to the regulation of atmospheric conditions that the twentieth-century house will possess the most decided advantages over the houses we live in now. The heating and cooling of the air as it will be brought in through screened openings will be done automatically by electricity. There will be electric heaters in winter and refrigerating coils in summer, and the interior of the dwelling, if the occupants so desire, will be kept at an even temperature the year round. Thus it will be possible to have any climate to order — warm or cool, moist or dry — and no doubt the adjustment of these conditions to individual needs will be an important part of the therapeutics of the future. If families cannot agree upon a uniform climate for the entire house, each member of the family can have the sort of climate he or she requires in his or her individual apartments.

The twentieth-century kitchen will delight the heart of the careful housewife. It will be as clean and perfect in all its fittings as a laboratory for the most delicate chemical processes, and, indeed, it will be a laboratory rather than a kitchen. Cooking by electricity will be an exact science. Along one side of the tiled room will be a series of asbestos-lined doors, with thermometric indicators on each door. Put in your materials properly prepared — that is where the art will come in — set the thermostat at the given mark for simmering, stewing, boiling or baking, leave it so for a stated time, and there you are! Food cooked to perfection, and no dust, no dirt, no surplus heat, no steam, no odor. Who would not be a cook in the electric kitchen when the twentieth-century house shall be built?

A Good Time Coming

IN ALMOST every big department store nowadays there is an exhibit of cooking by electricity. No dirt, no ashes, no dust, no superfluous heat, no fire; nothing but as high a temperature as you want in the cooking apparatus, and that only just so long as you want it.

Partly because invention lags, chiefly because we have let short-sighted monopolists get control of electricity — and perhaps that's why invention is lagging — we can't afford to cook by electricity yet. But soon — for monopolies and monopolists do die — we shall be emancipated from the present superheated, dirty and crude system.

What a world — from the standpoint of comfort — this is bound to become after a century or so more of the sort of progress that began only about a hundred years ago. And how much of the "good time that's coming" we might anticipate if we weren't too lazy to think and too stupid to act.

RESTFUL NOOKS AND COZY CORNERS

Illustrations Suggesting How a Lounging-Place Can Be Arranged In Almost Any Room of the House

Here is an excellent suggestion for the young woman who has but little money to devote to the cozy-corner fad. In a nook of this kind a variety of cushions is the essential feature.

This nook in the home of Lieutenant-General Nelson A. Miles reveals the possibilities of the Indian corner. The background is formed by highly colored Navajo blankets, and trinkets.

A pretty and unpretentious cozy corner in the home of Mrs. U. S. Grant, at Washington, D. C. The drapery is Japanese silk hangings, and the majority of the cushions are covered with silk.

THE CITY HOUSE OF TO-DAY.

The ready-made dwelling—built to rent—in the first half of the century in New York compares with the ready-made dwelling of to-day in the metropolis as the flail of Franklin's time compares with the modern threshing-machine. In nothing that is outside the line of the revolutionary inventions of the age has progress made such strides as it has in ministering to the comfort of those who dwell in cities. The rented house of the first half of the century was larger than it has become, but it was a mere empty box, after all—usually it was a part of a monotonous row of such boxes. Now such dwellings are tastefully designed, and an effort is made to give each an individual character. Within they are illuminated by great plate-glass windows, decorated with a liberal finish of ornamental hard-wood, fitted with sanitary safeguards in the plumbing and ventilating fixtures, and completed by modern improvements of many useful kinds. In each is a house telephone, with mouth pieces and electric buttons in every room. The dumb-waiter of such a house reaches to the first bedroom floor, if not to the top of the building.

The mantel-pieces have cabinet tops, and are built above grate fireplaces that contain gas-logs, or false but showy fuel made of asbestos veined with perforated gas-pipes. The doors slide into the walls, so as not to take up any of the too little space in the small modern rooms. A showy china cabinet is a fixture in the breakfast-room, and a refrigerator is built in one of the walls near the kitchen. In madame's bedroom and in her parlor is a cheval glass. An apron of iron over the kitchen-range promises to rid the house of the smells of cooking, and good draughts for the fires are guaranteed by flues of iron piping instead of brick. Wardrobes, which are really dress-closets, with great doors, are fixed in the walls, and for the clothing of men the closet drawers of old are turned into shelves fronted by doors that drop open upon hinges at the bottom thereof. The dining-room has moved up stairs into the back parlor, and is one-quarter furnished by having a pretentious sideboard built in a niche in the walls. Stationary tubs are housed in an annex of the kitchen, and the *fin de siècle* bath-room has become a beautiful chamber lined and walled with brick, ventilated by an air-shaft and sky-light, and fitted with tubs and other equipments that are either porcelain-lined or made of crockery. Electric lights are distributed throughout the house, and all doors to yard and street are doubled, to save coal and the internal heat of the dwelling.

Thus the modern Cornelia is provided with what we may call fixed comforts. But she is not content with these. Therefore with the modern dwelling goes the man who keeps the street clean by an arrangement with the householders of each block. With it also goes he who attends to the furnace and rolls the ash-barrels out to the curb-stone. The private watchman gives first aid to the insufficient police, or the automatic burglar-alarm stands in that relation to him.

The laundryman long ago joined the letter-carrier, butcher, milkman, grocer, and baker in their periodical visits to the basement door; and whenever madame shuts up her house—all barred and bolted and chained as it has been by the builders—she turns it over to a sort of care-taking or watchman's company. If she moves out of a house, there are companies to send packers who will bundle up her belongings with professional skill, and that will store them for her by carrying them in padded vans to fire-proof warehouses. Her rugs and carpets are now beaten by machinery, and she may hire her spring house-cleaning done precisely as she gives out her washing. Before she rents a house she may order it inspected by a private company, that will report upon the character of its construction and its plumbing, and this company also offers to proceed at law against all nuisances in otherwise nice neighborhoods. Thus has vanished the necessity for drawing water, hewing wood, keeping a cow, churning, laundering clothes, cleaning house, beating carpets, and very much of the rest of the onerous duties of housekeeping as our mothers knew it. The out-of-town reader may fancy that the latter-day metropolitan house-wife now needs only to climb stairs, to sew, and to supervise the cooking of the household meals. But only a little of even this is true. She need not know a needle from a plough, and there are dwellings into which meals are now sent from the kitchens of hotels and large apartment-houses, in connection with which such dwellings are maintained.

It is not useless to put on record, at the conclusion of the century, even so hasty a summary of the changes that housekeeping has undergone. It may assist the future historian in determining why we of this era have crowded into the cities, or help him to sum up the means by which the cities attracted and held the people who abandoned the farms and villages. JULIAN RALPH.

Palm Nook in the Hall

The Dining-Room

An Elaborate Mantel and Chimney-Breast

A View in the Hall

Exterior of the Residence

THE NEW RESIDENCE OF HENRY W

The Breakfast-Room

The Staircase

The Beautiful Music-Room

Cozy Corner and Fireplace

The Twenty-first Street Window

The Library

POOR, GRAMERCY PARK, NEW YORK

No. 95013. Banquet Lamp.
This is another of the beautiful and popular styles of Cupid banquet lamps. The Cupid is of extra size, silver plated, and mounted on a very large cast open work base. The head is handsomely embossed and has No. 2 center draft burner. Both head and vase are finished in gilt. The lamp is completed with an elegant silk shade, in three colors; lemon, orange, or Nile green, with deep lace flounce. Height of lamp to top of burner is 20 in.
Lamp complete..........$5.65
Lamp only................ 3.30
Shade only............... 2.35

No. 95013.

Our $5.90 Bed.

No. 1T2444 Head is 72 inches high, foot 59 inches high. The pillars are $1\frac{7}{8}$ inches in diameter, the spindles, cross rods and ornamental iron work $\frac{5}{16}$ inch in diameter; pillars are surmounted by handsome brass knobs and have brass tips and rosettes. The extended foot rail adds to its already handsome appearance. We furnish this bed 4 feet 6 inches wide by 6 feet long, finished white enamel of best quality. Shipping weight, 110 pounds.
Our special price................................**$5.90**

OUR $14.95 5-PIECE UPHOLSTERED PARLOR SUITE.

AT $14.95 we offer this parlor suite as the greatest value ever furnished in this line.

HOW WE CAN MAKE THIS HERETOFORE UNHEARD OF PRICE of $14.95 is fully explained under the heading of new designs in High Grade Couches. It is made in the one factory that makes nothing but these suites and our upholstered couches. Our $14.95 price is below the lowest wholesale price, much lower than dealers can buy in the largest quantities.

BELOW WE QUOTE PRICES ON **SINGLE PIECES**, making it possible to order a **THREE-PIECE, FOUR-PIECE OR SIX-PIECE SUITE.**

THIS SUITE CONSISTS OF THE FOLLOWING FIVE HANDSOME PIECES: One large sofa, 36 inches high, 23 inches wide and 52 inches long; one large rocker, 33 inches high and 28 inches wide; one large easy chair, 34 inches high and 28 inches wide; and two large parlor chairs, each 31 inches high and 20 inches wide. Weight, packed for shipment, 200 pounds.

$14.95

SHIPPED DIRECT FROM OUR FACTORY, NEAR CHICAGO, FROM WHICH POINT THE CUSTOMER PAYS THE FREIGHT.

THESE SUITES are made on the very latest style hardwood frames. They are made extra strong, extra well braced throughout. Springs are the genuine Eagleton highest grade tempered steel springs. The suite is upholstered in the highest style of the art. We use the genuine Welton three-tone velours upholstering cloth and imported French Gobelin tapestry in the very latest style patterns and colorings, at least three different shades in each suite, all harmonizing perfectly. Each piece is fully overstuffed, handsomely decorated and finished, with deep fringe, fancy binding, and decorated with a handsome rococo brass gimp ornamentation.

PRICES FOR COMPLETE SUITE OF FIVE PIECES:
No. 1T6094 Upholstered in High Colored Velours........$14.95
No. 1T6096 Upholstered in French Gobelin Tapestry..... 17.40

PRICES FOR SINGLE PIECES:

	Colored Velours	French Gobelin Tapestry
Sofa	$4.95	$5.80
Arm Chair	3.10	3.55
Rocker	3.60	4.15
Reception Chair	1.65	1.95

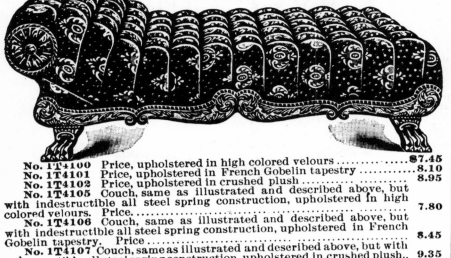
Wanted: A Man's Room

THERE are in the United States more than a million men who study and write in their homes. Their number has been vastly increased by the astonishing rise of the correspondence school, by the wonderful growth of the Chautauqua movements, by the multiplication of reading circles and literary organizations, by the widening opportunities for profitable writing and by the intensified interest in all public questions. The average man of this generation is a student, and there never was so much serious and earnest thought as there is to-day.

These men build homes. The very tendencies that make them book-lovers make them home-lovers. A respectable number can build without much regard for expense, can erect mansions in which a quiet and secluded room is easily possible. But the great majority of them are in moderate circumstances and a house that costs over five thousand dollars is beyond their reach. Some may say that if they want to read or to write they will rise above their environments. Lincoln lying on the floor before the open fire and forgetting everything but the printed words; the learned blacksmith working and reading at the same forge; the scholarly shoemaker mending and learning, and all the other cases of application and time-saving might be cited. But they belong to the past. The man of to-day needs and deserves comfort — and quiet.

Now, it is most extraordinary that in the thousands and thousands of plans for new houses published in architectural journals and in family magazines there is an obliviousness of man that is really pathetic. He has facilities to eat, to sleep, to bathe, to hang pictures, to shovel coal, to build fires and to entertain company, but if he wants to settle down for an evening of study or to do a piece of writing that necessitates close application and uninterrupted thought, what becomes of him? Where is he to go? In ninety-nine one-hundredths of moderate-priced houses the library is a grim and grinning sarcasm. It is the storm centre of the home, and its infrequent calms generally happen when the man is away. The president of one of the leading universities some time ago arranged a model library, so that he could do more of his work at home. Some months later a friend asked him how it worked. "Beautifully," was his reply. "It's the most popular room in the house — nursery, storeroom, sewing-room, smoking-room, every old kind of a room. They haven't eaten up there yet, but the restaurant and kitchen extensions will come later." "Where do you do your work?" "In the faculty office, just as before."

Of course this is another phase of a vexed question, but it does not absolve the architects. Judging from their plans most of them must be men who like to go out at night. Or they may be pessimists who look upon all husbands as failures. They riot in women's rooms, children's rooms and servants' rooms, but they seldom give a thought to the man. It would be a safe venture to say that not one house in a hundred contains a serious proposition for the man who wants to study and write. All pretend they have, but, as a matter of fact, they haven't. The library downstairs is a courtesy title for a sitting-room. The study upstairs is an emergency bedroom without a lock. All this is man's fault, of course. He has not asserted his rights. Being an animal that does not like to do what is best for himself he has vacillated and procrastinated. But the reform must come, and the architect who provides a safe, quiet and well-protected room for the man will deserve well of his fellow-beings. There is, too, an important moral bearing in this matter. The satisfying of the man means more happiness for the whole family, fewer domestic differences and longer lives. From every viewpoint, therefore, it is wise to provide a sequestered and upholstered den for that indispensable creature whom Mrs. Elisabeth in the book about her German Garden called The Man of Wrath.

A Bride, a Groom and a Bundle of Shingles

A TRUE STORY

By CHARLES BARNARD

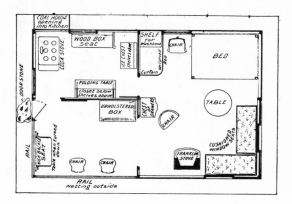

S HE was a college woman and he a college man, and the day they became engaged the thoughts of the young man turned lightly to their wedding journey. When and where?

When, in due season, the matter of a wedding journey was laid before the girl, she, being of a thrifty mind, asked how much wedding journeys cost. A liberal estimate for a little modest journey, as befitted young people just starting out in life, would be one hundred and fifty dollars. Why go on a journey? Why not build a house and go from the church to their own home? Verily, why not take the wedding journey money and build a home?

ॐ

THE idea was attractive and impossible. One hundred and fifty dollars would hardly build the piazza or dig the cellar. But why have a cellar? Why not reduce the house to the real essentials? The young people discussed the matter among their friends. Begin, begin, they all said. Beware of the dreadful boarding-house. Keep house, if in only one room.

Suddenly the first wedding present arrived—a bundle of shingles. Shingles! So suggestive, so poetic, so practical, "from storms a shelter and from heat a shade." The bride declared the gift providential and inspiring. She would build 'a house that should be a home. With great

moral courage the young people decided promptly that they would forego their wedding journey, ,and with the money and the shingles start a home.

Naturally, the first problem was the land. Happily, the bride lived in the country and land could be rented. A pasture on a hillside near the water offered an ideal spot for a home. A lease for five years, with the right to remove the house at any time, was secured, and the foundations of the home were laid with appropriate ceremonies.

ॐ

THE foundations were cedar posts sunk in the ground. On these posts was laid a floor twelve by twenty feet. Then a frame of scantling was erected and the rooftree laid. The donor of that suggestive bundle of shingles joyfully added a few more and the roof was finished.

Two sides of the building were inclosed with matched boards. The two other sides, south and west, were half inclosed, leaving the southwest corner open. This square space under the roof and open at the sides made the piazza. The siding, with two doors, finished the walls at the back of the piazza. Then a short partition inside divided the whole house into three parts—the piazza, a little kitchen, and a combination chamber and sitting-room.

The entire structure was built in a week, and cost, without the shingles, one hundred and twenty-five dollars, including doors, windows and two drainpipe chimneys.

When one begins anything, everybody helps. All the wedding presents were designed to fit the new home. A lovely little stove, furniture, glass, china, linen, silver, kitchen ware—everything fitted in admirably. Every one

took the deepest interest in this, the beginning of a home. Bride and bridegroom, with their own hands, added every little convenience that any housekeeper could ask, and on the morning of the wedding the delighted guests flocked to see the new house, and every one said it was a very good thing. The wedding over, the reception finished at the home of the bride, the young people walked across the fields in the gloaming to their own home.

ॐ

E VERYTHING has its limitations, and the limitations of this new home are as follows : It is strictly a summer residence ; the bride must be her own housekeeper, and the bridegroom must be the handy man around the house. There was no servant, no laundry, no guest-chamber, no drawing-room—none of the luxuries of a house. The bridegroom went in town every day and returned at night. The bride was cook, waitress, maid and housekeeper. On the other hand, the young people had a real home. They could and did entertain friends, and the friends flocked to see this unique and charming home and were delighted to take tea in the combination piazza and dining-room. In winter the young people can live in town, but they have a home of their own, and they have already proved the wisdom of the old proverb that " the happiest people live in the smallest houses."

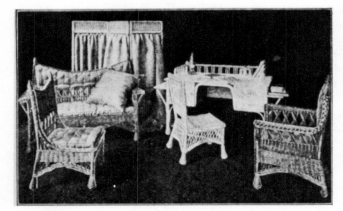

TIFFANY STVDIOS

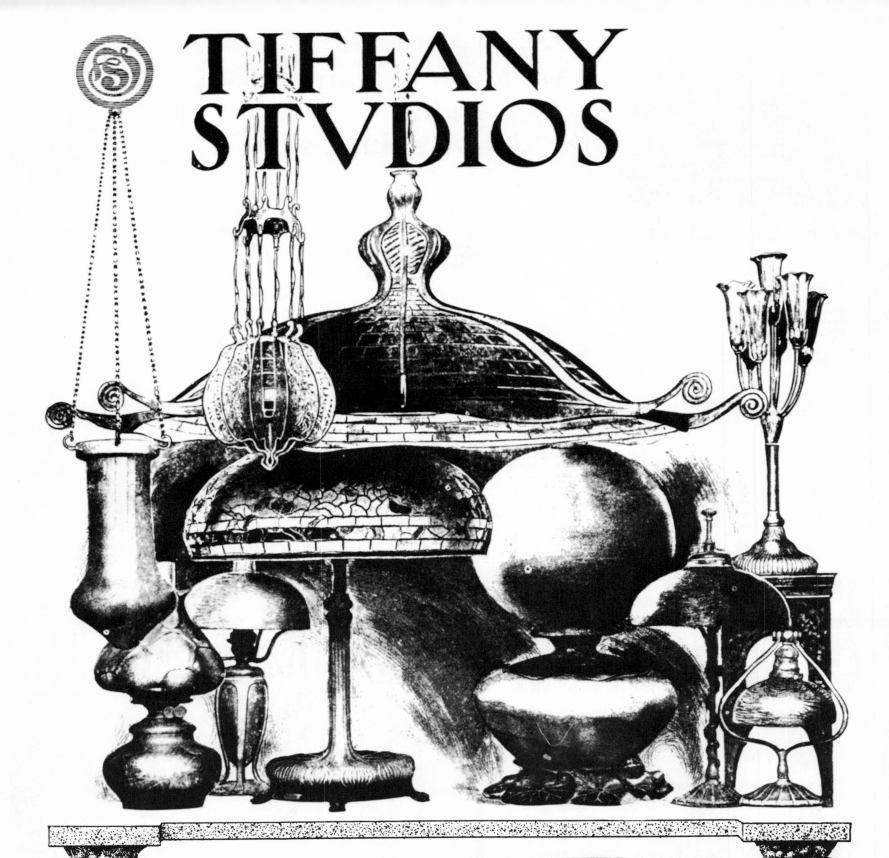

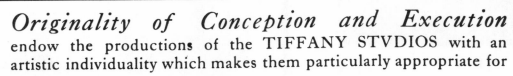

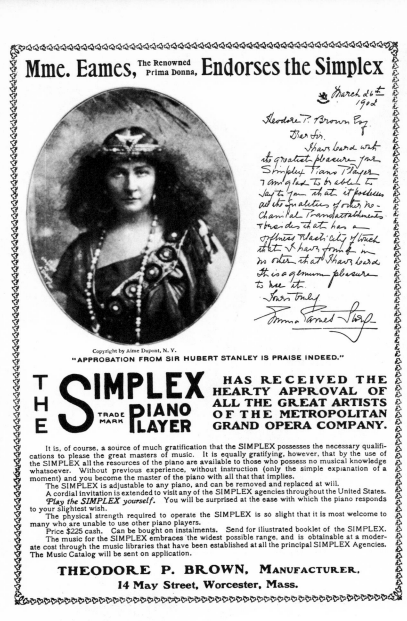
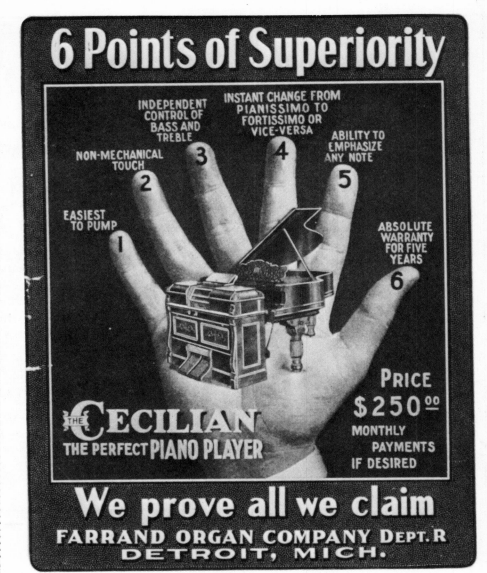

Housework and Machinery

Discussing Mrs. Lane's article in an English review on "The Extravagant Economy of Women," the Springfield *Republican* suggests that if the men of the United States should be compelled by statute to do, themselves, all the housework of the country for ten years there would be such a shaking up of methods as twenty centuries have not brought about. When the women came to their own again, they would find that for the first time in history there were really adequate tools for carrying on the conduct of home life.

We would like to see it tried—after we are dead. The *Republican* thinks that household economy is not at all on a twentieth-century basis. If housework were put on to the men, heat would be turned on by pressing a button, suction-pumps would draw all the dust out of the house, and a lot of methods and devices would be perfected for the relief of that large group of families in our society which can afford only one servant. The house of 2005, says our contemporary, ought to be no more like the house of 1905 than a motor-car is like an ox-cart.

For our part we are not so sanguine that invention is going to help so prodigiously in housekeeping. Women, for some reason, are not very good at tending machines. When the women got back to housework after their ten years' release they would promptly let the men's more intricate machines get out of order, and presently throw them out. House heating and lighting have already been simplified for persons who can afford the simplifications. In some streets of some cities heat can be let in from street mains by turning a cock. Modern plumbing is all a labor-saving apparatus, and an important one, and it is in general use in all American cities. Housework *has* been simplified somewhat by machinery; let us see what there is left to do.

The chief things that houseworkers do are to keep houses clean, to cook and serve meals, to wash and mend clothes, and to keep things in order. There is a machine that comes to sweep by suction. Four or five men bring it on a dray. Only rich people can afford to have it come. There is no prospect that houses ever will be kept clean by machinery. Nothing but human hands deals successfully with daily dust in such a city as New York.

As for cooking, the Philadelphia *Record* reports the installation of a pie-making machine in a bakery in that town, but pie, at best, is a mechanical sort of food. There are breakfast foods that come cooked or are guaranteed to be good to eat raw, and a vast line of nourishments come in cans, but household cooking requires brains as well as hands, and there is no hope that it will ever be done by machinery. It is an art. You cannot get art results by pressing a button.

As for clothes-washing, there are laundries and laundry machinery aplenty. Most of us would a little rather send our clothes out to be washed by machinery at a laundry than go naked, so most of our clothes are now washed in that way. But to wash clothes properly, so that they retain their proper hues, dimensions, qualities, and shapes, requires an intelligence so nearly human that it is easiest come by in a human being.

No, there is not much more to hope for from labor-saving household appliances. The reasons are good why more has not been done to make homes self-regulating and automatic. If servants are to be scarcer and dearer the relief must come by the simplification of living; by elimination of household possessions, and not by increase of household machinery.

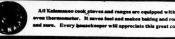

MISCELLANEOUS GOODS.

Lamp Chimney Cleaners.

No. 15054. This article is useful for many purposes, but for cleaning lamp chimneys it is the best invention yet brought out. The illustration shows how it brings the wiping cloth in contact with every part of the chimney.

Each 3c
Per doz.............30c

No. 15055. Wire Chimney Cleaner, Dish Cloth Holder, Cork Puller, etc.
Price each, 6c; per doz...........56c

Pot Cleaners.

Pot Chain or wire ring Dish Cloth.
No. 15056. Small size.
Each 5c
Per doz........54c
No. 15057. Large size.
Each 7c
Per doz........75c

No. 15058. Handled Pot Chain or wire Dish Cloth. Turned wire handle, bright wire rings.
Price each, 8c; per doz...........85c

No. 15059. The Sensible Pot Chain and Scraper is a new and useful article; each ring is double, which makes it very durable. The handle is malleable iron; the blade is steel; the handle and scraper are tinned. Weight, 4 oz. Price each, 10c; per doz...........$1.06

No. 15060. Wash your dishes without putting your hands into hot water. This dish mop is made of cotton and is securely fastened to handle. Length, 12 inches; weight, 4 ounces. Price, each, 8c; per doz...........87c

The Anthony Wayne Washer.

No. 16744. The Improved Anthony Wayne Washer No. 2. This machine is of the same capacity as the No. 2 Western Star. Made out of white pine, painted and grained an ash color. The staves and bottom are corrugated. Wringer can be attached. Shipping weight, 46 lbs. Price each........................$2.50

DIRECTIONS.
How to Use Either the "Anthony Wayne" or "Western Star" Washer and Do a Quick and Clean Washing Without the Use of a Washboard.

On the evening before wash-day place all the clothes you wish to wash in a tub, fill the same up with water (rain water preferred), so that they may be thoroughly soaked over night. On the following morning fill your wash boiler three-fourths full of rain water, put the same to boiling and cut into it one-half bar of hard soap and one teacupful of washing fluid, the recipe of which is found below. When boiling put in your clothes and boil from 10 to 15 minutes, after which wring them out, place them in the machine, work them from 5 to 10 minutes in the same, wring your clothes into the basket, rinse them through clear water, blue and hang on the line.

Do not put over five shirts or four sheets at a time into the machine, and see that the same is kept well filled with soap suds; the more water you can put in your machine and the freer the clothes will work in the water, the easier the machine will work.

We warrant, if these directions are followed closely, that the washing will be as clean as any lady can desire them. Proceed with all the rest like above and the largest washing can be done in two or three hours. The suds need not be removed every time, but can be used until they become too dirty; but always add hot water, soap and compound in proportion and keep the machine well filled.

Recipe for the Anthony Wayne Washing Fluid.—Take 1 pound of potash, 1 ounce of salts of tartar, 1 ounce of ammonia, place the potash into a large crock or earthen vessel and pour a gallon of hot water slowly into this vessel. Wait until this cools, then add the salts of tartar and the ammonia, and when all is fully dissolved bottle the fluid for use. All the ingredients can be bought at any drug store at a cost not to exceed 25 cents.

Send for our special washing machine circular. It is free for the asking.

Lamp Chimney Stoves.

No. 15100. Lamp Chimney Stove, fits any ordinary crimped top lamp chimney, as shown in cut. Water may be boiled in a few minutes.
Each 3c
Per doz.........35c

Fire Kindler.

No. 15101. The Indestructible Fire Kindler and oil can is used for starting wood fires, burning brush and marshes, burning insects and worms from trees, thawing water pipes and many other purposes which will suggest themselves to the user. Length, 12 inches; weight, 5 oz. Price, each...........25c

Hog Scrapers.

No. 15075. Hog Scraper. Will pay for itself the first time used. Wood handle with bolt extending through Scraper made of No. 18 sheet steel. Price, each..18c
No. 15076. Hog Scraper, made of No. 20 sheet iron. Price, each.............8c

Pinking Irons.

No. 15078. Pinking Iron, diamond tooth, ⅜, ½, ⅝, ¾, ⅞ or 1 inch. Price, each, 6c; per doz., assorted...........65c

STOVE FURNISHINGS.

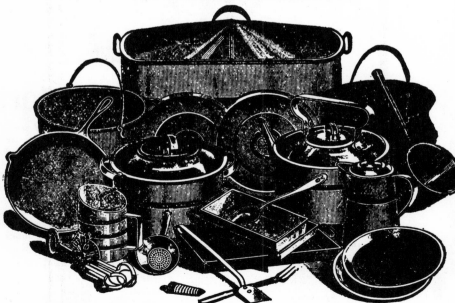

Complete Kitchen Furniture Assortment.

Our facilities for furnishing all sorts of kitchen utensils are unequaled, and in the outfits named below we offer you an assortment which contains not a single article but what is a very necessary part of household furniture. **We handle no seconds.** All our utensils are first quality and guaranteed perfect. When you order your stove from this list be sure to include the assortment that goes with the size wanted.

We have quoted our stoves without furniture, for the reason that many people wanting a stove are already supplied with the necessary utensils.

Order from us and get more for your money than from any other house.

In ordering Stove Furniture be sure and buy same size as your stove.

No. 15984.

1 Copper bottom tin Wash Boiler.	1 Box Grater.
1 Copper bottom tin Tea Kettle.	1 Biscuit Cutter.
1 Cast iron Stove Kettle.	1 Dover Egg Beater.
1 Cast iron Spider.	1 Doz. 3-inch plain Patty Pans.
1 Wrought iron Fry Pan, 10 inch.	½ Doz. 9-inch tin Pie Plates.
1 4-pint tin Tea Pot.	1 14-inch tin Basting Spoon.
1 5-quart tin Coffee Pot.	1 Cake Turner.
1 10-quart retinned Dish Pan.	1 1-quart tin Cup.
2 Black Dripping Pans, 10x12 and 10x14.	1 Vegetable Fork.
1 Tin Bread Pan, 5¾x10¾x3.	1 Tin Dipper.
2 Common square Bread Tins, 7¾x11¾x1½.	1 Flat handled Skimmer.
1 Revolving Flour Sifter.	1 Fire Shovel.
	1 Tin Wash Basin.
	1 Tube Cake Pan, 10 inch.

Price above assortment, No. 7 or 8........................$3.50
Price above assortment, No. 9....................3.75

No. 15985.

1 Heavy 1X-tin copper bottom Wash Boiler.	3 Tin Bread Pans.
1 Iron Stove Kettle.	2 Tin Cake Pans.
1 Tin Cover to fit.	1 Doz. assorted Patty Pans.
1 Iron Tea Kettle.	1 Basting Spoon.
1 Iron Spider.	1 Cake Turner.
1 Fry Pan.	1 Steamer.
1 Stove Shovel.	1 Retinned Cullender.
1 Nickel plated copper 5-pints Coffee Pot.	1 Cake Cutter.
1 Nickel plated copper 4-pints Tea Pot.	1 Biscuit Cutter.
1 Retinned Preserving Kettle.	1 Doughnut Cutter.
1 Cover to fit.	1 Nutmeg Grater.
1 Retinned Saucepan.	1 Large Grater.
1 Cover to fit.	1 Patent Flour Sifter.
1 Tin Muffin Frame, 12 cups.	1 Dover Egg Beater.
½ Doz. tin Pie Plates, 9 inch.	1 Covered japanned Dust Pan.
1 Extra heavy retinned Dish Pan.	1 Butcher Knife.
1 Pieced tin Cup, 1 pint.	1 Paring Knife.
1 Galvanized Water Dipper, 2 quarts.	1 Mincing Knife, double blades.
1 Flat handled Skimmer.	1 Bread Board.
1 Vegetable Fork.	1 Rolling Pin.
2 Drip Pans (give size of oven).	1 Wood Potato Masher.
	1 Oval hardwood Chopping Tray.
	1 Set Mrs. Potts' Sad Irons.

Price above assortment, No. 7...........$6.00
Price above assortment, No. 8...........6.25
Price above assortment, No. 9...........7.00

Turkish Tidies.

No. 23218 Fancy colored Turkish Tidies, figured center and border in variegated colors, long knotted fringe. Size, 16x35 inches. Price each............11c

Very Handsome Turkish Tidies.

No. 23219 Very Handsome Turkish Tidies, fringe on both ends, with very fancy and attractive center. Very pretty and will give excellent satisfaction. Size 15½ by 40.

Price each.. $0.15
Per dozen.. 1.70

Genuine Marseilles Turkish Tidy.

No. 23220 Genuine Marseilles Turkish Tidy, made in new and beautiful raised patterns; choice assortment of strictly up to date designs. With double knotted fringe; size 19½x41.
Price, each..25c
½ dozen... $1.40

No. 23320.

No. 23222 This is an exceptionally heavy and Fine Genuine Turkish Tidy, comes in the following beautiful colors, pink, white, nile green and canary, with beautiful contrasting floral designs on both ends; handsomely finished with fringe at ends, size 18x60.
Price each, 35c
Three for... $2.00

No. 23321.

No. 23222 This is a beautiful Turkish Stand Cover; comes made with white centers, and beautiful bright colored borders, finished with knotted fringe all around. Never before sold at less than 50c. Price each........ $0.35; Three for....... $1.00

Turkish Face Cloths.

No. 23223 Bleached Face Cloth. Size, 15x15, full bleached, plain white or with stripe.
Price............ 5c; Per dozen...........56c
No. 23225 Fancy Pattern Face Cloth. Size, 16x16, full bleached goods fancy block pattern center with striped border.
Each............... 9c; Per dozen..............80c

A Christmas Cozy Corner

These Papier Maché Decorations make unique Xmas gifts for fitting up cozy corners, dens, oriental rooms, libraries, etc. Being extremely light in weight, they can be held in place with a small tack. They do not break or chip off like iron or plaster, and are practically indestructible.

Armor 806, is 32x30 inches, finish antique or bright iron, by express prepaid, **$5.00**

Oriental Heads 852, 853, 854 and 856, are life size in colors, weight six oz., express prepaid, . each **$2.00**

Send for "Artistic Decorations," a booklet showing other designs. If your dealer will not supply you, remit direct to us. Reference, First National Bank, Milwaukee.

NATIONAL PAPIER MACHÉ WORKS
397 E. Water Street, **Milwaukee, Wis.**

OUR NEWPORT TOILET SET AT $3.75

OUR NEWPORT TOILET SET is one of the very latest and handsomest patterns put on the market, beautifully decorated with yellow and pink chrysanthemum blossoms and foliage as shown in the illustration, in addition to which every piece is heavily decorated with gold. The gold decorations are not simply lines and tracings as are usually put on toilet sets, but a heavy deep stippled effect which gives the toilet set a most luxurious appearance. We consider this set one of the handsomest we have ever been able to furnish, and being made by one of the most reliable potteries in America, we can guarantee it to be strictly high grade.

Each set is carefully packed complete in a barrel to insure safe delivery and shipped direct from the pottery in Western West Virginia.
No. 2T402 10-Piece Toilet Set, consisting of wash bowl, pitcher, covered chamber (2 pieces), covered soap dish (3 pieces), hot water pitcher, brush vase and mug. Shipping weight, 70 pounds.
Our special price..$3.75
No. 2T404 12-Piece Toilet Set, same assortment as the 10-piece toilet set No. 2T402, with a large slop jar and cover added, as illustrated. Shipping weight, 70 pounds. Our special price........ ....$5.45

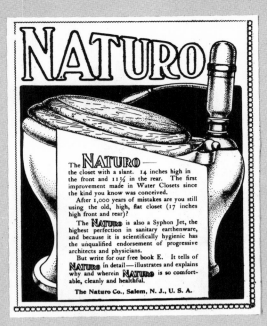
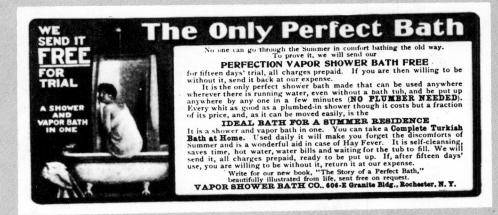

8 Growing Up

One is not greatly enlightened about childhood in the first few years of the 1900's by reading the magazines of the times. Perhaps the editors were operating under the old principle that children should be seen but not heard (or read about), or possibly they were bachelors who did not know what to do with the subject. As the pages of this section testify, most of the public concern about the young boy or girl centered on his education. The chancellor of the University of Nebraska writes about "The Public School of the Twentieth Century." He suggests that unless the quality of instruction in public schools is improved, unhappy taxpayers may refuse to give the school system sufficient financial support and thus eventually kill public schooling. Even though the author discards this prospect as unlikely, it is surprising to find that less than seventy years ago the public school system was on such a shaky footing that its demise could be considered as a possibility.

Some further statements on the condition of the schools during this period appear in the feature entitled "Publick Occurrences"; one learns that twenty-nine states and two territories had compulsory school laws (there were forty-five states and four territories in 1900), but that many of the laws were very weakly enforced. One is also told that twenty million children were attending school—eighteen million in public and two million in private schools; the figure seems rather large, for the total population of the United States was only seventy-six million when the 1900 census was taken. Some of the editorializing was probably a bit starry-eyed, for a great many public school students were getting sketchy educations at best, especially in farming regions where it was the custom to let children go to school only from the time the last harvest was over in the fall until early spring planting began. Moreover, the quality of teaching very often left much to be desired, especially in rural areas where the one-room schoolhouse survived—the little red schoolhouse of song and story—with children from the first to the eighth grade in one room under a teacher sometimes younger than her (or his) oldest pupil. It is depressing that today, these many decades later, we are still em-

broiled in debate over the quality of our youngsters' schooling.

On another subject Robert Shackleton, whose background is not revealed, tells "How Boys Earn Money." Mr. Shackleton appears not to have decided just exactly what his point of view was going to be: part of the time he tells of the hopeless situation for young working boys in New York City, and then he gives examples of how hard-working, plucky little chaps came through like heroes from a Horatio Alger book.

But even at his gloomiest, Mr. Shackleton did not begin to portray the situation as it actually existed. When H. G. Wells visited America in 1904, he was appalled at the kind of work to which children were put. Small boys barely in their teens were uniformed messengers working late into the night and going into unwholesome parts of New York. Children sold newspapers, often being forced to fight rivals to hold their street corners or other stations and frequently sleeping in flophouses because they had no homes or because what family they did have turned their tenement homes into boozy nightmares. Bootblacks were New York's other large class of boy workers. Many of them were Italian because of the system by which a *padrone* virtually bought boys from their parents in Italy, brought them to America, and then forced them to work for him. The eagle of laissez faire was soaring rather high at the turn of the century, but even so, New York State did feel that some aspects of child labor were getting out of hand. It roused itself enough to pass laws against letting children carry messages for patrons or inmates of brothels. But the laws were never enforced, so they changed nothing.

These were not the only shameful situations. The use of child labor had just about reached its peak in 1900. Industrialization was going ahead at a rapid rate in the nation, and there was much that a young boy or girl could do, especially since his labor cost very little. Large numbers of children worked in Eastern sweatshops. They worked in textile mills—their little hands could reach in among the bobbins and threads better than an adult's—especially in the South, where the textile industry was migrating from

New England because it did not have to pay so much for wages. In Pennsylvania small boys worked outside the shafts of coal mines, picking pieces of rock out of the coal that went by in chutes, filling their lungs with dust through a long and wearisome day. According to the census of 1900, one out of every twenty-five nonfarm jobs was held by a child between ten and fifteen.

In 1900 it was not against any law in most states to send children ten years old or younger into a mill and keep them there at work for any number of hours. That same year "less than a dozen states were seriously attempting to limit the labor of children in mills, mines, factories, or stores, in sweatshops or street trades." Those states that had some sort of child labor laws seldom made much attempt to enforce them.

The turning point came just after the new century began. Since the states were disinclined to do much about the situation, crusaders advocated national legislation. The agitation against exploitation of children made itself felt so quickly that in 1910 there were only about half as many children working at nonagricultural jobs as there had been ten years earlier. Within a few years compulsory school laws in most states made it difficult to use children in factories. The advocates of national child labor laws were never completely successful though, for the Supreme Court struck down such laws, saying that this was a matter for the states to legislate. An attempt to pass a child labor amendment in 1924 finally died when not enough states ratified it. But eventually the barring of the products of child labor from interstate commerce helped to wipe out child labor except in agricultural work.

This brief glimpse at the child labor situation does not mean that all American children passed gloomy childhoods at the turn of the century. Indeed, most of them remembered their early years as a time of fishing and swimming, of shady lawns and country roads, and of the smell of lilacs during the parade on Memorial Day.

The Talent in the Napkin

"AMERICA," said a visiting foreigner, "is a land where the men are sacrificed to the women and the men and the women to the children."

There is truth in this criticism, if criticism it was. No doubt "papa" manages to have a pretty good time withal; and as for "mamma," she is not miserable every moment that she is escorting the children about to places where they can enjoy themselves. But the fierce days of our pioneer ancestors have put their stamp upon us. Then everything was of necessity for the future—what was then in the present beside hardship but hope? And so we have the hereditary habit of sacrificing the present to the future.

Like every other habit, this in excess is a vice. And is there not, with many of us, too little recognition of the rights of the present? Do we not forget that each individual is here as the custodian of certain talents, certain potentialities, and that he or she can best serve others not by wrapping them in a napkin and burying them and permitting himself or herself to wink out as an individuality, but by bringing them to their full development?

This does not mean that papa ought to have a larger part of his earnings for drinks and cigars. Nor does it mean that mamma ought to spend more money in finery and more time in gadding and gossiping. It means that each owes it to future generations as well as to himself to develop his own intelligence and character. The best possible gift parents can give their children is the example and the memory of them as intelligent, independent, life-enjoying persons skilled in that high and rare art, the art of living. What could be worse for children than to see and to remember a father who was a mere breadwinner, a mother who was a mere household drudge?

The Boisterous American Child

IT IS true that the American child is the most boisterous in the world, and the least regardful of the peaceful conversation of its elders; but somewhat too much has been made of the fact. The comparison frequently made with English children does not impress one much. The young Briton's submission is the result of nursery-governess, "preparatory" school, public school and university. From childhood to maturity, his main life is outside of what we know as the family circle, and in an atmosphere the very breath of which is submission to authority. The conformity to tradition in thought and conduct, which goes so far toward making English society dull, is largely the result of the national attitude toward the child in the home—or, rather, out of it.

The comparison with the Japanese is vastly more interesting, for here the effacement of child before parent seems to be the result, not of estrangement or indifference, but of an intimate reverence that has many of the attributes of a religious sentiment. But as yet it is too early to judge fully of the virtues of Japanese family life. That it produces the highest type of discipline and devotion is manifest; but what of its result on the development of variety and intensity of character? We shall know better when the Japanese have had time to show whether they are as able to contribute as individuals to the world's civilization as they are as a nation to make use of what others have developed.

Meantime, the freedom of American family life, so often obnoxious to the stranger, has this virtue, that it gives full scope to the development of each individual under the eyes of his parent, and in collision with brothers and sisters and the children on the street. The American parent has his child dinned into him, but he knows him, and, if he is wise, checks his development, or aids it, sympathetically and wisely. It is good to bear in mind the prejudices and the nerves of one's neighbors; and it is better to make sure that freedom of development in the individual is always limited by due regard to society and the state. But it would be a bad bargain if we were to gain outward conformity at the expense of inward force.

The Power of Association

A LITTLE boy fell into the habit of setting up a fearful howling whenever a banana-cart came into the neighborhood, and would not be calm until his mother had bought him bananas. A little girl who lived next door watched this performance until she had reasoned it out. When the banana-cart again appeared she burst into a shrieking which made the clamor of the boy seem in comparison a polite and demure appeal. The mother of the little girl promptly withdrew with her to a secluded room and gave her the one spanking of her life. "When you see a banana-cart again, my precious," the mother said in conclusion, "don't think how much you want a banana, but how little you want a spanking."

The power of association of ideas is one of the great moral faculties—if rightly cultivated.

The Fountain of Eternal Youth

LIKE pretty much everything else, this matter of having children has two sides to it. As a great many children are failures and as children are the joint product of heredity and environment, both elements preponderantly under parental control, it would seem more sensible to say that there were too many people undertaking parental responsibility instead of too few. And further, parenthood has many cares and sorrows and exasperations. Still, when all is said, how many persons who found themselves childless at forty-five have been able honestly to congratulate themselves?

Children have a use as an assurance against destitution and loneliness in old age. They are satisfactory to the vanity for family immortality. But more than these and all other advantages is the advantage of prolonging one's life. Growing children will keep any proper man or woman young in spirit and in mind, will retard the development of that sour yet complacent cynicism which curses old age both for one's self and for those about one.

The man or the woman—again, the right sort of man or woman—who has children drinks every day a deep draught at the fountain of eternal youth.

Mental Diets

INVENTIONS are, one might almost say, under way by means of which sea-travel will be as rapid and as easy as the fastest land-travel now is—land-travel so swift that while one sleeps in his bed half a continent will be spanned, and men separated by thousands of miles will see each other and each other's surroundings as they talk wirelessly. It would be impossible to exaggerate the inevitable development from the marvels already discerned.

But it would be easily possible to exaggerate in certain directions the resulting benefits. The reason the child bred in small town and country surpasses the city-bred child is chiefly the dazing and deadening of the city child's mind by the ceaseless impact of impressions too swift and too numerous to be noted and digested. With the whole human race brought jam up against our eyes, with the roar of the whole world's activity bellowing in our very ears, there is danger that we shall see little and hear less.

It is not the quantity of food within reach which makes the body capable; it is the quality and the amount properly assimilated. Neither is it the quantity of available mental food that makes the mind capable; again, it is quality and assimilation.

The Memoirs of a Baby
By JOSEPHINE DASKAM

NEVER before has the dignified title of "Memoirs" graced so funny a book as this. The sorry side of life—the tribulations of the little tots—have no place in this irresistibly amusing record of the home life of a typical young American couple. All the various incidents of a lively youngster's babyhood here find portrayal such as only Josephine Daskam can give.

The profuse pen-and-ink drawings of F. Y. Cory are done in the spirit of the narrative. The book will provoke the laughter of any one who simply turns the pages.

Cloth, $1.50

A REBUKE.

SHE.— What 's de matter wit' youse? Ain't youse got no manners dat youse must stare yer eyes out at every pretty girl youse see?

192

From the painting by
Jessie Willcox Smith.

A Good Foundation

A careful builder insures the permanency and strength of his building by laying foundations of the best materials. The good housewife lays a foundation of Ivory Soap and rests upon it the cleanliness and comfort of the family. It pays to use the best materials and the Ivory is the best Soap.

It Floats

How we love to have our children "look nice!"

From "The Luxury of Children."
Copyright, 1904, by Harper & Brothers.

THE LUXURY OF CHILDREN
BY E. S. MARTIN

With a genial charm and humor akin to that of Charles Lamb,
Mr. Martin has written a series of essays which have to do with the
many sweet, loving phases of child-life in the home. The book will
delight all fathers and mothers. Its quiet good-humor and charming
style make it a beautiful tribute to home life.

*With Eight Illustrations in Color and Marginal Decorations
in Tint by Sarah S. Stilwell. Square 8vo, in box. $1.75 net*

HARPER & BROTHERS, PUBLISHERS, NEW YORK

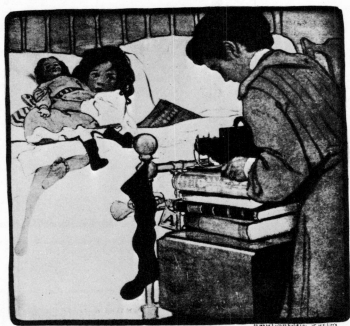

The Dearth of Children

THERE is great complaint about the scarcity of babies in the families of native-born Americans. There is no need to quote statistics. Every one knows the conclusion that the statistics lead to, which is that the native Americans seem less and less inclined every year to replenish the earth with new individuals of their own species. As concerns them, the birth-rate is constantly falling. Writers in foreign reviews—British reviews especially—comment on it as the sign of an awful defect in us and our civilization. Married Americans who ought to raise eight children, raise four; those who ought to raise four, raise two; those who ought to raise two, raise none, or content themselves with a single lonely sample of offspring. Also, a great many Americans who ought to marry, don't. The consequence is that the statisticians take gloomy views of the future of our race, and that thoughtful observers discuss the reason for American sterility, and possible methods of alleviating it.

President Roosevelt has recorded his views on the subject. Americans, he says, who are so cold-hearted and so selfish as to dislike having children, "are in effect criminals against the race, and should be objects of contemptuous abhorrence to all healthy people." President Eliot of Harvard has been thinking about it too. In his annual report he tells of looking up the records of the six Harvard classes which have been graduated from twenty-five to thirty-one years, and finding that the married members had no more than two surviving children each, and that twenty-eight per cent. of the members had not married. He thinks college graduates should marry earlier in life, and to that end is trying to get his young men out of college and through the professional schools sooner, so that they can earn money to marry on.

But men who don't marry until they are thirty have time enough to raise families as large as the country expects of them, if only they and their wives have the will and the good luck. The trouble is that both men and women who defer marriage until late form habits which they cannot reconcile to full nurseries and limited incomes. Youth is rash and imperfectly provident. Maturity has more prudence, and in the matter of children is apt to have too much. There need be no regret that people who cannot provide decently for large families do not have them. Such persons may have too many children as it is. The trouble is with people who can well afford to raise families of a decent size, and who neglect that privilege for fear that they will come to want, or because they want to spend their time and their money on other things.

The great thing that keeps the size of American families down is social and pecuniary ambition. There are a few thrifty parents in the land—farmers, miners, mill-workers, and the like—who look upon children as a potential source of income, and raise a good many because their keep costs little, and their labor is valuable. We don't approve of persons of that way of thinking. Our American feeling is that the parents should work for the children, but not the children for the parents, except in cases of special necessity. Almost all of us want our children to be better off than we are ourselves. We would rather have two children and give them what we consider special advantages of nurture and education, than have five and be unable to do for all of them what we want done. We are impatient of the common lot. Unless our children can rise above it, we think it a doubtful advantage to have secured them an entry in this world.

Now that is not altogether a bad characteristic. It makes for progress to a certain extent, but we carry it too far. We are too prudent, too selfish, for both ourselves and our offspring. It is by no means the children who have the most "advantages" that do best in the world, but those, rather, who are born with the best brains and bodies, and are hardest prodded by the spur of necessity. For the sake of pampering two children we forfeit the chance of drawing a great prize among the three others that we might have and don't.

It is too bad about us Americans. The hope of our amendment lies in the possibility that we may come to a better appreciation of the pleasure there is in raising good children as compared with any other rival interest that attracts us. We never will raise large families for the good of the country; never. The race may go hang, for all of us. But if more of us can come to feel, what is true, that the right kind of children pay enormously in love, in entertainment, in all things that make life desirable, we may come to raise more of them.

The Public School of the Twentieth Century *By* E. Benjamin Andrews

Chancellor of the University of Nebraska

IN A RECENT work on finance, Henry C. Adams says, in substance, that if this Republic is to continue free, all grades of education must be provided for at the general cost. This for the reason that in privately endowed schools the teaching is shaded to suit the social classes from which the benefactors hail. Consciously or unconsciously the bias of the class which maintains these institutions is displayed in their work. There is a great truth in this. The instruction given in privately endowed schools is usually not intended to be prejudiced, and yet a certain prejudice it cannot avoid. Questions vital to the masses are either not discussed at all, or only superficially and one-sidedly. This being so, the inquiry what is to be the character of the public schools in the twentieth century becomes most interesting and important. In so brief an article we can touch only the salient points in the coming change.

Could we not hope for betterment in the present condition of the public school system the outlook would not be bright. There would be good ground to fear that the public school system would pass away, its unfruitfulness being its ruin. Recalcitrant taxpayers, even now sometimes to be met with, disinclined to bear the burdens imposed on them for education, would grow in numbers, and, on becoming a majority, would deprive the system of all means to sustain a rich life, at last killing it altogether. But I have hope, as all true Americans must have. The public school is the foundation whereon shall arise a civic life of superb accomplishments. The betterment to come is to take effect in several forms.

The public schools of the future will have saner administration than is possible now. The educational report which the commission appointed by Mayor Harrison, of Chicago, recently put forth contains bright foregleams of the changes in the administrative methods of the public schools destined to characterize the new century. There will be some modifications in the propositions of the commission, but the central reforms it recommended will be worked out. Some of the changes proposed at first seem extreme; on study all are seen to be necessary and imperative. Indeed at some points the commission fails to go far enough.

Responsible Management by Specialists

Nearly all boards of education are unwieldy. Their meetings are not conferences with sincere desire to dispatch necessary business, but political debates wherein sides are taken and speeches made to the galleries. Many members, little interested, are so ignorant that designing colleagues easily use them in perpetrating jobs. In a board of six or seven members such evils could hardly appear; witness the history of the State universities, nearly every one of which is governed by a very small board, meeting for honest, earnest, efficient conference. Business is transacted rapidly, nearly all votes are unanimous, and jobs are practically unknown.

Early in the new century men will find that the interests of the pupils and teachers, also the interests of the public, the taxpaying body supporting the schools, can be best served by conducting the schools upon the same lines of central and expert responsibility on which banks, railroads and other great business institutions are conducted. The management of a bank, a wholesale mercantile establishment or a railroad is always placed in expert hands. Men of the keenest sagacity and the widest experience are sought for such executive positions, and then all business matters are resigned to them, directors and stockholders keeping their hands off. The officers come to their duties with breadth of mind, the courage of their convictions, brain power and tested ability. The citizen of the early future will insist that the public school system shall in the same way have expert and really responsible functionaries for Superintendent and Business Manager, to whom shall be committed all business of an administrative nature, to be attended to without interference on the part of board committees or members.

In most boards of education a mixed system prevails, which, besides being the cause of endless annoyance, is death to all really effective management. There is incessant, pernicious meddling with the administration—by members of the board as individuals, upon whom, in that character, no responsibility rests for the conduct of the schools. Some of these officious persons mean well, no doubt. They think the ark must be steadied. They believe that they have an office to fulfill which cannot be delegated. They do not see what good management involves. Not seldom, however, the disturbance is as vicious in its motive as in its results. Executive heads of educational systems ought not to be interfered with save when they fail in the performance of the duties imposed upon them. It is best that specialist talent should control the administration even at the risk of occasional errors.

It is delightful to see that the fussy and pernicious activity referred to is decreasing. One of the great drawbacks to ideal public education in America is thus nearing an end. Very pronounced is the growth of good public thought on this subject in Chicago—the most American city of the nation; the one in which the vital problems of the twentieth century will first attain solution. In every progressive city there is less and less disposition to interfere with a school official whose aim is to perform his duty; more and more determination to hold him accountable for his acts, and, until he fails, permit his judgment to prevail. This is a tremendous improvement, which will rapidly reach consummation. Among the American people reform movements, after their first inception, do not move slowly.

Those are in error who think of training each child by himself as the ideal method. For average pupils class teaching is the best. Example, emulation, comradeship count for much. The good teacher that is to be will, however, keep the classes well down to thirty each, and make special provision both for very brilliant and for pronouncedly dull pupils. The bright will not be held back nor permitted to skip the work of any grade; the backward will not be discouraged by failure in tasks beyond their power. In a school of usual size, both these sorts of pupils will be taught in one ungraded room. A large school will have two such rooms, one for each set. For both the teaching will be the very best which money can provide. When possible the instruction will still be groupwise, though in a few cases it may need to be individual.

The Present a Period of Advancement

The new century school will be better taught than now, as well as better administered and graded. When the press criticises our common schools it tells much truth, yet at the same time misses much truth. Instance what is said in criticism of "fads"—that is, music, drawing, manual training and the household arts. This criticism is often just, but not so in the way meant. Misapprehension of the nature of the so-called fads leads many to denounce them who would not do so if informed. We are passing through an era of pedagogical changes, few of which are perfectly worked out; all of which, however, are creditable. Our very crudity is our glory, a case of what Professor Palmer might call the "glory of the imperfect." Household art, manual training, drawing and music have been added to our courses of study, but it is to be admitted that most of these disciplines have not yet been brought into final congruence with the old work or with one another. Correlation is in progress, but takes its time, and we must wait the outcome. Few geniuses engage in teaching. Results must be reached by patient study of conditions and the practical application of such resources as we can command.

The work performed by the child in manual training, for instance, is worth all its cost as a knack or sleight-of-hand, and ten times its cost as an aid to motor efficiency and morality. No other pedagogical agency equals it in awakening the dull or in reforming the vicious. Proper manual training is at bottom mental; it does not retard but advances mental attainments. Still more is this true of color work, drawing and the various attempts at art. They are educative in a great variety of ways, exerting a manual, a mental, an æsthetic and a moral influence. An almost spontaneous art power resides in many children, which needs only cultivation to become a benign factor in their lives.

Handicapped as we are by imperfect correlation we are teaching the old studies better than could be done before "fads" were introduced; so that whatever widening of horizon, elixir of life or bent toward high character and aims we are now imparting is clear gain. If so much is true already, what may we not expect when full correlation is reached?

Twentieth century school teaching will blend into due harmony what I may denominate the pedagogy of gush and the pedagogy of grind. Teachers of a certain sort, very numerous, and on the whole highly successful, deem it the Alpha and Omega of their work to tap pupils' spontaneity, to call forth their interest, turning it, whenever necessary, from voluntary to involuntary, to arouse tremendous enthusiasm in them, to keep them pitched in the highest key.

Over against this method of holding a child's mind to his school work, depending wholly on involuntary interest, there is still in vogue the pedagogy of grind, which minimizes spontaneity and involuntary interest and places all the stress upon voluntary interest. Devotees of this system nearly all bewail the passing of the birch. It might well be called "birch pedagogy;" it is, at any rate, wooden. Extremes in the pedagogy of grind and extremes in the pedagogy of gush are alike to be avoided. These two pedagogies must be blended into a single rational method.

The teacher, for his part, should certainly try to be a source of interest to the pupil, but woe to the pupil if he depend for motive on this foreign source. The work of life is not always pleasant. Usually, interest in your work cannot be supplied by another, and when, perchance, it is, there is a lessening of your own strength, a growth of dependence, a loss of manliness. The power of pupils' initiative must be developed by self-reliance and a capacity to act independently.

No greater virtue can exist in a child than the inspiration to finish an unpleasant task. The old-fashioned country school excelled in its insistence on self-reliance. Some of its methods will find place in the schools of the next century.

A Return to the School of the Wilderness

One result of too much dependence upon involuntary attention is to keep pupils from paying close attention to the logical elements of knowledge, training their minds to incoherence, discontinuity, the avoidance of details, and the disuse of the reasoning power. Logical continuity in mental work at last becomes impossible, though in the way of fact knowledge the pupil may veritably heap Pelion on Ossa, figuring as a walking encyclopædia, equally ludicrous and useless. In studying general nature, animal life, the mineral world, or the vegetable kingdom, he uses only his eyes, jumbling together masses of observations. Thinking, he does not learn. We need a return to the methods of the school in the wilderness forty years ago, when the book and the pupil's hard study of it made him a man.

Not alone light but strenuous reading should be urged—essays, history, science, philosophy, books that test and books that drill. Noble passages should be memorized, and the most cardinal dates of human history learned once for all. This sort of study requires will-power, but it is indispensable, and should be insisted upon. A pupil should on graduation have not only an open mind and a beautiful nature, but a resolute will and an amount of absolutely correct information in detail.

Too many boys and girls after leaving school show evident disinclination to make strenuous effort of any kind. They lack the power of strong exertion, courage, resolution, grit—"sand." They are afraid to take the initiative. The school teaching of the next century will correct this, developing the strenuous qualities in children. The pupil will cease to feel that he must be extraneously interested before he can act. Instead of looking to his teacher for interest, as the pedagogy of gush has taught him, he will learn to find that quality within himself. It will no longer be beaten into his mind that his teacher must amuse him, keep him attentive. A suggested task may be never so dull or hard, he will still be able to think of it as required, as having claims upon him. Plenty of the tonic of driving the will to perform unpleasant duties will continually be given him.

Good Morals Part of the Curriculum

The time seems near at hand when public schools will be able to teach the elements of morality in a positive way. Hitherto they have not been permitted to attempt this because the simplest moral teaching has been thought to involve dogma. This fear is now seen to be groundless. All are becoming aware that for practical purposes morality can be taught without dipping into religion.

Public sentiment would even now sanction the positive and regular teaching in the public schools of cleanliness in body, speech and thought, of temperance, of the rights and laws of property, of public spirit, love of country, regard for parents, the aged, the feeble, the unfortunate. There are no parents who do not wish their children schooled in these vastly important duties.

All the common virtues need to be inculcated in the school as well as at home. This is a work that the school of the twentieth century is going to undertake and successfully carry out. A most useful code of morals will be taught in the schools, which will fasten upon the child at the very beginning of his mental life the principles that tend to produce good citizenship, the end and aim of the public school system.

When the common virtues are thus taught in the public schools as part of their regular office, when we bring before all children in this effective way the difference between right and wrong, and the royal claims of duty, the schools will take on a new relation to the people now patronizing various forms of private schools. Then, without quarrel or dispute, it will be seen that all children can be safely placed under the auspices of the public school system, sectwise divisions among elementary schools being no longer necessary. This reform in public schooling is, in my opinion, destined to bring about universal interest and a common faith in them, all citizens, without distinction of creed, applauding them with one voice.

Public Schools and Private

BOURKE COCKRAN, representing the Twelfth New York District in Congress, denounces the public schools on religious grounds—as "agnostic" and "anti-Christian." Here is a matter of opinion; and the fact that Mr. Cockran's opinion is in the minority entitles him, if anything, to a more respectful hearing. But when he goes on to assert that "every man of any consequence sends his children to private school," and that "the public school is becoming, as it is in Europe, the poor school," he states propositions which are matters either of fact or fiction.

So far as Europe is concerned, the decline of the private school and the rapid rise of the public school is one of the interesting and important politico-social-industrial phenomena. The chief reason is that the progressive states of Western Europe—Germany, France, Switzerland, Holland, Belgium, Italy—are now providing better education than could possibly be got in private schools.

In our own country we are in the transition stage. Formerly the public school was not only the best but also the one source of primary education. But since the Civil War, and until recently, the state let itself be outstripped, especially in the cities and larger towns; the superior mobility and progressiveness of private enterprise put it to shame. Now, however, a reaction is setting in, and throughout the country the state is striving to regain the ground lost, chiefly because it so long had a monopoly.

Probably Mr. Cockran, being from New York City with its proverbially narrow horizon, had in mind the private schools which snobbishness started and which snobbishness maintains. These, however, need concern no friend of the public-school system. They give an inferior education and will never attract the children of parents who think and wish their progeny to succeed in life. The important private schools are those started because the public education provided was not satisfactory. These are not so numerous as they were a quarter of a century ago. They will grow fewer and fewer as the people become wider and wider awake on the subject of education.

We have the wealth to make our public schools the best schools in the world. And that they should be, and must be!

The Dunce of His Class

MANY a boy has been a dullard at school and has made a failure of his after life simply because there was some defect in his ears which made it impossible for him to hear distinctly or some defect in his eyes which made it impossible for him to see things as they are. The brain gets not only the most of its information through the ears and the eyes, but also the most of its skill in the all-important faculty of judgment. And if the ears do not hear well and the eyes do not see correctly, both information and training are necessarily defective and awry.

These facts are obvious; yet thousands on thousands grow up, struggle, fail wholly or partially, die without knowing the simple and perhaps easily curable why of their misfortunes. And in every school to-day there are these curable so-called dullards.

Every pair of young eyes and young ears should be suspected until they have been competently examined.

When the School Year Ends

THE school year is about to close. What is the "school year"?

First, let us see what it is not. Take off for the long vacation, ninety days; for fall, winter and spring Saturdays and Sundays, seventy-six days; for the Christmas holidays, less Saturdays and Sundays already counted, ten days; for the Easter recess, less its Saturday and Sunday already counted, five days; for legal holidays, at best three days. Total, with no duplications, one hundred and eighty-four days!

From three hundred and sixty-five take one hundred and eighty-four. Remainder, one hundred and eighty-one. The "school year," then, is less than half the year!

In the days when learning was something unattractive and almost useless, and had to be birched into a child, this may have been all very well. But is it so well in this day, when properly taught children, if properly encouraged, like school almost as well as they like play?

No wonder so many children are so reluctant to learn. They would be as reluctant to play if we gave them as little chance to form the play habit.

Competition for Students

ONE of the singular and significant movements of these months lies in the struggle which colleges and professional schools are making for students. Each academy and high school from Portland, Oregon, to Portland, Maine, is canvassed for candidates for the freshman class of hundreds of our colleges. The colleges, too, especially in the senior and junior classes, are canvassed by the professional schools of law and medicine for candidates for their first-year classes.

The movement is at once good and bad. It is good, for many students would not go to college at all if they were not urged to go to a particular college. They need the impulse of some strong exterior force. The movement is bad, because the college is presented to many students after the manner of the commercial traveler drumming up trade.

In this competition for college students the various fraternities and athletic associations of the college coöperate with the official authorities. They, too, like to get the best fellows and the best football players for their organizations.

What's Wrong With the Schools?

WE HAVE about 27,000,000 children and youths of school age. There is an average daily attendance at the public and private schools of about 12,000,000 and an enrollment at the colleges and academies of less than 300,000. Again, with 11,000,000 youths of academy and college age, we have in attendance upon the institutions of higher education less than 300,000, of whom less than 175,000 are in colleges and universities.

Of course, the attendance would probably be much larger if the instruction at our higher institutions, both as to matter and as to method, were not of such a nature that it is an open question, to say the least of it, whether the young men and women students do not give a great deal of valuable time in exchange for very little that is of use. Yet the central truth remains—we are not doing anything like what we should do to make the oncoming generations successful at doing the things which we, in our ignorance, have done so bunglingly or have left altogether undone.

Less than half the children of school age at school! Less than three per cent. of our youths at college! What is the matter with the parents? What is the matter with the schools and colleges?

Country Boy and City Boy

NOT the least pressing question raised by the amazing modern concentration of population in the cities is where our good and great men are to come from when there is no longer an overproduction of virtue and ambition in the country. If the canals have need of all their canal boys, whence the future President? Without the splitting of rails how shall the Union be preserved?

Dr. J. H. Finley, president of the College of the City of New York—himself a country boy, and a disciple of virtue and ambition—is doing his best to soothe our fears: "The moral atmosphere, even in such a city as this, is much superior to the moral atmosphere of the average village, East and West. And think of what the boy in this city has in the 640 acres he may call his home. He has the whole history of humanity and the best men in the country within earshot. As far as the comparative health is concerned, I will say that most of the prairie boys I used to know in my youth are now under the sod."

These words may have been colored by the fact that they were addressed to city boys. But there is the tonic of wholesome truth in them. While we are reckoning the farm boys who have become philanthropists, let us not forget that the greed which created Standard Oil was nourished in a barnyard, and that Jay Gould's arrival on Broadway with ten cents and a harmless, necessary mousetrap in his pocket was the symbol of much subsequent setting and baiting of the sublime but very unnecessary mousetrap of frenzied finance.

Dalrymple.

DESTROYING

AMERICAN SCHOOL BOY AND GIRL. — Hold on, M

THE IDEALS.

...conoclast! Can't you leave us one Fairy Tale?

"Publick Occurrences"

DR. G. STANLEY HALL

PHOTO BY F. GUTEKUNST, PHILADELPHIA

DR. EDWARD BROOKS

An Army of Twenty Millions

Within a few days nearly twenty million boys and girls will be enrolled in the public and private schools of the United States, forming the greatest army of its kind the world has ever known. About two million of these will be in the private and incorporated institutions, and nearly eighteen million in the public schools. There will be nearly a half million in the city evening schools, the private kindergartens, the Indian and business schools, and others. The private schools always show a larger proportion of increase in good times because the parents then have more money with which to educate their children. But at their best these private schools have only about one-eighth or one-ninth of the total of the public schools. The public school system is therefore our chief educational fact and factor. It is the greatest single institution of the country. Its teachers number nearly one-half a million — about three-fourths are women — and these carry on their work in nearly 300,000 schoolhouses. To pay for all these requires upward of two hundred million dollars a year, and the value of the school property is between five and six hundred millions.

These enormous figures increase every year; increase more rapidly, in fact, than the population itself, for the school expenditure per inhabitant is larger every year, and the teachers' salaries are being raised; rather too slowly, it is true, but surely. In the past twenty years the public school expenditures in this country have increased two and one-half times for property and nearly three times for salaries and other expenses. It costs fifty per cent. more to-day to educate an American boy or girl than it did twenty years ago, but the quality of education is fully one hundred per cent. improved. No one objects to spending money on the schools, provided it is used by men who know what they are doing.

One good result that has been achieved, too, has been the lengthening of the school term, and this must go on until the schools in the rural districts are kept open at least nine of the twelve months. At present, with all the improvements, some of them are open only three or four months.

Among the progressive educators the idea is general that the school term should be shortened during the day and spread over as much of the year as possible. The average child in a long vacation forgets a great deal.

To Compel Children to Attend School

In twenty-nine States and two Territories of the United States and in all the civilized countries of the world, with few exceptions, there are compulsory school laws. This country differs from the rest of the world in that it exacts a longer period for school attendance. The penalties for parents and guardians offer interesting contrasts. In Europe the fines are small, and those laws which inflict imprisonment generally confine it to a few days. In this country the fines are larger and the terms of possible imprisonment are longer. The Pennsylvania law is one of the mildest. For the first offense the maximum fine is $2, and upon each subsequent offense the maximum fine is $5. Nevada is the most stringent. For the first offense the fine is from $50 to $100, and for each subsequent offense from $100 to $200. New York has a maximum fine of $5 for the first offense, and a maximum of $50 for each subsequent offense, or imprisonment at the longest for thirty days. Connecticut has a different sort of law. It puts a fine on each week's neglect, the rate per week being a maximum of $5. In Indiana the parent or guardian may be imprisoned as long as ninety days. Ohio has a system of fines ranging from $5 to $20.

These penalties may sound harsh, but very rarely have they been imposed, although tens of thousands of children stay away from school.

Looking Out for Little Truants

An educated population means a safe country. So the problem is more than to provide facilities for education; it is to compel every new generation to study. The compulsory statutes did little good because they were not enforced, but that is easily explained. The sentiment of those whom they were intended to reach defeated them. But gradually better things have come and the lagging schoolboy has had to quicken his pace. Take Chicago, for instance. Illinois has had a compulsory school law for a number of years, but until a year ago it was much of a farce, especially in Chicago. The city was then thoroughly organized, truant officers were detailed for their work and many homes were visited. The consequence was that since September of last year 16,791 children were placed in the schools; 31,593 cases of non-attendance were investigated, and 692 children who could not attend school for lack of shoes and clothing were relieved. The law was not pushed except in flagrant instances, of which there were thirty-five, all of which were won by the department. The results were augmented by the establishment of schools in the big stores and elsewhere that wage-earning children might receive instruction each day. Nor did the work stop here. A 'bus line was established for hauling crippled children to school, and altogether these labors offered one of the best illustrations of the value of a compulsory law which this country has yet known.

Schools Cheaper Than Penitentiaries

In Philadelphia the law of compulsory attendance has been in operation for a little over two years, and under the superintendence of Dr. Edward Brooks, who is at the head of the public school system of the city, it has been developed in several interesting ways. Doctor Brooks has devoted his life to educational work, and his dictum is, "Schools are cheaper than penitentiaries, and we need special schools that bar the way to the penitentiaries." Under him the law has achieved these results: Thousands of children have been taken off the streets and placed in schools. Two special schools have been established for backward and diffident children; two classes of the school children of the city have been taken, and the public sentiment which was so hostile to the law has been won to its favor. The city was divided into thirty attendance districts with one officer assigned to each district, and nearly 35,000 visits were made to homes and to employers.

It was in the establishment of the special schools that the great work was done. There were many children whose education had been neglected and who could easily be placed in school, but who would have to be put in lower grades of the regular schools with children much younger than themselves. To meet this difficulty special ungraded schools were suggested. Another class was composed of children who were backward on account of their own or their parents' carelessness. To accommodate such children several cities have instituted special schools so that they may catch up.

How Slow Children are Pushed Ahead

There is still another class — the difficult children: those who have been dismissed as being incorrigible, but many of whom are not really vicious. It is with this class that excellent work has been done in Philadelphia. "Indeed," says Doctor Brooks, "one of these schools became so popular in the neighborhood that a number of boys attending the regular schools made application to be admitted into the special school."

Somewhat in the same line, but yet different, is the Parental School, which is designed for the thousands of children loose upon the streets, absolutely beyond the control of their parents, and growing up in ignorance and vice, who, unless removed from their surroundings and properly trained, will belong to the criminal class when they become men and women. For these children a school of detention is commended; a reform school, but a kindly institution that is well described by the term Parental School. Such a school has been supported in Boston and its work is being watched with interest. Brooklyn, too, has tried this, and satisfactory results are reported. Other cities are joining in line, and thus education is being carried not only with kindness but with authority to the neglected children, the habitual truants, the difficult children and the ignorant and vicious children of the cities.

Never was education so ambitious and so active in every direction as it is to-day.

Great credit is due to the men and women who are planning and toiling in behalf of public education. There is no class so unselfish in work or so zealous in the effort to secure larger and better results. They do not receive pay commensurate with the value of their labors and the time must come when their salaries will be largely increased, for in no department of the world's activity is a high grade of intelligence so underpaid. The school teacher is easily the most important individual of our country.

The School for the Four-Year-Old

There is a world of interest in the developments of the public education idea. It spans the whole life of the pupil from infancy to the time when he is old enough to vote. For instance, there are nearly two thousand kindergartens, with over one hundred thousand pupils, in this country. To St. Louis belongs the honor of being the first city to incorporate the kindergarten with its public school system. To-day nearly two hundred cities are conducting kindergartens which are absolutely free to the little boys and girls. Almost one-half the States have laws authorizing kindergartens connected with the public schools. The age at which the school tries to take the pupil is generally four, and it seeks to develop him until he is in the neighborhood of twenty. In the upper grades some of our high schools are equal to the smaller colleges, and in many instances the pupil may step from them into the leading universities. In a practical way there are manual training schools which are doing a vast amount of good, and cooking schools and others which are being increased all the time.

The importance of facilities for the broader and more special education of women is proven by the larger participation which they are taking in the activities of the times. Thirty years ago about one hundred occupations were open to women. To-day the number is over four hundred, and it is increasing all the time.

Training for the Trade of the World

Whatever our course may be as to world politics there is no doubt that we have entered into the markets of the world with a determination to conquer. In so doing we have made competition beyond anything we have hitherto known. We have the advantage in the quality of our products, for they are unquestionably the best, but in some other respects we are not so fortunate. For years commercial schools have been maintained in Germany and Great Britain, and the commercial advance of Germany has probably been due to the broad training which its commercial agents and missionaries have enjoyed. It has been only a year or two since the world awoke to the wonderful advance of Germany in the trade of the world, but there is no question about the fact. An interesting illustration of the difference between the men of the two countries when they meet on foreign soil to sell goods is given in a recent report of Mr. George W. Bell, our consul at Sydney.

"German methods are superior to ours," he says. "The American agent too often says, 'You want this; it is the latest and best thing out.' And while he is arguing his customer into a good humor, the German says, 'Tell me just what you want and you shall have it by the next steamer.' The American wants to satisfy himself. The German wants to satisfy his customer. The German is a merchant while too often the American is a commissioner. If the Germans would improve the qualities of their wares and give one-half as much attention to style as Americans do we should have to look out for our laurels."

This difference, of course, while important, is not at all fatal. It will be easier to train our men to sell goods by pleasing their customers than it will for Germany to equal the standards of American products. At the same time facts like these ought to give a great impetus to the founding of practical commercial schools in the United States. They would be a vast aid to the advancement and extension of the American trade.

In commercial schools we see the tendency of the world toward special training in every department of trade and commerce. In order to succeed nowadays quickest and best the young man or the young woman must have a special education in the direction of the particular line of business. To meet this the special schools are being organized in different parts of the world.

The Study of the Child

Just about twenty years ago one of the most serious psychologists and philosophers of the country, Dr. G. Stanley Hall, began to take scientific observations of child life, concentrating upon the study psychology, philosophy and ethics. Thus arose the child study movement. In the words of Doctor Hall, it is a work "for the study of the mind, not unlike that which Darwin did for the methods of Nature study, or that embryology has done for anatomy, viz.: cross-questioning the old methods of analysis, classification of the powers and activities of the adult consciousness by bringing to it a genetic method based, not upon abstractions like Spencer's, but on a copious collection of carefully made and critically sifted objective data."

Child study is not nearly so solemn as these heavy words would seem to indicate. It is watching the child's growth and asking him questions. Some of the information that was elicited from numerous investigations is most interesting. For instance, in Boston a large number of school children of tender age were asked about familiar things. Not one-half of them knew what a sheep was. Only one in ten knew growing wheat. Three-fourths of them did not know an oak tree. Nine out of ten did not know where their own ribs or hearts were. But the most astonishing thing was that in Boston seven out of ten did not know beans.

Over a thousand school children in Washington were examined, and there were many interesting conclusions. For instance, as the circumference of the head increases, mental ability increases; the heads of boys are larger than those of girls; bright boys are in general taller and heavier than are dull boys; girls are superior to boys in their studies; as the age increases, brightness decreases in most studies; defects of speech are much more frequent in boys than in girls; boys are more unruly and lazy than girls, and so on through the list.

The conclusion of the best students and examiners is a natural one, that the complete education of the child depends mainly upon getting it when young and in encouraging the developments along the best lines. After all, the lesson comes back to the home, and the parents who do not do their duty by their boys and girls not only rob them of valuable time and opportunity, but cheat the world of the intelligence and effectiveness which they would develop if properly guided and aided.

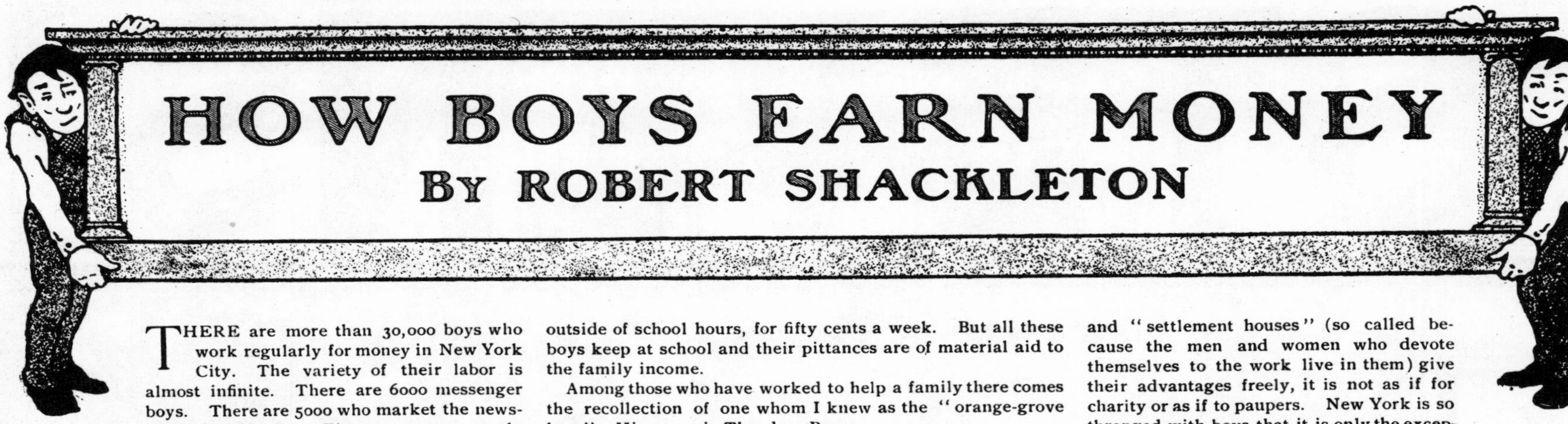

HOW BOYS EARN MONEY

By ROBERT SHACKLETON

THERE are more than 30,000 boys who work regularly for money in New York City. The variety of their labor is almost infinite. There are 6000 messenger boys. There are 5000 who market the newspapers of the city. There are 1500, mostly Italians, who shine the city's shoes, although Italian men are steadily pushing boys out of this employment. In spite of factory laws there are over 3000 boys under fifteen years of age in sweatshops, though this fact is better known to the law's evaders than to the official inspectors.

Of the 30,000 youthful workers it must necessarily be that the majority toil at dull daily routine, but there are also a host of individual cases of special ability and resourcefulness.

Just before sunrise, one day last winter, a wet and heavy snow began to fall. The sidewalks were soon covered. An army of men were quickly engaged in clearing off the snow, for otherwise the business of the city would be congested. It was the opportunity for which Larry Scott, a tenement boy of sixteen, had been waiting. He hastily gathered together a half-dozen boys of his immediate neighborhood with whom a previous arrangement had been made, and the little squad hurried off under his command.

A boy of less confidence than Larry would have supposed that, under the conditions of life in New York, each shop would have men ready to shovel snow and every apartment-house its janitor, but Larry knew that there were plenty of chances. A natural-born leader, his little company followed him devotedly; with snap and a pleasing briskness, he made the bargains for the squad, and soon he had all of them at work.

The snow continued. New cleanings were necessary. All forenoon the snow fell. Once in a while, when the six were busy, Larry used a shovel himself, and worked harder and faster than any of the others, showing that he was ready to use his hands as well as his head. When the snow ceased and there was no more cleaning to do he found that his morning's work, including his own shoveling and what was left after paying the other boys, had cleared him almost three dollars—a good sum for a forenoon for a boy of sixteen.

That was not the first day that Larry had worked. In fact, he had worked at one thing or another, in the intervals of schooling, ever since he could remember, and at the time of the snowstorm he happened to be a "tail-end boy" temporarily out of a job.

Now, a "tail-end boy" is not one who is behind, except in a certain limited and literal sense. A "tail-end boy" is an assistant on the big delivery wagons and he receives his designation from the part of the wagon where he sits. The wages are not high. Most boys receive no more than two dollars and fifty cents or three dollars a week. Larry received four dollars, for he was an exceptional boy.

Through that morning's work in the snow Larry received a good start, for one who noticed his clever scheme interested himself in the lad and secured him a position in which his resourcefulness and managerial capacity will steadily advance him.

But the boy who wants to earn money in New York must not look for a snowstorm. There are more boys than work. Many cannot find work at all. A boy must train his mind, he must cultivate skill, he must get education, he must have perseverance, he must be quick to use brain or hands at whatever opportunity offers. He must make opportunities. Larry would have won in some other way if the snow had not given him a chance.

Work Out of School Hours

IT IS well to realize what small wages many boys receive, and especially such as attend the day schools and work after school hours.

One boy washes bottles and pastes labels in a drug store every afternoon from three to six for one dollar a week. Another, who clerks at a street stand every afternoon and during all of Saturday, is paid seventy cents when Saturday night comes. Tony Saldi, thirteen years old, delivers bread for a bakery for two hours every day before school begins and for several hours after school is over. His work is among the poorest class of tenements, where it is necessary to climb numberless stairs every day. He is paid one dollar and fifty cents a week. There are boys who work in cigarette factories, outside of school hours, for fifty cents a week. But all these boys keep at school and their pittances are of material aid to the family income.

Among those who have worked to help a family there comes the recollection of one whom I knew as the "orange-grove boy." His name is Theodore Barnes.

He was sixteen years old. With a widowed mother and a younger brother he had gone from New York to Florida, where the family put all their capital into an orange grove and awaited results. The first result was a good crop. The second was a frost so destructive that the crop was utterly ruined and every tree had to be chopped back to the roots. The family faced ruin.

How Theodore Barnes Won Out

THEN it was that Theodore displayed his pluck. Leaving his mother and brother in Florida to care for the grove he returned to New York. He secured a place as delivery boy for a laundry. He worked early and late. Having the reponsibility of money as well as packages, and also the care of a horse, he earned five dollars a week. He asked his employers how much he could have as commissions for new customers. "Fifteen cents apiece," was the careless reply. They had had experience with other boys and did not expect very many customers from that source. But they did not know Theodore. He set himself to win customers, and it was astonishing to see how many packages from new households he turned in every week.

He lived with extremest economy. At the end of the first year his wages were increased a dollar a week. Knowing New York, he was able to pick up money now and then from other sources. Every week he sent money to those in Florida, and with this, and some chickens and vegetables that they raised, the two who were there were able to live along and to tend the orange trees.

It was a three years' task, for it took that long for the frosted trees to bear again, and at the end of that time Theodore went back victorious, earning his way as far as Jekyll Island by caring for a horse in a box car. He had saved the family fortunes.

But it is not every one who is so situated as to earn as much money as did the "orange-grove boy." "Basting-pullers," for example, rarely earn two dollars a week, and many earn no more than one dollar. A vast number of little chaps from nine to fifteen years of age work eleven hours a day at the wearisome and monotonous task of pulling basting threads from cloaks and coats. This is in defiance of factory laws, but the East Side laughs at inspectors who cannot speak the language of the people whose shops they inspect, and it is easy to pass warnings to get little boys out of sight under the very nose of the official. A "basting-puller" must be able to pull the bastings from one hundred and twenty coats a day. The air is thick-laden with the smell that wool gives out under a hot iron; there is usually little light, because the older workers monopolize the best places; the boys look forward to the time when they, too, can bend their shoulders over the heavy, clattering sewing-machines. Few of these workers reach the age of fifty and a sweatshop coatmaker of sixty is unknown. Boys are driven into this hard and wretchedly-paid work by the cupidity or poverty of their parents, and in most cases it is poverty. When one knows of conditions such as these he ceases to wonder at cases of stunted growth and at boy faces that are over-old.

In the poor districts of the East Side the children of eight families out of every ten go to work at the earliest age they can, or as early as the law can be evaded to allow.

On the streets of these districts; those crowded streets whose pavements are the gathering places of the people; the boys who work can readily be distinguished from the few who do not, for the responsibilities of wage-earning and the stress of long hours have given their faces a curious touch of earnestness which differentiates them from the natural "boy."

A boy who has not the advantage of good connections and and education should, if possible, ally himself with some "settlement house," or with one of the boys' clubs, or with one of the associations that interest themselves in the welfare of youth. There are many such philanthropies, and a boy not only obtains educational and training advantages during certain hours of the day or evening, but if he shows himself bright and capable he stands a far better chance of obtaining profitable employment. At the same time, too, his feeling of independence is maintained, for though these associations and "settlement houses" (so called because the men and women who devote themselves to the work live in them) give their advantages freely, it is not as if for charity or as if to paupers. New York is so thronged with boys that it is only the exceptionally able or the exceptionally fortunate who win more than small returns. New York is a city to which boys ought never to come from other parts of the country on the mere chance of finding something to do. This warning cannot be too strongly put. It is time enough to face New York when one has a capital of experience and acquaintance and money. But for the boys who live here and who must look for a livelihood here, the problem should be faced cheerfully and with the determination to succeed.

A boy of fifteen, of good character and with some recommendation or introduction, can be reasonably sure of earning three dollars a week. There are boys of that age who earn more, especially those who are messengers or office boys, but none can be sure of doing so. And three dollars a week is not a temptingly large amount if a boy must earn his own living. For steady workers, steady though small advances may be depended upon.

Of course, though, all questions of wages are relative. A bright Italian boy, sixteen years old, who has been in the United States less than four years but who has already learned to speak the language well, said to me:

"I work in a factory, making boxes. I work ten hours each day, and get three dollars and twenty cents a week. In Sicily, in a week, I might not earn more than five cents."

Children Who Support Their Parents

A CURIOUS feature of New York life is that of the boys who work to support parents whose earning power is small through inability to speak our language.

Children acquire a language with ease, whereas to adults it is a difficult and sometimes impossible task. The result is that there are a great number of foreign-born parents in New York who can speak little or no English but whose children, even though foreign-born, speak it fluently. Many cases of devotion can be found among this class.

John Lero, who earns five dollars a week in a factory where buttons of pearl, bone and vegetable ivory are made, was offered an attractive situation at a home in the country, but though he would there have good clothes, good food and good opportunities, there was to be less actual money, and he declined the chance.

The man who offered it was much surprised, for he had taken an interest in the lad and wished to better his condition. "Why won't you come?" he said.

"Because my father would starve," was the quiet reply. The father was a Greek who, barred from profitable employment by lack of knowledge of English, was forced to depend on his son, and young Lero, like other boys who are thus wage-earners for their elders, accepted the situation quite as a matter of course and a simple duty.

Many boys are fascinated by occupations which not only give uniforms or livery but which seem to have a certain air of picturesqueness. The "tiger," for example, is envied of many—the jaunty little chap, all high hat and fine coat and long boots and bright buttons, who, high-perched, has the same air of nothing-to-do as has the lower-seated occupant of the carriage. The boy who gets such a place is apt to receive good wages in addition to tips proportioned to his ability to please; but even the most fortunately-situated "tiger" cannot hope to retain his place forever, because he cannot forever remain a boy.

"Buttons" is constantly becoming a figure of more and more importance among New York boys. His little bench is in the hallway of every apartment-house of the better class; he opens the door of numberless doctors' offices; he receives the clients of art dealers and milliners; he is in evidence at the door of many a smart shop. Though his pay may not be large he has numerous opportunities of making friends among the class who employ office assistants, and he is sure to be well-remembered at Christmas.

"Front," in hotels, is usually bright-witted, and if he possesses the happy manner which, when he shows a room, makes the guest overlook the fact that it is next to the elevator and looks into a court, he has in him the essential qualities. His place permits of advancement through various grades of checker and steward to the august glory of hotel clerk.

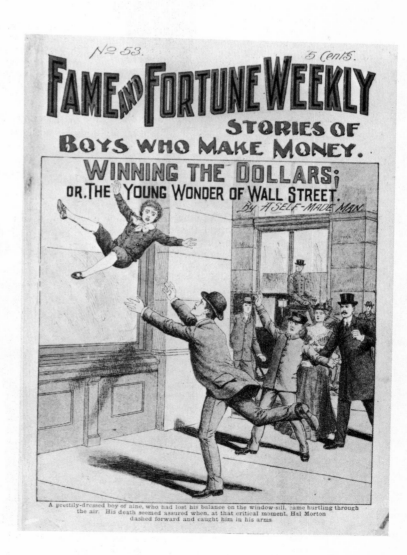

Heavy Weight Blue Cheviot Vestee Suit, $2.50.

This material is strictly all wool and is always popular as a dressy and warm suit and of exceptional good value. The coat is cut in the latest round cut sack style for little men, vest double breasted of same material and provided with a red flannel dickey with silk monogram worked in center. Lapels of coat are faced with satin. Pants are made with double seat and knees. The suit is well trimmed and finished throughout. We know that you cannot buy as good a suit at retail at anything like the price.

No. 40T854 Price for boys' vestee suit. ages 3 to 8 years... ..$2.50

Fancy Dark Mixed Cheviot Norfolk Suit, $2.50.

A handsome mixture of all wool material in blue, green and olive, made in Norfolk jacket and pants style as shown in illustration. This style has become very popular and we doubt if an all wool suit has ever been offered in this style at our price. The suit consists of two pieces, a jacket and pants. The jacket is cut with square corners, two box plaits down front and one in back, and has a belt of same material attached. Pants are made in our usual substantial manner with taped and double sewed crotch and double seat and knees.

No. 40T856 Price for boys' Norfolk jacket and pants, ages 4 to 10 years (no larger or smaller sizes)..........$2.50

Fancy All Wool Cheviot Vestee Suit, $2.75.

We especially recommend this number as an excellent wearing, medium colored suit, in heavy weight material. A suit which is bound to give satisfaction in every respect and which is certainly a great bargain at our price. The coat is made in the fashionable Kitchener yoke style, with a double breasted vest and shield with fancy embroidered emblem in center. Pants have double knees and seat, and the whole suit is thoroughly well lined and trimmed. The color of the goods is a bluish gray, green and olive mixture in a pinhead effect, relieved by an overplaid of red.

No. 40T858 Price for boys' vestee suit,

ages 3 to 8 years $2.75

Jacob Wendell & Co.'s Fancy Cassimere Vestee Suit, $2.75.

Another very pretty pattern which cannot fail to please you. It is a mixture of green and blue, very dark, and has a hairline overplaid in dark maroon. We have made this suit up in a very pretty style with a plaited front, double stitched all round, double breasted vest with a red flannel dickey which has a silk emblem embroidered in the center. It certainly makes a very handsome garment for the little fellows. The pants are made with closed front, have double knees and seat and a steel buckle at knee.

No. 40T860 Price for boys' vestee suit, ages 3 to 8 years....$2.75

Fancy Light Colored Vestee Suit, $3.00.

This is a heavy weight very natty pattern in a mixture of light gray, blue and green, relieved by single threads of orange about one inch apart. One of the prettiest combinations of colors imaginable and strictly pure wool and would be considered cheap at nearly double our price. The suit is made in the latest round cut sack style, lapels faced with gray satin, single breasted vest with a fancy embroidered detachable dickey. Pants are double sewed throughout and have two side and one hip pocket.

No. 40T862 Price for boys' vestee suit, ages 3 to 8 years...............$3.00

Fancy Kitchener Yoke Norfolk Jacket and Pants, $3.50.

A very handsome scotch cheviot in a brown and olive mixture, relieved by single threads of green and red. An ideal pattern for a Norfolk suit. The coat is made exactly as shown by opposite illustration with the popular Kitchener yoke effect, two box plaits down front and one in the back and a belt of same material. If you fancy this style of garment you will never be able to find a prettier suit and your boy will certainly be proud of it. The pants are made with double knees and seat, double sewed and taped crotch and two side and one hip pocket.

No. 40T864 Price for boys' Norfolk jacket and pants, ages 4 to 10 years $3.50

Blue Tricot Vestee Suit, $4.00.

This all wool, heavy weight navy blue tricot is a very desirable material for little boys' vestee suits and our designer has certainly produced a beautiful garment. Coat is made with round corners, large silk faced lapels and trimmed with cluster and loops in place of buttons. The vest is made of blue velvet with a double row of white ivory buttons and with a detachable white flannel dickey with a handsome embroidered silk emblem in center. Pants have two white ivory buttons and a fancy steel buckle at knee.

No. 40T866 Price for boys' vestee suit, ages 3 to 8 years......$4.00

All Wool, Fancy Green Mixed Vestee Suit, $4.50.

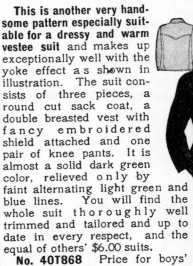

This is another very handsome pattern especially suitable for a dressy and warm vestee suit and makes up exceptionally well with the yoke effect as shown in illustration. The suit consists of three pieces, a round cut sack coat, a double breasted vest with fancy embroidered shield attached and one pair of knee pants. It is almost a solid dark green color, relieved only by faint alternating light green and blue lines. You will find the whole suit thoroughly well trimmed and tailored and up to date in every respect, and the equal of others' $6.00 suits.

No. 40T868 Price for boys' vestee suit, ages 3 to 8 years (no smaller or larger sizes)...................$4.50

Fancy Worsted Vestee Suit, $4.50.

Strictly all wool pure worsted goods warranted to wear and always keep its color, one of the nicest patterns we have ever been able to secure and equal, if not superior, to the best vestee suit that can be bought anywhere. It is an indistinct small check pattern in dark brown and olive, occasionally relieved by dotted green lines. If your boy needs a very dressy Sunday suit we would recommend this number. The coat is made in round cut sack style of the latest pattern, double stitched and elegantly lined. Vest is cut double breasted without collar, and has a handsome embroidered dickey attached. Pants are double sewed throughout, have double seat and double knees and closed front.

No. 40T870 Price for boys' vestee suit, ages 3 to 8 years.....................$4.50

Clothes for the Girl of Awkward Age

By Grace Margaret Gould
Illustrations by Anna May Cooper

No. 202—ALBERTINE SHIRT-WAIST

No. 201—LE ROY COAT

THE most important dress problem for mothers to solve is how to fittingly gown their daughters during what is usually termed the "awkward age." The wise mother knows that dress can, and should, compensate for the defects of immaturity. It should, however, do more than this. It should inculcate a graceful carriage and a personal style which would be both permanent and characteristic. On this page will be found not only the latest fashions for girls from twelve to eighteen, but styles which have been carefully selected to hide the defects and bring out the good points of a young girl's undeveloped figure.

No. 201—Le Roy Coat

This smart-looking box-coat is good style for a girl from twelve to sixteen. It is made with a cape trimmed with a stitched cloth strap over each shoulder. The mannish little turn-over collar and the cuffs are of velvet, while rows of stitching are used as the trimming. Made of tan-colored fine melton cloth, with dark brown velvet collar and cuffs, this coat would be a decidedly smart-looking little garment, and could be used for a best coat with good reason. For every-day wear it might be made of dark blue rough tweed, with the velvet the same shade, but the lining should be of some pretty, gay-looking Tartan plaid silk.

No. 202—Albertine Shirt-Waist

Here is a shirt-waist sure to be in demand, as it is something new, and that is what every girl is looking for these days. It is a shirt-waist of cotton vesting, which is the material that is most fashionable this year for the making of the winter shirt-waists. This model is made with four box-plaits in front, caught down with straps. The plaits are let out just above the bust to give a becoming fullness to the waist in front. The sleeve is a full bishop with a very deep tight-fitting cuff. The straps should also be of the vesting, and are most effective when matching in color the dot or the design in the material of the waist. The way the necktie is held under the two straps which are fastened at the front of the waist is a novel and pretty fashion for a girl to copy. This model can also be used for a silk waist, with straps and buttons of velvet, and the necktie of chiffon. The pattern for the Albertine shirt-waist is cut in 14, 16 and 18 year sizes.

No. 203—Mae Waist
No. 204—Minturn Skirt

For a dancing-school or a party dress nothing could be prettier or more simple than this girlish frock. It should be made of some dainty soft material like Liberty gauze, which though sheer has

No. 203—MAE WAIST
No. 204—MINTURN SKIRT

tion tucked at the sides, the fine tucks extending around the back, where the skirt is finished with an inverted plait at each side of the center back. The pattern for the Mae waist is cut in 12, 14 and 16 year sizes. The pattern for the Minturn skirt is also cut in 12, 14 and 16 year sizes.

No. 205—Sibyl Waist
No. 206—Lansing Skirt

This stylish every-day dress is made of dark blue short-haired zibeline. The waist has a group of plaits back and front reaching from the shoulder-seam to the waist. The bishop-sleeve is also made with plaits, which are stitched down from the shoulder to the cuff. The waist is made with a round, slightly low-cut neck to show a finely plaited deep collar of some sheer material like nainsook or fine grass-cloth. The waist buttons down the front. The skirt is an exceedingly stylish model, and one which can also satisfactorily serve duty as a separate skirt to be worn with shirt-waists.

No. 205—SIBYL WAIST
No. 206—LANSING SKIRT

a certain good reputation for durability; or of Clair de Lune, which is like a satin crêpe, or in fact any of the new crêpes, which are known by the names of Crêpe Egeria, Crêpe Meteor or Crêpe Mignon. The feature of the Mae waist, with its fine tucks and wide, straight-around belt, is the pretty, quaint way it is cut at the neck. The top of the three-quarter sleeve is cut out in a deep V to show the shoulder and also to give the fashionable sloping 1830 effect. The neck of the waist back and front, as well as the V of the sleeve, is outlined with band lace, and three narrow little straps of black velvet ribbon tie in bows at the shoulder, and assist in holding the waist in place. The fine tucks are let out to form a little fullness both for the front and back of the waist. The sleeve is an exceptionally graceful model, with its fine tucks at the top, and its full puff which droops below the elbow. It is finished with a narrow band of lace matching that used on the waist and the skirt. The tunic skirt has its upper por-

No. 207—MORRISON NORFOLK JACKET
No. 208—JANSEN SKIRT

9 The College Man

College for the class of 1905 was not much like college today. In those days the student body was a docile one, seemingly satisfied both with college administrations and with the Establishment in general. If there were unhappy students, there was certainly no hint of public complaint, much less demonstrations or riots. The average college student of the early 1900's was not greatly interested in reforming the world; he appears to have been rather crassly motivated, thinking of his education in terms of how much money it might get him. This is perfectly understandable, for as the introduction to Section 2, "The Breadwinner," has already discussed, this was a period when money was glorified.

The student of the time was also very much of a rah-rah boy. This was hardly unique to his period, but he seemed to bring it to a little finer frenzy and to surround it with more of a mystique; during these years the Frank Merriwell series and *Stover at Yale* beguiled millions of young readers.

Before the Revolution the leading families of the Colonies had sent their sons to college in the firm conviction that an education was necessary to a complete man. Yet more than a century and a quarter later the intellectual climate in America had declined so much that our journals were discussing whether it was even worthwhile for a boy—or girl—to go to college. When *The Saturday Evening Post* prevailed upon former President Grover Cleveland to write an article (the first he had ever written) on college education, the subject agreed on was not the overall value of an education, but the completely blunt "Does a College Education Pay?" It is pleasant to discover that President Cleveland, though self-educated and ignorant of the inside of colleges, makes the point that wealth is not the only measure of success and that "many a college-bred man labors in the field of usefulness without either wealth or honors. . . ." However, that was not the universal point of view at the time.

The reasons that college was held in such low esteem at the turn of the century had their roots deep in American history. It is enough to note that after the Civil War, and especially during the corrupt Grant administration, the obsession with money became crass and absorbing, and there was no longer any morality limiting the way money was acquired. There were big fortunes to be made by tricky deals in Western railroads, by cornering the gold market, by illegal operations in public lands, by buying senators and congressmen, by watering the stocks of a corporation—

for a thoroughly unscrupulous and acquisitive man the avenues to profit were limited only by his ingenuity.

This moral climate of predatoriness and lax ethics pretty much permeated business and industry at the turn of the century. While some of the pieces in the next few pages were being written, Ida Tarbell was preparing her famous exposé of the business practices of the Standard Oil Company, other muckrakers were exposing ruthless practices by other enterprises, and President Theodore Roosevelt was on the eve of his career of trustbusting. The tradition of the time was that the spoils went to the hard-driving, self-made man. Aggressive young men were eager to get into the hurly-burly as soon as possible and make their own marks. And the successful men they observed and took as models seemed living proof that a college education was a waste of time.

Against this background some of the turn-of-the-century opinions about college are easier to understand. Thus we find Charles M. Schwab, fresh from taking a principal part in forming the United States Steel Corporation, saying that a college education is a disadvantage to a businessman. On the other hand, another great steel man, Andrew Carnegie, thought highly of education and gave millions so that poor boys could have the education he had been denied. Charlie Schwab was a self-made man and so was Carnegie; yet while one despised higher education, the other endowed it. The difference may be that Schwab had been born and raised in the United States, where the ideal of the do-it-yourself frontiersman was still very much alive, while Carnegie had spent his formative years in Scotland, where education was something to be cherished.

The same bias against college education comes through strong in the article "Should Railroad Men Be College Men?" The author, though the president of a university and a college, does not seem to have very strong convictions himself; he devotes only two sentences to a weak statement of principles: "I suppose that in all the current discussion regarding the function of the college no one questions but that a college does aid one in becoming a gentleman. I suppose, also, that usually it is granted that a college education does aid one in becoming an efficient member of society." This seems a rather poor recommendation for higher education, especially from a college president, but undoubtedly college presidents too were on the defensive in the money-oriented society of the early 1900's.

One of the railroad officials interviewed by the good Dr. Thwing, author of the article, was blunt in saying that a college education would be a detriment to the aspiring railroad magnate because he would lose four precious years in getting started in his field. Several others thought an education would not hurt him if he was willing to work hard to catch up with the man who had not paused to go to college. And two or three men of advanced ideas believed that some higher education would be a definite advantage. But none considered it necessary.

If there was doubt about the value of college for men, it was hardly worth mentioning where women were concerned. The brief editorial pieces on the subject on the following pages are all that were turned up by a reasonably assiduous search. However, it is encouraging that even then enlightened men were saying, "Send your daughter to college."

One searches in vain for mention of scholarship or research or the love of learning. However, one can infer that a college education must have meant a great deal to some young men. "Through Harvard on Fifty Cents" tells of some of the scrounging and scrimping and ingenuity that put one penniless student through college. Unhappily, there is no clue as to why he wanted an education so badly. To be a philosopher? A writer? A railroad man? But he could be a railroad man without a higher education. Perhaps the love of learning was deeper and stronger then than the outward evidence would lead us to believe; perhaps the mass circulation magazines were saying only what they thought their readers wanted to hear.

The articles on college athletics need no exegesis; the same arguments, with various shifts in emphasis, have gone on ever since and will undoubtedly continue. And inevitably an article by Old Grad turns up, this one on hazing. He is, of course, in favor of it, because he went through it—it will make a better man of you, my boy, and you will be glad afterward. And like all Old Grads, he forgets the exact point of his story and relates incidents in which the hazed make fools of the hazers. If the article proves anything, it is merely that Old Grads should not sell stories to magazines.

Does a College Education Pay

By
Grover Cleveland

THOSE who antagonize collegiate education are always with us; and we often hear them inveighing, with differing degrees of emphasis, against the expenditure of time, money and effort which such an education exacts. We ought not to be surprised at the volume of these attacks when we recall the different sorts of people enrolled in the opposition; nor should we be astonished at the pertinacity of the onslaught when we consider how naturally self-conscious inferiority derives satisfaction from disparaging assaults of this nature. It is not difficult to classify the various forces engaged in these attacks; and if we examine their positions and offensive operations, we shall be entirely satisfied that the high point of vantage occupied by our universities and colleges is, or at least ought to be, absolutely impregnable.

As we look over the field, we first discover, standing on open and exposed ground, a collection of the enemy, who have a kind of sullen, sodden hatred of all education above the lowest and most rudimentary variety. They are tough, awkward and undisciplined fighters, always ready to make an assault, which can by no possibility injure any one but themselves. These we may properly disregard, with the wish that an intelligent environment may improve their condition.

The Peculiar Logic of Certain Self-Made Men

We find others among the antagonists of collegiate training who are recruited from the body of our so-called self-made men. These are posted behind the infirm defense of the things they have achieved without the aid of a liberal education; and they confuse the contention by much noise and thick clouds of smoke. They maintain a steadfast complacency among themselves by recounting the difficulties and trials they have overcome; while by some unaccountable but not uncommon mental process, or want of process, they connect in the relation of cause and effect their lack of education with their success. These are very often useful, active men in the business world, whose general recognition of duty as citizens and neighbors, as well as their frequent manifestations of benevolence and generosity in certain directions, must be cheerfully conceded.

They are, however, afflicted with two unfortunate difficulties which they seem unable to overcome, and which detract from their completeness of character and prevent their reaching the highest grade of liberal thought. One of these is the binding, fettering imagination that their own success indicates that the slight education they have been able to gather, and which has answered their needs, must be sufficient to compass success in all other cases. Their second difficulty is so intimately related to the first that it might be treated as a branch of it. It consists in their failure to recognize the extent of the revolution in the conditions of success that has taken place since they struggled and conquered. They seem to be strangely slow in comprehending how fast the world moves, and how certainly all who strive for rewards must move with it, or be left high and dry on the shoals of failure and disappointment. It certainly should not escape their notice that the methods profitably employed in every enterprise and occupation have so changed within the last fifty years that a necessity has arisen for an advanced grade of intelligence and education in the use of these methods; and that as this necessity has been supplied, a new competition has been created which easily distances the young man who is no better equipped for the race than our self-satisfied, self-made man. Therefore, while the perseverance, industry and thrift which entered into their early struggles can never become obsolete, and as factors of success can never be abandoned, it will hardly do for them to say that, notwithstanding new methods and new activities, it is undesirable to supplement these traits by the best attainable education. There are Indians in our Western country who, though surrounded by civilization, still wear the blankets and feathers to which they were long ago accustomed, and hold in utter contempt all observance of present-day customs; but while they wander about, still sullenly proud of their blankets and feathers and lead lives of vagabondage, younger men are making railroads through their lands and building houses which they might have built and occupied.

Our criticism of those who have joined the opponents of liberal education, from the large mass of our successful fellow-citizens who have lacked its advantages, should not, however, prevent our acknowledging cheerfully and heartily the different inclination of those who, though belonging to that general class, do not share the notions we deprecate. These are they who, in taking stock of their achievements and successes, plainly see in their lack of education a lack of opportunity, and regretfully place in the column of loss the diminution this deficiency has caused in the things they might otherwise have accomplished for themselves and for others. This appreciation of lost opportunity, accompanied as it must be by a correct apprehension of the changed conditions in the struggle of life, insures the enlistment of these candid and thoughtful men on the side of the best education. Consequently their sons are found among the students in our universities and colleges, and their influence and aid are frequently forthcoming in efforts to enlarge the opportunities of these institutions.

Another contingent arrayed against college education is made up of those who suppose they are in the occupation of strong ground when they point out the numerous failures in life among college graduates, and the slight impress often made in ordinary affairs by of them as may be considered to a greater or less de successful.

Differing Standards of Success

Of course the arguments with which their opponents make their attack are neither entirely just nor fair. In the first place we can confidently claim that whatever may be included in their conception of failures, their proportion among graduates of our universities and colleges is certainly less than among the aggregate of non-graduates. Beyond this, we are entitled to a distinct definition of the words *failure* and *success;* and when we are told that failure is indicated by the lack of wealth or honors, and that their acquirement proves success, it is quite pertinent for us to reply that the rewards of liberal education are not thus limited. Many a college-bred man labors in the field of usefulness without either wealth or honors, and frequently with but scant recognition of any kind, and yet achieves successes which, unseen and unknown by the sordid and cynical, will bloom in the hearts and minds of men longer than the prizes of wealth or honors can endure.

We must remember, however, that it is never wise to underrate our adversary's position; and that a dogged, wholesale denial of all truth or merit in an opponent's argument usually fails to meet the needs of discussion. Let it be admitted, then, that there are absolute and properly defined failures among university and college graduates; and let it be further admitted that, after making allowance for those foredoomed by their inherent slothfulness and mental deficiencies, these failures are more numerous than they ought to be. What is the result? Are we thus driven to the confession that a thorough course of college training is unprofitable? It is only necessary for us to point to its triumphs and achievements, plainly seen on every side and in every walk of life, to avoid such a confession. The limit of all needful concession is reached when these failures are admitted, with the qualifying suggestion that our universities and colleges cannot attempt to supply the requisites of success which should result from judicious home training, or which can only be cultivated and developed by the student himself.

Parents should never send their sons to college simply for the purpose of educational ornamentation. The fact that parents have the fate of a son largely in their keeping should not only enlist their parental love and pride, but should, at the same

MR. CLEVELAND IN HIS LIBRARY AT PRINCETON

COPYRIGHT, 1900, BY THE CURTIS PUBLISHING COMPANY.

time, stimulate their parental judgment. Furthermore, they should be constantly mindful that they have in charge not only a son, but an uncompleted man, who is soon to become their contribution to the manhood of the world. They therefore owe a dual duty, which demands on the one hand that the education of the son be undertaken as a help to his success in life, and on the other that this education shall promise for the maturing man the equipment necessary to insure his value as an addition to civilized humanity. Before he leaves home to enter upon his student life his sympathy with these purposes should be fully aroused, and he should be impressed with the importance of keeping them steadily in view. He should also take with him to his new surroundings a love of truth and honor, a cheerful, manly disposition and truly democratic inclinations. With these his collegiate advent must be auspicious, and his future life well guarded against failure. Lacking these, his way is made immensely more difficult and uncertain.

But whether well or ill accoutred, and without ignoring the influences for good that meet the student at the threshold of every well-regulated university or college, it is still true in a general sense that he himself must remain the responsible factor in the success or failure that waits upon the close of his collegiate career. As we are attempting to account for failures after graduation, we must assume a class standing sufficiently satisfactory to earn a degree. Therefore, we have no reference to deficiencies in studies when we assert that such failures may be charged, with considerable certainty, to stumbling-blocks in the student's path that he might have avoided, and to the neglect of certain aids incident to his college life which he ought to have appreciated and cultivated.

Two Extremes to be Avoided

There is such a thing as a sour and morose pursuit of study which leads to a sour and unsympathetic temper. This threatens unfitness for a profitable association with the outside world which is a handicap in dealing with every-day affairs. An opposite extreme is reached by a superficial and light-headed skimming of studies, which leaves in the mind just enough to meet the requirements of recitation and examination. This practice brings about self-deception and so unsubstantial an acquaintance with the subjects studied as to be almost useless. A loose habit of thought and conduct is also thus contracted, which must certainly stand in the way of success.

Another and constant source of some of the difficulties that lessen the graduate's chances of success remains to be mentioned. It may properly be called the introversion of college life. This term is here used to define a very natural inclination among collegians not only to look upon their student association as an independent world, but to permit it to completely encompass and limit their interests, their thoughts, their ambitions, their social relations, and nearly all things that seem to them worth having.

It would be a sad and brutal decree that unreservedly condemned a condition that lends to a college community its cheerfulness and happiness. The obliteration of a fervid attachment on the part of students for this world of theirs, and the destruction of the enthusiasm which its pleasures and incidents arouse, would usher in a time when the pursuit of higher education would be a forbidding and cheerless task. It is only a too profound and exclusive introversion that we deprecate; and it is only a wholesome dilution of college-world devotion, and its admixture with an interest in the affairs of the greater outside world, that, for the sake of the student's future success, we advocate.

It will not be denied that a constant and substantially unbroken confinement of our students in their thoughts and associations to the things that environ them, during their years of college study, produces a sentiment of separateness, which by a natural process is apt to lead, first to ignorance of movements and currents beyond their circle, next to a feeling of self-satisfied superiority, and frequently, at last, to a supercilious distrust of the intelligence of all who are not members of their order.

These conditions may not be general, nor even usual; but if they exist at all, and if in any number of cases, however small, they present obstacles to success, they are worthy of attention and correction.

When it is recalled that a college course is undertaken as a preparation for a prosperous career, and to fit the student to meet the requirements of manhood and citizenship, it cannot be denied for a moment that ignorance of the situation which awaits the graduate in the world's great field is an obstacle in his path; and inasmuch as his career must be wrought out, and the obligations of manhood and citizenship must be discharged in contact and coöperation with his fellow-men of every degree, it is worse than folly to say that any real or even suspected assumption of arrogant superiority does not interfere with his success.

The mention that has been made of some of the causes of the failures of college-bred men, which constitute the stock in argument of certain opponents of higher education, suggest natural and easily applied remedies.

Let the students in our colleges go beyond their studies and their sports, and with as much zeal and industry as they devote to either of these things, let them cultivate an interest in all that stirs and influences the great outside world, into whose strifes and struggles they must soon enter.

COPYRIGHT 1900 BY THE CURTIS PUBLISHING COMPANY

PHOTOGRAPHED ESPECIALLY FOR THE SATURDAY EVENING POST

MR. CLEVELAND ON THE VERANDA OF HIS HOUSE AT PRINCETON

And since no more congenial soil can be found for the cultivation of a truly democratic spirit than our well-organized and conducted universities and colleges, let their students rid themselves of the notion that this spirit can safely be limited to their college world and its especial conditions. Let them rather cherish it as a lasting possession, which in the larger world lying beyond college pursuits and associations will constitute a ready help in every relation of life and an unfailing safeguard against self-pride and arrogant behavior.

What, then, is the conclusion of the matter? Shall the value of a college education be impeached because a measure of success may be attained without it, or because there are failures among those who have had the advantage of such an education? Shall these things prevail against the leadership which the graduates of our universities and colleges have maintained in all things that elevate and improve mankind? This would be strangely irrational.

While the training of the mental powers paves the way to success in every occupation; as long as pioneer work is needed in every extension of our progress and civilization; as long as our national safety rests upon the intelligence of our people; and as long as we require in our public service pure patriotism, obedience to quickened conscience and disinterested discharge of duty, a college education will pay.

The College Man's Advantage in the Coming Century

By David Starr Jordan

PRESIDENT OF LELAND STANFORD, JR., UNIVERSITY

THE best time to be a boy the world has ever known is just this time — just at the outstart of a great, vigorous, forceful, wisdom-loving century. And just the best place to be a boy is right here in the United States, the one part of the earth where a boy can grow up with a reasonable chance of making the most of himself. "America means opportunity," says Emerson, and to the right kind of a boy this is the main thing.

Now, to the right kind of a boy, a boy with something in him, the best advice that anybody can give is summed up in these two sentences: Keep yourself clean. Go to college.

As to the first, cleanliness is strength. The various forms of evil mostly show themselves as short-cuts to happiness. Gambling and stealing are short-cuts to wealth. But they do not often lead thither and, when they do, wealth does not bring happiness. You cannot have a really good time in life unless you earn it, unless you deserve it. So with immorality and intemperance in all their various forms. They promise pleasure; they do not bring happiness. A spurious pleasure is not permanent; it leaves "a dark brown taste in the mouth," "it is different in the morning." Real happiness makes room for more happiness. The joy of action, the beauties of Nature, the pleasure of accomplishment, the charm of congenial society, the strength of being clean — all these delights grow on us with our enjoyment of them. They take nothing away, but leave us with still greater strength.

"We may," says President Ripley, of the Santa Fé Railroad, speaking of the demands of "a soulless corporation" on its employees, "we may be perfectly sure that the man who walks with truthfulness, sobriety and morality, who is what the world calls straight, and who can look everybody in the eye, will command the respect of his neighbors and himself, and will be infinitely happier in the world than the man who does not."

To go to college is to seek the training which will fit for the duties of life. It should be to find the secret of power. A man may be educated, and well educated, without darkening the college doors. But he is educated in the longest and slowest way. He has lost valuable time and wasted much effort.

A college is a device to bring students together that they may educate each other and that older and wiser students may educate them. "It brings," says Emerson, "every ray of genius to its hospitable halls, that their combined influence may strike the heart of the youth in flame."

The college should train through personal influence of professor and of student. "The fellow-feeling among free spirits" has long been famous in the universities of Germany. It was said of Doctor Nott, of Union College, that "he took the sweepings of other colleges and sent them back to society pure gold," such was his influence on young men. Something of the same influence is exerted for good in every college. The great teacher never fails to leave a great mark on every student whose life he touches.

The college and the university train men for definite ends in life. The graduate of the well-ordered college in these times knows some one thing very well and he can make his knowledge practical. The best teachers, the best lawyers, the best electricians, the best statesmen are those the university sends out. To excel in knowledge and action is to insure a fair salary and a worthy position in society.

Avoid the Middlemen of Education

The college gives a man a scholar's horizon. It enables him to see things which lie beyond his trade. A shoemaker is likely to measure the world by shoestrings, a grocer to think in terms of tea and sugar, a carpenter to put his universe together by rule of thumb. A scholar wherever placed should look beyond his profession and should see the affairs of the world in their true perspective. This should save him from bigotry, from intolerance, from selfishness. This should make him a more helpful member of society as well as better company to himself. This last fact alone is reason enough to justify a man in spending ten years of his life in higher education.

The higher education should make him a better citizen. It should give him the courage of his convictions, for only the educated man has any real convictions. Education shows how convictions should be formed. What the scholar believes he takes on his own evidence, not because it is the creed of his church or the platform of his party. So he, and he alone, counts as a unit in the community. "To see things as they really are" is the crowning privilege of the educated man. To help others to see them so is the greatest service he can render to the community. A tried beacon in the swaying tides of democracy is the educated man wherever he may be. You will go to college — where shall you go? The answer to this is simple. Get the best you can. You have but one chance for a college education. You cannot afford to waste that chance on an inferior school. Libraries, laboratories, rules, regulations, names and numbers do not make a university. It is the men who teach. Go where the masters are in whatever line you mean to work. Go to that school, in whatever State or county, under whatever name or control, that will serve your purposes best, that will give you the best return for the money you have to spend. Do not stop with the middlemen. Go to the men who know.

READY.

"Father," said the graduate, "it occurs to me that you might make a donation to Alma Mater."

"All right," said the old gentleman. "How much do you think it would cost to equip the new dormitory with poker tables, chips and similar paraphernalia?"

HIGH LIFE AND THE HIGHER EDUCATION

THE growth of luxury in the life of American college men was very dramatically pointed out not long ago by the head of one of the smaller colleges in New York. The undergraduates, he said, were every year finding new and more expensive sports, affecting more extensive and varied wardrobes, building larger and more commodious club and fraternity houses—often accustoming themselves to indulgences they had never known at home and could not have after leaving college. Meanwhile the men of character and learning, charged with their moral and intellectual welfare, were doomed to live on a mere pittance, often supporting large families on less than individual pupils spent upon themselves. A similar outcry against luxury has lately been raised at Yale, where the dormitories of the eighteenth century are rapidly giving place to splendid abodes of twentieth century comfort. It needed only a vivid protest or two to fix in the popular mind the notion that all our institutions of learning are hotbeds of corruption and decay. The prejudice against college life, which is always striving for mastery in American character with the prejudice in favor of college training, has for the moment got the upper hand.

The First Blast of the Trumpet

THE increase in luxury has been rapid enough. It is not yet twenty years since the charge of overindulgence, now trumpeted from a small inland college, was first prominently urged against the oldest and the largest of our institutions of learning in the phrases "The rich man's college," and "The fast set at Harvard." Mr. Post's Harvard Stories have been in print a single decade; yet they reflect a time when the fashionable undergraduate preferred to live in the bare, austere dormitories of the college yard. Even if he lived in Holworthy, the best of these, he warmed his three spacious chambers with a single open fire, while wintry blasts rattled his storm windows and raged at his hall door. He had no hot water, even to shave with, except such as he heated in a pipkin shivering over his grate; and if he insisted on the luxury of a flat tin bathtub tucked under his bed, as some few men did, he was not able to get more than a single pitcher of water for all day, except by a special arrangement with the porter. One of the buildings of that time, it is true, was an abode of luxury, where men had not only bathtubs, but could, if they chose, keep a valet, as some men did. But Beck Hall was then looked down upon as the abode of rich and unpopular men whose rooms far excelled their company. An old graduate at that time declared in a letter to The Crimson that Harvard could never hope to beat Yale as long as the men in Beck had window-boxes of flowers. He found a ready ear.

Only five years later, when Mr. Flandrau's Harvard Episodes was printed, Beck Hall was old-fashioned. The flourishing undergraduates lived in a building fully furnished with steam heat and porcelain tubs and glorying in a marble bathing tank in the cellar. Who can ever forget how, in the deliciously absurd Class Day Idyll, the disheveled, apoplectic, hard-breathing, middle-aged romancer of a Class Day girl called for Bill and claimed his hospitality as a relative, and how he was found in the tank-room, where he had been skating himself over the slippery floor on his back, and dragged out in a wrapper to meet her in the hall!

These two books only mark the crisis in a long period of increasing luxury. Unless one misreads the anecdote of the youth of John Fiske, he made his own bed. Under the motherly eye of a goody he would hardly have been allowed to go without sheets and spend the money on a set of the works of Voltaire! And it was not unusual for an undergraduate to make his own fire and to fetch his own water from the college pump, as some few men do still who need to save the expense of a porter. On the other hand, the era of growing indulgence seems by no means closed. The man with a valet has become less and less a nine days' wonder; and the time will no doubt come when tank-rooms will be so planned that the luxurious youth who is dragged out of them in a bath wrapper will be able to regain his raiment and his right mind before encountering his female relatives, real or alleged, on the staircase.

MEMORIAL HALL, HARVARD COLLEGE

Is the Growth of Luxury a Menace in American Colleges?

By JOHN CORBIN

Very few of the pursuits of mankind are as alluring as lamenting the birds in last year's nests. The ideal of a college where low living joins hands with high thinking, where the difference between man and man is scarcely seen, or not at all, has a charm that can be appreciated even without the striking perspective given it by the insufficiencies of professorial salaries. The thought of young Ralph Waldo Emerson meeting the richest and the greatest of his classmates at the college pump, where all have collected to draw water for the morning bath (we will give them the benefit of the doubt as to ablutions) floats before one in a transcendental haze of glory. But did such scenes ever take place? One has his doubts. It is true that in rural America, at least in the North, what is now regarded as service, for generations bore no mark of inferiority; and this is still the case in districts remote from the march of wealth. The farmer did his chores; his wife cooked and kept house. If an extra hand was needed, a neighbor's son or daughter was called in, who lived in the house on terms of perfect equality. When a boy went to college from such surroundings it was only natural that he should do his own fetching and carrying. To have a porter would have been as immorally luxurious as for the sons of a modern business man to have a valet. But even at that time the old and rich families in the towns had long been accustomed to personal service, and their sons in college enjoyed the attention of goody and porter for an extra fee. Farther back still, in the Colonial days, there was the sharpest of social differences between the merchants, whose portraits in flowing silks and turbans were painted by Copley, and the rugged farmer—the difference between those who did and those who did not do their own chores. Is it not largely the glittering foreground of marble tanks and steam heat that makes the past seem democratic?

That folly and vice exist is not denied. Many silly youths spend their four years in seeking the companionship of richer and more fashionable classmates for no other reason than that they are richer and more fashionable. They waste their fathers' money and the opportunity of building up mind and body, only to acquire habits of thought and of living that, harmless in themselves, perhaps, are for them false and vicious. They end by being that most repulsive of all reptiles, the toady snob. Too often the men they emulate are themselves positively bad. Mr. F. J. Stimpson's Guerndale (by "J. S. of Dale") is one of the earliest pictures of the fast American college man, abounding in adventures of gambling and carousal, and stifling with the atmosphere of debauch.

A year or two ago I happened to see in the study of a graduate of the Guerndale period a photograph of his comrades in one of the most fashionable college clubs, the members of which are supposed to have furnished Mr. Stimpson with the originals of his reckless undergraduates. I asked whether the picture of Harvard life in Guerndale were overdrawn. My friend shook his head, and went over the lives of his old clubmates one by one. It was not an edifying recital. Idleness and gambling, ruin and divorce, delirium tremens and suicide, were the outcome of the lives of almost a majority of the fellows who looked so promising in that fading old photograph. But it is to be added that not all of those young men went wrong in college; and many of them have lived to be the best of citizens. My informant is one of the sincerest and one of the most high-minded and able of modern American men of letters. Besides, the doings of his classmates established a record of recklessness that has long endured. Twenty years later the class of Seventy-blank was a byword at Harvard for the extreme of debauchery.

The Question of Large Allowances

YET the Guerndale type of undergraduate exists to-day. The rapid increase of vast private fortunes has quadrupled the number of young men who are thrown on the college world with bank accounts all out of proportion to their legitimate needs. Eight, ten, even twelve thousand dollars a year is no unusual sum. This is not so much as it may seem. Certain of the undergraduate clubs add upward of a thousand dollars a year to a man's expenses, and the regular athletic sports, to say nothing of yachting and polo, are the cause of heavy drains. Yet, at the best, such sums are madly in excess. As long as youth and human nature are what they are, the spending of so much money can only lead to vicious self-indulgence. Why do parents give such allowances? In part, perhaps, because having been poor themselves, they do not realize how surely too much money corrupts. More often their folly is the result of social ambition. With sudden wealth far beyond their desires they find themselves debarred from the life of gayety and fashion, and they wish to provide better for their children. They know that the great colleges afford the easiest field for their sons to make brilliant acquaintances. If a young man is bright and companionable, and not too much of a boor, he can go anywhere in the undergraduate world, and especially if he has had the advantage of making friends in the more democratic atmosphere of the fashionable preparatory schools—Saint Paul's, Lawrenceville, Groton, Saint Mark's, Exeter and Andover. And many parents whose wealth is older, whose social position has long been assured, are equally unwise. In certain colleges the Guerndale type of undergraduate is in a measure characteristic of the most exclusive clubs. Young men whose families live in the atmosphere of smart New York society, and who spend their summers at Newport and Bar Harbor, are not likely to transform their ideas of life to suit the more solid traditions of Harvard or Yale or Columbia. The standards of their classmates are much more likely to be bent to theirs. For the discipline of honest scholarship such men have no liking. Even the joy of manly sports has little charm. Yet in the purely social world they are the leaders, and they succeed to a considerable extent in perverting fellows of a far sounder stamp. Year after year good scholars and good athletes, in proportion as they are more and more closely assimilated by the leading clubs, are seen to fall little by little out of the general life of the college. At Oxford, in England, there is the Bullingdon Club, the chief sport of which is fox hunting, and the members of which belong mainly to the nobility, and which is known positively to discourage such athletic sports—rowing, running, football—as require careful and self-denying training. It is not quite so bad as that yet anywhere in America, but we are tending dangerously in that direction. Some one remarked some years ago that the exclusive clubs at Harvard were becoming more and more a sort of pool pocket, so that the moment a man got into them he was permanently out of the game of undergraduate life.

Bad as all this is, it is by no means certain that the proportion of wrong-doing is greater than in the fabled Golden Age.

In the picturesque sense, of course, there is a difference between those who drink too much hard cider in a village back yard and those who drink too much champagne at Delmonico's, between those who squander a parent's money for a porter's service and those who squander it for a valet and for a marble swimming-tank, between those who toady to the son of an East India merchant and those who toady to the son of a king of the trusts. But in their effect upon character these follies are all the same. In a university of four thousand, those who lead loose and luxurious lives are far more numerous, far more prominently organized than in a college of two hundred; but it does not follow that in proportion they are more important. Is not the present one of those instances in which the fledglings of last year's nest seem fairer than those in the apple tree by the window?

It will not do, moreover, to stigmatize every man who learns new standards of living at college. The four undergraduate years are the richest of all in opportunities for making friends, and the friends made in college are those that last longest. If one happens to fall in with fellows who have more money and a larger experience of life, as many a lad does on the athletic field and in the classroom, is it not worth some sacrifice to keep them as friends? I have known men who thought so, and whenever these have been men of ability the friends they sought for their own sake proved in the end worth while on the most prudent grounds. When a lad has his way to make in the world his most valuable asset, next to his character and education, is a personal address that puts him everywhere at his ease, and a close acquaintance with the men who are likely to become employers and the friends of employers.

Twelve Hundred a Year Spells Riches

IT MAY be put down, as a rule, that the charges of luxury and debauchery set forth in the newspapers, and even in the most stately reviews, are exaggerated. Some years ago, at the season when Princeton alumni gather at Old Nassau for commencement, the members of a recently graduated class were seated, according to the custom, in a little amphitheatre in the campus, discussing affairs of state. The orator of the occasion was discoursing on this same eternal question of the increase of undergraduate luxury, and was taking the side which those who have been through the mill almost invariably take. "They say that the undergraduate of to-day," he asseverated, "has discarded the democratic and odoriferous sweater of our time for knickerbockers and golf-blazers. Yonder goes one of the moderns" (pointing to a youth who was sauntering by in full uniform). "To our eyes he is a popinjay. But look at those pants. It cost him fifty cents to have a pair of fringed and baggy old trousers chopped off at the knee by a basement tailor. Look at that blazer! Any one of us can get one like it at a department store for five forty-nine!" Careful canvasses of the expenses of undergraduates in the leading Eastern universities have shown that, while the extreme of luxury has unquestionably risen, the average of expenses is gaining very slowly. With twelve hundred dollars a year a man of proper tastes is positively rich; with eight hundred a year he is well-to-do; many fellows get an education with only five hundred dollars a year, and I have known men to earn their own way through Harvard and yet belong to all but the most expensive clubs.

Alfred the Great and His Tin Tub

AT THE worst the increase of luxury is only a symptom of what is happening the world over. There is a popular superstition, and especially in America, that the morning tub was invented by Alfred the Great, and that for over a thousand years any true-born Englishman was liable to shrivel up and die if he were deprived of it. But in the archives of a certain Oxford college there is record of a test case that came before the master as late as the second half of the century just past. A certain undergraduate insisted that his "scout" bring him a pail of water every morning for his flat tin tub. The scout held there was no precedent for the demand. After mature deliberation the master decided in favor of the tub.

At Harvard a similar case arose fifteen years ago, and was decided against the cause of comfort and cleanliness, with disastrous results. Two of the older buildings afforded none of the conveniences of the bathroom, and even the palatial Holworthy, abode of well-to-do seniors, had not even a shower-bath. Time and again the undergraduates demanded bathrooms in every building. None were put in. The college said it could not afford them. Private capitalists read the signs of the times more shrewdly, and erected building after building on the most magnificent plan. That was what made the difference between the Harvard of Mr. Post and the Harvard of Mr. Flandrau. The rooms in the old buildings, for which there had once been the keenest competition among all sorts and conditions of men, were many of them unrented year after year at a loss very far in excess of what baths would have cost. The college yard, which had for centuries been the centre of the college life and the college traditions, in which the poorest lived on terms of something like equality with the richest, was given over to men of limited means. More than ever, the college tended to split up into cliques, greatly to the detriment of all that was best in its traditions.

Such circumstances give color to the often repeated charge that in our great universities it is only the very rich who can succeed in making themselves recognized. It would be futile to deny the power of money. The economists tell us that it is the lubricant of trade, without which the wheels soon grate and stop. But in society, as in trade, it is only the lubricant. No type is commoner than the millionaire's son whose life is as isolated as that of the poorest "grind." While reading under-

graduate compositions I became the confessor of several such. They were right-thinking and friendly fellows, but they had no abilities in athletics, in writing for the college papers, or in debating, and they lacked the social charm to make themselves liked for themselves alone. Their known wealth only served to emphasize their lack of friends. On the other hand, many of the richest and most popular fellows, and especially those in whose families wealth and cultivation were a tradition, dress simply, live in the barest rooms and are the most eager to seek out friends for their own sake. At Harvard, and everywhere else, I suppose, no type of undergraduate is commoner than fellows belonging to the richest and most cultivated families who are simple and democratic in their dress and sometimes—though not always—in their manners.

The Best Kind of College

WOULD it have been better if our colleges had maintained in its integrity the much-lauded standard of low living and high thinking, granting that such a standard ever obtained? It may be doubted. If they are to accomplish their mission, it must be by keeping in immediate and vital contact with all strata of American life. Any effort to alter radically the standard of living must result, as it resulted with regard to the baths in Holworthy, in throwing the more important functions of the undergraduate world out of gear. It is a decided limitation in the more conservative class of American parents that they regard education only as so much book learning and mental training. Quite as important to the average youth is the development of a sound knowledge of the world and of effective character. These can be best attained in a college where every phase of our life and character is fully represented. Sooner or later one has to accustom himself to the fact that men are richer, more luxurious and more evil than one wishes they were. Whether a young fellow is to go into business, law or the ministry, his best asset, next to his education, is a knowledge of the world of men, and the age of eighteen or nineteen is none too early to begin it. A young man who cannot keep his balance then has little chance of doing so when he is thrown up against life in the more trying temptations of bread-winning. As for the outcry I have used as a text, if it discloses any great evil it is the underpayment of our college professors. Many of the instructors at our richest university receive only five hundred dollars a year. Few of the professors receive more than four thousand. While the cost of living and the standard of living have advanced to the elevation of the porcelain bath, their incomes have remained at the level of the flat tin tub. Instead of telling the American parent that the colleges are hot-beds of luxury, it would seem wiser for the professor to say simply and with dignity that the college faculty is the abode of poverty.

There is, however, a very great evil in American undergraduate life. Its origin is not in wealth or in character, but in the system which is at the base of the social order. In the old college of two or three hundred men, all living in a single set of buildings and dining in the same hall, there was every chance for a free mingling of all sorts of men. It was not only easy to make acquaintance, but impossible to avoid them. The result was a compact and friendly college life that insured strength and permanency to the college traditions. In the modern universities of three and four thousand no such interplay of social forces is possible. The tendency is for the rich to know only the rich and the poor only the poor—a tendency which is equally unfortunate for both. When a man succeeds in becoming intimate with his classmates of all kinds it is only by means of a rare combination of ability, address and, one may add, good fortune. Vigorous efforts have been made to insure a closer social union, and with some success. But the problem as a whole is as yet unsolved. There is a strong and, I think, a growing tendency to find the ultimate solution in the English idea of dividing the university into a number of small colleges, each of which is a unit socially and in athletics. All the primary needs of life are supplied by the college—rooms, board, friends, clubs and sports. That a man shall make friends and acquaintances in college is all but inevitable, and when he shows especial capabilities, the way out into the greater life of the university is open to him through the friends he has made in college. The English system is certainly much pleasanter. In effect it is far more democratic, in that it makes it possible for any man, almost without regard to his poverty or wealth, to become a vital part of the life about him.

Furnishing a College Room. By Herbert Copeland

The room of Cunha, the Hawaiian athlete, at Yale

A Junior's room at Yale

A Senior's room at Yale

ONE of the first of the many delights to come to "a college man" is the fitting up of his quarters. As soon as the room is decided on the fun begins—and, in a way, it keeps up all the four years. In nine cases out of ten it is the first room he has ever "done" personally for himself; for, while he may have had a room of his own at home, it has mostly been arranged by the mother or the sisters, and has always been on inspection by the family. In his college room he can keep things, to a certain extent, as he wants them; at least he need not have them as *other* people want them; certain feminine niceties may be abandoned, as he, or he and a chum, will be sole occupants and inspectors—save always the ubiquitous "goody."

In furnishing a college room the first thing to be decided is, of course, how much money a man can afford to spend. The other things—the kind of a room he wants, whether it shall look like a library, like "a college room," like a "sporty den," or just like any comfortable sitting-room—will of necessity come later. A Freshman without developed tastes—and how few have them!—can tell nothing about these things. Let him just get the necessary furniture and let the rest come—it will, fast enough—as he sees other rooms and gets his bearings.

In this paper I shall consider the furnishing of a room as cheaply as practicable with a due regard for comfort and attractiveness, since any one knows that if an article *can* be bought for ten dollars it *may* be bought from there all the way up to the hundreds.

Almost all college rooms are in suites of two or three—a study and bedroom, or study and two bedrooms; and in the more luxurious and modern buildings a bath is included. The prices vary from sixty dollars a year up to $1000. If the quarters consist of only one room it will be more convenient to curtain off a portion for a bedroom, and have the study a thing of itself, even if very small.

As to the bedroom, almost all men prefer this to be furnished simply and plainly. A bed, bureau, chiffonier, washstand, a small rug and two chairs are the essentials. A brass or iron bed is far better than anything else; the style of the other things makes little difference, so long as the articles are strong and plain, for college rooms necessarily get hard wear. Thin cotton or muslin curtains always lend an air of retirement to a room, and are to be had for but little extra expense.

A bedroom thus furnished may cost as little as fifty dollars. In the following list the articles are all new and of fair value:

Bed ...	$20	Rug and Curtains	$ 5
Bureau or Chiffonier	15		
Washstand	5	Total	$50
Two Chairs	5		

Mothers, sisters and friends are only too glad to furnish from the home stock, or the pin-money purse, the small bedroom comforts to which "the dear boy" has been accustomed.

A great many men, on leaving college, wish to sell their furniture—that is, such things as beds, bureaus, chairs, curtains and the like. This may seem to give the entering Freshman a chance to buy cheap, but let him beware! In nine cases out of ten it does not pay: four years of college wear weaken things pretty badly, and before another four years have gone there won't be any furniture left, and the foolish buyer will have to replace just as he is beginning to want all his money for things other than beds and chairs. Then, too, it is a part of the game to charge the unsuspecting "Freshie" more than the stuff cost in the beginning. I personally know of one who paid twice as much for shabby curtains and shades as they cost when new, and the shades belonged with the room, anyway. For all such little games the wise Freshman—if this be not too much of a paradox—must be on the lookout. But if he gets caught, let him not be offended; it is legitimate. Like the fagging and beating in the English schools—one grows to it.

Attractiveness Gained with Small Cost

The making of an attractive room with a small outlay is an art worthy of the study of all men; or with a large outlay, for that matter, it is not so easy for the novice. I trust that the few following suggestions, derived from experience, may be of use to some one engaged in the sometimes puzzling but always agreeable task of "getting a room together."

To begin with, let no one sneer at the idea of an attractive room being important to a college man. The beginning of the college course, when one is meeting new men daily, is the time to attract acquaintances, to make friends of them and to begin to hold them—and the making and holding of college friends counts for all life—and a pleasant loafing place is a large factor in attracting. Above all, primarily, secondarily and finally, don't let the Freshman be fussy about his room—that is, after it is furnished. Don't mind if a chair is broken, don't notice if a match is scratched on the wrong place, or something laid where it ought not to be; better go with broken furniture forever, or a burnt carpet, than that two men, after leaving your room, say, "What a fuss Blank is!" They will not come back. But this is another story, only all the taste and beauty in the world will not make a college room attractive if the owner is fussy—a word to the wise! But to go back to the furnishing of the study.

First of all there must be a desk—a "library table" with drawers is the most convenient. Secondly, or almost firstly, a lounge or couch of some sort, also a window-seat. On these two, and the fire (fortunately nearly all college rooms are furnished with a grate or fireplace), depends everything. A desk-chair seems almost a necessity, though I'd choose, if I couldn't have both, a couch, and sit on the head of it to do my writing; also an easy-chair and two other chairs are advisable. If one has the courage of a rocking-chair, it will always be in use, and always be sneered at. One needs, too, a bookcase of some sort; wooden boxes, such as librarians move books in and often use for stacks in small libraries, are most convenient. As books increase, another and another box may be bought, adding little expense at the time. Any carpenter will make these boxes of the size desired and stain them any color to suit for a small amount of money.

The papering of the room is a matter on which little can be said. If it is ugly, change it if you can afford to—a room with an ugly paper will always be ugly, of course.

The best thing for the floor is a rug, almost as square as the room. These can be bought in good color and design, of ordinary American make, as low as fifteen dollars and still be fairly serviceable. If one can afford a heavier one, of course it is better. A foreign rug is best of all, but these, in any large size, can hardly be bought for less than one hundred dollars, though good rugs can often be bought at auction remarkably cheap; also odd chairs and desks may be got at a bargain. I know of an admirable desk being bought for two dollars, and a really splendid mahogany bookcase with glass doors, felt-lined shelves and drawers, ten feet over all, brought at the same sale but twenty dollars. However, these

A "library room" at Harvard

A Senior's room at Harvard

Furnishing a College Room

bargains will come later; it does not pay to wait for them at the first furnishing.

Absolutely necessary furnishings may be bought at the following prices—the articles all new and in good taste—and the prices quoted are those of good, reliable shops, not those which advertise to "furnish rooms for college boys."

Desk	$15
Couch	12
Window-seat	15
Three Chairs	12
Two Book Boxes	8
Rug	15
Curtains	6
	$83

Thus much for the larger necessities; but, of course, no room can be attractive or really furnished without a few pictures and ornaments of some sort. My first advice is, however, to go without either unless you can have something that you really like.

Gifts that Were Better Not Made If a friend or relative wants to give you something "for your room" ask him to let you select for yourself, otherwise you may have some awful unsuitability put upon you, some Bodenhausen Madonna, a Delft windmill clock that won't go, or a "smoker's set" on tip-tilted tripodical legs, with immovable gilt ash trays, brass-bound boxes and patent lighter.

A man naturally likes to select his own pictures and ornaments, but there are many little things that add a great deal to the comfort and attractiveness of a college room which it is safe to mention as desirable "tokens of esteem," or "Christmas remembrances," to those who wish to know of such, and who cannot be asked to allow "self-selection." There are a lot of things one does not think of for some time, but which it would be well to have, even early in the year. For instance, a small table is convenient, and if it has a double shelf it is doubly useful. A cabinet of some sort to keep dishes in is always handy, and dishes, too. Every one soon finds out it is often very agreeable to be able to make tea or coffee "on the premises," hence a Vienna coffee-pot and some cups and saucers are excellent things to mention to inquiring friends. Also stone mugs will be useful; and a fire set, a brass coal hod, and some knives and forks and spoons are far better than a silver desk-set or an embroidered head-rest.

A student lamp is on the line between a necessity and a luxury, or any pretty lamp that is not too fancy—only beware of the admirers of onyx. A blazer is a desirable possession, for he who can make a good rabbit has a hold on the affections of his friends. And last, but not least, comes the sofa-pillow; any number will not be amiss so long as they are not too dainty. Care should be taken to express a fondness for dark colors, not too much embroidered and distinctly not beruffled; for ruffles tear easily, and a torn ruffle is an abomination to a self-respecting cushion; so is a gilt cord to a tired head.

The pictures of Harvard rooms accompanying this article are fair samples, from the typical college room to the elaborate study.

The first is a view of a Senior's room, taken just before graduation, with the accumulation of four years in it.

The second is an example of one of the most elaborate study rooms. The heavy oak bookshelves are built into the room after the manner of a "real library." The whole woodwork of the room has been changed to correspond with the shelves, and the fireplace and mantel have been remodeled. The furniture is of oak and leather, the hangings are rare old Persian shawls of deep red with elaborate borders. The china and the few ornaments are of the choicest, and the floor is covered with a heavy Turkish rug. The whole effect of the room is rich and splendid in color and design. Few men, of course, have the taste, the books, the money or the ambition to go into things quite so heavily as has been done in this case.

But elaborate rooms are distinct exceptions to the rule. Seven-eighths of the rooms are still known as "college rooms." And while it is distinctly a barbarian, or boyish, love of adornment which produces these rooms, it is healthy and sound. One would suspect a college of "decadence" if the more refined type of room prevailed—and judging by appearances the colleges are safe from that cry for many years yet.

Through HARVARD on FIFTY Cents

By Garrison Williams

FOR at least a century Harvard has been known as "the rich man's college." The implication of that phrase has doubtless deterred many a poor young man from an attempt to enter her portals. The implication is that Harvard is a decidedly uncomfortable place for the student not possessed of much money; that he had far better look elsewhere.

The contrary is the truth. Wealth by no means assures success at Harvard. Though it is true that the cost of living is greater than the cost of living at Oxford, at Heidelberg, or the other foreign universities, it is none the less possible to secure all of the advantages which the catalogue has to offer for an expenditure seemingly impossible. To have a room in Dunster or Claverly Hall, to furnish one's rooms richly, to keep a stable and belong to the costly clubs of the college, is to spend in the neighborhood of $10,000 a year. But given pluck and brains to pit against the dollars of his more fortunate (or would you say *un*fortunate?) fellows, the poor man can work his way through Harvard with very little money and very great self-satisfaction, and graduate with honors far beyond the reach of men who waste their time as they waste the parental allowance, virtually buying their diplomas in the end.

THE ANCIENT AND HONORABLE ORDER OF TUTORS

When I say buying their diplomas I do not, of course, mean actual purchase and sale. There is, however, a regularly established system, politely called tutoring, by which students who disdain study may hurriedly absorb such knowledge as they are likely to be questioned about at forthcoming examinations. Among the indolent and well-to-do the "mid-years" and "finals" are bound to find many who are forced to have recourse to printed notes, syllabuses, seminars, and other aids and abetments of laziness. This is the "cramming" of the English colleges, and though the faculty openly discourages it, so long as there are quick wits on one side and long purses on the other some sort of bargain will be struck despite the most awful fulminations of the Dean. Legitimate tutoring is officially recognized. The growth of the University has largely eliminated from all but the most advanced and zealously guarded "starred" courses the personal element of guidance. To meet this lapse the heads of departments post upon the department bulletin boards the names of authorized tutors to the departments, chosen from the poor and brilliant scholars—at once an honor and an aid. The charges vary with the experience and ability of the tutor. The best work brings three dollars the hour, and from there down, as necessity and opportunity may determine.

That the poorest student has an equal chance for education with the richest is evidenced in my own experiences. Poverty, unless it is of the abject, helpless and hopeless kind, should never deter any young man from seeking knowledge at the fountain-head. For those who have no family resources Harvard offers many inducements in the way of scholarships and beneficiary funds. There are open no less than 206 scholarships, with grants ranging from $30 to $300. Every kind of premium is placed upon good scholarship. Had it not been for this fact, I, for one, could never have passed through Harvard. I doubt if any young man ever entered upon a college career under more unfavorable, nay, disheartening circumstances than I did. I was handicapped by ill health, a poor memory, and a reticent demeanor that I could not seem to conquer, be as bold as I might. My record as a student was so mean and unimpressive that I received upon my entrance to the University the maximum number of conditions.

WHAT MAY BE ACCOMPLISHED AGAINST ODDS

I had come to Cambridge with recommendations as a faithful and ambitious student, though I was from a new and therefore supposedly inefficient preparatory school. Somehow I floundered through my examination books, evoking, I am certain, the sympathy of the proctors in charge of the room. You may easily believe I was a happy youth when I saw my name posted in University Hall as admitted. Burdened though I was with drawbacks, my dogged determination had won for me the first step in the realization of all my boyhood dreams—a career at Harvard.

My plight upon arrival was bad enough, but added to my other shortcomings was the lack of funds for my immediate and pressing wants. From the moment I stepped off the car in Cambridge until the hour I crossed the yard for the last time I was thrown entirely upon my own resources in meeting the expenses of my course. Like an ominous spirit, foreboding evil, there arose constantly before me that old cry, "Harvard is the rich man's college." Now I can look back and smile at those first, fearful days, so full of apprehension for the future, so darkened by my worry as to how and where I was to obtain my equipment of books and furniture. I should not like to repeat the experiences of my first quarter-year at Harvard, helpful as those experiences were in making me resourceful and self-reliant. Because of my absolute poverty I learned to know the hard, outside business world much more intimately than do most students. I developed a keen commercial acumen along with intellectual breadth.

When I left Boston for Cambridge I had precisely fifty cents in my waistcoat pocket! I did not dare to spend any part of that huge wealth for food. To complicate matters, I had no idea as to where I should spend the night. I was totally unacquainted with the town. I found myself in the late afternoon in Harvard Square, as hungry and homeless as any tramp. I was travel-stained and footsore. I did not know that a mere inquiry would have set me on the right track to both food and shelter.

A FRESHMAN'S FIRST NIGHT AT CAMBRIDGE

Aimlessly I wandered through Cambridge with about the same feeling of desolation that would have possessed the soul of John Harvard—who knew the old town only as Newtown—had he linked arms with me that memorable evening and gone in search of a room. Through Cambridge Street and Holyoke Street I strolled, "sizing up" the houses in which I had been told rooms were to let. The New England spirit of enterprise that has turned every third dwelling in Cambridge into a lodging-house for students prevented me from securing a room "on trust." My sole baggage was the hand satchel I carried. Finally, in a far corner of Kirkland Street I found a kindly woman who seemed willing to take me in on speculation. I went to bed supperless but not wholly miserable.

I had left my native Pennsylvania town with enough to pay traveling expenses, plus my treasured fifty-cent piece and the

DRAWN BY
WILL CRAWFORD

Would he allow me to display my extraordinary skill as a window decorator?

promise of a loan of $175 from an intimate friend of my father. The latter was also one of my bondsmen, depositing in due time and order with the Bursar one-half the required $400 as a guarantee against my possible failure to meet all bills. The loaned $175 I fully expected to receive the day after my arrival. My representations to my trusting landlady were based on this assurance. The next day came, but the money did not. I haunted the express office through which it was to be delivered, and thought I saw in the face of the affable clerk the positive traces of criminal tendencies. I was plainly in pawn.

AN APPRENTICESHIP IN PRACTICAL ARCHITECTURE

It was late in the afternoon of my second day when I screwed up sufficient courage to approach the proprietor of one of the Boston bookstores and propose that I should dress up his shop windows with the new books, stationery and writing materials he offered for sale. I spoke very rapidly and earnestly to hide my confusion and humiliation, and declared I could attract in one day more customers by my handiwork than had come into his store in a week. Would he allow me to display my extraordinary skill as a window decorator? He finally consented to my proposition, and the price agreed upon was three dollars if my work proved wholly satisfactory. My impromptu effort was a revelation to myself. I think I did not arrange those books and things with any regard to harmonious blending of colors, but I built up some wonderful arches with paper boxes, and made some striking if inartistic rosettes with a bundle of pen-wipers and a stock of pencils. It is true that some of my geometrical effects in books were marred by placing them so that the casual spectator would have to stand on his or her head in order to read the titles. The chief thing of moment was that I received three dollars for my work. That night I dined—dined luxuriously, it seemed to me—and walked to my room with my chest out and my nose high in the air.

Then came my examinations, and if the borrowed money had not arrived at about the same time I should have flung myself into the Charles River. To be poor of pocket and poor of brain and still have enough perception left to realize one's state of hopeless demoralization seemed to me the very essence of ironical fate. Two of the three dollars earned as a window decorator went to my landlady—a sop to Cerberus. There was left of my original half-dollar just one lonely five-cent piece when my borrowed $175 came along to lift me from my slough of despond.

I felt secure with only my room rent of $2.50 the week to pay and a chance to live gayly on at least $125, allowing $50 for the payment of my first tuition bill in the coming February, which seemed almost far away enough to make me reckless. But I had counted without my host, as the phrase runs. There were incidentals to be paid for, which made the payment something more than a mere incident in my early college life.

I found that for $2.50 the week I could dine at the Foxcroft Club in a way that passeth human belief; with good roast beef at fifteen cents the plate, and side dishes at three and five cents each, topping off with good coffee and the inevitable piece of pie for eight cents, you may dine *à la* Foxcroft with true epicurean gusto and satisfaction. But what I found was reasonable enough in the way of inexpensive catering to the inner man, I soon discovered was offset by a monopoly in text-books. To-day all this is changed. The Coöperative—familiarly known as "The Coop"—managed by the students themselves, furnishes all necessaries to its members at cost prices.

A SCHOLASTIC MONOPOLY

Text-books were purchasable at but one place, and that place in Cambridge. There were many reasons why it was impossible to buy one's necessary books in any shop other than the Cambridge place, but it must suffice to tell that in the latter establishment text-books could only be bought and paid for at such prices as would appall the bookseller familiar with competition. My text-books did all but send me into absolute bankruptcy. I thanked Heaven my room rent was paid up some weeks in advance, though I trembled for myself when I thought of the likelihood of starving to death. The idea of starvation first came to me as an airy fancy; later, I was confronted by it as a grim and terribly real spectre. My original capital of $175 had dwindled to a $20 bill before I had actually fallen into the routine of my first term at college. In later years I realized what was not evident to me at the start—that the first months, necessitating as they do the purchase of many things used throughout the four years of college life, makes an initial expense larger in proportion than that of succeeding years.

HOW TO LIVE IN LUXURY AT $2.50 THE WEEK

Before the expiration of the spring term of my Freshman year I had imbibed much wisdom other than that printed in my text-books. I had learned how to live more economically than I had been doing, and how to make money within college grounds. Two-thirds of my original "pile" had gone by that time for tuition and text-books, and the balance paid for a few weeks' board and lodging. For the cost of the latter I had no complaint. My landlady was a second mother to me. There were three other student lodgers in the house, but somehow I did not affiliate with them, and none of us saw much of each other.

My quarters were remarkably cozy and homelike; I am certain no such comforts can be found at a cost so low outside of Cambridge. My home (as I soon came to call it) was one of those numerous houses where student lodgers had been catered to for two or three generations. I found that my motherly landlady, though keen enough at a bargain, had supported herself for years by means of her rented rooms. Conceive, if you will, a large, square room, in the old style, the door and window trimmings of Colonial design and painted white, and you have an outline sketch of the place I called home. Nothing was there that might be called luxurious, but everything was useful and some things were beautiful. An old-time mahogany dresser stood between the two windows of the room, and atop of this very dignified bit of furniture an oval mirror tilted between supports. A bamboo bookrack rose from the floor at one corner. There was an open fireplace with grate and fender. In a far corner stood my bed—an iron-framed affair, immaculately spread, and in the centre of the room was the study table, round and heavy, standing on its supports with a suggestion of being built all of a piece with the house itself. I was rich in chairs—four of them; two thickly upholstered ones, a walnut rocker, and the inevitable "Harvard chair"—a compromise between a steamer, a dentist's and a Morris chair, with the virtues of all these and an individuality of its own. For all this ease and comfort I paid the munificent sum of $2.50 the week. I could have lived out the whole of my college life in this sunny, cheerful apartment, but for the fact that it was inconveniently distant from the University, and I felt the need of keeping in hourly touch with congenial fellow-students. It was for this last reason mainly that I removed my few small belongings from the Kirkland Street house, bade my foster-mother a regretful adieu, and made my home for the rest of my Freshman and the whole of my Sophomore year in Divinity Hall, where as one of some half-dozen laymen—a clannish, irreverent but studious crew—I was happy, if poor.

WHEN THINGS LOOKED AT THEIR BLACKEST

The means by which I eked out my early college days, after my borrowed money was gone and I had succeeded in accumulating a number of bothersome debts, can perhaps be imagined by a recital of a few of my adventures in search of the elusive dollar. One day when I was completely stranded, with no hope of earning immediate cash (I could not bring myself to borrow from my classmates), I walked through the yard doing some hard thinking. Mechanically I drew out my watch to see the time. Here was my salvation. I would pawn it.

It was with the assurance of ignorance that I hurried into a Boston loan-office and asked for $50—$10 less than the original price. The struggle between my pride and my insistent hunger was sharp, but brief. I received $15 and left my watch. Later I pawned two rings and some silver toilet articles. These latter yielded me $7.50. This was the darkest hour of my college life. In a day of black extremity it was announced that I had won one of several prizes on the Bowdoin foundation, which meant $100, payable at an early date. Later I contested successfully for the Boylston prize for elocution, which yielded me $45. You may guess my condition of mind when I found these honors and (what was more to the point at the time) the accompanying helpful dollars showered upon me. This success changed my whole point of view and gave me a new inspiration to work for success. I determined not only to pay my way as I went, but to lay up riches for the future. I found this latter resolve impossible of realization. I worked and studied as only an ambitious youth can.

AN OPENING CAREER AS POLITICIAN AND CATERER

Another poor student, to whom I had been attracted by that same affinity which draws into congenial groups by themselves tramps, railroad Presidents and house-breakers, had a marvelous possession in a typewriter machine. I was a good operator, and my skill enabled me to earn enough for an entire new outfit of clothing and a few—just a few—little luxuries: a new briar pipe, for example, and a couple of pounds of good tobacco. Upon my borrowed machine I wrote, at a reduced rate per folio, letters, manuscripts and circulars—everything that can be expressed by the characters of the alphabet. For a Boston politician I wrote an address which he afterward delivered to his constituents amid awed praise and wild applause ($10). For a student's dinner-party I turned off twenty decorated menu cards, making the floral borders, etc., with combinations of the X and O signs of my writing instrument (result, $5). A greater part of my work was writing manuscripts for some of the professors, which, though laborious and exacting, was liberally paid for and helpful where the manuscript to be typewritten touched upon a subject in which I was interested. From such jobs I earned about $70. To do this work I had to sacrifice many sleeping hours and permitted myself no recreation. For the rest of my first year I virtually pounded out my living expenses on the typewriter, which I was soon able to rent at a low rate from my friend, who seldom used the machine and needed the money. Only once since I had secured the typewriter was I in actual need of money. That gloomy time came when my machine collapsed (from overwork, I presume) and had to be laid off for repairs for nearly a week.

DRAWN BY
WILL CRAWFORD
For a Boston politician I wrote an address which he afterward delivered

A VACATION OF HARD WORK

My vacation was a mere word, for during the summer I worked ten hours a day as porter in a country hotel. There were many humiliations attached to the position, but these were as nothing to the severe ankle sprain I received in handling a big trunk that slipped my grasp and threw me, neck and heels, as a broncho throws an inexperienced horseman, down a flight of steps. I was "docked" a day's earnings for my "carelessness," though my employer, a gruff man with a heart only partially ossified by worrisome years of hotel management, paid my doctor's fee, revoked the penalty, and gave me a fortnight's rest on full pay. At the beginning of my Sophomore year I had earned enough to pay my tuition fee, but that was all. From the loan fund of the college I borrowed $75 from the beneficiary funds I collected another $75 for some newspaper correspondence I received $30, and with small jobs, such as painting a fellow-student's blackened eye to a normal hue, bill-posting, song and speech writing, and my usual typewriting performances, I pulled through free and clear, with a few dollars left in my purse. This was gratifying, because my expenses were considerably higher than those of the previous year. I had bought myself a few luxuries, and had added a number of choice volumes to my growing library. When I moved into Divinity Hall I had hired my furniture and was given the privilege of paying the bill at Commencement. This I was able to do. I had indulged myself in Boston plays, and had spent some money on mild luxuries, and still was on the safe side of the ledger.

WILL CRAWFORD
My vacation was a mere word

A PROSPEROUS AND BUSY JUNIOR YEAR

During my Junior year my receipts were close upon $600. This good showing I was able to make by doing manuscript typewriting of a technical nature for one of the best-known professors at Harvard. He turned over to me the manuscript sheets of two books, and I translated his scrawl into intelligible English copy for the printer. One of the queer means by which I earned a quick $5 was the removal of a calf's intestines for the use of a professor in the medical school. All was fish that came to my net.

Students are necessarily debarred from the numerous scholarships offered until they have behind them a year's attendance and the records—recitation and examination—of their work. Finding myself eligible for certain prizes, I at once set about competing for them. My success was out of all proportion with my effort, for I attempted to secure everything available, and received—besides $200 from the Price Greenleaf Aid—a $250 award in the Bigelow scholarship, another $250 from the Bowditch scholarship, and a trifle over $50 for coaching a number of well-to-do idlers. Toward the end of my Junior year I secured quite a corner on the "private tutoring" business by forming classes convening for an hour or an hour and a half at a time and putting the delinquents through a rapid "course of sprouts," giving them valuable tips on questions, and bringing them into condition for the examinations. Bunching them together in this fashion, I was enabled to charge from fifty cents to $2 per capita (according to the difficulty of the studies), and as I conducted my educational kalsomining business on a strictly cash basis I made money until the arrival of examination days put an end to my monopoly.

With an increased income I bought better clothes, paying $30 for a measured suit where formerly a $12 ready-made outfit had to suffice. I began to feel less like an outcast. It is true I joined none of the expensive clubs—like the Porcellian—nor did I become connected with any of the numerous societies which form a social network around Harvard. I kept no high-bred dogs and horses, and had no drains upon my pocketbook from the dues of the athletic clubs, but college life was sweet to me, and the companionships I formed in Cambridge are still as strong as in the early days.

A TRIFLE THAT DETERMINED A CAREER

I began the summer following my Junior year with a brave attempt at driving a buckboard, but soon proved myself worthy of nobler occupation and was elevated to the proud position of hotel clerk—minus the traditional diamond shirt-stud and "loud" clothing. I became so prosperous on $15 a week (board and room free) that I was tempted to embark on the profession of hotel clerk and drop my aspirations to the bar. Something happened which deterred me from adopting a stand behind hotel counters. It was a foolish little incident, but it determined my future occupation, and I am sure I have not yet had cause to regret the choice. A great political discussion had arisen in the country town of which the hotel where I was employed was the chief hostelry. The discussion centred upon whether or not a new and more commodious town hall should be erected to supplant the Noah's Ark box which served as the present seat of municipal business. It was a momentous subject, and the opponents of the new edifice were in the majority—close-fisted farmers, for the most part. A mass-meeting was arranged so that the most eloquent advocates of the town hall question should furnish opinions for the townsmen to act upon at the forthcoming election. More for the fun of the thing than for any other motive, I volunteered to speak in favor of erecting a public structure "in keeping with the beauty and prosperity of the community." To those who opposed the innovation my proposed address was of no consequence. Being a "rank outsider," I was not looked upon with much enthusiasm by those who accepted my services, but they were short of speakers and I "might fill in a gap."

The great night came, and every man of the place who could walk or be carried came to the little toy town hall. I had worked up interest in the verbal contest of the evening among the half-hundred male guests of the hotel, and they helped swell the throng. Speeches in varying degree convincing and ungrammatical had been made when there came a lull in the proceedings.

ATTIC RHETORIC FROM A BARREL HEAD

This was my chance. Mounted on a barrel just outside the door, I began to harangue the crowd which struggled in vain to get through the doorway of the hall. There were almost as many persons outside the building as were within. I began in a loud voice to call attention to the inadequacy of the old structure on such occasions as the present one. I talked of the "penny wise, pound foolish" policy of town and village government. I appealed to the native's pride of citizenship and to his patriotism. I piled quotation on quotation, and hurled Latin and Greek at them in rolling periods. I finally wound up my peroration with a pat and amusing story, and retired amid the cheers of both progressives and conservatives. I had drawn out most of the audience from the hall by the mere vigor of my voice. There was nothing too good for me in the town after that night. A new town hall was unanimously agreed upon. I could have had a political office for the asking. They wanted me to open a law office in the town at once, and said I could enjoy a monopoly of the county's legal business if I would settle there. I think so much flattery turned my head, for I went back to Harvard determined to be a great legal luminary in one of the big cities. One thing saved me from conceit. It was the remark of my employer at the hotel: "You may be a pretty glib talker, an' you may know all about law an' politics, young man, but you're a mighty poor hotel clerk."

My Senior year at Harvard, as was and is the case with every earnest student, found every hour of the day, and many hours of the night, occupied with profitable work, equally profitable schemes, or study. I do not think I squandered a single minute. While, perforce, I studied more sedulously, I also contrived to earn more money than in previous years. This was no easy task. Besides keeping up my "coaching parties," I captured four scholarship prizes amounting in monetary value to $525. I do not think I possess an especial talent for profound thought, and am not much concerned about the elegance of my spoken or written thought. I was as much surprised as any one to find that I could win honors and dollars by working a few hours overtime on prize dissertations. I have the knack of conveying my ideas plainly in straightforward English, and a gift of words was provided for me upon my arrival in the world; and these have done much for me as student and lawyer.

THE PATH TO PROMINENCE AT LAST OPENS

I made an assistant of my fellow-student, whose typewriter I eventually bought outright, and turned out of hand a lot of work by proxy. I found myself respected by the fellows who from the start had stepped naturally into prominence, and not infrequently went to their rooms as a guest. This means something in a community where a student may keep himself as isolated as Crusoe on his island, and where social distinctions of rich and poor, idlers and workers, are as clearly marked as though the University were a big town. What with my several sources of income, my growing name (and its consequent benefit) as a tutor and general utility man, I made my final year at Harvard yield me large dividends. At the beginning of my Senior term I forsook Divinity Hall and moved over to better quarters in the yard. I felt that my larger income warranted this extravagance. Whenever I increased my expenditures I made it a rule to add an equal amount to my income. Thus I made up the added expense of new quarters by acting as the agent for a Boston theatre in the selection of intelligent " supers." I found no difficulty in getting students anxious enough to swell " the mob without " and willing to pay for the privilege.

❧

JUST WHAT ONE YEAR AT HARVARD REALLY COSTS

I do not propose narrating every detail of my life during the four fruitful years I lived under the protection of Alma Mater. It is enough to tell that at the end of my Freshman year I was out of debt, and had made my way, an unaided stranger, with an initial capital of fifty cents and a determination to succeed in my endeavor to get an education. I have always been methodical. I believe in the kind of genius which takes pains in doing things. From my first day at Harvard I began to keep an itemized account of my expenditures and receipts. From my memorandum books I have copied the following figures, which, as campaign orators are fond of saying, are " interesting and instructive." These are my Freshman-year expenditures:

Tuition (in three installments of $50 each)	$150.00
Room (in Cambridge; 26 weeks at $2.50 the week)	65.00
Room (in Divinity Hall; 13 weeks at $3.00 the week)	39.00
Board (at the Foxcroft; 38 weeks at $2.50 the week)	95.00
Text-books	30.00
Fuel and light (one large oil lamp)	11.00
Clothes	35.00
Typewriter hire (32 weeks at 25c. the week)	8.00
Typewriter repairs	3.00
Incidentals (including stationery, stamps, etc.)	23.00
	$459.00

These items cover only necessary expenses. For the greater part of my first year I was barely able to make both ends meet. I did my washing and ironing and performed similar menial duties for myself which, though unpleasant, were obligatory. (Of course this was the crucial period in my college career, but it incited me to further effort rather than discouraged me.) My receipts for the first year offer a still more picturesque array of facts and figures, each item the frame of some incident burned in upon my memory as with a branding-iron. Here are my Freshman-year receipts:

Borrowed	$175.00
Window dressing	3.00
Pawned articles	22.50
Bowdoin prize	100.00
Boylston prize	45.00
Small loans	12.00
Typewriting	102.50
	$460.00

At the end of my first academic year I had worked my way to an honorable place in the University, and had one lonely dollar with which to start out on my vacation. That amount, however, was just twice as much as I had when I landed in Cambridge, and I was at least fifty cents " ahead of the game," plus a year's tuition and the honor of being a full-fledged collegian.

❧

CLASS DAY TO A POOR STUDENT

On class day I " spread " modestly. My reception was a poor little effort, compared with the larger affairs of the societies, at the Pudding and the Hemenway Gymnasium, or the brilliant illumination of Beck, with its curtained inclosure and orchestra, but to these my friends had sent me cards, and from my own windows I could look out upon the fairest sight of all, the lantern-hung yard; and the sweetest music of the day, the farewell songs of the glee club, Lena Dear, and the Arion, were equally mine with all the world.

Having graduated, I faced the future with all my debts paid and a record of good scholarship, good behavior, and the good will of faculty and students alike. I returned home with $25 tucked away in my wallet—that money the grown-up child of my poor, little fifty-cent piece of four years before. My university training had cost me less than $2000. I make no boast of this fact, however, for others have gone through for less money, though none, I am sure, ever began a college career in Cambridge as I began mine, with no home resources, no cash in hand, indifferent mental training, and poor health. For my education at Harvard I spent less than many young men spend for pleasures during the same period.

By taking advantage of every opportunity offered to needy students—such helps as the Loan, Library and Furniture Associations; by hard work and earnest effort in securing some of the many cash prizes in which the corporation is especially generous; by keeping alert, cheerful, clear-headed and tactful, any determined young man can secure with economy and honor all the advantages of a university education.

A PROSPECT

Sixty-Eight Million Dollars Were Given for Colleg
We May Soon Exp

OVER-EDUCATION.

t Year;—if the Mania for College Education Continues
e Above State of Affairs.

Should Railroad Men Be College Men?

By Charles F. Thwing, LL.D.

President of Western Reserve University and Adelbert College, Cleveland

DRAWN BY GUERNSEY MOORE

THE members of every calling are in peril of becoming unduly prejudiced in favor of their calling as a necessary means or method for the improvement of man. It is well, therefore, for them frequently and justly to test the worth of their calling by a direct appeal to life itself. From such professional idolatry college officers are not free. From such professional idolatry college officers should use every endeavor to keep themselves free. The American college should constantly demand of the American people an answer to the question whether it is doing the utmost for the betterment of American life.

For the purpose of getting a more adequate understanding of the relation existing between the college and an important department of American life I have lately conferred with representative officers of many American railroads. Two questions I have submitted to the President or General Manager of one hundred leading railroads of the United States:

"What are (*a*) the advantages, (*b*) the disadvantages, possessed by a college graduate in entering the railroad service, not possessed by a graduate of the high school or the grammar school?"

"On the whole, would you advise a boy of eighteen, of intellectual habits, of apparently efficient administrative abilities, who has graduated at a high school and who desires to enter any branch of the railroad service, to go to college?"

To these letters, in the majority of cases, answers have been received.

I suppose that in all the current discussion regarding the function of the college no one questions but that a college education does aid one in being or becoming a gentleman. I suppose, also, that usually it is granted that a college education does aid one in being or becoming an efficient member of society. The exceptions to these two principles are so infrequent that one may eliminate them from the discussion regarding the worth of the college. But the general advantages which are supposed to accrue through a college education do not touch, in the view of certain good and wise persons, the fundamental question of the advantages or disadvantages possessed by the college graduate entering business as a life career. Touching the question of the worth or the worthlessness of a college course as a preparation for business no more vital method of discussion can be arrived at than one which shall limit an appeal to the question of railroad service; for the railroad service is the largest field for the employment of labor, and also it unites several diverse kinds of labor, as financial, executive, legal and mechanical.

Four Disadvantages of College Training

It is not to be denied that there are disadvantages placed upon those who enter the railroad service after the completion of a college course. One of these disadvantages arises from the environment which the college is supposed to represent. The college represents to most men an atmosphere of leisure, of wealth, and frequently of the extravagant, unwise use of wealth. This disadvantage touches those entering any form of service as well as those entering that of the railroad. The General Manager of the Atchison, Topeka and Santa Fe Railway Company says: "Unfortunately a majority of the young men who pass through college are financially able to live on a scale which they cannot hope to do in railroad service and are apt to contract expensive habits, and few of them are willing thereafter to begin railroad work at the very bottom, or, if they do, find the work too irksome and do not persevere therein. This, in my judgment, is the principal reason why so many prominent railway officials come from boys of moderate education and particularly from boys who begin the work while very young."

A still more obvious disadvantage springs from the time, later by four years, at which one is able to begin the railroad service. This disadvantage is direct, positive, and plain as the alphabet. "If he desires to enter railroad work, and is eighteen years of age, he won't have time to go to college if he desires and expects to reach the top before he dies. Consider that it takes an average of over thirty years' actual service to make a railroad president, which, of course, is considered the top of the ladder, so no time is to be wasted if the top is to be attained." Thus writes the General Manager of the Boston and Albany Railroad.

The President of the Ann Arbor Railroad says: "The college graduate is at a disadvantage compared with the graduate of the high school and the grammar school for this reason: that he has usually spent from three to five years of his life at college, and consequently is that much older and has less opportunity for improving himself in the branches that would fit him for railroading or any other commercial business." The President and General Manager of the Monon Route says: "Should the high school graduate, however, enter the service directly after graduation he would have at least four years' advantage in practical experience at the time the college graduate would enter the service, and in my judgment the college graduate would not be equal to the high school graduate until he had at least five years' practical experience."

A third disadvantage, which should not be passed over, lies in that condition of human nature which is inclined to depreciate advantages richer than those enjoyed by one's self, and to be willing to lessen the apparent worth of men who have had larger opportunities than one's self. Prejudice does exist still among many railroad people against the college graduate. Prejudice is becoming less, but it is not yet wholly eliminated.

A fourth disadvantage should not be omitted. This disadvantage lies in the arrogance and cockyism of certain college men. One, of course, emphasizes the word certain, for cockyism or arrogance is not the prevailing characteristic of college men, any more than it is the prevailing characteristic of humanity itself, but some college men are cocky. The General Manager of the Grand Trunk says: "A college education, I believe, leads a young man, on entering railroad service, to think that he 'knows it all;' of course, theoretically, he may, but any one who has such an idea rarely succeeds."

College men are usually willing to begin at the bottom of the ladder and climb up step by step, if this method of progress represents their duty. I know of a graduate of Harvard College who wished to learn the business of making steel. He was directed to shovel coal beneath boilers. At the time he received his first month's pay he was asked how he liked his job. "I have nothing to complain of," he remarked, "but I wish to ask: Why is it necessary for me to keep shoveling coal in order to learn to make steel?"

"For you to learn the business of making steel you must learn how coal behaves when it is on fire; you can in no way learn how coal behaves when on fire so well as by shoveling coal into the furnace."

Men Who Make Themselves Felt Anywhere

These four disadvantages which I name—soft environment, time, prejudice of officers or workmen, and arrogance in one's self—are disadvantages touching more or less strongly the college graduate who enters the railroad service. The summing up of the advantages and disadvantages is very well made by Mr. Cutts, General Passenger Agent of the Minneapolis and St. Louis Railroad. Mr. Cutts says: "At the present time civil-service rules are so generally observed, except perhaps in the professional branches of railroad service, such as the legal, medical and engineering departments, that it is usually quite difficult for a young man to get an opening except in the lowest grades; consequently the boy who begins with a high school education at, say, seventeen, will, by the time he is twenty-three, be much further advanced than the young man of twenty-three who entered on leaving college at twenty-one; and if we allow that they are of equal mental and business capacity the boy who started at seventeen will always remain in advance. Hence it seems fair to conclude that the four years between seventeen and twenty-one will prove to have been more profitably spent in gaining experience in the rudiments of the business than at college. The men who have made the greatest successes in the railroad field have generally been men without much schooling, but with great capacity for the absorption of knowledge, tireless workers, men who would make themselves felt anywhere, not born into the railroad business, but, getting there by chance, men who have improved every opportunity and overcome every obstacle, rising by sheer force of ability to a point where they attract the notice of the management and then later of the capitalists, who are always in search of tried men in whom to repose confidence and responsibility. After all, it is the man and not the years spent at school that tells, and perhaps in the class referred to the struggle of obtaining an education by reading and by observation while performing their daily work is just the kind of exercise best calculated to develop the remarkable characteristics which they bear."

The Atchison and Lehigh Valley Favor the Colleges

And yet more than a score of my correspondents directly affirm that a college education is of advantage, and usually of great advantage, to one who purposes to become a railroad man. Mr. Mudge, of the Atchison, Topeka and Santa Fe Railway, says: "On the whole, I would advise a boy of eighteen to take a college course before entering railroad work, provided he feels satisfied that he will still be willing to commence at the lowest round of the ladder and persevere in the work as thoroughly as he would have done had he commenced it four years earlier."

The President of the Lehigh Valley Railroad says: "Railroad work, as all other work of a similar character, has reached that point in its development where the man who has the best-trained mind, other things being equal, has the greatest chances for success. If a boy is so situated in life that he can continue his studies, after graduating at a high school, by taking a course through college, it will be decidedly to his advantage in the end. What seems to be needed at this time in young men who decide to follow railroad work as their career, is not so much any special knowledge as a thoroughly well-trained mind."

An officer of the Southern Railway Company says: "I am a staunch believer in education in its broadest sense, and I would infinitely rather have any young man in whom I am interested possessed of a college education and thrown upon his own resources at that time, than to have him start on his life's work earlier and with a small capital at his command, which, being controlled by one without experience, might be easily lost and not available when there has been acquired the experience to control it properly. One of the strongest arguments, I think, in favor of a college education for a young man is the fact that most, if not all, successful business or professional men who have themselves been deprived of the advantages of a college education insist upon their own sons enjoying those advantages."

The President of the Michigan Central Railroad says: "The transportation business of this country is becoming more and more every year an exact science, and the advantages of a college education in disciplining and developing the mind cannot be overestimated. I believe that in the future, as a rule, the managers of the different railroads in this country will prefer to employ young men who have obtained a thorough collegiate education, rather than those who have not gone beyond the limit of a grammar or a high school. My advice to a young man who desires to enter the railroad service would be, after he had finished his course at a high school, to take a course of three or four years at some scientific college, and while this would seem to put off the day when he would enter the railroad service, I am satisfied that in the end, all other things being equal, he will rise to a higher plane than if he had not obtained such an education."

The Views of Some High Officials

Lucius Tuttle, President of the Boston and Maine Railroad, says: "The years of mental training that the college graduate has secured will enable him to accomplish more in a shorter time than is possible for the young man who has not had these advantages; and, everything else being equal, I think that the college graduate in the end will be more successful in any class of business than the young man who enters service after a common or high school education."

Mr. Axtell, Vice-President of the Chesapeake and Ohio Railway, says: "The chief officers of a railway company need the training and the perfect command of the action of the mind which a collegiate course is supposed to, and I believe does, afford. They must be able to deal with and contend with the best-trained intellects in the country, and to do this it is proper that they should have all the advantages of a complete education. I therefore think that any boy aspiring to a chief position in a railroad should go to college if he can; it will help him. Many cannot go who still by strenuous effort reach high places, but in such instances they have a full realization of the difficulties they have contended with."

The President of the Wabash Railroad says: "To *enter* any of the other departments, a college education is not necessary, but if the young man has the right sort of material in him he will be advanced, and as he reaches the higher positions he will find that his college training, if he has had the advantage of it, will be of great benefit to him. On the whole, I am decidedly of the opinion that a man with a college education has the advantage of one without, not only in the railroad service but in any walk of life; and socially as well, and I would say to any young man that if he has an opportunity to secure a college education he should take advantage of it, no matter whether he expects to become a railroader, to enter one of the professions, or to adopt a mercantile career.''

These statements which I quote at length, and other statements also which, if space allowed, I should be glad to print, contain certain common lines of truth either expressed or implied. One of these elements refers to the character and power of the boy himself. One might say all depends upon the kind of boy who goes to college; all depends upon the kind of boy who enters the railroad service.

The General Superintendent of the Fort Worth and Denver City Railway Company says: '' Primarily it can be stated that whether or not a college education would be of any assistance to a young man would depend largely upon himself. In railroad business in almost any department there is undoubtedly room for young men of good education, but with it they must have a desire for the class of work they have selected, or rather the work that is found in the department to which they have gone, and a willingness to start at the bottom of the ladder and perform what might appear to them to be unimportant duties with the same degree of care as would be exercised in the higher branches. Railroad business requires assiduous application on the part of the employee, and success will depend largely on how well he may do his work, his ability for organization and administrative capacity, and for mastering the details of the work assigned. In the mechanical and engineering departments a great many technical questions come up that could be quickly solved by a young man with a college education if he had applied himself in that direction. A college education, perhaps, is not essential to one's success in the railroad business; but any man possessing the same, with opportunities to succeed in railroad business, would, I consider, be doubly equipped.''

Mr. Marvin Hughitt, the President of the Chicago and Northwestern Railway Company, says: '' Whether it be to the disadvantage of a young man to devote the time necessary in obtaining a collegiate education, in preference to going at once into railroad or other work, depends to a very great degree, if not wholly, upon the 'make-up' of the young man. And in the consideration of the advisability of the one course or the other this question of the kind of 'timber' a young man may be becomes a most important factor, in my judgment, in reaching a conclusion, considered both with regard to his school life and to his discharge of the duties pertaining to whatever line of work he may undertake; for one young man's mental equipment may be such, as compared with his fellow-worker, that when he has finished grammar or high school he will have reached a point in mental discipline and training that many of his coworkers can only hope to reach at the end of a thorough college course.''

Every Boy an Individual Case

One boy is better fitted to take up life and work on his graduation at the high school than is another boy on his graduation at college. Much depends not only on educational power, but the *morale* of the boy himself. His regard for the cardinal virtues has as great value as his respect for the cardinal verities. Moral honesty is as important as intellectual honesty. The love and practice of justice is more elemental than a sound intellectual interpretation of the origin and nature of justice. One boy who never goes to college may, by reason of his intellectual and ethical power, reach a far higher place than one who does go. Nature did for the one who finished his education with the high school more than both nature and the college did for the other. But of course the proper method is not to compare man with man, but to compare man with himself. The question is not whether a college education will make one man more efficient than another man, but whether it will make any man more efficient than he would have been without it.

In these remarks, too, is found a certain general inference to the effect that the value of education lies in the securing of a trained mind. It is also to be said that a trained mind is a mind trained to think. The railroad presidents, managers and superintendents who are most valuable are the men who can think. One of the railroad managers of the Northwest had a somewhat unique experience. The railroad of which he was superintendent was sold. The purchaser visited him in his office. He found him before a desk covered with papers writing or signing letters. The purchaser remarked:

'' Mr. W——, you and I will not get on together.''

'' Why, sir?''

'' Because you are so busy with your correspondence that you have no time to give to me. I don't want a man writing letters or signing them about ordinary business. For labor of that sort I can get a man for a thousand dollars. I want you to be free from this business and spend your time thinking about improvement in the efficiency of this railroad.''

The superintendent took the hint. The next time the owner of the road came to see him he was in his office, his desk clear of papers, apparently doing nothing, but really doing much and most. The power which the great railroad man of this country possesses is the power to think, and it is that power which the railroad system of this country opens every opportunity for using. Be it said that this is the power which the American college is ordained to develop.

A Technical or '' Liberal '' Education?

An important question emerges at this point. Should the education which the railroad man is to receive be a general college education or a technical one? This question is part of a still broader question whether a man should enter into the period of preparation for his profession immediately upon the close of his high school or academy course? The lawyer, the minister, the doctor pursues his professional study after his college course. The engineer, in all the various lines of engineering, usually makes his undergraduate course and his professional course identical. The technical school is supposed to take the place of both the liberal and the professional course. In general, if a man can afford the time, I am sure it is well for him to take up his technical course after his liberal education. But the expense in both time and money is great. Without entering into a discussion of the question, I am confident that it is best for a man proposing to enter the railroad service to enter the regular college; but while pursuing his course in the regular college to give to this course a scientific or technical relation. Let him, for instance, make special study of physics, chemistry, geology, economics and sociology. Such studies pursued in a college of liberal arts and sciences will prove to be at once liberalizing and also sufficiently professional.

The history of the administration of railroads of the United States is the history of a development. In the beginning the management of railroads was committed to their owners. This form of administration gave way presently to an administration carried on by those who had been trained in actual service. At the time of this form of administration legislators aroused themselves to the problems touching the public weal and wealth which the railroad had created. Strikes also came in and destroyed valuable railroad property. For meeting such conditions practical men had little or no knowledge. There arose a demand for men who could and can take a large view of the problems presented by the railroad service, and who can do much, through their power, for the solving of these problems. At this period in the development the college man was called into the service.

There can be no doubt, I think, that the problems created by the American railroad are increasing in number and difficulty. The need, therefore, of the properly and nobly trained mind in the solving of these problems is to become yet more and more urgent. Mr. Frank Trumbull, President of the Colorado Road, says: '' In my opinion the time is near at hand when the untrained boy, with moderate capital, will have a smaller relative chance for success, and the scientifically trained young man will be more in demand than ever before in the world's history: this because of the natural growth of combinations of capital and labor, and the impossibility of manufacturing or monopolizing brains.''

This paper has already become too lengthy. But I wish still to take space in order to say that success in the administration of the railroads, as in administration of any business, belongs, first, to the man of sound physical health; second, to the man of noble moral character; third, to the man who is a gentleman; fourth, to the man who, having a general education, is able to weigh evidence, to observe, to compare, to infer, to think; fifth, to the man of special education, who is able to apply his general power of thinking to the solution of problems immediately presented in and by his vocation; and, sixth, to the man who, having all these powers and finding himself face to face with opportunities, is willing through hard, diligent, noble work to apply his abilities in doing the duty which the opportunities lay upon him.

FRANCIS L. PATTON

Should a Business Man Have a College Education?

By Francis L. Patton
PRESIDENT OF PRINCETON UNIVERSITY

A BOY fifteen or sixteen years of age, let us suppose, has decided on a business career, but wishes to know whether it would be better for him to go to college first. This is a very important question and he must settle it soon, for unless he is at one of the schools which are specially intended to fit boys for college he may find that his school curriculum, however excellent in its way, is not of the kind to open to him the doors of many of our universities.

It is rather unfortunate that there are two types of secondary education in this land, one having in view '' the entrance requirements '' of the leading universities, and the other intended to fit men for the activities of life in the various avenues of employment. The High School principal says very naturally that he must plan his curriculum with reference to the wants of the great mass of his pupils who, when they leave school, must earn their living, and who cannot go, or at all events do not intend to go, to the university. He must see to it, therefore, that certain studies which are not included in the college entrance requirements, but that are, as he supposes, important factors in fitting boys to be good citizens and in enabling them to earn a livelihood, are incorporated in the High School's schedule of studies. If, therefore, a boy discovers toward the close of his career at the High School that he wishes to go to college it may easily happen that he will find that he has learned the things that he ought not to have learned and left unlearned the things that he ought to have learned. It is a pity that through lack of a proper articulation of the High School and the universities so few of the High School graduates go up to the universities. This condition of things is not likely to last, and there are indications now of an approximation of the High School curriculum to the requirements for admission to our colleges and universities. This approximation would go on more rapidly, perhaps, if there were, on the one hand, a little more elasticity in the construction of entrance requirements, so that a liberal substitution of '' equivalents '' would be allowed, and particularly if, on the other hand, the custodians of High School education would more commonly recognize the fact that the general mental discipline which fits a boy for college is the best discipline also to qualify for the work of life.

ALONE AT LAST!

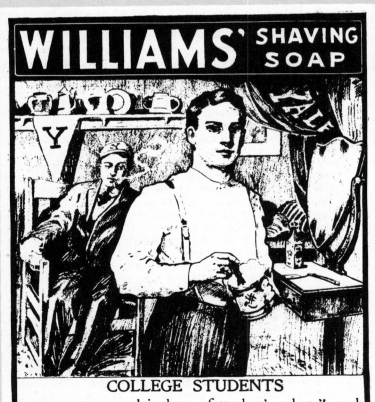
Are College Men Barbarians?

ON THE whole, despite apparent exceptions, college men were never more intellectual, never more eager in their pursuit of culture, and never more moral in practice than they are to-day. But in making this general statement certain discriminations are also to be made. More men are going to college than ever before. The proportion of college students to the whole population has vastly increased in the last fifty years. Courses of study are more numerous. The field of scholarship is wider. Scholarly experts are occupying teachers' chairs. The result is, first, that the best men in college classes are better than the best men of the earlier time. The result is, secondly, that the poorest men are poorer in scholarship and ability than the poorest men of the earlier times. The result is, thirdly, that the ordinary college man is now more scholarly than was his father twenty-five or thirty years ago. He is, on the whole, a better scholar; but he is not a better thinker. He has gained in scholarship; he has lost in thoughtfulness.

To say, as is sometimes done, that college students are barbarians is to speak in extreme terms. College men do at times give that impression. The newspaper reports of their actions often add color to such an opinion. But the reports are essentially false. The facts are not put in just proportion and perspective. The actions of college men that give the impression of barbarism are not characteristic. This conduct is accidental, incidental, not essential. It represents the bubbling over of animal spirits. Marching, cheering, singing represent the outpourings of vigorous, healthy life.

Essentially the college man respects the dignity and fitness of things. He is more devoted to books than to pranks. He respects scholarship more than ignorance. He honors courtesy. He despises boorishness and abominates the boor. He has regard for historic results, forces, conditions. His fun is without malice, and his sport has no evil intent.

●

Wanted: A Course in Courtesy

LAST week a feeble, gray-haired man boarded a car in which four sturdy young fellows, undergraduates in one of our universities, were seated. He rode standing for ten squares. None of them offered him a seat. He is a man distinguished for his learning, and they probably reasoned that he had distinction, scholarship and the respect of the community, and they had only their seats, worth five cents apiece, and the legal right to keep them.

Or, more probably, they belonged to a class that never has had a chance to learn the courtesies of life, and it did not occur to them that they had any duty to perform in the matter.

On the same day a member of the senior class in one of our principal woman's colleges wrote to a woman of advanced age, whom she never had seen, as follows:

Miss Blank proposes to form a collection of autographs and wishes to have yours. Indite your name in the middle of a page and return the book promptly to Miss Blank. Miss Blank incloses stamps for you to use.

Which proved that Miss Blank had some sense of honesty, if not of courtesy.

Why should not our public schools and colleges teach good manners? We make the proposal in all seriousness.

There are a thousand little customs or rules which a well-bred man observes when he walks or talks or eats, in the house or the street or the train. If he fortunately has learned them in his childhood he is as unconscious of them as he is of the act of breathing. But he cannot sit in a room or a car near you for a half-hour, though he does not speak a word, without betraying whether he has learned them or not. There can be, too, no doubt that his lack of good breeding will be more offensive to a stranger than his lack of good morals.

Now, our schools and colleges are filled with quick-witted girls and boys, many of whom, because of poverty, never have had the chance to learn the simple rules of good breeding which will be as necessary to them in pushing themselves up in the world as the Freemason's secret signs are to him in opening the lodge doors. We teach them gratuitously science, literature and countless ways of earning their living. Why do we refuse to teach them the little observances which will win for them friends, influence and power?

We open to all of our boys and girls the way to the position and the power of "ladies" and "gentlemen." Why not fit them to fill the parts? No success will compensate them for the want of good breeding. We have had able women, and men too, in the White House who have been wretched failures for the lack of that ease and simplicity of manner which a little training in childhood would have given to them.

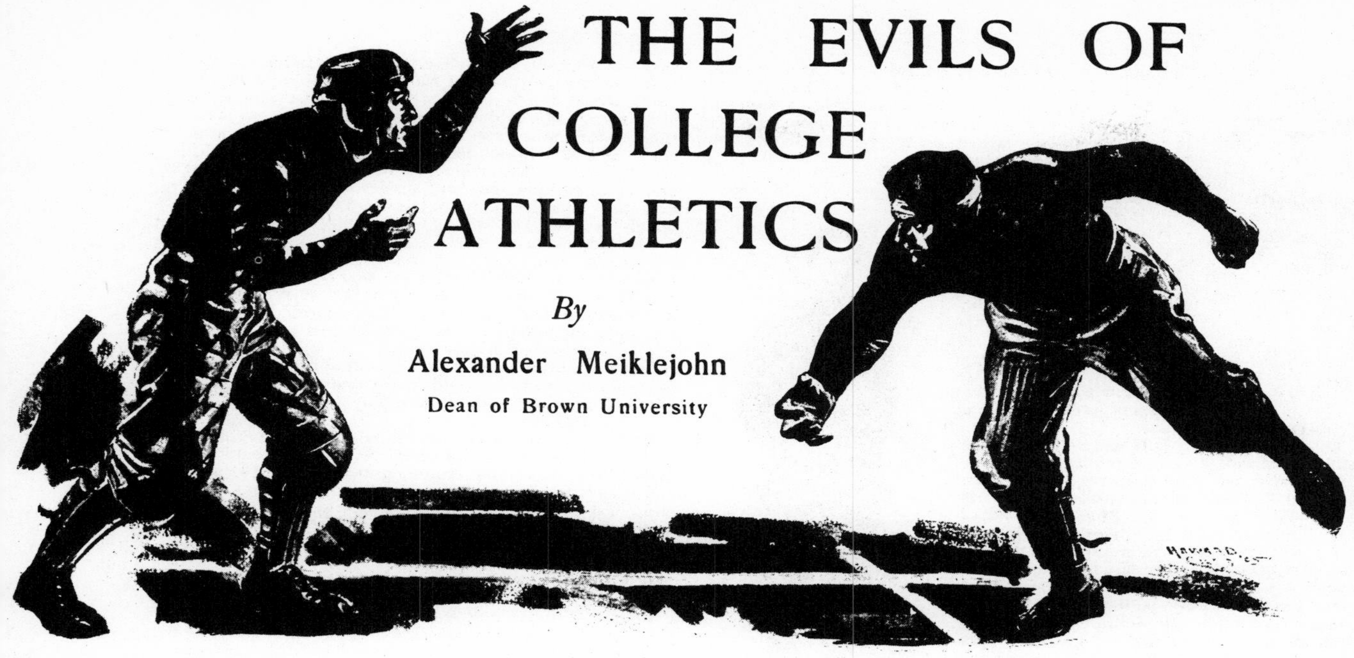

THE EVILS OF COLLEGE ATHLETICS

By

Alexander Meiklejohn

Dean of Brown University

WHETHER for good or for ill, intercollegiate athletics is to-day the most powerful social influence in the life of the Eastern college. Its influence for good in the development of the undergraduate is more decisive than that of any other factor except the intellectual leader-hip of high-minded teachers. Its influence for evil is becoming so pparent in the forms of unfairness, untruthfulness, and brutality s to threaten the most vital interests of the college training.

This contrast of the good and the evil comes out most clearly in "big" game of football, such as I saw during the last season. It 'as a glorious contest—one of those battles in which, with teams lmost equal in strength, the stronger fights its way, plunge by lunge, through the opposing line, often thrown back, but still ghting on, keen, remorseless, persistent; while the weaker team, oomed from the start, simply will not be beaten till the finish, oping to the last for victory. The joy of that struggle is with me et; the power of the winners, the gallantry of the losers, the oyalty of the boys who cheered their fellows in victory or defeat. and when, at the end, the men of the losing college gathered to-ether on the stands and cheered their players one by one, and nally, with bared heads, sang the song of their Alma Mater, they nd we had an experience worth the having. Those boys may not ave known what ideal it was they were cheering, but it was some ideal," and they were better for the worship of it.

But as we went from the field a friend began to ask me ques-ions. "Do you consider that sport healthy and normal?" he sked. "Did you see the slugging? Did you notice that the boys 'ere cheering to drown out the other team's signals? Is it true hat there were men on each team who had no right to play, under he rules? Do the students condone and encourage evasion of the ules? Is it true that preparatory-school players are attracted to he colleges by 'inducements'? Aren't there lots of other evils?" and when to all these questions I had reluctantly assented, he de-manded: "Why, then, do you college men permit such things; why on't you stop athletics altogether? Isn't it better to have no ames at all than to have them at the cost of fairness and honesty?" Before such questions as these the joy and inspiration of intercol-egiate athletics disappear. This certainly is true—whatever the alue of athletics, the evils of the present situation are simply in-olerable.

First, then, why should we have intercollegiate competition at ll? So far as football, baseball, and rowing are concerned, it is either good exercise nor good fun for the participants. The train-ng to which the men are subjected is far too severe and pro-onged to be good exercise for a student. Games within the col-ege, games between classes, dormitories, fraternities—these are ar better forms of exercise from the standpoint of health and un than is intercollegiate competition. These games should be de-eloped and facilities should be provided for them. But the value f intercollegiate competition is quite distinct from theirs—a value which justifies the sacrifice of fun, of time, of strength, and even, o some extent, of health. It is the value of furnishing a dominant ocial interest, of fusing together the members of a college com-nunity, of developing a college democracy, of creating a "college pirit." The importance of this service appears from several points f view.

In the first place, the service is one which no other factor in col-ege life can render. Nothing else can so get hold of the spirit f the college as the physical struggle of an intercollegiate game. t is war; it is conflict—a trial of skill, of strength, of endurance, n which the chosen champions of either group go forth to battle or the glory of Alma Mater. What our young men glory in is war—the war of muscle and wit, the fighting of chosen athletes or supremacy. Nothing else can so appeal to the imagination of body of young Americans.

Again, a common conflict with a common foe is of value in its emand for cooperation, for leadership, for subordination, for self-acrifice and self-control—the virtues of a democracy. It is good raining for the poor man and the rich to find themselves houlder to shoulder, whether in the field or on the stands—omrades in a common cause. Athletic competition tends to keep he personal life of the whole student body sane and pure. Those who are out of touch with student life often fail to realize just what it means to bring together in college dormitories five hun-red or a thousand boys. At a time when the physical tempta-ions begin to reveal themselves and when the restraints of home life are wholly withdrawn, it is worth something that the mere excellencies of the body should be exalted. It is worth something that within the very "college spirit" itself there should be es-tablished admiration for strength of body, for the conservation and development of the physical powers.

Now what are the evils of the situation?

In the first place, college teams do not fairly represent their colleges. To offer an outsider as your representative is not only a lie, but it is also destruction of true sport. But this is just what our colleges are doing. From the "urging" of preparatory-school athletes to the outright hiring of players, this practice is prevalent throughout the Eastern institutions. There is not an Eastern col-lege, important in athletics, which does not make a more or less systematic canvass of the schools. In some of the institutions thousands of dollars are expended annually in the work of se-curing for the teams men who have no right to play on them what-ever. This is an evil harmful alike to the schoolboy and to the college man. It is growing steadily year by year, and little has been done to check it.

A second evil, which has caused much public comment of late, is the evasion of rules. If games are to be played there must obviously be some agreement between the competitors as to the conditions of the contest. It is a lamentable fact that these agree-ments are not kept with loyalty nor even with honesty. There is not an Eastern college in which the "professional" rule has not been broken again and again in recent years. In many of the col-leges the students do not wish to see this rule enforced, and they condone and encourage the lying by which it is evaded. The same evil presents itself in the evasion of rules of play. The players are taught by their coaches to win, and they are encouraged and di-rected to win by unfair means if fair means fail. The war is made *real war*, and the generous rivalry of a friendly contest is lost from sight in the spirit which tries to "rattle the pitcher," to "put a good man out of the game," to "block a runner," or to drown the signals by well-timed cheering. Such tactics are mean and ungenerous. In their pettiness they are often more distressing than deliberate unfairness and deceit.

The third and most fundamental evil is a misapprehension of the place of athletics in college life. After all, athletics is sim-ply one of the student activities. It is more important than the others in social value, but not essentially different from them in any respect. In these recent years, however, it has been exalted to a place in the general university policy—it has become a *method of advertising*. Winning teams pay, we are told; they attract stu-dents, and with more students come better athletics, and so the fame and welfare of Alma Mater are assured. In this scheme of athletics the aim must be not clean, manly sport, but victories. This is the evil which is most fundamental, most subtle, most dan-gerous of all. Until this evil is done away with little will be ac-complished in the purifying of the athletic system.

Whatever the faults of the American student, the real source of athletic evils is not to be found in his character. It lies rather in a system of athletic control which has taken from the student the management of his own games. In most of the institutions the di-rection of athletics has been placed in the hands of a board, con-sisting of representatives of the faculty, alumni, and undergrad-uates in equal numbers, and appointed, wholly or in part, by the trustees of the university. The theoretical defects of this system are obvious. It was based upon the principle that the students cannot be trusted to man-age their own contests. But if this were true it would follow, not that we should impose fairness upon them, but that the games should be stopped altogether. Again, the system makes no adequate provision for in-tercollegiate cooperation in the management of games. It has been blind to the funda-mental principle of all sport, that there shall be mutual understanding and coopera-tion between competitors for the keeping of such agreements as are necessary for the wel-fare of the sport. It is curious to see how these defects in theory have revealed them-selves in the practical working of the sys-tem, so that it has perpetuated and increased the evils it was intended to destroy.

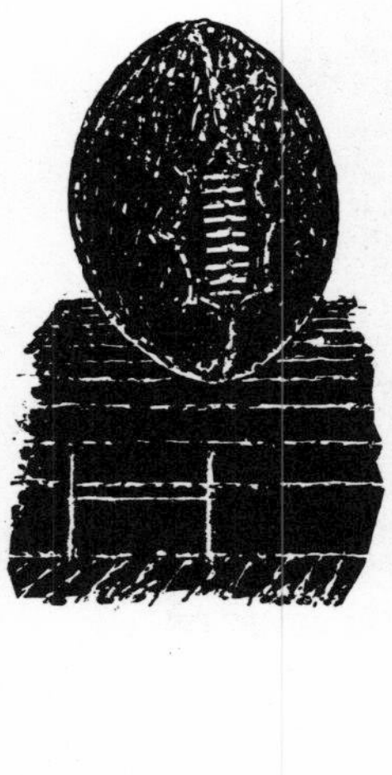

The first practical defect of the system is its inefficiency. How, for example, is the professional rule to be enforced? Practically all that a faculty member can do to secure enforcement is to ask each candidate the direct question, "Are you eligible for the team under the rules?"

Why Students Answer Falsely

If it be asked why the students lie in replying to this, the answer can be found. In the ordinary undergraduate scheme of morality any faculty rule may be broken and the punishment evaded under two conditions: First, if the rule lacks adequate enforcement, so that "everybody breaks it"; and, second, if the rule itself seems essentially unfair and unjust. The fulfilment of the first condi-tion I have heard described in the words of one of the cleanest boys I have ever known. He said: "Before I came to college they told me it would be all right, but when I came out for the team and found that ques-tion staring me in the face I couldn't stand it, and I left the squad. But then I heard that the fellows I had played with during the summer were all out for other college teams, and so I went back. I'm sorry I did it." He had done wrong, and he knew it. But his moral iniquity was not equal to that of the system which forced the situa-tion upon him by making a rule with no adequate provision for its enforcement.

The second condition is also amply ful-filled. Many of the players are in need of money, and it does not seem to them fair that they be debarred from college teams be-cause of their earning money by athletic skill. But, more than this, while the faculty member is asking, "Have you been paid for playing elsewhere?" alumni and under-graduates are asking, "What will you charge to play for us?" One can hardly expect clear moral vision from a boy who is for-bidden to accept his board for playing in the summer, but who is offered the managership of an eating club or a score-card privilege worth hundreds of dollars for playing on the college team. The boy is not a natural liar. But the whole situation seems to him a farce. A second practical indictment of the pres-ent system is that is has done more to cause misapprehension regarding the place of ath-letics than has any other factor.

Undergraduate Control Advised

Now, what is to be done? The under-graduates should be given control of their own games. It should be recognized that if this cannot be done the justification for the existence of the games is gone. None but undergraduates should be allowed to play upon the teams. Men in the graduate and professional departments have no proper place in college life in the sense in which that life needs athletics; they are "out-siders," and have no right to "represent" the college. Neither graduates nor pro-fessional coaches should have any part in the management or coaching of teams.

The attitude of the faculty should be ex-actly the same as toward other student activities. It should take no active part in athletic affairs, but should preserve its own ultimate authority over all college enter-prises. It should provide for careful super-vision of athletic finances. It should recog-nize the fact that at present athletics is taking altogether too much of the time of the players and managers, and should so reduce the schedules of games as to bring the situation within the limits of under-graduate time and wisdom. In general, it must keep the proper balance between ath-letic and other student activities, and must hold before the student the ideals of clean, honest, generous sport.

The one practical movement needed is the formation of a general board of undergrad-uate representatives of the Eastern colleges to take full charge of the athletic situation. Such an action would be theoretically sound in its recognition of principles and it would be efficient in practical administration. It would give for the first time a definite scheme of intercollegiate cooperation; it would ren-der evasion impossible by placing control in the hands of those who know the facts; it would appeal to the student sense of loy-alty to a voluntary agreement; it would call upon one of the strongest elements of the character of the American youth—the sense of efficiency and personal responsibility for his enterprise.

AMATEUR·SPORT

1896. ALL-AMERICA ELEVEN.

Baird (Princeton), full-back.
Kelley (Princeton) and Wrightington (Harvard), half-backs.
Fincke (Yale), quarter and captain.
Gailey (Princeton), centre.
Wharton and Woodruff (Pennsylvania), guards.
Church (Princeton) and Murphy (Yale), tackles.
Gelbert (Pennsylvania) and Cabot (Harvard), ends.

SUBSTITUTES.

In the line.

Cochran (Princeton), Rinehart (Lafayette).
F. Shaw and Wheeler (Harvard).

Back of the line.

Smith (Princeton), Minds (Pennsylvania).
Brown and Dunlop (Harvard).

THE FOOTBALL SEASON OF '96 provided interesting and brilliant illustration of the impossibility, under the present rules, of insuring an open game. And yet the rules of '96, revised under the auspices of the University Athletic Club by a most competent committee, were the best rules which by the light of past experience could at that time have been made. American football, however, is continuously growing, and we must keep pace with its development by accepting the lessons of each season's play, and by recasting our rules in accordance.

For several years the tendency to more or less close play has been marked; two years ago mass plays were the rule, last year much of them was eliminated, and this year the five-yard rule abolished actual mass formation, but left abundant room for close play, and failed to open the game, as most of us had wished it might do.

The lesson taught by the '96 season is, therefore, that the rule reading,

When the ball is put in play, at least five men must be on the line of the scrimmage. If, when the ball is put in play, five players, not including the quarter-back, be behind the line of scrimmage and inside of the positions occupied by players at end of said line, then two of these players must be at least five yards back of said line,

has partially failed in its purpose, and that it does not entirely proscribe mass formations, nor give us the open games so very much desired.

IT WOULD BE UNWISE, I think, to go further in prohibitive legislation in so far as the formation of the eleven is concerned. It seems to me the captain should be bound in that respect to no greater extent than the present rule holds him. Moreover, we do not wish the strategic element of football destroyed, because it is one of its most fascina-

ting qualities. Unless very radical and altogether undesirable rules were made, it is more than probable the ingenuity of captains and coaches would devise a means of getting around any rule in favor of some play which relied for its success largely on mere physical exertion. Nor would it be desirable, in my opinion, forever to expel close play from the captain's catalogue.

What we do wish is to make the play more open. Not because close play is more fruitful of injury, nor because it is not scientific, but because it rather makes of mere brute force an ascendant quality, and tends to the introduction of plays that show too wide a discrepancy between mind and matter.

It is not well for the future of football that its development should be along only the strength-requiring lines. Much physical effort is needful in all the plays of football, but a close adherence to wedges, turtlebacks, and other mass plays would soon destroy the traditions of the game and the interest of the spectators. And it is well to bear this in mind.

RATHER THAN TO GO further in the prohibition of close plays, it seems to me the advisable course of legislation lies in suggesting rules that will make close plays less valuable to the side using them. Experi-

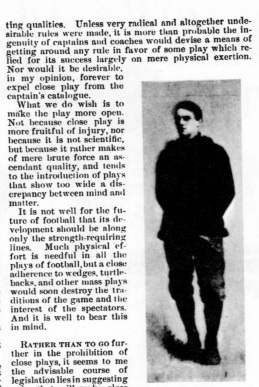

BAIRD, PRINCETON,
Full-back.

ence has taught us that a close play at its uttermost perfection is more often than not sure to gain the requisite five yards in four downs. It may be argued that a team which attains such skilful development in this direction is entitled to the reward, and in a general way this is of course true. But that brings us back to the point from which we started, and from which we wish to diverge. Given two teams of equal physical strength using mass plays, and the game would resolve itself into a pushing-match.

The only apparent solution appears to be through increasing the number of yards that must, in order to retain possession of the ball, be gained in four downs.

It is not probable that greater skill in close plays will be developed than has already been shown, so we are safe in taking what has been accomplished in the past as a basis in providing for the future. If, therefore, it were ruled that a team must gain ten instead of five yards in four downs, we should undoubtedly attain the open game without entirely abolishing close play.

INCREASING THE DISTANCE to be gained would not, so far as I can see, make the game harder. It would naturally make a faster game, and certainly give us plenty of kicking and some of the old long passing and the criss-crosses. Instead of depending on close play almost entirely, it would be reserved for a supreme effort when near the opponents' goal, or tried for a down, or perhaps for even two, on first possession of the ball; but a kick or some brilliant open play would beyond doubt be necessary to making the required ten yards.

Besides, it would relieve the present wear and tear on the men in a hard match. Take, for instance, that "revolving tandem" which Princeton worked this year on Yale to a consummate degree of perfection. It is beyond human possibilities for a tackle—even though he were eight feet tall and weighed a ton—to stand up, not to say to resist, that catapult when directed against him. Any team that perfected such a play would drive through any given point of any opposing line; it is simply the concentration of several men on one man of the opponents' line, towards whom they are whirled in single file. The strength of this play is in the rapidity of the whirling and the contiguity of the men in the whirl. It is the philosophy of shooting a tallow candle through an inch board applied to football. Princeton did it superbly, and wore Yale's line men to a standstill. If Yale had had the same play, and played it so well, Princeton would have found it as impossible to stop as Yale did.

We do not want to lose plays like this, but neither do we want the afternoon devoted to them; because they are practically unstoppable, and if all the teams employed

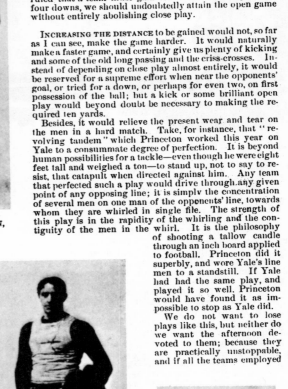

CABOT, HARVARD,
End.

KELLEY, PRINCETON,
Half-back.

FINCKE, YALE,
Captain and Quarter.

GELBERT, PENNSYLVANIA,
End.

WRIGHTINGTON, HARVARD,
Half-back.

MURPHY, YALE,
Tackle.

WOODRUFF, PENNSYLVANIA,
Guard.

GAILEY, PRINCETON,
Centre.

WHARTON, PENNSYLVANIA,
Guard.

CHURCH, PRINCETON,
Tackle.

THE ALL-AMERICA ELEVEN OF 1896.

them, as undoubtedly they will if permitted, we may give over all hope of ever getting more open play.

Perhaps the most satisfactory feature of the past season was the sportsmanly bearing that marked players generally, and especially in the Eastern big games. In no year has there been so little unnecessary roughness. Not a man was ruled out of the important games for slugging, and I saw only one throughout the season who deserved to be. A similar improvement has been noticeable also in the West, and, generally speaking, in the South, although there was one incident in the latter section which would have disgraced the game and the participating colleges but for the prompt action of the interested faculties. Youth and some trouble-making spectators were responsible for the one exception to the Southern rule of clean games manfully played.

Football play of '96 cannot be said to have shown any special improvement on '95, and with the exception of Princeton and Lafayette and the Carlisle Indian School, no Eastern college surpassed its previous efforts, and a few failed even to equal them.

Pennsylvania's eleven, for aggressive strength, was perhaps the most formidable in the history of that university, but as a team it was not so strong as the one of '95. The famous "guards back" interference of '95 was unaffected by the '96 rules, and proved the most valuable of Pennsylvania's methods of advancing the ball. The team was strong, too, on the defence, but in kicking weaker than any of the other leading teams. For the first half of the season Pennsylvania's play was very poor, fumbling and inharmony of action marking her general work; but she immeasurably improved during the last half, and met Harvard at her best, although that best was not up to the previous year's standard. I attribute Pennsylvania's poor showing for half the season to too great a confidence in the benefits of a preliminary training season—a fallacy which will not lead her astray another year, I fancy.

If Harvard's ailment were no more serious, her sons would have occasion for genuine rejoicing. But the verdict of wasted opportunity in '96 was also the verdict on the close of '95, and seems likely to continue for evermore, unless some radical change puts the preparation of the elevens on a more intelligent basis. It is so doleful to repeat the same old story, and yet there is none other to tell. However, I shall make it brief, and so clearly to the point that I hope it may lead to some urgent and consonant action by the men who are nearest to Harvard's athletics. In a word,—Harvard's football eleven was the victim of wretched management, which affected both its training and coaching. Because of improper training, half the team was out of practice on account of injuries most of the season, and actually nine of the eleven that played Pennsylvania were not fit for the supreme effort of so important a game. Because of its inadequate coaching, the possibilities of the team were not fully realized.

This is not to be taken as a criticism on the coaching of Waters and Newell, who gave Harvard one of the strongest lines in her history, but on the policy (and its sponsors) that expects two line men, be they never so expert, to round out a team; that ignores the first principles of training, and sets by the ears all the *alumni* who might, if sensibly encouraged, inaugurate a rational system of coaching.

Waters and Newell were given no substantial assistance from beginning to ending of the season. It will be hardly credited, I am sure, when I say that after the Princeton game, which revealed Harvard's weaknesses, only one football *alumnus* went out to help in the coaching! and all through the season the backs and quarterbacks and ends had the benefit of especial and expert coaching on only three or four occasions!

What result could be expected from such a policy? Harvard simply did not make the most of her material, which was as good as if not the best she ever had. That the team did so well reflects great credit upon Waters and Newell, and more particularly upon the men themselves; I never saw men so handicapped play so well or struggle on more pluckily under such disadvantages.

Whether Harvard's ailment be indifferent *alumni*, or *alumni* and coaches and trainers pulling at cross-purposes, or an improper system of training, or inefficient or insufficient coaching—Harvard football elevens suffer nevertheless, while we all look in vain for the inauguration of that "sensible" policy which we have long heard was forth-coming.

It appears to have become popular to refer to Yale's '96 eleven as the weakest one that ever came from New Haven—a deduction from superficial observation, as are most popular vogues. There have not been so many Yale teams stronger than that of '96, and some have been weaker. In fact, this year's team could not be called weak at all. It was not a star team, but an evenly developed one, and while not so strong as the '95 eleven, was far from deserving the general assertion of weakness. The common mistake made in discussing the respective merits of the larger college elevens is in taking, three or four years ago, the superiority of Yale as a basis for comparisons to-day.

It should be remembered that Yale has been the leader in the development of scientific football, and that the others, in the last three years particularly, have been catching up with her. Two years ago Pennsylvania caught and last year passed her, and Yale's '95 team was about as strong a one as has come from New Haven. This year a lower average of skill behind the line still further lessened Yale prestige, and she has been passed certainly by Princeton and Pennsylvania, and, in actual strength of play, most probably by Harvard also. But that does not indicate retrogression in Yale football; it means improvement in Harvard and Princeton and Pennsylvania.

Last year the Pennsylvania eleven was the strongest we had ever viewed on any field; this year Princeton has developed the most remarkable team in American football history; and this year, too, Harvard had the material which, properly handled, would have very closely contested the season's second honors. Last year Yale used the revolving tandem; this year Princeton has carried it to a superlative degree of development. The days of Yale's undoubted superiority in football have passed, and in the years to come her teams must be satisfied with a share, rather than a preponderance, of victories.

Reasons for Belief in the Value of Exercise and Athletics

By J. William White

John Rhea Barton Professor of Surgery, University of Pennsylvania

THE usual complaints about the abuses of athletics—the distraction of the student's attention from his educational curriculum, the danger of certain sports, the strain in others, have all been answered and re-answered, and there is not much that is new to say about them. They are not all groundless. We do tend to excess in competition; to jealousy and heart-burning and exaggerated rivalry; we think too much of winning; we incline to develop athletic specialists; and we do thereby detract to an extent from the usefulness of athletics to the whole mass of undergraduates. All these matters, however, are the objects of keen and unremitting criticism, and are being steadily bettered in this country. The number and severity of the injuries—in football, for example—have been greatly exaggerated; the frequency of serious strain—as from rowing or sprinting—has been overestimated; the collateral evils of betting, drinking and the like are obviously less than they were when the "great" games took place in cities and not on college grounds.

But the opponents of athletics die hard. In a recent number of a leading periodical is an article which contains within the compass of two pages more ludicrous misstatements than are often seen in such space, and yet it is evidently written by an earnest believer who feels that he has a message for the world. The writer asserts that college athletes upon reaching middle life experience "in a majority of cases what has been called 'the premature decay of physical endurance.'" He quotes an authority—to me unknown—as saying that "athletes do die young." He says that "the lungs also seem often to have suffered some deterioration of cellular tissue, so that pulmonary consumption is not an infrequent disease with adult athletes." He goes on to talk of "early exhaustion of vital energy which was intended to supply the body for seventy years or more," as if he were writing of an oil well or a coal mine; he quotes "some physicians"—discreetly leaving them unnamed—as "pronouncing," "excessive enlargement of special muscles and parts of the body a diseased growth somewhat like a hard tumor. And they say," he continues, with what is the real gem of the article, that "in the end the result will be the same as with other diseased growths—a pernicious anæmia, or consumption of the blood." It would all be too absurd for notice if it had not been put before thousands of non-medical readers by one of the best periodicals of this country, and thus made potentially the cause for alarm on the part of parents, guardians and educators of youth.

Real College Football

By David Starr Jordan

No college president is more popular with the student body over which he presides than is the president of Stanford University. Because of his sympathetic attitude, his estimates of collegiate affairs are highly valued

COLLEGE football has come to stay. It has its advantages, its dangers, and its evils, but it fills a place which no other game can take. Its strength lies in team work, not in individual plays. Its members are bound together by the strongest of ties, the tie of college spirit. A football match is to the loyal spectators the crash of one beloved organization against another. A professional team has no such ties; there are, therefore, no successful football teams outside the colleges. Non-collegiate teams represent nothing. The public is only bored by the victories of local teams or athletic clubs. But a struggle of Harvard against Yale, or Michigan against Wisconsin, fires the imagination and touches the deeper feelings of college men, and through them the greater world whose imagination they direct. Whether this ought to be the case or not does not matter. This is the fact, and none of the more individual sports, as baseball or track athletics, has this effect.

The evils of football mainly centre around the use of money as an aid to winning. When money is used, no matter how subtly, it is no longer a matter of students playing; it is not an outflow of animal spirits; it takes its rank among the game agencies of demoralization. Against this tendency, student committees can not stand alone. It takes the full force of the college authorities. When the Faculty has failed to put its whole strength on the side of clean football, some form of corruption has appeared.

It is vitally essential then that the football men should be held to their work just as severely as any other students and at all times. It is necessary that no football man should be allowed to receive money from any source in consideration of his playing. This excludes him from scholarships, from receiving gifts from alumni or citizens, from occupying sinecure summer positions provided by interested friends, from any of the hundred opportunities of attending college without paying its cost. Every financial aid, each academic leniency given to athletics, tends toward the demoralization of college athletics. In baseball, a professional or hired team may defeat any college team composed of those who play only for sport. In like fashion, an invincible football team might be hired by direct or indirect means, if the Faculty would wink at its employment and supplement this wink by convenient and lenient re-examinations of the athlete too dull or too busy to attend to his classes.

The future of football depends on the conscience of the college authorities. If these are satisfied with victory and indifferent as to other considerations, we shall have in football a source of progressive demoralization. If they insist on clean games played by clean players, the game of football will endure to the delight of our grandchildren, an unfailing source of that joy and good fellowship called college spirit, which, if not the highest academic product, is really a thing worth having and worth cultivating.

Endowing the College Athlete

THE proposal of certain Cornell alumni, to establish a scholarship to be awarded on the basis of scholastic attainments, character and athletics combined, opens up vistas of delight to the comic spirit. On the face of it, the proposal is identical with the Cecil Rhodes bequest; but whereas that was received with joy this is opposed with reprobation, and especially at Ithaca.

If it is right for an English university to reward sportsmanlike prowess with a stipend, why is it wrong for an American university? Simply because it is. There athletics is, and always has been, primarily a pastime. Here we make of it first and last a business. In England the authorities are not for a moment to be suspected of a tendency to swerve from the line of rectitude in order to further the chances of beating the rival university. At Cambridge, it is true, there once were signs of pique over the sudden influx of tried athletes at Oxford, but the occasion was at the worst one of half-satirical jest. In America we know by bitter experience that even college faculties are prone to cultivate success on the field as a mere advertisement. Once legalize the endowed athlete, and the way is opened up to a hideous orgy of professionalism in masquerade.

FRANK MERRIWELL AT YALE AGAIN

OR BATTLING FOR THE BLUE.

BY BURT L. STANDISH

If football dominated American universities, *Life* predicted in 1904, future college presidents would look like this.

This cartoon also accused colleges of placing too much emphasis on "Soc et Tuum" athletics.

Homer and the Housemaids

WE ASKED a question the other day of the ordinary college graduate: "Except for making a front, how much use have your Latin and Greek or your analytic geometry been to you?"

It was not a question likely to receive prompt or enthusiastic answers. Americans have made a fetish of the unregulated book-drilling which they give to the minds of their children and call Education. They will not tolerate any criticism of it. They hold it to be so indubitably a good thing that a dose of it will permanently uplift any boy or girl. It is like the old patent medicines warranted to cure every disease in every patient.

Just look at the facts. Here we have millions of foreign children: Swedes, Russians, Irish and German, besides the swarming myriads of natives, red, white and black, to fit for their future lives. Of this multitude will come a few leaders and teachers for the next generation. Now we give to them all a smattering of the education of teachers and leaders—bits of recondite knowledge: a taste of Greek, a nibble of international law, a whiff of the higher mathematics. We seem to have an idea that any man may be seized on any day by Fate and put into command, and we give them all this ragged coat of shreds and patches of learning so that no man may feel intellectually naked when he is dumped into the White House or on the Supreme Bench.

The plain fact is that three-fourths of these children will be tradesmen, mechanics, laborers, cooks and shopwomen. They have but four short years to master the training which will enable them to earn a living by these trades and to live with intelligence and dignity. Why rob them of this chance to better and widen their lives by cramming them with scraps of knowledge which by no possibility can be of any service to them hereafter? What use can Joe Pratt, who means to be a plumber, make of Homer? Or why should his sister, who is to be a trained nurse, go to a woman's college to study the Semitic tongues?

A few despairing housekeepers in a city in Iowa the other day petitioned the authorities to close the high school, " in order to leave some women in the town who were not unfitted by it for work in the house and kitchen." The appeal was copied throughout the country as a huge joke.

And yet? Has not the old fine art of homemaking fallen into disgrace among us, simply because the popular education of woman makes them despise the skilled trades of the needle and the kitchen range? After all, does the well-being of the nation depend on the skill of its women in cookery and baby-raising or on their knowledge of psychology and freehand drawing?

Somebody proposed lately that the boys in a certain high school should be given a course in drainage and sanitary science instead of philosophy, and that the girls in a woman's college should be taught nursing and housekeeping between the courses in the ancient Frisian dialect and Celtic poetry. But the proposal was laughed to scorn.

Our idea of education apparently still is to hint to the pupil what knowledge he will need should he ever develop wings, but to leave him totally unfit to use his hands and feet.

A Nation of College Graduates

MR. SCHWAB thinks that a college education is a disadvantage to a business man. Mr. Carnegie, the discoverer of Mr. Schwab, thinks so much to the contrary that he has given ten or fifteen million dollars to enable more Scotchmen to have the benefits of which he himself was deprived in his youth.

It appears as if Mr. Carnegie's views were rather more popular than Mr. Schwab's. Every commencement season sees more college graduates turned loose upon the world. Every new academic year finds college walls strained by increasing crowds of students. Where is it going to end?

Well, there is no reason why it should end at all, short of the collegiate education of every person in the community. A hundred years ago the function of the college was thought to be to train candidates for the ministry. Preachers were the only persons who really needed a college education, and that education, by the way, was less advanced in most respects than a high school training is now. Besides the ministers, it was thought that lawyers and doctors might get some benefit from a higher education, but in their case it was not at all necessary. The candidate for one of those professions might very well start in as a boy sweeping out the office of an old practitioner, and pick up a knowledge of the business in his odd moments. Outside of the three learned professions nobody had any real occasion for the things that were taught in college. Indeed, the education of that day was carefully designed to be as unpractical as possible. It gave no assistance in anything so sordid as the art of getting a living; nor did it help appreciably to expand the student's knowledge of the world in which he lived. It ran in a narrow groove, and made no concessions to varying tastes or aptitudes.

But now the whole meaning of education has been transformed. It is no longer a matter of learning to make quotations from Horace. It touches life on every side. It meets every possible need and aspiration, practical or ideal. In the hundreds of courses offered by the great American universities, with their thousands of possible permutations and combinations, there is something to fit every individual mind. There is not only the opportunity for intellectual culture beyond anything dreamed of in the old education, but there is the most practical sort of training for an infinite variety of gainful occupations as new as the modern education itself. A single electrical company this year offered positions to the entire graduating class in the department of mechanical science at Cornell.

Evidently, Mr. Schwab's ideas are not universally held in the business world.

Even now the higher education reaches directly only an insignificant fraction of the population, but there is no reason why, in time, it should not reach all. A few years ago there was a justifiable fear that an increase in the number of college students might mean the creation of a swarm of superfluous ministers, doctors and lawyers, and the subtraction from productive pursuits of numbers of young men who ought to be working with their hands. But now the young man who works with his hands can find in college plenty of material to give him pleasure and inspiration in his calling. The higher education in this country no longer tends to produce a parasitic intellectual aristocracy. The American college is the most powerful ally of American democracy.

HAZING—By Jesse Lynch Williams

IN WHICH AN "OLD GRAD" RISES TO MAKE A FEW REMARKS ON AN ANCIENT COLLEGE INSTITUTION

SO THE sophomores have been making it interesting for you, have they? I'm glad of it; that's one of the things you came to college for. You will agree with me after you get out, if not sooner. What's that? Well, let me illustrate.

Once upon a time during the old days of free, untrammeled hazing—real hazing, I mean, not mere persiflage and pamphlets containing formal freshman-year restrictions—there was a certain professor's son. And he thought his father was a greater man than the president—the president of the college, I mean, for the president of the country was a mere Philistine and did not count. The son should not be blamed for this, because the father would have been inclined to agree with him. I should add that not all professors take themselves so hard. There is a system of hazing that goes on with them, too, even to-day. When a young instructor comes back from Germany weighted down with the dignity of his Ph. D. and feeling sorry for the United States and its deplorable lack of real scholarship —— But about this boy:

"They'd better not try to haze me," he remarked the day he matriculated. "My father is a professor."

It was hard to secure him because he lived at his father's home, and the sophomores did not dare go there after him, even in those days.

"They don't dare haze me," he announced to his classmates as he crossed the campus; "I am the son of Professor Blank." (He always pronounced the capital P in Professor Blank.)

After painstaking efforts Fate delivered him into the sophomores' hands by night. He smiled a kindly warning at them. "Evidently you do not realize who I am," he said, as if to break it gently.

"Um," said his captors gloatingly, "it is hard to realize that we've got you at last." And they hurried him along over the dark road toward the canal.

"You'd better not," he announced; "my father is Professor Blank."

"We know that," was the answer; "that's the reason. Now then," they added, "here's for your father," as they ducked him in a businesslike manner under the cool, moonlit ripples of the canal. "And here," they repeated as he came up spluttering, "is one for you. Now will you be good?"

"You will suffer for this," he roared when he got breath enough; "my father——"

"Ah? then here's for our suffering. *Now* will you be good?" In the course of time he said he would, and he was. He has been a better man for it ever since. They saw to it that he had exercise enough on the way home to keep from dying of pneumonia, and he has lived to return thanks for it—as father used to tell us we should do, you may remember, when he led the way into his study and closed the door.

The canal cure reminds me of the celebrated case of young Pollington, and I tell you this to show you that even I acknowledge that too much medicine is worse than none.

You may have heard the public version of this story; the papers were full of it.

I don't know what was the matter with Pollington; perhaps it was because he came to college with a reputation as an expert swimmer and they did not want him to get out of practice. Some say they gave him more encouragement to swim than he deserved—at any rate, it was more than he wanted, for one dark night, as they loosed their hold of him while he took off his clothes, he slipped out of their reach and plunged head first into the water and—that was all. He did not reappear above the surface. The sophomores waited seconds which seemed like hours, looking up and down the stream. They saw nothing. He was gone.

And they were responsible. That was what came upon them now like a thunderbolt as they ran up to the village for help. But even grappling hooks brought nothing to the surface. Only his clothes were on the bank where they had made him take them off, a pathetic little pile of clothes it seemed now. When carried back to his room a letter was found in the coat pocket. It was addressed to his classmates

and said, "I cannot stand it longer. Good-by." The authorities were aroused. The college became excited. The newspapers got hold of it. It was telegraphed all over the country—big headlines, many editorials. Detectives were put on the case. Finally all but one or two of the sophomores were rounded up. First they were brought in for a hearing before the President and expelled from college. The culprits were about to be turned over to the civil authorities, waiting outside the faculty-room. Pollington himself walked in.

He had swum under water across the canal and had come up noiselessly—a trick known to many swimmers—in the shadow of some bushes on the opposite bank. Then waiting there with only his nose above water until the sophomores left in a panic, he quietly put on a change of clothing which he had hidden in the bushes during the afternoon, and spent the night at a farmhouse, then took an early morning train for a little holiday at home. The hazers had been badly enough hazed already and got off rather easily.

I know of a different case which did not get into the papers. It has never been told before.

Usually the hazing was deserved, and in almost all cases the hazers were reasonable, decent enough chaps who did their harmless tricks—the canal cure was seldom employed—if not as a duty to their younger brothers, at least as a harmless pleasure for themselves. Occasionally, however, there was a bully, like Bum Batter. He was a big, thick-headed brute, as strong as an ox and quite as slow. His special delight was goading nice, innocent, hardworking freshmen, nervous, sensitive little fellows, whose superior sense and sensibilities probably riled up all the bully in big, stupid Batter. Little Harrison Sinclair stood it patiently for a while because he wanted to get everything that was coming to him as a college man. But finally this is what happened:

Did you ever hear of Ike Weir, the "Belfast Spider"? There used to be much about him in the sporting columns of the newspapers, in the old days when he was champion featherweight of the world. By this time he had

THEY WERE BROUGHT IN FOR A HEARING BEFORE THE PRESIDENT

reached the boxing-lessons stage of his career and was called "The Professor" at the Athletic Club of which Sinclair was a junior member. Sinclair wrote a long letter that brought the Belfast Spider down to visit his former pupil. That night Bum Batter and a noisy little nuisance named Channing came around to have their usual sport with their victims. "Another skinny little poler, eh?" drawled Channing, sticking his finger under Ike Weir's face. "You must have been looking for trouble to come into this room." The pugilist had a lean, intelligent face and had borrowed Sinclair's glasses and a cap for the occasion. "Take off your hat, freshman," bawled Batter.

The Belfast Spider kept staring at a Greek book which he held upside down, though he didn't know that.

"Take it off for him, Channing," growled Batter, implying

that this was really too easy for the great Batter to bother with.

"With pleasure," said Channing, and tried to.

Ike in his palmy days had a very pretty way of doing these things. It was so quick that all they saw was the pseudo-freshman springing up from his chair, the flash of a fist, and then Channing thoughtfully picking himself up on the far side of the room, with a red welt forming on his jaw. The pugilist had sat down again and assumed his rôle of the studious student.

"Well! this won't do at all. I'll have to take a hand in this myself," said Batter, rather pleased at the excuse. "Now then, freshman," in a mighty voice, "let's see you take off that hat and apologize to Mr. Channing." No reply; only a quiet, catlike glance. "Here, here! Take it off, I tell you!" Batter now shook his fists.

"Aw! g'wan!" said the Spider. He had been coached not to talk, but forgot in the enthusiasm of his art.

Batter thought the "lanky little poler" was guying his own rather uncouth enunciation, and it made him furious. The real freshmen were chuckling expectantly by this time —which also was contrary to rehearsal—and that made Batter still more furious. "You miserable little pup," he bawled, drawing back his left, "I'll teach you once for all to be impudent to *me*. Take that!"

The Spider quickly moved his head six inches to one side without changing his expression. "Slower'n I sized you up to be," he grinned. And then the inevitable happened. Down and up. Down and up. Then down and out, and hazing was all over in North Entry.

Usually when a boy was hazed much his need was great. These last two cases were merely exceptions to prove the rule, and I have yet to hear of a graduate regretting that he was hazed. But I have recalled these bits of history chiefly to show you how much more conscientious sophomores used to be in the rough-and-ready days of old and to make you feel a little more pleased with the present methods.

Oh, I know you haven't kicked. If you had I shouldn't respect you enough to take the trouble to talk to you. But I can tell from the tenor of your letters, enthusiastic though they be, that you think it rather hard luck, now that you are free from the irksome restraint of schooldays, that a big boy like you, in college at last and called a man by courtesy, cannot do exactly as he pleases and stick out his chest like the college men he used to see at football games.

You have sense enough to smile about it, I see, but you can't quite understand why you should be made to feel so insignificant. When you stop to think of it, you *are* pretty insignificant, to be sure, but you don't see why you shouldn't be allowed on the street after nine o'clock, and you no doubt think you'd feel a lot more like a real college man if they let you smoke a pipe. You don't fancy making way, and even stepping off the walk at times, for every one on the campus except other freshmen. You think it rather absurd that in a college which has grown up into a university and is supposed to have put away childish things that you can wear no other style of head covering than a mild form of black cap.

But it only lasts a year, this rather pleasant purgatory; and you'll appreciate your blatant blessedness all the more when you, in turn, are a sophomore, covered with the college colors, and are yawping terribly at next year's frightened freshmen. Then I fancy you won't think all this so absurd.

Even the sophomores, you'll find, have to give way to the juniors, and the juniors to the seniors, and the seniors, who seem to you to own the campus, if not the earth, touch their hats respectfully to the instructors, and the instructors to the assistant professors, and so on up the scale of academic dignity. It seems rather absurd sometimes to people outside, and so it is, but there is bound to be some kind of ranking here as there is all over the world, even in America where we are supposed to be free and equal, but never were nor shall be, and certainly the best class distinction for a college is the distinction of classes—academic seniority. With human nature as it is there is bound to be some kind, and if not this kind there might be distinctions that harked back to money or social position.

And if such were the case, Dick, you might never learn certain valuable life lessons which every man ought clearly to understand.

Athletics for Girls

THE development of a fondness for athletics among girls has been a noteworthy feature of life in this country during the last decade, and it is not strange that it should be attended by manifestations of misdirected energy and bad taste. From anxious mothers, from teachers and from physicians earnest protests are being made against the tendency to encourage girls to think that they are just as well adapted to the athletic life as boys are.

As to the adaptability of girls to physical exercise, there is something to say on both sides, but the weightier opinion on the part of physicians seems to be that the girl is so different from the boy in temperament and constitution that though a moderate amount of exercise of the right kind and under the right conditions is immensely beneficial, excessive training, overexertion, and the influences of publicity are detrimental to her physical and mental well-being.

All this ought to be sufficiently obvious to any intelligent person who stops to reason about the matter. The trouble is that when athletics for girls became the fashion the majority of parents did not stop to reason about it, but allowed their daughters to do as the other girls did; and there were always enough girls of independent ideas to take the lead and set an example that the others were only too ready to follow.

A reaction against this state of things was sure to come, however, and it has already begun. Even basket-ball—a game supposed to be particularly suited to girls—has come under the ban. Miss Lucille Eaton Hill, director of physical training in Wellesley College, is convinced that competitive athletic contests for young girls, and especially interscholastic basket-ball matches, are exceedingly injurious to the players physically, and tend to "a general lowering of the standards of womanly reticence and refinement." Miss Hill has been studying the conditions of athletics for girls in some of the New England schools, and she finds a great deal to condemn. In one school the girls had formed an association and were training themselves in running and jumping with the aid of boy coaches and without supervision by the school authorities.

The moral of all this is that if parents desire their daughters to be given the right sort of physical training to fit them for lives of usefulness and honor, they must see that the task is intrusted to competent instructors.

Send the Girl to College

AN EXCEEDINGLY shrewd Chinaman, Sir Chentung Liung Cheng, said the other day: "In all our seaports they are now establishing schools for girls. That is the foundation of the reform (of China). Just wait a few years and see what will happen when our educated girls are grown up and become mothers. It is no longer the case in China that the girls are regarded lightly in the family. We are coming to think more of our daughters than of our boys."

Thus it appears that in their study of the Occident the Chinese have hit upon one of its secrets which it too often overlooks itself — possibly because its men do almost all its public talking and public writing. Especially is this secret important to us — the democracy whose mission seems to be to lead the world in the march upward to that Arcady where every human unit shall have the chance to count as one.

Our extensive and expanding system of higher education for women is often bitterly assailed by educated men, even by educators. Bourbonism, especially when bulwarked by vanity, does not yield easily; and it will be many a day before death reaps the last man with the passion for looking down on his fellow-creatures. To avoid unprofitable dispute, grant that woman should look up to man. Still, there remains unimpaired the truth that woman's two highest functions are to be the companion of man and the mother of men. The helpful and profitable companion for an educated man must be an educated woman—educated not merely for man's "hours of ease," nor for his happily infrequent hours "when pain and anguish rack the brow," but also for the hours of development and endeavor.

So long as so-called education consisted in a little Latin and less Greek, forgotten as speedily as the business of life could crowd it from the mind, higher education was as unimportant to women as—well, as it was to man. But now that education consists in teaching not how the Greeks and Romans lived but how "you and I" must live to-day and to-morrow, the gap between the man who has had higher education and the woman who has not had it and has not supplied the deficiency is wide indeed, and will grow wider. If as much attention were given to the relations between men and women from five years after marriage on to the end as is given to their relations during the purely sentimental and transitory mating season, this difference would appear in its true importance.

The same point of view fits for woman as a mother. So long as the training of children centred around the slipper and the switch, an ignorant mother was not at a great disadvantage—the best educated mother knew too little. But nowadays the child of the highly educated mother has an enormous advantage—other things being equal.

No education in the mother will compensate for lack of character. Character without education is infinitely better than education without character. But character plus education is the true ideal—and it is attainable.

If we are to enter more and more fully into the rich promised land which freedom and science open to us, we must have not only the man who knows but also the woman who knows. After all, is it not our ultimate excuse for being alive that we are the parents of the next generation? And there the woman, with practically absolute control over the next generation at its vital formative age, has the better of the man. If anything, she needs the higher education even more than does man. By all means send the girl to college.

●

The American Schoolma'am

WELL, the blow has fallen where expected least. It has struck with equal hand two sentiments that seemed fixed among the accepted ideas: one, that our women teachers exercised a desirable influence over the youth of the nation; second, that foreigners had some reason for their criticism that American boys were too masculine, too combative, too boisterous.

A few months ago Mr. Moseley's commission arrived to inspect the American people and to find out the causes of their greatness. The commissioners were neither aristocratic snobs nor impressionist artists; they were not seekers of the grotesque or the sensational for book material, not persons prone to banquets tendered by leading citizens. They were real workers, educated men of common-sense and intelligent observation. They came; they saw; they have reported. They hold up our educational system to Great Britain as worthy of imitation, but twenty-four of the twenty-six investigators unite in declaring that there are too many women

teachers; that their influence upon American boys involves a tendency to effeminacy, "to a sexless tone of thought," as one writer puts it. "The boy in America," writes Professor Armstrong, "is not being brought up to punch another's head or have his own punched in a healthy and proper manner."

Now, what are we to do? Doctor Harris, the United States Commissioner of Education, in his latest statement now before us, says that the teachers of the 16,000,000 pupils enrolled in the public schools of the country show 317,204 females to 122,392 males. Counting the female teachers in other schools, we get a total approaching a round half million. That is not all. Twenty-five years ago male teachers formed forty-three per cent. of the total. To-day they comprise less than twenty-eight per cent. In other words, the teaching force of American public schools is seventy-two per cent. female—and the proportion increases every year. The average monthly wages for males is about fifty dollars and for females about forty dollars—both disgracefully inadequate.

Of course, the evident reform is to pay more money and thus to draw more males into the work. Another scheme would be to present to the minds of the males the opportunities that come to teachers. Take, for instance, our Presidents for the past forty years. Who were they? Nearly all of them school teachers. Who have been our Cabinet officers? Our Senators? Our Representatives? School teachers. Who became millionaires, and great authors, and bank presidents, and railroad officials, and leading citizens? School teachers. Where may you best find the secrets that lead to success? In the schoolroom. Teach school and win the world's prizes. If you would hit the larger mark cultivate your aim by showing the young idea how to shoot.

At the same time we shall not accept the verdict of our British critics. We decline to say a word against the schoolma'am. We loved her when it was safe to love, and no true American could possibly go back on his first sweetheart.

●

A Taboo on the College Girl

A COLLEGE girl, exasperated by the comments of the community in which she went to live after graduating, made a few remarks the other day which probably voice the minds of her kind everywhere. She was accused, she said, of never forgetting the peculiarity of her education, whereas the fact was that it was her friends who were always reminding her of it. If she was light-hearted and given to fun, as she had learned to be in the undergraduate world, she was asked if *that* was all the good her education had done her. If she spoke seriously of serious things, she was rebuked for pedantry. The one accomplishment she had learned in her four years which her friends were capable of appreciating was how to make fudge. She threatened to devote her life to making fudge, though she confessed that her temptation was to devote her life to saying it.

The day has come to raise the taboo on the educated woman. The time was when learning sat heavily upon our sisters. In order to demonstrate the masculine might of her intellect, she gave herself over to the highest of higher mathematics and the most deeply buried Greek roots; and, absorbed in much ground and lofty intellectual tumbling, she became a stranger to normal ways of girls of her age. When she emerged she was likely to be a strange and uncouth creature, versed in unintelligible lore and ignorant of all the amenities of small talk, amusement and gowns. An ordinary man would have as soon thought of making love to an encyclopædia bound in calf. The maker of perverted proverbs was quite justified in objecting that girls would be boys.

It took some years for the college woman to learn that one way for girls to be like boys was for them to have all the fun that was going, and that a better way was to be simply themselves. The young graduate of our anecdote is the prophet of a new generation. The time is coming when the better sort of college woman will be as intelligently simple and unconscious as the better sort of college man, and wisdom will be justified of her children, female as well as male.

"PUBLICK OCCURRENCES"

COLONEL A. L. MILLS — PRESIDENT RICHARD T. ELY — PROVOST C. C. HARRISON

A Great College Year

This will be the greatest college year that the United States or any other country has ever known. THE SATURDAY EVENING POST has taken some trouble to collect the returns from the different institutions of the country, and there is scarcely an exception to the report of an unprecedented increase in the number of students. This affects not only the Universities, so called, but all the colleges of every class and size throughout the Union.

Such an institution as Princeton, for instance, reports an increase of forty per cent. in the Freshman class. Harvard has the largest Freshman class in the history of any American institution. Columbia has an unprecedented increase. Yale has six hundred Freshmen, with an increase of more than ten per cent. in every department, and the Western colleges are fully as prosperous. The collegiate institutions of the country, some four hundred in all, have a combined attendance of between one and two hundred thousand, and the total is not far from the two-hundred-thousand mark.

During and after all periods of prosperity the private schools and the colleges secure an increased membership, for the evident reason that people are better prepared to pay for the instruction of their children. That the figures have this year gone far beyond anything ever before known is, of course, largely accounted for by the increase in population; but, while allowing fully for all that, it is still true that the number has greatly exceeded any former proportion in the population statistics of the country.

It may be well to explain that the word college, as referring to American institutions, is on the average more true than the word University. There are, in name, more than one hundred Universities in the United States. Actually, however, there are not a half dozen; but in these days, when a "professor" may be anything from a bootblack to a Sanscrit scholar, it would be idle to quarrel with mere names.

The great thing is that the rush for higher education was never so strong or so general as it is in the present day.

Better Looking Students

The practical men who manage the business of the colleges report in a personal and confidential way that the students are better dressed and better appearing than at any time in their experience. The era of bathtubs and sanitation and good living has had its effect upon American youth. To-day if young Ben Franklin should come to Philadelphia to try his fortunes, it is quite likely that he would not march up the street munching his cheap loaf, but would be riding comfortably and handsomely in an automobile toward a scholarship, possibly pausing on his way to get a well-balanced luncheon at a fashionable café.

The whole tone of college life has been wonderfully raised within the past few years, and if one desires to see a set of well-groomed young men he should attend the opening proceedings of a modern college. Their clothes are not only new and well made, but their complexions are clear.

Better Order Among the Students

Generally at the opening of the college year there are disturbances between certain of the classes and in some instances there have been outbreaks among the students in general. Several rushes and class contests occurred this autumn, but they were fewer than for ten years past.

To some extent the improvement was due to the extra precautions taken by the Faculties, but a great deal of the credit undoubtedly belonged to the students, who have grown no longer to look upon violent horseplay as either instructive or amusing.

In other ways the student of to-day shows that he is manlier, more orderly, and more regardful of the things in conduct and appetite which make for useful manhood. He is the best young man in any country or of any period in the world's history, and he will do big things and do them well.

PROFESSOR JOSIAH ROYCE

Does a College Education Pay?

Last spring, in THE SATURDAY EVENING POST, in the only article which former President Cleveland had at that time ever contributed to a magazine, he asked and answered the question: Does a College Education Pay? His conclusion, expressed with his usual clearness and vigor, was that it did. When some people get a surplus of money they are apt to think themselves above mere mercenary motives or conditions, and thence comes a certain self-satisfied feeling of superiority. Mr. Cleveland proved that education, even when measured by mercenary standards, shows large profits.

Curiously, the messages that came this month from the leading collegiate institutions all agreed upon one point, and that was the wonderful recognition among leading men of the monetary value of higher and skilled education. They have found that the college really does pay. The self-made man, who has been boasting that he got along in the world without a college education, finds not only that his son is better off with these additional opportunities, but that he himself profits more largely by having college men in his employment.

Here is an illustration. It comes from two of the technical departments—those of chemistry and mechanical engineering—of one of the leading Universities of the world. Last June these two departments turned out about fifty graduates. Every single one of them secured a remunerative position at once, and the applications from leading concerns would have taken nearly as many more. A young graduate, not yet turned twenty, became the chemist of a company in one of the large cities. There were certain by-products which were an entire waste to the company. He was asked to experiment with them, and to see if he could get anything from them. Within three months he had succeeded with one of the products and at once received a handsome increase of salary.

"The coal regions," said the professor who read the young man's letter in which he told of this experience, "are full of waste products that must be utilized for the benefit and profit of their owners, and it is the same in all other sections and in all other businesses."

Education is becoming so popular, not only because it is the best thing in itself, but also because, when reduced to dollars and cents, it pays, and that with some is the test.

The Broadening of the Colleges

This recognition of the practical value of a college education has had a very positive effect in the colleges. It has caused them to cater more to the real, practical needs of the times. More young men than ever before now go to college to learn how best to do special things. The idea of the all-round training and experience is by no means abandoned, and the classical departments have their quota, but the most marked increase is in the special departments in which young men are taught to be experts.

Hence there is a broadening and quickening in the colleges themselves. The men at the head of our institutions are studying as never before the facts of progress and the requirements of the new generation, and colleges are improving their equipment in order to give to young men facilities for the largest and most direct results. Thus we have colleges for commerce, colleges for diplomacy, colleges for business—and the departures have just begun. The fact that each new school of this kind gets immediate recognition and attracts encouraging attendance shows how quick the new generation is to appreciate the effort to give better service.

False Charges Against Athletics

A great deal of good-natured fun has been poked at the athletic exuberance of the modern University, and there have been jokes galore upon the theme that the young men go to college for the games and that the studies are merely incidental.

No doubt the modern college boy wants sport, and he is very proud if he can gain eminence in any prominent contest of skill and endurance, but, at the same time, never in the country's history was the college student really more serious than he is to-day.

The surface indications may not always seem to bear this out, but that does not alter the truth. We are in the midst of a very quick and instant age. Things must be done promptly or somebody else will do them and get all the credit. They must be done with skill or somebody else will do them better. The young man knows this, and while he may have, as he should have, his lighter hours and his recreations, deep down in his thoughts and purposes is a simple and triumphant earnestness.

Then again, college athletics have done vast good in improving the physical quality of the students. After all the sins are counted against it—and they are not too few—the credit side of the ledger is preponderatingly favorable to college sport.

It has encouraged and produced a higher manliness.

The Modern College Man

There is one thing that we should always remember as the best proof of college life, and that is the fine quality of the college man, his capacity for work, and his interest in the better things of life.

Take, for instance, four men on this page. Doctor Harrison, Provost of the University of Pennsylvania, can work from nine in the morning until after midnight all through the college course, and set a pace which the young men find hard to follow.

Dr. Richard T. Ely, of the University of Wisconsin, is a man of incessant activity, which accounts for his ability not only to gather the facts of the world's advance, but to analyze them and write about them in books and to do more than three or four ordinary men achieve.

Professor Josiah Royce, of Harvard, is another great worker, whose capacity for toil is unlimited; and there is not at West Point a young cadet who has a more vigorous step, a clearer eye, or a keener interest in everything going on than Colonel Mills, the Superintendent.

So it goes with other college presidents and professors. They are a remarkably fine set of men, and in accounting for the improvement among the students we should not forget their influence and example. Both have been powerful.

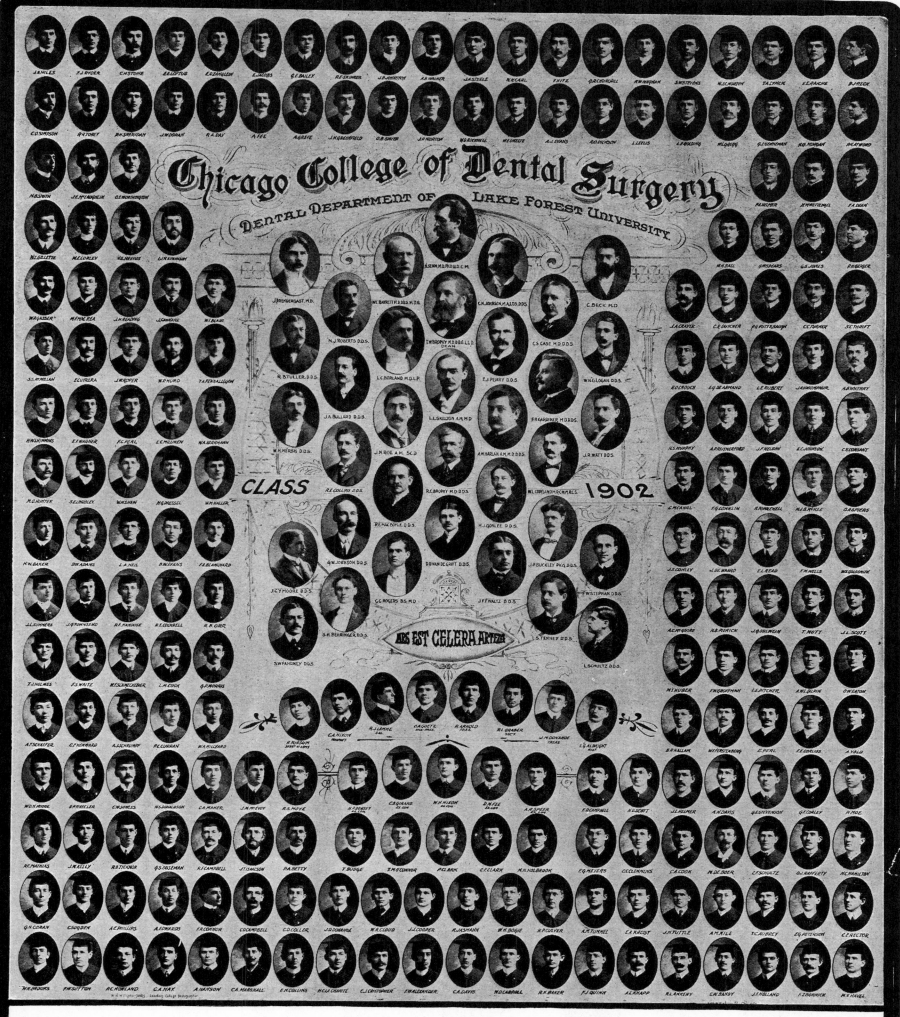

The above is a reproduction of the Class Picture of the senior class session of 1901-1902 of the Chicago College of Dental Surgery.

10 The World Beyond Our

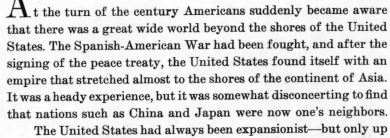

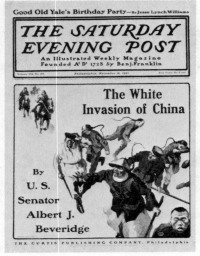

At the turn of the century Americans suddenly became aware that there was a great wide world beyond the shores of the United States. The Spanish-American War had been fought, and after the signing of the peace treaty, the United States found itself with an empire that stretched almost to the shores of the continent of Asia. It was a heady experience, but it was somewhat disconcerting to find that nations such as China and Japan were now one's neighbors.

The United States had always been expansionist—but only up to a point. Before the Civil War the cry of manifest destiny was popular, but to most citizens it meant only that the manifest destiny of the American people was to settle the continent as far as the Pacific coast. Few took seriously the expansionists who orated about taking Mexico and Central America, much less those who said that it was the duty of the United States to take over everything from the North Pole to the southern tip of Argentina. There were many, among them Abraham Lincoln, who opposed the war against Mexico as shamelessly imperialistic.

The war against Spain was something different. The Cubans, fighting for their freedom as the American colonists had done at Lexington and Concord, won the sympathy of their neighbors to the north. It was true that Spain had misgoverned Cuba; but few Americans knew that many of the stories of Spanish atrocities against the Cubans were being fabricated by political refugees in New York apartments and by American newspapers. Fewer yet knew that Spain had made concession after concession to avoid war with the United States, but that the popular mood of belligerency was by then so strong that the irresolute President McKinley did not have the courage *not* to ask Congress to declare war.

And so there was war, and it was the most patriotic, roman-candle-shooting, brass-band-and-marching, everyone-united-against-the-enemy war the United States has ever fought. Democrats joined with Republicans in rushing to the colors; two former Confederate generals were made generals in command of volunteers. But it was an inept war. Only with the greatest difficulty and bungling was the Army able to transport a force to Cuba to defeat a brave but even more clumsily mishandled Spanish army. The Navy did better; it annihilated an antiquated Spanish fleet in Manila Bay and another off Cuba, at a total cost of one American life. A few days after the second Spanish squadron had been destroyed, virtually ending the war, John Jay, ambassador to Great Britain, wrote to Colonel Theodore Roosevelt, who had led his horseless Rough Riders in a well-publicized dash against enemy works: "It has been a splendid little war; begun with the highest motives, carried on with magnificent intelligence and spirit, favored by that spirit which loves the brave. It is now to be concluded, I hope, with that fine good nature which is, after all, the distinguishing trait of our American character."

During the "splendid little war" thirteen of every fourteen

Shores

deaths were caused by disease rather than battle wounds. American soldiers were fed tinned meat—"embalmed beef"—that made many of them retch, and they were sent into the heat of Cuba wearing woolen uniforms. But perhaps the worst element of all was the national upsurge of imperialism, a feeling that we too had every right to pick what we could off the colonial bush. The brief war had hardly ended—active hostilities lasted only slightly more than two months—before voices were raised demanding that the United States grab everything not fastened down. Typical of the new imperialists was the Chicago *Times-Herald,* which wrote: "... We find that we want the Philippines. ... We also want Porto Rico. ... We may want the Carolines, the Ladrones, the Pelew, and the Marianna groups. If we do we will take them. ... Much as we deplore the necessity for territorial acquisition, the people now believe that the United States owes it to civilization to accept the responsibilities imposed upon it by the fortunes of war."

By the Treaty of Paris, Spain agreed to free Cuba, to turn over Guam and Puerto Rico to the United States, and also, after some protest, to cede the Philippine Islands to this country. The Cubans were given command of their own destiny—after a short period of interim guidance—but Uncle Sam decided to stay in the Philippines. However, the Filipinos had been fighting for their freedom from Spain and saw no reason why they should exchange one master for another. A great body of opinion in the United States agreed that we should let the islands go their own way, that an exercise in imperialism that would put us so definitely in Asia was to be avoided. Feelings ran high, and the debate in Congress was bitter, but McKinley, who had to make the final decision, chose to keep the islands. A year or so later he told a group of Methodist churchmen that one night when he had been distraught and sleepless trying to decide whether to annex all or some or none of the islands, God had come to him and had told him "to take them all and to educate the Filipinos, and uplift and civilize and Christianize them." McKinley's God was poorly informed, for he did not know that the great majority of Filipinos were Roman Catholics.

It was a fateful decision. The Filipinos continued against the Americans the insurrection they had been carrying on against the Spanish, and to stamp out the last guerrilla resistance took until 1902 and cost more American lives than had the war with Spain. Far more important, American presence in the islands at once involved this country in Asian power politics. Its first fruit came in 1900: the United States was caught up in the Boxer Rebellion, when the long-suffering Chinese attempted to throw all foreigners out. Some of its more recent effects have been American involvement in a war with Japan and more lately in an interminable action in Vietnam—these and other Oriental entanglements had

their beginnings on the night the sleepless McKinley heard God tell him to retain the Philippines.

In the flush of imperialism of the time, the Hawaiian Islands were annexed in 1898 and at once made a territory, little Wake Island was swept up at about the same time, and in 1899 the Samoan island group was divided among Great Britain, Germany, and the United States.

President Theodore Roosevelt was responsible for one of this country's most flagrant acts of imperialism during the opening years of the century. The United States was eager to start building a canal across the Isthmus of Panama, then a part of Colombia, but Colombia was reluctant to agree to the terms offered by the United States. A minor revolution, organized with American knowledge, broke out in Panama in 1903. An American cruiser that was conveniently on hand landed marines to prevent Colombian troops from restoring order, and with almost indecent haste the United States recognized the Republic of Panama. The new nation, of course, speedily approved construction of the canal. In after years Roosevelt boasted, "I took the Canal." It was a costly act. Had the United States been a little more patient, Colombia would have granted passage rights; instead, Colombia is still resentful, other Central American nations became suspicious of American intentions, and Panama has often been a prickly neighbor to the Panama Canal.

The length of this chapter compared with others in this volume is some measure of the interest of the popular magazines—and therefore of the people—in the outside world. With its victory over Spain the United States had become a world power—and Americans wanted to find out what kind of world it was.

It is bootless to try to analyze the relevance of the following articles and editorials to events in the United States at the beginning of the century. Sometimes there was a clear relation: "Panama and Suez" certainly was inspired by the intense interest in the canal, which was just getting under way. But what of something like "Russia and Her Rulers," which had very little connection with American foreign relations? The answer appears quite obvious: the majority of citizens of this country were so exuberantly interested in the novelty of the outside world that they would very likely have read with fascination an account of the raising of ponies in the Shetland Islands.

There are on the following pages a number of articles whose views of the future have proved surprisingly prescient. Some, however, were dishearteningly incorrect. Among them is one stating that mankind had become so civilized that future wars seemed unlikely. In truth, two world wars and countless lesser ones lay ahead.

A CENTURY HENCE

By Charles Johnston

Bengal Civil Service (Retired)

IN every community there are a few men who count; the rest take their direction from these. In society, a small number of women of originality and power take the lead in everything, while the rest are glad to follow suit. So in the greater society, the greater community of the world, a few nations or races count, and the rest are ruled by these; not only politically, but in thought, feeling, genius, and inspiration.

In looking forward to see what a century may bring forth, the first matter to get clear is which of the nations count, and which are, as the Sanskrit proverb says, "mere empty measures, filling up the granary." One sound and practical way is to see which races have succeeded in establishing sovereignty over a large number of individuals; in other words, to begin with the largest empires, numerically, and to work down from these to the lesser powers. For to establish an imperium over a vast body of men is one of the very strongest symptoms of effectiveness in a race. The most populous of all states is what our statisticians, most deceptively, call "the Chinese Empire." Let us, then, begin by facing the Yellow Peril. Where will it stand in a hundred years?

Our statistics are deceptive because, strictly speaking, there is no Chinese Empire—that is, the imperium, or sovereign power, is nowhere in Chinese hands. The Chinese cannot even rule themselves, much less do they rule any one else. The imperium among them is held by a handful of stiff-necked Manchu Tartars, men of much the same race as the great mediæval conquerors, Genghis Khan, and Timur the Lame, whom Dryden called Tamerlane, and Coleridge's friend, Kublai Khan, who did a stately pleasure dome decree. These Manchu Tartars undoubtedly had the gift of sovereignty, the genius of rule, the great binding power of collective will, without which even hundreds of millions can no more hold together than so many grains of dry sand. They also had the cementing quality that makes empires, the quality which the true Chinaman so conspicuously lacks.

The Chinamen are an immense heap of human grains of sand, without binding power, without collective will; therefore they have no political weight at all. And with a race so old, so definitely crystallized psychically, so to speak, there is no great chance of their gaining this quality within a hundred years, or thrice a hundred. They are no peril at all politically, so long as they try to stand by themselves. And the Chinese are the first to recognize it. Therefore they tolerated the Manchu Tartars these three hundred years, having already had a Mongol dynasty, cousins of the Tartars, for several centuries before. There was a brief interlude of Chinese rule between the true nomad Mongols and the Manchus, but it ended badly, with the last dynast hanging himself on an acacia-tree. So perished Chinese sovereignty.

Manchuria is in fact a Russian province, whatever it may be in law. Politically, therefore, the Chinese can never count. Commercially, however, they will count in an ever-increasing degree. The commercial growth of Japan will be a drop in the ocean compared with China. Our capitalists and laborers should agree with each other quickly, while they are in the way, lest they be delivered into the hands of the Chinaman. Let them ask the English merchants and officials of Singapore or Hong-kong what the Chinaman can do, economically, and be wise in time.

The so-called Chinese Empire is estimated to number just over four hundred millions. The British Empire is something under the same figure. The two together make up half mankind. We may now look more closely at the British Empire, to recognize the elements of which it really consists.

First comes India, with its three hundred millions of half-starved brown people, who for long centuries have not counted in the world's destinies, nor will they ever count again. There are a few millions of red or white race who do count, but we must pass over them now. Governing these three hundred millions stand some nine hundred inhabitants of the British Isles, many of the most gifted coming from Scotland or Ireland, just as all the soldiers of genius in the British army, the Wolseleys, Kitcheners, Robertses, and the like, are of Irish birth. A small army of English, Irish, and Scotch regiments backs up the nine hundred rulers of India—and, incidentally, consumes the revenues in "punitive expeditions" across the frontiers. Thus in world politics three-fourths of the British Empire does not count at all, or counts as a liability rather than as an asset.

Of the remaining hundred million or so, under British rule, forty millions are Africans, whether Kaffirs or negroes, and, politically, these also may be left out. Then there is an indeterminate fringe of some ten millions; then, and lastly, a residue of about fifty millions of white race, and these last alone count in the politics of the world. Seven or eight millions of these, being in Ireland or of Irish birth, are negatively electrified toward the empire, so to speak, and against them we may count off some seven or eight millions of Scotch birth or descent, leaving some thirty-five million Englishmen.

Here at last we have our British unit, for the purposes of prognostication. And we are instantly faced by one most significant and tremendous fact: that the rate of increase among these men of English race has been dwindling decade after decade, so that they are rapidly approaching the French standard, where births exactly equal deaths, and there is no increase in population at all. This is true not only in England, but also in Canada, Australia, and South Africa, and is, ethnically speaking, the most ominous and overshadowing fact in our whole inquiry.

It points to the eclipse of a race-stock which has played a very large part in recent centuries, and by which the nineteenth century was practically dominated. The pure English race-stock is dwindling and dying out, and will be a constantly diminishing factor in world politics throughout the twentieth century. And the great self-governing colonies like Canada and Australia are swiftly becoming sovereign states, rather than fractions of the empire; so that here all indications point the same way.

In a hundred years the pure English race will be nothing like the world factor that it is to-day. Perhaps Mr. Stead is right in thinking that, long before that, the British Isles will be added to the Insular Dependencies of the United States; in which case England will count about as much as Ohio and Illinois in the total counsels of the nations.

We come now to Russia, at present third among the states of the world, with a population of one hundred and thirty millions. Here the contrast to England is almost total. First of all, nearly all of these are of pure Slavonic race; and the rest are of transitional subraces, closely akin to ·the Russians, and willing to be absorbed in them. To-day Russia stands first among the white nations of the earth, with a population almost double that of her nearest competitor. More than this, and in striking contrast to the pure English race, Russia has the largest birth - rate in the world, being about fifty per thousand, as against something like twenty - three for France and thirty-three for England. But the Russian death - rate is also abnormally large, through causes which are being gradually eliminated by progress, such as bad food and unhealthy houses. So that Russia takes between fifty and sixty years to double in population, the pure Slavonic element being the most robust, vital, and prolific, and thus evidently destined to absorb and assimilate the whole mass.

Now for our significant fact: Within twenty-seven years, at the present rate of increase, we shall have two hundred millions of Russians. Within eighty years, we shall have four hundred millions; and within the century we shall have a half-billion of Russions, of nearly pure Slavonic blood. This becomes not a menace, but a promise, when we see that sympathy is the true key-note of the Slav, who is far more hopeful soil for the ethics of the Sermon on the Mount than in the self-assertive and dominating Teuton.

Nor will this exhaust the Slavonic area. Draw a line from Rügen on the Baltic to Venice; nearly everything to the east of this line is ethnically Slav. Hence the dire apprehensions of the Prussian and Austrian Pan-Germans, who feel and fear the rising tide. Count von Bülow recently expressed the matter in a nutshell, by comparing the Slavs to rabbits, and the Teutons to hares, for their power of reproduction; beginning with equal numbers, you will have a hundred rabbits before you have a score of hares. So it is with Slav and Teuton. Therefore all eastern Europe, as well as most of Asia, may be added to the Slavonic area.

We come now to the fourth of the great world powers, our worshipful selves. It is evidently impossible to do the subject justice in a paragraph or two. We can only express with the utmost brevity a series of conclusions slowly and laboriously reached.

We at present number some ninety millions, less than seventy millions being of white or nearly white race; a large influx of the inhabitants of southern Europe being amongst the nearly white, the olive races, like the Sicilians or Neapolitans.

We speak of these seventy millions as Anglo-Saxons, using this as a synonym of English - speaking. But even England was never Anglo - Saxon in race. We all nominally speak "English," but some of it is very queer English, from the standpoint of Mayfair, where the court tongue of England is most uniformly spoken: But Anglo-Saxon in race this country is not. And here, as everywhere else in the English area, the pure English race has a dwindling birth-rate, and is rapidly .approximating the condition already reached by the French, where births just equal deaths. Mr. Roosevelt's recent letter suggests some of the causes of this; in any case, they are not occult.

At the present moment there are probably between twenty and twenty-five millions of Irish in this country, and, as they are recruited from the most vigorous portion of the Irish race, their birth-rate is unusually high, approaching the Russian standard. So that they will decidedly count in the larger world a century hence. We have also strong elements drawn from Germany, many of Slavonic race; and a large contingent from other Slavonic areas, like Austria and Poland; .add to these our immigrants from the Latin countries, and it is evident that the American of a hundred years hence will be the quintessence, the final distillation, of all the European races. The Teutonic element, with its bullying proclivities, will be pretty well drilled out by that time; and the Celtic element will be greatly strengthened. We shall have a type more sympathetic, more psychic, very creative, and with a rich promise of good for the remainder of the world.

The German Empire stands next, and is a strong and vital factor. It cannot extend in Europe, yet extend it undoubtedly will. So·we may logically apportion to it a population of a hundred and fifty millions, largely represented in the temperate zone of South America. A subtemperate zone may belong to the Latin races; while we may look to see the red race reassert itself, and dominate tropical South America, as well as most of Central America. But doubtless the whole of the New World will be in touch, joined in a loose confederacy, with this country as a very influential factor.

These are the races which chiefly count, and a century hence they will stand somewhat thus:

First, we shall have the Russian realm, with a population of not less than five hundred millions,—equal to a third of the whole human race at the present time. This .population will be of almost pure Slavonic blood, and the small extraneous elements in it will be made up for by the strong kindred Slavonic element at present beyond the borders of Russia.

Second in numbers, we shall have the new American race, in extent about two hundred millions. The birth - rate in the United States tends to decrease, but the number of immigrants tends to increase; and this, of course, means an increasing departure from the first race-type. All evidence points to the thought that, while Russia will without doubt tend to become Americanized, by the devolution of responsibility to ever-widening circles of the population, the opposite course will prevail in America,—a more collective consciousness growing up, and gradually approaching the Slavonic moral standard, with its sympathetic general consciousness. Thus the two greatest world powers will approach each other. the one growing in individual responsibility, while the other increases in the power of sympathetic feeling.

Next in order we shall probably have a hundred and fifty millions of pure Teutons, divided between central Europe and temperate South America, a race whom we should look on as the intellectual heirs of Goethe and Wagner, of Kant and Schopenhauer, the masters of great realms of the noblest thought and art, and therefore a treasure-house of one of the great heritages of mankind.

The English race is evidently destined to dwindle, as did the Spanish power which overshadowed the world three centuries ago. Even now, India is an element of sheer weakness, a mass of magnificent misery; while the great self-governing commonwealths of Canada and Australia are only nominally subject to England, and with every year will more and more become sovereign states. The destiny of Canada evidently is a part of the general destiny of the New World; and, as the English type in Canada, as elsewhere, is dying out, we may add the Dominion to the area of the new American race. The present American invasion of the Northwest Territory shows how this will practically come about. Australia may be expected to remain more English in type.

To apply this to the map of the world: Russia, foremost of the white powers, will extend down to the borders of China proper, covering a vast tract in central Asia equal to about two million square miles. Russia will extend her influence over Slavonic Austria and the Balkan peninsula, down to the borders of Hellas, which will also depend on the greatest power in the Eastern Church.

The American states will doubtless reap, in a fuller and closer federation, that sowing of common interest and feeling which the Monroe Doctrine is bringing about, and which includes Canada just as much as it includes Venezuela. We may, therefore, confidently forecast a federation of the New World, with this country as preponderant member. In this federation, a great German state in South America will doubtless be included, and German political power will absorb a part of western Austria, gaining a port on the Adriatic, and stretching from the Baltic to the Mediterranean.

Whether India is destined to continue its present relation to England, or whether its poverty and distress will become a burden on some other land, is a question mainly interesting to the millions of India, but of no weight in world politics. The strictly English area may, therefore, be limited to England and Australia, with a joint population of under fifty millions.

Looking Toward the Future

Lord Lytton said: "Civilization obeys the same law as the ocean; it has its ebb and its flow; and when it advances on one shore it recedes on the other."

A hundred years ago Spain was greater in possessions and population than the United States, but during the century just ending its fortunes were long at an ebb and the flood has been with the United States. Similar changes have gone on in other nations and in other parts of the world. China has had the ebb; Japan has had the flow.

Thousands of years ago there were countries with great civilizations. To-day some of them are wild deserts.

What is the quality that will hold, that will make a nation strong and sure? "No civilization," said Bismarck, himself one of the great makers of modern history—"No civilization other than that which is Christian is worth seeking or possessing." This idea is shared by most of the great men of the world. Furthermore, it is proven by history itself. Wherever Christianity goes it takes civilization with it. Where it rules, civilization thrives. It is the permanent force in the world. Time will not wreck it, because it has that positive moral quality which is stronger than the ages.

THE YELLOW PERIL IS BUT ONE of many which afflict the heated imagination, or which entertain the excitement-loving mind. From a prominent organ of thought in Naples we learn that "the terrible Yankees wish to seize the entire globe." When we have pierced the Isthmus, seized the commerce of the Pacific, and made of that ocean a lake, "the poor Atlantic will be no more than a ditch," and "as to the Mediterranean, by Bacchus, it will be reduced to the condition of a basin in which children sail toy vessels under their nurse's eye." Europe, decrepit, in this view, faces "the yellow peril on one side, the American peril on the other," and possibilities more remote threaten from Africa and from South America, to say nothing of the Slav. Alertness to approaching danger, consciousness of a crumbling world, seem keenest among the so-called Latin nations, which began to practice these qualms some years ago apropos **PERILS EVERYWHERE** of Anglo-Saxon strength. Each race and nation identifies its own cause with that of "civilization." To the Japanese and Chinese the menace is from the barbaric West, and the situation is like that in the later centuries of the Roman Empire. The Anglo-Saxons think they and progress are inseparable and one. The Slav sees in himself the herald of a brighter day. The Latins, while they admit loss of relative brute power, assume as an axiom that in their races reposes what is best in human thought, in art, and civilized refinement. To a mind detached from prejudices of race, these conflicting perils are but guesses at the unknown, indulged in partly to lend spice to current news. They have, nevertheless, deeply affected serious minds, and among those who have used the yellow peril to support vast armaments in Europe have been men of such different and distinguished understanding as the philosopher RENAN and our foremost naval authority, Captain MAHAN. Japan is now applying to the white peril a similar line of argument.

The Passing of the "Foreigners"

THE tendency toward a new use of an important word—a slight tendency as yet and apparently unconscious on the part of those who are newly employing it—has become apparent since the beginning of the troubles in China.

The word is "foreigner," and the new tendency is to use it as descriptive of those who are not citizens of countries of modern civilization.

Should there, after all, be a long and desperate war in which the United Powers shall stand against the semi-civilization of the East, there is no doubt that, by the end of the war, the word would be accepted in its new sense.

And all this would be but the natural evolution of its meaning. Long ago it did not designate merely the native or citizen of another country. A foreigner was, perhaps, only a native or citizen of an adjoining town.

Two hundred years ago a foreigner, to a schoolboy, was a lad who had received his education in a school of another parish. It was in 1660 that Harrow School began to receive such "foreigners" as pupils. "The touns, the countes, the foreyns, all aboute," an old chronicle reads, thus grouping together things that were not local.

The words native and foreigner are even yet used by some in an old-fashioned, narrow sense. "Are these native berries?" asked a would-be purchaser of a market woman in Duxbury the other day. "Lawsy, no!" said the dame, "them ben't native Duxbury; them be foreign! Them be from South Duxbury!"

The use of the word native and foreign gradually broadened. It was not so long ago that a war between England and Scotland was a "foreign" war. In our own country there have never been narrow lines, but it must not be forgotten that in "foreign" war we won California and that in defiance of "foreign" opposition our early statesmen were determined to open the Mississippi.

The narrow use of "foreigner" has long ceased, and broader usage has been steadily strengthening. For some time past, owing to the closer drawing together of England and the United States, a considerable number have unconsciously referred to the English as practically part of ourselves, and only to men of the rest of Europe and of the world when they employed the word "foreigners."

Foreigners have been driven farther and farther away, as national and friendly associations have advanced. And now may come the still broader change—a change that some time was certain to come in the evolution working out through the centuries. If all the nations of Europe stand side by side with America under such a stress as to weld close the ties of brotherly feeling, the word "foreigner" will no longer be used as it has been.

To the Chinese we are all classed together as foreigners. To the uncivilized, the civilized will be the only foreigners; to the civilized, the uncivilized will in time be the only foreigners.

And the evolution will continue. There must come a time when there will be no longer any but civilized peoples, and then there no longer will be any "foreigners."

Disappearing Barbarism

WE STILL have military shows; the young people, and not a few of the older ones, crowd to see them, and the gold lace and the bands set the spines a-tingling. But there's no doubt about it, the taste for that sort of thing is on the decline. It is going the way of the once almost universal taste for cock-fights and prize-fights. At one of the biggest military shows recently they fired the guns as usual, but they didn't let the men drop dead. "We can't make the battles realistic any more," explained the management. "The people won't stand for it." Apparently, instead of being thrilled nowadays by seeing men shot down wholesale, people are coming to be shocked and disgusted.

No doubt the growth of the humanitarian spirit is in part responsible for this change, and there must also be taken into account the education of the masses away from childishness. At bottom, the military spectacle is barbaric; and what is the barbarian but a child?

THE UNITED STATES TO-DAY IN THE FAMILY OF NATIONS

By Shelby M. Cullom

United States Senator, Chairman of the Committee on Foreign Relations

SO LONG and persistently has the course of empire set westward that poetic fancy has become conviction, founded, like so many theories, on the recurrence of misunderstood incidents.

Long before the Louisiana Purchase brought the Mississippi into better light than Indian lore, and before the vast possibilities of its vicinage entered into the dreams of pioneers, we were as sure as now of America's ultimate supremacy. It was not so much without self-assurance as it was without rational ground. There are many, even to-day, who consider this theory of the westward tendency of empire fully substantiated and a good and sufficient ground for our present position in the family of nations. At the same time, they are prone to place reliance wholly upon the army and navy to sustain the nation in the position they have gained for her and to lift her to higher—to the highest of all —places, which we are assured is her eventual destiny.

For the moment it will strike such people as heresy— almost as treason—to assert that there is no Western magnetic pole holding the needle of the compass and guiding the helm of empire, or to declare that armies and navies never made or created anything or ever did more than defend the power which created and sustained them—the power of resource, only limited by the limitations of supply. Yet, throughout the world's history, when the resources failed, the army and navy, no matter how mighty, have always failed with them, and the apparent supremacy has disappeared, not because the armies were vanquished, or because empire must keep on to the westward, but because the internal element of strength was exhausted.

Supply not only seeks out demand, but finds that demand offering the best compensation. It creates an economic system, growing from local to national and international, and that in turn creates competitive economic systems, which in the end test, not the battalions in the field but the strength of the resources behind the competition—whether between two lines of steamers, two farmers raising corn, or two armies encamped against each other. And the country possessing the greatest resource and the best facility of distribution is the country which absorbs the compensation and therefore dominates. It is the country which in the necessary course of events becomes the rich and powerful nation.

According with this law, the United States entered the competition, with the multitude, the variety and the inexhaustible quality of her resources. It was not that she stood at the end of new worlds with nothing unexplored beyond but what she possessed within her own boundaries. It was the previously unknown condition and situation which alone could and inevitably must drop the anchor of empire fast and forever in an unlimited resource.

The United States is the one great commercial watershed of the world, sending streams from its eternal reservoir north, south, east and west, without the possibility of contact with any other source of perennial supply which can be more than competitive—only in some limited field, at most, and in a limited kind of resource. That is, no other source of supply can ever create a permanently dominant economic system. Nothing but the disintegration of the United States can ever touch this source of power and weaken the validity of our supremacy. May no one ever live to see the day of such disruption.

A combination of natural conditions has given to the United States this possibility in the family of nations. Considered from this viewpoint, legislative and diplomatic wranglings seem almost a waste of time and mental energy at first thought, but upon consideration they assume an importance unparalleled as the factor, guarding, protecting and making best available the resources we possess as the one means of establishing the nation in the position which it occupies, or may dream of ever occupying, among the controlling powers of earth.

Legislation and diplomacy are supported, but they are neither guided nor manipulated—save in exceptional and most regrettable instances—by the power of the nation's resources. They are the mind and brain. The resources are the body and brawn. They rise and broaden—they *must*, if we make the best of our position—not only in proportion but a little in advance of the strides of the body as it moves forward. They are not to be credited with the powers of its brute strength, or accounted responsible for the blunders of its unappreciated muscular development, but they are fully accountable for its progress in the right direction, for its wise development, its character at home and its influence among the thinking powers abroad.

The hand which carries food to the mouth on a knife-blade may be able to strike a ponderous blow. We may respect the blow and fear provoking it, but not the refinement of the owner. Much more is the dignity of his position impaired if the hand be found in another man's pocket. The physical position which America holds to-day among the nations is one to thrill with pride the sportsman quality in every loyal citizen; but no less, though less appreciated as a matter for patriotic congratulation, is the high position of influence accorded to us by our sister powers. For this we are indebted to the earnest labors, the honest convictions and the untiring efforts of those who have guided the nation in the past, not only in its dealings with foreign powers but—and more important—in its dealings at home; not only for what they have done but for what they have had to fight to leave undone.

Not many years ago such a thing as the Peace Conference at The Hague would have seemed preposterous, and as late as 1897 the idea of arbitration treaties was so vigorously fought that the subject was dropped; but to-day the United States is the acknowledged leader in measures surely tending to a world adoption of a perpetual alternative for war.

There are some who still believe that all of this is simply because the brute strength of our nation has at last been recognized and that the course of events was enforced by what we termed our filibustering tendencies; but no one can view our position to-day with thought and common-sense and not realize that it was distinctly *in spite* of those tendencies; that in competitive jurisprudence we have been advancing as steadily as in all other competitive systems. So many, too, have but recently aroused to an appreciative sense of our position among the nations that it is hardly surprising to find the very general opinion that we suddenly leaped into prominence as a world-power; but to gather such sentiments from intelligent newspapers is astonishing, for they are wholly erroneous. America did not suddenly become either more or less at any period of her career. It has been a slow, persistent, undeviating growth in prominence. The history of our diplomatic intercourse is one of constantly widening influence and broadening intelligence; and the danger which most threatens us to-day is not from inexperience, bravado or arrogance in anything like the degree that it is from neglect of vital interests and from tendencies to insincerity.

In the counsels of nations the United States now plays an important part. The voice of America is heard with deference and respect upon all subjects of world interest. More than once in the near past we have been solicited to act, as the nation which would bear the greatest weight of influence in some emergency. Nothing is more suggestive of our social position than a glance at the diplomatic circles representing foreign nations in Washington. The men whom the world sends to us to-day are masters in their art. There is no capital on earth which can claim such a convention of ability.

This is the victory of peace, and in peace and honor we shall better sustain and enlarge our field than by any force of arms or display of filibustering. It is not, however, a cause for glory, but rather for caution. It demands more earnest endeavor than ever before marked the course of legislation. It is true that the United States never stood so high in the esteem of all nations; but it is also true—consequently true —that she never stood in a more difficult, problematic and critical position. It is the more difficult and complicated because in the process of expansion we stand where many new questions must be met and answered, establishing our policy in matters which never before came under serious discussion. There are questions in which the world is interested, our treatment of which will indicate our sense of honor and international as well as internal integrity. There are questions where lack of wisdom, or sinister ambitions, would create doubt and uncertainty in the convictions of the world. Opinions will always differ. Parties will rise and fall. Policies may even radically change without material effect. Circumstances alter cases with the whole as well as with the individual; but the vital principles of truth, honor, justice, equity and patriotism must remain fixed and immutable.

Natural conditions have given us dominance which we shall never lose so long as we possess the strength of unity. But dominance does not signify precedence. The nations must always consider us, but they need not always respect us. To-day the country stands socially even in advance of her commercial ascendency, because the secret of precedence lies in legislation and diplomacy, not in brute energy.

The prominence of the United States in the family of nations has been attained by her integrity of purpose to use wisely and well her natural predominance. She will retain the position so long as she continues in that course. She will forfeit it in the moment when she deviates. God forbid that private interests with sinister motives ever invade our State Legislatures, reach out into the Congress of the United States, or taint our international transactions.

Uncle Sam's Best Customers

IT IS well for us to keep on conquering foreign markets and taking vigilant precautions against any interference with them, but we may have the consoling reflection that our permanent prosperity is not dependent upon the good will of foreign customers and not accessible to the jealous attacks of foreign governments.

Our total export trade, which seems such a tremendous thing to us and to our European rivals, amounts to only about twenty dollars for each one of our population. A very little improvement in the consuming and purchasing power of our poeple would reduce that trade to insignificance.

Mr. Fred A. McKenzie, the author of The American Invaders, invites England to shudder because we sell American typewriters to her to the amount of over $20,000 a week. That is a trade worth having, of course, but there are people enough in New York City alone who need typewriters, and have not yet bought them, to double it.

There is nobody in the United States, outside of the list of millionaires, who would not like to have more or better clothes. If every person in the country were able to spend on an average $10 a year more for clothes than he spends now the volume of trade in that line would be increased by nearly $800,000,000 annually, or more than half the amount of our combined exports of every kind.

If every American family could live in a neat, comfortable cottage of moderate cost, the lumber, iron, steel, glass, paint, plumbing and building trades would have a boom so colossal as to dwarf everything known in the field of foreign commerce. If every American family could have all the meat it wanted, three times a day, the American farmer would have no need to concern himself about the German tariff.

And so on around the whole circle of our industries. Would it not be worth while for our field-marshals of business to give some attention to this curious situation? The American garment-maker is trying to induce the savages of Africa and Polynesia to wear clothes which they are much more comfortable without, because if he cannot sell his goods to them his workers will not be able to buy anything to eat. The American farmer is loaded down with things to eat, and he is trying to force them upon the protesting Germans because, if they do not take them off his hands, he will not be able to buy anything to wear. Why cannot the farmer with his ragged overalls and the garment-maker with his pinched stomach make a trade? Why cannot the people who make bicycles and automobiles find buyers among the people who make hats and shoes?

The consuming power of this country is absolutely unlimited. Nobody's wants are ever satisfied. The more one has the more he thinks he needs. The only reason why we do not all live in palaces, with mosaic floors, silken upholsteries and marble baths, and have fast horses, automobiles and yachts, is that we cannot produce enough to pay for them. Will anybody explain, then, why it is that we are always complaining of under-consumption and over-production?

Why People Talk About Us

IT IS not strange that we Americans are pleased and flattered by the amount and the kind of attention we have been attracting in Europe during the past five years. But it is somewhat astonishing that we should permit a very small part of the American people to appropriate all the credit for the outburst of admiring envy.

Europe became acutely aware of us in 1898 — a year of two events for us:

First: We ousted an ancient and impotent cripple whose presence in our neighborhood had become most offensive, and incidentally we relieved him of an Asiatic insular burden that had almost exhausted the last drops of his vitality.

Second: We entered the full tide of that material prosperity which began in the spring of 1896, and we were floated by it into a dominating position in the markets of Europe.

If we had fought the Spanish war and had remained commercially insignificant in the European markets, does any one who gives the matter thought fancy that Europe would be talking about us now? International gossips, professional fighting men and schoolboy statesmen excepted, both America and Europe know that the only European nation with which we could carry on a real war is England. And England has shown that she would endure much at our hands rather than provoke us to that extremity. With the only Power which could possibly war with us thus friendly, why attach importance to the shrieks of German and Austrian irresponsibles who chatter only because there isn't a discernible human probability of a serious attempt at a war? Why heed silly talk of the little German Navy—or a big one, should Germany build it—steaming four thousand miles from a coal supply to attack us? The German Emperor may be eccentric, but he isn't crazy; and, if he were, there are statesmen in Germany.

No, but for the second great and overshadowingly important fact of 1898, Europe would have continued to have small interest in us. Here are two conclusions from statistics which show the tremendous significance of the inauguration of our commercial supremacy:

First: In these four years of our growing European fame the *excess* of our exports, chiefly to Europe, over our imports was *nearly three thousand million* dollars. This excess was greater than for the entire twenty previous years combined.

Second: While our exports of foodstuffs are about twice what they were twenty years ago, our exports of manufactured goods are more than *seven* times as great as they were twenty years ago. And like our foodstuffs, these manufactures go for the most part to Europe.

There we see why there is hardly a home in Europe where we are not talked about nearly every day. The farmers are talking about the competition of American foodstuffs. The manufacturers and their workmen are talking about the competition of American manufactures. And the shopkeepers are selling and the people are buying American-made goods —and talking about the country from which these new and cheaper and better articles come. They have forgotten Dewey at Manila, Roosevelt at San Juan; they know nothing of the vast outpourings of Congressional eloquence for the saving and prosperity of the country which daily find their swift way into the lost river of the Congressional Record. But they are incessantly reminded of the energy of American merchants and the skill of American workmen.

Machinery—using the word in its broadest sense—has made business the chief concern of the whole world. It has transformed politics into business, has made statesmen and politicians and kings and ambassadors and ministers the agents and servants of business. And we are attracting world-attention because we have been acting upon, and are now teaching other nations to act upon, the maxim that universal prosperity is the first and vital step toward universal progress.

Nor need we fear "trade wars" that menace the imagination of our whangdoodle "conservative statesmen." Those to whom we sell good goods at low prices aren't going to fight us. Those whom we teach to make better goods at low prices are going to be too busy to quarrel. Those who won't learn are going the way of all failures. Machinery is multiplying the capacity of the earth for population. It is multiplying markets as fast as it is multiplying products. Those who talk of world-markets as if they were narrow and growing narrower talk without thinking. On the contrary, in the world-markets there is room for all, there will be room for all—and there will always be an unlimited number of vacant stalls waiting for newcomers with the brains and the goods.

And when the people reduce political and military and journalistic busybodies to their proper station, the peaceful and progressive interchange of material and mental commodities will be less often impeded and interrupted. To the rear with the man who talks and threatens! To the fore with the man who thinks and works!

Why is the Anglo-Saxon Disliked?

OUR new citizens, or subjects, in the tropics East and West, have but to become acquainted with us to become fond of us—so we think. The black man and the brown, the process of assimilation or of subjugation once completed, cannot know us but to love us nor name us but to praise—such is our naïve belief. We like ourselves; other people should like us too.

This flattering unction will go for nothing. No people, least of all a subordinated one, ever really liked another. No people ever will. And we, of all peoples—we, the Anglo-Saxons—are the least likely to make ourselves endeared. The Continental nations have come to look upon the Englishman as being not a "good European"; he is as much set apart by his morale as by his topographical situation. The American, once tolerantly viewed as a kind of juvenile Englishman, is to-day judged with the severity that maturity invites. The two halves of our race are now set together and frowned upon in common.

Why are we disliked? Because we are successful. Or, more exactly, because we are prosperous. The question then becomes, Why are we prosperous?

We are prosperous because, more fully and more readily than any other stock, and with smaller sense of loss or of incompleteness, we can disembarrass ourselves of certain elements that are in general looked upon as normal in the make-up of the average human being, but that do not promote his progress in the world. We can subordinate passion, and we can elbow aside the amenities. With the Italian, for example, love is a pursuit and an occupation in itself; and the Frenchman expects to "cherchez la femme" as a matter of course. Boulanger was neither the first nor the last of them to get entangled, to his own undoing, in the hem of a petticoat. The Anglo-Saxon, of all men, is least likely to have the plans of a cool head upset by the pranks of a hot heart. This peculiarity is recognized the world over as abnormal; and the advantage it gives under the modern conditions of rivalry is more or less resented.

Again, *savoir-faire* is no great part of the Anglo-Saxon outfit; *suaviter in modo* does not always find a close translation into English. We carry a crude, brutal directness with us all over the world. We are always ready to leave the gravel walk and cut across the grass—an informality that calls forth protest. Of all peoples we are the crudest when away from home—and the barbarian, even the savage, is very likely not to be crude at all. Travelers assure us that nowhere do good manners count for more than in the jungle.

If the Englishman is held to be not a good European, the Anglo-Saxon may easily come to be held as not a good human being. Our blood circulates on a plan of its own—a plan that promotes the cool head, the clear vision, the firm will. The Anglo-Saxon may be looked upon as a specialist highly effective in his one department—the domain of the practical. The fair, all-round development on a general emotional basis he leaves to men of different blood.

The emotional manifestations of our race (as in the arts) do not interest the outside world. The whole Caucasian tribe has heed for Maupassant, or Mascagni, but will not listen to us save on matters practical. No Englishman since Byron has had a real vogue on the Continent. The only Americans who are recognized abroad as having any true value and any actual bearing on the fundamental concerns of life are Whitman and Poe—those daring and passionate reprobates that are still banned by our respectables. Our self-conscious drawing-room proprieties amuse the big round world, but hardly interest it. We are too self-righteous to secure its sympathy—too calmly expert in avoiding the pitfalls that beset the feet of Manon, and Gretchen, and Santuzza, and Des Grieux, and Hulot, and Chardon.

The Anglo-Saxon is the cool, determined, calculating person who prospers, but who does not endear himself. The Filipino has already found the American as tyrannous as the Spaniard, and not nearly so agreeable personally. If the "lesser breeds" must toe the line, there is a choice of manners to employ in bringing them to it; and if we may believe the voice of Experience, the pleasantest manner that we can assume will be the one best calculated to minimize our tribulations. Surely we do not admire ourselves so heartily that the admiring good will of the rest of mankind may be dispensed with. —HENRY B. FULLER.

SOME very able men are taking Zionism seriously, though, to be sure, very able men have taken seriously before now scores of movements that came to naught. One man who is credited with having become an enthusiastic Zionist is Mr. Zangwill, the novelist. A recent despatch from London quotes him as expressing confidence that the charter for Palestine will very soon be obtained from the Sultan, if indeed Dr. Herzl, who has been negotiating for it, has not got it already. And once the charter is in hand, Mr. Zangwill thinks, the Zionist movement will go forward with vastly quickened speed, and subscriptions come in much bigger and faster. Mr. Zangwill's idea is that the selection of colonists for the budding Jewish settlement must be very careful. Palestine must by no means be allowed to become a refuge for needy Jews who can't make a living. Only skilled workmen should be admitted.

The Zionists have now accumulated about a million dollars. Money is pretty common nowadays, and the Sultan always needs it. Like enough the idea either of selling a charter at a good price or of finding a profit in the increased prosperity of Palestine would be acceptable to him. Yet the Zionist idea seems to be largely based on sentiment, and the Sultan may develop a counter-sentiment which will be obstructive. The cry of "Jerusalem for the Jews" may not fall gratefully upon his ears. It is a cry that no longer stirs the least jealousy in Christian Europe, and yet it is only six centuries since the last of the crusades.

THERE is said to be a project on foot to admit Alaska into the Union as a State. We cannot regard this suggestion as seriously made, and we are sure that Congress will not seriously entertain it. The enactment of a law conferring Statehood on Alaska would be a confession by Congress of its own incompetency to provide a government for distant territories. Alaska has been a possession of the United States for thirty-two years. During all that time it has been without a properly organized government. During the last Congress a large number of bills were introduced in both Houses to provide a government for Alaska, or to regulate and better the administration of justice. The best thing that Congress can do for Alaska is to take up one of these bills and pass it after proper amendment and full debate. The debate itself would be educational, and would lead to a wider and more thorough understanding among Congressmen of the principles on which colonial government should be based. The lesson must be learned, and that soon, and the subject of government for Alaska is a good theme for practice. Moreover, the people of Alaska, who may be called "old inhabitants," are not practised in the arts of self-government. They have not made their own laws. In a word, they have not yet had that schooling, insufficient though it has generally been, which we have required of the people of the Territories contiguous to the States whose Union they were eventually to join. Alaska is at present mainly a mining-camp, whose population is not the best foundation for a State, and is likely to diminish. We have had our sad experience with Nevada, and are not ready for a repetition, or worse.

Our Light Colonial Load

THE Census Bureau has issued a statement, showing that the total population under the Government of the United States is 84,233,069. Of these, 6,961,339 belong to the Philippines, 953,243 to Porto Rico, 154,001 to Hawaii, 9000 to Guam, 6100 to Samoa, and the rest to the old United States.

Compared with other Powers, our share of the "white man's burden" does not appear to be unduly heavy. The only real burden we are carrying is in the Philippines, and the entire population of that group is only one-eleventh of our own. And it is in only half of the Philippines that we are having any serious trouble. The southern islands have been ostensibly friendly to us from the start, and as our Government there goes on the principle of asking nothing from them but "civility, and little of that," this satisfactory situation seems very likely to continue.

Great Britain, with a population of about 40,000,000, rules 300,000,000 in India and many millions more in other parts of the world. France rules about as many dark-skinned subjects as she has Frenchmen at home. Holland governs dependencies containing about seven times her own population. Even Portugal manages, after a fashion, to keep her flag flying over distant territories of more than the population of her kingdom and of nearly thirty times its area.

Compared with these top-heavy colonial empires, the system of the United States is solidly based. All of our colonies together have less than one-sixth the population and one-thirtieth of the area of the mother country. Evidently, there is no danger that our centre of gravity will shift. We may make blunders in dealing with the Philippines and Porto Rico; we may do things we should rather have left undone; but whatever our mistakes may be they can cost us nothing more than humiliation. So long as the huge majority of the people under our flag are participants in the Government, our system will be in too stable equilibrium to be shaken.

Moreover, a disaster that should strip us of our colonies, if such a thing were conceivable, would do us no serious harm. We should still be where we were four years ago, with the great bulk of our resources unimpaired.

Imagine the British Empire cut down to the little islands in the North Atlantic, or Holland reduced to the half-drowned strip of land on the German Ocean! To such Powers as these the loss of their colonial empires would be a disaster that would change their whole position in the world. To us, it would be merely an annoyance in which many people would see a benefit.

Inevitable Revolution

IN RUSSIA the supporters, which means the beneficiaries, of the present "government" of loot and shoot are calling for peace and submission at home on the ground that the revolutionary agitation is "bad for business." And so it is. But there comes a time in a disordered society—whether the disorder proceed from caste tyranny or the oppressions of monopoly—when the only way to save business from utter destruction is doing the things that do temporarily seem to aggravate the ills they seek to cure. That time has come to Russia; and so, some sort of revolution is inevitable.

Even at this early stage, the Czar is himself authorizing measures which it would have been revolutionary treason to hint at, much less propose, a year ago. Not always in cataclysms of blood and chaos do revolutions come about. Often, most increasingly often in this day of press and people, the most radical changes are made so peacefully that Revolution hardly recognizes her own well-behaved, innocent-faced children.

RUSSIA AND HER RULERS

BY W. T. STEAD

The Revolutionary Usurpers

RUSSIA has always been subject to the plague of revolutionary usurpers. But never until the twentieth century have they been anonymous. The peculiarity of the present malady which threatens the disruption of the Russian Empire is that the Revolutionists are men whose names are unknown. The Revolution in Russia, like the Veiled Prophet of Khorassan in Lalla Rookh, hides its features behind a veil removed neither by night nor by day. We hear darkly of Social Democrats, of Social Revolutionaries, of the "War Department," of the Peasants' Union, of Strike Committees, of Councils of Workmen's delegates, but in none of these organizations does authority concentrate sufficiently into a single hand for any individual to be so much as named. Probably if any one were named to-day he would disappear to-morrow. For the Revolution now, as in the olden time, has a saturnine appetite for its own children. But whatever may be the cause, the anonymity of the Revolution is one of the elements of its terrorism. Who is this impalpable foe, all pervading as the fog, against which emperors and dictators contend in vain? No one knows. The leader of to-day is but like a foam bubble on the crest of a wave. The bubble bursts, but the momentum of the wave is unimpaired.

From one point of view this anonymity, this intangibility of the Revolution, is an advantage. It at least eliminates one element of error into which rulers invariably fall. Whenever any leader arises who becomes conspicuous in organizing disaffection, Authority always mistakes effect for cause and declares that if only the leader were got rid of discontent would disappear. So, in the days when Russia was devastated by revolution, the trouble was always attributed, now to the false Dimitri, then to Stenka Razin, and still later to Pugatchef. To few was it given to realize as did General Bibikoff, who said: "Pugatchef is only a bugbear worked by the Cossacks. It is not Pugatchef who is important, but the general discontent." There is no Pugatchef to-day. General Discontent is the only Commander-in-chief of the Revolution. But his name is Legion.

Russia from the dawn of her history has been the happy hunting-ground of all kinds of adventurers. Lying midway between Europe and Asia, she has been plundered to the bone alternately by each Continent. Her history begins with the despairing appeal of her harried and helpless Russians of the Northwest to the Varangians of Rurik: "Our country is large; we have everything in abundance, but we lack order and justice. Come and take possession of it and govern us." Seven centuries pass, and again, the Slavonian anarchy having broken loose, the boyards appeal to the foreigner this time—to Poland—with the same despairing cry: "Our country is large, but we have no justice. Come and govern us." To-day we are witnessing the same phenomenon. The Slavonian anarchy is once more abroad in the land. And although there is no appeal by tangible, visible, audible leaders to a foreign sovereign, there is raised the same old wail: "Our country is large, but we have no justice," and this time the vast, multitudinous, anonymous, myriad-headed revolutionary movement cries to "Universal Suffrage" to come over and deliver them. Always salvation is sought from without. Yet Russians are convinced that they are the people who have nothing to learn from the decaying nations of the West.

The Changeless Elements of Terrorism and Violence

THE tendency of the Russian social organism to go to pieces is the historical justification for the Autocracy. Anarchy below begets Despotism as its corrective. The two produce as their natural progeny the present state of things in Russia. Despotism has accustomed Russians to bow submissively before Authority. Anarchy, always indigenous in the Slavonian land, makes this very submissiveness its most potent weapon against the Autocracy. But it has always been so in Russia. As Victor Berard says in his Russia and Czarism: "During the whole of the eighteenth century, as in the sixteenth and in the seventeenth, and for that matter in the nineteenth and the twentieth—in the year 1905—it is quite enough for a gilded coat or a uniform to show the peasants a paper authorizing the massacre of the nobles and the pillaging of their estates, for an impostor, in a single day, to find a numerous following."

The first and most famous of these impostors was the false Dimitri, who declared himself the son of Ivan the Terrible, a kind of Russian Perkin Warbeck, and who, at the beginning of the seventeenth century, headed a rising which, with Polish aid, seated him for a brief period on the throne of Muscovy. The second was the revolt of Stenka Razin, a freebooter who, in the latter half of the seventeenth century, raised an army of 200,000 men and founded a bandit empire that stretched from Nijni Novgorod to Astrakhan: "I come to fight the boyards and the rich. I am the friend of all the poor, the friend of the people. You fight for those traitors the boyards, but I and my Cossacks are fighting for our Lord the Czar." Stenka Razin, multiplied a hundredfold, is alive again to-day. He says "bureaucracy" instead of "boyards," but otherwise his phraseology is unaltered.

The third and the best known of the revolutionary usurpers of Russia was Pugatchef, a Cossack of the Don, who, in the last quarter of the eighteenth century, declared himself to be the Czar Peter III, and raised an insurrection on the Volga which was accompanied by all the horrors of a servile war. The peasants rose at his bidding and burned and pillaged and slew just as they are doing to-day. At last Bibikoff defeated him, and a Scotch soldier of fortune ultimately succeeded in capturing him at Simbirsk. The false Peter III was clapped into an iron cage and carted like some captive wild beast to Moscow. There—like the false Dimitri who was murdered, and like Stenka Razin who was executed—Pugatchef met a violent death at the hands of the executioner.

Since then there have been few revolutionary usurpers. But to-day Russia is full of them. They usurp authority not in the name of any false Dimitri or Peter, but in the name of the Revolution. They justify their usurpation by glozing pleas of liberty and independence, but they use unhesitatingly the methods as well as the phrases of Stenka Razin. They do not fling generals and bishops from the tops of their castles and steeples; they blow them to pieces with dynamite or shoot them with revolvers.

The details vary, the essential elements of terrorism and violence never change. And to-day, as in the previous centuries, success of the revolutionary usurper is possible only because of the widespread misery and discontent of the masses of the people.

Blind Obedience the Foundation on which the Revolution Rests

THERE is no pretense about the matter. The Revolution is the product of social discontent and political disaffection. But it is nurtured by lies and triumphs by terrorism. There has been a great deal said concerning the pacific methods of the Russian revolutionist: "Look how wonderful it is, the conquest of the people, gained by means of passive resistance! Revolution by voluntary starvation!" And there is, of course, a good deal of truth in it. But revolutions have their secret methods like monarchies, and when you come to look closely into the astonishing unanimity of the pacific strike, you promptly discover that there would be no unanimity if there were no terrorism.

The Revolution is prompt to assail Authority by its own weapons. The Terrorism from above is combated by Terrorism from below. The Government shoots mutinous soldiers who refuse to execute sentences of court martial. The Revolution kills and burns and pillages to enforce obedience to its commands. The unanimity of the railway strike was obtained, Prince Hilkoff assured me, by the simple process of sending a gang of rowdies, primed with vodka and paid at so much a head, into the machine-shops and railway stations with orders to stop work on menace of bad treatment. The unanimity of the St. Petersburg strike was obtained by the threat to smash the windows of shops that refused to close, and to burn down factories whose workmen persisted in remaining at work. Of course, unless there was a widespread sympathy with the movement these terrorist tactics would have been useless. But it is only honest to admit that, without the terrorism, the strike would have been a failure. Terrorism is the disciplinary method of the Revolution, and it is applied unhesitatingly.

The audacity, the nerve—I think that when I was in Chicago they called it the "gall"—of these revolutionary usurpers almost passes belief. Nothing but the helpless readiness of Russians to submit to Authority can explain the promptitude with which the orders of the Revolutionists are obeyed. Into the office of the Novoe Vremya, the leading daily newspaper in Russia, in the Nevski Prospect, one fine afternoon when the strike was brewing, there walked three strangers, who ordered the office to be closed at once.

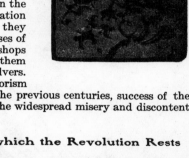

"And who are you?" asked the manager.

"We are the representatives of the Social Democratic Revolutionary Committee," was the answer, "and we are to see that this office is closed, or else——"

The manager promptly put up his shutters.

The Nevski is the chief thoroughfare in the capital of St. Petersburg. A word on the telephone would have brought the police to arrest the criminals who were intimidating a law-abiding citizen. But sheer impudence carried the day and the office was closed. On another occasion the Strike Committee improved upon this precedent. They boldly took possession of the Novoe Vremya office, and used its type and machinery for the production of their official gazette. When the editor was permitted to resume the publication of his paper he congratulated the strikers upon their audacity and commended their spirit to the Minister of the Interior as worthy of all imitation.

The appetite grows by what it feeds on. On the day I left St. Petersburg—October 28—the Strike Committee was sending around delegates to all the banks ordering them to close. Some obeyed the command; others—notably the foreign banks—resisted the order to close. But the audacity of the strikers knew no bounds. Half a dozen girls entered the Russo-Chinese Bank and imperiously ordered the officials to close the doors. "If you don't," they said, "others will come and make you."

In some banks the intimidating deputation scoffed at the police and were removed only by military force.

In the case of the factories the usual threat is to destroy the machinery or to burn the whole building. As a rule, the employer and the workmen give in. The same tactics that were employed to extort the constitution are now being used to punish the employers for refusing to pay ten hours' wages for eight hours' work. Seventy-two firms had joined in the lockout. They were informed that one of their number would be selected by lot and his factory fired to teach him to behave.

The whole *modus operandi* is singularly like the operations of the Land League in Ireland twenty years ago. There we had the same spectacle of a disaffected peasantry willingly consenting to be terrorized by "village ruffians" and "midnight murderers" into a refusal to pay rent.

And in Ireland, also, the whole moral authority was with the law-breakers and not with the law-makers. I remember saying, after visiting Ireland in 1886, that the trouble was that the Land League was so positively certain that it was in the right that it never hesitated to kill a man, even if he were innocent, whereas the English Government in Ireland was so keenly conscious that it was in a false position that it hesitated to kill a man even when it knew he was guilty. It is just so in Russia. The Government hesitates to enforce its own laws, even when they are just. The Revolution never hesitates to execute its edicts, no matter how unjust they may be.

The control of the revolutionary forces in St. Petersburg has fallen more and more into the hands of a body calling itself the Council of Workmen's Delegates, one-fourth of whom are neither workmen nor workmen's delegates. Three-fourths of the Council is supposed to be elected by the St. Petersburg workingmen in the proportion of one delegate to every 500 members. There are about 600 members of the Council, which would give it a constituency of about 200,000 workmen. One-fourth of the number is appointed by various Socialist groups—the Socialist majority, the Socialist minority, and the Socialist Revolutionists. The nerve with which this Council arrogates to itself a right to threaten the whole nation with a general strike whenever it is displeased with any action of the Government is superb.

The Social Democrats have few supporters outside the large towns, and the first thing that needs to be borne constantly in mind is that in all Russia there are only twenty towns with more than 100,000 inhabitants. Russia is a huge farm. Three-fourths of the Russian people live in wooden huts, thatched for the most part, all of which, it is said, are burned down on an average once every fourteen years. The methods of the revolutionary usurpers in dealing with the town populations are of small importance compared with their tactics in the country. It is in the country among the peasants that the revolutionary usurper has ever achieved his most disastrous successes. For the method of the Revolutionist is to incite the peasant to burn, to steal and to slay by telling him lies in the usurped name of the Czar. In the eyes of the Revolutionist, the end justifies the means. To him everything is fair in revolution

as in war. But to the onlooker it is difficult to conceive more hideous cruelty achieved by more detestable means.

The method of the revolutionary usurpers who have at this moment let hell loose over vast provinces in Russia is simplicity itself. The Russian peasant is a simple, ignorant fellow, who with all his simplicity and ignorance holds fast to two fundamental ideas. The first is that no one ought to have more land than he can till, and the second is that the Czar is the Vice-gerent of Almighty God. The peasants are wretchedly poor. The protectionist policy by which Count Witte fostered into precarious existence Russia's infant industries told cruelly upon the agricultural population. They have been taxed to the bone, and this year more than a dozen governments in the granary of Europe are in the grip of a terrible famine. They have been profoundly shaken by the disasters of the war.

Something, it is evident, has gone wrong. The Government, once apparently omnipotent, has not even been able to hold its own against the Japanese in the far-away East. Thus a deep, vague, but tormenting moral doubt has seized the peasant at the same time that his crops have failed and his children are dying of famine typhus. Just at this psychological moment a sudden excitement breaks out in his village. A great general in gorgeous uniform, accompanied by two or three other men in uniform, summons the starosta and bids him call together the mir or village community to hear the ukase that has been issued by the Czar. The peasants flock in from their fields, and stand with bare heads to listen to the will of the Little Father. When they are all assembled, the pseudo-general with great parade reads aloud a forged ukase which solemnly declares that Nicholas Alexandrovitch, the great and mighty Czar, has decreed that all the lands and goods of the landowners are henceforth to be made over to the peasants, and, further, that on the following morning at eight o'clock these particular peasants must assemble with carts and horses at the neighboring estate of Prince A. B., and assist the peasants from the other villages in removing the goods, farm stuff, farm stock and other possessions of the landowner in order that they may be divided among themselves. "And," continues the

MAP OF ~~ASIA~~ RUSSIA PUBLISHED AT ST. PETERSBURG

pseudo-general, "it is the Czar's will that you shall burn the prince's house and all the farm buildings to the ground. Only when you have pulled down the nests the crows will fly away." Having finished his reading the "General" and his staff drive off to another village where the same ceremony is gone through. The whole countryside is agog with the great news. All the rest of the day is spent in repairing harness, in making ready the carts and providing teams so that they may not be late at the rendezvous fixed by the Czar.

The next morning, long before daylight, every road leading to the doomed estate is thronged with carts all driving to the rendezvous. Prince Obolenski, who two years ago had a terrible time in stamping out a jacquerie that had broken out in the sugar-producing districts of Kharkoff, described such a scene to me as resembling nothing so much as a huge anthill. In every direction carts were driving to a common centre, and other carts were returning full. In one case there were 2500 carts busily engaged in carting off the sugar, and they succeeded in removing three hundred tons of it before the Cossacks arrived. The usual plan of operations is for the marauding peasants—each in his simple heart exultant that the Czar has at last given the land to his people —to approach the landowner's house and demand his keys. They say that the Czar has given everything to them, and that if the keys are given over to them they will not maltreat anybody. If, however, he refuses, they will be obliged to kill him and burn his house over his head.

Looting the Landowners

Picture the position of such a landowner, summoned at daybreak, to stand and deliver by thousands of peasants firmly persuaded they are doing the Czar's bidding and with their mouths watering for their prey! What can he do? Summon the Authorities? Alas, the nearest Authority may be fifty miles away and the roads at this season are mere quagmire! Besides, even if he could reach them, and few country houses have telegraph or telephone, what could they do? The Authority might or might not have a few Cossacks. The nearest garrison may be hundreds of miles away. There are no police. There are a few village constables here and there elected by the peasants, but what can they do, even if they tried, against the multitude? Besides, they as constables would be the first to obey the Czar's order.

But, it may be asked, can the landowner not rely upon his own peasants? If he does, he relies upon a broken reed. His own peasants will never begin the pillage. They stand aloof, watching curiously the colloquy between their master and the strange peasants who come in the name of the Czar to take the land. Undecided, anxious, torn by conflicting feelings of devotion to their landlord and their inbred longing for the land, they wait until the parley is over and the pillage has begun. Then, as they see strangers carrying off the sheaves that they have reaped, and staggering under the weight of furniture with which they have been familiar from childhood, a confused murmur breaks out: "We have more right to it than these fellows!" And in another moment your peasants have joined the pillagers and are looting with the best. In a very few hours the place is skinned to the bone. The live stock are often butchered on the spot. Everything that is portable is removed. Then, as a climax, the torch is applied to the buildings and the ruined proprietor is left with his children to warm himself by the flames of his ancestral home.

That is the Revolution in Russia—the real Revolution which hides its grim and blood-red features behind no end of pretty masks of pleas for freedom and justice. There is no personal animus against the landed proprietors. In all the cases of agrarian outrage reported, I do not remember to have seen one in which the action of the peasants was excused or defended on the ground that they had legitimate grievances against the landlord. In many cases the peasants expressed and apparently felt the greatest regret that they had to plunder the property of one who had been their best friend. In the case of Prince Dolgoroukoff's estate, the whole proceeds of which were every year devoted to the upkeep of no fewer than seventy-four schools for the children of the peasants, the peasants wrecked everything, weeping as they plundered: "We wept, Little Father, we wept bitterly when we were doing it, for it went terribly against the grain, but we could not help it. We were told to do it, and so we did." A leading Liberal landowner of Novgorod, residing in St. Petersburg, was surprised to receive a deputation of his peasants who had traveled all the way to St. Petersburg to beseech him not to return now to Novgorod, because if he did they would beat him and destroy his property, and they would rather commit any crime than that, but they had no choice.

Social Revolutionists

The Social Revolutionists confine their propaganda chiefly to the peasants. But, as the peasant does not cease to be a peasant when he goes to town to work, the Social Revolutionists are busy both in town and in country. Between them and the Social Democrats there is a general understanding rather than a working agreement. The Social Revolutionist was less dissatisfied with the Douma than the Social Democrat, and for obvious reasons. The peasant is the predominant elector in the Douma. The town workman, excepting so far as he is a peasant, was left out in the cold. The Peasants' Union, a recently formed organization, controlled chiefly by revolutionary schoolmasters and peasants who were living in towns, has adopted an agrarian program hardly distinguishable from that of the Social Revolutionaries. This led to the arrest of its members, who, though they say that they represent nearly 400,000 peasants, only represent them in so far as they give articulate expression to their craving for more land.

The best organized of all the revolutionary organizations in Russia is the Jewish Bund. The Jews are at once the most oppressed and the brainiest people in Russia. Every now and then a savage stimulus is given to their zeal by massacre and outrage. The Bund is therefore the most *bona-fide* organization of the kind in Russia. The Jews, however, have enough energy and enthusiasm to spare after organizing the Bund, and in all the revolutionary organizations in Russia you always find the Jews well to the front. After the Bund, the Social Democrats with their republican aspirations come next, and then the Social Revolutionists. Mixed up between these are the purely economic Trades Unions, or Workmen's Associations, which, however economic they may be at their foundation, inevitably gravitate into politics. Of that the most remarkable illustration was the Railway Employees' Union which precipitated, almost by accident, the great political strike of October immediately preceding the grant of the constitution. In February the demands of the railway men were of the usual trades-unionist description: more wages, shorter hours of work, and the removal of grievances. But in October all these economic demands were submerged in the demand for a constitution.

The most serious of all the revolutionary movements in Russia is that which aims at permeating the armed forces of the empire with revolutionary ideas. When once the Government cannot rely upon its soldiers and its sailors the game is up. Hence the most strenuous efforts have been made to penetrate the naval and military barracks. Owing to the absence of the regular army in Manchuria, the barracks were filled with reservists, many of whom brought with them from their villages sullen discontent, and a readiness to listen to any foes of the existing Government.

The Union of Unions was an attempt to federate all the existing professional and other associations. Its president, Professor Milukoff, and his committee were promptly arrested and thrown into jail. After remaining in prison untried and even unaccused for five weeks, Professor Milukoff was released. But although from time to time meetings of the Union of Unions, or League of Leagues, have been held, the expectation entertained that it would develop into a kind of illegal but national committee capable of coördinating all the developments of the revolutionary movement has not been realized. At the end of October we heard a good deal about the Council of Workmen's Delegates in St. Petersburg, and something about the Peasants' Union of Moscow, but the League of Leagues seemed to have receded somewhat into the background. It would be a good thing for Russia and for Humanity if the revolutionary movement were capable of being controlled by any representative committee, especially by a committee presided over by a man as sane, as reasonable and as practical as Professor Milukoff. But the actions of the revolutionary "movement" appear to be incapable of control.

The Storm-Winds Gather

The probability is that, if the revolutionary forces succeed in upsetting the Czar, Russia itself will burst like a great bomb. As long as the Czar is on his throne there is only one authority. If once he disappears, the last semblance of authority will perish and Russia will be plunged into a bloody anarchy, in which regiments would find themselves on opposite sides and all the centrifugal forces would have full play. In Poland there are, besides the Social Democrats and the Jewish Bund, the Polish National League and the Polish Proletarian party. There is a revolutionary party among the Little Russians, and very formidable revolutionary committees among the Letts and the Courlanders of the Baltic provinces. Finland has recovered her ancient constitution, but if Russia went to pieces there are many Finlanders who would be glad to see Finland lord in her own house. In the Caucasus there are Armenian and Georgian and Tartar leagues mutually hostile, whose feuds have filled the whole of that beautiful land with bloodshed and misery. If once the Czar went, the keystone of the arch would disappear. There is no one as yet visible above the horizon who has the standing, the influence or the following to enable him to organize a government which would be recognized everywhere throughout the Russian Empire. The immediate future would seem to promise nothing but limitless confusion. A myriad of beggars on horseback are riding swiftly by as many different roads to the common inevitable destination. There will be attempts to organize governments more or less provisional in the southeast and in the southwest. Foreign intervention will be implored in the Caucasus, in Poland, and in the Baltic provinces. In the absence of a Czar the Cossacks may attempt to reestablish their ancient republic. Everywhere there will be arson, pillage and massacre on a scale such as this generation has not witnessed.

THE VACANT PLATE.

TURKEY.—Ha! Ha! How disappointed they look! Now I have lots to be thankful for.

RUSSIA & AMERICA
The Two Youths · Among the Nations
By ALBERT J. BEVERIDGE

IT WAS Emerson who called attention to the fact that with nations, as with men, it is all a question of heart beats, all a matter of arterial circulation. It is an obvious and yet a very profound truth that men wear out, and so do nations wear out, since nations are merely aggregations of men. And it is a very simple deduction that the whole problem of life is to preserve youth. Everybody knows that youth means growth, means the doing of things, means creation, construction, expansion. Conversely, age means decay, disintegration, the return to the original elements out of which the aging man or nation was first formed. After all, we cannot get away from the biological basis. And so it is quite clear that the duty of statesmanship is to preserve the youth of the people it serves. And youth is preserved by preserving the processes of youth — by building, growing, keeping active the creative energies. Youth is synthetic and imaginative; age is analytic, reminiscent and reflective. Youth seeks new fields to cultivate; age retreats even from the old ones; and this is just as true of nations as of men. Take the testimony of our American philosopher again. Says Emerson: "A good deal of our politics is physiological. . . . In England there is always some man of wealth and large connection, planting himself, during all his years of health, on the side of progress, who, as soon as he begins to die, checks his forward play, calls in his troops and becomes conservative. All conservatives are such from physical defects. They have been effeminated by position or Nature, born halt or blind through luxury of their parents, and can only, like invalids, act on the defensive. But strong natures, backwoodsmen, New Hampshire giants, Napoleons, Burkes, Broughams, Websters, Kossuths, are inevitable patriots until their life ebbs, and their defects and gout, palsy and money warp them." Thus Emerson — and while it seems to be untrue of individuals, it is certainly true of nations. The advantages of youth are well-nigh terrible in peoples and in individuals. No matter how completely the older peoples may occupy all of the present positions of superiority; no matter how the guns may be trained upon us to-day, we know that to-morrow those guns will be rust, the hands that trained them will have vanished, and that we shall be occupying still stronger positions than they do now, still higher up the steeps of power.

The Man to Plan the To-morrow of America

It was the perception of this elemental truth that made Peter the Great one of the most far-sighted statesman who ever lived. He knew that Russia would degenerate utterly if confined within mere land boundaries. He knew that nations breathe only through the sea — ports are breathing places. He knew that the more Russia touched the rest of the world the greater she would be. He conceived the simple but grand idea of Russia as an ever-growing, ever-expanding, and therefore ever-youth-renewing power. Or let us rather say that he was the incarnation of the desire of the Russian people — the personification of their racial purpose. To effectuate this great conception he laid down certain broad lines of national procedure that reached farther into futurity than any statesman, perhaps, who ever planned beyond his own immediate day. All the Russian statesmen since the period of Peter have largely been the executors of the great idea of the mighty man, whose vast intellect and burning activity made men in his day call him mad. It is this same conception which to-day is dominating the mind of the American people. And America will respond to the man who adequately gives expression to our master instinct. The intelligence of our people is so unusual that their common thought is larger and truer than that of any one man, and penetrates deeper into the coming centuries; and he will best plan the to-morrow of the American people who is the truest interpreter of their tendencies and purposes.

The same thing, and fundamentally from the same cause, is true of the great Russian Empire and of the great American Republic. We are the two youths of the world. We are the two entirely unexhausted peoples. We are the two expanding powers — the two powers, that is, that will continue to grow and develop in the coming centuries. And this is no reflection on the other great nations — perhaps to-day greater nations. They have achieved their development. But the period of American development is already here; and the development of Russia is beginning. Neither of us has achieved so much in art, philosophy; literature, law or even commerce as at least three of the other of the great, and one may say splendid, nations of to-day; but we have the advantage of youth. We hold the future in our hands. Not that England and Germany and other nations do not hold a noble future in their hands, too. (In Africa, England is securing room for great development also.) And let England thank God for her Cecil Rhodes, her Lord Cromers, and for all those other material and constructive minds who seek, find or create new fields for English constructive enterprise, for commerce and for the continuation of England's world-work. It is good to read of a man who lives on the earth to-day similar to those of whom the Bible speaks when it says, "And he founded a city." It is good to know that there are men who are founding something, planting something, building

something, creating something, and so long as England has those daring souls who prefer the wilds of Africa to the wiles of London, who prefer the jungle and the mountains of hazard to the ease of society, she will not fail — no, nor falter.

The Similarity of Russian and American Types

No traveler can fail to be fascinated with the singular charm of the harbor of Nagasaki, in Japan. It has few superiors in beauty and convenience in the world. The greatest ships move in deep water up to within a stone's throw of the shore. The hills, pine-clad and shrouded with that blue haze that so softens and beautifies the Japanese landscape, holds the harbor of still bluer water in loving embrace. Wooded islands stand like sentinels at its entrance — and they are sentinels indeed, fortified with the heaviest and most modern guns. Many days I have spent in this harbor, and I have never seen a time when Russian vessels of war were not anchored there. Once I was a guest on one of the noblest of these ships. A middle-aged officer, speaking English, thoroughly familiar with the geography, climate, products and politics of the United States, entertained with instructive talk. He was strangely American in appearance, manner, apparently in ideas. Two of the subaltern officers arrived from shore leave during the visit. One of them was of the Royal family of the Romanoffs. Their light hair, blue eyes, straight nose (anything but Tartar; and why do people mentally associate them with Tartar blood — they have none), thin nostril, delicate lip and singular alertness of manner and idea would have convinced you that they were American. They were of the type of the young American in appearance and in mental attitude.

I was not greatly interested in the ship, although one of Russia's latest; in course of time it will be archaic, as will all present vessels of war of every nation. But the men — they were of fundamental interest. They will not be archaic in a few years, nor their nation! Or will they? That is the question which is of infinitely more importance than ships, or guns, or commerce, or possessions, or geography. I asked to see the men. They were superb. They were young men, of course, but they were youthful young men. They were not old young men. They were young men of a race in its youth; in short, they were like our own young men. They made one think of the appearance of the people who fill the common coaches of the American railway trains; and there is no better place to study the characteristics of our people and to get the inspiration of their vast and youthful vitality. This similarity in youthfulness of the two peoples — the American and Russian — will impress any one who looks beneath surface differences.

One day, on the boat from Cologne to Mayence on the Rhine, I appeared to be the only American — was the only American. I had asked the German band on board if they would not render a certain German national composition. The request drew forth a remark from a gentleman I had not noticed before, and I was sure I had found a compatriot. He looked like an American professional man. Later I was presented to his wife and daughter — they, too, looked like Americans. As a matter of fact, he is an eminent Russian physician of St. Petersburg.

The Bond Between America and Russia

The similarity is startlingly apparent in the history of Russian and American expansion. The fascinating stories of the Russian Cossack exploration and settlement eastward and of the American pioneer expansion to the westward are so similar that, with the change of dates and names, one might be substituted for the other. Instead of the Stornganoffs we had Astor and the Hudson Bay Company; instead of Lewis and Cass and Fremont, the Russians had Yermak, Atlasoff and Khabaroff. There is nothing in American history so full of vitality, of racial inspiration as the story of Boone and Crockett and Carson, and all that company of fearless hearts who sought solitude and courted death to extend the dominion of the American flag on our own continent; and their story, which so thrills our blood to-day, can be reproduced in the recital of the adventures of the pioneers of Russia, who swept across "the girdle of the world," as the Ural Mountains were called, dared the unknown, seized Siberia, captured the Ameer, and, in a word, obeyed the instincts of the Russian people of which they, in their way, were merely the servants and forerunners. Frozen, starved, murdered by savage tribes in the new lands which they explored, the American and Russian pioneers have reached out in the centuries that are past, one toward the East and the other toward the West, in precisely the same manner, asking nothing better than an unmarked grave as their reward for extending the dominion of their respective peoples.

"Yes, I think undoubtedly that you Americans will control things for the next three hundred years, perhaps the next five hundred years," said the Russian naval officer, as we discussed the world and events on the deck of this great destroyer in Nagasaki. "But after that it will be our turn.

We are not ready yet. We are not sufficiently developed yet. We have youth without development; you have youth with development. Our business for the next three hundred years, anyhow, will be development. Our business will be getting ready. You are ready now." His casual words were deeply true. They are a statement of the conclusion to which every inquiring and thinking mind arrives.

Russia is like a world in formation. We are like a world newly formed, and full of vast productive energies. The conclusion from these two great facts states itself. Russia is, and for a long time yet will be, one of the choicest fields for our activities. Siberia is to be developed — her forests felled, her mines opened, her fields tilled; and Siberia's natural resources are tremendous — minerals, woods, agricultural possibilities. Already the number of her inhabitants is very considerable. Her population within the next hundred years will run into the tens of millions. Russia herself — I mean European Russia — is still undeveloped. Some person has got to develop that great dominion. Some person has got to build the railroads, furnish the machinery, construct the public and private works, manufacture and sell the goods, supply all the increasing wants of the Russian people and every part and dependency of the Russian Empire. None of the European nations is in so fortunate a position as the United States to do all this, because of the conflicts, jealousies, hatreds, and the scores of complications of Old World politics, springing out of present conditions and inherited from the conditions of a recent and remote past. The American Republic alone stands in an unrivaled position to supply the needs of the Russian Empire during the period of its development. The Russians prefer to buy from us what they cannot make or raise themselves. They prefer that we should build their railroads, that we should construct their buildings, that we should make their machinery, that we should sell them their clothing, that we should do all of the great work of development which they themselves cannot do. The reason for this is twofold. First, Russia has nothing to fear from us — for a century at least, as she thinks. Second, there is a fraternal feeling which has been fostered for a hundred years by both American and Russian statesmen and which has created a sentiment which is and will always be an invaluable asset in international dealings, whether political or commercial. But there is yet a third reason, which has its roots deeper than the policy of statesmen, in the soil of a common youth among the nations of the world and of a common certainty of future mastery. It is the same law which draws young men together in politics, or in business effort at the beginning of their careers.

Our Common Growth on Parallel Lines

Development! Development! Development! That is the thing upon which the Russian mind is intent. It is the thing to which her location, resources and the period now reached in the progress of her people force her. And it is the thing upon which the American mind should fasten itself, not in fear nor in envy, but with a realization of the opportunity it brings us. Of course the irresistible expansion of the Russian Empire, the sure, gradual, even perhaps slow, but manifestly mighty awakening of the Russian people, may cause alarm in the minds of the statesmen and people of other nations of the world. But it should not cause uneasiness in our minds. It should not even cause jealousy. If it makes other nations jealous or uneasy that is not an unfortunate fact for us. The Russian people are proceeding along the same lines upon which we are proceeding, more slowly than we, and far behind us. They have the same right to develop, to expand, to work out their destiny that we have. Indeed, it is hardly a question of "right," used in the narrow sense; for Russian expansion and development in the future, like American expansion and development in the present, and British expansion and development, which seemed to have reached its limit till Rhodes came with his misunderstood but imperial mind, and Roman expansion and development in her period, are merely great forces of Nature working themselves out in human society and civilization. And these forces will continue to work out their — shall we not say predestined? — results, no matter who is pleased or saddened by those results.

Russian Energy No Menace to America

Russia's great Trans-Siberian Railway, then, which is the most apparent and striking example of present Russian effort, should not alarm us. To the thoughtful mind, seeking new fields for American enterprise, the employment of American capital and markets for the product of American labor, that railway might well be built at our expense, for the benefit of American commerce alone. But when it is finished, will it not be the commercial highway by which Russia will ship her goods into China and the far East? Yes. But not now. Not for some decades yet; for Russia has not the factories, the mills, the machinery with which to supply her own population. She will have in a hundred years — perhaps fifty years — but in the meantime the Siberian Railway, from the viewpoint of American commerce, is merely the channel by which American goods, clothing, implements, machinery, rails, engines and practically all the products of our manufactories, mines and farms will find their way to the Siberian people. So that this railway, which is but a repetition by the Russian Government of the achievements by which American private enterprise has belted our own continent with many similar trunk lines, is for the present, at least, merely another American commercial opportunity.

If it is objected that the completion of this railway and the general progress of Russian development will bring her all the earlier into final competition with us, the answer is that the Russian progress cannot be stayed by our dissent. The Siberian Railway will be, is being, completed. New provinces will be, are being, added to the empire. Seaports have been, are being, and still others will be, acquired by the government of the Czar. We cannot stop it. No power can stop it. It is as inevitable as our own development; and it is profitless to argue about it — weak and absurd to complain of it. The wise and strong thing to do is to take advantage of it. For many years many of the wants of the Russian people must be supplied from without. I have suggested the reason why other nations are not in so good position as the American Republic to supply those wants. While the opportunity exists there, nay, while it invites us, it would be the very insanity of jealousy not to avail ourselves of it.

It must be remembered that the wants of the Russian people will increase as their progress increases. The civilized man (as the word civilized is now understood) means the man with the most wants. When a railroad has once penetrated to a previously isolated section of the world, the wants, the desires, the necessities of the people of that section immensely increase.

Commercial Duties that Await Us in Russia

The Trans-Siberian Railway is the largest material fact — or rather, perhaps, suggestion — in the world to-day, except our own recent acquisitions of territory. It is the beginning of a development of a mighty people and a mighty physical empire. Within the lives of the next generation railways will penetrate every portion of European Russia; and branch lines will extend, like nerves from the spinal cord, on either side of the Trans-Siberian line to the fields and mines and forests of that great dominion of Asiatic Russia. It appears to me that here is a new field for American enterprise which that fortunate series of circumstances that is now blessing us makes almost exclusively ours. Next to the immense trade of the Orient it is our most obvious and easy market; and since it is our business to find work for our hands to do — constructive, developing work — it would appear that the commercial conquest of Russia is an opportunity so great as to become almost a commercial duty.

There are three great and new fields for American enterprise — three great and new markets for our products. One is Central and South America; another is the far East, and especially China; the third is the Russian Empire. Instead of wasting time upon non-constructive theories, we should bend every energy of inventive and practical statesmanship toward commercial supremacy in these three fields. So much has been said concerning the Oriental market that awaits us and, though not recently, concerning the South and Central American markets which should be ours, that extended reference to any one would be out of proportion in this paper. But, singularly, little attention seems to have been given to the great Russian opportunity for the investment of American capital and the sale of American goods, and, in short, the conquest by American thought and energy of the great Russian market. Has not the time arrived to give this vital opportunity our earnest attention? To occupy this field does not mean that we shall leave our other European markets. We have those markets, and they should be fostered as carefully as any merchant would nurture the trade which he has once secured. And, in the nature of things, the European markets which we now possess must continue to be ours; although, aside from markets for breadstuffs, these markets must continue to be ours in a comparatively decreasing degree. In all manufactured goods, England and the countries of Western Europe will more and more make for themselves all they need. It is to the new fields that the American people and, as their agent, the American statesman must look. And of these new fields, the three that are ours by natural conditions and all the other circumstances that create and foster commercial intercourse, are the countries of the American continent, of the far East and of the great developing Russian world.

This conquest of Russian markets is not material alone. It has its aspect of glory as well. Perhaps it is the latter to which the historian of a thousand years from now, tracing out the influence of the American people in their great world-work, will give the most, if not exclusive, attention. For it is so very simple and plain a fact that its very simplicity obscures it, that a conquest of markets means, in the end, a conquest of ideas as well. Where our merchants go our speech goes, our manners are grafted, our civilization takes root. The very act of selling produces a dominating influence over the mind of the purchaser — otherwise he would not buy. Civilization follows commerce; liberty follows commerce, too. Civilization began when people began to exchange their mutual products and possessions. Men cannot exchange their products without exchanging their ideas, and so it may be that the American commercial conquest of Russia will also be the conquest of American ideas, manners, and, in the very distant end, perhaps American institutions among the Russian people. Or will you have it that, conversely, it may be in the end the triumph of Russian ideas, manners and institutions over us? I answer that such a result is impossible, unless Russian ideas, manners and government are the superior type. For nothing is surer than this, that the fittest type in manners, laws, ideas and government will finally survive. The law of evolution is much more apparent in the intellectual world than it is in the material world.

The Progressive Instinct of the Russian People

I have never been impressed with the idea which seems to oppress or gladden many minds that the Russian Government was destined to crumble and finally disappear — perhaps, as some writers have suggested, in a second "terror," surpassing the awful days of the French Revolution. Such talk appears to me to be wild, absurd, ill-informed. There is nothing more interesting or useful at present for Americans than the study of Russia, Russian history and government. The Russian Government is singularly elastic, remarkably progressive. The aspirations of the Russian people, as a people, are obeyed and realized by the Russian Government with remarkable fidelity. It was a great Russian financier who is reported recently to have uttered this significant truth.

"No," said he, "the Siberian Railway does not pay along the entire line, and perhaps will not pay for some time, although all other Russian railways pay heavily. But Siberia must be developed before that greatest railway of the world returns dividends upon its whole length, and when that occurs it will be the best paying property in the world. The development of Siberia is a great work — a hard work." (Even the Siberian Railway is said to be profitable on certain divisions now.) "Our whole development toward the Pacific is arduous and expensive. Neither this generation nor the next will reap the greatest benefit from that. Why, then, are we doing all this? We are doing it because we cannot help it. We are doing it in obedience to an instinct of the Russian people. We are obeying the common thought and common determination of the millions; or rather, I should not say their common thought, but their common instinct. We are moved as by the voice upon the face of the waters; we are moved as you are moved, and by the same great elemental power. In a word, we are growing. We are making ready a home for our future tens of millions. We are getting in touch with the world of to-day and the world of to-morrow also."

"Russia will be your great competitor in a few years. That is the conclusion of the whole syllogism of her progress toward the Pacific. That is the meaning of Port Arthur, of the Siberian Railway, of her movement toward the Persian Gulf. It is merely the movement of her people for the opportunities of trade, to create, to construct, to do. Your expansion, which is much more rapid than Russia's, is the same thing. Do you not see, therefore, that every step of Russian progress in the far East brings your final great competitor closer to you?" Thus spoke the ablest English financier in the far East; and one cannot quarrel with the sense and truth of his words. But admitting their correctness does not negative the plain fact of our commercial opportunity, involved in that very development of Russia, so far, at least, as the present and the next few decades are concerned. Will refusal to trade with Russia retard her progress appreciably? And if we do not trade with her, will not others? And if wealth is to be drawn from this commercial course, why should we not absorb it? And if we acquire wealth, strength, commercial greatness from this source, shall we not have been strengthened for the final conflict which some think they perceive, even by the very antagonist they fear?

Why Russia Will Avoid a Conflict

"What are you going to do," said my English friend in Hongkong, "when finally you and Russia are face to face as serious competitors in the far Eastern market?" The answer is that it is a situation which will take care of itself when it arrives. I have long had my own ideas as to what will occur; but it is not fruitful to discuss any situation so far in the future that we can neither act upon it nor prepare in a definite and tangible way for it. To go to war to protect commercial rights is not a shocking proposition; but to undertake conflict where the struggle itself would destroy the trade advantages which are yours under peaceful conditions is an impossible thought. It may be that other nations may invite and finally compel such a conflict with Russia. But there is nothing in the present situation to indicate that Americans will become involved in any such controversy for several generations at least, if ever; and the conflicts of others are something with which we have nothing to do except as those conflicts may affect our rights, present or prospective. I hardly look, however, for armed conflict between Russia and any power whatever for a very long time to come.

The remark of the Russian naval officer in Nagasaki harbor is the expression of all Russian thought, and one might say of all intelligent people everywhere on this subject. Russia is developing, growing. She needs her money for railways, for naval stations, for ships, for development, and has none for war.

The Argument for Commercial Conquest

All this theory of trade opportunities is "cold-blooded," we are told. One sometimes even hears it called "sordid." It is a matter of no importance to the ongoing of the American people whether these unkind adjectives are applicable or not. It is our business to find employment for every American. It is our business to discover new fields which the American mind and progress may enter and develop. It is our business to keep our productive energies active. It is our business to keep alive the constructive tendencies of the American people. In a word, it is our business to preserve our national youth — to keep growing in wealth, in power and in that kind of civilization which does not also mean decay. There are many offensive things about the ruggedness of Philistinism, but at least it has virility and perpetuity. It will not be a fortunate day for this virile republic when the bold spirit of our pioneers, who explored our continent and established our empire even in the wilderness, the audacity of our great constructive minds who have built our railroads, finished our bridges, launched our ships, and all our masculine, daring and synthetic character, is succeeded by the merely interrogative intellect, by a disposition to introspection, or even by the refined methods of art — for the ethnologist has pointed out for so many centuries that art is the beautiful flower that springs from the soil of decay, that that proposition may be taken now as *res adjudicata;* and one must be excused for preferring life, even if it is rugged, even if it is a selfish life, rather than death, no matter how beautiful.

How the Eternal Analogy Holds

There is no disputing the theory of progress by the law of rhythms. Olive Schreiner never said anything half so great as that "the Eternal analogy holds." Human progress is by mighty impulses, just as is everything else in Nature. And human progress, by impulses instead of by a steady and continuous current, takes the form of the predominance, the sovereignty, the mastery of successive peoples during successive periods. A mere glance at history suggests this; careful study confirms it. It is this period of mastery, of dominion, which the American people have reached to-day. Our whole policy as a nation should be shaped from the viewpoint of this great truth. The whole problem of our statesmanship, largely considered, is to extend this period — to render it permanent, if such a glad dream were possible, and let us not deny that it is.

England's sagacity during the past seventy-five years in these lines commands the admiration of her bitterest enemy; and it is this which has made her great, and which has kept her young. It will be a departure from these lines which will mark the beginning of her decline. Fortune has favored us in these great material particulars in a manner that compels a belief that it is the purpose of Providence to make us the master people of the world for a long period immediately before us. One cannot stop to quarrel or argue with him who holds the other view. It is like arguing against the coming of spring, or the ripening of corn in summer. It is like quarreling with the progresses of the suns. It is like — nay it is — disputing with a fact — and who can dispute successfully with facts? Our productive energies are unequaled in the history of the world; this is merely a fact. Our geographical position between the two great oceans is imperial beyond that of any other country on earth; that is merely a fact. The possession of Puerto Rico, the canal, Hawaii, the Philippines gives us a series of bases — commercial, naval and military — equaled only by two or three of the choice positions held by England; this is merely a fact. In politics we are through with childhood; through with petty disputations about State rights, about fanciful standards of money, about paralytic feebleness under the Constitution. These as practical questions are in the past, and the American people have reached that stage in their evolution where they are a Nation, a consolidated, indivisible People — a great, single, human Power; all this is merely a fact. In short, we have at last got ready for our work — and our work awaits us; it will continue to develop before us as our capacity for doing it develops, until our period as the sovereign people of the world has ended. "Yes, I think undoubtedly that you Americans will control things for the next three hundred years, perhaps five hundred years," as the Russian officer said in the beautiful harbor of South Japan. The American people think so, too, and it will be our business to make that five hundred years a thousand.

There is nothing discouraging in this program to the devotee of mere ideals. Ideals are nothing unless they are effectuated, and it has been pointed out before that ideals and ideas are not extended merely by talking about them. Nature has its methods of the propaganda of civilization. It is by the great and simple methods of growth. It is by making two blades of grass grow where one grew before. It is by the planting of trees, the building of roads, the setting of ships upon the waters, the manufacture of things of human use. It is by carrying merchandise to the peoples who need it. It is by the great law of service, for with these things go our thought, our speech, our religion, our institutions. "Faith without works is dead," and it is written that, "Man shall not live by bread alone, but by every word that proceedeth out of the mouth of God."

The Greatest

—1819–1900—

Queen

in the World

By Marie Corelli

AFTER THE STATUE BY GEORGE FRAMPTON, A. R. A.

"SHOW me, then, whether there be more to come than is past, or more past than is to come!"

Such was the prayer of the prophet Esdras, in Babylon, to the Angel who was sent from Heaven to instruct him. We, in our generation, may ask the same question to-day of the Recording Angel of the world's history, who stands forever among us, mute but observant: "Show us whether there be more to come than is past, or more past than is to come!"

For it is difficult to grasp the idea of any more perfect monarch's reign than that of our beloved Queen and Empress; it is well-nigh impossible to imagine a more magnificent Empire than the one over which she holds her dominion. All the great kingdoms of ancient days fade into insignificance beside the grandeur, the progress, the steadfast making for Truth, Justice and Freedom which preëminently distinguish the British rule; and the power, the brute force, the barbaric ostentation of conquest and egotism of the Roman Cæsars vanish like a mist of the marshes when confronted and compared with the one clear light of unsullied goodness in the heart of the "Mother of Nations"—the simple woman who, by pure love and faith, has done more than countless legions of fighting men could ever do for the glory of the country, and has fulfilled a far higher destiny and won a far greater fame than any conqueror who ever ruled by fear. Victories are hers by sea and land; victories not only over territories and peoples, but over barbarous systems of slavery, superstition and prejudice; victories of enlightenment and civilization; victories in science, in discovery, in learning, in education and national advancement—these cluster around her throne and adorn it more brilliantly than priceless jewels can adorn her imperial crown.

But her influence is of that deep and gentle and convincing nature which is felt more than seen, and it extends, not only through her own "Happy Isles," but away out to the younger children of her love, those far-off and faithful Colonies, springing up in their youthful and splendid vigor to take active part in the grand work of supporting and maintaining at their highest culmination the dignity and honor of Great Britain. It is an influence which appeals to the best instincts of all men and all women, the home-influence, the mother-love. In all history we can find no king or queen of England who has been so much and so truly the head of the national home as Queen Victoria. She is truly the Greatest Queen in the World.

It is a curious fact that there are very few civilized countries where woman's work is made such a butt for men's contemptuous ridicule as in England. The Englishman is ever quick to sneer at woman's advancement in art, in literature, in scholarship and general intellectual ability, yet all the while 'tis a woman who rules him, and to a woman alone he is compelled to bend the knee! Off goes his hat at sight of the Queen! cheers break from his throat at the proclaimed words, "the Queen!" "knights and earls, and knaves and churls" bow their heads to "the Queen!" And with all peoples and in all countries there seems to be only one Queen to whom the article "the" can be applied without further modification. Other Queens are qualified in their estate by the land over which they rule—as, for example, Queen of Italy, Queen of Greece, Empress of Germany, Empress of Russia; but when "the Queen" is said every one means England's Victoria. Of all queens the greatest, she is of all women the simplest, and herein gives matchless example to her sex. Above the splendors of her position and enthronement, she is preëminently woman in the sweetest and most womanly sense of the word—one who is gifted with quick, fine sympathies, and who has the supreme and exquisite tact which is, or should be, inherent in every true and unselfish feminine nature, combined with perfect self-command, flawless purity and a strong, personal potency for good. Throned and crowned and sceptred in the fierce light of the whole world's constant observation, she yet remains as unaffected and sincere of soul as the most unsophisticated of her subjects and is in very truth one with them in the ordinary round of their daily existence.

Are we bereaved of our best-beloved? So is the Queen. Have we suffered from evil-speaking and misjudgment? So has the Queen. And in our joys is she not equally one with us there? Do we find rest and pleasure in the natural beauty of the world, the perfume and color of flowers, the songs of birds? So does the Queen. Do we understand the winsome ways of little children and take delight in making them happy? So does the Queen.

In all quiet, natural and innocent pleasures the Queen is one with her subjects; it is only in social vice and folly that she takes no part.

Perhaps there was never a time more convincingly marked by the Queen's mother-love for her people than now, while the war in South Africa is still claiming the lives of many whom England can ill afford to lose. Her grief for the brave fellows who have fallen, her sympathy and care for the bereaved ones left to face their desolate lives alone, her interest in every detail of the campaign,

her anxiety for every scrap of news from the front, her simple, womanly regret for the whole deadly quarrel, all this shows what a true and tender friend Englishmen have in their beloved Monarch. And when one remembers her great age, which she bears so cheerily and courageously, giving herself up without hesitation to whatever duties of state call her forth into public evidence, one's reverence is mingled with wonder and admiration that she can and will do so much to still more endear herself to all hearts. The soldiers might all be the sons of her blood from the tenderness she expresses concerning them. They are "My poor soldiers!" with her; they are not mere food for powder and shot as they have often been considered by former Sovereigns of England. "My poor soldiers!" Their wounds, their losses, their pains, their troubles are hers, too; she feels them with an acute sympathy, and her kind heart aches for Tommy's weariness, fevers, excitements and general irritation when he is "sent home invalided" and craves to go out again. There is in her gentle, noble nature none of the indifference to his fate suggested in the verse:

"What did you get to eat and drink,
Johnnie, Johnnie?"
"Standing water as thick as ink,
Johnnie, my Johnnie, aha!
A bit o' beef that were three year stored,
A bit o' mutton as tough as a board,
And a fowl we killed with a sergeant's sword,
When the widow give the party."

This is scarcely the right spirit to foster between the sovereign and her fighting men. When the warriors of old time shaped England's greatness and laid down the lines of glory and honor for future generations to follow, they did not count up personal troubles or hardships, they never complained of long marches or scant fare, nor, let it be well remembered, have they ever complained at all of any of their sufferings—not now, or at any time. They have never "begged" the nation's charity—not now, or at any time. Two or three newspapers in want of "copy" may complain and beg *for* them, but they themselves have nothing to say but one thing—Duty! They have never called *themselves* "beggars." If they once began to take this low estimate of their profession, the prestige of the army would soon be at an end. If they started grumbling at "barbarious wars," or at their rations "when the widow give the party," there would soon be seething rebellion, where there is now loyalty, devotion and heroic indifference to merely physical inconvenience. But they know themselves and their calling too well to do this. They know, each and every man of them, that there is no one who feels greater sympathy for them than the Queen they serve; and that when she thanks her brave men for brave deeds bravely done, her gratitude comes from the heart and not from the lips alone. Her recent visits to the hospitals where her wounded soldiers lie have borne ample evidence to this. Her instincts are all those of sympathy, gentleness and love.

Whenever the Queen acts upon her own initiative, something good, something generous, something graceful is the result. How much the country may have to regret from interference with her inward wishes we shall perhaps never know, but this is very certain, that if Her Gracious Majesty had been able to do as her own fine feeling dictated she would have gone to Ireland long ago. She would, without doubt, have visited it as often as she visited the French Riviera, and we may be quite sure that the Irish people would never have returned her kindness by insult as the French have done. For though we do not consider the low boulevard press as representing the voice of France, one would like to see a more general rising of warm protest among the French at the offense perpetrated by one, or a few, of their countrymen against the Queen, whose noble reputation, as well as whose reverend age, should insure her safety from this kind of coarse indignity.

The Queen's Aloofness from Smart Society

One wonders, glancing back through the history of the triumphant reign of this great and good Sovereign, how things might have been if the Prince Consort had lived! If the Queen, instead of being driven by deep grief and heartbreak to retire into more or less privacy, had continually appeared at the head and front of society and taken enthusiastic part in all its doings! Certainly there would have been a very different state of things to that which exists at present. We venture to think divorces would not be so common. And it is just possible that some of the aristocracy would be leading very different lives, and that so many of them would not be seen at Monte Carlo season after season, gambling away their reputations and virtues together. The Queen's steadfast, beautiful example of life would have been more faithfully followed by the majority than it is, and the entrée into the Upper Ten would not have been given to the newest South African millionaire. To be presented at Court would have been really a distinctive sign of honor and high standing, not a mere form of social custom and usage in which flaunting Vice rubs shoulders with modest Virtue. The atrocious vulgarity, slang and open licentiousness of the so-called "smart set" would never have disgraced our English breeding; in fact, it is extremely doubtful whether this same "smart set" would have existed at all—or if it had existed, it would not have been termed "smart," but rather the contrary. The personal friends of the Queen are men and women of upright and honorable life, and there is a very strong, visible line of demarcation between Her Majesty's guests and what is called "society." In London this line of demarcation is not so quickly and generally observable as it is in the provinces. London is a seething whirlpool of incessant excitement, incessant "rush," incessant competition; and perhaps one of the fiercest struggles going on in it to-day is the fight between Honor and Disgrace—whether to live well or live ill—whether to sell the soul to Mammon or keep it clean for God; and between the great houses that "receive" the Phrynes and Aspasias of the stage and those who pay servile worship to the speculator there is very little to choose. And to many of the more thoughtful among Her Majesty's subjects the untimely death of the Prince Consort is the only cloud upon the brightness of her glorious reign—not only because of the irremediable grief it caused to the Queen, but also because it has deprived the social world of that closer influence and more constant guidance which from her would have been of such inestimable advantage not only to us but to all nations. However, despite the sorrows which have separated her in certain ways from the world of fashion and amusement, she remains the guiding light of everything good in our society.

Queen Victoria's Visit to Ireland

How warmly and heartily the Irish people appreciate the firm courage and womanly grace of Her Majesty's visit need not here be emphasized. Those who are inclined to indulge in rankling thoughts of the past and to dwell on old injuries and bitterness should try to feel and to realize that it is not their gentle and gracious Queen who has of her own will and wish appeared to neglect them. It should be remembered that she is a constitutional Sovereign and must generally do as her Ministers bid. Never has such an opportunity occurred for her boldly to take her own initiative as now, when the dauntless, high-spirited sons of Erin have fought and died for her cause. With that fine perception and instinctive tact inherent in her nature, the Queen has recognized that now or never must her children of the Emerald Isle learn that the mother love of her heart is as warm for them as it is for all her glorious Household of Nations, and that the loss of her Irish sons who have been stricken down in battle for her honor has caused her as much grief and as many tears as even they, in their passionate exigency of need and clamor for love, could demand. Great was the joy and pride of England on this last St. Patrick's Day, when the bright green flag emblazoned with the Harp of Erin floated beside the Royal Standard from many a window in many a city and town, and willingly and with light hearts did the people, one and all, obey their Queen-Mother's command and wear the bright little shamrock on their breasts as a sign of affection not only for their Sovereign but for their sister island. Lovely Ireland, with its purple hills, deep green valleys, lakes and streams, has been for a long time like the "ugly duckling" of the fairy fable; but we must not forget how that much-tormented bird, whom none of its brothers and sisters could understand on account of its "strange ways," turned out to be the fairest of the brood, after all, and developed into the graceful beauty of the swan. With tenderness, with care, with affection where there has been mistrust, with fraternity where there has been dispute, Erin will realize this transfiguration in herself and mark the days on which her great Queen-Mother came to rest under her protection as a golden time in her calendar. No brighter daughter of the home does Victoria possess than Erin; her face is one of the sweetest, her heart one of the staunchest. Poetry, romance, beauty distinguish her; and when she sends her warriors out to fight there are few that can match them or resist them. Little need be said for the Irish women, whose standard for upright living and chastity is the highest in the world, or for the sweet, wild Irish girls with their bright eyes and dark tangles of hair and lovely, laughing, animated faces. The Queen, in her good heart, cannot but rejoice to know of such fresh youth and beauty and unspoilt innocence, flourishing as the flowers flourish in this mossy dell-like corner

of her Empire. The gallant Irish heroes who have fallen in the fight have not perished in vain, if their memory brings the Queen closer to Irish hearts and makes her one of them.

What the Queen Has Done for Her Own Sex

With the summer that is now breaking in upon us we may hope that peace will come like the dove of the ark, flying across the troubled waters and bringing good news of rest. For the Queen's sake we pray that this may be; and that the clouds which have darkened the skies so threateningly may disperse in clear sunshine. England wants all nations to understand that she desires brotherhood rather than enmity, love instead of hatred. The country has been blessed abundantly with good things, and it will be impossible for future history to chronicle a more glorious era of advancement in good works and good feeling than that of Victoria, Queen and Empress.

A universal charity has prevailed throughout the realm; never have the poor had so much done for them, never have the sick been so carefully housed and tended, never has any one with skill and determination had better chances of fortune than now. And, despite the fact previously alluded to, that there is no civilized country where woman's work meets with so much flippant ridicule from the casual man as in England, the intellectual progress of woman under a woman's government has been steady and triumphant. This fact alone is a distinctive mark of the Queen's great epoch. This may or may not be due to the Queen's influence, or the consciousness that all have, that the Sovereign, though the ruler of the most magnificent Empire in existence, is still—only a woman! Whatever may be the cause, the fact is there; and the intellectual capacity of women workers in Great Britain is bound to reach a very high level.

Everything has advanced and made for the better in Victoria's reign, and only one section of society persistently harks back to the worser morals and manners of Charles the Second's period. That, however, is a small section, and by the natural course of events is gradually beginning to destroy itself. And when history writes the record of Victoria's long and brilliant reign the small blots on society's scutcheon will vanish as though they had never been, and the persons who have made those blots will be "passed over" as unimportant items of ill-assorted fare in a full feast of plenty. And the glorious name and fame of the one Queen in England's history who is truly the mother of her people will shine like the sun in a cloudless sky. There is no one so good as she is, so simple, so kind, so thoughtful of her subjects. Her little hand holds a great Empire in the gentle grasp of loving-kindness. She is the bond of union between the Old World and the New. Her spirit is with her brave soldiers on the field of battle, and, whenever she can, she takes her welcome presence to them when they are brought home wounded and disabled. She evinces a constant, active interest in the work of foreign peoples despite foreign insult; she sends her greeting to the sons and daughters of her loyal Colonies with all the tenderness she truly feels; and wherever her name is spoken it is received with veneration and homage. Unique in goodness, unique in power, unique in history, she is, in her great age and continued vigor, the crowning splendor of her splendid reign.

"God save the Queen" is no mere formula; it is the prayer of a mighty people, a people of various climes and colors and creeds, all differing in opinion but all banded together in one great family of union and defense under the one mother whose love has never failed them and never will fail them, Victoria, the greatest Queen in the world!

"PUBLICK OCCURRENCES" *That are Making HISTORY*

Copyright by London Stereoscopic Co., London

GENERAL LORD ROBERTS

The Price of British Empire in India

After the defeats in South Africa many of the English newspapers, including the London Times, said it was the most serious setback since the mutiny in India. For centuries this revolt of a subjugated people will be a subject of history and romance. The war and the things that followed gave Rudyard Kipling his material and opportunity. It is an interesting fact about most great wars that the origin or the climax was trivial, and in the case of the Indian mutiny this was peculiarly the case. No historian has ever yet been able to find adequate cause. Of course there were the national antagonisms between the races, but that did not count for everything. Disaffection existed, and in the crisis there was a rumor that the cartridges which had been served out to the native soldiers were greased with the fat of animals unclean alike to Hindu and Mohammedan. The slaughter began. On Sunday afternoon, May 10, 1857, the Sepoys broke in open mutiny, and then for two years the war went on, with the loss of thousands of lives.

When the Boers Whipped the British on Majuba Hill

We never know how much history we have forgotten until some disturbance brings out the details bearing upon great events. In thousands of journals and newspapers it has been asserted over and over again in the past several years that the idea of a South African Empire, holding somewhat the same relations as Canada to Great Britain, was originated, suggested and formulated by Cecil Rhodes and Joseph Chamberlain. As a matter of fact, the credit belongs to Lord Carnarvon, who, after seeing the effects of the confederation act in Canada, suggested that all the European settlements of South Africa be united under similar confederate government. The scheme was adopted, and the British agents in South Africa simply went ahead to annex things in their own peculiar way. It was not until April, 1877, that the Transvaal was nominally added to the British Throne. In order to make the annexations more valid, excuses were found and wars were started to sustain them. The cost was a great many millions of dollars and a number of good English lives. The natives were mowed down, and the whole desperate business made sad chapters in African history. The Boers, who had fled to escape British aggression, at last made their stand. The open troubles began in 1880.

In December, 1880, the South African Republic was proclaimed, with Kruger as President, Joubert Commandant-General, Jorissen Attorney-General, and Bok acting State Secretary. Pretorius joined Kruger and Joubert in the direction of affairs. The English lost heavily during the war. It astonished them beyond measure that they were defeated by such small numbers of the Boers. They made a final stand on the Majuba Mountain, which commanded the Boers' position, but this did not dismay the hardy Dutch, who on February 27, 1881, carried the place by storm, killed 83, including the British Commander, Sir George Pomeroy Colley, and disabled and captured 183. Sir Frederick Roberts—the present Roberts in command—was appointed Commander-in-General, and 15,000 troops were sent to South Africa from all parts of the British Empire. But before they arrived an armistice had been arranged and gradually peace was reached.

Copyright by Elliott & Fry, London

GENERAL LORD METHUEN

It is a fact in history, however, that after the conclusion of the preliminary settlement, while the Boers departed to their farms, the British not only did not decrease their forces, but made open preparations for the renewal of the war. In that contest Europe, outside of Great Britain, was practically one in sympathy with the Boers, and leading men in the Continental countries signed petitions pleading that the Transvaal be recognized as an independent State. With the effect of the defeats and the insistence of the sentiment of the world, Great Britain gave in. No one has ever said a word against the bravery of the Boers in that wonderful fight on Majuba Hill, and it is one of the distinct defeats that befell the English in all their long experiences in war.

Copyright by Messrs. Bassano, London

GENERAL LORD KITCHENER

Some Famous Setbacks to English Arms

Many interesting parallels have been drawn between the American Revolution and the present contest of the South African Republic. Whether or not the merits of the case are similar must of course be left to future historians, for not even the best of men is competent to judge at short range as to absolutely where the right and wrong belong. History needs plenty of distance.

Possibly there are more contrasts than parallels in these two wars. Great Britain has sent, and is sending, to South Africa more troops than she sent to America during the seven years of the conflict, for in that time the number of British troops and hirelings who crossed the Atlantic was only about 112,000 soldiers and 22,000 seamen. The United States had forces during the same period of 232,000 Continental soldiers and 56,000 militiamen.

Many of us have forgotten that the war against the American Colonies was so unpopular that King George could not raise enough troops in his own country, and had to hire men from the Continent. The present war was at first unpopular with the people of Great Britain, but there has been no lack of readiness on their part to supply men and munitions, although it has been necessary to call heavily upon the colonies for assistance. The history of the Revolution is pretty familiar to all. We whipped the English at the North and in the Middle States, and finally in the South. After the brilliant feats by American armies the climax came in the surrender of Cornwallis. Cornwallis surrendered 7247 men, 75 brass cannon, and 69 iron guns, while several vessels with 900 men and officers were surrendered to the French fleet. Already in the few months' fight in Africa the Boers have killed, captured and disabled almost as many men as the entire forces surrendered to the Americans on October 19, 1781, which sealed our independence.

In some respects there is a better parallel in the War of 1812. Great Britain sent three armies under three Generals to the different sections of the country, and they were defeated even more disastrously than the first armies in South Africa. The most famous of the battles took place actually after the treaty of peace was signed. It was at New Orleans. Twelve thousand picked British troops were defeated by 5000 Americans, the British losing 2000 in killed, wounded and prisoners, while the American loss was only a few men. In that case General Andrew Jackson and his sturdy troops found even greater safety behind cotton bales than the Boers are finding in their mountain fastnesses. This war on the part of the United States was in some respects the most remarkable of the century because it began with a bankrupt treasury and an army of only 10,000 men.

One of the Great Tragedies of the Century

Since the American Revolution England has not been fighting all the time, but she has been in trouble most of the time. Her brilliant victories in the Napoleonic wars make stupendous reading. To all parts of the world have her soldiers gone, and she has contributed marvelous chapters to civilization; yet her finest experiences have not been without their tragedies, although in the end, except in three or four instances, she has known some of the greatest victories in the records of the world.

In the beginning of the forties there was trouble in Afghanistan. "Disaster after disaster occurred, not without misconduct," says one of the most serious of English authorities. The English Army at that time comprised between 15,000 and 20,000 men, of whom many were English soldiers and officers, and the attempt was made in 1841 to force the Khaibar Pass. It was not a success. Then began the retreat. It was in the high altitudes, and the winter was one of the severest ever known. The troops were entirely demoralized, and the march back—or to give it another name, the retreat—was marked by the greatest confusion, and by the most indescribable suffering. Of all this great number, one wounded and half-dead man, Doctor Brydone, reached Jelalabad, and afterward 95 prisoners were recovered. The terrible loss of life was one of the worst disasters in the history of armies. The fact that the Khaibar Pass was afterward forced and England won the day showed the resolution of a nation which, although it may be badly beaten, seldom admits defeat.

The British Reverses in the South African War

Often the sayings of a General become more familiar to the great public than the details of his victories or his defeats. For instance, it has been printed all over the world that Sir Redvers Buller had vauntingly proclaimed before leaving England that he would eat his Christmas dinner in Pretoria, the capital of the South African Republic. It distinctly lowered him in the estimation of those who liked to think of him as a great fighter, and it hurt him personally. But since it has gone its rounds there has come a letter with his signature in which he said: "I was never foolish enough to make any such statement as has been attributed to me. There is an old saying which has sound sense in it; 'Never prophesy unless you know.'" More foolish were the speculators of the London Stock Exchange who, on the declaration of war, sent a message to President Kruger saying, "May the Lord make you thankful for what you are about to receive," and who two months later saw their fortunes toppling like buildings in a cyclone, and themselves shaking and shivering in the midst of ruin.

There were two sides from the English standpoint. One was the every-day, joyous feeling that the war would be simply a picnic march to the stronghold of the Boers. The other was—and this was that of those best informed and conservative—that the South Africans had built up, and were building up, a strong military establishment, with splendid modern equipments, with expert officers from Continental countries, and with all the resources for a modern conflict with a powerful nation. The events since October 10 have more than corroborated this suspicion.

It may be several months before we shall know exactly the official figures of the various battles that were fought, but we do know that the three divisions of the English fighting forces were each defeated in turn; that ending with the year more than 900 English troops were killed, nearly 4000 were wounded, and between 2000 and 3000 were missing: altogether a casualty list in the neighborhood of 7000. Adding those incapacitated by illness this total now exceeds 10,000. When the smaller Generals, such as White and Gatacre and Methuen, were driven back, Great Britain, with that admirable confidence in her men which she has always shown, waited with perfect patience for Commanding-General Buller to force a magnificent victory and thus retrieve the disgrace. Instead of that, he met the Boers with disastrous results, with a loss of over 1000 men and of a dozen guns, and with a shock to British pride that was felt throughout the world.

Britain's Position as a Great Power at Stake

Immediately the true size of the war was appreciated. The London Times, which is never given to sensation and always speaks conservatively for England, declared: "We are fighting not merely for supremacy in South Africa, but our position as a great Power. We know we have miscalculated the strength of our foe, and we are resolved not to make future miscalculations." The English Government called out the available troops of the Empire. People, while they differed as to the justice or the reason of the war, agreed that their flag must be upheld, and on top of all the War Office appointed Baron Roberts Commander-in-Chief, with Lord Kitchener as Chief-of-Staff. These two are the greatest fighters in the English Army—Roberts, who did wonders in India, and Kitchener, who did marvels in Africa, both men of infinite courage and infinite persistence, knowing nothing save duty, and never wearying until victory is won. At once the spirits of the British nation arose, and to-day the English are confident that when the new commanders and the new troops begin their campaign the triumph of British arms will not be long postponed.

But the Boers are not dismayed. In a letter written since the war began their commander, General Joubert, said: "Up to the present time our enemies have fought bravely; but when they begin to suffer the privations of war, demoralization will come upon them, and they will weaken. We are convinced of our own ultimate triumph and of God's aid in this war, as in our preceding wars with the same foes. The blood that must be shed in this struggle, which will last probably more than a year, will not be upon the heads of our children. We fight for our creed and country."

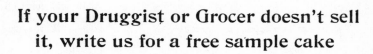

THREE BLOODLESS REVOLUTIONS

The Middle Classes of England, France and Germany are to-day Contending for the Basic Principles of the American Republic

By DAVID GRAHAM PHILLIPS

THE European rulers who have been doing so much visiting of late are preening themselves upon the present almost unparalleled state of tranquillity in the foreign affairs departments of the nations of Western Europe. The fact is that they had no more to do with it than election and weather prophets have to do with the events which they just happened to forecast. The reason the statesmen of Europe are unable to make the several peoples shake their fists and mutter at each other across the boundary lines is that domestic affairs are so absorbing. "We, the people," are becoming tremendously self-conscious in the Twentieth Century Europe and refuse to respond to the once potent cries of foreign devilism. They are thinking more about the devils of caste and privilege at home.

To begin with England, there the Tory or Conservative party, ruled by and for the most hidebound, most bigoted of English upper classmen, has found through a renegade middle classman a new issue for throwing dust into the eyes of the people. Of course the real issue in the skillful but cruel oligarchy called England is now as always that oligarchy itself—how to abolish the distinctions and privileges of caste which enable the upper class few to loll in comfort and luxury upon the backs of the many. And the problem with the upper class is how to confuse and shunt this issue. With the close of the Boer war, so ruthlessly brought on by the upper class and so shockingly mismanaged by it, this issue threatened to come to the fore more strongly than at any time since Mr. Gladstone shelved it with his Home Rule scheme.

But Mr. Chamberlain, the real leader of the Tories, came to the rescue. The two great leaders and preservers of the Tory party in the past half-century have been Mr. Disraeli and Mr. Chamberlain—both men of "low" origin, both renegade radicals, both prevailing by dressing up Toryism in a clever radical disguise.

Chamberlain's Paternalistic Policy

MR. CHAMBERLAIN'S issue is an expansion of the doctrine of imperialism. Imperialism was "Empire for Englishmen." Mr. Chamberlain's new edition of it is, "Englishmen for the Empire"—though, of course, he does not put it just that way. For, while Englishmen listened complacently, even enthusiastically, to proposals to sacrifice other peoples for the sake of spreading their own domain, they would not rise to the height of self-sacrifice necessary to the carrying out of imperialism's inevitable corollary—Englishmen sacrificed for the sake of the empty glory of the imperial name.

Mr. Chamberlain's proposition is: The basis of the unity of the component parts of any empire must be mutual advantage in the union in matters of trade and commerce. As England has free trade, it cannot offer to its colonies any such advantages, but on the one hand gives and on the other hand gets no commercial advantages beyond those of foreign nations. If this state of affairs continues the empire must perish, because commercially the colonies will continue to look on each other and on England as so many foreign nations. The remedy, the one remedy, is a protective tariff walling the empire round; free trade or an approach to it within the wall, protection against the foreign nations outside it.

The contention of the opponents of Great Britain is: The commerce between England and the colonies is a mere trifle in the total foreign trade of England, and if England got all the colonial trade, it is still so small that it would not compensate her for what she would lose. Free trade has made England. Whether or no foreign nations and English colonies continue to be stupid enough to fancy that by levying on themselves the plausible predatory taxes of that relic of barbarism, the protective tariff, England should be wise enough to continue in the intelligent course. While the foreign trade of England has fallen off somewhat, it has fallen amazingly little considering the fact that where thirty years ago she was practically the only manufacturing nation in the world, to-day she is one of four great manufacturing nations—England, the United States, France and Germany. As to the colonies and the mother country, no policy that would ruin England could possibly make her dearer to them, and the ties of political protection, of blood and language and patriotism, with no really strong disrupting force acting against them, are quite sufficient to hold the empire together. That the new policy would ruin England is certain, because it would mean a tax upon the food of the people, upon their bread, upon their meat, and a tax upon their clothing and shelter, with no possible corresponding rise in wages. For, if wages rose, how could the manufactures, necessarily produced at greater cost, be sold in England's great markets, the markets of foreign nations?

By raising this question of basic policy Mr. Chamberlain has dissolved the old parties of England which have been slowly dying since Mr. Gladstone split the Liberal Party with his Home Rule program. Mr. Chamberlain has held on to all the old-line Tories—how could they revolt from him when he alone offers them another and long lease of life for caste and privilege? He has won over a probably large body of liberals of the "imperial" or "jingo" type. And he has bid for the skilled laborer by promising him that the money raised by taxing his food shall be used in giving him an old-age pension.

As Liberalism stands in the main for equality before the law, for abolition of privilege, for curtailing the powers of the government, for compelling every man to shift self-respectingly for himself, Mr. Chamberlain's paternalistic program makes him at last an out-and-out Tory. The taint of socialism which his opponents find in his projects need trouble no Tory. The difference between paternalist and socialist is merely a difference of opinion as to the right name for the bounty-distributing central power, and doubtless Tory craft, aided by the stolidity of the English masses, can indefinitely postpone serious discussion of that difference. In Germany, the domestic question that absorbs people and public men is on the surface socialism. In face of the savage open attacks of the Emperor upon the Social Democrats as traitors and rascals, they have polled a vote which even under the unrepresentative electoral system of the German Empire has made them the largest party but one in the Reichstag, and that one is the anti-government Clerical or Catholic party. If there were equality of representation in Germany, the Socialists would have nearly half the Reichstag. For the election showed that nearly one-half of William's subjects are, by his own definition, traitors.

The Social Democrats in Germany

BUT the fact is that the socialist victory does not mean a victory for socialism. In the first place, the German Government is so paternalistic that to an American it looks like a state where socialism prevails in all but name. Again, the program of the Social Democratic party, once revolutionary, democratic, violently radical from the viewpoint of such a divine-right ruler as the Kaiser, is now in its practical paragraphs little more than a protest against William's assumption that he is a shepherd and the German people so many extremely helpless sheep intrusted to his care, and a protest against William's fantastic militarism and costly and profitless expansion. Finally, the indignation of the less subservient section of the German people who are not in the least attracted by the Social Democratic projects was so great against the Emperor and the bigoted, arrogant army officers and junker or "country squire" aristocrats that they voted with the Social Democrats as the best way of expressing their weariness and disgust.

The prospect is that the Social Democrats, striving to hold these new voters, will still further broaden and de-socialize their platform and policy. The Social Democratic party will become the nucleus of a vigorous agitation for a true Constitutional monarchy with a sovereign as free from notions of "divine right" as a "ruler" of England is in presence of a prime minister come to tell him what to say and do. But for the present the shrewd Emperor can be relied upon to keep his "mailed fist" full as heavy as ever upon the German people, from time immemorial accustomed to an autocratic "war lord" over them.

While Germany is thus wondering what the haughty, quick-tempered Emperor will do now that the worm has, not indeed turned, but rather wriggled impertinently, the French are wondering what will become of Combes.

From the standpoint of M. Combes, the Prime Minister of France, and the overwhelming majority of the supporters of the Republic in the French parliament, the present French situation is as follows: Ever since the revolution, or for more than a century, France has been trying to establish firmly a true republic. She has had all the monarchies of Europe against her. She has had the established church, in so far as it is represented by the great religious orders, against her.

When she made her first attempt, Europe combined to re-seat the Bourbons, and she had to create a military dictator who made himself Emperor and went crazy. When combined Europe expelled him and restored the Bourbons, she got rid of them as soon as possible and reëstablished the republic, disguising it, for various cogent reasons in domestic and foreign conditions, as a monarchy—Louis Philippe, "King of the French." Then came the throwing off of the disguise and the establishment of the republic with Napoleon "the Little" as President. Again monarchic wiles proved too strong for the republican majority of France, and there was the fraudulent "Third Empire." This fell at Sedan, and once more the republic was established.

At first the republic was a "party," but it has steadily gained ground until it is no longer merely the most powerful party among several parties but is the nation—almost.

The Contest Against Caste

NOW, according to the men in control of the party which represents the most numerous body of republicans, the party to which an actual majority of Frenchmen belong, the one remaining dangerous internal foe of the republic is, or rather was, the great religious orders within the Catholic Church of France. Not the Catholic Church itself, for these republicans insist that the mass of parish priests and of prelates of the Church who work among the people is as bitterly hostile to the great, powerful orders as they are.

The republican contention is that these orders, established of old by the kings of France, and in large part composed of the sons and daughters of the old noblesse and of men and women of the families loyal to noble and king, have been toiling for a restoration of monarchy. The allegation is that in the schools of these orders, notably in the fashionable schools all under their complete control, the flower of the youth of France, the future fathers and mothers of the most enlightened and influential citizenship of France, was trained in royalism, in hatred of and contempt for the republic. "To establish the republic for the future," said the republicans, "we must stamp out these hotbeds of royalism. These orders either must act in the open, must give in public and in private the same teachings, or they must go." And they have gone—the orders teaching the girls of France, the mothers of the Frenchmen of to-morrow, were expelled by the narrowest vote of all.

This same situation, from the standpoint of the active and angry minority, may be stated thus: France is a republic. It pretends to be free. Yet a faction of fanatical republicans, thinly disguising hostility to all religion under profuse professions of solicitude for "true religion" and for the "downtrodden parish priest," has changed France into a despotism in which freedom of speech and action are denied and forbidden. If the republic is so strong, why does it have to resort to such tyrannies to maintain itself?

Between these two parties stands a third, whose strength has not yet been tested at the polls. This third party says: "M. Combes and his followers are in the main right. The great orders have been too arrogant in their pride and wealth. They have opposed the republic, have carried on a secret and covert propaganda for restoration of monarchy. But M. Combes is trying to do in one day what should have been done by slow stages in a period of many years. In his overzeal he is putting the republic in jeopardy, is building up a sentiment that may lead to a disheartening reaction."

At bottom in all these nations—England, Germany, France—the issue is the same, though the forms in which it presents itself are deceptively different. France is contending over the old, old question of privilege, of caste, transmitted to her from that dark and bloody past in which the splendid French intellect, the finest and the most aspiring in Europe, fought so valiantly and so successfully for the rights of man.

And in Germany, what is Social Democrat against Emperor but the common man struggling to win a little more ground from the hierarchy of blood and sword which at once robs and rules him? And in England, is it not again privilege, rank and birth and law-entrenched caste, striving adroitly to devise new schemes for keeping the mind of the people off of the great, black basic wrong, the legal inequality of men through the accident of birth?

Personal Christianity

A Special Translation Made With the Express Approval of His Majesty the German Emperor, of an Address to His Sons, the Princes August-Wilhelm and Oscar, on the Day of Their Confirmation

By Kaiser Wilhelm II

Copyright, 1904, by Horace Markley

DRAWN BY J. J. GOULD

MY DEAR SONS: At the present time, in which we are about to drain our glasses to your health and to express our congratulations that you have joined us in the congregation of the Lord as men who have a fervid desire to work therein, I should like, as your father, to make a few remarks to you as to the attainment of this aim. This day, in a spiritual sense, is for you similar to the day on which the officer or the soldier takes the oath of loyalty to his colors. As Princes of the Royal House you have the privilege of wearing a uniform from the tenth year of your age. To this I desire to compare your confirmation. You are selected as fighters for Christ. With the present day you have, so to speak, come of age in your faith. The defense and weapons, as well as the armor, which you will have to use have been taught you and prepared for you by a skilled hand. Their use in all the situations of life is left to you from now on. But in this, though it will also be possible to instruct you further, remember that finally, however, every one must learn for himself how to use weapons. It is the same with the spiritual ones which are intrusted to you. I intentionally speak in a military sense, as I presume you know the beautiful parable in which the Christian is compared to a warrior, in which the weapons that the Lord has placed at his disposal are left to his choice. Certainly you will find later an opportunity to use one or the other of those weapons, and you will surely carry out what you have this day so well promised in your pledge. Your religious teacher has to-day emphasized, and quite correctly, to you the idea of what is to be expected from you—that is, that you must become "personalities." This is just the point on which, in my opinion, the most depends for a Christian in the struggle of life. For there can be no doubt whatever, when referring to the person of our Lord, we can say He has been the "most personal personality" that has ever wandered about on this earth among the children of men.

In school you have read and heard, and you will read and hear in the future, of many great men—savants, statesmen, kings, princes, and also poets. You have read words and sayings of many of them which ennobled you and even filled you with enthusiasm. To be sure! Is there a German youth who would not feel inspired and enthusiastic by such songs as those of our poet Koerner? And yet they are all the mere words of men. Not one of them is to be compared to any single word spoken by our Lord. And this is said to you so that you will be in a position to defend it, as soon as you find yourselves in the struggle of life and hear exchanges of opinions and also exchange opinions yourselves regarding religion, and, above all, regarding the person of our Savior.

The word of man has never been able uniformly to inspire people of all races and of all nations to attain the same aim, to endeavor to be like Him, and even to give their lives for Him. This miracle can only be explained from the fact that the words He spoke were the words from the living God, which awaken life and which remain alive even after a period of many thousands of years, while the words of the savants are long forgotten.

Now, when I look back on my personal experience, I can only assure you—and your experience will be the same—that the cardinal and main object of human life, and principally that of a life full of responsibility and activity—this has become clearer to me from year to year —lies solely and alone in the position we take regarding our Lord and Savior. I have called Him the most personal of personalities, and thus rightly. For it cannot be otherwise in human life. And as happens with us all, so it was also with Him. There have been disputes regarding opinions of Him: some were for Him, some were in doubt, and many were against Him. But about this there can be no doubt whatever, and the severest foe and denier

of the Lord is but a proof of the fact: The Lord is still living at the present time as a complete personality which cannot be ignored. His heavenly form is still walking about among us, visible only to our mental eye, and perceptible only to our soul: comforting, helping, strengthening, but also awakening contradiction and persecution; and because He cannot be ignored every human being is compelled, whether he be aware of it or not, to compare the life he leads, the office he holds, the work he does, with the angle of vision in which he stands toward our Savior; and if his work is done in the sight of the Lord, whether it be agreeable to Him or whether it be to the contrary, his conscience, if it be still alive, will always thus direct him.

In fact, I firmly believe that many people are of the opinion that it is inconceivable in our nowadays "modern" life, with its multifarious duties and its many situations full of responsibility, that one could give such particular attention to the personality of our Savior and have so much regard for Him as there was felt for Him in former times. And mankind has filled Heaven with many beautiful figures, other than that of our Lord, with pious Christians, who are called saints, and to whom man prays for help. But all this is only an incident and a vanity. The only Helper and Redeemer is now, and will always be, the Savior.

There is only one thing I can advise you, with all my heart, regarding the life that lies before you: toil and work without intermission; this is the essential part of the Christian life. It was thus He lived before us! Glance at the Scriptures and read the parables of our Savior. The severest punishment is for the one who does nothing, who sits idle, or floats with the stream, and allows others to do the work, as in the parable of the talents. Whatsoever be your passions or your gifts, every one should try to do the best in his power and in his province to become a personality, to grow into his duties, to toil in them, and to further them in accordance with the example of our Savior. Above all, in everything you commence, strive to make it, if possible, of benefit to your fellow-men, for it is the most beautiful thing to rejoice with others, and where this is not possible, try to have your work at least of benefit to your fellow-men, the same as was exemplified in the life full of work and the acts of our Lord. In so doing you will have fulfilled what is expected from you. Then you will become good German men, capable Princes of my house, who are able to share in the great work left to us all.

That you may be fitted to carry out such a work to its accomplishment with blessings, and that the help of God and our Savior be with you in this task—to this we drain our glasses.

Germany's Covetous Eye

By Frederic Courtland Penfield

The Kaiser's Systematic Play
for Trade Supremacy in China

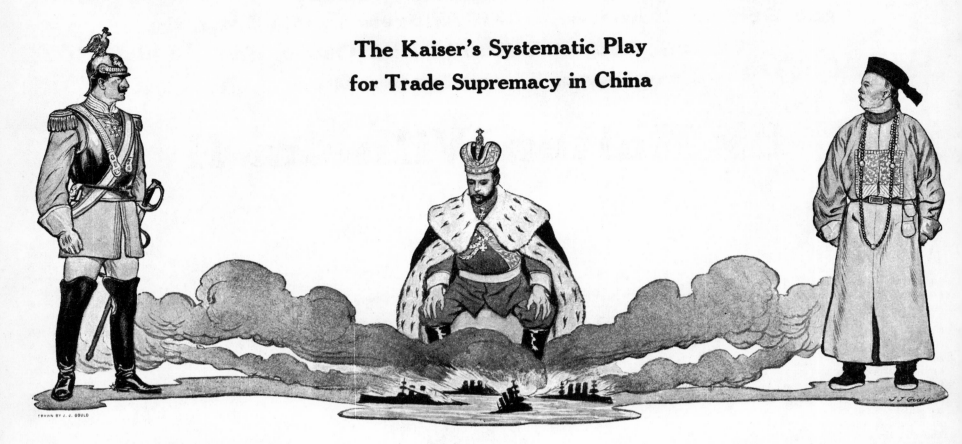

DRAWN BY J. J. GOULD

FRANCE had no choice but to espouse Russia's side in the conflict in Asia, for it was compelled by her alliance with the Czar's Government. But of Germany's interest in the conflict, the Germany of paramount military importance, bound by no alliance, and having no voice in the controversy leading to war, the Germany that should have been neutral in the strictest sense of the word—what of that country?

It is a fact incontrovertible that, from the commencement of hostilities between Russia and Japan, the German Emperor has been as pro-Russian as any wearer of the Czar's uniform. And bankers of Berlin, most of them, have been equally pro-Russian in their conduct and sympathy. And shipowners of Hamburg and Bremen, taking their cue from the capital, have devotedly supported the Russian side, many of them finding it easy to view situations of international procedure in a manner allowing them to reap golden benefits; for whenever Russia was forced to purchase ships to augment her armed fleet these were always found in Germany. When Russian squadrons were dispatched to the Far East they were coaled practically throughout that long journey from German colliers. And in other helpful ways Germany has officiated as the handmaiden of Russia.

The Kaiser's favoritism for Russia was infectious throughout his empire, as suggested, and six months ago his people were practically unanimous for the cause of their neighbors on the north. Had the contending armies and fleets in the Far East been equally matched, with the outcome hanging in the balance, the influence of William II could have swayed the continent of Europe in Russia's favor; and, things in Manchuria and on the sea being equal between Russia and Japan, an advantage would thereby have accrued to Russia difficult to overcome. Why? Because the Kaiser is the strongest, most influential and cleverest potentate in Europe. Splendid exemplar of the war-lord idea, he is really the peer of diplomatists, a ruler whose utterances are weighed and discussed as those of none other in Continental Europe. Understanding the value of words, and a coiner of subtle phrases, an epigram from the Kaiser contrasting the destiny and rights of the "white man" and the "yellow man" would probably have left the British Japan's only sympathizers in the Old World.

But the psychological moment never came—there was a hitch somewhere in Asia, and Kuropatkin's genius was expended in masterly retreats; all the triumphs on land and sea were those of the little men under the sun-flag. Finally came a mighty engagement, and William hastened to decorate the Russian loser and the Japanese victor. But the point was strained; the public perceived this. As a result, the incident fell flatter than the anti-climax of a melodrama played to empty seats.

The Kaiser's chagrin was great. But it need not have been, for the march of events in the East was proving him simply to be mortal—he had failed to pick the winner, and was gradually becoming aware of it. A plunger in a sporting event perceives an error of judgment in a few minutes, usually. With the War-Lord of Germany it required the lapse of months to bring the sad fact to his understanding that Japan would win in the great struggle.

Why War-Lord, as an appellation for the august William? Adept in the art of warfare he surely is; but have not the Fatherland's victories under his rule been those of peace only? Has Germany been involved in strife possessing the dignity of war since he came to the throne? Has she not, on the other hand, made headway in trade and sea transportation under his guidance that has no parallel in the history of a European state? And are not the words "Made in Germany" so painfully familiar throughout two-thirds of the globe, especially in Great Britain and her possessions, that they strike terror to Britons who study with apprehension the statistics of England's waning trade? All this is true, and Suez Canal returns prove that the users of the waterway under Britain's red flag are yearly less numerous, while the number of German ships is steadily growing.

Then why not Trade-Lord? This is what the German Emperor is. It is the better of the appellations,[1] and more truthfully descriptive. It surely is creditable to the German people that their national progress is due to habits of industry and thrift, rather than to military display: the artisan, not the drill-master, is making Germany great.

And could Trade-Lord William be honestly called "astute" if he overlooked the fact, obvious as a mountain, that one of the stakes in the Russo-Japanese conflict would be the privilege, amounting almost to right, to exploit commercially the most populous country on God's footstool—China? More than one-fourth of the people of the earth are Chinese, and their country in this year 1905 is more primitive, in the absence of railways, telegraphs and other public utilities, and every provision conducing to comfort and common-sense in living, than any other land pretending to civilization. It is a fact that outside of Shanghai, Canton, Peking and Tientsin, the people do not want many of the products of the outer world; but it also is a truism that much profit accrues from teaching Asiatics to "want" modern products.

The German Emperor foresaw that China could not much longer resist the invasion of outside enterprise and trade; and to his mind there could have been no suspicion of doubt that the victor in the awful contest could and would dictate trade terms and privileges everywhere in the Celestial Empire. If Japan won, the Japanese would surely exploit commercially their great neighbor, whose written language is nearly identical with their own—this would be but natural to the Mikado's people, teeming with aptitude as manufacturers and traders, and recognizing the necessity for recouping outlay in the war.

If Russia were successful, her reward would be the validating of her hold upon Manchuria, the bundling of the Japs out of Korea, and the attainment to a position of controlling influence in China's political affairs. The supplying of articles of general manufacture and commerce to the 400,000,000 people of China could have been no part of Russia's program, for the simple reason that Russia is not a manufacturing country and has but little to sell. Even her enormous tea bill is paid yearly in money to China. A nation aspiring in time to control the whole of Asia couldn't bother with commercial matters—certainly not. Yet one of the fruits of victory in the war would have been the splendid opportunity to exploit trade everywhere in China—a privilege of priceless value.

What country was to benefit through this, with Russia's moral support and permission?

France? Hardly; for the French were bound by hard-and-fast alliance, and it had never been the policy at St. Petersburg to give anything material to France. Uncle Sam, whose people had financed half the war loans of Japan, could scarcely hope to extend his business in China with Russia's coöperation; nor could Japan's ally and moral supporter, John Bull.

Who, then, could stand in a likelier position to become legatee of this valued privilege than the Trade-Lord of Germany? The Emperor William had been Russia's "best friend" from the inception of the war, and was admittedly an adept in promoting trade, for his people had attained in a few years to an envied position in the commerce of the world. A quarter of the trade of "awakened" China would make Germany a vast workshop, a hive of industry.

And this was precisely what the astute Hohenzollern saw through the smoke of battle in far-away Manchuria. He saw a prosperous Germany if the Slav crushed the yellow man. To say he did not would be a libel upon a giant intellect.

Any one disposed to review practically certain incidents in the recent history of Germany may develop a dozen reasons why the Emperor should seek to make his country all important through trade conquest. Let it be remembered that the Kaiser chafes at barriers of every kind, and that there is a restlessness in his nature at times trying to his patience to restrain. He looks at the map of the German Empire and painfully admits that the present frontiers are practically those bequeathed by the Great William. To a divine-right monarch this is exasperating. The loftiest ambition of an ordinary sovereign, governing perfunctorily, even, is to have the national area expand under his rule.

William's mediæval temperament shudders at the crowded condition of the earth in this twentieth century, when all frontiers appear immovable. Had he lived in the days of the Crusaders his valiant sword would probably have brought all Palestine under German control; and had he been a free agent when Bonapartism collapsed he most likely would have carried the German standard to the Mediterranean, perhaps to Stamboul. The ironical fact is that the German Emperor has had rebuffs and disappointments in his efforts to expand his realm. The Monroe Doctrine, excluding his empire from even a coaling station in this hemisphere, is to the Kaiser a perpetual nightmare. Sturdy sons of the Fatherland control the trade of more than one state in South and Central America, but nowhere is it possible to unfurl the standard of Germany over "colony" or "sphere of influence." Even to forcibly back up her subjects' rights the approval of the Government at Washington has first to be obtained. In his heart, the Kaiser loathes the Doctrine of Monroe—that is certain.

It is twenty years since Germany began to build up a colonial empire in Africa, and the net result is that, after spending some hundred million dollars, she has acquired over a hundred million square miles of territory, with a sparsely scattered German population of between five and six thousand souls—men, women and children. A third of the adult male population is represented by officials and soldiers. Militarism is rampant everywhere, with the result that the white settler shuns German colonies as he would the plague. The keen-witted Kaiser long ago saw that empire-building in the Dark Continent could produce nothing but expense during his lifetime.

"To perdition with the Monroe Doctrine, and with African tribes blind to the excellence of German-made wares," the Kaiser might have said ten years ago. "I'll have sweet revenge upon all and sundry by capturing trade everywhere. I'll make Germany the workshop of the universe. Keep your territory, if you like; I'll get the trade!"

The Kaiser Looks Eastward

THE resolute Trade-Lord then turned his face to the East, the bountiful Orient, pregnant with resource beyond the dreams of avarice, teeming with hundreds of millions of people. The East had made England dominant in the world's affairs.

Keeping his soldiers at home the Kaiser hurled a legion of trade-getters into the Far East, planting commercial outposts in Ceylon, sending a flying column of bagmen and negotiators to India and the Straits Settlements, and distributing a numerical division of business agents throughout China. The Empire of the Celestials was made the focal point of a great propaganda, openly espoused by the Emperor.

It was readily demonstrated that Great Britain had no permanent control of commerce in the East, not even in her own possessions. The Teuton, for a time content with trifling profit, underbid all rivals—and orders and contracts poured into Germany. Belgian products competed only in price; and American manufacturers seemed too busy in providing goods for home use to try seriously for business in Asia—they booked orders coming practically unsought, that was about all.

The Chino-Japanese conflict of ten years ago, although disastrous to China's army, stimulated the absorbing power of the Chinese for goods of Western manufacture, and Germany sold her wares right and left.

Important steamship lines were now subsidized by the German Government to maintain regular services between Germany and the Far East, carrying goods and passengers at reasonable charges; and it was known that in his personal capacity the Emperor had become a large shareholder in one of them. Germany was prospering, and the Trade-Lord and his lieutenants were happy. All recognized the possibilities of Oriental business. China was preparing to throw off the conservatism and lethargy of centuries, and trade was the keynote of everything pertaining to Germany's relations with the Peking Government. German diplomatists on service in China were

instructed to employ every good office to induce German business, and the Kaiser himself selected and instructed consular officials going to the Flowery Kingdom. Able commercial attachés, with capacity for describing trade conditions, were maintained there, and expected to be as industrious as beavers. For trade-promoting capacity German consuls in China have no equal—and they all know that the Kaiser's interest in Chinese trade amounts to mania.

The assassination in the streets of Peking, in 1900, of Minister von Kettler, Germany's envoy, and the subsequent sending of an imperial prince of China to Berlin to express the regrets of the Chinese Government, strengthened materially the Kaiser's hold upon Chinese affairs. Reiteration from Washington of the "open door" in China struck no terror in the Kaiser's heart, justified in believing he could hold his position against all comers. As proof of this belief, he might point to German steamers in Hongkong and Shanghai literally vomiting forth each week thousands of tons of goods "Made in Germany," penetrating every section of China even to the upper waters of the Yang-tse. A few years ago nearly all this trade was exclusively British.

The question of Chinese exclusion and the threatened boycott of American goods by China has recently been the occasion of anxiety in this country—but none in Germany. It is well appreciated that the spread of the sentiment in the East that the United States is unjust to Chinamen of the better class might undo the splendid work of Secretary Hay in cultivating the friendship of the Celestial Empire by standing fast for China's administrative entity and insisting on the "open door" policy.

When China Wakes

KNOWING that the "awakening" of China would be one of the results of the war, the Master Mind in Berlin had not long to consider where the interest of Germany lay, for he well knew that if they conquered, the Japs would in a few years supply the kindred Chinese with practically every article needed from abroad.

If Russia won, then "Best Friend" William of Germany, one of the most irresistible forces in the world, would have a freer hand in China than ever—and this would mean a prosperous Germany for years to come.

By directing the sympathies of the German people to the Russian side the Kaiser played a trump card in statecraft, certainly. As a soldier, William II must have known the fighting ability and prowess of the little men of Japan, for German officers had for years been the instructors of the Mikado's army—but the public attitude of the head of a government must ever be that which best serves the State. Whatever the chagrin at Berlin over Russia's defeat, a battle royal will be needed for Japan to overcome Germany's lead in Chinese trade; but in time Japan will have this, provided she is well advised and has the fortune to be backed by Uncle Sam.

What of the German colony in China—Kiau-chau, on the east coast of the Shantung peninsula, whose forts frown upon the Yellow Sea? Is there anything like it, strategically and tradewise, in the East? No. When the Kaiser's glance falls upon the map of Kiau-chau, and he recalls the ease with which he segregated from Peking's rule a goodly piece of old China, he may be irreverently moved to the extent of again snapping his fingers at the Monroe Doctrine, and at millions of simple Africans who refuse to eat German foods and wear not a stitch of German fabrics. Kiau-chau represents the cleverest feat of empire-building the world has seen since the Great Powers declared a closure to land-grabbing in the East.

When some German missionaries were murdered a few years since in China, the Kaiser, ever an opportunist, was justly angry, and Peking shuddered at the possibility of national castigation. Could the Mighty One at Berlin condone the offense if China gave Germany a harbor to be used as coaling station and naval headquarters? Possibly; but how can China bestow territory in view of the American Government's certainty to insist that there be no parceling of China—none whatever?

"Easily managed," was the reply. "It need not be a transfer of territory, but a 'lease,' say for ninety-nine years. This would save China's 'face,' and not disturb the Powers."

Hence a "lease" was prepared for all the territory bounded in a semicircle drawn fifteen miles from Kiau-chau Bay—a goodly piece, in all conscience. Then came *pourparlers* for greater German authority, and for more territory. As a consequence, in a second document signed at Peking, it was additionally agreed that "in a further zone thirty miles from all points of the leased territory the Chinese Government shall no longer, for a space of ninety-nine years, be entitled to take any step without previous authorization from the German Government."

This amounted in substance to saying farewell on China's part to a slice of domain in all more than twice the size of the State of Rhode Island. The "sphere of influence," so called, measures 2750 square miles. Germany was given, as well, the equivalent of sovereignty over the

harbor of Kiau-chau, no end of mining and railway rights, and other privileges. The lease dates from March 6, 1898.

Kiau-chau harbor is one of the most spacious and best protected on the coast of China. The small native town of Tsing-tau, admirably situated on the harbor, was adopted by Germany as the seat of government, and all the appurtenances of a military and naval station have been erected. A look of permanency characterizes every structure. The house of the naval governor is even pretentious. The capital is laid out with generous regard to broad streets, designated on name-plates as "strasses." A bank and a hotel await the coming of business. The harbor has been dredged, and two miles of the best wharves in Asia constructed of masonry. Warehouses, barracks, hospitals, administrative buildings and coal-sheds are there, all in German style, and intended to last hundreds of years.

A Firm Foothold

TSING-TAU as a seat of deputed government may not have found its way into schoolbooks, but the inquisitive traveler in North China readily learns of its existence. Perhaps it is meant to be complimentary to China to retain the name Tsing-tau—but that is all about the place that is Chinese, save the coolies executing the white man's behest. There are 2500 Europeans, almost exclusively Germans, in William's capital on Kiau-chau Bay. Soldiers and officials predominate, of course, but merchant and industrial expert are in the pioneer band in conspicuous numbers.

And what of the "hinterland," compassed by the forty-five-mile semicircle, dotted with thirty-odd native towns, the whole having a population of 1,200,000? This patch of China is surely in process of being awakened; there are numerous schools wherein European missionaries are teaching the German language, and enterprise greets the eye everywhere. Locomotives "Made in Germany" screech warnings to Chinese yokels to clear the way for trains heavy with merchandise of German origin—and this is but an incident in the great scheme of Germanizing the Chinese Empire. Incidentally, it is provided by the agreement between the Peking and Berlin Governments that a native landowner in the leased section can sell only to the German authorities. This ruling conveys a meaning perfectly clear.

Less than a hundred miles up-country are the enormous coal-fields of Weihsien and Poshan, by agreement worked with German capital, and connected with the harbor by railways built with German money, and so devoted to Teutonic interests that the name of the company is spread on the cars in the language of the dear old Fatherland. The whole is a magnificent piece of propagandism, surely.

And what is back of it? What is the purpose of the appropriation of 14,000,000 marks for Kiau-chau in this year's official budget of the German Government? Trade, little else; and Trade spelled best with a large T.

It was an interesting occasion, on a clear, bright day in April last, when his Royal Highness Prince Friedrich Leopold of Prussia and his brilliant military suite were landed on the quay at Tsing-tau. The great steamer that had brought them from Europe, dodging derelict Russian mines all the way from Shanghai, was the first Imperial mail-ship to enter Kiau-chau harbor. Tsing-tau was in gala mood and dress, naturally, and the princely brother-in-law of the Kaiser debarked amid cheers from German throats and the bellowing of brass instruments on shore, and the booming of guns on warships assembled in the harbor.

No function could have been more German anywhere. At home there would have been a different background to the picture. In Hamburg there would have been no interned Russian battleship under repairs, like the Czarevitch, at a neighboring jetty; no flotilla of torpedo-boat destroyers that had escaped from Port Arthur, glad to find safety in a friendly harbor, and supposed to be "out of commission"; certainly no trainload of American petroleum in cases, destined for up-country use in China. It is a truism that the Light of Asia is American petroleum. And the four-masted Yankee schooner discharging Oregon pine at a nearby pier—that couldn't be seen in a German port. Otherwise, picture, setting and frame were intensely German.

And the twenty or thirty packing-cases with the Imperial cipher on their lids? What do they contain? Presents from the German Emperor to the Emperor and Dowager Empress of China, that's all—and wholly "Made in Germany."

It was a subtle move in the coquetry going on between the courts of Berlin and Peking to land a carload of gifts at Germany's seaport in China and have them convoyed to the Chinese capital by a princely messenger almost a member of the Kaiser's household.

And its significance? Trade, again with a large T. Looked at superficially, it might be thought a diplomatic cementing of the ties of amity between the nations. But Germany has a program to be carried out in the Celestial Empire, be it remembered, somewhat difficult of execution now that Japan has arrested the Russian advance.

The Partition of China

THE natural course of events in China seems to be moving along with celerity. The news is that the great powers, meaning England, Russia, Germany, and France, are about to agree upon a delimitation of spheres of influence. This government is not expected to become a party to any treaty that may be made in this behalf, partly, it is said, because, as the Senate would have to act on such a treaty, there would necessarily be delay and probably embarrassment to the treaty-making power—that is, to the executive. It is said also that the administration favors the proposed delimitation because it has assurances, from replies, already received or expected to Secretary HAY's request to the powers concerned, as to their attitude towards the policy of the "open door," that, in the event of the making of the convention, the treaty rights of this country in China would be preserved.

We do not know, of course, what the powers propose to do in the matter of changing the government of China. It may be that the English idea is to prevail, and that the general government will remain in the control of the Chinese, and even in the hands of the present dynasty, the authority of the viceroys being limited or destroyed. Or it may be that it is the intention of the powers to assume a suzerainty over the whole of China and to govern it through their own agents. China herself, if we are to draw our conclusion from the good-humored, but really pathetic, criticism on the news which was made by the clever Chinese minister to this country, has not been consulted on the proposed partition. What we do know is that China will inevitably be forced to do business with the world on modern and liberal principles, and that no ideals of justice will be permitted to stand in the way of the advancement of trade interests. Judged from the ideal point of view, China has the right to complain, to employ the minister's metaphor, of any proposition to divide up her house among her neighbors without her consent. But the minister does not state the case accurately.

China contains much more potential wealth than any unexploited country in the world. Perhaps we would be within bounds in saying that if her resources were developed by modern methods and modern men she would be naturally the richest country in the world, the United States excepted. Her government has pretended to throw open her great resources, to a certain extent, to the commercial powers, including this country. She has entered into treaties with those powers. She has pretended to simplify her tariff policy and her port and local charges, with a view to relieving those who trade with her from the uncertain and onerous exactions of local authorities, and to afford national protection to the foreign traders. These treaties have been violated, and the English have especially the right to complain of her failure to observe her obligations. Even if these obligations were observed, much the greater part of China would be still closed to development, but as it is, the Peking government cannot or will not control the viceroys, and trade is consequently hampered. Now the trading world says, in effect, to China, "You must trade with us, and you must permit us to turn your potential into actual wealth." If China were wise, she would accede to this demand without pressure. It is true that those who would reap the greatest benefit would, in the first instance, be the hated and distrusted foreigners, but in the end the Chinese themselves would enormously benefit by the change. Indeed, if we are correctly informed as to the commercial and industrial character of the Chinese, they would be the greatest beneficiaries of the application of modern methods to the development of their rich mineral and agricultural resources, and of the possibilities opened up through the establishment of manufactures and the extension of commerce. But the Chinese are not wise, in this direction at all events, and they strenuously resist the bestowal of riches upon them by force.

Not many months ago it seemed as if the movement, which cannot long be delayed, of modernizing and Europeanizing China would be forced forward by war; but now it seems as if the result would be effected through peaceful but not less effective pressure. This may be prevented, of course, by Japan, but perhaps Japan will be invited to take a share in the division, and will thus gain the fruits of her victory over China of which she was deprived by Russia. If China can be opened peaceably it will be a great gain for civilization, provided she is not actually robbed of her rights. If she can be persuaded to yield wisely, the outcome will be altogether good. The world needs her wealth, and when that wealth is made obtainable this country will doubtless be benefited by the revolution more than any other country than Great Britain—eventually even more than Great Britain. It is to be hoped that Secretary HAY will see to it that the United States do not connive at any injustice to China. We want our share of her resources, but we do not want it at the expense of our self-respect. China will be better off than she is by the adoption of the policy of "spheres of influence," and the world will be better off too, not only if that policy is adopted, but if its success is not the result of war. The great value of the assemblage or the alliance of the powers is that it makes for the avoidance of war, but the avoidance of war will not be a blessing if it is effected through an unjust ignoring of the rights of the Chinese. We are quite sure, however, that Chinese rights can be safeguarded by the co-operation of the American and English governments, and that is an object for the attainment of which Secretary HAY may well exercise his unquestioned powers of diplomacy.

The Shark in the Yellow Sea

THE "chancelleries of the world," of which, since we have become a "world power," we may call our State Department one, are groping timidly and not very hopefully for a way out of the thorny Chinese thicket. No doubt the Powers will blunder through to some sort of tolerable standing ground, but the difficulties in the way are staggering. The task of ruling China through foreign officials would be one of such immensity that the most buoyant bearers of the white man's burden might be excused for shrinking from it. The partition of the Empire would mean that each of the Powers would have to govern seventy or eighty millions of the most refractory subjects on earth.

There is a third course which will not be adopted, unless it should be forced upon the Powers by the impossibility of carrying out any other program, but which would have certain rather marked advantages. That is the plan of taking the Chinese at their word and letting them alone—first, of course, exacting due reparation for the crimes of the present summer.

The western world in former times got along very well without intercourse with China. We are concerned now about Chinese markets, but it would take the profits on a good many years of Chinese trade to pay the cost of the present little unpleasantness. A good deal of that Chinese commerce upon which the civilized world has been congratulating itself has been the sale of Krupp guns, Mauser rifles and cartridges.

The "Yellow Terror" that has been the nightmare of some ingenious writers is the product of the attempt to break down the seclusion of China by force. The Chinese have not displayed any inclination to disturb Europe. All they seem to want is to be let alone. Some day the western world may consider seriously whether it would not be best to let them have their way in that respect. Imagine China wiped off from the map—every foreign minister, consul, missionary and trader withdrawn from Chinese soil, every Chinese representative abroad sent home, and all the 150,000 Chinese inhabitants of the United States deported. It would make considerable disturbance in the present arrangements of the world, but possibly less than would be produced by a China awake, armed, and stirred to ambitious activity. A country that could put ten million men in the field without missing them from the ordinary activities of life, and whose rule of warfare is to give no quarter to man, woman or child, is one whose desire for "splendid isolation" might, perhaps, be more profitably encouraged by civilized powers than suppressed.

Probably such a policy could be substantially carried out without an entire sacrifice of Chinese trade. The bulk of that trade now goes through a few ports, such as Shanghai and Canton, where the local populace has become accustomed to foreigners, and these points of contact might be preserved even if all relations between the western world and China as a whole were abandoned. If we should give up the attempt to force our civilization upon the rest of the country, China might settle back into the torpor of ages, and the yellow peril might be forgotten.

Of course it is annoying to have to hold your hand just as you are about to throw your harpoon into a whale. But what if the whale turns out to be a shark?

—SAMUEL E. MOFFETT.

Earl Li and General Grant

Li Hung Chang still loves to speak of General Grant. "He was a friend to China," he said the other day; "I wish he were still alive."

The great Chinaman loves to remember also that he and Grant were of the same age. "And he won his first success in a great war that ended in April of 1865, while I won my first great success as leader of the Imperial army in a war almost, if not quite, as stupendous—the Taiping Rebellion—which ended in July of 1865. And my own name, Li, is pronounced the same as that of General Grant's chief adversary.

"I admired General Grant," continued the Chinese statesman, "and I remember how closely I looked at his face when we first met. I had anticipated that first meeting with great interest, and was convinced, in advance, that General Grant and I were to be the close friends that we really became."

Earl Li remembers with a reminiscent grin that Grant did not like either of those two Chinese delicacies, birds' nest soup or sharks' fins.

"When I pressed him to tell me frankly just what he thought of those dishes, he said that the soup didn't seem to have any taste at all, and that the prepared fins, somehow, seemed to be mostly oil."

General Grant urged Li Hung Chang to visit the United States. "He told me how much he would be delighted to make my visit to his country pleasant, but it did not seem then that I could ever go; and when I did go my friend was dead, but I saw that all America honored his memory. I was taken to his tomb, beside that noble river, and I felt so grieved and sad, as I was there, to think that he was really dead."

Li Hung Chang likes to tell, too, how Grant amazed a mandarin who asked question after question about the United States.

"And how should I travel to get there?" the mandarin finally asked.

"Dig a deep enough hole right under your feet," responded the American general.

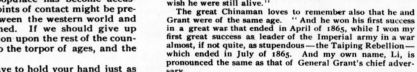

LI HUNG CHANG AND GENERAL GRANT

"PUBLICK OCCURRENCES"

The Curious Prejudices of Some People

One of the most famous lawyers, after undertaking a big case, always first directed his attention to the opposition. He studied it thoroughly and conscientiously, and then, when he had reached a full understanding of it, he began to attack it from his own side. Perhaps it might be well for the average person to pursue some such a program in considering the tragedy which has begun in the Chinese Empire. In other countries rowdies have maltreated and killed inoffensive Chinamen, have slaughtered them on occasion without justification.

Another thing. Minister Wu Ting-fang, Chinese Minister to the United States, in a public statement said: "Confucianism, Buddhism, and Mohammedanism have existed side by side for centuries in China without persecuting each other," and he added that the Chinese, who are a very conservative people, cannot understand the zeal of the American missionaries.

He drew a picture of what might happen if Chinese missionaries should come to this country and should attempt to spread the teachings of Confucius and Buddha, and to prevail upon our people to tear down their churches. He thought they would be mobbed. This, of course, is his view.

Practically all of these people can read and write, yet they are ignorant and superstitious, and there is a belief running through the lower classes that the foreigners want their eyes for medical purposes. Said Minister Wu: "I remember assuring the Emperor himself at an audience I had with him that there was no foundation for such a rumor." Then, too, if there is one reverence that the Chinese have it is for the sacredness of their graveyards. And the foreign engineers run railroads through them.

revenue of about eighty million dollars, and the trade amounts to many hundreds of millions each year.

Not least interesting, these people have in their dictionary from 40,000 to 60,000 characters, of which we are gravely told 25,000 have "the sanction of good usage."

Twenty Million Lives Lost in One Rebellion

It has been said that every nation needs a shaking up every fifty years, and this recalls the fact that it was just fifty years ago that the great Taiping Rebellion began in South China and spread over fifteen of the eighteen provinces, resulting in the sacrifice of the almost incredible number of twenty million lives. It is well to bear in mind, too, that this was a kind of Christianity, although corrupted and debased. The Manchu dynasty had ruled for over three hundred years. A schoolmaster named Hung Siu Chuen, born in 1813, from some Christian tracts and other books evolved a new religion. He had a vision, and he claimed that these words were addressed to him: "All human beings in the world are produced and sustained by Me; they eat My bread and wear My clothes, but not one among them has the heart to venerate and remember Me; they take My gifts and therewith worship demons; they rebel against Me and arouse My anger." After this a sword was given to Hung—so he said—and he was commanded to exterminate the demons. He claimed that this command came from God, and that Christ stood by his side and told him how to act. His preaching led to thousands of converts and "The Church of God" was established. Then followed the demolition of

The Meaning of the Boxer Movement

In the choice lot of information and misinformation about China we have no better example than the various definitions of the Boxers. Professor F. W. Williams, of the chair of Modern Oriental History at Yale, is quoted as follows: "The term Boxers is derived from the Chinese word about equivalent to the English term for rough classes. The Chinese term is 'Yi Ho Chuan,' which may be interpreted as 'righteousness, harmony and fists.'" Another authority drawing his information from the missionary sources states: "Boxers is the new name for the Society of the Great or Strong Sword (in Chinese, Ta Too Why). Its members kill and rob foreigners without discrimination on the slightest provocation, and oftentimes on no provocation whatever." Still another authority says: "The Boxers were first organized in Shantung province about a year ago as a sort of protection against thieves and robbers, the Boxers being allowed to carry swords and to have them in their possession. Their first demonstration was the murder of a missionary, and finally the attack on the Belgian engineers, which led to the present outbreaks." Other accounts describe them variously as belonging to the lower and the upper classes, as having the friendship of the authorities and being opposed by them. On top of all this comes the declaration of Minister Wu, who said the Boxers are not an organized society, but simply "a mob of fanatics," and he states that he never heard of them until the present trouble began. There is no reference whatever in any books to the Boxers or the Boxer movement; it is something new, and about all that we know definitely of it is that it is directed against all "foreign devils." In its way, it is a part of the turbulence which means the eventual disruption of the Chinese Empire.

SIR CLAUDE MACDONALD.

LI HUNG CHANG.

WU TING-FANG.

EDWIN H. CONGER.

An Educated Nation Without a Census

"In point of intellect, as in business and diplomacy, the Chinese are the equals of the ablest and most civilized nations of Christendom." This is the deliberate judgment of the latest, and in some respects the most judicial, of the encyclopædias.

And yet with all this intelligence China has never had a census. That is why the figures you read about the population of the empire vary so wonderfully. Millions are handled in Chinese guesses as if they were the veriest trifles. You will read in one authority that the population is 350,-000,000 and in another that it is over 400,000,000. Fifty million Chinamen more or less do not seem to count.

The very latest figures that seem at all dependable—if guesses can ever be dependable—show some extraordinary totals. China proper—that is, Central China—has 1,322,841 square miles and 383,000,000 population. Manchuria—including what Russia has grabbed—has 362,310 square miles and 18,000,000 population. Mongolia has 1,288,000 square miles and 2,000,000 population. Ili, comprising several countries, has 579,750 square miles and 1,180,000 population; and Thibet has 362,310 square miles and 6,000,-000 population. Add all these together and you will have what has been known as the Chinese Empire.

No nation in the world can produce such totals. No nation can adduce such a variety and wealth of natural products. China has a range of climate as great as that of the United States. In China proper every acre of land is cultivated—it is the most thoroughly cultivated country on the globe. It has all the cereals and all the fruits; it has both anthracite and bituminous coal, and it is rich in gold, silver, lead, tin, copper, petroleum and natural gas. Its great river—the Yang-tse-Kiang—is open to foreign trade for 1700 miles, 600 miles of which is navigable by the largest ocean-going ships and 500 miles more of which is navigable by steamers. Out of the eighteen provinces of Central China there is an annual

temples and idols and the great rebellion which did not end for fourteen years, or until "Chinese" Gordon won his great victory and Hung himself committed suicide by poison.

The Division of the Jellyfish

Land bigness and enormous population do not make a nation. Education does not make a nation. The necessary things are, reasonably honest government, public spirit and character. Theoretically, China is a perfect government of the monarchical kind—it is modeled on the home—but actually it is a tyranny debased, with corruption in all its ramifications and with intrigue in all its operations. Thus even education adds to the weakness, because instead of contributing to the higher impulses and interests of the people it makes the corruption more insidious and effective, and the intrigue deeper and more dangerous. China is a wonderful mass—the great jellyfish of nations it has been called—but it lacks the power of progress. Of all nations in the world it is the most helpless and the most hopeless.

Thus come the opportunities. This is a century of land grabbing, a century of extension and expansion, and the morality of the greatest government of Europe does not go much beyond the saving clause of a pretext on which to hang its plans and purposes. No one fancies for a moment that the internal outbreaks in China are the main concern of the great Powers. They have happened rather unexpectedly—very unfortunately for Great Britain, with all her best troops in South Africa; not very opportunely for Russia, with her trans-Siberian railroad uncompleted, and not any too well for Japan, who will have to depend upon the friendship of Great Britain. But the grab game has begun, and it is easy to see that Russia is leading. The Cossack is getting more first mortgages on the Celestial than any other grabber.

The Policy of the United States

Lord Rosebery has declared that the next big war will be fought for commercial supremacy, and only three months ago Marquis Ito, the greatest statesman in Japan, in announcing his opposition to any scheme of partitioning the Middle Kingdom of China, said: "If the United States is to have the commerce of the world, she must mix in foreign politics." There never was a more delicate situation for our diplomatists, and the policy so far ordered by the Administration, and executed by Minister Conger, seems to be the only safe course. The marines landed under Captain McCalla have been used simply for the protection of life and of American interests. Any coöperation in political schemes has been avoided. The marines were landed because there were American lives and property to be saved.

This nation is unique in that its interference in any foreign complication or situation has been for the good of all nations and of humanity in general. Great Britain opened China largely to get a market for the opium products of India. The United States opened Japan for the commerce and the profit and the progress of the whole world. The European Powers drew their "spheres of influence" on Chinese territory before beginning to plot for the downfall of the empire. The United States, by a splendid stroke of diplomacy and insistence, secured the "open door" in China for the weak nations as well as the strong, an act which such a wise statesman as Senator Davis, of Minnesota, places next to the treaty which Franklin negotiated securing the independence of the United States. The position of this country, therefore, is that of unselfishness unparalleled in history, with no axes to grind, with no land schemes to execute, and with only the broader interest of humanity and commerce to protect and advance. It all goes to show that Washington was right, and that Uncle Sam is never so strong as when he keeps out of entangling alliances with other nations, and stands alone for right and reason.

John Chinaman at Home

His Queer Beliefs

By Rev. Francis E. Clark, D.D.

His Ridiculous Army

THE army of China is the laughing-stock of the world, and no wonder. It is a synonym for cowardice and not for courage. It is a rabble picked up in the slums, ill-equipped, ill-fed, ill-clothed, ill-paid or paid not at all. Even the Chinese laugh at their own soldiers.

At a recent public meeting the speaker, an American, urged Christian courage and fortitude, saying that his hearers must endure hardship and be brave like good soldiers. When his Chinese interpreter came to translate this passage he interpolated the remark: "Of course he does not mean Chinese soldiers."

Why should they be brave? They have no high motive to urge them to heroism. Patriotism, as we understand it, does not exist. Pride of race there is, but no love of country or government. A race of Manchu robbers has been in power for two hundred and fifty years. Their authority is tottering on the brink of ruin. What soldier would risk his life unnecessarily for such a gang of bandits?

Moreover, these soldiers know that they are constantly starved in rations and cheated in arms and munitions of war by their superior officers. Tons and tons of gunpowder are filched every year from Chinese forts and magazines and sold to the firecracker makers, and doubtless a large proportion of the noisy little fuses with which American youngsters usher in the Fourth of July are made of stolen powder. At the time of the Japanese war hundreds of government rifles and even some cannon were in the pawn-shops, where they had been placed by patriotic officers who did not have time to get them out before the war was finished.

During the early "Boxer" troubles a squad of Chinese soldiers was detailed from a fort to guard the premises of some friends of mine at Paoting-fu, near Peking. Night after night the soldiers marched into my friend's compound and camped in one of his outhouses. At last it occurred to him to request the soldiers to fire a salute, so that all ill-disposed persons might know of their presence. To this they gravely replied that they would gladly do so had any powder been given them, but that before the next night they would get some powder and fire the salute at nine o'clock. Thereafter, for a week or more, promptly at the appointed hour, the welkin rang with a tremendous discharge of small arms. But one night it was omitted, and my friend, inquiring the reason, was told that the soldiers were out of wadding. It was afterward discovered that when the soldiers had powder and wadding they had no bullets.

The fact that flint-locks are still made and sold in China—as well as the huge, antiquated harquebuses that require two men to hold and fire, the long barrel resting on the shoulders of one man while the second touches off the fuse—speaks volumes for the inefficiency of the Chinese sharpshooter. But the most amusing

TRAINING FOR THE CAVALRY

SIDETRACKING THE SPIRITS

SPIRIT SIGN-POSTS

E K

SPIRIT-PROOF ROOF

PHOTOS TAKEN BY DOCTOR AND MRS. CLARK

MANDARIN'S TOMB

spectacle which the martial defenders of the Celestial Empire make of themselves is at their drill, especially when practicing for military degrees. There are military as well as literary degrees conferred by the Emperor, and these coveted honors are given largely for skill. But not for skill with a Mauser or Henri-Martini, not for accuracy of rifled cannon practice or daring horsemanship, but — save the mark! — for skill in archery, and that in the closing year of the nineteenth century! Evidently China has not yet heard that the bow and arrow are out of date. The favorite practice is shooting from horseback, and this idea seems to retain something of the romance of chivalry until we see the manœuvres for ourselves. Then the possibly sublime quickly subsides into the ridiculous. A trench is dug for the archers, and the old hacks which they mount amble along in this ditch while the bowmen, as they slowly pass the target, discharge their arrows at it. Even under these easy conditions the target is rarely hit.

In the Treasurer's Yamen at Foochow, as in other cities, are stored implements which the candidates for the military degree use in their practice — huge stone mallets which they learn to throw, great cleavers and spears and three-pronged tridents which they learn to wield. Most amusing of all is a hobby-horse of gaunt and knobby build which the aspirant for a degree mounts and practices upon before he is allowed to mount the real horse in the ditch. When I visited the Yamen one of these would-be soldiers, for a small silver consideration, obligingly mounted his wooden horse and struck a martial attitude with his bow, while a friend snapped a camera at him.

At the entrance to this Yamen is a long white wall on which are painted heroic scenes from Chinese history. These are reproductions of historic events that occurred a thousand years ago, and they represent the brave general on his horse twanging his bow at the fleeing enemy.

Fooling the Malevolent Spirits

No small part of a Chinaman's time is spent in fooling the spirits. Many of the gods in his Pantheon are malevolent deities who must be appeased or deceived. Apparently, too, they are very stupid spirits, who can be imposed upon by the most trifling impostures. Most of them seem to be knaves, and all, without exception, fools. The character of his belief has done not a little to add to the heavy burden under which the Chinese peasant is groaning.

For instance, in order to mislead the spirits there are few straight roads in China. How many millions of years of toil in the aggregate has this effort to turn aside malevolent spirits added to the poor burden-bearer of China! You cannot go a dozen rods without coming to a sharp corner. Even the roads through the rice fields zigzag back and forth in a most perplexing corkscrew fashion, while in the cities one is continually winding in and out and out and in as though the road had been laid out on the ram's-horn principle. Moreover, the road often goes out of its way to climb a hill, up which the broken-backed coolie with his heavy load must climb only to make his way toilsomely down again, when the road might have been kept on a flat and level plain.

Blind Man's Buff in the Highways

The reason for all these turnings and windings is simply that the spirits may be fooled and turned out of their path, and may not reach their destination. It is well known in China that spirits travel in a straight line and on level ground, so, if they come to an obstructing wall or a turn in the road, they simply go straight ahead and do not find the party they are after and whom they wish to plague in some uncanny way. Because of this superstition the lot of the laboring man in China, always hard, is almost doubled in severity, and the number of useless "foot pounds," if we can express it mathematically, which he raises every day in absurd deference to the spirits must be calculated by the billion.

When you enter the gate of a city there are usually two entrances in adjacent walls, but they are never opposite one another. In order to find the second you must turn a corner. This is in order that the spirits may lose themselves in getting in. Often these gates are built of massive stones and are highly ornamented and cost large sums of money, but nothing is too costly to deceive the spirits.

Playing at Handball with Evil Spirits

In front of a temple one frequently sees a great stone screen, which is built to deflect the spirits and turn them aside from the ancestral hall. The roofs of the temples and many of the houses turn up at the end instead of sloping down as roofs do in civilized countries. This is not for the picturesqueness of the effect, as might be supposed though this effect is undeniable, but in order that the spirits may depart into the upper air when they come to the curving roof tree, instead of falling into the courtyard below.

On a boat in some parts of China the cook will be very angry if you cross your chopsticks on top of your bowl of rice, for the word in his language for crossed chopsticks is the same as for overturning the boat. Neither must you ask him in the Ningpo language, "When do we arrive?" because to arrive is the same word as "shipwreck." A friend one day pointed out to me a rude picture of a turtle chalked on a wall with some Chinese characters near it, and told me that the owner of the wall, in order to preserve his premises from defacement, had written, "If you hurt this wall you are a turtle," which was the heaviest curse that could be pronounced upon the superstitious passer-by, who wished to be anything but a turtle in the next world. Hence his walls were preserved intact.

"You are a cow," says one woman to another in the height of her uncontrollable anger, and nothing worse can be said to her neighbor, for if she is to be a cow in the future state of existence she will have to drink all the dirty water she has made in her ablutions in this world.

Hoodwinking the Demons with Names

In the matter of their children, parents are continually trying to fool the spirits. They frequently call them by most opprobrious names in order that the spirits may not know how much they love them, as "little slave," "little dog," and "good-for-nothing brat." Of course if the spirits hear them called by these names they will suppose that they are not worth harming. As boys are esteemed much more highly than girls they are frequently given girls' names so that the spirits may think they are girls and deem them too worthless to kill.

The other day I saw upon the street a very boyish-looking little girl, of ten years old or so, with an earring in one ear, an anklet on one ankle and her hair combed in bangs in front. I asked the mother if it was a little girl, for I had my suspicions, and she responded, "Oh, no, he is a boy, but we make him look like a girl so that the spirits will not run off with him."

At the grave's mouth these superstitions naturally reach the climax of absurdity, for there it is important to deceive the spirits in every possible way. So piles and piles of paper money are burned at the proper season in order that the departed may have passage-money into spirit land, roast pigs and pheasants and all kinds of delicacies are offered to his manes in order that he may have enough to eat and drink, paper houses are provided for him to live in, and paper horses for him to ride. Then all are burned, for this is the approved way of sending the supplies to the other world. Great care is taken in the selection of a site for the grave, which is always decided by the geomancer, and if good luck comes to the family of the deceased others are likely to plant their graves near by that they may share in the good influences.

All these superstitions have their sad and pathetic side, for they show the depth of the spiritual blackness into which these people are plunged. Nowhere is the pathetic side more strongly brought out than when death comes to a household and the poor mother, with an aching heart, bends over the cradle of the little boy who is breathing his last, and cries out in anguish: "You are a little girl! You are a little girl! You are a pig! You are a slave! At best you are nothing but a little girl!" But the spirits do not heed, and the pride of her heart is taken away, and the joy of her eyes is quenched forever, for the spirit of death can no man fool even in China.

Editor's Note — This paper, by the Rev. Francis E. Clark, President of the Young People's Society of Christian Endeavor, is based upon information gathered on the spot, during the author's journey around the world, only a few days before the landing of Admiral Kempff's marines.

The Threat of the Yellow People

ISOLATION or subjugation — these are the alternatives in China. Compromise would be the supreme folly of years of weakness in dealing with Pekin. Now that the first mission of the allied armies has been accomplished, when full reparation has been made to the countries concerned, China should be left to grovel in the slime of centuries before her monstrous gods; or the breach in the Great Wall should be widened with bayonets and the Law of Civilization crammed down the throats of the Chinese.

But to reëstablish the old order, to keep on taking gold for priceless blood, to return our Ministers under the cowardly fiction that they are representatives of subject powers, to send forth our citizens anew to massacre and outrage, would be intolerable and not to be borne. It would mean more profitable trade with China — in battleships, in ordnance, in firearms, in high explosives. It would mean new opportunities for White Men who put money before country to build forts, to establish manufactories of munitions of war for the Yellow People. It would mean a few years of doubtful profit and uneasy peace — then new risings, fresh atrocities and greater massacres. Each time the Chinese rose would find them better drilled, better equipped, more determined. Where we had only the raw ferocity of a rabble to fear, we should have to fight organized armies in whom the brutal barbarism of the centuries before Christ would be reënforced and made terribly potent for evil by the most devilish inventions of modern ingenuity. Each time we should avenge our citizens more dearly and buy back our Ministers at a greater price in blood.

We are at the parting of the ways. The easy and the obvious thing to do is to demand our dollars and then let China alone. Nor does this policy lack for advocates. There are people of the tenements who ask nothing of the authorities but to be left to live on in their disease-breeding dirt, and there are those who would not disturb them. China is a plague spot among the nations, a threat against their peace and prosperity. The indemnity for the past must be paid, and a guarantee for the future be given. And a guarantee cannot be had by leaving China to herself. Not partition, but a government of and by the Chinese, under the direct supervision of the Powers, is one plan proposed, and a good plan. So may the sting of the dragon be drawn.

Is China's Case Hopeless?

IF THERE is any truth in the fancy that ears will burn while their owner is being talked about, the collective ears of China must have been ablaze during the past few weeks. Everything ever written derogatory to Chinese character and capacity has been dragged again into print, and the civilized world has been assured that China is determined to remain suspicious, semi-barbarous, tricky, isolated and unchanging.

Within the memory of men not yet old the world was talking in exactly the same way of Japan, a nation then less known and less progressive than the China of to-day. The first modern treaty with Japan was extorted about forty-five years ago, and literally at the cannon's mouth. At that time the feudal system prevailed, the great lords fought one another for amusement or spoils and frequently rose against the general government, which was as weak as that of China. The Emperor, like the nominal ruler of China, was an autocrat and "The Son of Heaven," at whom no ordinary mortal was allowed to look; like China's Emperor he was also a puppet in the hands of a real ruler and a court circle. The people were as ill-fed, ignorant and suspicious as the Chinese of to-day; neither their lives nor possessions were respected. They dressed in long gowns like the Chinese, wore their hair in a manner compared with which the Celestial's pigtail is a thing of beauty, regarded magic as an actual and transcendent power and believed all foreigners were "devils." The members of the first Japanese Embassy to the United States were in appearance as comical as any band of buffoons, and their manner was as conceited, stolid and suspicious as that of a lot of prairie Indians. For years after the treaty ports were opened there was intense hatred of the foreigner and his religion. Yet to-day Japan ranks with the civilized nations; the Emperor, who is his own master, dresses like an American gentleman, as do most of his subjects who can afford it; he has granted a constitution, of which his people are very proud and fond, the rights of rich and poor alike are protected by law, cruel punishments have been abolished, the foreigner's life is as safe as it would be in any civilized country, all religions are tolerated, some vices and bad customs supposed to be inherent are abating rapidly, all good customs of civilization are being accepted and most of the bad ones are being avoided. The changes, which were not effected without friction, began at the top, among the great nobles, and the other classes followed their leaders.

China is known to contain many would-be reformers, some of whom are men of natural force and high character. Their task is no greater than was that of the men who reconstructed Japan, for when they become predominant at court, as they almost were a year ago and would now be but for the reactionary measures of the Dowager Empress, reform by edict will be sudden, as it was in Japan.

With our knowledge of Japan's marvelous and rapid change for the better, the American mind can well afford to believe that China, too, will suddenly and at no distant date assume an honorable place among the great nations.

— JOHN HABBERTON.

Japan After the War

By Frederic Courtland Penfield

Victory of Arms the Prelude to a Greater Struggle for Trade Throughout the East

DRAWN BY JAMES PRESTON

UNTIL recently, Japan has never been taken seriously. Now it is the country upon which the gaze of the world is centred, the nation whose deeds and utterances are discussed almost to the exclusion of other topics. Japan is a little country manifestly playing for big things, and seems destined to attain them; but to speak of her as a "world power" is extravagantly untrue. After the capitulation of Port Arthur and the destruction of Rojestvensky's fleet, half the newspapers of America and England bristled with the phrases "world power," "first-class power," and the like, when to have called Japan a good fighter would have been precisely descriptive.

Within a decade Japan has conquered China with her millions, and defeated, in a manner without parallel in brilliant warfare, what was regarded a great power of northern Europe. But neither victory conferred title upon Japan as a great power. History affords no evidence that a nation has attained to lasting greatness through the agency of the sword; there is, on the contrary, the pathetic story of the empire of Napoleon, dazzling for a time, but collapsing eventually like a house of cards.

Japan is aware that excessive employment of superlatives imparts nothing helpful in placing her upon a basis of permanent security, and it is a matter of observation that the person who fights well does little else. Does Japan hope to become powerful, and take high place in the family of nations, for no other reason than the possession of military prowess? If the answer could be echoed from Tokyo and Yokohama it would be "No, a thousand times, no!"

It may truthfully be said of Japan that her humane conduct of the campaign, her treatment of prisoners, and the magnanimous abstention from rejoicing over victories, earned almost universal approval. These are among the small things that stamp a people. For months past, whenever peace was suggested by any statesman representing a neutral government, convinced that prolongation of hostilities could not affect the outcome, the Japanese always signified with promptness their willingness to sheathe the sword. These facts become illuminative to the impartial investigator seeking to determine whether Japan's ascendency is merited and will be advantageous to human progress.

The fact cannot be gainsaid that a great force is rising in that portion of Asia washed by the Pacific, a force that in a few years may become dominant in Oriental politics and commerce. But the defeat of the Czar's armies and fleets by the Japanese should be taken only as an earnest of what is to follow. Japan has much to achieve before she becomes a power, either "great" or "first-class." It requires no clairvoyance to see that five years from now she will be a factor for the good of the world—to record this opinion is but common justice.

To prosecute the war and finance the Japanese Government in other directions, approximately $588,000,000 has been consumed; and the fact that but a fraction of this was wasted and none diverted by processes of "graft," places the Japs upon a lofty pedestal as examples to the rest of mankind. Before the outbreak of hostilities the public debt was $282,000,000. It is now, consequently, $870,000,000. Can this be considered a serious burden? Coming in great measure as the price of their awakening, it may more readily be made effective by the Japanese people as a stimulant than as a deterrent, for Japan has acquired qualities that cannot be gauged in figures—ambition and aroused energy.

Japan's Well-Filled Cash-Box

THE pro rata public indebtedness amounts to only $18.51. That of the United States, fast diminishing, is $10.93 per person; but every subject of Great Britain dwelling in the United Kingdom bears a bonded indebtedness of $91.80, and every citizen of France $151.70. It is fair comment that if a nation has no debt it likewise has no commerce, and amounts to but little in world affairs; and that whether a debt be burdensome or otherwise depends upon the character of the people. To the sons of New Japan, with conflict ended and a career of industry entered upon, a pro rata obligation of $18.51 will be the merest bagatelle.

Japan's cash-box is well stocked by reason of the recent four and a half per cent. loan. In Tokyo it was admitted that this latest bond issue in America, England and Germany was unnecessary; but it was deemed wise to take advantage of market conditions to secure at a low rate a fund with which to pay off internal obligations, that there might be money in the country to develop industries immediately the war terminates. While the gross indebtedness of Japan may not be reduced for many years, its weight upon the people may readily be lightened by redemptions and conversions in the next four or five years. As the country's credit strengthens, the rate of interest on borrowings automatically decreases. There is no longer need for paying six per cent. for financial aid, and there will consequently be numerous funding operations in the future. It is a fact that Japan has debentures upon which capital was secured for early railway construction still paying ten per cent. interest. When these mature, new loans may be substituted at home upon a five per cent. basis, and possibly lower. In a word, Japan's financial position is extremely sound, and she will carry easily her existing debt.

Whatever the indemnity from Russia, its payment is certain to spread over a term of years. It will place Japanese bonds in a position of enviable soundness, no doubt. As a rule, war indemnities accomplish little for victorious nations beyond reëstablishing their credit, and are rarely completed in the same generation with the conflict. It would be unfortunate for the cause of peace if a conquering nation received its indemnity in spot cash, as successful pugilists are supposed to do on leaving the roped arena.

Japan's greatest asset unquestionably is the energy of her people, aroused now to an inordinate degree by success in two wars, and the fact that they are shrewd enough to perceive that there can be victories greater than those of arms. This energy is further accentuated as a national resource by the imitative power of the people, their remarkable industry, willingness to toil for a low wage, and ability to live on an inexpensive diet of rice and fish.

A Country Athirst for Western Knowledge

THE Mikado's subjects demand no luxury of food, dress or home surrounding; they have no dissipations that absorb an undue amount of time or money, and the percentage of adults who may be described as belonging to the idle class—through affluence, indolence or disability—is probably the smallest in the world. There are not ten great fortunes in the land. A Japanese home, sheltering a family, costs no more to own than the rent of a laborer's house in this country. These facts consolidate into a concrete quality of definite security value. It was the best security back of America's and England's loans to the Japanese Government, aggregating $360,000,000—not a "quick asset," like railways, docks and public buildings, but something of the highest conceivable importance, nevertheless.

The custom of speaking of our friends of the Island Empire as "the little Japanese" is a fault that should be promptly mended. Japan is small, it is true, but the people are numerous to the point of wonderment. Consequently, it can do no harm to memorize these facts: That Japan has an area actually 27,000 square miles greater than the British Isles, and 5,000,000 more inhabitants; in other words, the population of Japan is 47,000,000, while that of Great Britain and Ireland is but 42,000,000. That Japan's population exceeds that of France by nearly 9,000,000, of Italy by 15,000,000, and of Austro-Hungary by 500,000. That outside of Asia there are but three countries in all the world with greater populations than Japan—Russia, the United States and Germany.

It is the judgment of many who have studied the Japanese at close range that they are endowed with attributes of mind and body which make them equal, man for man, with the people of America and of Great Britain. Asiatic though they are, it will be unwise to permit the brain to become clogged with the idea that they are "Asiatics" in the popular acceptance of the word. The Japan of the present is the antithesis of "Asiatic," and the Japan of the near future promises to be a country to be best measured by Western standards.

The Japanese are athirst for knowledge, and impatient for the time to arrive when the world will estimate them at their intellectual value, and forget to speak of them as th little "yellow" men of the East. This is manifested to visitor many times a day. Their greatest craving is to kno English, not merely well enough to carry on trade advan tageously, but to read understandingly books that de with the moderate sciences, and other works generall benefiting. Yokohama and Tokyo possess a score establishments where practically every important volum of instruction, whether it be English or American, is repr duced in inexpensive form and widely sold. For man years English has been taught in Japan's schools, but thou sands of boys and men in cities and towns are each ye acquiring the language by study in odd hours.

Examine the dog-eared pamphlet in the hands of the la assisting in the shop where you are purchasing somethin and you are almost certain to find it an elementary Englis book. Merchants know English well, as a rule; but wi many of them the desire for knowledge is not satisfied wit the acquisition of English—they desire to know oth languages. In Yokohama I know a merchant of importan whose English is so good that one is drawn to inquire whe he learned it. The answer will be that he studied at od hours at home and when not serving customers. And th visitor may further be informed by this man that he is al studying German and French. A teacher of German go to his house at six o'clock each morning and for two hou drills him in the language. Then, in the evening, after long day spent at business, a French teacher instructs hi in the graceful language of France. And this merchant but a type of thousands of Japanese who are daily garneri knowledge.

It is a pleasing incident for the visitor from America read of a meeting in the Japanese capital of the local Ya Alumni Association—quite as pleasing as to see baseba played in every vacant field convenient to a large tow Returning schoolboys have carried the game home their companions, and in the voyage across the Pacific has lost none of its fine points. For thirty years and long the Japs have been learning English with the industry beavers. And ambition has been responsible for this, th dogged determination to be somebody, and the patriot wish to see Japan stand with the progressive nations the earth. The power to keep such a people down do not exist. Preparation is a subject never absent from th thoughts of the Japanese. It was preparation that ga them victory after victory over the creatures of the Cza Now they are preparing for a brilliant career in trade a commerce.

New Conditions and New Wants

TO SPEAK in strict honesty of Japan's natural resource one must admit that they are disappointingly fe Perhaps no country is less promising agriculturally, unle it be Norway or Greece. The arable soil of the Mikado empire is sorely limited, for it aggregates something le than sixteen per cent. of an area about equal to that of th State of California. Much of the country's surface is d nied to cultivation by mountains and volcanic tract The valleys and bottom lands spreading from the foothil to the coast are absorbed in rice culture, and provide th bulk of the staple of the people. If the rice crop might b sent to market it would produce $200,000,000 each yea But no food crop can be raised for export; and with th conformation here indicated, there can be little room f forests or grazing land for flocks and herds. To afford sustenance to the inhabitants of Japan it was necessary last year to purchase from other countries upward of $47,000,000 worth of food supplies, mainly rice and sugar. With thoughtful Japanese it is a saddening fact that the soil of their country is not able to feed the fast increasing population, for it is admitted that if the sea were not compelled to contribute generously to the nation's needs there would be hunger in the land.

The requirements of the Japanese are growing at a rate outstripping the ratio of increase of population, for the adoption of Western ideas has carried with it many added tastes. The native of twenty years ago might subsist on what his country gave him, but not so the subject of the Japan of the armored battleship and soldier whose genius halts the advance of a mighty European nation. This modern must have hundreds of articles that his forefathers never dreamed of. Incidentally, he wants yearly three hundred thousand tons of sugar, a half million bales of cotton, thousands of tons of wool, besides cargoes of flour and petroleum, and he produces none of them, or next to none. The rousing of a people from the sleep of centuries creates new situations which perplex great minds.

"If Japan were blessed with deposits of coal and iron," you remark to a native statesman, perceiving the extraordinary industry of the masses, "her development after the war might be rapid."

"We have both," insists the patriotic Japanese.

Acknowledging that England's strength has secure basis in her iron and coal, and aware that America's richness in these staggers comprehension, you go in quest of the facts as they exist. But you discover that only technically can Japan be included in the list of coal and iron producing nations. She has a fair supply of good bituminous coal, that is clean to handle, produces great heat, and is used by Japanese commercial and Government vessels; but the market for it elsewhere has to compete with Chinese and Indian coals. It is Nagasaki and Kobe opinion that the supply may last two hundred years. Were it mined on the scale of English or American coal it would probably be exhausted in a generation. To meet last year's abnormal demand, coal was raised to the value of $8,000,000, a sum exceeding slightly the value of all other minerals produced in the twelve months. With endless water power, and processes of converting this into electricity, there will be an abundance of inexpensive energy always in Japan.

The country can never be an important producer of iron. The greatest efforts have been made to develop the industry in the province of Rihuchuu, but unattended with success. At a cost in excess of its market value, a paltry 18,000 tons of iron was smelted last year; and the only important steel works in Japan, fostered by the Government, has failed through the necessity of bringing pig iron from China. A plausible rumor obtains in official Tokyo that the Government is not to abandon its effort to force success in iron and steel making; and in responsible quarters the assertion is made that a long lease has been secured on an important ore tract in China, the product of which will blend advantageously with Mexican or Californian hematite. And further, Japan is said already to have secured in Manchuria a seam of coal fifty feet in thickness, covered by a few feet of soil, that is contiguous to transportation, and that cannot be exhausted for centuries.

DRAWN BY JAMES PRESTON

The investigator whose verdict should possess no bias is obliged to say that the prospect of Japanese prosperity through mineral production at home is but little more encouraging than through agriculture. Experience has many times demonstrated that iron and steel are profitably produced only when deposits of coal and ore are fairly close neighbors. For two thousand years Japan has been a producer of copper in a moderate way, and the mining of that metal is carried on at present with some profit. Since the outbreak of hostilities, gold mining has been encouraged by the Government, to aid the specie-reserve fund. Including the yield of the island of Formosa, Japan has produced in gold about $7,000,000 in the past year.

In what manner, then, may the aroused Jap, poor in everything but ambition and enterprise, create for his beloved country a position of security in the fast-rushing, selfish world? He knows the hopelessness of agriculture, and is likewise aware that other natural resources of his land are unlikely to yield a competence. He must do something immediately the war ends, for it is now or never with the Jap, and he is aware of this. His craving to be admitted into permanent brotherhood with progressive nations, and the necessity to achieve a career of profitable usefulness for his beloved Nippon, make a force as uncontrollable as that of Niagara.

A New Era for a New Japan

THE day that peace is made certain between Russia and Japan will mark a new era in the Mikado's empire, for that day will begin seriously the work of upbuilding Japan. Manufacturing and trade conquest are to be united in a campaign enlisting the coöperation of every patriotic subject. The Japanese of the immediate future are to be manufacturers, carrying the articles of their fabrication to Asiatic markets in their own vessels; and this they will do as effectively as they fought. Five years hence the world will see in Japan a country wherein the whirr of machinery will remind one of New England, and the construction of ships suggest the Clyde or Mersey. Japan's program is an elaborate one, but it will succeed, for it is the creation of the Mikado's Government. The last borrowing of $150,000,000—not required for war purposes, obviously—was probably the commencement of operations in the campaign that is to convert Japan into a vast workshop.

There are two countries which the Japanese look upon with admiration and envy, the United States and England; and for thirty years they have been assiduously studying the commercial methods of both. Painfully aware of the narrowness of Nature's gifts in their own land, the Japs turn now to England as a nation to be patterned from. They know that England long ago forsook agriculture for manufacturing, and that the great industrial communities have been built up at the expense of the farms. The Japanese are aware that the energies of the country, years ago devoted to agriculture, are now given over to the iron and shipbuilding and textile industries; and that the English people find it more profitable to run a workshop for the universe and buy their food from abroad with the product of their manufacturing. Herein is the text of the New Japan. Any visitor to the Japanese capital may divine it; and, if mingling with men of finance and shipping, he would know it. The anticipation of events is admittedly a trait of the Japanese character; and a few months hence America and Europe may marvel at Japan's preparation for a commercial propaganda, as they did at her preparedness for war. The Japanese have an acute sense of fact, let it be borne in mind, and do nothing from impulse.

It is no more than fair to Japanese astuteness to assume that the program of Japan's intentions is familiar to every representative of the Mikado's Government in commercial Europe and America. The Japanese Minister at London, Viscount Hyashi, talked very close to something in his mind when saying to an interviewer that "Japan's greater proximity to China proper and to Manchuria will enable her to secure trade on exceptionally favorable terms; and the Japanese surely are not to be blamed if they happen to be geographically well placed for trading in their immediate neighborhood."

And at a public dinner in New York, Consul-General Uchida gave evidence of familiarity with the program when he said: "We are going to adopt American methods of making money; we like to use American machinery, and we find your cotton the best in the world. We expect a great industrial and commercial boom as soon as the war is over. We will then have to make up the expenses of the war in industries, and for that purpose we must import American machinery and raw materials."

The words of the diplomatist in London join perfectly with those of the consular official in America. They sum up Japan's policy in a line. She is to commercialize China and Manchuria with an endless variety of goods manufactured from American raw materials by American machinery. No program could be simpler. One of Japan's greatest statesmen, a member of several ministries, hesitates not to say that it offers the shortest possible cut to prosperity. "Remember," he insists, "that we are justified in emulating the United States, for is not Japan her god-child?"

In a very few years Japan may be spinning a third of the cotton worn by the millions of Asia—this is the ambition, at least, of powerful Japanese capitalists. And the idea is by no means chimerical, when it is known that Japan ceased three or four years since to purchase cotton save in a raw state. America had formerly a good customer in Japan for cotton fabrics. Now she buys the cotton from us by the bale, spins and weaves for her own use, and sends to China and Korea cloth and cotton yarns to an enormous extent. The value of the cotton yarn spun last year in Japan was $47,000,000, and next year it may be nearly twice as much.

There is so much logic in selecting cotton-spinning for a great Japanese industry that one is led to speculate as to the permanence of the business in England. Japanese labor is as good as British, and cheaper, and Japan has the markets of Asia almost at her door. Easily can she secure the trade of China, and in time she may invade India itself with her "Manchester goods." If so, it will be unfortunate for Manchester, for the Japs will enjoy certain advantages over British spinners. The escaping of Suez Canal charges might be sufficient to give Japan a considerable control of the Indian market. Japan desires an industry that may become national in its ramifications. Natural and economic conditions are making this the cotton industry.

A fruit of Japan's victory is the silencing of Russian disapproval of her aspirations in Korea, and she is left in a position of influence amounting to dictatorship over this peninsula. As the military campaign progressed, yielding with each event a measure of success to Japan, the Government of the Mikado kept pace by tightening with every victory its hold on the political affairs of the hermit country.

So dominant is Japan's sway at Seoul that Korea might be the vassal of Japan. Japanese diplomatists guide the Korean policy and Japanese officers direct military affairs. Korea's representatives abroad, many of them, have been called home, for Japan is willing to look after the foreign interests of her neighbor gratuitously.

Japan can derive immeasurable benefit from her ward, for Korea offers a solution to the troublous problem of ever-increasing population and lack of foodstuffs. The hermit kingdom, amazingly rich in agriculture, richer still in mineral wealth, and but sparsely settled, presents a tempting opportunity, for the possession of the country seems indispensable to Japan's play for greatness.

And when the dispersing smoke of war reveals a bruised and neglected Manchuria, it will be discovered that Japan possesses sufficient influence at Peking to secure privileges for exploiting a vast section of southern Manchuria—and Manchuria is as prodigal in natural resources as Korea. Count Okuma, thrice premier of Japan, has an alluring scheme for "colonial development" in Manchuria and Korea, an item of which is to make Manchuria compete with Germany as a beet-sugar producer by means of Japanese energy.

Five years hence Japan will industrially be well-to-do; ten years hence, industrially affluent as well as politically powerful. And ten years is not long for a busy nation to wait, when the reward earned is the undisputed position of a World Power—to a country immersed in business, ten years is like a day in a man's life.

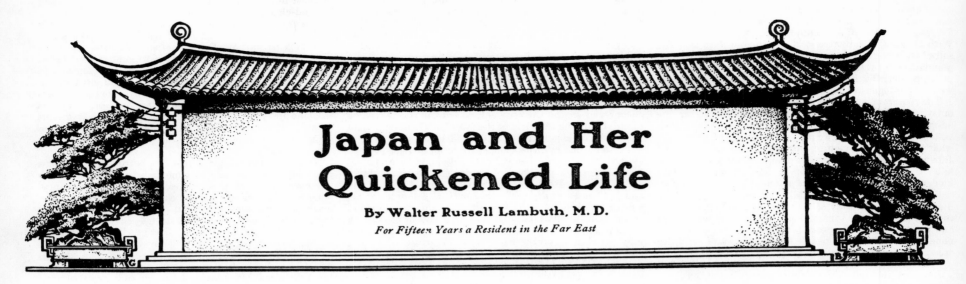

Japan and Her Quickened Life

By Walter Russell Lambuth, M. D.

For Fifteen Years a Resident in the Far East

IT WAS Sir John Lubbock who gave utterance to the words, "Great battles are really won before they are actually fought." In the Franco-Prussian War of 1870 the victory of Germany, so swift and overwhelming, was achieved by forces that were wrought out in the schoolhouse and in the university. It was the character and qualification of the German soldier in the ranks as much as the military strategy of Von Moltke that won enduring fame for the German arms.

In her terrific struggle with her huge antagonist in Manchuria it has not been otherwise with Japan. The little Island Empire, just emerged from a feudal system which required absolute obedience, has been for a generation under further discipline and training, from the kindergarten up to the great University of Tokyo. The best war maps in the world are those which have been made by her own military engineers since the first capture of Port Arthur ten years ago. Every foot of the Korean peninsula and of Manchuria has been triangulated and the height of every mountain range accurately measured. Nothing has been left to chance or to the fortunes of war. It is not a matter of astonishment, then, that Japanese artillerymen, whether upon the south bank of the Yalu at Wiju, or upon the hilltops of Kinchow, have trained their guns with such scientific precision. If there be any doubt about the process which has yielded such results let the would-be skeptic make a careful examination of the Japanese educational exhibit at the St. Louis Exposition. When a nation just out of its swaddling clothes can show such figures one must acknowledge that tremendous forces are at work in the social and educational life of a nation. In 1873 only fifteen per cent. of the females in Japan

could read and write; in 1893 there were eighty-seven per cent. In 1873 only forty per cent. of the males could read and write, and in 1903 the number had grown to ninety-six per cent. From the educational and scientific standpoint, these keen-eyed, clear-headed little islanders seem to be fully abreast of the twentieth century, into the arena of which they have leaped with a single bound.

Japan has truly awakened to the consciousness of her power, and, with the restless activity which prevails among her young men, there is in some quarters no little uneasiness over the so-called "yellow peril." We are told that at the recent exposition in Osaka the emphasis was placed upon "guns and brains"; that the Engineering School of the Imperial University turned out 500 graduates last year, and many of these are being employed by the Chinese authorities, who have dismissed their European teachers and sought the leadership and counsel of those who are near akin to them by tradition and by blood. It is pointed out that drillmasters have been invited to China by the provincial governors to discipline their soldiers, and that in the Japanese army and navy, out of which these drillmasters have come, not one American or European is to be found.

The writer has had no fear of the "yellow peril." The leaders of the Empire of the Rising Sun — such men as Ito, Okuma, Inouye and others, with Mutsu-hito, the benevolent man, at their head — are far more peacefully inclined than Western nations have given them credit for. Their supreme desire has been to enter upon an industrial era that will enable Japan to manufacture and supply the goods which may enter the open door both in Korea and China. To this policy she is as much committed as the United States, and is

in full sympathy with the statesmanship of Secretary Hay. Her present fight is for her life. Mr. Takahira, the Japanese Minister to Washington, has, in a recent magazine article, made this perfectly clear. The war into which the nation has been plunged is not one of aggression. Japan, though at present sweeping the sea and forcing the fighting on land, is acting on the defensive. She stands for the independence of Korea and the integrity of China. Ambitious to align herself with Western nations, she will no more take sides with the Mongolian in the future than she did during the Boxer movement, when her troops marched with the allied forces upon Peking.

The influence of Christianity in the Japanese Empire is far greater than a casual observer would suppose. One writer has recently observed that Christianity is giving Japan her new ideals. Marquis Ito at one time asserted that a nation did not need a religion, and deliberately advised the elimination of all religious and moral instruction in the education of the youth of his country. He has recently shifted his position and declared that his people, who adopted the civilization of the West, must now seek for its foundation. Nor does the Marquis stand alone in his revised opinion. Baron Maejima, an ex-Cabinet officer of Japan, says of Christianity: "No matter how large an army or navy we may have, unless we have righteousness at the foundation of our national existence we shall fall short of success.

"I do not hesitate to say that we must rely upon religion for our highest welfare. And when I look about me and see on what religion we may best rely, I am convinced that the religion of Christ is the one most full of strength and of promise for the nation."

Are We Getting Japanitis?

THE time is coming for some one to tell us the whole truth about the Japanese. Aristides lost caste because people always would call him the Just, and if the mind of the nation is to be kept firmly fixed upon the example of the latest in the family of great nations we must make sure that excessive admiration does not bring in the malady of Japanitis. A recent traveler with an eye for the picturesque and the jocose tells of an innkeeper who gave him a long "song-and-dance" (or the Oriental equivalent therefor) about the purity of a bottle of wine he was serving. The label of the bottle read: "Sauternes, Bordeaux & Co." Our own labels are no more veracious, perhaps; but we do the trick with greater sleight of hand.

The anecdote, we are inclined to think, is characteristic. According to an American tea-merchant who has done a large business in the Orient for over a quarter of a century, the Chinese trader can be trusted to the last scruple, but the heathen Japanese is past master at all the ways that are dark and the tricks that are vain. The Chinaman, he says, moreover, has an imagination for large enterprises, while the Jap is timid and procrastinating.

In the war, it is true, there have been no false labels and petty huckstering. But one swallow is no excuse for duck trousers. In the whole history of the world there has been no period of national advance as rapid, intense and thorough as that through which Japan has passed in the last quarter of a century. It is more than possible that what we have lately seen is only the crest of the wave. The

place of the nation in history will depend upon its ability to transmute the present enthusiasm into steady-going and permanent character.

A Race of "Stand-Patters"

THAT distinguished Japanese man of public affairs, the Baron Kantaro Kaneko, giving his views on matters American and Japanese, adventured into prophecy — which, as George Eliot so sagely observed, is the most gratuitous of all the forms of errors. "The United States," said he, "will always be a democratic republic; the only possible alternative is an oligarchy. Japan will never be a republic."

Never, some one has said, is a long time. No longer, however, than always. Alas, if there are any two matters about which it is neither worth while nor wise for a short-lived mortal to concern himself, they are what is going to happen in the never and what is going to happen in the always!

Of one thing we may be certain — that the state of affairs which is will not be the state of affairs even so short a distance away as to-morrow. We are a race of "stand-patters." Experience seems unable to cure us of the habit of thinking that what is will continue to be. The sensible man is he who has no theories, no especial concern even, as to the future, but concentrates himself upon doing his level best with the present moment which will be gone forever, and forever lost, unless it is instantly attended to.

SMASHED!

Will the Philippines Pay?

By Augustus O. Bacon, United States Senator from Georgia

THOSE who approve the acquisition of the Philippine Islands by the United States, as well as those who favor their permanent retention, are not agreed in the motives and reasons assigned therefor. Some there are who base their advocacy upon the very high ground that, in wresting these islands from the dominion of Spain, we assumed a responsibility, permanent in duration, for the maintenance of orderly government in the same, and with it an obligation, mandatory and not to be avoided, to lift these ten millions of Asiatics through educational processes, moral, religious, industrial and political, to a plane of civilization which shall approximate at least that which we have ourselves attained. Those of this mind recognize that this responsibility and this obligation must be met and discharged without flinching — even though they involve, for several generations, if not for an indefinite period, an annual expenditure of seventy-five or a hundred millions of dollars by the United States. Those of this heroically philanthropic view are not appalled either by such consideration, or by that of the no less certain consequence of the loss of the lives of many officers and soldiers of the American Army, to say nothing of the sacrifices of the vast host who will return year after year broken in health, thereafter necessarily dependent upon the public for support.

The large majority, however, base their advocacy upon the less philanthropic and more practical proposition that the possession of these islands will pay in dollars and cents. The suggestion is not without reasonable foundation, that even those who compose the minority first mentioned are deceiving themselves in their conception of their unselfish and philanthropic impulses, and that, though perhaps not fully recognized by themselves, they share with others the anticipations of golden gains, the hope of which is so candidly expressed by those of the majority.

A Glance at the Debit Side of the Ledger

It is a low plane upon which to base the judgment of the American people in regard to that which is really the weightiest and most overshadowing question of the day — whether the United States shall be permanently committed to the policy and the task of possessing and dominating trans-Pacific colonies of many millions of Asiatics in a vast and difficult territory. And yet it is difficult for one who weighs the utterances of men in every-day intercourse, as well as much of the outgivings of the press, to rid himself of the conviction that the most potent factor in determining this most pregnant question is the answer which shall be rendered to the inquiry, "Will it pay?" If the final conclusion in the public mind is that the possession of these islands will pay, and that their retention under our domination will result in profitable money return, there is reason to apprehend that the political ideals of the past hundred years will make but slow progress in the effort to secure the transfer of these islands to the dominion of their own people. These political ideals will continue to be revered in theory, but many eyes will be blind to the fact that the preservation or practical overthrow of these ideals is involved in the question.

It is a remark very frequently heard, "We have got the islands and there is no way in which we can honorably get rid of them." That remark is generally made by the inconsiderate or uninformed, or by those who for other reasons are unwilling to give them up. Whenever in the lapse of time it is shown conclusively that the continued possession of these islands will not pay from a pecuniary or business standpoint,

but that, on the contrary, for an indefinite period — a period the limit of which no man can fix with any reasonable probability — their retention will, under the most favorable conditions, entail annually a net loss of many tens of millions of dollars, thus adding every year a vast sum to the more than $300,000,000 already lost by the United States on this account, there will speedily be found a way through which the connection will be sundered without dishonor to the American people. This will have a most speedy, practical demonstration if such conclusion be reached in a time of general business depression and of stringency or panic in the money market — a period the recurrence of which in the not remote future our repeated experience in the past leaves us little room to doubt.

What the Philippines Have Already Cost

Indeed a less weighty influence would accomplish such a result, for it will be recalled that, before the decision of the "Insular Cases," the statement was freely made in dominant circles that, if the Supreme Court should hold that no tariff could be imposed upon the products of the Philippine Islands when brought to the United States, we would get rid of the Archipelago. It was in the confidence that such action would promptly follow such a decision, as well as in the maintenance of what they believed to be the correct constitutional construction, that many were most anxious that the Supreme Court should so decide.

If the same care is exercised as that which is observed by men in the determination and management of their private business, the people of the United States should be able satisfactorily to answer the inquiry, "Will the Philippines pay?"

It is necessary to consider two sides of an account in order to determine where the balance shall be placed. There may be a large income, but, if the expenditure exceeds it, the balance must be on the debit side.

By many it is confidently estimated that we have already expended more that $400,000,000 on account of the Philippine Islands. There can be no doubt that the expenditure has exceeded $300,000,000. What has been the full expenditure on this account it is difficult to determine with accuracy, but it is not difficult to determine a minimum beyond which it has certainly gone. If all the expenditures, both directly and indirectly, due to our connection with the Philippines — including in this way all the expenditures which would not have been made if we had not this connection — could be accurately ascertained, the amount would far exceed that which appears as directly chargeable to that account.

For instance, it would appear at first glance that only the expenditures on account of the army actually in the Philippines should be charged against that account. But the fact is that the same soldiers cannot be kept all the time in that climate, and, in consequence, a large reserve must be kept at home with which to replace the troops which, at the end of certain periods, must be brought home for recuperation. In consequence, even if that reserve does not exceed the number of troops which would otherwise be required in the United States, the annual transportation of many thousands of troops to and from the Philippines involves an immense expenditure not only while on the Pacific, but also while on the land between the Pacific Coast and the various posts throughout the United States. Again, military service in the Philippines involves a large waste of men through death and broken health, causing vacant places which must be filled by new recruits. One man goes out and another is recruited and

takes his place. The two count as one in estimating the number in the army, but the cost of recruiting, equipment and transportation to the Philippines has been that of two men instead of one.

Another illustration is found in the matter of expenditures on account of the transports other than their running expenses. These transports would be practically unknown to our service but for the Philippines. A huge sum has been expended in the purchase of ships and in refitting them for the service. When they are sold scarce fifty per cent. of this expenditure is received for them and the difference is a dead loss incurred on account of the Philippines. If the suggestion of the War Department for the sale of the transports should be adopted, and the transportation of the troops and supplies should hereafter be undertaken by the commercial lines, there will be a speedy liquidation of this loss, running up into the figures of many millions. And thus there could be specified dozens of similar classes of expenditure indirectly made, and of losses incurred, on account of the Philippines, which, if added to the direct expenditures, would enlarge the amount of the latter by many millions.

Looking Ahead for Ten Years

Thus considered, $300,000,000 is not only a conservative estimate but doubtless an underestimate in large degree of the expenditures already made by the United States on account of the Philippines. This may safely be taken as a minimum estimate in stating the account. If there were no future expenditures to be taken into the account, and expenditures already made were finally to end at this figure, there would be no reasonable ground to hope for a return of the amount from the Philippines in a generation to come. But by no means is this to be the end of the expenditure. There is well-founded reason for the belief that in ten years, if conditions continue as at present, and as those having the best opportunity to be accurately informed believe they will, this expenditure will be at least trebled. With $1,000,000,000, then, charged to the debit side of the Philippines' account, if the statements hereinafter made as to the probable business of the Archipelago are well founded, a century will not see it or any respectable proportion of it returned to the United States by any receipts of revenue of any kind from the Archipelago, or indirectly to the general public through profit derived from trade or business of any kind with the islands. That it is not practicable to estimate with accuracy the future annual expenditure of money by the United States Government which the retention of the Philippines will make necessary must, of course, be recognized. Nevertheless the minimum annual expenditure can be estimated at a figure so low as to be reliable for the purpose of the statement of this account of debit and credit.

The latest report from General Wheaton, a most able and conservative officer, is that 50,000 troops will be required in the Philippines for the next five years, and in this opinion, so far as it relates to the number of men, so many officers who have seen service in the islands agree with him as to leave little room for reasonable suggestion that it is too high; and the general expression among them is that this large army will be required, not only for five years, but for a generation. Even if this estimate is discounted and the number put at 40,000, below which practically all the officers are agreed it cannot safely be reduced, the cost directly and indirectly of that army for the Philippines will be about $60,000,000 a year. A soldier in time of war or in foreign service costs the Government about fifty per cent. more than a soldier at home in time of peace. The last analysis of all the organization, equipment and paraphernalia of the War Department is the fighting man. All the expenditures of the Department, from the salary of the Secretary of War down to the least important, at last relate to this fighting man as a conclusion. In this view the estimate is that each soldier at home in time of peace costs annually about a thousand dollars; and that in time of war and in foreign service this cost is increased to about fifteen hundred dollars. If to this there be added the many attendant expenditures above suggested and a reasonable estimate of the increased naval armament and expenditure made necessary in the Philippine service, the annual expenditures can be shown to be reasonably between $75,000,000 and $100,000,000. But, leaving out of the calculation all of the items which would thus swell it, there can be no reasonable doubt that with 40,000 soldiers in the islands the expense of the army and navy required by the Philippine service will at the lowest possible minimum be annually $60,000,000. That it will largely exceed this there is little reason to doubt, but limiting it to $60,000,000 a year, the aggregate in five years will be $300,000,000. This, added to the $300,000,000 already spent, makes a total of $600,000,000.

The army requiring this vast annual expenditure will not be needed to crush out organized armed resistance to the American authority, for that has already been nearly accomplished; but in the generally hostile temper of the Filipinos it will be needed to guard every nook and corner of the Archipelago and thus to repress the revolt which would threaten in the absence of military force. It is no reply to say that we now have a large army—one greater than is required for service in the United States—that it must be stationed somewhere and may as well be in the Philippines as elsewhere. A partial rejoinder is found in the statement already made that the cost of the army in the Philippines is much greater than would be the cost of the same army if stationed in the United States. But the complete answer is in the fact that that army would not be needed were it not for the requirement of the service in the Philippines. It will not be forgotten that, in the Fifty-sixth Congress, the argument in favor of the army bill which was most strongly pressed was that the large increase in the army was required for service in the Philippines. It was indeed practically the only argument of those who advocated the bill, as will readily be seen by reference to the published debates. That the increase was not required for domestic service is abundantly shown by the fact that the country is now getting along satisfactorily without the forty or fifty thousand soldiers now seven thousand miles away on the other side of the Pacific Ocean, a month's sail from our shores. So that it would seem to be a legitimate conclusion that the cost of the army in the Philippines is properly chargeable to the debit side of the Philippine account.

No place is given in this account to the loss of life among our trained military officers and the young men who compose the files of our army, but, limiting the consideration solely to the cold question of money, those who believe it to be from this standpoint a bad venture feel that they can with confidence challenge those who think otherwise to furnish the figures which will show how this money thus already expended, and that inevitably to be expended, can ever be repaid to the United States either in money or its equivalent.

But suppose the calculation be based upon the anticipations of the optimists that within a few years, or even immediately, the army can be reduced to twenty thousand men, there would, in five years, adding to the yearly expenditure the amount already spent, be an aggregate of $450,000,000 or $500,000,000, an amount for the repayment of which it is thought that the challenge may be safely made for the production of figures showing how it can be reasonably done.

A most serious item of expense directly chargeable to the Philippines is the certain and enormous increase in pensions to be paid. We have already sent 120,000 soldiers to the islands. Every year will add to their number and, in a few years, with each annual addition, the names of several hundred thousand men will be upon the rolls of those who have seen service there. The large majority of them will sooner or later be on the pension rolls, and properly so. Among them few will escape ultimate disease directly caused by military service in that tropical climate. If the necessity for the expense of the presence of the army there should ever cease, the cost of its maintenance will only be transferred to the payment of the increased pension rolls. That cost ever continuing for the next fifty years will in the aggregate amount to hundreds of millions of dollars. What may be expected in the way of pension claims by soldiers who serve in a tropical climate is shown in the last report of the Commissioner of Pensions. On page 47 he gives as an illustration the history of what he terms a "crack" regiment of 937 men which served in the Cuban War. He says that they were "a fine body of men," that there were no battlefield casualties, but that, when mustered out of the service, only five per cent. were in as good physical condition as at the time of enlistment, and that seventy per cent. were diseased. Of the number, 477 have filed claims for pensions, and they are doubtless entitled to receive them.

There are several ways in which expenditure on account of the Philippine Islands may be repaid if enough is secured thereby. Among them are:

1. By the acquisition of military and naval bases such as sites for garrisons, naval stations, coaling stations, etc.
2. By money directly paid to the Government.
3. Through the profits to the general public in increased trade and in the development of the productive resources of the country.

Confining the inquiry for the present to the compensation directly to the Government, the first above mentioned may here be passed without other mention than that the United States, by their selection, can in the Philippines take such harbors and sites for those purposes as they may deem proper and no one can or will say them nay; but no one will contend that the value of such sites will balance the account.

As to the subject of the compensation of a government for war expenditure, the fact is recalled that during the past year Mr. Chamberlain submitted to the House of Commons a statement of the plan for the reimbursement of the British Government for the expenditures in the Boer War by issuing bonds for the full amount which were to be entirely paid by exactions levied upon property situated within the territory formerly comprising the two South African Republics. The Government of the United States cannot in this case reimburse itself by that method. A war indemnity cannot properly be exacted from the Philippines as in the case of a defeated foreign country, and, for that and other reasons, the plan will not be at all considered by the United States. If the contrary were true, such indemnity could not be collected because the possible resources of the islands would not only be insufficient for the repayment of the hundreds of millions of dollars already expended, but by the most grinding exactions there could not annually be wrung from the Filipinos an amount sufficient to repay one-third of the sum which the United States must continue to spend on account of our possession and domination of the Philippines.

———

Editor's Note—This paper will be concluded next week.

The Bat Mightier Than the Sword

SOME of us have felt a little doubt on the question how far "benevolent assimilation" in the Philippines assimilates, but the latest news from the islands ought to reassure us. The work of education begun by the American school-teacher is being completed by the American game of baseball. A six-club league has been organized at Manila, representing different branches of the public service, and the whole population turns out at the semi-weekly games. Baseball is as wild a fad in Manila now as Ibsen in Boston or the cake-walk in Paris. Even the English have been captured by it, which seems to show that as a colonizing people our branch of the race is even stronger than the other. You can usually trace the limits of English colonization by the cricket-fields, and hereafter you will be able to bound greater America by its baseball grounds.

In Manila the Filipinos have taken to the game so enthusiastically that they have organized clubs of their own, which play on the league grounds before and after the regular matches. The crowds on the bleachers have acquired all the baseball technicalities and do their "rooting" in English.

Think of the power of that lever for the Americanization of the islands! We might perhaps remain unmoved by shouts of "*Desliza! Kelly, desliza!*" or "*Matad el arbitrador!*" but how can we fail to feel at home when we hear the same sentiments expressed in the familiar words, hallowed by sweet associations, "Slide! Kelly, Slide!" and "Kill the umpire!"?

Mr. Chamberlain has been inviting Boers and Britons to shake hands over the bloody chasm in South Africa, and has not apparently met with the most flattering success. A good deal of blood has flowed in the Philippines, but baseball may prove a better peacemaker than Mr. Chamberlain. Certainly a Filipino who can deliver a good drop curve is not a member of an inferior race, but a man to be respected by his conquerors, and the conqueror who can bat a home run with two out and three men on bases is not a loathsome oppressor but a being to be loved by any Tagal patriot who has money up on his team.

When the Filipinos were devoted to cock-fighting, and General Otis was trying to suppress that sport on the ground that it was inconsistent with the moral standards of Brookline, Massachusetts, the situation was dangerous. If the brown men had stuck to cock-fighting and the white men to poker there would have remained a gap between the races that all the diplomacy of Governor Taft might not have been able to bridge. But baseball may make diplomacy unnecessary. It is gratifying to have the Filipinos taught to sing The Star-Spangled Banner in school, but when of their own accord they pick up Casey at the Bat in English they may be considered thoroughly assimilated.

THE FUTURE OF CUBA

BY CARL SCHURZ.

NOTHING could be more natural than the sympathy of Americans with other Americans who struggle against oppression, and with those poor victims of the struggle who, in consequence of it, are reduced to starvation and misery. That the bloody and destructive conflict in Cuba be brought to a speedy conclusion, and be followed by a reign of liberty, law, and order, is therefore the sincere wish of all the good people of this country. That wish springs from a generous sentiment, and it is strengthened by a just appreciation of the annoyances, commercial and other, which are caused by the frequent recurrence of distracting disorders at our very doors. The thought that it may be the business of this republic to put an end to the trouble by friendly counsel and mediation, or, if that be of no avail, by forcible interference, finds, under such circumstances, much favor, even among persons who do not think lightly of a war with its incalculable sacrifices in blood and treasure which interference by force would bring on. But it is by no means inconsistent with so generous a disposition calmly to examine, aside from other considerations of right or of interest, the question whether the attainment of the immediate object of such interference, the abolishment of Spanish rule in Cuba, would really have the desired effect of securing to the people of that island the blessings of peace, liberty, and a fair measure of good government. In this respect we are not without valuable experience.

In the early part of this century the efforts of the Spanish colonies on the American continent to achieve their independence excited much sympathy in the United States. HENRY CLAY championed their cause with characteristic fervor. Those efforts appeared to him like a repetition of our own Revolutionary war. He attributed to the struggling South Americans all the political capacities of his own people. He thought that as to their "fitness for freedom" the people of South America were "in some particulars even in advance of us." He fiercely attacked the MONROE administration for not aiding them effectively. He urged the repeal of our neutrality laws for their benefit, and insisted that their independence be formally recognized while the struggle was yet undecided. He predicted for them a glorious future. His glowing speeches created a great stir in the country, but the administration remained firm in its conservative attitude.

In March, 1821, HENRY CLAY had an interview on the subject with the Secretary of State, JOHN QUINCY ADAMS, who thus recorded his part of the conversation in his diary: "I regretted the difference between his [CLAY'S] views and those of the administration upon South American affairs. That the final issue of their present struggle would be their entire independence of Spain I had never doubted. That it was our true policy and duty to take no part in the contest was equally clear. The principle of neutrality in *all* foreign wars was, in my opinion, fundamental to the continuance of our liberties and our Union. So far as they were contend-

ing for independence I wished well to their cause; but I had seen, and yet see, no prospect that they would establish free or liberal institutions of government.... Arbitrary power, military and ecclesiastical, was stamped upon their education, upon their habits, and upon all their institutions. Civil dissension was infused into all their seminal principles. War and mutual destruction were in every member of their organization, moral, political, and physical.... Of these opinions, both his [CLAY'S] and mine, time must be the test."

Time has been the test, and it is now generally recognized that JOHN QUINCY ADAMS'S predictions have proved far more correct than those of HENRY CLAY. In fact, seven years after the interview, CLAY himself, in answering a complimentary letter from BOLIVAR, the famous South American leader, could not refrain from giving words to his disappointment, saying that the people of the United States were still anxiously looking for the realization of their hope that with the independence of the South American republics free institutions would be established, "insuring all the blessings of liberty." He might say the same thing now.

The question whether the population of Cuba, consisting of Spaniards, white Creoles, and one-third of negroes and mulattoes, is in any essential respect superior to that of the American republics south of us, and whether better things may be expected of it, is certainly one of far-reaching importance. That question is by no means answered by the statement upon which an esteemed contemporary lays great stress—that the insurgents in Cuba have exhibited splendid fighting qualities, and that they may therefore be trusted with equal capacities for self-government. The fighting in the Spanish South American colonies was in its time quite as respectable as the fighting now is in Cuba; and considering that the national origin of the two insurgent forces as to the white source is the same—there being an Indian admixture in South America and a strong negro element in Cuba—and considering further that the two populations have grown up under similar tropical conditions of climate and under similar traditional influences, religious, social, and political, it is not unreasonable to apprehend that their conduct after the achievement of independence will be similar also. In other words, it is very probable, if not certain, that in Cuba, as in South America, when the war against the Spaniards ends, wars of factions will begin. And inasmuch as in Cuba a large part of the revolutionary forces consists of negroes and mulattoes, high places of command being held by men of color, who, having done their share of fighting, will claim their share in "running" the government, those wars of factions are likely to become embittered by race antagonisms of peculiar acrimony.

Those of us who by warlike intervention—that is, by shedding the blood of our own people and by sacrificing the treasure of our own country for the purpose of "liberating" Cuba—expect to stop bloodshed and destructive disorder, and to establish

civil liberty, peace, and prosperity there, may thus meet with a disappointment as keen as that of HENRY CLAY was. To accomplish their humanitarian end entirely, more intervention by force will probably be required against the factious disturbers. The same men whom our first intervention had liberated would then hate and fight their friends and liberators of yesterday as their enemies and oppressors of to-day. Whoever regards this as an overdrawn picture need only read the history of the American republics south of us, and imagine that the United States had helped them against the Spaniard by warlike intervention, and then attempted to establish and maintain peace and orderly government within their borders. Such a study will convince every candid mind of the complexities of the task. And nobody can foretell how far, after we had once embarked in such a task, our sense of responsibility—not to speak of the growth of a reckless spirit of adventure—would drive us on.

Would not then the annexation of Cuba to the United States appear as the only remaining shift? Probably it would. This would mean the incorporation in our political system of a country, with a population of over 1,500,000 souls, which is essentially uncongenial, if not positively hostile, to our political and social principles, ways of thinking, and habits; a country the climatic conditions of which are such that its principal laboring force—that is, the bulk of its citizenship—can never consist of people of Anglo-Saxon, or, more broadly speaking, of Germanic, blood; a country that is sure to breed interminable race antagonisms—an evil of which we already have more than enough; a country in every way unfitted for the building up of a well-ordered democracy as we understand it. The idea of embodying in our political system such a country with such a population, of making ourselves responsible for "maintaining a republican form of government" and peace and order there, and of permitting such a State—for a State it would become—to take an important part in governing our whole republic, is so appalling that every thinking American may well hesitate before venturing upon any step likely to lead us on to it.

It may be said that all this is mere conjecture. If so, it is conjecture based upon historical experience which no serious man will make light of—the experience that no American republic south of us has ever enjoyed many years of internal peace and prosperity, except under such a government as that of POFIRIO DIAZ in Mexico—an intelligent and vigorous martial dictatorship clad in republican garb—for such it is—a kind of government which, although the best Mexico or any southern republic ever had, we would surely not tolerate in this country, and which we could never exercise over others without fatal injury to our own free institutions. In the face of so grave a situation as the present, it is not ungenerous and certainly not unpatriotic to consider the future of our own country at least as much as that of any other.

"PUBLICK OCCURRENCES"

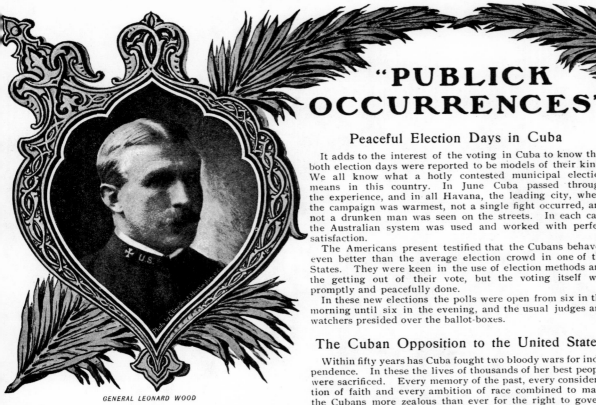

GENERAL LEONARD WOOD

MAJOR-GENERAL JOHN R. BROOKE

Peaceful Election Days in Cuba

It adds to the interest of the voting in Cuba to know that both election days were reported to be models of their kind. We all know what a hotly contested municipal election means in this country. In June Cuba passed through the experience, and in all Havana, the leading city, where the campaign was warmest, not a single fight occurred, and not a drunken man was seen on the streets. In each case the Australian system was used and worked with perfect satisfaction.

The Americans present testified that the Cubans behaved even better than the average election crowd in one of the States. They were keen in the use of election methods and the getting out of their vote, but the voting itself was promptly and peacefully done.

In these new elections the polls were open from six in the morning until six in the evening, and the usual judges and watchers presided over the ballot-boxes.

The Progress of Freedom in Cuba

The first Monday of November, which will be the fifth day of the month, will be a red-letter day in the history of Cuba. Then will begin the convention to frame a constitution for the island. The men who will participate and who will do the work are those elected on the fifteenth of September from the six provinces of the island. The election itself and the personality of the men make the event one of importance in the records of free government and constitutional progress. The convention will be composed of seven members from the province of Santiago, two members from the province of Puerto Principe, seven members from the province of Santa Clara, four members from the province of Matanzas, eight members from the province of Havana, and three members from the province of Pinar del Rio—thirty-one delegates in all.

Nothing can better illustrate the plans and purposes of this convention than the following, which was promulgated by the Military Governor of Cuba in announcing the date and the conditions of the election:

"*Whereas*, the Congress of the United States by its joint resolution of April 20, 1898, declared

"'That the people of the Island of Cuba are, and of right ought to be, free and independent;'

"'That the United States hereby disclaims any disposition or intention to exercise sovereignty, jurisdiction or control over said Island except for the pacification thereof, and asserts its determination, when that is accomplished, to leave the government and control of the Island to its people;'

"*And, Whereas*, the people of Cuba have established municipal governments, deriving their authority from the suffrages of the people given under just and equal laws, and are now ready, in like manner, to proceed to the establishment of a general government which shall assume and exercise sovereignty, jurisdiction and control over the Island;

"*Therefore, it is ordered* that a general election be held in the Island of Cuba on the third Saturday of September, in the year nineteen hundred, to elect delegates to a convention to meet in the city of Havana, at twelve o'clock noon on the first Monday of November, in the year nineteen hundred, to frame and adopt a constitution for the people of Cuba, and, as a part thereof, to provide for and agree with the Government of the United States upon the relations to exist between that Government and the Government of Cuba, and to provide for the election by the people of officers under such constitution and the transfer of government to the officers so elected."

Illiteracy Among the Cubans

In the early part of the present year a census of Cuba was taken, under the authority and direction of the United States War Department. The principal purpose was to ascertain how many males there were of twenty-one years of age and over and to classify them according to race, nationality, citizenship, literacy and superior education.

It was found that in Cuba the total number of male citizens of voting age was 417,993, of whom 187,813 were whites born in Cuba, 96,088 whites born in Spain, 6794 whites born in other countries, and 127,298 colored, including blacks, mixed and Chinese.

More than one-half of the white Cuban citizens were unable to read, and of the colored Cuban citizens three out of four were illiterates. Altogether about one-half of the voting population were able to read.

The total population of Cuba is placed at 1,572,797, of whom 910,298 are native whites, and 234,638 are negroes. The foreign whites bring the total white population to 1,052,516. Of both sexes over thirty-five per cent. can read and write, and about twenty thousand are highly educated.

The Cuban Opposition to the United States

Within fifty years has Cuba fought two bloody wars for independence. In these the lives of thousands of her best people were sacrificed. Every memory of the past, every consideration of faith and every ambition of race combined to make the Cubans more zealous than ever for the right to govern themselves. Señor Salvador Cisneros y Betancourt, who was twice President of the Island Republic, came to the United States two weeks before the election and laid before President McKinley a protest against the United States taking any part in the Constitutional Convention. In articles and interviews he called for the immediate withdrawal of the United States troops from Cuba. The petition itself states that the Cubans have demonstrated to the world that they are a law-abiding people fully capable of self-government and entitled to absolute independence. "The time has come," it recites, "for the intervention of the United States to cease, and the Government of the United States to leave the Cubans to enjoy fully their sovereignty and absolute independence by withdrawing from Cuba all the American troops."

Señor Cisneros did not hesitate to attack the rule of the United States in Cuba. He charged that the military authorities had been arbitrary, acting as conquerors in a conquered land; that they discriminated against the Cuban people and in favor of carpet-baggers from the United States; that they had used patronage for their favorites and robbed the public treasury; that hundreds of thousands of dollars had been stolen; and his arraignment included the following:

"It is a fact, however humiliating its admission must be both to Cubans and Americans, that a great deal less has been done by the military government in Cuba to repair the ravages of war and to restore to the country its lost prosperity than was done by the Government of Spain during the same period of time at the close of the bloody ten years' war."

Not a Pleasant Record

This sounds very serious, and there is no doubt that the Americans have not reflected much credit on the United States by the quality of some of the administration and economy which they have displayed in Cuba. The pilfering of the postal revenues and the legal delays that have followed are an acknowledged disgrace to this country.

The very fact that Governor-General Wood, after his appointment, was able to save $100,000 a year in lopping off superfluities shows the condition of things, and it is being freely charged in our own campaign that the investigation into Cuban scandals ordered by the United States Senate has been postponed, for party reasons, until after the Presidential election.

Some Work to Be Done

Most people would probably like to see the United States leave Cuba at once and hand it over to its own citizens, but there again we come against grave obstacles. The party feeling has been running high among the Cubans, and instead of electing the men best qualified to consider constitutional questions there was a disposition to fill the convention with extremists who knew more about guerilla warfare than they did about statesmanship. There were exceptions to this rule, of course, but in a public speech General Wood felt constrained to say: "Your delegates must be competent to draft a constitution, and it is the duty you owe yourselves and your fellow-patriots to see that your representatives are without party prejudice. Bear in mind that no constitution which does not provide for a stable government will be accepted by the United States. You want liberty for all, and for no particular party. The United States insists that you have it."

The very fact that in this General Wood set a standard which was probably beyond the people of his own country does not make so very much difference.

The main purport was that the United States intends to supervise the convention, to keep track of its proceedings, to see whether or not its work is satisfactory, and to hold Cuba until it is reasonably satisfied that it can get along by itself.

And this supervision the Cubans vigorously resent.

Suffrage Qualifications in Cuba

The figures of illiteracy make all the more interesting the elections which have been held in Cuba during the present year, and especially the conditions which govern them. We have been reading a great deal and hearing a great deal about the qualifications for the suffrage in our own country. Some of the Southern States have come in for a large share of criticism over the new laws which practically disfranchise the negroes. It happens, however, that some of the Northern States have educational and property qualifications, although not intended for racial distinctions. The rules and regulations for the election of September 15 were formulated and promulgated by the War Department of the United States Government, being printed in both English and Spanish, and signed by J. B. Hickey, the Assistant Adjutant-General. We quote from the official announcement:

"Voters at this election must possess one of the following qualifications: (a) Ability to read and write; (b) ownership of real or personal property to the value of two hundred and fifty dollars, American gold; (c) service in the Cuban army prior to July 18, 1898, and honorable discharge therefrom whether a native Cuban or not."

It is furthermore provided that the voter must be a native male Cuban or the son of a native male Cuban, or a Spaniard included within the provisions of the Treaty of Paris, who has not made declaration of his decision to preserve his allegiance to the Crown of Spain.

It can thus be seen that the conditions of the suffrage in Cuba were more strict in both of the elections than in any State of the United States. In other words, the Government itself has in Cuba set an example of qualified suffrage, and the result is that only one out of three male adults can exercise the voting privilege at the polls.

The Financial Outlook of the Island

It will probably take the convention several months to get through its work. Then will follow the usual delays in the editing of its report and in putting it into force, if indeed it is accepted by the United States. We shall have Cuba under our charge for at least a small part of the twentieth century.

The great fear is that if this country lets go too soon it will have to take hold again. The conditions are not altogether promising and one fact is especially disturbing. Over eighty million dollars is claimed by the native troops, and with this pressure from all parts of the island it is feared that there might be issues of bonds and securities that would rapidly and permanently cripple the finances of the island. The revenues are now between seventeen and twenty million dollars a year, and they will not exceed the latter sum for several years to come.

The Good Done by Americans

An impartial judgment of American rule in Cuba, begun under the governorship of General Brooke, is that despite its deficiencies it has done wonderful good. You cannot in a day overturn an old system and put a new civilization on its foundations. There must be the trusting of new men, and the fact that a few are recreant to their duties should not convict the whole policy of a great and impartial Government.

The men from the United States have done several great things. They have organized the police admirably; they have administered the finances more ably than ever before in Cuba's history; they have taken a complete census; they have banished actual suffering, and worked heroically for the best interests of the island. In the courts improvements have been made, and in the public schools and the postal service Cuba has been changed as if by magic. So taking all in all the Cuba of to-day is in better condition, and in a better position, than it ever has been in the past.

CHRISTMAS ON

THE ISTHMUS

South America and the Big Stick

SOME of the European ill-wishers of this country assert that the Monroe Doctrine is so unpopular among our Latin neighbors that the idea of making the southern continent independent of our protection through the creation of a United States of South America is making rapid progress.

Let us hope that the latter part, at least, of this allegation may be true. We are not keeping up the Monroe Doctrine for fun, and if the South Americans can learn to take care of themselves without our assistance, every sensible Gringo will wish them joy.

Ten jangling little South American republics need a Monroe Doctrine with a big stick behind it, but one great South American republic could swing an adequate stick of its own. It would have forty million people to start with, and if it were governed with decent honesty and common-sense it would rank as one of the great powers of the world.

Perhaps the continental idea is a little too big to be easily put into effect, considering the fact that Brazil, which occupies the heart of the continent, speaks a different language from its neighbors. But even a reduction in the number of South American republics from ten to four would make a wonderful difference in their standing before the world. Chile and Argentina are manifestly two severed halves of one country. Each of them has a sea-coast that the other needs. United, together with Paraguay and Uruguay, they would make a compact and respectable power. If the nine Spanish-speaking republics in South America do not feel quite up to the task of creating a United States it would be a great thing for them to create three Mexicos. But they would have to begin looking for men of the Diaz calibre. If they are going to keep on being ruled by their Castros and Marroquins their present responsibilities are large enough, and even too large.

ᐁ

The Indestructible Monroe Doctrine

SEVEN years ago there was a row over Venezuela, and certain papers in London announced that the Monroe Doctrine was wiped out forever. But when the trouble was settled the Monroe Doctrine was found to be in unusually good health. A few weeks ago Venezuela again became a first-page subject in the world's news, and the Italian Parliament was informed by one of its members that England and Germany had knocked the Monroe Doctrine sky-high. This information seemed to be credited, for Italy hastened to subscribe for a ground-floor allotment of stock in the Anglo-German blockade. The international syndicate is now in liquidation, and the subscribers are anxiously looking for an opportunity to dispose of their shares at a discount. Meanwhile the Monroe Doctrine remains an ugly and immovable fact. If it is "sky-high" it is also bedrock-deep, and all the way between.

Intelligent Americans have never claimed for the Monroe Doctrine a place in international law. They have been content to regard it as a declaration of American policy, good just so long as we have the will and the power to enforce it. But the current of events may yet carry it into the law of nations, without any effort on our part to put it there. International law is merely a collection of the usages commonly observed by civilized Powers, and it includes some things queerer than the Monroe Doctrine.

All the American republics, with the possible exception of Chile, have already recognized that Doctrine as part of the public law of the Western Hemisphere. England, in practice and in all but explicit terms, has accepted it as an inviolable principle. Germany has repeatedly disclaimed any intention of violating it. Russia and Spain, which used to have American possessions, have given them up—the former voluntarily, the latter under pressure. France accepted a practical application of the Doctrine thirty-six years ago, and has never displayed any desire to experience another. Austria refrained from sending troops to the help of Maximilian when we pointed to our "No Trespassing" signboard. Italy was careful to assure us that she had no designs on South American real estate when she joined the blockade of Venezuela. Finally The Hague treaty, signed by all the principal Powers of the world, carries a codicil by which our traditional policy toward American questions is reserved.

Since the Monroe Doctrine was first announced, eighty years ago, no attempt to violate it has ever been consummated. The chance that any such attempt ever will be consummated is less now than ever before. If undisturbed possession for from five to twenty years will give a man a title to a farm by prescription, how long a period of unbroken acquiescence in a certain doctrine by the whole world will it take to give that doctrine the force of international law?

Our Unnamed Colony

NOW that we have actually enacted a law, after three-quarters of a century of agitation, providing for the construction of an Isthmian canal by the United States, we are giving most of our attention to the ditch we are about to dig. We do not fully realize that before we get that ditch we shall have something else hardly less important—to wit, a new colony.

The law, as passed, provides that before we begin the construction of the canal we must secure the perpetual, exclusive control of a strip of territory, at least six miles wide, from sea to sea. If that cannot be obtained from Colombia we must try to get it from Nicaragua and Costa Rica. There can be no canal without it.

Now, "exclusive and perpetual control" may sound better in Latin-American ears than "annexation," but in substance it is the same thing. Practically what we propose to do is to annex a strip of territory six miles wide along the line of the canal. On the Panama route that would give us about 270 square miles of land; on the Nicaragua route about 1000. In the one case we should have a colony about four times the size of the District of Columbia; in the other we should have one almost as large as Rhode Island.

This will be the first isolated outpost we have ever planted on the southern mainland of America. With Alaska on the north, it will put a pair of Yankee clamps on the whole continent. It will make the Stars and Stripes more than ever the "American flag," for that will be the flag the traveler will see in every zone of North America, from the steaming swamps of Panama to the ice-bound rocks of Point Barrow. Other countries may be sandwiched in here and there—there may be a wedge of British territory between Alaska and Washington and half a dozen republics between Texas and Panama—but the one universal American Power will be more than ever the United States. There will be inspiration for every patriotic citizen of this republic in merely looking at the map.

It is a satisfaction to feel that the prosperity of our new colony is assured from the start. There will be no hanging around the doors of the Capitol waiting for Congress to perform its "plain duty" in the matter of the tariff. The canal, first in construction and then in operation, will make perennial good times on the Isthmus. The commerce of the world will flow, year by year, through that six-mile strip. American towns will spring up along the great ditch and reach out for the trade of the Southern continent. And on the principle that "to him that hath shall be given" Congress will probably decide to take off the duties on Isthmian sugar. Good luck to the youngest of Uncle Sam's infants!

Perhaps Colombia and Nicaragua and Costa Rica may all refuse to give us that exclusive perpetual concession. But let us hope not. Our new Isthmian colony would be a neighbor for whose presence any Latin-American republic could well afford to give a six-mile strip of land.

PANAMA AND SUEZ

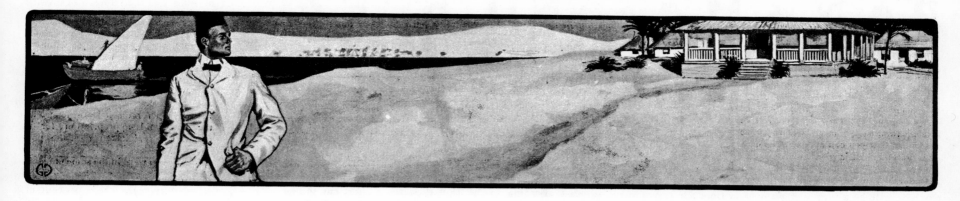

A Comparison and a Forecast
By Frederic Courtland Penfield

Former United States Diplomatic Agent and Consul-General to Egypt
Author of Present-Day Egypt

THE Government is being memorialized almost daily by labor organizations to employ Americans exclusively in constructing the Panama Canal; and at least one labor convention has urged President Roosevelt in a group of resolutions solemnized by "whereases" and "wherefores" to permit the great waterway to be completed only by members of recognized American labor unions. Were this done it would lead not only to the undoing of trade-unionism, but literally to the demise of most of the unionists sent to the isthmus.

The sentiment reflected in these appeals to the Executive is laudable, for it is distinctly patriotic. But canal-digging at Panama with pick and shovel is not a vocation for the adopted or native American—his services are worth more at home. Considerations of humanity must take precedence of those of patriotism in this gigantic undertaking, and the canal must perforce be finished by laborers greatly inferior in more than one respect to American workmen. They must be men raised in the tropics, accustomed as nearly as possible to climatic conditions of the isthmus, and possibly immune to more than one disease that in a few months might decimate an army of workers reared in northern latitudes. To attempt to predict the death-rate, otherwise, would be folly.

The Most Perplexing Problem of the Enterprise

WHO—what nationality, what race of men—will supply the brawn and muscle? "Chinese," will be the answer of three out of four persons giving the problem passing thought. There are physical as well as political reasons why Chinamen cannot consistently be employed. They are not indigenous to the tropics, for they come from a country having practically the range of latitude of the United States; when transplanted to a latitude near the equator they lack the stamina requisite for severe manual effort, and bring with them racial vices and unclean customs not wanted in a land that is going to be near kin to Uncle Sam. De Lesseps had them on the isthmus, and the bones of thousands are there to-day. Most of the labor in building the Panama railroad was Chinese, it is true; but it is as inevitable to the passenger to be told by conductor or chance acquaintance that every sleeper on the line marks the grave of a Mongol as it is to pay his fare. And, much to the point, the digging of a governmental canal on the equivalent of American soil by a race excluded from our domain by law would be a grave anomaly, for the United States cannot readily control men having no legal existence under its statutes.

Chinese labor, probably, is out of the question. Panama City and Colon have long complained of the presence of Chinese on the isthmus, and for numerous reasons they are held undesirable; but they have been there since the time of De Lesseps, and control certain lines of trade and do many things for the Panamanian. Their savings always go to China, and when their "pile" is accumulated they go, too. It would be better to go to Southern India, to the neighborhood of Madras, for laborers than to China. Indian coolie labor has much to commend it. The English Government has proved this in British Guiana, where indentured coolies, working the sugar plantations, have saved the colony from bankruptcy. These East Indians toil like beavers, frown upon miscegenation, and at the end of their five years' contract are taken back to India with practically every farthing earned during their exile. The native Africans brought by De Lesseps to cut the canal left beriberi and other diseases on the isthmus.

But Asiatics and blacks from Africa are neither necessary nor desirable to the great work soon to be taken in hand. The question of labor is the most perplexing problem associated with the enterprise, doubtless; but the Western World can supply the men needed. It is asserted generally by those writing on the subject that to complete the canal will require the services of 50,000 men for eight years. This calculation is mellowed by age: it was the estimate a dozen years ago. I would like to compliment that form of American genius that produces dredgers, rock-cutters and excavators, steam navvies and drills by believing that if 50,000 workers were necessary a decade ago under foreign guidance to finish the canal, that 40,000 can now perform the task in eight years. That would be allowing a paltry twenty per cent. benefit to the American inventor and mechanic.

If this hypothesis is reasonable, the Government has a solution of the labor feature at its door—or at the canal's door—in the British West Indies. It is the blacks and half-breeds of the Caribbean archipelago who must be looked to by the United States Government. A few thousand West Indians are now working for the French company, and presumably a few thousands of the flotsam and jetsam of humanity would gravitate toward the isthmus directly operations began. Some toilers will be drawn, naturally, from the Gulf States, and from Italy and other southern countries of Europe; but few will come from the Latin-American neighbors of the republic of Panama—inhabitants of these will prefer politics and revolutions to good wages.

Probably ninety per cent. of the laborers must be drawn from King Edward's island possessions. Jamaica, with its agricultural depression and other misfortunes, should spare a reasonable number of its 750,000 people. The authorities may question the wisdom of letting laborers in large numbers leave the island; but the opportunity to earn a white man's wage will probably stampede the Jamaicans in their desire to work for Uncle Sam. At home they are lazy, at times troublesome; but when working on Costa Rican banana plantations or for the French canal company they have ever been tractable and industrious. Reared in a latitude only six hundred miles north of the isthmus, they would go there immune from certain fevers and disorders.

The Choice and Care of the Workmen

ANOTHER island from which important drafts of blacks may be made is Barbados, the most populous spot according to area in this hemisphere. Barbados, only three hundred miles north of Panama, has 200,000 people, averaging 1178 to the square mile. Barbadian negroes are scattered over the American tropics; Trinidad is full of them, and few island villages are without some representatives, explained by the fact that Barbados is practically without industries. A few laborers would come from the Bahamas, and some from the Danish West Indies. Trinidad, St. Lucia, St. Vincent, St. Christopher and other British islands would send quotas; but practically none would be contributed by strife-loving Hayti and Santo Domingo. With Porto Rico fairly started on a career of prosperity, few men could be spared from the island, and the same situation exists in Cuba.

The British islands accessible to Colon have, approximately, 1,500,000 people; and it is a fact unfortunate to their welfare that since the collapse of the sugar industry the scheme of existence has not always been with them a simple matter. These poor blacks and mulattos must be jubilant over the prospect of remunerative occupation. The Washington Government as a paymaster would have an impelling influence with them not easily checked. Assuredly three or four per cent. of this population of about 1,500,000 would be available, and might be spared from the islands without creating local shortages of workmen; probably the movement might secure the coöperation of the administrators of the islands. The men are there and ready enough to work for Uncle Sam. The task of getting them may present certain difficulties, but not unsurmountable.

Obviously an industrial army of 35,000 might be attracted from the Caribbean archipelago. The workers should be chosen with the same care as that devoted to recruiting for the army and navy. If rigorous and exhaustive, a physical examination would contribute to the lessening of the death-rate on the isthmus; and this should take place in the islands, that none but sound men be engaged. A condition should be an agreement to remain on the isthmus for a period of three or four months at a time, and not longer. They should then be replaced by a fresh draft of men, interchange and transportation being systematically arranged by agents of our Government. We possess the requisites for this part of the work. The interoceanic canal, to be governmental property, is entitled to all needed assistance from the army, navy and transport service. If there is no precedent for the program herein sketched, it is because no truly great canal has been constructed by a government.

The effect upon the islands from which the laborers are drawn should be beneficial. Apathy and indolence reign everywhere in the West Indies; planters and traders once rich are now poor, and among the blacks there is a painful absence of money. Prostration of the sugar industry is directly responsible for this. A few years' remunerative labor, with attendant quickening of intellect and energies, can have but one effect upon the moral and material welfare of the negroes. They are capable of any work where their task is outlined by superior intelligence. What they need is encouragement, something more encouraging than their prevailing rate of compensation, two shillings or less a day. These facts are certain to be perceived by the British Government, and this might produce an understanding with the American Government amounting almost to coöperation.

Here is something that should be better understood: that under United States rule the isthmus will not be the pest-hole it has been ever since the demands of travel and commerce turned it into a highway. The advent of American rule will improve the hygiene of the region, the methods of living, perhaps the climate. Of the French millions spent and squandered on the isthmus, very little was devoted to improving sanitary conditions. Abundant provision was made for caring for those stricken by disease, but little was done in the direction of minimizing the chance of a workman being overtaken by illness through unwholesome and unsanitary conditions.

The Plague Spot of the Western World

THE Chagres River makes the isthmus the unhealthiest spot on the American continent; it might well be called the River of Death. Overflowing its banks and flooding the low swamp lands annually, or following a torrential rain, it leaves vegetable and animal matter to decay under the scorching tropical sun, breeding swift and strange death. It is the source of the most dangerous fever known, tenfold more dangerous than yellow fever. Thousands of native African and Chinese laborers have been victims of Chagres fever. Complaining at their toil of not feeling well, they would lie on the bank to rest for a moment—and would never rise. If there has been a fall of rain, however moderate, or if the atmosphere is heavy with moisture, the penalty for venturing out of doors after nightfall is generally death—death within a few hours. Mile upon mile of the country between Colon and Panama is a mass of underbrush so thick that nothing but animals and reptiles can penetrate it; where this jungle is broken the spaces are covered by water surfaced with green, wherein loathsome reptiles and poisonous insects thrive.

(Continued)

PANAMA AND SUEZ

Men skilled in hygienic science must correct many failings of Nature within the canal zone. Engineers, medical officers and sanitary experts must precede the man with the shovel and "clean up" the isthmus. This is imperative. A year devoted to the task would probably shorten the constructive work by two years. Colon and Panama must be cleansed, scores of fever-breeding swamps drained, stagnant sink-holes obliterated, and decaying nature looked after. A vital prerequisite will be a supply of pure water from one end of the canal to the other. To my mind greater care should be exercised in selecting health officers for the isthmus than engineers to lead the canal-makers: the responsibilities of the former will be greater than those of the latter, and the success of the former greater than any utilitarian victory can possibly be.

For months the Washington Government has had Colonel W. M. Black on the isthmus. This modest officer is one of the ablest sanitary engineers in our army. He helped General Wood to clean up Cuba, working out the details of many suggestions that reduced the mortality at a rate almost amazing. If Colonel Black and his assistants are to forerun the civil engineers and the laborers with picks and shovels the death-rate should be tremendously lessened from what it was under the French company. Perhaps they may reduce the annual mortality to five per cent.; some who are familiar with Colonel Black's capabilities say the death-rate should be under this figure, provided the greater share of workpeople come from the Caribbean islands.

Our Government will have better natural conditions to deal with at Panama than those that De Lesseps and the later French company contended with. Uncle Sam finds the canal nearly two-fifths dug—eleven miles of "wet" cutting on the Atlantic side and nine miles of the same on the Pacific side being practically completed. But the remaining twenty-seven miles of "dry" cutting will try his powers, for it calls for the reducing of the Culebra (meaning snake—everything on the isthmus is named from something vile and poisonous) hill to a depth where locks may be introduced. This elevated cutting cannot be half so fatal to life as was the work in the low regions.

The cost? It will be enormous—say $225,000,000, including the payment of $40,000,000 to the French company and $10,000,000 to the republic of Panama. Bear in mind, please, that citizens of France have spent and squandered fully $265,000,000 over the Panama scheme—but not half this found its way to the isthmus, presumably, for Paris swindlers had fat pickings for many years in the name of Panama. The Suez Canal, just under a hundred miles in length, cost a round $100,000,000; but that presented no engineering difficulties, demanded no deep cuttings, no locks. Hundreds of thousands of Egyptian fellaheen working without pay simply scooped out the desert sand by basketfuls along a line traced by the gold-headed cane of Ferdinand de Lesseps. The engineering features, after it was demonstrated that the Mediterranean and Red Seas were of the same level, might almost have been dealt with by a bright schoolboy.

The Panama Canal will make the United States the trade arbiter of the universe; but it will "pay" only indirectly. It is going to be expensive to construct and expensive to operate; and for a great many years the tolls cannot be expected to defray the cost. With its artificial harbors the Nicaraguan Canal would cost more to construct and operate,

and could never be very successful. In these times the Egyptian Canal collects $20,000,000 a year from its traffic, but thirty years ago the receipts were half this sum; frequently reduced, its tariff is now $1.70 per ton of freight and $2 for each passenger. Last year the number of steamships (there were no sailing vessels) passing through the Suez Canal averaged ten a day.

The Panama enterprise will indirectly bring golden reward through affording to the United States a short cut to new markets at present almost unknown to American products. The entire west coast of South America—where British and German trade is paramount—will be brought into close commercial relations, and ships using the waterway will make Australia and the Orient neighbors of the Atlantic seaboard. The construction of the Suez Canal altered the conditions of trade of the Eastern Hemisphere, and the completion of the Panama Canal will correspondingly revolutionize Western World commerce. The shortening of water distance between our own Atlantic ports and those of the Pacific Coast is not the purpose of the isthmian canal, for it cannot logically be made a competitor with rival transcontinental railroads.

This being an age of public utilities, and with American statesmen devoting profound thought to reëstablishing the Stars and Stripes on the sea, it is reasonable to believe that the canal will not be in operation many years before the best intelligence of the land will agitate for free privileges to United States ships. Indeed, it would be strange if one or both of the great political parties did not make a Presidential campaign attractive by a "free canal" plank—that is, free use of the canal to the flag of the United States, with the expense to the nation defrayed from a public appropriation, perhaps that supporting rivers and harbors. Toll roads and bridges had to yield to the sentiment against them.

No one not gifted with prescience may venture to pronounce when the canal will be finished; but it is reasonable belief that it should be opened to traffic during the winter of 1911-12. Canal-building as an industry depends upon too many controlling influences to make it possible to determine long in advance when an enterprise will be consummated. Here are five cardinal elements that the mind may fancy as represented by the star in the flag of Panama: Health, labor, engineering, politics, money. It is the last-mentioned only that possesses no germ of delay, when Uncle Sam fairly starts with spade and pick; and it is hoped that politics will not enter into the project, for it should be the canal of the nation, irrespective of faction or party. The remaining elements are beyond human control, but alertness, forethought and experience may minimize the possibility of delay therewith. If matters run smoothly the turnstile between oceans should be ready for use by 1911; if only fairly well, then 1912 would be a safer prediction. A rational compromise is to say "during the winter of 1911-12." Should an outbreak of plague, cholera or yellow fever ever get beyond control of the medical authorities on the isthmus, prognostications as to when the canal will be completed would have to be revised.

It was thirteen years from the date of obtaining the concession by De Lesseps, in 1856, before the Suez Canal was finished—but only a minor share of this period was represented by constructive work. De Lesseps' obstacles were not those of engineering, but of financiering and political opposition. In

later life he came to be considered as an engineer, but first of all was he a diplomatist, and the bringing of the waters of the seas together at Suez was the triumph of finance and negotiation. Diplomacy was back of it all, the diplomacy of olden times, in contradistinction to the straightforward variety known in these days as "the new diplomacy." Manipulation, intrigue, chicanery, wire-pulling and bribery built the Suez Canal. The *corvée* of Egyptian peasants, toiling under a parching sun, with hundreds of thousands dying of disease and neglect, was incidental to the great scheme, nothing more.

When De Lesseps obtained the Suez concession Egypt had no debt. He persuaded the rulers of Egypt that the canal would elevate the country to a prominent place among nations—and they need not subscribe to the undertaking, and until 1968 the Cairo government would receive fifteen per cent. of the canal's takings. Viceroy Said was the first subscriber, borrowing, however, $17,000,000 for the purpose. Succeeding to the khediviate, Ismail Pasha was consumed with longing for greatness, and at first voluntarily, and then involuntarily, subscribed generously to the canal enterprise; he had but to sign papers obligingly prepared in Europe to get the cash. More than half the money stuck to the hands of the financial agents.

Where England Came In

The canal project meanwhile engendered the hostility of England, for the British Government objected to any short cut to India that might be used by any Tom, Dick or Harry: and the English press teemed with accounts of horrible conditions along the canal route, where Egyptians were dying like flies. Petitions poured in upon the Sultan of Turkey—actual sovereign of Egypt—to halt the inhumanity. These obstacles naturally produced a radical cramp in the canal company's finances; and whichever way he turned De Lesseps found a stone wall ahead of him. But his ability as a negotiator appeased Constantinople, then one European capital after another. He wrung from Ismail more subscriptions, that merry monarch borrowing in Europe with profligate hand, not only for the canal, but for his government and himself. At last, to secure the small amount required to complete the waterway, the Egyptian Government, through Ismail, signed away the right to participate in the canal's income.

But Ismail was forgiving, and he spent $21,000,000 of the people's money celebrating the opening of the canal. This made De Lesseps the Great Frenchman; but Egypt now had a paper debt of more than $500,000,000, and nothing to pay with. Not relishing an insolvent creditor, England induced the Sultan to dethrone Khedive Ismail; and his successor soon had a rebellion on his hands, led by a fanatic who had coined the phrase "Egypt for the Egyptians!" England sent troops to quell the revolution and "reëstablish the authority of the khedive," declaring vaguely that her army of occupation would remain but six months. It has been there twenty-one years, and students are growing old in their endeavor to find the precise difference between "occupation" and "annexation." But England has given Egypt a measure of prosperity unique in history. Uncle Sam similarly "occupied" Cuba, but kept his promise to restore the island to the Cubans.

The Suez Canal proving a success, the last security that Ismail parted with before his exile was his personal holding in the company. Disraeli bought the shares by cable, and to-day they are worth ten times the amount paid. They give England control of the canal, but she lets France manage the enterprise.

Is it a misfortune for a country to possess a site for an interoceanic canal, the construction of which is demanded by the necessities of the world's commerce? Egyptians have decided views on this subject, and Colombians might give a ready reply to the question.

The Suez Canal yields nothing to the country through which it runs.

Only a Few Wars Left

IT IS just a quarter of a century since Beaconsfield at Berlin gave the Turk a new lease of life in Europe, and every winter since that time the political almanacs have predicted an uprising in the spring to complete the work then unfortunately interrupted. The "war-cloud" in the Balkans is a little blacker now than usual, and perhaps it may break at last.

Whatever may happen just now, the country of Alexander the Great is a region of unfailing interest because it is one of the few spots on the globe—perhaps the only one—over which a great war is still a logical probability. Notwithstanding the tremendous competition in armaments it is a fact that war on a great scale is becoming obsolete. Business and humanity combined are growing too powerful to permit the peace of the world to be seriously endangered except for very grave cause. It may be said with confidence that if four unsettled questions were out of the way the idea of a great war anywhere in the world could be permanently dismissed.

The first and most serious of these is the Turkish question. That is almost certain to bring on a collision sooner or later: because Russia considers Constantinople and its surroundings worth a war, because the Turks would certainly fight rather than be driven out of Europe, and the condition of the Christian subjects of the Porte is a cause of war always available whenever Russia thinks the time opportune for making use of it. A war involving Russia, Turkey and the Balkan peoples would be a great one, even if it went no further, and it would be hard for some, at least, of the other Powers to keep out of it.

The second danger point is the far East, where there is a prospect that Japan may sooner or later come into collision with Russia, with possible consequences of which the Anglo-Japanese Alliance gives a hint. The third, where the chance of averting the trouble is much better, is Morocco, and the fourth is Austria, where Pan-Germanism and Pan-Slavism are arousing passions that may overcome the tendency of business and civilization toward peace.

These are the only points at which issues are at stake which the great Powers would consider worth fighting about. Some people might add a fifth possibility—the chance of war in America over the Monroe Doctrine. But if we are well prepared, that is a contingency that need not cause any serious uneasiness. There will be no more great wars except when substantial existing interests clash. All the Powers of Europe have too many troubles of their own on hand to go out of their way to hunt new ones over here.

When We Go to War

MR. ROOSEVELT has now as his adviser and manager for foreign affairs a man whose chief characteristic is an excellent mind to an extraordinary degree free from passion. Mr. Root is as calm and as cold as an adding machine. Further, Mr. Roosevelt makes no secret of his enormous confidence in "Elihu's judgment." Whatever may or may not be the effect of Mr. Root's influence, so far as domestic affairs—notably Mr. Root's friends and clients, the "captains of industry"—are concerned, every one will feel that the distinguished, powerful office of Secretary of State, while he occupies it, will neither inaugurate nor promote any provocative policy in heat and thoughtlessness.

If we ever have a foreign war it will be because we ourselves wish it, as no nation on earth would dream of the madness of attacking us. Therefore, if we should have foreign trouble while "Elihu's judgment" is at the helm, we should know that "Elihu's judgment" was that we needed a foreign war to take our minds off our home troubles.

Promise of Peace in the Horrors of War

Many lurid pictures have been drawn of airships flying over forts and cities and dropping high explosives. The idea is by no means an exaggeration, and it must be left to the imagination to appreciate what awful havoc in life and property would result.

Almost as terrible would be the work of these submarine boats creeping under the naval monsters and blowing the great machines with their hundreds of men to destruction and death.

Indeed, war may yet be made so horrible that the world will have the peace for which it prays.

No More Worlds to Conquer

THOUGH more men are now under arms than there ever were in any other period of the world's history, and the devices for killing soldiers are varied and effective to a degree that would have driven any of the great conquerors wild with envy, there is an utter lack of new worlds to conquer, and this lack promises to continue until means can be devised for sending military expeditions to some of the other planets. Russia has appropriated everything worth having in Central Asia, Africa has been divided into "spheres of influence" in which the nominal holders have their hands full and running over, the South American countries have been extending their borders inland ever since they got rid of the Spaniards and Portuguese, and even the smallest isles of the sea that were worth stealing have been snatched from the natives by big bullies calling themselves, in their superior wisdom, civilized nations.

It cannot be denied that there remain many possibilities of fighting, but they are a disheartening lot to would-be conquerors, for plunder—or ownership, which amounts to the same thing—is no longer possible in the old and popular manner. Time was when a great nation desiring possession of a smaller one marched in and took it, but now the permission of several other great nations must first be obtained, and such permission is likely to cost more than the prize is worth. Even were it not so, the probable cost would be discouraging. In the days of Alexander, Xerxes, Timour and Genghis Khan men by thousands were gathered into bands, made their own bows and arrows, javelins and spears, and ate what they could find by the way; their pay consisted of what they could steal. Even in Napoleon's day the cost of cannon, pound for pound, was no greater than that of other castings of iron or brass, but nowadays a single battery of field guns costs as much as was paid for all of Napoleon's artillery. When "Old Ironsides" and other American frigates were taking an incalculable mass of conceit out of the British navy it cost only two or three dollars to fire one of their heaviest cannon, but when our thirteen-inch guns thundered at Cervera's fleet the expense of each shot was many hundreds of dollars. Britain's conquest of India, or such part of it as was effected by fighting, cost but a trifle, and there was much to show for it, but her struggle with a few thousand Boers has been costing more than a million dollars per day for half a year and the expense will continue at this rate until the war ends, when her gain, aside from a lot of grazing land which our Western cattle men would think dear at a dollar an acre, will have been merely "prestige" of a kind over which the thoughtful Briton will not do much crowing. The partitioning of China may sound well to soldiers who long for stations, but the hatred in which India holds Britain is likely to warn other Powers against trying to assimilate countless millions of a civilization far older than their own.

World-conquering after the old fashion is a dead business; nothing can bring it to life again. Nations may continue to fight, but very few and small are they that will disappear in the maw of their victors. The real conquests of the future will be made by the traders, the teachers and the missionaries who follow new flags into old lands. The United States are setting the example in Cuba, Porto Rico and the Philippines, and the robber-nations of Europe are too wise not to profit by it. —JOHN HABBERTON.

11 The Body Beautiful

The historian usually finds contemporary journals a rich source of information about a given period. But if one were to judge by the evidence presented by magazines during the first few years of this century, he might well gain the impression that the art of healing had fallen into a kind of limbo. The publications of those years discuss the subject of disease only superficially and barely mention such important topics as new developments in surgery.

The omissions seem strange to a generation accustomed to reading daily of miraculous drugs, organ transplants, and even gene manipulations. But medical reporting for the general public was scant in those first years after the turn of the century. Health seems to have been viewed largely in terms of exercise and cold showers, the search for a sound mind in a sound body. The only people who talked of disease and ill health were the advertisers; they promised cures for everything from cancer to stones in the bladder and relief from chilblains and rheumatism. Even the brewers claimed health-giving qualities for their beers.

It was not as though nothing was happening in the art of healing during those years. In 1900 Walter Reed and his associates carried out the brave experiments (at the cost of the life of one man and the crippling of another) that proved that yellow fever was transmitted by mosquitoes. Between 1904 and 1906 Colonel William Gorgas put Reed's experiments to use and virtually eliminated yellow fever in the Panama Canal Zone, making possible the building of the canal. Radium was being used to treat cancer by 1903. Steady advances were being made in surgery, and the details of operative procedure could not have failed to fascinate a public to which the world of medicine and surgery was still largely a mystery.

Undoubtedly the publications were chiefly responsible for the lack of informative articles on such subjects. The magazines could not have had many correspondents with the background necessary to write a story about medicine that would be intelligible and interesting to laymen. Some Victorian prudery was probably also involved: when one began to discuss disease and operations it was almost always necessary to mention parts of the body below the neck and above the knees. Rather than get into such predicaments, it was better to avoid the subject entirely.

Nor did the medical profession encourage journalists. Organized medicine even today has not entirely discarded the witch-doctor concept that it is privy to secrets that must be retained within a select circle of the initiated and not be revealed, under any circumstances, to the common people. This philosophy made the medical profession a poor source of news in the early 1900's;

its instinct was to withhold even stories that showed it in a shining light.

Among the pieces that follow there is only one major article on a medical subject (this does not mean that others were not published during the period, but it does indicate that they were hard to find): an explanation entitled "How Vaccination Protects Us Against Smallpox." The editors found a doctor to write the article for them; they could have had a smart high-school student do the job because the subject was a hoary one. Edward Jenner had discovered a vaccine against smallpox in the 1790's, and the story of how he had made his discovery had become a classic and was undoubtedly told in the science classes of high schools at the beginning of the century. That a major magazine, *The Saturday Evening Post,* felt it necessary to have a doctor retell this century-old story is a sorry comment on the low state of the reporting of medical news at the time.

The editors of various journals did pontificate from time to time on matters of health and medicine, but their sources of news were poor in most cases, their choice of items on which to comment was uninspired, and the ability of their staff writers to interpret what they read was hardly superlative. As a result, one finds pieces like "Sunlight and Health Fads," in which the editor cheers on the Surgeon of the Army, who has claimed that Northerners should be cautious about living or vacationing near the equator, should not go out in the noonday sun, and should even view with suspicion the "sunny, well-lit room" described not only in Victorian books on health but in any number of country novels. Another editorial writer has come upon—and passed on to his readers —an item about an English doctor who thinks that doorknobs, especially in railway coaches, are larger than they need be and so pass an unnecessarily large number of microbes from person to person. The good doctor proposes a simpler door latch, one that would require contact with perhaps only one finger and thumb. The notion is perhaps a meritorious one, but hardly the stuff with which a national magazine should have been filling its pages.

Items such as the two cited above indicate a frivolous attitude toward medical news. The advertising columns are even more illustrative of a lack of standards. Ads for cancer cures as well as for other nostrums abound. It was in 1906, soon after most of these advertisements appeared, that the first Pure Food and Drug Act was enacted. The new law required a listing of any narcotics, stimulants, or other dangerous ingredients contained in patent medicines, but it was only a halfway measure: many people did not know whether the drugs named in small print on the side of their favorite elixir were dangerous or not. Nor did the law stop the purveying of quack nostrums. An amendment in 1913 did forbid false claims about the curative value of medicines and so put a stop to the most flagrant advertising of such things as cancer cures. But being a federal law, it covered only substances that moved across state lines, and unless it was backed up by a state law, it left plenty of opportunity for trafficking in human suffering.

The journals of the time were on more comfortable ground when they talked about exercise and sports. They are subjects with few pitfalls; just as everyone is against sin, everyone is for exercise. In 1903 an article on "skeeing" so excited the editors of *Country Life in America,* a publication long dead and forgotten, that they not only let the author ramble on with descriptions of what a "skee" was, but suffered him to go into careful descriptions of how a "skeer" dressed for his sport.

The reader will also find in the following section a piece reporting that many American horsewomen were abandoning the sidesaddle in favor of the "cross-saddle" (the term must have had a short life for it is not in dictionaries today). There is an article on gymnastics for businessmen, with illustrations that would repel most businessmen, and a truly interesting article on the game of rackets, illustrated with sketches of a wooden player.

If anyone doubts the value of exercise, an academic professor of surgery removes all uncertainties with his "Reasons for Belief in the Value of Exercise and Athletics." One may not be swayed by the good professor's arguments, but he is certain to be vastly impressed by the professor's ability to go on and on, endlessly citing great men in centuries past who combined a sound mind with an athletic body.

One should not overlook Eustace H. Miles's "How to Improve Your Health in Odd Moments." This is a treasure of odds and ends. "The color even of the underclothing is said to have an effect upon the skin: red is thought to be warming and exciting; blue cooling and quieting." Was there, then, a sound reason for the popularity of red flannel underwear? Miles also advocates sun baths—but with the head covered; he does not explain why. And he offers a large number of simple remedies: to help your brain, lie on your back with the back of your head in a basin of cold water. Before you snicker, think back over some of your own remedies for an overtaxed brain. Perhaps some of Mr. Miles's simple remedies are worth trying before we discard him out of hand as the relic of a bygone era.

Doctoring—Oriental and Occidental

TRAVELERS have long made merry over the paradoxical Chinese custom of paying physicians only when in health and suspending payment as long as a fit of illness continues. But in two recent instances Occidental communities have unconsciously imitated the custom—which indicates that it is far from being as absurd as it seems.

In certain rural districts of the South the doctors have begun to hire their services by the year, guaranteeing medical attendance for five dollars a head—no inconsiderable sum in those parts. The canton of Zurich, in Switzerland, according to report, is about to create a public medical bureau by taxing each citizen eighty-six cents a year.

In both cases the medical profession, through its special press, has objected. From the point of view of the skeptical layman, this is not the least convincing argument in favor of the innovations. One objection is that contract labor can be of only inferior quality. Maybe, and maybe not. In any case, the patient has always resort to the higher talent. An objection which at first sight seems more valid is that of the thousand natural ills that flesh is heir to, nine hundred and ninety-nine are imaginary. The medical journals would have us believe that the Swiss State physicians will be doomed to a life of metaphorically holding the hands of females who cherish the delusion of an unappreciated malady.

The medical scribes forget, however, that a physician paid by the State will be under no obligation to prescribe Florida or the Riviera for discontented wives, nor to treat society leaders for nervous breakdown between an Ibsen afternoon and a midnight ball.

"Madam," the public practitioner will say, "all you need is a close and devoted attention to your duties as a wife and a mother"—or, "Madam, douse the fake intellectual end of the candle, and blow out the wick of social climbing, and you will be all right." Some gentle souls may not take to this sort of thing; but many husbands will quietly smile as they unloose their purse-strings to the yearly tune of eighty-six cents.

Sunlight and Health Fads

EVERY year brings its bit of evidence to show that health-fads are to physical well-being what get-rich-quick schemes are to industry. A dozen years ago a diet-quack advertised his system by declaring that those who practiced it so educated their stomachs that, in time, a saucer of rice would bring on acute indigestion. He had a host of disciples—who now remember him with digestions hopelessly weakened and perverted. The bath enthusiasts are learning that the exhilarating shock of cold bathing, often repeated, brings on a general exhaustion of the nerves in reaction, while much hot bathing debilitates the skin. Specialists in digestion are finding out that the chief effect of the water-cure is to weaken the stomach and intestines by flushing out the juices necessary to digestion. Exercise and fresh air themselves are very easily overdone.

The latest superstition to be laid is that sunlight is a universal curative. In his recent work on "The Effect of Tropical Light on White Men," Major Charles E. Woodruff, Surgeon in the United States Army, does much more than show that we of the North are weakened and destroyed by life near the Equator. He proves, or comes precious near to proving, that any race braves extinction when it migrates to a climate the natural result of which is a greater or less degree of dermal pigmentation. More than this, he shows that, even in his own climate, a man may suffer as severely by living much in the sun as by living little in it. He even questions the universal good of the much-desired "sunny, well-lit room." Nocturnal animals who never see the day are as well and strong as those who roost and wake in the twilight. The youths and maidens who have gone bareheaded through the past summers are now finding out that their hair has dried and lost freshness of color, and is even threatening to fall out prematurely.

All this is not to deny the value of diet and Christian cheerfulness, exercise, water, air and sun. Each in its way is invaluable, and the use of it may be greatly enhanced by wise cultivation. The important thing is to use none in excess, but all in natural conjunction. The human system is the product of billions of years of reaction upon environment, and nothing is more immediately disastrous to it than a sudden or radical change in a hereditary mode of life. Health, like wealth, is the result of slow, wise and temperate activity day by day.

Your Servants' Health

IN A SERIES of rules for long life and health, a French doctor put very conspicuously these two: If you live in city or town, sleep as high up in the air as possible; see to it that your servants sleep in thoroughly sanitary quarters.

Many people who try to live healthfully fail because they neglect the two chief sources of disease—what comes in from the streets and what comes down from the servants' rooms which the mistress of the house never visits, never even thinks of. The mistress of the house says that she gives "the girl" or "the servants as good as they have been used to at home," and is content with herself. Putting wholly aside the moral question of having a slum or a near-slum under one's roof, there remains the cold fact of the dangerous unhealthfulness of it. The servants should, for prudence's sake, have not "as good as they've been used to," but as good as the laws of health dictate—and that is very good indeed.

Fat Men and Automobiles

AN INTERESTING companion puzzle to that of the red-haired woman and the white horse is the conjunction of the fat man and the automobile. If you will note the occupants of every automobile in any day, and will keep a record of the total number of persons and the total number of over-weights, you will be astonished by the result. Are people of big bulk also above the average of prosperity and so able to enjoy the newest and most fascinating of luxuries? Or does the habit of coursing about in the automobile superinduce the fat-assimilation which ends in ponderous preponderance of adipose?

Does getting fat improve one's chances of owning an auto and having the leisure to use it? Does owning an auto improve one's chances of getting fat?

The Extinction of the Life Insurance Agent

THE reading world will receive with conflicting emotions the reports of Professor Mentchikoff's endeavors to prolong life. The experimenter denies the original story, which was to the effect that he had found the long-sought elixir of life; we, therefore, who are truly good need not fear that certain of the wicked may infest the earth forever. But the experimenter intimated, in his recent communication to the French Academy of Medicine, that though his researches are still in the initial stage it is really possible to arrest for a long time the tendency to physical decay after the prime of life has been passed. He says there is no biological proof that death is absolutely necessary. Stripped of verbiage which is alarming to any one who is not also an advanced physiologist, the Mentchikoff report indicates that as death is due to conflicts between different classes of cells in the human system, it can be postponed, at least, and possibly for a long period, by limiting the reproductive power of such of the cells as prey upon others.

Nothing can absolutely assure us against death, for we shall continue to have with us the deadly cigarette, the pneumonia-inducing draught in which we all like to sit in hot weather, the reckless trolley-car, the pistol supposed not to be loaded, the midnight rarebit, the morning cocktail, unripe fruit, over-ripe ditto, the unguarded railway crossing, and scores of other deadly menaces, to say nothing of political campaigns and other murderous struggles.

Yet, even if the prudent may survive in the struggle with old age, humanity will be the gainer in many ways. For instance, we shall no longer be obliged to hear of the good which people would do could they live their lives over again. The life insurance agent will be shorn of his terror, for the final event on which he enlarges would be so remote, and the annual cost of insurance be so greatly reduced, that neither would affright. There would be no excuse for forcing very young persons into society, marriage, and even the learned professions, nor for forcing statesmen out of politics on the plea that they are growing old, nor for shelving judges, physicians, clergymen and teachers at about the time when they have acquired the experience necessary to usefulness.

Some interests might suffer; quite a number of undertakers would change their business, cemetery trustees' faces would be as gloomy as their bills, and there would be misery for the uncanny people who wait for dead men's shoes. On the other hand, the thousands of well-to-do people who are saving money with which to do good—after they are dead— will become so impatient while waiting that they will be compelled to superintend the projected beneficences instead of leaving their money for trustees, lawyers and "next of kin" to fight over in the dim future. Good luck, Mentchikoff! —JOHN HABBERTON.

THE ENDLESS SEARCH.

PONCE DE LEON. — They laugh at me, but they still keep it up!

An Unsolved Mystery

IT IS a most unpleasant truth that during the last thirty years the death rate from cancer has nearly doubled, and that as yet there has been no effective treatment found for it.

In England and Wales in the year 1876, out of every thousand deaths, twenty-three were from cancer, while in 1899 this had increased to forty-six per thousand, and the proportion is still increasing with greater rapidity. The foregoing considers the sexes together, but when we separate the statistics we find that women are much more subject than men. In 1899, thirty-four deaths out of every thousand for men, and fifty-six out of every thousand for women, was cancer's record. Cancer is at present perhaps the worst disease that attacks adults of mature years, those under twenty-five years being practically free from it, and as yet no cause can be definitely assigned.

During a good many years, the opinion has been stated by physicians that cancer can be caused by too much meat eating, or by an overfed condition, accompanied by indolence, and statistics seem to bear out this conclusion.

That Terrible Business Strain

THE Chicago Board of Health has compiled some interesting statistics which show that deaths from nervous disorders have materially decreased in the Windy City of late years. This is not at all because the business pace has slackened or because men are less burdened with affairs. It is because golf and country clubs have come into vogue, and, as a rule, business men are conducting themselves more sensibly when away from their desks.

The dragon of overwork, which is represented as annually devouring the flower of our commercial manhood in the great centres, is in sober fact hardly more deadly than his papier-mâché brother in the opera of Siegfried. Ninety-nine times out of a hundred it isn't what you do when in the office, but what you do when away from it, that determines the state of your nervous system. The bartender and other servitors of the lower nature could throw a great flood of light on those horrifying stories about the devastation wrought by business strain.

Not long ago the builder of a large commercial enterprise was gathered to his fathers in middle age and in a very shattered condition. The fact furnished a text for various preachments about the deadliness of modern business — in which, however, no mention was made of the two pints of whisky, the twenty black cigars and the several hours' devotion to the poker-table which figured in the daily regimen of the deceased, and which presumably had something to do with the wreck of his nerves.

Every Man His Own Doctor

AT A CONVENTION of doctors in Washington, recently, the chairman said that there were too many doctors, too many schools for doctors, too much doctoring.

Just the reverse is the truth, if the matter be looked at a little more broadly. Every man should be a doctor; every school should be first of all a school of medicine; every one should be doctoring all the time.

But — Doctor should not mean a person engaged in putting unsightly patches upon the human machine; a school of medicine should not mean a place where common-sense is smothered in useless and even dangerous accumulations of more or less inaccurate observations on the surface symptoms of disease and on the methods of making those surface symptoms disappear; doctoring should not mean dosing with drugs that leave weakness and woe behind them in a dismal trail on their way to give disease a battle that, with its violence, shakes the very foundations of health.

If from earliest childhood we were taught and were got into the habit of practicing the only certain truths of medicine — that disease cannot fasten upon the body that is well aired, well carried, well fed with real food taken slowly and in moderation, well treated in the matter of regularity — if this millennium should arrive, such of the doctors as did not turn surgeons would seek employment as experts upon sanitation.

Disease is not a cause. It is an effect. Its best, its only true, doctor is Doctor Prevention.

The more savage the penalties of ignorance, the faster the spread of intelligence. The multiplication of bad professional doctors, shaking as it does blind public confidence in cures and professional curers, is not a cloud without traces of silver lining.

How to Improve Your Health in Odd Moments

By **Eustace H. Miles**

Formerly Lecturer and Honours Coach at Cambridge University, England

NO LONGER do we live the healthy outdoor life which our ancestors lived. We are not so healthy in body as they were, though we may be stronger in intellect. To counteract the nervous exhaustion and other evils of city life we have to use means which at first seem artificial rather than natural; but it is better to use them than to be ill. I wish to suggest a few of the simplest here. They will be no great tax upon time or money.

First of all comes exercise; and a few kinds of exercise, out of some hundreds, may be discussed here. Those which necessitate a strain—that is to say, exercises of strength—often make people slow as well as making them muscular; and they may produce a large chest without producing a large expansive power of the chest: by this I mean that the chest may always be large, but not have the capacity of being larger when it is filled with air.

These exercises of strain or strength are generally bad for the young, who—owing to the relative size of their heart and arteries—need, instead, many exercises of speed. Nevertheless they have their use. But exercises of activity are better, and should be practiced in the early morning. The body should be stripped. A man should have his windows open, so that he may have not only the benefit of the exercises, but also of the light and air bath, which is so cheap and yet so valuable. A sun-bath, with the head covered, is even better—when we can get it.

The Value of Systematic Breathing

One of the best kinds of exercise is breathing. The mouth may be kept closed, or a quill may be put in it. Anyhow, the breathing should be done slowly, chiefly through the nose, because the nose is meant to filter and warm the air. Standing with the chin back and the shoulders back, breathe in slowly, upward; then hold the breath and pat the chest all over; then let the breath out slowly and quietly. A friend of mine assures me that his chest expansion increased several inches owing to this exercise alone. One can test the growth of the chest by the tightness of the coat or waistcoat.

This will be valuable for the lungs and for the chest, and will be valuable for the whole body, because through the whole body runs the blood, and the blood is purified by the oxygen of the air. Such an exercise will also strengthen the heart. The commonest exercises to accompany the in-breathing and out-breathing may be summarized as follows. The beginner should do the in-breathing with the in-breathing exercises; afterward, when he has become skillful at breathing, he may reverse the process, and do the in-breathing with the out-breathing exercises, and vice versa.

Now, let us take one of the many exercises for the stomach. Lie down flat on your back and raise both your legs as high as possible many times. You will be surprised to find how few times, at first, you can do this. The legs may be kept straight, or may be bent as they come up.

Another good exercise, for other organs besides the stomach, is also one of the best (though one of the least known) for reducing weight in a short time. By its means a boxer has put himself into training almost immediately, and it is wonderful to notice how the muscles of the stomach begin to appear. Take a plank and lean it up against a wall, or incline it in some other way. If possible, have a small platform at the top of the plank. Walk up the plank; then turn round and walk down it. If you begin quietly and at a gradual inclination this is a good exercise for the heart. Instead of climbing perpetually, you are alternately climbing and descending. I can cordially recommend this for many purposes.

We have considered, then, the lungs and the stomach. Now let us have something which will help the kidneys. Bend forward and, with the palms of your hands behind you, pat and slap the body where the kidneys are. This will help them considerably, and may be tried several times during the day—if no one is looking.

Helpful Baths and Injurious Use of Soap

All these exercises are good for the heart, and the blood generally, and so is anything which will produce a sweat—for example, a Turkish bath. The best kind, of course, is one which leaves the head exposed to the open air.

A game of squash is fine, quick exercise for sweating purposes. It can be played by artificial light. The more you perspire through the skin, the more you relieve the kidneys of extra work, for poisons go out through the skin, as well as through the mouth, and so forth.

The skin itself is helped by the air-bath mentioned above, for the skin breathes in and out. Tar over a dog and it will die, because it cannot breathe through its skin, even though it can still breathe through its mouth. The perspiration will also be good for the skin, for the tiny pores of the body will be kept open. The unwary person often closes these pores with soap. I believe it is by far the safest plan to wet any part before you soap it; soap it, and then remove the soap; but do not put the soap on the dry skin. Of course, the skin is always helped by ordinary washing. It should be rubbed well—for instance, with loofah; a wet towel is nearly as good. By the way, when one is abroad and cannot get a bath, a wet towel rubbed all over the body is almost as good. The color even of the underclothing is said to have an effect upon the skin: red is thought to be warming and exciting; blue cooling and quieting. Color affects not only the eyes but also the surface of the body.

A helpful exercise is to twist the body. Stand with the heels together and with the hands on the hips; then, keeping the feet rigid, twist the shoulders round upon the hips as upon a pivot. This is a fine exercise for many games, such as golf, cricket and lawn tennis. You may vary the exercise by keeping the top part of the body rigid and moving the lower part of the body with a twisting movement.

Food that Stimulates the Brain

We have now mentioned some of the most important organs: the lungs and chest, the heart, the stomach and the kidneys. We now come to the brain. Any exercise may help the brain by purifying the blood, so that all the above exercises will be beneficial to it. The blood circulates everywhere, and no one part can be benefited without every other part being benefited also.

I believe that food affects the brain more than anything else does. Of course, we need phosphates. It seems that the phosphates from wheat and other sources have an equal value with the phosphates from fish. This has been my personal experience. But, far more important than phosphates, which are so easy to get (for example, in Graham bread), is the use of pure proteid. Its importance has scarcely been realized.

The proteid must be pure and, if possible, free from stimulants. It is remarkable that, if we can feed the rest of the body, the brain seems to be able to feed itself. Apparently the brain is the last part of us to stop working. If we eat nothing, we use up, first, our fat, then our cells and tissues. Everything has to give up its energy to the brain, as if the brain were the king of the city, and all the other inhabitants had to starve, if necessary, so that the king might be fed.

Another help for the brain is the use of cold water for the feet. It will draw the blood away from the brain itself. Walking barefoot on wet grass gives one of the most refreshing feelings that I know. Treading water in bath or basin is almost as good. Alternate hot and cold baths for the feet, or warm and cool baths, are an excellent cure for cold feet, and the same applied to the hands may serve as a cure for cold hands. And here I may mention a very simple way of keeping warm in cold weather. After you have had your bath and have dried yourself, wet yourself again before you put on your clothes. You will not catch cold if you do a few exercises afterward, but you will get a wonderful glow and harden yourself against catching a cold at all.

It may be convenient to mention, while we are on the subject of baths, a few rules for cold-water bathing. Do not use cold water until you are warm. Warm yourself, before you use cold water, by warm water or exercise or massage. The second rule is always to use cold (or at least cool) water after using hot or warm water, unless you have had a very, very hot bath; that is the sole exception, I believe. After a very, very hot bath you do not need cold water. The third rule is to get warm *after* using cold water as well as before using it; you can get warm by exercise or massage.

Coming back to baths that help the brain: one of them is the cold or cool bath for the head. Lie down on your back and let the back of your head rest in a basin partly filled with cool water. This can last two, or three, or even fifteen minutes. Cold water poured down the spine is one of the best of tonics.

Packs and rubbings are invaluable. They are liberally used in the nature-cure establishments in England, Austria, Germany and America. Partial packs are the best. For example, you have a cold. When you go to bed you can take a towel or a piece of material of a similar kind. Wet it thoroughly in cold water; wring it out; put it round your waist, not too tightly, yet not too loosely; over this, and overlapping it on both sides, put two or three thicknesses of flannel; tie the whole thing up safely. You will soon get a most delightful feeling of comfort after the first cold shock, and sleep will be induced. In the morning, or if you wake up at night, take off the two bandages, wash the place well, dry it carefully, and rub it.

Sleep is invaluable for the brain, and one help toward sleep is massage of the head. The head can easily be massaged either by the hand or by the massage-roller. The motion should be up the forehead from above the eyes.

Kicking is another good exercise for the brain, and a good time for kicking is the early morning, as soon as you get up. If you are tired with work, stand and kick about for half a minute.

Early rising, followed by the alternate walk and run, which is less exhausting than a continued run, is of course magnificent for the health all round.

Economy as a Help to Health

It seems strange to speak of economy as a help to health, and yet it is. Though it may not bring actual joy, it may do the next best thing—it may prevent worry, and thus prevent the bad effects of worry upon the blood, digestion, etc. You can economize in clothing by wearing few clothes. Those who wear few clothes are less liable to catch cold than those who wrap themselves up so carefully; and the washable clothes are often the cheapest. But the best means toward economy is the diet. It is curious that I should have found, after a very wide experience, that the very best foods for health, work and training are also the very cheapest and the easiest to regulate. The basis of my own food supply is milk-proteid, which is free from germs of typhoid, etc. It is not stimulating, as meat is, and is very, very rich in blood-forming elements.

People should eat slowly. Fast eating is a terrible curse in America; and, if you wish to eat slowly, you must begin by masticating consciously. Soon the slow mastication will develop into a habit even when you go out to luncheon downtown! That is the supreme test. You must concentrate your will, your whole energy, on the subject of mastication, and bite your food, let us say, thirty times for the mouthful.

Practice concentration of will in all things; that is also a great source of health. When you brush your hair, think of that, and that only: let your mind, as it were, move into the muscles which you are using. When you have a bath, think of that, and that only. When you play a game, you think of the game; when you work, you think of the work; and you should extend this experience to almost all things in life. When you go through some of the commonest acts you should think of them; put your whole soul into them. Of course, this can be carried too far; but the commonest fault is never to try it at all.

The Helpful Practice of Image-Making

Another help for the mind, and therefore for the health, is to practice image-forming in the mind. When you read, form mental pictures of some one doing something—only, of course, what you read must be pure and ennobling. How little we try to supplement and correct our character by image-forming. Yet, after all, a man's acts must largely depend upon the images which have been formed in his mind. Should not a coward study the images of brave men and get them into his mind as an everlasting possession? Should not the impure study the figures of purity? Should not the restless and anxious study the figures of restfulness and peacefulness till they get these figures into their minds and can imitate them? There is not the slightest doubt that we can fill our minds with certain images, and afterward recall these at will, and, with these, recall the state of mind which they represent. We must have the power of bringing up before our minds any given picture. In order to aid this power, so little developed as we grow older, we should try to draw from memory; then correct the drawing, and draw again. This is good practice for odd moments.

The most important image for the American mind is that of relaxation. We must practice getting ourselves into a position of relaxation even when there is no need for such a position, just as we practice for a game long before the competition itself. Let a person stand with bent legs and with a smile on the face and with arms and hands and fingers hanging down limp: let him remain thus for a few minutes each day when he feels fresh, happy and restful; then, when he feels tired or unhappy or restless he can resort to this position, and a feeling of contentment and repose will follow, "as the night the day."

Medical science has been wont to exaggerate the importance of internal remedies, but these are not to be neglected. Of these the greatest is water. If one is well, cool water may be best, and, anyhow, the times for drinking water are the early morning and the late evening—that is, just after and just before sleeping. If the blood is impure, the early morning water may have in it a little table salt. After this, there should be exercise before the meal. Again, if the blood is impure, hot water, the last thing at night or the first thing in the morning, may be the best. Here, again, one should not eat near the time when one drinks water.

One of the best forms of water is in fruit—for instance, apples; for here the water is soft and pure. Other fruits, vegetables, etc., have their various uses. Among these, onions and lemons may be mentioned. But the apple is the prince of fruits, partly because it has valuable salts, and also fibre, which our systems need.

What else shall we take besides pure water in some form or other? Is there any drug which is valuable? There are some who take salicylate of soda the last thing at night. This breaks up the uric acid in the blood. There are others who take aromatic spirits of ammonia, especially in some effervescent water. There are others who take bran-tea, which is good for the brain, or oat-tea, or tea made from almost any sort of fruit—for example, apple tea or black currant tea; but for a person in perfect health water is generally sufficient.

HOW VACCINATION PROTECTS US AGAINST SMALLPOX

Laboratory for the study of disease-producing germs

By Joseph McFarland M. D.

Professor of Pathology
Medico-Chirurgical College
Philadelphia

THE recent outbreak of smallpox in our country has aroused unusual activity among the health authorities in securing for us the advantages of vaccination. This has been followed by a revival of efforts among persons who, though often actuated by sincere motives, are sometimes influenced by personal prejudices, and in nearly all cases by lack of information, to destroy confidence in this greatest of all prophylactic measures. This sentiment is almost entirely confined to the laity.

A survey of the conditions existing in the Middle Ages, and indeed in our own times to within a half-century ago, reveals a state of affairs almost incredible. Smallpox existed in nearly every civilized community almost all the time, and broke out in occasional epidemics by which a great part of the population of a city or village was destroyed. Every one had or expected to have smallpox, and faces unmarked by it were rare. What a change one half-century has made! At the present time smallpox is a rare disease in Europe and America, though in Oriental countries it is as common to-day as it formerly was in Europe; and there is no reason to believe it would not be so common as formerly in our own country had not vaccination become universally approved and been made more or less obligatory.

It is incontrovertible that in countries in which vaccination is practiced smallpox is not common; in countries in which it is widely practiced it is rare, and in that country in which it is universally practiced, Germany, it scarcely exists. The opponents of vaccination attribute the reduction in the smallpox mortality in civilized countries to the generally improved sanitary conditions. This theory is not borne out by fact. Smallpox may occur, under the very best sanitary conditions, in communities not protected by vaccination. In Germany, where the lower class live to-day under conditions almost identical with those of one hundred years ago, smallpox does not exist. Furthermore, nearly all of those persons who have suffered from smallpox during the present epidemic have not been properly, successfully or sufficiently vaccinated.

Immunity and What It Is

The protection which vaccination affords depends upon a condition, observed in nearly all of the infectious diseases, known as immunity. Immunity means *power to resist disease*. Some animals are immune by nature, sometimes against one, sometimes against many diseases, this being known as natural immunity. Dogs, for example, are immune against smallpox; and its cause, therefore, is unable to affect them. We do not know through what means the tissues of the dog are able to protect themselves against the smallpox germ. Man, horses, mice and guinea-pigs are susceptible to tetanus or lockjaw, and when the microörganism of lockjaw enters one of them through some wound, it meets with no hindrance, is able to grow and produce its specific poison which, acting upon the nerve centres of the brain and spinal cord, produces violent muscular spasms, which cause death. Fowls of various kinds are immune against tetanus; and even if the germs of the disease are intentionally introduced into their bodies they are able to resist these organisms and show no disease from their presence. Human beings, guinea-pigs and various other animals are susceptible to diphtheria, but rats are naturally immune, and though enough diphtheria poison to kill a human being be introduced into a rat, it produces no disease. Among susceptible animals, we find occasional individuals resisting disease better than others. Thus, among human beings certain infectious diseases occur chiefly in childhood and are known as children's diseases—adults, through some change that takes place in their vital activities, becoming immune. Again, it is found that during an epidemic of any infectious disease, some persons resist the disease because of an individual immunity that they possess.

Immunity, not natural, may be acquired in various ways. Thus, by having had certain diseases we become immune against future attacks. This is *acquired immunity*. Every one knows how common it is for children to suffer from second attacks of measles, chicken-pox, scarlet fever and mumps. Among adults second attacks of typhoid fever are rare and second attacks of yellow fever almost unknown. In the course of these diseases, therefore, the body is, in some way, changed so that it remains subsequently protected, or, to use the technical expression, has an *acquired immunity*.

Editor's Note—A second paper on this subject, answering the objections to vaccination as a preventive measure, will appear next week.

A few diseases leave no immunity; thus, diphtheria may occur repeatedly. A few diseases confer no immunity, but leave the patient predisposed to future attacks, rheumatism being a type of this class. Acquired immunity is of variable duration: after yellow fever and smallpox it is almost permanent; measles leaves a much less permanent immunity, and nearly all of us count among our acquaintance children who have had two attacks; diphtheria leaves almost no immunity, and after the lapse of a few weeks the protection afforded by an attack of the disease may disappear.

Immunity Artificially Produced

Laboratory experiments show that immunity can be conferred by a variety of artificial means, among which may be mentioned the production of a mild form of disease by the inoculation of the body with what are called attenuated germs. Thus, the anti-cholera vaccination which has been tried with good results in India, and the anti-anthrax vaccinations by which thousands of cattle are every year saved from death from splenic fever, are accomplished by the introduction, into the bodies of the men and animals to be protected, of attenuated, living organisms of the respective diseases. Bacteria can be attenuated by exposure to heat or injurious chemical agents, and then produce a mild infection more or less closely resembling the original disease. Without doing any serious harm to the individual, they change his constitution precisely in the same manner as an attack of the disease would do and confer upon him an immunity identical with that resulting from an attack of the disease. To accomplish the production of this artificial immunity it may not be necessary to introduce live bacteria at all, the introduction of their products frequently sufficing to confer immunity upon the individual. This is well illustrated in the vaccination against plague, suggested by Haffkine, who found that when a small quantity of a very poisonous dead culture of the plague bacillus is introduced into the body, it produces a mild illness, succeeded for a number of weeks by immunity.

Vaccination, or vaccination against smallpox, as we must now specify it, since various other forms of vaccination have been mentioned, brings about a form of immunity similar to some of the forms already mentioned. It confers upon the vaccinated individual a resistance or immunity against smallpox which depends upon the occurrence of vaccinia, a disease related to smallpox and possibly at one time identical with it, but differing from it in its mildness, its local manifestations and its lack of contagiousness.

Before anything was known about vaccination against smallpox, and from unknown antiquity, a form of prophylaxis, or disease prevention, was practiced in China and other of the Oriental countries. The result was the occurrence of an attack of smallpox which sometimes proved fatal, though usually it was very mild.

The practice of inoculation or variolation, was introduced into Western Europe from Turkey, in 1718, by Lady Montagu. The history of vaccination is so well known that but a brief mention of it is necessary. When smallpox was an everyday disease domestic animals occasionally suffered from eruptive, epidemic diseases, which bore a certain resemblance to it. Among these may be cited vaccinia of the cow and ovinia of the sheep.

Edward Jenner and His Discovery

A brief digression must now be made to call attention to the fact that the microörganisms of disease produce different manifestations in different animals, and that in those cases in which we can successfully inoculate the diseases of man into the domestic animals, the maladies from which they suffer bear but a partial resemblance to the diseases as we know them in man. Thus, though in man smallpox takes the form of a general febrile affection with an eruption all over the skin, the cow when invaded by the same disease germs suffers from a pustular eruption limited to the udder and teats. From its location and the contact with the fingers of milkers it was not an uncommon accident that this modified disease should be communicated to the hands of the milkmaids and dairymen. Curiously enough, those who suffered from this modified and local affection acquired from the cow were found by experience to be immune against smallpox. A number of physicians both in Germany and in England confirmed this observation and early recorded it, but it remained for the genius of Edward Jenner to suggest, in 1798, a practical and systematic use of it. Having learned the particulars known to the dairymen and milkmaids, Jenner made an experimental inoculation upon a young lad who had not had the smallpox, inoculating him on the arm with the disease contracted from the udder of a cow. He watched the progress of the resulting lesion through its various stages, and after the boy's complete recovery inoculated him with smallpox and found him entirely immune. This led to a prolonged series of investigations and experimental inoculations on the part of Jenner, whose publications and contributions to various learned societies shortly attracted widespread attention and interest. It is entirely through the efforts of Jenner that the vaccination against smallpox has become a practical and valuable measure.

From experiments which have been recently made there can be no doubt of the close relationship which exists between vaccinia, the disease of the cow, and variola, the smallpox of man. The dissimilarity of the diseases depends upon the difference between the constitution of the cow and the human being. It is the same kind of difference that permits certain animals to be susceptible, other animals to be occasionally susceptible, and still other animals to be immune against a disease. The cow does not acquire smallpox, but its modified form called cowpox. The cow does not suffer from the general disease, variola, but from the local disease, vaccinia. In what way the constitution of the cow determines that the disease shall be local instead of general cannot at present be explained. The difference in the behavior of the organism in the man and in the cow depends upon the difference in environment. In the unfavorable environment of the cow's tissues the smallpox germs become changed, crippled or "attenuated" as it is called, and are thus rendered less able to grow in man than they originally were, so that when they reënter man, instead of producing smallpox, they produce vaccinia or cowpox. It is cowpox which confers upon him a certain degree of immunity to virulent smallpox germs and enables him to resist any ordinary infection. The immunity which thus results from vaccination is subject to the usual variations—that is to say, in some cases it is almost permanent, in other cases it is of prolonged, in still other cases of short duration. The duration varies according to conditions that can be neither regulated nor predetermined, but rest entirely upon the peculiarity of the individual. It is on this account that revaccination is necessary, for experience has shown that the immunity frequently wanes in the course of five or seven years, so that a vaccination performed in infancy may cease to be useful about the time a child is ready to go to school. A second vaccination usually confers an immunity that persists throughout life, though perhaps for safety it is better to have a third operation in early adult life, and, as the permanence of immunity is uncertain, those who have not been successfully vaccinated for years should have the operation repeated whenever a serious epidemic occurs.

Why Vaccination is Sometimes Unsuccessful

Interesting variations may be observed. Some persons seem to possess a natural immunity to vaccinia, and though often repeated, vaccination upon them never "takes." It is commonly supposed that such persons are also immune to smallpox, though this is not necessarily true, as the virulence of the unmodified smallpox germs is so much greater than that of the vaccinia germs that they may successfully infect, though the latter fail. In other cases the duration of the immunity following the primary or original vaccination lasts so many years that it may be late in life before vaccination can be successfully repeated. In still other cases the duration of immunity may be so short that a "take" results almost as often as the vaccination is performed and the individual is afforded very little protection by it. Such cases are, however, exceptional, and the average individual, having been successfully vaccinated in infancy and again in childhood, thereafter remains immune to smallpox for many years. The exceptions not being understood by the laity, and even by some of the medical profession, furnish the grounds for controversy concerning the value of vaccination. To the thoughtful individual vaccination is not so much a protection to the individual as to the community, so that though any vaccinated individual may be an exception to the rule, in not being immune to smallpox, in a thoroughly vaccinated community so few such exceptions really occur that his chance of accidental exposure to the disease is reduced to a minimum.

"WHEN DOCTORS DISAGREE."

MEDICINE MAN. — There ought to be a law passed to squelch you humbugs!
MENTAL HEALER. — I'm no more a humbug than you are.   Neither of us is infallible; but I do far less harm than you do!

The Danger of Door-knobs

AN English medical authority has lately published an emphatic protest against the use of door-knobs, which, he asserts, are active agents in the spread of disease. Unless they are kept immaculately clean, it is claimed, they should be abolished in favor of foot levers. The danger is especially marked in the case of the door-handles of railway trains. One company has adopted a short handle, to turn which requires only a small effort, owing to the operation of a lever inside the lock. "The lock may be easily released by a slight pressure of the thumb and the forefinger, and only a slight soiling of the fingers is involved. Most railway-carriage door-handles, however, are large and clumsy, requiring a complete grip with the whole hand before any effect upon the lock can be obtained. In such a case the fouling of the hand is complete. Surely such a disagreeable system of opening the doors of railway carriages could be replaced by some much less objectionable method. Dirt is, of course, largely inseparable from the railway train, but we think that this particular and offensive evidence of it might easily be minimized. At all events, no contrivance for the purpose could be better adapted to soil the hands of the passenger than the handles in use at the present time by most of our railway companies."

The Greatest Destroyer of Life

IN EVERY country in Europe except one consumption kills more people than any other disease. The one exception is England, where out of every 10,000 deaths, 1100 are caused by consumption and 1150 by bronchitis. In France consumption kills twenty-five per cent. more people than any other disease, and, excepting pneumonia and typhoid fever, nearly sixty per cent. more than any other. In Germany out of 10,000 deaths 1270 are caused by consumption, while the next highest is typhoid fever with 450. In Russia out of 10,000 deaths consumption causes 1960. According to the last census in the United States, out of 872,944 deaths for 1890, consumption caused 102,199, or twenty-five per cent. more than pneumonia, which came next with 76,496.

No statistics of war have such awful meaning as these frightful figures. For years consumption has killed more people than all the conflicts of nations; more than any of the pestilences, more than any of the diseases which attack and destroy human life. And it was not until the present generation began that any doctor dared to assert that consumption could be cured. Certainly in the latter half of this century no profession has made such magnificent strides, such splendid discoveries, or exhibited such skill, self-sacrifice and persistence as the physicians'.

Dr. Alfred Meyer, of New York, in a recent article in the Medical Record, gives a most interesting account of a sanitarium established by the State of Massachusetts for the cure of consumptives. In 1895 the Legislature appointed a Board of five trustees and appropriated $150,000. A site was chosen at Rutland, 1160 feet above the sea, and sheltered by a hill one hundred feet higher. The hospital grounds included two hundred acres of land. The institution was opened in 1898. In the first six months of its existence there were 224 patients, a very large number of whom were improved by an average stay of four months only. At present there are between 150 and 200 patients, male and female. These patients, or the counties sending them, pay five dollars each the week. They live an out-of-door life in the higher altitude, build their winter camps, and manage to have a pretty good time. The temperature of the wards when they sleep indoors is seldom above forty degrees Fahrenheit all winter. According to Doctor Meyer, the consumptive under these circumstances has from twenty-five to thirty-five more chances of getting well than he would have had.

In the New York Legislature this year a bill will be introduced to appropriate $200,000 for the establishment of a similar sanitarium in the Adirondacks. The prediction is made that there will come a time when the States will have their consumptive hospitals just as they do their asylums for the insane, and with results that will be an enormous gain in public health. But private philanthropy is doing even more while the States hesitate to act. In nearly every country of Europe there are institutions of this kind for the rich and the poor, especially in Germany and France, and they are very rapidly increasing.

Japan was one of the first to establish such an enterprise, and it was under the patronage of the Empress. An Italian Countess has recently given to the Italian Hygienic Society all her wealth for a sanitarium for consumptives. In nearly every city of this country there are movements on hand, and in most of them the homes are already in operation. Certainly there could be no nobler way in which the public spirit and generosity of the people could be shown, for it saves human despair, makes life better, brighter and happier, and becomes a source of truest economy in the real wealth and welfare of the world. —LYNN ROBY MEEKINS.

The Home of the Microbes

IF ST. PAUL could have foreseen the time when 96,000,000 microbes would be found on a single greenback he would have been more than ever convinced that the love of money is the root of all evil. The health authorities throughout the country are becoming aroused to the dangers of disease-carrying currency, and Health Commissioner Darlington, of New York, proposes that every piece of money in circulation shall be frequently disinfected. At the same time Congress is asked to pass an act compelling the Government to destroy all the bills it takes in and pay out none but new ones.

Of course, nothing ought to be allowed to stand in the way of health, but it is worth while to remember that, under this arrangement, bills of small denominations would be an extremely expensive luxury for our Uncle Samuel. It costs the Government a little over a cent and two-thirds to print, issue and redeem a note, regardless of its size. That is over one and two-thirds per cent. of the value of a dollar bill. If the notes were purely fiat—issued with nothing but the public credit behind them—the Government would, in effect, be borrowing at three and one-third per cent. if they were redeemed twice a year, six and two-thirds per cent. if they were redeemed quarterly, and twenty per cent. if they were renewed monthly. But, in addition, it loses the interest on a huge gold reserve and an enormous mass of silver bullion, most of the small bills being silver certificates.

The cost of printing and handling is insignificant in proportion to the value of large bills, but it is very heavy in proportion to that of small ones. The Bank of England, which never pays out an old note, issues no notes for less than twenty-five dollars. In the number of pieces our bills above that figure are not worth counting.

What we really need is a handy coin to take the place of the one-dollar and two-dollar bills. The silver dollar is too clumsy.

If somebody will show us how to make a dollar of about the size and weight of a quarter, durable, distinctive in appearance and not easily counterfeited, we can retire all our small paper currency, and several trillion microbes will be out of a job.

The Danger of Early Rising.

Yet another venerable superstition has met its doom at the hands of the irrepressible "scientist," says the London World. Until now people have been content to accept, if not to act upon, the theory that early rising—in conjunction, of course, with a correspondingly early habit of going to bed—is conducive not only to wealth and wisdom, but also to health. Indeed, a familiar rhymed adage protests as much in so many words. But, like many another primitive belief, it has been ruthlessly shattered by the scientific iconoclasts, one of whom now claims to have discovered that people who get up early go mad much more readily than others. In support of his theory he points to the undoubted prevalence of insanity among those engaged in agricultural pursuits. Though it is sad to see a time-honored doctrine thus exploded, one is disposed to favor the new opinion at the expense of the old. In any case, there can be no harm in being on the safe side, and, after all, it is so easy not to get up early.

Too High a Price for Life

THERE is no reason to doubt that, by following any one of a dozen of the current recipes for long life, one could keep himself on earth a hundred years or a hundred and fifty. But in each and every recipe there is this flaw—it would take such an interminable deal of bother to follow it. One would have to go about the world thermometer and food-scales in hand, wholly centred in one's self, with no time for wife or children or friends. As for fun, that would be out of the question.

There isn't anything, not even life, for which one could not pay more than it was worth. And the scientifically correct regimen would mean not a century or a century and a half of life, but a dreary waste of centuries—long years of death in life.

Until some more attractive plan for centenarianism is found the most of us will prefer to take the chances and think at least part of the time of something else besides microbes.

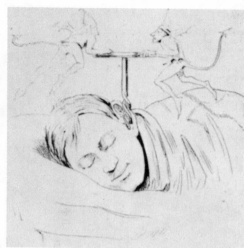
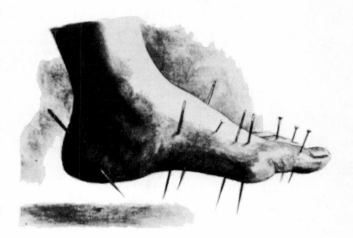

Funny Fads in Food

SCARCELY a year runs its course without contributing to the great budget of food-fads that has been accumulating ever since the days of the first man who possessed at one and the same time an uncertain digestion, an impressible mind, and the means of pleasing his palate. Had any of the results been of general application the experimenting might have ended, but none seem to have been satisfactory except to the experimenter and his special followers, who formed but a small fraction of the race. Persons that are curious on the subject may read of classes whose only food was meat, others who ate only fish, and some who subsisted solely on vegetable diet, but they will be hopelessly puzzled if they attempt to discover which of the three became preëminent among their fellow-men. Reasoning by analogy, the meat-eaters point with pride to lions and tigers, the most masterful of beasts, yet the vegetarians show that larger frames and better tempers are found in the elephant and hippopotamus, and that larger and stronger than half a dozen lions, tigers, hippopotami and elephants combined is the whale, which subsists solely on fish, and which has a larger head, in proportion to body, than any other animal.

The newest food-fad is that human life can be maintained best by food that itself is living. Like other alleged discoveries, this is not really new, for the supreme dish at a Japanese feast is a live fish, and we Americans, who are not to be outdone by any older race, consume millions of live oysters daily through nine months of every twelve. As to that, who is there that does not delight in eating cherries direct from the tree and berries from the bush? To be consistent, however, the believers in live food should take their wheat and other grain-food green and direct, in the field, and sweeten their meals by chewing green cane and sugar-beets.

One of the most notable exemplars of peculiar dietary custom is an American army officer of good physique, who, in several years of exacting service at an out-of-the-way Western post, subsisted entirely on "canned goods." It was his custom to open cans at haphazard, a single can for each meal; whether the contents were fish, fowl or flesh, vegetables or fruit, he ate that and nothing more, and he lives to tell the tale. But he was always active, physically and mentally, except when asleep, and he breathed fresh air twenty-four hours of every day.

A Good Secret to Know

A MAN went to a nose and throat specialist the other day to have his cold cured. As he was paying a not small sum for the first treatment he said: "How long does it take you to cure a cold?"

"Three weeks," said the specialist.

"And how long would it take me to get well if I didn't come to you?" asked the alarmed patient.

"Twenty-one days," said the specialist.

And it wasn't until the patient was half-way home that he suddenly stopped and wondered whether he ought to laugh or get angry. He finally decided that perhaps the secret he had learned was worth the price he had paid for it. It's a good secret to know.

Poisoned "Food"

THE makers of poison for adulterating food and the users of those poisons in adulterating food were powerful enough with the national machines of both political parties to prevent Congress from enacting a law protecting the people. But out in South Dakota their lobby was defeated. The legislature of that State has passed, and Governor Elrod has signed, a bill which, so far as can be judged from reading it, is a model of pure-food legislation. If the newly-created Food and Dairy Commissioner does his duty, the people of South Dakota will know what they are eating and drinking, and poisoners for dividends will not do business in that State.

If a citizen of the United States dies from eating a poisoned "food," why should not the president of the corporation of poisoners for dividends that manufacture that "food" be arrested, tried and hanged, like any other poisoner? Why should he be exempt because he doesn't happen personally to know his victim?

Less Work for the Doctors

FAR more important and encouraging as "signs of the times" than any developments in politics or industry are the advertisements of physical culture systems and health foods and other means for promoting a sound body. The enormous increase in this kind of advertising within the past five years means a sudden enormous increase in intelligent public interest in health. And that means oncoming generations with purer, stronger blood and therefore with clearer, more active, more courageous brains. And that, in turn, means that all the problems of living, personal, social, political, will be met and taken care of.

Some one once said that the peoples of Asia were enslaved because they did not know how to say " No." But back of this vacillation lay poor health—the universal Asiatic complaint, due to a universal neglect of health, mitigated though it was by the sanitary regulations imposed under the guise of religious ordinances. No physically robust people was ever enslaved or was ever retrogressive. The first warning of the downfall of the Roman Empire before the hardier Northern races was the wretched throngs of weaklings in the pestilence-haunted cities of the Mediterranean. Heretofore in the world's history civilization has meant decay, because it has meant taking a nation's best from the healthful open-air toil of the country and decaying and degenerating it in noisome cities where the very ideals of happiness involved destruction of health.

And our civilization of overabundant food, of exercise-ending street cars, and of all manner of muscle-saving and therefore muscle-decaying machinery would have meant speedy ruin to us of the modern world had it not been for the progress of sanitary science and of interest in things sanitary.

The first fruit of this progress has been the doctrine of the relative importance of drugs and the passing of the "family doctor"—two developments that are so rapid that we hardly appreciate them as yet. The other day Sir William Treves, the eminent English surgeon, announced what England seemed to regard as the amazing discovery that pain is not an evil, but a good—a friendly sentinel rousing the garrison to repel the invader, disease.

It is a grand advance that we have made in discovering that the body does not wish to get sick, does not accidentally get sick, but on the contrary wishes to stay well, and will stay well if its owner is not ignorant or reckless. This discovery will make two great changes in our system of education.

The first will be the teaching of breathing. To breathe properly means health, long life, capacity for work. Yet to-day how many people know how to breathe, have learned how to supplement Nature's somewhat clumsy device for carrying on the breathing function automatically? How many people, of the millions who are anxious that their children should learn spelling and reading and ciphering and manners, give a thought to their children's learning to breathe?

The second great educational change will be in the matter of diet. In this country and in nearly all of Europe except France we are still eating the things our forefathers managed to digest when they were toiling and sweating terribly in the open air.

Nature made the appetite for food keen because she had to deal with conditions in which the food supply was short and hard to reach, and, if the appetite had not been keen, the animal would have easily given over the struggle. We ignore the changed conditions and use Nature's no longer necessary bait as an excuse for stuffing ourselves three times a day and eating between meals. If it weren't that sanitation is so much better nowadays, and cooking also, the consequences would be even severer than they are. As it is, we suffer a great deal from "overwork" and "nervous prostration," don't we?

It is pleasant to eat to satiation. It is comfortable to take no exercise and to breathe lazily in one corner of the lungs. But it isn't the way to be long-lived and healthy. And it is the way to let the other fellow who breathes and exercises and eats properly distance us. Hence the growth of interest in health and the decline of interest in drugs and doctors.

I WANT to personally invite each of the 600,000 readers of THE SATURDAY EVENING POST to join "The 'FORCE' Society." It already has more than two million members — besides myself. Its object will be clear to you when you read the Creed below.

The membership is limited strictly to those who want to be happier than they are.

Each member is entitled to an "M. F. S." after his name — and to enroll other members if he thinks enough of them.

The Creed is simple — I wrote it myself.

❧ *I believe that to be happy is all I want.*

❧ *I believe that I was never unhappy until I thought I was, and that, therefore, I can never be happy until I think I am.*

❧ *I believe there's no use trying to think happiness with my mind when my stomach is arguing the question with my body.*

❧ *I believe that if I ate the food my stomach liked the best there wouldn't be any question to argue.*

❧ *I believe, therefore, that before I think about being happy I've got to settle this food problem.*

That's all there is to the Creed.

You see, it stops rather abruptly, because that's where you join the Society, and when you've joined, you *have* settled the food problem.

I know of but one food that makes the Creed livable.

It is the food that made me sunny.

The secret of the Society's rapid growth is that this sunny food I make has the quality in it that makes those who eat it tell of its sunniness to lots of others — the first thing.

From the very beginning "FORCE" was a success. Its sales were soon greater than those of all other foods. Then the ordinary competition of advertising and good salesmanship gave way to an underhand method of attack, and one that was very hard to meet.

A rumor was circulated that "FORCE" contained some harmful ingredient. It gained ground, evidently because some people made it their duty to see that it was circulated.

I first tried to meet this malicious report quietly by the publication of analyses by chemists of the highest standing. Then I decided that the only way to kill a rumor was to fight it in the open.

I spent fifty thousand dollars in advertising throughout the whole country my offer of a reward of $5000.00 each to any man, woman or child, to any professional chemist or private citizen, to any grocer or his customer, who could prove that there was anything in any package of "FORCE" bought in the open market but wheat, barley-malt and salt.

This offer has been published in nearly every newspaper in the United States. I will keep on publishing it until everyone knows what I know — *that "FORCE" is synonymous with absolute purity.*

The point is, that I am not simply offering proof that there is no harmful substance in "FORCE." I am proving that *there is no substance in it that ought not to be there!*

The World's New Motto

The two words "Be Sunny" shall be my text hereafter. I am going to show the members of The "FORCE" Society that sunniness is more "worth while" than anything else ; that just as soon as the body is freed from unnecessary drags upon it one begins to feel better — and so does everyone else in one's neighborhood ; that most of us are bound down by wrong or badly chosen foods, and that "FORCE" is a good food for everybody every day, but particularly *for you, today !*

I am also going to show you that your thoughts have a good deal to do with your health and your happiness — more than you think for.

And I want to show you a new way of thinking that is as good for your happiness as "FORCE" is for your health. To do this I have had to add a new word to the language — "FORCE-thought." It's the quality which marks the members The "FORCE" Society.

Force-thought is something like fore-thought, only it begins sooner and goes further.

Force-thought is the kind of thinking that when put into action accomplishes things — makes them easier.

It is the sort of thinking that nets a profit to the thinker.

It recognizes that in order to think for profit, — to think hard and clearly with one's mind — one must begin with one's body and eat the sort of food that nourishes the body without burdening the stomach and supplies the brain with the food it needs to think with.

The one food which best helps clear, concentrated thinking is "FORCE."

The first principle of Force-thought, therefore, is eating "FORCE."

But there's more to it — which I haven't time to tell you this week.

"The Gentle Art of Using Force"

Meanwhile, the best way to join The "FORCE" Society is to send for a copy of my new book.

It treats of two subjects : how to serve "FORCE" in many ways, and how to be sunny — always.

I think the recipe for being sunny is the best one in the book.

It's the first book I've ever written, so I have had it lithographed in six colors, and think it will prove one of the most popular books of the year, for I have already had to publish one million copies to supply the demand.

I will mail you one on receipt of a 2-cent stamp.

Yours truly,

Sunny Jim

(To be continued.)

"Publick Occurrences"

PEOPLE die faster in cities than in the country, yet in every part of the world people are flocking to the cities more and more every year. In New York there are, on the general average, fourteen persons in each dwelling-house, while the proportion of population to the square mile for the United States is only about twenty-two. There are tenements in that city that contain more men, women and children than an ordinary town which calls itself a city. Other centres are not so crowded, but the jam is increasing constantly, and in some instances where little houses are spread over a large area the conditions are worse, because the health officers reach them less effectively than if they were congregated in larger structures.

Add to all this thronging, all this congestion, the bald, fateful fact that nine out of ten of the people have taken little or no interest in sanitation, and have been disposed to resent the advice and visits of the health authorities.

But now the health department is in most cities considered a vital and necessary branch of municipal government, second in importance to none other.

Its modern development has taken place within the past quarter of a century, and its finest growth within the past decade. Coming closer, the past five years have been notable in achievements. What is the result of all this? Simply that in the half century the average of human life in this country has been lengthened about three years.

Multiply our 75,000,000 population by three and you get a gain of 225,000,000 years. Well, figure out the rest for yourself. If you put it in dollars even Mr. Rockefeller and Mr. Morgan would seem poor.

How Lives are Saved

It has been the keeping of the little white hearse in the stable more than it used to stay there that has done more than anything else to bring up the average of life. "Save the children!" is the cry of modern humanity and of the modern health department.

Here is an illustration—one of many which could be cited: Last summer the Health Department of Rochester, New York—we take one of the cities of the second class so as to make the illustration the more impressive —established in the most crowded parts of the city five stations where the purest milk could be obtained for infants, each station being in charge of a trained nurse. Doctor Goler, the Health Commissioner, states that a thousand lives were saved.

In New York City a generous merchant has been supplying pure milk to the poor for several years, and in every instance the mortality in the sections where the stations were located was lowered.

"There is nothing so cheap as human life" has long been the declaration of the pessimist, and many good people have accepted it, if not entirely at least in part. If a machine is broken, they say, it takes money to repair or to replace it, and the lost time of the machine is valuable; but if a workman is maimed or killed there is another workman ready to step into his place and the mill grinds on.

But this is not the enlightened or the true view; it is not the modern creed. Every child born has its financial weight. We estimate every immigrant to be worth $1000 to the country, and surely our own babies are as valuable. The duty, then, as well as the problem, is not only to save the life of the tot but to bring it up under such conditions and with such encouragements and protection as will enable it to get a strong hold on life and to become one of the country's wage earners and wealth builders.

The Importance of Milk

In all this milk plays a leading part, and milk is very much like the little nursery girl who was good when she was good and horrid when she was bad. In Baltimore, a few years ago, the Health Department suddenly ordered inspectors to investigate the milk supply, and for a day or two the sewers ran white. The details were sickening, and yet the people had been drinking the impurities for years. Almost every city has had an experience of a similar sort, and even now no city in the country gives sufficient attention to its milk supply.

Just what the inspection of milk and the watching of milk dealers means is instructively shown in a recent incident in Buffalo.

Health Commissioner Wende invented a system by which he was able to trace promptly the source of bad or infected milk. Six cases of scarlet fever broke out in one section of the city. The system was put into operation, and in a few hours the cause of the disease was located in a certain milk peddler's wagon, and the source of contagion was at once cut off.

If the large centres of population could have no milk except pure milk served thousands of lives would be saved or prolonged.

The Rush for Fresh Air

But even children cannot live by milk alone. There must be other things, pure water and fresh air among them. Of all the great cities of the United States, Philadelphia has the worst water, and the result is that its people run constant risks of typhoid and other diseases.

Other cities are doing better, and there is no doubt that, taken together, the water supplies of the cities are being improved. Even Philadelphia is spending millions for filtration plants to separate the solid ingredients of the Schuylkill River from the fluid.

But the great thing in summer philanthropy is fresh air. First come the public parks. There are 159 cities in this country that have over 25,000 inhabitants. Of these 122 have public parks. In some parks are fine playhouses for children, erected at a cost of thousands of dollars; in one or more there are nurseries where babies may be kept.

Then we begin to count the various enterprises outside the park systems and the list is almost endless. Several cities have floating hospitals; others have chartered boats; others give the use of their ice boats for free summer excursions, the expenses in almost every instance being borne by public contributions and gifts of supplies. The assiduous care to keep infection from these heterogeneous crowds, the demand for tickets, the happiness of the mothers and children taken from the darkness and foulness of alleys and by-streets into the beauty and freshness of the open air, make a story that beggars words.

The pity is that after centuries of civilization such things should be necessary, and a worse pity yet is that it seems to be growing more necessary as the world progresses.

In every part of the country are summer homes for the poor women and children. With scarcely an exception they are filled, and the applications are far beyond the accommodations.

You who skip away on the first warm wave seldom pause to think that for every person who can escape from a big city in summer four or five have to remain, and that out of this proportion there are literally thousands in every city who cannot afford to pay twenty-five cents for a day's excursion.

From that fact has arisen a most excellent form of summer philanthropy—the sending of the poor, especially the children, to the country or the seashore. There are various associations for this sort of work, and in many cases the members—including women of wealth and culture—take turns in accompanying their guests and in providing for their wants.

Two Great Health Problems

In this age of problems it is hard to discriminate, but there are two upon which all may agree. Just now they lead.

The first is in regard to consumption. Some one has said that it has "killed more people than all the wars and plagues and scourges of history put together." Doctor Biggs, the New York expert, declares that of every four New Yorkers who die between the ages of fifteen and sixty-five one dies of consumption, that there are 20,000 cases in that city constantly, and that the deaths last year numbered more than 9000. According to a New York newspaper, one specialist asserts that of this country's population 10,000,000 "must inevitably expect to die of consumption."

The other problem is to get the small cities of the United States to awake to the importance of sanitation. Nearly all of them do nothing until threatened by an epidemic, and then the zeal is only temporary. To arouse these communities to the importance of constant watchfulness and of preventive measures will be to increase the average of life for the whole nation.

We have been dazzled by the outburst of wealth in the new century, but these strivings for health are worth all the dollars that have passed through Wall Street.

Keep Young

THIS rapid lowering of the death-rate everywhere means an enormous change in mankind in the near future. A few centuries ago a man's useful years were in the average not more than fifteen. As each generation has to be taught everything over again, is it not astonishing that an average of only fifteen years of real capacity—from twenty-five to forty—should have been able to lift us from savagery? Now the average, at least among the most competent classes, is upward of twenty-five years—for the death-rate is heaviest among the ignorant and incompetent. In fact, taking superior education into account, we have to-day a race that has recently *doubled* its period for assimilating and applying knowledge and wisdom. Think what an effect will be produced when the average man lives in the prime of his powers half a century, or sixty, or seventy years!

Teach the science of health! Encourage the youth to leave off folly for manhood earlier! Encourage the old to avoid stiffness and sadness and regretful reminiscence, and to keep the head and the heart of intelligent, vigorous youth!

Where Germicides Wont Work

THE Germans have found an antitoxin for the "laziness germ." They claim that it will transform any man of sluggish and slothful habit into an energetic person to whom "that tired feeling" is unknown. This is the reduction of the germ theory to its logical absurdity.

Germs are not the only cause of disease. Germs simply multiply in depleted or diseased tissue. True, when these germs have got a good hold they must be overcome before the damaged tissue can be restored. But that restoration is not a work for drugs only but for Nature as well. To get well, the sick person must stop doing the things that made him ill, must "cut out" the inordinate indulgences that at last drove his long-suffering system into revolt.

Germicide or no germicide, beer and fried food will continue to produce sluggards in Germany; and in our own country the rapid-fire lunch and three to six meals a day will continue to make men old at forty and women old at thirty.

Appendicitis and Ping-Pong

DISEASES, no less than games, seem to have their periods of popular favor. And just now appendicitis is the ping-pong of the medical world.

Ten years ago, nine men out of ten didn't know that they had such a thing as an appendix; to-day, the nine men know all about it and go pale whenever they have a stomach-ache on the right side, and the tenth man has lost his. There is an appendicitis club even, with an initiation fee of one appendix—your own, not transferable—and it is not a poor man's club, either. For an appendix, worthless in its proper place, costs anywhere from fifty to a thousand dollars, according to the reputation and conscience of the attending surgeon, when you receive it in alcohol as a guarantee of good faith.

Of course, the popularity of appendicitis is due largely to its being a novelty, though people used to have it, under another name presumably. A story which is going the rounds illuminates the attitude of the public toward the new fad.

It seems that an ambulance brought to one of our hospitals a man who had been picked up in the streets in an unconscious condition. After a hasty examination the house physician decided that the man was suffering from acute appendicitis and ordered him on the operating table.

While he was still unconscious an attendent started to remove the patient's clothes, and the doctor's attention was arrested by this sentence tattooed on his chest:

"If found unconscious, do not operate for appendicitis. Have had it taken out twice."

Some surgeons are more conservative, as is shown by another story, one which is being told of an appendicitis specialist, a man of great skill, who rarely loses a case. Some one was calling on him a while back, and noticed that his pet poodle was moping about disconsolately, ears drooping and tail down.

"What's the matter with that dog, Doctor?" the visitor asked. "He seems sick."

"Well, I guess he is sick. That dog has appendicitis."

"Appendicitis!" exclaimed the visitor. "Then why don't you operate on him?"

"Operate on that dog!" exclaimed the doctor. "Well, I guess not; why, he cost a hundred dollars!"

Still, if you really have it, you would better have it out.

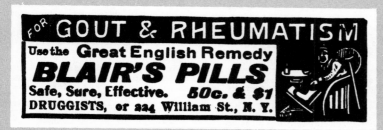

OUR

$18.00 Giant Power Heidelberg Electric Belt

FOR ONLY $18.00 WE OFFER THE GENUINE 80-GAUGE CURRENT HEIDELBERG ALTERNATING, SELF-REGULATING and ADJUSTING ELECTRIC BELT AS THE HIGHEST GRADE, VERY FINEST ELECTRIC BELT EVER MADE, AS THE ONLY SUCCESSFUL ELECTRIC BELT TREATMENT, as the most wonderful relief and cure of all chronic and nervous diseases, all diseases, disorders and weaknesses peculiar to men, NO MATTER FROM WHAT CAUSE OR HOW LONG STANDING.

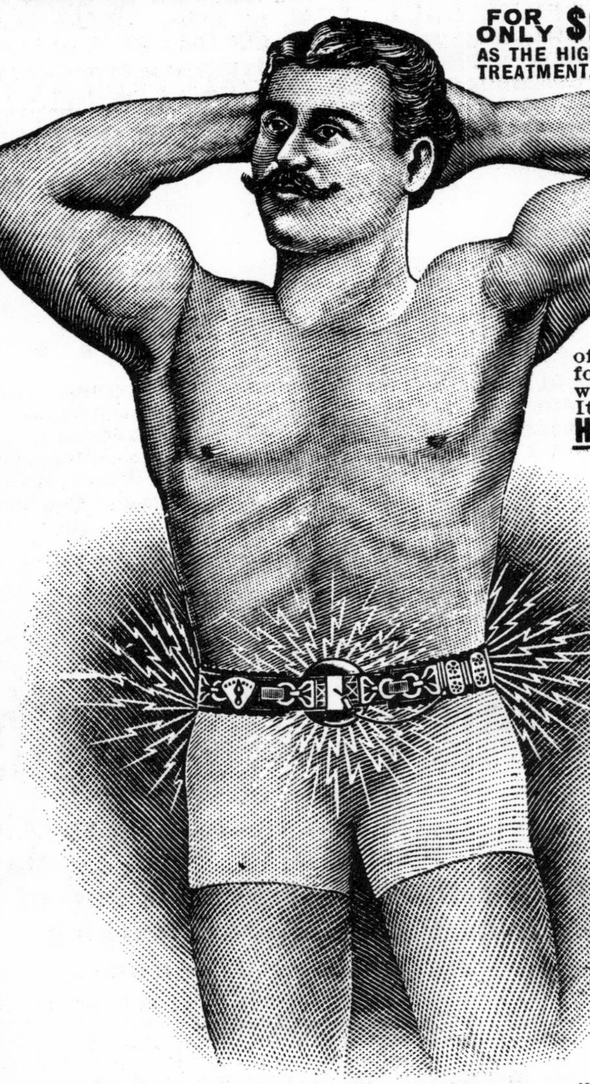

Sent on 10 Days' Free Trial

$18.00 IS OUR LOW PRICE, based on the actual cost to manufacture, for this highest grade electric belt, a superior belt to those usually sold at $30.00 to $50.00. **Our $18.00 Giant Power Belt is the result of years of scientific study and experiment,** it is the very highest grade, a belt that has all the best features of other electric belts without their drawbacks, defects and discomforts, with exclusive and distinctive advantages not found in other makes. Positively wonderful in its quick cure of all nervous and organic disorders arising from any cause, whether natural weakness, excesses, indiscretions, etc. The nerve building, health giving, vigor restoring current penetrates and permeates the affected parts; every nerve, tissue and fiber responds at once to its healing, vitalizing power; health, strength, superb manliness, youthful vigor is the result.

OUR GIANT POWER **80-gauge Current Genuine Heidelberg Alternating Electric Belt at $18.00** will do you more good in one week than six months of doctoring. The Heidelberg Electric Belt for disorders of the nerves, stomach, liver and kidneys, for weakness, diseased or debilitated condition of the sexual organs from any cause whatever, is worth all the drugs and chemicals, pills, tablets, washes, injections and other remedies put together. Its strengthening, healing and vitalizing power is magical—never before equaled.

HAVE YOU DOCTORED? **Have you perhaps written to some quack, so called institute or self styled men's physician,** have you tried various so called remedies for your peculiar trouble without success, without getting any help, perhaps not even temporary relief. Perhaps you are discouraged; maybe hopeless. **Don't give up. Don't despair. You may yet be cured.** The Giant Power Heidelberg Electric Belt is just what you need. Just what you should wear. Send for our Giant Power 80-gauge Current Heidelberg Electric Belt at once, wear it according to directions. In a day you will feel a difference, in two days there will be a marked change for the better, in three days you will experience relief, in a week or two weeks your system will be filled with the grand health giving current, in a month **you will be a new man.**

OUR GIANT POWER 80-GAUGE HEIDELBERG ELECTRIC BELT AT $18.00 **comes complete with the finest stomach attachment and most perfect, comfortable electric sack suspensory ever produced.** The lower illustration shows the style of these attachments, but you must see and examine, wear them, to appreciate the comfort and convenience. The suspensory encircles the organ, carries the vitalizing, soothing current direct to these delicate nerves and fibers, strengthens and enlarges this part in a most wonderful manner. The sack suspensory forms part of the circuit. The electric current must traverse every one of the innumerable nerves and fibers. Every wearing brings the current in contact with the organ; every wearing means that part of the organ is traversed through and through with the strengthening, healing current; means a liveliness imparted, a vigor induced, a tone returned, a joy restored that thousands of dollars' worth of medicine and doctors' prescriptions would never give.

DON'T SUFFER IN SILENCE, **don't endure in secret.** $18.00 will buy our Giant Power 80-Gauge Current Genuine Heidelberg Electric Belt. $18.00 will enable you to face the world anew. $18.00 will bring to you health and strength, vigor, manliness and happiness, a bigger measure for your money, a greater bargain than you could ever possibly secure in any other purchase.

ARE YOU IN DOUBT? **Have you tried so called remedies without avail and fear to take advantage of this great offer?** Do you hesitate because some unreliable firm or doctor took advantage of you? With us you run no possible risk. **Let us send you one of our Genuine Giant Power 80-gauge Heidelberg Electric Belts under the liberal condition of our offer.** We will send you the belt, then after ten days' fair trial if you have any reason to be dissatisfied, if you are not greatly benefited, return the belt to us and we will refund your money.

HOW THE 80-GAUGE HEIDELBERG ELECTRIC BELT IS MADE. **Every $18.00 80-Gauge Electric Belt of the Heidelberg make is the very finest belt that can be manufactured,** made of the highest grade materials money will buy, put together by scientific, skilled mechanics, hand made and finished in every part. The casing for the battery of cells is made of an extra quality very fine selected satin, a grade prepared particularly for this purpose, absolutely non-conducting, lined with a genuine Brighton insulating flannel, and then a layer of close woven non-conducting duck, forming the very best and perfect insulating case possible.

THE BATTERY **In our $18.00 Giant Power Heidelberg Electric Belt we furnish the new and genuine Heidelberg battery,** consisting of triple cells, producing an 80-gauge current. The battery is made of a secret, highly excitable, metal alloy and composition of silver and copper, a combination producing the quickest, most powerful and lasting current. **No battery in any other make can compare in any respect to the Heidelberg.** One cell of a Heidelberg battery, with its distinctive triple construction and special composition, has more strength, produces more current, than two cells of the ordinary **electric belts usually advertised.**

ELECTRODES. **Four large and one extra large (five in all) electrodes secure a fine equal distribution of the current** to the proper organs and affected parts. The electrodes are large size, splendid conducting surface, extra full and finely silver plated. The four electrodes in back are 2 inches across, the front and largest electrode is 5 inches across. Wonderful in its treatment of diseases of the stomach, liver and kidneys. Carries the life giving electric fluid straight to the affected parts. The big current bearing electrodes can be adjusted for any position, any part, any organ, bringing it in the direct route of the current. **For a weak or deranged nervous system the electric treatment has splendid results.** It stops losses, repairs waste, gives tone to every tissue and muscle. The whole body feels the good effect. No words can describe the change in health, feeling, vitality, even character, from the result of wearing a **genuine Heidelberg Giant Power Electric Belt.**

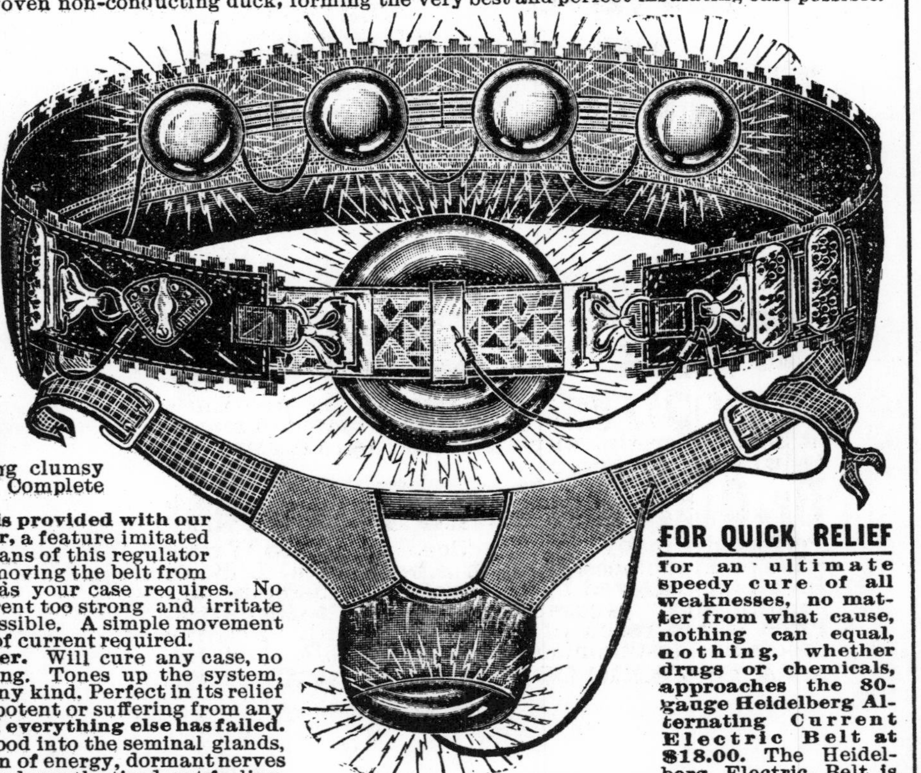

EVERY BELT IS PUT OUT UNDER OUR BINDING GUARANTEE **for more current, more power, more and quicker relief than any belt sold at three times the price. Simple, comfortable, efficient.** Nothing clumsy about the belt, nothing uncomfortable. No one can tell if you wear it. Complete instructions for use and wear sent with every belt.

CURRENT REGULATOR. **Every 80-gauge Heidelberg Electric Belt is provided with our own special and perfect current regulator,** a feature imitated (but not successfully) by every electric belt maker in the country. By means of this regulator the current can be instantly adjusted to any strength desired without removing the belt from the body. You can make it mild, medium or strong, just as you like, just as your case requires. No possibility of your receiving an unpleasant shock, no chance to get a current too strong and irritate tender parts. Six different strengths, different degrees of current are possible. A simple movement of a tiny one-inch lever does it. You get just the strength, just the gauge of current required.

THE 80-GAUGE CURRENT **is marvelous, really magical in its power.** Will cure any case, no matter how obstinate, how long standing. Tones up the system, drives out disease, fortifies the body against cold, against sick attacks of any kind. Perfect in its relief and cure of the peculiar diseases of men. For those sexually weak or impotent or suffering from any trouble of the sexual organs the **Giant 80-gauge Belt affords relief when everything else has failed.** The stimulating alternating current forces a vigorous circulation of blood into the seminal glands, enlivening them into a healthy glow. They quickly respond to this infusion of energy, dormant nerves wake up and expand, general circulation is produced, youthful vigor displaces the tired out feeling, natural power returns. In most cases of sexual weakness the full power of this belt is required, but a cure is certain. The 80-gauge current absolutely doubles the sexual force and power.

No. 8R3020 OUR 80-GAUGE CURRENT BELT..............$18.00

FOR QUICK RELIEF **for an ultimate speedy cure of all weaknesses, no matter from what cause, nothing can equal, nothing, whether drugs or chemicals, approaches the 80-gauge Heidelberg Alternating Current Electric Belt at $18.00.** The Heidelberg Electric Belt is the best, most reliable, most harmless yet powerful, most efficient and the cheapest cure possible. Don't let a specialist bleed you. Don't pay $25.00, $30.00 or $50.00 for an electric belt not one-half as good as the **Genuine 80-gauge Giant Power Alternating Current Heidelberg Electric Belt at $18.00. Send for one of our $18.00 belts immediately. Throw physic to the dogs. Strengthen and cure yourself at once.**

Home Gymnastics *for the* Business Man
By Dudley A. Sargent, M.D.
Director of Physical Culture at Harvard College

Fig. 1

WE ARE living in an age of rapid transit. The telegraph, the telephone, and the swift-flying mail train and ocean liner have quickened the pulses of life and revolutionized the methods of doing business. How to keep pace with this rapid method of doing things is getting to be a very serious problem with a great many people. Unfortunately, the human organism cannot be too suddenly changed to meet the new requirements to which it may be subjected. A sudden rise or fall in the temperature may bring on a fit of sickness in many persons, and the difficulty in adjusting one's self to a new climate is familiar to all.

The difficulty of adapting one's self to new methods of thinking and acting are no less trying and severe, and a host of persons are breaking down annually in their efforts to do so. It would be the height of folly for a young man to enter an athletic contest at the present day without taking a course of preparatory training to get himself in condition. But the pursuit of a trade, business or profession is no less a struggle, in which those who are best prepared and keep themselves in the best working condition win success, while those who are poorly prepared through lack of a good inheritance or education, or who neglect to keep themselves in fine physical condition, drop out of the contest and give up the race. Surely it must be apparent to every one that in order not only to attain eminence, but even to hold one's own in the struggles of the business world, a man must always be at his best.

How to keep one's self physically fit to meet the duties and responsibilities of every-day life is a question worthy of consideration. When bicycles are so cheap, gymnasiums so accessible, and boat, golf, riding, tennis, baseball, bowling and other athletic organizations are so numerous, there is no excuse for not attending to the body's needs on the ground that some particular form of exercise is not in itself interesting or attractive. But there are many who do find a ready excuse—usually lack of time or money—for not availing themselves of those golden opportunities to keep strong and well. To this large class of individuals who find themselves for one reason or another unattached to any of the numerous athletic organizations, I offer a few hints and suggestions on home exercise. If these are faithfully carried out they will meet the condition of the average man, and render him better fitted in every way to meet the daily wear and tear of a mentally active, though physically inactive, life.

These exercises which I am about to

Fig. 3

Fig. 5

recommend are exceedingly simple, and the only requirement on the part of the individual is courage and persistency enough to do them. If these qualities are present—and but little can be accomplished without them—good results are sure to follow. This is the course:

Arise in the morning in time to allow yourself about one hour before breakfast. Do not bathe even the hands or face, but put on at once a loose pair of flannel drawers, a flannel shirt and a pair of woolen golf stockings. Do not wear garters or slippers for this occasion, as the garters interfere with the free circulation of the blood in the legs, and the slippers prevent the proper action of the toes, upon which a well-poised body depends. Open the windows in your sleeping-room, or, preferably, go into a room where the windows have been open all night and the air is as fresh and pure as possible.

First Exercise.—Stand between two chairs which you have placed back to back about thirty inches apart (see Figure 1). From this position bend the knees and the arms, allowing the body to sink between the chairs to a depth of about twelve inches; then extend both arms and legs energetically, bringing the body to an upright position. Be sure to keep the head and shoulders well back, and to lessen the resistance put upon the muscles of the arms and chest by doing the greater part of the work with the legs. In no case is it advisable to try to lift the weight of the body between the chairs by the use of the arms alone. Repeat this exercise from twenty to one hundred times.

Second Exercise.—Stand with the feet about twelve inches apart, with the arms extended outward from the sides in a horizontal position (see Figure 2). From this position turn as far round as possible to the left, keeping the left arm fully extended, but allowing the right arm to fold across the chest until the fingers touch the left shoulder (see Figure 2A); now reverse the movement, turning quickly to the right, swinging the right arm well back in a horizontal plane, and allowing the left arm to fold across the chest until the fingers touch the right shoulder.

In doing this exercise concentrate the attention about the muscles of the waist and loins, but use the arms and legs in swaying from side to side in such a way as to modify or intensify the strain put upon the centre of the body. Repeat from twenty to one hundred times in each direction.

Third Exercise.—Stand with feet about twenty inches apart, with the arms held in a vertical position above the head with the backs of the hands touching (see Figure 3). From this position bring the arms downward and sideward, turning the body slightly to the right and bending both the trunk and knees until the hands can be clapped between the legs (see Figure 3A); then raise the arms upward and sideward, extending

Fig. 6

at the same time both the trunk and legs, until the hands are placed back to back again over the head as in the original position. Now do the same exercise turning to the left side, and repeat alternately from right to left from twenty to one hundred times.

Fig. 4

Fourth Exercise.—Stand with feet about twenty inches apart, with tips of the fingers placed upon the shoulders (see Figure 4). From this position thrust the hands and arms downward, bending the knees and rising on the toes until the fingers touch the floor midway between the feet (see Figure 4A). Now come to an upright position, bringing the fingers to the shoulders, and thrust the hands and arms upward to a vertical position above the head. Bring the fingers again to the shoulders, thrust downward to the floor, and return again to the thrust over the head. Repeat from ten to fifty times.

Fifth Exercise.—Stand in a natural position with elbows at the sides and finger-points touching just under the chin. Raise the elbows out from the sides as high as possible, keeping the fingers of both hands in contact under the chin, and elevate the right knee to a horizontal position in front of the body (see Figure 5). Return to the original standing position with elbows at the sides and raise the elbows and left knee. Repeat alternately from forty to one hundred times.

Fig. 2A

Sixth Exercise.—Stand with the right foot advanced diagonally forward about thirty inches, with the left arm folded across the small of the back and the right arm extended upward over the head as far as possible (see Figure 6). From this position incline forward, pivoting at the hips, and touch the floor in front of the right foot with the fingers of the right hand (see Figure 6A). Return again to the original position, keeping the right arm rigidly extended and carry it backward as far as possible. Repeat from ten to fifty times, then try the same movement with the left foot advanced, the right arm behind the back and the left arm extended upward and backward.

Seventh Exercise.—Stand with the feet about twenty-four inches apart, with the weight thrown on the right leg and the right arm extended upward and the left arm down by the left side (see Figure 7). From this position bring the left arm sideways and upward and carry the right arm sideways and downward, throwing the weight of the body at the same time on to the left foot (see Figure 7A).

Fig. 4A

Fig. 6A

The Stone Method

FREDERICK W. STONE

Athletic Instructor of The Stone School of Scientific Physical Culture

Was formerly athletic director of Columbia College and the Knickerbocker Athletic Ass'n, New York. At present he is the athletic instructor of the Chicago Athletic Ass'n, where he has classes daily from 12 to 1, and from 4 to 6. He established the world's record for 100 yards sprint (9 4-5 seconds) and held it unbeaten until 1902. As Mr. Stone has been an athlete and an instructor in physical culture for 32 years, and is himself a physically perfect man at 52 years of age, it will readily be admitted that he is thoroughly capable of teaching others the science of self-development.

No apparatus whatever required and does not overtax the heart

WE are successfully teaching The Stone Method of Scientific Physical Culture to men and women in every part of the world. It requires only 10 minutes each day, in your own room, just before retiring, or upon arising, and you will be put to no expense aside from our modest fee.

The Stone Method is a system of concentrated exertion, by which more exercise is actually obtained in 10 minutes than by the use of apparatus two hours. The exercises are rational, moderate, and are taught by an instructor who is thoroughly versed in physiology. Our pupils are of both sexes and range in age from 5 to 85 years. The Stone Method embraces a thorough course in deep breathing without extra expense.

We take into consideration your present condition, occupation, habits, mode of living and object which you wish to attain, and give you instructions accordingly. You will follow the instructions one week, and then report, stating what the effect has been and what results you have accomplished, when instructions for another week will be sent you, and so on until the course is completed. We thus keep in touch with your progress and are enabled to advise you intelligently. Your case will be given the same careful consideration as though you were the only pupil.

FOR MEN

Conscientiously and systematically follow our instructions and we can promise you a fine, strong, well-developed physique, which bears every evidence of perfect manhood; a clear brain; a light step; a splendid circulation that will make itself known in a ruddy complexion; bright eyes; sound, easy-working lungs, with plenty of room in which to expand; an increased appetite, good digestion; an active liver; sound, restful sleep; a cheerful disposition; an erect carriage. If you are too fat we can reduce your weight to normal, and if you are too thin we can increase your weight to what it should be. In a word, we give you greater strength, better health, LONGER LIFE. Individual instruction is given in every case.

Children

Proper exercise early in life will prevent and correct stooped shoulders and develop children into strong, healthy, robust men and women. Our breathing exercises will overcome mouth breathing, the cause of chronic Catarrh. Proper exercise will also correct many deformities in children.

FOR WOMEN

Women receive quite as much benefit from The Stone Method as men. We can insure perfect health, a good complexion, and, when desired, an increased chest development; we can increase the weight or reduce it; we can fill out those hollow places and give the form that beautiful contour so much desired; we can also reduce the abdomen as surely as day follows night.

Mr. Stone is the only physical instructor paying special attention to women and children. He is ably assisted in this department by Mrs. Ellen Walker, who has had a very extensive experience, and who alone opens and answers letters of a private nature. Confidential letters may be addressed

"Mrs. Ellen Walker, care The Stone School."

It is impossible, in this limited space, to convey an adequate idea of the manifold advantages of **The Stone Method** of Physical Culture. We have prepared a booklet for men and one for women, which explain the system in detail and our plan of mail instruction, and we will send them **Free,** with Measurement Blanks and Testimonials, to any person who is interested. These booklets contain many photographs from life of those who have perfected themselves physically by **The Stone Method.** They show what YOU can attain. Write to-day. The booklets will prove interesting whether you wish to take instruction or not.

The Stone School of Physical Culture

1668 MASONIC TEMPLE, CHICAGO, ILL.

LONDON: 4 Bloomsbury Street, Near New Oxford Street, W. C.

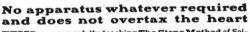

Reasons for Belief in the Value of Exercise and Athletics

By J. William White

John Rhea Barton Professor of Surgery, University of Pennsylvania

IT IS constantly forgotten by those who are lukewarm adherents, or actual opponents of athletics, that education of the body is always education of the mind, and, not infrequently, of the spirit. It was not alone or even chiefly by reason of the strength and endurance of their men and the vigor of their women that Sparta first, and then all Greece, assumed a commanding and for years an impregnable position among the nations of antiquity. It was because in acquiring those qualities it was imperatively necessary to cultivate the kindred ones of sobriety, cleanliness, self-restraint, temperance, moderation and regularity in all things—necessary to observe scrupulously all the rules of health as they were then understood. In other words, then as now the cultivation of the muscular power for certain purposes, even though the latter were in themselves trivial, brought not only strength but health, and not only health but increased intellectual vigor and activity, and augmented moral power.

This association between physical, intellectual and moral strength is a natural one, unchangeable in its essential principles, though subject, of course, to individual exception, and quite as applicable to our own community to-day as to that of any Grecian village two thousand years ago. It furnishes one of the strongest arguments for the assertion that we have, in the widespread diffusion of physical culture, one of the most potent factors at our command, even in these days of progressive sanitary science, for increasing the average of public health and longevity, diminishing disease, both by prevention and by cure, augmenting the world's power for work by adding to the usefulness and activity of the individual, and promoting indirectly at the same time the material prosperity, the happiness, and even the morality of the race.

The two most common arguments urged by well-meaning people against athletics, or "physical culture," using the terms as synonymous, are:

First. That the assiduous cultivation of bodily strength is not compatible with a proper degree of attention to the mental faculties.

Second. That athletics are frequently, or perhaps even usually, hurtful and productive of disease.

The first of these objections, that of the opposition between physical and mental development, is as old as Plato, who, recognizing the evils as well as the benefits of athletics, described some of the athletes of his time as "sleeping away their lives"; or as Galen, who speaks of both Greek and Roman athletes as "heavy and stupid." Their words applied, however, then, as they would apply now in many instances, to the man who gave up his life exclusively to the cultivation of his body, neglecting all mental discipline or acquirements. It may be admitted at once that in that sense, and with such people, athletics are far from exerting a beneficial influence; nor is it probable that they ever conduce to the avoidance of disease or the promotion of longevity unless the requirements of the mind are recognized as of more than equal importance with those of the body. We must not be misled, however, into believing the exception to be the type of the class. There may be such instances of mental or moral deterioration favored and fostered by athletics as are dramatically portrayed in the novel of Man and Wife, by Wilkie Collins, one of the leaders in the crusade against the so-called abuse of physical training. There are unquestionably instances of men who from the start were incapable of high intellectual cultivation, but who are endowed with, or have acquired, enormous bodily strength, without at the same time developing the virtues which have been described as more or less closely associated with, and brought out by, physical culture. But, though we may have occasional Geoffrey Delamaynes among gentlemen, and will never be without the Bill Sykes type among brutes, the records of art, of literature, of science show an intimate association between brain-power and bodily vigor, which is of itself sufficient answer to all such hasty generalization.

Editor's Note — Professor White's first paper on Exercise and Athletics appeared in The Saturday Evening Post of November 24.

Famous Examples in History

Samson, though he seems to have lacked discretion, was a judge in Israel. Pompey was the equal of any soldier in his command in feats of strength. Sallust says of him: "*Cum alacribus saltu, cum velocibus cursu, cum validis certabat.*" Cæsar was naturally of a delicate constitution, suffering from severe headaches, and probably epileptic, but by continual exercise he became an athlete, "admirable in all manly sports," and surpassed by none in enduring the fatigues and hardships of a military life. Lycurgus not only laid down the laws which for five hundred years made Lacedæmon the chief city of Greece, but was able to outrun all the mob who persecuted him and forced him to seek refuge in a sanctuary. Cicero is described by Plutarch as at one time thin, weak and dyspeptic, but as having been so strengthened by gymnastic exercises at Athens as to have become robust and vigorous. Coriolanus' successes were attributed by his enemies to his strength of body, he having so exercised and inured himself to all sorts of activity that he "combined the lightness of a racer with an extraordinary weight in close seizures and wrestlings." Alcibiades, according to Herodotus, became master of the Athenians, in spite of his excesses, by reason of his "force of eloquence, grace of person and strength of body"; and from the same authority we learn that Alexander had unusual endurance. Themistocles, Socrates and Plato excelled in gymnastic exercises; Sertorius swam the Rhone in full armor; Marcellus was "of a strong body"; Pelopidas "delighted in exercise"; Marius never missed a day on the Campus Martius; Cato "maintained his character and persisted in his exercise to the very last"; and even the mythological heroes — Theseus, Romulus and Remus — are accredited with "strength of body and bravery equal to the quickness and force of their understanding."

Numberless instances might be adduced in the records of ancient and mediæval history, which, whatever their authenticity, serve to show the close relation believed by the chroniclers of those days to exist between great physical strength and the intellectual powers which lead men to positions of command.

Athletic Leaders Lead in Intellect

This was, of course, due in part to the preëminence of physical force and of personal achievements in those ages; but in our own time we find that many of the most successful men in the various learned professions, in literature and in statesmanship have been lifelong devotees of some form of athletics, or have at least in their younger days taken prominent part among the athletes of their schools or colleges. Doctor Morgan, in his excellent work on University Oars, calls attention to the fact that of the one hundred and forty-seven Cambridge men who constituted the crews between 1829 and 1869, twenty-eight per cent. bore off honors in more important contests than those of the river, taking in some cases the very highest academical distinctions, and proving, according to Doctor Morgan, that mind and muscle, provided only they be judiciously guided, are not unequal yokefellows, but are well able to work together with reciprocal advantage. Among the aquatic champions whom he mentions were three bishops, two judges, one learned and world-renowned historian, and many others filling posts of honor and intellectual distinction. The general average of class men at Oxford was about thirty per cent., while among cricketers it rose to forty-two, and among rowing men to forty-five per cent.

At the present day the average age reached by those who attain their majority is fifty. In a list of five hundred of the greatest men in history, prepared not to show their longevity, but in order to determine at what time of life men do their best work, it was found that the average age at death was about sixty-two years. Madden, in his curious work on the Infirmities of Genius, gives a list of two hundred and forty illustrious names, with their ages at death, the average being about sixty-six years.

We see thus that, on the one hand, many of the great men of the past have been noted not only for their mental but for their physical power as well; and that, on the other, in the development of their bodies, the time given to athletics and to exercise tended to produce at once increased tenure of life and the highest and best intellectual capacity.

Here again, were it desirable, example might be indefinitely multiplied. It is easy to recall that Sir Walter Scott was unusually robust and physically active until overtaken by fatal disease; that Burns in his youth was an athlete of no mean prowess; that Byron, despite his deformity, excelled in feats of strength, and that he prided himself as much upon having swum the Hellespont as upon having written Childe Harold; that Dickens considered himself at a great intellectual disadvantage if compelled to forego his daily ten-mile walk at four miles an hour, regardless of weather; that George Sand preferred to work far into the night so that she might have some hours of daylight for her walks in the country; that Goethe swam, skated, rode and was passionately fond of all forms of exercise; that Humboldt prepared himself for his explorations by systematic exercise to the point of fatigue; that Leonardo da Vinci was a devoted equestrian; that Wordsworth was an indefatigable pedestrian; that Kant allowed nothing to interfere with his daily afternoon walk; that Gladstone lost no opportunity for out-of-door exercise; that Bismarck all his life was fond of sport and exercise, and as indefatigable in their pursuit as in his diplomatic work; and that among living authors, orators and statesmen we have many equally conspicuous examples of the same great truth.

The Relation Between Brain and Brawn

This association of exercise with intellectual power may not seem so difficult to understand if it is remembered that modern science has apparently shown that there is even closer relation between brain and muscle than was hitherto suspected even by the most earnest believer in exercise.

It is asserted now that "there is no brain stimulus except that which comes through muscles." It is certain that when muscles cannot for any reason act from early youth the corresponding brain area does not develop. Each nerve cell is now supposed to have a special function; to do only its own work and respond only to the stimulus originating in the muscle with which its nerve fibre is connected. Every action of the nervous system without exception expends itself in its turn in muscular action.

The coarser lower nerve cells are associated with the corresponding muscular movements — like walking — and develop earliest. Even a congenital idiot or imbecile can usually walk. The cells associated with motions requiring precision of movement, rapid muscular contraction, accuracy in employing separate muscles or groups of muscles, develop later and in exact proportion to the demand for them. If this demand is not made until the organism is too mature and the developmental period has passed, the result, so far as the brain centres are concerned, is less complete, though the general bodily effect may be satisfactory.

The easily noticed difference in mental power between the plowman or the day laborer and the skilled artisan is often — perhaps almost always — the result, not the cause, of their avocations. The relation of these facts to the principles governing educational systems is obvious, but its full consideration would carry me beyond the limitations of this paper.

In my opinion exercise is beneficial in proportion to what Hamerton calls the "faith" in exercise — the firm conviction of its value and necessity which makes one go out in all weathers, or take time under all circumstances for the discipline and hardening of the body, even leaving for that purpose the most urgent intellectual labors. When we hear that William Cullen Bryant, a most remarkable example of the preservation of undiminished mental and physical vigor to advanced years, attributed this to a habit formed in early life of devoting the first hour or two after leaving his bed in the morning to "moderate gymnastic exercise," his allowance of which he had not reduced "the width of a thumb-nail" in his eighty-fourth year; when we read that Mr. Gladstone, on the morning that he introduced his Home Rule bill, while all England, indeed the whole world, was to be his audience in a few hours, and while the fate of great parties and of an entire race was involved in his presentment of his case, "spent an hour at exercise, after which he bathed and ate a light breakfast" — we must acknowledge that exercise has something to commend it to thoughtful attention.

I believe that as a rule it does not receive this attention to the degree it merits, either from my profession, from parents or guardians, or from the governing bodies of educational institutions. Physicians and surgeons too often advise it in a merely perfunctory manner, and, their real indifference being reflected in the conduct of the patient, turn to drugs to stimulate skin, or kidneys, or heart, or lungs — work infinitely better done by exercise.

The generally accepted axiom of to-day, that too much food is one of the most notable factors in causing fatal disease, should, in the majority of cases, read, "too much food relatively to the amount of exercise." Less food, even in the absence of exercise, would save many lives; the same amount of food with abundant exercise would save many more; but the most useful text from which to preach to modern communities would be "much less food and much more exercise."

The most practical application of all this which can be made in a nation where compulsory military service does not exist is in relation to the thousands of undergraduates, who, at a period of life when either the greatest good or the greatest harm may most easily be wrought, are under control of the boards of the various colleges and universities.

A Summary of Vital Suggestions

If I were suddenly invested with supreme power, say as Dictator of Physical Culture in all Educational Institutions, my first pronunciamento would consist of a series of propositions somewhat as follows:

Whereas: From time immemorial until now, health and strength have depended on a sufficiency of sunlight, oxygen, food and exercise;

And whereas: Circumstances have deprived the human race of nineteen-twentieths of the sunlight, and three-fourths of the oxygen to which our forebears for myriads of years were accustomed; have reduced the necessity for exercise for the purpose of the mere maintenance of life to one thousandth of that formerly needed; and have made food so easily procurable that much more is eaten than is required for the repair of waste, additional strain being thus thrown on the heart, liver, lungs, kidneys, blood vessels, skin and brain;

And whereas: Associated circumstances make the present demands upon the nervous system (which should be understood to include the mind and the morals) far greater than in times past, both during the educational period and in after life;

And whereas: In the former period, extending from childhood to early adult life, must, if ever, be laid the foundation of the health and strength without which later effective work becomes impossible;

And whereas: No thinking or observant educator who has been so situated as to know of the personal life of large numbers of boys and of young men can fail to be convinced of the value of strenuous physical endeavor in aiding them to avoid various pitfalls which beset the steps of youth and adolescence — as well as of more advanced age.

WHY AMERICA WINS

By Eustace Miles, M. A.

Formerly Scholar of Kings College, Cambridge
Amateur Champion at Tennis, Racquets and Squash Tennis, 1900

IT IS said that lookers-on see most of the game. This is not quite true. People who wait till things have shifted into their proper proportions see still more of the game. Players who also occasionally are lookers-on, and always are waiting till things shift into proportion, see still more of the game. It is in all three capacities that I offer this short article on that question (more interesting, perhaps, to the English than to the Americans) why the Americans win in so many branches, not only of sport but also of commerce and life.

Without being egotistical, I shall have to explain first why the Americans did not beat me at my three favorite games. The first reason was that they have not played these games long enough. In England we are trained for them by ballplay in almost every school and in both our universities. Now that the Americans are adopting these three games we may reasonably expect them to beat us here also, especially as racquets, tennis and squash tennis are among the best exercises for the well-to-do, and, if they are cheapened, for the masses of the people as well. Add to them fives (or hand-fives), and we have a quartet which is bound to spread throughout the United States and to do great good wherever it spreads.

The second reason is still more important: namely, that I have long been practicing the American methods of learning these games. It is by arduous and constant preparation for play, as being thoroughly worth while, that I have managed to win. It is not from any superior skill; it is almost entirely from superior advantages and practice; for here we have opportunities of play everywhere.

The Americans win chiefly in sprints; the hundred yards is their typical distance. They win also where victory depends largely on knack, on the acquirement of some better, quicker, easier way of doing something. Rapidity and technique and adaptation of new devices—these are sources of American success in sport as in business.

In business, however, it is more than likely that the Americans will win where it is a matter of lasting as well as of sprinting. There is at present no prospect of similar victories in sport. We still hold the upper hand in the long distances.

The Contrast Between Typical Methods

THE contrast between typical English and American methods, to which there will always be exceptions, is seen most clearly when we contrast the English university athlete and the American college athlete. The Englishman is going to run for his university; let us say that the race is a quarter of a mile or something less. He practices starting now and then; he is rather careful about what he eats and drinks and smokes; he does not work *too* hard with his brain; he does not worry himself too much; but his chief training is to run the actual distance or part of the distance. A few take considerably more care. The majority take just about this much, no more and no less.

The American college athlete also practices running his distance; but, in addition, he practices the art of starting till he has nearly perfected it. There are many different positions from which to start at an advantage. The American is likely to practice all, in order that he may find out which is best for him; that one he will make his very own by constant repetition. How arduous, yet, when he looks back ten years later (that is the supreme test), how well worth while. Then he will probably practice the beginning of the race, the middle of the race, the end of the race. He will diet himself with considerably more scrupulous attention. He will give more of his soul to the practice. Probably he will not work much more than an Englishman does: he may work a great deal less; but for his particular end—victory in his race—he considers every sort of advantage and habit worth while; *he grudges no labor spent in acquiring the habit.* Before the race he will be massaged, so that his limbs and muscles may be warmed and rendered more flexible and lithe, less cold and stiff and awkward. Most Englishmen despise this, to their great disadvantage. They think that they are going to "get along somehow" without this apparently trivial item. They are finding in sport and in business that such apparently trivial items make just the difference between victory and defeat.

The American first decides that he is going to do the thing. Otherwise—and he probably discusses the matter very carefully with himself and his friends—probably he does not do the thing at all. But, having decided, he does it with all his might. The Englishman does not think much about whether it is worth while; doing it, he does it with all his might, too. But the American practices it with all his might and with all his mind. He studies it also. How can he better the present method or absence of method? That is worth working out. *He invests far more time and trouble on his apprenticeship for success.* That gets almost at the root of the matter. The Englishman thinks that he will learn by doing. The American, unless he is a genius, knows that he will not; he knows that he will learn partly by doing, but partly also by studying and practicing; he outlays more time in preparation and he gets his interest and capital in return.

The Old Story of Follow it Up

I HAVE had lately considerable experience of English methods in advertising, and the usual business manager is still uneducated enough to ask himself that ridiculous question, How much will it cost? He does not mind spending a few shillings or pounds, but he draws the line at a large sum; he would sooner sink his shillings and pounds with no return and no profit than lay out his pounds or hundreds of pounds with an absolute certainty of two hundred per cent. coming back within a year or two. He asks, Will it cost *much?* The American does not. He asks, Will it pay? If so, where shall I advertise? Suppose I have a school for boys. Where shall I advertise that school? Who decides to which school the boy shall go? For the most part, the parents do. What paper do parents see? Perhaps the mothers rather than the fathers; but both, if possible. The answer is one that perhaps has not occurred to the Englishman, *because he has never asked himself the question.* The answer may be some woman's paper in which the English schoolmaster would never dream of inserting his ad. Then the American asks himself, How shall I advertise? with what wording, with what spacing, with what if any illustration, with what type, and so on? Next he asks himself, How shall I follow it up? For how long shall I follow up, and at what intervals? I have heard more than five business men in one particular branch of trade remark to the effect that they were going to try *one* advertisement in this or that paper. The absurdity of it—one advertisement! Why, the very essence of advertising is repetition: the "hammer, hammer, hammer" of constant impression. This shows precisely the difference between English and American ways. We are only beginning to learn the art of advertising; we are only beginning to learn the art of practice and preparation.

I said above that I had been using the American method, though I am bound to say that I used it before I knew anything about America—certainly long before I went there. It is amazing how much the Americans know about us (and profit by knowing it), and how little we know about them. In my own games much of the success depends upon the positions and movements of the body and, therefore, of its pedestals, the feet. Without the correct pose of feet the body is at an incredible disadvantage. So I devised a foot drill for my games, and practiced it thousands of times in my bedroom and elsewhere. I have now made it mechanical, an inseparable part of me, about which I never have to trouble while I am actually playing. It works itself; it is an acquired habit, a secondary instinct. But it was acquired through conscious and repeated practice. I do not see how it could have been acquired otherwise, for I am by nature a "duffer" at games. Most other players fail to recognize their weakness as I did, and go on playing and playing scarcely at all better than before. They think that they will succeed because they repeat; they think that practice makes perfect. As a matter of fact, practice of a bad habit only establishes that habit and makes it harder and harder to remove. It pushes success farther and farther away.

When the Englishman takes up a pursuit he asks himself no question about method; he asks himself, How do most people do it in England? And the answer to that will be nearly the same as the answer to the question, How have most people done it in England? The American does not ask himself this as an important question; he asks himself, How can I better the way in which most people have done it anywhere?

In answering the question the Americans creep right up along the borderland of the law everywhere; they occasionally swerve beyond the law into the land of the not-law; but, as a rule, they sail very close to the wind, but just on the safe side, technically. Englishmen, as a rule, keep on the inside.

There is another radical difference between English and American causes of success. It is seen very clearly in public education. In England our well-to-do classes get a fairly good education at what we call Public Schools—they are really large private schools, more of the type of Groton, St. Mark's and St. Paul's in America. Also our Poor-Law or Workhouse School boys and girls and our Reformatory Industrial School boys and girls get a really excellent education. But our majority, between the well-to-do and the lowest children, and, indeed, our majority of the lowest children after a certain age, get scarcely any education at all. In America there is a far more widespread education, a far more sensible and interesting education, a far more all-round education (including manual training), and a far more practical education, including among its best qualities an education in patriotism. *While we attend to the richest, the poorest and the most criminal children,* America does not confine itself to children. It educates children of all classes almost equally well, and continues education beyond childhood well into manhood.

Is the Game Worth the Candle?

THE Americans win—not because their methods are faultless: they win because they concentrate on the work and invest their time in preparation for it. They have more patience because their reason is convinced that patience pays. Their desire is victory, and, for the sake of that, they undergo drudgery. The typical Englishman does not ask his reason any questions; he asks, What are the other people doing? He does what other people are doing.

As the result of the two systems, I should say that there is nothing quite so good as the best Englishman who uses his reason sensibly: whose life is not one succession of smart, snappy jerks. The Englishman occasionally wins, but it is a rarity. Most of us, in what are known as the serious things of life (business and many branches of games and athletics), are beaten by the Americans because they are desperately anxious to win. When they have won they cannot rest. America is not a land of contentment.

We win, as a nation, in what is equally important—repose. We find our kindred in Philadelphia rather than in New York. And as a nation, and as individuals, we shall continue to be comparatively contented, if not happy—unless we are ruined financially first. In that case, I suppose, we shall at length become Americanized.

We, too, shall want to win; we, too, shall become desperately anxious; our calmer faces and our gentler voices and our quieter extremities will then leave us. That is where we are superior at present.

In two respects we are both losers. Both the English and the Americans lose in every way by eating abominably fast; and the more we hustle the faster we eat. It is there that the Japanese beat us both. Possibly the future of the world, though it may be thousands of years ahead, will rest with the slow eaters. For they shall have patience and placidity. They shall grow reasonably.

BREAKING THE RECORD

By Henry Harrison Lewis

MR. CHARLES R. FLINT'S instructions to his yacht-builder were terse and to the point. When the man came prepared with plans and specifications, Mr. Flint waved them aside. "I want the fastest boat afloat," he said. "I do not care how you build it or what it will cost. Build for me a craft that will break the speed record."

When the *Arrow* was delivered to Mr. Flint a number of months later, the magnate took her out for a trial trip over a measured-mile course. The lithe, slim, low-lying craft with its raking, squat funnel and sharp bow darted through the water like a greyhound. She seemed fairly to leap from one wave-crest to another. The torpedo-boat stern was smothered in foam, and against the knife-like edge of the bow curled an enormous "bone" which wet the forward deck with spray. Her owner stood aft with watch in hand. In affairs of commerce he was always cool and collected. His deals were executed with the *sang froid* of a Napoleon.

Now he was transformed. His usually imperturbable face revealed an intense eagerness not at all characteristic of the man. He alternately eyed the second-hand of his watch and the red-painted buoys marking the course. As one after another was passed he laughed aloud. Then when the last buoy faded astern he clapped his hands in an ecstasy of triumph.

"Forty-five miles an hour!" he cried. "That beats the record!"

When Charles R. Flint stood on the deck of his boat, and saw her travel faster than any other craft had traveled before, he typified in himself the spirit that seems to be born in man—and especially in Americans. The desire to do something a little better than any one else has done, to move a little faster by train or boat, in running or swimming or driving, is inherent in a great many human beings.

The citizens of St. Louis claim that their coming exposition will be the best and most important ever held. "It will be a record-breaker among expositions," they assert. Boston is building a remarkable waterworks system. "The reservoir will exceed five thousand acres in extent," her citizens claim. "It will break the record in reservoirs."

One of the transportation companies of New York erected a power-house with a chimney-stack so enormous that a dinner was given in its base to several hundred persons. "Our smoke-stack is the largest on earth," says the superintendent. "It holds the record."

An official attached to the ordnance department of the United States Army conceived the idea of excelling his predecessors by building the largest gun ever cast in the country. Finally, after much effort, he succeeded in having a bill passed in Congress appropriating money to build a sixteen-inch gun, the "first of ten." The enormous piece of ordnance, which weighs one hundred and fifty tons and is forty-nine feet in length, is now mounted at Sandy Hook at the entrance to New York harbor. Its trial was successful, because the gun was fired without bursting, but it is safe to say that the remaining nine will never be finished. The needs of the service do not reach to the extent of hurling a ton of metal a distance of twenty-one miles.

The "Arrow," Charles R. Flint's Famous Yacht, the Fastest Boat on Earth. Making the World's Record of 45 Miles in One Hour

COPYRIGHT, 1902, BY W. P. ROBERTSON

"Heatherbloom," the World's Champion High-Jumping Horse, Clearing the Bars at 8 Feet 3 1-2 Inches, the Highest Jump on Record of any Horse with Rider

C. W. Murphy Making the World's Bicycle Record of One Mile, Paced by a Locomotive, in 57 4-5 Seconds

A. Duffy (Second from Left of Picture) of World's Amateur Running Record for

Still the gun is a "record-breaker," and thus serves a purpose.

The record in bicycle speed held by C. W. Murphy was achieved under the most spectacular conditions. To make a mile in the really remarkable record time of

fifty-seven and four fifths seconds it was necessary to use a locomotive and railway-car as a pacing-machine. The locomotive itself had to speed at more than a mile a minute, which is usually considered fast traveling even for a thing of

Each Achievement the Greatest of Its Kind

D. S. Horton of Princeton University Breaking the Pole-Vaulting Record (Amateur) of the World. Height, 11 Feet 10 3-4 Inches

The "Atlantic City Flier," the Fastest Railway-Train in the World. Which Makes Regular Trips at a Speed of 62.2 Miles an Hour

The Largest and Most Powerful Gun Ever Made in the United States. This Record-Breaking Piece of Ordnance is 49 Feet Long, 16 Inches Diameter of Bore, Weighs 150 Tons, and Fires a Projectile Weighing 2,400 Pounds a Distance of 21 Miles

The Greatest Record-Breaking Achievement of 1903. Lou Dillon Making the Phenomenal World's Trotting Record of One Mile in 2 Minutes Flat, at Readville, Massachusetts, August 24, 1903

Georgetown University Making the 100-Yard Dash in 9 3-5 Seconds

Barney Oldfield Breaking the One-Mile-Automobile Record at The Empire Track, Yonkers, N. Y., in 55 4-5 Seconds

Ray W. Ewry Making the Record for Three Jumps without Weights. Distance, 35 Feet, 7 1-4 Inches

steam and steel. How much more wonderful is the achievement of a man on a frail bicycle.

Somewhat different is Barney Oldfield's exploit in automobile-driving. There is something of tangible value in annihilating distance with a wagon or car. The perfection of the automobile is of distinct advantage to transportation, and although Mr. Oldfield's machine was constructed especially for racing purposes, its creation represents a gain in the perfection of mechanism.

It is interesting to note that the majority of world's records are held by Americans. The desire to excel, so prominent in our commercial life, can also be found in our athletics.

Hill-climbing on skees by the stair method—a rather slow process. The ordinary ways are tacking at sufficient angles to keep from sliding back, or going straight up the hillside by keeping the feet at right angles to each other

SKEEING, A NEW SPORT FOR AMERICA

AN EXHILARATING PASTIME THAT ANY ONE CAN ENJOY WHEREVER THERE IS SNOW— THE THRILLING JUMPING CONTESTS IN UPPER MICHIGAN— SKEEING AS A USEFUL MODE OF LOCOMOTION

By JOHN A. GADE

NO SPORT is more invigorating or better develops all the muscles of the body than a day's run on skees. It beats horseback riding, it beats Swoboda. Nansen and his men could never have endured the hardships of their Arctic expedition had they not been gradually toughened from childhood by days spent on skees. During the last ten years skeeing has grown to be almost as much of a winter sport in the northern and northwestern states as tobogganing in Canada. Where the snowfall of one night is frequently too deep to be cleared away (as in Oregon, Nevada, Michigan and Wisconsin), and lies on the ground for weeks together to the depth of several feet, skees virtually become the life-preservers of the inhabitants. They furnish the only means by which the mail-carriers can reach the inaccessible and outlying mountain districts of the Rockies. A pair of skees makes an excellent Christmas present, as skeeing can be practiced wherever there is snow.

The object of the skee is twofold: first, to keep the wearer from sinking into the snow, and secondly, to maintain an advantageous rate of progress.

The weight of a man's body, standing on the soles of his feet, rests on about sixty square inches; on the skee it is distributed over more than six hundred and fifty, so that even in soft snow the skee-runner seldom sinks in more than a couple of inches, and is able to advance rapidly. The same is true of the Canadian snow-shoe in a lesser degree, but, for speed, the latter are snails compared to the former. The western skee-runner can cover on an average about four miles an hour, while the mountaineers and guides, experts in running, can sometimes make eight miles an hour. To the natural step made by the foot, the great length of the skee, as well as the slipperiness of its under surface, always adds several inches, obliging the pedestrian, even along a level road, to break into a dog-trot, if he wishes to keep up with a skee-runner. Down hill an experienced runner can let himself go, but for a beginner it would be like turning on the clutch-valve of an automobile without knowing where the break was.

Skees differ radically from the Canadian or Indian snow-shoe. They are about seven feet long, four inches broad, and taper from an inch thick at the center to three-quarters of an inch at the back and three-eighths of an inch in front. This gives a slight total swelling toward the center of about a quarter of an inch in the whole length. In front they curve upward about a foot, so as to ride easily on the snow instead of sinking into it. This curve has been made by steaming the wood during the process of the manufacture of the skees, and subsequently by placing them in a frame, until the bend remains permanent. After using, they are naturally wet, from their long contact with the snow, and tend to unbend again. Their points should then be tied down by a stout piece of string to one of the straps in the center and not be released until the next time the skees are to be used.

All the surfaces of the wood are varnished, except the bottom, which is grooved in the center to aid in keeping the balance, and waxed smooth as a good razor-strop prior to using. The best materials are naturally the woods which combine strength with flexibility and lightness. The ideal skees are those which, like well-tempered steel, bend without breaking. Ash and oak make the best as well as the most expensive, those of oak being a little heavier and more brittle. A good pair of skees costs from four to five dollars, while a pair of poor ones may be had for two and a half. Price and quality depend somewhat on where they are bought.

On the upper side of the skee, just where the foot rests, a piece of undressed cow- or deer-hide, or ribbed rubber, is attached, this making a firmer resting-place than the wood, which soon becomes wet or icy and slippery. The method of attaching the foot to the skee is by far the most important factor in determing whether the day's sport is to be pleasure or disappointment. Hundreds of amateurs have given up skeeing in disgust, or declared it was an art that must be acquired from childhood, merely because they have not understood how to fasten the skees, first, so securely to the foot that together they work as one member, and secondly, so that the foot remains flexible in every muscle. This can be accomplished only by starting fundamentally right. Over the every-day stocking a second one, coarsely knit, with a garter top, should be drawn. In Norway, socks one and a half inches thick, made of goat-hair, are used. The ordinary thick winter boot is as useless as a pair of carpet slippers for riding.

A specially constructed shoe is necessary. It should be made of one piece of leather, practically without a sole, to ensure perfect flexibility, so that it bears much resemblance to a moccasin. Under the heel alone a second piece of thin leather projects out behind to catch

A Nevada trapper off for a day's catch

the back strap of the fastenings. If any one wishes to procure the best possible shoes, the best idea is to send to Norway for a pair. The next best, is to order a pair of shoes made, sewn as far as possible in one piece, of the height of a pair of ordinary high lace-shoes. Have the lacing as short as possible, in order to keep out the snow. Make them of pig-skin, and keep them limber by constant oiling or rubbing with melted fat. Make them without soles, the leather under the foot being of the same thickness as the sides. For a heel, sew a secondary piece of leather one-quarter of an inch thick, projecting triangularly toward a point about an inch from the back of the shoe.

The foot should be bound to the skee by two sets of straps. The front one, of tough leather, one and a half inches wide, passes over the foot higher than the toes and through a hole bored half-way down through the sides of the skee to receive it. The best back straps are made of two pieces of selected and steamed bamboo, about one-quarter of an inch in diameter; these are laid side by side, wound around with copper wire, and then wrapped in strong leather. They are attached by non-rusting screws to the upper surface of the skee, directly in front of the foot, running through the front strap and back around the heel of the shoe, where they are kept from slipping off by the piece of leather which projects beyond the heel. That is the whole mechanism.

A pole is often used to give the runner an additional push when going on a level, or to act as a brake when going down hill. This is about an inch in diameter, so as to be held easily, and four feet six inches long. A few inches from its bottom it should be run through a circular disk of either wood, leather or metal, five or six inches in diameter, to hinder the stick from sinking into the snow when used. In jumping, the stick is never used, owing to the danger of falling on it. The best runners in Norway never use one, looking upon its aid as effeminate.

The best snow for the sport is the hard-packed snow that is dry and powdery on top. The skees skim over this without sinking in or breaking through the crust that is formed when sudden cold follows a thaw. With a temperature about freezing point there is little pleasure in skeeing; the sticky snow clogs and adheres in big lumps to the skees until the feet feel like lead.

A great many of the skee clubs have built their special club-houses or huts. These generally lie outside the towns or cities, in the shelter of the woods. This should be near some hill that is capital for jumping, i. e., at least

Winter fishing through the ice in Nevada, made possible by crossing the snow-bound hills on skees

a hundred yards long and considerably steeper above than below the position of the jump. The members straggle out to the hut, when they have finished their Saturday afternoon's work, and gather around the crackling logs of the huge stone fire-place for the evening meal. Everything is of the most primitive nature. One of the members acts as cook, while others carry water or wood, or toast the bread. The walls and roof are built of rough-hewn logs. There is simply one large room, with a smaller store-room behind. Two large cupboards, one on each side of the chimney-breast act as skee lockers, containing plenty of extra pairs of skees and straps in case of necessity. In the center of the room is a large deal table, covered with pewter mugs. Roughly constructed camp-chairs stand around it. Sunday morning, as soon as it is light, all the member are up; the last man out locks the door and all are off for the hill.

The great event of the skeeing clubs of the western states is the jumping contest. Every one has skeed at top speed out to the big hill where the tournament is to be held. At the foot of the hill they are steaming like oxen.

Some tack up it, bending forward sufficiently not to slide backward. Others climb up stair-fashion, and others again mount in the true Norwegian way, putting each skee in front of, and at a right angle to the other, while keeping the body at an incline of forty-five degrees to the skee. In the middle of the hill the runners collect to build the "take off," a mound of pine boughs, over which snow is shoveled, packed and patted firm and smooth.

The track-makers are the first to descend to make a smooth course. When this is finished all assemble at the top, except the judges and the measurer.

Only a skee-runner knows the sensation as he tightens the straps for the last time. Below, the endless hill seems to stretch on forever into the expanse of the valley, the steepness of the incline lost in its whiteness.

A long breath filled with airy snowflakes, cap off, a cramping of the fists, and you start. Faster and faster you go, till suddenly a flash of green in front, and the jump is coming! Crouching until your knees almost touch your skees, with muscles strained till your calves and loins ache with the tension, out into the air you sail!

School-boys at Alta, California, tacking up a hill

Off for the winter camp—boys with packs on their backs crossing a Californian valley on which the snow is several feet deep

A strange lightness and feebleness take possession of your limbs, and your spirit shares the intoxication of soaring into space, when you are suddenly called back to earth, for half a second softly, but then hard as iron an electric shock passes up your spine to the back of your head. You wobble helplessly from right to left, each foot seems glued to the ground and still in the air, but you have kept your balance and are shooting forward, while the ten-foot measuring stakes rush kaleidoscopically by you. At last you catch your first breath like a hiccough, then a longer one. You are master of the field with a jump of a hundred feet or more, and finish the victorious course in a neatly rounded curve.

The finest runners are naturally those that have gained their balance on skees very soon after learning to keep it on their natural underpinnings.

Youngsters drop down on their skees from high jumps as confidently and securely as a cat does from a fence; and children too poor for a real pair clatter down the snow-slides of

Down hill slowly — braking with the poles

A tremendous jump — over ninety feet! At Ishpeming, Mich.

their cellar doors on a pair of barrel staves tied on with cords.

If the present enthusiasm for skeeing in America continues, the great winter carnivals of Canada may some day be rivaled by a great American skee race similar to the famous one held every winter outside the Norwegian capital.

Skees were first known to have been used in the thirteenth century. Eight centuries passed before the trappers, lumbermen and wood-choppers of America learned the vast superiority of the skee over the Canadian snow-shoe. In a century more, the latter will be looked at in museums as the clumsy implement of the by-gone age. Whereas, some years ago only a few Scandinavian experts made a scanty living by selling their manufacture to enthusiastic countrymen, skees of all qualities may now be found at any place in the Northwest during the winter season.

What a revelation it would be to an easterner to follow one of the great skee clubs of the West, such as the "Red Wing," of Minnesota, on a regular winter outing!

A skeeing tournament in the upper peninsula of Michigan. The thousands of Scandinavians employed in the mines at Ishpeming and Negaunee have brought their native sport with them

Cross-Saddle Seats for Women

CROSS-SADDLE riding by ladies is no longer a fad; it has become a fashion, not only in the Western States, but in New York and Boston and Washington, and in other centres of what is considered culture, and where the correct way of riding is certainly known. Cross-saddle riding is not only unquestionably the more comfortable way of riding for the equestrienne, but it is admittedly the most healthful; not only for these

Irwin, of Cheyenne, a dainty and petite lady, the last one who would be picked out as possessing the seat of a Centaur, a nerve of iron, and a grip of steel. Mrs. Irwin has never turned to cattle-roping and bronco-busting, but she has ridden many vicious animals, and has ridden them so well that she was given a loving-cup at the last Frontier-day celebration in Cheyenne.

One of the best-known women riders of the West is Dora

Mrs. George Barnard, of Boston, one of the Pioneers in using the Cross-seat

Miss Chestie, of London, who carries the Cross-seat to the Extreme

reasons, but because she is a far more attractive figure riding her horse astride than in any other way, and because she knows this fact, has the up-to-date woman adopted the man's seat in the saddle.

But it is from the Western States that the cross-saddle seat comes, and to the Western woman, who loves the saddle, it is a surprise that riding astride has had so slow a growth to popularity. The Western woman has no use for the side-saddle, and in the Western school of riding utility is the first consideration; in fact, utility is the basis of all Western riding. The Western woman has naturally taken the cowboy as her model, and there is not a thing in the cowboy's trappings that is not an absolute necessity. He needs every ounce of blanket and leather his horse carries, and naturally he has the style of riding that gives the least fatigue and the most natural grace. Were the cowboy to shorten his stirrups and sit bolt-upright he would not last an hour, but the long stirrup and the limp seat in the saddle seem to make the horse and its rider a unit.

From the cowboy the Western woman has learned her lesson in riding, and the cross-saddle and the divided skirt have given her equal privileges, of which she has not failed to take advantage. There is in the West, to-day, a school of equestriennes, whose equals cannot be found in the entire world, made up of daring, dashing, natural riders, as much at home in the saddle as any cowboy. Many of these take part in the great cattle round-ups; some have even acquired fame as steer ropers and branders. To such women a bucking bronco is a mere plaything, and they regard a tussle with such an animal as the best kind of good sport.

The present championship of Wyoming is held by Mrs. W. H.

Mrs. Thomas Hitchcock, Jr. at the Meadowbrook Club, Long Island

Chiquita, of Santa Rosa, New Mexico; she is a genuine cowgirl, and declares that she was brought up in the saddle. She is part Indian, and it is owing to this fact that she is called "Cherokee Dora" all over the Southwest. Dora performs a score of daring feats in the saddle, and she is a champion at the "chicken-plucking" contests, a cowboy sport in her part of the country. "Chicken-plucking" consists in burying a chicken in the sand until only its head and neck protrude. The contestants then ride at full gallop, bending from the saddle and endeavoring to grasp the neck of the chicken as they pass at great speed. Miss Cherokee Dora has beaten the most skilled Mexican vaqueros at their own game, and is the acknowledged champion.

But this cross-saddle seat does not belong to the West alone. On Long Island, where some of the society women of New York follow the hounds during the spring and fall of each year, the cross-saddle seat is slowly forcing its way into popularity. Mrs. Thomas Hitchcock, Jr., an admirable horsewoman herself, and the wife of one of the authorities in America on hunting, frequently uses the cross-saddle with a riding-habit that is an admirable utilitarian costume that does not sacrifice feminity. For 'cross-country riding there can be no question of the superiority of the man's saddle, since the horse going over a fence is helped by the position, the rider leaning forward on the take-off, and backward on the fall, keeping his or her centre of gravity over the point of least resistance to the progress of the horse. In the side-saddle this can never be accomplished, however expert the rider may be.

In Boston, too, the cross-saddle seat seems to be gaining ground, and one of the best of New England riders, Mrs. George Barnard, has for some time been using the man's saddle.

RACKETS,
A GAME FOR EX-ATHLETES

THE English game of rackets made its way to New York as early as 1793, and maintained a feeble and fitful existence there until, more than a hundred years ago, the New York Racket Club gave it a permanent hold. Outside of New York the game has had no popularity in the United States until recently; but in the last five years courts have been built in New York, Philadelphia, Boston, and Chicago. The reason for this sudden development in the game is not far to seek, for it has come in the wake of the college athletic spirit. Rackets is pre-eminently the game of the ex-athlete. Without such a sport to relieve the physical torpor of winter life in the city he would not only lose the best results of his early training, but in many cases would be positively the worse for his highly developed physique.

The discovery of this fact is one of the few happy results of the many crusades against athletics. After the charge that manly sports are an immediate danger to life and limbs had been thoroughly disproved, the opposition, shifting ground, pointed to instances where famous oars and football-players have succumbed in later life to heart, lung, and stomach diseases. Competent physicians, moreover, declare that a sedentary life immediately following three or four years of hard training is a constant menace to health. Not only does the training-table appetite follow one long after its only excuse, the training itself, is a thing of the past, but heart and lung diseases that normally developed organs would repel find easy lodgment in the degenerating tissues of an ex-athlete. When a famous oar is carried off by peritonitis, heart or lung disease, the fault will usually be found to lie with the torpor of his later years, not with the activity of his youth. The highly developed body, like any delicate machine, rusts out at once, though it would not wear out in years. This fact, which ex-athletes have long recognized, consciously or unconsciously, in the craving for winter exercise, has lain at the root of the recent development in rackets, and is to-day the significant feature of the game.

The first impression one receives of a game of rackets is that it is a very dull substitute for lawn-tennis. It has the appearance of being played in a dungeon, and has been ridiculed as "lawn-tennis in jail." There is a certain whimsical touch in this, for the oldest English court was in the Debtors' Prison, London (Fleet), familiar to readers of Dickens, in which the game was played in an open court against a single wall. It is a curious fact that the modern dungeonlike court came into use the moment the game was free of the Fleet Prison, so that rackets has never been, as it were, at large. Yet, as the author of the excellent article on English rackets in the Badminton Library remarks, "stone walls do not a prison make." The very fact that rackets is an in-door game, and consequently a winter game, constitutes its chief value, on the side of the athlete at least; and though it may lack the open air, the grass, trees, and sky, that give charm to lawn-tennis, it makes up, as every player will testify, in rapidity and excitement. Even the Tabasco flavor of personal danger is not lacking, for if the ball were to hit the wrong part of a player's skull, the result would be what is sometimes called a "sundowner." Such accidents are easily avoided by the expedient of shielding the

BACKHAND SERVICE.

head with the catgut of the bat when the ball is about to be struck from behind. Yet this will not prevent flesh bruises, and these, though scarcely larger than a Mexican dollar, often rival a carbuncle in making themselves disliked. The most serious accident is a sprained ankle from stepping on one of the discarded balls with which the front of the court is often littered. Yet, though the element of danger lends a zest to the sport unknown to tennis, accidents of any kind are extremely rare.

The salient point of a game of rackets is easily grasped by any one familiar with lawn-tennis and handball. It is, in fact, handball played with an adapted lawn-tennis racket. The ball is served alternately from the boxes a and b, so as to fly directly to the front wall, ×, strike above a line eight feet from the floor, and then rebound into the court a when served from a, or into b when served from b. The ball must be returned to the front wall before it has struck the floor more than once, though it may, and usually does, hit either the side or the back wall of the court, or both. After the service the ball may strike any place on any wall, except that it must reach the front wall above the "telltale," a hollow sounding footboard. As on the service, it must not strike the floor more than once, and this must be after it has struck the front wall. The fine point in serving consists in giving the ball a twist, so that it will rebound at unexpected angles, or return in such a way that it will be impossible to get the bat behind it. This is often so successfully managed that the ball skims about the court, hugging the walls, whereas the angle of incidence in each case would lead one to expect it to bound free of the wall. Yet the full value of these twisting services is lost unless the server is able to direct the ball accurately. There are a number of strange though well-authenticated anecdotes that illustrate the accuracy of a first-rate racketer's strokes. An English player once undertook to quiz Henry Fairs (Punch), then the professional champion of England, about his marksmanship, and volunteered his head as a target at the end of the court. Fairs accepted, but limited himself to his quizzical friend's nose. On the first shot he took it square on the bridge and broke it. A shot on the temple would have made sorry work of their fooling. Another story, about the celebrated William Grey, is evidence of still greater skill. The marker of the court where Grey practised used to keep the mice he caught until Grey came, and would then let them run in the court. Grey would kill a mouse with a single shot almost without fail.

Brilliant as the service may be, however, the thorough racketer is always more proud of his skill in the "bully," that is, in the play that succeeds the service. Here his utmost marksmanship is required, and in addition those mental qualities most valued by the sportsman,

RETREATING AFTER FOREHAND SERVICE—DANGER FROM THE REAR.

absolute presence of mind in unexpected turns, and bodily activity to match it. When two players are equally good in the "bully" it often happens that every motion they make is so direct and unerring that they appear to be going through a carefully planned drill, rather than acting in each motion on the exigency of the instant. It is related of William Grey that he seldom put forth his full strength in the service, because he preferred to contest each point in the "bully." This is thoroughly characteristic of English sportsmanship, which places as much value on the style of winning as on the victory.

The chief characteristic of the game, as a whole, it must now be evident, is swiftness. The tough little ball is

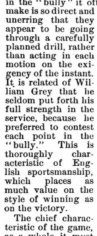

WAITING FOR THE FOREHAND SERVICE.

shot at its utmost speed by the tightly strung bat, and the floor and walls of the court are so prepared as to give it the sharpest possible rebound. It is said that in England when a court is to be put in prime condition it is swatted out with bullocks' blood to harden the surfaces; and in almost any court the ball travels so fast as to be invisible to the untrained eye, except at the point where it rebounds from the walls. In fact, the strokes are so hard and frequent that though the balls are made as tough and compact as possible, a score of them and more are often burst open in a single set, or are so deadened as to be useless. But the chief factor in quickening the game is the amount of ground to cover, which is almost twice what it is in lawn-tennis; and as the object in each return is, of course, to place the ball where the opponent will be least likely to reach it, the "bully" not infrequently resolves itself into a series of ten-yard dashes.

Such a game is little short of violent, and in this, of course, lies its virtue as a winter sport for ex-athletes. It quickens the heart, brings the lungs into play, and opens the pores of the skin. It thus throws off all impurities from the blood, cleanses the stomach, and stimulates a more wholesome appetite than the mere brain-worker can ever enjoy. To lose a pound and a half or two pounds weight in half an hour's play is no uncommon thing, even for a slender person. This flesh is, of course, mostly put on again at the next meal; but a week of such exercise makes one literally a new man. Best of all, the game is violent enough to renovate thoroughly the most highly developed heart and lungs, placing them beyond the danger of disease.

FOREHAND SERVICE.

These qualities which commend rackets to ex-athletes commend it also to men who have taken on fat; in fact, in too many cases an individual represents both classes. And, strange though it may appear, such an individual need by no means be a duffer at the game, as any one who has witnessed the American racket championship of late will testify. The explanation of this lies in the fact that a series of short spurts is not beyond the power of any man, however fat, whose muscles have not degenerated, provided only that he is given short intervals of rest. It is interesting to note also that the solid men have the swiftest strokes (which are generally the hardest to return), perhaps in accordance with

BACKHAND VOLLEYING.

the same wise provision of nature by which fat batsmen are able to drive a baseball far enough to allow them to reach first base. No one who has not passed the two-hundred-and-fifty mark should despair of rackets; in fact, it would be almost as just to speak of it as the fat man's game as the game for ex-athletes.

From what I have said it may be supposed that the price one pays for youthful training is life service in racket jails. This is far from the case, though many a worse fate might befall one. Although the exercise is violent, the frequent pauses between services keep it from being a continuous strain, so that in spite of the fact that the vital organs are constantly kept clear and sound, they diminish gradually in development, and in a few years shrink to the bare requirements of rackets. After this, if the game grows irksome, it is only a step to the constitutional; and if the worst comes to the worst, even this may be given up to the excess of business and irrational pleasures which are the bane of American life. In this event the only difference between the ex-athlete and the non-athlete will be that the former has lived, for a time at least, as a healthy man should live, and is proportionately stronger, not only to ward off disease, but to succeed in the usual walks of life.

JOHN CORBIN.

BACKHAND HALF-VOLLEY OFF THE BACK WALL.

BACKHAND HALF-VOLLEY.

Is Our National Game Doomed?

By James A. Hart

President Chicago League Ball Club

NOT since the first league game was played has this country seen so much professional baseball as in the present year. This is the best answer that can be made to the question: "Is our national game doomed?"—a question which crops out at frequent intervals in all quarters of the field.

Another convincing reply to this inquiry is to point to the fact that every school yard, village common and vacant city lot is a perpetual drill-ground for baseball, where Young America acquires a practical knowledge of the game as intuitively as he learns how to whistle. He does not have to be taught—and what is still more significant, he unconsciously acquires a loyalty for this splendid sport which time cannot alter. As he grows older and takes his place in the business world he finds the diamond of his boyhood playground the centre of cherished associations. These come sweeping back upon him with peculiar force and vividness when he knocks off work on a Saturday afternoon and joins in the shouting throng in grandstand or bleachers.

But why does this wave of fear that the popularity of baseball is seriously threatened recur just at this time, when every league has gone through the entire season and all material proofs substantiate the claim that baseball was never stronger in public favor than at the present moment?

Strife between the National and American Leagues, resulting in temporarily unsettled conditions in the governing powers, is the main cause, and perhaps the only one that needs be taken into account.

Heretofore professional baseball has been governed by a compact known as the National Agreement. This document designates the National League as "party of the first part" and all other leagues as "parties of the second part." A desire for expansion and for greater swing and prominence led the American League to recede from this compact, and this precipitated the present disturbed conditions which are accountable for the recurrence of the public timidity and doubt regarding the future of baseball.

That a new adjustment will be effected which will put professional ball on a sounder and better basis than it has ever before occupied I cannot doubt. This can only be effected by the creation of a strong central organization which shall absolutely control the entire field and also command the unqualified confidence of the public.

Those who look upon baseball affairs solely from the sportsman's viewpoint fail to consider the peculiar obstacles which beset the business and legislative end of the sport.

When it is remembered that it costs $700 a game to keep a National League team in the field it will be seen that some one must pay considerable attention to the business phase of the sport. No business in the world presents conditions as paradoxical as the baseball business. In illustration of this phase, let it be said that every team has its opponent as a partner in the matter of income, but not of outgo. Then, too, there is a constant shifting of opponents. Only one team in a league can stand at the head, but several of them can be simultaneously at the foot, so far as the opinion of the public is concerned.

Again, the public invariably cries to the management of a team not in the forefront: "Why don't you go out and get men who can play?" This natural but generally unreasonable reproach fails to take into account the fact that the management is hedged about by a multiplicity of restrictions regarding the engagement of players. These restrictions are absolutely necessary to keep the game clean, fair and above reproach. In this connection the public should always, in fairness, keep in mind the fact that the natural tendency of any professional sport is downward. In other words, it will be abused and debased unless protected by restrictions increasingly rigid and of a fearless, progressive character.

Baseball has been thus protected, and to this is largely due the high place which it has in the field of sports. It has been kept clean, and the American people are proud of it.

Any attempt to account for the irrepressible popularity of baseball will be inadequate which does not recognize the fundamental characteristics of the game itself. A league game presents a certainty of from ninety to one hundred and twenty minutes of entertainment, the exact nature of which cannot be forecast by the shrewdest "fan," or even by the star players. Consequently it always offers the attraction which attaches to the element of chance, to the possibility of some surprising incident, to the certainty that its every step must be a spontaneous development.

Baseball is the best game in the world; it is American to the backbone—clean, honest and active; and our people are fonder of it to-day than ever before.

OUR NATIONAL GAME IN 2005 A. D.

THE TRIUMPH OF THE ATHLETIC GIRL.

Copyrighted by Byron

Midland Beach
Now for a Dip

Tub Race
Pulling Hard

Midday on the Board-
walk at Asbury
Park

The
Bathing
Atlantic

The Funny Things They
See—Narragansett
Pier

Cape May

AND BATHERS

at Larchmont on the Home Stretch

Bathing at Newport, R. I.
A Quiet Hour at Newport

The Receding Tide
Santa Monica

Hour at City

Copyrighted by Byron
Far Rockaway -"Getting on to the Ropes"

12 The American Way

In 1900 there were seventy-six million Americans. By 1905 their number had increased to almost eighty-four million. They were an active people, constantly on the go. They built skyscrapers and bridges, argued about politics, worried about their health, took vacations, invented things, got into trouble. Most of their activities and interests can be fitted into more or less neat categories—the City, College, Women, and the like—and thus they have been divided in the sections of this book. But many of their ideas and enterprises at the beginning of the century ranged too widely to be encompassed in any classification. They are therefore assembled in this chapter under the heading "The American Way," a title indicating that such concerns were, in composite, a measure of the quality of life in the United States.

And what was the American way of life? The magazines of the time did not quite agree. A 1902 editorial, "The American Commercial Spirit," freely admitted that the prevailing spirit of the time was unabashed commercialism. However, it found that fact good and proper and called on the Bible and on classical authorities to prove that the man of much substance not only was a person to be admired but very likely was among those blessed by the Lord.

A less money-oriented but more biting view of the American way of life is provided by a cartoon in *Puck* depicting a Chinese Foreign Mission Society collecting funds to help civilize the heathen Americans. No one missed the point then, when every church had a mission society collecting funds to Christianize the Chinese. Inset drawings show the savage American practices that the Chinese missionaries hoped to alleviate: feuds in Kentucky, lynching of Negroes, labor riots, the scourge of the Tammany tiger in New York City, and anti-Chinese riots in the West. *Puck* was a humorous magazine, but sometimes its humor had a sharp cutting edge. There are no riots against Chinese today, and feuds in the Cumberlands are likewise things of the past, but all is not yet serene. New problems have arisen; today student radicals and black militants confront the police, and anarchy is no stranger to the national scene.

By the beginning of the century labor unions had already become part of the American way; advertisements urged the public to buy only clothing with the union label, and the article "The Business Side of the Big Unions," on the following pages, shows that at least some of the unions had gotten a strong foothold in the economy. There is a tendency to think of unions as still fighting for existence at the beginning of the twentieth century, whereas here the building trades unions are portrayed as already engaging in some of the restrictive practices for which they are being castigated today. The article tells of plumbers limited by union rules to installing only one bathtub per day and of plasterers held to doing nine square feet when they could easily finish forty. Also discussed are the rigid division of labor among unions that still exists, labor's opposition to the introduction of machinery, and its attempts to limit the number of apprentices in order to keep membership in trade unions small and wages high.

If one is surprised to find unions so sophisticated at such an early date, one is equally unprepared for the attitude of the author of the article. The nation was business-oriented at the time; most magazines spoke to the solid middle class, and the middle class had a tendency to equate unionism with anarchy (a tendency it has not completely shed today). Yet the author recognized that only in united action could the worker exert any power, especially in the face of ever-growing trusts and combines in business and industry. A listing in this chapter of the great American trusts indicates how gigantic some combinations were becoming. The time was long past when a worker with a problem could walk in to see the owner, for in a hundred-million-dollar trust the office of the president might not even be in the same city as the factory of the worker.

Among these varied and far-ranging expressions of what was on the mind of Americans are articles on such subjects as the victimization of American tourists by rapacious Europeans, the Mafia, and the prevalence of "unclean" dramas on the American stage. The author of the article on the fleecing that awaited American travelers must have had a very unhappy experience himself, for he insists that virtually every innkeeper, shopkeeper, porter, and other European was lying in wait for the unwary American tourist. Although the unsophisticated small-town American has always been considered fair game by the more avaricious Europeans, the description given in the article does appear exaggerated. On the other hand, even today there are tourists who return from abroad complaining that they have been overcharged every inch of the way. Those same people would probably have a hard time with some New York taxi drivers and restaurateurs.

The account of the Mafia appears to tell of a simpler day when the secret society carried out its vendettas and murdered its victims almost entirely in Sicily and Italy; the United States was involved in its intrigues only when the long arm of the society reached across the ocean to murder someone who had immigrated in an attempt to escape its revenge. That may indeed have been the situation at the turn of the century. More likely the Mafia (or Cosa Nostra) had already entrenched itself more deeply in American crime than the author was able to learn; even today the society is very reluctant to yield up its secrets.

A familiar echo from the past is the argument about what should appear on the American stage. An editorial tells of a producer who has said that he will henceforth have nothing to do with plays that hold America up to ridicule; his attitude was too chauvinistic for the editorial writer, who felt that some constructive self-criticism was a good thing. Another writer takes issue with the charge that American playwrights were "morbid, abnormal, audacious, startling, or unclean." Not so, says the writer. It is not American but foreign playwrights who pollute the country. "While there is an audience for unclean plays, there is a larger audience for those that are clean": good American plays like *The Little Minister, Barbara Fritchie, The Old Homestead, Way Down East.* Here, certainly, is a tendency that has changed drastically over the years; audiences today stand in line to buy tickets for the "unclean" plays. Or possibly it is only because there is not much choice; perhaps in their hearts today's theatergoers yearn for a simpler time when there were plays about staunch, brave, and handsome boys meeting loyal, understanding, and beautiful girls and winning them in the third act without either having taken off any clothes.

But even in that long-ago day a few inspired crystal-ball gazers sensed the shape of the future of the drama. On one of the following pages is a drawing of two ladies in very low décolletage attending the theater of some future decade. On the stage actors are cavorting through what is apparently a Greek drama. They could not be more naked if they were appearing on Broadway in 1970.

One very important matter that was beginning to worry perceptive Americans early in the century should be commented on. From the time of the first settlements the land and water and forests had been exploited as though they were limitless and as though there would be no tomorrow and no day of reckoning. But as one cartoon on the following pages proves, there was already awareness in the early 1900's that at least some of our natural wonders were being exploited and despoiled out of existence. The cartoon appeared in 1905, when conservation was still a virtually unknown word, three years before President Theodore Roosevelt started seriously to preach the gospel of preserving our national resources. It is from *Life,* the old humor magazine, but the joke is a wry one: Niagara Falls harnessed and festooned with power lines, Yosemite Park a monstrous billboard, Mammoth Cave in use as a subway tunnel, Yellowstone Park turned into a source of steam for heating and laundries. We have largely saved these four natural wonders and we can claim to our credit many other bits of grandeur or beauty set aside and saved from exploitation. But by and large it has been a losing fight since 1905. The once common wonders of sparkling brooks, quiet woods, and crisp air have gone or are going fast. In many aspects the American way has not improved in almost three quarters of a century.

The Times Not Out of Joint

IF AMERICAN history were truthfully written and conscientiously taught, we should hear less ignorant lamenting over the degeneracy of the present and the dreadful outlook for the future. The melancholy but cheering truth is that our ancestors, with all their good points, had many failings. Lynching, tar and feathering, disheartening miscarriages of justice, unworthy public conduct of all kinds, were painfully near to characteristic of us in all our past.

The journey to the lofty goal of self-government and profound reverence for one's neighbor's rights is long and steep and full of dips and twists. But we are headed in the right direction, and, eighty millions strong, we march more rapidly than we did when we were but two or three million "revolutionary heroes."

The American Commercial Spirit

WE ARE living in a commercial age. That the spirit of the day is of too commercial a character may be admitted. But we must not think, as many would have us think, that our present condition is something unprecedented and that the ideals of Americans have been altogether lowered — that our ambitions and aims are of a new and contemptible kind.

Before passing sweeping condemnation on present-day Americanism, let us look at a few facts that are overlooked by our critics. Let us see if there is anything inconsistent with natural human nature, with laudable human ambitions, in our national desire to be rich and successful.

The Book of Job is one of the most ancient and beautiful of human productions, and Job himself is the ideal man and the ideal philosopher. Yet, in beginning the book, we find that he is pictured as being a man of substance, owning "seven thousand sheep, and three thousand camels, and five hundred yoke of oxen, and five hundred she asses," and this inventory is followed by the significant words, "So that this man was the greatest of all the men of the East." And, in closing the book, we find that, after his tribulations, "The Lord blessed the latter end of Job more than his beginning; for — (and note the significance of that word "for") — he had fourteen thousand sheep, and six thousand camels, and a thousand yoke of oxen, and a thousand she asses."

And it was nearly as many centuries before the Christian Era as it is now after that era — it was so far back that we can scarcely imagine land as possessing any value, but as being the free possession of whomsoever would take it — that we find Abraham paying down for a place of burial for his wife Sarah, "four hundred shekels of silver, current money with the merchant."

A consideration of facts like these, of conditions such as these, existing thousands of years ago, gives a new meaning to the word "commercialism" and affords a new viewpoint from which to consider our own "commercial age."

After this, it is surely needless to multiply examples; yet, for any who may still be tempted to look upon America as unprecedentedly "commercial," let us quote some words of the great merchant Dinde Desponde. To the Duke of Burgundy he once said — and that was a century before Columbus reached the shores of America, and so it cannot be ascribed to American influence — "Trade, my lord, finds its way everywhere and rules the world. There is nothing but may be accomplished with money."

So let us not think of ourselves as of a nation set apart in low ambitions. And we may remember that all the world at present is as commercial in spirit as is America — only not so successful. That, after all, is the only difference. And we may retort upon critics that not only have other nations shown as much of a commercial spirit as has our own, but that other nations have fought destructive wars for the sake of financial aggrandizement. — ROBERT SHACKLETON.

The Basis of Civilization

ROBERT HUNTER'S plausible assertion, in his book on poverty, that there are 10,000,000 Americans on the ragged edge of want continues to cause comment and, in some quarters, agitation. It has already been noted in these columns that a very large part of this extreme poverty is among immigrants not yet "fitted in," and that another large part comes under the head of incurable — the poor who are so through one or more of the four great causes of poverty — ignorance, intemperance, incompetence and inertia.

Further, over against the evils which come from privation must be set the evils which come from superfluity. It is no mere theory that poverty is more likely to produce useful members of the next generation than is prosperity, and extreme poverty is more favorable than extreme prosperity. And while it is sad and deplorable that any considerable number of us should want, it is not so sad, not so deplorable or so menacing as the fact that so very many Americans are now being brought up in the most enervating luxury and with ideals which centre about the means of continuing that luxury.

Property may be the basis of civilization; but unless property rests upon character, the loftier the civilization the shakier and the rottener it is.

No Fear of Faults Disclosed

TO LISTEN to some of our stump speakers one would think that patriotism was a virtue not unlike that of the Scotchman who was eating asparagus for the first time. He chewed toilsomely away at the thick end. His friend said: "Wullum, t'other eend!" But "Wullum" held doggedly to the thick end, saying: "Mon, I prefair it!" Happily we are reduced to no such straits of valiant lying to justify our love and faith. We love our country so much and so intelligently that we long to know its faults and to correct them. We believe in it so profoundly that we fear no disclosures of flaw, but only concealment. And we honor it so highly that we shall never be content until it is the perfect instrument for the development of the human race. We have no need to be blind and prejudiced in our love and faith and honor.

An Accomplished Gentleman

THE American believes that all men were created free and equal except himself, who was born when the earth was in perihelion.

He is the enterprising reformer who pleads for the simple life, and pays ten dollars a plate for a banquet that would test the digestive abilities of an ostrich.

He proclaims himself the boss of the world, and keeps awake at night trying to devise means to escape the bossism of the little politicians.

He stands ready to supply liberty to all mankind, and commits the government of his great cities to a lot of men to whom he would not lend a hundred dollars without collateral.

He cultivates the lowly and contrite spirit, and promptly threatens to thrash any European nation that touches the Monroe Doctrine, behind which hide the little bankrupt bullies of Central and South America.

He takes pride in the fact that he is the author of "Millions for defense, but not one cent for tribute," and fees everybody and keeps the grafters prosperous.

He attends mass meetings to promote the ends of justice, and stops on his way home to swear off his taxes.

Still, he is about the best of the lot at present claiming the globe, and while the millennium may catch him before he is perfect, it is going to find him pushing along in the general direction of better things.

THE WEALTH OF THE UNITED STATES.

Writing of this country more than a century ago, Talleyrand said that it was "impossible to move a step without feeling convinced that the irresistible progressive march of nature requires an immense population to cultivate some day this large extent of ground lying idle now, indeed, but which only wants the hand of man to produce everything in abundance." The fugitive from the French republic saw clearly that the new American republic was to be one of the great and fruitful countries of the world. Probably he foresaw that it was to be the richest country in the world. He evidently feared to give utterance to all that his imagination pictured, for he added, "I leave to others the satisfaction of foretelling the prospects of those countries."

Clear as Talleyrand's vision was, and whatever his imagination may have pictured, he could not have begun to realize the truth as it is now presented by the British statistician Mulhall in the current number of the *North American Review*. Mr. Mulhall begins by saying that "if we take a survey of mankind in ancient or modern times as regards the physical, mechanical, and intellectual force of nations, we find nothing to compare with the United States in this present year of 1895." It is flattering to our pride that this foreign economist should tell us the news of our successful struggle. The demands of nature in what Talleyrand calls her "irresistible progressive march" have been more than met. The great population is here; but more than that, the genius of the race that inhabits the country has vastly multiplied the productive powers of the individual. Since 1840 the working power of the individual in this country has been almost doubled through useful inventions. The working power measured in foot-tons is 1940 tons daily, while the working power of an individual in Great Britain is 1470 tons. The working power of a single person in this country is twice that of a German or of a Frenchman, more than three times that of an Austrian, and five times that of an Italian.

In 1890 we produced 350 bushels of grain and 1230 pounds of meat per hand employed, while each hand employed in similar tasks in the United Kingdom produced only 119 bushels of grain and 1090 pounds of meat. In France this production amounted to only 98 bushels of grain and 350 pounds of meat; while in Germany, Austria, and Italy it was still less. As Mr. Mulhall puts it, "An ordinary farm hand in the United States raises as much grain as three in England, four in France, five in Germany, or six in Austria, which shows what an enormous waste of labor occurs in Europe because farmers are not possessed of the same mechanical appliances as in the United States."

Speaking of our educational statistics in the census of 1890, Mr. Mulhall says, "It may be fearlessly asserted that in the history of the human race no nation ever before possessed 41,000,000 instructed citizens." The annual school expenditure in this country is $2 40 per inhabitant. Great Britain comes next, with an expenditure a little more than half as much. France spends only 80 cents; Germany, 50 cents; Austria, 30 cents; and Italy, 25 cents.

This country is also the richest in the world. Its wealth exceeds that of Great Britain by thirty-five per cent. The gains and wages of both rural and urban working people have also increased. From 1861 to 1870 the yearly accumulations of an urban worker amounted to $48 30, and of a rural worker to $17 90. In the period from 1881 to 1890 these annual accumulations amounted to $73 30 and $47 30 respectively. In 1860 the average yearly wage of an American operative amounted to $289.

An interesting fact is that agricultural wealth has greatly increased in this country. "In fact," says Mr. Mulhall, "if the United States had no urban population or industries whatever, the advance of agricultural interests would be enough to claim the admiration of mankind, for it has no parallel in history."

The statistics which Mr. Mulhall has taken from our own census confound the prophets of evil, the socialists, the communists, the currency tinkers, and those who believe that the American man is so incompetent and America is so poor a country that competition with the rest of the world on even terms is impossible. Our enormous wealth has saved us from what otherwise would have been the disastrous consequences of our trifling with the laws of nature; but the result of wasting money in the purchase of silver bullion shows us that there is a limit beyond which even the rich republic cannot safely go in the effort to repeal the universal laws that govern trade and money by experimental human statutes.

Concerning Your Neighbor's Business

MANY and varied are the alleged occupations that give a plausible excuse for neglecting one's own immediate work of the home and the day. None—not even minding one's neighbor's business—is so fascinating and dignified as searching the horizon for the mast-tops of remote calamities. It invests one with the air of patriotic concern. It gets one the reputation of being a thinker and a prophet—who remembers the shivery predictions of "calamity howlers" long enough to jeer at them as false prophets? And no one suspects that the "thinker" and "prophet" is simply an idle fellow who cannot endure the drudgery of useful work.

Just now this class of thinkers is greatly concerned, and has induced many busy people to be greatly concerned, over the growth of socialism and kindred isms. "Look at the socialist vote," they say. "Look at the strikes. Look at the attacks upon the right to work. Look at the acquiescence of press and politicians."

It is true there is an unprecedented amount of socialistic activity, and there was last November a socialist vote of 300,-000, and there are many unpleasant signs of an unwholesome discontent. But when these matters are rightly considered, is there any cause in them for alarm, or even for amazement or even for astonishment? Is not the wonder rather that there has been and is so little unhealthy and un-American discontent?

Within the last fifteen years the rising standards of the European masses and the increasing burden of caste, monarchy and militarism have caused the socialistic propaganda which Karl Marx started with his Das Kapital to spread with the swiftness of a prairie fire in dry weather among the working-classes of the various European nations. And within the past ten years there have poured into this country from the fiercest "hotbeds" of European discontent—from Italy, from the most socialistic parts of Germany, Russia and Austria— no less than five million immigrants, almost all from the oppressed laboring class. They were wretchedly poor; they were densely ignorant; they were bitter against the social order as they have known it all their lives. And instead of spreading out over the country, on farms and in the villages, as did former immigrants, they have huddled together in the cities and larger towns, each successive billow pushing in upon those that preceded it.

Within this mass is vaguely outlined a vast collection of foreigners in spirit as well as in language—a multitude who do not know their new country in its history, in its laws, in its customs, in its ideas. They are full of political and social notions natural to the oppressed of their native lands, but wholly alien to us. They exaggerate every small discomfort into an outcropping here of the conditions from which they fled; they fancy that only the most drastic remedies will cure these largely imaginary grievances. They blame their new country for misfortunes chargeable to their own lack of knowledge of its ways. And their leaders are, of course, saturated with socialistic theories. Finally, these theories are tolerated and encouraged by scholarly and philanthropic persons who have unfortunately read European history and sociology to the neglect of the history and sociology of their own democratic Republic. These facts do not constitute a menacing or even an especially difficult problem. On the contrary, the problem is one which time and common-sense and the fifty-odd million native Americans and the millions of assimilated foreign-born and native-born of foreign parentage will readily solve. If the Republic were not founded wholly upon principles of justice and right, if there were radical wrongs of iron caste and entrenched privilege, if we had not schools and colleges in abundance and the atmosphere of reasonableness, there might be cause for jangling the alarm bells. But we started right nationally, we are still in business for the benefit of the common man; and the most blinded and prejudiced cannot fail to see it after a while.

Childish Hands and Brains

THERE are cases of child labor in this country that would make even a "clamorer for dividends" heartsick. There are instances of executive and legislative corruption in connection with this matter of child labor that would almost cause a sensation in Russia. And it is not surprising that those who are devoting their lives to this particular phase of philanthropy are often moved to violent language.

But, on the other hand, it must be evident that the question of child labor is not easy to settle by statute. Theoretically, a child ought to be at school, ought to be getting an education, including a knowledge of a trade or trades. Practically, this is not always possible at present; and the employment of children at certain kinds of work saves them from the bad influences of the streets, from contracting idle and vicious habits, from being the slaves of the ignorant caprices of unfit parents.

The man who employs a child at healthful labor that aids in its education is a public benefactor. The man who uses child labor to make dividends for himself and weak and ignorant citizens for the State is among the vilest of the vile. How draw a statute that will encourage the one kind of employer and will send the other kind to prison?

That is the problem. Meanwhile, let us vote more and more money to our public schools, to expand their activities in every wise direction so that they shall provide a magnificent all-around education for every sovereign American.

The Lesson of the Post-Office

FOR many years the advocates of public ownership of several utilities have used our own experiment in that direction, the Post-Office Department, as their stock illustration. Well? Why this sudden recent silence?

Because, within six months, the Post-Office Department has been shown to be:

Inefficient;
Behind the times;
Honeycombed with corruption;
Preposterously expensive.

It is hard to escape the conclusion that we had better wait a while before we give the politicians any more "utilities."

Pure Air and Pure Politics

OF THE fifty-one and a half million people living in the North, the West and the Far West, twenty-four and a half millions, or almost fifty per cent., are dwellers in cities and towns; and in the almost purely agricultural South the urban tendency grows steadily stronger.

These facts point the vast importance of municipal problems to the American people. Most of these problems are, perhaps unfortunately, involved in political partisanship; but there are two—and these of the very first rank—that are so clear that no partisan, however bigoted, can befuddle them: pure air and pure water.

The rural districts have by no means solved them—bad water and badly ventilated bed and sitting rooms are not unknown among farmers. But Nature helps there; she is excluded from the city and town. The urban dwellers, if they care intelligently for their own health and for the health of the children, will fight for air that is not merely breathable but health-giving, for water that is not merely sightly and free from odors and germs but is a strong wine of health. It would not be easy to degenerate a race that had, pouring through its veins, the spirits that pure air and pure water put into a man.

The Stormy Sea of Liberty

THESE sentences sound as if they were from a speech or an editorial of yesterday:

"Increasing disregard for law pervades the country—the growing disposition to substitute the wild and furious passions in lieu of the sober judgment of courts, and the worse than savage mobs for the executive ministers of justice. Accounts of outrages committed by mobs form the every-day news of the times. They have pervaded the country from New England to Louisiana; they are not the creature of climate. Whatever their course may be, it is common to the whole country."

But those sentences, descriptive of conditions which would generally and profoundly alarm us did they exist to-day, are taken from a speech by Lincoln delivered in 1837, a quarter of a century before the Civil War and sixty years ago.

And still we stagger on; and the things that make our pessimists stew and sweat to-day are so much less formidable than the things that justly alarmed sober, unhysterical men for free institutions in our earlier days. The sea of liberty is indeed stormy, as Jefferson said! But ours is a ship that was built for storms.

A National Educational Problem
By Francis G. Peabody

For the last twenty years Prof. Peabody has occupied the Chair of Christian Morals at Harvard University. He has contributed a number of valuable books to ethical literature, and has been an educational leader

AT the gathering this year in New York City of a notable company representing the interests of education from Maine to Texas two conclusions seemed to be agreed upon by all present: first, the extreme need in the South of elementary schools for whites as well as blacks; second, the duty of the North to lighten the burden borne by the South in its new crusade against illiteracy. The South is deeply stirred by this new demand for leadership and sacrifice. Instead of "war governors" we hear of "education governors," with a new campaign cry, "Free schools for all the people." Lack of schools is not the fault of the South; it is the sorrow of the South. The South has been tested by almost every trial—by the desolation of war, by the equally desolating effects of reconstruction, by humbled pride, by poverty. It is now being tried by the slavery of illiteracy, and nothing is more gallant in the records of the South than the enlistment of its representative men in this new war of emancipation. Yet, the situation, as President Dabney of the University of Tennessee has summed it up, is still grave. "In schoolhouses costing on an average $276, under teachers paid on an average $25 a month, the average Southern child gets five cents' worth of education a day for eighty-seven days in the year." Southern education is thus not a race question or even a Southern question, still less a top-heavy question concerned with the higher education. It is a question of citizenship and of the primary school as the basis of an intelligent suffrage.

If chattel-slavery appeared to the North so inconsistent with American democracy as to justify war, not less inconsistent with national self-respect is the slavery of ignorance. Behind the problem of Southern education lies the question of perpetuity for a government of and by the people. The education of one part of the country is essential to the whole country. Democracy, as Mr. Lowell said, means not "I am as good as you are, but you are as good as I am." Democracy assumes that the more favored can not thrive without lifting with them the less fortunate, that there can be no survival of the fit without a revival of the unfit, that the North can not say of the South, or the white of the black, "I have no need of thee." Of this moral idealism, on which democracy rests, the common-school is the first expression, and of it Jefferson wrote: "Were it necessary to give up the Primary or the University, I would rather abandon the last; it is safer to have a whole people respectably enlightened than a few in a high state of science and the rest in ignorance." The education of the South is not a cause that invites philanthropy and patronage, but it is an education of the North in the ideals on which national prosperity finally rests.

The South's Largest Gain

FOR a decade a remarkable change has been going on in the South. The manifestations have been local but the results bear the semblance of a great movement. After the war the South had almost as many drinking-places as it had stores. To-day more than one-half of the counties below Mason and Dixon's line prohibit the sale of liquor. For instance, almost sixty per cent. of Texas, nearly eighty per cent. of Georgia, ninety per cent. of Mississippi and all of Tennessee except eight cities have voted out the saloon, while even in Kentucky forty-seven counties are under prohibition rule.

There is nothing of particular political importance in these facts, but there is in them a vast deal of social and personal significance. In literature pretending to represent the life of the South the mint julep figures as conspicuously as the genial sunshine or the climbing roses, when, as a matter of fact, ice-water or lemonade might be more realistic. The Southern "majah, sah!" with some of his old manner, still hangs on, but the Southern man of to-day is quite another kind of person. This may be a loss to romance, for, even to the abstainer, there is fragrance in the mention of mint which lemonade fails to suggest, and the major with his large manner and contempt for statistics fills more of the atmosphere than the quiet, agile worker who thinks of crops, cotton mills and stock quotations instead of the lost cause and its battles.

But the same qualities of grit, endurance, fidelity and cheerfulness which made splendid records in war are bravely at work solving the problems of peace. In most cases the liquor question has been handled as a plain business proposition. The saloon balked enterprise, reduced the labor supply, increased lawlessness and kept communities poor; worse still, it played havoc with the individual. In more than four hundred counties the good citizenship of all parties arose and banished it.

Behold the benefits! This year the South has more money than it has ever known, more money for spending; so much of it in fact that three of the great cities of the North have formed special business organizations to secure Southern trade, while the cities of the West have met the competition by the most alluring inducements. But the larger gain is in the general uplift of the population. Despite the occasional outbreaks of crime—in most cases where the saloons still exist—the whole trend of the South is steadily toward wise and safe conservatism, and the evolution of Southern personality is producing broad-minded Americans who live clean lives, do good work and carry no chips on their shoulders.

It has been said that had it not been for whisky there would have been no Civil War. Hard drinking, both North and South, inflamed the passions engendered by slavery. It follows as a most hopeful fact that in the consideration of the race question, which lingers long after the abolition of human bondage, the work of conciliation and adjustment will be done by men of temperate habits and temperate minds. In the new conditions being wrought by the South itself there must come higher character and achievement than its oldest and finest chivalry could show.

"THE BIG STICK"

"WITH THIS STICK I COULD 'LATHER' THE WORLD."

WILLIAMS' SHAVING STICK

Uncle Sam is not anxious to "lather" the world, but he *does* insist on lathering his own face comfortably and safely. **LATHER** either makes or unmakes a shaving soap. It's the great essential, the "Sine qua non." No other feature counts for much. If the lather dries quickly, it will smart and irritate the face. If it is not absolutely pure and neutral, or if the soap is highly perfumed, it poisons the delicate face tissues.

Rich, Creamy Lather

has for three-quarters of a century been the distinguishing characteristic of Williams' Shaving Soap. It's the kind a man *feels safe* in putting on his face, and enjoys using. It stays on the face, penetrates and softens each particular hair, and

makes shaving easy; above all, it leaves the face cool, soothed and refreshed. It's unique. There's no other like it. Your face is too valuable to experiment on with inferior kinds. Insist on the old, reliable WILLIAMS' SHAVING SOAPS.

Send 4 cents in stamps for (Trial) Shaving Stick

THE J. B. WILLIAMS COMPANY, = Glastonbury, Conn., U. S. A.

The Drift of Our Drama

AN EDITORIAL in a recent number of a popular magazine on the degradation of the stage in America has been widely quoted and freely commented upon. It is a vigorous arraignment of the sensational drama, the writer arguing that the scheme is "to make money by pandering to vice at the cost of the wholesale demoralization of the youth who are to be the backbone of the American nation of the future." A London newspaper in commenting upon this editorial says that "the writer charges American dramatists with being not only incapable of appreciating what is intellectual, instructive, wholesome or inspiring, but addicted naturally to what is morbid, abnormal, audacious, startling or unclean."

The writer of the editorial does nothing of the sort. It is the American manager whom he accuses of pandering to vice. He does not mention the American dramatist. He knows that it is the foreign playwright who pollutes our stage. The American playwrights, with one or two conspicuous exceptions, write clean plays. Bronson Howard, William Gillette, Augustus Thomas, James A. Herne, shining lights in the American galaxy, have never touched upon the "morbid, abnormal, audacious, startling or unclean." Their plays are wholesome, and, I am glad to add, popular. Unclean plays have their little day, usually in New York; then they go, and are forgotten. But only one of them has been the work of an American dramatist.

While there is an audience for unclean plays, there is a larger audience for those that are clean. The greatest successes have been made with such plays as The Little Minister, Barbara Frietchie, The Prisoner of Zenda, The Pride of Jennico, The Old Homestead, Shore Acres, Way Down East, Shenandoah, and to go farther back, Hazel Kirke and Young Mrs. Winthrop. Any manager will tell you that there is a fortune in plays of homely life. It is because of its homeliness that Caleb West has been made into a play.

All the "book-plays" that are announced for early production are clean—To Have and To Hold, Richard Carvel, Janice Meredith, David Harum and The Adventures of François. All of these are American plays, which goes to prove that, given a chance, the American dramatist will redeem the condition of the theatre, which by some is now regarded as a "national peril."

—JEANNETTE L. GILDER.

A Bad Taste in the Mouth

MR. CHARLES FROHMAN lately announced that in future he will produce no plays that satirize Americans—or, as he expresses it, hold them up to ridicule. Mr. George Ade, already one of our leading playwrights, announces it as his mission to make his countrymen think well of themselves.

On business grounds the purpose of both is to be commended. Nothing is commoner than the man who says that he reads or goes to a play to be amused, and who objects to works of art that, as he expresses it, leave a bad taste in his mouth. Lately, two very able plays by Mr. Clyde Fitch have failed, the one largely because it satirized the foibles of women shopping, and the other largely because it showed the seamy side of marriages in which wholesome American girls sell themselves for foreign titles. The public of the veracious and satirical Mr. Howells and Mr. James numbers thousands, while novels that deal with commercial drummers who make themselves kings sell by hundreds of thousands.

But is the purpose proclaimed by the manager and the playwright as patriotic as it sounds? There is much, of course, in educating a national self-respect; but is there nothing in the gift which Burns wished the gods would "gie us"? Isn't it rather that most of us lack the intellectual faculty of enjoying veracity in art? Time was, and not so very long ago, when honest folk loudly proclaimed that there was more beauty in Home, Sweet Home than in all Beethoven and Wagner. An optimist might hope that those who now abhor the bad taste in the mouth will some day be just a little ashamed of proclaiming their preference for crude art—even if they still prefer it, which they probably will.

The criterion of a play or a novel is not whether it makes us think well of ourselves, but whether it makes us think truly and deeply. No one enjoys the bad taste in his mouth, or if he does his taste is quite perverted. But all who have real minds enjoy thinking real thoughts. "There ought never to be more pain," said Coleridge, speaking on a very similar subject, "than is compatible with a coexisting pleasure, and to be amply repaid by thought." A false satire or a brutal tragedy is the worst of art; but true satire and intellectual or spiritual tragedy is a mental tonic to all who have minds.

This cartoon from an 1897 issue of *Life* foreshadowed stage nudity of the 1970's. The caption read: "Glimpses of the Future. The Stage in the Twentieth Century, as Promised by Present Indications."

The Safety of the President
By Ex-President Grover Cleveland

THE dastardly and now thrice-repeated assassination of a President of the United States, and the terrible circumstances attending the crime, have filled the popular mind with shock and trepidation. This has given rise to a universal demand among our citizens that at this late day something more shall be done by way of protecting the life of our Chief Executive than is accomplished by the deterrent effect of the conviction and execution of the miserable and loathsome creatures who strike the fatal blow. This demand is intensified by the fact that even the restraint that follows this exhibition of stern retributive justice is lost if the foul deed happens to be committed within the jurisdiction of a State whose laws do not denounce the crime of murder with the punishment of death. Thus the chance is by no means remote that our Chief Executive may be assassinated and a great nation be staggered by direful fear and apprehension, and yet that the foul life of the murderer may be saved, to heroize assassination in the imagination of the enemies of social order and to become a centre of sympathy and pity among those who disseminate vicious discontent. It is at this time a perfectly natural and justifiable cause of satisfaction that the hopeless and self-convicted perpetrator of the infamous crime which now darkens with mourning every honest American household can anticipate nothing more gratifying to his brutal self-conceit, and nothing more heroically notorious or sensational, than a shameful death under the law.

Our people have not forgotten that hardly more than a year ago a plot was hatched on American soil which culminated in the assassination of a European King ; and now that the continuance of such plotting has forced the poisoned chalice to our own lips, it is insisted on all sides with an earnestness that will not subside with the present acute excitement, that not only should such terrible crimes be adequately and certainly punished in all their branches of execution, instigation and encouragement, but that the opportunity for murderous conference should be prevented, and the bloody counsels of assassination be placed under the ban and watchfulness of the law. It is hardly conceivable that our countrymen will long condone a failure on the part of those intrusted with national interests to take such steps in this direction as will indicate the solicitous care of our people for their constituted Government, and express their determination that the faithful discharge of the highest public duty shall not provoke the peril of violent death.

It is suggested that the safety of the President can be much increased by curtailing his accessibility to the public. It is even said that the custom which has always permitted to the people large latitude in meeting and greeting their Chief Executive, by taking him by the hand, is absurdly dangerous.

A radical diminution of the popular enjoyment of those privileges would be much more difficult of accomplishment than at first blush is apparent. The relations between all the decent people of the land and the President are very close. On the part of the people this situation is the outgrowth of their feeling that they have a more direct proprietary interest in the Presidential office than in any other instrumentality of their Government. They have determined by their united and simultaneous suffrages who the President shall be. In his high office they regard him as the representative of their sovereignty and self-government; and, as the administrator of laws made for their welfare and advantage, they look upon him as their near friend—alive to their needs and anxious for their prosperity and happiness. Closely allied to these sentiments and perhaps directly resulting from them there is an immensely strong band of attachment between all good citizens and their President which, though difficult to define, is nevertheless unmistakably real and distinctively American. In the minds of all law-abiding people, excepting an insignificant minority whose love of country is selfish or who make party scheming an occupation, this attachment overreaches party affiliations and crowds out of memory the exciting incidents of party strife. It may be said to rest upon a feeling of sincere and generous good-fellowship or comradeship which includes the idea that, though the President has been clothed with high honor by his fellow-countrymen, he is still one of the people, that he still needs their support and approbation, and that he is still in sympathy with them in every condition of their daily life.

This attachment and affection of our plain and honest people for their President is not only manifested by their desire to see, hear and greet him, but these kindly sentiments are stimulated and strengthened by every indulgence of this desire. When danger is charged against this indulgence let us remember that, while only one of our three Presidential assassinations can be in any way related to a public opportunity for the people to greet the President, such opportunity has in many millions of honest hearts rekindled wholesome Americanism, and made more deep and warm patriotic impulse. Against one miscreant who, with a desperate foolhardiness that can hardly be again anticipated, has through access to the head of our Nation accomplished a murderous purpose, we should not forget the countless numbers of those who in the privilege of like access would prevent such accomplishment with their lives.

Mr. Cleveland in his library

All things considered it is a serious question, even at a time when all are aroused to the need of better protection of the President, whether a serious limitation of the people's public access to him is justified as either necessary or effective.

It is not amiss to add that in discussing the curtailment of the privileges long accorded to the public in this regard the President himself must be reckoned with. We shall never have a President who is not fond of the great mass of his countrymen and who is not willing to trust them. His close contact with them is inspiring and encouraging. Their friendly greeting and hearty grasp of his hand, with no favors to ask and no selfish cause to urge, bring pleasant relief from official perplexities and annoying importunities. The people have enjoyed a generous access to their President for more than a hundred years. Weighing the remote chance of harm against the benefit and gratification of such access both to himself and the people, it can hardly be predicted that a project for its abolition would be sanctioned by any incumbents of the Presidential office.

It is by no means intended to suggest that this access should be unregulated and entirely free from all precaution. Those charged with care for the President on such occasions should never in the least degree tolerate the idea that there can be a harmless person of unsound mind ; nor should they relax their watch for such persons and for all others that may properly be suspected of a liability to do harm. Every doubtful case should be determined on the side of safety and all suspicious movements or conduct should challenge prompt and effective caution. Such precautions can be taken quietly and

unostentatiously. It may be safely said, however, that among the millions interested in having such precautions for Presidential safety adopted, the President himself will be the least anxious concerning them. This will always be so.

The fact is not overlooked that we have fallen upon a time when the danger of Presidential assassination, growing out of conditions and causes to which our thoughts have been somewhat accustomed, is nearly forgotten as we are confronted face to face with another menace more dreadful in intent, more secret in machination, and more cunning and unrelenting in execution than any other. We can no longer doubt the existence and growth of a spirit of anarchy in our midst. It seems to need no especial exciting cause to rouse it to deadly activity, but deliberately plans murder in high places — senseless and useless except to indulge its love for blood and its hatred of every agency of human government. Though of foreign parentage it has been permitted to pass our gates, and has been too long allowed to construe American freedom of speech and action as meaning unbridled and destructive license to disseminate the doctrines of hate and social disorder, and to teach assassination.

Our people in their grief and indignation are asking why this should continue ; and they are inquiring whether their belief in free institutions compels them to tolerate the deadly infection of anarchy. They have been taught that nations, like individuals, possess inherently the right of self-defense. They see this right exercised by the exclusion from our country of diseased persons and of criminals and persons under contract to labor here to the detriment of our workingmen. They have seen substantially the entire Chinese race excluded from our shores upon grounds that seem almost trivial in comparison with the reasons that cry out against the admission of anarchists. It appears to them perfectly palpable that when the personal character and behavior of aliens seeking to mingle with our population may involve our peace and security, it would be only a wise safeguard to exact evidence of their previous decent life and orderly disposition as a condition of their reception.

Nor will these questioners be satisfied with mere relief from the future importation of the dangers of anarchy. They are asking if our popular Government would be subjected to monarchical taint if strong and effective remedies were applied to the suppression of the machinations of anarchists who have already a foothold among us. They see vagrants, common gamblers, suspected criminals and disorderly persons in the hands of the law for the harm they may do of a feeble kind and within narrow limits ; and they cannot understand why anarchists, whose diabolical character and teachings are or ought to be well known, are allowed to plot and conspire until bloody assassination strikes down the embodiment of beneficent rule and shakes the foundations of lawful authority. Our people love liberty and are devoted to every guaranty of freedom to which their Government is pledged. In dealing with anarchy, however, they impatiently chafe under the restraint which bids them to wait for the tragedy it prepares, and to content themselves with visiting retribution upon its worthless and miserable tools. If to suppress and punish those who directly or by suggestion incite assassination savors of monarchy, they are prepared to take the departure.

A serious and thorough consideration of the peril which has so shockingly broken in upon the peace of our national life would be incomplete in its lesson and warning if it failed to lead to an honest self-examination and a frank inquiry whether there are not causes other than anarchistic teachings, and perhaps near our own doors, whose tendency, to say the least, is in the wrong direction. Have not some of our public journals, under the guise of wholesome criticism of official conduct, descended to such mendacious and scandalous personal abuse as might well suggest hatred of those holding public place? Has not the ridicule of the coarse and indecent cartoon indicated to those of low instincts that no respect is due to official station? Have not lying accusations on the stump and even in the halls of Congress, charging executive dishonesty, given a hint to those of warped judgment and weak intellect that the President is an enemy to the well-being of the people?

Many good men who are tearful now, and who sincerely mourn the cruel murder of a kindly, faithful and honest President, have perhaps from partisan feeling or through heedless disregard of responsibility supported and encouraged such things. They may recall it now and realize the fact that the agents of assassination are incited to their work by suggestion, and this suggestion need not necessarily be confined to the dark councils of anarchy.

Not the least among the safeguards against Presidential peril is that which would follow a revival of genuine American love for fairness, decency and unsensational truth.

AS THE HEATHEN SEE US.—A MEETING

OF THE CHINESE FOREIGN MISSIONS SOCIETY.

Are Great Men Fatalists?

RECENTLY, when President Roosevelt was gently taken to task by a friend for rashly exposing himself to danger, the President replied that he did not foolishly court danger. "There is only one way to protect me," he is reported to have said. "Surround me with a couple of regiments of infantry, make them form a hollow square and keep the people five hundred feet away, and then ——" The President, it is reported, did not finish his sentence, but doubtless he knew he could leave it to the imagination of his auditor to complete it. It is easy enough to fill in that blank. In the first place no American President would resort to such excessive and unwarranted precautions; in the second place, when one remembers how European rulers have been assassinated, protected as they are at all times by guards and detectives, the futility of trying to prevent a fanatic or madman from carrying out the design born in his warped brain is obvious.

People who think from accounts in the newpapers that President Roosevelt is rash or reckless do not know him. He is not rash, but rational. Because he is President he declines to become a hermit; partly because it is not in his nature, partly, perhaps, because he remembers the fable of the king's son whose death, an astrologer predicted, would be caused by a lion. To defy the prediction the king shut up his son in a castle. One day the young man, tired of his confinement, dashed his hand in the face of a painted lion. Behind the lion was a rusty nail, which so injured the prince's hand that he died of blood-poisoning. Behold, a lion had caused his death! What Fate has willed man cannot defy.

Yet the President does not recklessly court danger. To a friend not long ago talking about riding vicious horses he said very simply: "I would not ride such a horse; I never would have ridden that horse, and of course not now; it is not my business to tame wild horses; it is my business to be President." Yet, on the other hand, he would not imitate the example of the king of fable. Shortly after the accident at Pittsfield which came so near to ending his life, it was suggested to him that perhaps at the next city he visited he would prefer having two to four horses to his carriage. The President said he didn't care in the least how many horses he had; the committee could do as it liked. This was not bravado or assumed indifference. The President fully realized the peril in which he had been placed, and doubtless he also realized that the puny hand of man could not thwart the mightier hand of destiny.

One often wonders if great men are fatalists; or are they great simply because they think not of themselves, and know that their lives are controlled by a Power so infinitely wise that it would be folly for them to attempt to interfere in whatever their destiny may hold in store for them?

A New Deal in Politics

THERE is going to be some extremely interesting politics in this country in the next four years. Each wing of the Democratic party has had its turn now, and each has proved that it cannot succeed without the other. In 1896 and 1900 the radicals tried to win without the conservatives, and failed. In 1904 the conservatives have failed to win without the radicals. What next?

American political history has shown that when a dominant party has destroyed all effective organized opposition there is likely to be a general shuffle and a new deal. So it was after 1820, when Monroe's almost unanimous second election was followed by the break-up of the too-successful Jeffersonian party and a contest among four Republican candidates at the next election. It was so after 1852, when Pierce's overpowering triumph led to the disappearance of the Whigs and the creation of the new Republican party. The Greeley rout of 1872 brought a revulsion of feeling that gave new life to the paralyzed Democracy.

To-day the signs of political readjustment are in the air. They are not confined to any one party — they cover the whole field of politics. Bryan and Cleveland were no more incongruous as members of the same party in 1892 than LaFollette and Spooner are in 1904. There is a great body of Republicans who really belong on the Democratic side, and a smaller, but still large, number of Democrats who ought to be Republicans. Party names no longer correspond to real things. An English visitor who was recently writing a profound essay on American politics for one of his home reviews turned helplessly to an American friend and asked: "What is the difference between the Republican and Democratic parties?" The informant could not tell, and the article had to go into print without that important information. There is good reason to believe that observers of the campaign of 1908 will not be confronted by any such difficulty.

President McKinley

EIGHTY million Americans unite in deploring the shooting of President McKinley. Eighty million voices cry aloud in detestation of the act. Eighty million citizens unite in doing honor to the manliness, the bravery, the patriotism of him who last March was for the second time made President of the United States. And with these eighty millions the whole world has joined.

That within forty years three Presidents should be thus attacked seems at first thought to be a black omen for the future of our land. Within these forty years the people have by their ballots chosen only seven men to fill the office of Chief Magistrate — and, of those seven, three have been marked by the assassin!

Yet, in truth, there is nothing in this that points to danger for the Republic or to a weakness in Republican institutions. Lincoln was the victim of the heats of a great conflict, but the man who struck the deadly blow was far from understanding the wishes or the feelings of any leader: the South as well as the North deplored the tragedy. Garfield was the victim of a man of unbalanced mind, inflamed by the heat of a partisan conflict. McKinley was the victim of one whose narrow brain had soaked in the poisonous teachings of the offscourings of Europe.

And it may well be that this will teach the makers and the administrators of our law to understand better the mighty difference between what is liberty and what is criminal license; it may well be that, henceforth, those who teach or who believe that the murder of rulers is a praiseworthy act shall be placed, with other enemies of society, where their evil beliefs can bear no evil fruit. But at this time it is to sorrow and sympathy rather than to retribution that we turn; to pity rather than to punishment.

It was the nation that was blindly aimed at when McKinley was struck down. He was not attacked because he was of the North or of the South, for gold or for silver, for expansion or for anti-expansion, a Republican or a Democrat. He was struck as the head of this Republic, and men of all parties, of all shades of opinion, were drawn together by a common grief. The nation felt the blow. The pulse of the nation beat in unison with that of its suffering leader. Eighty million American hearts beat as one.

The Vice-Presidency

THEODORE ROOSEVELT is the fifth Vice-President to succeed to the Chief Magistracy by the death of the elected President. If he lives to complete his term the Presidency will have been administered by men attaining it through such substitution for nearly eighteen out of the 116 years of our constitutional history. In other words, there are fifteen chances out of a hundred that in any given time the Government may be in the hands of a Vice-President.

In reality the chances are much greater. No President died in office before 1841. Of the sixty-four years from that time to 1905, Vice-Presidential administrations will have covered nearly eighteen, or over 27 per cent. The proportion will have been almost precisely the same for the forty years from 1865 to 1905, and will have been over 29 per cent. for the twenty-four years beginning with 1881.

That is to say, when we elect a Vice-President we ought to do so with an eye to the fact that there is at least one chance in four that we are electing a President.

Under the system in vogue in the early years of the Republic statesmen of Presidential grade were elected to the Vice-Presidency. John Adams, Thomas Jefferson and George Clinton were all Vice-Presidents. About the time when it began to seem unnecessary to treat the Vice-Presidency seriously, and the office began to be treated as a consolation prize for small-calibred "favorite sons," the Presidents began to die in office, and the Vice-Presidency began to fulfill the great function which had been designed for it by the framers of the Constitution.

Of the five Vice-Presidents who have succeeded to the Presidency since 1840, Mr. Roosevelt is the only one, with the possible exception of Fillmore, whose accession has not caused a shock of surprise and disappointment. Mr. Roosevelt is recognized on all sides as a man of Presidential calibre. He was a leading candidate for the next nomination before the dreadful event which prematurely placed the office in his hands. But Arthur, although, as it turned out, he made an excellent President, would never have been considered seriously for that position in advance, and nobody would have thought of nominating Tyler or Johnson for the second place if his accession to the first had been regarded as likely.

It is quite time that the good example set by the nomination of Roosevelt should be generally followed. If we are to have accidental Presidents a quarter of the time there is no reason why they should be of inferior quality to those who administer the Government for the other three quarters. Let us cease to regard the Vice-Presidency as an office that anybody can consider it beneath his dignity to fill. The greatest statesman we can produce need not regard himself as belittled by accepting a place that has been held by Adams and Jefferson, and that has given five out of its last sixteen holders the control of the Government.

Familiarity that Breeds Danger

THE late President McKinley is reported to have said shortly before his assassination that there could be no safeguard, in this country, with our institutions, against such happenings as that of the sixth of September. What the President clearly had in mind was the unavoidable danger to which the American institution of hand-shaking as administered to the Administration exposes the Chief Executive.

It has long been notorious that the ordeal inflicted upon the President at every public function is not only fatiguing in the extreme but even physically painful. What, then, must be the mental attitude of the victim toward his tormentors? Can it be one of good-fellowship? And how must those who have pulled and battered him like the schoolboy captain of a winning team be affected? Do they carry away with them the awe of a great presence and a sense of the majesty of an august office?

Spectators of the Philadelphia National Convention who saw the treatment received by the then Vice-Presidential candidate at the hands of Republican stalwarts cannot think so. He was hustled, bunted, bruised, trod upon and beaten between the shoulders much more like a captured pickpocket than the chosen candidate for the second highest honors in the gift of the Nation. The expression of his face was a curious commingling of resistance, anger, deprecation and disgust. The police rushed in and the incident was closed, but thoughtful persons went home wondering what the people had really assembled for — to choose candidates for our highest offices or to play a rough game.

Though the intention in all this is undoubtedly good, the effect is none the less bad.

Criticism is part of our Government. It can never be suppressed and it may only be abated with much caution. But horse-play and scurrility undoubtedly pave the way to a cheapening of respect from which dangerous abuses of freedom may grow.

Our Haphazard Cabinet

IN THE Republican platform is this: "In the interest of our expanding commerce we recommend that Congress create a department of commerce and industries in the charge of a secretary with a seat in the Cabinet." In the Democratic platform is this: "In the interest of American labor, and the uplifting of the working man as the cornerstone of the prosperity of our country, we recommend that Congress create a department of labor in charge of a secretary with a seat in the Cabinet."

When Washington began the Presidency in 1789 his Cabinet consisted of four — Secretary of State, Secretary of the Treasury, Secretary of War, and Attorney-General. In 1798 a Secretary of the Navy was added; in 1829 the Postmaster-Generalship was created; in 1849 the Secretary of Interior became the eighth member, and in 1890 the Secretary of Agriculture completed the present list of the President's official advisers. Within the past decade no less than four new Cabinet officials have been seriously proposed. Measures for some of them have been introduced in Congress, and now the great parties officially recommend two. The British Cabinet has eighteen members, so that if we try to keep up with that country in numbers we shall have plentiful opportunity for additions. Of course there will be a demand for all possible vacancies. Education, navigation, public works, and other important interests will want places at the Cabinet table.

Among the serious students of government the conviction is general that there must come a time when the whole Cabinet scheme will have to be revised and systematized. The enormous growth of the country has given it a haphazard increase. The Interior Department, although one of the latest created, has more things and interests to handle than any other. Some of the bureaus of the Treasury have more work than several of the entire departments.

The one common and curious fact in the Cabinets of both the United States and Great Britain is that they are not Cabinets. Our own arrangement is more like a consultation board whose proceedings are seldom known to the public. The Cabinet of Great Britain has no official existence and no records are kept of its proceedings. Dicey in his history says "that the Government of England is in the hands of men whose position is legally undefined: that though the Cabinet is a word of every-day use no lawyer can say what the Cabinet is." The successful party calls a Prime Minister. The Prime Minister appoints his Cabinet and the administration stands or falls upon its work. Our Cabinet is different, and yet it is not a Cabinet in the real political purport of the term, and each Cabinet officer, with the exception of the Postmaster-General and the Attorney-General, and probably the Secretary of State, has under him important matters which are entirely foreign to his special sphere of work.

We all recall the gale of ridicule that blew from one end of the country to the other when the Department of Agriculture was being fought through a doubting Congress, and it is possible that some similar opposition will appear when the bills for the new positions reach the fighting stage. But unquestionably there must come a time when a great constructive statesman will do for the administration branch of the Government what John Marshall did for the laws in the first part of the century. Our national machine is getting so big that it will need improvement for smooth running and the best results. — LYNN ROBY MEEKINS.

STAMPING-OUT ANARCHY.

The Third Term Bogey

NINE Presidents have been elected for two terms — Washington, Jefferson, Madison, Monroe, Jackson, Lincoln, Grant, Cleveland and McKinley, all of them except Cleveland for two successive terms. Two of the nine did not live to complete their second terms — Lincoln and McKinley. Of the remaining seven, four have been talked of for a third term — two, Washington and Jefferson, for a third successive term; two, Grant and Cleveland, for a third term after an interval. In the cases of the remaining three — Madison, Monroe and Jackson — there was no talk of a third successive term partly because precedent was against it, chiefly because the men themselves were not eligible in the exciting political conditions, Jackson for other reasons, as well as because he was seventy and very infirm at the end of his second term.

It is generally supposed that Washington refused a third term because he was against it on principle. It is true, at that early day in the history of the Republic, indeed in the history of the democratic-republican form of government, there was a feeling that it was necessary in every formal way to emphasize the difference between the elective or votative principle and the hereditary principle. But Washington was not influenced by this feeling. In that immortal Farewell Address he apologizes for not accepting a third term, assures his countrymen that he is "influenced by no diminution of zeal for your future interest, no deficiency of grateful respect for past kindness." In the case of Jefferson, the declination of a third *successive* term was through dread of the monarchic idea. It is through Jefferson's adroit use of the precedent set by Washington that the impression exists that Washington declined a third successive term because he wished to safeguard against the possible future rise of a reigning family. Jefferson nowhere expressed himself on a third *not-successive* term; and he was succeeded by two of his devoted disciples who maintained his policies for four terms, or until long after he was dead.

Finally, the makers of the Constitution, having devised the four years' term, felt that they had done all that was possible to enable the people to rebuke a usurper and left them free to reëlect as many times as they might choose.

Grant had the first real opportunity in our history for a third not-successive term. The movement to get it for him was organized and managed and wholly inspired by a group of politicians — his private misfortunes combined with the unsatisfactory nature of his second term made the people, even the party rank and file, hostile or indifferent.

And now we again hear talk of a third not-successive term for Mr. Cleveland, in splendid health, returning to popularity, sixty-six years young, a large political factor both among independents and among democrats.

There are also other considerations in the matter besides precedent. But the precedent — Jefferson's imitation of Washington's example for a reason which Washington would have repudiated, and that an imitation as to three *successive* terms only — does not seem so strong on analysis as it is popularly supposed to be.

The People and the Senate

ONE of the insistent but seemingly futile demands for a change in our Government is that regarding the manner of electing United States Senators. It is an old and familiar subject, and it is to the fore once more, with results slightly better than has marked its course heretofore. In previous years its fate has had a distressing monotony. Some State Legislatures declared for the election of Senators by the popular vote; many of the Representatives in Congress were committed to the movement; the bill for the proper amendment of the Constitution went through the House of Representatives — and then it was promptly buried in the pigeonholes of the Senate.

But, like all movements that have conviction and public sentiment behind them, this one fails to be discouraged. It grows on its defeats. Many States have declared for the change. The newspapers have printed thousands of columns in favor of it. They have shown that certain men have become members of the Senate by money or manipulation, or both, and that Senatorial fights in Legislatures have been responsible not only for flagrant corruption but for serious interference with the work of State legislation. Furthermore, it has been demonstrated that the men who won or bought Senatorial prizes could never have been chosen to such high places if they had depended upon the suffrages of the whole people.

Arguments such as these, and other arguments similar to them, are continually increasing in number and in force, and every few years we have striking illustrations which show the degrading effects of a money contest for a place in the Senate — effects which degrade not only the Legislature which makes the choice, but which act strongly upon the people and upon the Senate as well.

It is this very persistence that has brought the topic from the Senate pigeonholes and led some of the Senators and the newspapers that support them into an open defense of the present system. Senator Hoar has discussed the matter in a speech of high intelligence and ability. He defends the election of Senators by Legislatures and declares that it is the only plan that gives us a true federated Government. To elect Senators by popular suffrage would, in his opinion, simply give us two Houses of Representatives, and would greatly impair the Senate's efficiency as a careful deliberative body.

Senator Penrose seeks apparently to ridicule the measure by a bill which he has introduced basing Senatorial representation on population, which would give dozens of Senators to the big States and only two to such commonwealths as Rhode Island and Delaware. Some of the advocates of the present method call it "a veritable cornerstone of the American Union."

The people have the power in their own hands. If they will elect to their Legislatures men who cannot be bought either by money, influence or office they will get better Senators. A change in the system might produce improved results, and it might not. Citizens who would vote to send a money-taker to the Legislature might also vote to send a money-spender to the Senate. All that may happen, for the new plan has never been tried. But it has happened, and it does happen constantly, that, when the people elect honest Legislatures, the honest Legislatures send acceptable men to the United States Senate.

So, until the change is made, the responsibility falls upon the citizens who elect the Legislatures as heavily as it falls upon the Legislatures which elect the United States Senators.

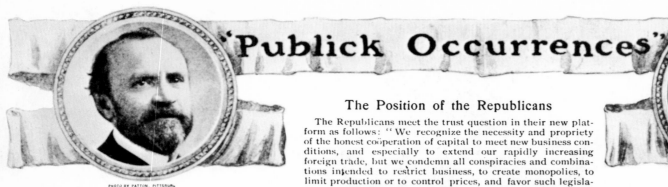

"Publick Occurrences"

PHOTO BY PATTON, PITTSBURG

HENRY PHIPPS

PHOTO BY HEMPERLEY STUDIO, PHILADELPHIA

CLEMENT A. GRISCOM

Six Billions in American Combines

Never before in our history was a Congressional Record so loaded up with tables of figures and reprinted speeches as in the closing days of the first session of the present Congress. It is the usual plan to do this on the eve of Presidential elections in order that the matter may be cheaply printed and franked through the mails. All the parties are equally guilty. Mr. Grosvenor, speaking for the Republicans, fills page after page in the finest type with tables and quotations from his party press. One speech of this kind, which is printed in the Record of June 13, would require the better part of a day for delivery, while as a matter of fact not more than ten or fifteen minutes of the time of the House was occupied, Mr. Grosvenor getting the usual leave to print for the remainder. In the same way Senator Allen in the Senate and Representative Cummings in the House, by the grace of leave to print, got the complete anti-trust speech of William J. Bryan in the proceedings of both branches. Likewise the Democrats in both the Senate and the House secured not only once but twice in the Record the insertion of a table filling four large pages, taken from the Commercial Year Book by Byron W. Holt, and entitled, Trusts and Combines in the United States. In offering it Senator Allen said:

"I want to call attention to the remarkable fact that more trusts have been formed since the fourth of March, 1897, up to this date, two to one, than in all the history of this country from its organization." There are nearly four hundred in the list, which will by virtue of its use in the official proceedings of Congress become familiar campaign literature in the Presidential contest. The total amount of money represented in all these trusts is placed at over six billions of dollars, or three times the annual commerce of the whole United States. Other trusts, organized since, add another billion.

Thirty Huge Combinations

In order that some idea may be obtained of these combines and the statistics given we will take those whose stock amounts to fifty million dollars and over:

	Common Stock	*Preferred Stock*
American Ice Company	$60,000,000	
American Steel and Wire Company of New Jersey	50,000,000	$40,000,000
American Sugar Refining Company	36,968,000	36,968,000
American Woolen Company	30,000,000	20,000,000
Atlantic Steamship Pool	100,000,000	
Bay State Gas Company	100,000,000	
Central Lumber Company	70,000,000	
Chemical Combine	50,000,000	
Consolidated Smelting and Refining Company	27,000,000	27,000,000
Continental Tobacco Company	30,000,000	30,000,000
Federal Steel Company	46,484,000	52,767,600
National Steel Company	32,000 000	27,000,000
National Tube Company	30,000,000	30,000,000
New England Insurance Exchange	58,537,167	
Anthracite Coal Trust	150,000,000	
Rubber Goods Manufacturing Company	25,000,000	25,000,000
Standard Oil Company	97,250,000	
Steel Rail Manufacturing Ass'n	50,000,000	
Underwriters' Association of N. Y.	56,428,711	
United States Leather Company	62,854,600	62,254,600
Western Union Telegraph	97,370,000	
Amalgamated Copper	75,000,000	
American Hide and Leather Company	40,000,000	30,000,000
American Plow Company	65,000,000	
American Smelting and Refining Company	27,400,000	27,400,000
Carnegie Steel Company	125,000,000	125,000,000
National Carpet Company	50,000,000	
Republic Iron and Steel Company	30,000,000	25,000,000
Soapmakers' Combination	25,000,000	25,000,000
Union Steel and Chain Company	30,000,000	30,000,000

Not Enough Money for the Trusts

The thirty combinations above are credited with capital amounting to two and one-third billions of dollars.

The entire general stock of money of all kinds in the United States, gold, silver, notes and certificates, amounts to about $2,700,000,000. So that if all the four hundred combines in the list should try to turn their capitalizations into cash they would use up every penny of the nation's money and then have only about forty per cent. of their demands. Indeed, the thirty corporations mentioned here would nearly use up all our cash. Of course, we know that business is transacted mostly on credit and this gives an entirely different view of the case, but the comparisons show the real financial hugeness of the modern combinations. It naturally follows that such a condition should become a political issue.

The Position of the Republicans

The Republicans meet the trust question in their new platform as follows: "We recognize the necessity and propriety of the honest coöperation of capital to meet new business conditions, and especially to extend our rapidly increasing foreign trade, but we condemn all conspiracies and combinations intended to restrict business, to create monopolies, to limit production or to control prices, and favor such legislation as will effectually restrain and prevent all such abuses, protect and promote competition, and secure the rights of producers, laborers and all who are engaged in industry and commerce."

An expression much more to the point was the speech of Senator Wolcott, the temporary chairman who outlined the Administration's policy, and who said that trusts were heard of only under Republican Administrations, because it was then that the people had confidence and that capital came forth to make prosperity, while under Democratic rule capital always went into hiding. This point was enthusiastically applauded by the Republican Convention.

No Good Trusts, Say the Democrats

The Democrats follow their leader, Colonel Bryan, who declared in his famous anti-trust speech:

"I want to start with the declaration that a monopoly in private hands is indefensible from any standpoint and intolerable. I make no exceptions to the rule. I do not divide monopolies in private into good monopolies and bad monopolies. There is no good monopoly in private hands. There can be no good monopoly in private hands until the Almighty sends us angels to preside over the monopoly."

Colonel Bryan in the same speech said:

"I was riding through Iowa and saw some hogs rooting in a field. The first thought that came to my mind was that those hogs were destroying a great deal in value, and then my mind ran back to the time when I lived upon a farm and we had hogs. I thought of the way in which we used to protect property from the hogs by putting rings in the noses of the hogs; and then the question came to me, why did we do it? Not to keep the hogs from getting fat, for we were more interested in their getting fat than they were; the sooner they got fat the sooner we killed them; the longer they were in getting fat the longer they lived. But why did we put the rings in their noses?

"So that while they were getting fat they would not destroy more than they were worth. And then the thought came to me that one of the great purposes of government was to put rings in the noses of hogs. I don't mean to say anything offensive, but we are all hoggish. In hours of temptation we are likely to trespass upon the rights of others."

When it was suggested that radical action might be unconstitutional he replied: "If it is unconstitutional, and is so declared by the Supreme Court, I am in favor of an amendment to the Constitution that will give Congress power to destroy every trust in the country."

The Democratic National Convention at Kansas City declared in its platform for 1900:

"We pledge the Democratic party to an unceasing warfare in nation, state and city against private monopoly in every form. Existing laws against trusts must be enforced and more stringent ones must be enacted providing for publicity as to the affairs of corporations engaged in interstate commerce, and requiring all corporations to show, before doing business outside of the State of their origin, that they have no water in their stock, and that they have not attempted, and are not attempting, to monopolize any branch of business or the production of any articles of merchandise, and the whole constitutional power of Congress over interstate commerce, the mails and all modes of interstate communication shall be exercised by the enactment of comprehensive laws upon the subject of trusts. Tariff laws should be amended by putting the products of trusts upon the free list to prevent monopoly under the plea of protection.

"Corporations should be protected in all their rights and their legitimate interests should be respected, but any attempt by corporations to interfere with the public affairs of the people or to control the sovereignty which creates them, should be forbidden under such penalties as will make such attempts impossible."

Other Parties Want Public Ownership

The other parties go further in their opposition to trusts, and some of them, especially the Populists, declare in favor of the public ownership and operation of all public utilities, including railroads, telegraph and telephone systems, coal mines, and so on.

In Chicago last February an anti-trust conference was held. It continued for three days and was addressed by prominent men from different sections of the country. A regular platform was adopted. It called on Congress to absorb the telegraph and telephone systems of the United States and run them in connection with the Post-Office Department; it sought to drive the private banks out of business; it demanded that Congress place on the free list all articles the sale of which in the United States was controlled by a trust; finally it resolved that the Government should take hold of and operate the railroads.

This conference, however, although prolific in discussions, did not make a deep impression upon the country.

Thirty Laws Against Trusts

When we get away from political rhetoric the trust problem grows even more interesting. Much of the best thought of the country is concentrated upon it. Among the students of financial and industrial questions and conditions there seems to be an idea that the trust is here to stay. Professor Day, of Columbia University, holds that it must be considered a permanent factor in modern civilization. Doctor Hadley, of Yale, and other eminent men do not express much hope in the solution of the problem by political platforms and campaign speeches. With the conservative men the idea seems to be that all legislation affecting corporations and combinations must be experimental; that permanent regulation will come through experience as sifted and made binding by the courts.

Congress and twenty-nine of the States have passed laws expressly designed and constructed to prohibit trusts, and yet the trusts have increased more rapidly since these laws were passed and have grown more in capitalization than ever before in the country's history.

"The trouble seems to be," says Doctor Whitten, "that any law drastic enough effectually to prohibit the trust will at the same time prohibit many forms of combination and organization recognized as highly beneficial. Thus far the labor organizations have been the principal sufferers from legislation intended solely to destroy trusts."

This, of course, is one of the extraordinary and totally unexpected developments of the situation.

No Uniformity in Trust Legislation

A still greater trouble is the lack of uniformity in the various laws. For instance, New Jersey, Delaware and West Virginia deliberately loosened and broadened their incorporation laws in order to increase the income of the State government by the fees. At the same time Massachusetts, which is said to have the best corporation law in the country, has a state commissioner of corporations to examine and approve the certificate of organization, and compels every corporation to pay in the whole amount of its capital stock before it can begin business, and after that to make annual statements to the state commissioner, giving the details of meetings, shareholders, capital stock, assets and liabilities.

The conviction is held by many that since the States will not adopt uniform laws the only remedy is for the National Government to take charge of the problem. As the first great step it is held that every corporation, every trust or combination shall be obliged to give full publicity to its affairs under heavy damages.

"Publicity serves the same function as street lighting," says one of these writers; "it furthers legitimate business and prevents crime."

All the serious students of the trust problem have declared that the first essential in the solution of it is this publicity.

The Good and Bad in Combinations

Everybody recognizes that there are good combinations as well as bad ones. An ice trust that doubled prices to the poorer classes when the warm weather began—as it did in New York—or a sugar trust that adds thirty million dollars to its profits by securing control of independent refineries, and then raising the price of sugar six times in five weeks—as it did in May and June last—naturally and inevitably arouses the indignation and opposition of the people; but there are industries and interests needing large capital that could not exist without organization or combination of some kind or other. For instance, it is probable that if the steamship interests, at the head of which is Clement A. Griscom, or the great Carnegie Mills, of which the Vice-President is Henry Phipps, did not have the means and the privileges of some sort of organization they could not reach the great results which are now easily, even if very profitably to those most interested, produced.

It is recognized universally that mere competition does not make trade. More money has been lost by rate cutting and under bidding and similar kinds of disorganization, which belong to competition carried to the extreme, than in any other way, and in the end the cost of it all has fallen upon the people—upon the small shareholders and the workers. So competition has its evils as well as organization.

Still for the next three months we shall hear little but denunciations of trusts in general. It is the stormiest period of their stormy existence. But mere denunciation does little good except to call attention to facts and to emphasize the necessity for meeting new forces and conditions in our political and industrial life. The problem, after all, will not be solved by the oratory of the hustings but by the calm thought and patriotic effort of the serious people of the country.

Too Much of a Good Thing

NOT a day passes without some more or less impressive instance of the uncertain state of our administration of justice. Now it is a criminal freed, though guilt is in every knot of the web of evidence which envelops him; again it is Judge Lynch executing the mandates of savage passion. Now it is men of power leering at the law from behind an impregnable corporate bulwark; again these men are executing upon their victims a law of sinister procurement. Of course, if the scales of justice were not in the main held even, if there were not mitigations of and compensations for the very worst miscarriages, the time for quiet discussion and warning would have passed. Fortunately for us all, that time is still ours.

It is no answer to the indictment to say that the evil will cure itself when it becomes a real menace. Nor is it an answer to say that justice is better administered than formerly or is more evenly administered in this Republic than anywhere else on earth. Both these statements are true; and it is also true that the grossest injustices of our time come from the fact that the law has not yet caught up with the astounding social and industrial development of the past half century, has not yet learned how to reach the new and most ingenious variations upon chicane and crime. But justice, as Webster well said, is man's chief earthly concern. So long as it does not prevail men cannot afford to relax their vigilance or their anxiety.

Curiously enough, the chief reason for the persistence of injustice, in face of the careful precautions of our fundamental law against it, is the industry and enthusiasm of our lawyers. Far more than the ministers, more even than the doctors, the lawyers have had a free hand in their profession. They have been left by the American people in completer custody of justice than by any other people or governmental power on earth. And with what may be conceded to be in the main the best intentions in the world, they have made of the plain highways of justice a maze so intricate, so confusing, so beset with bogs and pitfalls of technicality, that they alone can thread it — no, not all of them, but only the shrewdest and most highly paid. It is not surprising that some hasty and unthinking citizens are moved to applaud Peter the Great's famous remark in England: " I have only two lawyers in my whole Empire, and I shall hang one of them as soon as I get home."

They cannot be justly blamed for this. It is human instinct to aggrandize and enshroud in mystery and difficulty one's own labor that one's achievement shall seem the more amazing to onlookers.

But, much and vigorous assertion to the contrary notwithstanding, not conscious corruption but the passion for nicety and technicality, for hair-splitting and word-twisting, is responsible for most of our injustice and imperfect justice.

Justice is the only begotten of the law — provided the law be begotten of common-sense and the common instinct of humanity as to right and wrong. By multiplying laws, judges are not constrained to do justice, but are tempted to forget justice in indulging the human passion for complexity and mystery. Multiplied and particularized laws hamper judges in establishing justice, create avenues of escape for offenders, place the poor man with his cheap lawyer at the mercy of the rich man with his expensive lawyer. Also they confuse or blunt the sense of justice of the whole community by bridging the abyss between right and wrong with an imposing structure of technicality.

Also, no matter what our ingenious lawyers may say, the law deals with *real persons only*—with human beings endowed with moral sensibilities, and by no means able to shift their responsibilities to a fictitious, unmoral, corporate personality of the lawyers' creating.

Not since the age of Tribonian and Justinian has the lawyers' ideal kind of law flourished as to-day in America. And while the lawyers call upon us to admire the work of Tribonian and Justinian, they forget that those twinned luminaries of law were twinned luminaries of a Roman world where justice lay prostrate and injustice jeered openly at a despairing and decaying civilization.

Punish Less and Reform More

TOO long the criminal has been a subject of public indifference. So that he is caught and punished, the majority of people care little what becomes of him after, nor do they often question whether or not his punishment is proportioned to his offense. But slowly the public attitude on this matter is changing. The work of the reformatories in curing criminals when mere punishments had only made them bitter, and the reluctance of juries to find just verdicts, lest the men on trial receive unjust sentences, have shown society to be wrong in its theories. Men who sin in ignorance are better lifted from their sins than forced to expiate them, when it is partly the fault of society that they are ignorant and sinful. A most significant change in the treatment of the criminal has been made in recent years by the introduction of the indeterminate sentence system in several of the States. This puts it into the power of men who may have been harshly judged in the first place, and whose mere conviction was penalty enough, to earn their freedom.

The hope of liberty is in itself a stimulus to effort in the reformatory schools and training classes, and the man reproved of the law goes back into the world stronger than when he left it.

In addition to the parole, or indeterminate sentence, a few of the States (Massachusetts, notably) have adopted a probation system which goes into operation before sentence. Certain men and women attend trials in the lower courts and act as intercessors in cases that promise reform. The probation officer is the opposite of the prosecuting attorney, in that the latter brings up everything bad against the prisoner, while the probation officer finds all that is good. It is no longer necessary to confine a man even if he is guilty: he can be placed on parole instead. These probation officers can, with a paroled man's consent, collect his wages and give them to his family. He then has no power to buy drink or squander his means, and if he misbehaves in anywise his liberty is forfeit and he can be sent to prison.

That the warning of an initial arrest suffices in a majority of cases is proved by the records, for few of the paroled ever imperil their liberty again, and something like 4000 persons are conditionally released in the State of Massachusetts every year. It will not be alleged in consequence of these mercies that Massachusetts makes a bad showing in respect to criminal records.

People who misunderstand the nature of these reforms cry out that the prisons are made too comfortable; that sin is encouraged by cleanliness, air, light, sufficient food, and the use of books and papers; that prisons ought to be made places of terror, so that the hesitating might be frightened from them. If mere punishment is the aim, then it were wiser to return to old methods and to whip and rack the offenders, put them into stocks and pillories, crop their ears, take away their property, divorce them from their families, deny their civil rights, even take their lives. But did those punishments prevent crime, or save society? No. The severer the laws the worse the behavior. When stealing was a capital offense thieves abounded in every city, they were in every street, they picked pockets in the church; property was not safe either in the home or on the person; highwaymen infested every road.

As laws modify and the sacredness of life is better appreciated, the causes of offense diminish. And deprivation of liberty is punishment enough.

A prison should not be an inferno, but a purgatory. The criminal is almost invariably weak of will and mind and body; he does not understand himself or his relation to society; his ideals are wrong, his passions have never known check. In this state of barbarism he is dangerous, and society in its own defense sends him into the exile of a prison. If it does no more, he returns, at the end of his sentence, worse than he went in. When it opens his cell door it must open the way to a new life. The prison must be a school, a shop, a church, rather than a place of penitence, for, till the mind and conscience are wakened, there will be no penitence: only anger and nursing of revenge. Mere punishment consigns its victim to darkness and hopelessness, but the probation officer and the reformatory bring him to the light.

—CHARLES M. SKINNER.

The Powers Behind the Throne

TWO changes on the bench of the Supreme Court of the United States — one practically accomplished, the other imminent — mean far more to the nation than a Presidential election.

Our government, being " of laws, not of men," is in the last analysis a government by the Supreme Court. For all laws that vitally affect our institutions or the deeper and broader inter-relations of citizens, state and nation go to the Supreme Court for interpretation. And a majority of those nine Justices decides the fundamental question at issue, which is not merely what the law means, but whether or not it is a law. If that majority says it is not a law, there is no practicable appeal — there is nothing to do but submit.

Sometimes students of our country wonder at the " marvelous elasticity " of our Constitution, at its equal fitness for three millions of people in the eighteenth century and for eighty millions in the twentieth century. A long look at Article III — wherein the judicial power is defined — may at least discourage the theory that the makers of the Constitution were endowed with supernatural wisdom. It is the Supreme Court that provides the elasticity and adaptability.

The Supreme Court not only can and does legislate like all other courts. It also — and here it is unique — can and does amend the very Constitution itself. Interpretation is legislation; it is also amendment. It could easily be essential abrogation and substitution.

Again, the world is astonished at the stability of our " experiment in democracy," at the comparative rigidity with which our Government has in the main confined itself to and contented itself with the modest authority consistent with popular freedom, and has refrained from flagrant acts of usurpation. Part of the secret of this stability of our liberties and this obedience of our Government to the popular will no doubt lies in the character of the American people, in the wholesome frequency of elections, and in the still more wholesome scattering and checking and counterchecking of power. But another, and perhaps a larger, part of that momentous secret will be disclosed to any one who will read the great decisions of the Supreme Court. There will be found evidence that, beginning at the very birth of the Republic, the Executive and the Legislative Departments have, in peace and in war, again and again tried to fly the track of democratic liberty. And nearly always they have been at the time sustained and urged on by the hot prejudices of a dominant faction of the people. Each time — to speak only of those instances in which the liberties and the rights of the individual citizen were boldly or insiduously assailed — the Supreme Court has intervened to protect; and the fiery faction, cooled by the long wait in the august court's calm, passionless chamber, has meekly subsided under its solemn, indisputable rebuke. Since one excess invariably and inevitably produces another and greater excess, we might, probably should, have gone far toward despotism as have all other great republics of the past had not the Supreme Court been there to forbid that fatal " first step " which counts heaviest.

Further, one has only to watch the current of public discussion for a short time to note how it is restrained and guided by the mere fact that the Supreme Court is known to be there, guarding the popular rights, ready to resist passion, subtle partisan intrigue, expediency's schemes that would sacrifice all to a plausible experiment.

The Supreme Court has made mistakes, has shown that even in its exalted atmosphere, so promotive of honest, impartial, far-seeing judgment, man is still fallible. But if its records are searched — not the famous cases alone, but also the many others where, often in obscurity, the very vitals of individual liberty, social, political, even economic, were attacked — that majestic tribunal becomes an object of reverence, of affection. And base indeed would be the man who, elevated to its dignity, could violate its tradition that an American citizen's rights are sacred and inviolable.

What Uncle Sam Will Give You

By René Bache

Merely to Help Fill the Pocketbooks of His People, He Employs Hundreds of Men and Distributes Millions of Dollars

DRAWN BY GUERNSEY MOORE

SO MUCH has been said about free Congressional seeds, $160,000 worth or so, which are distributed annually among grateful farmers—half a dozen ounce-packets going to each recipient—that one might imagine this to be the only gift bestowed by a generous Government upon the citizens of this country. As a matter of fact, however, the generosity of Uncle Sam is most comprehensive, and he gives away an immense number of things of other kinds, supplementing such tangible presents with information that is of actual money-value to people in all walks of life. Indeed, there is scarcely an individual who does not profit in one way or another, where his pocketbook is directly concerned, by such openhandedness on the part of the Federal management.

Even the immigrant, on first reaching our shores, has an opportunity to notice an example of this liberality. A ferry, on which no fare is charged, is maintained for his benefit between Ellis Island and Manhattan, the boat running every hour, and his friends are thus enabled to visit him without paying a cent. During the period of his detention he has free lodging; though he is obliged to pay twenty-four cents a day for board, it is cost price, and, when he goes away, he is at liberty to take with him all the food he can carry, purchasing it at about one-third the rate an American housewife would reckon upon for the same provender.

Much of the business of the new-fledged Department of Commerce relates, as a matter of course, to foreign trade. One of its bureaus, recently organized, is that of Manufactures, which seeks to show the Yankee merchant where he can sell his goods to greatest advantage abroad, and where he can buy them best and cheapest. It proposes, in a word, to put money into the pockets of our exporters by helping them to find foreign markets, and to place them in touch with possible buyers all over the world. With this end in view, expert agents are immediately to be sent out to Europe, Asia, South America and Africa, to procure information which, when it has been gathered, will be distributed gratis to all applicants.

It is probable that the Bureau of Manufactures will soon absorb the Tariff Division, which makes a study of foreign tariffs, and the Bureau of Statistics. The latter bureau not only compiles all sorts of data relating to imports and exports, for the benefit of American merchants, but also utilizes, for the gathering of the latest commercial information, the greatest corps of reporters in the world, publishing their reports in the only daily paper that is issued by any Government. This daily paper costs nothing a year, and anybody may receive it at that price who so desires. The contributors, or reporters, are the consuls of the United States, who are stationed in every seaport of importance on the globe.

Have Your Scales Tested

MUCH more noteworthy than might be supposed, as a distributor of free information worth dollars to the everyday citizen, is the Bureau of Standards. The duty of giving to each State of the Union, and to each of the agricultural colleges in the country, a full set of accurate weights and measures is merely an incidental part of the business of this branch of the Government. At merely nominal cost, any mercantile establishment or other business concern may have its measures and weights tested—a matter of the utmost importance, inasmuch as nowadays all commercial industries, as well as all of the sciences, depend fundamentally upon the correctness of measurements of one kind or another. To such an extent is accuracy in these matters carried that, whereas an inch divided into 10,000 parts would have satisfied all requirements a few decades ago, to-day it must be split into 1,000,000 parts.

The Bureau of Standards maintains a huge refrigerating plant, by the help of which it is enabled to conduct experiments independently of the season, any room being kept at any required temperature for an indefinite period. It will determine the error of your thermometer by comparing it with the ideal instrument, in which the glass tube is occupied by air instead of mercury. Before long it will be ready to furnish standards of electrical units, such as ohms, amperes and watts; and, meanwhile, it is ascertaining with absolute accuracy the candle-power of lamps and the relative intensities of various kinds of light. Of sound no exact measurement has as yet been made. We speak of a "volume" of sound, but nothing definite is meant. Nevertheless, we shall certainly have a standard unit of sound some day—a discovery not less important than the method of measuring by light-waves, which the bureau has already adopted.

The United States Geological Survey is starting in to spend $20,000,000 in the building of dams and reservoirs to irrigate dry regions in the West. People who use the stored water will be obliged to pay for it, but all of the money thus obtained will be used for the construction of new irrigation works, making the gift in a manner continuous. This Government bureau is even now operating, on the World's Fair grounds in St. Louis, a huge plant for the washing of coal. Producers deliver the raw coal—hundreds of tons of it daily—and the impurities, such as slate and pyrite, are separated from it in water by a gravity process, the pure fuel being returned to the owners without the charge of a cent for the work.

Teaching Economy of Coal

THE Government is trying to show the people how to save money by the economical use of fuels. It maintains a chemical laboratory for analyzing samples of coal, the "fuel value" being ascertained by a special contrivance in which a small quantity is burned in pure oxygen. So delicate is the process that the operator watches the thermometer gauge from a distance through a little telescope, lest the heat of his body, if he went near, might affect the apparatus. Other tests are made for steam-production, for gas-generation, for coking and for briquetting. Coal briquettes (waste cemented with coal-tar pitch or other "binder") are coming into quite general use for domestic purposes, taking the form of eggs or small bricks, and larger ones, weighing twenty-five pounds apiece, are employed for locomotives.

Such tests the Geological Survey will make for anybody free of charge, and, in like manner, it will determine the qualities of cements. It is coöperating with the Department of Agriculture in the work of testing road materials and pottery clays—a branch of investigation which is expected to develop to such an extent that a Bureau of Structural Materials will have to be established. Meanwhile anybody who has road-stuff or clay that he wants examined has only to send it to Washington, and a report on it will be returned without expense to himself. Samples of rocks submitted will be examined in the same way, and expert opinions given, together with whatever information may be desired in regard to mining possibilities.

The Forest Bureau, in addition to planting hundreds of thousands of trees on sand dunes, naked hillsides and other barren areas, without charging anything for the service, gives to owners of timber-lands working plans for the management of such forests. Its agents first examine the lands, and upon their report are based the recommendations which are finally made to the proprietor. In such matters the bureau acts in an advisory capacity, the chief end in view being to furnish profitable object-lessons to the people. If A sees that his neighbor B is making money out of a wooded tract by the adoption of certain simple methods, he is likely to undertake similar methods in the foresting of a tract of his own. In the same way the Forest Bureau coöperates with stock-raisers in trying to solve problems which relate to grazing in the forest reserves; and it is also helping the railroads to find out how timber for ties and the butt ends of telegraph poles may be rendered more durable and decay-proof by saturation with chemicals.

The United States Naval Observatory at Washington gives away annually, as has been estimated, a million dollars' worth of time. At noon every day it sets all the electric clocks in the United States, the circuits of telegraph companies being thrown open for that purpose, and, at the same instant, by the pressure of a button, it drops "time balls" at every one of our seaports, in order that mariners may be enabled to set their chronometers.

Moreover, the Weather Bureau is keeping a benevolent watch on these same mariners, and, if a storm threatens, detains them in port by a prompt warning. At any Weather Bureau station a skipper may, without paying a cent, have his barometer tested for accuracy. But, of course, though many valuable cargoes—not to mention human lives—are saved by warnings furnished to shipmasters by the Government, the greatest usefulness of such advance information, free to everybody, appears in the case of impending warm waves or "freezes." Shippers sending perishable merchandise long distances often escape great loss by keeping an eye on the forecasts, which, though so frequently in error as regards rain or shine from day to day, are wonderfully accurate where "spells" of heat or cold are concerned. To this fact testimony would readily be given by truck-growers, especially in Florida, where the prompt adoption of precautions, in response to warning of expected frost, has saved many a crop.

Some of the most valuable of our fisheries depend for their maintenance on the fresh supplies of young fishes which the Fisheries Bureau annually contributes to the waters. A conspicuous example in point is the shad-fisheries, which would be practically non-existent at the present time if it were not for the billions of "fry" which the Government has poured into the rivers. All of these fishes are a free gift to the people; but, for that matter, anybody who has a pond or a stream on his land may have it stocked free of charge with trout or bass or crappie by Uncle Sam. All he has to do is to put in an application, indorsed by his Congressman, and he will promptly receive as many "fry" as are required for "brood stock." In starting in to raise poultry, one begins usually with a rooster and four or five hens; similarly, a thousand bass or crappie may, at the outset, serve for a good-sized pond. The owner of the pond or stream will be furnished gratis with pamphlets containing full instructions for feeding, and all he is asked to do in return is to report results three years later.

Get a Free Box of Microbes

ANY farmer who wishes to grow peas or beans or clover may obtain from the Plant Bureau, for the asking, a small pasteboard box containing microbes of the nitrogen-gathering kind, for inoculating the soil. Properly used, they may be expected to increase the crop largely, enabling the plants to draw sustenance from the air. If you would like to go into the business of raising silkworms, the Bureau of Entomology will send you five thousand eggs, ready for hatching; and, in case you have no mulberry trees to furnish food for the insects, a few little ones will be supplied on request. In all likelihood, if you are an agriculturist, some pestiferous bug is attacking your fields, and in that case the Department of Agriculture will gladly supply you with a few specimens of some predaceous beetle, or other enemy of that particular bug, to eat the invader. Only the other day the Government imported from northern China an insect that looks like a hedgehog in miniature, which is expected to wipe out the destructive San José scale, and at the present moment Dr. L. O. Howard, the chief official expert, is in Europe collecting parasites of the dreaded gipsy moth.

Uncle Sam breeds these beneficial bugs, and is delighted to give them away to applicants.

The Right Sort of Voters

WE SEE in our experiences with our new island possessions the absolute necessity of restrictions upon the suffrage, so that the interests of the Government may be kept in the hands of capable men. When the Government drew up the regulations for the first elections in Cuba and Porto Rico, it made strict qualifications in regard to education and property ownership, and widened the electoral privilege only so far as to include citizens who had served in the armies.

The Commission that went to Hawaii saw the condition of things there and recommended that Congress limit the suffrage, by a property qualification, to the intelligent whites and the respectable natives. Congress, however, was influenced by the conditions that prevail in our own States and made the law much broader. What might have been expected soon happened. The eleven thousand unintelligent voters overwhelmed the three thousand intelligent people, and then followed the troubles which have since kept the islands in more or less of a ferment.

In Massachusetts the suffrage is restricted by intelligence, thus keeping the Government within responsible bounds. Massachusetts has its politics, but the administration of its affairs both in State and city is far above the average in cleanliness and competency.

Many of the States have recently held or are holding conventions to frame new constitutions, and in every instance we find recognition of the importance of making the vote intelligent by keeping it in the hands of intelligent citizens. The South has the greater problem to handle because of the prevailing ignorance among the colored people. Outside of the admitted purpose to disfranchise the negroes as far as it can be done by legislative expedients is the real fact that the white people have both the intelligence and the property. The injustice of the new provisions in the South is that they do not discriminate in favor of those negroes who hold property or who have acquired enough education to entitle them to the ballot.

If President Grant's recommendation to Congress, nearly thirty years ago, had been followed there would be few illiterates at the polls to-day, for he declared in favor of an educational qualification after the year 1890. Other Presidents have shared the same view, and there is no doubt that the great majority of Americans cordially favor it. The matter is brought to every voter when he finds his ballot of no more account than that of the most ignorant person or of the most worthless vagabond who sells his vote for a few dollars.

With the increase of educational facilities and the vast expenditure of millions to save the generations from ignorance, the Government and the States have done and are doing their duty nobly, and it is right to expect that all this provision should have its effect in a better and worthier citizenship.

Socialism as a Live Issue

WITH a suddenness that must be startling to those who note only the surface of events, Socialism has become a factor in our moral, political and industrial life. The Socialist vote for President last fall attracted a good deal of attention—more, perhaps, than in itself it deserved—but it was in no way a measure of the importance of the Socialistic movement. And year by year, as science compels consolidations and coöperations on a scale impossible in the past, the collectivist proposals formulated by the German Jew, Karl Marx, out of the theorizings of the great French economists of the eighteenth century, are bound to receive more and more attention.

Whatever one believes about it, he must inform himself. For, while Mark Hanna's prediction that Socialism would be the storm centre of the next great political battle in this country seemed exaggerated when he made it a few years ago, his farsightedness is already vindicated. To fight for Socialism, you must understand it; to fight against Socialism, you must understand it.

IF MONEY CAN MAKE A CANDIDATE for the highest office in our free government, why not go to the top and start a boom for ROCKEFELLER? Think what a boom he could purchase if only he could be persuaded that political advertisement would be worth the price that he could pay. He could afford a ROCKEFELLER club in every village in America. He could buy a dozen times seven newspapers and keep them all busy printing his name in green and crimson ink. He would be the real thing. A few millions spent in advertising would seem like a still, small voice if ROCKEFELLER should once properly turn his billion into sound. Nor does he lack other qualifications for the place. If Mr. HEARST, for instance, can claim to be a newspaper trust all by

WHY NOT ROCKEFELLER? himself, Mr. ROCKEFELLER is greater in the combination line also. In holiness, too, he seems to our unbiased vision at least the equal of his rival. One of our readers writes indignantly that "no man in the Christian era" is to be compared for good work with Mr. HEARST, and others draw analogies which our sense of reverence renders it impossible to quote. Against this spiritual exaltation of the one citizen, however, we pit the long religious history of the other. Mr. HEARST, as we have magnanimously declared, is competent to pay the salaries of able men, and it has been suggested that a substitute candidate be found in MI. BRISBANE, in whom resides the majority of his chieftain's brains. It would be more logical to choose a man who surpasses Mr. HEARST in that power which is his very own, namely money. We wish to be as fair as if conviction were an emotion foreign to our nature, and it is on the ground of logic purely that we launch a boom for the richest man of all.

A GROWING MENACE

Uncle Sam's Last Big Lottery

A TYPICAL SOUTH DAKOTA FARM SCENE

The August Allotment of Home-steads in South Dakota

By F. A. MILLER

WHEN President Roosevelt signed the proclamation opening the Sioux Indian lands of the Rosebud Reservation, in South Dakota, he made possible the transformation of 382,000 acres of wild and uncultivated land into one of the most productive and quickly populated sections of farm land in the United States. That this possibility is already realized and that all previous records for travel to a new "land of promise" will be broken by the Rosebud movement, in July of this year, is clearly apparent from the great number of inquiries received by the United States Land Office at Chamberlain, South Dakota, and by the Western railroads.

Probably never before in the history of the Northwest has there been an equal interest in the opening to settlement of any other tract of Government lands. The reasons for this intense interest are not far to seek. The cities of the East and the Central West are closely crowded. These centres of population contain a large class of discontented inhabitants, a struggling multitude weary of the dreary turmoil and competition of the denser communities. They are anxious to acquire farms of their own, the products of which will support them in comfort, provide for their children, and insure for themselves, in their declining years, a substantial competency. Perhaps a still larger class attracted to the opening of the Rosebud Reservation is recruited from the juniors of the American farmers. Certainly the junior farmer will be numerously in evidence and will make a model settler. His father has done well and prospered on a farm in one of the Central States, and would gladly give each of his boys a good start on the highway to independence; but he finds that land in their home county has quadrupled in value since he "settled," and that to buy farms there for his sons does not appear to be the wisest investment. The opening of Uncle Sam's big land lottery, however, offers an ideal opportunity for the farmer's son. Trained on the home farm, backed with sufficient capital to make his first payment of one dollar an acre on 160 acres, and perhaps double that amount for necessary buildings, implements and other items of equipment, he starts under peculiar advantages in a State whose fertile farms have given it a preëminent rank.

In a recent letter to me, Governor Charles N. Herreid, of South Dakota, concisely covered the subject under consideration in these words:

"Here the fortunate homeseeker may secure some of the best land in the Northwest. Here homes may be established, not in some far-off wilderness, but adjacent to organized, prosperous communities, having the advantages of modern rural civilization. On every quarter section (of Rosebud Reservation land) before next Thanksgiving Day will be found some enterprising homesteader. Several houses and churches will spring up as if by magic. The hunting grounds of the Indian braves will soon be the scene of marvelous activity and prosperity.

"During the last six years South Dakota has produced annually more wealth per capita than any other State in the Union. Why? Because we have the energy, intelligence, enterprise and natural advantages."

Land on the Installment Plan

UNCLE SAM, evidently imbued with the spirit of the times, has provided that the sale of these newest bargains shall be made upon the modern installment, or "easy-payment," plan. "A dollar down and seventy-five cents a year on each acre, for four years," in a general way covers the advertisement of this Federal installment offering. No fee whatever is required to register for one of the quarter-section land bargains; but those who are fortunate in the drawing and make "final entry" must pay the land office fees, amounting to fourteen dollars, for 160 acres, in addition to the first payment of one dollar an acre.

In the opening of the Rosebud Reservation there will be no picturesque and chaotic race from the border line, with horses, bicycles and automobiles as pacemakers. Uncle Sam has tried this undignified and barbaric experiment in opening other reservations and has decided to submit the question of selection to chance rather than to speed and violence. To those who anticipate a mighty rush and a quick grab for the best lands he will say: "Back to the land office! There will be no race to-day."

It is unnecessary to quote the act of Congress or the President's proclamation opening the Rosebud Reservation to settlement in order to show just what must be done to obtain one of these farms of 160 acres. The clearest statement of all the rules and qualifications comes from the Government Land Commissioner at Chamberlain, South Dakota, and is, in brief, as follows:

None but persons qualified to make entry will be permitted to register for the Rosebud lands in Gregory County, South Dakota.

Qualifications to make a homestead are: Not the owner of more than 160 acres of land in any State or Territory; a citizen of the United States, native born or naturalized by first or second papers; over the age of twenty-one years or the head of a family; *bona fide* intentions to make entry and comply with the homestead laws of the United States for own use and benefit *and not directly or indirectly for the use or benefit of any other person;* has not since August 30, 1890, entered under the public land laws of the United States a quantity of land which, with a legal homestead, would make more than 320 acres; has not heretofore perfected or abandoned an entry under the homestead laws of the United States.

Honorably discharged soldiers and sailors of the Civil or Spanish-American Wars, or their widows, may, by power of attorney, appoint an agent and furnish him with a copy of discharge or other competent evidence of military service and honorable discharge. Such agent can register for one person so appointing him only, and for himself.

No person will be permitted to register more than once, or in any other than his true name. Any person who shall transfer his registration certificate will thereby lose all benefits of the registration, and will be precluded from entering or settling upon any of said lands during the first sixty days.

As soon as registered each person will be given a certificate of registration which will entitle him to go upon and examine the land. This certificate must be preserved and presented with application by those entitled to make entry.

Dates of registration—July 5 to July 23, 1904, both days inclusive.

Places of registration—Chamberlain, Yankton, Fairfax and Bonesteel, South Dakota.

Manner of registration—In person at the time and places mentioned.

Drawing for right of entry begins July 28, 1904, at Chamberlain, and continues until the names of all persons registered have been drawn. Each person will be notified by postal-card, at the address given by him when he registers, of the drawing of his name, and of the time he must present his application to make entry.

The drawing will be under the supervision and management of the Secretary of the Interior, through the Commissioner of the General Land Office, and a committee appointed by him. Every safeguard to insure fairness will be adopted. It is not essential that persons registered shall be present at the drawing unless they wish. No one will gain or lose anything by the time, place or order of his registration.

Persons whose names are drawn thereby secure the right to make selection of the lands, and homestead entry therefore, in the order of drawing, beginning with number one.

Entries begin August 8, 1904, at nine o'clock A. M., at Bonesteel, South Dakota. The names of the first 100 drawn will be called on that day; the second 100 on the following day, and in like manner 100 on each day until the lands are exhausted.

If at the time of considering his regular application to make entry it shall be found that any applicant is disqualified from making homestead entry his application will be rejected, notwithstanding his prior registration.

Within six months after making entry the homestead claimant must establish a residence in a house on his claim, and thereafter reside continuously upon the land and cultivate the same for the period of five years.

No fee whatever is required at the time of registration. Each person must procure and execute the proper and necessary papers for registration, for which notaries and other proper officers will be permitted to make a reasonable charge of twenty-five cents for each person. The executed papers must be presented by the person to the registering officer.

Those who become entitled by the drawing to make entry must, at the time of filing their homestead applications, pay the land office fees, which amount to fourteen dollars for 160 acres, and in addition thereto one dollar per acre for the amount of land embraced in the application. The fee for a soldier's declaratory statement is two dollars, payable at the time of filing the same, which must be in the order of the drawing.

At the end of two years, three years, four years, and within six months after the expiration of five years respectively from the date of making entry, the claimant must pay seventy-five cents per acre for the land embraced in his entry. Default in any payment at the time it becomes due forfeits all right to the land, and the entry will be canceled.

At any time after fourteen months of continuous residence and cultivation any person who shall have made a homestead entry for the lands in question may make a commutation proof upon such entry, upon payment of the balance of the purchase price for the land then remaining unpaid, the land office fees and commissions, and, in addition thereto, one dollar and twenty-five cents per acre for the land, for the privilege of such commutation. Upon lands filed upon within the first three months after August 8, 1904, the commutation price will be five dollars and twenty-five cents per acre, besides fees and commissions.

No person will be allowed to settle upon any of the Rosebud lands until after October 8, 1904, except those who shall make entry therefor pursuant to the act and proclamation.

"Is it worth while?" do you ask? A thousand times "Yes!" The Government has surrounded its bargain counter with only such conditions as will keep away those who would speculate in its generosity. The provisions given above are all for the interest of the honest homeseeker who would in good faith follow Horace Greeley's famous advice. When the reader considers that the Rosebud lands are bounded on three sides by splendidly developed farm lands, with communities of well-to-do farmers owning substantial and permanent homes and farms valued at fifteen dollars to thirty-five dollars an acre, he can best judge of the rich promise the immediate future holds in store for the settler on the Rosebud Reservation lands.

What the Country is Like

THE country to be opened is adapted to diversified farming. The land is too valuable to be used to any extent for grazing. Those who wish land for a cattle range would do well to go directly west of Chamberlain, South Dakota, in Lyman County, where 400,000 acres of land are now open to homestead entry.

General farming in South Dakota includes the growing of corn, wheat, oats, hay, barley, rye, flax, of potatoes and other vegetables, and of fruits, the raising of poultry and the pursuit of dairying.

Gently undulating prairie land forms about half of the tract to be opened; the other half is rough and broken. The bottom lands along the Missouri River and the lands near the numerous large creeks are narrow and the land is rough. Back from the river the uplands are 700 to 800 feet above the level of the Missouri River, or about 2000 feet above sea level.

With the exception of about a dozen sandy sections, all of the 382,000 acres are well adapted to farming. Near the Missouri River the soil consists of a loose but rich black loam, free from sand or "grit," and underlaid by a loose yellow clay. The entire reservation is well watered from numerous creeks, rivers and many permanent springs. On the uplands an abundant supply of water is furnished from tubular wells, and flowing artesian wells have been sunk along the Missouri and Whetstone rivers. Along all the streams considerable timber is found. Rainfall is ample, and the climate is most delightful, being identical with that of the eastern parts of South Dakota and Nebraska and northwestern Iowa. As a rule, little snow falls before the holidays, and cattle and horses find green grass until December. The long Indian summer gives opportunity to care for all crops during pleasant weather. The heavy falls of snow during midwinter are followed by sunshine. No greater tribute could be paid South Dakota climate than to state that thousands of cattle subsist through the entire winter without shelter or without food other than the grass of the prairies.

It is natural for the prospective settler to indulge in the fancy of drawing first choice in Uncle Sam's last big lottery and prospectively to build not merely a castle but an entire city. And yet there are populous towns and cities already built on the land recently opened to settlement in the Territory of Oklahoma. Those who are fortunate enough to secure, at an initial cost of one dollar an acre, the sites on which the towns of the Rosebud tract will be founded undoubtedly will win a rich prize.

Is there any way by which these town sites can be foretold? None that I know of—personal inspection of the reservation and a study of its local geography ought best to fit the settler to choose the land he wishes when his name is drawn "out of the hat" at Chamberlain in July. There are but 2400 quarter-sections on the Rosebud Reservation to be given out by Uncle Sam; the number who have already indicated an intention to register for these lands is more than 25,000. It is altogether probable that many who register but are not "lucky on the draw" will take up less valuable homesteads in Lyman County or make other settlement in South Dakota. Such an increase in the population means more than an increase in the number of farmers and cattlemen. There will be a corresponding demand for carpenters, blacksmiths and other tradespeople. The sudden transformation of an Indian reservation into a civilized agricultural community presents unusual opportunities for success in every important trade, calling and profession.

The Rosebud Reservation will be opened without scenes of disorder. The abolition of the grand rush is a wise precaution to that end. Steps have been taken to prevent congestion of transportation facilities and to save the towns of Chamberlain, Yankton, Geddes, Platte and others from having their populations multiplied many times during one or two days at the time of registry. The railroads, instead of making low rates for one or two days only, announce them for every day from July 1 to 23, inclusive, with a return limit on the tickets of August 31.

How to Get There

FOR transportation to the reservation from the nearest towns hundreds of horses and carriages have been secured. The distances vary from six to twenty miles. As Chamberlain, Geddes, Platte and Yankton have for five years been central points in South Dakota land movements their stage lines and livery facilities will be equal to the demand. Many settlers in going to the Reservation will go directly from the Government Land Office at Chamberlain to the Reservation by boat down the Missouri River. Five steamboats will make this trip of thirty miles down stream and provide an easy means of access for those who do not care to ride or drive by road.

To appreciate the prospective development of the present Indian tract it is worth while to consider what South Dakota, outside the reservation, has done in recent years.

South Dakota is long on wealth but short on people. For the sixth consecutive year South Dakota in 1903 led all other States in the Union in the production of per capita wealth. This is a good sign for the prospective settler, who naturally prefers to avoid communities that are crowded and lands that do not yield rich and profitable returns.

South Dakota is larger by one-fourth than the area of all the New England States, but its population is only about half a million people, or approximately six to the square mile.

In studying the 1903 crop report of South Dakota one is impressed with these returns of new wealth produced: Live stock, $35,950,164; wheat, $29,422,900; corn, $15,819,200; hay and fodder, $13,840,000; minerals, stone and cement, $10,000,000. The fact that the 1903 table of products amounts to $14,939,264 more than the 1902 total shows by what bounds the Sunshine State has been leaping forward.

Modern Wonder Workers

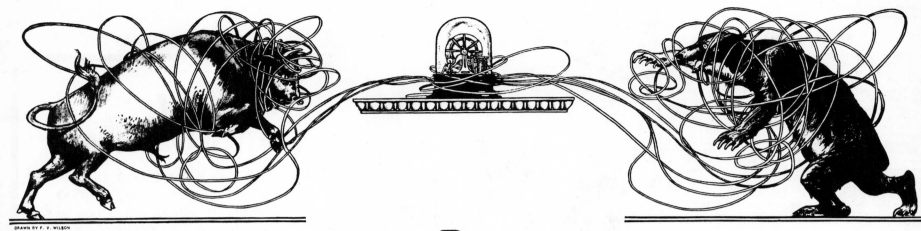

DRAWN BY F. V. WILSON

By
EDWIN LEFÈVRE

WALL STREET has made financial history with a vengeance these past few years. The great boom in business caused not a greater but a more spectacular boom in stock, and with the latter came certain tendencies which culminated in "epoch-making" deals, the full import of which is not yet realized. The country has beheld the wholesale creation of trusts, from the Chewing-gum "combine" to the United States Steel Corporation, some of them obeying the manifest economic tendency of the times and others merely the manifest stock-market necessities of great gamblers. Wonderful days these have been and wonderful men. The thoughts of the nation have been colored by the wonderful prosperity and the lives of thousands influenced or governed by the vagaries of the ticker. A magic name—Wall Street!—and it conjures visions of sudden fortunes, plunging, reckless exploits, golden successes of men who have in superabundance the money that means comforts and power these days; or the brains and constructive abilities that have made the name of American respected by the less strenuous nations. But to understand these financial generals, and the thrilling romances of their lives fully, one must realize their opportunities. They came from the boom. It is well to consider in turn what the boom came from and what it meant.

In times of abundance wise men prepare for scarcity. In times of scarcity wise men wait for abundance. Joseph saw, in Pharaoh's dream, the "signs of the times" —seven fat years to be followed by the seven lean. He cornered wheat when fat crops made the quotation low, and waited to sell till the crop failures that followed made the staple scarce and valuable. Probably before Joseph's time—certainly after —there has been this logical alternation of "good" times and "hard," and financial students have been struck with the regularity of these changes. In this country we have had a boom every twenty years, with corresponding depression periods, when men sink into extremes of pessimism, and there come panics, unnecessary losses, broken confidence, hopelessness. Memory being short with most of us, when good times come again men rise to extreme heights of optimism, the sun of prosperity tips every cloud with gold, and long after the sun has ceased to shine the eyes remain dazzled; so that even when they are closed the gold glitters on. Thus, till darkness comes.

Humanity has never witnessed so remarkable a period of prosperity as has blessed this country since 1896, remarkable not only for magnitude but for duration. That it has

Editor's Note—This is the first of a series of articles by Mr. Lefèvre on Wall Street and Prosperity.

stamped itself deeply on our people's habit of thought, engendered recklessness, created new social, financial and industrial conditions, is natural. When we are prosperous we are apt to be extravagant. But that the development of certain new tendencies—to mention but one, the wholesale formation of trusts—must exert lasting influence upon the national life, is far more important. The extravagant simply pay for their extravagance and there's an end to it. Individual extravagance is punished with individual ruin and corporate extravagance with receiverships. But none can foretell whither the concentration of vast power in few hands may lead. Trusts will not produce hard times; they dislike nothing so much; and yet the danger that a financial oligarchy may dominate the republic does not seem imaginary to some observers. At the moment, combined labor is doing its utmost to divert the public's attention from combined capital. But the sense of danger will awaken again when hunger pinches the workingmen. Trusts may stifle competition and increase prices, but if their employees are kept busy enough

THE NEW YORK STOCK EXCHANGE

and fairly paid, the grievances against them in good times are mostly academic. It is when the pendulum swings downward that the mob will blame the trusts. Economic problems, financial precedents, the history of the nation's commerce and the fluctuations of trade are not understood by the many; but the desire for scapegoats is one of the universal traits. Yet economy of energy being the keynote of modern life, the development of the trust is as logical as the development of the specialization of knowledge. What struggles may arise before the place and functions of the trust are definitely fixed in the economy of the nation, what abuses may inflame prejudice against them all and lead to hostile developments, that is what none may say.

The country itself with its stupendous wealth has created the prosperity in which we have been living these past six or seven years. Heretofore this wealth was largely potential; of late it has become actual. For a hundred years this nation grew with the help of Europe. From Germany, from France, from Great Britain, skilled labor came because there were better opportunities in a free country, unfettered by precedent and possessing unparalleled natural resources. The irresistible attraction toward America gave us what we lacked. There were no caste bounds to hamper. Any man could become as good as the better if he had it in him in like measure. It was the country of fair play.

But it was not the rapid growth of mere population alone; it was the amazing growth of a *productive* population that made us great. We took good men from Europe and we borrowed Europe's money. Uncle Sam, a young man embarking in business, asked for financial assistance, giving as collateral mortgages on his railroads, on his farms, on his factories, till his business grew so that he paid off his debts. For a hundred years he worked hard, and now having a better and bigger property than his cousins, he feels richer than all of them, which he is.

The last period of depression, ending in 1896, was accompanied by the usual phenomena: sluggish commerce, semi-paralyzed industry; money was coming out from strong boxes, if at all, fearfully; men would not venture in new enterprises. Timidity is contagious and in those dark years it seemed wisdom to the many. We suffered from nervous prostration and were taking the rest cure, while Nature, the handmaid of Providence, was working for us. The country was growing, becoming greater, richer, stronger in every respect. When it awoke it was incredibly rich. It resumed work in earnest; with its tremendous pent-up energy, repressed for years, it was able to accomplish more than had ever been dreamed possible. The traffic from the more populous territories, the demand from the increased population which had consumed so little during the lean years, the carrying out of cherished projects, long delayed, all meant stupendous business. It was not because the country had been idle that it became busy. It was primarily because there were bounteous crops here, short harvests elsewhere. In the year ending June 30, 1897, we sold to Europe $267,271,000 more than Europe sold to us. Bear in mind that it was an accession of wealth from out the wheat fields of the Northwest, the corn fields of the Middle West, the cotton fields of the South. It was not old wealth changing hands; it was new wealth plucked from the ground, the transmutation of sunlight, rain and the sweat of men's brows into gold by the alchemist, Nature. The first year of the good times was remarkable; the second was a wonder. The goddess, Fortune, was paying America a real visit; she had taken off her street wraps, sat down and refused to budge. We sold the world much at profitable prices. We fed Europe. There was a great strike of mechanics in Great Britain when her industrial activity was curtailed and her old customers became ours. There was a great expansion in electrical enterprises; copper was needed and we supplied it. We sold copper to help run Europe's trolleys. The American copper producer was making money out of the illumination of Great Britain's streets as well as out of the darkness of Boer farms in the shape of copper wire and brass rifle-shells. These are only instances that could be multiplied indefinitely. For example, we had begun by buying our steel in England; then we bought English machinery and manufactured our own rails — much more expensively than in England. Then we built our own improved machinery, and having greater resources, made rails cheaper. So with other things. In 1890 our yearly tin-plate product was practically nil. In 1898 we produced 18,071 tons, valued at $1,162,930; three boom years later we turned out 399,291 tons, valued at $35,776,474! And so through the catalogue of industries. Always the natural wealth, the push and activity of the American people, the blossoming of the tree of freedom.

The Distribution of Prosperity

THERE was a third wonderful year, and a fourth, and a fifth; we are upon the seventh. There were ups and downs; the downs for years were pygmean and the ups gigantic. Lately the downs have been ominous. In the five fiscal years of the United States Treasury Department from June, 1896, to June, 1901, we bought from the world $3,750,542,752; we sold to the world during the same five years $6,277,196,032. The balance in our favor was $2,526,653,280. It was more than all the present gold mines of the entire world at the current rate of output could produce in twenty-five years! There wasn't enough cash available to pay for Europe's purchases of American products; so Europe began to send back the old American I. O. U's — the mortgages on our railroads, on our farms, on our factories. American securities came back to America.

For the first time in history industrial America found itself free of foreign debt. Optimists grew doubtful at this unexampled and continued prosperity. Three years ago the shrewdest men, thinking the upward swing of the pendulum had gone far enough, looked for the downward stroke. To-day many do not think it has begun.

Prosperity has not been equally distributed — it never is; but the entire nation has lived well, and a few have grown stupendously rich. Five years ago a prominent newspaper of the metropolis had a standing rule that the death of a man who left a million dollars behind him was to be chronicled on the first page. To-day, nobody having less than fifteen millions of dollars is entitled to that exquisite posthumous distinction. Ordinary one-millionaires are so common that you bump against them in the street, and as a friend of mine, telling of a dinner at which he had been, said, you could not throw a toothpick around the table without hitting a millionaire. A man died in a New York hotel a few months ago. Nobody knew him. When his will was probated it was discovered that he had left a fortune greater than was possessed twenty years ago by any American, excepting possibly Mr. Vanderbilt or Mr. Astor. A quiet old man named Smith, of whom nobody had ever heard, died at a ripe old age. Yet the State received in fees from the inheritance tax something like $2,000,000, of itself a vast fortune as fortunes went a dozen years ago. It was mostly in St. Paul stock. A man named Jones died in Florida. But he was from Pittsburg; he made iron. He left $60,000,000. Thus, while the poor have not grown poorer, the rich have grown flamboyantly richer. They say in Wall Street slang *flim-flam-boyantly* richer. The old-time fortunes, begotten of the fulfilled dreams of a realty-mad family like the Astors, or of the building and development of railways, like the Vanderbilts, or of fortunate bonanza-strikers, like the Mackays, are relegated to the second rank by the bank accounts of the latest American type, the Stock Market Millionaire. Where the Fisks and the Drews and other Wall Street freebooters of a by-gone generation operated in one or another stock involving fifty or seventy-five thousand shares, the financier of to-day deals in whole railway systems involving fifty or seventy-five millions of dollars, or combines an entire industry into a single corporation having a capitalization greater than the national debt of the United States.

The Turning of the Tide

THESE men are the wonder workers of modern finance. Some belong to old finance; the majority are new men whose prominence dates from yesterday. New and old achieve miracles, and revolutionize our very methods of doing business. That the magnitude of their operations is unprecedented is certain; but it is the development of certain tendencies along new lines which need cause deep concern. Modern financial practice has indeed been carried on in strange and not altogether reassuring ways. Good has been done. There has been the elimination of vexatious problems, of the demoralization attendant upon senseless and wasteful trade fights or rate wars. There has been the more economical because more scientific operation of railways and manufactures, the suppression of expensive methods of distribution, rendered unnecessary by consolidation; there has been an expansion in the fields of usefulness, the establishment of commercial independence, the clearer understanding of the necessities of the export trade, and a certain independence of thought, a confidence which has, for example, sent an American to build, and what is more, to control, an electrical street railway in London, like Mr. Yerkes, or has made an American buy and control the most important lines of British and German, as well as American steamships, like Mr. Morgan, or has made Americans, representing other Americans, determined to supply Paris with better gas, like Mr. Brady and Mr. Billings, otherwise famous as the owner of Lou Dillon. Foreign economists write seriously of the "American peril."

If the United States has become a world-power it is largely because of its captains of industry. It is a fact that no bond issue could have been floated exclusively in this country ten short years ago, either by the Federal Government or by the strongest railroads. European help was absolutely indispensable.

Since the present boom began Great Britain "allotted" a part of its war loan to America. Imperial German and Austrian bonds, and German and Swiss and Swedish municipal bonds were and are offered for sale in New York by various firms; the Russian Government "listed" on the New York Stock Exchange 2,310,000,000 rubles of its four per cent. bonds for American investors. The Mexican national debt was "converted" by New York bankers. All this before the boom made bonds difficult to sell by making bond manufacturers overgreedy.

Why Wall Street Thinks Well of Itself

WALL STREET allows itself to think at times that it is America. This is because it is American intensely and typically, and because in it dwell the men who have done the most to harness the upbuilding, wealth-making forces of the country, who have planned and carried out the "deals" which have brought on the new conditions. Apart from the stock speculating end of the existing condition of affairs, one must go to Wall Street to get at the fountain-head of affairs.

For example, the United States Steel Corporation, the dominant power in the iron and steel industry of the United States, may in time be the dominant power in the iron and steel industry of the world. Mr. Morgan begot it. He is in Wall Street. The railways of the United States, the most important industry of the country, are under the control of a scant score of men, and the scant score of men have offices in Wall Street.

Thus, if the causes which led to the establishment of the United States as a world-power did not originate in Wall Street, the leaders of the various enterprises which make the United States a world-power are there. The spirit of the times has found expression in every city in the land, but in Wall Street it is expressed through a megaphone. Also, in Wall Street is the great security market that is the Court of Last Resort. In Wall Street the trusts have been formed — *with an eye on the stock market;* there railroads have absorbed other railroads — *with an eye on the stock market.* Some years ago promoters of American enterprises took their bonds and stocks to Europe for European bankers to sell to the European public. During the boom the promoters took their nice new bonds and stocks to the New York Stock Exchange to sell to the American public. The American public at large is affected by the trusts rather than by the stock market; but the makers of the trusts are the slaves of the ticker; not that they are speculating blindly, but that they must float the stocks they manufacture. Hence this vital importance of the stock market. It was Morgan, the Wall Street man, not Carnegie, the iron master, who floated the Steel Trust. Hundreds of thousands of men, depending for a livelihood upon the Steel Trust, are employed in its coal and iron mines, in its furnaces, in its steamers, in its limestone quarries, in its docks, in its railways, in its cooking ovens, in its mills, in its offices. Millions depend upon the use of its products for their livelihood — builders of bridges, of edifices, of safes, of toy pistols — users of iron and steel in every form. Why and how Mr. Morgan organized the trust became important. It is the same in other "revolutionizing" creations and consolidations. A dozen years ago this was the most individualistic nation in the world; and individuality and individualism were encouraged. Government ownership of railroads seemed practically impossible. There were then too many owners, too many interests.

The present concentration of power in few hands makes the Socialist's dream realizable. Uncle Sam might walk into a room, where seated about a table he might find Messrs. Morgan, Hill, Cassatt, Harriman, Schiff, Vanderbilt, Gould, Rockefeller, Reid, and for good measure, three more. And Uncle Sam could in five minutes arrange for the purchase of all the railroads of the country!

The Financial Sin of the Eighties

IN THE previous boom (1880-84) our great sin had been the over-building, on borrowed money, of railroads, so flimsily constructed that they could not be operated with profit. The insolvency of those roads during the subsequent hard times was a foregone conclusion. The price of this error had to be paid. The lesson was nevertheless a bitter one, and as a direct result of it almost all of the reorganizations of this last bankrupt period, when the American people had got down to "hard pan," were carried along scientific and conservative lines.

Although confident of the return of better times, our financiers were powerfully affected by the scarcity of cash and the reluctance of many of the hoarders to buy securities, and willingly or not they were forced to be conservative. The reorganizations of bankrupt railroads were therefore carried on in the strongest possible manner, the roads being often capitalized below their real values.

In the present boom there was, on the contrary, no over-construction, but plenty of over-capitalization. The profits even, which in this wave of prosperity were enormous, were capitalized. Men of great imagination, optimists by nature and by business, they even went on to capitalize their hopes! In the end the greatest of them all, Mr. Morgan, acknowledged that they had over-manufactured securities. They were "undigested." They ought to be. If the securities new and old "listed" on the New York Stock Exchange in the last five years should return interest or dividends at the rate of four per cent. per annum, it would mean an annual disbursement of about fifty millions on the bonds and nearly seventy-five millions on the stocks, practically a total of $125,000,000 yearly.

These figures tell the story of the country's prosperity and of the tremendous stock operations. The story of the stock operators must be told in another article.

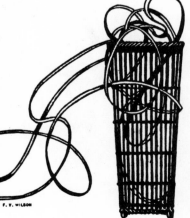

THE MUNICIPAL BIG STICK.

FATHER KNICKERBOCKER. — I hate to use this, but —

The Promoter's Obscuration

BUSINESS in the United States is at flood-tide. All the stock indications show it. If the thing could be exactly measured it would no doubt be proved that material prosperity is even now at the highest pitch ever known. Yet you hear very little of that prosperity tout, the promoter, who was cutting so great a figure some seven years ago. No new industrial flotations are proposed. None of importance has been offered this year.

Six and seven years ago nearly all the industries of the country were taken in hand by the promoter, who combined them and capitalized them into preferred and common stock to the amount of five billions or so. Surveying his handiwork to-day one might suppose that it had been struck by a tornado, instead of having enjoyed a long summer of splendid commercial weather. Out of a hundred companies that were floated in the halcyon days of trust-building, perhaps six will now be found paying a dividend on the common stock, while some have been unable even to earn the stipulated rate on the preferred shares and others have gone hopelessly to wreck.

This is not the fault of the times or of any general condition. It is the fault of a persistently crude imagination. We ought to know by this time that the sky is actually unattainable by man; that the tower of Babel would have failed to reach the empyrean dome even without the harsh expedient which was thought advisable in that case. The greatest of the promoters declared that deductions drawn from past experience no longer counted—in other words, we were going to build right into Heaven. The financial public was in a frame of mind to believe it then. That is why the promoter no longer attracts attention to himself, but, on the contrary, is mostly engaged in trying to live it down.

Good times have the expansive effect of sunshine. There may be moments when the blue looks only three-quarters of a mile away and solid as rock; but, if you are tempted to order building material, pause and reread some of the prospectuses of 1898.

The Outrage of Taxation

NOT since Boston threw the tea overboard has there been a greater up-welling of passionate protest against a tax than is now on exhibition in New York.

The Legislature proposes to tax stock transfers at the rate of two dollars for each hundred shares. As the face value of a hundred shares of stock is usually $10,000, the tax would amount to about two one-hundredths of one per cent. Thus to many innocent people it looks trivial.

The truly diabolical nature of the impost appears only to the initiate who know that last year 187,312,065 shares were transferred on the New York Stock Exchange, and that, in a really bang-up year for business like 1901, the number of shares handled exceeded 265,000,000. There are gentlemen of the Exchange called room-traders who will buy or sell some 10,000 shares in a fairly busy day and go home at night only $17 richer or poorer, as the case may be. Upon their frail shoulders this monstrous tax would fall with crushing weight.

To a man who wished to invest $10,000 in stocks, or to realize upon an investment of that size, the little addition of two dollars would make no difference. But, if only the man who wishes to invest or to realize upon his investment were to be considered, the beautiful home of the Exchange would be for rent next week. It is the man who is playing for a two-point turn who makes the colossal totals which are the just boast of the Exchange and who pays the freight, and to that man two dollars in real money makes a lot of difference. It is a realization of this rather painful fact that makes the "Street" take the tax so much to heart.

Probably the Legislature would be willing to raise the needed revenue by taxing the farms, as the "Street" insists it should, but it foresees that such a course would bring an equally cyclonic outburst from the farmers.

We began by declaring that, so long as we had a drop of blood to shed, we would never submit to taxation without representation. That was a mistake The qualifying words should have been left out. For no body of free-born Americans who are at all worthy of their glorious heritage ever think of submitting to taxation of any sort, with or without representation, except after making a roar that shakes the circumambient air.

CONCERNING A SMALL STREET. SINCE the recent fall in the stock market, the relation of Wall Street to the rest of the country is pretty well understood. When this nation is really *en route* to ruin, with ticket bought and passport viséd, we doubt not that Wall Street, along with other thoroughfares, will join it. That is inevitable. But we think it is now established, and quite to the general satisfaction, that if Wall Street seeks the road to ruin, on a special train of its own contriving, there is no particular reason why the rest of our geography should pack up and accompany it, any more than if Pine Street or East Broadway should elect to go. When race goers, form players, *et al*, see track odds moving restlessly, they do not claim, as a rule, that the safety of the Republic is directly involved. Even the defeat of five favorites, a dire calamity in itself, would not necessarily spread the report that national prosperity was endangered. In fact, the racing fraternity, gamblers though they be, possess an accurate sense of their true significance, in the national regime.

Taking Long Chances

A VAST deal has been said about the pernicious influence of horse-racing, but, singularly enough, the most dangerous effect of such exhibitions has been quite overlooked, and this particular evil should have all the greater attention because it menaces the innocent bystander to a peculiar degree.

It is well known that Wall Street is the guardian of the business interests of the country. The vast extent of its trust in this regard need not be commented upon. But Wall Street is so unfortunately constituted that it simply cannot resist a horse-race. It feels its responsibility to the nation. It knows that the material well-being of nearly eighty million people rests in its perspiring hands. But if there is an "event" at Sheepshead Bay it shuts up shop and goes.

So far fortune has been kind to the country. No supreme business crisis has ever fallen on the day when there was a big horse-race. If such a conjunction ever happened there would, apparently, be no hope for the public. Its fiscal guardian would certainly go to the race.

A Costly Twist on the Lion's Tail

THE success of the American manufacturer in the British Islands during the past year or two has been so great that he is coming to look upon those countries as his natural possession. Indeed a prominent American recently startled a London dinner-party by referring to the Revolutionary War as "that unfortunate affair by which we lost England!"—a reversal surely of all previous descriptions of the episode. But commercial statistics undoubtedly justify not only pride in present achievements but enormous faith in the future. Foreign markets are unquestionably marked as ours; but meanwhile the student of the ways by which we acquire them may occasionally point out methods by which it is not advisable to approach the foreigners, and give warning that tact is as useful sometimes in opening a door to commerce as it is in private life in opening doors to dinner-parties.

The autumn in England was marked by a determined effort on the part of an American combination to control the English cigarette trade. This effort may yet succeed; but in the beginning there can be no question that great harm was done by the way in which the Americans advertised their plans. To reporters from all the newspapers they declared that they were going to drive every British manufacturer out of business, and that within a few months the American cigarette would reign supreme. Now this, when cabled to America, is very good advertising, but naturally enough its appeal was not so strong in Britain. The native manufacturers put huge advertisements in the papers in which was shown the British lion reclining on a rock by the Atlantic and smoking a London-rolled cigarette while he repelled the attempt of an army of evil-looking American cigarettes to enter his country. The result is unquestionably that, at the moment, a great number of people in England insist on having the English product.

If the Americans had kept only reasonably quiet probably this would never have happened. In questions of trade patriotism is not easy to rouse. The Parisian cries, "*Vivent les Boërs*"—and dashes into an English tailor's to order his clothes. The English Imperialist calls loudly for measures against the Teuton, and then goes out and fills his house with things "made in Germany." Nations, however, may resent being told by foreigners that there is no hope for them.

An Age of Minor Frauds

IT IS an age of adulterations and substitutions. From the newest drug to the oldest picture all things are subject to imitation. Of course imitations are not commonly equal to the original, unless one accepts such a case as that of Bol, who imitated Rembrandt so well that one cannot tell his pictures from that of his master, or of Trouillebert, who is said to have painted rather better Corots than Corot painted himself, or of Byron, who, revering Pope and regarding him as a model, wrote twice as well as Pope knew how to write. But it is not the duplication of Van Marckes and Daubignys and Diazes for the cheap auction marts that need vex the ordinary citizen, for as a rule he is not a heavy investor in such art, and when he does buy a Millet he insists on bargain prices. It is the minor frauds in material that have become common. He buys a picture, does our patron, which was painted to order by some promising young townsman with a conscience, and after it is hung up at home it begins to look less bright. The color not only sinks and dulls beyond the remedy of varnish, but it changes and fades. The crimson he so admired in the sunset becomes a rusty brown. The yellow in the robe grows green. The blue of the sky turns into a zinnober. The materials have been adulterated.

The citizen no doubt owns a book that is a matter of pride to him: a limited edition of some favorite author, with special plates and a tasteful binding. He keeps it on his shelf where he can see the outside of it, and reads something else, because it is too fine to handle. After some years he notices that the edges of the leaves are turning brown; after another while the paper begins to chip and the print to look muddy; one day he cracks a leaf through, while bending it. Lo! the paper is made of wood pulp, and is worthless.

He buys a handsome chair in one of the shops where they sell everything from collar buttons to pulpits, and assembles the family to admire it. It is pretty, and no mistake, with its gracefully wrought arms, its neatly tapering legs, its soft cushion in delicate colors, its carven back. He puts it near the register, the radiator or the fireplace, and in time he finds that the veneer which represented rosewood, mahogany or cherry is peeling off, that the carving on the back is composition, that the rep in the seat is sleazy, that the whole thing is drying and becoming disjoined.

He orders a frame for one of his pictures and the gold blackens, the carving cracks off because it is not carved, and the wood cracks. It is raw wood and bogus gold.

He finds a charming little French bronze: a nymph with draperies floating about her and rising so lightly that she seems about to fly. One day he drops her and she breaks like a piece of coal. He finds that he has paid $150 for a figure in spelter.

His son collects postage stamps until he buys a bunch of rarities at a high figure, or pays ten cents for a new, uncanceled issue from Samoa that has a face value of a dollar. Then somebody tells him that it is an easy matter to copy stamps in photogravure and print them in color, and he drops into a chair and thinks quite hard.

The victim of commercial enterprise sits at his fireside on a chair warranted to last for five years, with his feet in paper-soled slippers and his plump form in an all-wool suit that came from a shoddy mill in Vermont, and tries to digest his dinner after drinking wine from California, enriched in France with water, fusel-oil and logwood, and coffee made of ochre, beef blood and peas, and he wonders if sin comes natural to people who sell things. He recalls masters in the museum that are as sound as if they had left their studios but fifty years ago; carved Buddhas in wood that after two centuries show no warp or crack; Amsterdam and Oxford prints, readable and tough, though nearly three centuries old; German and Italian furniture that can be used every day, yet was made before the soldiers were born who fought in our Revolution; oriental rugs that have done duty in Eastern palaces for four centuries and have not yet lost their color. Then he turns to Bellamy and hopes that things will be different in 2000. —CHARLES M. SKINNER.

THE FOX. — I knew those hens would be attracted by my advertisement promising Tinted Trading Stamps.

THE OWL.—So you are making money?
THE EAGLE.—Yes, lots of it. I've started a scheme for teaching people how to fly by correspondence.

The Gentle Art of Tax-Dodging

NEWPORT will be less gay this summer. The assessor has discovered and listed for taxation $13,313,100 of personal property which has not been taxed before.

The amount of the tax, if grossly measured in dollars and cents, is a bagatelle to Newport, but the galling fact that these particular owners of personal property were unable to escape paying these taxes must sadden and humiliate them as often as they recall it—intruding its grinning head at their richest feasts and derisively poking them in the ribs as they lie on their downy beds. It is something that few self-respecting property-owners can stand. Many millionaires have been driven from their homes by it, and gone wandering from State to State and township to township in order to escape.

Once there was a resident of Chicago who listed all her personal property for taxation. The local newspapers put it on the front page under scare heads. Such a thing had never happened before. People date reminiscences from it now, as from the year of the great fire, or the winter of the deep snow. Opinion was divided. Some thought this miraculous property-owner was merely eccentric, others argued for insanity. It was pointed out that the total personal property returned for taxation was less than it had been thirty years before when the city had a third of the population and a sixth of the wealth. The episode made a record, as they say in sporting circles. To date nobody seems ambitious to match it.

There is a trifling formality in connection with the personal property schedule. It consists of the affidavit at the bottom where the property-owner does solemnly swear that he has listed above all his taxable possessions. On account of this some timorous gentlemen draw their balances out of the bank the day before, put the money in a safe deposit vault, and with a free mind swear that they haven't it. For all they know the vault was robbed over night. The like devices by which the sensitive salve their consciences for the perjury are infinite. But the sensitive are in the minority. The hardier majority just swear their way through it and have it over with.

The art of tax-dodging has developed to a point where the man who tells the assessor the truth must pay anywhere from five to twenty times his just proportion of taxes. Everybody is acquainted with the system, but we appear satisfied with it, for nothing worth mentioning is done to change it.

The Marriage of Cheats and Dupes

AN HONEST and conservative metropolitan real-estate agent lately gave it as his experience that there is a natural affinity between the cheat and the dupe. The world is full of opportunities for large and certain gains in investment, he said; but it is quite impossible to interest the natural-born dupe in any of them. He instanced a case where he vainly urged an investment now regularly netting twelve per cent. upon a man who the next day dropped his pile—or hoisted it—into the promotion of an airship company. Both dupe and cheat have imagination—the one unbalanced by common-sense, and the other unbalanced by honesty.

There is a limit, however, to the imagination of even the most willing dupe. A case was reported the other day of a widow who gave to a friendly spiritualist sums ranging from $50 to $250, and aggregating $1100, which, as she readily believed, her departed husband had need of in the other world. When the graft was at its best the wife of the spiritualist called on the dupe and said that the departed husband had expressed a desire for a pair of bisque figurines that adorned her mantelpiece. At this the widow revolted, and, her suspicions aroused, haled the spiritualist into court. The limit of her imagination was her bisque figurines.

A play was given some time ago in London in which a politician, who had won his way by dropping gold sovereigns into the contribution-box on Sundays, became a boodler, as we should say, and was rebuked by the spirits of dead statesmen, who stepped out of their frames in the lordly mansion he had bought with his boodle. One spectator left the pit in high dudgeon. "I don't say there ain't no sperruts, and all that," he remarked; "but that a man should drup a suvring into the contribution, that ain't in 'uman natur'!"

Have we not all of us, even the greatest sharps, an element of the dupe? Cæsar groveled in superstitious abasement before the statue of a goddess he imagined he had offended; and Napoleon at least half believed that theatrical rubbish about his star. The greater and more philosophical the mind, in fact, the more surely it recognizes that in all human affairs the element of the unknown, the mystical, is vastly in excess of the known and the knowable.

Yet there is the clearest of all distinctions between the Napoleons and the repositories of gold bricks. When the Napoleons are in action they never forget that Providence is on the side of the strongest battalions. They reserve their talk about their stars for idle moments.

The Hole in Your Purse

WITH spring just out of sight beyond the approaching horizon, laboring men are beginning to talk of increases of wages and of strike projects and plans. It is a good idea to talk and think of higher wages — the next best thing to talking and thinking of doing one's work more intelligently and more faithfully. But does it ever occur to wage-earners that it is useless — and even a little silly — to arrange for more money to flow into your pocket when there is a large and unguarded hole in the bottom of it?

Wages absorb the attention of workers. *Prices* — how little attention, comparatively, they pay to them! If the increase of wages is more than balanced by the increase of prices enhanced to make good the increase of wages, how does the wage-earner benefit?

People Who Save

IT IS frequently said that the working class, so called, is the first to suffer from a panic or other cause of business stagnation and the last to recover from such misfortune; it is further said that in good times this class spends as fast as it earns. If this be true, there must be something radically wrong in the reports of the savings banks of the several States, as collated and published by the Comptroller of the Currency.

From the Comptroller's statistics it appears that in 1892, the year before the last panic began, the savings banks had about four and three-quarter million depositors, with more than seventeen hundred million dollars to their credit. In 1893—the panic year—the number of depositors increased nearly sixty thousand, with a credit of almost seventy million dollars. In 1894, the hardest year of the period of depression, the number of depositors was reduced by less than five thousand, and the deposits decreased only thirty-seven million dollars. In 1895, while the depression still continued, the number of depositors exceeded that of any preceding year by about forty-five thousand, and the deposits became about twenty-five million dollars greater than in any year before. In 1896, business still being stagnant and a Presidential contest under way, about two hundred thousand additional depositors appeared, with nearly one hundred millions in money. In 1897 and 1898 there were large gains, while last year brought the savings banks about three hundred thousand new depositors, and the moneys on deposit increased by more than one hundred and sixty millions, the grand total for the year being more than five and one-half million depositors and twenty-two hundred and thirty million dollars.

In all the years named—the bad as well as the good—the average of the money on deposit exceeded three hundred and fifty dollars per individual. It has often been said that the working class in America is not so economical and prudent as the same class in Europe. On the other side of the Atlantic the number of savings bank depositors, in proportion to population, is greater than here; nevertheless, the entire sum on deposit in all European savings banks is not twice as great as that in the United States, the average per individual is not half so great as it is here, nor does the average of the most prosperous European states much exceed one-half of our own, although in these states the small farmers use the savings banks to an extent unknown in farming sections of the United States.

These figures prove beyond doubt that the working class in the United States does not squander its money, and that it is so successful at accumulating that even a long period of business depression cannot ruin it, for, as is shown above, the worst year of the recent "hard times" reduced the aggregate of savings bank depositors by only about two per cent., and this, too, at a time when in every State of the Union the bank balances of thousands of persons supposed to be well-to-do dwindled and disappeared. It is true that not all savings bank depositors belong to what is called the working class. It is also true that some working men drink their possible surplus instead of saving it, but after all possible exceptions and allowances are made, the savings bank statements indicate that as a rule the American workingman is well paid, industrious, provident, economical and thrifty; he is better off than the champions of his own class admit, and he has far more self-denial, self-command and character than are attributed to him by his critics.

—JOHN HABBERTON.

Living on Pennies

THIS is the golden age of the economist. Nothing in life is so interesting as experiments. We like to compare great poverty with great wealth, great sorrow with great happiness, the purity of our own candidate for office with the demagoguery of the opposition leader, the perfect manner of our own preacher with the sensational person who is vulgarizing the spirituality of the other church.

And so in the very exuberance of prosperity, in the most wonderful expansion era the world has ever known since Alexander wanted the whole earth, and at the time when the apotheosis of civilization is the full dinner-pail, we find these dealers in statistics and these reformers in ideas and manners glorying in the real smallness of the cost of living when practiced from the standpoint of the economists who love the fractions of cents.

We have in Boston a most excellent gentleman who offers to keep a family alive on $2.00 a week. And in the South we have another excellent gentleman who is general secretary for a Society for the Improvement of the Conditions of the Poor, who presents menus and figures to show that a family of six can live on $1.50 a week. An idea of the bill of fare can be obtained from the items for Wednesday. For breakfast a family of six have oatmeal, bread, syrup and coffee; for dinner they have hominy and bread; for supper they have bread, sausage and tea. For every breakfast during the week they have oatmeal, and at only two meals do they have anything resembling meat, when it is entered as sausage or white pudding, each of which is an indefinite term. There is a wonderful interest in all the lists, but the supper for Monday and Wednesday and Saturday, consisting of bread, syrup and tea, is the most interesting. For $2.00 a week such luxuries as cabbage, cold meat and pork are offered, and there is also a slight promise of a few codfish cakes.

It would be unjust as well as unwise to discourage these experiments, for there is undoubtedly behind them a strong and serious purpose. The value of starvation has been scientifically demonstrated in many cases, and the usefulness of cutting people down to a plain diet has its merits. We observe, however, that most of these scientists take other people to practice their theories on, and it is furthermore established that when a family, which is paying $1.50 to $2.00 a week for riotous living, is able to leave home and go to a good restaurant for a wider selection of dishes, there is likely to be no one at home to answer the door-bell during meal hours. Unquestionably the reform, as the opposite of the tendency of high living, may accomplish something. It may correct the American stomach and save it from dyspepsia; it may reduce formal dinners and banquets to sensible proportions; it may cause a decline in the demand for pepsin tablets and those patent concoctions which are warranted to digest anything from cheap cheese to a party platform.

But, after all, the average man, and for that matter the average woman, not to mention the average child, is disposed to get about the best the purse can afford. It is out of the order of civilization and entirely contrary to the spirit of the human race not to prefer canvas-back duck to scrapple, or quail to tame goose. Good food is a factor in all growth. Make it coarse and insufficient and those who eat it deteriorate. Make it sufficient and sensible and you get a better population, a better culture and a much finer-looking lot of people. Instead of trying to live on $1.50 the average family would do much better to earn $30 a week and get what is best for nourishment and satisfaction.

But of course the scientists will keep on investigating, and after they have proven their conclusions by indisputable figures they will, like sensible men, go to their homes or their clubs and enjoy the best that the market affords.

THE AMOUNT OF SALARY or wages is frequently treated in connection with the pension question, as it was, for instance, when the letter carriers were endeavoring to induce the Committee on Post-Offices and Post-Roads of the House of Representatives to take steps toward increasing their recompense. We should much rather see conditions improved in any ordinary employment by an increase in salary or wages than by an extension of the pension system. Every cent that can be paid to labor, up to the point where only so much goes to capital as will reconcile it to the risks of industry, is a nearer approach to righteous distribution. The highest wages possible to any business are a matter of mere justice, and high wages make for self-respect and better standards of living. Pensions, on the other hand, in ordinary cases too much resemble alms. Pensioner is not a sturdy word. For cases of actual injury, whether in battle for the Government or in a factory in private employment, a pension is the only possible mode of recompense, because the accident can not be foreseen, and there are special employments where retirement on a pension has its justification. In ordinary cases, however, money that can be afforded for pensions might much better be given as salary. Providing for old age is a wholesome need, and a man ought not as a matter of course to be supported because he has grown old.

WAGES AND PENSIONS

DISCRIMINATE AGAINST

INFERIOR UNCLEAN SWEAT-SHOP CLOTHING.

INSIST UPON THIS LABEL

ENDORSED BY ALL TRADES UNIONS AND LEADING REFORM SOCIETIES.

UNION LABEL used by 180 representative wholesale manufacturers in the United States and Canada, making all grades and styles of clothing. For information, apply to HENRY WHITE, General Secretary, Bible House, New York, N.Y.

The Business Side of the Big Unions

By I. K. FRIEDMAN

"YOU TOOK THE WRONG JOB"

"REST UP," ANSWERED THE PLUMBER

JUST after the formation of the Steel Trust the superintendent of one of the big plants of the corporation sent for the head roller and remarked, "Tom, your salary ran up to three thousand dollars more than mine last year and I'll have to cut you down."

"I don't see why," retorted the roller; "the only trouble with you is that you took the wrong job."

However much or little truth there may be in this anecdote that has gone the rounds of the steel industry, it serves not only to illustrate the truism that everything depends on how one looks at it, but it also reflects in a rough-and-ready way the attitude of mind of labor and capital—the two camps that ever have been at loggerheads. The bone of contention is but one of profits, and the whole quarrel is over the division of the product of united industry; and the great clash will come inevitably when labor demands for its share more than capital can grant and sustain its existence as such. Our superintendent evidently thought he was entitled to more money than the roller for his work of direction, and the latter was not bashful in declaring that he performed a more necessary function and was therefore entitled to a greater wage.

The anecdote, moreover—to use it as a text—makes it clear that labor is demanding more and more of the social product, taking it for granted everywhere, in Europe as well as in America, that it deserves more. On what the demand is based, on the evolution of it, with its justice or its injustice, with its wisdom or its folly, the limits of this article forbid discussion. It is only to be pointed out here that trades unions were fashioned merely for the end of wresting a greater share of production from industry. They had their birth in the economic logic of events, just exactly as the mammoth trusts were born of the same sources. It was the union that put the magnate of the rolls in a position to feel sorry for the mistaken choice of his boss. Both organizations went up to the music of the dollar and both business epics are written in the poetry of money.

And side by side with the "trustification" of our industries has gone on the unionization of our labor, the end and aim of both being practically the same—the establishing of a monopolistic price for their products of labor and commodities, to oust the old law of price evolved from supply and demand. "Supply and demand!" exclaimed the arrogant member of a union committee to an employer. "There isn't a word about that in our constitution. You supply what we demand, or we strike; that's the only supply and demand that I know anything about."

However mistaken, however arbitrary, the restrictions of the unions on labor have all emanated from the same ideas that inspired the trust to restrict trade. When the building unions of Chicago went to the extreme length of forbidding the plumbers to set more than one tub a day and wipe no more than four joints, when a lather capable of laying about forty square yards a day was held down to nine, when the laws of his union made the plumber refuse to touch a task that he could finish in a minute merely to give the steamfitter a half-day's work—all of these unjust rules were made with the notion that there was but a given amount of work at a given time, and the trick was to put the price for it up as high as it would go while the work lasted. When building was hampered until it stagnated the restrictions were removed. On about the same principles the trust juggles with the interests of the public. Theoretically, both sides should keep an eye wide open for permanent as against merely temporary benefits, but practically both of them are willing to grab what they can and let the future take care of itself.

"See here, my friend," said a wiseacre to a plumber, "don't you know that in only wiping four joints a day, when you can do three times as much without hurting yourself, that you are limiting the productivity of capital, and if this keeps up there will be no money invested in building and that you will be out of work? What will you do then?"

"Rest up," answered the plumber.

The insistence of the unions on a minimum wage is the only practical method by which any wage scale can be enforced by the unions. The minimum wage lumps abilities and strikes an average between the ordinary and the exceptional worker, and though here and there it may handicap the gifted mechanic it more than compensates for the injustice to him by its protection of the mass. Often the employer resorted to the trick of putting a "rusher" on a job, paying him an unusually high rate, and then requiring the same output from those who received a far lower compensation. Often where unorganized labor is employed a machine answers all the purposes of the "rusher," and the man who feeds or tends it must keep up with the mechanism or quit his job; but the moment the men are organized the union steps in to insist on a "dead-line" that, in a certain sense, regulates the revolution of the wheels. The linotyper in Chicago, for instance, who delivers thirty-two hundred "ems" an hour is declared a competent union workman; he has the full liberty of setting up more if he chooses, and, as a matter of fact, he will average four thousand, but no employer can discharge a man who observes the limit without calling down the wrath of the union upon his head.

This may be as good a place as another to insist on the false reasoning of those who would claim that our tendency toward shorter and shorter hours will end by transforming our toilers into a shiftless and good-for-nothing race. Professor Jacques Loeb in his brilliant book, The Comparative Physiology of the Brain, full of interesting excursions on our social problems, points out that man is a worker by the force of his instincts and that if he idles his blood accumulates chemicals that make him uncomfortable and wretched, and his only release from misery is the satisfaction of instinct through employment.

The man who is a perfect artist at doing nothing is abnormal, degenerate and out of consideration. All those who have studied the question are ready to admit that the way to the saloon is lengthened by shorter hours, and that overwork and overtaxation of the system cause more drunkenness than leisure and sloth. In the normal, and not to say ideal, social system an abbreviation of hours in factory and mill ought to lead to a gratification of individual tastes through a change of occupation. Nor is work, as some philosophers would have us believe, the be-all and end-all of man.

The Fight for a Reduced Output

BUT to return to our muttons: The fight of the labor unions against the installation of new machinery is a monopolistic attempt to regulate the supply and demand of its sole product—labor. The hostility of the printers to the introduction of the linotype machines in the Government printing offices at Washington causes an extra and unnecessary expense of thousands of dollars annually—most of it as much of an economic loss as if it were dumped into the sea. But the enmity of American labor to new inventions has been comparatively slight and is steadily on the wane. The unions recognize, with the most stupid of us, that new machinery creates new wants and opens to the worker new fields of an unlimited acreage; that the typewriter, the telegraph, the railroad and what not have given hosts employment in the mere making of implements, not to mention the running of them, and that the displacement caused by the innovations is small enough to be negligible.

When the unions hold that a surplus of apprentices will end by making a deficit of work; that it is far better to keep a boy from learning a trade than to let him master it only to find himself out of a job in his manhood—when the unions argue thus they are consistently monopolistic, and blind to the fact that nothing makes work like work. Yet, without taking the time to delve into it, one can see how even this severe limitation of apprentices is self-regulative, in the long run, by the same law as that the trust must in the end pay the penalty for trifling too flippantly with the natural price of commodities.

The story is told of a walking delegate who entered a machinist's shop and commanded: "Here, I want that new boy to quit. You've got more apprentices at work now than the law allows."

"But he is my son," explained the proprietor.

"What! that little red-headed guy?" retorted the surprised delegate. "Well, he probably hasn't got brains enough to make a mechanic, anyway. Better let him play marbles."

To put their wares on the market, and to sell them, to win customers, the unions employ about the same methods as the alert merchants of our day. Men want something for their money; they must be shown why it is to their advantage to change over from one house to another, and these advantages must not only be claimed but they must be proved as well; and so trained organizers, like wide-awake drummers, are kept on the road to preach unionism and promulgate its doctrines. Union papers go out to their trade by the carload; circulars, advertisements of all descriptions burden the mails. The Cigar Makers' International Union of America appeals to converts with the following:

> Do you know that capital (employers) has combined in our trade, in trusts and other ways, and that the natural tendency of wages, owing to the fierce competition, is always downward, and that wages are constantly being reduced except in cases where we are organized and protected by the Cigar Makers' International Union? Do you fully realize that many of our large manufacturers have become millionaires and that they live in palaces, own fast horses and yachts, and that they spend in a minute for luxuries more than you earn in a month? Do you fully realize that, owing to your unorganized condition, you are getting from two dollars to ten dollars per thousand less than is received by union men? Did you ever stop to consider the fact that by your action you are preventing the organized portion of our craft from making further and more substantial gains? . . . Do you think you are doing justice to yourself, to yours, to your wife and children, by standing alone, thus permitting your employer to reap all the benefits and profits of the trade—to clothe his wife and children in silks and to give them the best of everything, while yours are scantily clothed and housed in ramshackles when compared with those of the average employer? . . . All we ask is that you carefully read what we have to say; talk this matter over with your wife and friends; ask your wife and children if they would not like you to earn better wages in order that you may enjoy more comfort and better conditions in life.

Vast sums of money are collected by the unions in the shape of dues, and since men don't expend unless they can secure an immediate and palpable return, vast sums are distributed in sick, death and strike benefits. In other ways the comparison just made will ring true; for no business through long experience builds up a finer mechanism for the transaction of its affairs than a successful union. Take, for example, the Cigar Makers' International Union of America, which has won by common consent the place of the model union in the world of labor. It has 43,000 members, each of whom contribute three dollars in initiation fees and thirty cents a week for dues to the treasury. The four hundred and eighty locals of the union hold their funds in trust for the International. Including the permanent balance, the organization handles over $1,200,000 a year. It pays a strike benefit of five dollars a week; a funeral benefit of fifty, a wife and widowed mother benefit of forty dollars, and a graduated death benefit running from $200 to $250. A member of the union who finds it necessary to travel from one place to another in order to secure work is entitled to a loan of twenty dollars. From 1879 to 1900 the International paid out almost five millions in benefits of all kinds. Money is as much the sinews of a strike as of a war, and in the big contests waged with the New York manufacturers the International

Editor's Note—This is the first of two papers on this subject by Mr. Friedman. The second will appear next week.

spent over $250,000 for purposes of offense and defense. These figures are interesting if for nothing more than to show what the union means in the social life of its adherents.

The officers of the union consist practically of a president, a secretary and an editor of the Journal, all of them represented in one person, and for these combined and trying services he receives the absurd salary of $1500. One sees at a glance the discrepancy between the responsibilities and powers of the office and the enormous temptations it would offer for dishonesty to all but the strongest among men.

The International meets in convention but once in eight years. Its laws are all made by the members themselves under the initiative and referendum system, and those who fail to vote in general elections are fined one dollar—a plan that contains more than a suggestion for those who advocate a general use of the initiative and referendum in our public affairs. When a member is fined for any reason he may take an appeal from his local to the president, and from the president to the executive board, and from the executive board to the referendum vote—a complicated mill that grinds slowly but exceedingly small. A conservative policy has made strikes infrequent, and the statistics of the International show that strikes and trade disputes grew fewer as the membership and wages increased; on the same grounds, one supposes, that a strong nation is more likely to contest its prowess with a weak nation than one of equal power and resource.

Strikes never are allowed except by the authority and consent of a popular vote. Every difficulty involving more than twenty-five members must be submitted at once by the president of the International to a vote of all the local unions, and no action is considered official unless approved by a majority of two-thirds.

The dissimilarity of the material with which it works compels a change in the organization of a union and accounts readily enough for any variation in type, just as a difference in economic institutions explains the correlative difference in the superstructure of its legal and political system. The billet is the basis for wages in the steel industry and the scale shifts with its value, and so the exigencies of the case compel the delegates of the Amalgamated Association of Iron, Steel and Tin Workers to assemble annually, whereas one convention in eight years answers the purposes of the cigar makers' union. The feature—one that apparently is neither to be changed nor altered—that distinguishes the Amalgamated Association from all the other unions is the expiration of all agreements with employers at midnight of

June the thirtieth. After the adjournment of the yearly May convention the representatives of the various mills and their superintendents meet to discuss the scale, and if there is any dissent the fires are drawn and the mills are closed (a procedure that is considered neither a strike nor a lockout) until the mooted point is settled.

Varying veins, hard and soft coal and local conditions put many obstacles in the way of the union of the United Mine Workers of America, but the genius of its leaders has evolved a plan that apparently has surmounted them all. This union likewise holds an annual convention and arranges its business for the year; but during the assembly the delegates from the several districts hold what may be termed side conventions to fix their own scale of wages and conditions of work, and these separate agreements must be passed on by the body of the whole before they become conclusive and binding. In the third week of the convention a joint meeting is held between the operators and the committees from their districts for the purpose of talking over the wage scales already drawn up. Thus the soft coal operators and district officers of Western Pennsylvania, Ohio, Indiana, Illinois, Iowa, part of Missouri and Michigan, a small patch of Maryland, and West Virginia fix their scales for varying veins, and when their conclusions are passed on by the body of the whole the remainder of the coal country—Alabama, Virginia, Arkansas and Indian Territory—convenes its operators and miners to indorse, with necessary changes, nearly the same articles of agreement.

Unions and "Class Distinction"

EXAMPLES might be quoted without end, but in the main the tendency of unionism is to conform to these three types, and perhaps enough has been said to show that the energy, the brain and the executive ability required to organize a huge union keep an even pace with the tax that the trust levies on the same abilities of its master minds. Americans point with pride to the rapid assimilation of the hordes from Europe as one of their chief national triumphs, and yet one of the seeming insuperable obstacles of trades unionism was the amalgamation of different peoples whose languages, customs, temperaments and characteristics, their ways of thinking and living, were even wider apart than the varied lands from which they came. The two processes have gone on hand in hand, the one helping the other.

Before its actual achievement the marshaling of "low" and unskilled labor—teamsters, flat-janitors, waiters, elevator

boys and what not—into the line of unionism would have seemed an absurdity. To-day the question is no longer what can be but what cannot be unionized, and the cannot is represented by a circle of rapidly diminishing circumference. Skilled labor learned how dependent it was on unskilled labor in times of trouble, and the ingenuity of the organizer was forced naturally and logically to strengthen the points easiest of attack.

The skilled labor employed on a building, for instance, had ten chances to one of winning their strike if the teamsters refused to haul material to the forbidden spot; and the teamsters in turn had triple the chance of winning their strike if the elevator boys and flat-janitors refused to accept goods from "scab" drivers.

"Union man?" asked the elevator boy, noticing the absence of a button in the teamster's coat.

"Nop," comes the answer.

"I'm sorry, but I can't take you upstairs. The elevator just broke, and I'm forbidden to carry more than twelve pounds, and I can't carry freight up while passengers are waiting. You'll find a stairway in the rear."

And so the marvelous process of amalgamation went on apace, wiping out fine distinctions as it went, teaching skilled labor and the public at large that the man who performs its meanest toil is just as necessary to the business of the community as its finest artisans. Let one waiter walk out of a restaurant and there is just one more unhappy individual in the community; let them all walk out together and a hungry public begins to scratch its head and think that a waiter amounts to something. This community of interests, this cohesion of member to member, gave labor a new dignity and a self-respect that it never had before—save in sermons on the dignity of toil.

In one way "class distinctions"—words detested by the bigoted and the sentimental—have been wiped out by the unions, and in another way class feeling has been intensified and solidified. To those who are willing to drop narrow prejudices, who can forget for a moment the bugaboos with which it has been associated, the term "class struggle" has all the significance of a beautiful epic. It means nothing more nor less than the upward and onward movement of the greater portion of our present society. It stands for the emancipation of the toiler, for better wages and a higher standard of living. In the march of the masses along the fields of economics, in the restless movement of the peoples, it symbolizes the same thing as equality in the triumphant advance of the nations across the realms of politics.

The Servant Question in America

A Man's Solution for a Woman's Problem
By Harrison Rhodes

IT MAY seem ridiculous, even impertinent, of any one, who has for some years avoided the problem by living abroad, to attack the question of domestic service in America. But one gets a fresh view coming back to it, and feels, perhaps, that there is something to be learned from a comparison of conditions here with conditions there. It is just possible that the American woman is at too close quarters with her difficulties to get any clear view of them in perspective. She is engaged in a veritable struggle for life and has neither time nor patience for calm reasoning. The small, technical details of the matter necessarily bulk large in her field of vision. She wonders how she can teach the cook to make the buckwheat cakes light, and how she can convince the housemaid that dusting with a soft cloth is the only effectual way, and that the feather-duster is a delusion and a snare. With such matters the present article is not to deal. The question is, broadly speaking, a social one—a problem of the relation of classes to each other; and some readjustment of these relations must, in my opinion, be brought about if things are to go any better below stairs in America. Upon this basis of investigation the value of a detached view is more apparent.

Let me clear the ground to a certain extent in the very beginning by stating that the incompetence and ignorance of servants has very little place in the discussion. Not incompetence, but indifference, is the difficulty. There are, of course, plenty of untrained servants, but the incompetent servant, when willing, becomes competent quickly enough. If the truth be acknowledged, there is no great amount of skill or intelligence necessary for the ordinary work about a house, and all that there is to know can be learned with no great difficulty. Cooking is, of course, scarcely to be included in this statement. But, after much study of the subject, one comes to feel that the ability to cook is largely a gift of the gods. Training helps, but people either are, or are not, born to be cooks. All the willingness in the world would not, it is true, enable some people to learn how to make soup. But, on the other hand, indifference and lack of interest will often lead a *cordon bleu* to send up uneatable meals. So that, even here, the wish to do well is, after all, the important thing.

Intelligence and capability are at a high level in America. We constantly proclaim this ourselves and the visitor from abroad almost invariably acknowledges it. The American stock itself is wonderfully efficient, and there can be no doubt that even the brain of the stupidest immigrant begins to move more quickly in our atmosphere. If American servants are bad it is not because they could not be good, but because they do not want to be.

This last statement would probably be echoed eagerly by thousands of embittered housekeepers. The other day a woman who is struggling to manage a New York flat said to me:

"Servants! Oh, they're just devils—that's all you can say about them!"

And as it appeared that the day before her housemaid had got drunk and had attacked her mistress, catching up and smashing a valuable little Sheraton table in the attempt to use it as a weapon, there seemed a shadow of reason for the statement. Yet, in spite of such incidents, I am convinced that it is, on the whole, the fault of the employers rather than of the employed that the problem of American domestic service is so acute a one.

The Search for the Impossible

WE ARE trying for the sort of servant we shall never be able to get. The employers seem to be struggling to force the employed into a relation which is wholly out of harmony with the spirit of our national life. The ideal of Americans would seem to be the impersonal, almost wholly commercial, arrangement which exists between the well-trained English servant and his master. Of course, the pompousness and the petrified politeness are not demanded; we have laughed at them for too many years in plays and comic papers. But the employers say to themselves: "We

are willing to pay good wages, to provide comfortable quarters and good food, and to ask only a reasonable amount of service. In return, we expect them to do their work, as they would in any other occupation, for the wages paid them. There is no degradation involved, since we do not consider the relation in any special way a personal one. We do not ask favors of them. We pay for what we want and we expect to receive it."

Now, this is all very logical. And in England, because class feeling still exists so enormously, there are servants who think it the natural and proper thing that they should perform menial services and do what they are paid to do. But even in England they will not do one bit more than that. The traditional code by which duties are assigned to the various servants in an English household is ridiculously minute. "Tweeny," in Mr. Barrie's delightful play, The Admirable Crichton, is an example. She was a "between-maid," and it was her function "to carry the dishes from one end of the kitchen table, where they are placed by cook, to the other end, where they pass into the charge of Thomas and John." What American could endure such unchanging and rigid laws as this? Should we like the English condition of armed neutrality even if we could get it? But we cannot.

For the American considers that personal services are degrading when he is asked to give them merely because some one else has more money than he and can afford to pay for them. This seems at once to establish a class distinction which he resents and to which he is determined not to submit. If what he gives is the result of a mere commercial bargain then he determines that he will get as much and give as little as possible. If England is armed neutrality, America is open war. Mistress and maid are enemies. No demand is too preposterous to be made by servants before deigning to accept a place.

"You send out the washing, of course," says a prospective cook.

"No," timidly begins the would-be mistress, who had meant to be firm that the cook should be laundress, too.

"What do you do with your soiled clothes, then?" is the sarcastic inquiry. "Throw them away every week?"

THE STRIKE BREAKER

Who He Is, Where He Comes From, How He Cares for His Forces and Organizes for Action

By ROBERT SHACKLETON

VERY recently I was looking over a roll of names in an office in New York. There were cards contained in drawers and arranged in classified departments. So far as appearances were concerned it was precisely the same as the card catalogue of a library; but as a matter of fact it was all prepared for a very different purpose.

On each card was written the name of a man, with his address and a statement of his occupation; and often there were a few words additional, in succinct comment as to record or character. There were some six hundred machinists listed, there were about as many boilermakers, there were carpenters, teamsters, printers and men of other vocations, and there were "handy men," capable of doing divers things, best in some particular line but fit for metamorphosis. There were some 3000 names in all, and men of widely separated localities were listed; but that room in New York represented potential organization.

In rolls such as that lies the power of the strike-breaker—a man whose class of work has but recently been established and which has still more recently reached an astonishing development.

It is a factor of singular interest, this which has so unexpectedly come to affect the relations of industry. It is too early, as yet, to gauge its final importance with much approach to certainty; but employers and employed feel an equal sense of its possible consequence, an equal concern in watching its further growth.

So naturally has the new development come about that it seems strange that it did not come long ago. It is a case of evolution; yet, though the processes of this evolution have been open to the sight of all, the final consummation has been unexpected.

For years the employed have been powerfully perfecting their organization. For years employers have been getting their own strength in hand. Long ago it seemed as if the lines were permanently drawn between the two, and that whenever a contest should come, developing into a strike, it would be only a question of whether employer or employed were in that particular instance the stronger.

But the new idea is to hold men in hand ready to proceed to any part of the country and prepared to take the place of strikers in any line of work: not unskilled men, picked up at random, after a need has arisen, but men of efficiency in the particular department of work in which they are called for. For a strike of carpenters, carpenters are to be ready; if builders or boilermakers are wanted there must be builders and boilermakers to fill the gap; if a street-railway line in any city finds itself minus its employees the strike-breaker is expected to see that new motormen and conductors materialize.

And all this is very different from efforts at strike-breaking which have obtained in the past: efforts made with the help of hastily gathered and unorganized men. For the very essence of the new movement is organization, and in the most recent developments the strike-breaker retains personal command of his men and does not merely turn over so many hundreds of them where needed.

In the carrying out of his plans the strike-breaker depends upon the potency of two forces, one old and one new. The new force, hitherto latent and unsuspected, has been discovered by himself, and the old force is one which is very old indeed but which has never before been used with anything of system in such a connection.

It is within the last five years—it is practically within the past three years—that the new system definitely began its development; it is very recently that its strength has begun to be realized. Formerly employment agencies were called upon at random, and men were sought out in the highways and hedges, so to speak, and advertisements for workers were published in distant cities. As the new system develops such aids will less and less be relied upon.

Necessarily, of the men who are regularly enrolled under the new system there will always be a proportion who will be unable to respond when a call is made; but the strike-breakers believe that by far the greater number can be depended upon.

There are at least two strike-breaking bureaus in New York that have adopted the elaborate system of keeping enrolled a force who await a demand for their services; there are two in Massachusetts; there is at least one in Chicago.

A New Captain in Industrial Warfare

AT THE head of one of those in New York is a man who, having served an apprenticeship with the concern to which I referred at the opening of this article, perceived a point in which the system could be importantly strengthened, and straightway set about the task.

It is he who has set the example of holding the strike-breaking force firmly under his own control, instead of being content with furnishing a certain number of men of a specified line of capability, and his example is sure to be followed, for it gives an element of centralized strength which was hitherto absent.

He not only retains command of his men, but assumes charge of matters of subsistence and daily management, and is himself the paymaster, thus bringing about an entire centralization of power. In his own case the strike-breaking efforts have thus far been applied solely in the direction of strikes of street-railway men, but there is no doubt that he, and the few others who are working along similar lines, will be ready to apply the latest developments of the new profession in any branch of business in which their services are called for.

A small number of men are held in hand, under pay, constantly, and till a strike arises are utilized in general work as private detectives or spies, and they make a nucleus around which reënforcements can be swiftly gathered. A few corporations have begun to pay regular retainers to one or another of the strike-breaking managers, and this renders somewhat of constant expenditure possible and indeed expected. The bulk of the men relied upon are scattered through the country, and most of them, at the time a summons comes, are busied with other vocations—work which they are expected to leave, although the prospect of double pay would seem to the average man but poor compensation. But that is just the point—the men are not of the average kind!

The strike-breaker knows that there are a large number of men, even in this twentieth century, who are as eager for a time of adventure as ever were the men of the Middle Ages. A certain number of such men become regular soldiers, but to most of them an army career is distasteful, on account of too much regularity and being tied too hard and fast, or else circumstances have not been such as to turn them in the direction of an enlistment. The love of adventurous excitement, with as much as possible of freedom still retained, is the feature of their character which is to be depended upon.

These are such men as those who, in the Middle Ages and even in much later times, went from one country to another as soldiers of fortune; men such as Dugald Dalgetty, or like those who followed the standard of Hawkwood from the territories of one prince to another, now taking part in one fight and now in another.

This principle in mankind is the ancient force which has been rediscovered and applied to their own uses by the professional breakers of strikes.

Numbers of the adventure-loving men are well-to-do; among them are some of really good education; as a class they average high as men to be depended upon to take risks and obey orders. Most of them are quite ready to leave good employment when a call comes, for the love of adventure irresistibly draws them, and as it is the "handy men" who principally form this class it can be readily understood why

they have little fear of not finding other work when their services in a strike, at unusually high pay, are no longer required.

But even more interesting is the latent and unsuspected force which has been discovered and applied—the organization of the unorganized!

Workingmen are now well organized. But heretofore it has not occurred to any one to organize, in antagonism to them, those who are outside of the unions.

There are men who have been dismissed from workingmen's unions; there are malcontents; there are some who are opposed to the unions from prejudice or principle; and there is the sadder class of those who, though they have been strong union men and still perhaps are so at heart, have found the unions unable to protect them, and, desirous of working at the trade for which they are best fitted, find themselves almost forced to join the hostile ranks—men, these, who have been active in the union cause in some strike, and afterward, when the strike is over and they have been taken back with others not so prominent, have found themselves discharged for some ostensible cause disconnected with anything for which their fellow-workers can take up their quarrel, and afterward find it impossible to find employment—for blacklisting, or what amounts to that, is an active force in certain lines. Upon this class the professional strike-breaker places great reliance, for it supplies him with a number of well-trained men.

The Present Strength of the New System

A RECENT happening in the city of New York was impressively illuminative in its exhibition of the present strength of the new system, which has already taken such swift root, and in its shadowing forth of possible greater strength in the future.

A strike was threatened on the lines of the elevated railway—and it will give an impression of the present power of the unions to explain that the strike was threatened by some 4000 men employed by the elevated system on account of dissatisfaction with the scale of wages announced for the employees of another system, the subway, controlled by the same capital, but which at that time had not begun operation. It would seem as if organization could go little further than for the men of one line to stand together in regard to the affairs of a line unopened. But strength was soon confronted with strength.

Silently into New York there came an army of a thousand men, each one qualified to work on an electric road. They came singly or in pairs, they came without ostentation, without the waving of banners and the flourish of trumpets. And these men came prepared to hold in their hands an important factor in the comfort of hundreds of thousands of citizens for as many days as should be necessary.

They all reported to one man, and he, like a general, saw to their organization and maintenance, their way of living, their comings and goings. There were cooks and waiters for the wants of the inner man; there were barbers for the outer. There were dormitories and cots. There was every preparation which could have been made for the maintenance of an actual army of that number of men.

It was known that at any hour the strike might be declared, and therefore it was arranged that on each of the elevated trains there were to be at least two men riding, unnoticed, as passengers, who were ready to assume the positions of motorman and guard. At the dormitories the men were drilled in the calling of the stations, and they were also drilled in the more important matter of the system of signals. And thus

the strike-breaker in charge of this little army was prepared to continue the operation of trains, no matter at what hour they might be deserted by the regular employees.

Nor was this all. There were preparations made for the aid of the possible injured, and there were lawyers retained, ready to proceed to the police courts, there to represent any of the strike-breaking force who might be arrested on whatever charge. Without this care the forces of the army might have been seriously depleted, especially if scenes of violence had occurred.

Now, it is probable that not every one of these details was part of the original plan of the leader. He must have adopted some suggestions made by the managers of the road. But he and other strike-breakers will doubtless make use of all of them, with new ideas additional, when the next case shall arise. As has been said, the whole thing has been a matter of development.

In this New York case strong political considerations operated to bring about a settlement, whereupon this army of a thousand folded their tents like the Arabs and stole away as silently as they had appeared.

This same man, under whose command there were such thorough preparations to break the impending strike in New York, has done other similar work within the last three years, but has till now been able to keep his light under a bushel, where he fain would still have it, for publicity is not a source of strength to him. A year or so ago he took three hundred men to San Francisco in anticipation of a strike, and there, too, the strike did not take place. These new conditions, and the centralization of strength on either side, operate to make all concerned more chary of a conflict.

The men of the unions are frankly dubious as to how best to meet these new developments. They are far from admitting that there is reason for downheartedness, but they say that their own plans of action must be matured with care. Thus far, in industrial questions as in all others, development on the part of an antagonistic force has entailed a sequent counter-development, and it will be interesting to know what form the opposition will take.

A system of spies is an important part of present-day strike-breaking. Corporations admit, unreservedly, that they pay men whose business it is to join the labor organizations and keep in touch with all their proceedings, and in particular to give timely warning of any intended strike. One large trust has for an important motto, "Avoid a strike if possible." Spies keep the managers of the mills informed; and in most cases, when a strike cannot otherwise be avoided, the mill where it is to occur is suddenly shut down, and the would-be strikers find themselves out of work without having had a chance to give voice to discontent or to formulate demands. With so many mills under its control this corporation can do temporarily without the use of any one, for the work can be turned into other channels.

On the whole, thus far the advent of the man who makes the breaking of strikes a business has operated to the discouragement of strikes; and when a strike occurs it is better to combat it by businesslike display of organized tactics than to make use of arbitrary power, and crush the industry of a town out of existence, as was done in a Pennsylvania town on the ground that it was a "hotbed of unionism." The mills were dismantled, the machinery was moved to other cities, and not a wheel has since been turned there, not a fire has been lighted; which is a severer form of punishment than even the most successful of strike-breakers has either the power or the desire to inflict.

The old-fashioned way of meeting a strike was for the owners to lock the mills, or shut down the works, and then for both parties to do a minimum of negotiation and a maximum of waiting, till at length one side or the other was tired and surrendered at more or less discretion.

But with the growth of business there came to the operators of large concerns a realizing sense of the magnitude of their loss by cessation of work, and so the putting to work of outside men was attempted.

That there are always tens of thousands out of work, or even hundreds of thousands, was the mainstay of this system, and men were gathered from all quarters; and some years ago a feature which plays a prominent part in the most recent strike-breaking began to be observed—that of segregating the men and providing them with food and quarters.

But the present-day strike-breakers utilize a radically different principle in their disregard, so far as possible, of men who are out of work, and their reliance upon such as are somewhere employed. They know that many an individual of most admirable character may be out of work, and with no fault of his own; but when they need to recruit hundreds they fear to recruit them from the idle. Anomalous though it seems, they trust to men who are to leave other employment. This feature clearly differentiates the strike-breaking bureau from the employment agency.

As part of the new system, there are corporations who have an understanding by which they are to aid one another with men in case of a strike. It has been said that they frankly lend, from one city to another, trusted employees who are entirely in the interests of the employers. This is strenuously denied by certain corporations that have been confronted with the charge; but it is a fact that although men are not actually lent, which would give great offense to the unions and needlessly aggravate ill-feeling, there is with some companies a system under which certain men may resign their places, for two weeks or a month at a time, and then—entirely by accident, of course—these men are soon working as strike-breaking employees in another city.

There are at least 15,000 men now enrolled at the headquarters of the strike-breakers. One bureau alone makes claim to the names of more than that, but rivals say that this must certainly be a premature estimate, as the system has not been in force sufficiently long to gain so many men who can be soberly relied upon. However that may be, the system promises to expand rapidly, and any premature estimate of to-day is likely to seem very small a few years hence.

The Working "People."

WILL THE WHITE SLAVE HAVE A LINCOLN?

A National Eight-Hour Day

AN IMPORTANT economic and sociological experiment now being carried out under the direction of the Navy Department will be watched with the keenest interest by political economists no less than sociologists. At the Brooklyn Navy Yard there is under construction a first-class battleship. The wages of men in Government yards, it is officially stated, are forty per cent. higher than those paid in private yards, and the Government employee is given a vacation every year on full pay; the man working in a private yard takes his vacation at his own expense. There is still another heavy item against the Government. The Government works its men only eight hours a day; the contractor has established a minimum of ten.

Clearly, then, the Government is at a disadvantage to the extent of over forty per cent. paid in wages and two-tenths less returned in labor reckoned in money cost and productiveness on the basis of a day's work, and with this handicap it must be hopelessly outclassed when brought in competition with private industry.

Yet it is claimed that the disadvantages are more apparent than real. The advocates of the eight-hour day assert that it is as profitable as the ten hour; that a man working eight hours is able to do better and more work than one who labors ten hours. In the one case he is fresher and more vigorous, and can keep up an even stroke from the moment the bell rings in the morning until he lays down his tools at night; in the other he is fagged out and loiters toward the end of his stint, or else he keeps going on his nerve instead of on his muscle. The building of this ship will perhaps throw some light on this complicated problem. The average day's labor has been, in less than a century, reduced from fourteen and twelve hours to ten, in some cases even to eight. It is admitted that labor to-day working ten hours is more effective than it was in the first quarter of the last century when it worked from two to four hours longer. Why may not the present century discover that eight hours are still more profitable than ten?

That is really the great sociological question involved in the building of the vessel. It is the beginning of the agitation for a national eight-hour day. The time and money required to build this ship may, in a measure, show whether higher wages and shorter hours have an economic value, or whether when a certain point is passed capital is simply making a gratuity to labor for which it can expect no financial return.

The Public Versus the Strike

IT STRONGLY behooves the public to ask by what authority either side to the great coal strike presumed to allow any stoppage of the coal supply. Similar difficulties are liable to occur at any time, and the public has a right to demand by what warrant any associations, whether of capital or of labor, so acted as to incommode the people, presume to tax the people with heavily increased prices, presume to make suffering and misery among millions who have no connection with the quarrel.

The fuel of a country is as much a public utility as its water, its food, its light, its air, its transportation facilities. No body of men should be allowed to interfere with the supply of any of these.

The right to get food at a fair price, the right to drink, and breathe and be warm and to travel, are basic rights. When such rights are abridged, when the rightful possessions of the people are withheld from them, liberty ceases.

The question of individual rights is simple. An owner has certain rights as to the hiring or discharging of men and the fixing of wages. A miner has certain rights as to accepting certain wages and agreeing to certain hours and rules. On either side are basic individual rights that must always be respected.

But the moment that owners or miners, controlling public utilities, act as a great body they must act with consideration for the public. They are no longer individuals with private rights, but bodies of men bound to render certain duties to the community. The community gives them law and order; it gives them all the benefits of government; and they, in turn, must not act contrary to the community's rights.

If owners and workers will not willingly recognize this, they must be made to. Laws that compel the reference of disputes to arbitration must be passed and enforced. Laws that permit but do not compel arbitration are worse than useless, for they serve to bring arbitration into disrepute.

To allow the exercise of supposed rights at the expense of the public is contrary to all real liberty. Bodies of men, whether employers or employed, who control heat or food or air or water or transportation, cannot safely be allowed to engage in quarrels in which the public must suffer.

A Revised Labor Problem

EXCEPT in those occupations which can be successfully pursued only after long training, strikes in cities are almost always failures. As soon as the men quit their jobs the towns and the country pour in hundreds to take their places. City wages seem big to the rural or semi-rural because they are big to the eye. And even though they prove to be far less big and even painfully small to the stomach, the would-be city dweller is content—for a time.

There is one explanation of the at-times ferocious arrogance of city labor unions. They have to keep employers cowed, for they know what is certain to be the result of a strike.

If civilization ever discovers a way of making the country fascinating as a place to live to the average man with small capacity and less desire for reflection and self-amusement, there will be a revised labor problem. Directors of great enterprises will be selected for their skill in entertaining laboring men and keeping them from returning to the ease and independence of the small farm.

Shortening Up the Working-Day

OF COURSE there is a limit to the reduction of the hours of labor, and that limit is set by the needs of society on the present level of social requirements. We cannot reduce work to three or four hours a day because our workers could not produce in that time what society requires. But it is a fair question whether, with our vast improvements in machinery and methods, we are not in a position to get on with less than ten hours' labor from them. Thus far those improvements have served mostly to reduce the prices of all sorts of commodities, and of course the workingman has shared in that benefit in his degree. But he would benefit still more if that progressive reduction of prices were checked somewhat, to give him time for intellectual improvement and social enjoyments. Where he is engaged in such monotonous employments as those of factories and mines, he has not the nervous energy left for the enjoyment of art, literature and science, even if he had the time. His relations with his family and his neighbors are unsatisfactory and formal. He is not a man, but a workman. He needs leisure as he did not need it in the varied, and therefore less exhaustive, employments of the workshop, and as he does not in the varied employments of the farm.

This is assuming, it may be objected, that he will make the best use of the time he gains by the reduction of the hours of labor; but what security have we that the time gained will not be spent in idleness or drunkenness? That is not our affair. If we can afford to let him have the time he is entitled to it, whatever use he may make of it. Do we refuse to pay a just debt because we think our creditor will spend it in drink or some other folly? If we are really concerned about the result of shortening the labor day, then let us show it by increasing the laborer's opportunities for making the best use of it. Our American wealth has not gone much toward that object. The number of places and institutions in which the American workingman can get access to intellectual employments of any kind is not so great as it ought to be—not so great as in many parts of Europe.

The present movement is not to be considered apart from the general and prolonged effort of labor to improve its condition. How great has been the success of that effort only they can judge who have looked closely into the history of the relations of labor and capital. That success is the safety-valve of our social system. No one is so much interested in seeing it fail as the Socialist or the Anarchist, who argues that labor cannot improve conditions except by destroying our social system.

For this reason those who want neither kind of destructive revolution should give every reasonable support and sympathy to efforts which aim at reasonable alterations demanded by labor.

Old Dogs and New Tricks

THERE has been much and savage criticism of the tendency among employers, both individual and corporate, to fix an age limit for employees—a maximum age at which they will take any one into their service. But the most of this criticism has been as intemperate as it has been unjust.

A German scientist announces, with plausibility, that on the average a human being stops his mental growth at almost thirty! How many years after a man has said, "I will learn no more; I know enough," would you say he would become absolutely useless, even though, through kindness of heart, his employer does not discharge him? On the other hand, for the man who keeps alive and keeps growing, what possible fear can there be of any age-limit regulation?

Any man who is an illustration of the proverb, "You can't teach an old dog new tricks," is likely to be fierce on the subject of age limits. Any man who awakens each morning with young enthusiasm and interest will not be likely to insist that business enterprises should be charitable institutions for persons who decide that any old way is a poor way to do their work.

OUR IMPORTED CRIMINALS
By BROUGHTON BRANDENBURG

The Truth About the Mafia

So widespread an interest has been aroused in this series of articles, which throw the first real light on the outrageous conditions existing among the alien criminal classes, that one of the leading publishing houses in New York has obtained the privilege of publishing them in book form. The two preceding articles dealt with naturalization frauds, smuggling, counterfeiting, revenue evasion, and the padroni bankers, and showed this country to be in many respects a veritable felon colony for Europe. The present paper deals with those mysterious murders, kidnappings, and other outrages variously laid to societies called the "Mafia" and the "Black Hand"

A SUBJECT of mystery, lending itself to stirring romance, which finds fresh food almost daily in Italian crimes in the United States, it is not to be wondered at that the "Mafia" is the cause of continual misrepresentation. The press bristles with sensational "Mafia," "Black Hand," and "Camorra" stories. What little attention the public has paid to the terrible influx of alien criminals into the country has been attracted by such things as the crime of the unspeakable beast at Buffalo; by the dastardly work of Brescia and Lucchini, foreign Anarchists, and the countless mysterious outrages among Italians laid to the door of the Mafia and the Black Hand. The condition is bad enough, but our misconception of it is worse, and I hope here to present and support my conviction, arising from my researches, that there is no such thing as an organized criminal secret society or Mafia in this country as yet, but that we are verging on worse things than Campania, Calabria, or Sicily ever knew.

It is difficult for an American to understand the Mafia, not as a society, but as a condition. It is only a name, a class reference, just as are "White Caps," "Hooligans," "Molly McGuires," and "Ku-Klux" with us. Its age does not add one whit to its definite character, and the very origin of the word is colloquial. It springs from *malviventi* (ones of the evil life), and has its variation in *mafite* (a bad man) and *mafiusi* (participants in *mafia*). These words again have their variations in the dialects of Italia Meridionale, the Calabrese, Basilicatese, Sicilian, Apulian, and Abruzzese.

Given a strong-hearted, hot-blooded race, such as are the black Italians of the south, and then given centuries of oppression, mulcting, malicious injustice from the north, and frequent changes of rulers and codes of laws, landlords, and economic conditions, and it is not surprising that the southern Italian became a social guerilla in behalf of himself and his kin against the rest of the world. So did the "Moonlighters" in Ireland. Respect for laws which afforded him no protection, whether under Greek, Roman, Byzantine, Moorish, Norman, Spanish, or French rule, became an unknown quantity. Disregard and contempt grew into a tradition, and not enough years have elapsed since Garibaldi's famous march for freedom to alter the southern nature. If it forbore in patience for centuries before it took to the knife in the terrible "Sicilian Vespers," these latter times of peace and security must as patiently work the reformation. Poverty, such as is incomprehensible in this country, and profound ignorance the statistics of which are appalling, serve to check the development of civic virtues—aided by the oppression of the priesthood and the grinding, crushing *latifonda*: the system of ownership of the land by a few, who compel the many (who must till those lands or starve) to give one-half of the crop for the privilege of producing it. These things have thrown the Italian of the south on the defensive against all men, and Heaven help his oppressors of

the north if ever he takes the aggressive! As a people I have said the worst of them when calling them ignorant and lawless, for the blood which arouses to fierce slaying heat on provocation is by the same token a blood of generous, loving, loyal, and tender hearts. They are industrious, honest, thrifty, eager to learn, keen in judgment, cautious in operations, and tenacious of those ideals common to the Catholic peasantry the world over. I firmly believe that, with proper appreciation and handling, the millions of Italians from the south coming to the United States will form one of our most reliable and conservative classes of general society, but if we continue to treat them as "dirty dagos," pay them for fraudulent naturalization and voting, expose them to the contamination, subversion, and depredation of their own criminal classes, we must expect such abasement of our institutions as the colonial founders never could have foreseen. One man in every ten who comes here as an immigrant had better, for the good of society, be pitched overboard in mid-ocean, for he aborts our benevolent assimilation of the other nine. He is like poison among them, and under our police systems, that are not one-tenth as severe as those of Italy, he fosters crime and thrives on the proceeds. So it will come about that our imported fellow-citizens will take our tools of a beneficent civilization and turn them into weapons against our civic rights, our property, and our lives. They are doing it now.

It is this one man in ten who is *mafite*. When he

comes from the country districts he comes from the *mafia di campagna*, and when he comes from the city he comes from the *mafia di citta*. If he have education, position, wealth, and high skill of legal, literary, medical, or technical sort, he is of the *mafia alta*; if from the classes of the ignorant and poor, he is of the *mafia bassa*.

The *mafia* has no laws, no written records, no membership rolls, and no organization more than comes from force of circumstance. It has no officers except as necessity dictates. Its leaders arise naturally, and its activity is spasmodic. It is at all times opportunist. The man who wishes to retire from the gang to respectability does so without asking consent of his fellows, and all that he need do is keep their secrets and stand ready to afford assistance in time of trouble. There are the following general punitive and other processes which are well understood: murder in order to silence, for punishment, or now and then for moral effect on the public; the alibi established by perjury; the anonymous letter of demand, threat, or warning, and false testimony or silence under all pressure in order to protect a comrade. Louis Troja, the Harlem banker, was killed as an example. Benedetto Madonia, whose body was found in a barrel in New York City, was killed to silence him.

During centuries these were the methods by which oppressed communities defended their rights against injustice and despotism, and, as I have said, age lent them virtue as they became ingrained, inbred, and traditional. Men of position, driven by political pressure, fled to the mountains and became bandits; by reason of superior gifts some became bandit chiefs, with here and there a common man, born a leader, who arose and outshone them all. The law of the knife became as virtuous as the law of the bullet among the mountaineers of Kentucky, West Virginia, and Tennessee to-day. There are thousands of men still living in Italy who were members of the bands that held the mountain roads before '70. Many, many of their compatriots are in the United States, and one eminently respectable Italian importer in New York whom I might mention had a name of dread in Basilicata. They called him "Il Lupo" ("The Wolf"), and now he is a member of the Italian Chamber of Commerce. But he is a good citizen.

Instances of blackmail and attempted blackmail have been reported to the police of the Eastern cities. A large number of them were perpetrated by Americans, some are practical jokes, and all but a few of those sent by Italians are nothing more than the work of small independent groups of budding thieves. The public rarely hears of instances where *scrocco* letters are received by men of wealth. If they are reported at all they do not get beyond Inspector McClusky or his right hand man in all Italian matters, Joseph Petrosino, a really great Italian detective. He and his partner Bannoil rank as detective sergeants on the New York force, and are worth their weight in gold to the department. Both are men who live under the constant shadow of death, swift and terrible. I shall never for-

ROOM IN WHICH THE RIVERDALE MURDERS WERE COMMITTED

Here on the night of September 19, 1904, unknown men shot down three Italians, Bruno, Viruso, and Scaccia, after they had received letters from New York warning them not to proceed on their intended visit to Italy

get how, when I met Petrosino for the first time, he showed himself to be always on the alert for the vengeance of his enemies. He entered a room, did not see me, and stood with his back to me a very few feet away.

"Somebody to see you, Joe," said a brother officer.

He whirled like a flash. His right hand went down into his overcoat pocket; he shot one quick glance *first* at my hands and then at my face—and stood at ease.

He and his running mate have on hand constantly cases of Black Hand and Mafia letters, and can very nearly tell when they see one whether it is sent by some cobbler to another cobbler to drive him out of the neighborhood, for small grafting, for adventure by youngsters incited by bad literature, or by the real thing in the way of *bassa mafia*. If the truth were known as to the amount given up by Italians of means as the result of threatening letters, it would be appalling. Out of my personal acquaintance, I have a list of more than twenty doctors, merchants, lawyers, and others who have given up sums ranging from $50 to $1,000. One doctor received a demand for $5,000. Instead he gave a balance sheet showing his previous year's practice and expenses, proof that he netted but a few hundred on the year. He heard nothing further, but has added to his practice a new and mysterious class of patients. Sometimes they come to him to have wounds dressed. He knows few of them by name, but believes they are of the *cosca* that sent him the letter.

The Riverdale Murders

I have given a list of cases where the shadow of secret organization lay athwart the circumstances. To some of these murders the *scrocco* letters are now referring, as examples of what will befall those who do not pay up. The Troja, Domando, and Cagliostro Bank cases are most frequently named, but in two important affairs already mentioned, that remain to be considered in detail, there is more significance than in any of the others.

On the 19th of last September there were living in a small cottage in Riverdale, on the outskirts of Chicago, three men who worked on the railroad. They had come there from Italy nearly two years before, a fourth man, Angelo Novello, being with them at that time. He started back to Palermo in August. I have been unable to find that he ever reached home. On the evening of the date mentioned the three were making their preparations to start for New York the next day to take a North German Lloyd steamer for Naples. That day they had bought knives and revolvers for each. They had received an anonymous letter warning them to prepare for a violent death, and one man had just got a farewell letter from his brother, who conveyed in veiled phrases his further warning of impending doom. Two were men of common fibre, the third a man of education. The two were asleep in different rooms, and the third sat at a table writing some letters. Suddenly a pane of glass in the room where the one man slept was shattered, and as he sprang to his feet he was shot dead. The other sleeper never rose from his couch, but died as he lay. The third man endeavored to make his escape, but the assassins entered and killed him also. They looked for the letter of warning, and left on it the print of bloody fingers. Several hundred dollars in the dead men's pockets were untouched. The police and newspaper men struggled in vain to get an opening in the case. From names on letters and hearsay of other Italians, names were given the men. No significance was found in their identity. The case became a mystery of the past, a Mafia crime. If there had been but one Italian officer working on the affair he could have instantly given astounding developments.

The Long-Armed Mafia

The men's names were, first Bartolo Scaccia, the educated man, and his letters came from Giuseppe and Andrea Scaccia, olive oil exporters of Casteldaccia, Sicily. The others were Antonio Viruzo and Vincenzo Bruno. Can any one who has read even the brief résumé I have given of the Palizzolo case compare the facts without a sudden quickening of interest and a growing conviction of connection between them? Here are the points of connection. The men come from Casteldaccia, one of the storm centres of the Palizzolo case. They left there at a time when many others connected with the case were leaving. The Scaccia family were arrayed with Palizzolo. A Vincenzo Bruno was suspected and accused with Fontana, Garufi, and the others. The crime is obviously a *mafia* crime. They could have belonged only to a *cosca* of Palizzolo's cohorts, coming from where they did. They set about returning

as soon as they heard of Palizzolo's acquittal and had received letters from their *compadres*.

Instead of being the ordinary gang murder of three Italians, I believe the Riverdale tragedy is one which should startle patriotic Americans—being an instance, probably the first, of the Grand Mafia of Sicily stretching its arm across the Atlantic and by murder silencing the lips and preventing the return of three men who might add by their presence in Italy to the danger of their chief. Done with ease, security, and without police comprehension in a land of liberty, law, and order.

A fascinating example of the operations of a limited gang, and of our inability to cope with such, let alone the Grand Mafia should it fasten upon us, is the famous "barrel murder."

On the night of April 13, 1903, a barrel was found on the street at Avenue D and Eleventh Street, on the East Side of New York, containing the body of a man, evidently an Italian, dressed in misfit clothes and with thirteen stab wounds in his neck and breast. The body was still warm when found. In an hour the police machinery was in full motion. A terrible gang murder had been done, but newspapers and police were at sea until District Chief Flynn, of the United States Secret Service, advised Inspector McClusky that his men had been for months shadowing a gang of Italian counterfeiters, and on Monday night of the date mentioned had seen the murdered man with them. To the Secret Service men, who knew the others, the man was known as "the newcomer." He was well dressed, and did not appear to be a laboring man. Inspector McClusky's men, acting on this tip, located the members of the gang, and, while the papers were full of the mystery, waited until they had all the important ones under their eyes. All were to be arrested at once. Inspector McClusky called in his men, put them in squads of fours, and, knowing the desperate task on which he was sending them, told them to "get their men but not to get hurt." On Wednesday night the greater portion of the twelve wanted were brought in. They were Giuseppe Morello, thirty-four, agent, 178 Chrystie Street, known as the chief of the band and a dangerous man: only one finger on his right hand; Giuseppe Fanaro, 25 Rivington Street; Antonio Genova, thirty-eight, importer, 514 Fifteenth Street; Lorenzo Lobieido, forty-two, merchant, 308 Mott Street; Vito Laduca, twenty-four, laborer, 308 Mott Street; Domenica Pecoraro, thirty-two, farmer, 182 Chrystie Street; Pietro Inzerillo, forty-four, confectioner, 226 Elizabeth Street; Tommaso Petto, twenty-four, a clothing presser, known as "The Ox," by reason of his strength; Ignacio Lupo, forty, importer, 433 West Fortieth Street; Giuseppe Lalamia, laborer, 308 Mott Street, and Giuseppe Guardano, twenty-two, laborer, 165 Mott Street.

Evidence, yet no Conviction

The newspapers said at the time that the prisoners were sullen, smiling, or confident, and uncommunicative, denying everything; but a scene quite the reverse and intensely dramatic occurred in the assembly room of the Detective Bureau that night. Four men were assigned to each prisoner, coats off and sleeves rolled up. The prisoners were hustled in, flung on the floor and ordered stripped in less than two minutes. Stricken with fear, in a panic that was a psychological study, they wept and prayed, each with his rosary in his hands, while the powerful officers tumbled them about, shaking huge *coltelli* and loaded revolvers from every one. Then they were put individually through the "Third Degree," but sought refuge in pretence of lack of knowledge of English. Some of the things found were cigars in the pockets of Petto and Morello identical with those on the dead man, and a pawn ticket for a watch that was later proved to be the dead man's. The shoes on the dead man were of the same sort as those worn by a member of the gang. After the victim had been more than once identified as some one else, it was proved that he was Benedetto Madonia of Buffalo, formerly a stone mason, but for some time connected with the gang, and once sent on a mission for it to Pittsburg, as proved by letters found in Morello's house. All the band denied knowing him. The collar on the dead man was found to be identical with Morello's. The barrel and sawdust were identical with those in Inzerillo's café, bearing the same marks in every way. It was found that Madonia had been with Salvatore Maculoso, a barber, at 406 East Houston Street, had told him that he had come to New York to see if his brother-in-law, Di Primo, a member of the gang, was not in trouble, and had found that Di Primo was already in prison. Going to him, Di Primo said the gang had deserted him and robbed him of his money. Madonia came to New York once more in his brother-in-law's interests and knew he was in danger. He was with the gang at its headquarters at 8 Prince Street and 16 Stanton Street, being

CAGLIOSTRO'S BANK AND SALOON

This place, 141 Mulberry Street, New York, opposite the "House of Blazes," was the scene of the daring and cold-blooded midday murder of a man supposed to be Andrea Andano

seen there by Secret Service men, who, when all seemed to have quieted down, left their watch for the night. A few hours later Madonia's body was found.

I have given the principal points adduced by the police and Secret Service. In the trial there was enough perjury to keep half the gang in prison for the next twenty years, but they were cleared one and all and pitched back into the lap of society. From my knowledge of conditions among the Italians in New York to-day, I am compelled to predict a terrible harvest from this sowing.

To exterminate the *bassa mafia* and prevent a *grand mafia*—*Make a death penalty for such conspiracy, create a sufficient Italian police Secret Service, and on resulting evidence deport about six shiploads.*

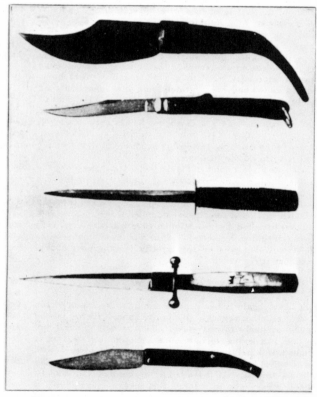

KNIVES TAKEN FROM ITALIAN CRIMINALS

The topmost knife is fully one hundred years old and is called a "grosso coltello." Below it is a vicious spring-back that was used by a Neapolitan murderer. The next is a typical stiletto. The white-handled dagger is "La Pugnale," the "official" weapon of the Malviventi. Engraved on the blade is a skull-and-crossbones, and the motto "Memento Mori." The lowest weapon is of home manufacture—made by the village blacksmith, and is very common among the lower classes of Italians. These pictures are about one-third actual size

The International Association of Brigands

DRAWN BY H. L. SAYEN

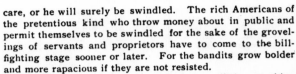

What the American Abroad May Look for from Innkeepers, Shopkeepers and Tradespeople in General

By David Graham Phillips

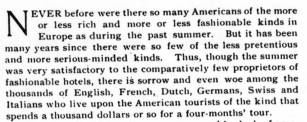

H. L. SAYEN

NEVER before were there so many Americans of the more or less rich and more or less fashionable kinds in Europe as during the past summer. But it has been many years since there were so few of the less pretentious and more serious-minded kinds. Thus, though the summer was very satisfactory to the comparatively few proprietors of fashionable hotels, there is sorrow and even woe among the thousands of English, French, Dutch, Germans, Swiss and Italians who live upon the American tourists of the kind that spends a thousand dollars or so for a four-months' tour.

This cruel disappointment was not caused by lack of prosperity among that kind of Americans, nor yet by lack of Americans who have not made the European tour. The cause is European rapacity, plain rapacity, and nothing else. The European tour for the inexperienced traveler has gradually developed into a grand scheme for swindling him, for getting as much money as possible for small and grudging service. And the news of this change of conditions has spread through America and is discouraging European travel. Those who have been don't care to repeat the experience. Those who have not been are being discouraged by the tales of returned travelers.

It is difficult for a European to understand the American. When a European is overcharged or otherwise despitefully used he makes a fearful row and the offense is repaired and is not repeated. But the American who doesn't like the way he has been treated usually says nothing, rarely gives any outward sign. He grins and bears it, goes his way—and doesn't come again. This mode of procedure is so directly the opposite of the European's expectation that he can't understand for the life of him why his good friend and valuable customer, the American, hasn't come back to be swindled again.

When an American of the inexperienced kind lands in Europe he is in high good humor and ready to enjoy everything, to believe in everybody. He is *en fête* and doesn't expect or especially wish to get off cheaply. And he is delighted with and most grateful for the unaccustomed deferential courtesy he receives on every hand. He had had no idea he was such an important person or so attractive to his fellow-beings. Talk to him when he has been in London or Paris two or three days only and he will be full of comparisons to the disparagement of the country and the people he has left behind him at home.

Then—he finds a hand in his pocket. He looks along the arm, the shoulder, until he comes to the face—it is the face of one of the most cordial and helpful of these new foreign friends of his. This gives him a shock, sets him to thinking and watching. And soon he is astounded that any European could ever have had the brazen impudence to accuse Americans of being sordid money-lovers. For, wherever he now looks with his unscaled eyes he sees greedy faces, greedy hands, fingers that fairly twitch.

Never, oh Never Again!

BUT never again is he the same trusting, credulous person he was before he caught that crafty hand. He has passed into the graduate tourist class. He conducts himself not like one journeying for pleasure but like one making a perilous and hateful passage through a land infested with thieves. He buttons his pockets. At sight of a friendly smile he frowns. At an attempt at courtesy he scowls. Where he gave absurdly large tips he now gives none at all and takes a gloomy joy in his meanness. He quarrels with the items in his hotel bill or restaurant bill, certain he is being robbed, though unable to put his finger on the cleverly concealed trap for his money. And he is hot for war between the United States and whatever country he happens to be traveling in. He hates; he is hated; he suffers; he is the cause of suffering in others. He loses sleep, he loses flesh, he loses respect for himself, he loses his naturally sunny disposition.

For many years now Europe has been full of these Americans every summer. Is it strange that there are fewer and fewer of them?

If the American visitor stays long enough in Europe or comes often enough he passes out of this stage. He learns to travel in Europe; he learns to discriminate; he learns to baffle the rogues and to keep his temper. He finds that Europeans of certain kinds are much like Americans of certain kinds in that they are unable to resist the temptation to impose upon those who invite it. He finds that in Europe, as in America, a man cannot have his rights unless he knows what they are and has the intelligence and the firmness to enforce them.

But, after all allowances are made, the fact remains that brigandage is by no means confined in Europe to a few bands in far Eastern and far Southern mountain fastnesses. Brigandage begins at every steamer landing—the brigands are waiting for their prey and pounce as the gangway falls. And brigands patrol every tourist-visited highway of Europe, city, town and country, preying upon strangers without interference from the Government, often with the Government's aid and encouragement.

When a foreigner, especially an American, appears, prices at once soar in all but a very, very few of the most respectable shops and hotels and restaurants—perhaps prices would soar there were they not already as high as the proprietors have dared to put them. If the American discovers and tries to get the treatment cheerfully given the native, surliness or open hostility is shown him. If he gives the same tips that the natives give he gets no service, or service that makes him wish he could wait upon himself. And the politeness native shows to native must be paid for handsomely, or he is punished for his stinginess.

Full as exasperating, even to the accustomed traveler, as the persistence of extortion are its pettiness and its slyness.

Extortion as a Fine Art

YOU go to a first-class hotel. In America at such an hotel all the guests would be treated alike—"shaken down" for whatever they might have in their pockets if you will, but still with a large, frank boldness of the "take it or leave it, as you please" kind. Not so in Europe. There, each arrival is a separate case receiving special study with a view to special treatment. And in a score, perhaps fifty, petty ways he will be robbed—the day of his arrival will be charged as a separate day, though he came late in the afternoon; a few cents will be tacked on to his breakfast bill, a shilling or a franc here and there on his luncheon bill, several shillings or francs on his dinner bill. If he has washing done and does not ask prices in advance, prices will be double or treble what they would have been if he had asked. If he sets a day for the return of the washing an extra price will be charged for that, although he could have had it done overnight without extra charge had he so arranged. If he does not ask the price of baths in advance he will not be surprised, when he gets his bill, that so little bathing is done anywhere in the world outside of America—for no one but an Englishman calls the English basin of cold water a bath.

He must get a specimen bill for his first twenty-four hours in the hotel, must ask for his bill every few days, must wrangle over it every time, must scrutinize it with the minutest care, or he will surely be swindled. The rich Americans of the pretentious kind who throw money about in public and permit themselves to be swindled for the sake of the grovelings of servants and proprietors have to come to the bill-fighting stage sooner or later. For the bandits grow bolder and more rapacious if they are not resisted.

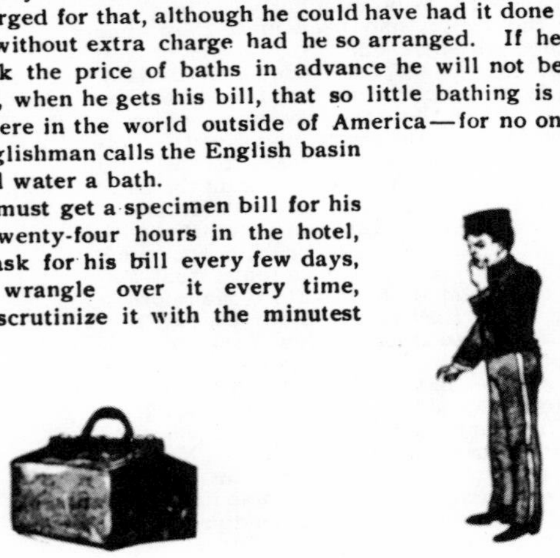

The other day an American who knew a little something about prices and practices in Europe went into one of the most famous of the first-class restaurants of Paris—one within sight of the Madeleine. As he ordered in English to a head waiter who realized that he was an American, and as he had not been in that particular restaurant for several years, and then infrequently, the management saw, or thought it saw, a chance.

As you may suspect from what has been said above, if you don't happen to know it from experience, the important person in a European hotel or restaurant is the man or woman who makes out the bill. Usually it is the proprietor or his wife. But sometimes the proprietor has no wife and feels that his mind is not subtle enough for the great work. In this particular restaurant—a fashionable establishment, mind you, where thousands of famous people dine from time to time—the proprietor himself does the petty plucking. As the American aforesaid was in a bit of a hurry to get away to the theatre with his companion he ordered a small dinner. The bill, including a $2.50 bottle of Bordeaux, should have been about twenty-five francs.

When it was presented, something in the waiter's bland face, something in the pair of eager eyes gazing dreamily in that direction from behind the cash desk made the American say to his companion: "I suspect that this bill is going to be a work of art."

A Price for Every Customer

BUT he was fairly startled when he saw the total—sixty francs! And the wine and the main dish were unchangeable, because their prices were marked on the cards presented in advance. With an ingenuity born of the desperation of a crafty mind working on a dull day well into the dull season, the proprietor had taken items which should have come to eight or nine francs and had inflated them to bear more than five times that amount.

The American, through admiration rather than through anger, studied the bill carefully. In detail it was perfect. No single item seemed outrageous, yet there was the scandalous total. Nothing is idler than generalities of criticism.

To be at all effective criticism must be pointedly, sharply detailed. The American paid the bill. The next night but one a French acquaintance of his ordered precisely the same dinner in the same restaurant, and got it for twenty-two francs. He complained of it as excessive and the proprietor took three francs off the price of the wine. Thus, his bill was less than one-third the American's bill.

But this is a small instance. Nor are these things done in Paris alone. It is London and Constantinople. It is Berlin and Rome. It is St. Petersburg and Madrid. It is grand continental, international brigandage. And it is gradually estopping Americans from going abroad.

In fashionable shops there is one price for the native, another somewhat higher for the experienced traveler, a third for the American, whether experienced or inexperienced. If the price happens to be marked on the article, often the clerk pleads that it is a mistake. Or, failing that, he shows that the quality of the article is poor and offers another of alleged better quality at an "American" price. But usually the bandits have no trouble with Americans. They pay if they must have whatever the thing may happen to be—a dinner or a dress. They pay, and they don't come again; or, if they do come, they buy as little as possible.

It has long been recognized in criminology that the criminal conceives a violent hatred for his intended victim and will plot a revenge upon him if he by chance escapes: even

though the escape was unconscious. So it is with the European bandits. Their dislike for those by whom they live and upon whom they prey is disguised beneath a veneer of servile politeness that causes the experienced to shudder. It is like the playfulness of the cat with the captive mouse, like the feasting of the missionary by the cannibal king who purposes to eat him.

In England and Germany and other northern countries where the bandits are more brutal and less adroit, the hostile attitude, soon discovered, frightens some Americans, angers others, fills others—they perhaps the most numerous—with a longing to placate at any cost the causeless hatred. In France, Italy and other Southern countries where the bandits, even though they be Germans by birth, are subtle, smooth and as searching and thorough as the best stilettos, one feels as if he were walking on a thin crust of flower-bed over a seething volcano.

In Switzerland—there the bandits are now so bold and open that there is vague talk of government interference to check them. They have made of the most beautiful country in the world a place where only the traveler willing and able to buy peace at any price can journey without feeling somewhat as if he were in the torture chamber of a prison. It is not the innate depravity of the Swiss or of the German hotel-keepers of Switzerland that is responsible for this state of affairs. So far as the Swiss are concerned, in their natural state they are about the finest people on earth—independent, simple, free from cant or snobbishness, passionately adoring freedom, singularly honest. No, the shocking conditions are due to the fact that, as more tourists have gone to Switzerland for long or longish stays than to any other country, the opportunities and temptations to brigandage have been greater than anywhere else.

If present European developments continue European travel will be undertaken only by those Americans who are very rich and very prodigal. There is hardly a doubt that, if Americans were tempted as Europeans are, they would develop as large and as industrious an army of brigands as Europe has. But this does not change the main facts:

That Americans of the most profitable class for the European business men of all kinds are going abroad less and less.

That, unless the brigands are checked, brigands and honest purveyors to tourists will alike be practically put out of business.

And it is idle for Europeans to say: "But you Americans must learn to travel in the European way." We do not care to learn it. We prefer our own easy-going way; we have no fancy for squabbling eternally over trivial sums. And if Europe wants us to come, she must take us as we are.

On This Day

ON THE Fourth of July we are prone to forget everything but the Declaration of Independence, the noise of fire-crackers, the picnics, the golf matches, the baseball games, the parades, the dollar excursions and the Flag.

But it is a day of other great anniversaries. Penn made the treaty with the Six Nations, the Wyoming massacre occurred, Nathaniel Hawthorne was born, work on the Erie Canal began, the corner-stone of the first American railroad was laid, Lincoln called for 500,000 troops, Vicksburg surrendered to Grant, three Presidents—Jefferson, Adams and Monroe—died, and the news of the destruction of Cervera's fleet was published—all on the Fourth of July. And the list could easily be lengthened.

Still, it is the day on which the proud bird of freedom screams the loudest, and so we accept it as the date of our patriotic pæans and hosannas. It has changed, as all things do and must. Home runs capture the plaudits the orators used to get, and the small boys are willing to trade their chances of becoming President for a few extra fireworks. The sweet girls who formerly sat in the shade looking unutterable nothings are swiping bits of balls over the undulating landscape, and the romantic swains who wrote verses and made pretty speeches are plunging into the woods or bounding o'er the deep.

This year, however, the day could be made a big one for the patriot. The figures of trade have rushed to the highest totals in the world's history; the recognition of this Government's power and influence has passed all the boundaries of earth; the increase in moral as well as material achievements and resources has been the largest ever known, and Prosperity is capitalized all over the national domain. It is a wonderful development we have reached when we can read of the losses of tens of millions in stock quotations, and from floods and fires and disasters on land and sea, and yet know that all the loss is not a serious fraction of the general gain.

Of course there are a few lamentations. We are getting too commercial; the dollar is our horizon; plutocracy runs rampant; the simplicity of our fathers has gone with their ruffled shirts and their altitudinous beavers, and race suicide is fitting the modern family to the city flat; but these lachrymations and suspirations belong to every age. Heraclitus, the weeping philosopher, is like the poor—he is always with us.

In point of fact, it is a pretty good age. It has its problems, its evils, its wickednesses and its bad tendencies, but on a general average it measures up a little better than it did a year ago or a hundred years ago. Life never was quite so good; it never had so many rewards, comforts or satisfactions. Mankind is higher. Better than that, ideals are loftier and purposes are less selfish.

The Significance of Our Flag

"I MIGHT love that Flag more if I saw it less," a good American said recently. He was offended by the frequency with which our national banner is flaunted from every schoolhouse and every public building, to say nothing of many private houses. The American use of the Flag is peculiar. In no other country is a parallel to be seen to this lavish display. The first thirteen years of my life were spent under the British Government, and in that time I saw the Union Jack but twice, and then at the head of recruiting parties during the Crimean War. When I saw America on the Glorious Fourth, I wondered at the display of patriotic bunting quite as much as at the glorious persistence of noise, dear to a boy's heart. And when the Civil War came, the city seemed to have put off its ordinary colors, and to have become red, white and blue.

There is much, however, to be said for the American abundance of the Flag. It is a sacrament of the national life—an outward and visible sign of the inward grace of nationality. The Nation is an unseen thing, making itself outwardly visible through such symbols. "The kingdom of Heaven is within you," some one quoted to Frederick Maurice. "Yes, and so is the kingdom of England," he answered. So is the American republic. But it naturally seeks expression in symbols, and the Flag, with us, takes the place of many symbols which are possessed by other countries, but not by us. Kingship is a symbol with which we dispense, although the disposition to fuss over our Presidents personally has grown of late years, and is essentially a monarchical tendency.

In most countries, soldiers and public edifices, and every official except those of the municipalities, represent the Nation. With us, this is reversed. The public officials, buildings and troops are commonly those of the State in which we live, and for the State we now feel only a modified and limited patriotism. For twenty years no body of United States troops was seen in my city, and when they did appear, in dirty and travel-worn uniforms, the popular interest in them far outran anything we had felt in our State militia.

The Flag stands for the Nation. It is the symbol of the bond which unites the whole country, from Alaska to Florida, from Campobello Island to the Golden Gate. It stands for that historic past whose life we share through participation in the life of the Nation. It identifies each of us with the whole American people, near and far, past and present, and even yet to come. Its forms are not things of beauty, for the straight line is not the line of beauty. But they have a historic sense which more than compensates for their lack of grace.

It speaks of the past, when the thirteen feeble Colonies arrayed themselves against the first empire of the world, and made the unlucky number forever fortunate. It speaks of the present, when the handful of corn on the tops of the mountain has grown to be a forest like the cedars of Lebanon. It tells us of triumph, of growth, of unity in willing submission to the lawful authority of a free government. Let it wave in the daily sight of every American citizen, for its significance is as inexhaustible as it is broadly democratic.

—ROBERT ELLIS THOMPSON.

The Yosemite Valley offers Unusual Advertising Advantages

The Mammouth Cave of Kentucky would make a fine Subway.

THE PRACTICE OF ANGLING FOR THE BLIND FISH—WHILE WAITING FOR EXPRESS TRAINS—WILL NO LONGER BE TOLERATED PASSENGERS RIDING ON TOPS OF CARS DURING THE RUSH-HOURS ARE CAUTIONED NOT TO BUMP THE STALACTITES

WHY STOP

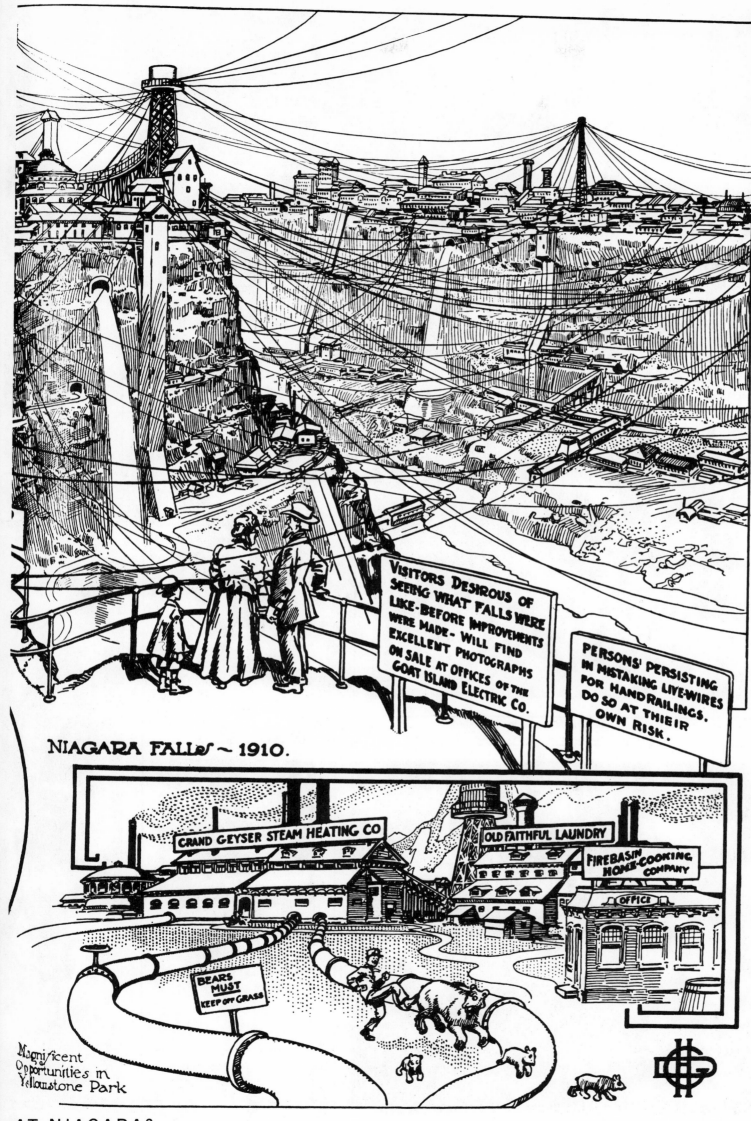

NIAGARA FALLS ~ 1910.

Magnificent Opportunities in Yellowstone Park

AT NIAGARA?

The Volunteers of America's Santa Claus

On the Great East Side the Bulk of the Christmas Shopping is Done in the Streets

Bringing Ho

Christmas-Time Means Night and Day Work for the Delivery-Wagons
of the Big Department Stores

The Hot-Chestnut Man
is the Sign of Winter

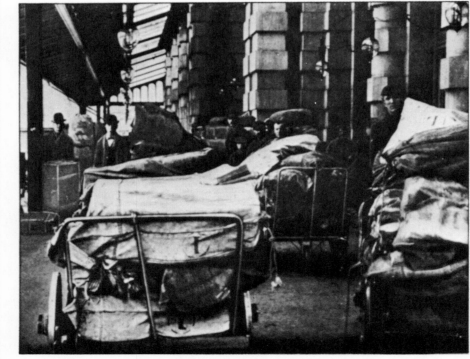

One Way of Getting Presents Home

The Post-Office is Swamped with Christmas Mail

A Salvation-

The Day before Christmas on Sixth Avenue, the Greatest Shopping-District in the World

A Familiar Living Advertisement

the Mistletoe

A Typical Shopping Crowd

These Christmas Trees Come All the Way from Maine

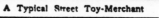

Army Santa Claus

Here's Your Christmas Holly

A Typical Street Toy-Merchant

THE FARMER TYPE OF THE PAST AND—

THE MODERN MACHINE FARM OPERATOR.

THE JOLLY OLD TIME JACK TAR AND—

YE ANCIENT STAGE COACH IS—

THE HORRIBLE PHOTO-PORTRAIT OF PRESENT AND—

DEAR OLD BROADWAY OF YORE AND—

THE PASSING OF

THE SEA STOKER OF TO-DAY.

THE OLD-TIME LANDLORD HAS—

GIVEN WAY TO THE CRISPY CLERK.

SUPPLANTED BY THE FLYING "MOBILE."

THE FINE OLD GILBERT STUART PORTRAIT OF YESTERDAY.

AS IT IS NOW.

THE PICTURESQUE.

J. OTTMANN LITH CO PUCK BLDG N.Y